T0189684

Lecture Notes in Artificial Intelligence   13458

Subseries of Lecture Notes in Computer Science

More information about this subseries at https://link.springer.com/bookseries/1244

Honghai Liu · Zhouping Yin · Lianqing Liu ·
Li Jiang · Guoying Gu · Xinyu Wu ·
Weihong Ren (Eds.)

Intelligent Robotics
and Applications

15th International Conference, ICIRA 2022
Harbin, China, August 1–3, 2022
Proceedings, Part IV

 Springer

Editors
Honghai Liu
Harbin Institute of Technology
Shenzhen, China

Lianqing Liu
Shenyang Institute of Automation
Shenyang, Liaoning, China

Guoying Gu
Shanghai Jiao Tong University
Shanghai, China

Weihong Ren
Harbin Institute of Technology
Shenzhen, China

Zhouping Yin
Huazhong University of Science
and Technology
Wuhan, China

Li Jiang
Harbin Institute of Technology
Harbin, China

Xinyu Wu
Shenzhen Institute of Advanced Technology
Shenzhen, China

ISSN 0302-9743   ISSN 1611-3349 (electronic)
Lecture Notes in Artificial Intelligence
ISBN 978-3-031-13840-9   ISBN 978-3-031-13841-6 (eBook)
https://doi.org/10.1007/978-3-031-13841-6

LNCS Sublibrary: SL7 – Artificial Intelligence

This Springer imprint is published by the registered company Springer Nature Switzerland AG
The registered company address is: Gewerbestrasse 11, 6330 Cham, Switzerland

Preface

With the theme "Smart Robotics for Society", the 15th International Conference on Intelligent Robotics and Applications (ICIRA 2022) was held in Harbin, China, August 1–3, 2022, and designed to encourage advancement in the field of robotics, automation, mechatronics, and applications. It aims to promote top-level research and globalize the quality research in general, making discussions, presentations more internationally competitive and focusing on the latest outstanding achievements, future trends, and demands.

ICIRA 2022 was organized by Harbin Institute of Technology, co-organized by Huazhong University of Science and Technology, Shanghai Jiao Tong University, and Shenyang Institute of Automation, Chinese Academy of Sciences, undertaken by State Key Laboratory of Robotics and Systems, State Key Laboratory of Digital Manufacturing Equipment and Technology, State Key Laboratory of Mechanical Systems and Vibration, and State Key Laboratory of Robotics. Also, ICIRA 2022 was technically co-sponsored by Springer. On this occasion, ICIRA 2022 was a successful event this year in spite of the COVID-19 pandemic. It attracted more than 440 submissions, and the Program Committee undertook a rigorous review process for selecting the most deserving research for publication. The advisory Committee gave advice for the conference program. Also, they help to organize special sections for ICIRA 2022. Finally, a total of 284 papers were selected for publication in 4 volumes of Springer's Lecture Note in Artificial Intelligence. For the review process, single-blind peer review was used. Each review took around 2–3 weeks, and each submission received at least 2 reviews and 1 meta-review.

In ICIRA 2022, 3 distinguished plenary speakers and 9 keynote speakers had delivered their outstanding research works in various fields of robotics. Participants gave a total of 171 oral presentations and 113 poster presentations, enjoying this excellent opportunity to share their latest research findings. Here, we would like to express our sincere appreciation to all the authors, participants, and distinguished plenary and keynote speakers. Special thanks are also extended to all members of the Organizing Committee, all reviewers for peer-review, all staffs of the conference affairs group, and all volunteers for their diligent work.

August 2022

Honghai Liu
Zhouping Yin
Lianqing Liu
Li Jiang
Guoying Gu
Xinyu Wu
Weihong Ren

Preface

Organization

Honorary Chair

Youlun Xiong — Huazhong University of Science and Technology, China

General Chairs

Honghai Liu — Harbin Institute of Technology, China
Zhouping Yin — Huazhong University of Science and Technology, China
Lianqing Liu — Shenyang Institute of Automation, Chinese Academy of Sciences, China

Program Chairs

Li Jiang — Harbin Institute of Technology, China
Guoying Gu — Shanghai Jiao Tong University, China
Xinyu Wu — Shenzhen Institute of Advanced Technology, Chinese Academy of Sciences, China

Publication Chair

Weihong Ren — Harbin Institute of Technology, China

Award Committee Chair

Limin Zhu — Shanghai Jiao Tong University, China

Regional Chairs

Zhiyong Chen — The University of Newcastle, Australia
Naoyuki Kubota — Tokyo Metropolitan University, Japan
Zhaojie Ju — The University of Portsmouth, UK
Eric Perreault — Northwestern University, USA
Peter Xu — The University of Auckland, New Zealand
Simon Yang — University of Guelph, Canada
Houxiang Zhang — Norwegian University of Science and Technology, Norway

Advisory Committee

Jorge Angeles	McGill University, Canada
Tamio Arai	University of Tokyo, Japan
Hegao Cai	Harbin Institute of Technology, China
Tianyou Chai	Northeastern University, China
Jie Chen	Tongji University, China
Jiansheng Dai	King's College London, UK
Zongquan Deng	Harbin Institute of Technology, China
Han Ding	Huazhong University of Science and Technology, China
Xilun Ding	Beihang University, China
Baoyan Duan	Xidian University, China
Xisheng Feng	Shenyang Institute of Automation, Chinese Academy of Sciences, China
Toshio Fukuda	Nagoya University, Japan
Jianda Han	Shenyang Institute of Automation, Chinese Academy of Sciences, China
Qiang Huang	Beijing Institute of Technology, China
Oussama Khatib	Stanford University, USA
Yinan Lai	National Natural Science Foundation of China, China
Jangmyung Lee	Pusan National University, South Korea
Zhongqin Lin	Shanghai Jiao Tong University, China
Hong Liu	Harbin Institute of Technology, China
Honghai Liu	The University of Portsmouth, UK
Shugen Ma	Ritsumeikan University, Japan
Daokui Qu	SIASUN, China
Min Tan	Institute of Automation, Chinese Academy of Sciences, China
Kevin Warwick	Coventry University, UK
Guobiao Wang	National Natural Science Foundation of China, China
Tianmiao Wang	Beihang University, China
Tianran Wang	Shenyang Institute of Automation, Chinese Academy of Sciences, China
Yuechao Wang	Shenyang Institute of Automation, Chinese Academy of Sciences, China
Bogdan M. Wilamowski	Auburn University, USA
Ming Xie	Nanyang Technological University, Singapore
Yangsheng Xu	The Chinese University of Hong Kong, SAR China
Huayong Yang	Zhejiang University, China

Jie Zhao   Harbin Institute of Technology, China
Nanning Zheng   Xi'an Jiaotong University, China
Xiangyang Zhu   Shanghai Jiao Tong University, China

Contents – Part IV

Data Processing and Image Analysis

Advanced Key Technologies in Intelligent Interactive Robots

Machine Learning in Human-Robot Collaboration

Multimodal Sensing and Understanding

Bio-inspired Healthcare Robotics and Technology

Robot Vision and Applications

Compliant Mechanisms and Robotic Applications

Active Control of Chatter for Five-Axis Milling Based on Piezoelectric Actuator

Shun Gao[1], Fangyu Peng[1,2], Xiaowei Tang[1(✉)], Rong Yan[1], Jiawei Wu[1], and Shihao Xin[1]

[1] School of Mechanical Science and Engineering, Huazhong University of Science and Technology, No.1037 LuoYu Road, Wuhan, China
{pengfy,tangxw,yanrong,d202080296}@hust.edu.cn
[2] State Key Lab of Digital Manufacturing Equipment and Technology, Huazhong University of Science and Technology, No.1037 LuoYu Road, Wuhan, China

Abstract. Five-axis milling is an important machining method for complex surface parts, and chatter is an important factor affecting its machining efficiency and quality. Stability boundary prediction can effectively optimize process parameters and avoid chattering, but it is difficult to actively improve the stability boundary. Therefore, in this paper, a research on active control of five-axis milling chatter based on piezoelectric actuators is carried out. A device for active control of chatter is designed, and a dynamic model of five-axis milling machining considering active vibration suppression is established. The fuzzy PD control method is used to simulate the chatter active control, and the effect of chatter suppression is analyzed by simulation, and the active control experiment is carried out to verify the effectiveness of the active chatter control device and method.

Keywords: Five-axis milling · Chatter · Fuzzy PD · Active control

1 Introduction

Five-axis milling is widely used in complex curved parts with overlapping blades, and chatter is the main factor restricting the efficiency of milling. When the depth of cut exceeds the stability boundary of a certain speed, chatter will occur. Active control to suppress chatter is an important measure to ensure machining stability and improve the surface quality of machined parts.

The active control of chatter in milling has been extensively studied. Wang et al. [1] designed an active control system with piezoelectric actuators for the problems of low workpiece stiffness and time-varying characteristics during milling of thin-walled parts. In order to ensure the best vibration suppression in the milling process performance, PD control parameters are changed according to the cutting position. Wan et al. [2] developed a two-degree-of-freedom non-contact electromagnetic actuator, integrated it into the milling spindle system, and adopted the differential drive method to make the output force and the control current have a linear relationship, which is convenient for control. Chen et al. [3] designed an electromagnetic actuator, which can provide radial

© The Author(s), under exclusive license to Springer Nature Switzerland AG 2022
H. Liu et al. (Eds.): ICIRA 2022, LNAI 13458, pp. 3–14, 2022.
https://doi.org/10.1007/978-3-031-13841-6_1

actuation force and circumferential torsion force, and control the damping and stiffness of the system in real time during processing. Paul et al. [4] used a PID controller combined with fuzzy logic to achieve chatter suppression, PID control targeting a static transfer function model, combined with fuzzy control to compensate for the nonlinear behavior in the milling system. Parus et al. [5] employed a Linear Quadratic Gaussian (LQG) control method combined with a piezoelectric actuator to control chatter during milling, and utilized a Kalman filter to estimate the current state of the system and perform feedback control. Wan et al. [6] integrated an electromagnetic actuator on the spindle system and used an active sliding mode controller to suppress milling chatter. Li et al. [7] used the vibration state of eliminating the spindle rotation frequency and its harmonic components for control, which reduced the control energy. Zhang et al. [8] used the Pade approximation to simplify the dynamic model of milling machining for robust control.

The existing researches on active chatter control are all aimed at three-axis milling. For large-scale curved parts such as ship propellers, five-axis milling is an essential processing method. Thus, this paper studies the active chatter control of five-axis milling. A chatter active control device for five-axis milling is designed. A dynamic model of chatter in five-axis milling is established. Finally, the fuzzy PD control method is used for active control of five-axis milling systems.

2   Design of Active Chatter Control Device

The ultimate purpose of active control of milling chatter is to suppress the relative vibration of the tool and the workpiece. The workpiece can be actuated by applying a force at the workpiece end to offset the relative motion of the two [9], but it needs to provide greater force and energy in the processing of large parts. Therefore, the use of actuators to control the vibration of the tool is the preferred solution. Smart materials are more widely used in the field of vibration control, among them, piezoelectric actuators have the advantages of small size, large power and fast response, and have gradually become the darling of the field of machining vibration control.

2.1   Active Chatter Control Device for Five-Axis Milling

For the five-axis machine, the tool axis vector is changed by rotating the A and C axis. Thus, a chatter active control device is designed, which is fixedly connected to the spindle and changes with the change of the spindle's posture. As the core component of the active control device, the piezoelectric actuator is used to control the vibration of the tool. The laser displacement sensor is used to measure the vibration state of the tool. During the milling process, the tool tip is in a cutting state, and the output force of the actuator cannot directly control the tool tip, so the position of the output force can only be placed at the tool bar. Similarly, the displacement sensor does not measure the vibration of the tool tip, but the vibration of the tool bar. The three-dimensional structure of the chatter active control device is shown in the Fig. 1. The piezoelectric actuator is placed in the groove of the bottom support. The fixed support plate and the machine spindle are fixedly connected by bolts distributed in the X and Y directions. The bottom support and the fixed bracket are fixedly connected by bolts. The spatial position of the fixed bracket can be adjusted by rotating the ball screw.

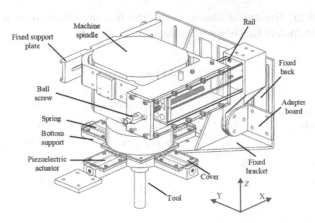

Fig. 1. Three-dimensional structure of chatter active control device.

2.2 Dynamic Model of the Control Device

The bracket of the chatter active control device for milling is fixedly connected to the spindle, and the actuator is connected to the bracket. In this paper, the dynamic characteristics of the bracket are considered for the accuracy of chatter control.

Considering the dynamics of the bracket, the dynamic model of the tool, actuator and bracket coupling is established as shown in Fig. 2, and the differential equation of motion is:

$$\begin{cases} m_1\ddot{x}_1(t) = -c_1\dot{x}_1(t) + c_2(\dot{x}_2(t) - \dot{x}_1(t)) - k_1x_1(t) + k_2(x_2(t) - x_1(t)) - F_d + F \\ m_2\ddot{x}_2(t) = -c_3\dot{x}_2(t) - c_2(\dot{x}_2(t) - \dot{x}_1(t)) - k_3x_2(t) - k_2(x_2(t) - x_1(t)) + F_d \end{cases}$$

(1)

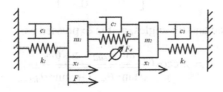

Fig. 2. Dynamic model of chatter active control device.

where m_1, c_1, k_1 are the equivalent mass, stiffness and damping of the tool, m_2 are the equivalent modal mass added by the actuator and the bracket, c_2, k_2, c_3, k_3 are the equivalent damping and stiffness of the actuator and the bracket. F is the external interference force, and F_d is the output force of the piezoelectric actuator. The Y direction is similar to the X direction. The modal characteristics of the piezoelectric actuator are calculated using the product catalog combined with the identification experiment [10]. The modal parameters of the bracket in the active chatter control device are obtained by finite element harmonic response analysis, which is simplified to a second-order differential system. The modal parameters of the tool are obtained by the modal test method. The parameters are shown in Table 1.

Table 1. Modal parameters.

Structure	Mass (kg)	Damping (N s/m)	Stiffness (N/m)
Mounting brackets	112.48	5.64×10^3	9.23×10^6
Actuator	0.05	2.5×103	8.25×10^7
Tool (X direction)	0.42	136.41	1.92×10^7
Tool (Y direction)	0.36	133.31	1.67×10^7

2.3 Dynamic Model of Five-Axis Milling

During five-axis milling, the tool axis vector is transformed, and the dynamic modeling of five-axis milling with cylindrical end mill needs to consider the influence of changes in lead and tilt angles. However, in five-axis milling, the frequency response function will not change significantly under different lead and tilt angles. This section uses the classical approach of five-axis dynamics modeling [11].

The modal parameters of the tool are defined in the frequency response coordinate system, and the milling force solution is defined in the tool coordinate system, they are no longer coincident during milling. Therefore, the two need to be unified in the process of dynamic modeling. The rotation transformation matrix of the tool coordinate system (TCS) and the frequency response coordinate system (FCS) can be expressed as:

$$
{}^{FCS}_{TCS}R = \begin{bmatrix} \cos\theta & -\sin\theta & 0 \\ \sin\theta & \cos\theta & 0 \\ 0 & 0 & 1 \end{bmatrix} \tag{2}
$$

θ is related to the lead and tilt angles, and is expressed as:

$$
\theta = \arccos(\frac{\tan\theta_{lead} \cdot \cos\theta_{tilt}}{\sqrt{\tan^2\theta_{lead} + \sin^2\theta_{tilt}}}) \tag{3}
$$

when $\theta_{lead} = 0, \theta_{tilt} = 0$, its denominator is 0. At this time, it is the case that the lead and tilt angles all are 0, which is three-axis milling.

Because the stiffness of the tool in the axial direction is large, the axial vibration of the tool is ignored. Only the dynamic cutting thickness is considered. The radial milling force in the tool coordinate system is:

$$
\begin{bmatrix} F_x \\ F_y \end{bmatrix}_{TCS} = \begin{bmatrix} a_{11} & a_{12} \\ a_{21} & a_{22} \end{bmatrix} \begin{bmatrix} \Delta x \\ \Delta y \end{bmatrix}_{TCS} = \begin{bmatrix} a_{11} & a_{12} \\ a_{21} & a_{22} \end{bmatrix} \begin{bmatrix} x_{TCS}(t) - x_{TCS}(t-T) \\ y_{TCS}(t) - y_{TCS}(t-T) \end{bmatrix} \tag{4}
$$

Among them, $a_{11}, a_{12}, a_{21}, a_{22}$ are the direction coefficients of the dynamic milling force.

The modal parameters are measured in the frequency response coordinate system. For five-axis machining, the vibration and dynamic milling force defined in the tool coordinate system need to be converted into the frequency response coordinate system. For the rotation transformation in the X and Y directions, may wish to set:

$$
{}^{FCS}_{TCS}\boldsymbol{R}' = \begin{bmatrix} \cos\theta & -\sin\theta \\ \sin\theta & \cos\theta \end{bmatrix}
\tag{5}
$$

According to the coordinate transformation relationship, the milling force in the frequency response coordinate system is:

$$
\begin{bmatrix} F_x \\ F_y \end{bmatrix}_{FCS} = {}^{FCS}_{TCS}\boldsymbol{R}' \begin{bmatrix} F_x \\ F_y \end{bmatrix}_{TCS} = {}^{FCS}_{TCS}\boldsymbol{R}' \begin{bmatrix} a_{11} & a_{12} \\ a_{21} & a_{22} \end{bmatrix} {}^{FCS}_{TCS}\boldsymbol{R}'^{-1} \begin{bmatrix} x_{FCS}(t) - x_{FCS}(t-T) \\ y_{FCS}(t) - y_{FCS}(t-T) \end{bmatrix}
\tag{6}
$$

The dynamic model of five-axis milling processing in the frequency response coordinate system is obtained as:

$$
\begin{aligned}
&\begin{bmatrix} M_{xx} & 0 \\ 0 & M_{yy} \end{bmatrix} \begin{bmatrix} \ddot{x}_{FCS}(t) \\ \ddot{y}_{FCS}(t) \end{bmatrix} + \begin{bmatrix} C_{xx} & 0 \\ 0 & C_{yy} \end{bmatrix} \begin{bmatrix} \dot{x}_{FCS}(t) \\ \dot{y}_{FCS}(t) \end{bmatrix} + \begin{bmatrix} K_{xx} & 0 \\ 0 & K_{yy} \end{bmatrix} \begin{bmatrix} x_{FCS}(t) \\ y_{FCS}(t) \end{bmatrix} \\
&= {}^{FCS}_{TCS}\boldsymbol{R}' \begin{bmatrix} a_{11} & a_{12} \\ a_{21} & a_{22} \end{bmatrix} {}^{FCS}_{TCS}\boldsymbol{R}'^{-1} \begin{bmatrix} x_{FCS}(t) - x_{FCS}(t-T) \\ y_{FCS}(t) - y_{FCS}(t-T) \end{bmatrix}
\end{aligned}
\tag{7}
$$

It can be seen that the transformation of the lead and tilt angles is equivalent to changing the dynamic milling direction force coefficient in the dynamic model. In the five-axis milling process, the system has a time-delay and time-varying nonlinear behavior.

The external interference force in formula (1) is related to the dynamic milling force, and the vibration state of the point where the tool and the actuator are in direct contact is related to the vibration state of the tool tip. F can be expressed as a function related to the vibrational state. From this, the dynamic equation of the coupling control force and the milling force is:

$$
\begin{cases}
m_1\ddot{x}_1(t) = -c_1\dot{x}_1(t) + c_2(\dot{x}_2(t) - \dot{x}_1(t)) - k_1x_1(t) + k_2(x_2(t) - x_1(t)) - F_d + F \\
m_2\ddot{x}_2(t) = -c_3\dot{x}_2(t) - c_2(\dot{x}_2(t) - \dot{x}_1(t)) - k_3x_2(t) - k_2(x_2(t) - x_1(t)) + F_d \\
\qquad F = f[(x_1(t) - x_1(t-T)), y_1(t) - y_1(t-T)]
\end{cases}
\tag{8}
$$

3 Design and Simulation of Fuzzy PD Controller

3.1 The Structure of Active Control System

The control model established considering the installation position of the actuator and the measurement position of the sensor is shown in Fig. 3.

The tool bar is the position where the piezoelectric actuator outputs the force, and the tool tip is the position where the milling force acts directly. The vibration of the two is affected by the milling force and control force. $G_{tt}(s)$ represents the transfer function

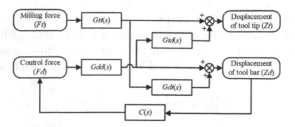

Fig. 3. Control model for five-axis milling

matrix from the milling force to the displacement of the tool tip, $G_{dd}(s)$ represents the transfer function matrix from the control force to the displacement of the tool bar measured by the displacement sensor. $G_{dt}(s)$ and $G_{td}(s)$ represent the transfer function matrix of the displacement of the tool bar and tool tip. The displacement of the tool bar due to the milling force is $G_{tt}(s) \cdot G_{dt}(s)$, and the displacement of the tool tip caused by the control force is $G_{dd}(s) \cdot G_{td}(s)$. $C(s)$ represents the transfer function of the control, then:

$$\begin{cases} Z_t(s) = G_{tt}(s) \cdot F_t(s) + G_{td}(s) \cdot G_{dd}(s)F_d(s) \\ Z_d(s) = G_{dd}(s) \cdot F_d(s) + G_{dt}(s) \cdot G_{tt}(s)F_t(s) \\ F_d(s) = C(s) \cdot Z_d(s) \end{cases} \qquad (9)$$

The frequency response function of the tool tip under control is:

$$\frac{Z_t(s)}{F_t(s)} = \frac{G_{tt}(s)}{1 - C(s)G_{dd}(s)}\{1 + C(s)G_{dd}(s)[G_{td}(s) \cdot G_{dt}(s) - 1]\} \qquad (10)$$

$G_{dd}(s)$ is the transfer function of the coupling tool and control device, expressed as:

$$G_{dd}(s) = \frac{x_1(s)}{F_d(s)} = \frac{-m_2s^2 - c_3s - k_3}{As^4 + Bs^3 + Cs^2 + Ds + E} \qquad (11)$$

The transfer function models in the X and Y directions are similar, and the control model in the X direction is taken as an example, in which:

$$\begin{cases} A = m_1m_2 \\ B = m_1(c_2 + c_3) + m_2(c_1 + c_2) \\ C = m_1(k_2 + k_3) + m_2(k_1 + k_2) + c_1c_2 + c_2c_3 + +c_1c_3 \\ D = c_1(k_2 + k_3) + c_2(k_1 + k_3) + c_3(k_1 + k_2) \\ E = k_1k_2 + +k_1k_3 + +k_2k_3 \end{cases} \qquad (12)$$

The transfer function between the tool tip and tool bar fluctuates around a fixed value in most of the frequency range, which is approximately a linear relationship, that is $G_{dt}(s) = 1/G_{td}(s) = c$, c is a constant. When $C(s) = 2 \times 10^8$ and $C(s) = 6 \times 10^8$, compared with the original tool tip frequency response function, Fig. 4 is the bode diagram.

It can be seen that after the feedback is applied, the amplitude-frequency characteristic is reduced compared with the original tool tip frequency response in most frequency

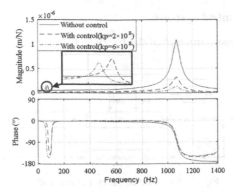

Fig. 4. The bode diagram of the tool tip system under control

ranges, and only increases around 73.5 Hz. Therefore, when the control is applied, the change trend of the vibration state will be complicated and difficult to judge.

In order to keep the amplitude-frequency characteristic variation under feedback control consistent within a specific frequency range, a notch filter is designed to adjust the control effect. The control first passes through a notch filter, it is taken as:

$$G_1 = \frac{1.276s^2 + 104.7s + 6.657 \times 10^5}{s^2 + 50.44s + 8.148 \times 10^4} \tag{13}$$

Compared with the original system, the tool tip transfer function characteristics of the system with series notch filter under control are shown in Fig. 5.

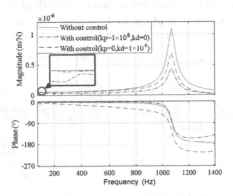

Fig. 5. Bode diagram of tool tip system with notch filter under control

It can be seen that when $kp = 1 \times 10^8$, $kd = 0$ and $kp = 0$, $kd = 1 \times 10^4$, the amplitude-frequency response of the system under feedback control is lower than that of the original system, and the effect on the amplitude response change is consistent between 0–1200 Hz, and there will be no sudden change in the effect characteristics in a certain frequency range.

3.2   Simulation of Control Systems

The Fig. 6 shows the basic structure of the fuzzy PD control.

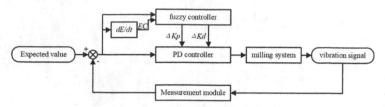

Fig. 6. Structure of fuzzy PD controller

The input of the fuzzy controller is the error and the rate of change of the error, and the output is the coefficient correction term of the PD control term. ΔKp and ΔKd are used to correct the Kp and Kd, that is:

$$Kp = Kp_0 + \Delta Kp$$
$$Kd = Kd_0 + \Delta Kd$$

(14)

The proportional and differential term coefficients change with the change of vibration displacement and speed, so as to compensate the change of the direction coefficient in the dynamic model caused by the change of the tool axis vector, that is, to change the modal characteristics of the tool in real time to suppress chatter.

The lead angle is 0°, the tilt angle is 30°, the rotation speed is 2000 r/min, the feed rate is 250 mm/min, and the depth of cut is 2.6 mm. Figure 7 shows the vibration displacement of the tool tip in X direction without and with fuzzy PD control. It can be seen that the X-direction vibration of the tool tip diverges, chatter occurs at this time. After adding fuzzy control for 0.15 s, the chatter state of the tool is suppressed.

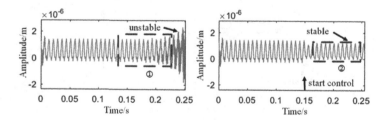

Fig. 7. Displacement of tool tip in X direction (left: without control; right: with control).

The displacement spectrum of tool tip in the X direction without control and with control is shown in Fig. 8. It can be seen that the chatter frequency is suppressed after adding fuzzy PD control. Therefore, when chatter occurs, fuzzy PD control can suppress the chatter state of the tool and reduce the vibration amplitude of the tool.

Numerical simulation of five-axis milling vibration is carried out, the critical depth of cut is shown in Table 2. It can be seen that under the same cutting conditions, the

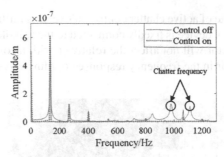

Fig. 8. Displacement spectrum of tool tip in X direction

fuzzy PD control has a better improvement effect on the critical depth of cut than the classical PD control, and the average improvement effect is 4.5%.

Table 2. Critical depth of cut

Rotating speed(r/min)	Critical depth of cut (mm)		
	Without control	PD	Fuzzy PD
2260	2.6	3.2	3.3
2500	1.6	2.4	2.5
2680	2.6	3.2	3.4
3000	1.5	2.4	2.5

4   Active Control Experiment of Milling Chatter

In order to verify the effectiveness of the control device and method in this paper, milling experiments were carried out. The workpiece material was aluminum alloy 6065. The parameters of milling tool are shown in Table 3.

Table 3. Parameters of milling tool

Milling tool parameter	Value
Teeth number	4
Diameter	8 mm
Overhang	125 mm
Natural frequency in the X direction	444.6 Hz

The experimental site of active chatter control in five-axis milling is shown in Fig. 9. The active chatter control device is fixedly connected to the spindle, and the transformation of the tool axis vector will not affect the relative positions of the two. The control force acts on the tool bar in the frequency response coordinate system.

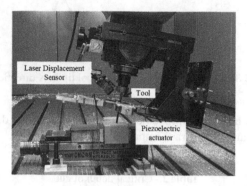

Fig. 9. Experimental site

All cutting parameters except the tool axis vector are kept unchanged, the rotation speed is 2400 r/min, the feed rate is 100 mm/min, the cutting depth is 1.5 mm. The experimental parameter settings for five-axis milling are shown in Table 4.

Table 4. Parameters of the lead and tilt angles

Number	Lead angle(°)	Tilt angle(°)
1	10.0	0.0
2	9.7	1.7

Figure 10 is the time-domain diagram of the vibration of the tool in the X-direction and its displacement spectrum diagram under the frequency response coordinate system obtained from the experiment. When the lead and tilt angles are 10° and 0°, the vibration amplitude is attenuated from 81 μm to 64 μm after adding the control, and the amplitude increases after the control is released. When the lead and tilt angles are 9.7° and 1.7°, the vibration amplitude in the X direction of the tool bar without control is 88 μm, and the vibration amplitude with control decreases to 73 μm. It can be seen from the vibration spectrum in which the low-frequency forced vibration signal is filtered out, the chatter frequency appears between 300 and 500 Hz when no control is added. After adding the control, the chatter frequency was suppressed. There was a significant forced vibration at the natural frequency of the device, which caused a large proportion of the vibration.

After adding control, the vibration state of the tool changes significantly compared with that without control. The experiment verifies the effectiveness of fuzzy PD control for five-axis milling chatter control, and fuzzy PD control also reduces the amplitude of forced vibration.

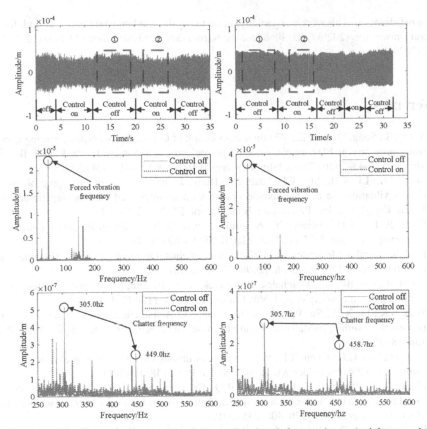

Fig. 10. Vibration displacement of tool bar in the X direction (left: experiment 1; right: experiment 2)

5 Conclusions

The chatter problem in multi-axis milling is an important reason for restricting the processing efficiency and processing quality. Using the active control method to apply a control force at the tool to suppress the relative movement between the tool and the workpiece is an important measure to ensure the processing quality. A chatter active control device based on piezoelectric actuators is proposed. A dynamic model of chatter in multi-axis milling is established, and an active control model is established considering the characteristic that the actuating force is concentrated at the tool bar. Aiming at the time-varying characteristics of multi-axis milling, the fuzzy PD control method is used to control the chatter. Compared with the classical PD control, the fuzzy PD control has a better effect on improving the chatter stability boundary of multi-axis machining. The experiment verifies the effectiveness of the active chatter control device and method studied in this paper for the active chatter control of multi-axis milling.

Acknowledgment. This work was partially supported by the Fundamental Research Funds for the Central Universities (2020kfyXJJS066) and the Natural Science Foundation of China (52175436, U20A20294).

References

1. Wang, S., Song, Q., Liu, Z.: Vibration suppression of thin-walled workpiece milling using a time-space varying PD control method via piezoelectric actuator. Int. J. Adv. Manuf. Technol. **105**(7–8), 2843–2856 (2019). https://doi.org/10.1007/s00170-019-04493-5
2. Wan, S.K., Li, X.H., Su, W.J., Yuan, J.P., Hong, J., Jin, X.L.: Active damping of milling chatter vibration via a novel spindle system with an integrated electromagnetic actuator. Precis. Eng.-J. Int. Soc. Precis. Eng. Nanotechnol. **57**, 203–210 (2019)
3. Chen, F., Lu, X.D., Altintas, Y.: A novel magnetic actuator design for active damping of machining tools. Int. J. Mach. Tools Manuf. **85**, 58–69 (2014)
4. Paul, S., Morales-Menendez, R.: Active control of chatter in milling process using intelligent PD/PID control. IEEE Access **6**, 72698–72713 (2018)
5. Parus, A., Powalka, B., Marchelek, K., Domek, S., Hoffmann, M.: Active vibration control in milling flexible workpieces. J. Vib. Control **19**, 1103–1120 (2013)
6. Wan, S.K., Li, X.H., Su, W.J., Yuan, J.P., Hong, J.: Active chatter suppression for milling process with sliding mode control and electromagnetic actuator. Mech. Syst. Signal Proc. **136**, 18 (2020)
7. Li, D.H., Cao, H.R., Chen, X.F.: Fuzzy control of milling chatter with piezoelectric actuators embedded to the tool holder. Mech. Syst. Signal Proc. **148**, 16 (2021)
8. Zhang, X.W., Wang, C.X., Liu, J., Yan, R.Q., Cao, H.R., Chen, X.F.: Robust active control based milling chatter suppression with perturbation model via piezoelectric stack actuators. Mech. Syst. Signal Proc. **120**, 808–835 (2019)
9. Puma-Araujo, S.D., Olvera-Trejo, D., Martinez-Romero, O., Urbikain, G., Elias-Zuniga, A., de Lacalle, L.N.L.: Semi-active magnetorheological damper device for chatter mitigation during milling of thin-floor components. Appl. Sci. Basel **10**, 16 (2020)
10. Li, P.D., Fu, J., Wang, Y., Xing, Z.W., Yu, M., IEEE: dynamic model and parameters identification of piezoelectric stack actuators. In: 26th Chinese Control and Decision Conference (CCDC), pp. 1918–1923. IEEE, NEW YORK (2014)
11. Tang, X.W., et al.: Stability prediction based effect analysis of tool orientation on machining efficiency for five-axis bull-nose end milling. J. Manuf. Sci. Eng. Trans. ASME **140**, 16 (2018)

A Robot-Assisted System for Dental Implantation

Xianglong Wu[1,2], Qirong Tang[2]($\boxtimes$), Fang Wang[3], Ruiqin Guo[2], Qing Zhu[1],
Shujun Li[1,2], Deyu Tu[1], and Qingyun Liu[1]

[1] School of Mechanical Engineering, Anhui University of Technology, Maanshan,
Anhui 243002, People's Republic of China
[2] Laboratory of Robotics and Multibody System, Tongji University,
Shanghai 201804, People's Republic of China
qirong.tang@outlook.com
[3] The Affiliated Stomatology Hospital of Tongji University,
Shanghai 200072, People's Republic of China

Abstract. For treating tooth defects or loss, dental implant technology is the main
treatment method because of its comfort, beauty, durability and no damage to the
adjacent teeth. Free-hand operation for dental implant surgery highly depends on
the clinical experience of the doctors and their state during the operation. Moreover, the training period is long. Additionally, dental implant surgery guided by
an implant guide plate also has some limitations, such as poor cooling effect, high
chance of thermal burn injury to the bone, blind operation, inability to make real-
time adjustments during the operation, etc. In this study, a robot-assisted dental
implant implantation system guided by the NOKOV optical motion capture system is presented, and the functions of each component of the system is introduced.
The kinematics of the system was analyzed, and the coordinate transformation
between the optical motion capture system and the manipulator was completed.
Finally, the motion planning of the manipulator was simulated according to the
pose recognized by the optical motion capture system. The results of the simulation
confirmed the effectiveness of the proposed robot-assisted system. Our findings
suggested that the system should be further investigated for practical applications
in the future.

Keywords: Anodontism · Dental implant surgery · Robot-assisted
implantation · Kinematic analysis

1 Introduction

Tooth loss affects chewing, appearance and healthy adjacent teeth. With improvements
in living standards and the popularization of oral implant technology, oral implantation
has become the main way to treat dentition loss and defects [1]. The steps of dental
implant surgery are mainly divided into the preparation the implant cavity, implantation
of the implant, installation of the abutment and installation of the dental crown. The
position, angle, and depth of the implant cavity determine the placement position of

© The Author(s), under exclusive license to Springer Nature Switzerland AG 2022
H. Liu et al. (Eds.): ICIRA 2022, LNAI 13458, pp. 15–28, 2022.
https://doi.org/10.1007/978-3-031-13841-6_2

the implant, which ultimately determines the utility and aesthetics of the implant [2]. Due to the continuous development and extensive application of computer-assisted technology in surgery, preoperative planning, dynamic navigation, and other techniques are being widely used in dental implant surgery [3]. There are mainly three ways to perform dental implant surgery: free-hand, digital surgical guide and dynamic navigation [4]. Free-hand operation is highly dependent on the clinical experience and personal state of the doctor during the operation, and only highly skilled doctors can perform such operations. Although a digital surgical guide plate can improve the precision of implantation, there are still several limitations. First, special surgical instruments are needed. Second, the cooling effect is poor during the operation, which might cause thermal burn injury to the bone. Third, the operation is performed under blindness, so doctors cannot make necessary adjustments according to the current condition of the alveolar bone [5]. When dynamic navigation is used for dental implant surgery, the current information on the implant and preoperative planning is displayed, which can help doctors to make adjustments and be in more control of the situation during the operation. However, doctors need to continuously stare at the computer screen instead of the operating area; thus, intuition is poor. With the help of preoperative planning and dynamic navigation technology, implantation surgery can be more accurate than free-hand operation [6].

With the advancement in medical science and technology, the robot-assisted system has been introduced to dental implant surgery. Some studies have shown that robot-assisted dental implant implantation can effectively improve the quality of surgery. Brief et al. developed a set of dental implant surgery robot system to assist doctors in preparing implant cavities on the patient's jaw according to the preoperatively planned position, angle, and depth [7]. Pries et al. constructed an oral implant robot system to study the effects of implant angle, implant position and implant diameter on implant force and jaw stress and to determine the best implant orientation and the number of implants [8]. Kim et al. designed a human-robot collaborative dental implant system. Surgical-assisted manipulators that complement possible surgical failures during implant surgery were studied based on hand tremors, fatigue, and the proficiency of the dentist [9]. Sun et al. applied the MELFARV-3S robotic arm with six degrees of freedom to construct a set of dental implant robot systems guided by CBCT (Cone Beam Computed Tomography) images. They used this system to conduct a simulation experiment. The implantation deviation of the system was 1.42 ± 0.70 mm [10]. Syed et al. built a robotic system for oral implantation based on force feedback technology. After establishing spatial mapping and the association between the force feedback device and the robot, the force feedback device could be used to remotely operate the manipulator during surgery [11]. Koyo applied the stereo vision-based navigation system to the three-degree-of-freedom dental implant robot, which could autonomously judge the distance from the robot to the preoperatively planned path and complete the action autonomously [12]. Li et al. proposed a new robotic arm system for dental surgery, which optimized the working space of the robotic arm to suit the needs of the human oral cavity. They proposed a robot-assisted dental cavity preparation system designed to improve the efficiency of dental procedures [13, 14]. Cao et al. developed an image-guided zygomatic implantation robot system. They used this system to conduct a simulation experiment. The results showed that the surgical entry point deviation of the robot was 0.72 ± 0.36 mm, the endpoint deviation was 1.37 ± 0.80 mm, and the angle of deviation was $1.66 \pm 0.50°$ [15]. Cheng et al. developed and tested a human-robot collaborative dental implant system, using a positioning method of manual guidance and contact position feedback for robot-guided oral implant surgery [16]. Zhao et al. developed an oral implant robot, determined the location of the patient's edentulous area through the navigation module, and planned the path based on the designed implant plan; the robot could actively control the implant instruments to complete the preparation of the implant cavity along the path [17].

In this study, an auxiliary implant placement system based on the NOKOV optical motion capture system was developed. First, the components of the system were introduced. Second, the kinematics of the manipulator was analyzed, and the coordinate conversion between the optical capture system and the manipulator was completed. Finally, the motion planning of the manipulator was simulated based on the position and pose recognized by the optical motion capture system. The results of the simulation showed that the manipulator could move to the specified position and pose.

2 Materials and Methods

The overall design scheme of a robot-assisted dental implant system was proposed according to the requirements of dental implant surgery. The robot-assisted system mainly consists of an implant system, an optical motion capture system, and control system. These are equivalent to the hands, eyes, and brain, respectively, as shown in Fig. 1. Robot-assisted dental implant implantation system maninly includes a trolley, realistic manikin, an implant system, an optical positioning system and a control system. The trolley plays a supporting role and connects all functional parts. The realistic manikin is the carrier of the implant experiment. The implant system comprises a mechanical arm and an end-effector. The end-effector is provided with a six-dimensional force sensor and a dental implant handpiece. The optical motion capture system captures the posture information of the implant system, and the positioning device, rigidly connected to the oral cavity, sends the information to the control system. According to the planting scheme and the information on the pose, the system controls the mechanical arm to move to the planting area. Finally, the planting operation is performed by the dental handpiece.

2.1 A Subsection Sample

The implant system consisted of a robot body, an end-effector, a dental implant mobile phone, and a six-dimensional force sensor (Fig. 2). The working space of dental implant surgery is narrow, and the implant cavity requires high precision. Thus, the robot arm needs high flexibility and accurate terminal movement. Therefore, the UR5 (Universal Robot 5) manipulator was selected as the robot body. The UR5 manipulator is a 6-DOF manipulator with a working radius of 850 mm, and the repetitive positioning accuracy can reach 0.01 mm. It met the high precision and safety requirements of the robot-assisted dental implant implantation system in this study. The six-dimensional force sensor constituted a force feedback system that could monitor the force on the end effector and dental implant handphone in real-time. The safety of the patient was guaranteed according to the monitoring force.

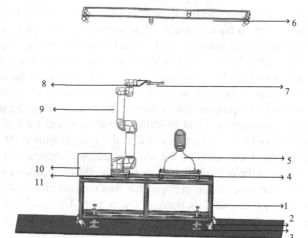

Fig. 1. Robot-assisted dental implant implantation system Here 1 is trolley, 2 is universal wheel, 3 is vacuum chuck, 4 is fixation frame, 5 is realistic manikin, 6 is optical positioning system, 7 is dental implant handpiece, 8 is six-dimensional F/T sensor, 9 is mechanical arm, 10 is control system, 11 is mechanical arm fixation frame.

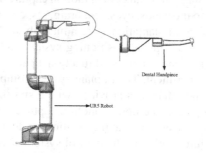

Fig. 2. Schematic diagram of implanting system

2.2 Selection of the Optical Positioning System

To enable the planting system to reach the planting area and complete the planting operation, it is necessary to add positioning equipment to the system for intraoperative navigation and positioning. In this study, a NOKOV optical motion capture system was used (Fig. 3). The positioning system consists of a motion capture lens and a reflective marking point. During the dental implant operation, the positioning system provides information on the pose in real-time for positioning. The system has a delay of 2.4–5.2 ms, and the positioning accuracy was ±0.3 mm, which meets the needs of dental implant surgery.

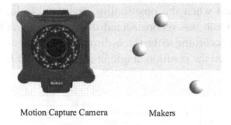

Motion Capture Camera   Makers

Fig. 3. NOKOV optical motion capture system

2.3 Selection of the Control System

The control system of the robot-assisted dental implant system controls the mechanical arm, performs motion planning, etc. However, the teaching control panel of UR5 can only realize simple road point design and cannot develop the rich functions of UR5. Therefore, the ROS (Robot Operating System) was used as the control system, using the MOVEIT! software in the ROS to plan the motion of the manipulator. The ROS fully supported the development of the UR5 manipulator, which improved the development efficiency of the system (Fig. 4).

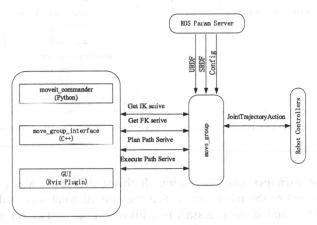

Fig. 4. Structure diagram of move_group node for MoveIt

2.4 Application Process of the Robot-Assisted Dental Implant Implantation System

The application process of the robot-assisted dental implant implantation system is shown in Fig. 5.

Preparation Before Dental Implantation. Before the operation, a positioning device with reflective marks was placed in the patient's mouth, and CT (Computed Tomography) scanning was performed when the positioning device was placed. Based on the CT images, the patient's mouth was reconstructed three-dimensionally. Finally, the doctor devised an implant plan according to the three-dimensional images of the patient's mouth, i.e., the doctor determined the position, angle, and depth of the implant cavity.

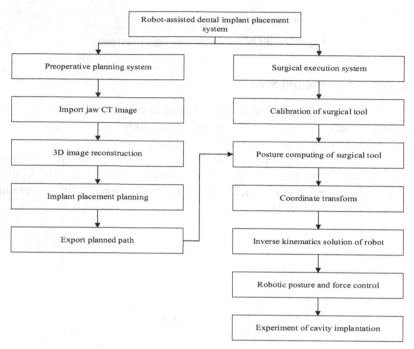

Fig. 5. Execute procedures of robot-assisted dental implant implantation system

Preparation of Intraoperative Positioning. In this study, the dental implant drill was installed at the end of the robot arm so that the control point was at the tip of the implant drill. Therefore, it was necessary to calibrate the surgical tools for this system. Direct measurements were used to calibrate the tools. After calibration, it is necessary to calculate the coordinate transformation between the optical motion capture system and the mechanical arm. Here, the marking frame, which consisted of optical marking points, was used to calibrate the two parts. Combined with the results of tool calibration and coordinate conversion, the position information of the implant in the optical motion capture system was converted to the coordinate system based on the mechanical arm. Through these steps, positioning and tracking were performed during dental implant surgery.

Robot Implant Surgery. The experimental framework of the robot-assisted dental implant system is shown in Fig. 6. The mechanical arm was controlled to move to the implant area according to the patient position information captured by the optical positioning system. Then, the implant cavity was prepared, and the dental implant was implanted according to the implant scheme.

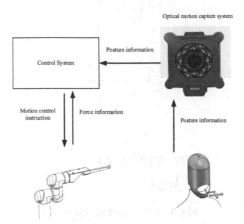

Fig. 6. Frame diagram of implant implantation experiment

3 Kinematics Analysis of the Robot-Assisted Dental Implant System

3.1 Forward Kinematics Analysis

Based on the configuration, the D-H method was used to establish the coordinate systems of each joint. The base coordinate system and the initial position and orientation of the mechanism were initially fixed (Fig. 7).

The standard D-H parameters were established according to the structure of UR5 (Table 1).

The transformation matrix of the coordinate system between neighboring joints can be expressed as

$$_i^{i-1}T = R(z, \theta_i)T(z, d_i)T(x, a_i)R(x, \alpha_i). \tag{1}$$

Here, $T(z, d_i)$ and $T(x, a_i)$ denote the translations; $R(z, \theta_i)$ and $R(x, \alpha_i)$ denote the rotations; and d_i, a_i, θ_i, and α_i are the D-H parameters of link i (see Table 1).

$$_i^{i-1}T = \begin{bmatrix} c\theta_i & -s\theta_i c\alpha_i & s\theta_i s\alpha_i & a_i c\theta_i \\ s\theta_i & c\theta_i c\alpha_i & -c\theta_i c\alpha_i & a_i s\theta_i \\ 0 & s\alpha_i & c\alpha_i & d_i \\ 0 & 0 & 0 & 1 \end{bmatrix}. \tag{2}$$

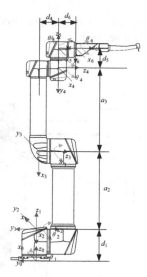

Fig. 7. UR5 structure diagram

Table 1. The UR5 Robot Standard D-H Parameters

Linkage i	θ_i (°)	a_i (mm)	d_i (mm)	α_i (°)
1	Θ	0	89.2	90
2	Θ	−425	0	0
3	Θ	−392	0	0
4	Θ	0	109.3	90
5	θ	0	94.75	−90
6	θ	0	82.5	0

Here, c = cos and s = sin. By substituting the parameters shown in Table 1 into Eq. (2), the transformation matrices were obtained as follows:

$$
{}_1^0T = \begin{bmatrix} c_1 & 0 & s_1 & 0 \\ s_1 & 0 & -c_1 & 0 \\ 0 & 1 & 0 & d_1 \\ 0 & 0 & 0 & 1 \end{bmatrix}
{}_2^1T = \begin{bmatrix} c_2 & -s_2 & 0 & a_2c_2 \\ s_2 & c_2 & 0 & a_2s_2 \\ 0 & 0 & 1 & 0 \\ 0 & 0 & 0 & 1 \end{bmatrix}
{}_3^2T = \begin{bmatrix} c_3 & -s_3 & 0 & a_3c_3 \\ s_3 & c_3 & 0 & a_3s_3 \\ 0 & 0 & 1 & 0 \\ 0 & 0 & 0 & 1 \end{bmatrix},
$$

$$
{}_4^3T = \begin{bmatrix} c_4 & 0 & s_4 & 0 \\ s_4 & 0 & c_4 & 0 \\ 0 & 1 & 0 & d_4 \\ 0 & 0 & 0 & 1 \end{bmatrix}
{}_5^4T = \begin{bmatrix} c_5 & 0 & -s_5 & 0 \\ s_5 & 0 & c_5 & 0 \\ 0 & -1 & 0 & d_5 \\ 0 & 0 & 0 & 1 \end{bmatrix}
{}_6^5T = \begin{bmatrix} c_6 & -s_6 & 0 & 0 \\ s_6 & c_6 & 0 & 0 \\ 0 & 1 & 1 & d_6 \\ 0 & 0 & 0 & 1 \end{bmatrix}.
$$

$$(3)$$

The forward kinematics of the end-tip for the base frame was determined by multiplying the six matrices in Eq. (3). An alternative representation of $_6^0T$ is,

$$
_6^0T = {}_1^0T{}_2^1T{}_3^2T{}_4^3T{}_5^4T{}_6^5T = \begin{bmatrix} n_x & o_x & a_x & p_x \\ n_y & o_y & a_y & p_y \\ n_z & o_z & a_z & p_z \\ 0 & 0 & 0 & 1 \end{bmatrix} \tag{4}
$$

Here, (n, o, a) represents the orientation of the Cartesian coordinate system, which is attached to the end-tip. The vector p in Eq. (4) defines the position of the end-tip of the robot manipulator.

The manipulator workspace was investigated by performing simulations in MAT-LAB using the above parameters. The results of the simulation are shown in Fig. 8; the blue cube represents the area that the tool end-tip could reach.

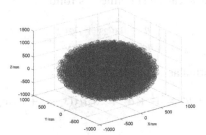

Fig. 8. Achievable working space of the end effector

3.2 Inverse Kinematics Analysis

The inverse kinematics solution is essential for determining the displacements of the prismatic joints and the rotation angles of the rotary joints of the robotic manipulator for a specific position and orientation of the tool end-tip.

$$
_1^0T^{-1}{}_6^0T{}_6^5T^{-1} = {}_3^1T{}_4^2T{}_5^3T{}^4T. \tag{5}
$$

Equation (6) can be derived from Eq. (5),

$$
\begin{cases} -p_y c_1 + d_6(a_y c_1 - a_x s_1) + p_x s_1 = d_4 \\ a_x s_1 - a_y c_1 = c_5 \\ s_6(o_y c_1 - o_x s_1) - c_6(n_y c_1 - n_x s_1) = s_5 \end{cases}. \tag{6}
$$

Thus, the joint θ_1, θ_5 and θ_6 can be obtained,

$$
\begin{cases} \theta_1 = a\tan 2(d_6 a_y - p_y, a_x d_6 - p_x) - a\tan 2\left(d_4, \pm\sqrt{(d_6 a_y - p_y)^2 + (a_x d_6 - p_x)^2 - d_4^2}\right) \\ \theta_5 = \pm acr\cos(a_x s_1 - a_y c_1) \\ \theta_6 = a\tan 2(n_x s_1 - n_y c_1, o_x s_1 - o_y c_1) - a\tan 2\left(s_5, \pm\sqrt{(n_x s_1 - n_y c_1)^2 + (o_x s_1 - o_y c_1)^2 - s_5^2}\right) \end{cases}.
$$

Additionally,

$$_1^0T\,_6^{-10}T\,_6^5T\,_5^{-14}T^{-1} = \,_4^1T.$$ (7)

Equation (8) can be derived from Eq. (7),

$$\begin{cases} d_6\big(s_6(n_xc_1 + n_ys_1) + c_6(o_xc_1 + o_ys_1)\big) - d_6(a_xc_1 + a_ys_1) + p_xc_1 + p_ys_1 = a_3c_{23} + a_2c_2 \\ p_z - d_1 - a_zd_6 + d_5(o_zc_6 + n_zs_6) = a_3s_{23} + a_2s_2 \end{cases}$$ (8)

Given,

$$\begin{cases} d_6\big(s_6(n_xc_1 + n_ys_1) + c_6(o_xc_1 + o_ys_1)\big) - d_6(a_xc_1 + a_ys_1) + p_xc_1 + p_ys_1 = m \\ p_z - d_1 - a_zd_6 + d_5(o_zc_6 + n_zs_6) = n \end{cases}.$$ (9)

The above two formulae can be simplified as follows

$$\begin{cases} m = a_3c_{23} + a_2c_2 \\ n = a_3s_{23} + a_2s_2 \end{cases}.$$ (10)

The squares of the formulae were added,

$$m^2 + n^2 = a_2^2 + a_3^2 + 2a_2a_3(s_{23}s_2 + c_{23}c_2).$$ (11)

Because,

$$s_{23}s_2 + c_{23}c_2 = c_3,$$ (12)

So,

$$\theta_3 = \pm\arccos\left(\frac{m^2 + n^2 - a_2^2 - a_3^2}{2a_2a_3}\right).$$ (13)

The formula was expanded,

$$\begin{cases} m = (a_3c_3 + a_2)c_2 - a_3s_3s_2 \\ n = a_3s_3a_2 + (a_3c_3 + a_2)s_2 \end{cases}.$$ (14)

The value fo θ_3 was substituted into the above formula,

$$\begin{cases} s_2 = \frac{(a_3c_3+a_2)n - a_3s_3m}{a_2^2 + a_3^2 + 2a_2a_3c_3} \\ c_2 = \frac{m + a_3s_3s_2}{a_3c_3 + a_2} \\ \theta_2 = a\tan 2(s_2, c_2) \end{cases}.$$ (15)

According to equation $_5^1T$, $\theta_2 + \theta_3 + \theta_4$ was obtained,

$$\begin{cases} s_{234} = -s_6(n_xc_1 + n_ys_1) - c_6(o_xc_1 + o_ys_1) \\ c_{234} = o_zc_6 + n_zs_6 \\ \theta_2 + \theta_3 + \theta_4 = a\tan 2\big(-s_6(n_xc_1 + n_ys_1) - c_6(o_xc_1 + o_ys_1), o_zc_6 + n_zs_6\big) \\ \theta_4 = a\tan 2\big(-s_6(n_xc_1 + n_ys_1) - c_6(o_xc_1 + o_ys_1), o_zc_6 + n_zs_6\big) - \theta_2 - \theta_3 \end{cases}.$$ (16)

The angles of the six joints of the manipulator were calculated.

$$
\begin{cases}
\theta_1 = a\tan 2\left(d_6 a_y - p_y, a_x d_6 - p_x\right) - a\tan 2\left(d_4, \pm\sqrt{\left(d_6 a_y - p_y\right)^2 + \left(a_x d_6 - p_x\right)^2 - d_4^2}\right) \\
\theta_2 = a\tan 2(s_2, c_2) \\
\theta_3 = \pm\arccos\left(\frac{m^2 + n^2 - a_2^2 - a_3^2}{2a_2 a_3}\right) \\
\theta_4 = a\tan 2\left(-s_6\left(n_x c_1 + n_y s_1\right) - c_6\left(o_x c_1 + o_y s_1\right), o_z c_6 + n_z s_6\right) - \theta_2 - \theta_3 \\
\theta_5 = \pm acr\cos\left(a_x s_1 - a_y c_1\right) \\
\theta_6 = a\tan 2\left(n_x s_1 - n_y c_1, o_x s_1 - o_y c_1\right) - a\tan 2\left(s_5, \pm\sqrt{\left(n_x s_1 - n_y c_1\right)^2 + \left(o_x s_1 - o_y c_1\right)^2 - s_5^2}\right)
\end{cases}
\tag{17}
$$

4 Coordinate System Conversion and Trajectory Planning

4.1 Coordinate System Transformation

This system included six important coordinate systems, i.e., the base coordinate system B, the end flange coordinate system E, the tool coordinate system T, the motion capture system coordinate system C, the marker ball coordinate system O and the implant coordinate system M. The relative pose relationship between the motion capture system coordinate system and the marker ball coordinate system $_O^C T$ can be obtained by NOKOV. The relationship between the end flange coordinate system and the base coordinate system can be obtained by the teaching control panel or the ROS. The posture relationship of the implant coordinate system in the marked ball coordinate system $_M^O T$ was measured using three-dimensional software. To realize the coordinate transformation of the system, it is necessary to determine the relative relationship between the coordinate system of the moving capture system and the coordinate system of the manipulator $_C^B T$, and the relative relationship between the tool coordinate system and the end flange coordinate system $_T^E T$.

The positional relationship between the coordinate system of the dynamic capture system and the base coordinate system of the manipulator was intended to be $(-0.360, 0.355, -0.635)$ based on measurements and calculations. Additionally, the attitude relationship is expressed as $(-90, 0, 180)$ as Euler angles. The tool coordinate system was calibrated to obtain the positional relationship between the tool coordinate system and the flange coordinate system $(0, -0.017, 0.297)$. The attitude relationship was expressed as $(90°, -90°, 0)$ as Euler angles. The pose relationship between the implant coordinate system and the robot arm coordinate system was expressed as,

$$
_M^B T = {_C^B T} {_O^C T} {_M^O T}.
\tag{18}
$$

4.2 Trajectory Planning

The MoveIt! tool in the ROS was used to realize the motion planning of the manipulator when the posture of the implant in the manipulator coordinate system was obtained based on the dynamic capture system. The RRT_Connect motion planning algorithm was selected to control the manipulator for reaching the specified position. In this study, one set of data was used to verify the feasibility of the system in the ROS. According to the above-mentioned method, the pose matrix of a group of dynamic capture marker ball supports in the robot arm base coordinate system was obtained,

$$
{}_{O}^{B}T = \begin{bmatrix} 0.4948 & -0.0313 & 0.8684 & -0.2670 \\ 0.8689 & 0.0283 & -0.4941 & -0.6766 \\ -0.0091 & 0.9991 & 0.0412 & 0.3450 \\ 0 & 0 & 0 & 1 \end{bmatrix}. \tag{19}
$$

As the end pose, the motion planning of the manipulator was simulated in the ROS, and the motion trajectory of the manipulator was obtained by joint space planning (see Fig. 9). Joint angles were described by the rqt_plot tool (see Fig. 10). The manipulator moved smoothly in the simulation process.

Running the command to view the actual position of the end-effector (see Fig. 11) and comparing it with the position in Eq. (19). We can find the end-effector of the robot could move to the expected position based on the information posture captured by the moving capture system. The results indicated the feasibility of the robot-assisted dental implant implantation system.

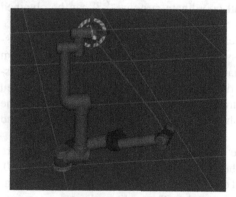

Fig. 9. Movement trajectory of the end-effector

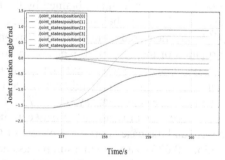

Fig. 10. Change curves of joints angles

```
rmb@rmb-Vostro-3670:~$ rosrun tf tf_echo /base /ee_link
At time 1650204676.657
- Translation: [-0.267, -0.677, 0.345]
- Rotation: in Quaternion [0.967, -0.256, 0.019, 0.010]
            in RPY (radian) [3.133, -0.041, -0.517]
            in RPY (degree) [179.494, -2.354, -29.615]
```

Fig. 11. Position of end-effector

Here, Translation is the position of end-effector, Rotation is the posture of end-effector.

5 Conclusion and Future Studied

In this study, a robot-assisted dental implant system was designed. Then, the functional components of the system were introduced, and the kinematics of the system was analyzed. The unique solution of the forward kinematics and the physically meaningful solution of the reverse kinematics of the system were obtained. Finally, based on NOKOV, the motion planning of the manipulator was simulated in the ROS. The results indicated the feasibility of the robot-assisted dental implant implantation system. Simulation experiments of dental implants need to be conducted on the head mold to further verify its accuracy.

Acknowledgment. This work is supported by the projects of National Natural Science Foundation of China (No.61873192; No.61603277), the Quick Support Project (No.61403110321), the Innovative Projects (No.20-163-00-TS-009-125-01; 21-163-00-TS-011-011-01; 2021-JCJQ-LB-010-11), and the Key Pre-Research Project of the 14th-Five-Year-Plan on Common Technology (No. 50912030501). Meanwhile, this work is also partially supported by the Fundamental Research Funds for the Central Universities and the "National High Level Talent Plan" project. It is also partially sponsored by International Joint Project Between Shanghai of China and Baden-Württemberg of Germany (No. 19510711100) within Shanghai Science and Technology Innovation Plan, as well as the project of Shanghai Key Laboratory of Spacecraft Mechanism (18DZ2272200), and Shanghai 2021 "Science and Technology Innovation Action Plan" special project of biomedical science and technology support(21S31902800). All these supports are highly appreciated.

References

1. Wu, Y., Zou, S.Q., Wang, X.: Preliminary application of dental implant robot in dental implant operations. Chin. J. Minim. Invasive Surg. **21**(09), 787–791 (2021)
2. Monaco, C., et al.: 2D/3D accuracies of implant position after guided surgery using different surgical protocols: a retrospective study. J. Prosthodont. Res. **64**(4), 424–430 (2020)
3. Block, M.S., Emery, R.W.: Static or dynamic navigation for implant placement—choosing the method of guidance. J. Oral Maxillofac. Surg. **74**(2), 269–277 (2016)
4. Panchal, N., Mahmood, L., Retana, A., Emery, R.: Dynamic navigation for dental implant surgery. Oral Maxillofac. Surg. Clin. North Am. **31**(4), 539–547 (2019)
5. Gargallo-Albiol, J., Barootchi, S., Salomó-Coll, O., Wang, H.: Advantages and disadvantages of implant navigation surgery. a systematicreview. Anatomischer Anzeiger Official Organ of the Anatomische Gesellschaft **225**, 1–10 (2019)
6. Jorba-Garcia, A., Figueiredo, R., Gonzalez-Barnadas, A., Camps-Font, O., Valmaseda-Castellon, E.: Accuracy and the role of experience in dynamic computer guided dental implant surgery: an in-vitro study. Medicina Oral, Patologia Oral y Cirugia Bucal **24**(1), 76–83 (2019)
7. Boesecke, R., et al.: Robot assistant for dental implantology. In: Niessen, W.J., Viergever, M.A. (eds.) MICCAI 2001. LNCS, vol. 2208, pp. 1302–1303. Springer, Heidelberg (2001). https://doi.org/10.1007/3-540-45468-3_204
8. Pires, J.N., Caramelo, F.J., Brito, P., Santos, J., Botelho, M.F.: Robotics in implant dentistry: stress/strain analysis. System overview and experiments. Ind. Rob. **33**(5), 373–380 (2006)
9. Kim, G., Seo, H., Im, S., Kang, D., Jeong, S.: A study on simulator of human-robot cooperative manipulator for dental implant surgery. In: IEEE International Symposium on Industrial Electronics, pp. 2159–2164. Insititute of Electrical and Electronics Engineers, Seoul, Korea (South) (2009)

10. Sun, X.Y., McKenzie, F.D., Bawab, S., Li, J., Yoon, Y., Huang, J.K.: Automated dental implantation using image-guided robotics: registration results. Int. J. Comput. Assist. Radiol. Surg. **6**(5), 627–634 (2011)
11. Syed, A.A., Soomro, A.M., Nighat, A., Duan, X.G., Qiang, H., Manzoor, F.: Telerobotic assisted dental implant surgery with virtual force feedback. Telkomnika Indonesian Journal of Electrical Engineering **12**(1), 450–458 (2013)
12. Yu, K., Uozumi, S., Ohnishi, K., Usuda, S., Kawana, H., Nakagawa, T.: Stereo vision based robot navigation system using modulated potential field for implant surgery. In: International Conference on Industrial Technology, pp. 493–498. Insititute of Electrical and Electronics Engineers, Seville, Spain (2015)
13. Li, J., Lam, W.Y.H., Chiu Hsung, R.T., Pow, E.H.N., Wang, Z.: A customizable, compact robotic manipulator for assisting multiple dental procedures. In: 2018 3rd International Conference on Advanced Robotics and Mechatronics, pp. 720–725. Insititute of Electrical and Electronics Engineers, Singapore, Singapore (2018)
14. Li, J., et al.: A compact dental robotic system using soft bracing technique. IEEE Robot. Autom. Lett. **4**(2), 1271–1278 (2019)
15. Cao, Z.G., et al.: Pilot study of a surgical robot system for zygomatic implant placement. Med. Eng. Phys. **75**, 72–78 (2020)
16. Cheng, K.J., et al.: Accuracy of dental implant surgery with robotic position feedback and registration algorithm: an in-vitro study. Comput. Biol. Med. **129**(2208) (2021)
17. Bai, S.Z., Zhao, Y.M.: Related research on dental implant robots. In: Handbook of the 15th National Symposium on Computer Applications in Stomatology, pp. 63–64. Guangxi China (2017)

Tri-axial Motion Sensing with Mechanomagnetic Effect for Human-Machine Interface

Zijie Liu, Chuxuan Guo, Hongwei Xue, and Jiajie Guo[✉]

The State Key Laboratory of Digital Manufacturing Equipment and Technology, School of Mechanical Science and Engineering, Huazhong University of Science and Technology, Wuhan 430074, China
jiajie.guo@hust.edu.cn

Abstract. Haptic sensing has been critical to human-machine interaction for wearable robotics, where interaction force sensing in the three-dimensional (3D) space play a key role in stimulating environmental proprioception, predicting human-motion intent and modulating robotic fine-motions. While normal pressure sensing has been widely explored in the uniaxial way, it is still a challenging task to capture shear forces along the tangential directions where typical capacitive or resistive sensing is difficult to implement. Moreover, integration of uniaxial force sensing modules in one unit would produce a bulky system that is impractical for wearable applications. Herein, this paper proposes a tri-axial motion sensing method based on mechanomagnetic effect, where both normal and shear forces can be captured through the magnetic field monitoring in the 3D space. A soft magnetic film was designed and fabricated to induce compliant deformations under tri-axial loads, and the flexible deformations can be captured through the magnetic flux changes via the hall-effect. Both simulation and experimental results are provided to justify the sensor performance and validate its potential applications to human-machine interaction.

Keywords: Tri-axial motion sensing · Flexible sensor · Mechanomagnetic effect · Wearable robotics · Human-machine interface (HMI)

1 Introduction

In the past decade, significant progress has been made in high-performance flexible sensors. Existing sensors are capable to capture uniaxial tension and compression with high sensitivity and wide sensing range [1, 2], however, in most practical applications in a three-dimensional (3D) space, loadings consisting of both normal and shear forces are featured with various directions. As one of the most important organs, human skin contains abundant mechanoreceptors, which can sense different types of external stimuli such as touch, pressure, sliding, twisting, and vibration by converting external mechanical stimuli into internal electrical signals. Dexterous robotic motions rely on tactile sensing [3], which the ability to measure normal and shear forces is critical for slip detection in real time. Besides, in medical practice, patients with severe diabetes will lose foot sensation, which further leads to skin rupture and infection on the feet in a

© The Author(s), under exclusive license to Springer Nature Switzerland AG 2022
H. Liu et al. (Eds.): ICIRA 2022, LNAI 13458, pp. 29–38, 2022.
https://doi.org/10.1007/978-3-031-13841-6_3

long run; related research suggests the shear force during walking as one of the main factors causing skin rupture [4]. It can be seen that monitoring multi-directional forces in the 3D space has been critical to both robotic and health care applications; however, it is still a challenging task to capture both normal and shear forces/deformations within one sensing unit. This paper proposes a tri-axial motion sensing method based on mechanomagnetic effect, where both normal and shear forces can be captured through the magnetic field monitoring in the 3D space.

Various novel sensors have been developed to capture pressures [5, 6], strains [7] and shear forces [3, 8] with excellent performance specifications. Flexible pressure sensors can be categorized as piezoresistive [10], capacitive [11], piezoelectric [12] and triboelectric [13] groups. Recent research on 3D flexible sensors focuses on the conductive materials and structural design. Conductive materials includes ultra-thin metal wires[4], nanomembrane [14, 15], liquid metals [16, 17], and nanoparticles [13]. Convex microstructures such as hemisphere [18] and pyramid [12] were employed in structural design of 3D force sensors to improve the sensitivity. However, most existing sensors target at uniaxial load measurement like normal force (pressure), and few attentions have been paid to measure shear or torsional deformations or combination of various loads. To address this issue, stacking different sensors to achieve multi-dimensional sensing becomes a competent candidate [19]; however, these solutions can be either complicated in structural design or time-consuming in data processing, which can lead to a high fabrication cost, low sampling rate, narrow communication bandwidth, or short battery life in practice.

To tackle the challenging problem of 3D force/deformation sensing with common flexible materials and simple structural designs, this paper proposes a flexible tri-axial motion sensor and its parametric solution model based on magnetics. The sensor is featured with a sandwich structure that consists of a flexible magnetic film, a silicone elastomer layer, and a Hall-effect sensor, where the soft magnetic film induces compliant deformations under tri-axial loads and its flexible deformations can be captured through the magnetic flux density changes via the hall-effect. The remainder of the paper offers the design principle of mechanomagnetic sensing, sensing model calibration, sensor performance characterization, and illustrative application to human-machine interface (HMI).

2 Principle of Mechanomagnetic Sensing

2.1 Bioinspired Design

Figure 1(a) shows the design concept of the proposed sensor inspired by skin mechanoreceptors. As the primary mechanoreceptors in the skin, Merkel disc under the spinosum is for pressure sensing and the Ruffini ending is for shear sensing [19], each of which works independently to detect mechanical stimuli in different directions. Inspired by the skin multi-dimensional force sensing, this paper proposes a flexible sensor based on the mechanomagnetic effect to emulate skin perception function. The permanent magnet magnetic field naturally has three-vector properties and spatial continuity. Therefore, the magnitude and direction of the 3D loads can be retrieved by measuring the magnetic flux density with the Hall-effect sensor which are highly compact and commercially available.

As shown in Fig. 1(b), the sensor consists of a magnetic film, compliant elastomer and commercial Hall-effect sensor (MELEXIS-MLX90393). When loads of different magnitudes and directions are applied to the sensor, the magnetic flux density around the Hall-effect sensor changes. Combined with the solution model proposed in Sect. 2.2, the spatial position change of the flexible magnetic film can be retrieved by monitoring the 3D magnetic field change, and then the 3D measurements can be further calibrated into 3D forces. Figure 1(c) shows the deformation of the elastomer under normal compression and shear force. As shown in Fig. 1(d), a normal load/deformation compresses the elastic layer along the axial direction, moving the magnetic film close to the Hall-effect sensor to increase the measured magnetic flux density. On the other hand, a shear force/deformation displaces the elastic layer in the radial direction, and the offset magnetic film will give rise to change of magnetic flux density in the corresponding direction. The same principle applies to cases with forces/deformations in the opposite directions. Considering the axial-symmetry of the sensor structure, the relation of B_x and U_x in Fig. 1(d) is also applicable to the case of B_y and U_y.

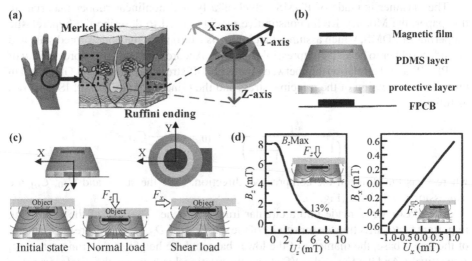

Fig. 1. Illustration of the 3D force sensor. (a) Illustration of the human skin structure. (Modified from Schmidt RF: Fundamentals of Sensory Physiology, 3rd ed. Berlin, Springer-Verlag, 1986) (b) Illustration of the 3D force sensor structure. (c) Illustration of the working principle of the 3D force sensor. (d) Left: The magnetic strength curve of the flexible magnet along the Z axis. Right: The magnetic strength curve of the flexible magnet along the X axis.

2.2 Mechanomagnetic Sensing and Parameter Optimization

In this section, a mechanomagnetic model based on the equivalent magnetic charge (EMC) model and the hyperelasticity model is established. The relationship between the magnetic flux density and the displacement of the magnetic film can be obtained from EMC model. The relationship between the displacement of magnetic film and the force can be obtained from the hyperelasticity model. Then the relationship between the force and the magnetic flux density can be obtained.

The expression of the EMC model is as follows:

$$
\begin{cases}
B_x = \frac{B_r}{4\pi} \int_0^t \int_0^{2\pi} \frac{(z-z_0)r_0 \cos\theta}{K} d\theta dz_0 \\
B_y = \frac{B_r}{4\pi} \int_0^t \int_0^{2\pi} \frac{(z-z_0)r_0 \sin\theta}{K} d\theta dz_0 \\
B_z = \frac{B_r}{4\pi} \int_0^t \int_0^{2\pi} \frac{r_0(r_0 \cos\theta - x)\cos\theta}{K} + \frac{r_0(r_0 \sin\theta - y)\cos\theta}{K} d\theta dz_0 \\
K = [(x - r_0 \cos\theta)^2 + (y - r_0 \sin\theta)^2 + (z - z_0)^2]^{\frac{3}{2}}
\end{cases}
\tag{1}
$$

where B_r is the remanent magnetization of the film, B_x, B_y and B_z are components of the magnetic flux density of the film along x, y, and z axes, t is the thickness of the film, (r_0, z_0) is the coordinates of the source, point and (x, y, z) is the coordinates of the film.

DNN is used to sole the inverse function because the expression involves a variety of complex caculations. Figure 2(a)(b)(c) show the specific parameters and the loss of the DNN. Figure 4(a)(b)(c) show the distribution of magnetic field strength in space.

The elastmer is made of PDMS, which is a typical nonlinear rubber material. In this paper, the Mooney-Rivlin constitutive model is used to describe the hyperelastic properties of PDMS, which assumes that rubber is isotropic in the undeformed state and considers rubber to be an incompressible material. According to the incompressibility of the PDMS and the relationship between the Kirchoff stress tensor and the Green strain tensor, the expression of the principal stress and the principal strain of PDMS is shown as follows:

$$
\frac{\delta_1}{2\left(1 - \varepsilon_1 - \frac{1}{(1-\varepsilon_1)^2}\right)} = C_{10} + \frac{1}{1 - \varepsilon_1} C_{01}
\tag{2}
$$

where ε_1 is the strain in the compressive direction, δ_1 is the stress and C_{10}, C_{01} are expression coefficients (Fig. 3).

The elastomer is made into a circular truncated cone. The size of the cone is an important factor affecting the sensitivity of the sensor. D_{up}, D_{down}, and h_0 are the diameter of the upper base, the diameter of the lower base and the height of the truncated cone, respectively. And the Fig. 4(d)(e)(f) shows the relationship between the displacement of the magnetic film and the force with the different size of the cone using FEA. Table 1 provides the relevant parameters involved in the model.

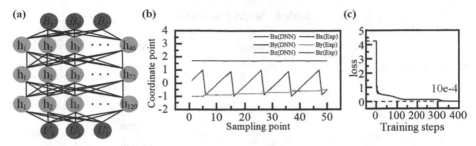

Fig. 2. (a) Illustration of the neural network model. (b) Comparison of DNN results and experimental results. (c) Training error curve of DNN

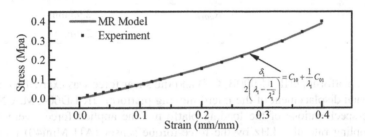

Fig. 3. Stress-strain curve of PDMS

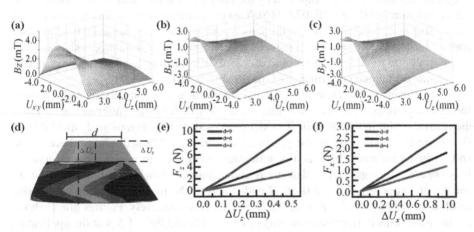

Fig. 4. (a) (b) (c) The magnetic strength curve of the flexible magnet along the z axis and x/y axis. (d) (e) (f) Force-displacement curves of circular cones of different sizes along the z/x axis.

3 Experimental Validation

3.1 Sensor Performance and Model Calibration

Figure 5(a) shows the compact size of the proposed tri-axial motion sensor against that of a commercial force-torque sensor (ATI Mini40). The loading test platform was setup as shown in Fig. 5(b), where the normal compression was vertically applied by

Table 1. Model parameters.

	Symbol	Value
Mechanical model	C_{01}	−0.03279
	C_{10}	0.14374
	D_{up}	6 mm
	D_{down}	9 mm
	h_0	4 mm
Magnetic field model	B_r	0.06 mT
	t	0.8 mm
	R_{corr}	2.95 mm
	r_0	2 mm

the loading platform (ZHIQU-990B, CN) and the shear force was exerted by adjusting the horizontal displacement of the micro-moving platform (JR-LD60-LM, CN). Table 2 lists the specifications of the loading platform. The applied forces were recorded at the sampling rate of 1 kHz by the force-torque sensor (ATI Mini40) through the data acquisition unit (National Instrument USB-6251, USA), and the corresponding magnetic flux densities were captured by the Hall-effect sensor and further collected by the microcontroller (STM32F407ZGT6). Two experiments were conducted to calibrate the sensing model and characterize the sensor performance: 1) In uniaxial loading tests, applied loads and corresponding magnetic flux densities were simultaneously measured to calibrate the force sensing model; and 2) Cyclic loading tests were performed to investigate the fatigue performance of the flexible sensor.

The calibration curves in Figs. 5(c, d) show linear relations between the applied forces and corresponding magnetic flux densities, which further calibrate the radius of the magnetic film in the theoretical model presented in the previous analysis (Table 1). Given the axial symmetry of the proposed sensor, the calibrated relation between B_y and F_y is not presented here as it is anticipated to be the same as that for B_x and F_x. It is observed in Figs. 5(c, d) that the sensing ranges for the normal compression F_z and shear forces (F_x, F_y) are 0–10 N and −1.5–1.5 N, respectively; and the sensing resolutions for F_z and (F_x, F_y) are 0.8 N and 0.4 N, respectively. Figures 5(e, f) shows the measurements during cyclic loading of Fz = 10 N and Fy = 1.5 N at the application frequency of 0.5 Hz for 800 times, which validates the sensing stability and repeatability of the flexible sensor (Table 3).

Table 2. Specification of experimental eqsuipment

Loading platform (ZHIQU-990B)

Loading velocity	Range of loading	Resolution of force	Accuracy of force
1–500 mm/min	0–50 N	0.001 N	<±1%

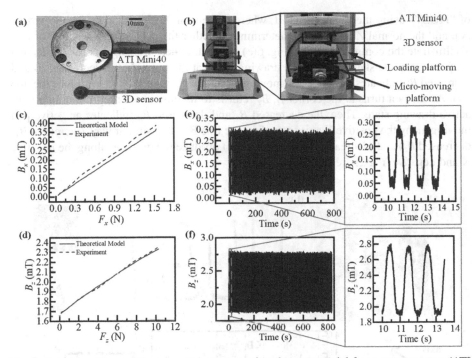

Fig. 5. (a) Comparison of the proposed sensor against the commercial force-torque sensor (ATI Mini 40). (b) Experimental setup for loading tests. (c) Measured B_x against the applied F_x. (d) Measured B_z against the applied F_z. (e) Cyclic test of the sensing unit at 10 N compression (800 times, loading frequency of 0.5 Hz). (f) Cyclic test of the sensing unit at 1.5 N shear force (800 times, loading frequency of 0.5 Hz).

Table 3. Specification of the flexible sensor

Range of loading on X/Y-axis	Range of loading on Z-axis	Resolution of force on X/Y-axis	Resolution of force on Z-axis
−1.5 N–1.5 N	0–10 N	0.4 N	0.8 N

3.2 Illustrative Application to HMI

Immediate application of the proposed flexible sensor is illustrated with the example of HMI that detects finger-tip planar motions and clicking operations to control a computer pointer to emulate manual sketch and writing with one finger. Figure 6(a) shows the prototype of the HMI, where two cable connects to the ground and power source while another two cables transmit the signals of magnetic flux densities. Given the above analysis, the 3D deformations of the compliant elastomer can be decoupled with the measured magnetic flux densities, and the finger-tip motions or loads can be retrieved as the reference command to the controlled pointer. Figure 6(b) demonstrates the writing of "HUST" using the finger-tip HMI, where the planar X-Y motion drives the virtual pen and the normal Z-axis motion determines whether the pen-writing is active or not. To illustrate the command details, Fig. 6(c) shows the measured signals for B_x, B_y and B_z for a rectangle sketch. When the drawing starts at the point A, the decreased B_z and increased B_y indicates an active pen moving along the positive Y axis to produce the line AB. As the pen turns at the corner B, B_z returns to its initial value representing a non-active drawing state. Then, the decreased B_z and decreased B_x indicates an active pen moving along the positive X axis to produce the line BC. In a similar way, (increased B_x, decreased B_z) and (decreased B_y, decreased B_z) produce the drawing along the negative X and negative Y axes, respectively.

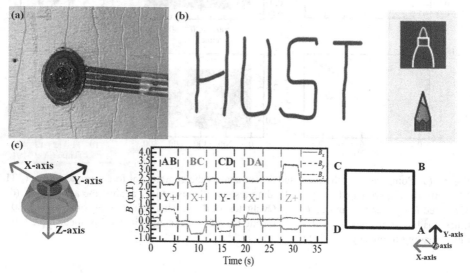

Fig. 6. Illustrative application to HMI. (a) The flexible tri-axial motion sensor. (b) "HUST" sketched with the flexible HMI. (c) Output signal of HMI.

4 Conclusion

This paper has developed a flexible sensor to capture tri-axial motions based on the mechanomagnetic effect, where the magnetic flux density changes with the compliant deformations of the magnetized film in an elastomer. The theoretical model has been employed to analyze the magnetic field, in which the Hall-effect sensor was used to capture the magnetic flux density vector in the three-dimensional space. Both numerical simulation and experimental results justify the high sensing resolution, good performance stability and low fabrication cost of the proposed tri-axial motion sensor. The immediate application of the tri-axial motion sensor is illustrated by the finger-tip control terminal that can achieve planar motion and clicking operations of a computer pointer to emulate manual sketch and writing with one finger. It is anticipated the proposed sensor has a wide application in potential for human-machine interaction, ranging from wearable robotics to medical rehabilitation, sport science, and so on.

Acknowledgements. This research was supported by the National Natural Science Foundation of China (Grant 51875221).

Appendix

Fabrication of Magnetic Film

The flexible magnetic film was fabricated with mixture of polydimethylsiloxane (PDMS; SYLGARD 184, Dow Corning) and NdFeB powders. The mass ratio of PDMS and NdFeB is 1:5. The mixture was cast into a thin film of the thickness about 0.3 mm using a knife coater. After curing for 30 min at 100 °C, the film was manually cut into a circular shape with the diameter of 4 mm and was automatically magnetized to saturation in the magnetization equipment (AMH-500 Hysteresisgraph, Laboratorio Elettrofisico).

Fabrication of Elastic Layer and Sensor Assembling

The elastic layer of the proposed sensor was made from PDMS (SYLGARD 184, Dow Corning) with the mass ratio of curing agents being 10:1. The air bubbles in the elastomer mixture was removed by the vacuum pump. Then the mixture was cast into a mold and cured for 30 min at 150 °C. After the magnetized film was cured, it was put into the groove on the upper surface of the elastomer, then the groove was filled with PDMS mixture to obtain the elastomer assembly that was cured for 5 min at 150 °C in an oven. Finally, the elastomer was bonded to the flexible circuit board with a silicone adhesive.

References

1. Palaniappan, V., et al.: Flexible m-tooth hybrid micro-structure-based capacitive pressure sensor with high sensitivity and wide sensing range. IEEE Sens. J. **21**(23), 26261–26268 (2021)
2. Xia, K., et al.: Carbonized chinese art paper-based high-performance wearable strain sensor for human activity monitoring. ACS Appl. Electron. Mater. **1**(11), 2415–2421 (2019)
3. Boutry, C.M., et al.: A hierarchically patterned, bioinspired e-skin able to detect the direction of applied pressure for robotics. Sci. Robot. **3**(24), eaau6914 (2018)
4. Shu, L., et al.: Monitoring diabetic patients by novel intelligent footwear system. In: 2012 International Conference on Computerized Healthcare (ICCH), pp. 91–94 (2012). https://doi.org/10.1109/ICCH.2012.6724478
5. Han, S., et al.: Battery-free, wireless sensors for full-body pressure and temperature mapping. Sci. Transl. Med. **10**(435), eaan4950 (2018)
6. Yang, J., et al.: Flexible, tunable, and ultrasensitive capacitive pressure sensor with microconformal graphene electrodes. ACS Appl. Mater. Interfaces **11**(16), 14997–15006 (2019)
7. Tan, C., et al.: A high performance wearable strain sensor with advanced thermal management for motion monitoring. Nat. Commun. **11**(1), 3530 (2020)
8. Liu, Y., et al.: E-textile battery-less displacement and strain sensor for human activities tracking. IEEE Internet Things J. **8**(22), 16486–16497 (2021)

9. Hongseok, O., Yi, G.-C., Yip, M., Dayeh, S.A.: Scalable tactile sensor arrays on flexible substrates with high spatiotemporal resolution enabling slip and grip for closed-loop robotics. Sci. Adv. **6**(46), eabd7795 (2020)
10. Ping, Y., Liu, W., Chunxin, G., Cheng, X., Xin, F.: Flexible piezoelectric tactile sensor array for dynamic three-axis force measurement. Sensors **16**(6), 819 (2016). https://doi.org/10.3390/s16060819
11. Choong, C.L., et al.: Highly stretchable resistive pressure sensors using a conductive elastomeric composite on a micropyramid array. Adv. Mater. **26**(21), 3451–3458 (2014)
12. Yue, W., et al.: Dynamic piezoelectric tactile sensor for tissue hardness measurement using symmetrical flexure hinges and anisotropic vibration modes. IEEE Sens. J. **21**(16), 17712–17722 (2021)
13. Sun, K., et al.: Hybrid architectures of heterogeneous carbon nanotube composite microstructures enable multiaxial strain perception with high sensitivity and ultrabroad sensing range. Small **14**(52), 1803411 (2018)
14. Kim, J., et al.: Stretchable silicon nanoribbon electronics for skin prosthesis. Nat. Commun. **5**, 5747 (2014)
15. Zhang, R.R., Lubin, J.A., Kuo, J.S.: Bioresorbable silicon electronic sensors for the brain. Neurosurgery **79**(4), N19 (2016)
16. Ponce Wong, R.D., Posner, J.D., Santos, V.J.: Flexible microfluidic normal force sensor skin for tactile feedback. Sens. Actuators, A **179**, 62–69 (2012)
17. Ali, S., et al.: Flexible capacitive pressure sensor based on PDMS substrate and ga-in liquid metal. IEEE Sens. J. **19**(1), 97–104 (2019)
18. Chen, S., et al.: Flexible piezoresistive three-dimensional force sensor based on interlocked structures. Sens. Actuators, A **330**, 112857 (2021)
19. Chen, H., et al.: Human skin-inspired integrated multidimensional sensors based on highly anisotropic structures. Mater. Horiz. **7**(9), 2378–2389 (2020)

Flexible or Continuum Robots
in Clinical Context

Model Predictive 6D Image-Based Visual Servoing for 3C Products Assembly

Ying Qu, Xiansheng Yang, Yixin Xie, and Yunjiang Lou[✉]

Harbin Institute of Technology Shenzhen, Shenzhen 518055, China
louyj@hit.edu.cn

Abstract. The application of visual servoing in robot assembly is very promising. In this paper, the 6-degree-of-freedom (DOF) image-based visual servoing (IBVS) control based on model predictive control (MPC) is implemented for 3C products assembly. Since the classical IBVS is calculated by multiplying the error times the pseudoinverse of an interaction matrix, it cannot handle constraints. Hence, the collision encountered in the process and the feature points out of the visual range cannot be solved well. Therefore, based on MPC, which can solve the servoing problems by transforming them into constrained optimization, this paper proposes a new MPC for the 3C products assembly system. In the new MPC, we estimate the depth information through image information, to solve the problem of deep collision, and propose a new cost function, which can better solve the problem of the system falling into a local optimal solution. Finally, the simulation verified in the ROS-Gazebo simulation results shows that the new control method is feasible and the control performance is more satisfactory.

Keywords: Image-based visual servoing (IBVS) · Model predictive control (MPC) · Assembly · Robot control

1 Introduction

Because of its fast speed and accuracy, the visual servoing is regarded as an effective method, which is widely used in the field of robotics, such as mobile multi-robot cooperative assembly tasks [1], unmanned aerial vehicles [2], physiological-motion tracking in medical robotics [3], and Railway fastener inspection [4], etc. The Vision-Based Control can be divided into three categories according to the feedback information: 1) position-based visual servoing (PBVS) which computes 3D information; 2) image-based visual servoing which uses directly 2D information extracted from images; 3) hybrid visual servoing (HBVS) which combines both 2D and 3D information in the same scheme. Since in the IBVS, the control input is dependent on the error between the current features and the desired features from the 2D image plane, simple proportion control can make the local convergence of visual features to obtain the desired effect. However,

This work was supported partially by the NSFC-Shenzhen Robotics Basic Research Center Program (No. U1913208) and partially by the Shenzhen Science and Technology Program (No. JSGG20210420091602008).

because traditional IBVS cannot handle constraints, the location may be far away from the expected area if the initial and desired locations are distant [5]. Hence the stability of the system is achieved only in the region near the desired location. At the same time, if feature loss occurs, it's difficult for the camera to regain the visual features, and then the visual servoing mission fails.

MPC can solve the above problems by transforming them into constrained optimization problems. Due to the form of optimization problems, constraints can be easily dealt with [5]. Because of this property, MPC is very suitable for robotic visual servoing systems with multiple constraints [6]. In [7], the MPC was proposed to tackle the under-actuation issues of the IBVS of a quadrotor, and the feasibility and stability of the MPC are guaranteed. Also, more and more researchers have applied the neural network in MPC [6], to solve a formulated optimization problem. By using a primal-dual neural network (PDNN) over a finite receding horizon, [8] iteratively solves a formulated QP problem to stabilize a physically constrained mobile robot. Also, in [9], PDNN is also utilized as a promising optimization tool to solve the QP problem, and the vision-based tube MPC was used in the control of multiple mobile robots, for handling the constraints and suppressing the disturbances. Based on the Model Predictive Path Integral control framework, [10] propose a real-time and inversion-free control method for IBVS, which can also be used in PBVS, without solving the online optimization problem which improves computing efficiency and reduce computing burden. In [11], by using tensor product model transformation, the constraints in MPC can be formulated as linear matrix inequalities and the success chance of visual servoing tasks increased. But for the assembly system, the main issue in these works is that the collision and the local optimal solution were not taken fully into account.

For MPC in IBVS, because the controller cannot directly obtain the depth information, it is easy to fall into the local optimal solution, i.e., the servoing is completed from the image features, while the actual servoing situation is not ideal. Meanwhile, in the servoing process of the assembly system, the collision between the moving assembly gripped part to the holding fixed part should be avoided. The above methods have not solved these problems.

In this paper, MPC based image visual servoing system will be considered in a 3C product assembly system. In the assembly process, if the initial deviation angle is too large, MPC is prone to fall into the local optimum, which leads to the further increase of the deviation angle, resulting in servoing failure. At the same time, during the assembly, the physical depth also needs to be guaranteed to prevent collisions during the assembly process. However, depth cannot be obtained directly from two-dimensional information of images, so it cannot be directly translated into constraint problems in MPC.

The main contributions of this paper include the following.

1) The depth constraint is expressed as the constraint of the state variables in the optimization problem, to carry out the depth constraint.
2) The cost function is proposed from a mode concerned only with the norm of the error vector to one also concerned with the difference of elements in the error vector. Therefore, the problem that is easy to fall into local optimization is solved to ensure the final servoing effect.

The paper is organized as follows. The 3C products assembly system and the main difficulties we had in the assembly are introduced in Sect. 2. Then, an MPC suitable for this assembly system is given in Sect. 3. In Sect. 4, the simulations illustrate the effectiveness of the proposed approach. Finally, the conclusion and future work are given in In Sect. 5.

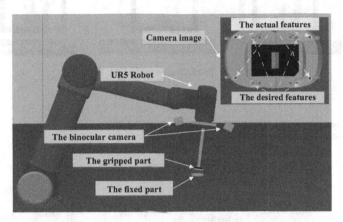

Fig. 1. Set up of robot assembly

2 System Description and Problem Statement

The main target of our system is to complete the accurate assembly of 3C products as shown in Fig. 2. After feature points are extracted from the camera, the error between the desired feature and the actual feature is calculated and input into MPC. Then according to the constraints of the predictive model and optimization function, MPC outputs the camera velocities to control the robot by minimizing the cost function. The visual servoing approach is shown in Fig. 3. This system is to complete the closed-loop control task through visual information.

The target of this paper is to use MPC to output the control input by minimizing the error. To independently verify the work of this target, image features are simplified into four points located at the four vertices of the assembly groove, as shown in Fig. 1. The task of this paper is to make the image information of the four actual feature points reach the position of the desired feature points, which image information comes from the binocular camera fixed on the mechanical arm with eye-in-hand configurations, to complete assembly.

Therefore, for the MPC, the goal is how to get the appropriate camera velocities through the two-dimensional information of the feature points, to minimize the error between the actual feature points and the desired feature points.

2.1 Depth Problem

In the servoing process, because there is only two-dimensional image information, and the system pays more attention to reducing the error of feature points, it's easy to occur

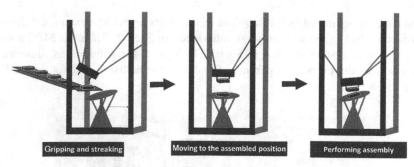

Fig. 2. 3C product assembly task flow

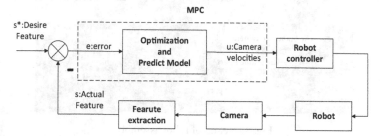

Fig. 3. The visual servoing approach

that the error is reduced from the perspective of the image plane as shown in Fig. 4., but the collision occurs in the actual process as shown in a 3D world, both in classical IBVS and general MPC.

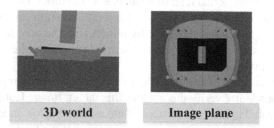

Fig. 4. From the image plane, the depth information cannot be seen directly. But from the 3D world coordinate system, it is obvious that the depth is over the physical constraint.

2.2 Local Optimal Solution

The main idea of MPC is to obtain the control input that minimizes the overall cost by predicting what will happen in a given unit of time, so if the prediction time is too short, say 1 or 2 periods, it is easy to fall into local optimum, namely to make cost down as soon as possible, by tilting, pretended to be completed the servoing from the image plane as shown in Fig. 5., but did not complete actually as shown in the 3D world. If the prediction time is too long, say thousands of periods, it will consume computing power and time, which is not conducive to real-time control.

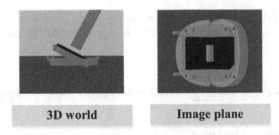

Fig. 5. From the image plane, the error between the actual feature points and the desired feature points is very small. But from the 3D world, it is obvious that the performance of the servoing task is poor.

3 Model Predictive Image-Base Visual Servoing for Six-DOF Robot Arm

3.1 Model Predictive Control

The goal of our system is to minimize the error

$$e(t) = s(t) - s^* \tag{1}$$

where $s(t) = [u_1(t), v_1(t), u_2(t), v_2(t), u_3(t), v_3(t), u_4(t), v_4(t)]^T$ is the four actual features in the image plane, and $[u_i(t), v_i(t)]$ is the actual feature of ith point at time t, and $s^*[u_1^*, v_1^*, u_2^*, v_2^*, u_3^*, v_3^*, u_4^*, v_4^*]^T$ is the desired features in the image plane.

To use MPC, a predictive model is necessary and it can get from the relationship between the time variation of the image feature $\dot{s}$ and the camera velocity can be written as [12]

$$\dot{s} = L_s \cdot u_c \tag{2}$$

where $u_c = [v_x, v_y, v_z, w_x, w_y, w_z]^T$ is the control input, and L_s is the interaction matrix. According to [12], the interaction matrix is written as follows:

$$L_s = \begin{bmatrix} -\frac{1}{Z} & 0 & \frac{u}{Z} & uv & -(1+u^2) & v \\ 0 & \frac{1}{Z} & \frac{v}{Z} & 1+v^2 & -uv & -u \end{bmatrix} \tag{3}$$

where Z is the depth of the feature to camera frame.

Let Z be constant and (2) can be approximated with the Newton-Euler method as

$$s(k+1) = s(k) + L_s T_e u_c(k) \tag{4}$$

where T_e. is the sample time.

Let the sample time $T_e = 1$ and therefore we obtain the predictive model as

$$s(k + 1|k) = s(k|k) + L_s u_c(k) \tag{5}$$

where $s(i|j)$ is the estimate for time i at time j.

Hence, at time k, the goal of our system is equivalent to the minimization of the following cost function.

$$J_{\mathrm{mpc}}(u) = \min \sum_{i=k+1}^{k+N} [s(i|k) - s^*]^T Q(i)[s(i|k) - s^*]|_{Q=I} \tag{6}$$

where N is the prediction horizon.

To express the camera speed explicitly in the cost function, we can let

$$x(i|j) = s(i|j) - s^* \tag{7}$$

According to (5) and (7), we can get

$$
\begin{bmatrix} x(k|k) \\ x(k+1|k) \\ \vdots \\ x(k+N|k) \end{bmatrix} = \begin{bmatrix} I \\ I \\ \vdots \\ I \end{bmatrix} x_k + \begin{bmatrix} 0 & 0 & \dots & 0 \\ L_s & 0 & \dots & 0 \\ L_s & L_s & \dots & 0 \\ \vdots & \vdots & \vdots & \vdots \\ L_s & L_s & \dots & L_s \end{bmatrix} \begin{bmatrix} u_c(k|k) \\ u_c(k+1|k) \\ u_c(k+2|k) \\ \vdots \\ u_c(k+N-1|k) \end{bmatrix} \tag{8}
$$

Further, (8) can be written as

$$X_K = M \cdot x_k + C \cdot U_K \tag{9}$$

And (6) becomes

$$
\begin{aligned}
& J_{\mathrm{mpc}}(u) \\
&= \min \sum_{i=k+1}^{k+N} [x(i|k)]^T Q[x(i|k)] \\
&= \min \begin{bmatrix} x(k|k) \\ x(k+1|k) \\ \vdots \\ x(k+N|k) \end{bmatrix}^T \begin{bmatrix} Q & & & 0 \\ & Q & & \\ & & \ddots & \\ 0 & & & Q \end{bmatrix} \begin{bmatrix} x(k|k) \\ x(k+1|k) \\ \vdots \\ x(k+N|k) \end{bmatrix} \\
&= \min X_K^T \cdot \tilde{Q} \cdot X_K \\
&= \min 2(x_k^T M^T \cdot \tilde{Q} \cdot C) \cdot U_K + U_K^T \cdot C^T \cdot \tilde{Q} \cdot C \cdot U_K + (x_k^T \cdot M^T \cdot \tilde{Q} \cdot M \cdot x_k)
\end{aligned} \tag{10}
$$

Since the last term of (10) is a constant, removing it does not affect the minimization of the optimization function, so that (10) can be simplified as

$$J_{\mathrm{mpc}}(u_c) = \min \frac{1}{2} U_K^T \cdot O \cdot U_K + P U_K|_{O=C^T \cdot \tilde{Q} \cdot C, P = x_k^T M^T \cdot \tilde{Q} \cdot C} \tag{11}$$

At this point, the camera speed can be expressed explicitly in the cost function, so it can be transformed into general quadratic programming for solving, such as a quadratic program (QP), and the constraints can be transformed into the optimization function. The standard expression of quadratic programming and constraint is

$$J_{\mathrm{mpc}}(u_c) = \min \frac{1}{2} U_K^T \cdot Q \cdot U_K + P U_K$$

$$\text{s.t. } lbA \leq A U_K \leq ubA$$

(12)

The constraints of feature points in the image plane can be expressed as

$$\begin{bmatrix} e(k|k) \\ e_{\min} \\ \vdots \\ e_{\min} \end{bmatrix} \leq \begin{bmatrix} e(k|k) \\ e(k+1|k) \\ \vdots \\ e(k+N|k) \end{bmatrix} \leq \begin{bmatrix} e(k|k) \\ e_{\max} \\ \vdots \\ e_{\max} \end{bmatrix}$$

(13)

where $e_{\min}$ and $e_{\max}$ are the limit on the minimum and maximum error.

To translate into the expression of optimization variables, (13) is further written as

$$E_{\min} \leq X_K \leq E_{\max}$$
$$E_{\min} \leq M \cdot x_k + C \cdot U_K \leq E_{\max}$$
$$E_{\min} - M \cdot x_k \leq C \cdot U_K \leq E_{\max} - M \cdot x_k$$

(14)

Hence in (12)

$$\begin{cases} lbA = E_{\min} - M \cdot x_k \\ ubA = E_{\max} - M \cdot x_k \\ A = C \end{cases}$$

(15)

3.2 Depth Constraint

In the servoing process, the depth can be expressed as

$$z(k) > z_{\min}$$

(16)

Since depth cannot be obtained directly, it is necessary to estimate depth information through image information [13].

Suppose there are two points in space, and their coordinates in camera coordinates are $P_1(X_1^c, Y_1^c, Z_1^c), P_2(X_2^c, Y_2^c, Z_2^c)$, then in the image plane, they can be expressed as

$$\begin{bmatrix} u_1 \\ v_1 \end{bmatrix} = \begin{bmatrix} f \frac{X_1^c}{Z_1^c} + u_0 \\ f \frac{Y_1^c}{Z_1^c} + v_0 \end{bmatrix}, \begin{bmatrix} u_2 \\ v_2 \end{bmatrix} = \begin{bmatrix} f \frac{X_2^c}{Z_2^c} + u_0 \\ f \frac{Y_2^c}{Z_2^c} + v_0 \end{bmatrix}$$

(17)

where f, u_0, v_0 are the known camera intrinsic.

Since the depth of the target point is similar in space under the system and $\sqrt{\Delta X^{c2} + \Delta Y^{c2}}$ can be viewed as a constant l, also the $\Delta u \approx 0$ in our system, it can be approximated as

$$\begin{cases} \Delta u = u_1 - u_2 = f\frac{X_1^c}{Z_1^c} - f\frac{X_2^c}{Z_2^c} \approx f\frac{X_1^c - X_2^c}{Z^C} = f\frac{\Delta X^c}{Z^C} \\ \Delta v = v_1 - v_2 = f\frac{Y_1^c}{Z_1^c} - f\frac{Y_2^c}{Z_2^c} \approx f\frac{Y_1^c - Y_2^c}{Z^C} = f\frac{\Delta Y^c}{Z^C} \end{cases} \tag{18}$$

Therefore,

$$\sqrt{\Delta u^2 + \Delta v^2} \approx \sqrt{\Delta v^2} \approx \frac{f}{Z^C}\sqrt{\Delta X^{c2} + \Delta Y^{c2}} \approx \frac{f \cdot l}{Z^C} \tag{19}$$

and

$$Z^C \approx f\frac{l}{\sqrt{\Delta v^2}} \stackrel{\Delta v > 0}{\approx} f\frac{l}{\Delta v} \tag{20}$$

We have now obtained the relationship between the estimate of depth and the image plane so that the depth constraint can be transformed as

$$f\frac{l}{\Delta v} > Z_{\min}^C \tag{21}$$

Since

$$\Delta v = v_1 - v_2 = (e_1 + v_1^*) - (e_2 + v_2^*) = e_1 - e_2 + v_1^* - v_2^* = e_1 - e_2 + \Delta v^* \tag{22}$$

where $e_1 = v_1 - v_1^*$, $e_2 = v_2 - v_2^*$

For P1 and P2, (21) can be further expressed as

$$\begin{bmatrix} 1 & -1 \end{bmatrix}\begin{bmatrix} e_1 \\ e_2 \end{bmatrix} < f\frac{l_1}{Z_{\min}^C} - \Delta v^* = z_{\text{limit}} \tag{23}$$

After extending (23) to the prediction horizon, the constraint can be expressed as

$$A \cdot X_K < Z_{\text{limit}} \tag{24}$$

where A is used to establish the relationship between the error of v, and Z_{limit} is made up of z_{limit}.

So far, the overall optimization function can be summarized as

$$\begin{aligned} J_{\text{mpc}}(u_c) &= \min \frac{1}{2}U_K^T \cdot O \cdot U_K + PU_K \\ s.t.\, E_{\min} - M \cdot x_k &\leq C \cdot U_K \leq E_{\max} - M \cdot x_k \\ A \cdot C \cdot U_K &< Z_{\text{limit}} - A \cdot M \cdot x_k \end{aligned} \tag{25}$$

3.3 Punishment for the Local Optimal Solution

We realize that when the local optimal situation occurs, although the overall error will decrease, the error difference of the same horizontal or vertical feature point will increase, so the new cost function needs to punish this situation.

Hence, the Q in (6) can change from I to

$$
\begin{aligned}
Q &= I + k_1 \cdot P_u + k_2 \cdot P_v \\
P_u &= p_{u12}^T \cdot p_{u12} + p_{u34}^T \cdot p_{u34} \\
P_v &= p_{v12}^T \cdot p_{v12} + p_{v34}^T \cdot p_{v34} \\
p_{u12} &= [0\ 1\ 0\ -1\ 0\ 0\ 0\ 0],\ p_{u34}= [0\ 0\ 0\ 0\ 0\ 1\ 0\ -1] \\
p_{v12} &= [1\ 0\ -1\ 0\ 0\ 0\ 0\ 0],\ p_{v34}= [0\ 0\ 0\ 0\ 1\ 0\ -1\ 0]
\end{aligned}
\tag{26}
$$

where $k_1, k_2 \in R$ can be adjusted according to the actual situation.

As shown in Fig. 6, measured by the original cost function, although the new MPC makes the value of the cost function higher (which is also the reason why the original cost function tends to fall into local optimal solution), the overall servoing effect is better. The specific results can be seen in Sect. 4. The reason is that when the initial angle is too large, if we want the parts back to horizontal, the cost function will increase. On the contrary, continuing to tilt can reduce the error in the image plane quickly, and therefore reduces the value of the cost function.

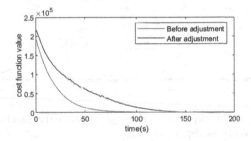

Fig. 6. The comparison of cost function values between the original MPC and new MPC

4 Simulations

To verify the effect of the new MPC adopted in this paper, the simulation will compare the effect of classical IBVS, original MPC, and new MPC from two aspects of deep collision and local optimum.

4.1 Simulation Environment

The simulation environment is shown in Fig. 1. A simulation experiment is carried out in ROS, and Gazebo is integrated into ROS as a physical simulation environment. A

6-DOF UR5 robot is used as the assembly robot in the simulation experiment. The robot is controlled in real-time, and the control frequency is 1000Hz.

A binocular camera is attached to the end-effector to obtain image information. The resolution of the camera is 1280 × 1024 and the pixel focal length is 3629.62. Since we only collect the image information near the assembly space, we crop the area of (640, 512) size including the assembly point.

4.2 Simulation of Depth Constrain Problems

With the same initial position, the effect of depth constrain is verified by comparing the classical IBVS, the original MPC, and the new MPC from the error in the image plane, the depth of features points, and the actual servoing effect. The results are shown is shown in Fig. 7. and Fig. 8.

Figure 7 shows that for the new MPC, the convergence of error in the image plane is better than that of the classical IBVS and the original MPC, and the depth of the features points for both the classical IBVS and the original MPC exceeds the minimum limit and the situation can be seen in Fig. 8 directly.

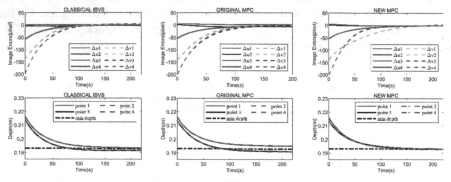

Fig. 7. The image error and the depth information (getting from the Gazebo) of four features for three IBVS methods to verify the depth constrain.

4.3 Simulation of the Local Optimal Solution

The setting of the experiment is the same as that in Sect. 4.2, but the setting of the initial position is changed. In this initial position, the local optimal solution is more obvious. The results are shown is shown in Fig. 9 and Fig. 10.

Compared with Fig. 7, the image error in Fig. 9 of the classical IBVS and the original MPC are similar to that in Fig. 7, but the over depth situation is more serious. It can also be seen from Fig. 10 that the actual feature points are not far from the desired points in the image plane, but the actual servoing situation is very poor, especially in the original MPC.

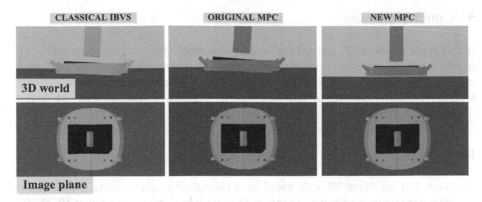

Fig. 8. The servoing result in the simulation world and the image plane for three IBVS methods.

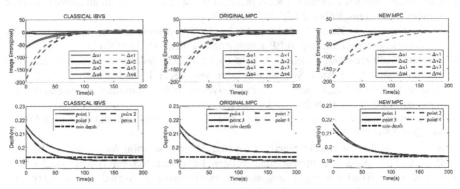

Fig. 9. The image error and the depth information (getting from the Gazebo) of four features for three IBVS methods to verify the solution of the local optimal solution.

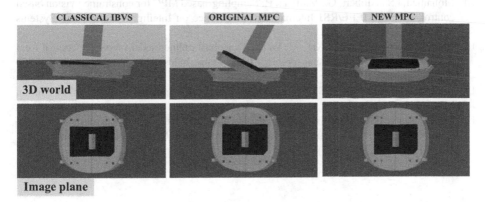

Fig. 10. The servoing result in the simulation world and the image plane for three IBVS methods.

5 Conclusion

In this paper, a new MPC method for the IBVS assembly system is proposed. By estimating depth, the system can complete the servoing task and solve the problem of depth expression in state variables, to realize its constraint. In addition, the problem of entering local optimization is avoided by verifying the cost function. Simulation results show that the new MPC is effective.

References

1. Wang, Y., Lang, H., de Silva, C.: Visual servo control and parameter calibration for mobile multi-robot cooperative assembly tasks. In: Proc. IEEE Int. Conf. Autom. Logist. (ICAL'08), pp. 635–639 (2008)
2. Guenard, N., Hamel, T., Mahony, R.: A practical visual servo control for an unmanned aerial vehicle. IEEE Trans. Robot. **24**(2), 331–340 (2008)
3. Ott, L., Nageotte, F., Zanne, P., de Mathelin, M.: Robotic assistance to flexible endoscopy by physiological-motion tracking. IEEE Trans. Robot. **27**(2), 346–359 (2011)
4. Aytekin, C., Rezaeitabar, Y., Dogru, S., Ulusoy, I.: Railway fastener inspection by real-time machine vision. IEEE Trans. Syst. Man Cybern. Syst. **45**(7), 1101–1107 (2015)
5. Allibert, G., Courtial, E., Chaumette, F.: Predictive control for constrained image-based visual servoing. IEEE Trans. Rob. **26**(5), 933–939 (2010)
6. Wu, J., et al.: A survey of learning-based control of robotic visual servoing systems. J. Frankl. Inst. **359**, 556–577 (2022)
7. Roque, R., et al.: Fast model predictive image-based visual servoing for quadrotors. In: 2020 IEEE/RSJ International Conference on Intelligent Robots and Systems (IROS). IEEE (2020)
8. Fan, K., et al.: Visual servoing of constrained mobile robots based on model predictive control. IEEE Trans. Sys. Man Cybernet. Sys. **47**(99), 1428–1438 (2016)
9. Li, Z., et al.: Robust vision-based tube model predictive control of multiple mobile robots for leader-follower formation. IEEE Trans. Indust. Electro. **99**, 1–1 (2019)
10. Mohamed, I.S., Allibert, G., Martinet, P.: Sampling-based MPC for constrained vision based control. In: 2021 IEEE/RSJ International Conference on Intelligent Robots and Systems (IROS), pp. 3753-3758 (2021)
11. Hajiloo, A., Keshmiri, M., Xie, W., Wang, T.: Robust online model predictive control for a constrained image-based visual servoing. IEEE Trans. Industr. Electron. **63**(4), 2242–2250 (2016)
12. Chaumette, F., Hutchinson, S.: Visual servo control. I. basic approaches. IEEE Robot. Autom. Mag. **13**(4), 82–90 (2006)
13. Wu, J., Cheng, M.: Depth estimation of objects with known geometric model for IBVS using an eye-in-hand camera. International Conference on Advanced Robotics and Intelligent Systems (ARIS) **2017**, 88–935 (2017)

3D Visual Servo Control of a Flexible Endoscope with RCM Constraint

Jian Li[1], Xue Zhang[1], Yisen Huang[1], Xiao Luo[3], Ke Xie[1], Yitian Xian[1], Philip Waiyan Chiu[1,2,3,4], and Zheng Li[1,2,3,4](✉)

[1] Department of Surgery, The Chinese University of Hong Kong, Hong Kong, China
lizheng@cuhk.edu.hk
[2] Chow Yuk Ho Technology Centre for Innovative Medicine, The Chinese University of Hong Kong, Hong Kong, China
[3] Multi-scale Medical Robotics Ltd., The Chinese University of Hong Kong, Hong Kong, China
[4] Li Ka Shing Institute of Health Science, The Chinese University of Hong Kong, Hong Kong, China

Abstract. In minimally invasive surgery, endoscopes provide visual guidance to surgical operations. To tackle the problems caused by traditional hand-held endoscope, robots are introduced to steer the endoscope.

Image based instrument tracking is an effective way to ease the human-robot-interaction. In this article, we aim to design a 3D visual servoing scheme for a robotic flexible surgical endoscope with algorithm-based RCM constraint. The endoscope consists of two identical cameras and is based on continuum mechanism, mounted on the tip of a UR5 robot arm.

This article conducts kinematic modeling of the flexible robotic endoscope to get the mapping from joint space to task space. Then the relationship between depth and joint variables is derived. Finally, to validate the constrained visual servoing scheme, simulation is conducted in V-REP. The results show that it is feasible and effective to achieve 3D visual servoing of the flexible robotic endoscope with RCM constraints.

Keywords: Robotic flexible endoscope · 3D visual servo control · Remote center of motion

1 Introduction

Minimally invasive surgery (MIS) is committed to minimizing surgical incisions, so as to reduce patient pain, shorten hospitalization, and reduce complications [1]. During MIS, endoscopes help surgeons to observe internal organs or tissue in details. Conventionally, the endoscope is held and operated by an assistant manually. But the endoscope assistant may not always work perfectly with the surgeons and faces problem of fatigue and misoperation, albeit through lengthy learning process. Thus, it is a practical way of introducing robotic system to simplify surgical procedure and enhance the stability of camera view.

© The Author(s), under exclusive license to Springer Nature Switzerland AG 2022
H. Liu et al. (Eds.): ICIRA 2022, LNAI 13458, pp. 53–63, 2022.
https://doi.org/10.1007/978-3-031-13841-6_5

Nowadays, a wide variety of endoscope systems integrated with robots have been developed, equipped with different kinds of novel human-robot interaction methods. Among these, the most popular technologies are teleoperation, voice control, eye tracking control, etc. [2]. These robots could replace endoscopy assistants. However, it shift the workload to the surgeons, forcing them to devote more attention to the endoscope control. So visual servo control scheme has been adopted to various commercially available robotic assisted endoscope systems to lower the surgeons' burden [3].

Recently, researchers has brought the continuum mechanism into endoscope system to enhance dexterity and safety [4–6]. These flexible endoscope systems outperform traditional rigid endoscopes in both dexterity and safety.

Robotic surgical system like da Vinci Surgical System, Senhance Robotic Operating System are specially designed for clinical usage, and their fancy prices prevent them from being widely used. Naturally, it is practical to integrate surgical systems into commercially available collaborative robot arms [4, 7]. However, when using cobots in MIS, the endoscope should be constrained by the remote center of motion (RCM), namely, the lateral speed of the endoscope should be set to zero at the RCM point. The RCM constraint aims to enable the endoscope inserting through the trocar.

Moreover, in most cases surgeons prefer to keep the instrument at the proper distance from the camera and to maintain it at a reasonable area in field of view (FOV). But traditional monocular endoscope can only obtain two-dimensional image information. Some researchers proposed a method based on image moment to realize visual tracking along the direction of depth [8], however, the depth information is still lacking and it is difficult for surgeons to set and adjust the desired value of image moment. Another way is to design a state observers to estimate depth information, provided that the monocular camera velocity needs to satisfy the constraints of the control system [9], which is not practical in clinical application.

Based on the issues above, in this paper, a flexible endoscope equipped with stereo vision and a collaborative robotic arm are combined to realize three-degree-of-freedom visual servoing under the RCM constraint. The remainder of this article is organized as follows. Section 2 establishes the kinematics model of the endoscope containing the UR5 robot and the flexible part. In Sect. 3, stereo vision for 3D visual tracking is introduced. In Sect. 4, the control framework together with the RCM constraint is detailed. In Sect. 5, the feasibility of the proposed method is verified through simulation. Finally, conclusions are given in Sect. 6.

2   Kinematic Modelling

In this section, the kinematic modelling of the robotic flexible endoscope is conducted. Figure 1 shows the outline of the system, in which the stereo camera is located at the tip of flexible part based on the UR5 robot arm. A rigid shaft inserts through the RCM point which is expressed with a red point, and the green ball in Fig. 1 represents the tracking target.

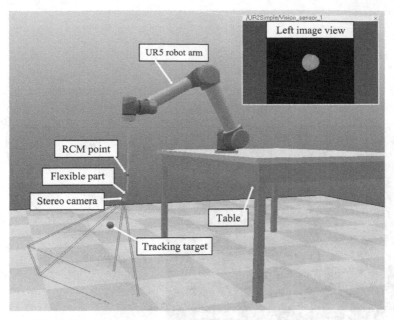

Fig. 1. Overview of robotic flexible endoscope with stereo camera

Based on the conventional Denavit–Hartenberg (DH) method [10], the coordinate frames of the system is shown in Fig. 2. For frames $\{O_0\}$ to $\{O_7\}$, the transformation matrices can be generated as:

$$T_i^{i-1} = \begin{bmatrix} c_{q_i} & -s_{q_i}c_{\alpha_i} & s_{q_i}s_{\alpha_i} & a_i c_{q_i} \\ s_{q_i} & c_{q_i}c_{\alpha_i} & -c_{q_i}s_{\alpha_i} & a_i s_{q_i} \\ 0 & s_{\alpha_i} & c_{\alpha_i} & d_i \\ 0 & 0 & 0 & 1 \end{bmatrix} \tag{1}$$

in which $i = 0, 1, \ldots, 7$ representing the number of frames, q_i, α_i, d_i, a_i are DH parameters of the robot, $c_{q_i}, s_{q_i}, c_{\alpha_i}, s_{\alpha_i}$ represent $\cos(q_i), \sin(q_i), \cos(\alpha_i), \sin(\alpha_i)$ correspondingly.

For the flexible part, the kinematics model is derived based on [11]:

$$T_8^7 = \begin{bmatrix} s_\varphi^2 + c_\theta c_\varphi^2 & -s_\varphi c_\varphi(1-c_\theta) & c_\varphi s_\theta & \frac{l}{\theta}(1-c_\theta)c_\varphi \\ -s_\varphi c_\varphi(1-c_\theta) & c^2\varphi + c_\theta s_\varphi^2 & s_\varphi s_\theta & \frac{l}{\theta}(1-c_\theta)s_\varphi \\ -c_\varphi s_\theta & -s_\varphi c_\theta & c_\theta & \frac{l}{\theta}(s_\theta) \\ 0 & 0 & 0 & 1 \end{bmatrix} \tag{2}$$

where φ quantifies the angle of bending direction and θ denotes the extent of bending, l is the length of the flexible part, and $c_\varphi, s_\varphi, c_\theta, s_\theta$ denote $\cos(\varphi), \sin(\varphi), \cos(\theta), \sin(\theta)$, accordingly.

Lastly, for the transformation from frame $\{O_8\}$ to $\{O_c\}$, the relationship is obvious:

$$T_c^8 = \begin{bmatrix} I & t_c \\ 0^T & 1 \end{bmatrix} \tag{3}$$

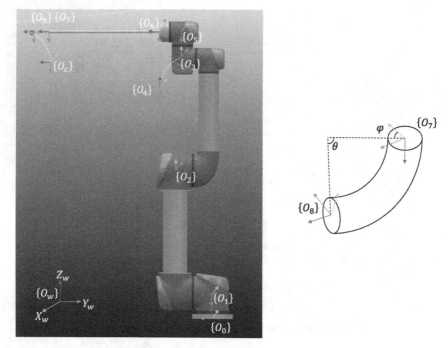

Fig. 2. Kinematic modelling of the flexible endoscope system

in which $I \in \mathbb{R}^{3\times3}$ is an identity rotation matrix, and $t_c = \begin{bmatrix} 0 & 0 & z_c \end{bmatrix}^T$ is the translation vector from frame $\{O_8\}$ to $\{O_c\}$.

After get the mapping from the base frame to camera frame, differential kinematics equation is utilized to get the relationship between the joint velocities and the end-effector(the stereo camera) linear and angular velocity:

$$\begin{bmatrix} v_c^0 \\ \omega_c^0 \end{bmatrix} = \begin{bmatrix} J_p \\ J_O \end{bmatrix} \dot{q} \tag{4}$$

where v_c^0 and ω_c^0 are the linear and angular velocity of the tip camera frame relative to the base frame of the system. $J_p \in \mathbb{R}^{3\times8}$ and $J_O \in \mathbb{R}^{3\times8}$ are geometric Jacobian matrices for linear and angular velocity, correspondingly; $\dot{q} = \begin{bmatrix} \dot{q}_1 & \dot{q}_2 & \dot{q}_3 & \dot{q}_4 & \dot{q}_5 & \dot{q}_6 & \dot{\varphi} & \dot{\theta} \end{bmatrix}^T \in \mathbb{R}^8$ representing the joint velocity of the robotic system.

3 3D Visual Tracking Scheme

This section shows the principle of both 2D visual servo control of classical monocular endoscope systems and 3D visual tracking with a stereo endoscope system. The basic goal for visual servo control in surgical application is tracking the surgical instrument to the appropriate position in the field of view by adjusting the motion of endoscope automatically.

3.1   Classical Image-Based Visual Servo for Monocular Camera

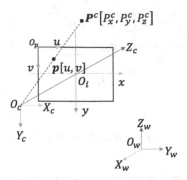

Fig. 3. Camera frame transformation

For a monocular camera, the image-based visual servo framework is to establish the relationship between the projection of the target point and the camera motion. As Fig. 3 shows, consider a point in camera frame $P^c = \left[P^c_x, P^c_y, P^c_z \right]$ and its projection onto the pixel frame of the camera $p = [u, v]$, the mapping between the velocity of the 2D point $\dot{p}$ that of the target point relative to the camera is derived based on [12]:

$$\dot{p} = \begin{bmatrix} \dot{u} \\ \dot{v} \end{bmatrix} = J_{img} \begin{bmatrix} v_c \\ \omega_c \end{bmatrix} \tag{5}$$

in which v_c and ω_c are the linear and angular velocity of the camera relative to the target point, and J_{img} is called image Jacobian matrix which is expressed as:

$$J_{img} = \begin{bmatrix} -\frac{f\alpha}{P^c_z} & 0 & \frac{(u-u_0)}{P^c_z} & \frac{(u-u_0)(v-v_0)}{f^2\alpha} & -\frac{f^2\alpha^2 + (u-u_0)^2}{f^2\alpha^2} & \frac{(v-v_0)}{f} \\ 0 & -\frac{f}{P^c_z} & \frac{(v-v_0)}{P^c_z} & \frac{f^2 + (v-v_0)^2}{f^2} & -\frac{(u-u_0)(v-v_0)}{f^2\alpha} & -\frac{(u-u_0)}{f} \end{bmatrix} \tag{6}$$

where f is the focal length of the camera, α is the ratio of the pixel dimensions, u_0, v_0 are the coordinates of the principal point.

3.2   Stereo Vision and 3D Visual Servoing Framework

For a stereo endoscope consisting of two identical cameras shown in Fig. 4, $\{O_{cl}\}$, $\{O_{il}\}$, $\{O_{pl}\}$ and $\{O_{cr}\}$, $\{O_{ir}\}$, $\{O_{pr}\}$ are camera frames, image frames and pixel frames of left and right view, respectively.

Similar to the case of image-based monocular visual servo control, the target point in left or right camera frame $P^c = \left[P^c_x, P^c_y, P^c_z \right]$ is projected onto left image and right image planes and get $p_l = [u_l, v_l]$ and $p_r = [u_r, v_r]$, accordingly, which denotes the projection onto left and right pixel frames.

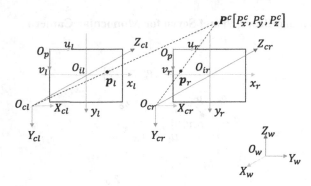

Fig. 4. Stereo camera frame transformation

In Fig. 4, $O_{cl}O_{cr} = b$ is the baseline of the stereo endoscope. Based on the principle of triangulation [13], the depth of the target point can be calculated by:

$$P_z^c = \frac{bf}{u_l - u_r} = \frac{bf}{d} \tag{7}$$

in which d means the disparity of the target point center in left and right pixel frames.

Inspired by [14], the goal of 3D visual servo is composed of two parts: keeping the projection of the target point in the left pixel frame in the middle of the field of view; keeping the camera at a suitable distance from the target point.

For the first goal, it is obvious to generate the relationship between joint space and velocity of target in pixel frame by classical 2D image-based visual servoing:

$$\frac{d}{d\dot{q}}\begin{bmatrix} \dot{u}_l \\ \dot{v}_l \end{bmatrix} = J_{imgl}\begin{bmatrix} R_0^c & 0 \\ 0 & R_0^c \end{bmatrix} J_{robot} \tag{8}$$

where J_{imgl} is the left image Jacobian matrix, $J_{robot} = \begin{bmatrix} J_p \\ J_O \end{bmatrix}$ represents the Jacobian matrix from the base frame to the tip camera frame of the robot system, R_0^c is the rotation matrix from the camera frame to the base frame.

The mapping between joint variables and the distance from target point to camera is derived by:

$$\frac{d\dot{P}_z^c}{d\dot{q}} = \left(\frac{\partial \dot{P}_z^c}{\partial \dot{p}_l}\frac{d\dot{p}_l}{d\dot{q}} + \frac{\partial \dot{P}_z^c}{\partial \dot{p}_r}\frac{d\dot{p}_r}{d\dot{q}} \right) = \left(\frac{\partial \dot{P}_z^c}{\partial \dot{p}_l} + \frac{\partial \dot{P}_z^c}{\partial \dot{p}_r} \right)\begin{bmatrix} J_{imgl} \\ J_{imgr} \end{bmatrix}\begin{bmatrix} R_0^c & 0 \\ 0 & R_0^c \end{bmatrix} J_{robot} \tag{9}$$

in which J_{imgr} represents the right image Jacobian matrix, and $\left(\frac{\partial \dot{P}_z^c}{\partial \dot{P}_l} + \frac{\partial \dot{P}_z^c}{\partial \dot{P}_r} \right) = \left[\frac{fb}{(u_l-u_r)^2}, 0, \frac{-fb}{(u_l-u_r)^2}, 0 \right]$.

Thus, the mapping from the 3D visual servo goal to joint space is:

$$\begin{bmatrix} \dot{u}_l \\ \dot{v}_l \\ \dot{P}_z^c \end{bmatrix} = J_{stereo}\begin{bmatrix} R_0^c & 0^{3\times3} \\ 0^{3\times3} & R_0^c \end{bmatrix} J_{robot}\dot{q} \tag{10}$$

where $J_{stereo} \in \mathbb{R}^{3\times6}$ is defined as the Jacobian matrix for stereo visual servo control:

$$J_{stereo} = \begin{bmatrix} 1 & 0 & 0 & 0 \\ 0 & 1 & 0 & 0 \\ \frac{fb}{(u_l-u_r)^2} & 0 & \frac{-fb}{(u_l-u_r)^2} & 0 \end{bmatrix} \begin{bmatrix} J_{imgl} \\ J_{imgr} \end{bmatrix} \tag{11}$$

4 Control Framework with RCM Constraint

4.1 Algorithm-Based RCM Constraint

In surgical robot systems, there are normally two ways to achieve the remote center of motion constraint, one is from the mechanism design [15, 16], and the other is algorithm-based method through the differential kinematics model [17, 18]. The mechanism-based RCM constraint is reliable but special design is required in the structure. Consequently, it is generally expensive and cannot be generalized between different systems. By contrast, the algorithm-based method suits different surgical systems well and it is convenient to realize.

In this paper, the kinematics-based RCM constraint is adopted illuminated by [17] and [19]. As for the system in this paper, the position and velocity of the actual RCM point is as follows:

$$p_{rcm} = p_6 + \mu(p_7 - p_6), 0 \leq \mu \leq 1 \tag{12}$$

where p_{rcm}, p_6 and $p_7 \in \mathbb{R}^3$ representing the special position of the RCM point, the sixth and seventh frame; $\mu \in \mathbb{R}$ is a scale factor reflecting the relative position of the RCM point in line segment $O_6 O_7$, which is treated as a joint variable.

The mapping of RCM motion control to augmented joint space is derived from (12):

$$\dot{p}_{rcm} = \begin{bmatrix} J_{p6} + \mu(J_{p7} - J_{p6}) & 0^{3\times2} & p_7 - p_6 \end{bmatrix} \begin{bmatrix} \dot{q} \\ \dot{\mu} \end{bmatrix} \tag{13}$$

The first matrix at the right side in (13) is defined as the RCM Jacobian matrix, $J_{RCM} \in \mathbb{R}^{3\times9}$, in which J_{p6} and J_{p6} are the Jacobian matrix. Hence, the RCM constraint can be achieved by a controller whose goal is to force the velocity of p_{rcm} to zero.

4.2 Control Framework for 3D Visual Servo with RCM Constraint

Based on Sec. 3 and Sec. 4.1, the total task space including the 3D visual servo and RCM constraint can be mapped to the augmented joint space. Also, while tracking the target automatically, it is expected to limit the motion range of the robotic arm, and to achieve the tasks more through the flexible joints to reduce the occupation and interference of the surgeons' operating space. Mathematically, the problem is expressed as:

$$\min \frac{1}{2}\dot{q}^T \Lambda \dot{q}$$

$$\text{s.t. } \dot{t}_d = J\dot{q}_{aug} \tag{14}$$

in which $\Lambda \in \mathbb{R}^{8\times 8}$ is a weighted matrix to regulate the extent of movement of each joint; $\dot{t}_d = \begin{bmatrix} \dot{u}_l & \dot{v}_l & \dot{P}_z^c & \dot{p}_{rcm}^T \end{bmatrix}^T$ represents the total task space for constrained 3D visual servoing; $J = \begin{bmatrix} J_{stereo} J_{robot} 0^{3\times 1} \\ J_{RCM} \end{bmatrix} \in \mathbb{R}^{6\times 9}$; $\dot{q}_{aug} = \begin{bmatrix} \dot{q} \\ \dot{\mu} \end{bmatrix}$ is the augmented joint space in velocity level.

The goal of the task space is to realize 3-DoF visual tracking and make the RCM point coincide with a fixed point in Cartesian frame, and the total error is expressed as:

$$e = \begin{bmatrix} u_l - u_l^* & v_l - v_l^* & P_z^c - P_z^{c*} & \left(p_{rcm} - p_{rcm}^* \right)^T \end{bmatrix}^T \tag{15}$$

in which u_l^*, v_l^*, P_z^{c*} and p_{rcm}^* are the desired value of u_l, v_l, P_z^c and p_{rcm}.

The controller for the system is designed based on the error function and the analytical solution of (14):

$$\dot{q} = \Lambda^{-1} J^T \left(J \Lambda^{-1} J^T \right)^{-1} K\dot{e} \tag{16}$$

5   Simulation Validations

The proposed scheme is verified through a kinematics simulation which applies the co-simulation of CoppeliaSim and MATLAB (Fig. 5).

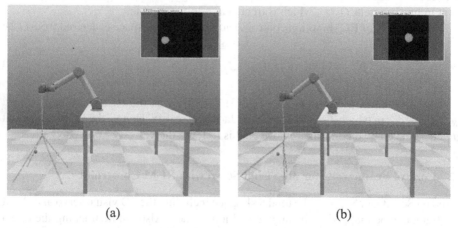

(a)   (b)

Fig. 5. Simulation of 3D visual tracking with RCM constraint. (a) Initial state. (b) Final state

In the simulation, initially, the tracking target is placed off-center of FOV. The robotic endoscope tracks the target and adjust the FOV automatically with the proposed scheme. Consequently, the target is kept at the center of FOV with a proper distance.

The initial value of the augmented joint vector is set to be $q_{aug0} = [0\ \frac{\pi}{6}\ \frac{\pi}{2}\ -\frac{\pi}{6}\ -\frac{\pi}{2}\ 0\ 0\ 0.001\ 0.7]^T$. For the stereo camera system, $f = 443.32$, $b = 0.01$, $u_0 = v_0 = 256$ and $\alpha = 1$. The weighted matrix is set as $\Lambda = \text{diag}([1\ 1\ 1\ 1\ 1\ 1\ \frac{1}{150}\ \frac{1}{150}])$. The proportional parameter in the controller $K = \text{diag}([20\ 18\ 15\ 200\ 200\ 200])$ and the desired depth $P_z^{c*} = 0.15\,\text{m}$.

The augmented joint variables are updated by means of Euler's method:

$$q_{aug}(t_{k+1}) = q_{aug}(t_k) + \dot{q}_{aug}(t_k)\Delta t$$

in which t_k is the time at k^{th} step, Δt is the unit time step size which is set as 0.005s in this paper.

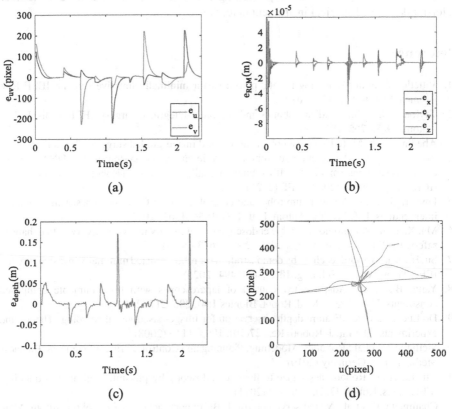

Fig. 6. Simulation results. (a) Tracking error of the pixel position. (b) Error of the RCM point. (c) Tracking error of the depth. (d) Trajectory of the target in pixel frame.

The simulation results are shown in Fig. 6. When manually moving the target in any direction in Cartesian space, the method proposed in this paper can always force the target quickly converge to the center of the FOV and maintain a desired distance under the RCM constraints.

6 Conclusion

This paper implemented 3D visual servo control with the RCM constraint on a flexible robotic endoscope. Using a binocular endoscope module, the mapping from depth of the target to robot joint space is analysed and the tracking scheme along the z-axis of the camera frame is realized. We adopted the algorithm-based RCM constraint which take the motion constraint as a secondary task except for visual tracking. The simulation results show the feasibility of the proposed method. This paper is a good attempt to combine the 3D visual tracking with programmable RCM and it is convenient to generalized to any other robotic endoscopes with stereo camera.

In future work, we will build the stereo endoscope system based on flexible mechanism and test the proposed method experimentally. Moreover, in order to promote the clinical application, deep learning methods will be introduced to replace color-marker-based surgical instrument detection.

References

1. Vitiello, V., et al.: Emerging robotic platforms for minimally invasive surgery. IEEE Rev. Biomed. Eng. **6**, 111–126 (2012)
2. Taylor, R.H., et al.: Medical robotics and computer-integrated surgery. IEEE Trans. Robot. Autom. **19**(5), 765–781 (2003)
3. Abedin-Nasab, M. (ed.): Handbook of robotic and image-guided surgery. Elsevier (2019)
4. Zhang, X., et al.: An autonomous robotic flexible endoscope system with a DNA-inspired continuum mechanism. In: 2021 IEEE International Conference on Robotics and Automation (ICRA), pp. 12055–12060. IEEE (2021)
5. Dwyer, G., et al.: A continuum robot and control interface for surgical assist in fetoscopic interventions. IEEE Robot. Autom. Lett. **2**(3), 1656–1663 (2017)
6. Ma, X., et al.: Autonomous flexible endoscope for minimally invasive surgery with enhanced safety. IEEE Robot. Autom. Lett. **4**(3), 2607–2613 (2019)
7. Su, H., et al.: Toward teaching by demonstration for robot-assisted minimally invasive surgery. IEEE Trans. Autom. Sci. Eng. **18**(2), 484–494 (2021)
8. Yang, B., et al.: Adaptive fov control of laparoscopes with programmable composed constraints. IEEE Trans. Med. Robot. Bionics **1**(4), 206–217 (2019)
9. De Luca, A., et al.: Feature depth observation for image-based visual servoing: Theory and experiments. The Int. J. Roboti. Res. **27**(10), 1093–1116 (2008)
10. Siciliano, B., et al.: Robotics: Modelling, Planning and Control. Springer Science & Business Media, Berlin, Germany (2010)
11. Ott, L., et al.: Robotic assistance to flexible endoscopy by physiological-motion tracking. IEEE Trans. Robot. **27**(2), 346–359 (2011)
12. Chaumette, F., et al.: Visual servo control. I. Basic approaches. IEEE Robot. Autom. Mag. **13**(4), 82–90 (2006)
13. Szeliski, R.: Computer vision: algorithms and applications. Springer Science & Business Media (2010)
14. Ma, X., et al.: Visual servo of a 6-DOF robotic stereo flexible endoscope based on da Vinci Research Kit (dVRK) system. IEEE Robot. Autom. Lett. **5**(2), 820–827 (2020)
15. Huang, Y., et al.: A surgeon preference-guided autonomous instrument tracking method with a robotic flexible endoscope based on dVRK platform. IEEE Robot. Autom. Lett. **7**(2), 2250–2257 (2022)

16. He, Y., et al.: Automatic surgical field of view control in robot-assisted nasal surgery. IEEE Robot. Autom. Lett. **6**(1), 247–254 (2020)
17. Aghakhani, N., et al.: Task control with remote center of motion constraint for minimally invasive robotic surgery. In: 2013 IEEE international conference on robotics and automation (ICRA), pp. 5807–5812. IEEE (2013)
18. Su, H., et al.: Bilateral teleoperation control of a redundant manipulator with an rcm kinematic constraint. In: 2020 IEEE International Conference on Robotics and Automation (ICRA), pp. 4477–4482. IEEE (2020)
19. Li, W., et al.: An accelerated finite-time convergent neural network for visual servoing of a flexible surgical endoscope with physical and RCM constraints. IEEE Trans. Neural Networks Learn. Syst. **31**(12), 5272–5284 (2020)

Automated Vein Segmentation from NIR Images Using a Mixer-UNet Model

Jiarui Ji[1] , Yibo Zhao[1] , Tenghui Xie[1] , Fuxin Du[2] , and Peng Qi[1(✉)]

[1] Tongji University, No. 1239, Siping Road, Shanghai 200092, China
pqi@tongji.edu.cn
[2] School of Mechanical Engineering, Shandong University, Jinan, China

Abstract. Accessing the venous bloodstream to obtain a blood sample is the most common clinical routine. Nevertheless, due to the reliance of venipuncture on manual technique, first-stick accuracy of venipuncture falls below 50% in difficult cases. A surge of research on robotic guidance for autonomous vascular access have been conducted. With regard to robotic venipuncture, efficiency and accuracy of vein segmentation is of much importance. This paper describes a method to accurately and efficiently segment, localize and track the topology of human veins from near-infrared (NIR) images. Both spatial and color augmentation are implemented on the dataset at first. Next, Mixer-UNet is used for identifying veins that would be hard to find in clinical visual assessment. The Mixer-UNet is developed on the basis of UNet and MLP-Mixer. Through the flexible information exchange through Token-mixing layer and Channel-mixing layer, Mixer-UNet can extract features from NIR images accurately. The performance of Mixer-UNet is validated on 270 NIR images, which are collected from 30 volunteers. Mixer-UNet reaches 93.07% on Accuracy indicator. Compared with the best-performing baseline, the F1-score indicator increases by 2.82%, reaching 78.37% in testing sample. The high accuracy and robustness of Mixer-UNet is expected to improve the vein segmentation of NIR images, and further contributes to the goal of an improved automated venipuncture robot.

Keywords: Medical robotics · Venipuncture robot · Vein segmentation model · MLP-Mixer · UNet

1 Introduction

Venipuncture is the most common clinical routine performed to collect blood samples, deliver fluids, and monitor patient health [1]. However, due to the reliance of venipuncture on manual technique, medical staff are often burdened

This work is supported by the National Natural Science Foundation of China (51905379), Shanghai Science and Technology Development Funds (20QC1400900), the Shanghai Municipal Science and Technology Major Project (2021SHZDZX0100) and the Fundamental Research Funds for the Central Universities.

with a heavy workload [2]. Moreover, finding a suitable cannulation site, particularly in patients with small veins, dark skin, or a high body weight is very difficult, and the success rate of first-stick accuracy of venipuncture falls below 50% in these cases [1]. To relieve the stress of medical staff as well as minimizing venipuncture-related adverse events, venipuncture robots attract lots of research interests.

In order to introduce a cannula into the center of the vein, automated venipuncture robot needs to locate a suitable vein or find correct venous access at first. To achieve this goal, visualizing the invisible palm-dorsa vein pattern is often adopted as a basis for automated venous access location.

The commonly used methods for visualizing human veins mainly fall into three categories: (1) Pressure-imaging based on force feedback. Through sensitive and spatially accurate pressure sensors, this technique has high sensitivity in mechanical deformation. While its imaging clarity is generally low due to low spatial resolution [3]. Carvalho *et al.* proposed a portable device that integrates force feedback and monocular NIR. The shape and actual distribution of human blood vessels are simplified in this work, resulting in low vein positioning accuracy [4]; (2) Ultrasound-imaging. Ultrasound imaging system is flexible, easy to use and low-cost. However, it has difficulty in displaying the transverse topology of blood vessels. (3) NIR-imaging. This kind of technology uses 700–1000 nm light from a laser to image the superficial blood vessels [1]. It is widely used thanks to its low price, clear-imaging ability, which clearly visualizes the cross-sectional topology of human blood vessels. However, the noise points and blurred edges in NIR images set up an obstacle to finding venous access.

Based on imaging technology for human veins, a surge of researches about automated venipuncture robot has been developed. In 2020, KUKA AG invented a robot arm for with ultrasound device and uses active contours to detect the vessels and it works well on phantoms [5]. Additionally, In 2017, Chen *et al.* proposed a 9-DoF puncture robot with the technology of ultrasound, NIR imaging, puncture force feedback, etc., which can steer needles and catheters into vessels with minimal supervision [6]. However, the huge size and high price of the robot has restrained its sales volume. In 2017, Chen *et al.* [7] developed a 2-DoF hand-held venipuncture device with the accuracy of 87%.

In previous studies, we have developed a 4-DoF venipuncture [8] and a 6-DoF automated venipuncture robot [9]. To visualize the invisible subcutaneous veins, our robot combines NIR-imaging and ultrasound-imaging to realize the function of vascular localization technology. Ultrasonic images are used for vein segmentation in the longitudinal direction, while NIR images are used for vein segmentation in a horizontal direction.

This paper focuses on the task of vein segmentation in the horizontal direction based on NIR-imaging technology. To extract the 3D position information of human vein, image semantic segmentation techniques from the field of computer vision is incorporated with NIR-imaging. In consideration of the noise points and blurred edges in NIR images this paper aims to address the issue by data augmentation and a novel neural network Mixer-UNet, so as to obtain the exact position for needle insertion. Our main contributions are as follows:

- The proposed model (Mixer-UNet) is constructed on the basis of UNet [10], which adopts an encoder-decoder architecture. The encoder part integrates MLP-Mixer [11] with convolution architecture, enabling effective information exchange through Token-mixing layer and Channel-mixing layer. The proposed architecture demonstrates significant improvement on vein segmentation from NIR-imaging images.
- The performance of Mixer-UNet is validated on 270 NIR images collected from 30 volunteers. Four different indicators (accuracy, precision, recall and F1) are adopted to evaluate Mixer-UNet. With an average improvement of 5% in F1-score and 7% in precision, Mixer-UNet is able to segment and locate vein region from NIR images accurately. The promising performance of Mixer-UNet certifies the superiority of the proposed method, providing a solid foundation for the implementation of automated venipuncture.

2   Research Methods

2.1   Venipuncture Robotic System

In order to realize automated venipuncture, our automated needle inserting robot combines ultrasound-imaging and NIR-imaging technology. In the aim of obtaining accurate 3D position information of human vein, ultrasound-imaging is used to detect the depth information and longitudinal inclination angle of blood vessel, and NIR-imaging technology is used to detect the topological distribution of blood vessel in the horizontal direction. As shown in Fig. 2, the NIR camera is placed directly above the human arm model.

The hardware architecture of the automated venipuncture robot is mainly composed of the control module and the execution module. As shown in Fig. 1, the control module uses the master-slave structure. Image signals from each sensor are processed by the main computer, and instructions from the master are transmitted by USB cable and STM32 controls the motion of motors and other actuators. The execution module uses a cantilever design with a total of 6-DoF. The mechanical structure of the robot is composed of a 4-DoF positioning unit and a 2-DoF end puncture unit. The positioning unit determines the position and adjusts the puncture angle by translation along the coordinate axis and rotation along the z-axis. The puncture unit controls the needle push rod and rotates the pitching angle. Ultrasonic and infrared devices are placed in the front of the robot. The overall structure adopts ergonomic design to capture clear images.

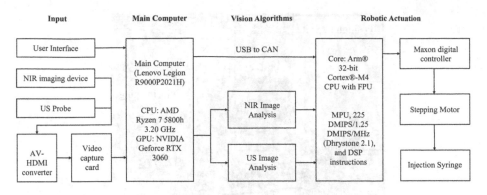

Fig. 1. Hardware system architecture design, depicting the process flow from image input, vision analysis, and robotic controls.

2.2   Automated Vein Segmentation from NIR Images

Data Composition. To verify the performance of the automated venipuncture robot [9] and the model we proposed in this paper, all the data used for training, testing and validation are collected by the NIR camera in the robot. The data we used are captured from 30 volunteers, including 17 males and 13 females with the aged between 18–70 years old. In total, we possess 270 NIR images (30 images per volunteer).

For the process of labeling ground truth of vein segmentation, we first used a self-defined pipeline consisting of several operations. The operations contain median filtering, eroding-dilating, brightness adjustment, adaptive histogram normalization and so on. We adjust the parameters of those algorithms image by image to obtain the optimal segmentation GT. The flow chart of the labeling process is shown in Fig. 4.

An illustration of the dataset is shown in Fig. 3. The binary graph represents ground truth for vein segmentation. As can be seen from the images, there are many noise points and blurring edges in the NIR images. Hairs on the skin, dark skin blemishes and so on may influence the segmentation accuracy, which makes the segmentation task challenging.

Data Processing Method. For the data augmentation part, due to the limited size of our dataset, we use several methods to achieve the goal of data augmentation. Our augmentation process mainly contains two parts, spatial augmentation and color augmentation. Spatial augmentation includes random resize crop, random horizontal flip and random rotation. Color augmentation includes sharpen, random brightness contrast and contrast limited adaptive histogram equalization. The aim of augmentation is to enhance the generalization ability of the model. The specific parameters of augmentation are illustrated in the Table 1.

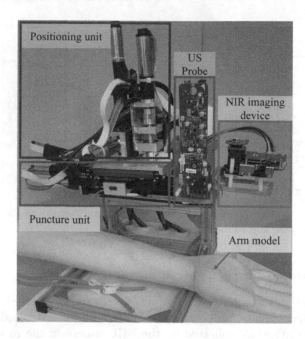

Fig. 2. Design and prototype of the automated venipuncture robot.

Table 1. Parameters of data augmentation procedure

Data augmentation		Value, probability
Position augmentation	RandomResizeCrop	0.5
	RandomHorizontalFlip	scale_limit=0.5, shift_limit=0.1
	Random Rotation	0.5
Color augmentation	Sharpen	0.2
	RandomBrightnessContrast	0.5
	CLAHE	0.3

The pre-processing part includes two processes. Firstly, the input image is resized into the size of 256×256. Normalization is implemented on the input picture as well.

Suitable Puncture Area. In order to select the appropriate region for puncture implementation, the vein region from the NIR image needs to be segmented. In the existing research on human vein segmentation, the most popular models include FPN [12], PSPNet [13], LinkNet [14] and so on. These neural network based on convolution, which can obtain sample features from a small number of data-sets and converge quickly. Their good performance is mainly due to the translation invariance in the convolutional neural network.

Although feature map information can be exchanged through convolution cores of different sizes. The information exchanged in total is still limited due to

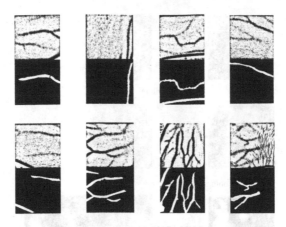

Fig. 3. Eight examples of NIR images (Top) and their ground truth (GT) label images (Bottom).

the locality of convolution. Based on the MLP-Mixer structure [11], the image is reshaped into a patch sequence. The MLP-Mixer structure enables the feature image information of token dimension to be exchanged through Token-mixing layer, and the feature image information of channel dimension can be exchanged through Channel-mixing layer.

In order to combine the advantages of previous models, we build a model with reference to the network architecture of the UNet [10]. The whole network adopts an encoder-decoder structure. In the encoder part, four Encoder-Blocks (three Conv-Block, one Mixer-Block) are used to reduce the image size and extract feature images of different scales. This process is called down-sampling.

In the first three layers of the Encoder-Blocks of encoder, convolution is adopted. In the last Encoder-Block, the MLP-Mixer structure is used to replace the convolution part in the original UNet network. MLP-Mixer accepts a series of linearly projected image patches (also known as tokens) as input.

In the decoder part, the corresponding four Decoder-Blocks are used to restore the picture into the size of the feature map. This process is called up-sampling. The parameters for these blocks are listed in Table 2, the size of the input sample is 256×256.

For the first three Conv-Blocks of the encoder part, their structures are generally similar. In each Conv-Block, the data is input into a max pooling layer (kernel size: 2) at first. The feature map of different sizes is extracted by double-convolution afterward. Double-convolution is carried out directly in the first Encoder-Block.

Double-convolution means performing the following process twice. After the feature extraction of the convolution layer is performed every time, the input information is normalized through batch-normalization, and then the nonlinear activation is performed through the Relu function to prevent the gradient from disappearing.

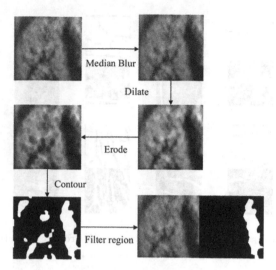

Fig. 4. The workflow of ground truth labeling process, including median blur, dilate, erode, contour and filter region.

For the last Encoder-Block of the encoder part, MLP-Mixer is adopted. For the feature image output from the third Conv-Block, the input image is first reshaped into a patch sequence, converted into feature embedding subsequently through per-patch fully-connected process. The sequence then goes through $depth = 12$ Mixer blocks for training. Finally, the normalization is carried out through layer-normalization.

In fact, the per-patch fully-connected process turns the picture into an embedded sequence. Assuming the size of the feature picture $W \times H$ and the number of channel is C, the patch size is A. Slice the picture and turn it into a picture with a resolution of $A \times A$. Then the original picture can be reshaped into a picture sequence of length $(N = \frac{W \times H}{A^2}, \mathbf{X} = [q_i^1; q_i^2; \cdots; q_i^N])$. The number of channels in each picture remains unchanged(C), $\mathbf{X} \in \mathbb{R}^{N \times C}$.

Mixer block of the MLP-Mixer is generally divided into two modules: Channel-mixing layer and Token-mixing layer. Channel-mixing layer allows communication between different channels; Token-mixing layer allows different spatial locations (tokens) to exchange information. These two types of layers are stacked alternately to facilitate the information exchange between two input dimensions [11].

Token-mixing layer acts on columns of $\mathbf{X}$ (i.e. it is applied to a transposed input table $\mathbf{X}^\top$), mapping $\mathbb{R}^S \mapsto \mathbb{R}^S$, which is shared in across columns. Channel-mixing layer acts on rows of $\mathbf{X}$, mapping $\mathbb{R}^C \mapsto \mathbb{R}^C$, which is shared across all rows [11].

As shown in the Fig. 5, after the four-stage down-sampling of the feature map in the encoder, the corresponding four-stage up-sampling is carried out afterward.

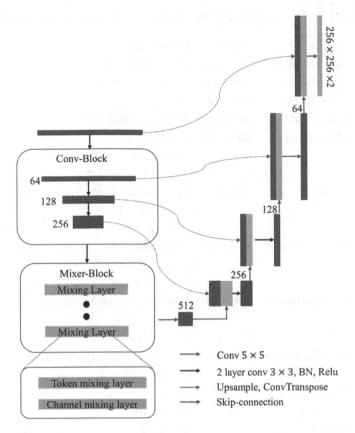

Fig. 5. The Structure of Mixer-UNet: four Encoder-Blocks (three Conv-Blocks, one Mixer-Block) and four Decoder-Blocks. The size of the input sample is 256×256

In the up-sampling process, the output feature map of MLP-Mixer is reshaped and the number of channels is recovered to 512 through convolution. Then, the feature map is input into the decoder part of Mixer-UNet, which consists of four Decoder-Blocks. Each Decoder-Block has two optional methods for down-sampling. One method is bilinear interpolation. The value of a pixel is calculated by the value of the pixel around the pixel. Firstly, through the surrounding pixels and single linear interpolation, some points with the same coordinate as the target point are calculated. Then, the pixel value of the target point is calculated through the single linear interpolation of these pixels. The other method is deconvolution. The convolution kernel ($[2 \times 2$, stride:2]) can enlarge the image shape and compress the dimension. One of the two methods can be selected for implementation.

Moreover, the idea of skip connection in UNet is adopted in network construction. The feature map obtained in each Decoder-Block will be in concatenated with the corresponding feature map of the same size in the Encoder-Block. Then, the feature map is input into the next Decoder-Block.

Table 2. Details of each layer in the basic network structure of Mixer-UNet.

Module	Output	Mixer-UNet
In-Convolution	256×64	$[3 \times 3, 64, 3] \times 2$
Conv-Block1	128×128	$[3 \times 3, 128, 64] \times 2$
Conv-Block2	64×256	$[3 \times 3, 256, 128] \times 2$
Conv-Block3	32×512	$[3 \times 3, 512, 256] \times 2$
Mixer-Block	32×512	$[5 \times 5, 512, 512] \times 2$
		MLPMixer, depth=12
		$[5 \times 5, 512, 512] \times 2$
Decoder-Block1	32×256	Upsample(scale=2), concatenate
		$[3 \times 3, 256, 512]$
		$[3 \times 3, 256, 256]$
Decoder-Block2	64×128	Upsample(scale=2), concatenate
		$[3 \times 3, 128, 256]$
		$[3 \times 3, 128, 128]$
Decoder-Block3	128×64	Upsample(scale=2), concatenate
		$[3 \times 3, 64, 128]$
		$[3 \times 3, 64, 64]$
Decoder-Block4	256×64	Upsample(scale=2), concatenate
		$[3 \times 3, 64, 64] \times 2$
Out-Convolution	256×2	$[1 \times 1, 64, 1] \times 2$
#params		197.7×10^5
FLOPs		39.9×10^9

In terms of loss function, we adopt the weighted loss method. The sum of cross entropy loss function and dice loss are taken as the final loss function, so as to optimize the expected accuracy of the model. For the activation function, we adopt the softmax function.

3   Experiments and Results

3.1   Experiments

The Mixer-UNet model is trained with 270 NIR images first. In order to avoid over-fitting and to improve the generalization ability of the model, data augmentation on the dataset is implemented. In the training process, the batch size for dataset is 8 and we use *GradScaler* to speed up the training process. Adam is chosen as the optimizer (Fig. 6).

3.2   Results

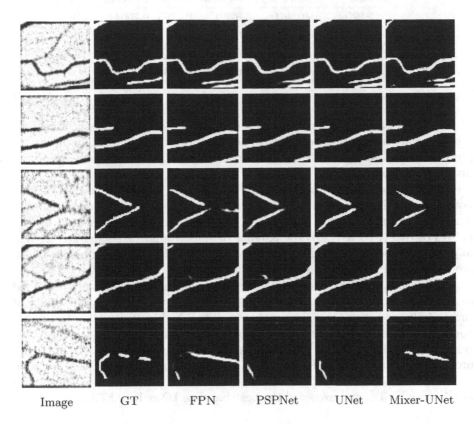

| Image | GT | FPN | PSPNet | UNet | Mixer-UNet |

Fig. 6. Vein segmentation results of FPN, UNet, PSPNet and Mixer-UNet. GT illustrates the label picture.

To show the superiority of our model, three different baseline models are trained using the same dataset. Since the size of parameters is different for these models, equal time is used to train all the models instead of even number of epochs. Adam optimizer is used for training to improve efficiency and reduce the consumption of memory. The learning rate is adjusted by the change of epochs. With epoch increasing, the learning rate gradually descends, leading to a better training result. All models are built based on Pytorch. The computer environment for experiment: GPU RTX 3080, CPU Xeon Gold 6142, memory 27.1 GB. Data augmentation is implemented at the same time.

Table 3. The performance of different models on Test-set.

Model	Accuracy	Precision	Recall	F1-score
PSPNet	0.9364	0.5750	0.7763	0.7004
UNet	0.9414	0.6350	0.9011	0.7450
FPN	0.9399	0.6516	0.7616	0.7555
Mixer-UNet	0.9307	0.6978	0.8938	0.7837

As shown in Table 3, the Mixer-UNet model has shown its superiority over other primary models in terms of five indicators. The indicator contains accuracy, precision, recall and F1-score, which are often used in evaluating the results of image segmentation.

True Positive (TP) means the number of pixels, which are marked as vein both in prediction picture and in GT; True Negative (TN) means the number of pixels, which are marked as background both in prediction picture and in GT; False Positive (FP) refers to the number of background pixels marked as vein in prediction picture; False Negative (FN) refers to the number of pixels, which are marked as background in GT but vein in prediction picture.

1) Precision reflects the share of vessel pixels in the pixels that are predicted to be vessels. Mixer-UNet has the highest precision, which means it's ability of successfully predicting the right puncture points is higher. 2) Recall indicates the ability of the model to locate vessels. In other words, whether the actual vein set is included in the identified vein set. Mixer-UNet has achieved 89.38% in recall, proved 8% on average. 3) F1-Score can simultaneously measure the precision and sensitivity of the model. As a result, Mixer-UNet outperforms other models in F1-score by 3%, and exceeded the best baseline UNet by 3.87%.

4   Conclusions

For the automated venipuncture robot, obtaining peripheral venous access is a critical prerequisite for inserting needles accurately. Vein segmentation method based on NIR-imaging is adopted in our robot, to get the exact vein access in the horizontal direction of human palm. In order to make vein segmentation and recognition more automatic as well as address the problems of multiple noise points in NIR-imaging images, this paper proposes a novel neural network Mixer-UNet to address this issue. At the same time, the image dataset is spatially and numerically enhanced to enlarge the learning range of Mixer-UNet. Based on UNet structure, Mixer-UNet adopts an encoder-decoder structure. It has shown promising performance in several indicators. Compared with the selected baselines, the Recall improves 8% on average; Compared with the best-performing baseline, the F1-score increases by 2.82%, reaching 78.37%. The accuracy and efficiency of Mixer-UNet in vein topology segmentation enables appropriate cannulation of the palm-dorsa vein.

References

1. Chen, A.: Image-guided robotics for autonomous venipuncture. Ph.D. dissertation, Department, BME, Rutgers University, New Brunswick (2016)
2. De Boer, T., Steinbuch, M., Neerken, S., Kharin, A.: Laboratory study on needle-tissue interaction: towards the development of an instrument for automatic venipuncture. J. Mech. Med. Biol. **07**(03), 325–335 (2007)
3. Lee, S., et al.: A transparent bending-insensitive pressure sensor. Nat. Nanotechnol. **11**(5), 472–478 (2016)
4. Paulo, C., Anurag, K., Sean, W., Patrick, F., Gregory, S.: Robotic assistive device for phlebotomy. In: Proceedings of International Design Engineering Technical Conferences and Computers and Information in Engineering Conference, Boston, Massachusetts, USA, vol. 57106, p. V003T14A012 (2015)
5. Unger, M., Berger, J., Gerold, B., Melzer, A.: Robot-assisted ultrasound-guided tracking of anatomical structures for the application of focused ultrasound. Curr. Dir. Biomed. Eng. **6**(3), 123–126 (2020)
6. Chen, A., Balter, M., Maguire, T., Yarmush, M.: Deep learning robotic guidance for autonomous vascular access. Nat. Mach. Intell. **2**(2), 104–115 (2020)
7. Balter, M.: Robotic devices for automated venipuncture and diagnostic blood analysis. Ph.D. dissertation, Department, BME, Rutgers University, New Brunswick (2017)
8. Huang, D., et al.: Autonomous robotic subcutaneous injection under near-infrared image guidance. In: International Design Engineering Technical Conferences and Computers and Information in Engineering Conference (2021)
9. Chen, Y., et al.: Semi-supervised vein segmentation of ultrasound images for autonomous venipuncture. In: Proceedings of IEEE/RSJ International Conference on Intelligent Robots and Systems (IROS), Prague, Czech Republic, pp. 9475–9481 (2021)
10. Ronneberger, O., Fischer, P., Brox, T.: U-Net: convolutional networks for biomedical image segmentation. In: Navab, N., Hornegger, J., Wells, W.M., Frangi, A.F. (eds.) MICCAI 2015. LNCS, vol. 9351, pp. 234–241. Springer, Cham (2015). https://doi.org/10.1007/978-3-319-24574-4_28
11. Tolstikhin, I., et al.: MLP-mixer: an all-MLP architecture for vision. In: Advances in Neural Information Processing Systems, vol. 34, pp. 24261–24272 (2021)
12. Lin, T., Dollar, P., Girshick, R., He, K., Hariharan, B., Belongie, S.: Feature pyramid networks for object detection. In: Proceedings of IEEE Conference on Computer Vision And Pattern Recognition, pp. 2117–2125 (2017)
13. Zhao, H., Shi, J., Qi, X., Wang, X., Jia, J.: Pyramid scene parsing network. In: Proceedings of IEEE Conference on Computer Vision and Pattern Recognition, USA, pp. 2881–2890 (2017)
14. Chaurasia, A., Culurciello, E.: LinkNet: exploiting encoder representations for efficient semantic segmentation. In: Proceedings of IEEE Visual Communications and Image Processing (VCIP), St. Petersburg, FL, USA, pp. 1–4 (2017)

A Novel Cable-Driven Manipulator with Constant-Curvature Deflections and Equal Displacements of the Antagonistic Cables

Yicheng Dai, Xiran Li, Xin Wang, and Han Yuan[✉]

Harbin Institute of Technology Shenzhen, Shenzhen 518055, China
yuanhan@hit.edu.cn

Abstract. The constant-curvature method can effectively reduce the complexity in kinematic modeling of the cable-driven manipulator and make the dynamic control easier. However, existing research has encountered some difficulties in modeling using this method. Due to the external load, the bending shape is not a constant-curvature arc. In this paper, a novel cable-driven serpentine manipulator is proposed, which can bend in accurate constant curvature under situations with or without external load. This manipulator is mainly composed of two parts, including arm segments and links. Both are with gear teeth. Two adjacent segments have a rolling motion by gear meshing, connected by an auxiliary link. The accurate constant curvature is realized by gear meshing of the links. Moreover, through the delicate position distribution of the gear center, the driving cables have equal antagonistic displacements, which means that a single pulley can control both cables. This feature can reduce the number of actuators significantly. Besides, the mapping between driving cable space and joint space can be linearized with a relatively small error, thanks to the special structure. Experiments in different conditions are carried out and the results show that the maximum tracking error and repeat positioning error are 4.9 mm and 4.87 mm while the average values are 1.52 mm and 1.04 mm, which are very small compared to the 272 mm long manipulators.

Keywords: Cable-driven manipulator · Constant curvature · Equal antagonistic displacements · Linearization

1 Introduction

Compared with traditional robots with rigid links or rigid joints, cable-driven serpentine manipulators have inherent flexibility due to the elasticity of the driving cable. Therefore, they have the potential to work in the environment of human-robot interaction with high demand for robot flexibility or high security [1]. However, it is a challenge to steer serpentine manipulators due to their flexible characteristics. It requires both models that describe the manipulator's shape and methods to measure the manipulator's shape during steering.

To accurately describe the shape of the manipulator under external load, scholars explored other methods, such as the Cosserate-rod method [2,3], and the finite element method [4]. Based on beam theory, a kinematic model was proposed to obtain the shape

H. Liu et al. (Eds.): ICIRA 2022, LNAI 13458, pp. 76–87, 2022.
https://doi.org/10.1007/978-3-031-13841-6_8

of the precurved-tube continuum robot [5]. In [6], a novel and unified analytic formulation for shape restoration of a multi-backbone continuum robot was presented. The modeling framework was based on elliptic integrals. Comprehensive statics model that considered the friction effect was also used in the shape reconstruction of continuum robots [7]. These methods have good performance but with a large increase in computation time, which makes them difficult using in real-time control. Methods based on sensors were also studied. Shape reconstruction method based electromagnetic (EM) sensors [8,9] and fiber Bragg grating sensors were introduced [10–12]. They have good measurement performance. But the complexity of the robot system is increased due to the added measuring instrument. All these conditions lead us to the advantage of constant-curvature approach. This method approximates the robot as a series of mutually tangent constant curvature arcs. It effectively reduces the difficulty of kinematic modeling and makes the dynamic response of the manipulator faster.

Some research relevant on this issue has been carried out, which are mainly focusing on structure design. A cable-driven manipulator which can bend in a constant curve was designed [13]. It was realized by the special multi-radius pulley, each segment was actuated by one antagonistic cable pair. The bending curve of the robot is approximated to a circular, but there are too many driving cables. Moreover, due to the cable elasticity, this design is not applicable for tasks where there exist external loads. In [14], a bionic tail was designed. The tail realized constant-curvature deflection through mounting gears on each side of the main segment. However, this mechanical tail has a complex structure. The number of the gears is twice as many as the segment. The cable routing is tortuous, which will cause large cable friction. In [15], a novel planar continuum manipulator, which mechanically constrains the redundancy by attaching the auxiliary links to the main continuum links were presented. However, this research didn't consider the problem of ensuring the equal antagonistic displacements of driving cables. On this issue, a simple method is to make the two-adjacent links have a rolling motion with a pivot at the middle link. In [16–18], an anthropomorphic seven-DOF cable-driven manipulator was proposed. But this design aims at a single joint. It remains to be studied in robots with multi-joint and multi-segment.

Existing research has improved the structure of the cable-driven continuous robot to a certain extent, but there are still some limitations. Bending in an accurate constant curve can reduce the complexity of robot kinematic modeling, which is important for real-time control [19]. Furthermore, the feature of equal antagonistic cable displacements is important for reducing the number of actuator, simplifying the diving box. Taking these two demands into consideration, a novel planar cable-driven serpentine manipulator is proposed in this paper. This manipulator is composed of multiple plane rotating segments with gears and connecting links. The installation method of its driving cables of different sections is the same with previous designs [20,21]. The features of the proposed novel design are summarized as follows.

– The proposed manipulator can realize accurate constant curvature by gear meshing of the links.
– It can achieve equal antagonistic displacements of driving cables through delicate position distribution of the gear center.
– The proposed manipulator has the potential of linearizing the mapping between driving cable space and joint space.

The organization of this paper is as follows. In Sect. 2, the structure of the proposed cable-driven serpentine manipulator is introduced and the kinematic model is derived. In Sect. 3, the working space is analyzed. In addition, the relationship between cable length and the deflection angle of a segment is analyzed, and the potential of linear mapping between driving cable space and joint space is discussed. In Sect. 4, experimental verifications are conducted and the results are analyzed. The comparison between the accuracy of the linear calculation and nonlinear calculation is carried out. Finally, conclusions are made in Sect. 5.

2   Modeling

2.1   Structure

The novel structure is shown in Fig. 1. (see Fig. 1) There are mainly two parts, including arm segments and auxiliary links, as shown in Fig. 1(a, b). Every two adjacent segments has a rolling motion by gear meshing. They are connected in the same plane through the auxiliary link, as shown in Fig. 1(c). The accurate constant curvature is realized by gear meshing of the links. The center of the gear is on the same line as the cable holes' ends on both sides exists. It is deliberate distributed to realize equal antagonistic displacements of driving cables. In other words, the change of the length between T_0' and T_1 is equal to the change of the length between P_0' and P_1. It indicates that a single pulley can control both cables, which will reduce the number of actuators and the size of driving box.

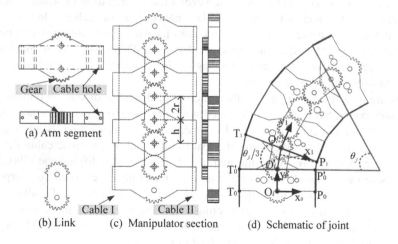

Fig. 1. Design of the new cable-driven continuum manipulator.

2.2   Kinematic Modeling

The cable-driven serpentine manipulator is composed of multiple arm segments and links. In order to control the robot effectively, kinematics must be studied, including forward kinematic and inverse kinematic. The forward kinematic is the mapping from driving space to working space, while the inverse kinematic is the opposite. For the cable-driven manipulator, forward kinematic is the process of finding the end pose, while knowing the cable lengths. In this paper, the deflection angle of the section will be used as an intermediary. Assuming the cable length is L, and the section angle is θ. Then the mapping from the driving space to the joint space can be expressed as:

$$\theta = f_{fwd}(\mathbf{L}) \tag{1}$$

After knowing the deflection angle of the section, the mapping from joint space can be obtained. As shown in Fig. 1(d), the gear teeth between the first arm segment and the second arm segment mesh to form a joint. Noting the deflection angle of the jth section as θ_j, and the number of the joint angle is n for each section. Noting the pitch circle of the gears is r, then the distance of the first gear center O_i' and the second gear center O_{i+1} is $2r$. The distance between the cable hole and the gear center is noted as R, and the depth of the cable hole is h. The transformation matrix from O_{i+1} to O_i can be expressed as:

$$^i\mathbf{T}_{i+1}^j = \begin{bmatrix} \cos(\frac{\theta_j}{2n}) & -\sin(\frac{\theta_j}{2n}) & -2r \cdot \sin(\frac{\theta_j}{2n}) \\ \sin(\frac{\theta_j}{2n}) & \cos(\frac{\theta_j}{2n}) & h + 2r \cdot \cos(\frac{\theta_j}{2n}) \\ 0 & 0 & 1 \end{bmatrix} \tag{2}$$

Then the transformation matrix from the end arm segment of the section to the first can be expressed as:

$$^0\mathbf{T}_n^j = {}^0\mathbf{T}_1^j \cdot {}^1\mathbf{T}_2^j, \cdots, {}^i\mathbf{T}_{i+1}^j, \cdots, {}^{n-2}\mathbf{T}_{n-1}^j \cdot {}^{n-1}\mathbf{T}_n^j \tag{3}$$

For a multi-section manipulator, the transformation matrix from the end to the base can be expressed as:

$$\mathbf{T} = {}^0\mathbf{T}_n^0 \cdot {}^0\mathbf{T}_n^1, \cdots, {}^0\mathbf{T}_n^j, \cdots, {}^0\mathbf{T}_n^{n-1} \cdot {}^0\mathbf{T}_n^n \tag{4}$$

Supposing the pose of the end effector is $\mathbf{X}_e$ in the local coordinate system, its expression in the base global coordinate system can be written as:

$$\mathbf{X} = \mathbf{T} \cdot \mathbf{X}_e \tag{5}$$

Noting that $\mathbf{T}$ is the function of the deflection angles $\theta(\theta_1, \theta_2, \cdots, \theta_j, \cdots, \theta_m)$.

For the novel manipulator proposed in this paper, the inverse kinematic is the process of finding the length of the driven cable $\mathbf{L}$ while the end pose $\mathbf{X} = [x_1, x_2, \cdots, x_n]$ is known.

$$\begin{bmatrix} f_1(\theta, x_1) \\ f_2(\theta, x_2) \\ \cdots \\ f_n(\theta, x_n) \end{bmatrix} = 0 \tag{6}$$

After obtaining the section angles, the cable length can be written as:

$$\mathbf{L} = f_{inv}(\boldsymbol{\theta}) \tag{7}$$

2.3 Simplification of Mapping Between Cable Length Change and Segment Angle

In the proposed manipulator, the cable length mainly includes two parts, as shown in Fig. 1. The first part is the cable in the hole of the arm segment, and the length keeps constant. The second part is the cable at the joint of two arm segments, and the length will change along with the joint angle. According to Fig. 1, the length change of the inconstant part can be written as:

$$\Delta L = 2R \cdot \sin(\frac{\theta_j}{2n}) \tag{8}$$

Supposing L_{int} is the initial cable length when the deflection angle is 0, the length of the driving cable can be expressed as:

$$L = L_{int} + 2nR \cdot \sin(\frac{\theta_j}{2n}) \tag{9}$$

On the contrary, the deflection angle of the section can be obtained after the cable length is known. it can be written as:

$$\theta_j = 2n \cdot \arcsin(\frac{L - L_{int}}{2nR}) \tag{10}$$

Compared with cable-driven serial robots with traditional hinged joint modules, like in [20, 21], the length calculation for the proposed manipulator is simple. This will surely improve the calculation efficiency between the shape and the cable length of the manipulator, which will lead to the improvement of the real-time control of the robot.

3 Motion Analysis

3.1 Working Space

In the design of the manipulator, the range of a single joint is $\pm 30°$. The maximum deflection angle of the whole section will be $90°$ when there are three joints. In this paper, a two-section cable-driven serpentine manipulator is designed, as shown in Fig. 2(a). The length of the manipulator can be extended by adding more sections or segments.

The workspace of the proposed manipulator is shown in Fig. 2(b). It shows that the manipulator has a big working space, which will ensure them meets various types of requirements. The joint angle is related to the parameter of R and r, which were introduced in Subsect. 2.2. If there exists a need to increase the joint angle, these two parameters can be changed so as to enlarge the workspace of the manipulator.

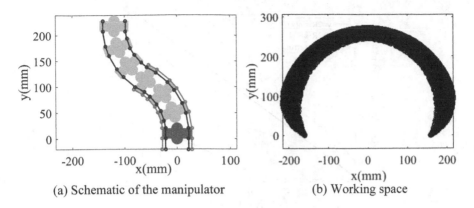

(a) Schematic of the manipulator   (b) Working space

Fig. 2. Analysis of the novel manipulator.

3.2 The Linear Mapping Between Cable Length and Segment Angle

In the simulation model, the manipulator is composed of two sections. Each section has a pair of antagonistic cables. There are four driving cables in the manipulator. Cable 1 and 2 are for the first section, while cable 3 and 4 are for the second section. The relationship between the cable length change and the joint angle is shown in Fig. 3. We can see that the length variations of the antagonistic cables are symmetrical about the x-axis. Since joint motions change the cable length by the same amount on opposite sides, a single pulley can control both cables. This design needs fewer actuators.

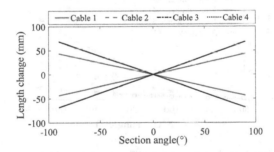

Fig. 3. The length change of the antagonistic cables.

According to the simulation results shown in Fig. 4, the relationship between the cable length change and the section angle is approximately linear. But as expressed in Eq. (8), the cable length change is a Sine function of the section angle, which is nonlinear.

In Eq. (8), note $\frac{\theta_j}{2n}$ as x, for the proposed novel manipulator with three sections, the maximum deflection angle of one section is $90°$, and when calculating the change of the driving cable, the maximum x value is $15°$. This value is very small which causing function $y = \sin(x)$ approximates to function $y = x$. Simulations are carried out to

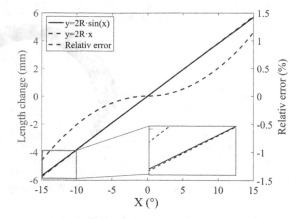

Fig. 4. The cable length change of the novel manipulator.

show the difference between these two functions. As shown in Fig. 4, the first function, represented in black solid line, is pretty close to the second one, represented in black dash line, when is in the range of ±15°. The maximum relative error is 1.15%, as represented in red dash line. As for the structure parameter of the manipulator proposed in this paper, where $R = 28$ mm, $r = 11$ mm, the absolute length error is 0.1965 mm, and the relative length error is 0.12%.

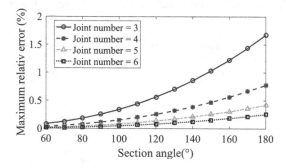

Fig. 5. The linearization error in different angle and joint number.

According to Eq. (8), the value of x is related to the deflection angle and the number of the joints. Simulations are carried out to analyze the influence of these two factors on the linearization of the sine function. According to the results shown in Fig. 5, the relative error increases with deflection angle and decreases with the number of joint. When the joint number is 3, the maximum relative errors are 0.82% and 1.675% for deflection angles of 60° and 180°. When increasing the joint number to 6, the maximum relative errors are 0.011% and 0.255%. According to the previous analysis, using the function $y = x$ to substitute the function $y = \sin(x)$, the linear mapping relationship from the driving cable space to the joint space can be realized.

The general hinged joint is shown in Fig. 6. The relationship between the cable length and the joint angel is complicated compared to the proposed novel structure. It can be written as:

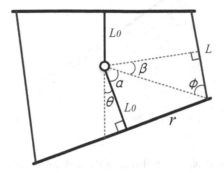

Fig. 6. The general hinged joint of traditional cable-driven snake robot.

$$L = 2\sqrt{r^2 + L_0^2} \cdot \sin\beta \tag{11}$$

Substituting $\beta = (\frac{\pi - \theta}{2} - \text{actan}\frac{r}{L_0})$, Eq. (11) can be written as:

$$L = 2\sqrt{r^2 + L_0^2} \cdot \sin(\frac{\pi - \theta}{2} - \text{actan}\frac{r}{L_0}) \tag{12}$$

When the joint angle is 0, the initial cable length is $2L_0$. The cable length change can be written as:

$$\Delta L = 2L_0 - 2\sqrt{r^2 + L_0^2} \cdot \sin(\frac{\pi - \theta}{2} - \text{actan}\frac{r}{L_0}) \tag{13}$$

Noting $B = 2\sqrt{r^2 + L_0^2}$, $x = \frac{\pi - \theta}{2} - \text{actan}\frac{r}{L_0}$, we have:

$$y = 2L_0 - B \cdot \sin(x) \tag{14}$$

Assuming the structural parameters of the traditional hinged joint are the same with the proposed manipulator, then we get that x is in the range of 6.5°–36.5° when the joint angle changes in the range of −30°–30°. The length change of the driving cable obtained by two calculation method is shown in Fig. 7. The black solid line represents the results of the length change, and the black dash line represents the results after linearizing the function. As we can see, the difference is obvious when x is a relatively large value. The maximum error is 114.69%, and the average error is 17.14%.

According to the linearization results of the mapping from driving cable space to joint space, the proposed structure has relative much small error compared with the traditional structure. It indicated that the linearization mapping has much higher feasibility in the proposed structure. This design will surely reduce the complexity of kinematic modeling of the manipulator, which is important for future real-time control.

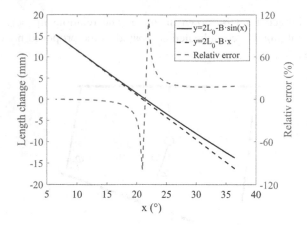

Fig. 7. The cable length change of the traditional hinged joint.

4   Experiment

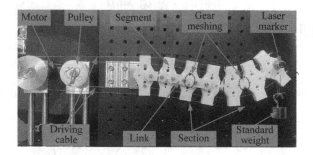

Fig. 8. The prototype of the proposed novel manipulator.

In order to verify the motion performance of the manipulator proposed in this paper, three groups of trajectory following experiments are carried out in this part. The first one is to use the original calculation method to obtain the cable length and control the manipulator, while the second one is to use the linear cable length calculation method. Different from the first experiment, the third one is carried out with an external load on the end. All these three groups of experiments are carried out in open-loop control mode, which will verify the accuracy of the model effectively. The two-section cable-driven serpentine manipulator prototype is shown in Fig. 8. There are four driving cables and each pair of antagonistic cables is routed around and fixed on one pulley, which is actuated by a motor.

As shown in Fig. 9, the planned trajectory consists of three parts, including two line segments and an arc. The expression of different line is shown in Fig. 9(a), and the start point and the endpoint is shown in Fig. 9(b). The green arrows represent the moving

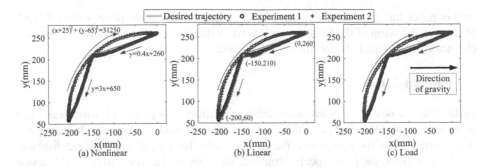

Fig. 9. Trajectory following experiments.

direction, and the black arrow represents the load direction. Each situation includes two experiments. According to the experimental results, the maximum value of repeat positioning error is 3.28 mm, 4.87 mm and 1 mm for these three different conditions respectively. Furthermore, the average repeat positioning errors are 0.53 mm, 1.04 mm and 0.45 mm. It should be noted that the error in experiments with load is relative small. The reason may be that the load make the structural of the robot fit more closely, and the error caused be assembly is reduced.

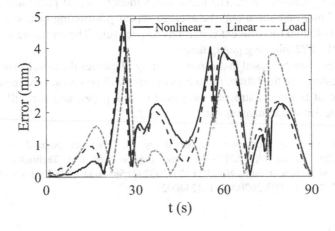

Fig. 10. Errors of trajectory following experiments.

The errors of trajectory following experiments are shown in Fig. 10. The maximum trajectory tracking errors are 4.9 mm, 4.8 mm and 4 mm, while the average tracking errors are 1.5245 mm, 1.48 mm and 1.3 mm for different situations respectively. They are very small compared to the 272 mm long manipulators. The control accuracy of the first and the second groups of experiments illustrate that, the mapping between driving cable space and the joint space has high feasibility. Comparisons of the first and the third groups of experiments indicate that the cable-driven serpentine manipulator proposed in this paper has good constant curvature bending performance under external load. Moreover, the setup of the actuation well verifies that the designed manipulator has the characteristic of equal displacements of the antagonistic cables.

5 Conclusion

In this paper, a novel cable-driven serpentine manipulator is proposed, which can bend in accurate constant curvature with or without external load. Though the delicate position distribution of the gear center, the driving cables have equal antagonistic displacements. Moreover, due to the special structure, the mapping between driving cable space and joint space can be simplified to a linear relationship with a relatively small error. According to the simulation results, the linearization error increases with deflection angle and decreases with the number of joint. When the joint number is 3, the maximum relative errors are 0.82% and 1.675% for deflection angles of 60° and 180°. When the joint number is 6, the maximum relative errors are 0.011% and 0.255%. The feature of linearization further reduces the complexity of kinematic modeling and improve the real-time control performance of the cable-driven serpentine manipulator.

To verify the kinematic model and the advantage of the manipulator, experimental verifications in different conditions are carried out. According to the results, the maximum tracking errors are 4.9 mm, 4.8 mm and 4 mm, and the average tracking error is 1.52 mm, 1.48 mm and 1.3 mm for different conditions respectively, compared to the 272 mm long manipulators. The maximum values of repeat positioning errors are 3.28 mm, 4.87 mm and 1 mm and the average repeat positioning errors are 0.53 mm, 1.04 mm and 0.45 mm for different conditions respectively. The errors are relative small compared to the 272 mm long manipulators.

This manipulator proposed in this paper mainly illustrates the novel structure of two layer gear meshing. In the future, more experiments will be carried out to demonstrate the advantage of the novel structure proposed in this paper, and we will extend this structure to the 3D space manipulators.

Acknowledgement. This work was supported by the National Natural Science Foundation of China (Grants No. 62173114), and the Science and Technology Innovation Committee of Shenzhen (Grants No. JCYJ20210324115812034, JCYJ20190809110415177, GXWD20201230155427003-20200821181254002).

References

1. Roesthuis, R.J., Misra, S.: Steering of multisegment continuum manipulators using rigid-link modeling and FBG-based shape sensing. IEEE Trans. Robot. **32**(2), 372–382 (2016)
2. Jones, B.A., Gray, R.L., Turlapati, K.: Three dimensional statics for continuum robotics. In: 2009 IEEE/RSJ International Conference on Intelligent Robots and Systems, pp. 2659–2664 (2009)
3. Trivedi, D., Lotfi, A., Rahn, C.D.: Geometrically exact models for soft robotic manipulators. IEEE Trans. Rob. **24**(4), 773–780 (2008)
4. Morales Bieze, T., Kruszewski, A., Carrez, B., Duriez, C.: Design, implementation, and control of a deformable manipulator robot based on a compliant spine. Int. J. Robot. Res. **39**(14), 1604–1619 (2020)

5. Webster, R.J., Romano, J.M., Cowan, N.J.: Mechanics of precurved-tube continuum robots. IEEE Trans. Rob. **25**(1), 67–78 (2008)
6. Xu, K., Simaan, N.: Analytic formulation for kinematics, statics, and shape restoration of multibackbone continuum robots via elliptic integrals. J. Mech. Robot. **2**(1) (2010)
7. Yuan, H., Zhou, L., Xu, W.: A comprehensive static model of cable-driven multi-section continuum robots considering friction effect. Mech. Mach. Theory **135**, 130–149 (2019)
8. Yuan, H., Chiu, P.W.Y., Li, Z.: Shape-reconstruction-based force sensing method for continuum surgical robots with large deformation. IEEE Robot. Autom. Lett. **2**(4), 1972–1979 (2017)
9. Song, S., Li, Z., Yu, H., Ren, H.: Shape reconstruction for wire-driven flexible robots based on Bézier curve and electromagnetic positioning. Mechatronics **29**, 28–35 (2015)
10. Henken, K., Van Gerwen, D., Dankelman, J., Van Den Dobbelsteen, J.: Accuracy of needle position measurements using fiber Bragg gratings. Minim. Invasive Ther. Allied Technol. **21**(6), 408–414 (2012)
11. Ryu, S.C., Dupont, P.E.: FBG-based shape sensing tubes for continuum robots. In: 2014 IEEE International Conference on Robotics and Automation (ICRA), pp. 3531–3537 (2014)
12. Moon, H., et al.: FBG-based polymer-molded shape sensor integrated with minimally invasive surgical robots. In: 2015 IEEE International Conference on Robotics and Automation (ICRA), pp. 1770–1775 (2015)
13. Racioppo, P., Ben-Tzvi, P.: Modeling and control of a cable driven modular snake robot. In: 2017 IEEE Conference on Control Technology and Applications (CCTA), pp. 468–473 (2017)
14. Saab, W., Rone, W.S., Kumar, A., Ben-Tzvi, P.: Design and integration of a novel spatial articulated robotic tail. IEEE/ASME Trans. Mechatron. **24**(2), 434–446 (2019)
15. Hwang, M., Kwon, D.-S.: Strong continuum manipulator for flexible endoscopic surgery. IEEE/ASME Trans. Mechatron. **24**(5), 2193–2203 (2019)
16. Kim, Y.-J.: Anthropomorphic low-inertia high-stiffness manipulator for high-speed safe interaction. IEEE Trans. Rob. **33**(6), 1358–1374 (2017)
17. Huang, Y., Chen, Y., Zhang, X., Zhang, H., Song, C., Ota, J.: A novel cable-driven 7-DOF anthropomorphic manipulator. IEEE/ASME Trans. Mechatron. **26**(4), 2174–2185 (2021)
18. Mustafa, S.K., Yang, G., Yeo, S.H., Lin, W., Chen, I.-M.: Self-calibration of a biologically inspired 7 DOF cable-driven robotic arm. IEEE/ASME Trans. Mechatron. **13**(1), 66–75 (2008)
19. Li, S., Hao, G.: Current trends and prospects in compliant continuum robots: a survey. In: Actuators, vol. 10, no. 7, pp. 145. Multidisciplinary Digital Publishing Institute (2021)
20. Yuan, H., Zhang, W., Dai, Y., Xu, W.: Analytical and numerical methods for the stiffness modeling of cable-driven serpentine manipulators. Mech. Mach. Theory **156**, 104179 (2021)
21. Xu, W., Liu, T., Li, Y.: Kinematics, dynamics, and control of a cable-driven hyper-redundant manipulator. IEEE/ASME Trans. Mechatron. **23**(4), 1693–1704 (2018)

Vessel Site Selection for Autonomous Cannulation Under NIR Image Guidance

Yibo Zhao[1] , Jiarui Ji[1] , Tenghui Xie[1] , Fuxin Du[2] , and Peng Qi[1,2]([✉])

[1] Tongji University, No. 1239, Siping Road, Shanghai 200092, China
pqi@tongji.edu.cn
[2] School of Mechanical Engineering, Shandong University, Jinan, China

Abstract. Venipuncture is a nearly ubiquitous part of modern clinical practice. However, currently venipuncture procedures are mainly applied by manual operation, whose the success rate might decrease below 50% in some situations, including pediatric, and geriatric patients. Thus, robotic technologies to guide autonomous vascular access attracts research attention. For venipuncture robots, near-infrared (NIR) images are widely used for real-time servoing and further to segment subcutaneous vessels for puncture with a series of deep convolutional neural networks. It has been realized that the success rate of puncture largely relies on the performance of segmentation models. However, the small size and low quality of NIR image dataset severely limit the accuracy and efficiency of segmentation models. This paper aims to address this issue by proposing a novel data processing method to improve the performance of segmentation models. With those novel image processing strategies, the segmentation results are improved. The Dice-mean value has increased by an average of 1.12%. Additionally, an algorithm of vessel site selection for puncture is proposed in this paper. Such data processing methods and the puncture site selection algorithm are expected to finally improve the performance of venipuncture robots.

Keywords: Venipuncture robot · Data augmentation · Image processing · The Bézier curve · Gaussian blur

1 Introduction

The technology of puncture plays an important role in the field of medical care and is critical for collecting blood samples, monitoring patient health and delivering fluids [1,2]. Nowadays, venipuncture procedures are mainly conducted manually, which means that successful venipuncture heavily depends on skill of the operator and physiological characteristics of patients [3]. The success rate

This work is supported by the National Natural Science Foundation of China (51905379), Shanghai Science and Technology Development Funds (20QC1400900), the Shanghai Municipal Science and Technology Major Project (2021SHZDZX0100) and the Fundamental Research Funds for the Central Universities.

of puncture can decrease in difficult populations, including patients with dark skin, young children, and obese patients [4,5]. The complications or adverse events might occur when puncture procedures fail [6,7].

To simplify the process of venipuncture and increase success rate of puncture, research on automatic venipuncture has been emerging in recent years. Perry *et al.* introduced a venipuncture robot based on ultrasound and stereovision, which is a 6-DoF machine with the success rate of 83% [8]. Balter *et al.* designed a venipuncture robot based on stereovision, ultrasound and force guidance [9]. In 2019, Leipheimer *et al.* developed a 6-DoF hand-held automated venipuncture device for rapid venous blood draws, with a success rate of 87% on all participants, a 97% success rate on non-difficult venous access participants [10]. In brief, the puncture robots improved the success rates and procedure times compared with manual works [11].

In previous studies, we proposed a 6-DoF image-guided automatic intravenous injection robot using near-infrared (NIR) and ultrasound [12]. Regards machine learning methods used in the venipuncture robot, it is critical to segment the vein region from NIR images.

The accuracy and efficiency of the robot are affected by the performance of vein segmentation model. However, there are some common problems caused by the small size of the training dataset, low image quality and noise points in NIR images, which influence the training effect of the model. Therefore, this paper proposed an image processing method to address these problems. For NIR images obtained from the robotic system, we first remove the noise points and perform image augmentation, while the original information of image is reserved at the same time. The pre-trained weight is used for transfer learning, so as to improve the accuracy of the model and the efficiency of machine puncture.

Moreover, on account of the angle error in puncture implementation, we then introduce a novel post-processing strategy and a vessel site selection algorithm. This helps to improve the safety and accuracy of venipuncture. The contributions of this paper are as follows:

A data pre processing method based on filtering, Gaussian blur and concatenate is proposed, which is combined with the method of transfer learning to improve the accuracy of the model.
- A novel post-processing method is studied. After the edge detection of the image recognition results, the edge smoothing processing is carried out through the Bézier curve, so as to remove the too small noise point area, bifurcation blood vessels and non-smooth edges. This step facilitates the selection of subsequent venipuncture points.
- A puncture point recognition algorithm based on connected domain recognition is investigated, and finally the most ideal position is selected from the recognition results.

2   Methods

2.1   Mechanical System

As shown in Fig. 1, a 6-DoF automatic venipuncture robot is designed with a reliable short transmission chain structure [12]. In details, the 4-DoF mechanism is used for the overall translation of the robot along the coordinate system in three directions and rotation in one direction. The other 2-DoF mechanisms are used to change the position and angle of the needle. The robot with the advantages of high axial stiffness of ball screw, high transmission accuracy, high mechanical efficiency, etc.

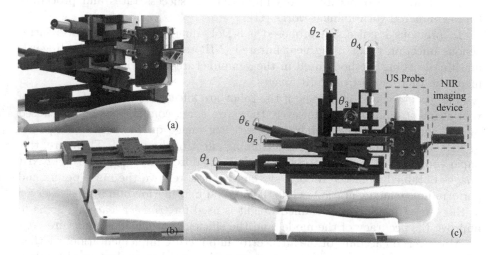

Fig. 1. An illustration of the automatic puncture robot. (a) Transmission design of robot; (b) Precision ball screw and maxon motor of the robot; (c) The Angle position of the robot's motor and image obtaining devices.

NIR images are used to provide information about the oxygen saturation of hemoglobin in the blood vessels [13]. The vessels are segmented to select the optimal puncture target from NIR images, while the x-y coordinates of the target are obtained. In order to locate the puncture point more accurately, the depth of puncture point was obtained by an ultrasound (US) probe. The venipuncture robot automatically punctures according to coordinates in 3D space.

As depicted in Fig. 2, the motor control scheme works as follows. First, the 3D coordinates of the selected target vein are provided from the NIR and US vein images processed by segmentation algorithm and inputted into the inverse kinematic equations. The robot has the ability to dynamically steer the needle in real time by tracking the injection site. For motor control, independent digital position controllers for each motor are utilized. Motors are operated with a controller area network protocol via 32-bit PWM signals.

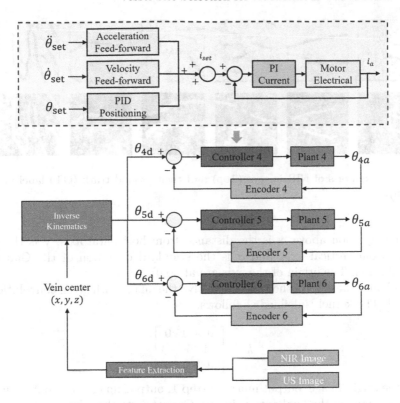

Fig. 2. Motor position feedback control and the target injection site is updated from the US 20 Hz. Plants 4–6 have different rotational inertias.

2.2 Data Composition

To verify the performance of the venipuncture robot and the proposed algorithm, all the data mentioned in this paper are collected by a NIR camera on the venipuncture robot. Experiments are carried out on 30 volunteers (17 males and 13 females) and 270 NIR images (30 images per volunteer) are collected. All images in dataset are grey scale image. The size of each image is 256 * 256. An illustration of dataset is shown in Fig. 3.

2.3 Image Preprocessing

Data Enhancement
The NIR image dataset was enhanced by the following steps:

1. Blur the image by a Gaussian function. The pixel in the output image is calculated as follows.

$$G(x, y) = \frac{1}{2\pi\sigma^2} e^{-\frac{x^2+y^2}{2\sigma^2}} \tag{1}$$

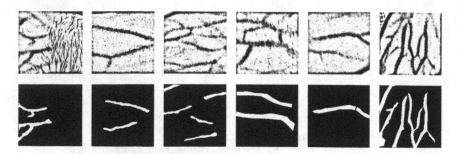

Fig. 3. Six examples of NIR images (Top) and their ground truth (GT) label images (Bottom).

In the equation above, x is the distance from horizontal axis, y is the distance from vertical axis, and σ is the standard deviation of the Gaussian distribution. The origin of the axis are at (0,0).

2. To enhance the edge of the vessel, convolve the image with given convolutional kernel. The kernel is defined as follows.

$$k = \begin{bmatrix} 0 & -1 & 0 \\ -1 & 5 & -1 \\ 0 & -1 & 0 \end{bmatrix} \tag{2}$$

3. Set the origin image, output image in step 1, output image in step 2 as the R, G, B channel of the final output image. Concatenate three images mentioned above to make the output image.

Data Augmentation

Due to the limited size of dataset, the model we trained might be a lack of generalization, which might lead to the unsatisfactory segmentation result. In order to address this problem, several data augmentation methods are applied to the dataset, including random resize crop and so on. The proposed data augmentation methods are demonstrated in Table 1.

Table 1. Parameters of data augmentation procedure

Data augmentation		Value, probability
Position augmentation	RandomResizeCrop	0.5
	RandomHorizontalFlip	scale_limit = 0.5, shift_limit = 0.1
	Random Rotation	0.5

2.4   Image Post-processing

After segmenting the vein from NIR image, the output results of the model still have problems such as noise points. The small blood vessel, abnormal protrusions at the edge of the blood vessel, and blurring at the edge of the blood vessel can lead to ineffective puncture implementation. In order to eliminate the subsequent influence of the problems mentioned above on the vein puncture point recognition, a series of image post-processing methods are adopted.

Firstly, the edge contour of the image is extracted. Then remove vascular areas that are too small to insert a needle by setting threshold. For the blurring of the edge and bifurcation problems, the Bézier curve is used to smooth the edges. For the smoothed images, the small regions are removed from the final pictures.

Since the area of blood vessels is likely to be expanded in the process of Bézier curve smoothing, the intersection will be taken on the pixel points of the blood vessel recognition image and the post-processing image. Only when the blood vessels are recognized both in post-processed picture and in the original segment picture, will they be marked. So as to ensure the safety of the puncture process.

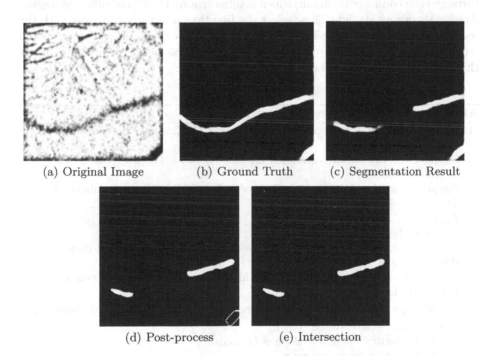

(a) Original Image   (b) Ground Truth   (c) Segmentation Result

(d) Post-process   (e) Intersection

Fig. 4. Image Post-processing: The original image, the ground truth of the image, the output of the segmentation model FPN, the result of post-process and the intersection result are shown in Fig. 4.

2.5 Vessel Site Selection

Ultimately, an accurate puncture site and position need to be calculated. For the puncture process, the intersection of veins, marginal protrusions, and too short blood vessels are not suitable for puncture implementation. In order to obtain the best puncture position and the most suitable vessel site, it is considered that only the vessels in line with the long and straight shape are suitable for puncture. To find these vessels, only performing ellipse fitting function on each vein section to get the corresponding angle is not enough. That's because this method does not consider the identification of long straight vessels in practical operation, which is difficult to implement in practical application and has large error.

In order to adapt to the complex and changeable vein topology of the human hand, the connected domain is extracted from the vein segmentation result picture. The Center of Gravity (CG) of each connected domain is calculated, which is treated as the possible puncture point set. If the CG is not inside the connected domain, the vein is discarded.

Assuming that the center point of each connected domain in the labeled blood vessel is $S = \{S_1, S_2, \cdots\cdots, S_n\}$. Multiple straight lines are used to pass through each connected domain, which rotates around the CG at different angles. Among the above straight lines, select the line that intersects the most with the connected domain set (S). Then select the CG corresponding to the extracted straight line as the target puncture point, and the slope of the straight line is the best puncture angle. The algorithm is as follows:

Algorithm 1. Puncture angle: connected domain algorithm

1: Suppose that the vein segmentation picture is Q. Extract the connected domain position of Q.

2: Suppose the size of the connected domain set is n; The set is labeled as $S = \{S_1, S_2, \cdots\cdots, S_n\}$.

3: Suppose that the CG corresponding to S_i is p_i; The CG set is labeled as $P = \{p_1, p_2, \cdots\cdots, p_n\}$.

4: **for** each $i \in [1,n]$ **do**

5:     **for** each p_i **do**

6:         using multiple straight lines passing through the connected domain S_i at different angles;

7:         Among these lines, the line that intersects most with the connected domain is selected, labeled as l_i.

8:     the slope of l_i. taken as the best puncture angle of the connected domain l_i

9: select $l_{optimal} = \max\{l_i, i \in [1, n]\}$

10: the best puncture angle: the slope of $l_{optimal}$

11: the best position for puncture: $p_{optimal}$

---

3   Experiments and Results

In order to verify the effectiveness and rationality of the proposed preprocessing method, five different backbones and three training methods are used.
The five backbones are MANet, UNET, PSPNet, FPN, and UNet++, which
are frequently-used classical models for segmentation tasks. The three different
training methods used in the experiment were model training without Imagenet
pre-trained weight, model training with Imagenet pre-trained weight and model
training loaded with Imagenet pre-trained weight and training with preprocessed
data. Three indicators, including dice similarity coefficient (DSC), Hausdorff distance (HD95) and intersection over Union (IOU) are used for the experimental
results. Through different performance indicators, we can show the performance
of this pre-processing method.

The training processes for the three methods and five backbones are totally
the same. The parameters used in the training process are illustrated in Table 2.

Table 2. Training parameters.

Training	Batch size	8
	Learning rate	0.0001
	Optimizer	Adam
	Epoch	100

The segmentation results of different training methods with the model of
Unet++ are shown in Fig. 5. Figure 5(a) shows the GT (Ground Truth) of the
segmentation task. Figure 5(b) shows the result of Unet++ trained with the original dataset. Figure 5(c) shows the result of Unet++ trained with Imagenet pre-
trained weight and the original dataset. Figure 5(d) shows the result of Unet++
trained with Imagenet pre-trained weight and the preprocessed dataset. As is
illustrated, the result in Fig. 5(d) is closer to the ground truth.

As we can see from Table 3, IOU only increased, with an average increase of
1.272 compared with the method without pre-training, 3.1524 compared with the
UNet model and 4.529 compared with the pre-trained PSPNet model. Compared
with the models pre-trained on Imagenet dataset, DSC increased by 0.004515,
while the FPN model increased by 0.01224; The HD95 index increased by 0.0001
on average, compared with the pre-trained MANET model increased by 0.0075.
We can see our preprocessing method, which can effectively improve the performance of models.

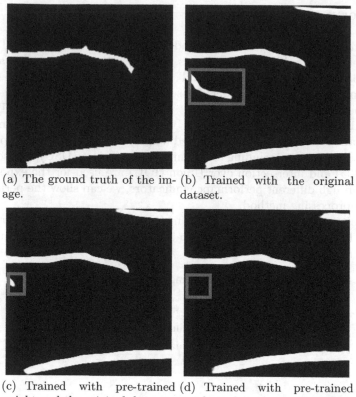

(a) The ground truth of the im- (b) Trained with the original
age.   dataset.

(c) Trained with pre-trained (d) Trained with pre-trained
weight and the original dataset. weight and preprocessed dataset.

Fig. 5. Experiment Results: The segmentation results of different training methods with the model of Unet++.

Table 3. DSC, HD95 and IOU metrics of the proposed preprocessing method on different baselines.

	Without pre-training			Pre-trained (Imagenet)			Preprocessed		
	DSC	HD95	IOU	DSC	HD95	IOU	DSC	HD95	IOU
UNet++	0.9280	0.5443	28.7276	0.9321	0.54612	45.8697	0.9382	0.5247	31.8256
MAnet	0.9293	0.5252	53.8857	0.9438	0.5177	41.3771	0.9353	0.5252	36.4116
FPN	0.8982	0.5441	33.6393	0.8862	0.5405	30.6170	0.8985	0.5418	32.4522
UNet	0.9221	0.5184	44.5188	0.9288	0.5131	38.7473	0.9322	0.5296	41.8997
PSPNet	0.8608	0.5099	39.3399	0.88419	0.5062	37.1357	0.8935	0.5028	41.6650

In order to remove the noise point in the output image and delete the regions that are not suitable for puncture, the post-processing methods are applied to the output images. As is illustrated in Fig. 6, the post-processing methods removed the region of small blood vessels, abnormal protrusions at the edge of the blood vessel and smoothed the edges of the vessels. After the intersection of segmentation result and the post-processing result, the output image reserved the regions that are suitable for puncture.

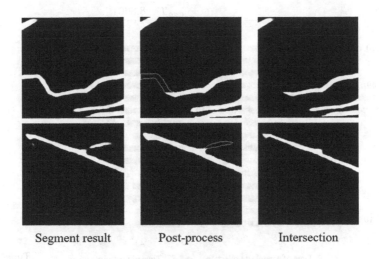

Segment result   Post-process   Intersection

Fig. 6. The Result of Post-processing.

The algorithm of vessel site selection for puncture is applied for select the appropriate puncture point and puncture position. As is shown in Fig. 7, the algorithm can select the appropriate puncture area and the puncture position after the post-processing procedure mentioned above. The result of the algorithm will be delivered to the mechanical systems of the puncture robots and the puncture process could be finished.

Fig. 7. The puncture point detection using the post processing result shown in the top of Fig. 5. $\angle theta = 5°$

In the experiment, we randomly selected 60 NIR images from the validation dataset to test the efficiency of the vessel site selection algorithm. Assume that the processing time of post-process is T_1, the processing time of vessel site selection is T_2, and the total time of T_1 and T_2 is T. The average of time cost is shown in Table 4. T and T_1 of 15 images are shown in Fig. 8.

Table 4. Average Processing Time.

Average time/s	$avg T_1$	0.007
	$avg T_2$	8.854
	$avg T$	8.860

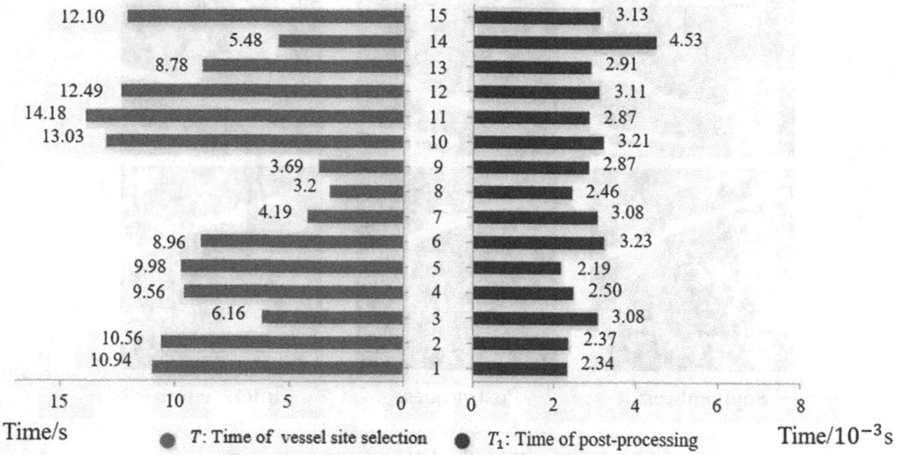

Fig. 8. The time of the vessel site selection algorithm and post-processing algorithm on 15 NIR images.

As shown in Table 4, the average of the processing time is less than 10 s. The average time of post-processing is less than 0.01 s. The main consumption part of time is vessel site algorithm. As shown in Fig. 8, the processing time of vessel site selection varies, but vessel site selection can be finished within 15 s. The procedure of post-processing can be finished within 0.01 s.

4   Conclusions

This paper discussed an image processing method for vein segmentation and an algorithm of vessel site selection for puncture. With the pre-trained ImageNet weight, data augmentation and image processing methods, the accuracy of vein segmentation models is improved, which is experimentally verified with several indicators. For example, the Dice-mean value is increased by an average of 1.12%. Additionally, the vessel site selection algorithm proposed in this paper calculates the accurate puncture site and position and then control the robot to achieve the autonomous puncture therapy.

References

1. Niska, R., Bhuiya, F., Xu, J.: National hospital ambulatory medical care survey: 2007 emergency department summary. Natl. Health Stat. Rep. **26**, 1–31 (2010)
2. Chen, A.: Image-guided robotics for autonomous venipuncture. Ph.D. dissertation, Department BME, Rutgers University, New Brunswick (2016)
3. Carr, P., et al.: Development of a clinical prediction rule to improve peripheral intravenous cannulae first attempt success in the emergency department and reduce post insertion failure rates: the Vascular Access Decisions in the Emergency Room (VADER) study protocol. BMJ Open **6**(2), e009196 (2016)
4. Jacobson, A., Winslow, E.: Variables influencing intravenous catheter insertion difficulty and failure: an analysis of 339 intravenous catheter insertions. Heart & Lung **34**(5), 345–359 (2005)
5. Kuensting, L., DeBoer, S., Holleran, R., Shultz, B., Steinmann, R., Venella, J.: Difficult venous access in children: taking control. J. Emerg. Nurs. **35**(5), 419–424 (2009)
6. Kennedy, R., Luhmann, J., Zempsky, W.: Clinical implications of unmanaged needle-insertion pain and distress in children. Pediatrics **122**(3), S130–S133 (2008)
7. Buowari, O.: Complications of venepuncture. Adv. Biosci. Biotechnol. **04**(01), 126–128 (2013)
8. Perry, T.: Profile: veebot [Resources_Start-ups]. IEEE Spectr. **50**(8), 23 (2013)
9. Balter, M., Chen, A., Maguire, T., Yarmush, M.: The system design and evaluation of a 7-DOF image-guided venipuncture robot. IEEE Trans. Rob. **31**(4), 1044–1053 (2015)
10. Li, F., Huang, Z., Xu, L.: Path planning of 6-DOF venipuncture robot arm based on improved a-star and collision detection algorithms. In: Proceedings of the 2019 IEEE International Conference on Robotics and Biomimetics, Dali, China, pp. 2971–2976 (2019)
11. Chen, A., Balter, M., Maguire, T., Yarmush, M.: Deep learning robotic guidance for autonomous vascular access. Nat. Mach. Intell. **2**(2), 104–115 (2020)
12. Chen, Y., et al.: Semi-supervised vein segmentation of ultrasound images for autonomous venipuncture. In: Proceedings of the IEEE/RSJ International Conference on Intelligent Robots and Systems, Prague, Czech Republic, pp. 9475–9481 (2021)
13. Beć, K.B., Grabska, J., Huck, C.W.: Principles and applications of miniaturized near-infrared (NIR) spectrometers. Chem. Eur. J. **27**(5), 1514–1532 (2021)

Data Processing and Image Analysis

Open-Set Fault Diagnosis Method for Industrial Process Based on Semi-supervised Learning

Jiaren Liu[1,2,3,4]($\boxtimes$) , Hong Song[1,2,3], and Jianguo Wang[5]

[1] Key Laboratory of Networked Control Systems, Chinese Academy of Sciences,
Shenyang 110016, China
liujiaren@sia.cn

[2] Shenyang Institute of Automation, Chinese Academy of Sciences, Shenyang 110016, China

[3] Institutes for Robotics and Intelligent Manufacturing, Chinese Academy of Sciences,
Shenyang 110169, China

[4] University of Chinese Academy of Sciences, Beijing 100049, China

[5] China Copper Co., Ltd., Kunming 650093, China

Abstract. Aiming at the inconsistent distribution of labeled and unlabeled data categories in the actual industrial production process, this paper proposes an open-set semi-supervised process fault diagnosis method based on uncertainty distribution alignment. Firstly, the proposed method forces the matching of the distribution of labeled data and unlabeled data. Then it combines a semi-supervised fault diagnosis model with the anomaly detection of one-vs-all classifier. The interior point (unlabeled samples in known class) is correctly classified while rejecting outliers to realize the fault diagnosis of open-set industrial process data. Finally, fault diagnosis experiments are carried out through numerical simulation and Tennessee-Eastman chemical process to verify the effectiveness and feasibility of the proposed method. Compared with temporal ensembling-dual student (TE-DS) and other semi-supervised fault diagnosis methods, it is proved that the proposed method is suitable for open-set fault diagnosis.

Keywords: Fault diagnosis · Industrial process · Semi-supervised learning · Open-set · Uncertainty distribution alignment

1 Introduction

A common assumption of semi-supervised learning (SSL) is that the tag space of tagged and untagged data is the same, but this assumption is often not satisfied in practice. Untagged data may contain new categories that cannot be seen in the tagged training data, which are often referred to as outliers. Because these abnormal values will seriously damage the performance of SSL algorithm [1], it is necessary to study the practicability of their detection in SSL. Ideally, the model should classify the samples of known categories (that is, interior points) into correct categories, and identify the samples of new categories as outliers. This task is called open-set semi-supervised learning (OSSL) [2]. However, most of the existing SSL methods [3, 4] are not suitable for OSSL. For example,

H. Liu et al. (Eds.): ICIRA 2022, LNAI 13458, pp. 103–112, 2022.
https://doi.org/10.1007/978-3-031-13841-6_10

the Fixmatch method [3] uses the model to generate pseudo-tags for the prediction of weakly enhanced untagged images, and trains the model to match its prediction for strongly enhanced images with pseudo-tags. This method takes advantage of pseudo-tags and uses the consistency between different enhanced images to standardize the model. However, in OSSL, it is possible to assign pseudo tags of known categories to outliers, thus reducing the accuracy of recognition. One feasible solution is to calculate the SSL target only for unlabeled samples that are considered to be interior points, in which the confidence threshold is used to select the interior point. For example, the multi-task curriculum (MTC) method [2] treats a certain proportion of samples as outliers by using Otsu thresholds [5], while the safe deep semi-supervised learning method [1] proposes meta-optimization, hoping to select untagged data that can help improve generalization performance. Although OSSL is a more realistic and practical scenario than standard SSL, it has not been widely explored, and it is not taken into account in current industrial fault methods using deep learning. Therefore, a fault diagnosis method based on open-set semi-supervised deep learning is proposed in this paper.

2 Distribution Alignment

Due to the limited sampling size, randomness and small sample size of labeled data, the empirical distribution of labeled data usually deviates from the real sample distribution, so it is difficult to judge the underlying distribution. This also leads to a big difference between labeled data and unlabeled data in empirical distribution, such as the existence of categories in unlabeled samples that have not appeared in labeled samples, which usually significantly reduces the performance of the model. In order to solve this problem, Wang et al. [6] proposed a semi-supervised learning method of augmented distribution alignment, which solved the imbalance of empirical distribution by countering distribution alignment. The core idea is to force the empirical distribution of labeled samples and unlabeled samples to be aligned by minimizing the loss function shown in formula (1).

$$\min_{g} d_{\mathcal{K}}(D_l, D_u) = \max_{g} \min_{h \in \mathcal{K}}[err(h, g, D_l) + err(h, g, D_u)] \tag{1}$$

where g is the feature extractor, h is the discriminator, and $\mathcal{K}$ is the measure of the divergence of the distribution between labeled samples and unlabeled samples, which can be expressed as shown in formula (2) [6].

$$d_{\mathcal{K}}(D_l, D_u) = 2\left\{1 - \min_{h \in \mathcal{K}}[err(h, g, D_l) + err(h, g, D_u)]\right\} \tag{2}$$

Let $err(h, g, D)$ indicate the prediction error of the discriminator to the sample x, and the calculation method is shown in formula (3) [6].

$$err(h, g, D) = \frac{1}{n}\sum_{x}[h(g(x)) \neq 0] \tag{3}$$

Inspired by Zhang [7], Wang [6] proposed a cross-set sample enhancement method to expand the training data set to make the learning process more stable and improve the robustness of the network model. The enhancement method is shown in formula (4)–(6) [6].

$$\tilde{x} = \lambda x^l + (1 - \lambda)x^u \tag{4}$$

$$\tilde{y} = \lambda y^l + (1 - \lambda)y^u \tag{5}$$

$$\tilde{z} = \lambda \cdot 0 + (1 - \lambda) \cdot 1 \tag{6}$$

where λ is a random variable that obeys a priori distribution, $\tilde{x}$ is an interpolation sample, $\tilde{y}$ is the corresponding label, and $\tilde{z}$ is the distribution discriminator tag.

Kurakin et al. [8] gave another idea of semi-supervised distribution alignment on the basis of the MixMatch method [9], forcing the predictive aggregation of unlabeled data to match the distribution. The basic idea of forced distribution alignment is to maximize the mutual information of unlabeled data between model input and output, that is, it is emphasized that excellent model prediction should depend on input as much as possible [10]. The goal can be formulated as shown in formula (7) [8].

$$\mathcal{J}(y;x) = H(E_x[p_{\text{model}}(y|x;\theta)]) - E_x[H(p_{\text{model}}(y|x;\theta))] \tag{7}$$

where $H(\cdot)$ represents entropy. Formula (7) encourages each individual model output to have low entropy, that is, high confidence for category labels and the model will predict each category at an equal frequency throughout the training set [8]. In the process of training, the average frequency $\tilde{p}(y)$ of the prediction category $q = p_{model}(y|x;\theta)$ of the model for unlabeled data is saved [8]. Given the prediction y of the model on the unlabeled sample u, q is scaled by the ratio $\frac{p(y)}{\tilde{p}(y)}$, and then the result is re-normalized to form an effective probability distribution so that the prediction of the label matches the distribution of the unlabeled data, as shown in formula (8) [8].

$$\tilde{q} = \text{Normalize}\left(q \times \frac{p(y)}{\tilde{p}(y)}\right) \tag{8}$$

3   Open-Set Semi-supervised Process Fault Diagnosis Strategy Based on Uncertainty Distribution Alignment

In order to solve the problem that the label categories in the labeled data collected in the industrial production process are incomplete, that is, the unlabeled data contains abnormal faults that do not exist in the tagged data, this paper combines semi-supervised fault diagnosis model with the anomaly detection of one-to-many (One Vs All, OVA) classifier. An open-set semi-supervised industrial process fault diagnosis strategy based on uncertain distribution alignment (UDA) is proposed. The overall framework of the OSSL-UDA model is shown in Fig. 1.

This paper realizes a further extension on the basis of semi-supervised fault diagnosis, mainly aiming at the semi-supervised fault diagnosis strategy for open-set industrial production process. Compared with the semi-supervised fault diagnosis method, the

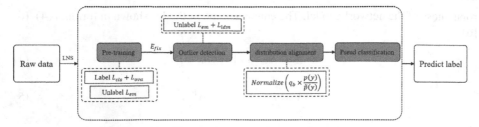

Fig. 1. OSSL-UDA method framework diagram

improvement of the proposed method in this paper is mainly reflected in two aspects. First, the practical problem that the distribution of labeled data and unlabeled data is actually unknown is considered in the fault diagnosis of semi-supervised industrial process. To solve this problem, a fault diagnosis method based on open-set semi-supervised learning is proposed. Then, in order to further force the consistency of the distribution between tagged and untagged data, an uncertain distribution alignment method is proposed to match the distribution of tagged datasets and untagged datasets.

For the fault diagnosis problem, given the standardized industrial process data $\mathcal{D} \in \mathbb{R}^{m \times n}$, $\mathcal{X} = \{(x_b, y_b):b \in (1, \ldots, B)\}$ denotes a batch of labeled samples randomly sampled from the labeled training set x_b, where $y_b \in (1, \ldots, K)$ is the corresponding label, and $\mathcal{U} = \{u_b:b \in (1, \ldots, B)\}$ denotes a batch of randomly sampled data from the unlabeled training set. At the same time, in order to solve the problem of open-set semi-supervised fault diagnosis, unlike the assumption that all unlabeled data come from K known classes in previous semi-supervised fault diagnosis tasks, the unlabeled data in the experimental setting of this paper may contain unknown classes. in order to achieve the correct classification of interior points while learning anomaly detection. The OSSL-UDA model contains three sub-modules. First, there is a shared feature extractor $F(\cdot)$, then an anomaly detector $D^j(\cdot)$, $j \in (1, \ldots, K)$ composed of K OVA sub-classifiers, and the last part is closed set classifier $C(\cdot)$, that is, a classifier without considering open-sets [11]. The classifier directly outputs the probability vectors of K categories corresponding to samples.

In order to solve the problem of open-set fault diagnosis, the model pre-training is carried out in the pre-E_{fix} batches. In this process, the OVA anomaly detection classifier is trained by labeled and unlabeled samples, and the anomaly threshold is obtained [11]. For the marked sample x, each sub-classifier of the exception detector outputs a distance, indicating the distance from the input sample to the corresponding category. The sub-classifier D^j corresponding to class j outputs two-dimensional vector $z_b^j = D^j(F(x_b))$, in which each dimension represents the probability of the sample x_b as the interior point score $p^j(t = 0|x_b)$ and the outlier score $p^j(t = 1|x_b)$, which is regarded as the interior point or outlier [11]. The L_{ova} is calculated by formula (9) [11].

$$\mathcal{L}_{\text{ova}}(\mathcal{X}) := \frac{1}{B} \sum_{b=1}^{B} -\log(p^{y_b}(t = 0|x_b)) - \min_{i \neq y_b} \log(p^i(t = 1|x_b)) \tag{9}$$

At the same time, the closed set sub-classifier $C(\cdot)$ is trained by cross-entropy loss L_{cls} minimization, and the OVA anomaly detection classifier and the corresponding closed set sub-classifier are obtained after E_{fix} batch training [11].

For unlabeled samples, entropy minimization is applied to OVA classifier, which is represented by L_{em} [11]. By minimizing the loss of unlabeled sample $\mathcal{U} = \{u_b\}_{b=1}^B$ in a given batch to enhance the distance between the outlier and the interior point, the L_{em} loss is calculated by formula (10) [11].

$$\mathcal{L}_{em}(\mathcal{U}) := -\frac{1}{B} \sum_{b=1}^B \sum_{j=1}^K p^j(t = 0|u_b) \log(p^{y_b}(t = 0|u_b))$$
$$+p^j(t = 1|u_b) \log(p^j(t = 1|u_b)) \tag{10}$$

After obtaining the pre-training model, the unlabeled samples are detected by the trained OVA anomaly detector [11]. If the outlier probability of the unlabeled sample u_b from the highest score class of all closed set sub-classifier $C(\cdot)$ in the OVA detector is higher than its probability as the interior point, then OVA regards the sample as an outlier, otherwise it is classified as a pseudo-interior point set $\mathcal{I}$. At the same time, the semi-supervised fault diagnosis method is used as the closed set classifier. The dual network training is carried out by constraining the consistency loss and stability loss of the selected pseudo interior point samples, and the closed set classifier is further trained [13]. This part of the constraint is collectively called $\mathcal{L}_{ldm}(\mathcal{I})$. In order to improve the success rate of outer point detection and apply uncertainty constraint to $\mathcal{L}_{ldm}$, the confidence threshold τ and uncertainty threshold κ are added. Only the pseudo interior point which is reliable enough is used to calculate the $\mathcal{L}_{ldm}$ loss. The final $\mathcal{L}_{ldm}$ calculation formula is shown in formula (11) [6, 8, 13].

$$\mathcal{L}_{ldm}(\mathcal{J}) = \sum_{i \in \mathcal{J}} \sum_{c=1}^K g_c^{(i)} \cdot (\mathcal{L}_{con} + \mathcal{L}_{std}) \tag{11}$$

$$g_c^{(i)} = [u(p_c^{(i)}(OVA)) \le \kappa][p_c^{(i)}(OVA) \ge \tau] \tag{12}$$

where $\boldsymbol{g}^{(i)} = [g_1^{(i)}, \ldots, g_K^{(i)}] \sqsubseteq \{0, 1\}^C$ indicates whether the sample $i_b \in \mathcal{I}$ is regarded as a pseudo interior point, and $g_K^{(i)} = 1$ indicates that the sample i_b is classified as a pseudo interior point of class K, $p_c^{(i)}(OVA)$ represents the output value of the OVA classifier, that is, the probability value that the OVA classifier regards the sample i_b as the interior point.

After screening out the outliers through the OVA anomaly detector, and the labeled samples and the unlabeled samples are forced to align the distribution to achieve distribution matching by formula (8) [8]. In each training batch, the model is saved in the past 128 batches. The predicted mean value $\tilde{p}(y)$ of the unlabeled data, and the predicted value of the current batch of unlabeled data is scaled by the mean value and the y-class distribution $p(y)$ in the labeled data set to implement forced distribution matching. The selected pseudo inliers are classified by the closed set classifier, and finally the fault diagnosis of the unlabeled samples of the known class is realized correctly when the outliers are rejected. The overall loss function representation of the final model is shown in formula (13), where λ_{em} and λ_{ldm} are the corresponding target weight parameters [6, 8, 13].

$$\mathcal{L}_{all}(\mathcal{X}, \mathcal{U}, \mathcal{J}) = \mathcal{L}_{cls}(\mathcal{X}) + \mathcal{L}_{ova}(\mathcal{X}) + \lambda_{em}\mathcal{L}_{em}(\mathcal{U}) + \lambda_{ldm}\mathcal{L}_{ldm}(\mathcal{J}) \quad (13)$$

4 Experiment

In order to verify the effectiveness of the open-set semi-supervised industrial process fault diagnosis method based on uncertainty distribution alignment, this section uses typical numerical simulation data [14] and Tennessee-Eastman process simulation data [15] for diagnosis experiments. Because the scenario of this paper is open-set semi-supervised fault diagnosis, that is, the categories of labeled samples and unlabeled samples are inconsistent, this paper selects two kinds of semi-supervised fault diagnosis models to verify the effectiveness of the method.

4.1 Numerical Simulation

The basic data of numerical simulation experiment [14] is multimode data. In order to satisfy the open-set semi-supervised learning scene, a class of unknown fault data not contained in the marked data are added to the marked data and test data, and finally the open-set data is obtained. The comparison methods are the dual student (DS) model [12] and the TE-DS [13] model. All the data are preprocessed by local nearest neighbors to eliminate multimode [14]. In order to enable the other two methods to deal with open-set data, the network model is used to predict whether the highest probability in the vector is greater than the abnormal threshold as an abnormal fault detector.

Table 1 shows the diagnostic accuracy of the DS, TE-DS and OSSL-UDA methods for 3 faults in open-set semi-supervised scenarios. It can be seen from the table that the proposed OSSL-UDA has achieved the highest accuracy in the diagnosis of the three faults, with an average accuracy of 82.95%. From the experimental results, we can see that the proposed OSSL-UDA method in open-set semi-supervised fault diagnosis, even with the interference of unknown types of faults, can still effectively and accurately classify the faults, and has a significant improvement compared with the DS and TE-DS methods.

Table 1. Open-set numerical simulation diagnostic accuracy (%)

Fault	DS	TE-DS	OSSL-UDA
1	75.50	76.50	**81.55**
2	76.75	80.25	**89.50**
3	69.26	69.00	**77.81**
Avg	73.84	75.25	**82.95**

4.2 Tennessee-Eastman Process

In order to further study the effectiveness of the proposed method in open-set fault diagnosis, simulation experiments are carried out on the Tennessee-Eastman platform [15]. The multimode scenario is further extended to open-set semi-supervised fault diagnosis. The single-class fault diagnosis and the multi-class joint fault diagnosis are also carried out, which are compared with DS [12] and TE-DS [13] methods. In the single-class fault diagnosis experiments, the unmarked data and test data of each fault condition add fault 15 as an unknown fault. The results of each method in single-class fault diagnosis experiments are shown in Table 2.

Table 2. Open-set single-class fault diagnosis test set accuracy (%)

Fault	DS	TE-DS	OSSL-UDA
1	95.71	99.67	**100.00**
2	76.98	88.21	**94.34**
3	55.32	57.28	**61.39**
4	93.26	95.53	**100.00**
5	81.34	80.10	**93.39**
6	76.52	93.10	**100.00**
7	99.58	99.68	**100.00**
8	84.99	91.70	**99.86**
9	62.31	55.59	**64.94**
10	59.21	61.57	**81.43**
11	**100.00**	95.39	100.00
12	89.23	97.01	**99.72**
13	98.97	92.76	**100.00**
14	**99.44**	87.86	92.83
Avg	83.77	85.39	**91.99**
Optimal	2	0	**13**

From the experimental results in Table 2, it can be seen that the proposed OSSL-UDA method in this paper has achieved the highest accuracy in 13 of the 14 single-class fault diagnosis experiments, in which fauls 1, 4, 6, 7, 11 and 13 all achieved 100% accuracy. It can be seen that the proposed method can achieve superior results in open-set semi-supervised fault diagnosis. In the single-class fault diagnosis experiment, because the analogy between the known class in the labeled sample and the unknown in the unlabeled sample is 1:1, the 3 semi-supervised fault diagnosis methods including the proposed OSSL-UDA method in this paper cannot effectively identify the unknown class, so it is easy to label the unknown class as the known class. In order to verify the ability of the OSSL-UDA model to identify unknown classes effectively when classifying known classes accurately in open-set semi-supervised fault diagnosis, multi-class joint fault diagnosis experiments are carried out, in which the ratio of labeled data known classes to unlabeled data unknown classes is 5:3.

The confusion matrix of the open-set semi-supervised fault diagnosis method in multi-class joint fault diagnosis is shown in Fig. 2. The experimental results of each method in open-set multi-class joint fault diagnosis are shown in Table 3. As can be seen from the experimental results in Table 3, the OSSL-UDA method proposed in this paper achieves the highest average accuracy of 92.11% in the open-set scene. In the diagnosis of four fault conditions in the five working conditions, the optimal diagnosis results have been obtained. But only in the normal working conditions, the diagnosis has not achieved high accuracy.

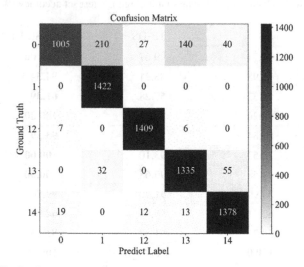

Fig. 2. Open-set multi-class joint fault diagnosis confusion matrix

Table 3. Open-set multi-class joint fault diagnosis accuracy (%)

	DS	TE-DS	OSSL-UDA
Normal	58.51	**100.00**	70.68
Fault 1	95.50	56.96	**100.00**
Fault 12	96.62	71.87	**99.09**
Fault 13	93.04	58.44	**93.88**
Fault 14	88.26	80.10	**96.91**
Avg acc	86.39	73.47	**92.11**
Outer acc	0.00	0.00	**79.79**

The multi-class joint fault diagnosis shown in Table 3 shows that the proposed method can effectively identify unknown fault types while accurately diagnosing known faults in open-set semi-supervised fault diagnosis scenarios. Compared with the other two methods, OSSL-UDA can identify 79.79% of unknown faults in multi-class joint faults. The results show that the proposed method is effective for the open-set semi-supervised fault diagnosis.

5 Conclusions

In view of the deficiency of labeled samples in the modern industrial production process and the inconsistent data distribution in the actual production process, this paper extends the semi-supervised fault diagnosis method to the open-set fault diagnosis scenario and proposes an open-set semi-supervised fault diagnosis strategy. In this method, the OVA abnormal fault detector is used to detect the abnormal fault of the unlabeled fault samples, and the pseudo interior points are selected from the unlabeled fault samples for closed set fault diagnosis classifier training. At the same time, confidence and uncertainty constraints are added to the training loss function of the closed set fault diagnosis classifier to ensure that enough reliable samples are selected from the pseudo interior point set for network training. After the outer point detection, the marked and unlabeled samples are forcibly distributed and aligned, so as to force the unmarked classification to align the labeled samples, so that the network model can accurately classify the known fault categories and identify unknown abnormal faults. Finally, experiments are carried out on the numerical simulation and the Tennessee-Eastman simulation. Through the comparative analysis of the experimental results, it is shown that the OSSL-UDA method proposed in this paper is effective fo open-set semi-supervised fault diagnosis.

Acknowledgements. This work was supported by the National Key R&D Program of China under Grant No. 2019YFB1706203.

References

1. Guo, L. Z., Zhang, Z. Y., Jiang, Y., Li, Y.-F., Zhou, Z.-H.: Safe deep semi-supervised learning for unseen-class unlabeled data. In: Proceedings of the 37th International Conference on Machine Learning, vol. 119, pp. 3897–3906. PMLR (2020)
2. Qing, Y., Ikami, D., Irie, G., Aizawa, K.: Multi-task curriculum framework for open-set semi-supervised learning. In: Vedaldi, A., Bischof, H., Brox, T., Frahm, J.-M. (eds.) ECCV 2020. LNCS, vol. 12357, pp. 438–454. Springer, Cham (2020). https://doi.org/10.1007/978-3-030-58610-2_26
3. Sohn, K., et al.: Fixmatch: Simplifying semi-supervised learning with consistency and confidence. Adv. Neural Inform. Process. Syst. **33**, 596–608 (2020)
4. Xie, Q., Dai, Z., Hovy, E., Luong, T., Le, Q.: Unsupervised data augmentation for consistency training. Adv. Neural. Inf. Process. Syst. **33**, 6256–6268 (2020)
5. Liu, D., Yu, J.: Otsu method and K-means. In: 2009 Ninth International Conference on Hybrid Intelligent Systems, pp. 344–349. IEEE (2009)
6. Wang, Q., Li, W., Gool, L.V.: Semi-supervised learning by augmented distribution alignment. In: International Conference on Computer Vision, pp. 1466–1475. IEEE/CVF. (2019)
7. Zhang, H., Cisse, M., Dauphin, Y. N., Lopez-Paz, D.: Mixup: beyond empirical risk minimization. In: International Conference on Learning Representations (2018)

8. Berthelot, D., et al.: ReMixMatch: Semi-Supervised Learning with Distribution Matching and Augmentation Anchoring. In: International Conference on Learning Representations (2019)

9. Berthelot, D., Carlini, N., Goodfellow, I., Papernot, N., Oliver, A., Raffeel, C.: MixMatch: a holistic approach to semi-supervised learning. In: Proceedings of the 33rd International Conference on Neural Information Processing Systems, pp. 5049–5059 (2019)

10. Grandvalet, Y., Bengio, Y.: Semi-supervised learning by entropy minimization. In: Proceedings of the 17th International Conference on Neural Information Processing Systems, pp. 529–536 (2014)

11. Saito, K., Saenko, K.: Ovanet: one-vs-all network for universal domain adaptation. In: International Conference on Computer Vision, pp. 9000–9009. IEEE/CVF (2021)

12. Ke, Z., Wang, D., Yan, Q., Ren, J.: Dual student: Breaking the limits of the teacher in semi-supervised learning. In: International Conference on Computer Vision, pp. 6728–6736. IEEE/CVF (2019)

13. Liu, J.R., Song, H., Li, S., et al.: Semi-supervised fault diagnosis method for chemical process based on TE-DS. Appl. Res. Comput. 39(01), 84–89 (2022)

14. Guo, J.Y., Liu, Y.C., Li, Y.: Fault detection of industrial process based on weighed local neighborhood standardization PCA. J. Shenyang Univ. Chem. Technol. 35(3), 265–274 (2021)

15. Li, H., Wang, H.G., Fan, W.H.: Multimode process fault detection based on local density ratio-weighted support vector data description. Ind. Eng. Chem. Res. 56(9), 2475–2491 (2017)

The Geometric Transformation Model of Two Views Based on the Line-Scan Camera Imaging Model

Lei Fang[1,2,3,4(✉)], Zelin Shi[1,2,3,4], Yunpeng Liu[2,3,4], Chenxi Li[2,3,4], and Enbo Zhao[2,3,4,5]

[1] Faculty of Robot Science and Engineering, Northeastern University, Shenyang 110169, China
fanglei@sia.cn
[2] Key Laboratory of Opto-Electronic Information Processing, Chinese Academy of Sciences, Shenyang 110016, China
[3] Shenyang Institute of Automation, Chinese Academy of Sciences, Shenyang 110016, China
[4] Institutes for Robotics and Intelligent Manufacturing, Chinese Academy of Sciences, Shenyang 110169, China
[5] University of Chinese Academy of Sciences, Beijing 100049, China

Abstract. With the increasing use of line-scan camera, it is difficult to ensure that its sensor is parallel to the target in imaging. This will make the target present a different appearance in linear array images. When two linear array images are registered, it is crucial to choose a suitable geometric transformation model. However, the imaging model of line-scan camera is different from that of frame camera, and the classical geometric transformation model of frame image, namely perspective transformation model, does not conform to geometric transformation of linear array image. Therefore, according to the imaging model of line-scan camera, the geometric transformation model of linear array image is derived in this paper. To obtain linear array images, an acquisition system is built. The geometric transformation model established in this paper and perspective transformation model are used to register the linear array images respectively. The registration results based on the geometric transformation model of linear array image show that the two linear array images can be completely aligned and the root mean square error of feature points is smaller. On the contrary, the registration results based on perspective transformation model show that the two images are not alignment, and the root mean square error of feature points is larger, which also indicates that it is not suitable for geometric transformation of linear array images.

Keywords: Line-scan camera · Imaging model · Geometric transformation model · Linear array image

1 Introduction

The line-scan camera is an imaging device with only one column sensor which has the characteristics of wide visual width and fast scanning frequency [1, 2]. It is mainly used in the aerospace field on account of high resolution images [3–6]. With the development

H. Liu et al. (Eds.): ICIRA 2022, LNAI 13458, pp. 113–124, 2022.
https://doi.org/10.1007/978-3-031-13841-6_11

of machine vision technology, the line-scan camera has been widely used in other fields [7, 8]. In rail transit, more and more attention has been paid to the safety of railway transportation [9–11]. To monitor the condition of train parts during operation, the trouble of moving electric-multiple-units detection system (TEDS) has been developed by the relevant department of China Railway. TEDS consists of 10 line-scan cameras to obtain a clear image of the train body at high speed, which is equipped on both sides and the bottom of the track [12]. When a train passes the TEDS station, the system is activated and collects the appearance of the train. At last, the relevant staff interprets the images according to prior knowledge to complete the operation inspection of trains.

To achieve automatic train fault detection through images, a lot of research has been studied by relevant departments. Lu et al. [13] compared the aligned train images to find out the differences between two train images, thus completing the automatic detection of train faults. It is indispensable to perform a geometric transformation to align two train images. Hence, it is very important whether the geometric transformation model can reflect the geometric transformation law of two linear array images. However, it is easy to ignore the pose difference of line-scan camera and only use translation or rigid geometric transformation model to align two linear array images, and the same situation also appears in Lu's paper. When the sensor of line-scan camera parallels to the target, the geometric transformation of different linear array images is simplified. This makes the geometric transformation models which are commonly used in the frame images also conform to the geometric transformation law of the linear array image. In practical application, it is difficult for different line-scan cameras to image at the same pose, which leads to a more complex geometric transformation on the linear array image. Meanwhile, the imaging model of line-scan camera is different from the model of frame camera, and we think that the geometric transformation model of linear array image is also different with that of frame image. Therefore, it is very important to establish the geometric transformation model of linear array images.

To solve the above problem, the geometric transformation model of linear array image based on the imaging model of line-scan camera is established, and a linear array image acquisition platform is built to obtain image data and verify the correctness of the established model. The geometric transformation model represents the mapping relationship between two images, the method based on feature points is used to register the linear array images, and the validity of the model is verified according to the registration results. At the same time, the perspective transformation model of the frame image is also used to register the same linear array images. Compare the results based on the two geometric transformation models, which verifies the correctness of the model established in this paper, and also verifies that the geometric transformation model of frame image does not conform to the geometric transformation law of linear array image.

The remainder of this paper is organized as follows. Section 2 reviews the imaging model of line-scan camera and derives the geometric transformation model of linear array image. Section 3 introduces the verification method for the established model. Meanwhile, the linear array images collected by the acquisition system built in this paper are shown. The compared verification experimental results are shown in Sect. 4. At last, Sect. 5 gives the conclusion of this paper.

2 The Geometric Transformation Model of Linear Array Image

2.1 The Imaging Model of Line-Scan Camera

The line-scan camera has only one line of photosensitive sensor which makes its imaging model different from that of frame camera, but the mapping relationship from target to image still conforms to the pinhole imaging model [14]. To describe this relationship, three coordinate systems are defined, namely the world coordinate system, the line-scan camera coordinate system and the image plane coordinate system, as shown in Fig. 1. The imaging process of line-scan camera is to transform the points in the world coordinate system to the camera coordinate system through rigid transformation, and then map them to the image plane coordinate system through the pinhole imaging model. The coordinate of a point P in the world coordinate system and the camera coordinate system are respectively represented as (X, Y, Z) and (x, y, z). Then the transformation of point P from the world coordinate system to the camera coordinate system can be expressed as:

$$\begin{pmatrix} x \\ y \\ z \\ 1 \end{pmatrix} = \begin{pmatrix} R_{3\times3} & T_{3\times1} \\ 0_{1\times3} & 1 \end{pmatrix} \begin{pmatrix} X \\ Y \\ Z \\ 1 \end{pmatrix} \tag{1}$$

where R and T are rotation matrix and translation matrix respectively.

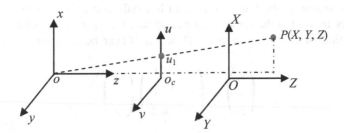

Fig. 1. A general view of geometry for line-scan camera imaging.

Point p in the camera coordinate system, which is P in the world coordinate system, is projected onto the image plane according to the pinhole model, and the coordinate of point p on the image plane is represented as (u_1, v_1). Since there is only one sensor column, one of the coordinates in the image plane coordinate system will be fixed. Assume that the sensor overlaps with u axis of the image plane, as shown in Fig. 1, according to similar triangles we can get:

$$\begin{cases} u_1 = \frac{f_1 x}{z} + p_v \\ v_1 = 1 \end{cases} \tag{2}$$

where $f_1 = f/dx$; f is the principal distance of the line-scan camera, dx represents the physical size of a pixel in the x-direction, and the p_v represents the principal offset in the sensor direction.

To obtain a useful linear array image, it is required relative motion between the line-scan camera and the target during imaging, and each line is spliced into a complete image. The v direction in the image coordinates will represent the count of imaging lines of the line-scan camera, i.e., $v = t \cdot F$, where t and F represent the sampling time and the sampling frequency of the line-scan camera respectively. Then, Eq. (2) is rewritten into the matrix form as:

$$
\begin{pmatrix} w_1 u_1 \\ v_1 \\ w_1 \end{pmatrix} = \begin{pmatrix} f_1 & 0 & p_v \\ 0 & F & 0 \\ 0 & 0 & 1 \end{pmatrix} \begin{pmatrix} x \\ t \\ z \end{pmatrix} \tag{3}
$$

Due to the relative motion between the line-scan camera and the target, the transformation relationship between the line-scan camera coordinate system and the world coordinate system will change with time. Therefore, the camera coordinate system at the first line imaging is selected as the reference coordinate system. Suppose that the velocity of the point relative to the line-scan camera is $V = -(v_x, v_y, v_z)$, then the coordinate relationship between point p in the camera coordinate system at time t and its coordinate in the reference coordinate system is:

$$
\begin{cases} x_i = x_1 - v_x t \\ y_i = y_1 - v_y t \\ z_i = z_1 - v_z t \end{cases} \tag{4}
$$

Since the sensor of the line-scan camera has only one column, it means that the target directly in front of the camera can be imaged, i.e., $y_i \equiv 0$. According to Eq. (4), the imaging time of ith line is $t = y_1/v_y$. Then, Eq. (4) can be rewritten as follows:

$$
\begin{pmatrix} x_i \\ t \\ z_i \end{pmatrix} = \begin{pmatrix} 1 & -\frac{v_x}{v_y} & 0 \\ 0 & \frac{1}{v_y} & 0 \\ 0 & -\frac{v_z}{v_y} & 1 \end{pmatrix} \begin{pmatrix} x_1 \\ y_1 \\ z_1 \end{pmatrix} \tag{5}
$$

Combining Eqs. (1), (2) and (5), the imaging model of line-scan camera can be obtained as follows:

$$
\begin{pmatrix} w_1 u_1 \\ v_1 \\ w_1 \end{pmatrix} = \begin{pmatrix} f_1 & 0 & p_v \\ 0 & F & 0 \\ 0 & 0 & 1 \end{pmatrix} \begin{pmatrix} 1 & -\frac{v_x}{v_y} & 0 \\ 0 & \frac{1}{v_y} & 0 \\ 0 & -\frac{v_z}{v_y} & 1 \end{pmatrix} \begin{pmatrix} 1 & 0 & 0 & 0 \\ 0 & 1 & 0 & 0 \\ 0 & 0 & 1 & 0 \end{pmatrix} \begin{pmatrix} R_{3\times3} & T_{3\times1} \\ 0_{1\times3} & 1 \end{pmatrix} \begin{pmatrix} X \\ Y \\ Z \\ 1 \end{pmatrix} \tag{6}
$$

In general, f_1, p_v and R, T are called the intrinsic parameters and extrinsic parameters respectively. By combining these matrices, a simplified representation camera imaging model is:

$$
\begin{pmatrix} wu \\ v \\ w \end{pmatrix} = \begin{pmatrix} m_{11} & m_{12} & m_{13} & m_{14} \\ m_{21} & m_{22} & m_{23} & m_{24} \\ m_{31} & m_{32} & m_{33} & m_{34} \end{pmatrix} \begin{pmatrix} X \\ Y \\ Z \\ 1 \end{pmatrix} \tag{7}
$$

It can be seen from the imaging model of line-scan camera that the scale factor w only affects one direction of linear array image, which is related to the corresponding direction of the sensor on the linear array image. As the sensor of frame camera is an array, the scale factor w in its imaging model will affect both the horizontal and vertical direction of the image. This is the main difference between the imaging model of line-scan camera and that of frame camera.

2.2   The Geometric Transformation Model of Two Views for Line-Scan Camera

The geometric transformation model describes the mapping relationship of the plane target on two images, which depends on the poses between the target and the camera. One image can be transformed by the model and geometrically consistent with the same target on the other image. However, the imaging model of line-scan camera is different from that of frame camera, and the geometric transformation model of frame image is not suitable for geometric transformation of linear array image. Therefore, by the imaging model of line-scan camera, the geometric transformation model of linear array image is deduced. Assume that line-scan camera I and line-scan camera II image a planar target which moves horizontally to the right at velocity V, as shown in Fig. 2. According to Eq. (7), the imaging model of line-scan camera I and line-scan camera II can be obtained as:

$$
\begin{cases}
\text{Line - scan camera I:} & \begin{pmatrix} w_1 u_1 \\ v_1 \\ w_1 \end{pmatrix} = \begin{pmatrix} m_{11} & m_{12} & m_{13} & m_{14} \\ m_{21} & m_{22} & m_{23} & m_{24} \\ m_{31} & m_{32} & m_{33} & m_{34} \end{pmatrix} \begin{pmatrix} X \\ Y \\ Z \\ 1 \end{pmatrix} \\[20pt]
\text{Line - scan camera II:} & \begin{pmatrix} w_2 u_2 \\ v_2 \\ w_2 \end{pmatrix} = \begin{pmatrix} n_{11} & n_{12} & n_{13} & n_{14} \\ n_{21} & n_{22} & n_{23} & n_{24} \\ n_{31} & n_{32} & n_{33} & n_{34} \end{pmatrix} \begin{pmatrix} X \\ Y \\ Z \\ 1 \end{pmatrix}
\end{cases} \tag{8}
$$

Since the world coordinate system can be set at any position, it is assumed that the XOY plane of the world coordinate system in Fig. 2 coincides with the target plane. This means that the value of the point on the target plane in the Z-axis direction is always 0, then Eq. (8) can be simplified as follows:

$$
\begin{cases}
\text{Line - scan camera I:} & \begin{pmatrix} w_1 u_1 \\ v_1 \\ w_1 \end{pmatrix} = \begin{pmatrix} m_{11} & m_{12} & m_{14} \\ m_{21} & m_{22} & m_{24} \\ m_{31} & m_{32} & m_{34} \end{pmatrix} \begin{pmatrix} X \\ Y \\ 1 \end{pmatrix} = M \begin{pmatrix} X \\ Y \\ 1 \end{pmatrix} \\[20pt]
\text{Line - scan camera II:} & \begin{pmatrix} w_2 u_2 \\ v_2 \\ w_2 \end{pmatrix} = \begin{pmatrix} n_{11} & n_{12} & n_{14} \\ n_{21} & n_{22} & n_{24} \\ n_{31} & n_{32} & n_{34} \end{pmatrix} \begin{pmatrix} X \\ Y \\ 1 \end{pmatrix} = N \begin{pmatrix} X \\ Y \\ 1 \end{pmatrix}
\end{cases} \tag{9}
$$

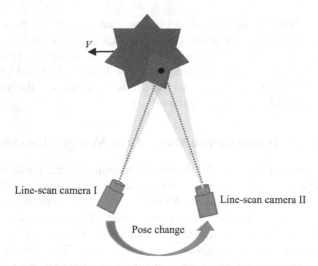

Fig. 2. Imaging by line-scan camera with different poses.

Suppose the inverse matrix of M exists; then, we can obtain:

$$\begin{pmatrix} X \\ Y \\ 1 \end{pmatrix} = M^{-1} \begin{pmatrix} w_1 u_1 \\ v_1 \\ w_1 \end{pmatrix}$$

$$w_1 = \frac{\det|M| - (m_{11}m_{32} - m_{31}m_{12})v_1}{(m_{21}m_{32} - m_{31}m_{22})u_1 + m_{11}m_{22} - m_{12}m_{31}}$$

(10)

Combine line-scan camera II in Eqs. (9) and (10) and eliminate the X and Y axes:

$$\begin{pmatrix} w_2 u_2 \\ v_2 \\ w_2 \end{pmatrix} = NM^{-1} \begin{pmatrix} w_1 u_1 \\ v_1 \\ w_1 \end{pmatrix}$$

(11)

By substituting w_1 in Eq. (10) into Eq. (11), the geometric transformation model of linear array image is obtained:

$$\begin{cases} u_2 = \frac{h_1 u_1 + h_2 u_1 v_1 + h_3 v_1 + h_4}{h_5 u_1 + h_6 u_1 v_1 + h_7 v_1 + 1} \\ v_2 = \frac{h_8 u_1 + h_9 u_1 v_1 + h_{10} v_1 + h_{11}}{h_{12} u_1 + 1} \end{cases}$$

(12)

where $h_1 \sim h_{12}$ are the combination of parameters in matrix M and matrix N, and these parameters have been determined at imaging. It means that the parameters in Eq. (12) are fixed. Therefore, for any two linear array images, the geometric transformation relationship between them can be represented by Eq. (12). Compared with the perspective transformation model of frame image, the geometric transformation model of linear array image has more parameters. Meanwhile, it has the same constraints as the perspective transformation model in the application that is only suitable for plane targets or approximate plane targets.

3 Verification Method of the Geometric Transformation Model of Linear Array Image

3.1 Verification Method

Image registration is the task of warping an image and making it consistent with another image geometrically. It is the key to image alignment that the model conforms to the geometric transformation law of the two images. Therefore, the linear array image registration will be used in this paper to verify whether the established geometric transformation model is correct. In general, two approaches have been proposed: the direct approaches and the feature-based [15]. The direct approaches use the value of all pixels of interest to establish an optimization objective and obtain the geometric transformation parameters by numerical optimization. However, this method is susceptible to the influence of initial value and optimization methods that cannot easily get the optimal solution. The method based on image feature points is to extract feature points from two images and then directly solve the parameters of geometric transformation model by feature point pairs which are matched. Hence, the linear array image is registered based on image feature points in this paper.

The goal of image registration is to find the geometric transformation parameters between two images. Then, change Eq. (12) to the following form:

$$\begin{cases} h_1 u_1 + h_2 u_1 v_1 + h_3 v_1 + h_4 - h_5 u_1 u_2 - h_6 u_1 v_1 u_2 - h_7 u_2 v_1 = u_2 \\ h_8 u_1 + h_9 u_1 v_1 + h_{10} v_1 + h_{11} - h_{12} u_1 v_2 = v_2 \end{cases} \tag{13}$$

There are 12 parameters to be solved in the geometric transformation model of linear array image established in this paper. According to Eq. (13), the parameters in u_2 and v_2 are not correlated, so 7 pairs of matching points are needed to solve the parameters in the model. Suppose that there are 7 matching point pairs (u_{1i}, v_{1i}), $i = 1...7$. The point coordinates can be substituted into Eq. (13) and written in the matrix form as follows:

$$\begin{cases} A_1 H_1 = B_1 \\ A_2 H_2 = B_2 \end{cases} \tag{14}$$

where

$$\begin{cases} A_1 = \begin{pmatrix} u_{11} & u_{11}v_{11} & v_{11} & 1 & -u_{11}u_{21} & -u_{11}v_{11}u_{21} & -u_{21}v_{11} \\ \vdots & \vdots & \vdots & \vdots & \vdots & \vdots & \vdots \\ u_{17} & u_{17}v_{17} & v_{17} & 1 & -u_{17}u_{27} & -u_{17}v_{17}u_{27} & -u_{27}v_{17} \end{pmatrix}_{7 \times 7} & B_1 = (u_{21}, ..., u_{27})^T_{7 \times 1} \\ A_2 = \begin{pmatrix} u_{11} & u_{11}v_{11} & v_{11} & 1 & -u_{11}v_{21} \\ \vdots & \vdots & \vdots & \vdots & \vdots \\ u_{15} & u_{15}v_{15} & v_{15} & 1 & -u_{15}v_{25} \end{pmatrix}_{5 \times 5} & B_2 = (v_{21}, ..., v_{25})^T_{5 \times 1} \end{cases}$$

$$H = (H_1, H_2)^T_{12 \times 1} = (h_1, ..., h_{12})^T_{12 \times 1}$$

Then, the parameters in the geometric transformation model of linear array image are:

$$\begin{cases} H_1 = A_1^{-1} \cdot B_1 \\ H_2 = A_2^{-1} \cdot B_2 \end{cases} \tag{15}$$

There are errors in the extraction and matching of image feature points, the optimal parameters for global geometric transformation cannot be obtained only by 7 feature point pairs. Therefore, iteration is adopted to get a globally optimal solution in this paper. Each iteration 7 feature point pairs are randomly selected and the geometric transformation parameters are calculated according to Eq. (15). Then the coordinate errors of other feature point pairs are calculated, and the number of errors less than the threshold is counted. Finally, the solution with the largest number is taken as the optimal geometric transformation parameters. The specific registration process is shown in Fig. 3.

Input: two linear array images which one is the target image and the other is the source image, iterations, the threshold of coordinate point error ε;

pre-compute:
1. extract the feature points from the two linear array images;
2. match the extracted feature points;

Iterate:
3. select 7 pairs of matched feature points randomly;
4. compute the geometric transformation parameters according to the Eq. 14 and Eq. 15;
5. evaluate the coordinates of feature points on the source image to the target image with Eq. 12;
6. calculate the coordinate errors of each feature point;
7. count the numbers N_{iter} of the coordinate error less than the threshold ε;
end
8. find the maximum from the N_{iter} and its corresponding geometric transformation parameters;

Output: the geometric transformation parameters of the two linear array images.

Fig. 3. The registration algorithm of linear array image based on feature points.

3.2   Experimental Data

To verify the geometric transformation model of linear array image, it is necessary to take the linear array image as experimental data. However, there is no public data set of linear array images. Therefore, a linear array image acquisition system is built in this paper and experimental data is collected by this system. As shown in Fig. 4, the system includes a line-scan camera, a one-dimensional motion platform, a tripod and a plane target. The platform passes through the front of the line-scan camera at a uniform speed from right to left and then completes the linear array image acquisition process of a planar target. By translation and rotation of the tripod, the line-scan camera can image the same target at different poses, and the different geometric transformations of the target can be produced on the image.

Figure 5 lists the linear array images collected by the acquisition system built in this paper. The content of linear array images is checkerboard which can extract the feature points with sub-pixel accuracy and obtain rich and evenly distributed feature points, and reduce the influence of image registration precision caused by the error of feature points.

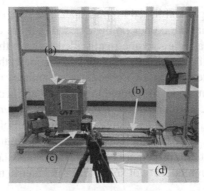

Fig. 4. Line-scan camera imaging system. (a) Imaged object. (b) One-dimension motion platform. (c) Line-scan camera. (d) Tripod.

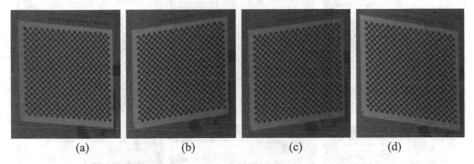

(a)   (b)   (c)   (d)

Fig. 5. The checkerboard linear array images collected by the acquisition system.

4   Experimental Results

The goal of the experiment is to verify the correctness of the geometric transformation model established in this paper according to the registration results of two linear array images. Meanwhile, in order to verify the perspective transformation model of frame image does not conform to the transformation law of linear array image, it will also be used to register the linear array image as a compared experiment. The registration process is the same as that in Fig. 3, except that the geometric transformation model of linear array image is replaced by the perspective transformation model of frame image. The number of iteration of the registration experiment is 1,00,000. Feature points in checkerboard images are extracted by the method in literature [16]. In this paper, the results of registration will be evaluated from two aspects. One is directly to observe the registration results, the feature points of the two images are drawn on their overlapped images. If the two checkerboard images are geometrically consistent, the feature points of the two images should also coincide. The other is to calculate the root mean square error of the image feature points, where the checkerboard feature points are the intersection points of each small box, a total of 899.

Take Fig. 5(a) as the template and register with Fig. 5(b)~(d) respectively. As shown in Fig. 6, the first row is the registration results based on the geometric transformation model of linear array image established in this paper. The pink corner points are almost invisible, which means that the corner points of each pair are completely overlapped, indicating that the two images are geometrically identical. On the contrary, as shown in the second row of Fig. 6, there are many pink and green points that do not coincide with each other, which indicate that the two checkerboard images registered based on the perspective transformation model of frame image are not aligned. The root mean square errors of the corner point coordinates after registration are shown in Table 1. The results of RMS errors based on the geometric transformation model of linear array image are less than 0.4 pixels, while based on the perspective transformation model are all more than 6 pixels. It means that the correctness of the model established in this paper, and the perspective transformation model is not suitable for geometric transformation of linear array image.

Fig. 6. The registration results of the checkerboard linear array image.

Table 1. The root mean square errors of corner points after registration.

Registration image pair	Based on the model established in this paper/pixels	Based on the perspective transformation model/pixels
(a)&(b)	0.1999	6.4958
(a)&(c)	0.2748	6.8646
(a)&(d)	0.3524	7.1378

5 Conclusion

As the line-scan camera is more and more widely used, it is difficult to make the sensor parallel to the target in the application, so the geometric changes of the target on the linear array image are different from those on the frame image. Therefore, according to the imaging model of line-scan camera, the geometric transformation model of linear array image is deduced in this paper. Experimental results show that the proposed geometric transformation model completely aligned two linear array images and the root mean square errors of feature point coordinates are about 0.4 pixels, the correctness of the model is verified. Meanwhile, the comparative experimental results show that the two linear array images register based on the perspective transformation model cannot be alignment, indicating that the model is no longer suitable for geometric transformation of linear array image.

Acknowledgement. This research was supposed by the Science and Technological Innovation Field Fund Projects (No. E01Z041101).

References

1. Hui, B.W., et al.: Line-scan camera calibration in close-range photogrammetry. Opt. Eng. **51**(5), 053602 (2012). https://doi.org/10.1117/1.OE.51.5.053602
2. Ye, Y.X., et al.: Robust registration of multimodal remote sensing images based on structural similarity. IEEE Trans. Geosci. Remote Sens. **55**(5), 2941–2958 (2017). https://doi.org/10.1109/TGRS.2017.2656380
3. Iwasaki, A., Fujisada, H.: ASTER geometric performance. IEEE Trans. Geosci. Remote Sens. **43**(12), 2700–2706 (2005). https://doi.org/10.1109/TGRS.2005.849055
4. Liu, C.C.: Processing of FORMOSAT-2 daily revisit imagery for site surveillance. IEEE Trans. Geosci. Remote Sens. **44**(11), 3206–3214 (2006). https://doi.org/10.1109/TGRS.2006.880625
5. Storey, J.C., Choate, M.J., Meyer, D.J.: A geometric performance assessment of the EO-1 advanced land imager. IEEE Trans. Geosci. Remote Sens. **42**(3), 602–607 (2004). https://doi.org/10.1109/TGRS.2003.820603
6. Zhu, Z.S., et al.: High precision matching and 3D surface reconstruction of Chang'E 1 lunar images. Acta Opt. Sin. **34**(2), 92–100 (2014)
7. Peng, W., et al.: A high performance real-time vision system for curved surface inspection. Optik **232**, 166514 (2021). https://doi.org/10.1016/j.ijleo.2021.166514
8. Usamentiaga, R., Garcia, D.F., de la Calle, F.J.: Line-scan camera calibration: a robust linear approach. Appl. Opt. **59**(30), 9443 (2020). https://doi.org/10.1364/AO.404774
9. Zhan, D., et al.: Study on high-speed and dynamic vision measurement approach for overhead catenary system geometric parameter inspection. Chin. J. Sci. Instrum. **35**(8), 1852–1859 (2014)
10. Xu, J.Y., et al.: Correction of rolling wheel images captured by a linear array camera. Appl. Opt. **54**, 9736–9740 (2015). https://doi.org/10.1364/AO.54.009736
11. Liu, L., Zhou, F.Q., He, Y.Z.: Automated visual inspection system for bogie block key under complex freight train environment. IEEE Trans. Instrum. Meas. **65**(1), 2–14 (2016). https://doi.org/10.1109/TIM.2015.2479101

12. Lu, S.F., Liu, Z.: Automatic visual inspection of a missing split pin in the China railway high-speed. Appl. Opt. **55**(30), 8395–8405 (2016). https://doi.org/10.1364/AO.55.008395
13. Lu, S.F., Liu, Z., Shen, Y.: Automatic fault detection of multiple targets in railway maintenance based on time-scale normalization. IEEE Trans. Instrum. Meas. **67**(4), 849–865 (2018). https://doi.org/10.1109/TIM.2018.2790498
14. Gupta, R., Hartley, R.I.: Linear pushbroom camera. IEEE Trans. Pattern Anal. Mach. Intell. **19**(9), 963–975 (1997). https://doi.org/10.1109/34.615446
15. Bartoli, A.: Groupwise geometric and photometric direct image registration. IEEE Trans. Pattern Anal. Mach. Intell. **30**(12), 2098–2108 (2008). https://doi.org/10.1109/TPAMI.2008.22
16. Geiger, A., et al.: Automatic camera and range sensor calibration using a single shot. In: IEEE International Conference on Robotics and Automation, pp. 3936–3943 (2012). https://doi.org/10.1109/ICRA.2012.6224570

Group Sparsity Regularized High Order Tensor for HSIs Super-Resolution

Xi'ai Chen[1,2(✉)], Siyu Guo[1,2,3], Huidi Jia[1,2,3], Baichen Liu[1,2,3], Zhenyu Li[1,2,4], and Zhi Han[1,2]

[1] State Key Laboratory of Robotics, Shenyang Institute of Automation, Chinese Academy of Sciences, Shenyang 110016, Liaoning, China
chenxiai@sia.cn
[2] Institutes for Robotics and Intelligent Manufacturing, Chinese Academy of Sciences, Shenyang 110169, Liaoning, China
[3] University of Chinese Academy of Sciences, Beijing 100049, China
[4] Shenyang University of Technology, Shenyang 110870, China

Abstract. Super-resolution of hyperspectral images is a crucial task in remote sensing applications. In this paper, we propose a group sparsity regularized high order tensor model for hyperspectral images super-resolution. In our model, a relaxed low tensor train rank estimation strategy is applied to exploit the correlations of local spatial structure along the spectral mode. Weighted group sparsity regularization is used to model the local group sparsity. An efficient algorithm is derived under the framework of alternative direction multiplier method. Extensive experimental results on public datasets have proved that the proposed method is effective compared with the state-of-art methods.

Keywords: High order tensor · Relaxed tensor train rank · Group sparsity · HSI super-resolution

1 Introduction

The value of Hyperspectral images (HSIs) lies in their high spectral range, which means higher precision in material identification. Because of the finite of the sun irradiance, current cameras inevitably need to consider the tradeoff between spectral resolution, spatial resolution, light throughput and etc. [1]. It means that in order to keep the high spectral resolution in need, HSIs are often acquired with lower spatial resolution. In various remote sensing tasks [2–9], high spatial quality of HSIs are in demanding.

Intuitively, the HSIs has three dimensions, namely width, height and spectral, which can be viewed as high order tensors. Low rank tensor theory has demonstrated its effectiveness in high order tensor representation. Li et al. [10]

Supported in part by the National Natural Science Foundation of China under Grant 61903358, Grant 61873259 and Grant 61821005, in part by the Youth Innovation Promotion Association of the Chinese Academy of Sciences under Grant 2022196 and Grant Y202051, National Science Foundation of Liaoning Province under Grant 2021-BS-023.

H. Liu et al. (Eds.): ICIRA 2022, LNAI 13458, pp. 125–137, 2022.
https://doi.org/10.1007/978-3-031-13841-6_12

formulate the HSIs super-resolution issue as coupled sparse tensor factorization, which updates sparse core tensor and the dictionaries of three modes of Tucker decomposition alternatively. Zhang et al. [11] propose a graph-regularized low rank Tucker decomposition method for HSI super-resolution, which utilize the spectral smoothness and spatial consistency and from the LR-HSI and HR-MSI, respectively. Ren [13] proposes a nonlocal sparse Tucker decomposition for HSI super-resolution. However, the performance of the Tucker decomposition based method is limited by the unbalance of its mode matrix. Tensor-train (TT) factorization is introduced to image processing and outperforms CAN-DECOMP/PARAFAC (CP) factorization and Tucker factorization benefiting from its relative balanced mode matrices [14,15]. The rank of TT decomposition consists of ranks of matrixes, which is formed by a well-balanced matricization scheme, i.e., matricizes the tensor along permutations of modes. The low TT rank (LTTR) prior has been proved to be effective in the color images and videos completion, and its performance is superior to Tucker rank based models [15]. In our model, we use TT decomposition to better represent the high order tensor.

Recently, the combination of low-rank tensor decomposition with spatial-spectral TV regularization [16] achieved great HSI recovery results because the HSI global spatial-spectral correlation and spatial-spectral smoothness can be considered simultaneously. However, there are still some problems with this approach. The models based bandby-band TV and spatial-spectral TV-regularized fully exploit the sparse prior of the spatial-spectral difference data, and usually use the convex l_1−norm to describe the sparse prior. In general, sparsity is a useful constraint to improve the piecewise smooth structure of each band. However, sparse prior only represents the number of nonzero elements, ignoring the local group structure of the nonzero elements. In this paper, we turn to incorporate the group sparsity term in SR model to exploit the local group sparse structure.

To better exploit the prior hidden in HSI images, in this paper, we propose an weighted group sparsity regularized low TT rank method for dealing with HSI super-resolution problem. The fusion strategy with Multispectral images (MSIs) is adopted in the SR model to facilitate the resolution in spatial domain. The relaxed low TT rank estimates the HR-HSI from the LR-HSI and HR-MSI by LTTR priors, and can effectively learn the correlations among the spectral, spatial and nonlocal modes of the similar HR-HSI cubes. Group sparse regularization of the spatial difference data is applied to model the local group sparsity in spatial.

The rest of paper is organized as follows: Sect. 2 introduces the tensor preliminaries. The proposed group sparsity regularized low TT rank tensor model for HSI SR problem and the derived algorithm to solve this model are given in Sect. 3 and 4, respectively. Section 5 and 6 provides the experimental results and conclusions, separately.

2   Preliminaries

In this section, tensor notations and operations are given in Table 1.

3 Model

We introduce a group sparsity regularized low rank tensor model for HSI image super-resolution, in this section.

The spatial structure of HSIs are often local repeated or correlated, which means that the HSIs possess nonlocal similarity property. To exploit this prior, k-means++ [18] technique is applied to cluster the similar spatial structural patches of the HSI images along the spectral mode. Through that, we obtain N_k similar 3-D cubes in each cluster, denoted as $\mathcal{X}^k \in \mathbb{R}^{I_1' \times I_2' \times I_3 \times N_k}$. And all the clusters form the original tensor $\sum_k^K \mathcal{X}^k = \mathcal{X} \in \mathbb{R}^{I_1 \times I_2 \times I_3}$. Then TT rank is used to exploit and measure the low rank property hidden in high order tensor. Since the direct optimization of TT rank is NP hard. We turn to use one of its nonconvex relaxed forms, i.e., log-sum norm, which has been validated more effective in approximating the rank [19].

Table 1. Tensor notations and operations.

Definition	Symbol
0-order tensor (scalar)	$x \in \mathbb{R}^0$
1-order tensor (vector)	$\mathbf{x} \in \mathbb{R}^{I_1}$
2-order tensor (matrix)	$X \in \mathbb{R}^{I_1 \times I_2}$
N-order tensor ($N \geq 3$)	$\mathcal{X} \in \mathbb{R}^{I_1 \times I_2 \times \cdots \times I_N} (N \geq 3)$
Tensor element	$x_{i_1, i_2, \ldots, i_N}$
Tensor fiber	$\mathcal{X}_{:, i_2, i_3, \ldots, i_N}$
Tensor slice	$\mathcal{X}_{:, :, i_3, \ldots, i_N}$
Tensor $n-$mode product	$\mathcal{Y} = \mathcal{X} \times_n U \in \mathbb{R}^{I_1 \times \cdots \times I_{n-1} \times J \times I_{n+1} \times \cdots \times I_N}$
Tensor $n-$mode product element	$\sum_{i_n} x_{i_1, \ldots, i_{n-1}, i_n, i_{n+1}, \ldots, i_N} u_{j_n, i_n}$
Tucker	$\mathcal{X} = \mathcal{G} \times_1 U^1 \times_2 U^2 \cdots \times_N U^N$
Tucker mode$-n$ unfolding matrix	$\mathcal{X}_{(n)} = unfold_n(\mathcal{X}) \in \mathbb{R}^{I_n \times \prod_{i=1, i \neq n}^N I_i}$
Tucker rank $(r_1, r_2, \ldots, r_N)$	$r_n = rank(\mathcal{X}_{(n)})$
Rank-1 tensor	$\mathcal{X} = \mathbf{x}^{(1)} \circ \mathbf{x}^{(2)} \circ \cdots \circ \mathbf{x}^{(N)}$
CANDECOMP/PARAFAC (CP)	$\mathcal{X} = \sum_r^R \mathbf{x}_r^{(1)} \circ \mathbf{x}_r^{(2)} \circ \cdots \circ \mathbf{x}_r^{(N)}$
Tensor Train (TT)	$\mathcal{X} = \sum_{r_0}^{R_0} \cdots \sum_{r_N}^{R_N} G_1(r_0, i_1, r_1) \cdots G_N(r_{N-1}, i_N, r_N)$
TT mode $-(1, 2, \ldots, n)$ unfolding matrix	$\mathcal{X}_{[n]} \in \mathbb{R}^{\prod_{i=1}^n I_i \times \prod_{i=n+1}^N I_i}$
TT rank $(r_1, r_2, \ldots, r_{N-1})$	$r_n = rank(\mathcal{X}_{[n]})$
Inner product	$\langle \mathcal{X}, \mathcal{Y} \rangle = \sum_{i_1, i_2, \ldots, i_N} x_{i_1, i_2, \ldots, i_N} y_{i_1, i_2, \ldots, i_N}$
ℓ_0 norm	$\|\mathcal{X}\|_0 = \#\{i_1, i_2, \ldots, i_N | x_{i_1, i_2, \ldots, i_N} \neq 0\}$
ℓ_1 norm	$\|\mathcal{X}\|_1 = \sum_{i_1, i_2, \ldots, i_N} |x_{i_1, i_2, \ldots, i_N}|$
$\ell_{2,1}$ norm	$\|\mathcal{X}\|_{2,1} = \sum_{i=1}^m \sum_{j=1}^n \|\mathcal{X}(i, j, :)\|_2 + \|\mathcal{X}(i, j, :)\|_2$
ℓ_F norm	$\|\mathcal{X}\|_F = \sqrt{\langle \mathcal{X}, \mathcal{X} \rangle} = \left(\sum_{i_1, i_2, \ldots, i_N} x_{i_1, i_2, \ldots, i_N}^2 \right)^{1/2}$

As in [20], the log-sum norm of the k-th cluster of the HSI tensor cubes, i.e., $\mathcal{X}^k$, in TT format can be written as

$$\|\mathcal{X}^k\|_{TT-LS} = \sum_{k=1}^{K} \sum_{n=1}^{N-1} \alpha_n \|\mathcal{X}^k_{[n]}\|_{LS} \tag{1}$$

where $\alpha_n = \frac{\min(\prod_{i=1}^{n} I_i, \prod_{i=n+1}^{N} I_i)}{\sum_{n=1}^{N-1} \min(\prod_{i=1}^{n} I_i, \prod_{i=n+1}^{N} I_i)}$ is the weight of mode-n matrix and it satisfies $\sum_{n=1}^{N-1} \alpha_n = 1$ and

$$\|\mathcal{X}^k_{[n]}\|_{LS} = \sum_{i} \log(\sigma^i_{\mathcal{X}^k_{[n]}} + \delta) \tag{2}$$

here $\sigma^i_{\mathcal{X}^k_{[n]}}$ is the ith singular value of matrix X and δ is a minimum scalar to avoid zero. For approximating the original tensor $\mathcal{X}_0$, each mode-n matrix in Eq. (2) has the following local minimum solution

$$\hat{\mathcal{X}}^k_{[n]} = U S_{\psi,\delta}(\Sigma_{\mathcal{X}^k_{[n]}}) V \tag{3}$$

where $U \Sigma_{\mathcal{X}^k_{[n]}} V$ is the SVD decomposition of $\mathcal{X}^k_{[n]}$, and the operator $S_{\psi,\delta}(\cdot)$ is defined as

$$S_{\psi,\delta}(x) = \begin{cases} \dfrac{a_1 + \sqrt{a_2}}{2}, & a_2 > 0 \\ 0, & a_2 \leq 0 \end{cases} \tag{4}$$

here $a_1 = |x| - \delta$ and $a_2 = a_1^2 - 4(\psi - \delta|x|)$.

Group sparsity has been validated as an effective way to model and promote the spatial local group structure of the nonzero elements [21]. Here, we applied the weighted group sparsity term to the SR model. The group sparsity regularization term is written as

$$\|W_g \odot D\mathcal{X}\|_{2,1} = \sum_{i=1}^{I_1} \sum_{j=1}^{I_2} \|W_{g_x}(i,j) D_x \mathcal{X}(i,j,:)\|_2 \tag{5}$$
$$+ \|W_{g_y}(i,j) D_y \mathcal{X}(i,j,:)\|_2$$

where W_g is the weighted matrix and D is the two differential operators, i.e., D_x and D_y, which computes the difference along the spatial modes

$$\|D_x \mathcal{X}(i,j,:)\|_2 = \mathcal{X}(i,j+1,k) - \mathcal{X}(i,j,k)$$
$$\|D_y \mathcal{X}(i,j,:)\|_2 = \mathcal{X}(i+1,j,k) - \mathcal{X}(i,j,k) \tag{6}$$

To sum up, with the relaxed low TT rank tensor and the weighted group sparsity of the spatial domain, we obtain the following HSIs super-resolution model

$$\min_{\mathcal{X}} \frac{1}{2} \|\mathcal{Y}_{h(3)} - \mathcal{X}_{(3)} BS\|_F^2 + \frac{1}{2} \|\mathcal{Y}_{m(3)} - R\mathcal{X}_{(3)}\|_F^2 \tag{7}$$
$$+ \lambda_r rank(\mathcal{X}) + \lambda_g \|W_g \odot D\mathcal{X}\|_{2,1}$$

where λ_r and λ_g are the positive trade-off parameters for balancing the low rank term and the group sparse term. Emperically, we set λ_r to $4e-4$ and λ_g to 1.2 in this paper. Specifically, with Eq. (1) and Eq. (5) we have the following equivalent objective model

$$
\min_{\mathcal{X}} \frac{1}{2} \left\| \mathcal{Y}_{h(3)} - \mathcal{X}_{(3)} BS \right\|_F^2 + \frac{1}{2} \left\| \mathcal{Y}_{m(3)} - R\mathcal{X}_{(3)} \right\|_F^2
$$
$$
+ \lambda_r \sum_{k=1}^{K} \sum_{n=1}^{N-1} \alpha_n \left\| \mathcal{X}_{[n]}^k \right\|_{LS} + \lambda_g \left\| W_g \odot D\mathcal{X} \right\|_{2,1} \tag{8}
$$

4   Algorithm

In this section, we derive an efficient algorithm to update each variables under the alternative direction multiplier method (ADMM) framework [22]. Auxiliary variables are induced to split the interdependent terms in updating each variables, i.e., $\mathcal{Z}_n = \mathcal{X}, (n = 1, 2, ..., N-1)$, $\mathcal{M} = \mathcal{X}$, $\mathcal{F} = D\mathcal{M}$. Then we have the following Lagrangian function for the subjective model (8)

$$
L(\mathcal{Z}_n, \mathcal{X}, \mathcal{M}, \mathcal{F}, \mathcal{Q}_n, \mathcal{J}_1, \mathcal{J}_2) = \frac{1}{2} \left\| \mathcal{Y}_{h(3)} - \mathcal{X}_{(3)} BS \right\|_F^2 + \frac{1}{2} \left\| \mathcal{Y}_{m(3)} - R\mathcal{X}_{(3)} \right\|_F^2
$$
$$
+ \sum_{k=1}^{K} \sum_{n=1}^{N-1} \left(\lambda_r \alpha_n \left\| \mathcal{Z}_{n[n]}^k \right\|_{LS} + \frac{\mu_1}{2} \left\| \mathcal{Z}_n - \mathcal{X} \right\|_F^2 + \langle \mathcal{Q}_n, \mathcal{Z}_n - \mathcal{X} \rangle \right)
$$
$$
+ \lambda_g \left\| W_g \odot \mathcal{F} \right\|_{2,1} + \frac{\mu_2}{2} \left\| \mathcal{F} - D\mathcal{M} \right\|_F^2 + \langle \mathcal{J}_1, \mathcal{F} - D\mathcal{M} \rangle
$$
$$
+ \frac{\mu_2}{2} \left\| \mathcal{M} - \mathcal{X} \right\|_F^2 + \langle \mathcal{J}_2, \mathcal{M} - \mathcal{X} \rangle \tag{9}
$$

where $\mathcal{Q}_n, \mathcal{J}_1, \mathcal{J}_2$ are the Lagrangian multipliers, and μ_1, μ_2 are the positive penalty parameters. In the experiment, we set $\mu_1 = 1e-4$ and $\mu_2 = 1e-6$, empirically.

Update $\mathcal{Z}_n$: with other variables fixed, the Lagrangian function Eq. (9) w.r.t $\mathcal{Z}_n$ is

$$
\operatorname*{argmin}_{\mathcal{Z}_n} L(\mathcal{Z}_n, \mathcal{X}, \mathcal{M}, \mathcal{F}, \mathcal{Q}_n, \mathcal{J}_1, \mathcal{J}_2)
$$
$$
= \operatorname*{argmin}_{\mathcal{Z}_n} \sum_{k=1}^{K} \sum_{n=1}^{N-1} \left(\lambda_r \alpha_n \left\| \mathcal{Z}_{n[n]}^k \right\|_{LS} + \frac{\mu_1}{2} \left\| \mathcal{Z}_n - \mathcal{X} \right\|_F^2 + \langle \mathcal{Q}_n, \mathcal{Z}_n - \mathcal{X} \rangle \right)
$$
$$
= \operatorname*{argmin}_{\mathcal{Z}_n} \sum_{k=1}^{K} \sum_{n=1}^{N-1} \left(\lambda_r \alpha_n \left\| \mathcal{Z}_{n[n]}^k \right\|_{LS} + \frac{\mu_1}{2} \left\| \mathcal{Z}_{n[n]}^k - \mathcal{X}_{[n]}^k \right\|_F^2 + \langle \mathcal{Q}_{[n]}^k, \mathcal{Z}_{n[n]}^k - \mathcal{X}_{[n]}^k \rangle \right)
$$
$$
= \operatorname*{argmin}_{\mathcal{Z}_n^k} \lambda_r \sum_{k=1}^{K} \sum_{n=1}^{N-1} \left(\alpha_n \left\| \mathcal{Z}_{n[n]}^k \right\|_{LS} + \frac{\mu_1}{2} \left\| \mathcal{Z}_{n[n]}^k - \mathcal{X}_{n[n]}^k + \frac{\mathcal{Q}_{n[n]}^k}{\mu_1} \right\|_F^2 \right) \tag{10}
$$

For $\mathcal{Z}^k_{n[n]}$, it can be updated via Eq. (3) as

$$\mathcal{Z}^k_{n[n]} = U^k_n S_{\psi,\delta}(\Sigma^k_n) V^k_n, \quad 1 \le k \le K \tag{11}$$

where $U^k_n \Sigma^k_n V^k_n = SVD\left(\mathcal{X}^k_{n[n]} - \frac{\mathcal{Q}^k_{n[n]}}{\mu_1}\right)$.

Update $\mathcal{X}$: the subproblem of $\mathcal{X}$ can be optimized by

$$
\begin{aligned}
&\underset{\mathcal{X}}{\operatorname{argmin}} L(\mathcal{Z}_n, \mathcal{X}, \mathcal{M}, \mathcal{F}, \mathcal{Q}_n, \mathcal{J}_1, \mathcal{J}_2) \\
&= \underset{\mathcal{X}}{\operatorname{argmin}} \frac{1}{2} \left\| \mathcal{Y}_{h(3)} - \mathcal{X}_{(3)} BS \right\|^2_F + \frac{1}{2} \left\| \mathcal{Y}_{m(3)} - R\mathcal{X}_{(3)} \right\|^2_F \\
&\quad + \sum_{k=1}^K \sum_{n=1}^{N-1} \left(\frac{\mu_1}{2} \left\| \mathcal{Z}_n - \mathcal{X} \right\|^2_F + \langle \mathcal{Q}_n, \mathcal{Z}_n - \mathcal{X} \rangle \right) \\
&\quad + \frac{\mu_2}{2} \left\| \mathcal{M} - \mathcal{X} \right\|^2_F + \langle \mathcal{J}_2, \mathcal{M} - \mathcal{X} \rangle \\
&= \underset{\mathcal{X}}{\operatorname{argmin}} \frac{1}{2} \left\| \mathcal{Y}_{h(3)} - \mathcal{X}_{(3)} BS \right\|^2_F + \frac{1}{2} \left\| \mathcal{Y}_{m(3)} - R\mathcal{X}_{(3)} \right\|^2_F \\
&\quad + \sum_{k=1}^K \sum_{n=1}^{N-1} \frac{\mu_1}{2} \left\| \mathcal{Z}_n - \mathcal{X} + \frac{\mathcal{Q}_n}{\mu_1} \right\|^2_F + \frac{\mu_2}{2} \left\| \mathcal{M} - \mathcal{X} + \frac{\mathcal{J}_2}{\mu_2} \right\|^2_F
\end{aligned}
\tag{12}
$$

Since Eq. (12) is convex, let the derivative w.r.t $\mathcal{X}_{(3)}$ is zero. Then we have

$$C_1 \mathcal{X}_{(3)} + \mathcal{X}_{(3)} C_2 = C_3 \tag{13}$$

where

$$
\begin{aligned}
C_1 &= R^T R + ((N-1)\mu_1 + \mu_2) I \\
C_2 &= (BS)(BS)^T \\
C_3 &= R^T \mathcal{Y}_{m(3)} + \mathcal{Y}_{h(3)}(BS)^T + \frac{\mu_1}{2} \sum_{n=1}^{N-1} \left(\mathcal{Z}_n + \frac{\mathcal{Q}_n}{\mu_1} \right) + \frac{\mu_2}{2} \left(\mathcal{M} + \frac{\mathcal{J}_2}{\mu_2} \right)
\end{aligned}
\tag{14}
$$

here I is the unit matrix. Equation (13) is a Sylvester equation which can be solved as demonstrated in [20, 23].

Update $\mathcal{M}$:

$$
\begin{aligned}
&\underset{\mathcal{M}}{\operatorname{argmin}} L(\mathcal{Z}_n, \mathcal{X}, \mathcal{M}, \mathcal{F}, \mathcal{Q}_n, \mathcal{J}_1, \mathcal{J}_2) \\
&= \underset{\mathcal{M}}{\operatorname{argmin}} \frac{\mu_2}{2} \left\| \mathcal{F} - D\mathcal{M} \right\|^2_F + \langle \mathcal{J}_1, \mathcal{F} - D\mathcal{M} \rangle + \frac{\mu_2}{2} \left\| \mathcal{M} - \mathcal{X} \right\|^2_F + \langle \mathcal{J}_2, \mathcal{M} - \mathcal{X} \rangle \\
&= \underset{\mathcal{M}}{\operatorname{argmin}} \frac{\mu_2}{2} \left\| \mathcal{F} - D\mathcal{M} + \frac{\mathcal{J}_1}{\mu_2} \right\|^2_F + \frac{\mu_2}{2} \left\| \mathcal{M} - \mathcal{X} + \frac{\mathcal{J}_2}{\mu_2} \right\|^2_F
\end{aligned}
\tag{15}
$$

By forcing the derivative of Eq. (15) w.r.t $\mathcal{M}$ to zero, we have

$$\left(\mathcal{I} + D^T D\right) \mathcal{M} = D^T \left(\mathcal{F} + \frac{\mathcal{J}_1}{\mu_2}\right) + \mathcal{X} - \frac{\mathcal{J}_2}{\mu_2} \tag{16}$$

here $\mathcal{I}$ is the unit tensor. As demonstrated in [21], we apply the efficient fast Fourier transform (FFT) to solve Eq. (16) as

$$\mathcal{M} = \text{ifftn} \left(\frac{D^T \left(\mathcal{F} + \frac{\mathcal{J}_1}{\mu_2}\right) + \mathcal{X} - \frac{\mathcal{J}_2}{\mu_2}}{\mu_2 1 + \mu_2 |\text{fftn}(D)|^2} \right) \tag{17}$$

Update $\mathcal{F}$: By fixing other variables in Eq. (9), the optimization problem of $\mathcal{F}$ is

$$\operatorname*{argmin}_{\mathcal{F}} L(\mathcal{Z}_n, \mathcal{X}, \mathcal{M}, \mathcal{F}, \mathcal{Q}_n, \mathcal{J}_1, \mathcal{J}_2)$$

$$= \operatorname*{argmin}_{\mathcal{F}} \lambda_g \|W_g \odot \mathcal{F}\|_{2,1} + \frac{\mu_2}{2} \|\mathcal{F} - D\mathcal{M}\|_F^2 + \langle \mathcal{J}_1, \mathcal{F} - D\mathcal{M}\rangle \tag{18}$$

$$= \operatorname*{argmin}_{\mathcal{F}} \lambda_g \|W_g \odot \mathcal{F}\|_{2,1} + \frac{\mu_2}{2} \left\|\mathcal{F} - D\mathcal{M} + \frac{\mathcal{J}_1}{\mu_2}\right\|_F^2$$

Let $\mathcal{R} = D\mathcal{M} - \frac{\mathcal{J}_1}{\mu_2}$, following [21,24], the tensor fibers of $\mathcal{F}$ is updated by

$$\mathcal{F}(i,j,:) = \begin{cases} \frac{\|\mathcal{R}(i,j,:)\|_2 - \frac{W_g(i,j)\lambda_1}{\beta}}{\|\mathcal{R}(i,j,:)\|_2} \mathcal{R}(i,j,:), & if \frac{W_g(i,j)\lambda_1}{\beta} < \|\mathcal{R}(i,j,:)\|_2 \\ 0, & \text{otherwise} \end{cases} \tag{19}$$

here the weight $W_g = 1/\left(\|(DQ + W_3/\beta)(i,j,:)\|_2 + \tau\right)$ with $\tau = 1e - 16$ used for avoiding zero as in [25].

Update $\mathcal{Q}_n, \mathcal{J}_1, \mathcal{J}_2$: the Lagrangian multipliers are updated by

$$\begin{aligned} \mathcal{Q}_n &= \mathcal{Q}_n + \mu_1(\mathcal{Z}_n - \mathcal{X}) \\ \mathcal{J}_1 &= \mathcal{J}_1 + \mu_2(\mathcal{F} - D\mathcal{M}) \\ \mathcal{J}_2 &= \mathcal{J}_2 + \mu_2(\mathcal{M} - \mathcal{X}) \end{aligned} \tag{20}$$

5 Experiments

5.1 Dataset

Most current HSIs super-resolution methods are tested on the ground-based CAVE dataset [26][1]. The images are captured by generalized assorted pixel camera of various real-world materials and objects. The database is divided into 5 sections and consists of 32 scenes. The spatial resolution is 512×512 pixel, the number of band is 31, the range of wavelength is 400 nm–700 nm at 10 nm steps. The $31st$ band of some scenes in CAVE dataset are shown in Fig. 1.

---

[1] http://www.cs.columbia.edu/CAVE/databases/multispectral/.

In experiments, the CAVE database are used as the HSIs ground truths. The LR-HSI image with size $8 \times 8 \times 31$ are simulated via Gaussian blur (7×7, zero mean, standard deviation 2) and downsampling factor (8×8). The corresponding scene HR-MSI HR-MSI is simulated by downsampling the reference HSI along the spectral dimension. The spectral downsampling filter is from the Nikon D700 camera response[2].

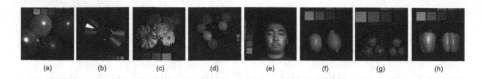

(a)   (b)   (c)   (d)   (e)   (f)   (g)   (h)

Fig. 1. Some sample bands of different scenes in the CAVE dataset

5.2   Compared Methods and Evaluation Indexes

In this section, we compare the proposed group sparse regularized high order tensor (GSHOT) method with three state-of-art HSIs super-resolution methods, including coupled spectral unmixing (CSU) [12], nonlocal sparse tensor factorization method (NLSTF) [13], and low tensor train rank method (LTTR) [20]. For quantitative comparison, we use five image evaluation indexes to assess the super-resolution performance of each method, including the peak signal-to-noise ratio (PSNR), the relative dimensionless global errorin synthesis (ERGAS) [27], the spectral angle mapper (SAM) [28], the universal image quality Index (UIQI) [29] and the degree of distortion (DD).

5.3   Qualitative and Quantitative Results

The qualitative results are provided in Fig. 2. It illustrates the best recovered band of each scene according to PSNR. From it we can see that all of the methods can recover the image structure, our GSHOT method has a relative better performance in the reconstruction of details, i.e., a sharp edge, compared with others. Especially in the second row of Fig. 2, our GSHOT performs best in reconstructing the white edge of the CD scene.

The quantitative results are showed in Table 2. For each scene, the values are obtained by averaging the index values of all bands. The best result are highlighted in bold. According to Table 2, our GSHOT method both can explicitly reconstruct the spatial structure and the spectral information.

To better compare the performance of each method in reconstructing each band, we plot the PSNR result curves obtained by each method in Fig. 3. All bands recovered by our method performs slightly better than the current best super-resolution method.

---

[2] https://www.maxmax.com/spectral_response.htm.

Fig. 2. Bands PSNR of (best 1 scene) recovered by each methods. (a) LR-HSI (b) CSU [12] (c) NLSTF [13] (d) LTTR [20] (e) GSHOT (f) Ground truth

Table 2. The quantitative values of each method in each scene.

Stuff scenes		CSU [12]	NLSTF [13]	LTTR [20]	GSHOT
Balloons	PSNR	42.158	43.186	50.022	**50.267**
	ERGAS	0.769	0.610	0.295	**0.290**
	SAM	4.653	2.721	2.249	**2.228**
	UIQI	0.945	0.961	0.967	**0.969**
	DD	1.161	0.758	0.389	**0.371**
CD	PSNR	32.349	37.076	41.170	**41.432**
	ERGAS	4.524	2.547	1.611	**1.571**
	SAM	6.059	5.017	3.416	**3.325**
	UIQI	0.845	0.856	0.899	**0.903**
	DD	1.908	1.210	0.642	**0.624**
Flowers	PSNR	44.013	40.337	47.992	**48.155**
	ERGAS	1.253	1.646	0.777	**0.769**
	SAM	14.652	7.288	5.899	**5.828**
	UIQI	0.779	0.848	0.861	**0.866**
	DD	1.124	1.176	0.534	**0.522**
Superballs	PSNR	42.509	42.112	48.633	**48.878**
	ERGAS	2.090	2.106	1.092	**1.065**
	SAM	9.033	7.094	5.763	**5.695**
	UIQI	0.863	0.882	0.904	**0.907**
	DD	1.071	0.808	0.467	**0.454**
Face	PSNR	42.777	40.485	47.033	**47.222**
	ERGAS	1.242	1.528	0.785	**0.776**
	SAM	8.108	5.441	4.916	**4.737**
	UIQI	0.830	0.887	0.889	**0.899**
	DD	0.803	0.915	0.449	**0.429**
Lemons	PSNR	45.055	43.080	50.315	**50.706**
	ERGAS	0.974	1.190	0.594	**0.581**
	SAM	4.884	3.816	3.145	**3.067**
	UIQI	0.774	0.824	0.843	**0.855**
	DD	0.670	0.690	0.345	**0.330**
Strawberries	PSNR	44.462	40.110	48.025	**48.253**
	ERGAS	1.107	1.743	0.785	**0.768**
	SAM	6.887	5.722	4.567	**4.506**
	UIQI	0.842	0.866	0.887	**0.893**
	DD	0.837	0.949	0.474	**0.459**
Peppers	PSNR	45.335	41.680	49.561	**49.900**
	ERGAS	0.806	1.185	0.552	**0.528**
	SAM	4.076	3.607	2.855	**2.750**
	UIQI	0.845	0.866	0.886	**0.894**
	DD	0.741	0.841	0.395	**0.374**

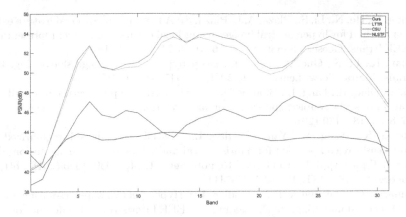

Fig. 3. Bands of Lemons recovered by each methods.

6 Conclusion

In this paper, we propose a group sparse regularized high order tensor method to deal with the problem of HSIs super-resolution. In this method, the group sparse is used to model the local group structure of nonzero elements in spatial and the tensor train representation in high order tensor enables the better exploiting of the low rank priority. The log-sum norm is applied as a relax version of the rank for better approximation. Experimental results validate the effectiveness of the proposed method compared with state-of-art methods.

References

1. Loncan, L., et al.: Hyperspectral pansharpening: a review. IEEE Geosci. Remote Sens. Mag. **3**(3), 27–46 (2015)
2. Bioucas-Dias, J.M., Plaza, A., Camps-Valls, G., Scheunders, P., Nasrabadi, N., Chanussot, J.: Hyperspectral remote sensing data analysis and future challenges. IEEE Geosci. Remote Sens. Mag. **1**(2), 6–36 (2013)
3. Gao, Y., Wang, X., Cheng, Y., Wang, Z.J.: Dimensionality reduction for hyperspectral data based on class-aware tensor neighborhood graph and patch alignment. IEEE Trans. Neural Netw. Learn. Syst. **26**(8), 1582–1593 (2015)
4. Akhtar, N., Mian, A.: Nonparametric coupled Bayesian dictionary and classifier learning for hyperspectral classification. IEEE Trans. Neural Netw. Learn. Syst. **29**(9), 4038–4050 (2018). https://doi.org/10.1109/TNNLS.2017.2742528
5. Wang, Q., Lin, J., Yuan, Y.: Salient band selection for hyperspectral image classification via manifold ranking. IEEE Trans. Neural Netw. Learn. Syst. **27**(6), 1279–1289 (2016)
6. Zhong, P., Wang, R.: Jointly learning the hybrid CRF and MLR model for simultaneous denoising and classification of hyperspectral imagery. IEEE Trans. Neural Netw. Learn. Syst. **25**(7), 1319–1334 (2014)
7. Fang, L., He, N., Li, S., Ghamisi, P., Benediktsson, J.A.: Extinction profiles fusion for hyperspectral images classification. IEEE Trans. Geosci. Remote Sens. **56**(3), 1803–1815 (2018)

8. Fang, L., He, N., Li, S., Plaza, A.J., Plaza, J.: A new spatial-spectral feature extraction method for hyperspectral images using local covariance matrix representation. IEEE Trans. Geosci. Remote Sens. **56**(6), 3534–3546 (2018)

9. Dian, R., Li, S., Guo, A., Fang, L.: Deep hyperspectral image sharpening. IEEE Trans. Neural Netw. Learn. Syst. **29**(11), 5345–5355 (2018)

10. Li, S., Dian, R., Fang, L., Bioucas-Dias, J.M.: Fusing hyperspectral and multispectral images via coupled sparse tensor factorization. IEEE Trans. Image Process. **27**(8), 4118–4130 (2018)

11. Zhang, K., Wang, M., Yang, S., Jiao, L.: Spatial-spectralgraph-regularized low-rank tensor decomposition for multispectral and hyperspectral image fusion. IEEE J. Sel. Topics Appl. Earth Observ. Remote Sens. **11**(4), 1030–1040 (2018). https://doi.org/10.1109/JSTARS.2017.2785411

12. Lanaras, C., Baltsavias, E., Schindler, K.: Hyperspectral superresolution by coupled spectral unmixing. In: Proceedings of IEEE International Conference on Computer Vision, pp. 3586–3594, December 2015

13. Dian, R., Fang, L., Li, S.: Hyperspectral image super-resolution via non-local sparse tensor factorization. In: Proceedings of IEEE Conference on Computer Vision and Pattern Recognition, pp. 3862–3871, July 2017

14. Oseledets, I.V.: Tensor-train decomposition. SIAM J. Sci. Comput. **33**(5), 2295–2317 (2011)

15. Bengua, J.A., Phien, H.N., Tuan, H.D., Do, M.N.: Efficient tensor completion for color image and video recovery: low-rank tensor train. IEEE Trans. Image Process. **26**(5), 2466–2479 (2017)

16. Xu, Y., Wu, Z., Chanussot, J., Wei, Z.: Nonlocal patch tensor sparse representation for hyperspectral image super-resolution. IEEE Trans. Image Process. **28**(6), 3034–3047 (2019)

17. Dong, W., et al.: Hyperspectral image super-resolution via non-negative structured sparse representation. IEEE Trans. Image Process. **25**(5), 2337–2352 (2016)

18. Arthur, D., Vassilvitskii, S.: K-means++: the advantages of careful seeding. In: Proceedings of Annual ACM-SIAM Symposium on Discrete Algorithms, pp. 1027–1035 (2007)

19. Xie, Q., et al.: Multispectral images denoising by intrinsic tensor sparsity regularization. In: Proceedings of the IEEE Conference on Computer Vision and Pattern Recognition, pp. 1692–1700, June 2016

20. Dian, R., Li, S., Fang, L.: Learning a low tensor-train rank representation for hyperspectral image super-resolution. IEEE Trans. Neural Netw. Learn. Syst. **30**(9), 2672–2683 (2019)

21. Chen, Y., He, W., Yokoya, N., et al.: Hyperspectral image restoration using weighted group sparsity-regularized low-rank tensor decomposition. IEEE Trans. Cybern. **50**(8), 3556–3570 (2019)

22. Boyd, S., Parikh, N., Chu, E., Peleato, B., Eckstein, J.: Distributed optimization and statistical learning via the alternating direction method of multipliers. Found. Trends Mach. Learn. **3**(1), 122 (2011)

23. Wei, Q., Dobigeon, N., Tourneret, J.-Y.: Fast fusion of multi-band images based on solving a Sylvester equation. IEEE Trans. Image Process. **24**(11), 4109–4121 (2015)

24. Liu, G., Lin, Z., Yan, S., Sun, J., Yu, Y., Ma, Y.: Robust recovery of subspace structures by low-rank representation. IEEE Trans. Pattern Anal. Mach. Intell. **35**(1), 171–184 (2013)

25. Huang, J., Huang, T.-Z., Deng, L.-J., Zhao, X.-L.: Joint-sparse-blocks and low-rank representation for hyperspectral unmixing. IEEE Trans. Geosci. Remote Sens. **57**(4), 2419–2438 (2019)
26. Yasuma, F., Mitsunaga, T., Iso, D., Nayar, S.K.: Generalized assorted pixel camera: postcapture control of resolution, dynamic range, and spectrum. IEEE Trans. Image Process. **19**(9), 2241–2253 (2010)
27. Wald, L.: Quality of high resolution synthesised images: is there a simple criterion? In: Proceedings of the International Conference on Fusion Earth Data, pp. 99–103, January 2000
28. Yuhas, R.H., Goetz, A.F.H., Boardman, J.W.: Discrimination among semi-arid landscape endmembers using the spectral angle mapper (SAM) algorithm. In: Proceedings of the 3rd Annual JPL Airborne Geoscience Workshop, vol. 1, pp. 147–149 (1992)
29. Wang, Z., Bovik, A.C.: A universal image quality index. IEEE Signal Process. Lett. **9**(3), 81–84 (2002)

Bearing Fault Diagnosis Method Based on Multi-sensor Feature Fusion Convolutional Neural Network

Xiaoyong Zhong, Xiangjin Song[✉], and Zhaowei Wang

School of Electrical and Information Engineering, Jiangsu University,
Zhenjiang 212013, China
songxiangjin@ujs.edu.cn

Abstract. Most existing deep learning models use a single sensor signal as input data, which makes them susceptible to external variables and cannot represent the operating state of a certain component. To achieve intelligent fault diagnosis of the rolling bearing in permanent magnet synchronous motors (PMSM) under cross-working conditions, a novel method based on a multi-sensor feature fusion convolutional neural network (MFFCN) is presented. The proposed model consists of a core network and two sub-networks to achieve information sharing and exchange. The deep features in multi-sensor signals are extracted by using dilated convolution blocks in the subnetwork. An attention mechanism is introduced in the core network to flexibly extract and fuse more effective features. The proposed model is verified by a fusion of vibration and current signal for bearing fault diagnosis of the PMSM. Experimental results show that the proposed model has higher diagnostic accuracy in fault diagnosis under various working conditions. In addition, the interpretability of the network model is improved through network visualization.

Keywords: Bearing fault diagnosis · Feature fusion · Attention mechanism

1 Introduction

Different types of motors are widely used in almost all modern industrial manufacturing. Rolling bearing is one of the most common key components in the motor, and its health status directly affects the service life of the motor. As a result, timely and precise diagnosis of bearing fault is essential to ensuring industrial production safety, increasing productivity, and eliminating hidden threats [1,2].

The research on bearing fault diagnostics based on machine learning algorithms has received considerable attention in recent years. Feature extraction and fault identification are the two main processes in these algorithms. Feature extraction primarily uses signal processing techniques to extract fault features from time domain, frequency domain or time-frequency domain in sensor

H. Liu et al. (Eds.): ICIRA 2022, LNAI 13458, pp. 138–149, 2022.
https://doi.org/10.1007/978-3-031-13841-6_13

data. The most commonly used signal processing techniques are variational mode decomposition [3], hilbert transform [4] and wavelet transform [5]. To classify the extracted features from the sensor data, k-nearest neighbors [6], support vector machines [7], and naive bayes [8] are commonly employed. The automatic identification and classification of different bearing faults are achieved by combining the above two stages. For example, Pandarakone et al. [9] proposed a method using fast Fourier transform an input to support vector network for classification of bearing faults. Hu et al. [10] proposed a fault diagnosis model based on wavelet packet transforms and support vector machines. However, these fault diagnosis scheme require the joint use of signal processing and machine learning algorithms on sensor data. The extracted features need to be selected manually, which limits the diagnostic accuracy of machine learning algorithms.

In recent years, the advancement of deep learning in automatic feature extraction from computer language, speech recognition and picture processing has provided beneficial ideas in the field of fault diagnosis. Chang et al. [11] proposed a parallel convolutional neural network (C-CNN) for turbine bearing fault diagnosis. Kao et al. [12] utilized a one-dimensional convolutional neural network (CNN) to identification of demagnetization and bearing faults in PMSM. Ye et al. [13] proposed an attention multi-scale network (AKR-Net), adding a channel attention block after each branch network to adaptively extract channel features. The deep learning-based fault diagnosis methods mentioned above are condition monitoring schemes with a single sensor. However, the application for single sensor data monitoring cannot fully explore the relationship between the fault data and the complicated bearing running state, resulting in incorrect diagnosis results.

Based on the aforementioned issues, a new multi-sensor feature fusion convolutional neural network (MFFCN) for bearing fault diagnosis is proposed. First, two sub-networks and a core network are created. The sub-network are utilized to automatically select the features of multiple sensor time series signals. The core network is utilized to combine the multiple sensor feature representations extracted by the sub-networks. Second, in order to realize the feature fusion process effectively, an attention mechanism is introduced into the feature fusion process to assign feature weights adaptively. Finally, the proposed model is evaluated using experimental vibration signal and stator current signal from PMSM. The experimental results show that the proposed model has obvious advantages in bearing fault diagnosis.

2   Flowchart of the Proposed Model

The proposed model structure is described in detail in this section. As seen in Fig. 1, the network is made up of two sub-networks and a core network. To begin with, the vibration signal and stator current signal is fed into each sub-network respectively through input layer to extract feature representations. The extracted shallow features are then fused, and the core network with attention mechanism method is used to adaptive deep feature extraction. Finally, the classification layer receives high-level feature representations to diagnose bearing faults.

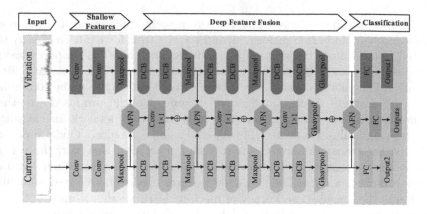

Fig. 1. Flowchart illustrating of the proposed MFFCN model.

2.1   Dilated Convolution Block

In traditional convolutional neural networks, the size of the convolution kernel is fixed, reducing the flexibility of the convolutional receptive field. Therefore, the dilated convolutional network is employed to extract the features of the vibration signal and stator current signal. As shown in Fig. 2, the dilated convolutional block (DCB) is made up of four parallel convolutional layers. Because multi-dilation rates are used, each convolutional layer's receptive field is distinct, thus multi-scale feature maps are obtained. When compared to the standard stacking convolutional network, the dilated convolutional block can use fewer parameters to provide a bigger receptive field, thus successfully reducing overfitting. Therefore, dilated convolutional blocks are used to extract high-level feature representations from single sensor data.

2.2   Multi-layer Fusion Network

The fusion strategy of the branch network and the core network is the key to effectively fusing the information contained in distinct sensor signals. The traditional data-level and decision-level network fusion tend to ignore the feature-level relationship between different signals, resulting in the loss of fault information. For that purpose, this study extracts feature information from two sub-networks. Then, a series of fusion points at multiple levels of the core network and sub-networks is developed to more thoroughly extract deep fault features.

As illustrated in Fig. 1, two convolutional layers and one pooling layer are utilized to extract shallow features in the sub-network, then dilated convolutional blocks are added to extract high-level feature representations for specific tasks. The features retrieved by the sub-networks are merged in the core network, and the merged features are sent back to each sub-network to realize the goal of information exchange and mutual sharing. It is worth mentioning that the

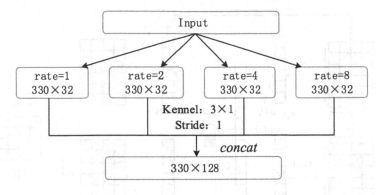

Fig. 2. The network structure of DCB.

output of the core network represents the final diagnosis result of the proposed model, and the output of each sub-network only reflects the diagnostic results of single sensor data.

2.3 Attention Fusion Network

Even if the small-scale DCB network is employed in this paper, the parameters of the proposed model are still extremely vast. Therefore, it is easy to generate irrelevant and redundant features. To address this issue, an attention method that can merge the features extracted by each sub-network is employed to select the relevant feature information and suppress the worthless feature information.

As illustrated in Fig. 3, this section takes the first fusion point as an example to explain the topology of the attention fusion network (AFN). Assuming that the features of vibration and stator current signals extracted by each sub-network are $\mathbf{F}_1 \in \mathbf{R}^{C \times L}$ and $\mathbf{F}_2 \in \mathbf{R}^{C \times L}$, respectively.

First, the compressed features are generated by passing $\mathbf{F}_1$ and $\mathbf{F}_2$ through a global average pooling layer (GAP):

$$z_1^c = \frac{1}{L} \sum_{i=1}^{L} F_1^c(i) \tag{1}$$

$$z_2^c = \frac{1}{L} \sum_{i=1}^{L} F_2^c(i) \tag{2}$$

where L denotes the feature's spatial dimension; C denotes the feature's channel dimension; $\mathbf{F}_1^c$ and $\mathbf{F}_2^c$ are the input feature of the c-th channel; z_1^c and z_2^c denotes the c-th channel compressed feature; $c = [1, 2, ..., C]$, $\mathbf{F}_1 = [F_1^1, F_1^2, ..., F_1^C]$, $\mathbf{F}_2 = [F_2^1, F_2^2, ..., F_2^C]$.

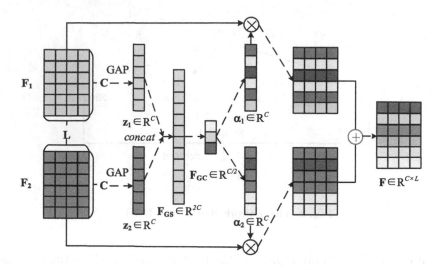

Fig. 3. The network structure of AFN.

Second, in the channel dimension, the compressed features of the two sensor signals are concatenated to form a global shared feature $\mathbf{F}_{GS} \in \mathbf{R}^{2C}$. A fully connected layer is employed to encode the feature channel and the globally encoded feature $\mathbf{F}_{GC} \in \mathbf{R}^{\frac{C}{2}}$ is obtained. The following is the relevant formula:

$$\mathbf{F}_{GS} = concat([\mathbf{z}_1, \mathbf{z}_2]) \tag{3}$$

$$\mathbf{F}_{GC} = \sigma(\mathbf{W}_{GC}\mathbf{F}_{GS} + \mathbf{b}_{GC}) \tag{4}$$

where $\mathbf{z}_1 \in \mathbf{R}^C$ and $\mathbf{z}_2 \in \mathbf{R}^C$ are the compressed features; $\mathbf{W}_{GC} \in \mathbf{R}^{2C}$ and $\mathbf{b}_{GC} \in \mathbf{R}^{2C}$ are the fully connected layer's weights and biases, respectively; and σ is the RELU activation function, $\mathbf{z}_1 = [z_1^1, z_1^2, ..., z_1^C]$, $\mathbf{z}_2 = [z_2^1, z_2^2, ..., z_2^C]$.

The fully connected layer is then used to construct the distribution of channel weights for different types of signals based on the feature $\mathbf{F}_{GC}$. The Sigmoid function is used to map the weight distribution from 0 to 1 in this case. The following is the specific calculation formula:

$$\boldsymbol{\alpha}_1 = f(\mathbf{W}_1\mathbf{F}_{GC} + \mathbf{b}_1) \tag{5}$$

$$\boldsymbol{\alpha}_2 = f(\mathbf{W}_2\mathbf{F}_{GC} + \mathbf{b}_2) \tag{6}$$

where $\boldsymbol{\alpha}_1 \in \mathbf{R}^C$ and $\boldsymbol{\alpha}_2 \in \mathbf{R}^C$ are the channel weights of features $\mathbf{F}_1$ and $\mathbf{F}_2$, respectively, $\mathbf{W}_1, \mathbf{W}_2 \in \mathbf{R}^{C \times \frac{C}{2}}$.

Finally, after the adaptive fusion of the core network, the $\boldsymbol{\alpha}_1$ and $\boldsymbol{\alpha}_2$ formed in the previous layer are channel-multiplied with the fusion point's input features $\mathbf{F}_1$ and $\mathbf{F}_2$ to generate the shared feature distribution $\mathbf{F} \in \mathbf{R}^{C \times L}$:

$$\mathbf{F} = \mathbf{F}_1 \otimes \boldsymbol{\alpha}_1 + \mathbf{F}_2 \otimes \boldsymbol{\alpha}_2 \tag{7}$$

2.4 Network Parameter Settings

The cross-entropy loss function is used by all networks, and the total network loss is the weighted sum of each network's loss. The parameters are updated using the Adam function [14]. The initial learning rate is set at 0.001, a dynamic learning rate is introduced, and the learning rate gradually approaches zero as the training time increases. A core network and two sub-networks are the key components of the proposed network model. Tables 1 and 2 show the specific parameter settings for the sub-network and the core network, respectively.

Table 1. Sub-net parameter settings.

Layers	Kernel number	Kernel size	Stride	Output size
Conv 1	32	33	1	1000×32
Conv 2	64	9	1	992×64
Max pool 1		3	3	330×64
DCB 1 and 2	32, 32, 32, 32	3	1	330×128
Max pool 2		3	3	110×128
DCB 3 and 4	64, 64, 64, 64	3	1	110×256
Max pool 3		3	3	36×256
DCB 5 and 6	128, 128, 128, 128	3	1	36×512
Global pool 1				1×512
FC layer 1				1×4

Table 2. Center network parameter settings.

Fusion points	Layers	Kernel number	Kernel size	Stride	Output size
1	Conv	128	1	1	330×128
	Max pool		3	3	110×128
2	Conv	256	1	1	110×256
	Max pool		3	3	36×256
3	Conv	512	1	1	36×512
	Global pool				1×512
4	FC layer				1×100
	Outputs				1×4

3 Experimental Verification

3.1 Experimental Platform Setup for Data Acquisition

This experimental platform is made up of three components: a power supply system, a motor driving system, and a data acquisition system. The frequency converter (MD500ET55GB-HP) is used to adjust the speed of PMSM (MS-180ST-M19015B-43P0). A magnetic powder brake (CZS) is coupled to the motor shaft in order to load the PMSM. The cDAQ-9178 USB data acquisition unit and NI -9215 voltage input module and NI-9232 sound and vibration input module by National Instruments are used to acquire the stator current and vibration signal. Tap drilling is used to simulate the localized bearing faults, and the hole diameters are 2 mm, 3 mm and 5 mm, respectively. The healthy and faulty bearings used in the experimental platform are shown in Fig. 4.

(a)   (b)   (c)   (d)

Fig. 4. Tested bearing. (a) healthy. (b) outer race fault 2 mm. (c) inner race fault 3 mm. (d) inner race fault 5 mm.

The experimental tests are performed with the healthy and faulty PMSM under two different rated loads (10%, 30%) and two different supply frequencies (15 Hz, 25 Hz). At every condition, 1000 signal segments are gathered. Both the stator current and vibration data are sampled at a frequency of 20 kHz.

In this paper, a sliding window approach is employed for time series segmentation. The length of each original sample and the step size of sliding segmentation are 10240 and 512, respectively. The fast Fourier transform is utilized to convert vibration and stator current signals from the time domain to the frequency domain, then low-frequency components is used as input to the proposed model. Furthermore, for the stator current signal, a notch filter is employed to eliminate fundamental wave component. For each signal segment, the first 1000 points of the low-frequency band are selected as the size of input vector. The proposed model is trained with the data set under one condition and tested with the data set under another condition. The detailed description is presented in Table 3.

Table 3. Detailed description of experimental data.

Label	Bearing status	Condition	Training	Testing
C1	Healthy	A(15 Hz, 10%) B(15 Hz, 30%) C(25 Hz, 30%)	800	200
C2	2 mm outer ring	A(15 Hz, 10%) B(15 Hz, 30%) C(25 Hz, 30%)	800	200
C3	3 mm inner ring	A(15 Hz, 10%) B(15 Hz, 30%) C(25 Hz, 30%)	800	200
C4	5 mm inner ring	A(15 Hz, 10%) B(15 Hz, 30%) C(25 Hz, 30%)	800	200

3.2   Performance Analysis of Different Sensor Signals

In order to validate the effectiveness of the proposed fusion network, the diagnostic accuracy of the single-sensor signal and the multi-sensor signal are compared in the frequency domain. As can be seen from Fig. 5, the diagnostic accuracy of the vibration signal is better than the current signal. These results match with existing studies. For bearing fault, the electrical signal contains less useful information than the mechanical signal. Furthermore, among the three different diagnostic systems for bearing fault diagnosis covered in this study, the core network showed the highest accuracy, followed by two sub-network. Therefore, the proposed model can fully explore the relationship between vibration signal, current signal and bearing running state. Hence, multi-sensor information fusion can improve fault diagnosis performance.

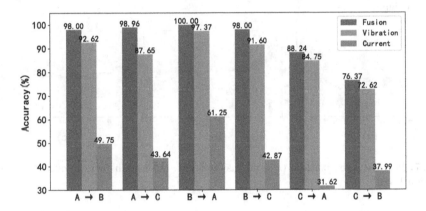

Fig. 5. Comparison of diagnostic accuracy with single sensor and multi-sensor signal.

3.3   The Accuracy of Time Domain and Frequency Domain Signals

This section focuses on the impact of time domain and frequency domain signals on the fault diagnosis performance of the proposed model. Figure 6 shows a comparison of the diagnostic accuracy of time domain and frequency domain signals. It can be seen from Fig. 6 that the frequency domain accuracy is greater than the time domain accuracy in all cross-conditional experimental validations. This means that in the cross-domain bearing fault diagnosis, the frequency domain signal is suitable as the input of the model.

3.4   Network Visualization

To comprehensively understand the feature extraction and classification mechanism of the proposed model, the t-distribution Stochastic Neighbour Embedding (t-SNE) technology is utilized to visualize the features extracted from the first fusion point, the fourth fusion point, and the core network classification layer.

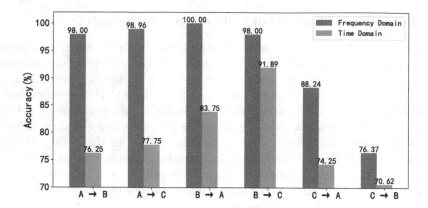

Fig. 6. Comparison of diagnostic accuracy with time domain signal and frequency domain signal.

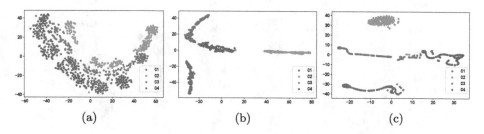

Fig. 7. Feature visualization. (a) first fusion point. (b) fourth fusion point. (c) classification layer.

As illustrated in Fig. 7, using working conditions C to A as an example, the high-dimensional signal is mapped into the two-dimensional space by t-SNE technology. As the network level deepens, the features gradually separate.

In particular, the output features of the first AFN layer are distributed disorderly in two dimensions. The output features of the fourth AFN layer are clearly separated, while individual features are misclassified. The output features of the core network classification layer have little overlap. This demonstrates that the proposed model has good feature extraction and generalization abilities.

3.5   Attention Fusion Network Analysis

This part visualizes the weight distribution of the attention mechanism after each fusion point to further understand the function of the AFN layer, and the results are given in Fig. 8. As shown in Fig. 8, the distribution of the channel attention weight α_1 of 3 mm (blue), 5 mm (orange) and 2 mm (green) in inner race fault and outer race fault of the bearing are represented.

It can be seen from Fig. 8 that at the shallow fusion point of the network, the attention weights of the channels are basically the same and evenly distributed

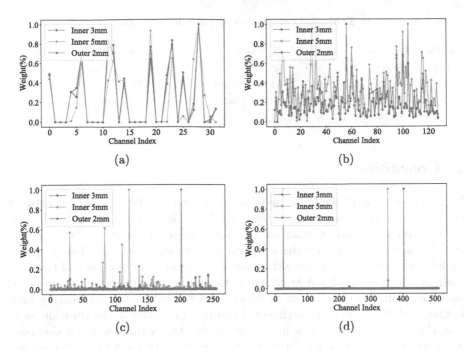

Fig. 8. Attention weight distribution. (a) first fusion point. (b) second fusion point. (c) third fusion point.(c) fourth fusion point. (Color figure online)

between 0 and 1. This shows that the shallow network has no ability to feature selection and a lot of redundant information is reserved. At the fourth fusion point, the attention weights of the channels are always close to 0 or 1, which may be explained by the fact that different kinds of bearing faults prefer different meaningful information in vibration signal or current signal for fusion between different channels. This further demonstrates that the attention mechanism is able to capture the critical fault feature information in multi-sensor signals.

3.6 Comparisons of Different Methods

To better analyze the diagnostic performance of the proposed method, the proposed MFFCN is compared with some existing methods, such as C-CNN [11], AKR-Net [13] and ECNN [15]. The results are shown in Table 4. As can be seen in Table 4, although the total training time and the number of parameters of C-CNN, AKR-Net and ECNN less than the proposed method, the proposed method can achieve much better accuracy in bearing condition identification under different cross-work conditions. This further verifies the effectiveness and generalization ability of the proposed method.

Table 4. Comparisons of different methods.

Method	A → B	A → C	B → A	B → C	C → A	C → B	Average	Time	Parameter
MFFCN	98.00	98.96	100	98	88.24	76.37	93.26	269.09 s	454.23w
C-CNN	88.35	89.46	95.24	93.74	85.00	78.42	86.56	195.68 s	225.47w
AKR-Net	80.43	81.32	82.74	80.32	86.34	71.47	80.44	106.59 s	322.15w
ECNN	83.74	59.62	85.00	74.37	62.25	70.24	72.53	50.83 s	32.10w

4 Conclusion

A novel bearing fault diagnosis method based on convolutional neural network with multi-sensor data fusion is proposed. The dilated convolution block combined with an attention mechanism is utilized to generate several fusion points in order to extract and fuse the features of multi-sensor signals. The proposed model can significantly improve the poor stability and low accuracy of the fault diagnosis methods with single sensor data. The effectiveness of the proposed model is verified by a fusion of vibration and current signals for bearing fault diagnosis of the PMSM. Experimental results and network visualization show that the proposed model has higher accuracy than vibration-based diagnosis and current-based diagnosis. In addition, the proposed model has two subnetworks and a core network, which can be easily expanded by adding additional subnetworks, which more types of sensor signals can be employed as network input.

Acknowledgements. Natural Science Foundation of Jiangsu Higher Education Institutions (20KJB510040); Natural Science Foundation of Jiangsu Province (BK20200887); the Doctor Program of Mass Entrepreneurship and Innovation of Jiangsu Province.

References

1. Wang, F., Liu, R., Hu, Q., Chen, X.: Cascade convolutional neural network with progressive optimization for motor fault diagnosis under nonstationary conditions. IEEE Trans. Ind. Inf. **17**(4), 2511–2521 (2020)
2. Xu, Z., Li, C., Yang, Y.: Fault diagnosis of rolling bearings using an improved multi-scale convolutional neural network with feature attention mechanism. ISA Trans. **110**, 379–393 (2021)
3. Dragomiretskiy, K., Zosso, D.: Variational mode decomposition. IEEE Trans. Signal Process. **62**(3), 531–544 (2013)
4. Batista, F.B., Lamim Filho, P.C.M., Pederiva, R., Silva, V.A.D.: An empirical demodulation for electrical fault detection in induction motors. IEEE Trans. Instrum. Meas. **65**(3), 559–569 (2016)
5. Peng, Z., Peter, W.T., Chu, F.: A comparison study of improved Hilbert-Huang transform and wavelet transform: application to fault diagnosis for rolling bearing. Mech. Syst. Signal Process. **19**(5), 974–988 (2005)

6. Wang, D.: K-nearest neighbors based methods for identification of different gear crack levels under different motor speeds and loads: revisited. Mech. Syst. Signal Process. **70**, 201–208 (2016)
7. Soualhi, A., Medjaher, K., Zerhouni, N.: Bearing health monitoring based on Hilbert-Huang transform, support vector machine, and regression. IEEE Trans. Instrum. Meas. **64**(1), 52–62 (2014)
8. Palácios, R.H.C., Da Silva, I.N., Goedtel, A., Godoy, W.F.: A comprehensive evaluation of intelligent classifiers for fault identification in three-phase induction motors. Electr. Power Syst. Res. **127**, 249–258 (2015)
9. Pandarakone, S.E., Mizuno, Y., Nakamura, H.: Evaluating the progression and orientation of scratches on outer-raceway bearing using a pattern recognition method. IEEE Trans. Ind. Electron. **66**(2), 1307–1314 (2018)
10. Hu, Q., He, Z., Zhang, Z., Zi, Y.: Fault diagnosis of rotating machinery based on improved wavelet package transform and SVMs ensemble. Mech. Syst. Signal Process. **21**(2), 688–705 (2007)
11. Chang, Y., Chen, J., Qu, C., Pan, T.: Intelligent fault diagnosis of wind turbines via a deep learning network using parallel convolution layers with multi-scale kernels. Renew. Energy **153**, 205–213 (2020)
12. Kao, I.H., Wang, W.J., Lai, Y.H., Perng, J.W.: Analysis of permanent magnet synchronous motor fault diagnosis based on learning. IEEE Trans. Instrum. Meas. **68**(2), 310–324 (2018)
13. Ye, Z., Yu, J.: AKRNet: a novel convolutional neural network with attentive kernel residual learning for feature learning of gearbox vibration signals. Neurocomputing **447**, 23–37 (2021)
14. Kingma, D.P., Ba, J.: Adam: a method for stochastic optimization. arXiv preprint arXiv:1412.6980 (2014)
15. Liu, Y., Yan, X., Zhang, C.A., Liu, W.: An ensemble convolutional neural networks for bearing fault diagnosis using multi-sensor data. Sensors **19**(23), 5300 (2019)

Effect of Foot Shape on Walking Performance of a Biped Robot Controlled by State Machine

Zhihao Zhou[1], Linqi Ye[1], Houde Liu[1(✉)], and Bin Liang[2]

[1] Tsinghua Shenzhen International Graduate School, Shenzhen 518055, China
liu.hd@sz.tsinghua.edu.cn
[2] Tsinghua University, Beijing 100084, China

Abstract. Bipedal robot is a multi-degree-of-freedom, high-dimensional, naturally unstable system. The control method based on kinematics and dynamics is complex in theory and implementation, and the control algorithm usually involves many parameters, which is difficult to design. In this paper, a control framework based on a state machine is designed to achieve stable walking of a 3D bipedal robot, which only involves 6 parameters to be designed. In terms of the structural design of biped robots, researcher's interests are mostly focused on legs, knees, and ankles, and there are few studies on the shape of the robot foot. In this paper, we build a three-dimensional biped robot model in Webots and use random searching method to find the control parameters that lead to stable walking. For the stable walking gaits, we compare the performance of five foot shapes in terms of the walking style, control efficiency, and stability. We found that the yaw angle is a key factor affecting the diversity of the robot's gait. In addition, it is found that the overall performance of the flat foot is most satisfying. The research in this paper can be helpful for the bipedal robot walking algorithm and the design of the foot shape.

Keywords: Biped robot · State machine · Foot shape

1 Introduction

The research of biped robot can be mainly divided into two fields, one is the control algorithm and the other is the structural design. Because biped robots are complex and naturally unstable, the control algorithm that enables biped robots to achieve stable walking is a primary premise. Kajita [1] proposed the LIP model and R. Blickhan [2] proposed the SLIP model. These model-based control methods reduce the order of the robot to a certain extent, but also bring errors on the model. Another common method is learning-based control. The Cassie robot from the Agility Robotics team used reinforcement learning to achieve a 5-km jog [3]. However, this method involves many parameters and the convergence is very slow. Raibert [4] proposed the control method by using a state machine, which can realize complex motion of the robot by simple feedback. This method is also used in the Altas robot.

Besides, the structural design of biped robots mostly focuses on the impact of legs, knee and ankle on motor performance [5–7]. There are few studies on the foot design,

H. Liu et al. (Eds.): ICIRA 2022, LNAI 13458, pp. 150–160, 2022.
https://doi.org/10.1007/978-3-031-13841-6_14

and most of them exist in passive walking research. Smyrli [8] studied the effects of the change in the lateral curvature of the semi-elliptical foot on the gait stability, walking speed, and energy efficiency, finding that the flat foot shape can make the gait more energy efficient. Subsequently, they expanded the foot shape to an arbitrary shape defined by a series of 2D points and established a mathematical model that verified the stability of the any convex foot geometry passive walking [9]. Kwan [10] used flat-foot and round-foot to simulate toe and heel strikes when walking, comparing the effects of foot length on walking speed, declination and centroid trajectory in long- and short-cycle gaits, respectively. And it is concluded that flat-foot and round-foot are more effective than point-foot. In terms of active robotics, Yamane [11] used the simplified model and collision dynamics to find the best walking parameters of the foot with a given shape. By comparison, they conclude that the curved feet can realize the walking speed of human beings more effectively than flat feet. Ouezdou [12] used the ADAMS physics simulation engine to compare the plate, flexible, active and hybrid flexible active feet, which differ in terms of total energy consumption and the normal contact force component, but did not change the shape of the foot. These articles are either based on passive walking robots rather than active robots, or use numerical simulation methods without physics engine simulation, or discuss them in a 2D plane rather than a 3D space. In general, there have been few studies on the impact of different foot shapes of three-dimensional, active robots on walking through physics engines.

This paper builds a three-dimensional active bipedal robot in Webots with 8 degrees of freedom that can be actively driven at each joint. The bipedal robot is controlled by a simple state machine control framework, which only involves 6 parameters. The foot shapes of Capsule, Cylinder, Box, Plane, and Flat are tested to achieve stable walking gaits by searching the control parameters randomly. Then their performance are compared in straight walking, lateral walking, in-place walking, as well as control efficiency and walking stability.

The remainder of this paper is arranged as follows. Section 2 describes the simulation model, including size, mass distribution, and joints. Section 3 introduces the control framework and control laws of the biped robot. Section 4 gives the experimental results and discussion. Conclusion is given in Sect. 5.

2 Simulation Model

2.1 Robot Model

We build a three-dimensional biped robot in the Webots software, as shown in Fig. 1a. The upper body, thigh, calf, and foot are distinguished by the hip joint, knee joint and ankle joint, respectively. The robot is 1.5 m high, 0.3 m wide, 0.13 m thick, and has a total mass of 29.84 kg. The densities of the robot are all distributed at 1000 kg/m^3, which is similar to that of humans. The mass of the robot is mainly concentrated in the upper body and thighs, and the volume and mass of each part of the robot are listed in Table 1. In order to better mimic human walking, the robot's center of mass is located in the center of the chest, at a height of about 1.02 m.

The robot has a total of eight degrees of freedom, and each leg has four degrees of freedom, all of which are active joints driven by motors. The specific distribution can

Table 1. Robot dimension and mass distribution.

Part	Dimension/m	Mass/kg
Upper body	0.3*0.13*0.43	16.77 kg
Hip	0.05*0.05*0.05	0.125
Thigh	0.13*0.14*0.34	6.188
Calf	0.04*0.04*0.04	0.06
Foot	0.05*0.14*0.01	0.07

be seen in Fig. 1b. There are two DOFs at the hip joint, which are the pitch joint and the roll joint. They are used to achieve fore-aft and side-swing of the thighs, respectively. The knee joint has a pitch joint for raising and lowering the calf. The ankle joint has a pitch joint that swings the foot up and down.

 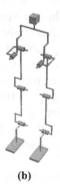

(a)   (b)

Fig. 1. The biped robot studied in this paper. (a) The simulation model of the robot. (b) The degrees of freedom of the robot.

2.2   Foot Shape

In this paper, five typical foot shapes are used, namely Capsule, Cylinder, Box, Plane, and Flat, as shown in Fig. 2. The size of each foot can be seen in Table 2. With these five shapes of feet applied to the robot, we use the same control framework and control law in Sect. 3 to find out the control parameters that can run stably with different shapes of feet. We found that under the parameters that can achieve a stable gait, different shapes of the foot exhibit different walking styles. And the walking performance of different foot shapes is also different, which is discussed in Sect. 4.

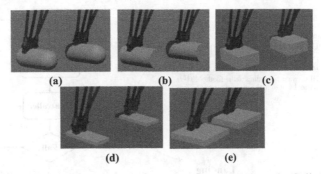

(a)   (b)   (c)

(d)   (e)

Fig. 2. Diagram of five foot shapes. (a), (b), (c), (d), (e) represent Capsule, Cylinder, Box, Plane, and Flat, respectively.

3 Control Method

3.1 Control Framework

This paper adopts the state machine control method proposed by Raibert [4], which is widely used in the control of legged robots because of its simplicity and effectiveness. As shown in Fig. 3a, the controller has four states, which are Swing stage of right leg, Landing stage of right leg, Swing stage of left leg, and Landing stage of left leg. The transition between states is triggered by two events, i.e., the step time and the swing leg touching the ground. The time of each step is set to 0.4 s, which is accumulated by the system time. The contact with the ground is judged by the touch sensors installed on the foot. The control laws for each joint in different states are given below.

There   are   six   parameters   involved   in the control laws, namely $c_1, c_2, a_1, a_2, d_1, d_2, d_3, d_4$. In the simulation, their ranges are set as:

$$c_1, c_2 \in (-0.1, 0.1)$$
$$a_1 \in (-0.2, 0.2), a_2 \in (0, 1)$$
$$d_1, d_2, d_3, d_4 \in (-0.25, 0.25$$

Each time a set of parameters is randomly selected within this range. If the robot can run without falling for 10s under this parameter, then this set of parameters is called as GoodData, recorded as G_p, and the next set of parameters is taken. The random number seed is the index of cycle, so that it will change every time, thus ensuring the randomness. The control flow chart is shown in Fig. 3b.

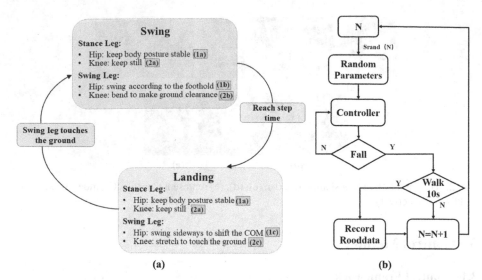

Fig. 3. The control framework. (a) The State Machine, (b) The control flow.

3.2 Low-Level Controllers

This section will discuss the control laws of the hip joint, knee joint and ankle joint respectively. Different states adopt different control laws, which are noted by a, b, c in Fig. 3. All joints adopt position control, which will not be declared in the following.

Hip Controller

- **(1a) Body posture controller**
  When a leg is the stance leg, its hip joint is used to maintain the stability of the body. The pitch joint of the hip is used to offset the pitch angle of body:

$$\theta_H^* = \theta_H + 2\theta_B \tag{1}$$

where θ_H^* is the desired angle of the hip pitch joint, θ_H is the current angle. θ_B is the current body pitch angle.

The roll joint of the hip is used to offset the roll angle of the body:

$$\varphi_H^* = \varphi_H - 2\varphi_B \tag{2}$$

where φ_H^* is the desired angle of the hip roll joint, φ_H is the current angle. φ_B is the current roll angle of the body.

- **(1b) Foothold controller**
  When a leg is the swing leg and is in the Swing state, its two joints at the hip of the leg are used to achieve the desired foothold. The choice of the foothold adopts the linear feedback of the body speed. The control laws of the two joints of the hip are:

$$\begin{aligned} \theta_H^* &= 0.2 - a_2 v_F + a_1 \\ \varphi_H^* &= c_1 - 0.5 v_L \end{aligned} \tag{3}$$

where, v_L is the lateral speed of the robot, v_F is the forward speed of the robot, both of which are approximated by the difference of the position obtained by GPS.

- **(1c) Landing controller**

When a leg is the swing leg and is in the Swing state, its roll joint of the hip moves a fixed angle, which is used to shift the COM of the body:

$$\varphi_H^* = c_2 \tag{4}$$

while the pitch joint no longer moves:

$$\theta_H^* = 0 \tag{5}$$

Knee Controller

- **(2a) Stance Leg Controller**

When a leg is the stance leg, its knee joint of the leg remains stationary to maintain upright of the leg:

$$\phi_K^* = 0 \tag{6}$$

where ϕ_K^* is the desired angle of knee pitch joint.

- **(2b) Swing Leg Swing Controller**

When a leg is the swing leg in the Swing state, its knee joint bends a fixed angle to make the foot off the ground:

$$\phi_K^* = -0.4 \tag{7}$$

- **(2c) Swing Leg Landing Controller**

When a leg is the swing leg in the Landing state, its knee joint is re-straighten to make the foot touch the ground and prepare for the next stance phase:

$$\phi_K^* = 0 \tag{8}$$

Ankle Controller

The ankle joint has only one pitch joint, and the control law is relatively simple, so it is not shown in Fig. 3a. Adjust the ankle to a certain angle at any stage to rotate the foot up and down.

- **(3a) Stance Leg Controller**

When a leg is the stance leg, its ankle joint is used to maintain body stability:

$$\gamma_{sS}^* = d_1, \gamma_{sL}^* = d_3 \tag{9}$$

where γ_{sS}^*, γ_{sL}^* are the stance leg's desired ankle angle when the other swing leg is in the Swing state and the Landing state, respectively.

- **(3b) Swing Leg Controller**

When a leg is the swing leg, its ankle joint rotates a certain angle to adjust the position of the foot to touch the ground:

$$\gamma_{wS}^* = d_2, \gamma_{wL}^* = d_4 \tag{10}$$

where γ_{wS}^*, γ_{wL}^* is the swing leg's desired ankle angle when it is in the Swing state and the Landing state, respectively.

4 Result

Based on the robot in Sect. 2.1, we use different foot shape described in Sect. 2.2, use the control method introduced in Sect. 3, run 6000 simulations on each foot shape, and finally obtain the GoodData P_G (not fall in 10s). Then using these GooDatas to control the robot, which make the robot walk stably without falling, we call them Stable Parameters, denoted as P_s (not fall in a long time). Record the total walking time of each foot shape for 6000 simulations, denoted as T (walking time before falling). The above parameters are listed in Table 2. Below we discuss the performance of these five foot shapes in straight walking, lateral walking, in-place walking, as well as control efficiency and stability.

Table 2. Simulation results of different foot shapes.

Shape	Size	P_G	P_s	T
Capsule	R = 0.03, H = 0.1	29	2	1015.234
Cylinder	R = 0.03, H = 0.14	16	4	1389.388
Box	X = 0.08, Y = 0.1, Z = 0.04	37	6	2486.380
Plane	X = 0.05, Y = 0.14, Z = 0.01	45	7	3248.828
Flat	X = 0.14, Y = 0.14, Z = 0.02	53	12	5238.526

4.1 Walking Performance

Control Efficiency
The same robot and control algorithm are used, and the random search method is used while the number of simulations is sufficient. The P_G and T generated by different shapes of the feet are different. Thus, we believe that the control efficiency of different foot shapes is different, and we define the control efficiency as follows:

$$E_i = \frac{P_{G_i}}{2 \sum P_{G_i}} + \frac{T_i}{2 \sum T_i} \qquad (11)$$

where E_i, P_{G_i}, T_i are the control efficiency, the number of P_G, and the total duration T of the i-th foot shape, respectively. The subscripts with i all represent the parameters of the i-th foot shape, which will not be repeated below. Although some parameters have not been recorded, the difference between the walking time and 10s is very small, so the control efficiency not only considers the GoodData, but also considers the total walking time.

Stability
We define the stability of each foot shape as:

$$S_i = \frac{P_{s_i}}{\sum P_{s_i}} \qquad (12)$$

From the number of P_s, it is obvious that Capsule is the most unstable one, and Flat is the most stable. Using the Capsule's P_s on Flat, it doesn't work for 10s. In the same way, if the P_s of a certain shape is applied to another, it is not possible to walk for 10s. Therefore, we can conclude that each shape has different characteristics, and its P_s is not universal.

4.2 Walking Gait

The control framework in Sect. 3 considers from the perspective of keeping the robot walking stably and not falling, and does not require the robot to achieve a specific gait such as straight walking, lateral stepping, turning, and stepping backward. We let the robot walk for ten minutes with each set of P_s using different foot shapes, and the obtained data is shown in Table 3. We found that the robot can achieve four kinds of gaits: straight walking, lateral walking, in-place walking, and backward walking with different foot shapes.

$\overline{|F|}$, $|F|_{max}$, $|F|_{min}$, are the average, maximum and minimum values of the forward distance's absolute value, respectively. $\overline{|L|}$, $|L|_{max}$, $|L|_{min}$ are the average, maximum and minimum values of lateral distance's absolute values, respectively.

Table 3. Gait data of different shapes

Shape	$\overline{|F|}$	$|F|_{max}$	$|F|_{min}$	$\overline{|L|}$	$|L|_{max}$	$|L|_{min}$
Capsule	71.99	108.29	35.68	2	65.15	5.61
Cylinder	37.9	79.39	13.69	4	9.56	5.14
Box	40.38	70.44	11.03	6	143.19	0.47
Plane	101.17	238.87	2.73	7	68.64	0.29
Flat	51.86	134.49	0.46	12	121.9	0.09

Straight Walking

The ability of straight walking is defined as:

$$\zeta_i = \frac{|F|_i}{|L|_{i\ max}} \tag{13}$$

where ζ_i is the straight walking ability of i-th foot, $|F|_i$ and $|L|_i$ are the forward and lateral walking distances under the same group of P_s.

We found that both the $\overline{|F|}$ and $|F|_{max}$ of the Plane foot are the largest. Therefore, we believe that the Plane foot has the greatest ability to walk forward. Denote the P_s of the Plane with the largest $|F|_{max}$ as P_{sF}. However, when the Plane foot walks forward, it also produces a large lateral displacement, which is a diagonal line instead of a straight line. While there is a set of P_s in the Flat foot, walking 92.79 m forward, with only 0.09 m laterally, which is a straight line. Denote this set of parameters as $P_{s\zeta}$.

Plot the IMU data of the robot when P_{sF} and $P_{s\zeta}$ are set on Plane and Flat feet, respectively, as shown in Fig. 4. It is found that the row angles of the robot are almost coincident, while the yaw angle of the Flat foot is almost 0, and the plane foot has fluctuations up and down, which is why the Flat foot can walk straighter.

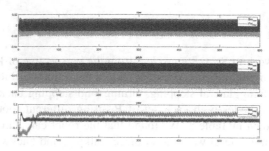

Fig. 4. IMU data for straight walking with Plane and Flat foot.

Lateral Walking

The ability of lateral walking is defined as:

$$\Gamma_i = \overline{|L|}_i + |L|_{\max i} \tag{14}$$

where Γ_i is the lateral walking ability of the i-th foot.

We found that Box foot has a significantly stronger lateral walking ability. It has a set of P_s that can walk 143.19 m laterally. Denote this set of parameters as P_{sLM}. Plot the IMU data of the robot when P_{sLM} and $P_{s\zeta}$ are set on Box and Flat feet, respectively, as shown in Fig. 5. It can be seen that the row angle and yaw angle of the Box foot are significantly larger than those of the Flat foot, which is the reason for the large lateral walking ability of the Box foot.

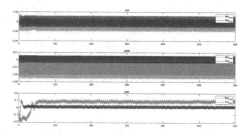

Fig. 5. IMU data for lateral walking with Box and Flat feet.

In-Place Walking

The ability of in-place walking is defined as:

$$\epsilon_i = \frac{1}{(|F| + |L|)_{min}} \tag{15}$$

where ϵ_i is the lateral walking ability of the i-th foot.

There is a set of P_s of Flat foot, which walks 4.6 m laterally and 0.49 m laterally in ten minutes, which can be approximately regarded as stepping in place. Denote this set of parameters as $P_{s\epsilon}$. Plot the IMU data of the robot when $P_{s\epsilon}$ and one random set of P_s are set on Box and Capsule foot, as shown in Fig. 6, we find that the yaw angle of $P_{s\epsilon}$ is a periodic polylines line, which is the reason why it can achieve in-place walking.

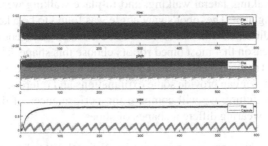

Fig. 6. IMU data for in-place walking with Capsule and Flat feet.

4.3 Discussion

According to the above analysis, we can find that the yaw angle is a key factor affecting the different walking gaits. This can also be seen from the control method. The pitch and roll angles of the robot are offset by the control law during the entire walking process to maintain stability, while the yaw angle is never controlled. Therefore, in the future, we can design different walking gaits by controlling the yaw angle of the robot.

The performance of the foot with different shapes is drawn on the radar chart as shown in Fig. 7. It can be found that the Flat feet are more prominent in straight walking, stability, and control efficiency. This can also explain why all well-known bipedal robots currently use the flat shape feet.

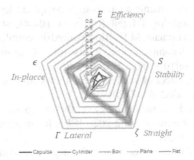

Fig. 7. Walking performance of different shapes of foot.

The video of simulation results for this article can be found in https://www.bilibili.com/video/BV1fv4y1K7nW/.

5 Conclusion

This paper builds a three-dimensional robot with eight degrees of freedom in Webots. A simple control framework based on a state machine is designed, and the whole algorithm only involves six parameters. Using the foot placement of speed feedback, the biped robot can walk continuously and stably without falling. On this basis, five shapes of feet were designed, and their performances in five aspects including control efficiency, stability, straight walking, lateral walking, and in-place walking were compared using the recorded walking data. The robot's yaw angle was found to be a key factor affecting gait diversity. In addition, the flat foot is found to be more advantageous in many aspects, which may be the reason that most biped robots choose this shape. The simple walking control law designed in this paper is helpful for bipedal walking control. What's more, the exploration in this paper can provide some explanations and references for the selection of robot feet. In the future, we will compare the performances of different feet from human experiments wearing different shapes of shoes.

Acknowledgements. This work was supported by National Natural Science Foundation of China (U1813216, 62003188), Shenzhen Science Fund for Distinguished Young Scholars (RCJC20210706091946001), and Guangdong Special Branch Plan for Young Talent with Scientific and Technological Innovation (2019TQ05Z111).

References

1. Kajita, S., et al.: Introduction to Humanoid Robotics. Introduction to Humanoid Robotics (2014)
2. Blickhan, R.: The spring-mass model for running and hopping. J. Biomech. **22**(11), 1217–1227 (1989)
3. Siekmann, J., et al.: Blind Bipedal Stair Traversal via Sim-to-Real Reinforcement Learning (2021)
4. Raibert, M.H.: Legged robots that balance. MIT press (1986)
5. Wang, K., et al.: Design and Control of SLIDER: An Ultra-lightweight, Knee-less, Low-cost Bipedal Walking Robot. In: 2020 IEEE/RSJ International Conference on Intelligent Robots and Systems (IROS) (2020)
6. Luo, G., et al.: Design and dynamic analysis of a compliant leg configuration towards the biped robot's spring-like walking. J. Intell. Rob. Syst. **104**(4), 64 (2022)
7. Yazdani, M., Salarieh, H., Foumani, M.S.: Bio-inspired decentralized architecture for walking of a 5-link biped robot with compliant knee joints. Int. J. Control Autom. Syst. **16**(6), 2935–2947 (2018). https://doi.org/10.1007/s12555-017-0578-0
8. Smyrli, A., et al.: On the effect of semielliptical foot shape on the energetic efficiency of passive bipedal gait *, pp. 6302–6307 (2019)
9. Smyrli, A., Papadopoulos, E.: A methodology for the incorporation of arbitrarily-shaped feet in passive bipedal walking dynamics. In: 2020 IEEE International Conference on Robotics and Automation (ICRA) (2020)
10. Kwan, M., Hubbard, M.: Optimal foot shape for a passive dynamic biped. J. Theor. Biol. **248**(2), 331–339 (2007)
11. Yamane, K., Trutoiu, L.: Effect of foot shape on locomotion of active biped robots. In: 2009 9th IEEE-RAS International Conference on Humanoid Robots. IEEE (2009)
12. Ouezdou, F.B., Alfayad, S., Almasri, B.: Comparison of several kinds of feet for humanoid robot, pp. 123–128 (2005)

Research on Part Image Segmentation Algorithm Based on Improved DeepLabV3+

Weiguang Hou[1,2,3], Shengpeng Fu[1,2(✉)], Xin Xia[1,2], Renbo Xia[1,2], and Jibin Zhao[1,2]

[1] State Key Laboratory of Robotics, Shenyang Institute of Automation, Chinese Academy of Sciences, Shenyang 110016, China
fushengpeng@sia.cn
[2] Institutes for Robotics and Intelligent Manufacturing, Chinese Academy of Sciences, Shenyang 110169, China
[3] College of Information Engineering, Shenyang University of Chemical Technology, Shenyang 110142, China

Abstract. Aiming at the problem of fuzzy edge segmentation and incomplete division in DeepLabV3+ segmentation results of parts, we propose an improved DeepLabV3+ semantic segmentation algorithm. Firstly, We replace Xception in the original network with lightweight MobileNet_V2 on the backbone network, improving the lightness of the network model. Then, channel attention is introduced into the backbone network to enhance the importance of effective feature information and enhance the learning ability of parts objective. After that, using feature fusion branches to adaptively learn spatial information of low-level features at different levels to obtain richer semantic information. Finally, the asymmetric convolution is used to replace the 3×3 convolution in the Decode-part to improve the processing ability of the convolution kernel and verify on the self-built mechanical parts dataset. The experimental results show that our method can achieve more precise semantic segmentation effect compared with the traditional deeplabv3+ and other segmentation methods.

Keywords: DeepLabV3+ · Channel attention · Adaptive spatial feature fusion · Asymmetric convolution

1 Introduction

Industrial robots are the products of modern scientific development, with the characteristics of versatility and intelligence, and are widely used in tasks such as handling and welding, which greatly improves production efficiency and quality. As an important part of the robot's intelligent grasping vision task, part segmentation will have a great impact on the smooth progress of the grasping task.

In the study of component area segmentation, Zhang Cong et al. [1] used the SIFT-SUSAN algorithm to extract features from part images, making great use of image edge point information. Han Chongjiao [2] used three geometric feature description operators to describe the contour characteristics of the component area, and obtains a good recognition effect. However, the accuracy of part feature recognition of these traditional methods

H. Liu et al. (Eds.): ICIRA 2022, LNAI 13458, pp. 161–170, 2022.
https://doi.org/10.1007/978-3-031-13841-6_15

mainly depends on the quality of the manual selection feature extraction method, and the recognition effect is poor in multi-target mechanical part images. As the convolution neural network algorithm is gradually proposed, the method of extracting component image region is often object detection or semantic segmentation. R-CNN [3], SSD [4] and YOLO series are commonly used in object detection methods. Zhang Jing et al. [5] used the K-means algorithm to recalculate the candidate box parameters, combined residual connection and the multi-scale method improve YOLOv3 to make it more suitable for small object classification detection. Yu Yongwei et al. [6] proposed a part identification method based on the Inception-SSD framework, taking into account the recognition accuracy and real-time. Yang Lin et al. [7] use the AdaBelief optimization algorithm, convex wrapping and minimal external rectangular box to improve positioning accuracy. Due to the wide variety of parts in the actual scene, the object detection method is difficult to extract the target outline and specific area, but the semantic segmentation method can be. The common methods are SegNet [8], UNet [9] and DeepLab series. Huang Haisong et al. [10] used convolutional neural networks to extract part image features and generate Mask segmentation masks, which split parts by example, but the problem of parts stacking on top of each other is not taken into account. Hong Qing et al. [11] use the DeepLabV3 network with the addition of custom Encoder-Decoder feature extraction structure, and at the same time use masks to mark the feature area, which has a good segmentation effect. Wang Yang [12] used the real dataset enriched by a virtual dataset set to train several convolutional neural networks optimized by the fully connected conditional random field, and achieved good results. However, these two methods do not consider the problem of real-time in the scene.

In this paper, for the problem that DeepLabV3+ [13] is not achieve satisfactory effect of segmenting the part area in industrial application scenarios, we propose an improved DeepLabV3+ model based on lightweight backbone. First, replace the Xceptions network of the original network with MobileNet_V2 to reduce the cost of training and prediction time for the model. Then, in order to enhance the learning ability of the model on the characteristics of the components area, channel attention is added to the backbone network to enhance important feature information. At the same time, the adaptive spatial feature fusion structure is used to strengthen the fusion of the different underlying features and improve the accuracy of model segmentation. Finally, asymmetric convolution is used to improve the processing ability of the convolution kernel. The model is trained and tested on a self-built dataset of mechanical parts. Experiments show that our approach achieves better performance compared with other some algorithms.

2   DeepLabV3+ Model

DeepLabV3+ uses atrous convolution to improve Xception as the backbone network for feature information extraction. Atrous convolution is added to control the resolution of the output feature map and the size of the receptive field of the convolution kernel. Set the convolution kernel to k, the input feature map is x, when atrous convolution acts on x, every position i in the output feature map y:

$$y[i] = \sum_m x[i + r \times m]k[m] \tag{1}$$

r is atrous rate. Atrous convolution is equivalent to up-sampling convolutional kernels by filling zero in the convolutional kernels.

The overall structure of DeepLabV3+ can be divided into two parts: Encode and Decode. In the Encode part, input image obtains the underlying feature of the original figure 1/4 size and the high-level semantic feature of the original figure 1/16 size through the backbone network, of which the high-level semantic features are input to the atrous spatial pyramid pool(ASPP). In the ASPP structure, the high-level semantic features go through 1 × 1 convolutions in parallel, and the 3 × 3 atrous convolution with atrous rate of 6, 12, 18 continues to extract the features and fuse the feature map after global average pooling, and then used 3 × 3 convolution to reduce the number of channels, resulting in a feature map into the Decode part.

In the Decode part, the feature map obtained by the Encode part is first sampled by 4 times bilinear interpolations, and then the underlying feature map generated by the backbone network is fused after 1 × 1 convolution, and then 4 times up-sampling operation after 3 × 3 convolution. Finally, the prediction result is obtained.

3   Improved DeepLabV3+ structure

In order to meet the needs of fast image segmentation in industrial application scenarios, we proposed a segmentation model that combines MobileNet_V2 [14] with improved DeepLabV3+. MobileNet_V2 network can solve the problems of large convolutional neural networks and insufficient hardware training in the training process of deep learning models [15]. Its core is deep separable convolution, which contains two parts: Depth-Wise convolution (DW) and Point-Wise convolution (PW). When the convolution kernel is the same size, it can greatly reduce the amount of calculation. The improved DeepLabV3+ network is shown in Fig. 1.

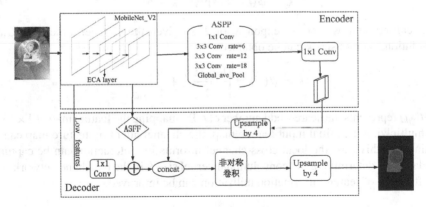

Fig. 1. Improved DeepLabV3+ structure

3.1   Channel Attention

As the convolutional layer deepens, the acquired semantic features become more abstract, influencing subsequent feature learning. Therefore, setting the degree of importance according to the influence of different feature channels on target prediction is conducive to strengthening the pertinence of feature learning. Efficient channel attention(ECA) [16] module can effectively establish the self-learning of the importance weights of each characteristic channel, and the overall structure is shown in Fig. 2.

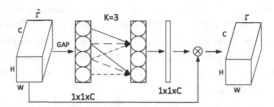

Fig. 2. Effective channel attention structure

For the feature map entered $\tau = R^{W \times H \times C}$, when considering only the interaction between the channel and the nearest neighbor k, the weight of the channel characteristic y_i is:

$$\omega_i = \sigma(\sum_{j=1}^{k} \alpha_i^j y_i^j), y_i^j \in \delta_i^k \tag{2}$$

δ_i^k represents the set of adjacent channels of y_i, and shares the weight parameter, then obtains a feature map of $1 \times 1 \times C$ after global average pooling. Since there is a mapping ϕ between the size of one-dimensional convolution k and channel dimension C:

$$C = \phi(k) \approx \exp(\gamma * k - b) \tag{3}$$

C can be seen as a power exponent of 2, so given the channel dimension C,the convolutional kernel size k can be obtained:

$$k = \psi(C) = \left| \frac{\log_2(C)}{\gamma} + \frac{b}{\gamma} \right|_{odd} \tag{4}$$

$|t|_{odd}$ represents the nearest odd number of t. By mapping the feature map of $1 \times 1 \times C$ and multiplying the initial input feature map, the channel attention feature map can be obtained. In this way, the local cross-channel information interaction can be captured by adaptively determining the convolutional kernel size k in the backbone network, and the efficiency of feature information utilization can be improved.

3.2 Adaptive Spatial Feature Fusion

Since Deeplabv3+ ignores different levels of feature information, it causes inaccuracies in subsequent network segmentations. Therefore, we use the Adaptive spatial feature fusion (ASFF) [17] structure to aggregate these different levels of information and improve network performance. ASFF structure is shown in Fig. 3.

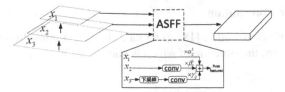

Fig. 3. Adaptive spatial feature fusion structure

The left side of Fig. 3 represents three different levels of feature maps, gradually increasing the resolution from top to bottom, and gradually reducing the number of channels, as shown in the solid wireframe in the figure. Take the feature map of 1 / 4, 1 / 8 and 1 / 16 generated by the backbone network as the input feature level of ASFF network, which is recorded as x_1, x_2 and x_3, and the corresponding number of input channels is 32, 24 and 16 respectively. Since y_1 has richer semantic information and spatial information, it is used as the output of this structure. The impact of different input and output levels on the performance of this module is shown in Table 1, the results show that the optimal ASFF training results can be obtained with the currently selected input and output.

Then, the size of the x_2 is adjusted to the same size as x_1 by 3×3 convolutional feature x_2 level, and then the 3×3 convolution is adjusted to x_1 size after the down-sampling operation of x_3 and then carry out adaptive spatial weight information fusion.Let $x_{ij}^{m \to l}$ represented as a feature vector at position (i, j) on the feature map adjusted to level m to level l.The formula for the corresponding l level fusion features is as follows:

$$y_{ij}^l = \alpha_{ij}^l \cdot x_{ij}^{1 \to l} + \beta_{ij}^l \cdot x_{ij}^{2 \to l} + \gamma_{ij}^l \cdot x_{ij}^{3 \to l} \tag{5}$$

y_{ij}^l represents the (i, j) feature vector of the output feature map y^l. α_{ij}^l, β_{ij}^l, γ_{ij}^l represents the spatial importance weights of the three different levels to the l level, and this article will take 1. The feature map of the output is upsampled and fused with the feature map after 1x1 convolution in the decoding layer.

Table 1. Influence of different input and output levels on network performance.

Input	Output	MIou/%
	y_1	92.58
1/2, 1/4, 1/8	y_2	92.43
	y_3	92.16
	y_1	**92.83**
1/4, 1/8, 1/16	y_2	92.77
	y_3	92.01

Note: the bold is the optimal result

3.3 Asymmetric Convolution

We use asymmetric convolution [18] to replace the 3×3 convolution in the original network Decode part, the structure of which is shown in Fig. 4.

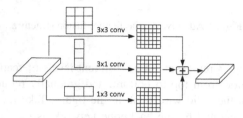

Fig. 4. Asymmetric convolutional structure

We assume $F \in \mathbb{R}^{H \times W \times D}$ represents convolution kernel. $M \in \mathbb{R}^{H \times W \times D}$ represents the input feature map, $O \in \mathbb{R}^{R \times T \times D}$ represents the output feature map. For the j-th convolutional kernel in this layer, the corresponding output feature mapping channel after batch normalization and linear transformation is:

$$O_{:,:,j} = (\sum_{k=1}^{C} M_{:,:,k} * F_{:,:,k}^{(j)} - \mu_j)\frac{\gamma_j}{\sigma_j} + \beta_j \tag{6}$$

$*$ is a two-dimensional convolutional operator, $M_{:,:,k}$ is a feature plot of size $U \times V$ on k th channel of M, $F_{:,:,k}^{(j)}$ represents a feature plot of size $H \times W$ on k th channel of $F^{(j)}$. μ_i and σ_i are channel means and standard deviation values for batch normalization. γ_i and β_i are the scaling factor and offset.

The asymmetric convolutional module contains three parallel convolutional layers with cores of $3 \times 3, 3 \times 1$ and 1×3, let $O_{:,:,j}, \overline{O}_{:,:,j}, \hat{O}_{:,:,j}$ be expressed as the outputs of the three branches $3 \times 3, 1 \times 3$ and 3×1, respectively, the result of the final fusion can be expressed as:

$$O_{:,:,j} + \overline{O}_{:,:,j} + \hat{O}_{:,:,j} = \sum_{k=1}^{C} M_{:,:,k} * F_{:,:,k}^{'(j)} + b_j \tag{7}$$

$F_{:,:,k}^{'(j)}$ can be simplified to $F^{'(j)}$ and b_j are shown in the following equation:

$$F^{'(j)} = \frac{\gamma_j}{\sigma_j}F^{(j)} \oplus \frac{\overline{\gamma}_j}{\overline{\sigma}_j}\overline{F}^{(j)} \oplus \frac{\hat{\gamma}_j}{\hat{\sigma}_j}\hat{F}^{(j)} \tag{8}$$

$$b_j = -\frac{\mu_j\gamma_j}{\sigma_j} - \frac{\overline{\mu}_j\overline{\gamma}_j}{\overline{\sigma}_j} - \frac{\hat{\mu}_j\hat{\gamma}_j}{\hat{\sigma}_j} + \beta_j + \overline{\beta}_j + \hat{\beta}_j \tag{9}$$

In formulas (8) and (9), $\overline{F}^{(j)}$, $\hat{F}^{(j)}$, $\overline{\gamma}_j$, $\hat{\gamma}_j$, $\overline{\beta}_j$, $\hat{\beta}_j$, $\overline{\mu}_j$, $\hat{\mu}_j$ and $\overline{\sigma}_j$, $\hat{\sigma}_j$ represent the output of the 1×3 and 3×1 convolutional kernel, the scaling factor, the offset, the channel mean of the batch normalization, and the standard deviation value, respectively.

Replacing the 3×3 convolutions in the Decode part with asymmetric convolutions can be understood as enhancing the kernel skeleton of convolution. The purpose is to enhance the processing ability of 3×3 convolution kernel, obtain more detailed information, and improve the accuracy of model.

4 Experimental

4.1 Experimental Platform and Parameter

Our experimental platform adopts Windows 10 system and PYTORCH deep learning framework. The CPU and GPU are Intel i5-10400H, NVIDIA GTX2070 with 8G memory. During training, some key parameters are set to use cross entropy loss function for 100 epochs. The initial learning rate and momentum are set to 0.007, 0.9. The learning strategy select poly. Due to the limited memory size, set batch size to 2 and optimize algorithm using the SGD to avoid falling into a local optimal solution.

4.2 Datasets and Evaluation Metrics

Since the experimental model in this paper is an improvement for the intelligent robot grasping scenario, it is necessary to make a corresponding dataset. Thercfore,we randomly arranged the positions of different mechanical parts in the engineering scenario, and use an industrial camera to obtain 2173 pictures with size of 2048×1536 pixels. We perform data enhancement operations on these images and expand them to 3000. After that, we use the Labelme to annotate the images, including 6 foreground categories and 1 background category, some of the sample images and labels are shown in Fig. 5. Then divided into training sets, validation sets and test sets according to 8:1:1, and the picture data is loaded in a VOC2007 format directory.

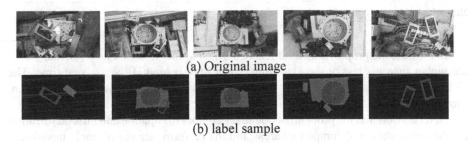

(a) Original image

(b) label sample

Fig. 5. Partial dataset sample

In this paper, the average prediction time, mean intersection over union (MIou) and pixel accuracy (PA) are used as the performance evaluation indicators of the semantic segmentation of mechanical parts. PA and MIou formulas are as follows:

$$PA = \frac{\sum_{i=0}^{n} P_{ii}}{\sum_{i=0}^{n} \sum_{j=0}^{n} P_{ij}} \tag{10}$$

$$MIoU = \frac{1}{n+1} \sum_{i=0}^{n} \frac{p_{ii}}{\sum_{j=0}^{n} p_{ij} + \sum_{j=0}^{n} p_{ji} - p_{ii}} \tag{11}$$

In the (10) and (11) formulas,n represents the number of categories,i represents the true value. The j represents the predicted value.p_{ij} indicates that it should be class i but is predicted to be class j, which is false negative.p_{ii} means to predict class i as class i,as true.p_{ji} indicates that it was originally class j.

4.3   Comparison of Results from Different Algorithms

Our method is compared with UNet, PSPNet [19], HRNet [20], DeepLabV3 [21], DeepLabV3+ and DeepLabV3+ (MobileNet_V2) on the self-built mechanical parts dataset, and the results are shown in Table 2.

Table 2. Comparison of different network performances.

Method	PA/%	MIou/%	Time/s
UNet	74.46	61.05	0.4553
PSPNet	88.83	78.62	0.5736
HRNet	96.15	90.46	**0.3574**
DeepLabV3	95.59	88.52	0.8206
DeepLabV3+	92.37	72.78	0.6749
DeepLabV3+ (MobileNet_V2)	97.24	92.23	0.4013
Our method	**98.64**	**93.65**	0.3972

Note: the bold is the optimal result

In the end, the proposed method reached 98.64% and 93.65% on PA, MIou, which are higher than the rest of the algorithm, but a little behind HRNet in real-time. The visualization results of our method with different semantic segmentation methods are shown in Fig. 6.

UNet network has the problem of boundary contour dissipation and misclassification for the segmentation of component areas and the performance is extremely unsatisfactory. PSPNet network segmentation effect is slightly stronger, but there are problems of segmentation discontinuity and blurred boundaries. HRNet segmentation has a good effect, but there is still a phenomenon of false segmentation. DeepLabV3 takes too much background into account. The traditional DeepLabV3+ method has a poor segmentation effect due to the similarity of the background to the part color and too much consideration of the shadow area. DeepLabV3+ with MobileNet_V2 segmentation works well, but there are still misclassifications and blurred boundaries. This method can reduce these problems and achieve better results for component image segmentation.

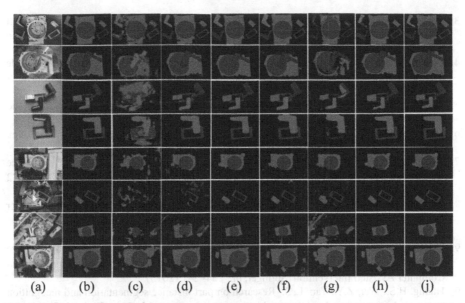

(a)　　(b)　　(c)　　(d)　　(e)　　(f)　　(g)　　(h)　　(j)

Fig. 6. Different network prediction results ((a):origin picture; (b):label image; (c):UNet; (d):PSPNet; (e)HRNet; (f)DeepLabV3; (g):DeepLabV3+; (h):DeepLabV3+ (MobileNet_V2); (j):our method)

5 Conclusion

In order to improve the accuracy of component segmentation in industrial application scenarios, we improved DeepLabV3+ network model of fusion MobileNet_V2 is used to semantically segment the component image. Experimental results show that the accuracy, mean intersection over union and average prediction time of the model on the dataset of self-built mechanical parts reach 98.64%, 93.65%, and 0.3972s, respectively, which can segment the parts feature region with better accuracy than other semantic segmentation methods. At the same time, feature fusion is used to enhance the utilization of the underlying information, but increase the amount of computation, so in the follow-up work, the model structure will continue to be optimized to improve the efficiency of computing.

Acknowledgment. This work is supported by the National Natural Science Foundation of China (52075532), the Nature Science Foundation of Liaoning Province (2020-MS-030), and the Youth Innovation Promotion Association of Chinese Academy of Sciences (2021199).

References

1. Zhang, C., Li, Y.G., Luo, L.F.: Parts image feature extraction based on SIFT-SUSAN algorithm. Manufacturing automation **36**(16), 81–85 (2014)
2. Han, Y.J.: Research on Geometric features-based Method for Workpiece recognition. Dalian University of Technology, Liaoning (2014)

3. Girshick, R., Donahue, J., Daeewll, T., Malik, J.: Rich feature hierarchies for accurate object detection and semantic segmentation. In: 2014 IEEE Conference on Computer Vision and Pattern Recognition, pp. 580–587. Columbus (2014)

4. Liu, W., Aanguelov, D., Erhan, D., Szegedy, C., Reed, S., Fu, C.Y., Berg, A.C.: SSD: single shot multi-Box detector. In: European Conference on Computer Vision, pp 21–37. Springer Verlag (2016)

5. Zhang, J., Liu, F.L., Wang, R.W.: Research on industrial parts recognition algorithm based on YOLOv3 in intelligent assembly. Photoelectron and laser **31**(10), 1054–1061 (2020)

6. Yu, Y.W., Han, X., Du, L.Q.: Target part recognition based on Inception-SSD algorithm. Optical precision engineering **28**(8), 1799–1809 (2020)

7. Yang, L., Chen, S.Y., Cui, G.H., Zhu, X.L.: Recognition and location method of workpiece based on improved YOLOv4. Modular machi. Tools and Autom. Machine. Technol. **10**, 28–32 (2021)

8. Badrinarayanan, V., Kendall, A., Cipolla, R.: SegNet: a deep convolutional encoder-decoder architecture for image segmentation. IEEE Transactions on Pattern Analysis Machine Intelligence, 2481–2495 (2017)

9. Ronneberger, O., Fischer, P., Brox, T.: U-Net: convolutional networks for biomedical image segmentation. In: Proceedings of International Conference on Medical Image Computing and Computer Assisted Intervention. Springer, pp. 234–241 (2015)

10. Huang, H.S., Wei, Z.Y., Yao, L.G.: Research on part instance segmentation and recognition based on deep learning. Modular machi. Tools and Automat. Machine. Technol. **5**, 122–125 (2019)

11. Hong, Q., Song, Q., Yang, C.T., Zhang, P., Chang, L.: Image segmentation technology of mechanical parts based on intelligent vision. J Machin. Manuf. Automa. **49**(5), 203–206 (2020)

12. Wang, Y.: Part segmentation in cluttered scene based on convolutional neural network. Qingdao Technology University, Shandong (2021)

13. Chen, L.C., Zhu, Y., Papandreou, G., Schroff, F., Adam, H.: Encoder-decoder with atrous separable convolution for semantic image segmentation. In: European Conference on Computer Vision, pp. 833–851. Berlin (2018)

14. Sandler, M., Howard, A., Zhu, M., Zhmoginov, A., Chen, L.C.: MobileNet_V2: Inverted residuals and linear bottlenecks. In: Meeting of the IEEE/CVF Conference on Computer Vision and Pattern Recognition, pp. 4510–4520. IEEE Computer Society (2018)

15. Li, Q.H., Li, C.P., Zang, J., Chen, H., Wang, S.Q.: Survey of compressed deep neural network. Computer Science **46**(9), 1–14 (2019)

16. Wang, Q., Wu, B., Zhu, P., Li, P., Hu, Q.: ECA-Net: efficient channel attention for deep convolutional neural networks. In: IEEE/CVF Conference on Computer Vision and Pattern Recognition, pp. 11531–11539. IEEE Computer Society (2020)

17. Liu, S.T., Huang, D., Wang, Y.H.: Learning spatial fusion for single-shot Object Detection https://arxiv.org/abs/1911.09516 (2020)

18. Ding, X., Guo, Y., Ding, G., Han, J.: ACNet: Strengthening the kernel skeletons for powerful CNN via asymmetric convolution blocks, pp. 1911–1920. Institude of Electrical and Electronics Engineers Inc (2019)

19. Zhao, H., Shi, J., Qi, X., Wang, X., Jia, J.: Pyramid scene parsing network. In: Proceedings of the IEEE Conference on Computer Vision and Pattern Recognition, pp 6230–6239. IEEE Press, Washington (2017)

20. Sun, K., Xiao, B., Liu, D., Wang, J.D.: Deep high-resolution representation learning for human pose estimation. In: 2019 IEEE/CVF Conference on Computer Vision and Pattern Recognition. pp. 5686–5696 (2019)

21. Chen, L.C., Papandreou, G., Schroff, F., Adam, H.: Rethinking atrous convolution for semantic image segmentation (2017). https://doi.org/10.48550/arXiv.1706.05587

Multiple Object Tracking by Joint Head, Body Detection and Re-Identification

Zuode Liu[1,2], Honghai Liu[1(✉)], Weihong Ren[1], Hui Chang[1,2], Yuhang Shi[1], Ruihan Lin[1], and Wenhao Wu[1]

[1] School of Mechanical Engineering and Automation, Harbin Institute of Technology, Shenzhen, China
honghai.liu@hit.edu.cn
[2] Peng Cheng Laboratory, Shenzhen, China

Abstract. Multi-object tracking (MOT) is an important problem in computer vision which has a wide range of applications. Formulating MOT as multi-task learning of object detection and re-Identification (re-ID) in a single network is appealing since it achieves real-time but effective inference on detection and tracking. However, in crowd scenes, the existing MOT methods usually fail to locate occluded objects, which also results in bad effects on the re-ID task. To solve people tracking in crowd scenes, we present a model called HBR (Head-Body-ReID Joint Tracking) to jointly formulates head detection, body detection and re-ID tasks into an uniform framework. Human heads are hardly affected by occlusions in crowd scenes, and they can provide informative clues for whole body detection. The experimental results on *MOT17* and *MOT20* show that our proposed model performs better than the state-of-the-arts.

Keywords: Multiple Object Tracking · Head detection · Person re-Identification

1 Introduction

Multi-Object Tracking (MOT), is an significant problem in visual scene understanding, which can be applied in many situations such as smart video analysis, autonomous driving and etc. The tracking-by-detection paradigm has been a dominant strategy that breaks MOT down to detection step and association step. Thus, the MOT system needs to perform detection and data association, separately [5,10,20,24,28]. However, the two-step models suffer from efficiency problems, and they cannot achieve real-time inference when there exists a large number of objects. In order to save computation and reduce running time, the detection and re-ID tasks are usually integrated into an uniform network as a multi-task learning model [17,19], but these methods usually fail to obtain long-term trajectories in crowded scenes due to the missed or wrongly detections.

In recent years, the focus of MOT has shifted towards people tracking in crowds of high density. As the density increases, the occlusion of people leads to

Supported by Peng Cheng Laboratory.

the ID switches and fragmentation of trajectories. In many practical pedestrian tracking scenes, the images are taken as a overhead viewing angle, and thus human heads can't be occluded in most cases. To track people efficiently in densely crowded situations, the human heads detection and tracking tasks were proposed [4,16], and these works focus on the detection of human heads and then use the existing tracking methods to associate them across different frames. In order to solve the occlusion problem, the people head and body detection should be considered in an uniform framework.

In this paper, we propose a MOT approach that jointly models Head detection, Body detection and Re-ID tasks (HBR) into a whole framework. Compared with the FairMOT [25] which only contains the body detection and re-ID branches, the added head detection branch contributes to detect the people whose body has been blocked and thus decreases the ID switches and fragmentation of trajectories. As shown in Fig. 1, our model has a simple network structure that consists of three homogeneous branches for human head, body detection and re-ID tasks, respectively. It has been proved that the network will be biased to the detection task if the anchor-based detection method is used [25], and thus the head and body detection branches in our model are based on the anchor-free object detection architecture CenterNet [27]. The human body detection branch estimates the people's body center and size, whereas the head detection branch only estimates the head center. The re-ID branch estimates the corresponding appearance embeddings of each people's center characterized as the measurement map pix, respectively.

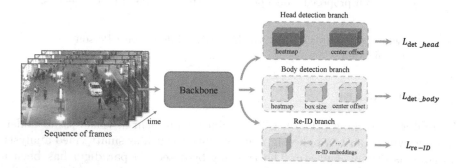

Fig. 1. The overall architecture of joint head detection, body detection and re-ID tasks. The input image is fed to the backbone (DLA34) to extract the feature maps. Then, we add three homogeneous branches to detect the pedestrian's head, body and corresponding re-ID appearance embeddings. Compared with the body detection branch, the head detection branch doesn't predict the box size.

We evaluate our model on MOT Challenge benchmark via the evaluation server. We obtain a significant improvement compared to the FairMOT without head detection branch. On public benchmark MOT20 where the images are taken from a top view, we obtain the MOTA of 68.1% (FairMOT: 61.8%). On MOT17 where the images are mostly taken from a heads-up perspective, identity switches (IDs) reduce to the one third of FairMOT and MOTA obtains the equivalent level.

In summary, this paper makes the following contributions:

(1) We present HBR that jointly formulates the head detection, body detection and re-ID tasks into an uniform network to solve the occlusion problem of tracking in crowd scenes.
(2) The experimental results on MOT20, MOT17 benchmarks show that HBR contributes to detect the people with occlusion and reduces the identity switches in tracking.

2 Related Work

This section briefly reviews the related works on tracking-by-detection MOT approaches, joint-detection-and-tracking MOT approaches and human head tracking approaches.

2.1 Tracking-By-Detection MOT Approaches

The tracking-by-detection MOT approaches separate models into two steps. Specifically, these models locate objects in each frame by detector firstly, and then associate the detections over time based on location and motion cues or appearance cues. Many popular detectors such as DPM [6], Faster R-CNN [13] and SDP [22] are used to detect pedestrians, and some works [10,20,24] use a large private pedestrians detection datasets to train their own detectors to boost the detection performance.

On the basic of detection, SORT [2] uses Kalman Filter [1] to estimate the object locations in next frame, computes their overlap with detections, and then associates detections to tracklets by Hungarian algorithm [8]. The trackers [2,3] based on motion and location cues may fail in crowded scenes and fast motion situations. Some works such as deepSORT [20], Poi [24] feed the detection region to re-ID networks to extract the appearance features and compute the similarity of detection in each frame to finish the data associations. However, the two-steps models can not achieve real-time inference for the two tasks don't share structure and parameters [19].

2.2 Joint-Detection-and-Tracking MOT Approaches

The joint-detection-tracking approaches learn the detection task and appearance feature embedding task in an unified deep model. JDE [19] is built on top of YOLOV3 and adds one re-ID branch to detector for extracting appearance feature, which nearly achieves real-time inference and obtains a comparable accuracy to these two-step approaches. FairMOT [25] demonstrates the anchor-based one-shot MOT architectures have limitations of learning re-ID features and adopts CenterNet [27] as basic detect structure to improve the problem and enhance the re-ID performance.

2.3 Head Detection and Tracking

Compared with the body detection, the human heads are hardly affected by occlusions in crowded scenes, and thus heads detection and tracking tasks begin to get more attention. The task of head detection combines the multi-scale and contextual object detection problem, [15] employs contextual and scale-invariant approaches to head detection. To compare the human head detection performance in dense crowd, [16] proposed a new dataset CroHD and a detector HeadHunter as the baseline. In head tracking task, the existing association methods are based on the appearance and motion cues, which suffers from the great challenge for the similarity and small region of human heads.

3 HBR: Joint Head, Body Detection and Re-ID Model

In this section, we introduce the HBR details including the backbone network, the human head and body detection branches, re-ID branch as well as training details.

3.1 Backbone Network

The detection tasks need more similar features for different instances while re-ID task needs more low-level features, and the enhanced Deep Layer Aggregation (DLA) [27] is used to alleviate this contradiction, for it has many hierarchical skip connections to fuse the multi-layers features. Original convolution layers in up-sampling layers are replaced by deformable convolution to dynamically adjust the receptive field. For an given image with the resolution of $H_{in} \times W_{in}$, the size of output feature map is $C \times H_{out} \times W_{out}$, where $H_{out} = H_{in}/4$ and $W_{out} = W_{in}/4$ in this model.

3.2 Head and Body Detection

The head and body detections are two parallel branches, and they are designed on top of CenterNet [27] which is an anchor-free detection architecture. There are three subtasks in human body detection branch, including heatmap estimation, body center offsets and bounding box sizes regression, and the head detection branch includes the above two subtasks expect bounding box sizes regression. To generate the final estimation targets in above five subtasks, the 3×3 convolutional layer with 256 channels is applied after the backbone, followed by a 1×1 convolutional layer.

As shown in Fig. 2, the locations of head and body center are estimated by heatmaps $\hat{M}^b_{xy}$, $\hat{M}^h_{xy} \in [0,1]^{H_{out} \times W_{out}}$. The response at a location in the heatmap is expected to be closer to one if it nears the ground-truth (GT) object center. For each people's body GT box $b^i = (x^i_1, y^i_1, w^i_1, h^i_1)$, the body center point (c^i_{bx}, c^i_{by}) is computed as $c^i_{bx} = x^i_1 + w^i_1/2$, $c^i_{by} = y^i_1 + h^i_1/2$, and the head center point (c^i_{hx}, c^i_{hy}) annotation is computed as $c^i_{hx} = x^i_1 + w^i_1/2$, $c^i_{hy} =$

Body detection   Head detection

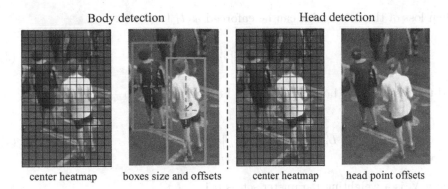

center heatmap   boxes size and offsets   center heatmap   head point offsets

Fig. 2. Two branches of body detection and head detection. The body detection branch includes heatmap, boxes size and offsets, and head detection branch includes heatmap and point offsets.

$y_1^i + h_1^i/12$, respectively. As the center point in image maps to the heatmap, the new coordinates of body and head center point in heatmap is $(\widetilde{c}_{bx}^i, \widetilde{c}_{by}^i) = (\lfloor \frac{c_{bx}^i}{4} \rfloor, \lfloor \frac{c_{by}^i}{4} \rfloor)$ and $(\widetilde{c}_{hx}^i, \widetilde{c}_{hy}^i) = (\lfloor \frac{c_{hx}^i}{4} \rfloor, \lfloor \frac{c_{hy}^i}{4} \rfloor)$. Then the body heatmap response at the location (x, y) is computed as:

$$M_{xy}^b = \sum_{i=1}^{N} \exp^{-\frac{(x-\widetilde{c}_{bx}^i)^2 + (y-\widetilde{c}_{by}^i)^2}{2\sigma_{cb}^2}}, \tag{1}$$

where N represents the number of objects in the image and σ_{cb} represents the standard deviation. Similarly, the head heatmap response M_{xy}^h can be computed, and the standard head deviation $\sigma_{ch} = \sigma_{cb}/3$. The body heatmap loss function is defined as pixel wise logistic regression with focal loss:

$$L_{heat}^b = -\frac{1}{N} \sum_{xy} \begin{cases} (1 - \hat{M}_{xy}^b)^\alpha \log(\hat{M}_{xy}^b), & M_{xy}^b = 1; \\ (1 - M_{xy}^b)^\beta (\hat{M}_{xy}^b)^\alpha \log(1 - \hat{M}_{xy}^b), & \text{otherwise}, \end{cases} \tag{2}$$

where $\hat{M}_{xy}^b$ is the body estimated heatmap, and α, β are the predetermined parameters in focal loss. The head heatmap loss function L_{heat}^h is computed in the same way.

As the location maping from object points in image to heatmap will introduce quantization errors up to four pixels, the offset subtasks of head and body detection branches are designed to locate objects more precisely. Denote the output of the body and head offsets as $\hat{O}_b, \hat{O}_h \in \mathbb{R}^{2 \times H \times W}$, for the body GT box and head center GT point, the body offset is computed as $o_b^i = (\frac{c_{bx}^i}{4}, \frac{c_{by}^i}{4}) - (\lfloor \frac{c_{bx}^i}{4} \rfloor, \lfloor \frac{c_{by}^i}{4} \rfloor)$ as well as head offset o_h^i. As for the boxes size of body, denote $\hat{S}_b \in \mathbb{R}^{2 \times H \times W}$, and the box size $s_b^i = (w_1^i, h_1^i)$ which is annotated in the body GT box, respectively.

Then loss of the head point can be enforced as l_1 loss:

$$L_p^h = \sum_{i=1}^{N} \|o_h^i - \hat{o}_h^i\|_1, \tag{3}$$

and the loss of body bounding box can be computed as:

$$L_{box}^b = \sum_{i=1}^{N} \|o_b^i - \hat{o}_b^i\|_1 + \lambda_s \|s_b^i - \hat{s}_b^i\|_1. \tag{4}$$

where λ_s is a weighting parameter set as 0.1.

In general, we can compute the human body and head detection loss:

$$L_{body} = L_{heat}^b + L_{box}^b, \tag{5}$$

$$L_{head} = L_{heat}^h + L_p^h. \tag{6}$$

where the L_{body} represents the human body detection loss and L_{head} represents the head detection loss.

3.3   Re-ID Task

The re-ID branch is designed for distinguishing people according to the appearance features in each frames. Ideally, the disparity of the same people's embedding is smaller than the different pairs, and to achieve this goal, a convolutional layer with 128 kernels is set on top of backbone features to extract re-ID features. Denote the embeddings feature map as $E \in \mathbb{R}^{128 \times H \times W}$, and the embedding of a pedestrian centered at (x, y) can be extracted as $E_{x,y} \in \mathbb{R}^{128}$.

To compute the re-ID loss, all the people with the same identity in the training dataset are set as the same class. For each body GT box $b^i = (x_1^i, y_1^i, w_1^i, h_1^i)$ and the corresponding center point $(\tilde{c}_{bx}^i, \tilde{c}_{by}^i)$ in body heatmap, we can extract re-ID embedding $E_{\tilde{c}_{bx}^i, \tilde{c}_{by}^i}$ and use a fully connected layer and a softmax operation to map it to a class distribution vector $P = \{p(k), k \in [1, K]\}$. The class label can be encoded as one-hot representation $L^i(k)$ and re-ID loss is computed as:

$$L_{id} = -\sum_{i=1}^{N} \sum_{k=1}^{K} L^i(k) \log(p(k)), \tag{7}$$

where K is the total number of identities in the training data. In the training process, only the embeddings located at the center of people are used.

3.4   Total Loss of Training

As the losses of three branches are computed above, the total loss is jointly computed together. To balance the three branches, the uncertainty loss proposed in [7] is used:

$$L_{total} = \frac{1}{2}\left(\frac{1}{e^{\omega_1}}L_{body} + \frac{1}{e^{\omega_2}}L_{head} + \frac{1}{e^{\omega_3}}L_{id} + \omega_1 + \omega_2 + \omega_3\right) \qquad (8)$$

where $\omega_1, \omega_2, \omega_3$ are learnable parameters to balance the three tasks. In the training processing, the heatmaps, boxes size map, center points offsets and one-hot representation for each object identity are generated firstly and then the total loss is computed between the GT labels and predicted outputs.

3.5 Online Association and Tracking

In the inference process, the images are resized to 1088×608 as input. We can obtain body detection estimated heatmap, and then we use 3×3 max pooling operation to perform non-maximum suppression based on the response scores for extracting the peak response points. In order to get the points that are more likely to have objects, we keep the keypoints whose heatmap response scores are larger than a threshold. Then, the corresponding bounding boxes of the remaining points can be computed on the top of body estimated offset and sizes as well as the identity embeddings. It is important to note that the head branch does not participate the inference process, that is to say, the head heatmap and offset will be computed but have none any final output in images.

As the bounding boxes and re-ID embeddings of objects are estimated in the inference process, we need to associate the objects with the same identity in each frames. To achieve this goal, we use a hierarchical online data association approach. Firstly, we use Kalman Filter [1] to estimate the location of each previous tracklet in the current frame. The distance D fuses the re-ID cosine distance D_r and Mahanlanobis distance D_m with the weighting parameter $\lambda = 0.98$: $D = \lambda D_r + (1-\lambda)D_m$. Then, the Hungarian algorithm with a threshold $\tau_1 = 0.4$ is used to complete matching. Secondly, we match the unmatched detections by the boxes overlap $\tau > 0.5$. The final unmatched tracklets after the two stages will be maintained for 30 frames and unmatched detections will be initialized as the new tracks.

4 Experiments

4.1 Datasets and Metrics

To train our model, we use the same datasets as FairMOT [25], including the ETH, the CityPerson, the CalTech, CUHK-SYSU, PRW, MOT17 and MOT20. For the datasets that don't include identity annotations, we treat the whole people as the different identity.

In order to evaluate our model in an unified measurement method, we implement our model in the testing sets of MOTchallenge benchmarks: MOT17 and MOT20. The objects detection metrics Average Precision AP is used to evaluate the detection performance, and then the common CLEAR MOT metrics such as $MOTA, IDs$ and $IDF1$ are used to evaluate tracking accuracy.

4.2   Implementation Details

To enhance the detection precision, we use the model parameters pre-trained on the COCO dataset to initialize our model. We use Adam optimizer to train our model for 30 epochs with the batch size of 12. The learning rate is set to 10^{-4} at the beginning and will decay to 10^{-5} from 20 epochs. The standard data augmentation techniques including rotation, scaling and color jittering are used to enhance the model performance. All the training process is finished on two Quadro RTX 6000 GPUs using Pytorch framework.

4.3   Evaluation on MOT Challenge

We evaluate our model on the MOT17 and MOT20 datasets, and compare the results with the recent one-stage approaches. The tracking results on MOT17 and MOT20 are shown in Table 1. All the results are from the related paper or MOT challenge. By adding the human head detection branch, our model get a significant improvement compared with the FairMOT [25], for MOT20, MOTA can be improved from 61.8 to 68.1. The reason for the great enhancement is that the images are taken from a top view on MOT20, and the added human head branch provides informative clues for the whole body detection, which can improve the occlusion problem in crowded scenes. The great reduction of IDs (2259 on MOT17 and 4513 on MOT20) shows that the head detection task enhances the ability of extracting the appearance feature embeddings.

Table 1. Comparison with the recent one-stage methods under the private detector protocol. The best results of each dataset are shown in bold.

Dataset	Tracker	MOTA↑	IDF1↑	MT↑	ML↓	IDs↓	FPS↑
MOT17	TubeTK [11]	63.0	58.6	31.2%	19.9%	4137	3.0
	CTrackerV1 [12]	66.6	57.4	32.2%	24.2%	5529	6.8
	CenterTrack [26]	67.8	64.7	34.6%	24.6%	2583	17.5
	TraDeS [21]	69.1	63.9	37.3%	20.0%	3555	22.3
	FairMOT [25]	73.7	72.3	**43.2%**	**17.3%**	3303	**25.9**
	HBR(Ours)	**73.7**	**74.1**	39.6%	20.4%	**2259**	22.1
MOT20	RTv1 [23]	60.6	67.9	**69.6%**	**7.3%**	5686	3.0
	FairMOT [25]	61.8	67.3	68.8%	7.6%	5243	13.2
	TransTrack [14]	65.0	59.4	50.1%	13.4%	3608	**14.9**
	CSTrack [9]	66.6	68.6	50.4%	15.5%	**3196**	4.5
	GSDT_V2 [18]	67.1	67.5	53.1%	13.2%	3230	1.5
	HBR(Ours)	**68.1**	**71.1**	62.6%	8.1%	4513	11.8

5   Summary and Future Work

In this paper, we put forward a multiple object tracking method that integrates the human head, body detection and re-ID tasks to solve the occlusion problem of tracking in densely crowded scenes. The experimental results show that the added head detection branch enhances the human detection task with occlusion and also improves the re-ID branch. Besides, our model can be optimized by adding the constrains between the head detection and body detection to increase the detection further in the future.

References

1. Basar, T.: A new approach to linear filtering and prediction problems, pp. 167–179 (2001)
2. Bewley, A., Ge, Z., Ott, L., Ramos, F., Upcroft, B.: Simple online and realtime tracking. In: 2016 IEEE International Conference on Image Processing (ICIP), pp. 3464–3468 (2016)
3. Bochinski, E., Eiselein, V., Sikora, T.: High-speed tracking-by-detection without using image information. In: 2017 14th IEEE International Conference on Advanced Video and Signal Based Surveillance (AVSS), pp. 1–6 (2017)
4. Cao, J., Weng, X., Khirodkar, R., Pang, J., Kitani, K.: Observation-centric SORT: rethinking SORT for robust multi-object tracking. arXiv preprint arXiv:2203.14360 (2022)
5. Fang, K., Xiang, Y., Li, X., Savarese, S.: Recurrent autoregressive networks for online multi-object tracking. In: 2018 IEEE Winter Conference on Applications of Computer Vision (WACV), pp. 466–475 (2018)
6. Felzenszwalb, P., McAllester, D., Ramanan, D.: A discriminatively trained, multi-scale, deformable part model. In: 2008 IEEE Conference on Computer Vision and Pattern Recognition, pp. 1–8 (2008)
7. Kendall, A., Gal, Y., Cipolla, R.: Multi-task learning using uncertainty to weigh losses for scene geometry and semantics. In: Proceedings of the IEEE Conference on Computer Vision and Pattern Recognition, pp. 7482–7491 (2018)
8. Kuhn, H.W.: The Hungarian method for the assignment problem. Naval Res. Logist. Q. **2**(1–2), 83–97 (1955)
9. Liang, C., Zhang, Z., Zhou, X., Li, B., Zhu, S., Hu, W.: Rethinking the competition between detection and ReID in multiobject tracking. IEEE Trans. Image Process. **31**, 3182–3196 (2022)
10. Mahmoudi, N., Ahadi, S.M., Rahmati, M.: Multi-target tracking using CNN-based features: CNNMTT. Multimed. Tools Appl. **78**(6), 7077–7096 (2018). https://doi.org/10.1007/s11042-018-6467-6
11. Pang, B., Li, Y., Zhang, Y., Li, M., Lu, C.: TubeTK: adopting tubes to track multi-object in a one-step training model. In: 2020 IEEE/CVF Conference on Computer Vision and Pattern Recognition (CVPR), pp. 6307–6317 (2020)
12. Peng, J., et al.: Chained-tracker: chaining paired attentive regression results for end-to-end joint multiple-object detection and tracking. In: Vedaldi, A., Bischof, H., Brox, T., Frahm, J.-M. (eds.) ECCV 2020. LNCS, vol. 12349, pp. 145–161. Springer, Cham (2020). https://doi.org/10.1007/978-3-030-58548-8_9

13. Ren, S., He, K., Girshick, R., Sun, J.: Faster R-CNN: towards real-time object detection with region proposal networks. IEEE Trans. Pattern Anal. Mach. Intell. 1137–1149 (2017)
14. Sun, P., et al.: TransTrack: multiple object tracking with transformer. arXiv preprint arXiv:2012.15460 (2020)
15. Sun, Z., Peng, D., Cai, Z., Chen, Z., Jin, L.: Scale mapping and dynamic redetecting in dense head detection. In: 2018 25th IEEE International Conference on Image Processing (ICIP), pp. 1902–1906 (2018)
16. Sundararaman, R., De Almeida Braga, C., Marchand, E., Pettre, J.: Tracking pedestrian heads in dense crowd. In: Proceedings of the IEEE/CVF Conference on Computer Vision and Pattern Recognition, pp. 3865–3875 (2021)
17. Voigtlaender, P., et al.: MOTS: multi-object tracking and segmentation. In: 2019 IEEE/CVF Conference on Computer Vision and Pattern Recognition (CVPR), pp. 7934–7943 (2019)
18. Wang, Y., Kitani, K., Weng, X.: Joint object detection and multi-object tracking with graph neural networks. In: 2021 IEEE International Conference on Robotics and Automation (ICRA), pp. 13708–13715. IEEE (2021)
19. Wang, Z., Zheng, L., Liu, Y., Li, Y., Wang, S.: Towards real-time multi-object tracking. In: Vedaldi, A., Bischof, H., Brox, T., Frahm, J.-M. (eds.) ECCV 2020. LNCS, vol. 12356, pp. 107–122. Springer, Cham (2020). https://doi.org/10.1007/978-3-030-58621-8_7
20. Wojke, N., Bewley, A., Paulus, D.: Simple online and realtime tracking with a deep association metric. In: 2017 IEEE International Conference on Image Processing (ICIP), pp. 3645–3649 (2017)
21. Wu, J., Cao, J., Song, L., Wang, Y., Yang, M., Yuan, J.: Track to detect and segment: an online multi-object tracker. In: 2021 IEEE/CVF Conference on Computer Vision and Pattern Recognition (CVPR), pp. 12347–12356 (2021)
22. Yang, F., Choi, W., Lin, Y.: Exploit all the layers: fast and accurate CNN object detector with scale dependent pooling and cascaded rejection classifiers. In: 2016 IEEE Conference on Computer Vision and Pattern Recognition (CVPR), pp. 2129–2137 (2016)
23. Yu, E., Li, Z., Han, S., Wang, H.: RelationTrack: relation-aware multiple object tracking with decoupled representation. CoRR (2021)
24. Yu, F., Li, W., Li, Q., Liu, Yu., Shi, X., Yan, J.: POI: multiple object tracking with high performance detection and appearance feature. In: Hua, G., Jégou, H. (eds.) ECCV 2016. LNCS, vol. 9914, pp. 36–42. Springer, Cham (2016). https://doi.org/10.1007/978-3-319-48881-3_3
25. Zhang, Y., Wang, C., Wang, X., Zeng, W., Liu, W.: FairMOT: on the fairness of detection and re-identification in multiple object tracking. Int. J. Comput. Vis. **129**(11), 3069–3087 (2021). https://doi.org/10.1007/s11263-021-01513-4
26. Zhou, X., Koltun, V., Krähenbühl, P.: Tracking objects as points. In: Vedaldi, A., Bischof, H., Brox, T., Frahm, J.-M. (eds.) ECCV 2020. LNCS, vol. 12349, pp. 474–490. Springer, Cham (2020). https://doi.org/10.1007/978-3-030-58548-8_28
27. Zhou, X., Wang, D., Krähenbühl, P.: Objects as points. arXiv preprint arXiv:1904.07850 (2019)
28. Zhou, Z., Xing, J., Zhang, M., Hu, W.: Online multi-target tracking with tensor-based high-order graph matching. In: 2018 24th International Conference on Pattern Recognition (ICPR) (2018)

Recognition of Blinding Diseases from Ocular OCT Images Based on Deep Learning

Rong Wang, Yaqi Wang$^{(\boxtimes)}$, Weiquan Yu, Suiyu Zhang, Jiaojiao Wang, and Dingguo Yu

College of Media Engineering, Communication University of Zhejiang, Hangzhou 310018, China
wangyaqi@cuz.edu.cn

Abstract. Age-Related Macular Degeneration (AMD) and Diabetes Macular Edema (DME) are eye diseases with the highest blinding rate. Optical Coherence Tomography (OCT) is widely used to diagnose different eye diseases. However, the lack of automatic image analysis tools to support disease diagnosis remains a problem. At present, the high-dimensional analysis of OCT medical images using Convolutional Neural Networks (CNN) has been widely used in the fields of visual field assessment of glaucoma and diabetes retinopathy. The method we proposed involves the transfer learning of Inception V3. The experiment includes two stages: (1) Firstly, using SinGAN to generate high-quality image samples and enhance the data; (2) Fine-tune and validate the Xception model generated using transfer learning. The research shows that the Xception model achieves 98.8% classification accuracy on the OCT2017 data set under the condition that the Xception model has the same parameter quantity as the Inception model, to realize a more accurate classification of OCT images of blinding diseases.

Keywords: OCT · Deep learning · Xception · SinGAN · Image classification

1 Introduction

In developed countries, AMD is the main blinding eye disease for people over 50 years old [1]. By 2040, about a 200million diabetes patients will develop Diabetes Retinopathy (DR) [2–4]. OCT generates cross-sectional or three-dimensional images by measuring echo delay and the size of backscattered or backscattered light. It was first applied in OCT imaging of the human retina in 1993 [5]. Deep Learning (DL) technology can quickly and accurately capture the characteristics of lesions and judge the types of diseases in the processing of medical images, to improve the accuracy and stability of diagnosis [6].

H. Liu et al. (Eds.): ICIRA 2022, LNAI 13458, pp. 181–190, 2022.
https://doi.org/10.1007/978-3-031-13841-6_17

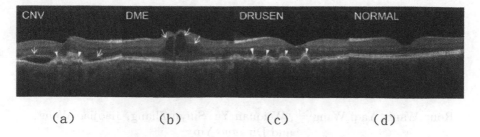

Fig. 1. Representative retinal OCT images

The specific lesion characteristics of age-related macular lesions are shown in Fig 1. The corresponding disease in figure (a) in the middle and late age macular disease. The corresponding focus is characterized by choroidal neovascularization (CNV) pointed by the solid triangle in the figure, that is, the proliferation of choroidal capillaries. At the same time, such patients will also produce subretinal effusion (SRF), that is, the position pointed by the white arrow. Clinicians will screen and judge whether the patient is in this kind of condition according to the characteristics of the two OCT images. The disease corresponding to figure (b) is DME, which is characterized by retinal swelling and thickening caused by subretinal effusion pointed by the white arrow in the figure; The corresponding disease in figure (c) is early AMD, and the corresponding lesion is characterized by multiple choroidal vitreous warts (drusen) at the position pointed by the solid triangle in the figure; figure (d) corresponds to the OCT image of normal retina, from which we can see that the retina maintains a concave contour, and there is no retinal effusion or swelling.

2   Related Research

In 2012, Krizhevsky [7] and others developed an image classification model called AlexNet CNN, which achieved a top-5 classification error rate of 15.3% on ImageNet. This breakthrough has aroused the interest of researchers in the research of image classification technology based on CNN. However, accurate blinding disease detection based on DL is still a challenging task because of their subtle differences in neuroimaging features during deterioration and insufficient samples. Presently, there are two popular methods to make up for the above defects.

The fundus OCT images were detected by customized CNN and data enhancement. For example, H. Chen et al. [8] used Inception V3 and image enhancement methods, including flipping, clipping, and horizontal scaling, to detect DR and achieved an accuracy of 80%. R. Sayres [9] et al. Used Inception V4 to classify DR and non-DR on the EYEPACS data set (five 1796 DR images of 1612 patients) and achieved an accuracy of 88.4%. M. Smaida [9] et al. Applied DCGAN for medical imaging, and tested and verified 1692 images from Kaggle and GON. The nonenhancement accuracy in the training and validation sets was 76.58% and 76.42% respectively.

The fundus OCT images were detected by model optimization and multi-layer model superposition. For example, Y. Peng et al. [10] developed DeepSeeNet for the automatic classification of AREDS patients (59302 images) and achieved an accuracy of 0.671. H. Jiang et al. [11] combined Inception V3, Reet152, and Inception ResNet V2 to enhance Dr detection on the private level 232244 image data set through tilt, rotation, translation, mirror image, brightness, sharpness, and contrast, with an accuracy of 88.21. Perdomo et al. [12] used OCT volume data set to evaluate the DME diagnosis of the OCTET model, which is an OCTET model based on CNN. At the same time, a missed cross-validation strategy was used in the experiment, and its accuracy, sensitivity, and specificity were 93.75%.

The above research shows that the application of deep structure in fundus images refreshes the accuracy of blinding disease detection. However, due to the high dependence of DL training on the quality of data sets, there is a high demand for locating anatomical structures and identifying lesions of blinding eye diseases [13], and the accuracy of automatic classification still needs to be further improved.

To overcome these limitations, a CNN model based on Xception and Sin-GAN is proposed in this paper, as shown in Fig. 2. Firstly, the experimental data is collected from Oct data sets provided by many authoritative institutions or ophthalmic centers at home and abroad (including CNV, DME, DURSEN, and normal folders), which meets the diversity and authority of the data set. Secondly, SinGAN is creatively used to generate high-resolution fundus images with local significance, and then the ophthalmic OCT images are accurately classified through the improved Xception model.

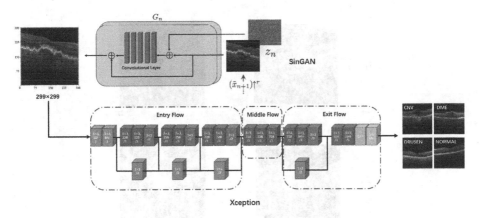

Fig. 2. CNN model based on Xception and SinGAN

3 Method

3.1 Crop and Adjust the Volume

Batch normalization (BN) was proposed by Sergey Ioffe and Christian Szegedy [14]. We have made the necessary simplification for each layer of input, where x_i represents a sample. First, the average value and variance of the elements in mini-patch are obtained, and then each scalar feature $X = [x_1, x_2, ..., x_n]$ normalized respectively:

$$x_i^{'} = \frac{x_i - \mu_B}{\sqrt{\sigma_B^2 + \epsilon}} \tag{1}$$

We introduce a pair of parameters for each activation function y_i scale and move the normalized values. By setting $\sqrt{\sigma_B^2 + \epsilon}$ and x' the network representation capability can be restored y_i the final output of the network. The data after data pretreatment is shown in Fig. 3:

$$y_i = y_i \cdot x_i^{'} + \beta_i \tag{2}$$

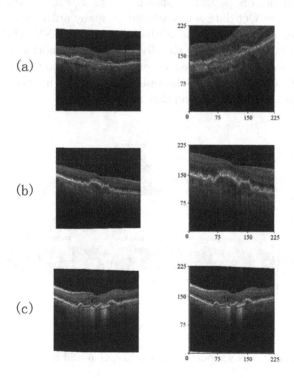

Fig. 3. Data preprocessing (a) Training set; (b) validation set; (c) Test set

3.2   Data Enhancement

SinGAN is an improved non conditional generative model based on generative countermeasure network, which can learn and train from a single natural image. The sampled images of fundus images with different sizes are input, and the distribution information of different scales is captured by Markov discriminant analysis (PatchGAN). The first image will output a random noise image, and then use the iterative idea to continuously learn the local details of the image, so as to generate a high-resolution fundus image. There are 12552 OCT images generated by SinGAN. With the original data set, the overall data is shown in Table 1.

Table 1. Specific classification of data sets

	Training set	Validation set	Test set	SinGAN	Total
CNV	37205	8	242	3724	41179
DME	11348	8	242	2863	14461
DRUSEN	8616	8	242	3244	12110
NORMAL	26315	8	242	2721	29286
TOTAL	83484	32	968	12552	84484

Keras provides a class of ImageDataGenerator to enhance the generalization ability of the model by enhancing the data of image samples. In this experiment, we randomly rotate the image sample by 90° and undergo a 0.25 shear and 0.3 zoom transformation, which can enlarge or reduce the image in equal proportion, and translate the corresponding $y(x)$ coordinate while the $x(y)$ coordinate remains unchanged. In addition, width is set_ shift_ Range and height_ shift_ Range, the parameter is a random floating-point number between $(-0.1, 0.1)$, as shown in Fig. 4:

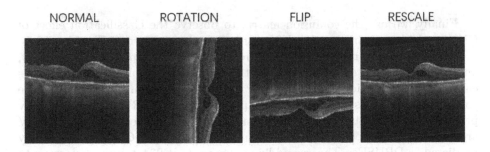

Fig. 4. Image data enhancement

3.3   Inception V3 Model

Inception V3 model uses a multi-layer small size filter to replace large size filter, which can reduce the over-fitting degree of the model and increase the performance of nonlinear expansion of the model. We passed nn.Sequential method to build the structure of the full connection layer of the Inception V3 model. Define a normalized function BN, use nn.Linear class to define the Linear layer of the model, complete the Linear transformation from the input layer to the hidden layer and use nn.ReLU class to define the activation function to achieve a four classification. Since we carry out a multi-classification task, the loss in the training process is calculated by CrossEntropyloss function. In gradient descent, each batch contained 128 samples, the number of iterations was set to 20 rounds, and the number of iterations was $128 \times 20 = 2560$ times. Finally, the CNN model based on Inception V3 achieved a classification accuracy of 92.5% on the OCT2017 data set, as shown in Fig. 5.

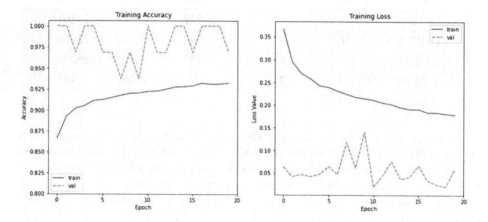

Fig. 5. Accuracy curve and loss curve of the model based on Inception V3 on the training set and verification set

Finally, we use the confusion matrix to observe the classification effect of CNN model based on Inception V3 on the test set, as shown in Fig. 6.

The sum of each row represents the real number of samples in this category, and the sum of each column represents the number of samples predicted in this category. The first line indicates that 241 samples belonging to DRUSEN are correctly predicted as a draft, and 1 sample belonging to DRUSEN is incorrectly predicted as CNV; The second line indicates that 239 samples belonging to CNV are correctly predicted as CNV and 3 samples belonging to CNV are incorrectly predicted as DRUSEN; The second line indicates that 234 samples belonging to normal are correctly predicted as NORMAL, and 8 samples belonging to normal are incorrectly predicted as DRUSEN; The fourth line indicates that 242 samples belonging to DME are correctly predicted as DME.

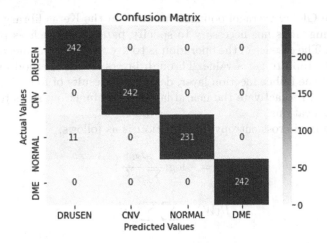

Fig. 6. Confusion matrix of the model based on Inception V3 on the test set

4   Experiment General Overview

4.1   Data Sets

Mendeley Data, including 84284 retinal OCT images from 4686 patients, which are divided into four categories (CNV, DRUSEN, DME, NORMAL), corresponding to "Choroidal neovascularization", "Drusen", "Diabetic Macular Edema" and "normal conditions" respectively. Specifically, the data set is divided into three main directories (test, train, val), representing the "test set", "training set", and "validation set" respectively. Each main directory contains sub-directories of four image lesion categories, in which each image label is (disease) - (random patient ID) - (image number of the patient).

The image data were collected using a Spectralis Frequency-domain OCT scanner from Heidelberg, Germany. Before training, each image was passed through a grading system. The system consists of several experienced professional graders and can effectively verify and correct the image labels. Each image imported into the database is started with a label matching the patient's latest diagnosis.

4.2   Process and Result

Xception model is another improvement for Inception V3 proposed by François Chollet in 2017. Its innovation is that when the convolution kernel acts on the multi-channel characteristic graph, the correlation and spatial correlation between channels can be completely separated. We create the model based on the CNN of Xception. First, we initialize the tensor of the input layer of the DL network through the input method in the Keras library, and define the resolution of the image as 224 and the corresponding batch processing parameter as

32. Then, the GlobalAveragePooling2D method in the Keras library is used for average pooling. It is not necessary to specify parameters such as pooling size and step size. The essence of the operation is to average each channel of the input characteristic graph to get a value. Through layers. Dense method modifies the parameters of the full connection layer, defines the results of four classifications, and uses sigmoid to activate the neural layer of the function, so as to carry out multiple classifications.

The formula of cross entropy loss function is as follows:

$$L_i = -\log(\frac{e^{f_{y_i}}}{\sum_j e^{f_j}}) \tag{3}$$

$$R(W) = \sum_k \sum_l w_{k,l}^2 \tag{4}$$

$$L = \frac{1}{N} \sum_i L_i + \alpha R(W) \tag{5}$$

The meanings of parameters in formulas (3) to (5) are: L_i is the loss value of the ith data. j is the number of categories, l is the number of layers, k is the number of neurons in layer k, N is the number of training data, α is the regularization coefficient, and L is the total loss value of training data.

In the training process, when the gradient drops, each batch contains 32 samples, the number of iterations is set to 30, and the number of iterations is $32 \times 20 = 640$ times. Finally, the CNN model based on Xception and SinGAN achieves a classification accuracy of 98.8% on the OCT2017 data set, as shown in Fig. 7.

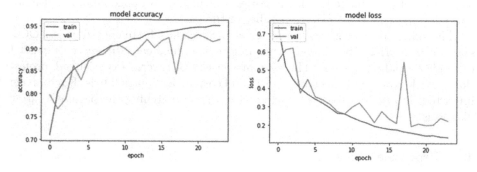

Fig. 7. Accuracy curve and loss curve of model based on Xception and SinGAN on training set and validation set

4.3   Comparative Experiment

We conducted a control experiment based on the same initial OCT image data set, and the specific work was as follows: Several typical network models in classical CNN were used respectively, including ResNet101, VGG19, and Inception V3 models. The comparison between the recognition experiment results in this paper and the above three related works is shown in Table 2. The accuracy and loss values obtained by the recognition of the training set, validation set, and test set of the OCT image data set by the four works are given in the table respectively. As can be seen from Table 2, although the accuracy of Xception in the validation set is slightly 0.03 lower than Inception V3 and ResNet101, the loss value of Xception in all data sets is the minimum, and the accuracy model in the training set and test set is higher than the other three models. The accuracy of the test set is up to 98.8%. In general, Xception's performance is undoubtedly optimal.

Table 2. Comparative experiment

Model	Training set		Validation set		Test set	
	Accuracy	Loss	Accuracy	Loss	Accuracy	Loss
ResNet101	0.925	0.66	0.939	0.59	0.913	0.71
VGG19	0.919	0.23	0.906	0.19	0.981	0.03
Inception V3	0.925	0.19	0.964	0.05	0.974	0.05
SinGAN+Xception (ours)	0.952	0.08	0.931	0.23	**0.988**	0.04

5   Conclusion

In this paper, we propose a method to identify and classify blinding eye diseases by optimizing the Xception model through transfer learning. In our method, SinGAN image generation and data enhancement are further carried out on the image to achieve the purpose of model generalization and compared with the traditional Inception V3 model. The research shows that the CNN based on Inception V3 achieves 92.5% classification accuracy on OCT2017 data set, while the CNN model based on Xception and SinGAN proposed in this paper achieves 98.8% classification accuracy on OCT2017 data set, realizing a more accurate classification of blinding diseases.

However, in clinical diagnosis, we should also obtain a wider number and level of image data to improve the overall detection ability. At the same time, due to the complexity of the types and severity of retinal diseases, the disease should be classified in detail to obtain a more perfect medical diagnosis. In the follow-up study, we will use the combination of OCT images and retinal color Doppler images to improve the reliability of classification.

Acknowledgement. This work is supported by the Natural Science Foundation of China (No. 62002316).

References

1. Shen, J., et al.: I and II wAMD-aided deep-learning grading algorithm based on oct. Chin. J. Optom. Ophthalmol. Vis. Sci. **23**(8), 615 (2021)
2. Yau, J.W.Y., et al.: Global prevalence and major risk factors of diabetic retinopathy. Diabet. Care **35**(3), 556–564 (2012)
3. Ting, D.S.W., Cheung, G.C.M., Wong, T.Y.: Diabetic retinopathy: global prevalence, major risk factors, screening practices and public health challenges: a review. Clin. Exp. Ophthalmol. **44**(4), 260–277 (2016)
4. Cheung, N., Mitchell, P.: Wong TYLancet. Diabet. Retinopathy **376**(9735), 124–36 (2010)
5. Drexler, W., Fujimoto, J.G.: State-of-the-art retinal optical coherence tomography. Progr. Retinal Eye Res. **27**(1), 45–88 (2008)
6. He, J., Wang, L., Zhang, R.: Optical coherence tomography based on deep learning for assisting diagnosis of common fundus diseases. Chin. J. Med. Imaging Technol. **37**(8), 1229–1233 (2021)
7. Krizhevsky, A., Sutskever, I., Hinton, G.: ImageNet classification with deep convolutional neural networks. Adv. Neural Inf. Proc. Syst. **25**(2) (2012)
8. Chen, H., Zeng, X., Luo, Y., Ye, W.: Detection of diabetic retinopathy using deep neural network. In: 2018 IEEE 23rd International Conference on Digital Signal Processing (DSP), pp. 1–5. IEEE (2018)
9. Sayres, R., et al.: Using a deep learning algorithm and integrated gradients explanation to assist grading for diabetic retinopathy. Ophthalmology **126**(4), 552–564 (2019)
10. Peng, Y., et al.: DeepSeeNet: a deep learning model for automated classification of patient-based age-related macular degeneration severity from color fundus photographs. Ophthalmology **126**(4), 565–575 (2019)
11. Jiang, H., Yang, K., Gao, M., Zhang, D., Ma, H., Qian, W.: An interpretable ensemble deep learning model for diabetic retinopathy disease classification. In: 2019 41st Annual International Conference of the IEEE Engineering in Medicine and Biology Society (EMBC), pp. 2045–2048. IEEE (2019)
12. Ghosh, R., Ghosh, K., Maitra, S.: Automatic detection and classification of diabetic retinopathy stages using CNN. In: 2017 4th International Conference on Signal Processing and Integrated Networks (SPIN), pp. 550–554. IEEE (2017)
13. Ng, W.Y., et al.: Updates in deep learning research in ophthalmology. Clin. Sci. **135**(20), 2357–2376 (2021)
14. Ioffe, S., Szegedy, C.: Batch normalization: accelerating deep network training by reducing internal covariate shift. In: International Conference on Machine Learning, pp. 448–456. PMLR (2015)

CTooth: A Fully Annotated 3D Dataset and Benchmark for Tooth Volume Segmentation on Cone Beam Computed Tomography Images

Weiwei Cui[2], Yaqi Wang[3(✉)], Qianni Zhang[2], Huiyu Zhou[4], Dan Song[5], Xingyong Zuo[5], Gangyong Jia[1], and Liaoyuan Zeng[5(✉)]

[1] Hangzhou Dianzi University, Hangzhou, China
[2] Queen Mary University of London, London, UK
[3] Communication University of Zhejiang, Hangzhou, China
wangyaqi@cuz.edu.cn
[4] University of Leicester, Leicester, UK
[5] University of Electronic Science and Technology of China, Chengdu, China
lyzeng@uestc.edu.cn

Abstract. 3D tooth segmentation is a prerequisite for computer-aided dental diagnosis and treatment. However, segmenting all tooth regions manually is subjective and time-consuming. Recently, deep learning-based segmentation methods produce convincing results and reduce manual annotation efforts, but it requires a large quantity of ground truth for training. To our knowledge, there are few tooth data available for the 3D segmentation study. In this paper, we establish a fully annotated cone beam computed tomography dataset CTooth with tooth gold standard. This dataset contains 22 volumes (7363 slices) with fine tooth labels annotated by experienced radiographic interpreters. To ensure a relative even data sampling distribution, data variance is included in the CTooth including missing teeth and dental restoration. Several state-of-the-art segmentation methods are evaluated on this dataset. Afterwards, we further summarise and apply a series of 3D attention-based Unet variants for segmenting tooth volumes. This work provides a new benchmark for the tooth volume segmentation task. Experimental evidence proves that attention modules of the 3D UNet structure boost responses in tooth areas and inhibit the influence of background and noise. The best performance is achieved by 3D Unet with SKNet attention module, of 88.04% Dice and 78.71% IOU, respectively. The attention-based Unet framework outperforms other state-of-the-art methods on the CTooth dataset. The codebase and dataset are released here.

Keywords: 3D dental dataset · Tooth segmentation · Attention

1 Introduction

Due to the low dose and high-definition vision, dental cone beam computed tomography (CBCT) film has been a standard to exam teeth conditions during

H. Liu et al. (Eds.): ICIRA 2022, LNAI 13458, pp. 191–200, 2022.
https://doi.org/10.1007/978-3-031-13841-6_18

the preoperative stage. 3D tooth segmentation for CBCT images is a prerequisite for the orthodontics surgery since it assists to reconstruct accurate 3D tooth models. However, manual tooth annotations requires domain knowledge of dental experts and it is time and labour-consuming. Therefore, automatic and precise tooth volume segmentation is essential.

Some shallow learning-based methods try to quickly segment teeth from X-ray or CBCT images such as region-based [15], threshold-based [2],boundary-based [7] and cluster-based [3] approaches. However, these methods present limited evaluation results on small or private datasets, and segmentation performances are highly dependent on the manual feature engineering. The main reason causing these problems is the lack of an open dental datasets with professional annotations. Dental X-ray Image dataset is the first public dental dataset published on the ISBI Grand Challenges 2015 mainly focusing on dental landmark detection and caries segmentation [25]. LNDb consists of annotated dental panoramic X-ray images. All teeth in patients' oral cavities are identified and marked [22]. Teeth_dataset is a relative small classification dataset, which presents single crowns and is labelled with or without caries [1]. We review two widely-used dental X ray datasets. However, the existing dental dataset all record 2D dental images and the spatial teeth information is compressed and distorted.

Recently, deep learning-based methods are available with an attempt to solve 3D tooth segmentation. Some methods apply Mask R-CNN on tooth segmentation and detection [5,11]. These approaches require accurate and specialised instance dental labels which are not always available. Other methods exploit 3D Unet with well-designed initial dental masks or complex backbones [27,28]. However, these segmentation methods are evaluated on private tooth datasets.

Attention mechanism has been widely used in computer vision tasks and achieve state-of-the-art performances on medical image segmentation tasks. To the best of our knowledge, attention based strategies [6,13,26] have not yet been applied in solving 3D tooth segmentation tasks on CBCT images mainly due to the annotated data limitation. Inspired by the success of attention mechanism on other medical image processing tasks, this paper's motivation is to explore the effectiveness of attention mechanisms in the tooth volume segmentation method.

In this work, we aim to (1) build the first open-source 3D CBCT dataset CTooth with dental annotations. Several state-of-the-art segmentation methods are evaluated on the CTooth. (2) propose an attention-based segmentation framework as a new benchmark. Experiment results show that the attention-based framework outperforms other 3D segmentation methods in this task.

2   CTooth Dataset: Fully Annotated Cone Beam Computed Tomography Tooth Dataset

2.1   Dataset Summary

Several 2D open-access dental datasets have been proposed, as shown in Table 1. Dental X-ray Image dataset contains 400 lateral cephalometry films and 120

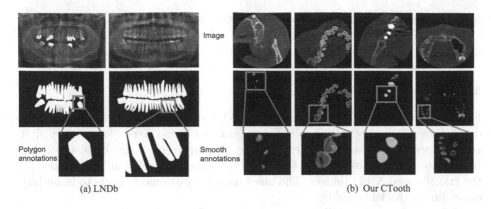

Fig. 1. Data comparison between the 2D LNDb dataset and our 3D Ctooth dataset.

bitewing images, and seven types of areas are marked, including caries, crown, enamel, dentin, pulp, root canal treatment and restoration [25]. LNDb consists of 1500 panoramic X-ray images categorized by 10 classes, with a resolution of 1991 by 1127 pixels for each image [22]. It is suitable for 2D tooth detection and semantic segmentation study. A small caries classification dataset Teeth_dataset with 77 intraoral images is proposed on Kaggle [1]. A shallow VGG network has easily handled the binary caries classification task on this dataset [23]. These dataset have limit quantity of images and not suitable for segmenting tooth volume by deep learning based method. Therefore, our first contribution is to build a 3D CBCT dental dataset with teeth annotations.

The images used in our data set were acquired on an OP300, manufactured by Instrumentarium Orthopantomograph®, and acquired at the University of Electronic Science and Technology of China Hospital. The radiographic images used for this research were coded in order to avoid identifying the patients. All CBCT slices originally obtained by the orthopantomography have 266 × 266 pixels in the axial view. The in-plane resolution is about 0.25 × 0.25 mm² and the slice thickness range from 0.25mm to 0.3 mm. The gathered data set consists of 5504 annotated CBCT images from 22 patients. There are in total

Table 1. Summary of publicly available dental datasets. To our knowledge, there are no 3D public dataset with tooth volume annotations.

Dataset	Year	Modality	Task	Scans
Dental X-ray Image [25]	2015	2D X ray	Caries segmentation Landmark detection	120 400
LNDb [22]	2016	2D X ray	Tooth segmentation and detection	1500
Teeth_dataset [1]	2020	2D RGB image	Caries classification	77
Our Ctooth	2022	3D CBCT	Tooth volume segmentation	7363

5803 CBCT slices, out of which 4243 contain tooth annotations. The images contain significant structural variations in relation to the teeth position, the number of teeth, restorations, implants, appliances, and the size of jaws.

2.2   Expert Annotation

Figure 1 illustrates a few samples of the LNDb dataset [22]. This is a 2D tooth dataset based on the panoramic X-ray images. These X-ray scans were first transformed to grey-scale images, causing a compressed range of pixel values. In addition, experts marked all tooth regions using the polygon annotations on the transformed X-ray images. The inaccurate polygon mode leads to boundary error during model training.

Different from the LNDb, all scans in the CTooth dataset are annotated in a smooth mode. Also, we only resize all CBCT slices to 256 × 256 resolution and do not process any transformation to change CT values. Four trainees from a dental association (with four years of experience) manually mark all teeth regions. They first use ITKSNAP [30] to delineate tooth regions slice-by-slice in axial view. Then the annotations are fine-tuned manually in the coronal view and sagittal view. In the annotation stage for each volume, it roughly takes 6 h to annotate all tooth regions and further requires 1 h to check and refine the annotations. The CTooth dataset took us around 10 months to collect, annotate and review. With its data amount and quality, we believe it is a valuable and desired asset to share in public for computer-aided tooth image research.

Table 2. Categories in the UCTooth dataset, the number of patients in each category, average number of teeth and slices per patient and the average statics of Hounsfield pixel values.

Category	# Volume	# Ave teeth	# Ave slices	Mean CT value
Missing teeth w appliance	6	13	217	140
Missing teeth w/o appliance	5	10	260	156
Teeth w appliance	6	16	351	144
Teeth w/o appliance	5	12	220	153

According to the features of the annotated tooth areas, all the CBCT volumes are categorized in to four different classes in terms of missing teeth and dental appliance. Table 2 summarises the basic statistics including average number of volumes in each category, average number of teeth, average slices per volume, and the mean pixel values (Hounsfield) for each category. According to the statistical results, we observe that the data distribution is balanced among four categories.

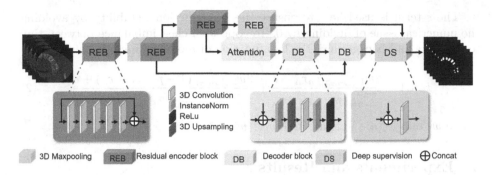

Fig. 2. The architecture of the proposed BM-Unet.

3 Attention-Based Tooth Volume Segmentation

3.1 Framework Design

To segment all tooth regions precisely, especially in small tooth roots, we propose an attention-based segmentation benchmark on the CTooth dataset as shown in Fig. 2. Inspired by the excellent performance of Unet based networks for medical image segmentation and classification, we extend the pipeline of Unet [21] to a 3D version as our base framework. Then we attempt to insert an attention branch at the bottleneck position of the base model to boost the tooth segmentation performances.

In the backbone feature extraction module, a batch of CBCT sub-volumes first pass through three Residual Encoder Blocks (REBs). Each REB contains 5 3D convolution layers with a shortcut connection, and is designed to collect tiny tooth features. The features from REB then go through a 3D maxpooling layer to increase the receptive field represented by each voxel. The encoded features with the largest receptive field are fed into an attention module and a bottleneck module (REB), separately. After that, the encoded tooth features from the bottleneck and the attention modules are reconstructed by a series of fully convolutional decoders (DB). The decoder design is the same as the decoder of 3D Unet including instanceNorm, 3D upsampling, 3D convolution and ReLu. Since the teeth size is relatively similar but with variation, we finally improve the response of the tooth areas with a deep supervision (DS) step. In the testing period, we attempt to explore the efficiency of various attention modules on our framework including channel attention, spatial attention and self attention.

3.2 Loss Function

Let $\mathbf{R}$ be the ground truth with voxel values r_n, and $\mathbf{P}$ be the predicted probabilistic map with the tooth label over N voxels p_n. The element-wise dice similarity coefficient (DSC) [17,24] between $\mathbf{R}$ and $\mathbf{P}$ is defined as follows:

$$\text{DSC} = \frac{2\sum_{n=1}^{N} p_n r_n + \epsilon}{\sum_{n=1}^{N} p_n + r_n + \epsilon} + \frac{2\sum_{n=1}^{N} (1 - p_n)(1 - r_n) + \epsilon}{\sum_{n=1}^{N} 2 - p_n - r_n + \epsilon}. \tag{1}$$

The ϵ term is used here to ensure the loss function's stability by avoiding the numerical issue of dividing by 0. To cope with class imbalance between tiny tooth roots and background, the loss function of model training is defined by:

$$L = 1 - \frac{2w_1 \sum_{n=1}^{N} p_n r_n + \epsilon}{\sum_{n=1}^{N} p_n + r_n + \epsilon} + \frac{2w_2 \sum_{n=1}^{N} (1 - p_n)(1 - r_n) + \epsilon}{\sum_{n=1}^{N} 2 - p_n - r_n + \epsilon}, \qquad (2)$$

where w_1 and w_2 are weights, and $w_1 + w_2 = 1$.

4   Experiments and Results

4.1   Evaluation Metrics on the CTooth

The segmentation inference results are evaluated using dice similarity coefficient (DSC), weighted dice similarity coefficient (WDSC), intersection over union (IoU), sensitivity (SEN), positive predictive value (PPV), Hausdorff distance (HD), average symmetric surface distance (ASSD), surface overlap (SO) and surface dice (SD) [9].

Two distance metrics (HD and ASSD) are evaluated on the surfaces of tooth volumes of $\mathbf{R}$ Let $\mathbf{S_R}$ be a set of surface voxels of $\mathbf{R}$, and the shortest distance of an arbitrary voxel p with $\mathbf{S_R}$ can be defined as follows:

$$d(p, \mathbf{S_R}) = \min_{s_R \in \mathbf{S_R}} \|p - s_R\|_2, \qquad (3)$$

where $s_R \in \mathbf{S_R}$ and $\|\|$ is the distance paradigm between point sets, e.g. Euclidean distance. Thus, HD is defined as follows:

$$HD = \max \left\{ \max_{s_R \in \mathbf{S_R}} d(s_R, \mathbf{S_P}) + \max_{s_P \in \mathbf{S_P}} d(s_P . \mathbf{S_R}) \right\}. \qquad (4)$$

The distance function is defined as:

$$D(\mathbf{S_R}, \mathbf{S_P}) = \Sigma_{s_R \in \mathbf{S_R}} d(s_R, \mathbf{S_P}). \qquad (5)$$

Moreover, the ASSD can be defined as follows:

$$\text{ASSD}(\mathbf{R}, \mathbf{P}) = \frac{1}{|\mathbf{S_R}| + |\mathbf{S_P}|} (D(\mathbf{S_R}, \mathbf{S_P}) + D(\mathbf{S_P}, \mathbf{S_R})), \qquad (6)$$

where $|\cdot|$ is the number of points of the set.

The surface overlapping values SO of $\mathbf{S_P}$ is calculated by

$$o(p) = \begin{cases} 1, & d(p, \mathbf{S_R}) < \theta \\ 0, & d(p, \mathbf{S_R}) > \theta \end{cases} \qquad (7)$$

$$SO(\mathbf{S_P}) = \frac{\sum_{n=1}^{M_\mathbf{P}} o(p_n)}{M_\mathbf{P}}, \qquad (8)$$

where θ is a maximal distance to determine whether two points have the same spatial positions. M_P is the number of points in the surface set S_P.

The surface overlapping dice values of S_R and S_P are calculated by:

$$SD = DC(r_m, p_m), \tag{9}$$

where $o(r_m) = 1$ and $o(p_m) = 1$.

4.2 Experimental Results

To reduce the noise and increase image contrast, we apply contrast limited adaptive histogram equalization [20] on image slices. The transformed input images are normalized to the range [0, 1] for each voxel. Kaiming initialization [8] is used for initializing all the weights of the proposed framework. The Adam optimizer is used with a batch size of 4 and a learning rate of 0.0004 with a step learning scheduler (with step size = 50 and $\gamma = 0.9$). The learning rate is decayed by multiplying 0.1 for every 100 epochs. The weighted dice loss is applied to guide the network backpropagation [16] with $w_1 = 0.1$ and $w_2 = 0.9$. The network is trained for 600 epochs using an Intel(R) i7-7700K desktop system with a 4.2 GHz processor, 16 GB memory, and 2 Nvidia GTX 1080Ti GPU machine. We implement this framework using the Pytorch library [19]. It takes 10 h to complete all the training and inference procedures.

Table 3. Evaluation comparison among different tooth volume segmentation methods on the CTooth dataset.

Method	WDSC	DSC	IOU	SEN	PPV
DenseVoxelNet [29]	79.92	57.61	49.12	89.61	51.25
3D HighResNet [12]	81.90	61.46	52.14	87.34	59.26
3D Unet [4]	82.00	62.30	52.98	88.57	60.00
VNet [17]	82.80	63.43	55.51	87.47	64.64
Ours	**95.14**	**88.04**	**78.71**	**94.71**	**82.30**

The proposed attention-based tooth segmentation framework outperforms several current 3D medical segmentation methods including DenseVoxelNet, 3D HighResNet, 3D Unet and VNet. As shown in Table 3, Our proposed method has more than 25% DSC gain, 20% IOU gain, 5% sensitivity gain and 18% PPV gain, respectively. One reason why the existing methods are not effective in this task is that these networks are all relatively deep and hard to train on CTooth with large data variance. The other reason is that current methods do not include components e.g. attention and deep supervision, or they do not allow certain configurations to extract tooth features in tiny regions. In the proposed framework, considering the teeth size is relatively small around roots, we reduce

Table 4. Ablation study results of choosing various attention modules in the proposed attention-based framework.

Attention	DSC	IOU	SEN	PPV	HD	ASSD	SO	SD
DANet [6]	59.45	43.27	75.88	52.45	15.12	2.37	73.98	66.41
SENet [10]	87.65	78.08	94.23	82.05	2.59	0.43	95.61	95.28
Attn Unet [18]	87.68	78.16	91.90	83.94	5.60	0.56	94.71	94.33
Polar [14]	87.81	78.36	91.32	**84.67**	**2.07**	**0.34**	95.44	95.21
CBAM [26]	87.82	78.34	93.80	82.77	2.35	0.36	95.89	95.56
SKNet [13]	**88.04**	**78.71**	**94.71**	82.30	2.70	0.44	**96.24**	**95.90**

the number of the down-sampling layers to avoid roots undetected compared to the 3D Unet.

Additionally, we augment the baseline network with several state-of-the-art attention modules. In Table 4, we present tooth volume segmentation results among various attention types including channel attention (SENet and SKNet), spatial attention (Attention Unet), channel and spatial attention (CBAM), and self attention (Polar and DANet). The base segmentation framework with self attention Polar achieves the best performance on 2 spatial surface distance metrics (HD and ASD). Channel attention SKNet fully exploits the automatic selection of important channels and achieve DSC 88.04%, IOU 78.71%, SEN 94.71%, SO 96.24% and SD 95.9% respectively. However, DANet cannot segment tooth volumes well as a large redundant quantity of matrix multiplication operations is required in DANet.

5   Conclusion

In this paper, we first introduce details of the CBCT dental dataset CTooth. This is the first open-source 3D dental CT dataset with full tooth annotations. We propose an attention-based benchmark to segment tooth regions on the CTooth dataset. Due to the fine design of the residual encoder, and the proper application of attention and deep supervision, the proposed framework achieves state-of-the-art performances compared with other 3D segmentation methods. In future, we will release more multi-organisation dental data on the next version of CTooth.

Acknowledgement. The work was supported by the National Natural Science Foundation of China under Grant No. U20A20386.

References

1. Pushkara, A.: Teeth dataset (2020). https://www.kaggle.com/pushkar34/teeth-dataset

2. Ajaz, A., Kathirvelu, D.: Dental biometrics: computer aided human identification system using the dental panoramic radiographs. In: 2013 International Conference on Communication and Signal Processing, pp. 717–721. IEEE (2013)

3. Alsmadi, M.K.: A hybrid fuzzy C-means and neutrosophic for jaw lesions segmentation. Ain Shams Eng. J. **9**(4), 697–706 (2018)

4. Çiçek, Ö., Abdulkadir, A., Lienkamp, S.S., Brox, T., Ronneberger, O.: 3D U-net: learning dense volumetric segmentation from sparse annotation. In: Ourselin, S., Joskowicz, L., Sabuncu, M.R., Unal, G., Wells, W. (eds.) MICCAI 2016. LNCS, vol. 9901, pp. 424–432. Springer, Cham (2016). https://doi.org/10.1007/978-3-319-46723-8_49

5. Cui, Z., Li, C., Wang, W.: ToothNet: automatic tooth instance segmentation and identification from cone beam CT images. In: Proceedings of the IEEE Conference on Computer Vision and Pattern Recognition, pp. 6368–6377 (2019)

6. Fu, J., et al.: Dual attention network for scene segmentation. In: Proceedings of the IEEE/CVF Conference on Computer Vision and Pattern Recognition, pp. 3146–3154 (2019)

7. Hasan, M.M., Ismail, W., Hassan, R., Yoshitaka, A.: Automatic segmentation of jaw from panoramic dental X-ray images using GVF snakes. In: 2016 World Automation Congress (WAC), pp. 1–6. IEEE (2016)

8. He, K., Zhang, X., Ren, S., Sun, J.: Delving deep into rectifiers: surpassing human-level performance on ImageNet classification. In: Proceedings of the IEEE International Conference on Computer Vision, pp. 1026–1034 (2015)

9. Heimann, T., et al.: Comparison and evaluation of methods for liver segmentation from CT datasets. IEEE Trans. Med. Imaging **28**(8), 1251–1265 (2009)

10. Hu, J., Shen, L., Sun, G.: Squeeze-and-excitation networks. In: Proceedings of the IEEE Conference on Computer Vision and Pattern Recognition, pp. 7132–7141 (2018)

11. Jader, G., Fontineli, J., Ruiz, M., Abdalla, K., Pithon, M., Oliveira, L.: Deep instance segmentation of teeth in panoramic X-ray images. In: 2018 31st SIBGRAPI Conference on Graphics, Patterns and Images (SIBGRAPI), pp. 400–407 (2018)

12. Li, W., Wang, G., Fidon, L., Ourselin, S., Cardoso, M.J., Vercauteren, T.: On the compactness, efficiency, and representation of 3D convolutional networks: brain parcellation as a pretext task. In: Niethammer, M., et al. (eds.) IPMI 2017. LNCS, vol. 10265, pp. 348–360. Springer, Cham (2017). https://doi.org/10.1007/978-3-319-59050-9_28

13. Li, X., Wang, W., Hu, X., Yang, J.: Selective kernel networks. In: Proceedings of the IEEE/CVF Conference on Computer Vision and Pattern Recognition, pp. 510–519 (2019)

14. Liu, H., Liu, F., Fan, X., Huang, D.: Polarized self-attention: towards high-quality pixel-wise regression. arXiv preprint arXiv:2107.00782 (2021)

15. Lurie, A., Tosoni, G.M., Tsimikas, J., Walker, F., Jr.: Recursive hierarchic segmentation analysis of bone mineral density changes on digital panoramic images. Oral Surg. Oral Med. Oral Pathol. Oral Radiol. **113**(4), 549–558 (2012)

16. Ma, J., et al.: Loss odyssey in medical image segmentation. Med. Image Anal. **71**, 102035 (2021)

17. Milletari, F., Navab, N., Ahmadi, S.A.: V-net: fully convolutional neural networks for volumetric medical image segmentation. In: 2016 Fourth International Conference on 3D Vision (3DV), pp. 565–571. IEEE (2016)

18. Oktay, O., et al.: Attention u-net: learning where to look for the pancreas. arXiv preprint arXiv:1804.03999 (2018)

19. Paszke, A., et al.: PyTorch: an imperative style, high-performance deep learning library. Adv. Neural. Inf. Process. Syst. **32**, 8026–8037 (2019)
20. Pisano, E.D., et al.: Contrast limited adaptive histogram equalization image processing to improve the detection of simulated spiculations in dense mammograms. J. Digit. Imaging **11**(4), 193 (1998)
21. Ronneberger, O., Fischer, P., Brox, T.: U-net: convolutional networks for biomedical image segmentation. In: Navab, N., Hornegger, J., Wells, W.M., Frangi, A.F. (eds.) MICCAI 2015. LNCS, vol. 9351, pp. 234–241. Springer, Cham (2015). https://doi.org/10.1007/978-3-319-24574-4_28
22. Silva, G., Oliveira, L., Pithon, M.: Automatic segmenting teeth in X-ray images: trends, a novel data set, benchmarking and future perspectives. Expert Syst. Appl. **107**, 15–31 (2018)
23. Simonyan, K., Zisserman, A.: Very deep convolutional networks for large-scale image recognition. arXiv preprint arXiv:1409.1556 (2014)
24. Sudre, C.H., Li, W., Vercauteren, T., Ourselin, S., Jorge Cardoso, M.: Generalised dice overlap as a deep learning loss function for highly unbalanced segmentations. In: Cardoso, M.J., et al. (eds.) DLMIA/ML-CDS -2017. LNCS, vol. 10553, pp. 240–248. Springer, Cham (2017). https://doi.org/10.1007/978-3-319-67558-9_28
25. Wang, C.W., et al.: A benchmark for comparison of dental radiography analysis algorithms. Med. Image Anal. **31**, 63–76 (2016)
26. Woo, S., Park, J., Lee, J.Y., Kweon, I.S.: CBAM: convolutional block attention module. In: Proceedings of the European Conference on Computer Vision (ECCV), pp. 3–19 (2018)
27. Wu, X., Chen, H., Huang, Y., Guo, H., Qiu, T., Wang, L.: Center-sensitive and boundary-aware tooth instance segmentation and classification from cone-beam CT. In: 2020 IEEE 17th International Symposium on Biomedical Imaging (ISBI), pp. 939–942. IEEE (2020)
28. Yang, S., et al.: A deep learning-based method for tooth segmentation on CBCT images affected by metal artifacts. In: 43rd Annual International Conference of the IEEE Engineering in Medicine and Biology Society (2021)
29. Yu, L., et al.: Automatic 3D cardiovascular MR segmentation with densely-connected volumetric convnets. In: Descoteaux, M., Maier-Hein, L., Franz, A., Jannin, P., Collins, D.L., Duchesne, S. (eds.) MICCAI 2017. LNCS, vol. 10434, pp. 287–295. Springer, Cham (2017). https://doi.org/10.1007/978-3-319-66185-8_33
30. Yushkevich, P.A., et al.: User-guided 3D active contour segmentation of anatomical structures: significantly improved efficiency and reliability. Neuroimage **31**(3), 1116–1128 (2006)

DU-Net Based Unsupervised Contrastive Learning for Cancer Segmentation in Histology Images

Yilong Li[2], Yaqi Wang[1(✉)], Huiyu Zhou[3], Huaqiong Wang[1], Gangyong Jia[4], and Qianni Zhang[2(✉)]

[1] Communication University of Zhejiang, Hangzhou, China
wangyaqi@cuz.edu.cn
[2] Queen Mary University of London, London, UK
qianni.zhang@qmul.ac.uk
[3] University of Leicester, Leicester, UK
[4] Hangzhou Dianzi University, Hangzhou, China

Abstract. In this paper, we introduce an unsupervised cancer segmentation framework for histology images. The framework involves an effective contrastive learning scheme for extracting distinctive visual representations for segmentation. The encoder is a Deep U-Net (DU-Net) structure which contains an extra fully convolution layer compared to the normal U-Net. A contrastive learning scheme is developed to solve the problem of lacking training sets with high-quality annotations on tumour boundaries. A specific set of data augmentation techniques are employed to improve the discriminability of the learned colour features from contrastive learning. Smoothing and noise elimination are conducted using convolutional Conditional Random Fields. The experiments demonstrate competitive performance in segmentation even better than some popular supervised networks.

Keywords: Unsupervised · Contrastive learning · Data augmentation · Tumour segmentation

1 Introduction

Histopathology images are considered as the gold standard for cancer diagnosis and grading. Depending on the type of cancer and the organ it is in, the assessment criteria varies, but the segmentation of tumour tissue out of the surrounding tissue is a fundamental step. This paper attempts to address the challenging problem of tumour segmenting in histopathology images. Recently, deep learning networks show superior performance in image segmentation tasks when they are appropriately trained with abundant image samples and corresponding annotation. However, if the quality and amount of annotation can not be guaranteed, the trained model's performance will be negatively impacted. This is often the case, unfortunately, due to the high requirement for time and resource

© The Author(s), under exclusive license to Springer Nature Switzerland AG 2022
H. Liu et al. (Eds.): ICIRA 2022, LNAI 13458, pp. 201–210, 2022.
https://doi.org/10.1007/978-3-031-13841-6_19

in such annotation process. In addition, the inter and intra-observer variability will generally lead to unsatisfactory training outcome. Therefore, unsupervised approaches which do not rely on manual annotated training data are highly desirable. Learning effective visual representations without human supervision is a long-standing goal. Most mainstream approaches fall into one of the two classes: generative or discriminative. Generative approaches learn to generate or otherwise model pixels in the input space [11]. In the generative approaches, pixel-level generation is computationally expensive and may not be necessary for representation learning. In comparison, discriminative methods learn representations using objective functions similar to those used for supervised learning, but train networks to perform tasks where both the inputs and labels are derived from an unlabeled dataset. Many of such approaches have relied on heuristics to design tasks [6, 8, 16, 20], which could limit the generality of the learned representations. Discriminative approaches based on contrastive learning in the latent space have recently shown great promise, achieving state-of-the-art results [1, 7, 9, 17].

In this work, we introduce a histopathology image segmentation framework named Deep U-Net with Contrastive Learning of visual Representations (DCLR). The core of the framework is a contrastive learning scheme which can work in a unsupervised manner, enabling learning of effective feature representations without relying on annotated boundaries [2, 13]. This framework is capable of using a learnable nonlinear transformation between the representation and the contrastive loss can substantially improve the quality of the learned representations. Besides, the representation learning with contrastive cross entropy loss benefits from normalized embeddings.

In this framework, the segmentation task is achieved through an unsupervised classification approach applied on patches extracted from whole slide images (WSIs). Based on the augmented data, the classification network first learns to classify the patches into tumour and non-tumour classes. The classified patches are then replaced into WSIs, and the segmentation boundaries of tumour parts are obtained. Finally, convolutional Conditional Random Fields (convCRFs) is applied to acquire smoother and more natural tumour region boundaries.

2   Methods

2.1   Data Augmentation

Data augmentation has not been considered as a systematic way to define the contrastive prediction task. Many existing approaches define contrastive prediction tasks by changing the architecture. We show that this complexity can be avoided by performing simple random cropping and with resizing of target images [15]. This simple design conveniently decouples the predictive task from other components such as the neural network. Broader contrastive prediction tasks can be defined by extending the family of augmentations and composing them stochastically.

Several common augmentation techniques are considered here, involving spatial/geometric transformation of data, such as cropping and resizing with flipping, rotation, and cutout. Since the operation of cropping and rotation are not significantly useful in histopathology images, this paper only considers employing resizing and cutout [5]. The other type of augmentation involves appearance transformation, such as colour distortion, including colour dropping, modifying brightness, contrast, saturation, hue, Gaussian blurring, and Sobel filtering [12,18]. Random colour distortion is an important augmentation technique specifically to the histology images. One common problem in histology image segmentation is that most patches from the tumour regions and non-tumour regions share a similar colour distribution. Neural networks may fail to extract distinctive features from the two types of regions due to the similar colour distributions. Therefore, it is critical to use colour distortion to relieve this problem and enable learning discriminative colour features to represent different types of regions. Strong colour augmentation substantially improves the performance of the learned unsupervised models. In this context, we argue that the simple cropping operation plus strong colour distortion can outperform some complicated methods, while it may not work as effectively in training supervised models, or even lead to negative effects. This argument is supported by experimental results presented in Sect. 3.

2.2   Network Structure

Generative approaches focus on pixel generation or modelling in the input space. However, pixel based generation is computationally expensive. In order to learn an effective representation with less computation cost, discriminative approaches use objective function and train networks to obtain the visual representation. Contrastive learning benefits from larger batch sizes and longer training. Discriminative approaches based on contrastive learning in the latent space show great promise, achieving state-of-the-art results in classification [19].

The proposed DCLR framework exploits contrastive learning of visual representations for histology image segmentation. It learns discriminative representations by maximizing the agreement between differently augmented views of the same data samples. At the same time, it learns representations by minimizing the agreement between augmented views of the different data samples from different classes based on a contrastive loss in the latent space. The learning process is illustrated in Fig. 1.

We define the batch size of the network input as b, and with contrastive prediction on pairs of augmented samples, the output of two augmentation operators are sized $2b$. A stochastic data augmentation module transforms any given data sample randomly, resulting in two correlated views of the same sample, denoted x_i and x_j, which are considered as a positive pair. We keep the positive pair of samples, and treat the remaining $2(b-1)$ example as negative samples. The proposed loss can guide the model to present agreement between differently augmented views of the same data sample. DCLR framework allows various choices of the network architecture. Here, we choose $f(\cdot) = \text{DU-Net}(\cdot)$ to encode the $2b$

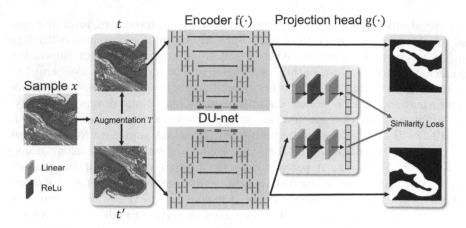

Fig. 1. An illustration of the DCLR framework. Two separate data augmentation operations t and t', selected from a series of augmentation operations T, are applied to the original data sample x. A base encoder network $f(\cdot)$ and a projection head $g(\cdot)$ are trained to maximize agreement using a contrastive loss. After the training is complete, we use the encoder $f(\cdot)$ and representation $g(\cdot)$ for downstream tasks.

correlated views. Thus $h_i = f(x_i) = \text{DU-Net}(x_i)$, where $h_i \in R^d$ is the output after the average pooling layer and d is the dimensions of network layers. Then a small neural network projection head $g(\cdot)$ is used in the space where contrastive loss is applied. After that, we use a Multi-Layer Perception(MLP) with one hidden layer to obtain $z_i = g(h_i) = W_2\sigma(W_1 \cdot h_i)$ where σ is a ReLU nonlinearity, and W_1, W_2 are weights.

In DU-Net, the separation border is computed using morphological operations. The weight map is then computed as

$$w(x) = w_c(x) + w_0 \cdot exp(-\frac{(d_1(x) + d_2(x))^2}{2\sigma^2}) \tag{1}$$

where $w_c : \Omega \to \mathbb{R}$ is the weight map to balance the class frequencies, $d_1 : \Omega \to \mathbb{R}$ denotes the distance to the border of the nearest cell and $d_2 : \Omega \to \mathbb{R}$ the distance to the border of the second nearest cell. In our experiments we set $w_0 = 10$ and $\sigma \approx 5$ pixels.

During training stage, the base encoder network $f(\cdot)$ and the projection head $g(\cdot)$ are constantly optimized in iterations to maximize the agreement using a contrastive loss. Let $s_{i,j} = z_i^T \cdot z_j / (\|z_i\| \cdot \|z_j\|)$ denote the dot product between normalized z_i and z_j (i.e. cosine similarity). Then the loss function of this network for a positive pair of examples (i, j) is defined as:

$$L_{i,j} = -log\frac{exp(sim(z_i, z_j)/\tau)}{\sum_{k=1}^{2N} H_{[k \neq i]}exp(sim(z_i, z_j)/\tau)}, \tag{2}$$

where $H_{[k \neq i]} \in \{0, 1\}$ is an indicator function evaluating to 1 if $k \neq i$ and τ denotes a temperature parameter. The final loss is computed across all positive pairs, both (i,j) and (j,i) are in a same batch. For each epoch, we update networks f and g to minimize L. After the training is complete, we discard the projection head $g(\cdot)$ and use the encoder $f(\cdot)$ and the representation $g(\cdot)$ for downstream tasks.

2.3   Post-processing

After the initial segmentation, a set of clear segmentation boundaries are obtained, but some noise remains. This is because the mask boundaries are mainly constructed using small patches of 512×512 pixels, leaving patch corners and edges in predicted boundaries. Moreover, the isolated tumour cells and fine details in boundaries are often not considered in human manual labeling, leading to very different ground truth boundaries compared to the predicted ones. To approximate the manner of manual labelled boundaries, a post-processing step based on convolutional Conditional Random Fields (CRF) is designed to adjust the obtained segmentation boundaries so that they are more inline with the hand-drawn boundaries.

All parameters of the convolutional CRFs are optimised using back propagation. The convolutional CRFs supplement full CRFs with a conditional independence assumption [14], which assumes that the label distribution of two pixels i and j are conditionally independent, if the Manhattan distance $d(i,j) > k$. Here, the hyper-parameter k is defined as the filter-size. This is a very strong assumption implying that the pairwise potential is zero, for all pairs of pixels whose distance exceed k. Consider an input $\mathbf{F}$, i.e. the probability map resulting from the unsupervised network with shape $[b, c, h, w]$, where b, c, h, w denote batch size, number of classes, input height and width, respectively, for a Gaussian kernel g defined by feature vectors $f_1, ..., f_d$, for each shape $[b, h, w]$, we define its kernel matrix as:

$$k_g[b, dx, dy, x, y] = exp(-\sum_{i=1}^{d} \frac{\Omega}{2\theta_i^2}). \tag{3}$$

where Ω is defined as:

$$\Omega = \left| f_i^{(d)}[b, x, y] - f_i^{(d)}[b, x - dx, y - dy] \right|^2, \tag{4}$$

where θ_i is a learnable parameter. For a set of Gaussian kernels $\{g_1...g_s\}$ we define the merged kernel matrix K as $K := \sum_{i=1}^{s} w_i \cdot g_i$, w_i is the weight of g_i. The resulting $\mathbf{Q}$ of the combined message passing of all s kernels is now given as:

$$\mathbf{Q}[b, c, x, y] = \sum_{dx,dy \leq k} \mathbf{K}[b, dx, dy, x, y] \cdot \mathbf{F}[b, c, x + dx, y + dy]. \tag{5}$$

The final output of the convolutional CRFs is the matrix $\mathbf{Q}$.

3 Experiments

3.1 Dataset

The proposed methodology is tested on a dataset of skin cancer histopathology scans. It is relatively difficult to decide the tumour region boundaries in such images, and some types of the skin cancer present nearly no colour difference between tumour and non-tumour regions. There are 3 types of skin cancer in this dataset, basal cell cancer (BCC), squamous cell cancer (SCC) and seborrheic keratosis cancer (SKC), each consisting of about 80 WSIs. Based on a random selection, 80% of the images are used for training and the remaining 20% are testing.

3.2 Preprocessing

To deal with WSIs in large resolution and limited annotations, we adopt the patch-based approach, which achieves WSI segmentation by firstly classifying small patches. Before patch extraction, the white background in WSIs is removed using a thresholding method on pixel intensities. For each patch in an annotated area, if 75% of it is annotated as the same tissue, this patch is defined as a sample of the corresponding category. As discussed before, a series of augmentation operations are applied, including resizing, cutout, colour distortion, Gaussian blurring, etc. The effects of these augmentation operations are illustrated in Fig. 2.

3.3 Network Training Details

The model is trained using stochastic gradient descent with an adaptive learning rate. The learning rate is 0.001, and the batch size is 64, it takes around 25 min for one epoch. The training is terminated if the validation accuracy does not increase for 20 epochs.

3.4 Post-processing

After network training, the patches are placed into the whole slide image with their class labels. The resulting segmentation boundary includes obvious patch edges which influence both the segmentation accuracy and visual impressions. So the convolutional CRFs is used to smooth the boundary and eliminate the noise. Some examples of segmentation results before and after the convolutional CRFs are shown in Fig. 3.

3.5 Result Evaluation

Table 1 shows the classification results by the proposed DCLR framework compared with three popular networks, simCLR [3], MoCo [10] and MoCo-v2 [4], on the dataset. Cases from the three types of skin cancer are treated separately. A

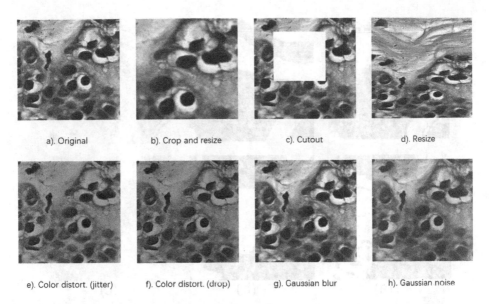

a). Original b). Crop and resize c). Cutout d). Resize

e). Color distort. (jitter) f). Color distort. (drop) g). Gaussian blur h). Gaussian noise

Fig. 2. Data augmentations: each augmentation can transform data stochastically with some internal parameters. The augmentation policy used to train the models includes random cropping with flipping and resizing, colour distortion, and Gaussian blurring.

model is trained for each cancer type. It can be seen that the accuracy of the proposed unsupervised classification method is on a competitive level with that of the other popular unsupervised classification networks. The training of the DCLR framework does not require any ground truth annotation, meaning that it can work in an unsupervised manner on un-annotated datasets.

After the classification on patches, segmentation masks of WSIs are produced by placing the patches back in whole images. The segmentation results of DCLR are compared with that of the patch based approaches relying on the three classification networks, as shown in Table 2.

Table 1. Classification results for the skin cancer dataset and the three sets of skin cancer: basal cell cancer (BCC), Squamous cell cancer (SCC), Seborrheic keratosis cancer (SKC)

Accuracy of classification				
Dataset	simCLR	MoCo	MoCo-v2	DCLR (our)
BCC	93.21	**94.94**	94.62	94.81
SCC	95.85	95.71	96.27	**96.62**
SKC	92.14	**94.81**	93.90	93.77

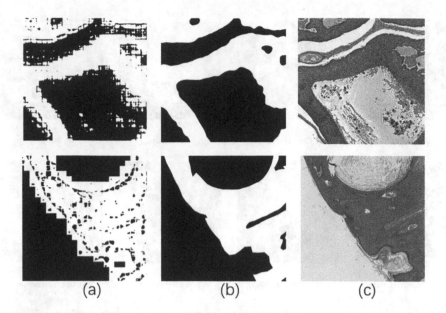

Fig. 3. Segmentation result: (a) the original patch-based segmentation masks; (b) the segmentation masks after post-processing; (c) the original image

The segmentation based on DCLR achieves the highest Dice coefficient in two classes, BCC and SCC, while it is lower than that of MoCo-v2 in SKC dataset with a small margin, mainly due to the patched edges and corners remaining in the segmentation boundary. To enhance the segmentation boundaries and remove the unwanted patch effects, the convolutional CRF based post-processing is applied on the boundaries. Table 3 compares the output of each method after post-processing. All the results of patch based methods are improved after the post-processing. DCLR performs the best in BCC and SCC classes, while MoCo-v2 still outperforms in the SKC class, but the margin is reduced.

Table 2. Segmentation results for skin cancer types

Dice coefficient				
Dataset	simCLR	MoCo	MoCo-v2	DCLR
BCC	60.70	61.02	61.76	**62.58**
SCC	60.53	58.86	60.88	**61.32**
SKC	60.31	60.97	**61.46**	61.19

Table 3. Segmentation result skin cancer after post-processing

Dice Coefficient (after post-processing)				
Dataset	simCLR	MoCo	MoCo-v2	DCLR
BCC	68.49	69.34	69.51	**69.76**
SCC	63.88	66.95	67.34	**67.61**
SKC	68.70	67.73	**69.26**	69.06

4 Conclusions

In this paper, we present a DCLR framework that exploits the contrastive visual representation learning scheme based on a DU-Net structure for unsupervised segmentation of histopathology images. We propose a dedicated series of data augmentation operations, a modified loss function to improve the segmentation performance of this unsupervised network and a deeper U-Net to improve the accuracy of the encoder. We carefully study its components, and show the effects of different design choices on the segmentation output. By combining our proposed methods, we achieve the state of the art segmentation performance in comparison against the popular unsupervised patch based or end-to-end segmentation methods. Overall, the unsupervised learning relieves the dependence on manually annotated segmentation as an essential requirement in conventional supervised learning, and is a highly desirable feature in computational histopathology.

In the future, we aim to follow the unsupervised learning stream and further improve the segmentation quality, especially focusing on data which presents less distinctive colours in tumour and non-tumour regions. One idea is to extract features from the last convolutional layer in order to discover more effective and discriminative features in such scenarios.

Acknowledgement. The work was partially supported by the National Key Research and Development Program under Grant No. 2019YFC0118404, the Basic Public Welfare Research Project of Zhejiang Province (LGF20H180001).

References

1. Bachman, P., Hjelm, R.D., Buchwalter, W.: Learning representations by maximizing mutual information across views. ArXiv abs/1906.00910 (2019)
2. Chaitanya, K., Erdil, E., Karani, N., Konukoglu, E.: Contrastive learning of global and local features for medical image segmentation with limited annotations. Adv. Neural. Inf. Process. Syst. **33**, 12546–12558 (2020)
3. Chen, T., Kornblith, S., Norouzi, M., Hinton, G.: A simple framework for contrastive learning of visual representations. In: International Conference on Machine Learning, pp. 1597–1607. PMLR (2020)
4. Chen, X., Fan, H., Girshick, R., He, K.: Improved baselines with momentum contrastive learning. arXiv preprint arXiv:2003.04297 (2020)

5. Devries, T., Taylor, G.: Improved regularization of convolutional neural networks with cutout. ArXiv abs/1708.04552 (2017)
6. Doersch, C., Gupta, A., Efros, A.: Unsupervised visual representation learning by context prediction. In: 2015 IEEE International Conference on Computer Vision (ICCV), pp. 1422–1430 (2015)
7. Dosovitskiy, A., Springenberg, J.T., Riedmiller, M., Brox, T.: Discriminative unsupervised feature learning with convolutional neural networks. In: NIPS (2014)
8. Gidaris, S., Singh, P., Komodakis, N.: Unsupervised representation learning by predicting image rotations. ArXiv abs/1803.07728 (2018)
9. Hadsell, R., Chopra, S., LeCun, Y.: Dimensionality reduction by learning an invariant mapping. In: 2006 IEEE Computer Society Conference on Computer Vision and Pattern Recognition (CVPR 2006), vol. 2, pp. 1735–1742 (2006)
10. He, K., Fan, H., Wu, Y., Xie, S., Girshick, R.: Momentum contrast for unsupervised visual representation learning. In: Proceedings of the IEEE/CVF Conference on Computer Vision and Pattern Recognition, pp. 9729–9738 (2020)
11. Hinton, G.E., Osindero, S., Teh, Y.: A fast learning algorithm for deep belief nets. Neural Comput. **18**, 1527–1554 (2006)
12. Howard, A.: Some improvements on deep convolutional neural network based image classification. CoRR abs/1312.5402 (2014)
13. Hu, H., Cui, J., Wang, L.: Region-aware contrastive learning for semantic segmentation. In: Proceedings of the IEEE/CVF International Conference on Computer Vision, pp. 16291–16301 (2021)
14. Krähenbühl, P., Koltun, V.: Efficient inference in fully connected CRFs with gaussian edge potentials. In: NIPS (2011)
15. Krizhevsky, A., Sutskever, I., Hinton, G.E.: ImageNet classification with deep convolutional neural networks. In: CACM (2017)
16. Noroozi, M., Favaro, P.: Unsupervised learning of visual representations by solving jigsaw puzzles. In: Leibe, B., Matas, J., Sebe, N., Welling, M. (eds.) ECCV 2016. LNCS, vol. 9910, pp. 69–84. Springer, Cham (2016). https://doi.org/10.1007/978-3-319-46466-4_5
17. Oord, A., Li, Y., Vinyals, O.: Representation learning with contrastive predictive coding. ArXiv abs/1807.03748 (2018)
18. Szegedy, C., et al.: Going deeper with convolutions. In: 2015 IEEE Conference on Computer Vision and Pattern Recognition (CVPR), pp. 1–9 (2015)
19. Wang, P., Han, K., Wei, X.S., Zhang, L., Wang, L.: Contrastive learning based hybrid networks for long-tailed image classification. In: Proceedings of the IEEE/CVF Conference on Computer Vision and Pattern Recognition, pp. 943–952 (2021)
20. Zhang, R., Isola, P., Efros, A.A.: Colorful image colorization. In: Leibe, B., Matas, J., Sebe, N., Welling, M. (eds.) ECCV 2016. LNCS, vol. 9907, pp. 649–666. Springer, Cham (2016). https://doi.org/10.1007/978-3-319-46487-9_40

Dual Path DNN Based Heterogenous Reference Image Quality Assessment via Decoupling the Quality Difference and Content Difference

Xiaoyu Ma[1], Yaqi Wang[2], Suiyu Zhang[2], and Dingguo Yu[1,2]

[1] Key Lab of Film and TV Media Technology of Zhejiang Province,
Communication University of Zhejiang, Hangzhou 310042, China
{maxiaoyu,yudg}@cuz.edu.cn
[2] Institute of Intelligent Media, Communication University of Zhejiang,
Hangzhou 310042, China
{wangyaqi,zhangsuiyu}@cuz.edu.cn

Abstract. Blind image quality assessment (BIQA) is a fundamental yet challenging task in the field of low-level computer vision. The difficulty is particularly due to the limited information, for which the corresponding reference for comparison is typically absent. In order to improve the accuracy and generalization ability of BIQA metrics, our work proposes a dual-path deep neural network (DNN) based heterogenous reference BIQA framework in which an arbitrarily selected pristine image is employed to provide important prior quality information for the IQA framework. The proposed IQA metric is still 'blind' since the corresponding reference image is unseen, but our metric could obtain more prior quality information than previous work with the help of heterogenous reference. Experimental results indicate that our proposed BIQA framework is as competitive as state-of-the-art BIQA models.

Keywords: Heterogenous reference · Deep neural networks · Image quality assessment

1 Introduction

Digital images could be distorted in any stage of their life cycle, from acquisition, compression, storage to transmission, which leads to the loss of received perceptual quality. Consequently, a reliable quality assessment metric of digital images is in great need to evaluate the quality of received image for the end users.

In the past decades, huge efforts have been devoted and a variety of IQA methods have been proposed. Especially as the emerging of Deep Learning (DL) techniques endows the BIQA is considered as one of the most challenging low-level image processing tasks because of the corresponding pristine images are

Supported by The Public Welfare Technology Application Research Project of Zhengjiang Province, China (LGF21F010001).

unavailable, the BIQA models are therefore blind to the prior quality information of pristine images and have no prior knowledge about what a 'perfect' image should be. Current state-of-the-art BIQA models tend to extract quality-aware features via deep neural networks by only the distorted image itself, such as [21–25]. This work presents an effective framework for BIQA models to extract more accurate quality-aware features, i.e., a pristine image whose contents are different from the distorted image is provided in order to afford the BIQA model with more prior knowledge about perceptual quality. The overall flowchart of our framework compared to traditional deep neural network (DNN) based BIAQ framework is described in Fig. 1.

The proposed framework is inspired by the observation that a pristine image with different content could also help to make more confident quality judgements during subjective experiments, which can be illustrated in Fig. 2. If viewers are asked to directly give an overall quality opinion to Fig. 2(a), it is very hard to say the image is perfect, or slightly contaminated; On the other hand, if Fig. 1(a) and Fig. 1(b) are simultaneously provided, it is easier to distinguish that the left image is more blurred compared to the right one. Since Fig. 2 indicates a randomly-selected pristine image with different content (referred to as Heterogenous Reference, HR) could help human observers to make more stable and accurate quality judgements, we think it is also feasible to stabilize and optimize the performance of BIQA model by providing heterogenous reference image to it.

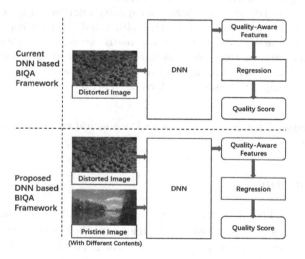

Fig. 1. Overall flowchart of our framework (lower) compared to traditional DNN based BIQA framework (upper).

It worth nothing that discrepancy between the heterogenous reference and distorted image results not only from their different quality level (quality difference) but also from that they share different contents (content difference),

(a)   **(b)**

Fig. 2. Pristine images with different content could also help observers to make a more stable and accurate quality judgement.

in another word, the quality difference and the content difference are tangled. The human visual system (HVS) could effectively capture the quality difference regardless of the interference of the tangled content difference, as illustrated in Fig. 2. However, the tangled quality and content difference would severely interfere the accuracy and robustness of the proposed BIQA framework.

In order to decouple the tangled quality difference and content difference between the heterogenous reference and distorted image, this work explores the inherent invariance of quality difference and content difference, then proposes an efficient decouple method implemented by multi-task dual-path DNN.

Our contributions are two-fold. Firstly, we employ a random selected pristine image (heterogenous reference) whose content is different from the distorted one, by which the proposed BIQA framework could capture more representative and stable quality-aware features and yield more accurate quality predicting scores; Secondly, we develop an efficient method to decouple the quality difference and content difference by analyzing the inherent invariance between them. Experimental results demonstrate that he heterogenous reference BIQA framework could capture more accurate quality-aware features and the predicting quality scores of our framework yields high correlation with human opinion scores.

The rest part is organized as follow: Sect. 2 introduces related BIQA algorithms; Sect. 3 illustrates our Heterogenous Reference BIQA based on decoupling of quality difference and content difference; Sect. 4 shows the experimental results; and Sect. 5 is conclusion.

2   Related Works

2.1   DNN Based Blind Image Qquality Assessment

Recent years have witnessed the significant development of BIQA models by exploring Deep Neural Networks for its better feature abstraction and representation ability. For example, Kang et al. [26,27] propose a multi-task shallow CNN to learns both the distortion type and the quality score; Kim and Lee [17] apply state-of-the-art FR-IQA methods to provide proxy quality scores for each image patch as the ground truth label in the pre-training stage, and the proposed network was fine-tuned by the Subjective annotations. Similarly, Da Pan et al. employ the U-Net to learn the local quality predicting scores previously calculated by Full-Reference IQA methods, several Dense layers were then incorporated to pool the local quality predicting scores into an overall perceptual quality score; Liang et al. [28] try to utilize similar scene as reference to provide more prior information for the IQA model; Liu et al. [20] propose to use RankNet to learn the quality rank information of image pairs in the training set, and then use the output of the second last layer to predict the quality score; Lin et al. [16] try to learn the corresponding unknown reference image from the distorted one by resorting the Generative Adversarial Networks, and to assess the perceptual quality by comparing the hallucinated reference image and the distorted image.

As described above, recent state-of-the-art BIQA methods [15–17,20] try to overcome the absence of reference image by digging the prior quality information from just the distorted image, e.g., [16] attempts to construct a hallucinated reference while [17] and [15] attempt to learn the FR-IQA score from just the distorted image. But is should be noticed that distorted images may have been suffered server contamination and not capable of reconstructing the corresponding reference of predicting the FR-IQA score by itself. Considering that, this work attempts to afford more prior quality information to the IQA model by providing a pristine image with different content (referred to as Heterogenous Reference).

2.2   IQA Using Similar Scene as Reference

Liang et al. [28] proposed to use similar scene as reference in order to measure the perceptual quality via dual-path DNN, their proposed IQA framework is similar as ours. But it should be noticed that their reference images share similar content with distorted images, resulting their model to be applied in limited IQA scenarios. Since the reference image in [28] is restricted to share similar contents, the content difference between the reference and distorted images are not significant, models in [28] therefore simply made use of dual-path DNN and need no further consideration of decoupling quality and content difference. On the contrary, our proposed BIQA framework aims to explore the prior quality-aware information in a randomly selected reference (heterogenous reference) whose content may quite different from the distorted one. As a result, our proposed BIQA framework explores the inherent invariant of quality difference and develops an efficient decouple method to relieve the interference of tangled content difference.

As described above, our proposed BIQA framework makes a further step than [28] by decoupling the quality difference and content difference and could be applied into wider IQA scenarios than that in [28].

3   Proposed Methods

3.1   Quality Difference Invariance and Content Difference Invariance

Given a distorted images x_d and a randomly selected heterogenous reference x_{HR}, we aim to obtain the quality difference representation $\phi_q(x_d, x_{HR})$ that detangled from the content difference representation $\phi_c(x_d, x_{HR})$, the $\phi_q(x_d, x_{HR})$ then could be utilized to regress the predicting quality score of the distorted image.

Intuitively, the $\phi_q(x_d, x_{HR})$ and $\phi_c(x_d, x_{HR})$ could be extracted by dual-path DNN with shared weights via multi-task training procedure, which would be thoroughly discussed in Sect. 3.2.

Now the key point, which is also our main contribution, is how to control the multi-task training procedure to guarantee the quality difference representation $\phi_q(x_d, x_{HR})$ and content difference representation $\phi_c(x_d, x_{HR})$ are detangled. It is of much importance to our BIQA framework because tangled $\phi_c(x_d, x_{HR})$ would interfere the accuracy of final predicting quality scores.

We observe the inherent relationship between $\phi_q(x_d, x_{HR})$ and $\phi_c(x_d, x_{HR})$ to derive constraints for the multi-task training procedure. Given two images x_{HR} and x'_{HR}, x_{HR} is a pristine image whose content is quite different from x_d whilst x'_{HR} is also a pristine image but its content is similar with x_d. The content difference representation of $\phi_c(x_d, x_{HR})$ and $\phi_c(x_d, x'_{HR})$ should have significant difference since x_d and x'_{HR} share similar contents whilst x_d and x_{HR} are quite different, i.e., $\phi_c(x_d, x_{HR}) \neq \phi_c(x_d, x'_{HR})$. On the other hand, considering the quality difference and content difference should be detangled and both x_{HR} and x'_{HR} are pristine images, their quality difference representation should be the same, i.e., $\phi_q(x_d, x_{HR}) = \phi_q(x_d, x'_{HR})$, which is referred to as the **quality difference invariance**.

Similarly, given two images and that share exactly the same content but suffer different degree of distortion, we can derive that $\phi_q(x_d, x_{HR}) \neq \phi_q(x_d, x'_{HR})$ whils $\phi_c(x_d, x_{HR}) = \phi_c(x_d, x'_{HR})$, which is referred to as **content difference invariance**.

Furthermore, we observe that quality difference invariance and content difference invariance act in an adversarial manner in dual-path DNN. Specifically, supposing the dual-path DNN splits into two branches in the k-th layer, one branch is used to capture $\phi_q(x_d, x_{HR})$ whilst the other is used to capture $\phi_c(x_d, x_{HR})$ (as shown in Fig. 3), the representation of the k-th layer is referred to as $\phi_k(x_d, x_{HR})$, then we can get

$$\phi_q(x_d, x_{HR}) = f_q(W_q \phi_k(x_d, x_{HR}))$$
$$\phi_c(x_d, x_{HR}) = f_c(W_c \phi_k(x_d, x_{HR})) \tag{1}$$

where the W_q and W_c denotes the weights of (k+1)-th layer in the two branches, f_q and f_c denotes the nonlinear transforms in two branches implemented by several fully-connected layers respectively.

Based on the inherent invariance of quality difference and content difference, if $\phi_q(x_d, x_{HR})$ and $\phi_c(x_d, x_{HR})$ are detangled, the W_c and W_q should share as little correlation C_qc as possible, where the C_qc could be defined as

$$C_qc = \frac{Vector(W_q)^T Vector(W_c)}{||Vector(W_q)||||Vector(W_c)||} \qquad (2)$$

where $Vector(\cdot)$ denotes the operation to vectorize a matrix into a column vector.

3.2   Implementation Details and Training Pipeline

The proposed heterogenous reference BIQA framework is illustrated as Fig. 3, the quality-aware features are extracted by dual-path DNN trained via multi-task labels. The training procedure includes 2 phases, i.e., Phase I pre-trains the DNN to extract detangled representations of quality difference $\phi_q(x_d, x_{HR})$ whilst Phase II trains a shallow network that could regress the $\phi_q(x_d, x_{HR})$ in to predicting quality scores.

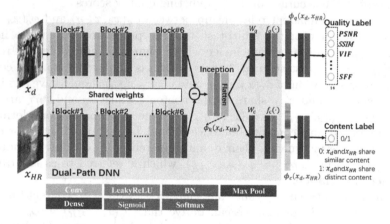

Fig. 3. An illustration of our proposed heterogenous reference BIQA framework.

As shown in Fig. 3, the proposed heterogenous reference BIQA framework takes two images as input, i.e., the distorted image x_d and a randomly selected heterogenous reference x_{HR}. Each path contains 6 blocks comprised of convolutional layers and batch normalization (BN). In addition, a max pool layer with size 2×2 is employed in the end of each block. The parameters in corresponding convolutional layers share the same weights and biases in both the upper path and lower path. The output of Bolock#6 in upper path and lower path is subtracted element-wise to get the discrepancy between x_d and x_{HR} in feature domain, the discrepancy is then fed into a convolutional layer to increase the channel-wise nonlinearity and then flattened into a one-dimension vector $\phi_k(x_d, x_{HR})$ representing the tangled discrepancy between x_d and x_{HR}, the quality difference $\phi_q(x_d, x_{HR})$ and content difference $\phi_c(x_d, x_{HR})$ is then obtained according to Eq. (1).

3.3   Training Sample Generating Procedure

In order to generate sufficient of training samples for Phase I, firstly we establish a training set containing large amount of distorted images, then generate training samples with multi-task labels in the form of $<x_1, x_2, l_q, l_c>$. (x_1 and x_2 are two input images denote the distorted image and the heterogenous reference respectively, l_q and l_c are multi-task labels denotes quality label and content label respectively).

Up to 500 high resolution pristine image are collected from digital cameras and online image resources, from which 200 images are manually selected as source image of the training set, images with ambiguous perceptual quality or similar contents would be excluded.

Considering that the proposed dual-path DNN is supposed to distinguish whether or not the distorted image and heterogenous reference share similar image content, current 200 source images could only provide image pairs that share either exactly the same or totally different image content. Such image pairs are easy to classified so that the content difference extractor would not be sufficiently trained.

In order to avoid the situation mentioned above, each of the 200 source images is generated into 7 versions according to the procedure illustrated in Fig. 4. The 7 versions share similar image contents since they are generated from the same source image, but they are not exactly the same in pixel domain. Such procedure could help to sufficiently train the quality difference extractor therefore help to detangle $\phi_q(x_d, x_{HR})$ and $\phi_c(x_d, x_{HR})$.

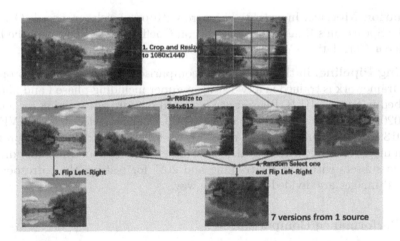

Fig. 4. Generating 7 similar pristine images from 1 single source image.

We could finally get 1400 pristine images with size 384×512. Up to 82 distortion types (including various intensions of Gaussian Blur, JPEG compression, Noise, Liminance Change, Color Distortion, etc.) are employed to deteriorate the quality of all 1400 pristine images, Therefore, finally we can obtain $1400 \times 82 =$ 114.8K distorted images together with their corresponding pristine images.

Each distorted image could generate 2 multi-task training samples in the training stage, i.e., $<x_d, x_{HR}^s, fr, 0>$ and $<x_d, x_{HR}^d, fr, 1>$, fr denotes the quality label obtained via various FR-IQA approaches such as PSNR, SSIM, etc., x_{HR}^s denotes the heterogenous reference randomly selected from the other 6 versions of pristine image that generated from the same source image as x_d, x_{HR}^d denotes the randomly selected heterogenous reference that generated from different source image. Therefore, the first training sample share similar image contents whilst the second training sample share distinct image contents, so their content labels are 0 and 1 respectively, and their quality labels are both fr.

Based on the generation procedure above, each distorted image could generate 2 multi-task training samples and finally 229.6K multi-task training samples are collected, which are utilized to training the dual-path DNN.

4   Experiments

4.1   Preconditions

Involved Datasets. Performance comparison experiments are conducted on 3 widespread IQA benchmark databases, i.e., LIVE [35], CSIQ [9], and TID2013 [36].

The ablation experiment that validate the effectiveness of our heterogenous framework is conducted on the training set we established in Sect. 3.3, namely CUZ2020.

Evaluation Metrics. In order to compare with previously proposed IQA metrics, the Spearman's Rank Order Correlation Coefficients (SRCC) and the Pearson Linear Correlation Coefficients (PLCC) are employed.

Training Pipeline. In the performance comparison experiments, the proposed BIQA framework is trained in a two-stage manner including phase I and phase II described in Section III-B. Phase I is conducted on our own training set namely CUZ2020, Phase II is conducted on existing IQA benchmarks such as LIVE and TID2013. In the training stage of phase II, we follow the experimental protocol used in most recent algorithms, where the reference images are randomly divided into two subsets with 80% for training and 20% for testing, the corresponding distorted images are divided in the same way.

4.2   Performance Comparison

Three state-of-the-art (SOTA) BIQA metrics i.e., HOSA [29], RankIQA (denoted as RIQA) [20], and Hallucinated-IQA (denoted as HIQA) [16] are involved in the performance comparison experiments. The entire performance comparison results on TID2013, LIVE, and CSIQ are shown in Table 1. Our heterogenous reference BIQA model achieves the highest performance in TID2013 in terms of PLCC and also achieves the highest performance in CSIQ in term of

SROCC. Our method achieves 15% improvement than RIQA in terms of PLCC in TID2013 and 2.4% improvement than HOSA in terms of PLCC in LIVE. These observations demonstrate our proposed mechanism increases the predicting accuracy from a novel perspective by employing heterogenous pristine image to the BIQA model.

Table 1. Performance comparison on three IQA image database

Method	TID2013		LIVE		CSIQ	
	PLCC	SRCC	PLCC	SRCC	PLCC	SRCC
HOSA	–	–	0.950	0.953	–	–
RIQA	0.779	0.780	**0.982**	0.981	0.825	0.838
HIQA	0.880	**0.879**	**0.982**	**0.982**	**0.910**	0.885
Ours	**0.897**	0.875	0.973	0.969	0.904	**0.892**

Our proposed BIQA model is as competitive as SOTA BIQA models such as HIQA. Such result is sensible because HIQA attempts to explore the prior knowledge of corresponding pristine image by a GAN, and our proposed BIQA model could also provide prior knowledge of pristine images by heterogenous reference.

In addition, Table 3 indicates that our proposed BIQA model is slightly overweighed by RIQA and HIQA in LIVE image database, we think that is mainly because our BIQA model is designed for a specific image resolution of 384×512, whilst images in LIVE own different resolution, we have to resize them into 384×512 before they are sent into the dual-path DNN, to some extent, such resize procedure would inferior the final accuracy. In the future work, we would propose a resolution independent DNN to fix this weakness.

4.3 Ablation Experiments

In order to distinguish what quality-aware features are more representative, we use FR-IQA scores as the proxy label, it is reasonable that a DNN could extract more representative quality-aware features means they could regress more accurate predictions for FR-IQA scores.

Our dual-path DNN are compared with the corresponding single-path DNN, which only takes distorted images as input and only yield predictions of FR-IQA i.e., without predictions of content difference. In the ablation experiments, both the single-path DNN and our proposed dual-path DNN with heterogenous reference are trained and tested in the newly established CUZ2020 described as Sect. 3.3. 50% reference images are used for training and the other 50% are used for testing, the corresponding distorted images are divided in the same way. The dual-path DNN are trained by multi-task label, the single-path DNN are trained directly by the 14-dimentional FR-IQA scores which are PSNR, SSIM,

SSIMC, VIF, VIFC, GMSD, GMADC, FSIM, FSIMC, MAD, VSI, MS-SSIM, MS-SSIMC, SFF, respectively (denoted as #1 to #14).

The output prediction of 14-dimentional FR-IQA scores from both the single-path DNN and the dual-path DNN are compared with the corresponding 14 ground truth FR-IQA scores, then the prediction accuracy in terms of PLCC are calculated as shown in Table 2.

Table 2. Performance comparison on three IQA image database

Metric	#1	#2	#3	#4	#5	#6	#7
Single	0.805	0.913	0.874	0.912	0.903	0.893	0.871
Dual	0.857	0.930	0.891	0.916	0.911	0.920	0.896
Metric	#8	#9	#10	#11	#12	#13	#14
Single	0.927	0.908	0.822	0.880	0.864	0.866	0.844
Dual	0.949	0.925	0.845	0.941	0.907	0.902	0.878

As shown from Table 2, the dual-path DNN achieves a significant improvement by a large margin. Specifically, our dual-path DNN outperform single-path DNN in FR-IQA metric #1–#14 by 6.4%, 1.9%, 1.9%, 0.4%, 0.9%, 3.0%, 2.9%, 2.4%, 1.9%, 2.8%, 6.9%, 5.0%, 4.2%, 4.0%, respectively.

5 Conclusion

In this work, a dual-path DNN based heterogenous reference BIQA framework is proposed to blindly measure the perceptual quality of distorted images. A randomly selected pristine images is employed as heterogenous reference to provide more prior quality information for the BIQA model. Both the performance comparison and ablation experiments have demonstrated the effectiveness of the proposed BIQA framework.

References

1. Author, F.: Article title. Journal **2**(5), 99–110 (2016)
2. Wang, Z., Bovik, A.C.: Modern image quality assessment. Synthesis Lect. Image Video Multimed. Process. 37–44 (2006)
3. Wang, Z., Bovik, A.C., Sheikh, H.R., et al.: Image quality assessment: from error visibility to structural similarity. IEEE Trans. Image Process. **13**(4), 600–612 (2004)
4. Sheikh, H.R., Bovik, A.C.: Image information and visual quality. IEEE Trans. Image Process. **15**(2), 430–444 (2006)
5. Xue, W., Zhan, L., Mou, X., et al.: Gradient magnitude similarity deviation: a highly efficient perceptual image quality index. IEEE Trans. Image Process. **23**(2), 684–695 (2014)

6. Zhang, L., Zhang, L., Mou, X., et al.: FSIM: a feature similarity index for image quality assessment. IEEE Trans. Image Process. **20**(8), 2378–2386 (2011)
7. Wang, Z., Simoncelli, E.P., Bovik, A.C.: Multiscale structural similarity for image quality assessment. In: 2004 Conference Record of the Thirty-Seventh Asilomar Conference on Signals, Systems and Computers, vol. 2, pp. 1398–1402. IEEE (2003)
8. Zhang, L., Shen, Y., Li, H.: VSI: a visual saliency-induced index for perceptual image quality assessment. IEEE Trans. Image Process. **23**(10), 4270–4281 (2014)
9. Li, S., Zhang, F., Ma, L., et al.: Image quality assessment by separately evaluating detail losses and additive impairments. IEEE Trans. Multimed. **13**(5), 935–949 (2011)
10. Larson, E.C., Chandler, D.M.: Most apparent distortion: full-reference image quality assessment and the role of strategy. J. Electron. Imaging **19**(1), 011006–011006-21 (2010)
11. Chang, H.W., Yang, H., Gan, Y., Wang, M.-H.: Sparse feature fidelity for perceptual image quality assessment. IEEE Trans. Image Process. **22**(10), 4007–4018 (2013)
12. Liu, T.J., Lin, W., Kuo, C.C.: Image quality assessment using multi-method fusion. IEEE Tran. Image Process. **22**(5), 1793–1807 (2013)
13. Wang, Z., Bovik, A.C.: Reduced-and no-reference image quality assessment. IEEE Signal Process. Mag. **28**(6), 29–40 (2011)
14. Rehman, A., Wang, Z.: Reduced-reference image quality assessment by structural similarity estimation. IEEE Trans. Image Process. **21**(8), 3378–3389 (2012)
15. Wang, Z., Simoncelli, E.P.: Reduced-reference image quality assessment using a wavelet-domain natural image statistic model. In: Human Vision and Electronic Imaging X. International Society for Optics and Photonics, vol. 5666, pp. 149–159 (2005)
16. Pan, D., Shi, P., Hou, M., Ying, Z., Fu, S., Zhang, Y.: Blind predicting similar quality map for image quality assessment. In: International Conference on Computer Vision and Pattern Recognition. IEEE (2018)
17. Lin, K.-Y., et al.: Hallucinated-IQA: no reference image quality assessment via adversarial learning. In: International Conference on Computer Vision and Pattern Recognition. IEEE (2018)
18. Kim, J., Lee, S.: Fully deep blind image quality predictor. IEEE J. Sel. Top. Signal Process. **11**(1), 206–220 (2017)
19. Talebi, H., Milanfar, P.: NIMA: neural image assessment. IEEE Trans. Image Process. **27**(8), 3998–4011 (2018)
20. Ma, K., et al.: dipIQ: blind image quality assessment by learning-to-rank discriminable image pairs. IEEE Trans. Image Process. **26**(8), 3951–3964 (2017)
21. Liu, X., van de Weijer, J., Bagdanov, A.D.: RankIQA: learning from rankings for no-reference image quality assessment. In: ICCV (2017)
22. Oszust, M.: Decision fusion for image quality assessment using an optimization approach. IEEE Signal Process. Lett. **23**(1), 65–69 (2016)
23. Pei, S.C., Chen, L.H.: Image quality assessment using human visual DoG model fused with random forest. IEEE Trans. Image Process. **24**(11), 3282–3292 (2015)
24. Gao, F., Wang, Y., Li, P., et al.: DeepSim: deep similarity for image quality assessment. Neurocomputing **257**, 104–114 (2017)
25. Simonyan, K., Zisserman, A.: Very deep convolutional networks for large-scale image recognition. arXiv preprint arXiv:1409.1556 (2014)
26. Bosse, S., Maniry, D., Müller, K., Wiegand, T., Samek, W.: Deep neural networks for no-reference and full-reference image quality assessment. IEEE Trans. Image Process. **27**(1), 206–219 (2018)

27. Kang, L., Ye, P., Li, Y., Doermann, D.: Convolutional neural networks for no-reference image quality assessment. In: CVPR (2014)
28. Kang, L., Ye, P., Li, Y., Doermann, D.S.: Simultaneous estimation of image quality and distortion via multi-task convolutional neural networks. In: ICIP (2015)
29. Liang, Y., Wang, J., Wan, X., Gong, Y., Zheng, N.: Image quality assessment using similar scene as reference. In: Leibe, B., Matas, J., Sebe, N., Welling, M. (eds.) ECCV 2016. LNCS, vol. 9909, pp. 3–18. Springer, Cham (2016). https://doi.org/10.1007/978-3-319-46454-1_1
30. Xu, J., Ye, P., Li, Q., Du, H., Liu, Y., Doermann, D.: Blind image quality assessment based on high order statistics aggregation. TIP **25**, 4444–4457 (2016)
31. Mittal, A., Moorthy, A.K., Bovik, A.C.: No-reference image quality assessment in the spatial domain. IEEE Trans. Image Process. **21**(12), 4695–4708 (2012)
32. Lin, Z., Zhang, L., Bovik, A.C.: A feature-enriched completely blind image quality evaluator. IEEE Trans. Image Process. **24**(8), 2579–2591 (2015)
33. Mittal, A., Soundararajan, R., Bovik, A.C.: Making a 'completely blind' image quality analyzer. IEEE Signal Process. Lett. **20**(3), 209–212 (2013)
34. Freitas, P.G., Akamine, W.Y.L., de Farias, M.C.Q.: Blind image quality assessment using local variant patterns. In: 2017 Brazilian Conference on Intelligent Systems (BRACIS), pp. 252–257. IEEE (2017)
35. Kim, J., Lee, S.: Deep blind image quality assessment by employing FR-IQA. In: 2017 IEEE International Conference on Image Processing (ICIP), pp. 3180–3184 (2017)
36. Sheikh, H.R., Sabir, M.F., Bovik, A.C.: A statistical evaluation of recent full reference image quality assessment algorithms. TIP **15**(11), 3440–3451 (2006)
37. Ponomarenko, N.: Color image database TID2013: peculiarities and preliminary results. In: Proceedings of 4th European Workshop on Visual Information Processing, pp. 106–111 (2014)
38. Glorot, X., Bengio, Y.: Understanding the difficulty of training deep feedforward neural networks. J. Mach. Learn. Res. - Proc. Track **9**, 249–256 (2010)

Automatic Segmentation of Kidney Computed Tomography Images Based on Generative Adversarial Networks

Tian Shan[1,2,3], Guoli Song[1,2(✉)], and Yiwen Zhao[1,2]

[1] State Key Laboratory of Robotics, Shenyang Institute of Automation, Chinese Academy of Sciences, Shenyang 110016, China
songgl@sia.cn
[2] Institutes for Robotics and Intelligent Manufacturing, Chinese Academy of Sciences, Shenyang 110169, China
[3] University of Chinese Academy of Sciences, Beijing 100049, China

Abstract. The morphometry of a renal tumor revealed by contrast-enhanced Computed Tomography (CT) imaging is an important factor in clinical decision making surrounding the lesion's diagnosis and treatment. Quantitative study of the relationship between renal tumor morphology and clinical outcomes is difficult due to data scarcity and the laborious nature of manually quantifying imaging predictors. Thus, we proposed an automatic kidney segmentation method, called SegK-GAN. The proposed method comprises a fully convolutional generation network of densely connected blocks and a discrimination network with multi-scale feature extraction. The objective function is optimized using mean absolute error and the dice coefficient. Compared with U-Net, FCN, and SegAN, SegKGAN achieved the highest DSC value of 92.28%, the lowest VOE value of 16.17%, the lowest ASD values of 0.56 mm. Our experimental results show that the SegKGAN model have the potential to improve the accuracy of CT-based kidney segmentation.

Keywords: Generative adversarial network · Kidney segmentation · CT image

1 Introduction

Renal tumor is one of the most common tumors in the urinary system. Most of them are malignant, and the incidence rate is increasing year by year. There were more than 400,000 kidney cancer diagnoses worldwide in 2018 resulting in more than 175,000 deaths [1], up from 208,000 diagnoses and 102,000 deaths in 2002 [2]. Since the segmentation results will affect the determination of disease and complications, segmentation accuracy should be further improved.

Traditionally, renal CT data were segmented manually in a time-consuming process that requires professional experience of the observer. To address this, various segmentation methods for renal CT images have been developed. Yan et al. took the spine as a marker, used the connected region labeling algorithm based on image intensity to determine the location information of the kidney, and then used the improved region

© The Author(s), under exclusive license to Springer Nature Switzerland AG 2022
H. Liu et al. (Eds.): ICIRA 2022, LNAI 13458, pp. 223–229, 2022.
https://doi.org/10.1007/978-3-031-13841-6_21

growth algorithm based on multi-scale morphology and labeling algorithm to segment the kidney [3]. Abirami et al. also used the spine as a marker to identify the position of the kidney through the connected region labeling algorithm. On this basis, the kidney region was extracted by adaptive region growth method [4]. Khalifa et al. proposed a random forest algorithm based on kidney shape prior information and high-order feature information to realize kidney segmentation and tissue classification [5]. Song et al. proposed a coarse to fine method to segment kidney from CT image [6].

In recent years, deep convolutional neural networks (CNN) have been frequently applied to medical image segmentation [7, 8].The fully convolution network (FCN) proposed by Shelhamer et al. [9] is an end-to-end network that classifies images at the pixel level, thereby solving the problem of semantic segmentation. Ronneberger et al. [10] applied a U-Net network to medical image segmentation. Sharma et al. [11] trained fully convolutional network for segmentation on slice-wise axial-CT sections. Ruan et al. [12] added a multi-scale feature extractor and a locator of the area of interest to GAN to achieve fast and accurate kidney tumor segmentation. Besides, Sandfort et al. [13] and Conze et al. [14] used GAN to achieve automatic multi-organ segmentation of abdominal CT and MR images, achieving effective simultaneous segmentation of multiple organs. However, due to the complexity of renal CT, we expect that the algorithm can learn more image features and perform well in different slices.

In this paper, we propose a SegKGAN, an end-to-end architecture for segmenting the kidney region. We improve the accuracy of kidney segmentation by adjusting the network structure and optimizing the objective function. The specific contributions of this work are as follows:

- In the generator network, we refer to an end-to-end full convolutional network similar to the U-Net structure as a network to generate segmentation result images.
- We choose to use densely connected blocks to create dense connections between the posterior layers and all anterior layers, which achieve feature reuse by connecting features in the channel dimension, enhance feature propagation, and greatly reduce the number of parameters.
- Multi-scale feature connections are designed in discriminator networks, and the L1 parametric form of the mean absolute error is added to the objective function as a regular term to prevent model overfitting and ensure sparsity.

2   Materials and Methods

Our proposed segmentation method consists of a generator G and a discriminator D. The generator is designed to learn the real data distribution and generate similar kidney images. The real are distinguished in discriminator and the results are fed back to the G. The images generated by the G are closer to the ground-truth images.

2.1   SegKGAN Architecture

Generator. The generator G is an end-to-end segmentation network as shown in Fig. 1. The overall structure of g is based on the encoder-decoder structure of the U-Net [10].

This network includes down-sampling and up-sampling processes. the down-sampling process includes a convolutional layer of 3 × 3 convolution Kernels, three maximum pooling layers, and three densely connected blocks. The up-sampling process includes three deconvolution layers and three densely connected blocks followed by a 1 × 1 convolution kernel.

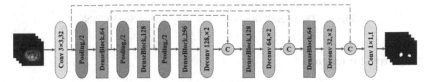

Fig. 1. The architecture of Generator

A dense block structure, as shown in Fig. 2, is introduced in the Generator network to achieve feature reuse by connecting features in the channel dimension.

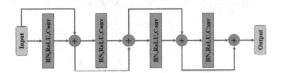

Fig. 2. The architecture of Dense Block

Discriminator. Discriminator is a multi-dimensional feature extraction network. Each layer includes a convolutional layer, a BN and a leaky ReLU activation layer. Figure 3 shows the structural details of the discriminator.

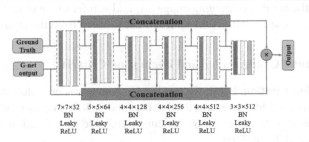

Fig. 3. The architecture of Discriminator

SegKGAN. The overall SegKGAN architecture (Fig. 4) consists of a generator, which provides the segmentation masks through the encoding and decoding layers, and a discriminator, which distinguishes whether a given segmentation mask is synthetic or real and evaluates it.

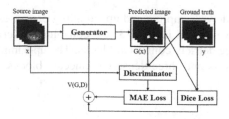

Fig. 4. The overall flow structure diagram of SegKGAN

2.2 Objective Function

The objective function includes the mapping term of the generator and the decision result term of the discriminator. Dice coefficient is an important metric used to evaluate the performance of segmentation. Mean absolute error (MAE) loss is more robust to outliers. Thus, the objective function is defined as:

$$\min_{G} \max_{D} V(G, D) = \frac{\lambda}{N} \sum_{i=1}^{N} \mathbb{E}_{dice}(G(x_i)y_i) + \frac{\delta}{N} \sum_{i=1}^{N} \mathbb{E}_{mae}(f_D(x_i, y_i), f_D(x_i, G(x_i)))$$

(1)

$$\mathbb{E}_{dice}(x_i, y_i) = -\frac{2 \sum_{i=1}^{N} x_i y_i + \varepsilon}{\sum_{i=1}^{N} (x_i + y_i) + \varepsilon}$$

(2)

$$\mathbb{E}_{dice}(x_i, y_i) = \frac{1}{N} \sum_{i=1}^{N} \|x_i - y_i\|_1$$

(3)

where N is the number of training images, x_i and y_i refer to the input CT images and ground truth. f_D is used to extract the hierarchical features from the input data x_i.

2.3 Experimental Configuration and Evaluation Criteria

Data and Implementation. Public dataset kits19, which was provided by 2019 Kidney Tumor Segmentation Challenge, was used to the model. 300 patients were selected. 150 patients were used as training set; 60 patients were used as validation set. training is based on Keras and TensorFlow.

Performance Metrics. DSC represents an ensemble similarity measure function that calculates the contour similarity in a pair of images, which is defined as:

$$DSC = \frac{2|A \cap B|}{|A \cup B|}$$

(4)

where A and B correspond with ground truth and segmentation results respectively. VOE is used to calculate the ratio between the intersection and joint points of two images, and its calculation method is as follows:

$$VOE(A, B) = \left(1 - \frac{|A \cap B|}{|A \cup B|}\right) \times 100\% \tag{5}$$

ASD is used to calculate the average surface distance between binary objects in two images, which is defined as follows:

$$ASD = \frac{1}{|S(A)| + |S(B)|}\left(\sum_{a \in S(A)} d(a, S(B)) + \sum_{b \in S(B)} d(b, S(A))\right) \tag{6}$$

where $S(A)$ and $S(B)$ denote surface voxels of ground truth and segmentation results. $d(\cdot)$ represents the shortest distance between the voxels from two images.

3 Result

SegKGAN showed a high segmentation performance. We evaluated the performance of the proposed method in qualitative and quantitative aspects.

3.1 Qualitative Evaluation

We conducted segmentation experiments using the SegKGAN model and other neural networks. As shown in the Fig. 5, we show the segmentation results. During the model training, the loss functions and dice coefficient are presented in Figs. 6 and 7.

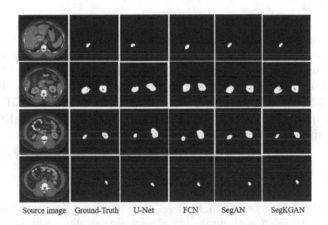

Source image   Ground-Truth   U-Net   FCN   SegAN   SegKGAN

Fig. 5. The segmentation results generated by different networks

3.2 Quantitative Evaluation

Our models SegKGAN and U-Net, FCN and SegAN models were evaluated according to the metrics listed in Sect. 2.3. All metrics for the four models were calculated using the Kits19 dataset, as shown in Table 1. Our SegKGAN model obtained the highest DSC value, the lowest VOE value, and the lowest ASD value.

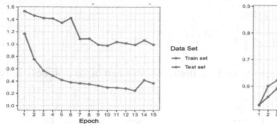

Fig. 6. Loss function

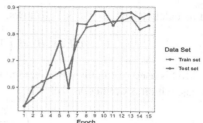

Fig. 7. Dice coefficient

Table 1. Quantitative assessment of U-Net, FCN, SegAN and SegKGAN in CT images for kidney segmentation. The results in bold indicate the first best score.

Model	VOE	ASD	DSC		
	(%)	(mm)	Maximum	Minimum	Mean
U-Net	18.74 ± 6.75	1.09 ± 0.46	93.12	54.23	89.68 ± 4.30
FCN	21.01 ± 5.82	0.87 ± 0.50	91.98	48.11	87.58 ± 7.54
SegAN	17.36 ± 2.43	0.68 ± 0.20	94.72	**63.16**	90.14 ± 6.71
SegKGAN	**16.17 ± 2.13**	**0.56 ± 0.21**	**95.26**	58.30	**1.28 ± 5.24**

4 Conclusion

In this paper, we propose a generative adversarial network-based image segmentation model called SegKGAN. In this model, we combine the encoder-decoder structure and densely connected blocks, and use the multi-scale convolutional network. Moreover, the respective loss functions are proposed to optimize the objective function. The segmentation results are close to the ground truth in kidney segmentation of CT images. By qualitative and quantitative comparisons, it can be concluded that the SegKGAN model is a more effective and robust CT segmentation algorithm.

References

1. Bray, F., Ferlay, J., Soerjomataram, I., Siegel, R.L., Torre, L.A., Jemal, A.: Global cancer statistics 2018: GLOBOCAN estimates of incidence and mortality worldwide for 36 cancers in 185 countries. CA: Cancer J. Clin. **68**(6), 394–24 (2018)
2. Parkin, D.M., Bray, M.F., Ferlay, M.J., et al.: Global cancer statistics, 2002. CA Cancer J. Clin. **55**(2), 74 (2005)
3. Gao, Y., Wang, B.: An automatic kidney segmentation from abdominal CT images. In: Proceedings of the IEEE international conference on intelligent computing & intelligent systems (2010)
4. Abirami, M.S., Sheela, T.: Kidney segmentation for finding its abnormalities in abdominal CT images. Int. J. Appl. Eng. Res. **10**(12), 32025–32034 (2015)

5. Khalifa, F., Soliman, A., Dwyer, A.C., et al.: A random forest-based framework for 3D kidney segmentation from dynamic contrast-enhanced CT images. In: Proceedings of the IEEE International Conference on Image Processing (2016)
6. Song, H., Kang, W., Zhang, Q., et al.: Kidney segmentation in CT sequences using SKFCM and improved GrowCut algorithm. BMC Syst. Biol. **9**(Suppl 5): S5 (2015)
7. Litjens, G., Kooi, T., Bejnordi, B.E., et al.: A survey on deep learning in medical image analysis. Med. Image Anal. **42**, 60–88 (2017)
8. Zhu, W., Huang, Y., et al.: AnatomyNet: Deep learning for fast and fully automated whole-volume segmentation of head and neck anatomy. Med. Phys. **46**(2), 576–589 (2019)
9. Long, J., Shelhamer, E., Darrell, T.: Fully convolutional networks for semantic segmentation. In: IEEE transactions on pattern analysis & machine intelligence (2017)
10. Ronneberger, O., Fischer, P., Brox, T.: U-Net: Convolutional Networks for Biomedical Image Segmentation. Springer International Publishing (2015)
11. Sharma, K., Rupprecht, C., Caroli, A., et al.: Automatic segmentation of kidneys using Deep Learning for total kidney volume quantification in autosomal dominant polycystic kidney disease. Sci. Rep. **7**(1), 2049 (2017)
12. Ruan, Y., Li, D., Marshall, H., et al.: MB-FSGAN: Joint segmentation and quantification of kidney tumor on CT by the multi-branch feature sharing generative adversarial network. Med. Image Anal. **64** (2020)
13. Sandfort, V., Yan, K., Pickhardt, P.J., et al.: Data augmentation using generative adversarial networks (CycleGAN) to improve generalizability in CT segmentation tasks. Sci. Rep. **9**(1) (2019)
14. Phca, B., Aek, C., Clgd, E., et al.: Abdominal multi-organ segmentation with cascaded convolutional and adversarial deep networks. Artif. Intell. Med. **117**, 102109 (2021)

Engineering Drawing Manager: A Smart Data Extractor and Management Software

Honglong Yang[1], Yang Du[1], Jingwei Guo[1], Shiyi Wei[1], and Hongbin Ma[1,2(✉)]

[1] School of Automation, Beijing Institute of Technology,
Beijing 100081, People's Republic of China
`mathmhb@139.com`
[2] State Key Laboratory of Intelligent Control and Decision of Complex Systems,
Beijing 100081, People's Republic of China

Abstract. Engineering drawings play an important role in fields such as architecture, industrial engineering, and electric engineering, within which tables contain essential data and structures. However, most engineering drawings exist in the form of scanned PDFs or images, which is inconvenient for data management and storage, especially for table information. Also, many industries are in urgent need of data management software for engineering drawings to improve the degree of digital preservation and management. To this end, a software, ED Manager which is based on the fusion of deep learning and traditional image processing, is presented to detect the position and structure of the table, split and recognize characters, and reconstruct the table in a digital form. Further, we extract crucial information and develop a user interface and database to construct a comprehensive model that fits most engineering drawings. Our software can accurately locate tables for various complex drawings, extract structured information from tables, and build a better data management software for engineering drawings.

Keywords: Engineering drawings · Table reconstruction · Table structure recognition · Optimal character recognition

1 Introduction

In the context of "Made in China 2025" [16] and industrial upgrading, various fields have the demand for transformation to digitalization, intellectualization, and internationalization. In this process, engineering drawings, as information carriers for design and manufacturing, play an important role. For example, in the field of architecture, manufacturing, and energy, engineering drawings contain important information on design structure and component details.

The data presented in the title blocks of engineering drawings record important information, including the designer, design date, product parameters, etc. Such information can be used as a reference for new products or can be used to improve directly on the original drawings, thus shortening production cycles and reducing research and development costs.

H. Liu et al. (Eds.): ICIRA 2022, LNAI 13458, pp. 230–241, 2022.
https://doi.org/10.1007/978-3-031-13841-6_22

Nowadays, with the development of the industrial manufacturing field, a huge number of engineering drawings have been accumulated. However, these drawings are difficult to manage. Although CAD software is widely used in the design process, most of the drawings in the fabrication plants exist in the form of scanned copies, prints, and other images. Since the title block, which contains unstructured information and is presented in various styles, cannot be directly recognized by computer system and can only be scanned and queried manually, it greatly reduces the efficiency of engineering drawings utilization and is not conducive to the digital preservation and management of engineering drawings. So far, there is no solution to this problem on the market. Therefore, the development of software that can provide a quick way to manage drawing information and a retrieval function is an urgent need. To achieve this solution, we combine methods including table detection, table line extraction, cell extraction, character segmentation, optical character recognition, and key information extraction.

For table recognition, many methods based on deep learning have been proposed. Gilani et al. [2] implemented and improved the Faster R-CNN [11] model and proposed an image transformation method that converts the table image to a natural image. Huang et al. [5] improved the precision of table recognition by introducing adaptive adjustments, an Anchor optimization strategy, and a post-processing method to the original YOLOv3 [10] model. Also, Qasim et al. [9] proposed an architecture based on graph networks for table recognition; and formulated the table recognition problem as a graph problem.

For table structure recognition, Suzuki et al. [1] proposed a border following algorithm to detect the borders of binary images, which can be used to detect the table cell well. Based on CNN, Siddiqui et al. [13] used semantic segmentation techniques based on FCN to recognize the rows and columns of tables well. Also, based on transformer architecture, Nassar et al. [8] presented a new end-to-end model by using a transformer-based decoder, which can solve complex column/row-header configurations, multiline rows, different variety of separation lines, missing entries, etc.

For character segmentation, many methods based on traditional image processing can segment images with merged characters, noise inference, and unknown size well. For instance, the Histogram-Based Character Segmentation method can both segment the horizontal and vertical characters with high accuracy. Many methods based on the connected components can also segment the characters well.

For optimal character recognition problems, many models based on recurrent neural networks and transformer architecture have been proposed to recognize characters of printed and natural images. SHI et al. [12] presented the CRNN model which can handle arbitrary lengths sequence without requiring character segmentation or horizontal scale normalization. Li et al. [7] proposed an end-to-end model named TrOCR, which is based on the transformer architecture without using CNN as the backbone.

The related studies mentioned above provide partial solutions to the problem of identifying and managing information in the table of engineering drawings and provide algorithmic processes for drawing information extraction. Although the software available in the market can achieve information extraction, content recognition, and text reconstruction of tables, they have some shortcomings. Firstly, they do not provide solutions in an engineering context. Secondly, they do not have an automatic positioning function to detect the table. Thirdly, they can only recognize tables with certain formats, such as title bars with less dense lines. In addition, they do not provide functions for data management and key information extraction.

The rest of the paper is organized as follows: Sect. 2 describes software structure. Section 3 explains the key algorithms used in ED Manager. Section 4 explicitly illustrates the improvement of the histogram projection method and an innovative algorithm called dots-connection method. Section 5 contains the software recognition results on different drawings and comparative analysis with other software. Section 6 concludes the software and provides some directions for future research.

The contributions of this paper are summarized as follows:

(1) we improved the character segmentation algorithm to extract words from a sentence with a traditional image processing method.
(2) we improved the table line extraction algorithm to avoid the problem of text misidentification due to text sticking.
(3) Based on deep learning and traditional image processing techniques, the software extracts both the structure information and content information, reconstructs the tables, and builds a data management supporting keywords search, which provides a solution to the problem of digital preservation and information management of engineering drawings.

2   Overview of ED Manager

2.1   Software Framework

Figure 1 shows the framework of ED Manager, which can be divided into three main parts: user interface layer, information processing layer and data management layer.

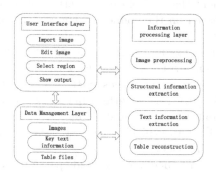

Fig. 1. Software framework

The user interface layer provides basic operating functions and interfaces of other layers' functions. After reading the instructions, the user can run the software through the interface layer such as importing and editing images, selecting processing regions, and viewing the final result.

The information processing layer reconstructs the table and extracts the key information through four main steps. The input of this layer is an selected image. The output is a html and csv file transmitted to the user interface layer for instant check and to the data management layer for long-term storage.

The data management layer defines several operations for users to add, delete, modify and require the stored data. These functions will be shown graphically on the user interface layer. The data management layer contains three kinds of data: image, text and table file. Image is from user input and used for long-term storage and checking results; text comes from the key information extraction in the information process layer; table file from the table reconstruction step in the information process layer includes both the text content and location information.

2.2   Workflow of Information Processing Layer

The workflow of the key algorithms is shown in the red box area of Fig. 2, and the four main steps are image preprocessing, structural information extraction, text information extraction and table reconstruction.

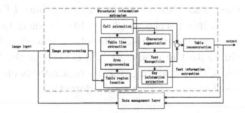

Fig. 2. Workflow of information processing layer

(1) Image preprocessing: At this stage, operations include image binarization, resizing, and enhancement of the whole image.
(2) Structural information extraction: The Structural information extraction includes four steps: table region location, area preprocessing, table line extraction, cell extraction. Table region location aims to automatically locate the tables on the image; also, the final table region can be chosen and modified manually. Table line extraction extracts the table line and reconstructs the table. The cell extraction extracts each cell by the findContours algorithm.
(3) Text information extraction: Character segmentation and text recognition are applied to each cell to convert the optical character into a digital format; after that, key information such as title, date and designers are identified, extracted and stored in the database.

(4) Table reconstruction: Table reconstruction combines the location information and text information to reconstruct the comprehensive information of the table.

3   Key Algorithms

3.1   Image Preprocessing

Image preprocessing aims to improve the effectiveness of information extraction and computational efficiency and is usually a necessary process to realize the key image processing algorithms. Specifically, grayscale and binarization are used to reduce the amount of calculation; erosion and dilation are used for filtering out the text and extracting the straight line; the median filter is used for removing noise points; image pyramid is used for expressing the image at multiple resolutions so the segment algorithm can fit images in various sizes. These methods mainly refer to the book *Digital Image Processing* [3]

3.2   Structure Information

Table Detection. In ED Manager, the detection of title blocks in the drawings is treated as a task of table detection, which means locating tables in an image using bounding boxes. We directly apply the X101 model trained on the dataset TableBank [6] to do this task. TableBank is an image-based table detection and recognition dataset, containing 417K high-quality labeled tables. X101 model is trained on this dataset with the object detection framework Detectron2 [14]. Faster R-CNN algorithm with the ResNeXt [15] is used as the backbone network architecture in training. Other training parameters are specified in [6]. Figure 3 shows the performance of the model on table detection.

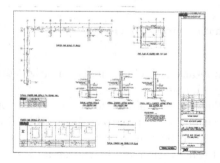 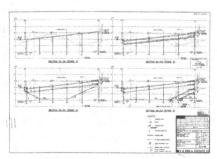

Fig. 3. Results of table detection

Table Line Extraction. In ED Manager, three methods based on traditional image processing, including Hough function method, dilating and eroding method, and an innovative dots-connection method, are used to implement table line extraction.

(1) The Hough transformation method uses the Hough function to transfer a line in the image coordinate $(x - y)$ into a point in the parametric coordinate $(\rho - \theta)$. The process of transformation is

$$y = kx + b \implies \rho = x\cos\theta + y\sin\theta \tag{1}$$

Specifically, the method can be divided into three steps: using the Hough function to transfer the discretized points; discretizing the parametric coordinate and generating a Hough matrix; finding the peak value of the Hough matrix.

The advantages of the Hough transformation method include strong anti-interference ability and high tolerance of gaps. The disadvantages include high time and space complexity and missing length information.

(2) The dilating and eroding method uses the OpenCV to set a specific kernel to extract the horizontal and vertical lines.

In order to extract the horizontal and vertical lines of images in different sizes, an adaptive algorithms is applied to choose appropriate kernel size. The algorithm can be described as

---

Algorithm 1. Adaptive Dilating and Eroding Algorithm for Line Extraction

---

Input: w: image width; h: image height; r: $\frac{w}{h}$
Output: k_w: kernal width; K_h: kernal height
 1: initial $k_w = w/15$; $k_h = h/15$
 2: **if** r $\leq$ 0.5 **then**
 3:     $k_w = w/15$
 4:     $k_h = h \times r/15$
 5: **else if** r $\geq$ 2 **then**
 6:     $k_w = w/(15 \times r)$
 7:     $k_h = h/15$
 8: **else**
 9:     $k_w = w/15$
10:     $k_h = h/15$
11: **end if**

---

(3) The innovative dots-connection method uses dilating and eroding method to extract the dots of the table, and uses the connected component method to delete the misidentified table lines. The method provides a way to eliminate the influence of the characters' size, table's aspect ratio, and complex structure on the table line extraction.

Cell Extraction. In ED Manager, the findContours function in OpenCV is used to extract the topological structure of a binary picture, and convert the picture into the border representation. FindContours is a boundary tracking algorithm that scans a binary image by the raster scan method and could distinguish between the outer border and the hole border. With this algorithm, we can extract the surrounding relationship between the boundaries, which corresponds to the surrounding relationship between the connected components [1].

In ED Manager, the function returns the inflection point information of the profile and saves the information in the contours vector. By finding the upper-left and lower-right corners of these returned contour inflection information, we can find the corresponding areas in the original map and intercept and save these areas, thus achieving cell extraction.

3.3   Content Information

Character Segmentation. The segmentation process consists of two parts: horizontal segmentation and vertical segmentation. The former divides the cell into lines of words; the latter segments a line into words. Both two parts apply the histogram projection method. This method counts the number of white pixels in each row (or column). If successive lines (or columns) contain a large number of white pixels in the histogram, it means there are characters in this area and those lines (or columns) should be cut out as a whole. Figure 4 shows the results of projected historgram, images after horizontal segmentation, and vertical segmentation.

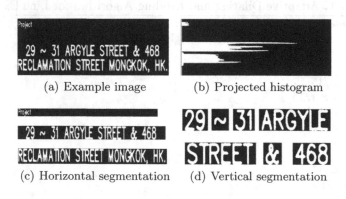

(a) Example image   (b) Projected histogram

(c) Horizontal segmentation   (d) Vertical segmentation

Fig. 4. Results of character segmentation

Character Recognition. In ED Manager, to recognize a word instead of a single character, the CRNN with LSTM [4] (long short-term memory) model is used to recognize arbitrary-length words with high accuracy. The principle of the CRNN-LSTM model is based on a feature extraction network and bidirectional LSTM, which can combine long-term memory and short-term memory to avoid the error back-flow problems. Therefore, the CRNN-LSTM model can efficiently recognize arbitrary words by considering the previous and subsequent input.

For ED Manager, we adopt three datasets to train the model. Firstly, an OCR dataset containing English words from Kaggle is implemented. Secondly, we use TRDG (TextRecognitionDataGenerator), a synthetic data generator for text recognition, and an English word list to generate more data. Thirdly, we use pygame to generate a dataset containing out-of-order characters. By combining the three different datasets, the CRNN-LSTM model can recognize various English words accurately. Figure 5 shows the characters that ED Manager is able to recognize.

```
0 1 2 3 4 5 6 7 8 9 a b c
d e f g h i j k l m n o p
q r s t u v w x y z A B C
D E F G H I J K L M N O P
Q R S T U V W X Y Z . ! /
? £ , % – \ € : ( ) + = $
ç ® @ # ^ * & ~ _ < > [ ]
` ; ‘ ’ ° { } " ‟ | – © é
ʃ æ ə ʌ ɔ ' \
```

Fig. 5. Supported recognized characters

Key Information Extraction. To construct an effective database, we extract five types of key information from the drawing: designer name, company name, project title, drawing date, and drawing number.

The key information is extracted by searching with proper keywords. For example, by searching for the characters 'No.', we can directly find the cell with the drawing number, as shown in Fig. 6.

Fig. 6. Examples of drawing number

4   Improvement

4.1   Improvement of the Histogram Projection Method

To achieve a better performance of character segmentation, we improve the histogram projection method in the following aspects:

(1) The top/bottom 10 rows (left/right 10 columns) are not considered in the histogram. This is because the extracted cell often has white table lines around the characters, which should be ignored for the purpose of character recognition. Otherwise, the white lines will be taken as characters and they may yield errors in the recognition process.

(2) We do horizontal dilation to the characters before vertical segmentation. The dilation operation makes the characters in a word closer to avoid cutting a word wrongly in the middle.

4.2 Dots-Connection Method

The dots-connection method combines the dilating and eroding method, connected components algorithm, and the prior knowledge of the table to extract the table line more robust and avoid extracting misidentified table lines, which are caused by some large size characters.

Figure 7 shows the workflow of the dots-connection method.

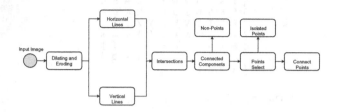

Fig. 7. Workflow of dots-connection method

In the workflow, the dots-connection algorithm can be divided into five steps. (1) Use dilating and eroding method to extract horizontal and vertical lines in advance. (2) With a bit-and logical operation obtain the intersections of vertical and horizontal lines. (3) Since the second step contains some misidentified areas which is the intersection of large size characters, we calculate the connected components areas and set a threshold value to delete the large areas. (4) To delete the misidentified corner points, we check whether each point is an isolated point. For a non-isolated point, there is at least one point in the same row and one point in the same column. To delete the isolated point, we set its coordinate equal to the previous point. (5) Connect those selected corner points to extract the table lines.

Step 3 and Step 4 are the major improvements of the dots-connection method. Since the intersections of large-size characters tend to be large size adhesion areas, and the corner points' areas are much smaller, the connected component algorithm can be used to calculate the area of intersections and delete the large parts. Also, with the prior knowledge that at least two points are needed to determine a line of tables, we can delete the misidentified corner points further.

Compared with the Hough function method and dilating and eroding method, our algorithm can get better performance, especially for tables with complex structures, extreme aspect ratios, and large size characters. Also, the time complexity and space complexity of our algorithm is smaller than the Hough function method.

Figure 8 shows different algorithms' performance for table with complex structures, extreme aspect ratios and large size characters. The experiement illustrates that the dots-connection method gets better performance since the former two methods cannot eliminate the misidentified lines caused by large size characters, which will affect the character segmentation and character recognition.

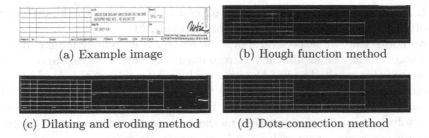

(a) Example image   (b) Hough function method

(c) Dilating and eroding method   (d) Dots-connection method

Fig. 8. Different algorithms' performance for tables with complex structures, extreme aspect ratio and large size characters

Furthermore, The dots-connection method not only improves the accuracy of extraction; but also guarantees the speed of extraction. Table 1 shows the comparison of the three algorithms on eight different tables (H represents Hough function method, D-E represents dilating dan eroding method, D-C represents dots-connection method). The experiement shows that the accuracy of the dots-connection method is greater than the other two methods in nearly all situations. Since the method relies on the dilating and eroding method to obtain the intersections, the speed is slower than it. Yet the method is faster than the Hough function method. The error rate is defined as the ratio of misidentified cells to the number of total cells.

Table 1. Results of three methods

Image pixels	Algorithm time (s)			Error rate (%)		
	H	D-E	D-C	H	D-E	D-C
1992 × 2952	0.49	0.045	0.12	37.5	25.0	16.7
1763 × 3893	0.18	0.074	0.18	6.8	2.2	0.0
1904 × 2010	0.13	0.024	0.086	3.6	3.6	3.6
16294 × 742	0.39	0.07	0.25	30.8	15.4	0.0
5441 × 557	0.076	0.016	0.068	17.3	15.4	0.0
2446 × 11498	0.33	0.41	0.81	14.3	0.0	0.0
886 × 4402	0.11	0.027	0.09	31.0	10.3	17.2
1008 × 4500	0.13	0.028	0.097	51.9	18.5	7.4

Table 2. Comparison of different software

Image	Total cell	Errors				
		Tencent	iFLYTEK	Baimiao	Youdao AI	ED Manager
1	44	0	8	0	29	0
2	58	1	1	1	34	0
3	29	1	–	1	23	1
4	52	8	31	10	32	0
5	58	1	4	1	39	0
6	160	1	0	0	–	0
7	13	3	–	3	–	1
8	17	6	0	4	9	0
9	36	5	0	5	14	0
10	58	0	0	0	25	1
11	26	2	1	5	6	8
Sum	551	28	45	30	211	11
ER	–	5.1%	8.8%	5.4%	55.8%	1.9%

5   Experiements and Analysis

To evaluate the performance of ED Manager in table reconstruction, we compare it with some other OCR software, including Tencent OCR, Baimiao OCR, Youdao AI and iFLYTEK AI.

For each of the software mentioned above, we test it with 11 images and count the number of cells which are not reconstructed correctly. The total number of cells of each image is also counted for reference. The results are shown in Table 2. ('–' means the table cannot be reconstructed at all, ER represents the error rate). As Table 2 illustrated, the error rate of ED Manager is the lowest among all software, which shows the accuracy of our algorithm.

We notice that the aspect ratio of some images is extremely large and some OCR software has great difficulty in reconstructing such images. However, the dots-connection method in ED Manager enables it to extract this kind of table structure information accurately. Figure 9 shows the reconstruction results for one image with extreme aspect ratio. The result shows that compared with other software, our dots-connection method can extract tables with complex structures, extreme aspect ratios and large characters well.

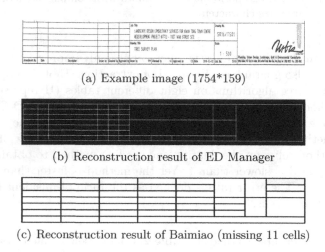

(a) Example image (1754*159)

(b) Reconstruction result of ED Manager

(c) Reconstruction result of Baimiao (missing 11 cells)

Fig. 9. Reconstruction results for images 4

6   Conclusion

In this work, we presented the ED Manager, a software based on the fusion of deep learning and traditional image processing, to detect, recognize, and manage the table of engineering drawings automatically with high speed and accuracy.

The ED Manager can finish various tasks including table detection, table structure extraction, table content recognition and table data management. For the table structure extraction, an improved method called dots-connection was presented to extract lines for tables with complex structures, extreme aspect ratios and large characters. And compared with both the existing methods and software, the dots-connection method achieves better performance.

In future work, we plan to enlarge the dataset of character recognition to improve the accuracy of CRNN-LSTM. Also, we intend to improve the dots-connection method to fit more situations such as tables without ruling lines. Furthermore, we hope to develop Android and ios application software, and a website to provide a variety of interfaces.

Acknowledgements. This work was partially funded by the National Key Research and Development Plan of China (No. 2018AAA0101000) and the National Natural Science Foundation of China under grant 62076028.

References

1. Abe, S.K.: Topological structural analysis of digitized binary images by border following. Graph. Image Process. Comput. Vis. **30**, 32–46 (1985)
2. Gilani, A., Qasim, S.R., Malik, I., Shafait, F.: Table detection using deep learning. In: 2017 14th IAPR International Conference on Document Analysis and Recognition (ICDAR), vol. 1, pp. 771–776. IEEE (2017)
3. Gonzalez, R.C., Woods, R.E.: Digital image processing. IEEE Trans. Acoust. Speech Signal Process. **28**(4), 484–486 (1980)
4. Hochreiter, S., Schmidhuber, J.: Long short-term memory. Neural Comput. **9**(8), 1735–1780 (1997)
5. Huang, Y., et al.: A yolo-based table detection method. In: 2019 International Conference on Document Analysis and Recognition (ICDAR) (2020)
6. Li, M., Cui, L., Huang, S., Wei, F., Zhou, M., Li, Z.: TableBank: a benchmark dataset for table detection and recognition. arXiv e-prints (2019)
7. Li, M., et al.: TrOCR: transformer-based optical character recognition with pre-trained models. arXiv e-prints (2021)
8. Nassar, A., Livathinos, N., Lysak, M., Staar, P.: TableFormer: table structure understanding with transformers. arXiv e-prints (2022)
9. Qasim, S.R., Mahmood, H., Shafait, F.: Rethinking table recognition using graph neural networks. In: 2019 International Conference on Document Analysis and Recognition (ICDAR) (2020)
10. Redmon, J., Farhadi, A.: YOLOv3: an incremental improvement. arXiv e-prints (2018)
11. Ren, S., He, K., Girshick, R., Sun, J.: Faster R-CNN: towards real-time object detection with region proposal networks. IEEE Trans. Pattern Anal. Mach. Intell. **39**(6), 1137–1149 (2017)
12. Shi, B., Bai, X., Yao, C.: An end-to-end trainable neural network for image-based sequence recognition and its application to scene text recognition. IEEE Trans. Pattern Anal. Mach. Intell. **39**, 2298–2304 (2017)
13. Siddiqui, S.A., Khan, P.I., Dengel, A., Ahmed, S.: Rethinking semantic segmentation for table structure recognition in documents. In: 2019 International Conference on Document Analysis and Recognition (ICDAR) (2019)
14. Wu, Y., Kirillov, A., Massa, F., Lo, W.Y., Girshick, R.: Detectron2 (2019). https://github.com/facebookresearch/detectron2
15. Xie, S., Girshick, R., Dollár, P., Tu, Z., He, K.: Aggregated residual transformations for deep neural networks. In: Proceedings of the IEEE Conference on Computer Vision and Pattern Recognition, pp. 1492–1500 (2017)
16. Zhou, J.: Intelligent manufacturing—main direction of "Made in China 2025". China Mech. Eng. **26**(17), 2273 (2015)

Advanced Key Technologies
in Intelligent Interactive Robots

Micro Vision-based Sharpening Quality Detection of Diamond Tools

Wen Xue, Chenyang Zhao[✉], Wenpeng Fu, Jianjun Du, and Yingxue Yao

School of Mechanical Engineering and Automation, Harbin Institute of Technology (Shenzhen), Shenzhen 518055, China
zhaochenyang@hit.edu.cn

Abstract. Ultra-precision grinding is the last critical step in diamond tool machining. At present, most of the tool quality detection methods in the grinding process are offline measurement, which will reduce production efficiency. The general tool condition monitoring (TCM) method is designed for the use of the tool for processing and production, and there are relatively few studies on the detection in the process of producing diamond tools. Referring to the general TCM method, this paper adopts the machine vision detection method based on deep learning to realize the on-machine detection of the grinding quality of diamond tools. The method proposed in this paper is optimized for the recognition of small-sized defect targets of diamond tools, and the impact of less data on the training of the recognition network is improved. First, an imaging system is built on an ultra-precision grinder to obtain information suitable for detecting defective targets. These tool images are then used to train an optimized object recognition network, resulting in an object recognition network model. Finally, the performance of the network on the task of diamond tool defect recognition is verified by experiments. The experimental results show that the method proposed in this paper can achieve an average accuracy of 87.3% for diamond tool detection and a 6.0% improvement in position accuracy.

Keywords: Diamond tools · Visual inspection · Tool condition monitoring

1 Introduction

Diamond tools are widely used in modern precision and ultra-precision machining. Especially in the new era of Industry 4.0, the quality of the cutting tools plays a vital role in the manufacturing industry. Due to the characteristics of high hardness, wear resistance and low thermal expansion coefficient, diamond tools have become the main material used in cutting tools.

The fine grinding of diamond tools is generally the last step in the tool processing. The ultra-precision grinding of diamond tools on a dedicated grinding machine can further reduce the surface roughness of the tool. After the diamond tool is put into production, due to the wear and tear of the diamond tool in production, it is also necessary to reprocess the diamond tool on a special grinding machine. Therefore, fine grinding of diamond tools, as the last step in the production of diamond tools, is a very important key step.

H. Liu et al. (Eds.): ICIRA 2022, LNAI 13458, pp. 245–252, 2022.
https://doi.org/10.1007/978-3-031-13841-6_23

In order to obtain the machining condition of the cutting tool in time, the monitoring of the tool condition in this process is necessary.

The general method to accurately determine the surface morphology of diamond tools is to use scanning electron microscopy (SEM) [1] or atomic force microscopy (AFM) [2] and their derivatives. Since diamond is non-conductive, it is necessary to coat a conductive film on its surface before using SEM to measure it. AFM determines the contour information of the tool by directly contacting the tool surface with the probe. Both of these methods are accurate measurement methods for determining tool parameters, and they are generally used for scientific research or to accurately determine a batch of tool parameters. In the actual production tool processing site, the more common way is to observe the processed tool under a microscope. If there is no obvious defect, it is a qualified tool. However, as the production batch of tools increases, this detection method brings some problems. Although this off-line detection method can screen out samples of tools that contain obvious tools, it is very time-consuming for these tools that need to be re-machined. Because the re-machining process has to reposition the tool, this increases the time cost. The manual detection method is far less efficient than automatic detection, which increases the labor cost. Considering these problems, and referring to the general tool state detection method.

The general tool condition monitoring methods can be divided into direct method and indirect method according to the contact mode. Analyzing tool state by measuring factors such as cutting force [3–5] or vibration [6, 7] during machining are common indirect method. Acoustic emission technology [8] is another way to detect tool wear. However, when the size of the tool is very small, environmental noise, processing temperature and chip may interfere with the sensor's signal acquisition, and it is difficult to obtain signals that can truly reflect the processing state from those collected signals. The direct method to obtain tool wear image by machine vision is another method to realize tool wear [9, 10] monitoring. The advance of image sensor technology and the fact that there is an interval in the actual working process make it possible to monitor the wear condition of the tool online [11]. We propose a method that combines machine vision and deep learning target recognition to realize the sharpening quality detection of diamond tools (named DDN).

Different from general target detection tasks, the chipping size of diamond tools is relatively small, and the number of samples with chipping is relatively small. In order to adapt the recognition network to the task of diamond tool detection, we optimized the network structure and parameters accordingly.

In this paper, we propose a method optimized for the problem of diamond tool defect identification during grinding. First, the structure of the identification network DDN and the basic optimization idea are proposed. Then, the experimental hardware platform setup and related preparations are introduced. Finally, we compare the performance of DDN and the non-optimized recognition network on the task of diamond tool defect detection, and analyze and summarize the experimental results.

2   Structure of the DDN

2.1   An Overview of DDN

The process of diamond tool defect detection is shown in Fig. 1. The deep learning method requires the surface image information of the diamond tool to be obtained first. These image information is fed into the neural network, and the parameters in the network are updated through the marked target information. After the above steps, a target detection network model suitable for diamond tool defect detection is obtained. Using this model, the image of the tool surface obtained in situ can be sent to the network in real time during diamond tool machining. If the model outputs the target information with defects, the defect target will be displayed on the relevant display device for the technicians to deal with in time. The defect detection network (DDN) is developed from the Faster RCNN [12] network. On the basis of inheriting its four parts: feature extraction network module, region proposal network module (RPN), region of interest pooling (RoI Pooling) module, and fully connected network module, part of the structure is improved to adapt to diamond tools characteristics of defect detection tasks.

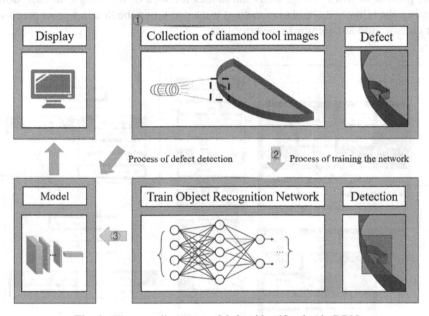

Fig. 1. The overall process of defect identification in DDN

2.2   DDN's Structure and Optimization

Figure 2 shows the network of the main modules of the DDN. The feature extraction network is the key link of the target recognition task. Its main task is to extract the specific features of different targets. After the image passes through the feature extraction network, a series of feature maps are output. The defects of diamond tools are generally relatively small. If the network is not optimized, some small features may disappear in the process of network transmission, resulting in a decrease in the accuracy of subsequent identification of the network. The feature extraction network of DDN continues the idea of ResNet50 [13] and introduces the block structure, which effectively solves the problem of gradient disappearance in the neural network. On this basis, the ResNet can increase a great depth, so as to extract the features of the target more efficiently. On this basis, DDN considers that the small-scale features will gradually disappear behind the network, so the feature maps of the first three stages are directly fused into the final output, so that these small-scale features can be preserved as much as possible. When retaining features, the DDN network introduces the concept of GoogleNet's [14] Inception, uses convolutional layers of different sizes of convolution kernels in parallel, and finally outputs them. DDN optimizes the size of the generated anchor in the RPN network. Because the role of the anchor is to predict the actual target position as much as possible. Therefore, if the difference between the anchor size and the actual target defect size is too large, the prediction error of the network will increase. DDN appropriately reduces the size of anchor generation so that RPN can generate accurate predicted positions. In the process of RoI Pooling, DDN introduces the idea of RoI Align. In each down sampling, the bilinear interpolation method is used to retain the floating-point precision after quantization and minimize the error loss.

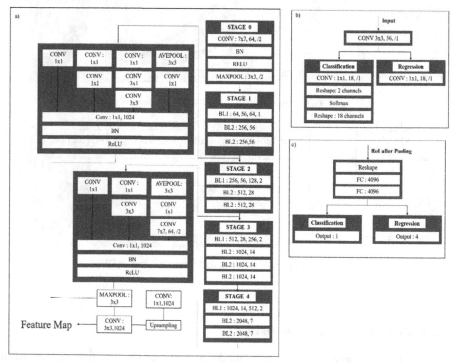

Fig. 2. DDN structure. a) Feature extraction network structure. b) RPN network structure. c) Classification and regression network structure

In addition to optimizing the network, considering the small sample size of diamond tool defect data, the idea of migration learning is adopted, and pre-training parameters are loaded at the beginning of training, which can make the network converge more quickly.

3   Experiment Setup

In order to obtain the image of the diamond tool surface, it is necessary to install an imaging system on the diamond tool sharpening machine. The imaging system include adjustment brackets, industrial cameras, industrial lenses and other hardware. Figure 3 shows the 3D model of the hardware. The zoom ratio of the imaging system is 1:10, which is to realize the function of tool setting under low magnification and the function of detecting diamond tool status under high magnification.

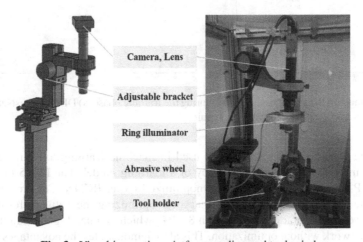

Fig. 3. Visual inspection platform on diamond tool grinder

Using the imaging system, a series of images of the diamond tool surface were obtained. According to the hardware parameters of the camera and lens we can obtain an image with a size of 2448 px × 2048 px, and these images contain both images with defects and images without defects. After this, screening of the images of diamond tools containing defects is performed. The images are cropped to 400 px × 400 px, and each image is guaranteed to contain at least one target piece of information. After obtaining the diamond tool image with defect information, the work of marking the location of these defects on the image is completed, which is also a key step in the production of the entire dataset. The tool used for labeling information is labelImg, in which the defect location is determined by a rectangular box.

4   Result and Discussion

When testing the network, control networks are added to show the performance of the DDN network more clearly. DDN, Faster RCNN based on ResNet50, and Faster RCNN without transfer learning are used respectively. The Fig. 4 shows the comparison of the losses of the three networks during the training process. It can be noticed that the network applying transfer learning can obtain relatively stable loss output on the validation set when the number of training rounds reaches about 80. This means that it is easier for your network to transfer the learned parameters to converge. As can be seen in the Fig. 4(c), the loss has been increasing, and in the first 100 epoch of iterative training, the network has not reached a state of convergence. This means that it takes many iterations for the network to converge on the training set. In the training of the first two networks, it can be seen that there are some fluctuations in the loss during 50 epoch of training. This is because the technology of freezing the network is used during network training, which can also make the network reach the convergence state faster.

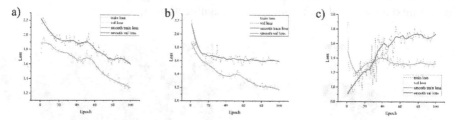

Fig. 4. Changes in the loss of each network during the training phase. a) DDN. b) ResNet50 based Faster RCNN. c) Faster RCNN without pretrain

Average Precision (AP) is generally used in machine learning to characterize the evaluation metric of the average accuracy of a learning model. The Fig. 5 (a) and (b) shows the P-R curves of DDN and the unoptimized Faster RCNN. The area under the curve is the AP value. It can be seen that after optimizing the network for diamond tools, the average accuracy rate can reach 87.3%, which is much higher than the target detection network without optimization. This also demonstrates the advantages of DDN for diamond tool inspection tasks (Table 1).

Table 1. Experimental data results.

Network	Average precision	Mean IoU
DDN	87.30%	0.8946
Faster RCNN	52.63%	0.8426

In order to illustrate that the prediction result of the DDN network is closer to the label value. All predictions generated on the test images are counted, where the IoU represents how close the predictions are to the real results. The closer the two are, the closer the value is to 1. It can be seen in Fig. 5(c) that the average closeness of the predicted boxes of DDN is higher than that of the unoptimized network. The DDN average IoU is 0.894, while the other network is 0.843, and the accuracy of the predicted result location is improved by 6.04%.

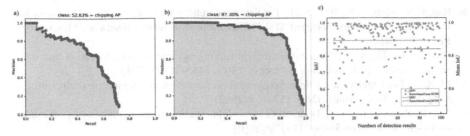

Fig. 5. a) AP curve of Faster RCNN. b) AP curve of DDN. c) Comparison of IoU of different networks

5 Conclusions

This article proposes an online monitoring method in the production process of diamond tools. Aiming at the tiny chipping that may occur in the grinding process of diamond tools, this paper proposes a small target feature extraction network suitable for diamond tools, and uses the idea of transfer learning to alleviate the influence of few data samples on the detection effect. Finally, an average accuracy rate of 87.3% for diamond tool defects was achieved. The detection precision is also 6.0% higher than that of the same type of network.

The problem of diamond tool defect detection has the characteristics of few data samples and small objects to be detected. Therefore, the general recognition network does not perform well on this task, and it is necessary to carry out targeted optimization. The experimental results demonstrate the good performance of DDN in the quality inspection of diamond tool sharpening defects. We will continue to optimize the network structure of DDN to further improve the recognition accuracy and verify its detection speed and other parameters. Finally, in order to solve the problem of the lack of experimental data, some methods of image data augmentation for diamond tool defects should also be discussed in the following work.

References

1. Zhang, K., Shimizu, Y., Matsukuma, H., Cai, Y., Gao, W.: An application of the edge reversal method for accurate reconstruction of the three-dimensional profile of a single-point diamond tool obtained by an atomic force microscope. Int. J. Adv. Manuf. Technol. **117**(9–10), 2883–2893 (2021). https://doi.org/10.1007/s00170-021-07879-6
2. Yang, N., Huang, W., Lei, D.: Diamond tool cutting edge measurement in consideration of the dilation induced by AFM probe tip. Measurement **139**, 403–410 (2019)
3. Azmi, A.: Monitoring of tool wear using measured machining forces and neuro-fuzzy modelling approaches during machining of GFRP composites. Adv. Eng. Softw. **82**, 53–64 (2015)
4. Kaya, B., Oysu, C., Ertunc, H.M.: Force-torque based on-line tool wear estimation system for CNC milling of Inconel 718 using neural networks. Adv. Eng. Softw. **42**(3), 76–84 (2011)
5. Wang, G., Yang, Y., Xie, Q., Zhang, Y.: Force based tool wear monitoring system for milling process based on relevance vector machine. Adv. Eng. Softw. **71**, 46–51 (2014)

6. Rao, K.V., Murthy, B., Rao, N.M.: Prediction of cutting tool wear, surface roughness and vibration of work piece in boring of AISI 316 steel with artificial neural network. Measurement **51**, 63–70 (2014)
7. Scheffer, C., Heyns, P.: Wear monitoring in turning operations using vibration and strain measurements. Mech. Syst. Signal Process. **15**(6), 1185–1202 (2001)
8. Li, X.: A brief review: acoustic emission method for tool wear monitoring during turning. Int. J. Mach. Tools Manuf. **42**(2), 157–165 (2002)
9. Teti, R., Jemielniak, K., O'Donnell, G., Dornfeld, D.: Advanced monitoring of machining operations. CIRP Ann. **59**(2), 717–739'(2010)
10. Peng, R., Pang, H., Jiang, H., Hu, Y.: Study of tool wear monitoring using machine vision. Autom. Control. Comput. Sci. **54**(3), 259–270 (2020)
11. Kurada, S., Bradley, C.: A review of machine vision sensors for tool condition monitoring. Comput. Ind. **34**(1), 55–72 (1997)
12. Girshick, R.: Fast r-CNN. In: Proceedings of the IEEE international conference on computer vision, pp. 1440–1448 (2015)
13. He, K., Zhang, X., Ren, S., Sun, J.: Deep residual learning for image recognition. In: Proceedings of the IEEE conference on computer vision and pattern recognition, pp. 770–778 (2016)
14. Szegedy, C., Liu, W., Jia, Y., et al.: Going deeper with convolutions. In: Proceedings of the IEEE conference on computer vision and pattern recognition, pp. 1–9 (2015)

Visual Alignment Method by Merging 2D/3D Data in Robot Automatic Drilling

Jiaying Wu[1], Xu Zhang[1,2(✉)], and Dawei Tu[1]

[1] School of Mechatronic Engineering and Automation, Shanghai University, Shanghai, China
zhangxu@hust-wuxi.com
[2] Huazhong University of Science and Technology Wuxi Research Institute, Jiangsu, China

Abstract. Aiming at the inconsistency between the coordinate system of target object and the theoretical coordinate system in robot automatic drilling, a visual alignment method by merging 2D/3D data is proposed. The 2D image data and 3D point cloud were acquired by the 3D Imaging System with Structured Light. An improved adaptive threshold and morphological processing algorithm were used to extract the edge features of datum holes. Edge discrimination and Euclidean clustering algorithm was used to calculate the projection points of the holes. Based on binocular stereo vision, the matching relationship between points in left and right images were established through the projection points, and the 3D coordinates of the center of the datum hole were obtained. The coordinate system transformation of the workpiece under the vision system was completed by the theoretical coordinates and the actual coordinates. Experimental results showed that the positioning accuracy of the datum hole of the proposed method was 0.05 mm, which was better than 10% of the traditional method that includes Canny edge detection and epipolar constraint.

Keywords: Binocular vision · Coordinate system alignment · Feature extraction · Point match · Datum hole position

1 Introduction

In aircraft assembly, the surface holes of aircraft components occupy an essential position. Traditional manual hole-making is difficult to take into account both efficiency and precision. However, the development of robot automated drilling technology makes it possible to address these issues [1]. Electroimpact and Airbus designed a robotic automatic drilling systems ONCE for Boeing F/A-18E/F for wing trailing edge flaps drilling, countersink, and detection [2]. An automatic vertical fuselage assembly system (FAUB) developed by KUKA for Boeing B-777X twin-aisle passenger aircraft used multiple bore-making robots to simultaneously carry out bore-making operations inside and outside the fuselage and can drill and rivet 60,000 fasteners per day [3]. Shenyang Aircraft Corporation and Beijing University of Aeronautics and Astronautics Cooperated to develop a hole-making end-effector. The robot drilling system drilled a 6 mm hole in a 7075-T6 aluminum alloy plate with an aperture error of ±0.04 mm and a

© The Author(s), under exclusive license to Springer Nature Switzerland AG 2022
H. Liu et al. (Eds.): ICIRA 2022, LNAI 13458, pp. 253–263, 2022.
https://doi.org/10.1007/978-3-031-13841-6_24

positioning accuracy of 0.3 mm [4]. Zhejiang University and NUAA of aeronautics and astronautics have also made remarkable achievements in developing automatic drilling and riveting machine [5, 6].

Automatic hole-making is based on the digital model of aircraft parts. Due to the influence of multi-source coupling assembly error in the actual assembly process, the shape of large flexible structural parts such as panels will inevitably deviate from the theoretical mathematical model. Therefore, the coordinate system alignment is an essential step before automatic drilling. Zhu et al. [7] constructed the bilinear error surface of the area to be prepared using the hole position deviation of the datum hole, and realized linear interpolation compensation for the hole position of the preparation hole. Shi et al. [8] predicted the hole location deviation to be prepared by establishing the Kriging model of the hole location deviation of the datum hole, providing a basis for the addition and arrangement of the datum hole.

Datum hole detection and location are the basis of complete coordinate system alignment. The workpiece surface usually sets several groups of datum holes. To correct the hole-making position, the vision system detects the offset of the actual datum hole position on the workpiece relative to the theoretical datum hole position. Zhou et al. [9] proposed a space such as the non-contact measurement of geometric parameters of the circle, Chen et al. [10], proposed a circular hole pose measurement method. Based on binocular stereo vision, the edge feature points are obtained by image processing, then the corresponding matching points of spatial circles are completed by epipolar constraints. Then the 2D contour is projected into 3D space, and the position and orientation are determined by spatial circle fitting. The 2D image processing technology is mature, high precision and fast operation speed. But for a plate with a large number of parallel holes, it is easy to mismatch by only relying on the epipolar constraint. Hole location by 3D point cloud data can be divided into direct and indirect methods [11]. The direct method directly extracts edge feature points from the 3D point cloud according to the spatial location between point sets. However, the direct method is highly dependent on the quality of point cloud data, so if there is a defect in point cloud, its exclusive features cannot be well-identified.. The indirect method converts the 3D point cloud into a 2D image and extracts the edge contours, then returns to the 3D point cloud edge contours [12]. Tan et al. [13] proposed a datum hole detection method based on linear laser scanning and 2D image. B. Steder et al. [14] proposed a novel extraction method for crucial points of interest, which operated on a range of images generated by any 3D point cloud. However, a 2D image edge representation of the point cloud edge will inevitably ignore the geometric advantages of the point cloud. However, it cannot avoid the problem of poor precision of hole location when the quality of the point cloud is not ideal.

This paper proposes a visual alignment method for datum holes, which integrates 2D images and a 3D point cloud. An improved adaptive threshold and morphological processing algorithm extract the edge features of datum holes and complete elliptic parameterization. Based on the projection model, Edge discrimination and Euclidean clustering algorithm were used to calculate the 3D centroid projection points of datum holes. Based on binocular stereo vision, the centroid projection point was used as the matching clue to obtain the corresponding matching point of the feature point under the left image and the right image. Then, the 3D coordinates of the center of the datum hole were calculated. The coordinate system transformation of the workpiece under the vision system was completed by the theoretical coordinates and actual coordinates.

2 Datum Location and Alignment Algorithm Based on 2D/3D Data Fusion

2.1 Datum Hole Edge Extraction

After the perspective transformation of the imaging lens, the rotundity-datum-aperture is oval. When capturing directly against the lens, the inner and outer gray value areas of the rotundity-datum-aperture are clear. There is only a small amount of noise caused by burrs, and the edge information is visible, as shown in Fig. 1a. However, In the actual processing process, the camera and the datum hole are often not directly against each other. Affected by the camera angle and lighting, the acquisition results include the inner wall information of the hole, so a large amount of false edge information is introduced into the imaging, as shown in Fig. 1b. Therefore, it is necessary to distinguish the actual edge and false edge of the datum hole contour to calculate the ellipse parameters that are more consistent with the real profile.

(a) Ideal datum hole   (b) Actual datum hole

Fig. 1. Datum hole.

Gradient-based methods were less affected by uneven illumination [15]. Define convolution kernels K_x and K_y to obtain all edge information of datum holes:

$$K_x = \begin{bmatrix} 0.3679 & 0.6065 & 0.3679 \\ 0 & 0 & 0 \\ -0.3679 & -0.6065 & -0.3679 \end{bmatrix} \tag{1}$$

$$K_y = \begin{bmatrix} 0.3679 & 0 & -0.3679 \\ 0.6065 & 0 & -0.6065 \\ 0.3679 & 0 & -0.3679 \end{bmatrix} \tag{2}$$

Get the gradient of the image in the X and Y directions:

$$G_x(i,j) = \sum_{m=0}^{M-1} \sum_{n=0}^{N-1} f(m,n) K_x(i-m, j-n) \tag{3}$$

$$G_y(i,j) = \sum_{m=0}^{M-1} \sum_{n=0}^{N-1} f(m,n) K_y(i-m, j-n) \tag{4}$$

where M and N were the number of rows and columns of two-dimensional array respectively, $x = 0, 1, 2, 3..., M - 1, y = 0, 1, 2, 3..., N - 1$. Obtain the gradient amplitude G of the region:

$$G = \sqrt{G_x^2 + G_y^2} \tag{5}$$

The adaptive threshold T_r of the datum hole region was constructed to deal with the edge search of the datum hole under different lighting:

$$T_r = \min val + \max val / \delta \tag{6}$$

where *minval* and *maxval* were the smallest and largest gradient amplitude, and δ was the additional threshold parameter. T_r was used as the threshold for image segmentation.

The final fitting target was an ellipse. The existence of outliers harmed the accuracy of ellipse fitting based on the least square method [16, 17]. As shown in Fig. 2a, the initial contour of the binary image *PSet1* contains more outliers. Thus, the edge points of datum holes were extracted by morphological processing to solve the problem of edge outliers. The plane ellipse parameterization based on the least square method is carried out for *PSet1*, and the ellipse was drawn on the new image of the same size to construct the constrained image. The open morphological operation was performed for *PSet1*, and the bitwise and bitwise operation were performed with the constrained image to produce the plot in Fig. 2b *PSet2*. Based on the least square method, the ellipse fitting of the *PSet2* was carried out, and the ellipse parameters more in line with the real contour were obtained.

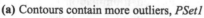

(a) Contours contain more outliers, *PSet1*　　　(b) Contours contain fewer outliers, *PSet2*

Fig. 2. Contours of datum hole.

2.2 Point Cloud Centroid Extraction

The function of point cloud data is to establish the corresponding point matching clue of left and right images. Large-scale down-sampling processing can be carried out for point cloud data. A voxel-based down-sampling process was carried out for the point cloud by bounding-box. Kd-tree was used to establish topological relations for point cloud data. All neighboring points, including within the radius of each index point, were obtained according to the topological structure. A local fitting plane of clustering of each point is constructed, and all neighboring points are projected into the fitting plane. Then, the maximum Angle calculation was used for boundary discrimination on the fitting plane.

To decide P_0 as the starting point, build the vector P_0P_i. To decide on P_0P_1 as X-axis, the perpendicular to P_0P_1 across P_2 as Y-axis, set up the coordinate system. To calculate the adjacent Angle α_i between each adjacent vector P_0P_i and P_0P_{i+1}. When $\alpha_i > \alpha_t$, the corresponding two neighboring points were boundary points, and the edge point cloud information of the datum hole was obtained. As shown in Fig. 3, reds are the boundary points, and blacks are the non-boundary points.

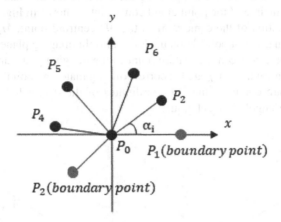

Fig. 3. Recognition of point cloud data boundary

The edge points of the point cloud were clustered to distinguish the set of edge points of the datum hole. The smallest Euclidean distance was the constraint condition to conduct the cluster search among the point clouds. Based on the topological structure, obtaining the set of all the nearest points within the radius of each index point, then calculating the three-dimensional centroid of the datum hole cluster.

2.3 Matching of Homonym Center Point and Calculation of Datum Hole Location

According to the basic principle of binocular stereo vision, projection matrix P represents the known transformation relationship between the 3D point M and the corresponding image point m on the camera imaging plane. Take the left projection matrix P_L of point M as an example:

$$P_L = K_L\{R_L|t_L\} = \begin{bmatrix} f_x & 0 & u \\ 0 & f_y & v \\ 0 & 0 & 1 \end{bmatrix} \begin{bmatrix} r_{00} & r_{01} & r_{02} & t_x \\ r_{10} & r_{11} & r_{12} & t_y \\ r_{20} & r_{21} & r_{22} & t_z \end{bmatrix} \tag{7}$$

where all parameters come from the left camera, K_L is a camera parameters matrix, f_x and f_y are focal length, (u, v) is the principal point, R_L is a rotation matrix, t_L is a translation vector, r_{00} to r_{22}, and t_x to t_z are specific parameters. The projection of the 3D centroid on the left image plane can be calculated:

$$m_L = P_L M \tag{8}$$

According to the basic theory of binocular stereo vision, the 3D centroid projection point shall coincide with the datum hole. However, due to elliptical parametric error and benchmark hole 3D centroid calculation error, the center of mass projection point and the datum holes can not be overlapped entirely. The matching constraint of the set of the center of the datum hole is that the point of the same name is closest to the projection point of the center of mass, which means the two points with the closest Euclidean distance to the projection point of the centroid are the matching points. The point matching principle of the point cloud constraint is shown in Fig. 4. O_L, O_R is the central optical position of the camera. M is the 3D centroid point. M_L, M_R is the 3D centroid projection point of point M on the left and right imaging plane, d_{min} represents the smallest distance between the feature point in the imaging plane and the projection point of the 3D centroid. C_L, C_R are the corresponding matching point. After the correct matching points are obtained, the 3D coordinates of the datum holes are calculated according to the triangulation technique.

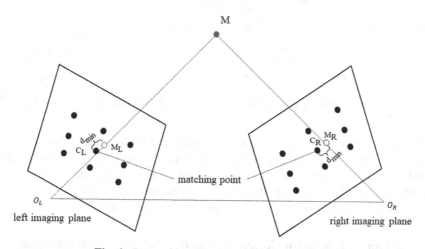

Fig. 4. Recognition of point cloud data boundary

Since the correct matching points were obtained, x_1 and x_2 are assumed to be the normalized coordinates of the two feature points according to the definition of polar geometry, which satisfy:

$$s_1x_1 = s_2Rx_2 + t \tag{9}$$

where, s_1 and s_2 are the depths of the two feature points to be solved, R is the rotation matrix of the cameras left to right, and t is the translation vector of the cameras left to right. The transformation can be obtained:

$$s_1\hat{x}_1x_1 = 0 = s_2\hat{x}_1Rx_2 + \hat{x}_1t \tag{10}$$

where $\hat{x}_1$ is the antisymmetric matrix, using the least square method to solve s_1 and s_2, then calculate the 3D coordinates of the datum hole.

2.4 Coordinate System Transformation

According to the deviation between the theoretical hole position of the datum hole and the actual datum hole position of visual positioning, the best actual machining coordinate system is determined by rotating and offsetting based on the theoretical coordinate system. Under the coordinate system of the robot vision system, the Theoretical mathematical model coordinate system frame {B}, obtained a series of datum point coordinates from Sect. 2.3. Selected three datum hole positions to establish the coordinate system frame {A}, the relationship between frame {B} and frame {A}:

$$A = \{{}_B^A R, {}^A P_{BROG}\}B = \begin{Bmatrix} \widehat{X_B} \cdot \widehat{X_A} & \widehat{Y_B} \cdot \widehat{X_A} & \widehat{Z_B} \cdot \widehat{X_A} & X_0 \\ \widehat{X_B} \cdot \widehat{Y_A} & \widehat{Y_B} \cdot \widehat{Y_A} & \widehat{Z_B} \cdot \widehat{Y_A} & Y_0 \\ \widehat{X_B} \cdot \widehat{Z_A} & \widehat{Y_B} \cdot \widehat{Z_A} & \widehat{Z_B} \cdot \widehat{Z_A} & Z_0 \end{Bmatrix} B \qquad (9)$$

where ${}_B^A R$ is the expression of the rotation matrix of {B} relative to {A}. $\widehat{X_A}, \widehat{Y_A}, \widehat{Z_A}$ represent the unit vector of the central axis direction of the coordinate system {A}. $\widehat{X_B}, \widehat{Y_B}, \widehat{Z_B}$ represents the unit vector of the central axis direction of the coordinate system {B}. ${}^A P_{BROG}$ is the position vector that determines the origin of the coordinate system {B}.

The rotation translation matrix of {B} relative to {A} was obtained by SVD, then the actual position of the hole to be made on the theoretical digital model was obtained, and the coordinate system alignment is completed.

3 Experiments

Three experiments were carried out to compare the new datum hole location algorithm to other approaches.

This paper adopts window10 64 bit operating system, visual studio 2015 C++ development platform, and opencv3.30 and pcl1.8.1 compilation environment. Provision250d structured light 3D imaging system, its measurement accuracy is 0.05 mm. ABB Robot controls the motion, its repeated positioning accuracy is 0.025 mm. The experimental piece is a flat circular hole. The parameter settings of the algorithm are shown in Table 1, and the experimental platform is shown in Fig. 5.

Table 1. Algorithm parameter setting.

Parameter	Value
ΔT	0
δ	6
r	1.25 mm
α_t	120°

Fig. 5. Experimental platform

Ten datum holes were used as experimental objects, as shown in Fig. 6. Firstly, measuring the center distance L of adjacent datum holes in each row by vernier caliper. Secondly, the traditional datum hole location algorithm which includes epipolar constraint and Canny edge detection was applied to calculate the center distance L_1 of two datum holes; the new datum hole location algorithm with *PSet1* to calculate the center distance L_2; the new datum hole location algorithm with *PSet2* to calculate the center distance L_3. The difference between L_i and L is the hole position detection error named ΔL_i. The experimental results are shown in Table 2.

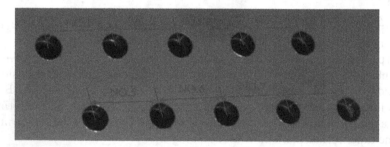

Fig. 6. Experiment object

Where, in group No.6, the traditional algorithm's positioning of the datum hole fails. The Comparison of hole spacing errors with other groups was shown in Fig. 7. The statistical data of the measurement results of the three hole-detection algorithms were shown in Table 3.

Table 2. Measurement results of hole center distance

NO	L/mm	Traditional algorithm		New algorithm/PSet1		New algorithm/PSet2	
		L_1/mm	ΔDL_1	L_2/mm	ΔDL_2	L_3/mm	ΔDL_3
1	12.94	13.011	0.071	12.979	0.039	12.979	0.039
2	12.92	12.944	0.024	12.904	−0.016	12.949	0.029
3	12.97	12.905	− 0.065	13.047	0.077	13.004	0.034
4	12.94	13.003	0.063	12.958	0.018	12.965	0.025
5	12.94	13.032	0.092	12.970	0.030	12.968	0.028
6	13.02	–	–	13.031	0.011	13.031	0.011
7	13.00	13.078	0.078	12.970	−0.030	12.972	−0.028
8	12.96	12.939	− 0.021	12.931	−0.029	12.930	−0.030

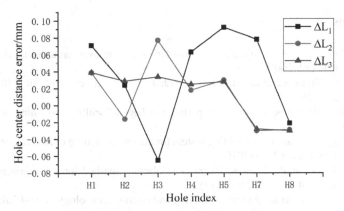

Fig. 7. Comparison of hole spacing errors

Table 3. Statistical data of measurement results of three hole-detection algorithms

Parameter	Error range/mm	Average/mm	Std Dev
ΔDL_1	[−0.035, 0.041]	0.034	0.054
ΔDL_2	[−0.030, 0.039]	0.013	0.034
ΔDL_3	[−0.030, 0.039]	0.013	0.026

4   Conclusion

Aiming at the problem of poor drilling accuracy caused by the inconsistency between the actual machined workpiece and the theoretical mathematical model in digital drilling, a visual alignment method by merging 2D image and 3D point cloud is proposed. The structured light 3D imaging system and ABB industrial manipulator were selected to build the datum hole detection and positioning system, and to carry out the datum hole contour detection experiment and hole position calculation experiment. The experimental results showed that compared with the traditional Canny edge detection and epipolar constraint hole positioning method, the detection results of the datum hole contour in this paper are more consistent with the actual datum hole contour. In this experimental environment, the matching success rate of corresponding points is 100%, the matching success rate is increased by 22.5%, the average value of hole spacing error is 0.13 mm, reduced by 10%, and the standard difference of hole spacing error is 0.026, reduced by 28%. Therefore, the positioning effect of this method on the datum hole is better than the traditional method, which can meet the requirements of automatic drilling in production and manufacturing.

Acknowledgements. This research is partially supported by the National Natural Science Foundation of China (Grant Nos. 62176149 and 51975344).

References

1. Bi, S., Liang, J., et al.: Application of robot technology in aviation industry. Aero. Manuf. Technol. **4**, 34–39 (2009)
2. Devlieg, R., Sitton, K., et al.: ONCE (One sided Cell End effector) robotic drilling system. SAE, 2002-01-2626
3. Waurzyniak, P.: Aerospace automation stretches beyond drilling and filling. Manuf. Eng. **154**(4), 73–86 (2015)
4. Du, B., Feng, Z., et al.: Robot drilling system for automatic drilling of aircraft parts. Aviation Manuf. Technol. **02**, 47–50 (2010)
5. Zhao, D., Bi, Y., et al.: A united kinematic calibration method for a dual-machine system. Assem. Autom. **38**(2), 226–238 (2017)
6. Chen, W., Jiang, L., et al.: Automatic drilling and riveting technology of Al–Li alloy panel of large aircraft. Aeronautical Manufacturing Technology **4**, 47–50 (2015)
7. Zhu, W., Qu, W., Cao, L., Yang, D., Ke, Y.: An off-line programming system for robotic drilling in aerospace manufacturing. Int. J. Adv. Manuf. Technol. **68**(9–12), 2535–2545 (2013). https://doi.org/10.1007/s00170-013-4873-5
8. Shi, X., Zhang, J., et al.: Hole position correction strategy based on Kriging model interpolation. Acta Aeronautica et Astronautica Sinica **41**(09), 325–333 (2020)
9. Zhou, F., Zhang, G., et al.: High accurate non-contact method for measuring geometric parameters of spatial circle. Chinese Journal of Scientific Instrument **05**, 604–607 (2004)
10. Chen, J, Zhiwei, G.: Circular hole pose measurement method based on binocular vision epipolar compensation. Laser Optoelectr. Prog. **58**(20), 432–438 (2021)
11. Li, H., Zhong, C., et al.: New methodologies for precise building boundary extraction from LiDAR data and high resolution image. Sens. Rev. **33**(2), 157–165 (2013)
12. Wang, Y., Ewert, D., et al.: Edge extraction by merging 3D point cloud and 2D image data. In: 2013 10th International Conference and Expo on Emerging Technologies for a Smarter World (CEWIT). IEEE, Melville, NY, pp. 1–6 (2013)
13. Tan, X., Tang, J., et al.: Research on reference hole detection technology based on line laser scanning and image processing. Modern Manuf. Eng. **04**, 115–121 (2019)
14. Steder, B., Rusu, R., et al.: Point feature extraction on 3D range scans taking into account object boundaries. In: Robotics and Automation (ICRA), pp. 2601–2608 (2011)

15. Ouellet, J.N., Hébert, P.: Precise ellipse estimation without contour point extraction. Mach. Vis. Appl. **21**(1), 59–67 (2009)
16. Fitzgibbon, A., Pilu, M., et al.: Direct least square fitting of ellipses. IEEE Trans. Pattern Anal. Mach. Intell. **21**(5), 476–480 (1999)
17. Liang, J., Zhang, M., et al.: Robust ellipse fitting based on sparse combination of data points. IEEE Trans. Image Process. **22**(6), 2207–2218 (2013)

CPC: Cable Parameters Calculation Based on 3D Point Cloud

Zhimin Fan[✉], Liefeng Guo, Yubao Chen, Feng Xiao, and Jianhua Zhang

Department of Computer Science, Tianjin University of Technology,
Tianijn 300384, China
fanzhiminmin@163.com

Abstract. We propose an innovative algorithm for cable parameters calculation based on the dense 3D Point Cloud. After finishing the aircraft cabin wiring work, the cable parameters need to be calculated to judge whether the wiring work is qualified or not. However, there are still some problems in calculating cable parameters for the robot applications. The cable is a deformable linear object without any specific shape and length, and its particular environment is also very complex. Therefore, What transpired in this paper is a cable parameters calculation algorithm based on relevant algorithms of dense point clouds with the aim of achieving accurate and efficient parameters calculation. First, the algorithm adopts the point cloud segmentation to get the cable, and the part of it is captured by the Octree Map. The minimum bounding box is also used to calculate the cable diameter. Then the path of the cable is created with the path finding algorithm, and the B-spline curve is fitted to the cable. Finally, after calculating the arc length of the curve through the numerical integration method, the feasibility of the algorithm is fully confirmed by experiments.

Keywords: Cable parameters · Point cloud · Computer vision

1 Introduction

As a critical technology of robot intelligence evaluation, Robot Computing has the advantages of solid controllability, high accuracy, and fast operation speed, which is widely used in parts processing, object measurement, and other industrial manufacturing fields [1–7]. The application of robots in manipulating deformable objects [8–12] is a popular topic in artificial intelligence. However, it is still challenging to apply robots in the cabin wiring [13] due to the complexity involved in the operational tasks of cables and the changeability of cable length and shape.

After the regular cabling work, the cables need to be evaluated to judge the qualification of the cabling operation. Because of the complex space environment of the cables and the high price and damage ratio of the cables used, manual estimation is used in this work currently, and the results of the manual assessment have some errors, which will have a negative impact on the subsequent

H. Liu et al. (Eds.): ICIRA 2022, LNAI 13458, pp. 264–271, 2022.
https://doi.org/10.1007/978-3-031-13841-6_25

cabling work. At present, the research on cable point cloud mainly focuses on each step in the process, such as point cloud segmentation, curve fitting, etc. There is no complete algorithm to calculate the calculation parameters of cable reconstruction. Moreover, the least square linear fitting algorithm is commonly used in cable curve fitting, which is complicated and inefficient. In this paper, an efficient and complete algorithm for computing cabin cable parameters is proposed, which can be applied to cables with various bends. In this algorithm, the point cloud image scanned by the depth camera is used as the input data, and a single instance of each cable is found by the point cloud segmentation [14,15]. In addition, the cable is surrounded by the minimum bounding box to calculate the diameter of the cable. Then, the Octree is constructed for the cable with the diameter as the resolution, and the optimal path is obtained by the improved A* routing algorithm. The center point of each Octree voxel in the direction is taken as a skeleton node so that the skeleton of the cable is obtained. Finally, the curve is fitted by B-spline interpolation [16,17] algorithm, and the length of the B-spline curve is calculated by the numerical integration. The main contributions of this work can be summarized as follows: 1) A complete and practical algorithm is provided to calculate the parameters for various bending cables; 2) A comprehensive experimental validation in terms of the parameters calculation and the curve fitting is made to ensure their accuracy.

2 Design of the Algorithm

In this section, we focus on the implementation details of our method, the main steps of the algorithm can be summarised as point cloud segmentation, diameter calculation, and length calculation. Figure 1 provides an overview of the algorithm.

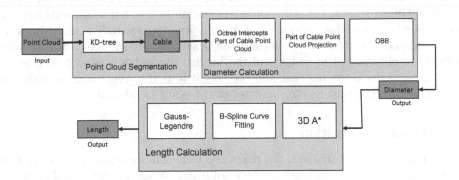

Fig. 1. An overview of the CPC.

2.1   Point Cloud Segmentation

As the starting point of the proposed algorithm, the KD-tree performs the point cloud segmentation of the input point cloud, producing the point cloud of the cables. First, a root node should be chosen on the cable. Then, the radius should be set as r and the adjacent points (the distance of points less than r to the root node) should be continuously added to the cable point cloud collection from the root node. Finally, the remaining points are the surrounding environment point cloud. In this way, the cable point cloud can be distinguished by choosing an appropriate r.

2.2   Diameter Calculation

First, the cable point cloud obtained after the point cloud segmentation is transformed into an Octree map, which is used to intercept part of the cable point cloud. Then we set the Octree resolution to a large number so that each Octree node contains as many point cloud points as possible. We Take out a point in the cable point cloud, then calculate its Octree node and then extract all the cloud points of the node so that we can get the part of the cable. We project the part of the cable to the two-dimensional plane. The plane is represented as:

$$Ax + By + Cz + D = 0 \tag{1}$$

If $A = 0$, $B = 0$, $C = 1$, $D = 0$, The projection of part of the cable point cloud to the XOY plane is obtained. Then the minimum bounding box is used to surround the part of the intercepted cable point cloud. The diameter of the cable point cloud is calculated to reduce the error in calculating the diameter of the very curved cable. The idea of generating OBB is to obtain the feature vector, that is, the principal axis of OBB, through the PCA (principal component analysis) according to the vertices of the object surface. The principal component analysis (PCA) is a kind of orthogonal transformation, which transforms a set of possible related variables into a set of linearly unrelated variables, namely principal components. After the bounding box is successfully surrounded, two valid values are obtained. The width and the height, the width is used to represent the length of the bounding box, and the height is used to represent the width of the bounding box, that is, the diameter of the point cloud cable.

2.3   Length Calculation

Optimal Path Generation. To make the Octree more regular, the Octree is constructed using the diameter as the resolution. We use the improved A* path finding algorithm to find the best path in the Octree. We need to determine where to start and where to end. All the Octree nodes are traversed, and the two Octree nodes with the maximum distance in Manhattan are taken as the starting point and the end point of the A* path finding algorithm.

$$m_{\text{dist}} = |x_{p_j} - x_{p_i}| + |y_{p_j} - y_{p_i}| + |z_{p_j} - z_{p_i}| \tag{2}$$

Among them, m_{dist} is the maximum length that we get by traversing the entire Octree, p_j is the end of the Octree that corresponds to this maximum length, p_i is the beginning of the Octree that corresponds to this maximum length, and x, y, z are their coordinates.

The core of the A* algorithm lies in the evaluation function. The specific implementation process of the improved A* three-dimensional searching Octree optimal path algorithm is as follows: (1) Starting from the beginning point p_j of the Octree, we add it to the O, which is the list of the vertical squares to be checked. (2) Ignoring the cubes that don't contain cloud points and the cubes in the E, which is the list of cubes that have been checked, we add the surrounding 26 cubes adjacent to the beginning point pi and accessible to the O. the beginning point p_i is set as the parent node of these cubes. (3) The beginning point p_i is removed from the O and added to the E, indicating that it is no longer concerned. (4) We take the newly obtained cube k with the smallest $f(k)$ value out of the O and put it in the E. (5) we ignore the cubes that don't contain cloud points and those in the E and check all cubes adjacent to k, then we add them to the O, and set our selected cube as their parent node. (6) If the cube adjacent to k is already in the O, we check whether it's $g(k)$ value is smaller. If not, do nothing. On the contrary, we set the current cube as a parent node, then recalculate the value of $g(k)$ and $f(k)$ of the current cube, and finally output the best path.

Cable Skeleton Acquisition. We find the center point (the coordinate values of all the cloud points in the node are added and averaged) of each Octree node in the best path and regard the point closest to the center point as a node of the tree skeleton and the control point of B-spline curve fitting. Figure 2 shows the process of generating the cable skeleton.

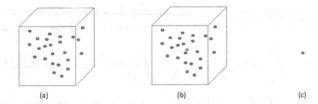

Fig. 2. (a) The point cloud point (blue) in an Octree node (cube). (b) The center point (yellow) and the closest point to the center point (red). (c) The extracted skeleton point. (Color figure online)

B-Spline Curve Fitting. Because our cable is not closed, the cable curve is fitted by the quadratic B-spline interpolation algorithm. The control points are obtained through the inverse calculation of the skeleton points, and the b-spline curve equation through the skeleton points is fitted. A quadratic B-spline curve is formed every three discrete points. Firstly, the skeleton points are smoothed onto the B-spline curve. Then we evenly insert the specified number of points between the skeleton points. Finally, the analytical expression of the quadratic B-spline curve of cable is obtained, which can be expressed as:

$$P(t) = \frac{1}{2}(1-t)^2 P_0 + \frac{1}{2}(-2t^2 + 2t + 1)P_1 + \frac{1}{2}t^2 P_2 \tag{3}$$

where P_0, P_1, P_2 are the three skeleton points for generating quadratic B-spline curves, and t is a parameter of the curve. The curve parameter t is divided into k equal parts, with t starting at 0 and interval $d * t$ up to $k * d * t$. In order to realize the coincidence between the two endpoints of the whole curve and the starting point P0 and the ending point P_n, it is necessary to take P0 and P_n as the mid-points and construct new points $P_{P1} = 2 * P_0 - P_1$ and $P_{P2} = 2 * P_n - P_{n-1}$ to replace P_0 and P_n respectively.

Length Calculation by the Numerical Integration. After the curve fitting is completed, the derivative of the quadratic B-spline curve in the parameter interval $[t_i, t_{i+1}]$ is:

$$P'(t) = (t-1)P_0 + (1-2t)P_1 + tP_2 \tag{4}$$

For any t in the definition domain, the value of $P'(t)$ can be obtained. The arc length of the curve corresponding to the interval can be obtained by the Gauss quadrature formula in the numerical integration. The error of the result is relatively small. The integral interval of the Gauss-Legendre formula is $[0, 1]$, and when the parameter interval is $[t_1, t_2]$, the formula is

$$\int_{t_2}^{t_1} f(x)dx = \frac{t_2 - t_1}{2} \int_{-1}^{1} f(\frac{t_2 - t_1}{2}u + \frac{t_2 + t_1}{2})|du \tag{5}$$

where u is a parameter. Therefore the arc length of the quadratic B-spline curve L in the interval $[t_1, t_2]$ is obtained by using the Gauss-Legendre formula.

$$L(t_1, t_2) = \int_{t_2}^{t_1} |P'(t)|dt = \frac{t_2 - t_1}{2} \int_{-1}^{1} |P'(\frac{t_2 - t_1}{2}x + \frac{t_2 + t_1}{2})|dx \tag{6}$$

After the arc length L of a quadratic B-spline curve is obtained, the arc length of each curve is calculated and their lengths are added. We get the total arc length S, $S = L_1 + L_2 + L_3 + ...L_n$,n is the total number of curves.

3   Experiments

In this section, we evaluate our method in terms of cable curve fitting and parameter calculation. The experiment is carried out on the analog cable data taken by the depth camera RealSense D455.

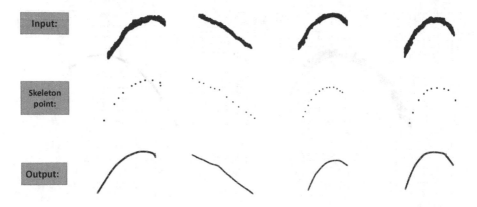

Fig. 3. Evaluation of the proposed algorithm using self-filmed cables with different lengths and shapes.

3.1 Curve Fitting

In this part, we show the effect of the CPC on cable B-spline curve fitting. We evaluate the method on three cables with different lengths and shapes. The original shape of each cable, the extracted skeleton points, and the quadratic B-spline curve fitting results are shown in Fig. 3, Fig. 4. The results show that the curve fitted by this method is the same as the length shape of the actual cable. At the same time, the skeleton points extracted by this method are smooth and suitable for curves with different degrees of curvature.

3.2 Parameter Calculation

We compare the parameters calculated by the CPC with the actual parameters of the cable. The results are shown in Table 1. The results show that among the three selected cables, the error between the length and diameter of the cable calculated by this method and that of the actual cable is controlled at the millimeter level, which reaches the error standard we want. This proves the accuracy of the algorithm.

Table 1. Comparison the actual cable parameters and the CPC calculated ones

Cables	Actual parameters		CPC	
	Diameter	Length	Diameter	Length
Cable1	0.024	1.556	0.023	1.555
Cable2	0.035	1.258	0.034	1.253
Cable3	0.03	1.653	0.03	1.658

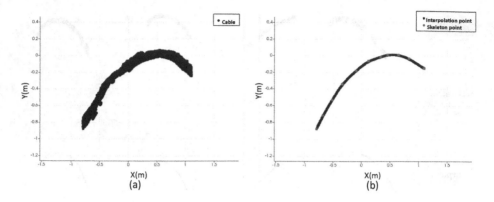

Fig. 4. Evaluation of the proposed algorithm using self-filmed cables. (a) The cable point cloud. (b) Skeleton points (red) and the fitted quadratic B-spline curve. (Color figure online)

4   Conclusion

In this paper, we propose the CPC, an algorithm for calculating cable parameters based on the point cloud. The experimental results show that the algorithm can accurately and efficiently calculate the length and diameter of cables with different bends and lengths. In addition, our algorithm can accurately fit the curve and visualize the shape of the curve, which lays a solid foundation for the subsequent robot routing work. In future research, we will improve the algorithm through more cable data to accurately calculate other parameters of the cable (such as the curvature) in practice.

References

1. Hermansson, T., Bohlin, R., Carlson, J.S., Söderberg, R.: Automatic assembly path planning for wiring harness installations. J. Manufact. Syst. **32**(3), 417–422 (2013)
2. Ramisa, A., Alenya, G., Moreno-Noguer, F., Torras, C.: Using depth and appearance features for informed robot grasping of highly wrinkled clothes. In: Proceedings of the ICRA, pp. 1703–1708 (2012)
3. Jayender, J., Patel, R.V., Nikumb, S.: Robot-assisted active catheter insertion: algorithms and experiments. Int. J. Robot. Res. **28**(9), 1101–1117 (2009)
4. Shah, A., Blumberg, L., Shah, J.: Planning for manipulation of interlinked deformable linear objects with applications to aircraft assembly. IEEE Trans. Autom. Sci. Eng. **15**(4), 1823–1838 (2018)
5. Jiang, X., Koo, K.-M., Kikuchi, K., Konno, A., Uchiyama, M.: Robotized assembly of a wire harness in a car production line. Adv. Robot. **25**(3–4), 473–489 (2011)
6. Salter, T., Werry, I., Michaud, F.: Going into the wild in child-robot interaction studies: issues in social robotic development. Intell. Serv. Robot. **1**, 93–108 (2008)
7. Behan, J., O'Keeffe, D.T.: The development of an autonomous service robot. Intell. Serv. Robot. **1**(1), 73–89 (2008)

8. Saha, M., Isto, P.: Manipulation planning for deformable linear objects. IEEE Trans. Robot. **23**(6), 1141–1150 (2007)
9. Pile, J., Wanna, G.B., Simaan, N.: Force-based flexible path plans for robotic electrode insertion. In: Proceedings of the ICRA, pp. 297–303 (2014)
10. Sanchez, J., Corrales, J.-A., Bouzgarrou, B.-C., Mezouar, Y.: Robotic manipulation and sensing of deformable objects in domestic and industrial applications: a survey. Int. J. Robot. Res. **37**, 688–716 (2018)
11. Wang, Y., McConachie, D., Berenson, D.: Tracking partially-occluded deformable objects while enforcing geometric constraints. In: 2021 IEEE International Conference on Robotics and Automation (ICRA), pp. 14199–14205. IEEE (2021)
12. Yan, M., Zhu, Y., Jin, N., Bohg, J.: Self-supervised learning of state estimation for manipulating deformable linear objects. IEEE Robot. Autom. Lett. **5**(2), 2372–2379 (2020)
13. Caporali, A., Zanella, R., De Gregorio, D., et al.: Ariadne+: deep learning-based augmented framework for the instance segmentation of wires. IEEE Trans. Ind. Inform. (2022)
14. Orlof, J., Nytko, M.: Determination of radial segmentation of point clouds using KD trees with the algorithm rejecting subtrees. Symmetry **11**(12), 1451 (2019)
15. Xu, H., Gossett, N., Chen, B.: Knowledge and heuristic-based modeling of laser-scanned trees. ACM Trans. Graph. (TOG) **26**(4), 19-es (2007)
16. Yao, G., Saltus, R., Dani, A.P.: Shape estimation for elongated deformable object using B-spline chained multiple random matrices model. Int. J. Intell. Robot. Appl. **4**(4), 429–440 (2020). https://doi.org/10.1007/s41315-020-00149-w
17. Tsuchie, S., Okamoto, K.: High-quality quadratic curve fitting for scanned data of styling design. Comput. Aided Des. **71**, 39–50 (2016)

Jacobian Estimation with Adaptive Kalman Filter for Uncalibrated Visual Servoing

Jiangping Wang[1], Zhaoxu Zhang[2], Shirong Liu[2(✉)], and Wei Song[1]

[1] Intelligent Robotic Research Center, Zhejiang Lab, Hangzhou, China
wangjiangping@zhejianglab.com
[2] School of Automation, Hangzhou Dianzi University, Hangzhou, China
liushirong@hdu.edu.cn

Abstract. An uncalibrated visual servo method based on Jacobian estimation with adaptive Kalman filter (AKF) is proposed in this paper. With less or no priori knowledge of the parameters of robotic manipulator and camera, the presented method introduces the projective Jacobian matrix estimated by an adaptive Kalman filter for noise covariance recursive estimation. By doing this, the Jacobian estimation adaptability can be greatly improved to achieve better tracking performance in UVS system. Finally, the simulation experiments are performed to evaluate the performance of the proposed method, indicating better performance compared with state-of-the-art UVS methods using standard Kalman filter (SKF).

Keywords: Uncalibrated visual servoing · Jacobian estimation · Adaptive Kalman filter

1 Introduction

Visual servoing (VS) is an approach to control the motion of a robot from the feedback of vision system, which is regarded as the basis of localization and recognition [1]. Classical robotic visual servoing methods rely heavily on the precision of calibrations of manipulator and camera [2]. Therefore, the visual servoing system should be recalibrated when the hand/eye relationship changed in robotic workspace. The inconvenience promotes the extensive research of uncalibrated visual servoing (UVS) in recent years.

In uncalibrated scenario, Image Based Uncalibrated Visual Servoing (IBUVS) is one of the mainstream strategies. However, a sufficiently large set of image features are need for hight accuracy and versatility, which will increase the size of Jacobian matrix to be estimated in IBUVS system. In [3], a novel visual servo strategy based on projection homography matrix is presented for a wheeled

Supported by China Postdoctoral Project (No. 2021M692960).

mobile robot. Furthermore, Gong [4] proposed a new approach to online Jacobian estimation, denoted as projective homography based uncalibrated visual servo (PHUVS). It is interesting to note that the size of Jacobian is fixed even if numerous of features are selected.

For UVS, the precision and stability primarily rely on the estimation of Jacobian. Massive estimation algorithms mainly use either nonlinear programming or state estimation. The earliest state estimation employing Kalman filter is by Qian and Su [5]. Specifically, several applications of modified Kalman filter could be used to estimate the Jacobian based on Qian and Su. In [6–8], the principle of standard Kalman filter (SKF) and the impact of estimation errors are analyzed to present the AKF principle and recursion formulas.

Various kinds of Jacobian matrices have been discussed in uncalibrated scenarios such as interaction matrix and image Jacobian matrix. Gong's work is very close to our research topic, where they mainly focus on the proposition of a novel method based on projective homography. However, a rigorous and sufficient online estimation algorithm has not been explored under the condition that the noise statistical characteristics are unknown. In this paper, we introduce the projection Jacobian matrix estimated by the adaptive Kalman filter to estimate the noise covariance recursively, which can obtain better tracking performance with less prior knowledge or without knowing the parameters of the robot and camera.

The major contributions of this paper are described as follows. Firstly, without camera parameters, hand/eye calibration and noise statistical characteristics, we conduct a updating method to estimate the noise covariance matrices. Secondly, the gain adaptive Kalman filter is applied for Jacobian estimation, where the gain matrix is related to the noise covariance by using covariance recursive estimation for achieving better tracking performance.

2   Theoretical Background

The block diagram of our UVS system is shown in Fig. 1. As mentioned, the projective Jacobian can be described as a mapping matrix between the error and camera velocity. In this diagram, Jacobian estimation is done with AKF algorithm instead of SKF one, which has two input vectors: end-effector velocity **V** and derivative of error matrix. And $\mathbf{J_E}$ refers to the estimated Jacobian.

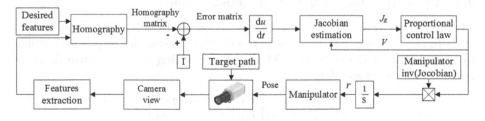

Fig. 1. System block diagram of our UVS system.

2.1   Geometry of Homography

Consider a point P extracted from the target presented in Fig. 2. P has two Euclidean coordinates $\mathbf{P_{C1}} = [X_1, Y_1, Z_1]^T$, $\mathbf{P_{C2}} = [X_2, Y_2, Z_2]^T$ in current and desired camera frame $\Re^1$ and $\Re^2$, respectively. The relationship between $\mathbf{P_{C1}}$ and $\mathbf{P_{C2}}$ can be expressed as:

$$\mathbf{P_{C1}} = \mathbf{R}\mathbf{P_{C2}} + \mathbf{t} \tag{1}$$

where $\mathbf{t} = [t_1, t_2, t_3]^T$ is the translation matrix from $\Re^1$ to $\Re^2$, and $\mathbf{R} \in \mathbb{SO}(3)$ is the rotation matrix of $\Re^2$ with respect to $\Re^1$. Thus, we have two normalized coordinates:

$$\mathbf{P_1} = \mathbf{P_{C1}}/Z_1, \mathbf{P_2} = \mathbf{P_{C2}}/Z_2 \tag{2}$$

As shown in Fig. 2, d_2 is the distance between π and the center of projection, $\mathbf{m}$ is the normal vector of plane π with length $\|\mathbf{m}\| = \sqrt{\mathbf{m}^T\mathbf{m}} = 1/d_2$, which also means $\mathbf{m}^T\mathbf{P_{C2}} = 1$. By substituting (2) and $\mathbf{m}^T\mathbf{P_{C2}} = 1$ into (1), we can obtain:

$$\mathbf{P_1} = \alpha(\mathbf{R} + \mathbf{t}\mathbf{m}^T)\mathbf{P_2} \tag{3}$$

where $\alpha = Z_2/Z_1$ is the depth ratio. And the Euclidean homography matrix can be expressed as:

$$\mathbf{H_E} = \mathbf{R} + \mathbf{t}\mathbf{m}^T \tag{4}$$

Let $\mathbf{p_1} = [u_1, v_1, 1]^T$ and $\mathbf{p_2} = [u_2, v_2, 1]^T$ be two image coordinates of current and reference camera, respectively. Suppose $\mathbf{K} \in \mathbb{R}^{3\times3}$ is the camera calibration matrix, thus

$$\mathbf{p_1} = \mathbf{K}\mathbf{P_1}, \mathbf{p_2} = \mathbf{K}\mathbf{P_2} \tag{5}$$

By using (3) and (5), we have:

$$\mathbf{p_1} = \alpha\mathbf{K}\mathbf{H_E}\mathbf{K}^{-1}\mathbf{p_2} \tag{6}$$

Accordingly, the projective homography matrix $\mathbf{H}$ can be denoted as:

$$\mathbf{H} = \mathbf{K}\mathbf{H_E}\mathbf{K}^{-1} \tag{7}$$

2.2   Projective Jacobian Matrix Construction

The aim of VS is to make $\Re^1$ coincide with $\Re^2$ if and only if $\mathbf{R}$ is equal to an identify matrix $\mathbf{I} \in \mathbb{I}^{3\times3}$, and $\mathbf{t}$ belongs to $\mathbb{O}^{3\times1}$. It means that $\mathbf{H_E}$ is isomorphic to $\mathbf{I}$ [4]. As the similarity between $\mathbf{H}$ and $\mathbf{H_E}$ according to (7), an error function can be constructed as follow:

$$\mathbf{E} = \mathbf{I} - \mathbf{H} = \begin{bmatrix} \mathbf{E_1} \\ \mathbf{E_2} \\ \mathbf{E_3} \end{bmatrix} = \begin{bmatrix} e_1 & e_2 & e_3 \\ e_4 & e_5 & e_6 \\ e_7 & e_8 & e_9 \end{bmatrix} \tag{8}$$

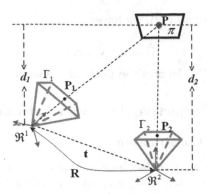

Fig. 2. Geometry of homography exhibiting two cameras with associated coordinate systems.

If $\mathbf{E} = \mathbb{O}^{3\times3}$, then $\mathbf{H}$ will converge to $\mathbf{I}$. Hence, the error function can be chosen as the objective function. By using (4), (7) and (8), $\mathbf{E}$ can be written as:

$$\mathbf{E} = \mathbf{I} - \mathbf{K}(\mathbf{R} + \mathbf{t}\mathbf{m}^T)\mathbf{K}^{-1} \tag{9}$$

By the derivative of (9), the following relationship are obtained:

$$\dot{\mathbf{E}} = -\mathbf{K}(\mathbf{S}\mathbf{K}^{-1}\mathbf{E} - (\mathbf{S} + \nu\mathbf{m}^T)\mathbf{K}^{-1}) \tag{10}$$

where $\nu \in \mathbb{R}^{3\times1}$ refers to the translation velocity of the camera, and $\mathbf{S}$ denotes a skew-symmetric matrix with the following form for three-dimensional cases

$$\mathbf{S} = \begin{bmatrix} 0 & -\omega_z & \omega_y \\ \omega_z & 0 & -\omega_x \\ -\omega_y & \omega_x & 0 \end{bmatrix} \tag{11}$$

Based on (8), we define an error matrix $\mathbf{G} = [\mathbf{E_1} \quad \mathbf{E_2} \quad \mathbf{F_3}]^T$. By matching the corresponding elements in left and right of (10), we can achieve an expression that relate the derivative of $\mathbf{G}$ and the camera velocity:

$$\dot{\mathbf{G}} = \mathbf{J_C}[\mathbf{v_c}, \omega_c]^T \tag{12}$$

where $\mathbf{J_C} \in \mathbb{R}^{9\times6}$ refers to the Jacobian matrix, $[\mathbf{v_c}, \omega_c]^T \in \mathbb{R}^{6\times1}$ denotes the camera velocity.

For eye-in-hand tracking system, the Jacobian matrix between camera velocity and end-effector velocity should also be considered in UVS system, which has the following relation:

$$[\mathbf{v_c}, \omega_c]^T = \mathbf{J_r}[\mathbf{v_r}, \omega_r]^T \tag{13}$$

where $\mathbf{J_r} \in \mathbb{R}^{6\times6}$ represents the hand-eye Jacobian, and $[\mathbf{v_r}, \omega_r]^T \in \mathbb{R}^{6\times1}$ denotes the end-effector velocity.

By insertion of (13) into (12), we have:

$$\dot{\mathbf{G}} = \mathbf{J_P}[\mathbf{v_r}, \omega_r]^T \tag{14}$$

where $\mathbf{J_P} = \mathbf{J_C J_r} \in \mathbb{R}^{9 \times 6}$ denotes the projective Jacobian.

3 AKF Based Projective Jacobian Estimation

3.1 Linear System Construction

It is obvious that the projective Jacobian matrix in (14) contains some elements that are difficult to get, such as d_2 and $\mathbf{m}$. According to [5], the elements of Jacobian can be regarded as states of a linear system. Thus, a linear system will be constructed in this part.

Let $\mathbf{r} = [r_1 \cdots r_n]_{n=6}^T$ represent the coordinates of end-effector in robotic workspace, then the relation of $\dot{\mathbf{G}}$ and $\dot{\mathbf{r}}$ can be described as a linear discrete equation:

$$\mathbf{G_{k+1}} - \mathbf{G_k} = \mathbf{J_P}(\mathbf{r}) \Delta \mathbf{r_k} \tag{15}$$

where $\Delta \mathbf{r_k}$ refers to the change of the coordinates of end-effector and k is iteration. Thus, $J_P(r)$ can be written as:

$$\mathbf{J_P}(\mathbf{r}) = \frac{\partial \mathbf{G}}{\partial \mathbf{r}} = \begin{bmatrix} \frac{\partial G_1}{\partial r_1} & \cdots & \frac{\partial G_1}{\partial r_6} \\ \vdots & \vdots & \vdots \\ \frac{\partial G_9}{\partial r_1} & \cdots & \frac{\partial G_9}{\partial r_6} \end{bmatrix}_{9 \times 6}$$

Based on (15), we can obtain a linear discrete system:

$$\begin{cases} \mathbf{x}_{k+1} = \mathbf{x}_k + \mathbf{w}'_k \\ \mathbf{z}_k = \mathbf{C}_k \mathbf{x}_k + \mathbf{v}'_k \end{cases} \tag{16}$$

where $\mathbf{z}_k \in \mathbb{R}^{9 \times 1}$ refers to the measurement vector. $\mathbf{w}'_k$ and $\mathbf{v}'_k$ are process and measurement noise matrix, which satisfy $E[\mathbf{w}'_k] = \mathbf{u}_k$ and $E[\mathbf{v}'_k] = \mathbf{h}_k$ respectively. Supposing that $\mathbf{W} \in \mathbb{R}^{54 \times 54}$ and $\mathbf{V} \in \mathbb{R}^{6 \times 6}$ denote the process and measurement noise covariances matrices, respectively. We have:

$$\begin{cases} E[(\mathbf{w}'_k - \mathbf{u}_k)(\mathbf{w}'_k - \mathbf{u}_k)^T] = \mathbf{W} \\ E[(\mathbf{v}'_k - \mathbf{h}_k)(\mathbf{v}'_k - \mathbf{h}_k)^T] = \mathbf{V} \end{cases} \tag{17}$$

$\mathbf{x}_k \in \mathbb{R}^{54 \times 1}$ represents the system state vector form of elements of $\mathbf{G}$:

$$\mathbf{x}_k = \begin{bmatrix} \frac{\partial G_1}{\partial \mathbf{r}} & \frac{\partial G_2}{\partial \mathbf{r}} & \cdots & \frac{\partial G_9}{\partial \mathbf{r}} \end{bmatrix}^T \tag{18}$$

where:

$$\frac{\partial G_i}{\partial \mathbf{r}} = \begin{bmatrix} \frac{\partial G_i}{\partial r_1} & \frac{\partial G_i}{\partial r_2} & \cdots & \frac{\partial G_i}{\partial r_6} \end{bmatrix}^T, i = 1 \cdots 9$$

And $\mathbf{C}_k \in \mathbb{R}^{9 \times 54}$ denotes the observation matrix composed of $\Delta \mathbf{r}_k$:

$$\mathbf{C}_k = \begin{bmatrix} \Delta \mathbf{r}_k^T & \cdots & 0 \\ \vdots & \vdots & \vdots \\ 0 & \cdots & \Delta \mathbf{r}_k^T \end{bmatrix}_{9 \times 54}$$

Finally, according to the above equations, (16) can be written as:

$$\begin{cases} \mathbf{x}_{k+1} = \mathbf{x}_k + \mathbf{u}_k + \mathbf{w}_k \\ \mathbf{z}_k = \mathbf{C}_k \mathbf{x}_k + \mathbf{h}_k + \mathbf{v}_k \end{cases} \tag{19}$$

where $\mathbf{w}_k$ and $\mathbf{v}_k$ are uncorrelated Gaussian white noise, which satisfy $\mathbf{w}_k \sim N(0, \mathbf{W}), \mathbf{v}_k \sim N(0, \mathbf{V})$ respectively.

3.2 Jacobian Estimation with AKF Using Recursive Estimation

System modeling error, image noise and features extraction error are usually unavoidable in UVS system. What's more, the noise statical characteristics are uncertainty or partially uncertainty in actual UVS system [7]. As the inconformity between actual statistical characteristics and given ones, a time-varying noise estimator is utilized in this work to attain the estimated values of the mean and covariance of process and measurement noises. The estimator uses the recursive estimation to adjust the Kalman gain for achieving better tracking performance.

Based on standard Kalman filter, the prediction and estimation of $\mathbf{x}_k$ are expressed as:

$$\begin{cases} \mathbf{x}_k^p = \mathbf{x}_{k-1}^e + \mathbf{u}_k \\ \mathbf{x}_k^e = \mathbf{x}_k^p + \mathbf{K_g} \tau \end{cases} \tag{20}$$

where $\mathbf{K_g}$ is the Kalman gain and τ represents the residual error vector:

$$\tau = \mathbf{z}_k - \mathbf{C}_k \mathbf{x}_k^p - \mathbf{h}_k \tag{21}$$

Based on (19) and (20) and (21), we can obtain:

$$E[\tau \tau^T] = \mathbf{L}_k + \mathbf{V}_k \tag{22}$$

where $\mathbf{L}_k = \mathbf{C}_k \mathbf{P}_k^p \mathbf{C}_k^T$ denotes the innovation matrix, and $\mathbf{P}_k^p$ represents the prediction of the state estimation error covariance matrix defined in Algorithm 1. The measurement noise can be written in the form of recursive estimation:

$$\mathbf{V}_k = (k-1)/k \mathbf{V}_{k-1} + 1/k \tau_k \tau_k^T - \Delta \mathbf{L}_k \tag{23}$$

Proof: The proof of (23) is shown in Appendix A.

Defined as $\gamma = (k-1)/k$, the Jacobian estimation with AKF algorithm can be concluded as Algorithm 1.

Algorithm 1: Jacobian matrix estimated by AKF

Given : $\mathbf{J}_P \in \mathbb{R}^{9 \times 6}; \mathbf{r} \in \mathbb{R}^{6 \times 1}; \mathbf{P} \in \mathbb{R}^{54 \times 54}; \mathbf{x}_k^e \leftarrow \mathbf{J}_i$

for $k = 1;\ k < iterations;\ k + +$ **do**

    Building measurement matrix $\mathbf{C}_k$ using $\triangle \mathbf{r}_k$;

    Recursive estimation:

        $\mathbf{h}_k = \gamma \mathbf{h}_{k-1} + (1 - \gamma)(\mathbf{z}_k - \mathbf{C}_k \mathbf{x}_k^p)$;

        $\mathbf{u}_k = \gamma \mathbf{u}_{k-1} + (1 - \gamma)(\mathbf{x}_k^e - \mathbf{x}_{k-1}^e)$;

        $\mathbf{W}_k = \gamma \mathbf{W}_{k-1} + (1 - \gamma)(\mathbf{K_g} \tau_k \tau_k^T \mathbf{K}_g^T + \Delta \mathbf{P}_k^e)$;

        $\mathbf{V}_k = (k - 1)/k \mathbf{V}_{k-1} + 1/k \tau_k \tau_k^T - \Delta \mathbf{L}_k$;

    Prediction cycle $\mathbf{x}_k^p = \mathbf{x}_{k-1}^e + \mathbf{u}_k$;

                 $\mathbf{P}_k^p = \mathbf{P}_{k-1}^e + \mathbf{W}$;

    Kalman gain $\mathbf{K_g} = \mathbf{P}_k^p \mathbf{C}_k^T (\mathbf{C}_k \mathbf{P}_k^p \mathbf{C}_k^T + \mathbf{V}_k)^{-1}$;

    Correction cycle $\mathbf{P}_k^e = (\mathbf{I} - \mathbf{K_g} \mathbf{C_k}) \mathbf{P}_k^p$;

                 $\mathbf{x}_k^e = \mathbf{x}_k^p + \mathbf{K_g} \tau$;

    Transform system state $\mathbf{x}_k^e$ to $\mathbf{J}_{Pk}$;

    Proportional control law

    $\triangle \mathbf{r}_k = -\mu (\mathbf{J}_{Pk}^T \mathbf{J}_{Pk})^{-1} \mathbf{J}_{Pk}^T (\mathbf{G}_k + \partial \mathbf{G}_k / \partial k \triangle k)$

end

Please note that $\mathbf{J}_i$ is the initial Jacobian acquired by orthogonal motions, and $\leftarrow$ represents the vector transformation. $\mathbf{P}_k^e$, $\mathbf{P}_k^p$ denote the estimation and prediction of state estimation error covariance matrix $\mathbf{P}_k$, respectively. μ is a positive factor.

4   Simulations and Analysis

In this section, AKF and SKF will be simulated and performed with PUMA560 that is a camera-mounted 6-DOF robotic arm demonstrated as Fig. 3a. And four features will be selected from the considered target illustrated in Fig. 3b. IBUVS and PHUVS will be used in UVS system to evaluate the performance of the proposed method comparing with IBVS.

4.1   Jacobian Estimation Under Static Positioning

This section is mainly devoted to test the performance of AKF applied in PHUVS and IBUVS. For static positioning, two kinds of motions demonstrated in Fig. 4 are used to compute position error, orientation error and image error. To reflect the performance of AKF objectively, the mean and covariance of process and measurement noises are set to random values. Figure 5 shows the end-effector velocity of PHUVS system under SKF and AKF.

It can be inferred that the end-effector velocity trajectory under AKF does not fluctuate as obvious as that of SKF. The main reason is that the AKF gain depends on the real-time estimation of measurement noise covariance and the innovation matrix concluded from Algorithm 1. If the tracking effect is not

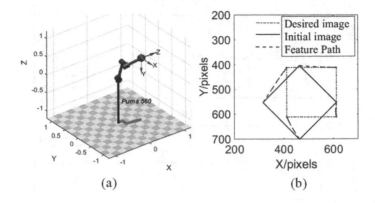

Fig. 3. (a) Robotic arm workspace. (b) Field of view and feature points trajectory.

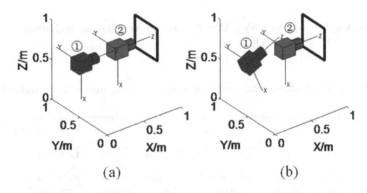

Fig. 4. Static positioning. Camera 1 is the initial position while camera 2 is the desired one. (a) Translation along x-axis. (b)Translation along x, y-axis.

satisfied, then the gain will not converge to a small number illustrated in Fig. 6. The performance of different VS methods used in VS system are also studied in this part. Effectivenesses of the PHUVS system based on AKF can be seen from these figures and results of the static positioning summarized in Table 1.

4.2   Jacobian Estimation Under Dynamic Tracking

To compare the effectiveness of UVS system for dynamic tracking [9], Mean-Square Error (MSE) and Jerk of robot joint value are introduced as the evaluation index in this paper. Besides, for the sake of reflecting the performance of each method objectively, 20 experiments are performed by different visual servo control strategies.

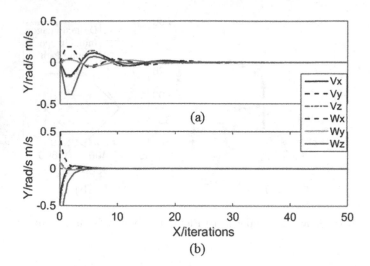

Fig. 5. $\mathbf{V}x, \mathbf{V}y, \mathbf{V}z$ and $\mathbf{W}x, \mathbf{W}y, \mathbf{W}z$ denote the translation and rotation velocity, respectively. (a) SKF. (b) AKF.

Table 1. Controller performance of static tracking under AKF and SKF

Task	Method	Standard Kalman filter			Adaptive Kalman filter		
		Position error	Orientation error	Image error	Position error	Orientation error	Image error
Translation along x-axis	IBUVS	0.2306	1.749×10^{-14}	1.2106	0.1508	1.679×10^{-15}	0.7736
	PHUVS	0.2197	8.679×10^{-15}	1.0023	0.1505	9.264×10^{-16}	0.6518
Translation and rotation	IBUVS	0.3468	10.648×10^{-8}	0.9787	0.2434	7.705×10^{-8}	0.554
	PHUVS	0.2961	9.467×10^{-8}	0.9106	0.2395	5.342×10^{-8}	0.2342

- MSE: Average closeness of current features and reference features can be measured by mean square error:

$$MSE = \frac{1}{M}\frac{1}{S}\sum_{i=1}^{M}\sum_{j=1}^{S} \| \triangle f_{i,j} \| \tag{24}$$

- Jerk: An abrupt change in the torque results in angular Jerk reflecting the rate of change of acceleration, the equation of which can be denoted as follows:

$$Jerk = \frac{1}{M-2}\frac{1}{S}\sum_{i=3}^{M}\sum_{j=1}^{S} \| \theta'''_{i,j} - \theta'''_{i-1,j} \| \tag{25}$$

where M is the number of iterations, $\triangle f$ refers to the features error, and θ denotes the joints angle of 6-DOF arm.

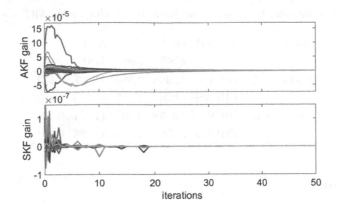

Fig. 6. The curves of the gain changes over time for AKF (Top) and SKF (Bottom). These two Kalman gains satisfy $\mathbf{K_g} \in \mathbb{R}^{54 \times 9}$, thus 54×9 curves included in each figure.

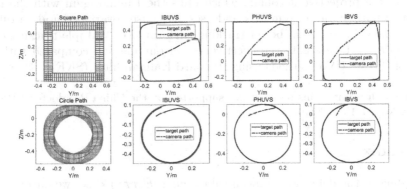

Fig. 7. Two different paths generated by a square target and tracked under IBUVS, PHUVS and IBVS by using AKF. The camera travels a distance of around 2.5 m and 2.4 m when the target moves along square line (Top) and circle line (Bottom), respectively.

In this section, different methods will be compared through dynamic tracking experiments. Figure 7 depicts the tracking results of different paths generated by a square target, showing that the camera trajectory by the PHUVS method with AKF in Cartesian space is optimal. This can also be further verified by the experimental results in Table 2. For different target paths, AKF has lower MSE and Jerk than SKF, especially when the target moves along a square path that has a sudden change of direction.

Table 2. Controller performance of dynamic tracking under AKF and SKF

Task	Method	SKF		AKF	
		MSE	*Jerk*	*MSE*	*Jerk*
Circle path	IBUVS	34.468	2.365	31.776	1.631
	PHUVS	10.267	1.915	7.6279	1.482
Square path	IBUVS	130.58	0.301	117.37	0.302
	PHUVS	26.561	0.185	15.186	0.201

5   Conclusions

UVS provides a method to control the motion of a robot by the error signals from the camera with appropriate control law. However, a rigorous and sufficient online estimation algorithm has not been explored under the condition that the noise statistical characteristics are unknown. In this paper, we use the AKF to estimate the projective Jacobian, which links the Kalman gain with the measurement noise covariance matrix and uses the noise covariance update rule to change the gain to obtain better tracking performance. Multiple tracking cases are performed to evaluate the effectiveness of our method compared with the state-of-the-art UVS methods using standard Kalman filter (SKF).

Acknowledgment. This research was supported by the China Postdoctoral Project (Grant No. 2021M692960).

Appendix

According to the definition of mean value, when $E(\tau\tau^T) < \infty$, we have:

$$\mathbf{E}_k(\tau\tau^T) = \lim_{k \to \infty} \frac{1}{k} \sum_{i=0}^{k} \tau_i \tau_i^T \tag{26}$$

Equation (26) can be transformed into

$$E_k(\tau\tau^T) = \frac{1}{k}\left(\sum_{i=0}^{k-1} \tau_i \tau_i^T + \tau_k \tau_k^T\right)$$
$$= 1/k((k-1)E_{k-1}(\tau\tau^T) + \tau_k \tau_k^T) \tag{27}$$

According to (21), we have:

$$E_{k-1}[\tau\tau^T] = \mathbf{C}_{k-1}\mathbf{P}_{k-1}^p\mathbf{C}_{k-1}^T + \mathbf{V}_{k-1} \tag{28}$$

Substituting (28) into (27), $E_k(\tau\tau^T)$ will be

$$(k+1)/k(\mathbf{C}_{k-1}\mathbf{P}_{k-1}^p\mathbf{C}_{k-1}^T + \mathbf{V}_{k-1}) + 1/k\tau_k \tau_k^T \tag{29}$$

Define $\mathbf{L}_k = \mathbf{C}_k \mathbf{P}_k^p \mathbf{C}_k^T$, then we will have:

$$\mathbf{L}_k + \mathbf{V}_k = \mathbf{L}_{k-1} - 1/k\mathbf{L}_{k-1} + (k-1)/k\mathbf{V}_{k-1} + 1/k\tau_k\tau_k^T \tag{30}$$

Finally, (30) can be written as:

$$\mathbf{V}_k = (k+1)/k\mathbf{V}_{k-1} + 1/k\tau_k\tau_k^T - \Delta\mathbf{L}_k - 1/k\mathbf{L}_{k-1} \tag{31}$$

With the increase of time, $\mathbf{V}_k$ depends on $\mathbf{V}_{k-1}$ much more than $\mathbf{L}_{k-1}$, the estimator of $\mathbf{V}_k$ can be rewritten as:

$$\mathbf{V}_k = (k-1)/k\mathbf{V}_{k-1} + 1/k\tau_k\tau_k^T - \Delta\mathbf{L}_k \tag{32}$$

References

1. Heshmati-Alamdari, S., Karras, G.C., Eqtami, A., et al.: A robust self triggered image based visual servo model predictive control scheme for small autonomous robots. In: Proceedings of the IEEE/RSJ International Conference on Intelligent Robots and Systems, pp. 5492–5497 (2015)
2. Pari, L., Angel, L., Traslosheros, A.: Uncalibrated visual servo using the fundamental matrix. Robot. Auton. Syst. **57**(1), 1–10 (2009)
3. Li, B., Fang, Y., Zhang, X.: Projection homography based uncalibrated visual servo of wheeled mobile robots. In: Proceedings of the IEEE Conference on Decision and Control, pp. 2167–2172 (2014)
4. Gong, Z., Tao, B., Yang, H.: An uncalibrated visual servo method based on projective homography. IEEE Trans. Autom. Sci. Eng. **15**(2), 806–817 (2018)
5. Qian, J., Su, J.: Online estimation of image Jacobian matrix by Kalman-Bucy filter for uncalibrated stereo vision feedback. In: Proceedings of the IEEE International Conference on Robotics and Automation, pp. 562–567 (2002)
6. Huang, Y., Zhang, Y., Wu, Z., et al.: A novel adaptive Kalman filter with inaccurate process and measurement noise covariance matrices. IEEE Trans. Autom. Control **63**(2), 594–601 (2017)
7. Sun, J., Xu, X., Liu, Y., et al.: FOG random drift signal denoising based on the improved AR model and modified Sage-Husa adaptive Kalman filter. Sensors **16**(7), 1073–1091 (2016)
8. Feng, B., Fu, M., Ma, H., et al.: Kalman filter with recursive covariance estimation-sequentially estimating process noise covariance. IEEE Trans. Ind. Electron. **61**(11), 6253–6263 (2014)
9. Fu, Q., Zhang, Z., Shi, J., et al.: Uncalibrated visual servo with obstacle avoidance using SQP method. In: Proceedings of the IEEE International Conference on Robotics and Automation, pp. 2031–2036 (2009)

Design of Wireless Synchronous sEMG Information Acquisition System

Nengyuan Cheng, Hongyu Yang, Hui Chang, Yifan Liu, Ruikai Cao, and Honghai Liu[✉]

State Key Laboratory of Robotics and System, Harbin Institute of Technology, Shenzhen, China
Honghai.liu@icloud.com

Abstract. The sEMG (surface electromyogram signal) reflects the degree of muscle activity, which contains a large amount of motion information about the human body. It has important research significance and application value in sports science, rehabilitation medicine, and so on. There are more and more products related to sEMG acquisition, which are mainly divided into wired and wireless. Compared with wired sEMG acquisition equipment, wireless sEMG acquisition equipment can free the subjects from the shackles of connecting lines and space, so it is more concerned by researchers. However, due to the independence among the wireless acquisition modules, synchronization time errors between each module inevitably occur, which will bring difficulties to the subsequent data analysis. To solve this problem, a synchronized four-channel sEMG data acquisition system is designed in this paper. The experimental results show that the synchronization time errors among the 7 modules are almost controlled below 30 us, which are better than similar products in the market (about 300 us), and it has high SNR (Signal Noise Ratio), so the effective data collected can be used for sEMG signal analysis and processing.

Keywords: sEMG · Synchronous · Wireless

1 Introduction

1.1 The Overview of sEMG

The sEMG is the spatiotemporal synthesis of action potentials generated at the skin surface during muscle contraction [7]. It is a one-dimensional temporal signal of voltage obtained by directing, amplifying, recording, and displaying bioelectric changes generated by single or multiple muscle cells or multiple muscle cells [2]. The frequency of its distribution is mainly concentrated 500 Hz and the amplitude of sEMG ranges from 0.01–10 mV [6]. When the body performs a set of actions, the corresponding muscle groups are stimulated by nerves and then contract. During the contraction period, the surface of the muscle cell is accompanied by a change in potential, generating sEMG signals. Since sEMG

H. Liu et al. (Eds.): ICIRA 2022, LNAI 13458, pp. 284–293, 2022.
https://doi.org/10.1007/978-3-031-13841-6_27

signals reflect changes in the contraction of the corresponding muscle groups, different muscle groups involved in different actions and different levels of health produce different sEMG signals. Hence, sEMG is one of the most significant biomedical signals for human behavior perception and has a great potential for application in neural control systems [3]. Besides, sEMG signals play an important role in action recognition, fatigue monitoring, and disease diagnosis [6,10].

1.2   The Overview of Wireless Synchronization

Synchronization between the various information acquisition modules within the system is a key technology for wireless sEMG acquisition and is the basis for subsequent data analysis. There are three main sources of synchronization error between devices. As shown in Fig. 1 (left), the first type of synchronization error is caused by the propagation of instruction. It means that when the server sends an instruction, the time when each acquisition module as a client receives the instruction is different. As shown in Fig. 1 (right),the second type of synchronization error is caused by minor differences between modules.It means that each acquisition module relies on the local crystal oscillator for timing, and there is inevitably a slight clock drift between each other. Even if propagation is synchronous, the time delay will also gradually increase, thus affecting the accuracy of data synchronization. As Fig. 3 shows, the third type of synchronization error is caused by packet loss. It means that during the data transmission process, the data packets of each module are lost at different times, resulting in the misalignment of data [2].

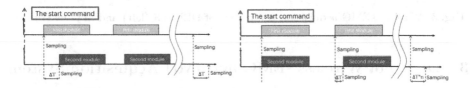

Fig. 1. Error due to propagation delay (left), error due to crystal difference (right)

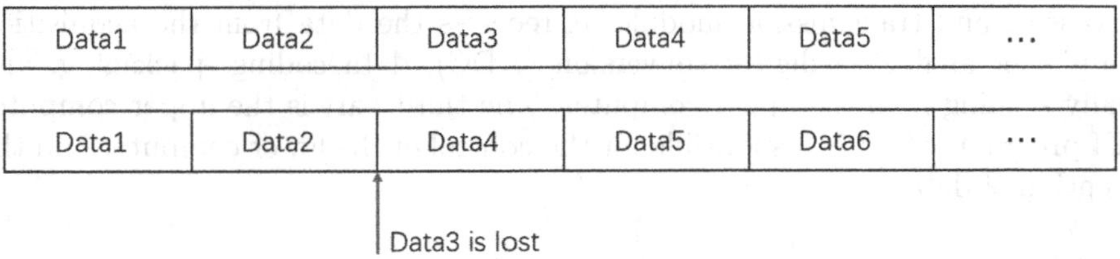

Data1	Data2	Data3	Data4	Data5	...

Data1	Data2	Data4	Data5	Data6	...

Data3 is lost

Fig. 2. Data alignment errors due to packet loss.

2   Related Works

With the development of wireless technology and the improvement of wireless protocols, multi-channel wireless sEMG acquisition devices are gradually available in the world. Wireless sEMG acquisition devices can free subjects from the constraints of acquisition lines and space, so the application scenarios have been greatly expanded. At present, the wireless surface sEMG acquisition devices on the market are mainly based on ZigBee, Bluetooth, WIFI, and some private protocols. Trigno (Fig. 1) of Delsys is based on WIFI or Bluetooth, which achieves a synchronization accuracy about 500 us and can collect data within 40 m. MYON 320 (Fig. 1) system is based on its private protocol, setting each device to communicate with the server at different frequencies to achieve a synchronization effect of less than 250 us. With a one-way broadcast and linear least-squares regression algorithm, Li et al. [2] achieved a synchronization accuracy of 500 us. Rong Zhou et al. [10] designed a wireless four-channel EMG acquisition device based on arduino.

Fig. 3. Wireless sEMG acquisition equipment of DELSYS (left) and MYON (right)

3   Design of Wireless sEMG and IMU Acquisition System

3.1   Overall System Architecture

As shown in Fig. 4, the wireless sEMG acquisition system consists of three parts. The first part consists of electrodes and signal lines. The second part is the data processing and transmission module. It receives the data from the acquisition module for analog to digital conversion (ADC), data coding, packaging, and finally sending it to the upper computer. The third part is the upper computer GUI program, which is responsible for the control of the lower computer and the reception of data.

3.2   Electrode Design

The electrodes are responsible for obtaining the sEMG signal, and they can be categorized into the dry electrode and the wet electrode. The contact resistance

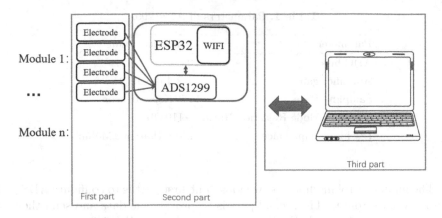

Fig. 4. The main frame of the system

of the wet electrode is usually several kilo-ohms, while the dry electrode relies on pressure and electrode synapse to ensure good contact with the skin, but the contact resistance is still higher than that of the wet electrode. The low contact resistance will make the signal energy consumed at the contact between electrode and skin low, which means the signal has a high SNR. To obtain high-quality signals, the wet electrodes are selected.

In terms of signal input mode, sEMG signal acquisition can be divided into single-ended input mode and differential input mode. Single-ended input mode is an absolute acquisition mode of sEMG signal amplitude, which inevitably retains the common-mode signal during the human muscle movement. Differential input mode is a differential amplification of the voltage between two differential electrodes, which largely suppresses common-mode interference such as power frequency interference and drift, so the differential input mode is selected [4].

3.3   Hardware Design

sEMG Collection Part. The ADS1299 is selected as the acquisition chip for sEMG signals in this system. The front-end of this chip integrates a low-noise programmable gain amplifier (PGA) and analog-to-digital conversion (ADC), which is especially suitable for the acquisition of electrophysiological signals and is widely used. It is used to collect ECG, sEMG, and EEG signals, and the key parameters of the ADS1299 are shown in the Table 1.

Main Control Module Design. ESP32-wroom32u is chosen as the main control chip, which is the WiFi chip developed by Lexin. The esp32-wroom32u is equipped with an Xtensa dual-core 32-bit processor that supports a maximum frequency of 240 MHz. It also supports 801.11b/g/n, with 801.11 n data rates up to 150 Mbps. [1].

Table 1. Parameters of ADS1299.

Parameter	Numerical value
ADC bits	24
Amplifier gain	1 2 4 6 8 12 24
Sampling Rate	250 Ksps–16 ksps
Common Mode Rejection Ratio	−110 Db
DC input impedance	More than 500 Mohm

The main control module has two jobs. The first part is to configure ADS1299 and read data from it. The second part is to process the data and send them to the upper computer via WIFI. The communication of ADS1299 needs to occupy a set of SPI and four GPIOs.

Data Transfer Module. Data transmission is realized by the WIFI function of the main control chip ESP32-wroom32u. ESP32 is a professional IoT chip with excellent RF performance. The key problem of a multi-channel wireless myoelectric acquisition device is to realize the synchronicity of data among each acquisition module. And the best solution is to realize one-to-many communication with the help of the UDP (User Datagram Protocol) broadcast function. The synchronization errors come from three aspects, which have been mentioned before. In contrast to the errors due to propagation, errors due to packet loss and clock differences can be programmed to control. So the key to the problem is to minimize the trigger error.

UDP is a connectionless transport protocol that provides a way for applications to send encapsulated IP packets without establishing a connection. Since no connection is established to transmit data, there is no need to maintain the connection state, including the sending and receiving state, so one server can transmit the same message to multiple clients at the same time. The broadcast function of UDP just meets the needs of the one-to-many communication of the system, and minimizes the trigger error. Therefore, in this system, the UDP broadcast function of ESP32 is used to send and receive instructions.

Design of Power Module. The system is powered by a 5 v battery. The power management module adjusts the raw voltage to the voltage required by each chip. The required voltage for this system is +3.3 V, ±2.5 V. 3.3 V is obtained by direct conversion from AMS117, +2.5 V is obtained by conversion using TPS73225, and −2.5 V is first converted to −5 V by TPS60403, and then converted to 2.5 V by TPS72325.

3.4   Program Design

The Design of the Lower Computer. The lower computer is responsible for collecting sEMG data, packaging, and sending to the upper computer. To ensure the stability of data transmission, the main function and data transfer function are configured on different threads.

In order to reduce the error caused by the propagation, the system uses the ayancUDP function. Compared with ordinary UDP, which repeatedly checks whether there are data packets in the loop, this function registers the UDP data reception event as a task, once there is a data packet, the callback function is executed immediately, eliminating the time error caused by cyclically checking data packets.

In order to control the problem because the crystal oscillator of each module has subtle differences, the upper computer will send data acquisition commands at 5 s intervals to ensure that the error will not increase too much.

In order to solve the data misalignment caused by packet loss, the last four bytes of the data are used to count the data packets to obtain the specific time of packet loss, the upper computer can align the data according to these four bytes.

The operation flow of the lower computer is shown in the following Fig. 5. The sampling frequency of the system configuration ADS1299 is 1000 Hz, which satisfies Shannon's sampling law. A transmission is a packet of 10 sampling nodes.

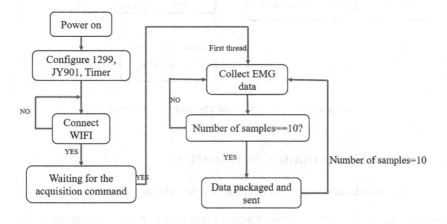

Fig. 5. Lower computer flow chart.

The Design of the Upper Computer. The main function of the upper computer is to process, visualize and store the sEMG data. The upper computer program is designed based on QT, a cross-platform development environment that supports Linux, Windows, and MACos.

The main functions are: 1) sending control instructions to the lower computer; 2) receiving sEMG data from the lower computer; 3) filtering the sEMG data at 50 frequency and displaying the sEMG waveforms on the interface; 4) saving the sEMG data for subsequent analysis.

Figure 6 shows the flow chart of the upper computer. After the program starts, it first displays the graphical interface, initializes the variables, and then establishes multiple UDP threads to listen for UDP packets. Each thread accepts the data of one acquisition module, which ensures the stability of data transmission. The received data is first decoded and then filtered 50 Hz. If the user wants to save the data, the data will be saved in a txt file.

It should be noted that we need to send a collection command every five seconds to align the clock of the lower computer.

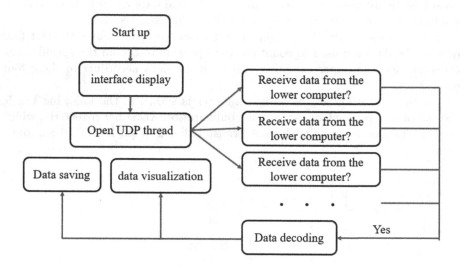

Fig. 6. The flow chart of the upper computer.

4   System Performance Verification

4.1   Synchronization Performance Verification

The experimental scheme of the synchronization accuracy experiment is to perform the pull-up and pull-down of a GPIO pin before and after each sample, and then use the logic analyzer to collect the level change of the pin and output the time difference.

The experiments tested the synchronization performance of 4 modules and 7 modules respectively. The data of 80 s were collected separately, and the synchronization effect is shown in Fig. 7. The synchronization accuracy of 4 modules is slightly better than that of 7 modules, and they both can almost be kept below 30 us, which is better than the synchronization accuracy on the market (around

300 us). It can meet the synchronization requirements of various experiments and it can also help solve the technical problems of wireless synchronization of multi-channel sensing nodes.

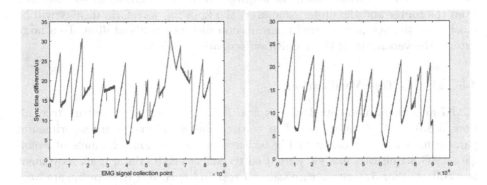

Fig. 7. Synchronization error of four channels (right) and seven channels (left).

4.2 sEMG Performance Test

Signal quality directly affects the results of subsequent data analysis, so SNR analysis of sEMG data is crucial. A pair of sEMG electrodes are placed on the lower arm, and the obvious waveform can be observed by making a fist, extending the index finger, and opening the five fingers, ok gesture, as shown in Fig. 8. The results show that the system has a high SNR.

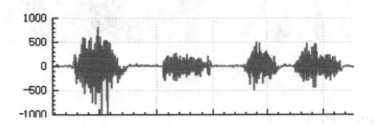

Fig. 8. The waveforms of the four gestures.

4.3 Data Transfer Performance Test

Compared with TCP, UDP is an unstable transmission protocol, so the packet loss rate needs to be tested. The packet loss rate test scheme is to add a counter to both the upper computer and the lower computer and then compare the values of the two counters after a period of time. The test result is that the packet loss rate is 0.01%.

4.4   Transmission Distance Test

The system uses a Xiaomi router as a hotspot. When each acquisition device and the upper computer join the hotspot, a local area network is built. During the experimental process, when the acquisition device is gradually moved away from the router and the upper computer, the knowing waveform display will be stuck, and the actual measured transmission distance is about 40m. To a large extent, the versatility of the acquisition scenario is solved.

4.5   sEMG Test Verification

sEMG and ultrasound signals are typical signal modalities in gesture recognition [5,8,9].So the system uses five gesture classifications as an experimental paradigm, which are shown in Fig. 9. First of all, the four channels of a single sEMG acquisition module were used to collect sEMG data. Each movement was collected for 5 s, with a three-second rest in between. Five movements were grouped together, and a total of 15 groups were performed. 10 groups were randomly selected as the training set, and the remaining 5 groups were used as the test set. Using SVM for classification, the recognition rate is 96%. Then, the two channels of the two modules are placed in the same position for the same process collection and classification, and the final recognition rate is 96%. The experimental results show that the system is effective in synchronous acquisition.

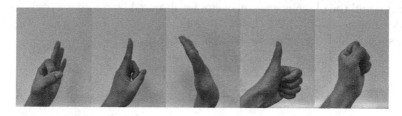

Fig. 9. The five actions used in gesture recognition.

5   Conclucion

This paper mainly designs a four-channel EMG acquisition system. The experimental results show that the synchronization accuracy of the system is much higher than that of similar devices on the market with a synchronization accuracy of 30 us. At the same time, it can meet the needs of data analysis in terms of transmission distance, packet loss rate, signal-to-noise ratio, etc. Finally, the effectiveness of the system is verified in gesture classification.

References

1. Barybin, O., Zaitseva, E., Brazhnyi, V.: Testing the security ESP32 internet of things devices. In: 2019 IEEE International Scientific-Practical Conference Problems of Infocommunications, Science and Technology (PIC S&T), pp. 143–146 (2019). https://doi.org/10.1109/PICST47496.2019.9061269
2. Li, W.: Study on multi-channel wireless sEMG simultaneous acquisition technology. Master's thesis, Zhejiang University (2018)
3. Sheng, Y., Zeng, J., Liu, J., Liu, H.: Metric-based muscle synergy consistency for upper limb motor functions. IEEE Trans. Instrum. Meas. **71**, 1–11 (2022). https://doi.org/10.1109/TIM.2021.3132345
4. Xuhui, W.: Research on high-density EEG/EMG wireless acquisition system
5. Yang, X., Yan, J., Fang, Y., Zhou, D., Liu, H.: Simultaneous prediction of wrist/hand motion via wearable ultrasound sensing. IEEE Trans. Neural Syst. Rehabil. Eng. **28**(4), 970–977 (2020)
6. Yu, Y., Jiang, H., Zhou, Y., Liu, H.: Analysis of stable SEMG features for bilateral upper limb motion. In: 2018 IEEE International Conference on Systems, Man, and Cybernetics (SMC), pp. 1945–1950 (2018). https://doi.org/10.1109/SMC.2018.00336
7. Zhou, Yu., Fang, Y., Zeng, J., Li, K., Liu, H.: A multi-channel EMG-driven FES solution for stroke rehabilitation. In: Chen, Z., Mendes, A., Yan, Y., Chen, S. (eds.) ICIRA 2018. LNCS (LNAI), vol. 10984, pp. 235–243. Springer, Cham (2018). https://doi.org/10.1007/978-3-319-97586-3_21
8. Zeng, J., Zhou, Y., Yang, Y., Yan, J., Liu, H.: Fatigue-sensitivity comparison of sEMG and A-mode ultrasound based hand gesture recognition. IEEE J. Biomed. Health Inform. **26**(4), 1718–1725 (2021)
9. Zeng, J., Zhou, Y., Yang, Y., Wang, J., Liu, H.: Feature fusion of sEMG and ultrasound signals in hand gesture recognition. In: 2020 IEEE International Conference on Systems, Man, and Cybernetics (SMC), pp. 3911–3916. IEEE (2020)
10. Zhou, R., Luo, Q., Feng, X., Li, C.: Design of a wireless multi-channel surface EMG signal acquisition system. In: 2017 3rd IEEE International Conference on Computer and Communications (ICCC), pp. 279–283 (2017). https://doi.org/10.1109/CompComm.2017.8322556

Augmented Graph Attention with Temporal Gradation and Reorganization for Human Motion Prediction

Shaobo Zhang[1], Sheng Liu[1(✉)], Fei Gao[1], and Shengyong Chen[2]

[1] College of Computer Science and Technology, Zhejiang University of Technology, Liuhe Road 288, Hangzhou, China
edliu@zjut.edu.cn
[2] Key Laboratory of Computer Vision and System, College of Computer Science and Engineering, Tianjin University of Technology, Tianjin, China

Abstract. Human motion prediction has progressed leap-forward by propulsion of many prior excellent work since its great significance for the promotion of various artificial intelligence applications. How to extract historical spatio-temporal feature better to reduce the discontinuity and long-term error accumulation of prediction motion are still the main challenge of current literature. In this work, a novel augmented graph attention with temporal gradation and reorganization method is proposed, which combines channel attention with graph attention and temporal convolution to be a integrated block for the first time on human motion prediction. The block learns 'what', 'where' and 'when' while capturing the spatial structure of human skeleton in the channel-spatial axes and temporal information in the sequential dimension, respectively. Furthermore, the mechanism of temporal gradation and reorganization can retain complicated and high dynamic temporal information effectively without selection of convolutional kernel size. Our experiments on Human3.6M datasets show that the proposed network performs higher prediction accuracy compared with state-of-the-art methods.

Keywords: Human motion prediction · Augmented graph attention · Temporal gradation and reorganization

1 Introduction

Perception, recognition and prediction of human motion are very important for robots to contact the outside world and assist human beings. Especially for human motion prediction, it is a fundamental technical support for intelligent robots to

Supported by National Key Research and Development Program of China (No. 2018 YFB1305200) and Science Technology Department of Zhejiang Province (No. LGG1 9F020010).

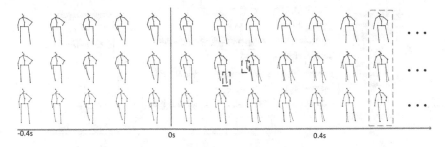

Fig. 1. Comparison of human motion prediction. Ground Truth (first row), predicted results of TIM [14] (middle row), and ours (bottom row) on the walkingdog action of the Human3.6M dataset are shown. The ground truth is also overlaid on the prediction results in gray to compare clearly. Discontinuous predicted joints indicated by the red boxes seriously impact the final accuracy of TIM. And poses in the green boxes show how errors gradually accumulate over time. Our network obviously outperforms TIM.

feedback human behavior in the procedure of human-robot interaction [7]. In addition, the development and application of this technology plays an indispensable role in the fields of autonomous driving [9], public safety [8,16], medical rehabilitation [7], motion detection [12], multimedia application [18] and so on, which must be a major trend in the future research of intelligent robots. However, for non-agent, it is not a simple thing to achieve natural and high-precision human motion prediction. The complexity of human behavior and the flexibility of human body lead to discontinuity and error accumulation of the predicted posture will greatly affect its practical application progress.

In response to these challenges, there have been many excellent preliminary work put forward different solutions. Methods for sequential data modeling is first proposed. RNN [20] and its subsequent LSTM and GRU have natural advantages for temporal information processing. However, high randomness, nonlinearity and uncertainty of human motion make it easy to trigger the error accumulation problem of simple sequential networks.

Furthermore, considering the inherent connection relationship of human body structure, the mathematical model of human skeleton is generally constructed based on the main joints of the human body [10]. Convolutional neural network(CNN) [13] has good spatial structure perception ability for two-dimensional regular data, but it cannot achieve good results usually on topological irregular data such as human skeleton. Graph convolution network (GCN) [19] can well construct and characterize irregular structure datas, the method of modeling human body structure by nodes and graph convolution has been gradually promoted. But the flexibility of human body determines that it is hard to represent local nodes movements by global skeleton modeling.

To tackle the above problems, we present the augmented graph attention with temporal gradation and reorganization method for human motion prediction. We follow the current mainstream ideas to extract the spatio-temporal information of human skeleton sequences. Inspired by the recent popular Transformer methods, which have achieved good performance in various fields, we characterize the spatial

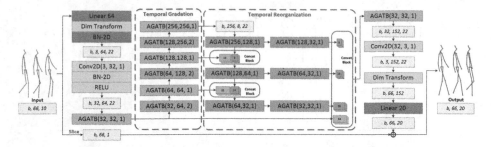

Fig. 2. An instantiation of our proposed augmented graph attention with temporal gradation and reorganization method for human motion prediction on Human3.6M dataset. The network is consisted of two main stages named temporal gradation stage and temporal reorganization stage. The parameters of AGATB represent in-channel, out-channeland convolutional stride, respectively. We set all convolutional kernel size as $(5, 1)$ in AGATB. Number in gray rectangle is the current data format, b presents batch size. $\oplus$ is element-wise addition. The effect of *ConcatBlock* is to concat two-levels or multi-levels features along sequential dimension, and processed by $BN - 2D$ and *RELU* in turn.

information by graph attention. In contrast to [19], the graph constructed based on skeleton joints in our work is regarded as a global connected graph. Moreover, we pay attention on local correlation and symmetry of joints based on the kinematic chain of a body skeleton [17] to fuse the global and local graph attention features. In addition, the difference between action categories is significant, so we introduce channel attention to learn 'what' is hidden in the poses of different actions. Simultaneously, we adopt tcn module [2] to extract temporal information, and combine it with the graph attention enhanced by channel attention to form augmented graph attention with temporal convolution block (AGATB), which better exploits the observable sequential data. Furthermore, we design a temporal gradation and reorganization framework based on the sensitivity of AGATB on temporal information. The temporal features are extracted from the low level to the high level in the gradation stage and recombined in the reorganization stage. It effectively avoids the serious dependence of kernel size of tcn network.

In summary, the main contributions of this paper are as follows:

- We propose an augmented graph attention with temporal convolution block (AGATB), which integrates channel attention into graph attention to form an augmented graph attention, and combines it with temporal convolutional network to simultaneously deal with the spatio-temporal feature representation for human motion prediction.
- We designed a gradaion and reorganization mechanism to deal with temporal information, which can effectively extract the temporal information from low level to high level, and integrate multi-level temporal feature for final prediction.
- Our experiments on the Human3.6M datasets show our network outperforms state-of-the-art (SOTA) methods.

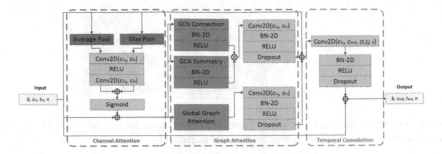

Fig. 3. Network of The Proposed AGATB. It contains channel attention, graph attention and temporal convolution three blocks. ⊕ is element-wise addition and ⊗ means concat operation along channel dimension.

2   Related Work

2.1   RNN Based Human Motion Prediction

Human motion prediction has developed for many years. During the exploration period, methods such as Hidden Markov Models [3] and linear dynamics system [23] are proposed to solve this problem, but these methods often require large amounts of data support, and can only deal with some simple repetitive motions as walking. The wide application of RRN in sequential data processing such as voice recognition [27] and machine translation [25] has inspired many researchers to apply it to the same sequential problem as human motion prediction. Fragkiadaki et al. [5] proposed a encoding-recurrent-decode framework to adopt the RNN to design a nonlinear spatial encoder for human motion prediction. Structural-RNN [11] based on an artificial spatio-temporal graph was designed. And they adopt noise to enhance the input data, so that the model has better robustness. Gui et al. [6] proposed an adversarial training method to generate smooth sequences to remove the human-pose artifacts that occur between the observable frames and predicted frames. Many methods [1,22] based on RNN have been optimized and explored in this domain. However, due to lack of intrinsic spatial structure representation of human body, the prediction results of RNN-based methods often have problems of discontinuity in adjacent frames and error accumulation with the extension of the predicted time.

2.2   Other Feed-Forward Methods

The traditional CNN network has good spatial information acquisition ability, and there are many methods [4,21] to realize human motion prediction using CNN. However, the characteristic of CNN determine that it has a natural disadvantage on topological irregular data of human skeleton. GCN essentially does the same thing as CNN, but GCN can well deal with the discontinuous and irregular human structural data by constructing human skeleton joints graph. And it is usually leveraged to establish the spatial connection of skeleton joints

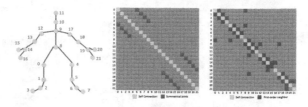

Fig. 4. The three images from left to right are skeleton of dataset human3.6M with 22 joints, symmetrical matrix $\widetilde{A}_s$ and adjacency matrix $\widetilde{A}_c$.

for pose estimation [17]. Li et al. [15] designed a new GCN named DMGNN, which contains a dynamic multiscale graph to represent the skeleton structure of the human body. Multiscale graph can fully simulate the internal relations of a human body. Mao et al. [19] encoded temporal information using discrete cosine transform (DCT), which converts temporal information to the frequency domain for calculation. A spatial-temporal architecture (LTD) was constructed in their work for high-precision predictions using a multi-layer GCN network. However, increasing the number of input sequences does not enhance the performance of LTD, which is contrary to common sense. On the basis of LTD [19], Lebailly et al. [14] presented the temporal inception module (TIM), which extracts and fuses multiscale temporal information in a more intuitive and understandable way, and used it instead of DCT as the input of a GCN. However, it is heavily dependent on the selection of the kernel size of the temporal convolution. They complete the fusion of multi-scale temporal information by using five groups of convolution kernels to extract temporal feature and combine them. In contrast, we propose an augmented graph attention with temporal convolution block to fuse spatio-temporal information, and use gradation and reorganization mechanism to grade and recombine temporal feature, which greatly reduces the dependence on temproal convolution kernel size of network.

3   Approach

The main task of human motion prediction is to predict human motion in the future based on limited observable historical data. Let $X_{-N:-1} = [x_{-N}, x_{-(N-1)}, \cdots, x_{-1}]$ denote the observed consecutive pose sequence, here N is the sequence number of input data. We aim to predict poses $[x_0 : x_{T-1}]$ in the next T frames. $x_t \in R^K$, with K denotes the number of joints in a pose, so we can use x_t^k to represent the coordinate of the k-th joint at time index t.

3.1   Network Structure

For the above purpose, we design a augmented graph attention with temporal gradation reorganization framework as shown in Fig. 2, which cantains two main stages named temporal gradation stage and temporal reorganization stage. In addition, in the network initialization phase, we use basic operations such as full connect network, 2d batch normalization, 2d convolution, activation function RELU to initialize the input observable pose sequence according to the network requirements, and use an AGATB to obtain the initial spatio-temporal feature. At the end of the network, we also use 2d convolution, full connect network and some dimensional transform operations as head of our framework to achieve the final output.

3.2   Temporal Gradation and Reorganization Mechanism

In the temporal gradation stage, we utilize 6 AGATBs for aggregating temporal features hierarchically. The gradation of temporal feature is mainly controlled by convolution stride. Setting stride as 2 each time can make the next layer temporal convolution have a larger receptive field to get high-level feature within the same convolution kernel size. This is our core strategy for temporal gadation. Throughout three similar operations, we can aggregate temporal feature from size 64 to 8, and the smaller size represents the higher global information conciseness. In the process of continuous aggregation of temporal information, the module also retains the temporal feature of each intermediate level, which provides a necessary condition for the reorganization of the next stage.

In temporal reorganization stage, we recombine the different level features generated in gradation stage along temporal dimension by concat operation, and normalize the recombined features using 2D batch normalization in concat block. After three concat block operations, high-level information absorbs low-level information which may contain strong geometric constraints to gradually extend temporal resolution, and the final feature map comprise abundant multi-scale temporal information.

3.3   Augmented Graph Attention with Temporal Convolution Block

As the core module throughout the network, AGATB can effectively aggregate spatial and temporal information shown in Fig. 3. It is worth noting that we integrate channel attention into graph attention to improve the representation ability of spatial feature and help the network learns 'what' and 'where' in the channel dimension while capturing spatial structure of human poses in the spatial dimension.

Channel Attention. In general, extraction of spatial and temporal features is the mainstream idea to deal with such 3D spatio-temporal structure data. Following this idea, we combine channel attention with graph attention in order to characterize hidden information contained in the channel, which can improve the spatial representation ability of graph attention mechanism. We formulate a 1D channel attention map $M_c \in R^{C \times 1 \times 1}$ to generate intermediate channel feature map for graph attention:

$$F^{'} = M_c(F) \otimes F,$$
(1)

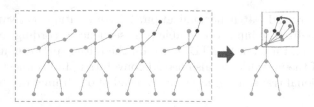

Fig. 5. Sketch of motion loss. We make a cross-product operation for the coordinate moving of the same joint within a certain time interval to form a motion, and add the motion of all joingts within all time intervals and subtract the motion of ground truth to form the final motion loss.

here $\otimes$ denotes element-wise multiplication, F is input and F' is the refined output. Woo et al. [26] aggregated spatial information of an image feature map by using average-pooling and max-pooling operations simultaneously. Likely, we impose average-pooling and max-pooling operations to aggregate spatial and temporal features in our application. A weight shared MLP is used to fuse the two feature descriptors to form final channel attention map as

$$M_c(F) = \sigma(MLP(AvgPool(F)) + MLP(MaxPool(F))), \qquad (2)$$

where σ denotes the sigmoid function.

Graph Attention. Graph attention is the major way we extract spatial feature. We follow Liu et al. [17] to construct our graph attention with local graph attention and global graph attention, respectively.

The initial graph of local graph attention is generated by a first-order adjacency matrix $A \in R^{K \times K}$ to represent the connections between joints and an identity matrix I to represent the self-connections, K means joints number in skeleton. So $\tilde{A} = (A + I)$ can denote convolutional kernel in our $GCNs$. The output of local graph attention can be expressed with

$$Y = \sigma(M \odot \tilde{A})XW, \qquad (3)$$

where $W \in R^{c_{in} \times c_{out}}$ is a learnable matrix used to transform output channels, $M \in R^{K \times K}$ is a learnable mask matrix. $\odot$ here is an element-wise multiplication operation, and σ is a softmax nonlinearity. Two different convolution kernels named symmetric matrix $\tilde{A}_s$ and adjacency $\tilde{A}_c$ are applied to generate two distinct $GCNs$ shown in Fig. 4.

The multi-head global attention is adopt to encode non-local relationships adaptively and effectively. The mechanism presents as

$$Y = \overset{I}{\underset{i=1}{\|}} (B_i + C_i)XW_i, \qquad (4)$$

where I is head number of attention, we set it as 4. $B_i \in R^{K \times K}$ is an adaptive global adjacency matrix, $C_i \in R^{K \times K}$ is learnable global adjacency matrix and $W_i \in R^{c_{in} \times (c_{in}/I)}$ is a transformed matrix shown in [17].

Table 1. Comparisons of test error on Human3.6M. Best results of each action on the corresponding timestamp are highlighted in bold. Our method outperforms the baselines on average and most actions for all timestamps.

Milliseconds	Walking					Eating					Smoking					Discussion				
	80	160	320	400	1000	80	160	320	400	1000	80	160	320	400	1000	80	160	320	400	1000
Res.Sup. [20]	23.2	40.9	61.0	66.1	79.1	16.8	31.5	53.5	61.7	98.0	18.9	34.7	57.5	65.4	102.1	25.7	47.8	80.0	91.3	131.8
ConvS2S [4]	17.7	33.5	56.3	63.6	82.3	11.0	22.4	40.7	48.4	87.1	11.6	22.8	41.3	48.9	81.7	17.1	34.5	64.8	77.6	129.3
TIM [14]	11.1	21.9	38.6	46.5	65.9	6.5	**14.6**	30.2	**38.6**	**76.4**	7.1	15.6	31.4	38.5	74.3	10.1	**23.8**	53.7	67.5	121.0
Ours	**10.6**	**21.6**	**38.3**	**44.4**	**60.2**	**6.5**	14.8	**29.4**	40.0	76.8	**7.0**	**15.3**	**30.8**	**37.7**	**71.6**	**10.0**	24.1	**53.0**	**66.7**	**117.9**

Milliseconds	Directions					Greeting					Phoning					Posing				
	80	160	320	400	1000	80	160	320	400	1000	80	160	320	400	1000	80	160	320	400	1000
Res.Sup. [20]	21.6	41.3	72.1	84.1	129.1	31.2	58.4	96.3	108.8	153.9	21.1	38.9	66.0	76.4	126.4	29.3	56.1	98.3	114.3	183.2
ConvS2S [4]	13.5	29.0	57.6	69.7	115.8	22.0	45.0	82.0	96.0	147.3	13.5	26.6	49.9	59.9	114.0	16.9	36.7	75.7	92.9	187.4
TIM [14]	**7.2**	**18.4**	**44.5**	56.6	109.4	14.3	31.8	66.7	81.8	140.0	8.5	**18.4**	**39.4**	**50.0**	108.1	9.9	24.8	60.1	77.4	171.5
Ours	7.3	19.0	44.9	**56.0**	**107.3**	**13.3**	**31.0**	**65.9**	**80.7**	**136.3**	**8.3**	18.5	39.8	50.1	**104.3**	**9.1**	**24.0**	**59.2**	**76.1**	**168.3**

Milliseconds	Purchases					Sitting					Sitting Down					Taking Photo				
	80	160	320	400	1000	80	160	320	400	1000	80	160	320	400	1000	80	160	320	400	1000
Res.Sup. [20]	28.7	52.4	86.9	100.7	154.0	23.8	44.7	78.0	91.2	152.6	31.7	58.3	96.7	112.0	187.4	21.9	41.4	74.0	87.6	153.9
ConvS2S [4]	20.3	41.8	76.5	89.9	151.5	13.5	27.0	52.0	63.1	120.7	20.7	40.6	70.4	82.7	150.3	12.7	26.0	52.1	63.6	128.1
TIM [14]	13.2	30.5	63.1	76.5	**136.8**	8.9	19.7	43.7	55.2	116.4	14.9	31.3	59.8	**72.6**	143.6	8.2	**18.7**	41.5	52.6	120.1
Ours	**12.4**	**29.1**	**61.9**	**76.2**	138.5	**8.6**	**19.2**	**43.1**	**54.7**	**114.5**	**14.4**	**30.7**	**60.1**	72.7	**142.7**	**8.4**	18.8	**41.2**	**51.8**	**116.8**

Milliseconds	Waiting					Walking Dog					Walking Together					Average				
	80	160	320	400	1000	80	160	320	400	1000	80	160	320	400	1000	80	160	320	400	1000
Res.Sup [20]	23.8	44.2	75.8	87.7	135.4	36.4	64.8	99.1	110.6	164.5	20.4	37.1	59.4	67.3	98.2	25.0	46.2	77.0	88.3	136.6
ConvS2S [4]	14.6	29.7	58.1	69.7	117.7	27.7	53.6	90.7	103.3	162.4	15.3	30.4	53.1	61.2	87.4	16.6	33.3	61.4	72.7	124.2
TIM [14]	8.6	19.7	45.3	57.5	108.0	20.6	42.0	75.7	89.5	**143.3**	9.3	20.0	38.6	47.2	70.5	10.6	23.4	48.8	60.5	113.8
Ours	**8.0**	**19.2**	**43.6**	**54.9**	**106.8**	**19.1**	**40.0**	**73.7**	**87.5**	150.1	**9.1**	**19.5**	**36.5**	**44.1**	**66.5**	**10.1**	**23.0**	**48.1**	**59.4**	**111.9**

Temporal Convolution Network. Temporal convolution network is a part of AGATB that is specially used to process temporal information. This part is a tcn unit, which is composed of a 2d convolution with temporal kernel, 2d batch normalization, RELU and dropout operation. The residual link reduces the possibility of gradient disappearance in the process of gradation and reorganization of temporal dimension.

3.4 Training

To train our network, we use mean per-joint position error (MPJPE) as the main loss function to minimize the error between predicted 3D human poses and ground truth. Following [10,19], the loss function can be expressed as

$$L_1 = \frac{1}{K(N+T)} \sum_{t=-N}^{T-1} \sum_{k=1}^{K} \left\| x'^{k}_t - x^k_t \right\|^2 . \tag{5}$$

In addition, to better supervise the optimization, we refer to Wang et al. [24] to construct a motion loss to better evaluate the prediction results, so as to better guide the network to evolve on better direction, shown in Fig. 5. Motion loss evaluates the motion of the same joint in different timestamp, and we use cross-prodcut to encode its motion. Meanwhile, considering that the movement rate of each joint varies greatly in differenet timestamp, we set four time intervals to better encode in a variety of time scales.

$$m_{t,k,i} = x^k_t \times x^k_{t+i}, \tag{6}$$

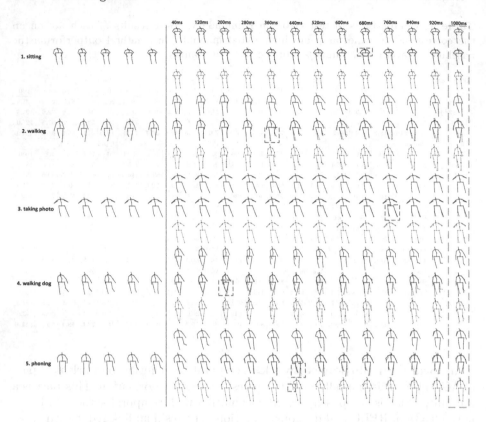

Fig. 6. Qualitative comparison on Human3.6M dataset. The image depicts the predicted human poses from time 40 ms to 1000 ms. Ground Truth, predicted results of TIM [14] and ours are shon from first row to third row for each action. The ground truth is also superimposed faintly in black with predicted results. Our network performs better on short-term and long-term prediction. Discontinuous poses occur suddenly in the red boxes impact final accuracy seriously. So we can see error accumulation in green boxes with extension of predicted time.

$$L_2 = \sum_{i \in S} \sum_{t=0}^{T-1-i} \sum_{k=1}^{K} \left\| m_{t,k,i} - m_{t,k,i}^{gt} \right\|, \tag{7}$$

where $m_{t,k,i}$ means the motion of joint x^k between timestamp t and $t+i$, S which i belongs to is the set of time intervals, we set is as $[4, 8, 12, 16]$. Our final loss function is combined by MPJPE and motion loss to supervise the network in an end-to-end manner.

$$L = L_1 + \lambda L_2, \tag{8}$$

we set λ as 0.002 in our application.

4   Experiments

4.1   DataSets

Human3.6M [10] involves 15 different scenarios of complex actions such as *smoking*, *purchase*, *eating*, *walkingdog* which were performed by eleven professional actors. It is almost the largest and challenging dataset for human motion analysis. Following the data processing of previous SOTA works [14, 19], the global rotations and translations are removed to retain 22 joints from 32 joints and the frame rate is down-sampled to 25 frames per second for training. The testing is performed on 256 random sub-sequences per action extracting from subject 5. So are the ablation experiments.

4.2   Baselines

We compare results with following baselines to evaluate the effectiveness of our approach: Res. sup. [20], convS2S [4], and TIM [14]. We evaluate our method with baselines using MPJPE described in training. The results of Res. sup., convS2S and TIM are all tested from their open source codes.

4.3   Results

Our motion prediction results on Human3.6M are shown in Table 1 and Fig. 6. We highlight the best results of each action on the corresponding timestamp in bold in Table 1. Our approach outperforms the baselines on average and most actions for all timestamps. Comparing to TIM, we have increased our average precision by about 2%.

4.4   Ablation Study

In order to better verify the effectiveness of our algorithm, ablation experiments are mainly focused on temporal gradation and reorganization mechanism. We conduct the ablation study in MPJPE metric with four relatively more complicated actions, namely *eating*, *directions*, *greeting* and *posing* of Human3.6M dataset in Table 2, Net-GR and Net-G represent our network and network without reorganization stage, respectively. The results indicates that temporal gradation and reorganization mechanism actually works effectively. Accuracy without reorganization stage decreases significantly compared to accuray of the full network. And we have not test that removing gradation operation by setting stride as 1, because we consider it makes no sense to extract low-level features in a loop, and it generates too many network parameters for training to our computers.

Table 2. Analysis of temporal gradation and reorganization mechanism. Net-GR and Net-G represent our network and network without reorganization stage. Better results of Net-GR comparing to Net-G show our temporal gradation and reorganization mechanism works effectively.

Milliseconds	Eating		Directions		Greeting		Posing		Average	
	560	1000	560	1000	560	1000	560	1000	560	1000
Net-G	55.6	81.3	78.2	108.8	106.3	139.1	109.3	170.6	87.4	125.0
Net-GR	**53.3**	**76.8**	**76.6**	**107.3**	**103.6**	**136.2**	**108.9**	**168.3**	**85.6**	**122.2**

5   Conclusions

In this paper, we propose a novel network to solve the problem of complex and variable human motion prediction. During the process of motion prediction, the proposed network can significantly reduce the error accumulation caused by the spatial-temporal discontinuity of human posture. In the proposed AGATB module, the channel attention is integrated into graph attention for building an augmented graph attention that provides better spatial feature extracting ability. Meanwhile, by fusing a TCN unit in AGATB, the temporal information is processed simultaneously. In addition, we build a gradation and reorganization mechanism in the proposed method for extracting abundant multi-scale temporal information, meanwhile, avoiding the dependence of convolution kernel size effectively. The experiments show that our work outperforms SOTAs on Human3.6M with better MPJPE, less discontinuity and error accumulation. Furthermore, we will focus on how to optimize our method to adapt the longer-term motion prediction.

References

1. Aksan, E., Kaufmann, M., Hilliges, O.: Structured prediction helps 3d human motion modelling (2019)
2. Bai, S., Kolter, J.Z., Koltun, V.: Trellis networks for sequence modeling (2018)
3. Brand, M., Hertzmann, A.: Style machines. In: Siggraph Computer Graphics Proceedings (2000)
4. Butepage, J., Black, M.J., Kragic, D., Kjellstrom, H.: Deep representation learning for human motion prediction and classification. In: IEEE Conference on Computer Vision & Pattern Recognition, pp. 1591–1599 (2017)
5. Fragkiadaki, K., Levine, S., Felsen, P., Malik, J.: Recurrent network models for human dynamics. In: IEEE (2015)
6. Gui, L.-Y., Wang, Y.-X., Liang, X., Moura, J.M.F.: Adversarial geometry-aware human motion prediction. In: Ferrari, V., Hebert, M., Sminchisescu, C., Weiss, Y. (eds.) ECCV 2018. LNCS, vol. 11208, pp. 823–842. Springer, Cham (2018). https://doi.org/10.1007/978-3-030-01225-0_48

7. Gui, L.Y., Zhang, K., Wang, Y.X., Liang, X., Veloso, M.: Teaching robots to predict human motion. In: 2018 IEEE/RSJ International Conference on Intelligent Robots and Systems (IROS) (2018)
8. Gupta, A., Martinez, J., Little, J.J., Woodham, R.J.: 3d pose from motion for cross-view action recognition via non-linear circulant temporal encoding. In: Computer Vision & Pattern Recognition (2014)
9. Habibi, G., Jaipuria, N., How, J.P.: Context-aware pedestrian motion prediction in urban intersections (2018)
10. Ionescu, C., Papava, D., Olaru, V., Sminchisescu, C.: Human3.6m: large scale datasets and predictive methods for 3d human sensing in natural environments. IEEE Trans. Pattern Anal. Mach. Intell. **36**(7), 1325–1339 (2014)
11. Jain, A., Zamir, A.R., Savarese, S., Saxena, A.: Structural-rnn: deep learning on spatio-temporal graphs. In: IEEE Conference on Computer Vision & Pattern Recognition (2015)
12. Kiciroglu, S., Rhodin, H., Sinha, S.N., Salzmann, M., Fua, P.: Activemocap: optimized viewpoint selection for active human motion capture. In: 2020 IEEE/CVF Conference on Computer Vision and Pattern Recognition (CVPR) (2020)
13. Knauf, K., Memmert, D., Brefeld, U.: Spatio-temporal convolution kernels. Mach. Learn. **102**(2), 247–273 (2015). https://doi.org/10.1007/s10994-015-5520-1
14. Lebailly, T., Kiciroglu, S., Salzmann, M., Fua, P., Wang, W.: Motion prediction using temporal inception module. In: Computer Vision–ACCV 2020 (2021)
15. Li, M., Chen, S., Zhao, Y., Zhang, Y., Tian, Q.: Dynamic multiscale graph neural networks for 3d skeleton based human motion prediction. In: 2020 IEEE/CVF Conference on Computer Vision and Pattern Recognition (CVPR) (2020)
16. Li, T., Liu, J., Zhang, W., Duan, L.Y.: Hard-net: hardness-aware discrimination network for 3d early activity prediction. In: European Conference on Computer Vision (ECCV) (2020)
17. Liu, J., Guang, Y., Rojas, J.: Gast-net: graph attention spatio-temporal convolutional networks for 3d human pose estimation in video. arXiv (2020)
18. Majoe, D., Widmer, L., Gutknecht, J.: Enhanced motion interaction for multimedia applications. In: International Conference on Advances in Mobile Computing and Multimedia (2009)
19. Mao, W., Liu, M., Salzmann, M., Li, H.: Learning trajectory dependencies for human motion prediction. In: 2019 IEEE/CVF International Conference on Computer Vision (ICCV) (2019)
20. Martinez, J., Black, M.J., Romero, J.: On human motion prediction using recurrent neural networks. In: 2017 IEEE Conference on Computer Vision and Pattern Recognition (CVPR) (2017)
21. Pavllo, D., Grangier, D., Auli, M.: Quaternet: a quaternion-based recurrent model for human motion (2018)
22. Tang, Y., Lin, M., Wei, L., Zheng, W.S.: Long-term human motion prediction by modeling motion context and enhancing motion dynamics. In: Twenty-Seventh International Joint Conference on Artificial Intelligence IJCAI-18 (2018)
23. Vladimir, P.C., Rehg, J.M., Maccormick, J.: Learning switching linear models of human motion. In: Advances in Neural Information Processing Systems 13, Papers from Neural Information Processing Systems (NIPS) 2000, Denver, CO, USA (2000)
24. Wang, J., Yan, S., Xiong, Y., Lin, D.: Motion guided 3d pose estimation from videos (2020)
25. Wang, R., Panju, M., Gohari, M.: Classification-based RNN machine translation using GRUs (2017)

26. Woo, S., Park, J., Lee, J.Y., Kweon, I.S.: Cbam: convolutional block attention module. In: European Conference on Computer Vision (2018)
27. Yao, J., Zhang, J., Li, J., Zhuo, L.: Anchor voiceprint recognition in live streaming via RawNet-SA and gated recurrent unit. EURASIP J. Audio Speech Music Process. **2021**(1), 1–18 (2021)

Highlight Detection and Removal Method Based on Bifurcated-CNN

Jingting Xu[ID], Sheng Liu[(✉)], Guanzhou Chen[ID], and Qianxi Liu[ID]

College of Computer Science and Technology, Zhejiang University of Technology, Liuhe Road 288, Hangzhou, China
edliu@zjut.edu.cn

Abstract. Many visual tasks of intelligent robots as object detection and tracking are very easily interfered by the specular highlights. Existing highlight detection and removal methods often suffer from low sensitivity in dealing with low saturation pixels and large-area highlight, and there are visual artifacts and information distortions in the compensated pixels. In this paper, we propose a novel two-stage convolution neural network (Bifurcated-CNN), to tackle the problem of specular highlight detection and removal on high-reflective materials. 1) The specular highlight features are extracted and removed in two stages from coarse to fine, so as to ensure the generation of diffuse images have no visual artifacts and information distortions. 2) We propose a bifurcated feature selection strategy (BFSS) to filter out the specular highlight features, which enhances the detection capability of our network. 3) Experimental results demonstrate that the proposed network is more effective to remove specular highlight with a $0.06 \times 1e^{-2}$ reduction in MSE, a 2.4831 improvement in PSNR, and almost the same in SSIM, compared with the state-of-the-arts. In addition, we build a large-scale transparent solid waste highlight dataset, which will help the solid waste sorting robots to solve the detection failure problems caused by specular highlight, and greatly contribute to accurate visual sorting in the plastic solid waste recycling industry. It is also helpful to evaluate and encourage new deep-learning methods. As we know, this is the first specular highlight dataset for the plastic solid waste recycling industry. The dataset will be made available at https://github.com/aobi12138/Bifurcated-CNN.

Keywords: Specular highlight removal · Intelligent robot · Object detection

1 Introduction

Specular highlight, as the bright spots on the surface of illuminated high-reflective materials, often causes information degradation. The information of specular highlight region, including color, texture, and structure, probably be degraded or completely lost. The damage caused by information degradation is fatal for many vision tasks of intelligent robots, such as object detection and tracking, text recognition, and AR-based surgical navigation.

Specular highlight detection and removal is an essential technology widely required. For example, an automatic sorting robot with accurate object detection technology can

© The Author(s), under exclusive license to Springer Nature Switzerland AG 2022
H. Liu et al. (Eds.): ICIRA 2022, LNAI 13458, pp. 307–318, 2022.
https://doi.org/10.1007/978-3-031-13841-6_29

significantly improve production efficiency in the plastic solid waste recycling industry. But the presence of specular highlight will seriously affect object detection accuracy. In particular, as a representative smooth and high-reflective material, plastic solid waste has many bright spots on its surface after being illuminated. The bright spot has remarkable similarity in shape with white label paper on plastic solid waste, leading to its mistaken identity as white label paper. So specular highlight will interfere with object detection, resulting in wrong results of solid waste classification. The negative impact inspires us to discover an effective way to detect and remove specular highlight.

Many researchers have been committed to detecting and removing specular highlight in recent years. The current methods can be divided into traditional model-based and deep learning-based methods. Furthermore, the former includes single-image and multiple-image methods. Single-image specular highlight detection and removal methods can be classified into: based on different forms of threshold [1], based on the assumption that only a tiny region of the image contains specular highlight [2], based on the inherent decomposition of the image [3], and based on the color-estimated [1], space-estimated, and illumination-estimated methods. Li et al. [1] proposed a specular highlight detection approach based on HSV channel thresholds in 2019. But such method cannot locate the specular highlight wholly due to the constraints of the thresholds. In 2018, Zhang et al. [2] proposed an approach based on the assumption that there is only a tiny specular highlight region in the image, regarding specular highlight detection as a sparse non-negative matrix factorization (NMF) problem. This method cannot deal with large areas of specular highlight. In addition, methods based on color, space, and illumination estimation often need to introduce corresponding prior models. Yang et al. [1] proposed a real-time highlight separation scheme in HSI color space for natural images. In addition to the color and space estimation-based methods, the illumination-estimated methods can also roughly remove specular highlight. The principle of the method basing on intrinsic image decomposition [3] is similar to theirs. However, the above methods probably fail under complex background and illumination.

To remove specular highlight under complex background and illumination, some multiple-image methods are proposed. In 2018, Wei et al. [5] proposed a multiple-image method for specular highlight detection and removal. They firstly collected multiple images by changing the camera perspective under fixed illumination, then estimated the position of the light source based on the assumption that the surface geometry is known, finally overlayed multiple images to filter out specular highlight. Although multiple-image methods can obtain more accurate specular highlight removal results than single-image methods, they are not practical because of their demand for large amounts of input data and the cost of computing resources. Therefore, single-image methods are the mainstream of this research field. The existing model-based single-image methods are efficient and easy to implement, but they fail easily when dealing with high reflectivity objects. To overcome these problems, people use modern deep learning tools and construct large-scale real-world datasets to obtain high-quality results.

In contrast, deep learning-based approaches perform better. Fu et al. [6] proposed a deep learning-based network in 2020 to detect highlight by using contextual contrast properties. In 2021, they continued this work and further presented a multi-task network for joint highlight detection and removal [7]. Compared to traditional model-based methods, deep learning-based methods are free from the constraints of the traditional model. They have made significant progress but still have some drawbacks, as shown in Fig. 1. 1) The ability of highlight detection in the low-saturation regions is weak. Depicted in the blue box of Fig. 1-(b), the specular highlights on the low-saturation metal surface are not detected. 2) The results of specular highlight removal are incomplete, as indicated by the red box in Fig. 1-(b). The large area of specular highlight is not wholly removed. 3) The compensated regions of the specular highlight removal results have visual artifacts and distortion in color, structure, and texture. It can be seen that the compensated region in the yellow box in Fig. 1-(b) is unrealistic.

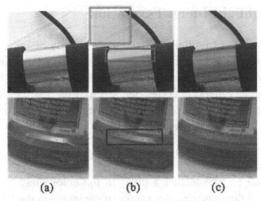

Fig. 1. Specular highlight removal results on real-world images [7]. (a) Input images with specular highlight, (b) specular highlight removal results by current method, (c) ground-truth.

The defects mentioned above lead to the residual specular highlight on the surface of highly reflective materials, which affected the efficiency of plastic solid waste sorting robots a lot. In addition, the lack of specular highlight dataset of plastic solid waste is also a significant obstacle. We build the first large-scale specular highlight dataset of transparent plastic solid waste for the plastic solid waste recycling industry, by collecting 10240 images captured on the solid waste recycling production line. The black belt of the production line with various transparent plastic bottles placed on it, is seen as the background. The light source and camera are fixed above the belt. As a typical object with a smooth and high-reflective surface, the transparent plastic solid waste will show many specular highlight areas of different sizes under illumination. We propose a novel single-image specular highlight detection and removal network, a two-stage convolutional neural network (Bifurcated-CNN), based on a bifurcated feature extraction strategy. Our network can detect and remove highlight simultaneously, and is progressively optimized for highlight removal from coarse to fine.

In summary, we make the following contributions.

- We establish the first large-scale specular highlight dataset by collecting pictures captured on transparent plastic solid waste, which helps distinguish specular highlight and white label paper on bottles for the plastic solid waste recycling industry. It is also helpful to evaluate and encourage new specular highlight detection and removal technologies.

- We propose a two-stage convolutional neural network (Bifurcated-CNN), to implement highlight detection and removal progressively. In the first stage, we present a bifurcated feature selection strategy (BFSS) to filter out specular highlight features. We enhance the ability to deal with specular highlight at different scales by extracting multi-scale highlight features. In the second stage, we achieve refined removal based on the specular highlight features roughly extracted in the first stage. The generated diffuse images have no visual artifacts and information distortions, experimentally verified to achieve state-of-the-art performance.

2 Specular Highlight Image Formation

The formation of specular highlight follows the principle of image reflection model. Tan et al. [11] proposed the classical two-color reflection model and pointed out that the reflected light on the surface of the object illuminated is the linear combination of diffuse and specular reflection components. From the two-color reflection model, without considering the influence of noise and other factors, it is known that an image with reflection can be represented as:

$$I(X) = D(X) + S(X) \tag{1}$$

where X denotes the coordinates of a pixel in the color image (x, y), and $I(X) = \{I_r(X), I_g(X), I_b(X)\}$ denotes the color vector of the image in the RGB channels. $D(X)$ represents the diffuse reflection component. $S(X)$ represents the specular reflection component. From Eq. (1), it can be concluded that the process of specular highlight removal is equivalent to separating the diffuse reflection layer $D(X)$ and specular reflection layer $S(X)$ in a given color image $I(X)$. But there are two shortcomings in this modeling approach. 1) No consideration is given to saturation, which causes low-saturation diffuse pixels misidentified as specular highlight pixels. Due to the great similarity in the appearance of low-saturation diffuse reflection and highlight, specifically on white material surfaces, the diffuse reflection is removed as specular highlight reflection, resulting in the loss of the original color, texture, and other information of the image. 2) Obvious inherent ambiguity between $D(X)$ and $S(X)$. Specular highlight in natural scenes usually have a random spatial distribution and a wide range of intensity values. This ambiguity makes the specular highlight reflection hard to be wholly detected, resulting in unsatisfactory highlight removal results.

To address these issues, we propose a novel specular highlight image model, denoted as:

$$I(X) = D_{detailed}(X) + S_{detailed}(X) \tag{2}$$

$$= D_{rough}(X) \otimes \alpha \left(S_{rough}(X) \| S_{detailed}(X) \right) + S_{detailed}(X)$$

where $D_{detailed}(X)$ and $S_{detailed}(X)$ denote the delicate diffuse image and highlight feature mask image. $D_{rough}(X)$ and $S_{rough}(X)$ denote the rough diffuse image and specular highlight feature mask, which describes the location of specular highlight in the image with the values of 0 and 1. $\otimes$ is a convolution operator, $\|$ denotes the concatenation operation, and α is the convolution layer. We introduce additional highlight features to supplement the missing detail information, and use a 1×1 convolution layer to fuse highlight features at different levels for delicate highlight removal. Equation (2), as an improved highlight model, is able to 1) directly solve the localization problem of highlight regions through highlight masks, which helps to improve specular highlight detection capability of the network; 2) distinguish highlight and diffuse regions, and handle differently on each region, thus avoiding the mutual contamination of features and optimizing specular highlight removal effect of the network.

3 Bifurcated Feature Selection-Based Two-Stage Network

Based on the proposed highlight model, a two-stage convolutional neural network (Bifurcated-CNN) with a bifurcated feature extraction strategy is proposed in this paper. Our network is able to achieve highlight removal significantly better. We propose the term "specular highlight feature", and filter specular highlight features from the original features by designing a bifurcated feature selection strategy (BFSS) combining an attention mechanism. We further implement a refinement processing module, Detailed Highlight Feature Removal (DFR), to generate delicate diffuse images.

3.1 Network Framework

The entire workflow of the proposed network (Bifurcated-CNN) is shown in Fig. 2. The two-stage network takes the real image $I \in R^{H \times W \times C}$ as the input, where C denotes the number of channels and H $\times$ W denotes the image spatial resolution.

In the first stage, we design a rough specular highlight feature extraction module (SFE) as shown in Fig. 2, to locate highlight region and generate diffuse images roughly. We can decouple the original feature map F into highlight feature map F_{spec} and diffuse feature map F_{diff}. After assuming that they satisfy the addition rule, $F : F = F_{spec} + F_{diff}$, the general idea of the SFE module can be expressed as Eq. (3):

$$F_{diff} = F - F_{spec} = \rho(I) - \Upsilon(\rho(I)) \tag{3}$$

where ρ denotes the process of saliency features extraction, and Υ denotes the process of highlight features extraction. Specifically, we filter the image to reduce the noise and extract the first order derivative extrema from the pixel points, considering that the specular highlight pixels satisfy the condition of "jump" or large change in pixel value. We can express specular feature as $F_{spec}(X) \equiv grad(f) \equiv \left[g_x \ g_y \right]^{-1} \equiv \left[\partial f / \partial x \ \partial f / \partial y \right]^{-1}$. In the SFE module, we extract specular highlight features, and roughly remove them by subtracting them from the original features, to generate a preliminary diffuse image and a highlight feature map.

The second stage of our Bifurcated-CNN implements detailed specular highlight removal (DSR), by introducing the rough diffuse image and highlight feature map from

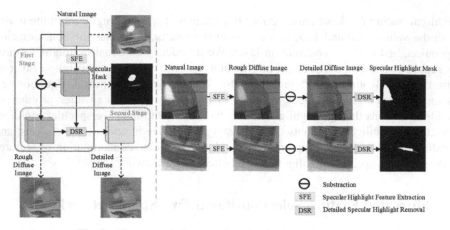

Fig. 2. The network framework and workflow of our method.

the first stage as priori information. We exploit the spatial information extraction capability of the full convolutional network, and take the coarse diffuse image as a prior, to detect specular highlight and compensate for degraded region.

We propose a novel two-stage network for highlight detection and removal, which is superior to other state-of-the-art methods. The model structure is shown in Fig. 3. We present the implementation details of the two stages in the following subsections.

3.2 Stage I: Rough Extraction Process of Specular Highlight Feature Based on BFSS

We propose the term "specular highlight feature" and the bifurcated specular highlight feature selection strategy (BFSS). By using BFSS and an attention mechanism, we construct the rough extraction stage of specular highlight features. As shown in the Fig. 3, this stage consists of three main steps. Firstly, we extract highlight features at five levels $f_{spec}^i (i = 1, 2, \ldots, 5)$ and iteratively improve the detailed information of the low-level features. From Eq. (3), we can see $f_{spec}^1 = \Upsilon(\rho(I))$, and express specular highlight features at the other levels as Eq. (4).

$$f_{spec}^i = \beta\left(f_{spec}^{i-1}\right), i = 2, 3, 4, 5 \tag{4}$$

Secondly, the expressiveness of highlight features is enhanced by combining the attention mechanism named CBAM to improve the ability of specular highlight detection. Finally, specular highlight features are subtracted from the original features f_{spec}^i to obtain $f_{diff}^k (k = i - 1)$. Our network outputs a rough diffuse image D_r and highlight feature map f_{spec} to achieve the coarse removal of specular highlight.

In the first stage, we extract highlight features at different levels, which have great randomness in size, shape and location. High-level features contain rich global contextual information that is conducive to location of specular highlight. In contrast, low-level features carry a large amount of detail information, which helps to generate fine diffuse

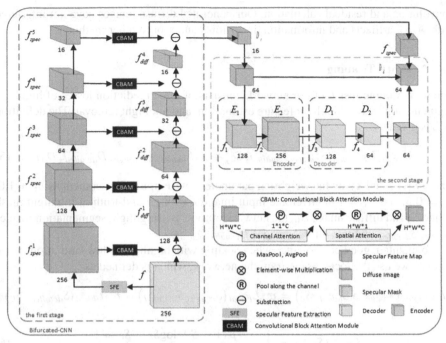

Fig. 3. The model structure based on proposed framework. It is a bifurcated feature selection-based two-stage network for specular highlight removal. The first stage is rough extraction of specular highlight feature. The second one is a delicate specular highlight removal stage.

images. Motivated by this, we iteratively supplement high-level features with the detail information of low-level features, to improve the robustness of processing specular highlight in different situations. By using the characteristics of different levels of features to effectively eliminate the noise of low-level features, we filter the specular highlights from the original features incrementally.

3.3 Stage 2: Delicate Removal Process of Specular Highlight Feature

The second stage makes full use of the spatial information acquisition capability of the full convolutional neural network to extract specular highlight in images through Encoder and Decoder structures. To enlarge the receptive fields of convolutional kernels, we augment Encoder with the inflated convolutional layers. Decoder is the combination of the up-sampling and convolutional layers. The features in Fig. 3, named f_2 and f_4, can be expressed as $f_2 = E(f_1) = Dilation(CONV(f_1))$, and $f_4 = D(f_3) = Upsample(CONV(f_3))$. Specular highlight removal is actually the process of image compensation. In particular, after obtaining the refined highlight mask image S_d, we assign different weights to different features, to avoid feature contamination between highlight and diffuse regions. In addition, we selectively retain useful features when fusing information in each layer for compensation of degenerated regions, by exploiting gated convolution and residual calculation. Our generated diffuse images have not interfered with visual artifacts and information distortions, superior to other methods.

3.4 Network Training

The total training loss L of our network consists of three prediction losses of highlight segmentation image, highlight feature estimation, and highlight removal. The definition of L is given by:

$$L = \lambda_1 L_{detection}(S_{rough}, S_{detailed}, S_0) + \lambda_2 L_{removal}(D_{rough}, D_{detailed}, D_0) \quad (5)$$

where λ_1, λ_2 and λ_3 are the weighting parameters, we empirically set them as $\lambda_1 = 1.0$, $\lambda_2 = 0.5$, and $\lambda_3 = 1.0$. Given the input image I with ground-truth of highlight mask image S_0 and diffuse image D_0, the network outputs two highlight segmentation images S_{rough}, $S_{detailed}$ and two diffuse images D_{rough}, $D_{detailed}$.

To maintain good performance when dealing with highlight in low-saturation image regions, we use the focal loss to train the network, which is defined as

$$L_{detection}(S_{rough}, S_{detailed}, S_0) = \varpi_1 L_{Focal}(S_{rough}, S_{0etailed}) + \varpi_2 L_{Flcal}(S_{detailed}, S_0)$$

$$L_{Focal}(S_i, S_0) = \begin{cases} -\mu(1 - S_i)^{\xi} \log S_i & S_0 = 1 \\ -(1 - \mu)S_i^{\xi} \log(1 - S_i) & S_0 = 0 \end{cases} \quad (6)$$

where S_i is a value in the set $\{S_r, S_d\}$. In Eq. (6), we set $\varpi_1 = 0.5$, $\varpi_2 = 1.0$, $\mu = 0.25$, and $\xi = 2.0$. In order to avoid highlight removal that distorts the color and texture of the image, we also use a pixel loss:

$$L_{removal}(D_{rough}, D_{diffuse}, D_0) = \varpi_1 L_{Pixel}(D_{rough}, D_0) + \varpi_2 L_{Pixel}(D_{detailed}, D_0)$$

$$L_{Pixel}(D_i, D_0) = \theta \cdot \|D_i - D_0\|_2^2 + \eta(\|\nabla_x D_i - \nabla_x D_0\|_1 + \|\nabla_y D_i - \nabla_y D_0\|_1) \quad (7)$$

where θ and η are set to 0.2 and 0.4, and D_i is a value in the set $\{D_r, D_d\}$.

3.5 Implementation Details

We have implemented Bifurcated-CNN in PyTorch on a PC equipped with a NVIDIA GeForce GTX Titan V graphics card and an Intel Xeon(R) W-2133 CPU (3.60 GHz), 8 GB RAM. We randomly divide the dataset into 10K for training and 3K for testing, and resize the input images to 256*256. We set the initial learning rate to 10^{-4}, and multiply the learning rate by 0.2 after every 5 epochs in the first 10 epochs. With batch size of 4, the whole training process requires about 2 days. In addition, we achieve data enhancement by using random mirror flip images and adding noise, to generate more images with different specular highlight for training.

4 Experimental Results and Discussion

We evaluate the proposed approach quantitatively and qualitatively on our self-built dataset and two publicly available datasets, SHIQ [7] and PSD [12], against six state-of-the-art methods, namely Multi-class GAN [8], Spec-CGAN [9], the method proposed by Shen et al. [4], the method proposed by Yamamoto et al. [10], the method proposed by Fu et al. [7], and the method proposed by Wu et al. [12]. We will provide more analysis of our method in this section.

4.1 Self-built Dataset

To verify the effectiveness of the proposed approach on the plastic bottle sorting assembly line, we build a real large-scale dataset by collecting pictures captured on the plastic bottles. In the visual area of the assembly line, we fixed the camera under the light source, and placed some plastic bottles on the black belt line.

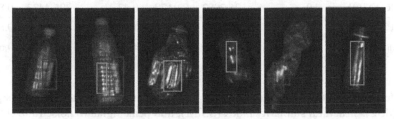

Fig. 4. Images from our self-built dataset

As the objects we selected to collect, transparent plastic bottles need to remove label papers due to the demands of industrial tasks. However, the removal of label papers is not perfect that some label papers will remain on the bottles because they are too sticky. The residual part of the label paper is usually pure white, as indicated by the red box in Fig. 4. Under the fixed light source in the visual area of the assembly line, many highlight will appear on the plastic bottle, and specular highlight are usually pure white, as indicated by the yellow box in Fig. 4.

Therefore, the residual label paper and specular highlight do not have apparent differences in color and texture characteristics. Moreover, it can be seen that the location distribution and size of specular highlight area have strong randomness. We selected the above plastic bottles as the source of data collection to prove the effectiveness of the method in this paper for specular highlight detection and removal.

4.2 Comparisons

To verify the advantages of the network in this paper, we quantitatively analyze it with five advanced highlight removal schemes, namely Multi-class GAN [8], Spec-CGAN [9], the methods proposed by Shen et al. [4], Yamamoto et al. [10], and Wu et al. [12], on the publicly available dataset PSD [12] and SHIQ [7].

Table 1. Quantitative comparison on PSD [12] and SHIQ [7]. The best result of each measurement is marked in **bold** font.

Dataset	PSD [12]			SHIQ [7]		
Metric	MSE/1e^{-2}↓	PSNR↑	SSIM↑	MSE/1e^{-2}↓	PSNR↑	SSIM↑
Ours	**0.08**	**32.9525**	0.9734	**0.11**	**31.6842**	**0.9716**
Wu et al. [12]	0.14	30.4694	**0.9916**	0.24	28.2384	0.9412
Multi-class GAN [8]	0.50	23.5240	0.8550	0.48	27.6318	0.8848
Spec-CGAN [9]	0.36	25.7082	0.9172	0.42	26.4423	0.8592
Shen et al. [4]	1.07	20.6226	0.8826	1.12	21.9024	0.8017
Yamamoto et al. [10]	8.46	11.8587	0.6264	4.76	19.5482	0.6375

In terms of accuracy, we compare the common metrics including mean-squared error (MSE), structural similarity index (SSIM), and peak signal to noise ratio (PSNR). In general, smaller MSE scores indicate better removal results. Larger PSNR and SSIM scores indicate better results. The statistical results are shown in Table 1.

Experimental results demonstrate that our proposed network obtains superior performance over state-of-the-arts. In particular, compared with state-of-the-arts on public datasets, it achieves a 2.4831 improvement in PSNR, a $0.06 \times 1e^{-2}$ reduction in MSE, and almost the same in SSIM on PSD dataset. The performance on SHIQ dataset is also improved significantly. From Fig. 5, we can see that most of the regions of specular highlight are detected in the final specular masks even for some challenging cases such as high reflectivity and low saturation. The diffuse images generated by our network are closer to the ground-truth than the existing advanced methods.

Experiments on our self-built dataset can also verify the effectiveness and usability of our network on the plastic bottle sorting assembly line. As depicted in Fig. 6, the diffuse images generated by our method are effective in dealing with transparent plastic bottles, which are made of highly reflective material. It obviously detects specular highlight areas of random location and size, and compensates the highlight areas with realistic texture and color. Our method effectively eliminates the interference of specular highlights in object detection, thus greatly contributes to accurate visual sorting in the plastic solid waste recycling industry.

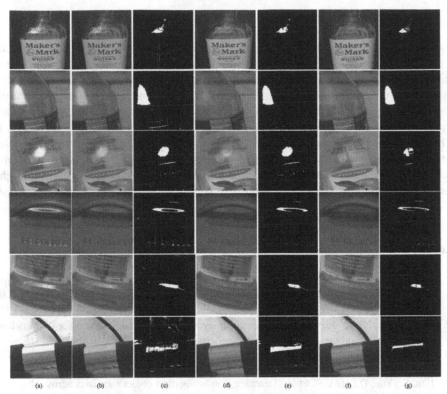

Fig. 5. Specular highlight removal results on real-world images. (a) input specular highlight images, (b) diffuse images by Wu et al. [12], (c) specular masks by Wu et al. [12], (d) diffuse images by our proposed method, (e) specular masks by our proposed method, (f) ground-truth of diffuse images, (g) ground-truth of specular masks.

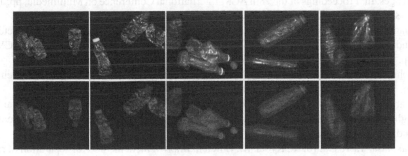

Fig. 6. The specular highlight removal results on our self-built dataset.

5 Conclusion

In this paper, we proposed a specular highlight removal network, Bifurcated-CNN, to tackle the problem of specular highlight detection and removal on high reflectivity materials, which greatly contributes to accurate visual sorting in the plastic solid waste recycling industry. In addition, we build a large-scale transparent plastic solid waste dataset, which is the first highlight dataset for the plastic solid waste recycling industry. Our proposed approach obtains superior performance over state-of-the-arts. In particular, it achieves a 2.4831 improvement in PSNR, a $0.06 \times 1e^{-2}$ reduction in MSE, and almost the same in SSIM, compared with the state-of-the-arts [12] on PSD dataset. It also performs well on SHIQ dataset. Our method can better deal with large-area specular highlight and low-saturation pixels, which has positive significance for the object detection task of robots.

References

1. Ranyang, L., Junjun, P., Yaqing, S., et al.: Specular reflections removal for endoscopic image sequences with adaptive-RPCA decomposition. IEEE Trans. Med. Imaging **39**(2), 328–340 (2019)
2. Wuming, Z., Xi, Z., Jean-Marie, M., et al.: Improving shadow suppression for illumination robust face recognition. IEEE Trans. Pattern Anal. Mach. Intell. **41**(3), 611–624 (2018)
3. Qingxiong, Y., Jinhui, T., Narendra, A.: Efficient and robust specular highlight removal. IEEE Trans. Pattern Anal. Mach. Intell. **37**(6), 1304–1311 (2014)
4. Jian, S., Yue, D., Hao, S., et al.: Learning non-lambertian object intrinsics across shapenet categories. In: IEEE Computer Vision and Pattern Recognition (CVPR), pp. 1685–1694 (2017)
5. Xing, W., Xiaobin, X., Jiawei, Z., et al.: Specular highlight reduction with known surface geometry. Comput. Vis. Image Underst. **168**, 132–144 (2018)
6. Gang, F., Qing, Z., Qifeng, L., et al.: Learning to detect specular highlight from real-world images. In: Proceedings of the 28th ACM International Conference on Multimedia, pp. 1873–1881. Association for Computing Machinery, New York (2020)
7. Gang, F., Qing, Z., Lei, Z., et al.: A multi-task network for joint specular highlight detection and removal. In: IEEE Conference on Computer Vision and Pattern Recognition (CVPR), pp. 7748–7757 (2021)
8. John, L., Mohamed, E., Mohamed, T., et al.: Deep multi-class adversarial specularity removal. In: Scandinavian Conference on Image Analysis, pp. 3–15 (2019)
9. Isabel, F., Sebastian, B., Carina, R., et al.: Generative adversarial networks for specular highlight removal in endoscopic images. In: Image-Guided Procedures, Robotic Interventions, and Modeling, p. 9 (2018)
10. Takahisa, Y., Toshihiro, K., Ryota, K.: Efficient improvement method for separation of reflection components based on an energy function. In: IEEE international Conference on Image Processing (ICIP), pp. 4222–4226 (2017)
11. Tan, R., Ikeuchi, K.: Separating reflection components of textured surfaces using a single image. IEEE Trans. Pattern Anal. Mach. Intell. **27**(2), 178–193 (2005)
12. Zhongqi, W., Chuanqing, Z., Jian, S., et al.: Single-image specular highlight removal via real-world dataset construction. IEEE Trans. Multimedia 1 (2021)

Two-Stream Adaptive Weight Convolutional Neural Network Based on Spatial Attention for Human Action Recognition

Guanzhou Chen[1]([✉]) [iD], Lu Yao[1], Jingting Xu[1] [iD], Qianxi Liu[1] [iD], and Shengyong Chen[2] [iD]

[1] College of Computer Science and Technology, Zhejiang University of Technology, Liuhe Road 288, Hangzhou, China
763483718@qq.com, edliu@zjut.edu.cn
[2] Key Laboratory of Computer Vision and System, College of Computer Science and Engineering, Tianjin University of Technology, Tianjin, China

Abstract. There is the problem of strong spatio-temporal complexity of actions and low differentiation of similar action features in Action Recognition. Unimodal input, such as RGB image, can provide rich appearance and context information, but background motion and object occlusion make it difficult to extract human motion information. Multimodal-based human action recognition methods can solve these problems. However, the problems of inadequate fusion of multimodal features lead to poor algorithm robustness and insufficient consideration of modal differences in existing multimodal-based human action recognition methods. We proposed a two-stream adaptive weight convolutional neural network based on spatial attention for human action recognition, SA-AWCNN, to achieve cross-modality feature complementarity. This method constructs a local feature interaction module from depth to RGB to effectively improve the network modal information interaction ability by using the complementarity between modes. At the same time, the spatial attention module is introduced to strengthen the spatial dimension feature information, and the effectiveness of network feature extraction is improved without increasing network parameters. Experiments show that the proposed method is effective in completing human action recognition tasks. The accuracy of our method on NTU RGB+ D dataset and SBU Kinect interaction dataset reaches 91.85% and 94.30%.

Keywords: Human action recognition · Multi-modality fusion · Attention module · Weight adaptation · Convolutional network

1 Introduction

In the field of human–computer interaction, human action recognition technology enables the machine to make corresponding feedback actions by identifying the type of human action and understanding the intention of the interaction. Therefore, it is crucial for the robot to accurately identify the actions of the interaction.

© The Author(s), under exclusive license to Springer Nature Switzerland AG 2022
H. Liu et al. (Eds.): ICIRA 2022, LNAI 13458, pp. 319–330, 2022.
https://doi.org/10.1007/978-3-031-13841-6_30

In the action recognition task, the original single RGB visual input is transformed into the input of human joint skeleton, spatial depth and infrared data, which greatly promotes the development of human action recognition research. Different modes have the same high-level semantics. After effective integration between modes, more abundant feature information can be provided for human action recognition than single mode. The research on the human action recognition method based on multi-modality can improve the accuracy of human action recognition by using the difference between modes for feature complementation. RGB is the basic input of visual tasks, and the human action recognition method based on multi-modality takes RGB image as one of the input modes.

Most of the existing multimodal human action recognition methods use simple struc-tured feature fusion, and tend to rely on RGB appearance information during the training process, leading to problems such as insufficient consideration of modal differences and poor robustness of the algorithm. This is due to the fact that the simple structured fea-ture fusion approach does not consider modal differences and correlations enough, and cannot fully utilize the modal characteristics for feature complementation. The method proposed in this paper provides a solution to these problems.

The innovation of this paper is as follows: We use RGB and depth data as algorithm inputs and propose a Two-stream Adaptive Weight Convolutional Neural Network based on Spatial Attention (SA-AWCNN) for human action recognition to enhance RGB and depth modal information interactions. The method builds a unidirectional local feature interaction module to establish a lateral connection from depth to RGB in order to take full advantage of the inter-modal complementarity to effectively improve the modal information interaction capability of the network. At the same time, a spatial attention module is introduced to enhance the spatial dimensional feature information, which significantly improves the effectiveness of network feature extraction without increasing the network parameters. To address the problem of training overfitting due to limited data volume, the data augmentation module is used to increase the number of training samples and improve the sample diversity, so as to enhance the generalization ability of the network model and prevent the serious overfitting phenomenon.

2 Related Work

With the development deep learning, researchers have tried to apply two-stream structural methods based on deep learning to the field of human action recognition to make up for the shortcomings of single-stream structural methods. Meanwhile, unimodal input, such as RGB image and depth image, has the problem of occlusion and self-occlusion, viewpoint changes, etc. And the above defects are not compensated by fusing different feature representations of one modality.

The late fusion approach [1] fuses the prediction scores after the single features are trained to obtain the prediction results. Although the late fusion approach can improve the network recognition performance to some extent, it does not take full advantage of the correlation and difference between different modalities. In contrast, early fusion app-roach based on deep learning can compensate for the lack of single-feature information by fusing different modal features. Methods [3] perform fusion operations at the fully connected layer in the later stages of the network, and while these methods have achieved significant success, their performance is still limited by the weaker spatio-temporal information representation and the learning ability of the convolutional network. Qin et al. [4] tried to divide the features into three parts: common features, RGB specific features and depth specific features. By calculating the distances of the three features separately, the distance-weighted sum is used to calculate the final distance result. Lu et al. [5] attempted to obtain the common and specific feature streams in a shallow convolutional layer rather than a deeper fully connected layer. The multimodal-based recognition method, to a large extent, ensures the integrity and diversity of the information feature representation and can effectively improve the network recognition performance.

The attention mechanism allows for more detailed information that can help in judgment, while suppressing useless information. Method [6] devoted to improving algorithm performance by developing more complex attention modules, but this inevitably increases the model complexity. Therefore Wang et al. [7] proposed a local cross-channel interaction strategy without dimensionality reduction, which can achieve efficient performance gain by one-dimensional convolution. The attention mechanism makes full use of different dimensional features with limited resources to achieve the effect of enhancing important features and suppressing non-important features.

3 Multimodal-Based Human Action Recognition

In this paper, we propose a two-stream adaptive weight convolutional neural network based on spatial attention for human action recognition (see Fig. 1), using RGB image and depth sequences acquired by a depth camera as the inputs. In the data preprocessing, data augmentation techniques such as random level flipping and multi-scale cropping are used to improve the diversity of data samples and reduce the overfitting phenomenon. In the feature extraction stage, in order to make full use of the complementarity between multimodal information, a new local feature interaction module is proposed in this paper to improve the network performance by establishing an interactive connection between RGB streams and depth streams to enhance the inter-modal information interaction. Meanwhile, a spatial attention mechanism is introduced to improve the ability of the model to extract key features. Finally, the fused action features are obtained by the feature fusion module, which transmits them to the action classifier to calculate and output the probability on the target class.

3.1 Feature Extraction Module

We propose a feature extraction module based on local feature interaction, which enhances the information interaction of modal features in the extraction stage by establishing a lateral connection from the depth stream to the RGB (see Fig. 1).

In the feature extraction module, the RGB stream and the depth stream are described as a single stream architecture sampled and run at two different frame rates. RGB images can provide richer spatial appearance information, and depth images can provide temporal motion information by increasing the sampling frame rate, and combining the two can obtain effective spatio-temporal feature information. In order to solve the speed difference of different subjects to complete the target action, this paper designs a non-fixed

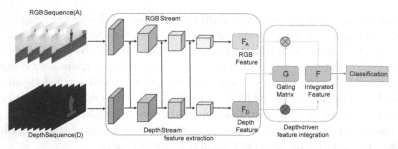

Fig. 1. The framework of two-stream adaptive weight convolution neural network based on spatial attention for human action recognition

step strategy: after randomly selecting the first frame, any frame within the step frame is chosen as the next frame. This sampling strategy can achieve variable frame extraction while keeping the number of frames constant to improve the generalization ability of the network and reduce the overfitting phenomenon.

The depth input sequence is sampled in small steps of τ/α when constructing the depth input sequence, where α is the frame rate ratio between the depth stream and the RGB stream, in this paper, we set $\alpha = 4$. According to the adjustment of the depth images size by the data augmentation module, the depth images input sequence can be represented as $D \in \mathbb{R}^{4T_A \times 1 \times H_A \times W_A}$, where T_A, H_A and W_A denote the number of frames, height and width of the RGB images sequence, respectively, and T_D, H_D and W_D denote the number of frames, height and width of the depth images sequence, respectively. The sub-module of RGB feature extraction uses the ResNet-50 [2] model as the base model of the convolutional neural network and adds the Temporal Shift Module (TSM) to each residual block of ResNet-50 to achieve efficient and effective spatio-temporal feature extraction. In the TSM module 1/8 of the input feature channels are shifted forward and the other 1/8 of the input feature channels are shifted backward [26]. The sub-module of depth feature extraction uses the ResNet-18 [2] + TSM model. Which reason is that the depth feature extraction network has a smaller number of channels, and although the spatial dimensional feature extraction capability is weakened, its temporal modeling capability is enhanced. The final output is RGB feature $F_A \in \mathbb{R}^{T_A \times C_A}$ and depth feature $F_D \in \mathbb{R}^{T_D \times C_D}$, where C_A and C_D are the number of channels for RGB and depth output features.

The network creates a lateral connection from the depth stream to the RGB stream to take advantage of the differences and complementarities between the modalities. The local feature interaction module attaches a lateral connection between the two paths of each "stage". Since the dimensions in the time and channel dimensions do not coincide, the time dimension is transformed into the channel dimension (TtoC) to achieve dimensional alignment in the time and channel dimensions before performing the local feature interaction operation. Specifically, we pack 4 frames of depth features into 1 frame of channels, and convert the depth phase features $F_D \in \mathbb{R}^{T \times C \times H \times W}$ to $F_D \in \mathbb{R}^{1/4T \times 4C \times H \times W}$. After extracted by the feature extraction module based on local feature interaction, RGB output features $F_A \in \mathbb{R}^{1/4T \times 4C}$ and depth output features $F_D \in \mathbb{R}^{T \times C}$ can be obtained.

3.2 Spatial Attention Module

We insert the spatial attention module (see Fig. 2) into the feature extraction module based on local feature interactions to generate a 2D spatial attention map $M_S \in \mathbb{R}^{1 \times 1 \times H \times W}$ in spatial dimensions, which can effectively encode the locations of spatial regions to be emphasized or suppressed.

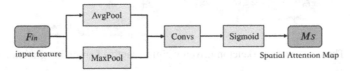

Fig. 2. The framework of spatial attention module

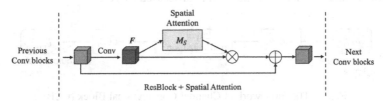

Fig. 3. The diagram of spatial attention module integrated with a ResBlock in ResNet

Based on the experience of inserting attention modules in convolutional neural networks [8], we inserted spatial attention modules after each convolutional block of the feature extraction base model (see Fig. 3). To further implement adaptive feature refinement, the input features are multiplied element-by-element with the spatial attention map to obtain the final output features.

3.3 Feature Fusion Module

To be able to efficiently fuse RGB features F_A and depth output features F_D generated by the dual-stream feature extraction module to obtain an adaptive and robust fused feature F, we propose a depth-driven weight-based adaptive feature fusion module (see Fig. 4).

In the depth-driven weight adaptive feature fusion module, firstly, the channel convolution module is used to perform semantic alignment operations on RGB and depth features to keep the same number of time and channel dimensions. Then, the depth features are used to drive the convolution gating module to generate the gating matrix. Finally, the gating matrix is used as a weight coordination factor in the adaptive feature fusion module to dynamically combine RGB and depth features.

RGB output feature $F_A \in \mathbb{R}^{1/4T \times 4C}$ and depth output feature $F_D \in \mathbb{R}^{T \times C}$ generated from the previous stage of feature extraction, we perform feature semantic alignment operations in the temporal and channel dimensions, respectively, in order to achieve consistent dimensionality of RGB and depth feature dimensions. In this paper, we propose a Channel Convolutional Block (CCB) to handle the channel dimension problem (see Fig. 5), where two channel features are output after convolutional layers of kernel size

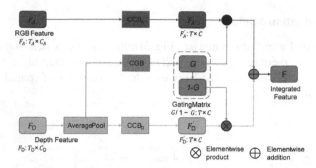

Fig. 4. The framework of skeleton-driven weight adaptive feature integration module

1, layer normalization and ReLU activation function, and the features have the same number of channels. The time dimension is processed as TtoC.

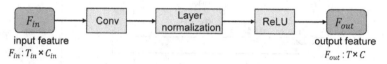

Fig. 5. The framework of Channel Convolutional Block (CCB)

Convolutional Gating Block. Before the feature fusion, we use a Convolutional Gating Block (CGB) to generate a gating matrix G that can be used as a weight coordination factor to dynamically fuse RGB and depth features to cope with changes in the dependence of the model on different modalities (see Fig. 6). The convolutional gating module takes the depth features $F_D \in \mathbb{R}^{T \times C}$, which have been semantically aligned in the time dimension, as input features, and computes a channeled gating matrix $G \in \mathbb{R}^{T \times C}$ and applies it to the features F_A' and F_D' that have achieved semantic alignment.

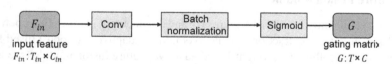

Fig. 6. The framework of Convolutional Gating Block (CGB)

Each element of the resulting gating matrix G lies between [0,1], and $1 - G$ is another gating matrix obtained by subtraction of G. $1 - G$ and G are intended to perform gating operations on features F_A' and F_D' from opposite directions, hat is, $G \otimes F_A'$ and $(1 - G) \otimes F_D'$, where $\otimes$ denotes element-by-element multiplication calculation.

Adaptive Feature Fusion Module. An adaptive and robust action feature $F \in \mathbb{R}^{T \times C}$ is generated by fusing the RGB features and depth features combined with the gating matrix. Action features are generated by the following equation:

$$F = G \otimes F_A' \oplus (1 - G) \otimes F_D' \tag{1}$$

where $\oplus$ denotes the element-by-element summation calculation.

To achieve feature fusion by adaptively changing the weights of RGB features and depth features to obtain adaptive and robust action features, we train the convolutional gating module by using a regularized loss function to force it to learn the priority of depth features:

$$L_{gate} = -log(1 - G) \tag{2}$$

The action features generated by the adaptive feature fusion module will be transferred to the action classifier to predict the probability of the target action class. We use a minimization loss function for network training:

$$L = \mathrm{L_{cls}} + \lambda \mathrm{L_{gate}} \tag{3}$$

where $\mathrm{L_{cls}}$ denotes the standard cross-entropy loss describing the loss of the true labels and the predicted distribution of the training model under all categories, $\mathrm{L_{gate}}$ denotes the gate regularization loss. λ is the weight factor of the regular term and the balance factor of the two loss functions. After several experiments, it is verified that the model has the best recognition performance when $\lambda = 1.5$.

4 Experiments

To verify the effectiveness of the two-stream adaptive weight convolutional neural network based on spatial attention for human action recognition and its component modules, this chapter introduces the NTU RGB + D dataset and the SBU interaction dataset as the benchmark dataset for each experiment.

4.1 Implementation Details

In this paper, we use ResNet-50 + TSM and ResNet-18 + TSM as the base models of convolutional neural networks for RGB streams and deep streams, respectively, and both initialize the ResNet models with publicly released weights pre-trained on the ImageNet dataset. For the NTU RGB + D dataset, set $T_A = 8, T_P = 32$ to sample and construct the input sequence. The final number of channels when all features are fused is $\mathbb{C} = 512$. The training parameters are: 60 training periods and an initial learning rate of 0.005 (reduced by a factor of 10 in the 20th and 40th periods). The weight decay is 1e-4, the batch size is 16, and the dropout is 0.5. The SBU interaction dataset is set to $T_A = 4$ and $T_D = 16$ to construct the input sequence because the sample sequence is too short. The final number of channels when all features are fused is $\mathbb{C} = 512$. The training parameters are: 100 training periods with an initial learning rate of 0.005 (reduced by a factor of 10 in the 50th and 80th periods). The weight decay is 1e-4, the batch size is 32, and the dropout is 0.5. The experiments were performed on two NVIDIA TITAN RTX GPUs for algorithm training. In the test phase, 1 clip clip is sampled for each video for accuracy verification.

4.2 Ablation Experiments

In this subsection, the effectiveness of each module in our method is examined through ablation experiments.

Data Augmentation Module. We increase the number of samples in the training dataset and improve the sample diversity of the dataset by adding a data enrichment module in the pre-processing stage of the dataset. In order to verify the effectiveness of the data enrichment module, we experimentally compare the recognition accuracy results of the proposed method before and after the addition of the data enrichment module, as shown in Table 1.

Table 1. Performance comparison of different data preprocessing methods in SA-AWCNN on NTU RGB + D dataset (Cross Subject) and SBU Kinect Interaction dataset

Method	NTU RGB + D (XSub)		SBU dataset
	Top-1 (%)	Top-5 (%)	Average rate (%)
–	90.11	98.56	92.97
+Data Augmentation Module	**91.85**	**99.24**	**94.30**

The experimental results show that adding the data broadening module to both NTU RGB + D and SBU benchmark datasets can effectively improve the model recognition accuracy. The main reason is that these two benchmark datasets are taken in a restricted laboratory environment with limited number of samples and small motion variations, which are prone to model overfitting. By means of data augmentation, the algorithm can effectively improve the model robustness and prevent serious overfitting.

Local feature interaction module. To better verify the effectiveness of the local feature interaction module, ablation experiments are first conducted for the one-stream structure and the simple two-stream structure, as shown in the first 3 rows of Table 2. The simple two-stream structure is that the generated features do not undergo feature interaction during feature extraction. The results of the deep features transformed by TtoC at the lateral connections are shown in the last row in Table 2.

The experimental results show that the accuracy of the two-stream structure model is better than that of the one-stream structure model in both cases, and the use of the TtoC lateral connection transformation makes the model even better. On the two benchmark datasets, the simple two-stream structure model achieves 89.74% and 91.50% recognition accuracy, which is slightly better than the RGB one-stream structure model by 0.44% and 0.41%. This indicates that the depth features can complement the RGB features to a certain extent. And the two-stream structure model with TtoC lateral connection transformation achieves the optimal accuracy, which is 2.11% and 1.80% better than the simple two-stream structure model. Therefore, it is verified that TtoC is effective as a lateral connection method.

Spatial Attention Module. In Table 3, the effectiveness of the spatial attention module is verified. The experimental results show that adding the spatial attention module can

Table 2. Performance comparison of different local feature interaction modules in SA-AWCNN on NTU RGB + D dataset (Cross Subject) and SBU Kinect Interaction dataset

Method	NTU RGB + D (XSub)		SBU dataset
	Top-1 (%)	Top-5 (%)	Average rate (%)
RGB-only	89.30	98.07	92.09
Depth-only	78.24	96.17	85.45
RGB + Depth	89.74	98.02	92.50
RGB + Depth + TtoC	91.85	99.24	94.30

obtain higher recognition accuracy on the NTU RGB + D dataset and the SBU interaction dataset, with 1.82% and 1.41% improvement over the unadded model. This indicates that spatial attention can prompt the network to extract more effective spatial feature information.

Table 3. Effectiveness verification of spatial attention module in SA-AWCNN on NTU RGB + D dataset (Cross Subject) and SBU Kinect Interaction dataset

Method	NTU RGB + D (XSub)		SBU dataset
	Top-1 (%)	Top-5 (%)	Average rate (%)
–	90.03	98.44	92.89
+Spatial attention	**91.85**	**99.24**	**94.30**

The effectiveness of each algorithm module proposed in the SA-AWCNN is verified by three ablation experiments.

4.3 Comparison Experiments

In this subsection, the performance effectiveness of the proposed SA-AWCNN method is compared with the existing mainstream human action recognition methods on the NTU RGB + D dataset and the SBU interaction dataset.

Tables 4 and 5 show the results of our SA-AWCNN on the NTU RGB + D dataset and the SBU dataset compared with the latest results of other existing mainstream algorithms. The experimental results show that the SA-AWCNN method performs better than other multimodal human action recognition algorithms. Among them, SA-AWCNN is 1.15% higher than the latest method 2s Shift-GCN [15], which is a dual-stream human action recognition method based on unimodality, and slightly improves 0.15% over the latest method IntegralAction [17], which is a multimodality-based two-stream human action recognition method. And its average recognition rate outperforms the Redius-margin [27] method by a margin of 0.9%. Attention modules are introduced in both methods [22, 24], but our spatial attention module achieves higher recognition accuracy.

Table 4. Top-1 accuracy of SA-AWCNN on NTU RGB + D dataset (Cross Subject)

Methods	Modality			XSub Top-1(%)
	RGB	Depth	Ske	
C3D [9]	✓	✓		79.6
TSN [10]	✓			84.7
MDiCNN [11]		✓		84.6
DDMNI [12]		✓		87.08
I3D [13]		✓		88.6
2s-AGCN [14]			✓	88.5
2s Shift-GCN [15]			✓	90.7
Pose-drive attention [16]	✓		✓	84.80
IntegralAction [17]	✓		✓	91.7
c-ConvNet [2]	✓	✓		86.42
ConvNets [3]	✓	✓		86.32
SA-AWCNN	✓	✓		**91.85**

Table 5. Average rate of SA-AWCNN on SBU Kinect Interaction dataset

Methods	Modality			Average rate (%)
	RGB	Depth	Ske	
DWT + Harris [20]	✓			91
MBEpicflow [21]	✓			94.23
3D MTG [22]			✓	90.40
Skeleton + LSTM [23]			✓	90.5
LSTM [24]			✓	91.5
Li et al. [25]			✓	94.15
Ijjina et al. [18]	✓	✓		90.98
Redius-margin [19]	✓	✓		93.4
SA-AWCNN	✓	✓		**94.30**

Through comparison experiments, it can be seen that our proposed SA-AWCNN method has significantly improved in recognition accuracy on both benchmark datasets, achieving optimal performance results.

5 Conclusion

This paper proposes a two-stream adaptive weight convolutional neural network based on spatial attention for human action recognition, SA-AWCNN. In the data preprocessing, the method introduces a data augmentation module to increase the number of training samples while improving the sample diversity to enhance the robustness of the algorithm model and prevent the serious overfitting phenomenon, in the feature extraction, a local feature interaction module is built to establish a lateral connection from depth to RGB to make full use of the inter-modal complementarity to effectively improve the network modal information. Meanwhile, a spatial attention module is introduced to improve the effectiveness of network spatial feature extraction, finally, a depth feature-driven weighted adaptive feature fusion module is used to dynamically fuse the feature RGB and depth features to generate the final fused features. Besides, the experiments show that the proposed method can effectively improve the recognition accuracy and achieve better performance.

References

1. Duan, J., Wan, J., Zhou, S., et al.: A unified framework for multi-modal isolated gesture recognition. ACM Trans. Multimed. Comput. Commun. Appl. **14**(1s), 1–16 (2018)
2. He, K., Zhang, X., Ren, S., et al.: Deep residual learning for image recognition. In: Proceedings of the IEEE/CVF Conference on Computer Vision and Pattern Recognition, pp. 770–778 (2016)
3. Ren, Z., Zhang, Q., Gao, X., et al.: Multi-modality learning for human action recognition. Multimedia Tools Appl. **80**(11), 16185–16203 (2021)
4. Qin, X., Ge, Y., Feng, J., et al.: DTMMN: deep transfer multi-metric network for RGB-D action recognition. Neurocomputing **406**, 127–134 (2020)
5. Lu, Y., Wu, Y., Liu, B., et al.: Cross-modality person re-identification with shared-specific feature transfer. In: Proceedings of the IEEE/CVF Conference on Computer Vision and Pattern Recognition, pp. 13379–13389 (2020)
6. Hu, J., Shen, L., Sun, G.: Squeeze-and-excitation networks. In: Proceedings of the IEEE/CVF Conference on Computer Vision and Pattern Recognition, pp. 7132–7141 (2018)
7. Wang, Q., Wu, B., Zhu, P., et al.: ECA-Net: efficient channel attention for deep convolutional neural networks. In: Proceedings of the IEEE/CVF Conference on Computer Vision and Pattern Recognition, pp. 11531–11539 (2020)
8. Woo, S., Park, J., Lee, J.-Y., Kweon, I.S.: CBAM: convolutional block attention module. In: Ferrari, V., Hebert, M., Sminchisescu, C., Weiss, Y. (eds.) ECCV 2018. LNCS, vol. 11211, pp. 3–19. Springer, Cham (2018). https://doi.org/10.1007/978-3-030-01234-2_1
9. Tran, D., Bourdev, L., Fergus, R., et al.: Learning spatiotemporal features with 3D convolutional networks. In: Proceedings of the IEEE/CVF International Conference on Computer Vision, pp. 4489–4497 (2015)
10. Wang, L., et al.: Temporal segment networks: towards good practices for deep action recognition. In: Leibe, B., Matas, J., Sebe, N., Welling, M. (eds.) ECCV 2016. LNCS, vol. 9912, pp. 20–36. Springer, Cham (2016). https://doi.org/10.1007/978-3-319-46484-8_2
11. Xiao, Y., Chen, J., Wang, Y., et al.: Action recognition for depth video using multi-view dynamic images. Inf. Sci. **480**, 287–304 (2019)
12. Wang, P., Li, W., Gao, Z., et al.: Depth pooling based large-scale 3D action recognition with convolutional neural networks. IEEE Trans. Multimedia **20**(5), 1051–1061 (2018)

13. Carreira, J., Zisserman, A.: Quo vadis, action recognition? A new model and the kinetics dataset. In: Proceedings of the IEEE/CVF Conference on Computer Vision and Pattern Recognition, pp. 6299–6308 (2017)
14. Shi, L., Zhang, Y., Cheng, J., et al.: Two-stream adaptive graph convolutional networks for skeleton-based action recognition. In: Proceedings of the IEEE/CVF Conference on Computer Vision and Pattern Recognition, pp. 12026–12035 (2019)
15. Cheng, K., Zhang, Y., He, X., et al.: Skeleton-based action recognition with shift graph convolutional network. In: Proceedings of the IEEE/CVF Conference on Computer Vision and Pattern Recognition, pp. 183–192 (2020)
16. Baradel, F., Wolf, C., Mille, J.: Human activity recognition with pose-driven attention to RGB. In: 29th British Machine Vision Conference, pp. 1–14 (2018)
17. Moon, G., Kwon, H., Lee, K.M., et al.: IntegralAction: pose-driven feature integration for robust human action recognition in videos. In: Proceedings of the IEEE/CVF Conference on Computer Vision and Pattern Recognition, pp. 3339–3348 (2021)
18. Ijjina, E.P., Chalavadi, K.M.: Human action recognition in RGB-D videos using motion sequence information and deep learning. Pattern Recogn. **72**, 504–516 (2017)
19. Lin, L., Wang, K., Zuo, W., et al.: A deep structured model with radius–margin bound for 3D human activity recognition. Int. J. Comput. Vision **118**(2), 256–273 (2016)
20. Berlin, S.J., John, M.: Particle swarm optimization with deep learning for human action recognition. Multimedia Tools Appl. **79**(25), 17349–17371 (2020)
21. Peng, C., Huang, H., Tsoi, A.C., et al.: Motion boundary emphasized optical flow method for human action recognition. IET Comput. Vision **14**(6), 378–390 (2020)
22. Liu, B., Yu, H., Zhou, X., et al.: Combining 3D joints moving trend and geometry property for human action recognition. In: Proceedings of the IEEE International Conference on Systems, Man, and Cybernetics, pp. 000332–000337 (2016)
23. Baradel, F., Wolf, C., Mille, J.: Pose-conditioned spatio-temporal attention for human action recognition. arXiv preprint arXiv:1703.10106 (2017)
24. Song, S., Lan, C., Xing, J., et al.: An end-to-end spatio-temporal attention model for human action recognition from skeleton data. In: Proceedings of the AAAI Conference on Artificial Intelligence, pp. 4263–4270 (2017)
25. Li, Y., Guo, T., Liu, X., et al.: Action status based novel relative feature representations for interaction recognition. Chin. J. Electron. **31**(1), 168–180 (2022)
26. Lin, J., Gan, C., Han, S.: TSM: temporal shift module for efficient video understanding. In: Proceedings of the IEEE/CVF International Conference on Computer Vision, pp. 7083–7093 (2019)

Sensing and Decoding of Biosignals for Human-Machine Interface

Desktop-Sized Lithium Battery Protection Printed Circuit Board Detection System Based on Visual Feedback Manipulator

Huang Xia⬤, Chenghong Pu⬤, Bangyu Wang⬤, Ziyang Liu⬤, and Yinfeng Fang$^{(\boxtimes)}$⬤

School of Communication Engineering, Hangzhou Dianzi University, Hangzhou, Zhejiang, China
yinfeng.fang@hdu.edu.cn

Abstract. At present, many small and medium factories which produce printed circuit board for lithium battery protection need to test products manually to determine whether they meet the production requirements due to the lack of a complete assembly line. The detecting efficiency is low. Combined with the current situation, this paper proposes a desktop-sized printed circuit board automatic detection system, which consists of four parts: camera, manipulator, PC and special tester. In order to improve the detection and location accuracy of detected points on printed circuit board, this paper proposed a detected point recognition algorithm based on YOLOv5 target detection algorithm, a hand-eye calibration algorithm based on neural network fitting and an approximate double-parallel scatter classification algorithm based on dynamic relaxation voting. Experimental results show that the average localisation error of the system is 0.71 ± 0.03 mm and the average image detected time is 2.88 s, which meet the design requirements.

Keywords: Desktop-sized automatic detection system · YOLOv5 target detection algorithm · Hand-eye calibration

1 Introduction

The lithium battery protection printed circuit board is an important part of the lithium battery module. The quality of the lithium battery protection circuit board directly affects the service life and safety of the lithium battery. After the factory produces the lithium battery protection printed circuit board, it needs to test the indicators of the printed circuit board to ensure the production quality. With the rapid development of automation control, desktop-sized manipulator are more and more widely used in industrial production. Compared with large-scale assembly lines, desktop-level detection systems are more cost-effective, and

Supported by the science and technology innovation activity plan for college students in Zhejiang Province in 2021 and the new talent plan (2021R407012).

H. Liu et al. (Eds.): ICIRA 2022, LNAI 13458, pp. 333–344, 2022.
https://doi.org/10.1007/978-3-031-13841-6_31

more popular in small and medium-sized factories. Based on the desktop-sized manipulator and supplemented by visual feedback, this paper designs and develops a desktop-sized lithium battery protection printed circuit board detection system.

In 2017, Liu Z [1] used principal component analysis and random Hough transform circle to locate the PCB board mark points on the basis of canny edge detection and give accurate positioning parameters. In 2019, Wu Z [2] proposed a precise positioning algorithm for circular marks on PCB based on sub-pixel edge detection and least squares fitting. Through template matching, edge detection roughly obtains the mark position then use least squares fitting and subpixel edge points for further accurate fitting. The positioning error is small. In 2021, Melnyk R [3] uses K-means clustering, filling and thinning algorithms to build skeletons and find pixels for special touch points. Cho T H [4] recognizes characters printed on PCB components by building an LPRNet neural network.

In 2015, Lu P [5] used the pinhole model and the four-coordinate relationship to solve the camera's internal and external parameter matrix by Zhang Zhengyou's plane calibration method, and then solved the camera distortion coefficient. The hand-eye transformation matrix is then determined by affine transformation. In 2019, Ali I [6] provided a mathematical method to study the minimization of pose error and reprojection error for the target for hand-eye calibration. In 2021, Li M [7] combined point cloud registration technology and adopted particle swarm optimization method to improve the calibration efficiency from the perspective of 3D reconstruction. Hua J [8] developed a neural network-based hand-eye calibration method to compensate for the nonlinear distortion of the camera lens.

This system is a desktop-sized device suitable for small and medium-sized factories. It is required that the system be as simple and easy to debug as possible under ensuring the detection accuracy. Combined with the above research, it is considered to construct a neural network-based visual detection and calibration system, which not only ensures the detection accuracy, but also reduces the cost of system construction and debugging.

2   System Composition and Detection Process

2.1   System Composition

The main purpose of the system design is to automatically detect whether the protection printed circuit board is qualified. This system consists of four modules: camera, manipulator, tester of protection printed circuit board and computer. The camera shoots the printed circuit board and transmits the image information to the computer for analysis; the manipulator carries the probe of the tester to move to the printed circuit board detected point; the tester of protection printed circuit board detects whether the relevant parameters of the protection printed circuit board meet the design requirements; The computer process the image information returned by the camera and control the manipulator and tester. The photo of system scenario is shown in Fig. 1.

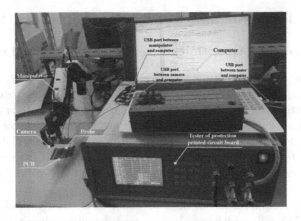

Fig. 1. Photo of system scenario

2.2 Detection Process

First, the camera shoots the board on the desktop, obtains the image information, and sends it to the computer through the USB serial port. The computer identifies the detected point of the printed circuit board through the detection algorithm of detected point, obtains the pixel coordinates of the detected point, and then gets the spatial coordinates of the detected points by the conversion relationship between the pixel coordinates and the space coordinates. After that, the computer controls the manipulator to move to the detected points, and at the same time controls the tester to start the test through the USB serial port. Finally, the tester returns the test result, prompting the worker whether the printed circuit protection board is qualified

In summary, the detection process of the system is shown in Fig. 2.

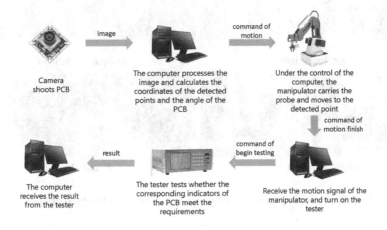

Fig. 2. Schematic diagram of detection process

3   System Principle and Corresponding Algorithm

3.1   The Detection Algorithm of Detected Point Based on YOLOv5

The Principle of Algorithm. Identifying the detected points of the printed circuit board captured by the camera is the basis of all subsequent operations, so correctly getting the pixel coordinates of the detected points is the key to the system. The traditional recognition methods are binarization, corrosion expansion and edge detection. However, the traditional methods will be affected by environmental factors, such as lighting, sundries in the shooting process etc., which often have a greater impact on the accuracy of detection, and the result of recognition is unstable.

Based on the requirements of high precision and strong stability, this paper adopts the YOLOv5 [9] which is a single-target detection algorithm for detecting the detected point. The algorithm has been widely used in PCB component detection [10,11] and defect detection [12,13].

Since only a single target, the detected point, needs to be detected, higher accuracy can be obtained with less training data and shorter training time.

Experiment and Result Analysis. We shoot images in the four scenarios(the circuit board is placed upright and the light is bright; the circuit board is placed upright and the light is dim; the circuit board is placed obliquely and the light is bright; the circuit board is placed obliquely and the light is dim), 6 pictures each, as a training set, and randomly shoot 6 images as a test set.

After 800 epochs, the final mAP@0.5 of the model on the training set is 0.995. Figure 3 shows the results of the YOLOv5 algorithm in different scenarios.

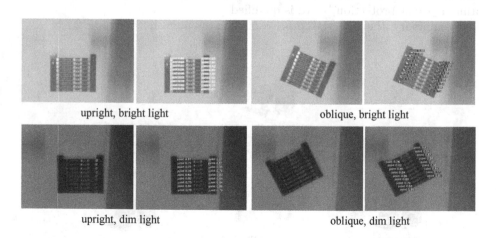

upright, bright light   oblique, bright light

upright, dim light   oblique, dim light

Fig. 3. Detection effect of Yolov5 algorithm in different scenarios

After inference, the detected target is selected by a rectangular frame, and the confidence(the number in Fig. 3) is displayed, that is the probability of the selected object is the target. The algorithm uses the center of the rectangular frame as the pixel coordinates of the detected target. It can be seen that the brightness of the light and the placement of the circuit board have no great influence on the final inference result of the YOLOv5 algorithm, indicating that the algorithm is not dependent on the scene, and the accuracy of detection in each scene is better and can detect all detected points.

In order to further test the accuracy and stability of the YOLOv5 algorithm in different scenarios, we use the success rate of the algorithm detected as the indicators of the accuracy and the confidence of the inference result as the indicators of the algorithm's stability. 20 experiments were carried out in each of four scenarios(the circuit board is placed upright and the light is bright; the circuit board is placed upright and the light is dim; the circuit board is placed obliquely and the light is bright; the circuit board is placed obliquely and the light is dim) and the detection confidence distribution and accuracy were obtained as shown in Fig. 4 in different scenarios, the accuracy of the algorithm is 100%, and the algorithm can accurately detect the detected points of the printed circuit board to meet the requirements of industrial production.

Figure 4 respectively studies the influence of light intensity and placement position on the stability of the algorithm. The confidences of most of the results are between 0.75–0.95, and only a few are between 0.65–0.7, indicating that the algorithm has strong stability in different scenarios.

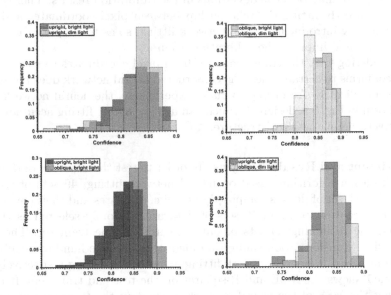

Fig. 4. Inference confidence distribution in different detection scenarios

Moreover, by analyzing and comparing the confidence distribution of the results in each scene in Fig. 4, it can be found that in the case of bright light, the confidence of the result is higher than that in the case of dim light; the confidence when board is places upright is higher than that when board is placed obliquely. It can be concluded that the confidence of the result is higher and the result is more stable when the light is bright and the printed circuit board is placed upright.

3.2   The Hand-Eye Calibration Algorithm Based on Neural Network Fitting

The Principle of Algorithm. Hand-eye calibration is the basis for realizing the transformation from pixel coordinates to space coordinates. The system requires the manipulator to carry a probe for detection, and the area of detected points is small (approximately $5\,mm \times 5\,mm$), so the system requires high positioning accuracy.

The traditional hand-eye calibration algorithm [14] generally calibrates the internal and external parameters of the camera to eliminate the influence of camera distortion, and then uses the affine change method for calibration, that is, by introducing a rotation matrix and a translation matrix.

However, because the calibration of internal and external parameters of the camera is too complicated, if the parameters are calibrated incorrectly, it will have a greater impact on the final result. Although the parameter calibration is accurate, there may be some deviations in the calibration results. Therefore, we considers directly fitting the relationship between pixel coordinates and space coordinates by introducing neural network fitting, so as to simplify the calibration process and improve the calibration accuracy.

Considering that the transformation from pixel coordinates to space coordinates conforms to certain rules, the constructed neural network does not need to be too complicated. According to many experiments, the neural network structure shown in Fig. 5 is designed, which can achieve better fitting accuracy under a relatively simple network structure.

Experiment and Result Analysis. In order to test the accuracy of the hand-eye calibration algorithm based on neural network fitting, 49 sets of data are sampled, each set of data is composed of pixel coordinates and their corresponding spatial coordinates, and 10 sets of data are randomly selected as the test set, and the remaining 39 sets of data are used as the train set. The traditional affine transformation calibration algorithm and the hand-eye calibration algorithm based on neural network fitting are used for testing respectively.

Table 1 shows the MSE and R-squares on the test and train sets. It can be seen that the MSE of the neural network method on the train set and the test set is much smaller than the affine variation method; the R-square of the neural network method on the training set and the test set is 0.99, which is far superior to the affine variation method. Figure 6 also more intuitively shows the fitting

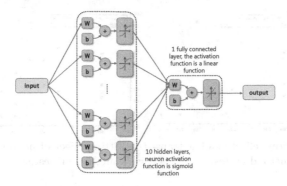

Fig. 5. Diagram of neural network structure

effect of the neural network method and the affine variation method on the test set. Combining the results in Table 1 and Fig. 6, both in the train set and the test set, the final fitting effect of the neural network method is far better than that of the affine variation method.

Table 1. Fitting effect of different calibration algorithms

Indicator	Affine transform	Neural network
MSE of train set	1.22	0.04
MSE of test set	1.75	0.14
R-square of train set	0.87	0.99
R-square of test set	0.84	0.99

3.3 The Algorithm of the Approximate Double-Parallel Scatters Classification Based on Dynamic Relaxation Voting

The Principle of Algorithm. Since the pixel coordinate set of the detected points returned after inference by the YOLOv5 algorithm is disordered, in order to ensure that detect points in sequence, and calculate the angle of the printed circuit board, it is necessary to classify the pixel coordinates. The problem can be transformed into an approximate double-parallel scatter classification problem: there is a point set P in the plane, find two sets of sub-point sets P_1, P_2, satisfying:

$$P_1 \bigcup P_2 = P, P_1 \bigcap P_2 = \oslash \tag{1}$$

And for any sub-point set, satisfy:

$$y_i = kx_i + b_i + \delta \tag{2}$$

where $(x_i, y_i) \in P_i$, δ is a normally distributed random error with mean 0.

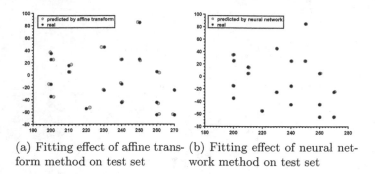

(a) Fitting effect of affine trans- (b) Fitting effect of neural net-
form method on test set   work method on test set

Fig. 6. The effect of affine transformation and neural network on test sets

In the field of image processing, Hough transform [15,16] is usually used to detect lines and circle in images. The approximate double-parallel scatter problem can be solved by using the Hough line detection algorithm.

The general idea of the algorithm is as follows: a straight line is determined according to two points, and each straight line is determined by two parameters, the slope k and the intercept b. First, create an empty parameter set Q. Secondly, every time the straight line parameter k, b determined by any two points in the coordinate set P is calculated, if the straight line parameter exists in the parameter set Q, the number of votes for this parameter is increased by 1, otherwise, the parameter is added to the parameter set Q. Finally, the two pairs of parameters with the most votes are selected as the parameters of the two parallel lines, and the coordinate set is classified according to the distance between each point and the two straight lines, and the final classification result is obtained.

There are two problems with the above algorithm idea:

– Since each coordinate point is not strictly located on a straight line, it may cause that the same parameters do not exist in the parameter set P, resulting in the failure of the voting mechanism. Therefore, it is necessary to introduce a certain relaxation judgment to improve the effectiveness of the voting mechanism.
– If the relaxation is introduced, when the slope of the parallel line is large, the calculated slope will have a large deviation due to the slight deviation of the coordinate points. If the relaxation is too small, the voting will also fail; If the relaxation is too large and the slope of the parallel line is small, it will cause wrong votes and the voting results will be invalid. Therefore, different relaxation at different slopes need to be considered.

Considering the above problems, on the basis of the original algorithm idea, dynamic relaxation is added to the voting part. If the currently calculated parameter is within the relaxation range of a parameter in the parameter set Q, the number of votes for this parameter increases by 1. The relaxation range is related to the slope parameter k in the currently calculated parameters. When k is larger, the relaxation range is larger; when k is smaller, the relaxation range is smaller.

To sum up, the pseudo code of the approximate double-parallel scatter classification algorithm based on dynamic voting is shown in Algorithm 1.

Algorithm 1: An approximate double-parallel scatter classification algorithm based on dynamic relaxation voting

---

Data: P

Result: G_1, G_2

1   **for** $p_i \in P$ **do**

2   **for** $p_j \in P, i \neq j$ **do**

3   **if** $x_j - x_i = 0$ **then**

4        $q' \leftarrow [\infty, \infty]$;

5   **else**

6        $q' \leftarrow \left[\frac{y_j - y_i}{x_j - x_i}, \frac{x_j y_i - x_i y_j}{x_i + y_i} \right]$;

7   **end**

8   **if** $q' \in \left[q - \delta \left(\frac{y_j - y_i}{x_j - x_i} \right), q + \delta \left(\frac{y_j - y_i}{x_j - x_i} \right) \right], q \in Q$ **then**

9        $N[q] \leftarrow N[q] + 1$;

10   **else**

11   add q' to Q, $N\left[q' \right] \leftarrow 1$;

12   **end**

13      $q_1 \leftarrow find(\max\{N[q]\})$;

14      $q_2 \leftarrow find(\max\{N[q], q \neq q_1\})$;

15   **for** $p_i \in P$ **do**

16   **if** $D(p_i, q_1) \leq D(p_i, q_2)$ **then**

17   add p_i to G_1

18   **else**

19   add p_i to G_2

20   **end**

21   **end**

22   **end**

23 **end**

Experiment and Result Analysis. In order to detect the effect of the algorithm, three sets of data which represent respectively the situation with different slopes of the parallel lines were generated. The results of experiment are shown in Fig. 7.

It can be seen from Fig. 7 that the algorithm can perform better classification whether it is a small slope or a large slope and provides help for the system to calculate the deflection angle of the printed circuit board and to detect sequentially.

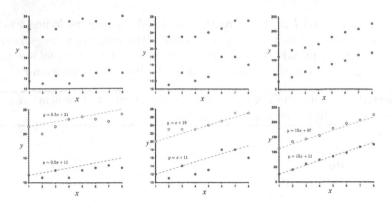

Fig. 7. Effect of scatter line classification algorithm

4   System Experiment and Effect Analysis

4.1   Experiment Platform

The software environment includes the deep learning framework torch1.10.1 and the operating system Windows 10 Professional Edition. The hardware development environment is the processor Intel(R) Core(TM) i7-6500U CPU @ 2.50 GHz 2.6 GHz, and the memory is 8G.

4.2   Experimental Metrics

The positioning accuracy error is used as the metric of accuracy, and the image recognition inference time and the moving time between two detected points are used as detection efficiency. The positioning accuracy error is defined as the Euclidean distance between the coordinates of the detected point calculated by the system and the coordinates of the actual detected point which is obtained through the feedback of the manipulator by the manual control. The image recognition inference time is defined as the time taken by the camera to capture the image and the system to obtain relevant information such as the coordinates and angles of the board. The moving time between two detected points is defined as the time required for the manipulator to move from the current detected point to the next detected point.

4.3   Experiment and Result Analysis

The experimental results are shown in Fig. 8 and Table 1. The results of 20 experiments are as followed: the average positioning accuracy error is 0.71 ± 0.03 mm, the average time of image inference is 2.88 ± 0.02 s, and the point-to-point moving average time is 1.20 ± 0.002 s, and all 20 experiments are successfully detected. The average error of positioning accuracy meets the requirements(5 mm $\times$ 5 mm), and the system detection time is short, and the efficiency is much higher than that of manual detection. The system design meets the requirements.

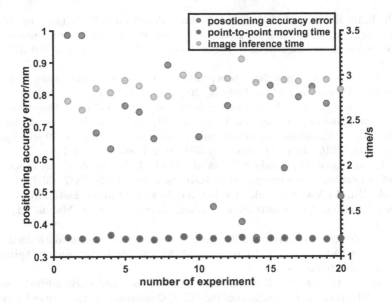

Fig. 8. Experimental result diagram

5   Conclusion

In view of the detection requirements of high accuracy and strong stability, a printed circuit board detected point detection algorithm, a hand-eye calibration algorithm and an approximate double- parallel scatter classification algorithm are proposed. The printed circuit board detection point detection algorithm based on YOLOv5 is less dependent on the scene and the amount of training data, and it can maintain high accuracy and strong stability. The hand-eye calibration algorithm based on neural network uses a simple neural network to fit the nonlinear transformation relationship. The accuracy is much better than the traditional algorithm. The approximate double-parallel scatter classification algorithm based on dynamic relaxation voting can quickly complete the clustering work for a few scatter points. In the final experiment of the whole machine, The experimental results show that the system meets the requirements in terms of accuracy and efficiency and the efficiency is far better than manual operation, which basically meets the requirements of desktop-level detection.

References

1. Liu, Z., Xiong, H., Xiao, S.L., et al.: Positioning of circular mark in PCB based on PCA and segment RHT. J. Chongqing Univ. Technol. (2017)
2. Wu, Z., Chen, F., Liang, G., et al.: Accurate localization of defective circular PCB mark based on sub-pixel edge detection and least square fitting. In: 2019 IEEE 8th Data Driven Control and Learning Systems Conference (DDCLS), pp. 465–470. IEEE (2019)

3. Melnyk, R., Hatsosh, D., Levus, Y.: Contacts detection in PCB image by thinning, clustering and flood-filling. In: 2021 IEEE 16th International Conference on Computer Sciences and Information Technologies (CSIT), vol. 1, pp. 370–374. IEEE (2021)

4. Cho, T.H.: Recognition of characters printed on PCB components using deep neural networks. J. Semicond. Disp. Technol. **20**(3), 6–10 (2021)

5. Lu, P., Liu, Q., Guo, J.: Camera calibration implementation based on Zhang Zhengyou plane method. In: Jia, Y., Du, J., Li, H., Zhang, W. (eds.) Proceedings of the 2015 Chinese Intelligent Systems Conference. LNEE, pp. 29–40. Springer, Heidelberg (2016). https://doi.org/10.1007/978-3-662-48386-2_4

6. Ali, I., Suominen, O., Gotchev, A., et al.: Methods for simultaneous robot-world-hand-eye calibration: a comparative study. Sensors **19**(12), 2837 (2019)

7. Li, M., Du, Z., Ma, X., et al.: A robot hand-eye calibration method of line laser sensor based on 3D reconstruction. Robot. Comput. -Integr. Manuf. **71**, 102136 (2021)

8. Hua, J., Zeng, L.: Hand-eye calibration algorithm based on an optimized neural network. In: Actuators, vol. 10, no. 4, p. 85.201920. Multidisciplinary Digital Publishing Institute (2021)

9. Redmon, J., Divvala, S., Girshick, R., et al.: You only look once: unified, real-time object detection. In: Proceedings of the IEEE Conference on Computer Vision And Pattern Recognition, pp. 779–788 (2016)

10. Lin, Y.L., Chiang, Y.M., Hsu, H.C.: Capacitor detection in PCB using YOLO algorithm. In: 2018 International Conference on System Science and Engineering (ICSSE), pp. 1–4. IEEE (2018)

11. Dou, Z.H., Liu, X.M., Yin, J.L., et al.: Mounted component inspection technology based on YOLO v3. Electron. Meas. Technol. **44**(13), 5 (2021)

12. Wu, J.G., Cheng, Y., Shao, J., et al.: A defect detection method for PCB based on the improved YOLOv4. Chin. J. Sci. Instrum. **42**(10), 8 (2021)

13. Li, J., Gu, J., Huang, Z., et al.: Application research of improved YOLO V3 algorithm in PCB electronic component detection. Appl. Sci. **9**(18), 3750 (2019)

14. Remy, S., Dhome, M., Lavest, J.M., et al.: Hand-eye calibration. In: Proceedings of the 1997 IEEE/RSJ International Conference on Intelligent Robot and Systems. Innovative Robotics for Real-World Applications. IROS 1997, vol. 2, pp. 1057–1065. IEEE (1997)

15. Duda, R.O., Hart, P.E.: Use of the Hough transformation to detect lines and curves in pictures. Commun. ACM **15**(1), 11–15 (1972)

16. Lu, C.H., Xu, S.H., Liu, C.H.: Application of digital image process in the detection of printed circuit board. Chin. J. Sci. Instrum. **22**, 426–429 (2021)

Continuous Finger Kinematics Estimation Based on sEMG and Attention-ConvGRU Network

Penghui Zhao, Chuang Lin[✉], Jianhua Zhang, Xinyue Niu, and Yanhong Liu

School of Information Science and Technology, Dalian Maritime University, 1 Linghai Rode, Ganjingzi District, Dalian 116026, People's Republic of China
linchuang_78@126.com

Abstract. sEMG is an efficient media for human-computer interactions, especially in the controlling of artificial limbs and other mechanical arms. In the paper, we propose a new Attention-ConvGRU model which can continuously estimate the finger joint angles based on sEMG when executing classical grasping motions. The experimental results show that the average correlation coefficient (CC) and the root mean square error (RMSE) of the proposed Attention-ConvGRU method are 0.8320 ± 0.04 and 8.8717 ± 0.98, respectively, which are significantly better than that of the GRU method (0.8093 ± 0.05, $p < 0.01$, 9.3716 ± 0.95, $p < 0.01$). Moreover, the training speed of Attention-ConvGRU is 4.5 times faster than that of GRU method.

Keywords: Finger joint angle · Surface electromyographic signal · Continuous estimation · Attention · Convolution · GRU

1 Introduction

The latest advances in deep neural networks (DNNs), coupled with the innovation and demands of rehabilitation technology, have led to a boom in the development of advanced electromyographic control [1]. Surface eletromyographic signal (sEMG) plays an important role in predicting human motion intentions and is wildly used in estimating kinematics of upper limb movements, especially hand movement, which is crucial in human daily life [2, 3]. Human hands are flexible and dexterous, which involves multiple degrees of freedom control, the estimation of finger kinematics is a challenging task. The motor estimation based on sEMG signal can be divided into two types: classification tasks and regression tasks. Classification tasks focus on discrete motion estimation, and there are many corresponding works such as Oskoei et al. [4], Phinyomark et al. [5], and Liu et al. [6]. The regression task is mainly to estimate the intention of continuous movement of the human body. Compared with the classification task, the regression task can achieve a more natural and intuitive control and is also more challenging. In recent years, more and more literature [7–10] began to pay attention to continuous motion estimation, while most of them can not keep the balance between accuracy and speed in practice.

© The Author(s), under exclusive license to Springer Nature Switzerland AG 2022
H. Liu et al. (Eds.): ICIRA 2022, LNAI 13458, pp. 345–353, 2022.
https://doi.org/10.1007/978-3-031-13841-6_32

To satisfy the requirements of both accuracy and speed in motor estimation, we propose a new method named Attention-ConvGRU (A-ConvGRU), which has a low computational cost also. The experimental results show that the proposed method can efficiently establish the relationship between sEMG and finger joint angles. The Ninapro dataset, a widely used public dataset, is used for evaluation. Compared with the fundamental GRU method, the proposed Attention-ConvGRU method has significant advantages in both accuracy and speed.

2   Method

2.1   Dataset

Ninapro [11] is a public data set for gesture recognition and continuous hand motion estimation. We selected the second group of data (experiment 2) from DB2 as the training set and testing set for this study. The selected dataset included 40 subjects, each subject performing 23 grips. We randomly selected 8 subjects (6 males/2 females, 25–31 years old, 52–75 kg weight, 158–187 cm height) and the most representative 8 movements, as shown in Fig. 1. Each movement was repeated 6 times for 5 s with a rest of 3 s. In DB2, sEMG was collected by the Delsys Trigno wireless system consisting of 12 wireless sEMG electrodes, which collected raw sEMG at a rate of 2 kHz. Hand kinematics were measured using CyberGlove II data gloves with 22 sensors. The position and number of sensors are shown in Fig. 2 [12]. We selected the Proximal Interphalangeal point (PIP), Metacarpophalangeal point (MCP), and two wrist joints as the estimated joints because they are the key movable joints in the grasping movement.

2.2   Data Preprocessing

The Ninapro data set has undergone some pre-processing operations, including Hampel filter to remove 50 Hz power frequency interference and timestamp synchronization of sEMG and joint angle data. Based on this processing, to reduce noise and simplify the calculation, we carry out RMS feature extraction for sEMG. The time window length of the sliding window is 100 ms, and the step size is 0.5 ms. The effect of data enhancement can be achieved by using a small step size to improve the generalization of the model.To speed up the training and improve the prediction accuracy, the μ-law transformation [1] is conducted for signal characteristics, where μ is set to 2^{20} and Minmax normalization is used for angle signals. The processed signal is then used as input to the model. Since each action in Ninapro was repeated 6 times, 4 of them were selected as the training set and the other two as the test set.

Fig. 1. Grasping action in 8 selected

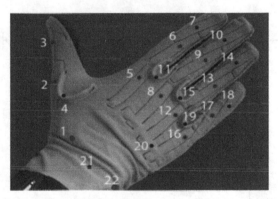

Fig. 2. CyberGlove II data-glove. The red dots represent the 12 angles we estimated [12]. (Color figure online)

2.3 Model

Gated Recurrent Unit (GRU)

Gated Recurrent Unit (GRU), a variant of traditional RNN, can effectively capture the semantic correlation between long sequences and relieve the phenomenon of gradient disappearance or explosion. Its core structure can be divided into two parts: update gate and reset gate. The internal structure of the GRU block is shown in Fig. 3. $r^{(t)}$ and $z^{(t)}$ represent values of the reset gate and update gate at time step t, respectively. $r^{(t)}$ represents how much information can be used to control the last time step. $z^{(t)}$ is used to control the extent to which the state information of the previous moment is brought into the current state. $x_i \in \mathbb{R}^n$ are one-dimensional vectors that are input in the time step t, and $\tilde{h}^{(t)}$ are the output candidate of the circular GRU block in the time step $t-1$, and the output is called $h^{(t)}$. Set as single-layer GRU, reset gate, update gate, output candidate and GRU output are calculated as follows [13]:

$$z^{(t)} = \sigma\left(W_z x^{(t)} + U_z h^{(t-1)} + b_z\right) \tag{1}$$

$$r^{(t)} = \sigma\left(W_r x^{(t)} + U_r h^{(t-1)} + b_r\right) \tag{2}$$

$$\tilde{h}^{(t)} = tanh\left(W x^{(t)} + U\left(r^{(t)} \odot h^{(t-1)}\right) + b\right) \tag{3}$$

$$h^{(t)} = \left(1 - z^{(t)}\right) \odot h^{(t-1)} + z^{(t)} \odot \tilde{h}^{(t)} \tag{4}$$

where W_z, W_r, W are feedforward weights, U_z, U_r, U are recurrent weights of update gate, reset gate and output candidate activation respectively, b_z, b_r and b are biases of reset gates and output candidate activation $h^{(t)}$.

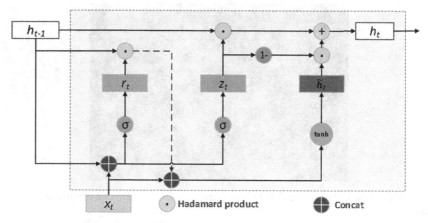

Fig. 3. The internal structure of GRU cell

Attention-ConvGRU (A-ConvGRU).
A-ConvGRU network mainly includes ConvGRU block, Attention block, and fully connected layer block. The network structure diagram is shown in Fig. 4.

The first is the ConvGRU block, which consists of three ConvGRU layers with hidden states of 64, 32, and 12. The internal structure of a single ConvGRU Cell is shown in Fig. 5. Different from the structure in Fig. 3 above, convolution is used to calculate each gate. Previous scholars proposed a similar idea [14], in which linear calculation was changed to 2D convolution to extract spatial information between sequence data. However, 2D convolution still has problems of large computation and slow training speed, and it is not suitable for processing one-dimensional time series such as sEMG. Therefore, we changed the linear computation in GRU to 1D convolution in the time dimension, which can not only better extract the local time-domain information of sEMG but also reduce the memory requirement and speed up the continuous estimation of hand movements. Therefore, it is more suitable for processing sEMG and other sequence problems. The key equations of ConvGRU are shown as follows, where '$*$' denotes the 1D convolution operator and '$\odot$', as before, denotes the Hadamard product:

$$z^{(t)} = \sigma\left(W_z * x^{(t)} + U_z * h^{(t-1)} + b_z\right) \tag{5}$$

$$r^{(t)} = \sigma\left(W_r * x^{(t)} + U_r * h^{(t-1)} + b_r\right) \tag{6}$$

$$\tilde{h}^{(t)} = tanh\left(W * x^{(t)} + U * \left(r^{(t)} \odot h^{(t-1)}\right) + b\right) \tag{7}$$

$$h^{(t)} = \left(1 - z^{(t)}\right) \odot h^{(t-1)} + z^{(t)} \odot \tilde{h}^{(t)} \tag{8}$$

To improve the model's ability to extract global sEMG information [15] and further improve the accuracy and robustness of model prediction, the Attention module was added after the ConvGRU block. The importance of information in sEMG can be well correlated with targets with higher importance values, and the higher the score, the more important it is for predictive performance. The corresponding calculation formula of the Attention module is as follows:

$$Attention(Q, K, V) = softmax\left(\frac{QK^T}{\sqrt{d_k}}\right)V \tag{9}$$

where d_k represents the dimension of the bond vector in matrix K. Q, K, V are query, key, and value vectors.

After the Attention module, there is a linear layer module, which contains two fully connected layers, FC1 and FC2. The number of neurons is 256 and 12 respectively, and the purpose is to output the predicted finger joint angles.

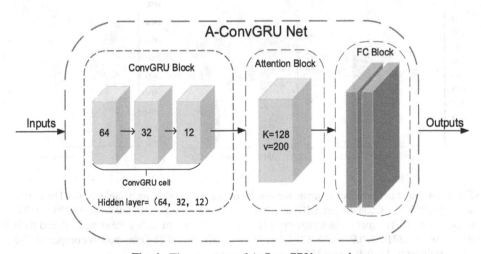

Fig. 4. The structure of A-ConvGRU network

3 Results

We built GRU and A-ConvGRU models on the Pytorch framework [16], trained on the same GPU (RTX 3090), and generated predicted joint angle information. The performance of continuous proportion estimation of finger motion was compared from the aspects of correlation coefficient (CC), RMSE and training convergence time. The convergence of the two models could be achieved after training 300 epochs, the batch size

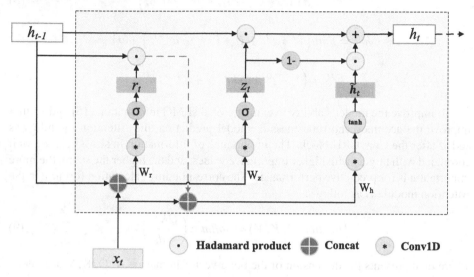

Fig. 5. The structure of the ConvGRU cell

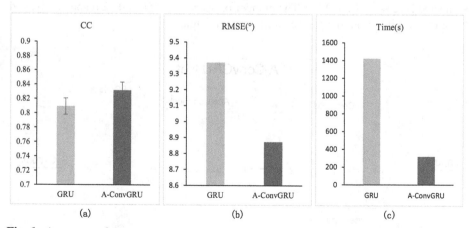

Fig. 6. Average performance comparison results of the two models on 8 subjects. (a) The correlation coefficients (CC) between GRU and A-ConvGRU were 0.8093 ± 0.05 and 0.8320 ± 0.04, respectively. (b) The root mean square error (RMSE) of the two models were compared, and their RMSE were 9.3716 ± 0.95 and 8.8717 ± 0.98, respectively; (c) The two models completed 300 epoch training in 1420.48 s and 317.98 s, respectively.

is 64, the iterator is Adam, and the loss function is the MSE loss function. The number of hidden layers of the GRU is 3, the size of the hidden unit is 128, and the size of the convolution kernel of the A-ConvGRU is 11.

Due to the limited number of subjects, the results of the two methods (RMSE and CC) were statistically analyzed first. Friedman test and Wilcoxon signed-Rank test (A-ConvGRU,GRU) were performed on the two methods respectively, and p values were

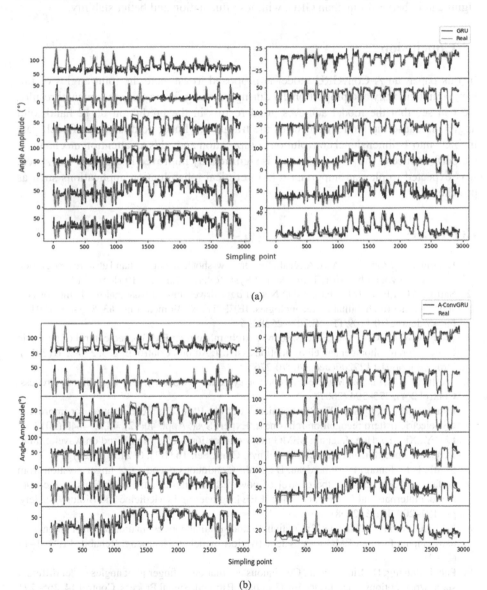

(a)

(b)

Fig. 7. (a) and (b) show the predicted and actual values of GRU and A-ConvGRU at 12 joints for 8 grasping motions, respectively.

all less than 0.05, indicating that the performance difference between the two methods was statistically significant and the performance of the proposed A-ConvGRU was significantly better than that of GRU.

The experimental results are shown in Fig. 6. It was clear that the A-ConvGRU outperformed the GRU in every aspect. Figure 7 shows the fitting of the real joint angles predicted by the two models. From the figure, we can see that A-ConvGRU has significantly better fitting than GRU, with less fluctuation and better stability.

4 Conclusion

In this paper, an A-ConvGRU model is proposed to estimate the joint angles of fingers simultaneously and proportionally during grasping. From the experimental results, we can see that the model achieves good results in the prediction of 12 hand joint angles. Because the model transforms the traditional linear computation of each gate in GRU into 1-dimensional convolution computation and adds an attention mechanism, the performance of the proposed model is significantly improved in accuracy and speed. It is expected to play an important role in clinical rehabilitation applications such as prosthetics.

References

1. Rahimian, E., Zabihi, S., Asif, A., et al.: Fs-her: few-shot learning for hand gesture recognition via electromyography. IEEE Trans. Neural Syst. Rehabil. Eng. **29**, 1004–1015 (2021)
2. Sartori, M., Llyod, D.G., Farina, D.: Neural data-driven musculoskeletal modeling for personalized neurorehabilitation technologies. IEEE Trans. Biomed. Eng. **63**, 879–893 (2016). https://doi.org/10.1109/TBME.2016.2538296
3. Rahman, M.H., Ochoa-luna, C., Saad, M., Archambault, P.: EMG based control of a robotic exoskeleton for shoulder and elbow motion assist. J. Autom. Control Eng. 3, 270–276 (2015). https://doi.org/10.12720/joace.3.4.270-276
4. Okoli, M.A., Hu, H.: Myoelectric control systems—A survey. Biomed. Signal Process. Control **2**(4), 275–294 (2007)
5. Phinyomark, A., Quaine, F., Charbonnier, S., et al.: EMG feature evaluation for improving myoelectric pattern recognition robustness. Expert Syst. Appl. **40**(12), 4832–4840 (2013)
6. Liu, Y., Xin, D., Hua, J., et al.: SEMG motion intention recognition based on wavelet time-frequency spectrum and convLSTM. J. Phys. Conf. Ser. **1631**(1), 012150 (2020)
7. Smith, R.J., Tenore, F., Huberdeau, D., et al.: Continuous decoding of finger position from surface EMG signals for the control of powered prostheses. In: Proceedings of the 30th Annual International Conference of the IEEE Engineering in Medicine and Biology Society, pp. 197–200. IEEE (2008)
8. Neo, J.G., Tamei, T., Shibata, T.: Continuous and simultaneous estimation of finger kinematics using inputs from an EMG-to-muscle activation model. J. Neuroeng. Rehabil. **11**(1), 1–14 (2014)
9. Pan, L., Zhang, D., Liu, J., et al.: Continuous estimation of finger joint angles under different static wrist motions from surface EMG signals. Biomed. Signal Process. Control **14**, 265–271 (2014)
10. Chen, C., Guo, W., Ma, C., et al.: sEMG-Based continuous estimation of finger kinematics via large-scale temporal convolutional network. Appl. Sci. **11**(10), 4678 (2021)

11. Atzori, M., et al.: Electromyography data for robotic hand prostheses. 1–13 (2014)
12. Guo, W., Ma, C., Wang, Z., et al.: Long exposure convolutional memory network for accurate estimation of finger kinematics from surface electromyographic signals. J. Neural Eng. **18**(2), 026027 (2021)
13. Chung, J., Gulcehre, C., Cho, K.H., et al.: Empirical evaluation of gated recurrent neural networks on sequence modeling. arXiv preprint arXiv:1412.3555 (2014)
14. Shi, X., Gao, Z., Lausen, L., et al.: Deep learning for precipitation nowcasting: a benchmark and a new model. Adv. Neural Inf. Process. Syst. **30** (2017)
15. Vaswani, A., Shazier, N., Parmar, N., et al.: Attention is all you need. Adv. Neural Inf. Process. Syst. **30** (2017)
16. Ketkar, N.: Introduction to PyTorch BT - Deep Learning with Python: A Hands-on Introduction. Apress, Berkeley, pp. 195–208 (2017)

Nonlinear Methods on HD-sEMG Signals for Aging Effect Evaluation During Isometric Contractions of the Biceps Brachii

Kawtar Ghiatt[1]([✉]), Ahmad Diab[1], Sofiane Boudaoud[1], Kiyoka Kinugawa[2], John McPhee[3], and Ning Jiang[4]

[1] Alliance Sorbonne University, Université de Technologie de Compiègne, CNRS, UMR 7338, Biomechanics and Bioengineering, Centre de Recherche de Royallieu, 60203 Compiègne cedex, France
kawtar.ghiatt@utc.fr
[2] Sorbonne University and AP-HP, Paris, France
[3] University of Waterloo, Waterloo, Canada
[4] National Clinical Research Center for Geriatrics, West China Hospital Sichuan University, and 11 the Med-X Center for Manufacturing, Sichuan University, Chengdu, Sichuan, China

Abstract. Muscle aging is associated with a loss of muscle mass and strength. Different factors are responsible, which can possibly lead to a modification of the complexity of the neuromuscular system. This may be reflected in electromyogram signals. In this study, we have tried to analyze the nonlinearity and chaotic characteristics of high-density surface electromyography (HD-sEMG) from Biceps Brachii (BB) during isometric contractions, at low and moderate levels, recorded from young and elderly people. For this purpose, three measures widely employed in nonlinearity detection were used: Time reversibility (Tr), Sample Entropy (SE), and Delay Vector Variance (DVV). For comparison purposes, the Root Mean Square amplitude (RMSA) was also computed. The results indicated that SE and Tr are significantly higher in elderly people. Furthermore, signal complexity decreases with contraction level for all categories.

Keywords: HD-sEMG signals · Aging muscle · Non-linear methods

1 Introduction

Muscle and strength loss are a natural process of aging. This contributes to the risk of fall, weakness and capacity to exercise [1]. Muscle aging is associated with a reduction in muscle fiber number and size. Numerous factors explain these changes in muscle such as replacement of muscle tissue by slower fibers, adipose and fibrous tissues, or disorders in the nervous system [2]. To adapt to these changes, the remained motor neuron innervates more muscle fibers, results in enlarged motor units and fiber-type grouping [3]. All these alterations may lead to modifications of the complexity of the generated muscle electrical activity according to contraction level [3]. To our knowledge, these aging effects are not yet taken in consideration in HD-sEMG applications like prosthetic control.

H. Liu et al. (Eds.): ICIRA 2022, LNAI 13458, pp. 354–362, 2022.
https://doi.org/10.1007/978-3-031-13841-6_33

In this study, we proposed to examine the complexity of HD-sEMG signals by using nonlinear measures. HD-sEMG signals were measured from the Biceps Brachii (BB), in 14 young and 14 older adults during an isometric contraction at 20% and 40% of maximum voluntary contraction (MVC). We computed the Time reversibility (Tr), Sample entropy (SE) and Delay Vector Variance (DVV) of each HD-sEMG signals and the Root Mean Square Amplitude (RMSA) for comparison. Nonlinear analysis was widely used to characterize biological signals such as EHG signals [4], effects of aging on the cardiovascular system in ECG signal [5], or disturbances in the complexity of EEG for schizophrenia [6]. Several applications of nonlinear analysis methods have been done on EMG signals. In [6], the authors investigated the complexity and coupling of HD-sEMG signals and grid misalignment estimation using nonlinear measures. The complexity of sEMG signals was examined during walking from four lower limbs muscles using sample entropy. The main objective of this study is to understand aging neuromuscular behavioral changes in isometric contraction, by measuring the effect of age on the complexity of muscle activation patterns during isometric contraction at different force levels. This can help to improve quality life of Elderly people, but also to adapt prosthesis model to aging muscle.

2   Material and Methods

2.1   Participants

Twenty-eight young and elderly subjects participated in the study after signing a participant consent form. All participants had no orthopedics, neurologic and cardiac disorders and were moderately active. There is no significant difference in BMI values between young and old subjects. This study has been reviewed and received ethics clearance through a University of Waterloo Research Ethics Committee (ORE#:2271).The characteristics of the participants are present in the following Table 1.

Table 1. Participants characteristics (YM: Young Men, YW: Young Women, EM: Elderly Men, EW: Elderly Women)

Group	Number	Age (years)	BMI (kg/m^2)
YM	5	25.2 ± 3.27	22.5 ± 2.13
YW	10	22.9 ± 3.6	21.9 ± 2.54
EM	4	73.2 ± 1.6	25.5 ± 4.61
EW	9	72.8 ± 3.6	24.17 ± 2.34

2.2   Torque and HD-sEMG Recording

At the beginning of the experimental exercise, the subject performed three BB maximum voluntary contractions for 5 s with two minutes of rest between each contraction. MVC is the maximum torque value of the dynamometer Biodex System Pro 4 (Biodex Medical Systems, Shirley, New York) obtained at the end of the three contractions. Then, the participant performed isometric contractions at 20% MVC and 40% MVC of BB muscle. The recording time was fifteen seconds to give time to reach the goal (20% or 40% MVC) and provide at least five seconds of reliable contraction. For each MVC level, subjects completed three trials with three-minute rest between them.

HD-sEMG signals were recorded simultaneously using an OT Bioelettronica manufactured 8x8 HD-sEMG grid from the dominant BB muscle, as depicted in Fig. 1. The sampling frequency was 2048 Hz. The grid was put over a line drawn between two anatomical landmarks: the acromion and the distal insertion of the BB tendon avoiding motor endplate and myotendineous junction vicinity (see Fig. 1). This placement was done according to SENIAM recommendation [7]. The ground and reference electrodes strips were placed on the wrist. A band-pass filter between 10 Hz and 500 Hz is applied to increase the signal to noise ratio (SNR) and reduce motion artefacts. Channels that were poorly connected or that had intermittent noise were discarded. Furthermore, channels with an SNR of less than 12 were removed. The SNR was computed as the following:

$$SNRc = 10\left(\frac{\sum_{i=1}^{N} S^2[i]}{N} \frac{P}{\sum_{i=1}^{P} R^2[i]}\right) \tag{1}$$

where S is the filtered sEMG recorded signal at a given channel c during the 5-s window. The value N is the number of samples in the 5-s time window. The value R is a 1-s surface EMG signal recorded at the same channel when the muscle is at rest (only noise is observed), and P is the number of samples in the signal R. The SNR was computed for each channel and for each three trials. The average of these three values was used as the mean SNR of the corresponding channel. Signal processing was achieved using MATLAB 2016a.

Fig. 1. Placement of the 64-electrode grid on the BB (left), HD-sEMG grid (right).

2.3 Methods

Four different measures (three nonlinear and one linear) were used to analyze the signals: Tr, SE, DVV, and RMSA. In the 15-s sEMG recorded signal, a five-second segment was selected. The retained five second signal is divided into five equal segments. The selected features were extracted from each channel and each segment of each participant. The mean and standard error of the mean (SEM) were calculated for each feature over the number of channels and number of segments and number of participants in each group.

At the end, we obtained a mean value over 64 channels for each group. Then, a two-tailed t-test was performed between the mean obtained for the younger participants and older participants of the same sex, for a given contraction level.

Time Reversibility

A time series is said to be reversible if and only if its probabilistic properties are invariant with respect to time reversal [8]. In [9], it was proposed a test for the null hypothesis to demonstrate that a time series is reversible. Rejection of the null hypothesis implies that a linear Gaussian random process cannot describe the time series, so time irreversibility is considered as a strong signature of nonlinearity. In this study, time asymmetry was simply measured by taking the first differences of the series to some power. In this study, non-linearity is computed by using time reversibility for Signal S, described as [4, 8]:

$$Tr(\tau) = \left(\frac{1}{N-\tau}\right) \sum_{n=r+1}^{N} (S_n - S_{n-\tau})^3, \tag{2}$$

where N is the signal length and τ is the time delay. The time delay is fixed at N−1.

Sample Entropy

Sample Entropy proposed in [10], is a refinement of Approximate Entropy [11], which quantifies the regularity and predictability of a signal. It can be defined how often different patterns of data are found in the dataset. It is the negative natural logarithm of the conditional probability that a dataset of length N, having repeated itself for m samples within a tolerance r, will also repeat itself for m + 1 samples[4]. Thus, a lower value of SE indicates more regularity in the time series. In this study, SE was computed as:

First, the time series of N points, $x1, x2, \ldots, x_N$, is embedded, in a delayed dimension, of length m, where the template vectors, given by:

$$y_i(m) = (x_1 + 1, \ldots, x_N + m - 1),$$

where $i = 1, 2, .., N - m + 1$. The probability $B^m(r)$ is the probability that two sequences are similar for m points, is computed by counting the average number of vector pairs, at distance lower than the tolerance r, without allowing self-counting. Similarly, Am(r) is defined for m + 1. The SE is then calculated as:

$$SE(x, m, r) = -\ln\left(\frac{A^m(r)}{B^m(r)}\right), \tag{3}$$

In this study, the tolerance r is defined as 0.25 of the standard deviation and m = 2.

Delay Vector Variance

The delay vector variance uses the predictability family to examine the determinism and nonlinearity in a time series [12]. Time series can be represented in phase space using time-delay embedding. When time delay is embedded into a time series, it can be represented by a set of delay vectors (DVs) of a given dimension m. The dimension of the delay vectors can then be expressed as $X(k) = [x_{(k-m\tau)} \ldots x_{(k-\tau)})]$ where τ is the time lag. For every DV $X(k)$, there is a corresponding target, namely the next sample x_k.

A set βk (m, d) is generated by grouping those DVs within a certain Euclidean distance d to DV X(k). For a given embedding dimension m, a measure of unpredictability σ^{*2} (target variance) is computed over all sets of βk. Then, the mean μd and standard deviation σd are measured over all pair-wise Euclidian distances between DVs as following d(i, j) = ∥ x(i) − x(j) ∥, (i ≠ j) [4].The sets βk (m, d) are obtained such that:

βk (m, d) = {x(i)} \∥x(k) − x(j) ∥ ≤ d} i.e., sets which consist of all DVs that lie closer to X (k) than a distance d, taken from the interval [μd − n_d * σd; μd + n_d * σd] where n_d is a parameter controlling the span over which to perform DVV method. For every set βk (m, d) the variance of the corresponding targets σ_k^2 (m, d) is computed. The average over the N sets βk (m, d) is divided by the variance of the time-series signal, σ_k gives the inverse measure of predictability, namely target variance σ^{*2}.:

$$\sigma^{*2} = \frac{\frac{1}{N}\sum_{k=1}^{N}\sigma_k^2}{\sigma_x^2}.$$ (4)

The delay and the dimension of the phase space are obtained automatically by the mutual information and the false nearest neighbor methods, respectively.

RMS Amplitude
The root mean square evaluates the magnitude of the sEMG signal, averaged over the grid to detect the activation of the muscle.

$$RMSA = \sqrt{\frac{1}{N_{total}}\sum_{i=1}^{Ntotal} S_i^2},$$ (5)

where N_{total} is the total number of samples recorded in the sEMG signal, and x_i is the i value of the sEMG signal for each channel.

3 Results

3.1 Torque

Table 2 displays the mean values ± SEM of the torque corresponding to the maximum voluntary contraction for each age and sex category. The average MVC is significantly lower for elderly women (YW = 31 Nm, EW = 47 Nm, p < 0.05). The average torque is not significantly different (p = 0.86) between young and elderly men.

Table 2. MVC repartition with age and gender

Group	MVC (Nm)	p-value
YM	63.6 ± 14.6	0.89 (n.s)
EM	63.4 ± 7.93	
YW	47 ± 13.54	0.04*
EW	31 ± 5.04	

3.2 Root Mean Square Amplitude (RMSA)

Figure 2 illustrates the changes in the mean ± SEM of RMS values of young and elderly people with increasing force. The values were significantly lower for elderly women in both 20% (YW = 50 mV, EW = 43 mV, p < 0.001) and 40% MVC (YW = 115 mV, EW = 80 mV, p < 0.001) but not for men.

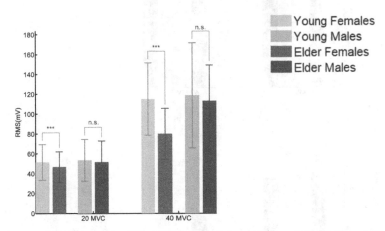

Fig. 2. Averaged RMSA for the BB of YW, EW, YM, and EM at 20% MVC and 40% MVC. "n.s" denotes "non-significant" (null hypothesis rejected), "*": p-value < 0.05, "**": p-value < 0.01, and "***" p-value < 0.001.

3.3 Nonlinear Measures

This part describes the results obtained for nonlinear methods. Figure 3 represents the mean ± SEM of Tr, SE and DVV of young and elderly people with increasing force, respectively. The average sample entropy and time reversibility decreased with increasing force. Elderly people show higher values (p < 0.001) of sample entropy and time reversibility in their respective categories. The values of SE and Tr decrease with the level of contraction in both gender categories.

If we examine now the DVV in Fig. 3-c, we cannot observe any common trend according to age category, even if the results are significantly different. There is no clear variation of the values between young and elderly. This is also the case when the force level increases.

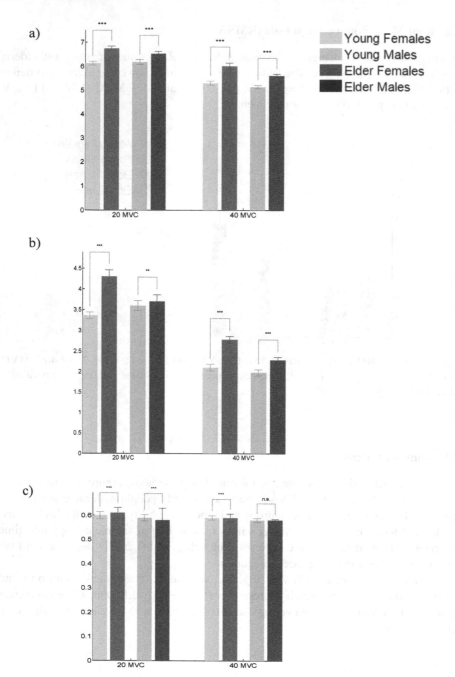

Fig. 3. Average Tr (a), SE (b) and DVV(c) for the BB of YW, EW, YM, and EM at 20% MVC and 40% MVC.

4   Results

Three nonlinear measures and one linear measure were applied to compare recorded HD-sEMG signals from young and elderly subjects during isometric contractions of the BB muscle at low and moderate contraction levels. The results indicate that elderly exhibited higher nonlinearity for both sex. Furthermore, this nonlinearity decreased with the contraction level. Concerning RMSA, the values are higher in the young cohorts, which not the case for the nonlinear descriptors. These observations seem to be related to both physiological and functional modifications of the neuromuscular system with aging. However, since this work is a preliminary study, it is hard and early to propose some hypothesis. Further studies are needed, combined to simulation for hypothesis testing, to better explain the observed results on larger cohorts.

5   Discussion

In this study, we attempted to characterize nonlinear properties of HD-sEMG signals of BB muscle during isometric contraction between young and elderly people. The obtained RMSA values of elderly women were lower than young women in both studied contraction levels. Elderly men exhibited also lower RMSA values than younger, but the difference is not significant. The lower values of RMSA in the elderly category can be explained by the loss of muscle mass with aging [2]. Elderly adults displayed higher values for time reversibility and sample entropy. Furthermore, the complexity seems to decrease with the level of isometric contraction. Concerning DVV, we did not see any particular trend between young and elderly people. Observed modifications of complexity, by using Tr and SE, should be related to functional and anatomical changes of the neuromuscular system with aging. We did not consider here that sample entropy could be affected by the high sampling rate. In a future work, we will distinguish a proper time lag. In addition, we will repeat the analysis at different time scales of the signal. However, the complexity increases with aging and its decrease with contraction intensity remains difficult to explain In fact, one study revealed that SE of sEMG signals are lower in the elderly for proximal muscles but not for Gastrocnemius muscle during treadmill walking [13]. It seems that complexity modification is specific to the studied muscle and the type of exercise. In this study, the HD-sEMG signals were recorded from Biceps Brachii muscle. This muscle is widely studied to characterize muscle activation and aging effect.This is mainly due to its size and fusiform shape that facilitate the electrode grid placement in alignment with muscle fibers. Finally, the obtained results should be further investigated and confirmed using a multiscale electrophysiological muscle model, especially after enlarging the experimental database.

Acknowledgment. This work was carried out and funded in the framework of the Labex MS2T. It was supported by the French Government, through the program "Investments for the future" managed by the National Agency for Research (Reference ANR-11-IDEX0004–02).

References

1. Kirk, B., Phu, S., Debruin, D.A., Hayes, A.D.: Aging muscle and sarcopenia. Encyclopedia of Biomedical Gerontology. Rattan, SIS, ed. Academic Press, USA, pp. 120–131 (2019)
2. Lexell, J., Henriksson-Larsén, K., Winblad, B., Sjöström, M.: Distribution of different fiber types in human skeletal muscles: effects of aging studied in whole muscle cross sections: aging and Skeletal Muscle Morphology. Muscle Nerve **6**(8), 588–595 (1983). https://doi.org/10.1002/mus.880060809
3. Piasecki, M., Ireland, A., Piasecki, J., Stashuk, D.W., McPhee, J.S., Jones, D.A.: The reliability of methods to estimate the number and size of human motor units and their use with large limb muscles. Eur. J. Appl. Physiol. **118**(4), 767–775 (2018). https://doi.org/10.1007/s00421-018-3811-5
4. Diab, A., Hassan, M., Marque, C., Karlsson, B.: Performance analysis of four nonlinearity analysis methods using a model with variable complexity and application to uterine EMG signals. Med. Eng. Phys. **36**(6), 761–767 (2014). https://doi.org/10.1016/j.medengphy.2014.01.009
5. Shiogai, Y., Stefanovska, A., McClintock, P.V.E.: Nonlinear dynamics of cardiovascular ageing. Phys. Rep. **488**(2–3), 51–110 (2010). https://doi.org/10.1016/j.physrep.2009.12.003
6. Kamath, C.: Analysis of EEG Dynamics in epileptic patients and healthy subjects using hilbert transform scatter plots. OALib **02**(01), 1–14 (2015). https://doi.org/10.4236/oalib.1100745
7. Hermens, H.J., et al.: European Recommendations for Surface ElectroMyoGraphy, p. 4 (1999)
8. Hassan, M., Terrien, J., Marque, C., Karlsson, B.: Comparison between approximate entropy, correntropy and time reversibility: application to uterine electromyogram signals. Med. Eng. Phys. **33**(8), 980–986 (2011). https://doi.org/10.1016/j.medengphy.2011.03.010
9. Diks, C., Vanhouwelingen, J.C., Takens, F., Degoede, J.: Reversibility as a criterion for discriminating time-series. Phys. Lett. **201**(2–3), 221–228 (1995)
10. Richman, J.S., Moorman, J.R.: Physiological time-series analysis using approximate entropy and sample entropy. Am. J. Physiol.-Heart Circ. Physiol. **278**(6), H2039–H2049 (2000). https://doi.org/10.1152/ajpheart.2000.278.6.H2039
11. Pincus, S.M.: Approximate entropy as a measure of system complexity. Proc. Natl. Acad. Sci. **88**(6), 2297–2301 (1991). https://doi.org/10.1073/pnas.88.6.2297
12. Kuntamalla, S., Reddy, R.G.L.: The effect of aging on nonlinearity and stochastic nature of heart rate variability signal computed using delay vector variance method. Int. J. Comput. Appl. **14**, 40–44 (2011)
13. Kang, H.G., Dingwell, J.B.: Differential changes with age in multiscale entropy of electromyography signals from leg muscles during treadmill walking. PLoS ONE **11**(8), e0162034 (2016). https://doi.org/10.1371/journal.pone.0162034

A Novel Preprocessing Approach with Soft Voting for Hand Gesture Recognition with A-Mode Ultrasound Sensing

Sheng Wei[1], Yue Zhang[1], Jie Pan[1], and Honghai Liu[2,3]

[1] College of Computer Science and Technology, Zhejiang University of Technology, Hangzhou, China

[2] School of Computing, University of Portsmouth, Portsmouth, UK
Honghai.liu@icloud.com

[3] State Key Laboratory of Robotics and Systems, Harbin Institute of Technology, Shenzhen, China

Abstract. To explore the potential of gesture recognition based on the A-mode ultrasound (AUS) interface in human-computer interaction (HCI), according to the characteristics of AUS signal, a novel preprocessing approach is designed, feature extraction is performed by the window analysis method, and four methods, Linear Discriminant Analysis (LDA), k-Nearest Neighbor (KNN), Support Vector Machine (SVM), and Artificial Neural Network (ANN) for classification. The experimental results show that the single feature with the best results can achieve 91.63% accuracy on KNN. Meanwhile, by feature combination, we can achieve 91.91% accuracy on the KNN classifier, it is 3.60% higher than the highest recognition rate of 88.03% among linear fitting features, called KB features. Further, we learn the integration of soft voting for four classifiers, LDA, KNN, SVM, and ANN, and achieve the highest recognition rate of 92.32% on single features and can achieve 93.09% decoding rate on combined features, which is 4.01% higher than 89.08% among KB features with the soft voting method. The experimental results show that AUS has outstanding performance in gesture decoding.

Keywords: A-mode ultrasound · Gesture recognition · Preprocessing · Feature extract · Classification method · Soft voting

1 Introduce

With the development of artificial intelligence and robotics, human-computer interaction (HCI) has gained widespread attention and application. In the field of HCI and machine control, biosignal-based interaction has been widely used. Currently, bioelectric signals that have been widely concerned include electromyographic (EMG) [10,16], electroencephalographic (EEG) [17], and electrooculography (EOG) [23], etc. In addition to bioelectric signals, Inertial Measurement

© The Author(s), under exclusive license to Springer Nature Switzerland AG 2022
H. Liu et al. (Eds.): ICIRA 2022, LNAI 13458, pp. 363–374, 2022.
https://doi.org/10.1007/978-3-031-13841-6_34

Unit (IMU) [7], near-infrared spectroscopy (NIRS) [13], pressure sensing [1], and ultrasound (US) [15,24] has been used in HCI, which is mostly non-invasive and can be better accepted by users. Among them, surface EMG (sEMG) signals have been widely used in HCI control due to their mature acquisition methods and good research base. However, it has the disadvantages of low signal-to-noise ratio and insensitivity to fine finger movements because it acquires weak electrical signals from the surface of human skin and is easily disturbed by external noise, while the muscles associated with fine finger movements are generally deeper in the arm [22]. Because US can acquire morphological information of deep muscles and tissues and it is non-invasive [3], we considered using US sensing as a signal source for gesture recognition to explore the possibility of its application in gesture recognition, especially its potential in the recognition of fine finger movements.

The US usually refers to mechanical waves with a vibration frequency of more than 20 kHz, which can propagate in different media such as solid and liquid. The propagation speed will be different in different media, and reflection and refraction will occur when encountering the interface of dissimilar media, it is commonly used in the detection and location of cracks in aviation and industry [19]. Because it can penetrate human muscle organs and other media, it is commonly used in various medical diagnoses. In medicine, it is often used for biological measurement of ophthalmology [12]. Just like visible light, it can image various tissues inside the human body, and it is convenient, intuitive and harmless to detect the health status of various parts of the human body. At present, the US used for the HCI is mainly A-mode ultrasound (AUS) [24] and B-mode ultrasound (BUS) [3], in which AUS is single-point US and BUS is array US.

The gesture recognition process is based on biological signals and mainly includes signal acquisition, data preprocessing, feature extraction, classifier training, testing, and other steps. After collecting the data, it is necessary to preprocess and extract the features according to the characteristics of different signals. At present, commonly used artificial features include time-domain features, frequency domain features, and time-frequency domain features. With the development of deep learning, many researchers have started to use convolutional neural networks to extract the abstract features of signals [4]. On the choice of classifiers, common machine learning classifiers include Linear Discriminant Analysis (LDA) [16], k-Nearest Neighbor (KNN) [2], Support Vector Machine (SVM) [2,10], and Artificial Neural Network (ANN) [16], decision tree [18], etc. Different classifiers have different characteristics, so we consider fusing the results of multiple classifiers to get more robust classification results.

The rest of the paper is organized as follows: Sect. 2 introduces the related works. Section 3 describes the methods and basic experimental setting. Section 4 shows the results and discussions. The last section gives a conclusion of this study.

2   Related Work

In the related work of wearable ultrasonic gesture recognition: Huang et al. [6] online gesture recognition based on BUS device, among 11 kinds of hand movements, the average online action selection time is (0.24 ± 0.15) s, the action completion time is (1.27 ± 0.19) s, the action completion rate is $(97 \pm 7)\%$, and the real-time accuracy rate is (95 ± 5). Li et al. [8] The average recognition rate of gesture recognition based on a single vibrator ultrasonic sensor for five finger movements is $(91.1 \pm 4.73)\%$. Sun et al. [20] put forward a man-machine interface technology based on a single-dual-frequency single vibrator ultrasonic probe (AUS probe). The four-channel recognition accuracy rate of three probes and two classifiers is 94.79% at the lowest. The muscle thickness was extracted to explore the relationship between muscle thickness, muscle strength, and muscle fatigue. Castellini et al. [3] found that muscle features are related to finger position through ultrasonic imaging, and moved the position of the point of interest by evaluating the optical flow at the key frame to prevent the shift error in the experimental process.

Xia et al. [22] arranged the two sensors at the same muscle location, which could acquire sEMG and AUS signals simultaneously, and the experimental results showed an average classification accuracy of $(68.59 \pm 5.20)\%$ for sEMG features and $(84.25 \pm 3.89)\%$ for AUS features, the recognition accuracy of AUS is higher than that of sEMG. Yang et al. [25] used a multichannel AUS lightweight device to evaluate the performance of finger motion recognition with an offline recognition accuracy of $(98.83 \pm 0.79)\%$. The real-time motion completion rate was $(95.4 \pm 8.7)\%$.

In related research on feature extraction of biological signals. In [14], researchers compared 37 sEMG features used for gesture classification. Among them, sample entropy is the best feature. In addition, the experimental results also show that the best three sEMG features can improve the recognition accuracy by more than 80%. Chen et al. [4] proposed a feature extraction method based on a convolutional neural network (CNNFeat) to improve the accuracy of gesture recognition. It was found that combining CNNFeat with traditional features could further improve the accuracy of SVM, LDA, and KNN, respectively, by 4.35%, 3.62%, and 4.7%. In addition, this work also demonstrates that CNNFeat can enhance model training through more data.

Voting is a common trick used in ensemble learning to help us improve the generalization ability of the model and reduce the error rate of the model [21]. It is an ensemble learning model that follows the principle of minority rule and reduces the variance by integrating multiple models, thus improving the robustness of the model. Ideally, the prediction of the voting method should outperform the prediction of any of the base models [11]. In classification, the voting method can be subdivided into the hard voting method and the soft voting method. The prediction result of hard voting is the class with the most occurrence of all voting results, while the prediction result of soft voting is the class with the largest probability sum of all voting results. Compared to hard voting, the soft voting method takes into account the additional information of prediction probability and therefore can produce more accurate prediction results than the hard voting method [9].

3   Method and Experiment

This experiment mainly includes AUS data acquisition, data preprocessing, artificial feature extraction, classifier training, etc. The flow chart of this experiment is shown in Fig. 1. A new preprocessing method for AUS data based on the characteristics of the collected AUS signal was designed, selected a batch of manual features commonly used in the field of sEMG, and used the data splitting window method to extract features from the AUS signal, and then fed the features into the LDA, KNN, SVM, and ANN classifiers for training to get the results. The final results are obtained based on the prediction probabilities of these four classifiers using the soft voting method. To demonstrate the effectiveness of our proposed preprocessing method and features, we compared them with KB feature which was proposed by previous researchers [25].

The experiments were performed on an i5-11400F CPU and 32 GB RAM Windows system PC. The scikit-learn software package written by Python was used as the machine learning toolkit in the experiment.

The data acquisition was approved by the ethics committee of the Zhejiang University of Technology. In this paper, all the experiments were carried out following the Declaration of Helsinki, and informed consent was obtained from all volunteers.

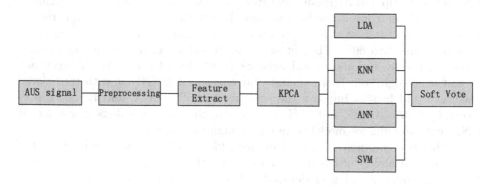

Fig. 1. Experimental flow chart.

3.1   Dataset

In this experiment, a four-channel US data set is utilized, and its sampling frequency 10 Hz, that is, each channel collects 10 frames of signals per second, and each frame of signals includes 1000 points. In the dataset, there are 20 gestures, as shown in Fig. 2. It includes: wrist flexion (WF), wrist extension (WE), wrist radial deviation (WRD), wrist ulnar deviation (WUD), wrist supination (WS), wrist pronation (WP), fist (FS), index point (IP), index and middle finger point (IMP), thumb and index finger flexion (TIF), thumb flexion (TF), fingers abduction (FA), thumb up (TU), index flexion (IF), middle finger flexion (MF), index and middle finger flexion (IMF), middle and ring finger flexion (MRF), ring and little finger flexion (RLF), pinch (PH) and rest state (RS). The above 20 movements are a set of movements, each of which lasts for 5 s, and there is no rest between movements. Each group of movements is completed continuously as an experiment, and each subject is required to conduct eight experiments continuously, with a rest time of 20 s between experiments. This dataset includes eight right-handed subjects (age: 22 ± 3, height: 175 ± 10 cm, weight: 65 ± 10 kg).

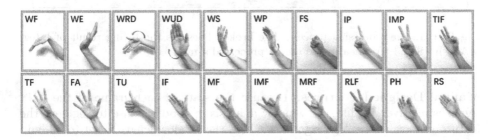

Fig. 2. Diagram of the twenty types of gestures in the dataset. The dataset includes six wrist movements, 13 fine finger movements and a rest state.

3.2 Methods

Data Pre-processing. For the original AUS data, because the AUS signal waveform is approximately symmetrical, we first adjust its value to be centered on zero and then pick up the absolute value to make all data non-negative. Log compression was used to reduce the absolute value of data. Because there are data with a value of zero, we add 1 to all data and then take the logarithm. This operation makes the data unchanged during processing, and compresses the data, which increases the weight of the small waveform at the back end of the signal, amplifies the deep muscle signal, and makes it more sensitive to the changes of the deep muscle without changing the relative relationship of the data.

The data pre-processing is shown in Fig. 3. As can be seen from the figure, those weak signals in the latter half of the signal that represent deep muscle states are amplified after pre-processing, which is very beneficial for the recognition of fine finger movements. From the feature fitting point of view, the features of the preprocessed signal are easier to be extracted.

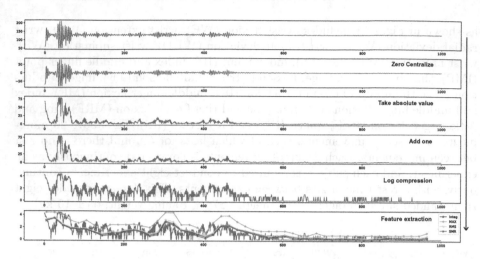

Fig. 3. Data pre-processing process. The broken lines are the fitting result of Integ, MAX, RMS and SMR feature to the preprocessed signal.

Manual Designed Features. Because the state of each frame of the AUS signal is relatively stable, the window analysis method was use to segment the feature window of the AUS signal, in which the window length is set to 30, and the increment interval is 20. Therefore, for the data with a frame length of 1000, there are 49 feature windows in each channel and 196 feature windows in four channels, and the features of each sample are composed of the feature values of each feature window. In the aspect of feature selection, some common time-domain and frequency-domain features in sEMG field were selected [5,14], those features were used in AUS signals for hand gesture recognition for the first time. The specific definitions and mathematical formulas are shown in the Table 1, in which S_i is defined as the signal value of AUS signal with a certain window length at different time points, and f_i represents the spectrum obtained by fast Fourier transform of intercepted signal S_i.

Because the extracted dimensions are too high and redundant, which is not conducive to the later multi-feature combination and has a great impact on the efficiency, it is necessary to reduce the dimensions of the data. Compared with the principal component analysis (PCA) method, kernel principal component analysis (KPCA) maps the original data to high-dimensional space through kernel function and then uses the KPCA algorithm to reduce the dimension, which can achieve better results, and the kernel function is cosine.

Machine Learning Classifiers. After the feature extraction, the obtained features need to be sent to the classifier for training, so the selection of the classifier is very important. In this experiment, we selected LDA, KNN, SVM, and ANN four typical machine learning classifiers, these classifiers have performed

Table 1. Description and mathematical equation of discrete features.

Name	Abbreviate	Equation
Integration	Integ	$\text{Integ} = \sum_{i=1}^{N} |x_i|$
Log detector	LOG	$\text{LOG} = e^{\frac{1}{N} \sum_{i=1}^{N} \log(|x_i|)}$
Mean absolute value	MAV	$\text{MAV} = \frac{1}{N} \sum_{i=1}^{N} |x_i|$
Max value	MAX	$\text{MAX} = max(x)$
Peak value	PK	$\text{PK} = max(x) - min(x)$
Root mean square	RMS	$\text{RMS} = \sqrt{\frac{1}{N} \sum_{i=1}^{N} x_i^2}$
Simple square integral	SSI	$\text{SSI} = \sum_{i=1}^{N} x_i^2$
Standard deviation	STD	$STD = \sqrt{\frac{1}{N} \sum_{i=1}^{N} (x_i - mean\,(x))^2}$
The 3rd temporal moment	TM3	$\text{TM3} = \left| \frac{1}{N} \sum_{i=1}^{N} x_i^3 \right|$
The 4rd temporal moment	TM4	$\text{TM4} = \frac{1}{N} \sum_{i=1}^{N} x_i^4$
The 5rd temporal moment	TM5	$\text{TM5} = \left| \frac{1}{N} \sum_{i=1}^{N} x_i^5 \right|$
Variance	VAR	$\text{VAR} = \frac{1}{N-1} \sum_{i=1}^{N} x_i^2$
Waveform length	WL	$\text{WL} = \sum_{i=1}^{N=1} |x_{i+1} - x_i|$
Square mean root	SMR	$\text{SMR} = \left[\frac{1}{N} \sum_{i=1}^{N} \sqrt{x_i} \right]^2$
Modified frequency mean	MFMD	$MFMN = \frac{\sum_{i=1}^{M} f_i S_i}{\sum_{i=1}^{M} S_i}$

well in previous studies, and then we selected their best hyperparameters for our experiment.

Because different classifiers have different emphases on feature classification, to take full advantage of the characteristics of different classifiers, we make soft voting on the classification results obtained by multiple classifiers and take the voting results as the classification basis. First, the extracted features were send to the selected four classifiers for training. Second, the test data were sent to each trained classifier to obtain the probability matrix of each classifier. Then add the probabilities of each category to get the final probability matrix, and then use the category with the highest probability as the result. The schematic diagram of the soft voting method is shown in Fig. 4.

3.3 Evaluation Method

The dataset in this experiment includes AUS data of eight trials collected by eight subjects in succession. For the eight experimental data of each subject, the first four trials were taken as the training set and the last four trials as the test set.

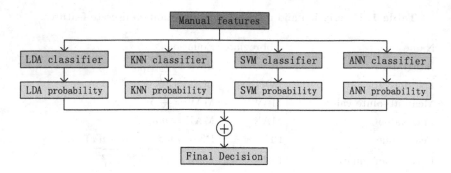

Fig. 4. The schematic diagram of soft voting method.

As a classification task, classification accuracy is the most commonly used evaluation index. The accuracy was used as the evaluation metric to evaluate our model. The formulas are shown below:

$$Accuracy = \frac{TP + FN}{TP + FP + TN + FN} \tag{1}$$

where TP is true positive, FP is false positive, FN is false negative, and TN is true negative.

4   Result and Discussion

4.1   Hyperparameter Tuning

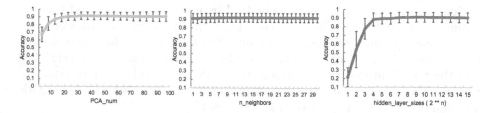

Fig. 5. The experimental results of hyperparameter fine-tuning, from left to right, are the tuning process of KPCA, KNN, ANN respectively.

In this research, the KPCA method was choose to reduce the dimension of data. Because the number of reduced dimension has a pronounced influence on the experiment, so we need to choose the appropriate dimension. Since the LDA algorithm has no super-parameters, RMS was use as the feature and LDA as the classifier to adjust the parameters of KPCA. The experimental results are shown in Fig. 5. It can be seen that the higher the dimension after dimensionality reduction, the higher the recognition rate, but at the same time, the higher the dimension, the lower the efficiency of the algorithm. Since the accuracy rate is not improved much after 40, we choose 40 as our dimensionality after dimensionality reduction.

The result of the KNN classifier is mainly impacted by the value of K, and the parameter that ANN needs to adjust is hidden_layer_sizes. We have experimented with hyperparameter adjustment when the dimension of KPCA is reduced to 40 dimensions, which is in a balance of effect and efficiency. Finally, we define the value of K of KNN to 13, the value of hidden_layer_sizes of ANN is 512, and the experimental results are also shown in Fig. 5. The kernel function of SVM is linear.

4.2 Single-Feature Results

The experimental results of the features in Table 1 in LDA, KNN, SVM, ANN, and soft voting methods respectively are shown in Table 2. In the case of single feature single classifier, the highest KB feature recognition rate was 88.03% using the SVM classifier, while in using our proposed preprocessing method and features, the combination with the best result is the extraction of Integ features and classification using KNN algorithm with 91.63% recognition accuracy, 3.60% improvement over KB features. This confirms the effectiveness of our proposed preprocessing method and features. For all single features, the recognition rate is improved after using the soft voting method, where the best result is the RMS feature reaching 92.32% and the least effective MAV feature also achieves an accuracy of 78.82%. It can be seen that AUS has an excellent performance in 20 categories including fine finger movements, which shows the effectiveness of AUS in fine finger gesture recognition.

4.3 Multi-feature Results

For the sake of experimental effectiveness and efficiency, we selected the five features with the highest recognition rate among the single features: Integ, MAX, RMS, SMR, and MFMD as the objects for feature fusion, spliced these five objects to obtain the fused features, and fed the fused features to each classifier for training. The experimental results are shown in Table 3. A comparison with the results of the single features shows that the fused features outperform the best performance of the single features in each classifier, the best result was achieved using the KNN classifier with 91.91%, which indicates that the fused features can represent the content of AUS more comprehensively and therefore obtain a higher recognition rate.

After using the soft voting method for the combined features, the recognition accuracy improved by 1.37%, 1.18%, 1.75%, and 1.53% over LDA, KNN, SVM, and ANN, respectively, reaching 93.09%. For each subject, the soft voting method outperformed the single classifier in most subjects and was also very close to the best performing classifier in subjects with lower performance than some single classifiers, indicating that the soft voting method can make good use

Table 2. Accuracy of single features with different classifiers and soft voting method.

	LDA	KNN	ANN	SVM	Soft voting
KB_Feature	87.96%	86.96%	83.86%	88.03%	**89.08%**
Integ	91.22%	91.63%	90.70%	91.32%	**92.07%**
LOG	88.37%	89.48%	88.60%	89.05%	**89.82%**
MAV	77.95%	69.67%	77.01%	76.65%	**78.82%**
MAX	90.66%	88.91%	89.34%	89.35%	**91.28%**
PK	87.61%	85.88%	86.95%	87.19%	**88.36%**
RMS	91.53%	91.61%	90.79%	90.86%	**92.32%**
SSI	89.66%	90.57%	89.04%	89.90%	**91.11%**
STD	86.00%	84.00%	84.44%	85.23%	**86.34%**
TM3	87.86%	88.32%	87.54%	88.18%	**89.26%**
TM4	85.77%	85.41%	85.60%	85.95%	**87.41%**
TM5	83.18%	82.99%	83.15%	83.52%	**84.88%**
VAR	89.66%	90.57%	89.04%	89.90%	**91.11%**
WL	82.26%	81.61%	81.04%	81.96%	**83.45%**
SMR	89.98%	90.89%	89.80%	90.31%	**90.98%**
MFMD	91.33%	90.08%	89.47%	89.88%	**91.82%**

of the characteristics of different classifiers to achieve better results. The above illustrates that the soft voting method is also applicable in fusion features.

Table 3. Accuracy of multi features with different classifiers and soft voting method.

Subject	1	2	3	4	5	6	7	8	Mean
LDA	92.79%	91.83%	91.71%	93.79%	78.13%	94.38%	97.88%	93.25%	91.72%
KNN	94.46%	90.46%	90.17%	92.58%	79.96%	**95.88%**	**99.08%**	92.67%	91.91%
ANN	94.58%	90.58%	88.04%	93.63%	81.71%	93.33%	98.54%	90.29%	91.34%
SVM	91.42%	91.54%	**91.96%**	93.38%	80.33%	92.42%	98.58%	92.88%	91.56%
Soft voting	**95.33%**	**92.54%**	91.79%	**95.29%**	**81.75%**	95.33%	98.50%	**94.17%**	**93.09%**

5   Conclusion

In this paper, a new data preprocessing method is designed for the characteristics of AUS signals, some common features in time and frequency domains are extracted, the KPCA method is used for data dimensionality reduction, and the single feature after dimensionality reduction achieves the highest accuracy of 91.63% in four typical machine learning classification algorithms, namely LDA, KNN, SVM, ANN, 3.60% higher than the highest recognition rate of 88.03% among KB features. The highest recognition rate of 92.32% was achieved for a single feature after using the soft voting method. In the case of feature combination, the combined features achieve up to 91.91% under the condition of a single classifier and up to 93.09% recognition rate after using the soft voting method, 4.01% higher than the highest recognition rate of 89.08% among KB features with the soft voting method. This experiment shows the applicability of the data preprocessing method proposed in this paper on AUS signals and the better results of the soft voting method compared to a single classifier when classifying AUS signals. Therefore, the AUS-based HCI has superiority in gesture recognition and has great potential for future applications.

References

1. Belbasis, A., Fuss, F.K.: Muscle performance investigated with a novel smart compression garment based on pressure sensor force myography and its validation against EMG. Front. Physiol. **9**, 408 (2018)
2. Bhusari, A., Gupta, N., Kambli, T., Kulkarni, S.: Comparison of SVM and KNN classifiers for palm movements using semg signals with different features. In: Proceedings of the 2019 3rd International Conference on Computing Methodologies and Communication (ICCMC 2019), pp. 881–885 (2019)
3. Castellini, C., Passig, G., Zarka, E.: Using ultrasound images of the forearm to predict finger positions. IEEE Trans. Neural Syst. Rehabil. Eng. **20**(6), 788–97 (2012)
4. Chen, H., Zhang, Y., Li, G., Fang, Y., Liu, H.: Surface electromyography feature extraction via convolutional neural network. Int. J. Mach. Learn. Cybern. **11**(1), 185–196 (2019). https://doi.org/10.1007/s13042-019-00966-x
5. Guo, S.X., Guo, C.H., Pang, M.Y.: A novel feature extraction method for semg signals using image processing. In: 2013 IEEE International Conference on Mechatronics and Automation (ICMA), pp. 1765–1770 (2013)
6. Huang, Y.J., Liu, H.H.: Performances of surface EMG and ultrasound signals in recognizing finger motion. In: 2016 9th International Conference on Human System Interactions (HSI), pp. 117–122 (2016)
7. Kim, J., Kim, M., Kim, K.: Development of a wearable HCI controller through SEMG & IMU sensor fusion. In: 2016 13th International Conference on Ubiquitous Robots and Ambient Intelligence (URAI), pp. 83–87 (2016)
8. Li, Y., Liu, H.: Gesture recognition system based on single vibration element ultrasonic sensor. Transducer Microsyst. Technol. **37**(2), 80–82 (2018)
9. Liu, L., Zhang, X., Liu, Y., Zhu, W.W., Zhao, B.X.: An ensemble of multiple boosting methods based on classifier-specific soft voting for intelligent vehicle crash injury severity prediction. In: 2020 IEEE Sixth International Conference on Big Data Computing Service and Applications (Bigdataservice 2020), pp. 17–24 (2020)
10. Majolo, M., Balbinot, A.: Proposal of a hardware SVM implementation for fast sEMG classification. In: Costa-Felix, R., Machado, J.C., Alvarenga, A.V. (eds.) XXVI Brazilian Congress on Biomedical Engineering. IP, vol. 70/2, pp. 381–386. Springer, Singapore (2019). https://doi.org/10.1007/978-981-13-2517-5_58
11. Nadeem, A., et al.: A novel integration of face-recognition algorithms with a soft voting scheme for efficiently tracking missing person in challenging large-gathering scenarios. Sensors **22**(3), 1153 (2022)

12. Nakhli, F.R.: Comparison of optical biometry and applanation ultrasound measurements of the axial length of the eye. Saudi J. Ophthalmol. : Official J. Saudi Ophthalmol. Soc. **28**(4), 287–91 (2014)
13. Ortega, P., Zhao, T., Faisal, A.A.: Hygrip: full-stack characterization of neurobehavioral signals (fNIRS, EEG, EMG, Force, and Breathing) during a bimanual grip force control task. Front. Neurosci. **14**, 919 (2020)
14. Phinyomark, A., Phukpattaranont, P., Limsakul, C.: Feature reduction and selection for emg signal classification. Expert Syst. Appl. **39**(8), 7420–7431 (2012)
15. Rabe, K.G., Jahanandish, M.H., Boehm, J.R., Fey, A.M., Hoyt, K., Fey, N.P.: Ultrasound sensing can improve continuous classification of discrete ambulation modes compared to surface electromyography. IEEE Trans. Biomed. Eng. **68**(4), 1379–1388 (2021)
16. Saeed, B., et al.: Leveraging ANN and lDA classifiers for characterizing different hand movements using EMG signals. Arab. J. Sci. Eng. **46**(2), 1761–1769 (2021). https://doi.org/10.1007/s13369-020-05044-x
17. Segning, C.M., Ezzaidi, H., da Silva, R.A., Ngomo, S.: A neurophysiological pattern as a precursor of work-related musculoskeletal disorders using EEG combined with EMG. Int. J. Environ. Res. Public Health **18**(4), 2001 (2021)
18. Song, W., et al.: Design of a flexible wearable smart semg recorder integrated gradient boosting decision tree based hand gesture recognition. IEEE Trans. Biomed. Circ. Syst. **13**(6), 1563–1574 (2019)
19. Sun, G.K., Zhou, Z.G., Li, G.K., Zhou, W.B.: Development of an optical fiber-guided robotic laser ultrasonic system for aeronautical composite structure testing. Optik **127**(12), 5135–5140 (2016)
20. Sun, X., Li, Y., Liu, H.: IEEE: muscle fatigue assessment using one-channel single-element ultrasound transducer. In: 8th International IEEE/EMBS Conference on Neural Engineering (NER), pp. 122–125. International IEEE EMBS Conference on Neural Engineering (2017)
21. Taha, A.: Intelligent ensemble learning approach for phishing website detection based on weighted soft voting. Mathematics **9**(21), 2799 (2021)
22. Xia, W., Zhou, Y., Yang, X., He, K., Liu, H.: Toward portable hybrid surface electromyography/a-mode ultrasound sensing for human-machine interface. IEEE Sens. J. **19**(13), 5219–5228 (2019)
23. Yan, M.M., Cheng, Y., Sakurai, K., Tamura, H., Tanno, K.: Mouse cursor-like control system in consideration of the DC-EOG signals using EOG-sEMG human interface. In: Icarob 2017 Proceedings of the 2017 International Conference on Artificial Life and Robotics, pp. P520–P523 (2017)
24. Yang, X., Zhou, D., Zhou, Y., Huang, Y., Liu, H.: Towards zero re-training for long-term hand gesture recognition via ultrasound sensing. IEEE J. Biomed. Health Inf. **23**(4), 1639–1646 (2019)
25. Yang, X.C., Sun, X.L., Zhou, D.L., Li, Y.F., Liu, H.H.: Towards wearable a-mode ultrasound sensing for real-time finger motion recognition. IEEE Trans. Neural Syst. Rehabil. Eng. **26**(6), 1199–1208 (2018)

Hand Gesture Recognition and Biometric Authentication Using a Multi-day Dataset

Ashirbad Pradhan[3] (iD), Jiayuan He[1,2], and Ning Jiang[1,2(✉)] (iD)

[1] National Clinical Research Center for Geriatrics, West China Hospital Sichuan University , Chengdu, Sichuan, China
jiangning21@wchscu.cn

[2] Med-X Center for Manufacturing, Sichuan University, Chengdu, Sichuan, China

[3] Engineering Bionics Lab, Department of Systems Design Engineering, University of Waterloo, Waterloo, Waterloo N2L 3G1, Canada

Abstract. Hand-gesture recognition (HGR) is one of the major applications of electromyography (EMG), specifically for controlling functional prosthetic hands. Recently, another application i.e. the EMG-based biometrics has found growing research interest due to its potential of addressing some conventional biometric limitations. It has been observed that for EMG-based applications, the translation of laboratory research to real-life applications suffers from two major limitations: 1) a small subject pool, and 2) limited to single-session data recordings. In this study, forearm, and wrist EMG data were collected from 43 participants over three different days with long separation (Days 1, 8, and 29) while they performed static hand/wrist gestures. The HGR evaluation resulted in a mean AUC of 0.948 ± 0.018 and 0.941 ± 0.021 for forearm data and wrist data, respectively. The biometric evaluation resulted in a mean EER of 0.028 ± 0.007 and 0.038 ± 0.006 for forearm data and wrist data, respectively. These results were comparable to the widely used Ninapro database DB2. The large-sample multi-day dataset would facilitate further research on EMG-based HGR and biometric applications.

Keywords: Electromyography · Hand gesture recognition · Biometrics · Multi-day

1 Introduction and Background Summary

Hand gesture recognition (HGR) via surface electromyographic (EMG) signals is a biomedical engineering application that received increasing attention recently, both in academia and industry. Advanced upper-limb prosthesis control systems have utilized such HGR in assisting upper limb amputees [1], and recent industrial applications have emerged using HGR for human-machine interactions in an industrial [2] and consumer applications scenarios [3, 4]. For the detection of hand gestures, the processed EMG signals reveal the extracted features which serve as inputs for standard pattern recognition techniques (PR) such as support vector machines (SVM) [5] and linear discriminant analysis (LDA) [6]. Currently, to achieve high classification accuracy even with simpler

H. Liu et al. (Eds.): ICIRA 2022, LNAI 13458, pp. 375–385, 2022.
https://doi.org/10.1007/978-3-031-13841-6_35

architectures advanced techniques such as deep neural networks (DNN) are employed [7, 8].

However, extensive investigation achieved poor cross-user transference performance for EMG-based HGR, suggesting lack of feasibility of a generalizable model [9]. Based on previous literature, such a calibration-free EMG-based HGR system that can generalize to un-seen users' EMG characteristics is hard to achieve, thus suggesting individual characteristics is an inherent feature embedded in surface EMG signals. This has encouraged the investigation of surface EMG as a potential novel biometric trait, which can be used for user authentication in security applications and user identification in forensics applications. One unique advantage of the EMG biometric trait, in particular for authentication applications, is the combination user-specific biometrics with user-defined gestures as passcodes, the latter of which is not possible with other bio-signals such as electroencephalogram (EEG) and electrocardiogram (ECG). Our past study set the foundation for the combination of these gestures (e.g. passcodes) to facilitate a dual-mode (password and biometrics) authentication system [10].

With high performance of both the HGR and biometric models we and others have demonstrated [10–14], it is natural to push the current technology from ideal laboratory settings to more realistic scenarios. It is well-known in the EMG processing literature; many non-stationary factors can affect the accuracy and consistency of an EMG processing system. These factors include electrode shifts, sweat, dry skin, and physical conditions, all of which have been investigated [15]. Therefore, to validate the effectiveness of EMG-based HGR and biometrics, a multi-day dataset with a large enough subject pool is warranted.

In the current study, we present an open-access Gesture Recognition and Biometrics electroMyography (GrabMyo) Dataset[1]. GrabMyo consists of 43 participants (subsequently termed as users), three sessions in three separate days (subsequently termed as sessions) of data collection, 16 hand and finger gestures each with seven repetitions (subsequently termed as trials). The EMG signals were recorded from both forearm and wrist positions. The sampling frequency of the recorded signals was selected as 2048 Hz. To obtain generalizable data, special effort was taken such as 1) electrode positioning protocol for reach session, 2) normal level force instruction, 3) rest duration for avoiding fatigue, 4) un-uniform interval between data collection sessions (Days 1, 8, and 29) and 5) data collection from healthy users (subjects with a single session of sickness have been eliminated from the study). These considerations are explained in greater detail in Sects. 2.2 and 2.3. The dataset provides a valuable resource for EMG-based HGR and biometrics research, particularly for improving algorithms' robustness in a multi-day scenario. Standard HGR and biometric analysis were performed, and the results were compared to those obtained from the widely used NinaPro Database (subsequently termed as Ninapro) [16].

---

[1] https://dx.doi.org/10.21227/82v9-2b79.

2   Methods

2.1   Participants

For the current database, 43 healthy participants (23 M, 20 F) with an average age of 26.35 ± 2.89, average forearm length (measured from the styloid process on the wrist to the olecranon on the elbow) of 25.15 ± 1.74 cm. All participants were informed of the procedures and signed an informed consent form before the experiment. The research protocol was approved by the Office of Research Ethics of the University of Waterloo (ORE# 31346) and the experimental protocol was conducted following the Declaration of Helsinki.

2.2   Experimental Setup

The experimental setup included a PC, a monitor, skin-adhesive pre-gelled monopolar sEMG electrodes (AM-N00S/E, Ambu, Denmark), and a commercial bio-signal amplifier (EMGUSB2 +, OT Bioelettronica, Italy). The sEMG signals were bandpass filtered between 10 Hz and 500 Hz, with a gain of 500, and then sampled at 2048 Hz.

   The participant's forearm length was measured as the distance between the olecranon process and the ulnar styloid process. The forearm circumference was measured at one-third of the forearm length from the olecranon process. The wrist circumference was measured at 2 cm away from the ulnar styloid process. After taking these measurements, the electrodes are placed on the forearm and wrist. For the forearm electrode placement, sixteen monopolar sEMG electrodes were placed in the form of two rings, each consisting of eight electrodes equally spaced around the forearm. The center-to-center distance between the two rings was maintained at 2 cm. For the wrist electrode setup, twelve monopolar sEMG electrodes of the same type as the forearm rings were placed in the form of two rings, each consisting of six electrodes equally spaced around the wrist. The center-to-center distance between the two rings was maintained at 2 cm, similar to the forearm setup. Therefore, a total of 28 monopolar sEMG electrodes were used for each session. A detailed pictorial representation of the electrodes' placement is provided in Fig. 1 while the actual electrode positions of one user is shown in Appendix I. To maintain consistency of the positions of the electrodes across all participants, the first electrode in each ring (total rings = 4) was anatomically positioned on the centerline of the elbow crease (see Fig. 3). [11, 14].

2.3   Experimental Protocol

In one experimental session, after instrumentation setup, the participant was seated comfortably on the chair with both their upper limbs in a resting position. Visual instructions for performing the gestures were provided on the computer screen placed in front of the participants. Sixteen hand and wrist gestures were included in the current study(see Fig. 3): Lateral prehension (LP), thumb adduction (TA), thumb and little finger opposition (TLFO), thumb and index finger opposition (TIFO), thumb and little finger extension (TLFE), thumb and index finger extension (TIFE), index and middle finger extension (IMFE), little finger extension (LFE), index finger extension (IFE), thumb extension

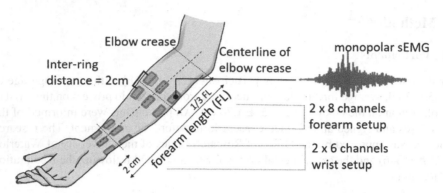

Fig. 1. Positions of the sixteen surface electrodes on the forearm and twelve electrodes on the wrist (dorsal view). The forearm electrodes formed two rings of eight electrodes each and the wrist electrodes formed two rings of six electrodes each. The monopolar EMG of each ring was acquired for subsequent processing and analysis.

(TE), wrist flexion (WF), wrist extension (WE), forearm supination (FS), forearm pronation (FP), hand open (HO), and hand close (HC). Resting (REST) trials were also added, making 17 tasks. Each user would perform the 17 tasks in a random order, during which each task was performed for five seconds and a ten-second relaxing period was provided between two consecutive tasks. All sEMG channels were continuously acquired, and one such continuous acquisition of 17 task, including the REST task and the relaxing periods, is called one run. Each user would perform seven runs, producing 119 trials or contractions (17 × 7) in one session. The user could also request additional rest between runs when they felt necessary. The entire session was repeated on day 8 (after 1 week) and day 29 (after 1 month) (Fig. 2).

2.4 NinaPro Database

The Ninapro database [16, 17] is an open-access dataset widely used as a benchmark for evaluating developed HGR models using multichannel forearm EMG signals. The database utilized for evaluating this work was the second Ninapro database DB2 [16]. The data for the DB2 database was collected using a Delsys Trigno Wireless EMG system with 12 wireless electrodes (channels), receiving electrical muscle activity at a rate of 2 kHz. The dataset is formed of collected signals from 40 participants (28 M; 12 F, age 29.9 ± 3.9 years). The DB2 dataset includes 50 gestures, however, exercise B comprising 17 hand gestures was selected for comparison with the present dataset due to their close similarities. The participants were instructed to repeat each gesture 6 times, each time holding the gesture for 5 s, followed by 3 s of rest. More details on the Ninapro database can be found in [16].

2.5 Signal Processing

For the proximal rings of the forearm setup (number of channels = 8) and the distal ring of the wrist setup (number of channels = 6), the monopolar sEMG signals were first re-referenced by a common average procedure. The processed signals were then segmented

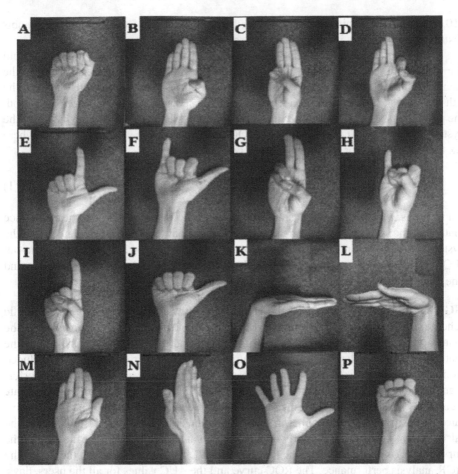

Fig. 2. Sixteen gesture classes investigated in the study: (A) lateral prehension (LP), (B) thumb adduction (TA), (C) thumb and little finger opposition (TLFO), (D) thumb and index finger opposition (TIFO), (E) thumb and little finger extension (TLFE), (F) thumb and index finger extension (TIFE), (G) index and middle finger extension (IMFE), (H) little finger extension (LFE), (I) index finger extension (IFE), (J) thumb extension (TE), (K) wrist flexion (WF), (L) wrist extension (WE), (M) forearm supination (FS), (N) forearm pronation (FP), (O) hand open (HO), (P) hand close (IIC).

into 200 ms width windows, with a 150 ms overlap. Each window was then processed using Hudgins's time-domain (TD) feature extraction [18]. Time-domain features (mean absolute value, zero crossing, slope sign changes, and waveform length) were extracted from filtered data [14]. Therefore, for a forearm setup, the feature vector consisted of $8 \times 4 = 32$ features, while the wrist setup consisted of $6 \times 4 = 24$ features. For the analysis of HGR using forearm EMG signals several PR and DNN techniques have been investigated. For the biometric analysis, a matching score, commonly the Mahalanobis distance, is used to assess if it's a match (access granted) or no match (access denied)

[10, 11, 14]. To maintain consistency in the HGR and biometric analyses, a Mahalanobis distance classifier was implemented as described below.

For a given feature vector sample p (the input), its similarity score, namely $S_{i,j}$, with the ith gesture and the jth user, was defined as the Mahalanobis distance between the sample and the class centroid is where $\mu_{i,j}$ is the centroid of the gesture i th class and the j th user and $\sum_{i,j}$ is the covariance matrix for the specific gesture and user class Both the parameters are calculated from the system training data and the sample p is from the system testing data. The leave-one-out (LOO) cross-validation scheme was used, where six trials were used for training and one trial for testing.

$$S_{i,j}(p) = \sqrt{\left(p - \mu_{i,j}\right)^{T} \Sigma_{i,j}^{-1} \left(p - \mu_{i,j}\right)}, \tag{1}$$

where $\mu_{i,j}$ is the centroid of the gesture i th class and the j th user and $\sum_{i,j}$ is the covariance matrix for the specific gesture and user class Both the parameters are calculated from the system training data and the sample p is from the system testing data. The leave-one-out (LOO) cross-validation scheme was used, where six trials were used for training and one trial for testing.

HGR Evaluation: In this study, the HGR analysis was performed in a user-specific scheme. For a particular user and a particular gesture, the true class consisted of the feature vectors from the target gesture of the user and the false class consisted of the feature vectors from the remaining 15 gestures of that user (the rest gesture was excluded from the HGR analysis to maintain consistency with biometric analysis). For the performance analysis a receiver operating characteristic (ROC), where the true positive rate (sensitivity) was plotted against the false positive rate (1 – specificity). The true positive rate or sensitivity represents the probability of detecting a correct gesture, while the false positive rate is the probability of detecting an incorrect gesture. The area under the curve (AUC) is calculated from the ROC curve [19]. The higher the AUC, the higher the HGR analysis performance. The ROC curve and the AUC values for all the users, days, and gestures are averaged and reported separately for the forearm and wrist electrode positions. The AUC values are then compared to those obtained from the Ninapro data with the same processing procedures.

Biometric Evaluation: In this study, the Verification mode of biometrics was used to demonstrate the feasibility of multi-day sEMG-based biometrics. In this mode, the claimant's identity and the corresponding gesture are known to the system. A more challenging and complex biometric mode, *i.e.* Identification, will be discussed in a separate study. As such, for a specific user (the Claimant), the true class consisted of the feature vectors from the target gesture (*e.g.* the passcode) of the Claimant and the false class consisted of the feature vectors of the other 15 gestures from the Claimant, as well as all gestures from the remaining 42 users. For the performance analysis a receiver operating characteristic (ROC), where the true positive rate (sensitivity) was plotted against the false positive rate (1 – specificity). The true positive rate or sensitivity represents the probability of detecting a correct hand gesture, while the false positive rate is the probability of detecting an incorrect hand gesture. The equal error rate (EER), is obtained from the ROC curve, where the false positive rate is equal to the false negative rate

(1 – sensitivity) [19]. The lower the EER, the higher the biometric performance. The ROC curve and the EER values for all the users, days, and gestures are averaged and reported separately for the forearm and wrist electrode positions. The EER values are then compared to the Ninapro data as described below.

2.6 Statistical Analysis

The current study aimed to evaluate the data quality of the GRABMyo dataset, using the HGR and biometric performance, as two example applications. Ninapro which has been widely used, was used as a reference database. The results from Ninapro data were compared with the two electrode positions. As such, for each of the two applications, *i.e.*, HGR and biometrics, a one-way ANOVA was performed on the AUC and EER, respectively, to determine if there were any significant differences among the three levels (Forearm, Wrist and Ninapro). In the case of a significant ANOVA, Bonferroni post-hoc analysis was performed to compare the three levels. All statistical tests were performed using RStudio 1.0. 136 (RStudio, Boston, MA).

3 Results

The ROC curve for the HGR and Biometric evaluation are reported (see Fig. 3).

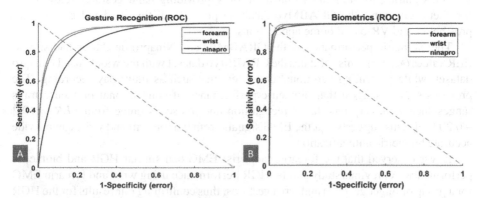

Fig. 3. The ROC curves are plotted for the HGR evaluation (A) and for biometric evaluation (B) for the forearm, wrist and ninapro data. The dotted line represents the point of intersection on the ROC curve from which the EER value is obtained.

Table 1 gives a summary of the mean and standard deviation of AUC and EER values for the HGR and Biometric evaluations respectively, for the Forearm, Wrist and Ninapro data. From the ANOVA, significant differences in the AUC values were found ($p < 0.001$, $F = 43.28$). Subsequent post-hoc analysis found these two pairs were significantly different: Forearm > NinaPro ($p < 0.001$, $F = 7.72$) and Wrist > NinaPro ($p < 0.001$, $F = 6.73$). This suggests that the HGR performance obtained using the GRABMyo data was significantly better than the Ninapro data. No such significance was found between forearm and wrist, indicating similar HGR performance for the two electrode positions. No significant difference between the EER values of the three datasets were obtained from the ANOVA ($p = 0.06$, $F = 2.8$) This indicates the biometric performance of the three datasets are similar.

Table 1. Mean (±STD) HGR and biometric performance

Electrode setup	HGR evaluation (AUC)	Biometric evaluation (EER)
Forearm	0.948 (±0.018)	0.028 (±0.007)
Wrist	0.941 (±0.021)	0.038 (±0.006)
Ninapro (Forearm)	0.875 (±0.034)	0.038 (±0.013)

4 Discussion

The above results suggest that the HGR performance is quite high as compared to the Ninapro database. The reported AUC of the Ninapro database (xx + xx) is similar to previous studies, thus corroborating our results. The lower performance of the Ninapro database might be due to the similar nature of the gestures listed in exercise B of the dataset. Contrary to the Ninapro database only providing hand gestures relevant for prosthetic functions, the GRABMyo database provides distinctive hand gestures for prosthetics and VR-based home applications.

The biometric performance of the GRABMyo and Ninapro databases had similar EER values (<0.04). This validates the GRABMyo dataset with the widely used Ninapro dataset, while presenting additional characteristics such as multi-day recording. The previous studies suggest that biometric performance of conventional biometric traits ranges such as fingerprints, facial recognition and iris scans range from $EER = 10^{-4}$ − 0.20 [20]. This suggests that the EMG signals from the forearm and wrist can provide accurate biometric authentication.

It was observed that the forearm and wrist EMG had similar HGR and biometric performance. A previous study similar HGR performance using wrist and forearm EMG for a group of finger gestures and wrist gestures, thus confirming our results for the HGR evaluation [21]. As accurate performance for both the electrode positions was achieved, a wearable bracelet or wristband device could be developed for commercial applications of HGR and biometric authentication. Future research using such devices could avoid the time-consuming experimental setup and facilitate biometrics-oriented large-scale data collection.

4.1 Limitations of the Study

The GRABMyo dataset presented a clear dominance in terms of subject-pool size and the number of recording sessions, however, there existed some limitations in this study. As compared to the previous study with around 50 gestures [22], the GRABMyo dataset included 16 more commonly used hand and finger gestures. Due to our large sample size, it was not timely feasible to include more gestures. For similar time constraints, multiple force levels were not collected for the same gesture. The subjects were instructed to perform the gestures at a comfortable level (the force with which they perform daily activities). Additionally, no electrode positions were marked for controlling the shift in electrode positions between sessions. The electrode placement protocol was generalized to the best of our ability, however, there might have been some electrode-shifts between the sessions. Although considered limitations, the force variations, and electrode-shifts are considered more realistic than in tightly controlled experimental settings.

4.2 Future Use of the Dataset

As discussed earlier, there exists a performance gap between real-life scenarios and the experimental settings for HGR and biometrics. EMG processing techniques that are robust to force-variations [23] and electrode-shifts [24], will be beneficial for HGR and biometric authentication in real-life applications and need to be investigated on this multi-day dataset. Other strategies to improve the authentication performance can be further investigated by implementing different fusion strategies [10]. Further, Identification, which is another authentication application of biometrics, can be explored in future studies. Furthermore, recent HGR research has focused on developing cross-user calibration-free models which reduce the training burden for real life applications [9, 25]. The presented large-sample dataset can provide resources for such calibration-free models.

5 Conclusion

To the best of our knowledge, the presented GRABMyo dataset is the largest multi-day dataset for EMG recordings while performing hand gestures. The key features of the GRABMyo dataset included: open-access, large subject-pool size, multiday recordings, commonly used hand gestures, and resemblance to real-life conditions. Standard analysis for HGR and biometric evaluation was performed, and it was observed that the GRABMyo dataset performed similarly, if not better, than the widely used Ninapro dataset. Furthermore, the high biometric performance suggested the feasibility of a novel biometric trait *i.e.* EMG signals from hand gestures for authentication applications. The forearm electrode setup demonstrated a similar HGR and biometric performance as the wrist setup, which could facilitate the development of wearable EMG-based bracelets and wrist bands for HGR and biometric applications. Therefore, the presented dataset and findings could facilitate further research on EMG-based biometrics and other gesture recognition-based applications.

References

1. Jiang, N., et al.: Myoelectric control of artificial limbs—is there a need to change focus? [In the spotlight]. IEEE Signal Process. Mag. **29**(5), 152–150 (2012)

2. Qureshi, F., Krishnan, S.: Wearable hardware design for the internet of medical things (IoMT). Sensors 18(11), 3812 (2018)
3. Wu, J., Sun, L., Jafari, R.: A wearable system for recognizing American sign language in real-time using IMU and surface EMG sensors. IEEE J. Biomed. Health Inform. 20(5), 1281–1290 (2016)
4. Dwivedi, A., Kwon, Y., Liarokapis, M.: Emg-based decoding of manipulation motions in virtual reality: towards immersive interfaces. In: 2020 IEEE International Conference on Systems, Man, and Cybernetics (SMC). IEEE (2020)
5. Tavakoli, M., et al.: Robust hand gesture recognition with a double channel surface EMG wearable armband and SVM classifier. Biomed. Signal Process. Control 46, 121–130 (2018)
6. Englehart, K., Hudgins, B.: A robust, real-time control scheme for multifunction myoelectric control. IEEE Trans. Biomed. Eng. 50(7), 848–854 (2003)
7. Clarke, A.K., et al.: Deep learning for robust decomposition of high-density surface EMG signals. IEEE Trans. Biomed. Eng. 68(2), 526–534 (2020)
8. Chen, L., et al.: Hand gesture recognition using compact CNN via surface electromyography signals. Sensors 20(3), 672 (2020)
9. Campbell, E., Phinyomark, A., Scheme, E.: Deep cross-user models reduce the training burden in myoelectric control. Front. Neurosci. 15, 595 (2021)
10. Pradhan, A., He, J., Jiang, N.: Score, rank, and decision-level fusion strategies of multicode electromyogram-based verification and identification biometrics. IEEE J. Biomed. Health Inf. 26, 1068–1079 (2021)
11. He, J., Jiang, N.: Biometric from surface electromyogram (sEMG): feasibility of user verification and identification based on gesture recognition. Front. Bioeng. Biotechnol. 8, 58 (2020)
12. Jiang, X., et al.: Enhancing IoT security via cancelable HD-sEMG-based biometric authentication password, encoded by gesture. IEEE Internet Things J. 8, 16535–16547 (2021)
13. Jiang, X., et al.: Cancelable HD-sEMG-based biometrics for cross-application discrepant personal identification. IEEE J. Biomed. Health Inform. 25(4), 1070–1079 (2020)
14. Pradhan, A., He, J., Jiang, N.: Performance optimization of surface electromyography based biometric sensing system for both verification and identification. IEEE Sens. J. 21, 21718–21729 (2021)
15. Benatti, S., et al.: Analysis of robust implementation of an EMG pattern recognition based Control. In: BIOSIGNALS (2014)
16. Atzori, M., et al.: Electromyography data for non-invasive naturally-controlled robotic hand prostheses. Sci. Data 1(1), 1–13 (2014)
17. Atzori, M., et al.: Characterization of a benchmark database for myoelectric movement classification. IEEE Trans. Neural Syst. Rehabil. Eng. 23(1), 73–83 (2014)
18. Hudgins, B., Parker, P., Scott, R.N.: A new strategy for multifunction myoelectric control. IEEE Trans. Biomed. Eng. 40(1), 82–94 (1993)
19. Bolle, R.M., et al.: Guide to Biometrics. Springer Science & Business Media, Heidelberg (2013)
20. Dahia, G., Jesus, L., Pamplona Segundo, M.: Continuous authentication using biometrics: an advanced review. Wiley Interdisc. Rev.: Data Min. Knowl. Discovery 10(4), e1365 (2020)
21. Botros, F.S., Phinyomark, A., Scheme, E.J.: Electromyography-based gesture recognition: is it time to change focus from the forearm to the wrist? IEEE Trans. Industr. Inf. 18(1), 174–184 (2020)
22. Jiang, X., et al.: Open access dataset, toolbox and benchmark processing results of high-density surface electromyogram recordings. IEEE Trans. Neural Syst. Rehabil. Eng. 29, 1035–1046 (2021)

23. Pradhan, A., et al.: Linear regression with frequency division technique for robust simultaneous and proportional myoelectric control during medium and high contraction-level variation. Biomed. Signal Process. Control **61**, 101984 (2020)
24. Prahm, C., et al.: Counteracting electrode shifts in upper-limb prosthesis control via transfer learning. IEEE Trans. Neural Syst. Rehabil. Eng. **27**(5), 956–962 (2019)
25. Côté-Allard, U., et al.: Unsupervised domain adversarial self-calibration for electromyography-based gesture recognition. IEEE Access **8**, 177941–177955 (2020)

EEG Generation of Virtual Channels Using an Improved Wasserstein Generative Adversarial Networks

Ling-Long Li🆔, Guang-Zhong Cao(✉)🆔, Hong-Jie Liang, Jiang-Cheng Chen, and Yue-Peng Zhang

Guangdong Key Laboratory of Electromagnetic Control and Intelligent Robots, College of Mechatronics and Control Engineering, Shenzhen University, Shenzhen 518060, China
gzcao@szu.edu.cn

Abstract. Aiming at enhancing classification performance and improving user experience of a brain-computer interface (BCI) system, this paper proposes an improved Wasserstein generative adversarial networks (WGAN) method to generate EEG samples in virtual channels. The feature extractor and the proposed WGAN model with a novel designed feature loss are trained. Then artificial EEG of virtual channels are generated by using the improved WGAN with EEG of multiple physical channels as the input. Motor imagery (MI) classification utilizing a CNN-based classifier is performed based on two EEG datasets. The experimental results show that the generated EEG of virtual channels are valid, which are similar to the ground truth as well as have learned important EEG features of other channels. The classification performance of the classifier with low-channel EEG has been significantly improved with the help with the generated EEG of virtual channels. Meanwhile, user experience on BCI application is also improved by low-channel EEG replacing multi-channel EEG. The feasibility and effectiveness of the proposed method are verified.

Keywords: Brain-computer interface · Wasserstein generative adversarial networks · EEG generation

1 Introduction

Brain-computer interface (BCI) system composes of signal acquisition, brain signals preprocessing, feature extraction, classification, and external device interface, which has been extensively applied to motor rehabilitation, medical diagnosis, and entertainment [1–3]. Electroencephalogram (EEG) is widely used as input signals in BCI as it's noninvasive, affordable, and high-resolution [4]. EEG paradigms on BCI mainly include motor imagery (MI), steady-state evoked potentials (SSEP), and event-related potential (ERP) [5, 6]. EEG-based BCI has broad applications like robot control, mental state monitoring, and neurorehabilitation [3]. The most popular metric for BCI is information transfer rate (ITR). However, low ITR is always a challenging problem affecting BCI performance [2]. BCI's ITR is related to target detection accuracy, class numbers, and

H. Liu et al. (Eds.): ICIRA 2022, LNAI 13458, pp. 386–399, 2022.
https://doi.org/10.1007/978-3-031-13841-6_36

detection time [7]. Generally, when class numbers of target classification increase, the detection accuracy may decrease. Enhancing classification accuracy is oneway to benefit the detection accuracy and further improve BCI's ITR [2, 7].

Related efforts mostly focused on deep learning (DL) technology to improve classification accuracy [5]. Whereas the DL-based methods largely rely on the quantity and quality of EEG datasets[3]. Recording EEG dataset involves multiple channels, but EEG acquisition equipment with high density is usually expensive and complicated to operate [8]. Note that when collecting subjects' EEG data using an EEG acquisition device with high-density wet electrodes (Ag/AgCl), each channel of electrode scalp needs insert conductive gel, the whole measurement process is long and complex, and the test experience for uses are poor. Thus reducing EEG channels of acquisition equipment for users is desired. Moreover, EEG with multiple channels contain feature redundancy, which may raise computational burden and interference. In practical BCI applications like medical diagnosis and neurological rehabilitation, electrode channels are often reduced to retain EEG quality for long time monitoring, which may degrade classification accuracy of EEG-based BCI [9]. Thus how to improve classification performance of BCI and user experience simutaneously is a meaningful task. Artificial EEG generation is a promising solution for these issues.

Lotte et al. [10] proposed three approaches to generate artificial EEG to enhance training data size for the BCI system, they were segmentation and recombination (S&R) in time domain and time-frequency domain, and analogies, respectively. But such conventional methods need multiple steps for implementation. Afterwards more advanced methods like variational autoencoder (VAE) and generative adversarial networks (GANs) were introduced. In [11] VAE was adopted to extract EEG features and remove noise in EEG channels for data augmentation (DA). Fahimi et al. [3] proposed a DCGANs-based model to generate artificial EEG for BCI users who were unable to pay attention in long period. Subject-specific artificial EEG were created via learning features of subject-independent, the generated data quality was improved, the performance of DCGANs outperformed S&R and VAE. Zhang et al. [6] proposed a deep convolutional GAN (DCGAN) to generate spectrograms EEG samples, convolutional neural network (CNN) was used to classify MI tasks. Compared with other baseline methods in terms of Freéchet inception distances (FIDs), analysis of variance, paired t-tests, and classification performance on two BCI EEG datasets, DCGAN obtained better augmentation performance than conventional methods like geometric transform, AE, and VAE. In addtion, the DCGAN could generate artificial EEG for small-scale datasets. In [3] and [6], GAN-based methods were used to enhance EEG datasets and had been proved superior to traditional baseline approaches. Hartmann et al. [12] improved Wasserstein GAN with gradient penalty (WGAN-GP) and designed an EEG-GAN framework, which showed that generating naturalistic EEG samples with GAN was possible. These studies reflected that GAN-based approaches have more potential ability in EEG generation than traditional methods. Luo et al. [8] used a WGAN model with Wasserstein distance and a spatial-temporal-frequency loss to generate EEG for high-sampling-sensitivity HSS-EEG reconstruction. Sawangjai et al. [4] designed a EEGANet model for time-series EEG generation to eliminate ocular noises in EEG preprocessing, which achieved competitive results compared with state-of-the-art methods. But the generaterd EEG had other artifacts need to be erased, and training EEG set from other EOG removing methods were still needed. Kan et al. [13] proposed a Graminan Temporal GAN with the form of Gramian Angular Field (GAF) to generate EEG for synthesis. EEG was decoded as three channel GAF images, GAN was used to create artificial multichannel GAF images. This method improved the accuracy of detecting anamalous images. Nevertheless, the generated GAF images also contained artifacts. To replace missing EEG with newly generated data, Lee et al. [14] proposed a GAN method to generate realistic EEG in terms of contextual imputation for missing sequence, via implanting latent features in the synthetic EEG, fake EEG samples were created, which looked natural and preserved contexual information.

In summary, there is a handful of GAN-based research on EEG generation, which are mainly for data augmentation, data reconstruction, data completion, and artifacts removal. But how to generate EEG samples of virtual channels from multi-channel EEG data has not been solved, and the user experience has not been considered to some extent. This paper proposes an improved Wasserstein GAN method for EEG generation of virtual channels based on multi-channel EEG data. The solution is concentrated on two concerned issues, one is to enhance the classification performance of the BCI system with low-channel EEG, the other is to improve BCI user experience by reducing EEG channel numbers. If low-channel EEG can replace multi-channel EEG for a BCI system and keep appropriate performance level unde the help of EEG of virtual channels, the ITR and user experience on the BCI system will be improved. The main contributions are listed as follows:

1. An improved Wasserstein GAN (WGAN) method is proposed for EEG generation and a novel feature loss function is designed to learn distinct features of EEG from multiple real channels;
2. The generated EEG of virtual channel not only resembles the ground truth; but also contains features of other related channels. Experimental results of MI classification on two EEG datasets show the classification performance is improved after adding the virtual-channel EEG as additional input;
3. The work preliminarily realizes low-channel EEG replacing multi-channel EEG for BCI related equipment. The fewer electrode channels in measurement process, the better experience for users.

2   The Proposed Method

2.1   The Improved Wasserstein GAN

GANs are composed of a generator G, and a discriminator D. In training process, G and D compete against each other by optimizing predefined loss function. G is trained to generate fake samples and continues optimizing samples until they can't be detected as fake by D. D is also trained to judge whether the generated samples are real [3, 15]. Nevertheless, GANs remain problems like training instability, mode collapse, and vanishing gradients [15, 16]. Considering this situation, many GAN-based improved versions (e. g., conditional GANs, DCGANs, WGAN) are designed. WGAN cures the problem of mode collapse, improves unstable training and gradient issues [17]. This paper proposes an improved WGAN model with a Wasserstein distance, a MSE loss, and a new designed feature loss, to generate virtual EEG based on raw EEG from multiple real channels. In WGAN model, the Wasserstein distance $W(P_r, P_g)$ is used to compare sample distributions [17, 18].

$$W(P_r, P_g) = \inf_{\gamma \in \prod(P_r, P_g)} E_{(x,y)\sim\gamma}[\|x - y\|] \tag{1}$$

where P_r is the real data distribution, P_g is the distribution of generated samples, $\prod(P_r, P_g)$ denotes all possible joint distributions, $\gamma\ (x, y)$ means transporting mass from x to y for transforming P_r into P_g. $W(P_r, P_g)$ shows the minimum cost for transportation. To preserve the contents of EEG, MSE loss function L_{MSE} is employed and shown as

$$L_{MSE} = \frac{1}{m} \sum_{i=1}^{m} \|x_i - \hat{x}_i\|^2 \tag{2}$$

where x is the real data, $\hat{x}$ is the newly generated data, m is the batch size.

In addition, deep features of EEG are taken into consideration, and a novel feature loss function is designed to help G to learn the internal features of the input EEG. The feature loss L_{FEA} is delimitated as

$$L_{FEA} = \frac{1}{m} \sum_{i=1}^{m} \|F(x_i) - F(\hat{x}_i)\|^2 \tag{3}$$

where F is the EEG features extracted from the pre-trained feature extractor.

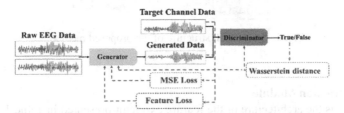

Fig. 1. The EEG generation process of the improved WGAN.

The objective function of WGAN [19] is defined as

$$\min_{G} \max_{D} L_{WGAN}(D, G) = -E_x[D(x)] + E_z[D(G(z))] \tag{4}$$

where E means the expectation operator, z denotes the input of multi-channel EEG, $D(x)$ is the possibility of x belonging to true, $G(z)$ is the generated EEG based on z. For the proposed improved WGAN model, the loss of G includes the amalgamation of the Wasserstein distance, the MSE loss, and the feature loss; the loss function of D is the Wasserstein distance. Combining Eq. (1) to (4) together, the optimization problem is

$$\min_{G} \max_{D} L_{W\,GAN}(D, G) = \lambda_1 W(P_r, P_g) + \lambda_2 L_{MSE} + \lambda_3 L_{FEA} \tag{5}$$

where λ_1, λ_2, and λ_3 are hyper parameters of the loss functions.

D and G are trained alternatively in the way of freezing one and updating the other. The EEG generation process of the proposed WGAN-based model is exhibited in Fig. 1.

2.2 Network Structure

The overall structure of the proposed method is depicted in Fig. 2, which consists of four parts to generate EEG of virtual channels from learning multi-channel EEG: 1) a feature extraction module, 2) a generator module, 3) a discriminator module, 4) a classifier. The input is EEG signals of multiple channels. The feature extraction module is handled to extract distinct features from the input EEG. The Deepconv layer is used to extract deep features of EEG. The generator is exploited to generate EEG of virtual channels in terms of the input EEG features. The discriminator is employed to distinguish the discrepancy between the generated EEG of the virtual channel and the real EEG. The classifier is designed to classify MI tasks based on the classified data.

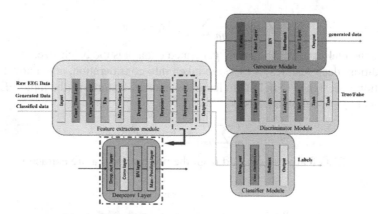

Fig. 2. The overall structure of the proposed method.

Feature Extraction Module

The first part is the architecture of the feature extractor presented in Table 1. To extract EEG features in a wide range, referring to [20], a deep ConvNet is developed to handle the input data, which composes of five light and deep convolution layers, and a max-pooling layer. The input is EEG samples with C channels (one channel corresponds to one electrode). The first two layers perform convolution over time and channel, note that exponential linear unit (ELU) activation function is used to improve fitting results in temporal convolution. Rectified linear unit (ReLU) activation function is adopted to fasten learning speed of the network. Then a max pooling layer is followed to pack the output data of spatial convolution layer. Finally, three groups of deep convolution layer and max pool layer are manipulated to encode EEG features, including operations of dropping out and batch normalization (BN).

Generator

The second part is the designed generator G based on multi-layer perceptron (MLP) structure, and the architecture is addressed in Table 2. G contains a flatten layer, two linear layers, and a BN layer. The input data are EEG features extracted from the raw EEG of multiple channels and have been flattened in one-dimensional sequence. The

Table 1. The architecture of feature extraction module.

Layers	Filter numbers	Kernel sizes	Strides	Activation	Output shapes
Input					$(1, C, 1000)$
Conv_Time layer	25	$(1, 10)$	$(1, 1)$	ELU	$(25, C, 991)$
Conv_Spat layer	25	$(1, C)$	$(1, 1)$		$(25, 1, 991)$
Max pooling layer		$(1, 3)$	$(1, 3)$		$(25, 1, 333)$
Deepconv 1 conv	50	$(1, 10)$	$(1, 1)$	ReLU	$(50, 1, 321)$
Deepconv 1 max pool		$(1, 3)$	$(1, 3)$		$(50, 1, 107)$
Deepconv 2 conv	100	$(1, 10)$	$(1, 1)$	ReLU	$(100, 1, 103)$
Deepconv 2 max pool		$(1, 3)$	$(1, 3)$		$(100, 1, 34)$
Deepconv 3 conv	200	$(1, 3)$	$(1, 1)$	ReLU	$(200, 1, 30)$
Deepconv 3 max pool		$(1, 3)$	$(1, 3)$		$(200, 1, 10)$

output is the generated EEG. Hardtanh activation function is empirically utilized to relieve zero tendencies of the generated samples.

Table 2. The architecture of the generator and discriminator.

Module	Layers	Neuron numbers	Activation	Output shapes
Generator	Input			$(200, 1, 10)$
	Flatten			(2000)
	Linear Layer	2000	Hardtanh	(2000)
	Linear Layer	1000		(1000)
Discriminator	Input			$(200, 1, 10)$
	Flatten			(2000)
	Linear Layer	1000	LeakyReLU	(2000)
	Linear Layer	2	Tanh	(1000)

Discriminator

The third part is the discriminator D also following MLP structure shown in Table 2. D contains a flatten layer, two linear layers, and a BN layer. The input is the flattening EEG features extracted from the generated EEG of virtual channel. The output is the judgement result true or false. The linear layers are leveraged to decide whether the generated EEG resemble the ground truth. The BN layer can relieve poor initialization.

Classfier

The fourth part is the CNN-based classifier, which comprises of classifier layer with N

convolution filters and is exploited to estimate the effectiveness of the generated EEG. The input is the feature vectors extracted from EEG. N convolution kernels (size 1×10, stride 1×1) with Softmax activation function are utilized to classify class labels of MI.

3 Experiments

3.1 Datasets

Experiments over two MI-EEG datasets BCI competition IV–2a [21] and IV–2b [22] are conducted to evaluate the proposed method, the details of the datasets are shown in Table 3. For the usage allocation for each dataset, 50% of the data train the improved WGAN, 40% of them train the classifier, and the remaining is leveraged for validation.

Table 3. The details of the used datasets.

Datasets	Number of subjects	Sampling rates (Hz)	EEG channels	MI class labels
BCI-C IV-2a	9	250	22	4 classes (left hand, right hand, feet, and tongue)
BCI-C IV-2b	9	250	3	2 classes (left hand, right hand)

3.2 Implementation Details

Data Preprocessing

To remove noise and unrelated components of the raw EEG, the data for MI tasks lasting 4 s are selected for each sample, the input data size is 1000 sample points per channel. The selected data are band pass filtered from 8 Hz to 38 Hz. Maximum absolute normalization is operated to fasten the network's learning rate.

Training and Implementation

The experiments are implemented in Python 3.7 with Pytorch 1.10.1, under the support of Nvidia RTX 3060 GPU. Based on the aforementioned datasets, the feature extractor is firstly well trained. Then the generator and the discriminator are trained in backpropagation according to the predefined loss functions, the pseudo code is described in Table 4. The classifier is trained and updated with cross-entropy loss function and dam optimizer, the learning rate is 0.00625.

EEG of three channels C3, Cz, and C4 are selected to conduct experiments on two datasets. As event-related synchronization (ERS) and event-related desynchronization (ERD) mode of MI mainly occurs surrounding sensory motor cortex, the regions of

C3, C4, and Cz mainly represent dynamic change of MI-EEG [2, 6, 23–25]. On BCI competition IV–2a, aiming to generate one virtual EEG sequence, which is not only analogous to the ground truth, but also learns representative features of EEG in C3, Cz, and C4. EEG samples collected from electrode 8, 10, and 12 (corresponding to C3, Cz, and C4) are the input of the generator. EEG samples of electrode 9 is treated as the ground truth. After training the proposed model, MI classification of four tasks is performed with classified data in four cases. Case 1: EEG signals of C3, Cz, and C4; Case 2: EEG signals of C3, Cz, and C4, and Gaussian noise; Case 3: EEG signals of C3, Cz, C4, and electrode 9; Case 4: EEG signals of C3, Cz, C4, and the EEG of virtual channel.

Table 4. The pseudo code of the improved WGAN.

Algorithm 1 the improved WGAN algorithm

Require: The learning rate α , the clipping parameter c, the batch size m, the weight parameter for Wasserstein distance loss λ_1 , the weight parameter for MSE loss λ_2 , the weight parameter for feature loss λ_3 , the pre-trained feature extractor F.

Require: initial discriminator's parameters ω_0 , initial generator's parameters θ_0

1: **while** θ has not converged **do**

2:   Sample a batch of real data: $\{x^{(i)}\}_{i=1}^{m} \sim P_r$

3:   Sample a batch of input data: $\{z^{(i)}\}_{i=1}^{m} \sim p(z)$

4:   a batch of generated data: $\tilde{x}^{(i)} = G_\theta(z^{(i)})$

5:   the loss of discriminator: $L_D^{(i)} = D_\omega(\tilde{x}^{(i)}) - D_\omega(x^{(i)})$

6:   Update D: $\omega \leftarrow \omega + \alpha \cdot \text{RMSProp}\left(\omega, \nabla\frac{1}{m}\sum_{i=0}^{m} L_D^{(i)}\right)$

7:   $\omega \leftarrow \text{clip}(\omega, -c, c)$

8:   $L_w^{(i)} = -D_\omega\left(G_\theta(z^{(i)})\right)$

9:   $L_{MSE}^{(i)} = \left\|x^{(i)} - \tilde{x}^{(i)}\right\|^2$

10:   $L_{FEA}^{(i)} = \left\|F(x^{(i)}) - F(\tilde{x}^{(i)})\right\|^2$

11:   the loss of generator: $L_G^{(i)} = \lambda_1 L_w^{(i)} + \lambda_2 L_{MSE}^{(i)} + \lambda_3 L_{FEA}^{(i)}$

12:   Update G: $\theta \leftarrow \theta + \alpha \cdot \text{RMSProp}\left(\theta, \nabla\frac{1}{m}\sum_{i=0}^{m} L_G^{(i)}\right)$

13: **end while**

On BCI competition IV-2b, with the same target, EEG samples of C3 and Cz are the input for the generator, the ground truth is EEG samples of C4. Based on the well-trained proposed model, MI classification of two tasks is carried out with the classified data under four cases. Case 1: EEG signals of C3 and Cz; case 2: EEG signals of C3 and Cz, and Gaussian noise; case 3: EEG signals of C3, Cz, and C4; case 4: EEG signals of C3, Cz, and the EEG of virtual channel.

3.3 Evaluation Metrics

Currently there is no unified and appropriate performance index to assess GAN-based model [12], only single metric could not give sufficient information for the quality [10]. This paper evaluates the proposed method from three aspects. The loss value of G and D during training process measures the training stability of the network. The visualization of the generation results appraises the quality of the generated EEG samples. The classification performance of accuracy and kappa value is calculated to verify the efficacy of the proposed WGAN-based EEG generation method.

4   Results and Discussion

4.1   Loss Variation of the Improved WGAN

To monitor the convergence situation of the improved WGAN model, the loss variation of the generator and the discriminator vs. epoch numbers on datasets BCI competition IV–2a and IV–2b are plotted in Fig. 3. All the loss values gradually tend to convergence after training about 300 epochs, and the generator and the discriminator maintain balanced, which indicates that the training ability of the improved WGAN is stable.

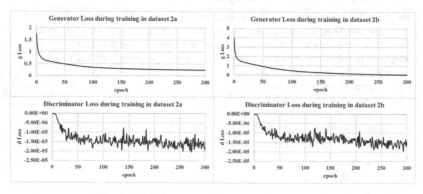

Fig. 3. The loss variation with respect to epochs.

4.2   Visualization of the Generated EEG

To estimate the quality of the generated EEG, the comparison results between the ground truth and the generated EEG in temporal domain and spectral domain are presented in Fig. 4 and Fig. 5, respectively. It's revealed that the data distribution on these two datasets are totally semblable; the basic trend of the generated EEG is in accordance with the original data in time and spectral domains, especially the distributions in spectral domain are closely similar. Though there are some peak and vibration points in temporal domain, distinguishable EEG features can still be mimicked.

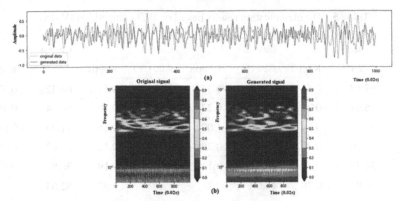

Fig. 4. Visualization of the original EEG and the generated EEG on BCI competition IV–2a. (a) Comparison results in temporal domain; (b) Comparison results in spectral domain.

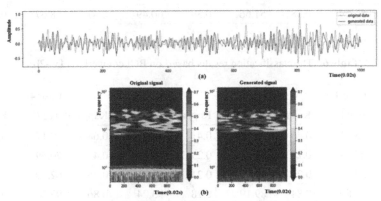

Fig. 5. Visualization of the original EEG and the generated EEG on BCI competition IV–2b. (a) Comparison results in temporal domain; (b) Comparison results in spectral domain.

4.3 Classification Results

To measure the MI-EEG classification performance based on the proposed method,

Tables 5–6 and Fig. 6 provide the classification results under four cases based on datasets BCI competition IV–2a and IV–2b, respectively. The four cases relevant to these two datasets are respectively defined in training and implementation part. As generating low-channel EEG from multi-channel EEG using GAN-based method remains relatively underexplored, no other comparison results present in this paper.

In Table 5 and Fig. 6 (a), the accuracy and kappa value in case 3 are obviously larger than the classification results of case 1 and case 2, which confirms that more data is helpful for obtaining better classification accuracy. The classification results achieved under case 4 are higher than case 1 and case 2, but close to the results under case 3. With the help of the generated EEG, the classification performance is improved compared to the results of case 1, the generated EEG are more useful than Gaussian noise as input in case 2. The classification performance based on EEG with three channels and

Table 5. The classification results based on BCI competition IV–2a.

Subjects	Case 1		Case 2		Case 3		Case 4	
	Acc (%)	Kappa	Acc (%)	Kappa	Acc (%)	Kappa	Acc (%)	Kappa
A01	67.83	0.57	52.17	0.36	70.83	0.61	68.42	0.57
A02	45.61	0.27	45.61	0.27	56.14	0.40	56.14	0.40
A03	73.04	0.64	73.91	1.00	73.96	0.65	71.93	0.64
A04	48.70	0.32	46.96	0.29	56.52	0.42	52.63	0.38
A05	34.78	0.14	33.04	0.11	39.58	0.19	36.84	0.18
A06	46.09	0.28	46.09	0.28	52.63	0.37	52.63	0.37
A07	50.88	0.36	50.88	0.36	64.91	0.53	61.40	0.49
A08	56.94	0.42	56.94	0.42	61.40	0.48	61.40	0.48
A09	59.38	0.46	59.38	0.46	68.40	0.58	66.67	0.56
Average	53.69	0.38	51.66	0.39	60.49	0.47	58.67	0.45

Table 6. The classification results based on BCI competition IV–2b.

Subjects	Case 1		Case 2		Case 3		Case 4	
	Acc (%)	Kappa	Acc (%)	Kappa	Acc (%)	Kappa	Acc (%)	Kappa
B01	73.61	0.46	72.22	0.41	84.72	0.68	79.17	0.55
B02	63.24	0.27	64.71	0.29	70.59	0.41	70.59	0.41
B03	59.72	0.21	59.72	0.21	62.50	0.25	62.50	0.26
B04	91.89	0.84	89.19	0.78	93.24	0.86	93.24	0.86
B05	85.14	0.70	74.32	0.49	95.95	0.92	93.24	0.86
B06	76.39	0.52	72.22	0.42	84.72	0.69	84.72	0.70
B07	80.56	0.60	79.17	0.57	91.67	0.82	87.50	0.74
B08	77.63	0.56	77.63	0.56	85.53	0.71	84.21	0.69
B09	83.33	0.67	79.17	0.59	86.11	0.72	86.11	0.72
Average	76.83	0.54	74.26	0.48	83.89	0.67	82.37	0.64

the generated EEG can maintain an approximate state in contrast to EEG with four channels to some extent. Hence, on BCI competition IV–2a with EEG data on C3, Cz, C4, and electrode 9, the proposed improved WGAN method improves the classification performance with the increasement of 4.98% for the average accuracy and 0.07 for the mean kappa value, compared to the case without virtual generated EEG.

From Table 6 and Fig. 6 (b), based on BCI competition IV-2b with EEG data on C3, Cz, and C4, the results show the analogical phenomena and variation tendency like Table 5. The classification results of case 4 are larger than case 1 and case 2, but approaching

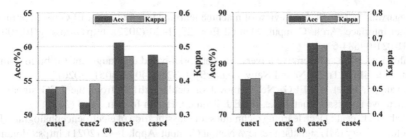

Fig. 6. Average accuracy and kappa value of four cases on datasets: (a) 2a (b) 2b.

the results of case 3. In total, the proposed improved WGAN method could generate valid one virtual-channel EEG signals, and benefits the classification performance with improvement of 5.54% for the average accuracy and 0.1 for the mean kappa value. Above all, the classification performance holds nearly the same even if the EEG channel is lessened under the support of the generated EEG of virtual channel.

In conclusion, the experimental results validate the feasibility and effectiveness of the proposed WGAN-based EEG generation method. This work explores EEG generation with multiple virtual channels based on multi-channel EEG, the proposed method can be extended to BCI system with other EEG paradigms in further.

5   Conclusion

This paper proposed an improved WGAN method for EEG generation of virtual channels based on multi-channel EEG. A novel feature loss was designed and added to the generator to constrain the network. Two MI-EEG datasets were used to verify the proposed method and assess the classification performance with the help of EEG generation of virtual channels. The results shown that the improved WGAN network can be trained steadily, and the generated EEG of virtual channels not only resembled the ground truth but also possessed distinctive features of the input EEG. The MI-EEG classification results indicated that the proposed method is feasible and effective to improve classification performance for a BCI system under the circumstance of EEG data with low channels. This method also improved user experience by using fewer electrode channels, it's potentially applied to customized BCI related equipment.

Acknowledgement. This work was supported in part by the National Natural Science Foundation of China under Grant NSFC U1813212, in part by the Science and Technology Planning Project of Guangdong Province, China under Grant 2020B121201012.

References

1. Volosyak, I., Gembler, F., Stawicki, P.: Age-related differences in SSVEP-based BCI performance. Neurocomputing **250**, 57–64 (2017)

2. Aggarwal, S., Chugh, N.: Review of machine learning techniques for EEG based brain computer interface. Arch. Comput. Method Eng. **29**, 1–20 (2022). https://doi.org/10.1007/s11831-021-09684-6
3. Fahimi, F., et al.: Generative adversarial networks-based data augment for brain-computer Interface. IEEE Trans. Neural Netw. Learn. Syst. **32**(9), 4039–4051 (2020)
4. Sawangjai, P., et al.: EEGANet: removal of ocular artifact from the EEG signal using generative adversarial networks. IEEE J. Biomed. Health Inform. 1–13 (2021)
5. Altaheri, H., et al.: Deep learning techniques for classification of electroencephalogram (EEG) motor imagery (MI) signals: a review. Neural Comput. Appl. 1–42 (2021). https://doi.org/10.1007/s00521-021-06352-5
6. Zhang, K., et al.: Data augmentation for motor imagery signal classification based on a hybrid neural network. Sensors **20**, 1–20 (2020). 4485
7. Ramadan, R.A., Vasilakos, A.V.: Brain computer interface: control signals review. Neurocomputing **223**, 26–44 (2017)
8. Luo T., et al.: EEG signal reconstruction using a generative adversarial network with wasserstein distance and temporal-spatial-frequency loss. Front. Neuroinform. 14(15) (2020)
9. Svantesson, M., et al.: Virtual EEG-electrodes: convolutional neural networks as a method for upsampling or restoring channels. J. Neurosci. Methods 355 (2021)
10. Lotte, F.: Signal processing approaches to minimize or suppress calibration time in oscillatory activity-based brain-computer interfaces. In: Proceedings of the IEEE, pp. 871–890 (2015)
11. Hwaidi, J.F., et al.: Classification of motor imagery EEG signals based on deep autoencoder and convolutional neural network approach. IEEE Access **10**, 48071–48081 (2022)
12. Hartmann, K.G., Schirrmeister, R.T., Ball, T.: EEG-GAN: generative adversarial networks for electroencephalograhic (EEG) brain signals. arXiv preprint arXiv:1806.01875 (2018)
13. Kan, C.N.E., Povinelli, R.J., Ye, D.H.: Enhancing multi-channel EEG classification with gramian temporal generative adversarial networks. In: ICASSP 2021–2021 IEEE International Conference on Acoustics, Speech and Signal Processing (ICASSP). IEEE, vol. 2021, pp. 1260–1264 (2021)
14. Lee, W., Lee, J., Kim, Y.: Contextual imputation with missing sequence of EEG signals using generative adversarial networks. IEEE Access **9**, 151753–151765 (2021)
15. Creswell, A., et al.: Generative adversarial networks: an overview. IEEE Signal Process. Mag. **35**(1), 53–65 (2018)
16. Gao, N., et al.: Generative adversarial networks for spatio-temporal data: a survey. ACM Trans. Intell. Syst. Technol. **13**(2), 1–25 (2022)
17. Arjovsky, M., Chintala, S., Bottou, L.: Wasserstein generative adversarial networks. In: International Conference on Machine Learning. PMLR, pp. 214–223 (2017)
18. Gulrajani, I., et al.: Improved training of wasserstein GANs. Adv. Neural Inf. Process. Syst. **30**, 1–11 (2017)
19. Yang, Q., et al.: Low-dose CT image denoising using a generative adversarial network with wasserstein distance and perceptual loss. IEEE Trans. Med. Imaging **37**(6), 1348–1357 (2018)
20. Schirrmeiste, R.T., et al.: Deep learning with convolutional neural networks for EEG decoding and visualization. Hum. Brain Mapp. **38**, 5391–5420 (2017)
21. Brunner, C., et al.: BCI competition 2008–Graz data set A. Inst. Knowl. Discov. Graz. Univ. Technol. **16**, 1–6 (2008)
22. Leeb, R., et al.: BCI competition 2008–Graz data set B. Inst. Knowl. Discov. Graz. Univ. Technol. 1–6 (2008)
23. Xu, B., et al.: Wavelet transform time-frequency image and convolutional network based motor imagery EEG classification. IEEE Access **7**, 6084–6093 (2018)
24. Pfurtscheller, G., et al.: Mu rhythm (de)synchronization and EEG single-trial classification of different motor imagery tasks. Neuroimage **31**(1), 153–159 (2006)

25. Liu, Y., Wang, Z., Huang, S., Wei, J., Li, X., Ming, D.: EEG Characteristic Investigation of the Sixth-Finger Motor Imagery. In: Liu, X.-J., Nie, Z., Yu, J., Xie, F., Song, R. (eds.) ICIRA 2021. LNCS (LNAI), vol. 13013, pp. 654–663. Springer, Cham (2021). https://doi.org/10. 1007/978-3-030-89095-7_62

Research on Compliant Rehabilitation Strategy of Upper Limb Rehabilitation Robot Based on sEMG

Hang Lyu[1,2,3], Ya-Lun Gu[1,3], Gao Lin[1,3], Dao-Hui Zhang[1,3(✉)], and Xin-Gang Zhao[1,3]

[1] State Key Laboratory of Robotics, Shenyang Institute of Automation, Chinese Academy of Sciences, Shenyang, China
zhangdaohui@sia.cn
[2] College of Information Science and Engineering, Northeastern University, Shenyang, China
[3] Institutes for Robotics and Intelligent Manufacturing, Chinese Academy of Sciences, Shenyang, China

Abstract. In this paper, a surface Electromyography (sEMG)-based compliant rehabilitation training method for the end traction upper limb rehabilitation robot is proposed. The sEMG signal of the forearm and upper arm on the affected side of the human body is collected by the electromyography sensor, and the sEMG signal is used to perform real-time force recognition through the end force estimation model, and the estimated force is used as the interactive force input in the admittance controller. Linear and circular compliance training trajectories were planned, and impedance parameter characteristics were analyzed to obtain admittance control parameters suitable for upper limb passive rehabilitation training. The results show that the force estimation method based on sEMG, combined with the compliance control strategy, improves the interactive ability of upper limb rehabilitation training, ensures the personal safety of users, and makes the training more scientific and effective.

Keywords: End traction · sEMG · Force estimation · Admittance control · Human-computer interaction

1 Introduction

Stroke is the leading cause of death and disability among Chinese residents, and its morbidity ranks first in the world. It has the characteristics of high morbidity, high mortality and high disability rate [1]. In China, one person has a stroke every 12 s, and one person dies of a stroke every 21 s [2]. Stroke survivors all have different degrees of motor dysfunction, and 80% of them have upper limb dysfunction [3]. Clinical studies have shown that rehabilitation training can effectively promote the functional recovery of patients. The traditional rehabilitation treatment is mainly a one-on-one, hand-in-hand way for therapists to rehabilitate patients, which will inevitably increase the workload of rehabilitation therapists [4, 5]. Rehabilitation equipment is needed to relieve the work pressure of

H. Liu et al. (Eds.): ICIRA 2022, LNAI 13458, pp. 400–409, 2022.
https://doi.org/10.1007/978-3-031-13841-6_37

rehabilitation therapists. Most of the traditional rehabilitation equipment adopts passive rehabilitation training and lacks the ability of human-computer interaction.

At present, many studies have been carried out on human-robot interaction methods for rehabilitation robots. Among them, sEMG is used in human-computer interaction in rehabilitation therapy and has achieved good evaluation because it has the characteristics of producing ahead of limb movement, and patients with complete upper limb hemiplegia can also produce EMG signals [6]. The upper limb rehabilitation robotic arm system developed by Harbin Institute of Technology collects the sEMG of the four muscles of the unaffected upper limb of the patient, and establishes the sEMG recognition model through the AR parameter model and the BP neural network [7]. The upper limb rehabilitation device designed by Wu Jun of Huazhong University of Science and Technology uses 4-channel sEMG signal for control, with active mode, passive mode and impedance mode [8]. The power-assisted robot HAL developed by the Cybernics Laboratory of the University of Tsukuba combines the joint torque estimated by sEMG and the lower limb motion reference model to construct a hybrid autonomous control system of HAL. The intention control based on sEMG makes the exoskeleton movement more flexible and natural. With the help of HAL, the subject can not only carry out normal daily life, but also complete more difficult tasks such as standing, walking, climbing, grasping, and lifting heavy objects.

In summary, the use of sEMG to achieve joint continuous force and motion estimation can achieve the safety and compliance of human-computer interaction. At present, there are few related studies and it has not been widely used. In this paper, a passive upper limb training method based on sEMG is proposed. The sEMG signal of the affected side is collected by the electromyography equipment, and the end force of the affected side is estimated in real time through the end force estimation model. Use the estimated force as the external force input to the admittance controller. Finally, the effectiveness of the method is verified by training experiments on straight lines and circles. The main contributions of this paper are as follows:

- Established a end force estimation model to achieve accurate force estimation for the upper limb end force.
- By introducing sEMG signals in passive training, the passive training that can only use the healthy side for interaction can be converted into passive interactive training only using the affected side, making the training more scientific and effective.

2   sEMG-Based Compliant Rehabilitation Method

2.1   Experimental Paradigm

For the linear motion and plane motion commonly used in upper limb rehabilitation training, the upper limb sEMG signal and force sensor data are collected during interaction. sEMG signal acquisition was performed using a Myo armband. Considering that the contact force is related to the upper forearm muscles, the Myo armbands are worn at the positions where the forearm muscles are located. The wearing method is shown in Fig. 1.

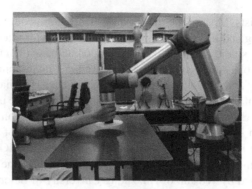

Fig. 1. Wearing mode

The force sensor adopts the six-dimensional force sensor of the UR5e robotic arm, which can measure the force and torque of six degrees of freedom, and the sampling frequency can reach up to 500 Hz. The selected sampling frequency is 200 Hz and the 30004 port is used to read the real-time data of the UR5e robotic arm end position and force sensor. Three male subjects (age: 23.7 ± 0.5 years old, mean ± SD) take part in the experiment. Subjects completed 3 linear motion and circular motion experiments. In the experiment, the Myo armband was used to collect the sEMG signal of the subject's right arm, and the sEMG information and the end force information of the robotic arm were recorded at the same time.

2.2 Force Estimation

After feature extraction of the collected sEMG signals, the NMF method is used to extract muscle synergy information, and the long-short-term memory neural network model is used to establish a end force estimation model for continuous force estimation during the interaction process (Fig. 2).

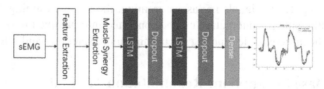

Fig. 2. Force estimation processing flow

After preprocessing the acquired sEMG signals, the EMG features for muscle synergy extraction were selected. It is generally believed that the level of muscle activity and EMG time-domain characteristics are approximately linear. The EMG time-domain features can be selected for muscle synergy extraction, and MAV features can be selected for subsequent muscle synergy extraction.

$$MAV = \frac{1}{N_t} \sum_{i=1}^{N_t} x_i \tag{1}$$

In this experiment, the non-negative matrix decomposition method was chosen to decompose for force estimation. The muscle activation level E can be expressed by the synergistic element matrix W and the activation coefficient matrix H:

$$E_{m \times n} = W_{m \times r} \times H_{r \times n} \tag{2}$$

Where m is the number of channels collected by sEMG, n is the number of sampling points, and R is the number of muscle synergy elements, which means that the muscle activation level is decomposed into R synergy elements.

Considering that the force continuous estimation is a time-varying sequence, this study chose to use a long short-term memory neural network model (LSTM) to build the end force estimation model. In this study, the tensor flow framework is used to build a force estimation model. The input of the model is the extracted muscle synergy information, and the dimension is n*5*16, where n is the number of samples. The network consists of five layers. The first layer is the LSTM layer, the second layer is the dropout layer to avoid model over fitting. The third layer is the LSTM layer, the fourth layer is the dropout layer, and the fifth layer is the full connection layer. The number of neurons is 3, which is the force output in the x, y and z directions.

2.3 Impedance Control Strategy

The impedance control of the rehabilitation robot is to adjust the impedance parame-ters to make the force and position of the robot end conform to a certain dynamic relationship. As an auxiliary robot, the rehabilitation robot is in direct contact with the human body and should be safe and flexible. There are two methods to realize im-pedance control. According to the realization method of target impedance, there are two methods, one is the force-based impedance control method, and the other is the position-based impedance control method. Active compliance of the joint with force-based impedance control.

The force-based impedance control strategy detects the force on the end of the ro-bot through the force sensor at the end of the robot, and then feeds the detected force information to the control model, outputs the position deviation, and corrects the desired position Xd. The admittance controller can be described as a spring-damper-mass system:

$$M_d \left(\ddot{X} - \ddot{X}_d \right) + B_d \left(\dot{X} - \dot{X}_d \right) + K_d (X - X_d) = F \tag{3}$$

Among them, M_d, B_d, K_d are the inertia parameters, damping parameters and stiff-ness parameters in the control model, respectively, F is the external environment force of the robot end, X, X_d are the actual motion trajectory and expected motion trajectory of the robot end.

For the linear motion and circular motion of the upper arm, different control strategies such as tracking the given trajectory and dynamically adjusting the power assist are proposed.

In the passive training mode, the end of the rehabilitation robot drives the patient's arm to move along a given trajectory. For patients in the early stage of rehabilitation, the muscle tension of the affected limb is high, which makes it impossible to complete the passive training along the set trajectory, and it is easy to damage the affected limb during exercise. It can be controlled by impedance. When the end is subjected to force in the vertical direction of motion, it will make a compliant motion in the corresponding direction to ensure safety (Fig. 3).

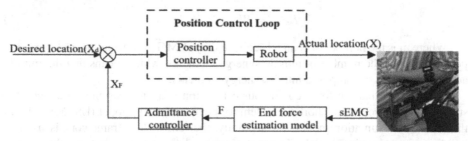

Fig. 3. Control strategy for tracking a given trajectory

X_d and X represent the expected trajectory and the actual trajectory of the robot. The force F is obtained through the end interactive force estimation model, and it can be converted into the position offset X_F after passing through the impedance model, so as to obtain the corrected position signal and input it to After the position control loop, the rehabilitation robot is controlled by the position controller, and the position control of the robot end is realized, thereby achieving the effect of compliant control.

In the assist training mode, it is hoped that the end assist of the rehabilitation robot can be dynamically adjusted. The deviation between the expected force and the force applied by the arm is regarded as the force provided by the end of the manipulator, and is converted into a position offset through impedance control to realize dynamic adjustment of power assistance. The patient can adjust the impedance parameters according to the rehabilitation situation, and select the appropriate interactive force for booster training (Fig. 4).

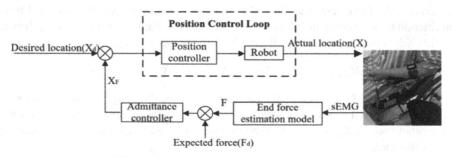

Fig. 4. Control strategy of dynamic adjustment assistance

3 Results and Analysis

For linear motion in the tracking given trajectory strategy, the end of the robot applies a vertical force F during the linear motion along a given direction, and the robot makes an active compliant motion while performing linear motion in the original direction. $\vec{F}$ is the external force received, $\vec{l}$ is the vertical motion direction vector, and the vertical direction force is calculated by projection.

$$Fn = \frac{\vec{F} \cdot \vec{l}}{\left|\vec{l}\right|} \tag{4}$$

Then get the position offset through impedance control:

$$M_d \Delta \ddot{p} + B_d \Delta \dot{p} + K_d \Delta p = Fn \tag{5}$$

Decompose into the x, y direction to get the corrected target position:

$$\begin{bmatrix} x \\ y \end{bmatrix} = \begin{bmatrix} x_d \\ y_d \end{bmatrix} + \frac{\Delta p}{\left|\vec{l}\right|}\vec{l} \tag{6}$$

The target position is then sent to the position controller to achieve compliance control in the corresponding direction. The force, motion position and trajectory diagram

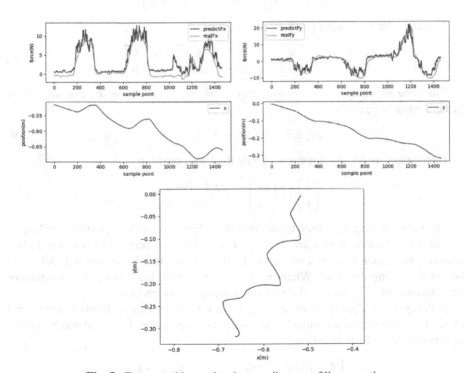

Fig. 5. Force, position and trajectory diagram of linear motion

of linear motion are shown in Fig. 5. It can be seen that when the applied force is perpendicular to the motion direction, the end of the manipulator will be offset in the corresponding direction. When the force is removed, the end of the robotic arm continues to move in the original direction.

For circular motion, during the movement of the robot end along the circular trajectory, a force F in the direction of the vertical velocity is applied, and the robot makes an active and compliant motion while tracking the trajectory motion (Fig. 6).

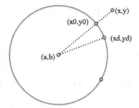

Fig. 6. Calculation of expected position of circular motion

Considering the trajectory offset during the movement process, first calculate the corresponding position on the circle through the current position:

$$\begin{bmatrix} x_0 \\ y_0 \end{bmatrix} = \begin{bmatrix} a \\ b \end{bmatrix} + r\frac{\vec{n}}{|\vec{n}|}, \ \vec{n} = \begin{bmatrix} x - a \\ y - b \end{bmatrix} \tag{7}$$

Calculate the next target position:

$$\begin{bmatrix} x_d \\ y_d \end{bmatrix} = \begin{bmatrix} a \\ b \end{bmatrix} + \begin{bmatrix} \cos\theta & -\sin\theta \\ \sin\theta & \cos\theta \end{bmatrix}\begin{bmatrix} x_0 - a \\ y_0 - b \end{bmatrix} \tag{8}$$

Calculate the radial force through projection, and then obtain the position offset through impedance control:

$$M_d\Delta\ddot{p} + B_d\Delta\dot{p} + K_d\Delta p = Fn \tag{9}$$

Decompose to the x, y direction, update the target position:

$$\begin{bmatrix} x \\ y \end{bmatrix} = \begin{bmatrix} x_d \\ y_d \end{bmatrix} + \frac{\Delta p}{r}\begin{bmatrix} x_d - a \\ y_d - b \end{bmatrix} \tag{10}$$

Then send the target position to the controller. The force, motion position and trajectory diagram of linear motion are shown in Fig. 7. It can be seen that when the applied force deviates from the center of the circle, the end of the robotic arm will deflect in the corresponding direction. When the force is removed, the end of the manipulator continues to complete the circular motion in the original direction.

In the dynamic adjustment assist strategy, the force F is obtained through the terminal interactive force estimation model, and the deviation between the calculated F and the set expected force F_d is as follows

$$\begin{cases} M_x\Delta\ddot{p}_x + B_x\Delta\dot{p}_x + K_x\Delta p_x = f_{xd} - f_x \\ M_y\Delta\ddot{p}_y + B_y\Delta\dot{p}_y + K_y\Delta p_y = f_{yd} - f_y \end{cases} \tag{11}$$

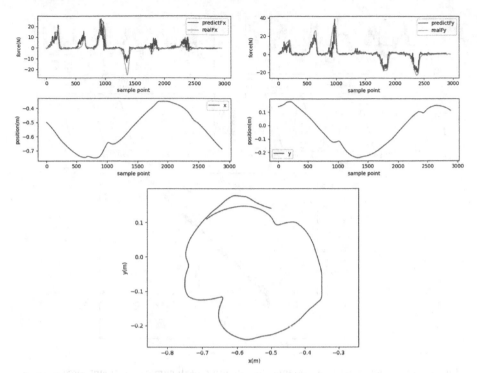

Fig. 7. Circular motion force, motion position and trajectory diagram

After passing through the impedance model, it can be converted into the position offset $\Delta X = \begin{bmatrix} \Delta p_x & \Delta p_y \end{bmatrix}^T$, so as to obtain the corrected position signal.

$$\begin{bmatrix} x \\ y \end{bmatrix} = \begin{bmatrix} x_d \\ y_d \end{bmatrix} + \begin{bmatrix} \Delta p_x \\ \Delta p_y \end{bmatrix} \tag{12}$$

After inputting it into the position control loop, the position controller is used to control the rehabilitation robot, realize the position control of the robot end, and realize the dynamic adjustment of the power assist. Figure 8 shows the force, motion position and trajectory of the dynamic adjustment assist strategy. It can be seen that when the applied force is less than the expected force, the end of the robotic arm will apply corresponding assistance.

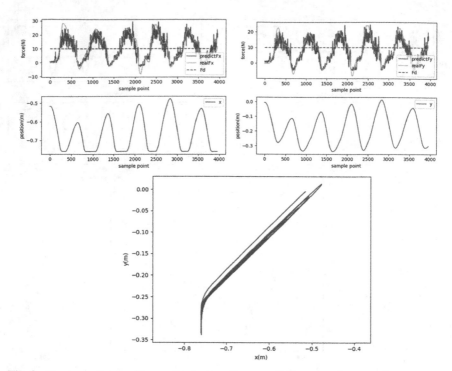

Fig. 8. Force, motion position and trajectory diagram of dynamic adjustment force strategy

4 Conclusion

In this paper, a passive upper limb training method based on sEMG is proposed. The EMG signal of the affected side is collected by the EMG equipment, the end force of the affected side is estimated in real time through the end force estimation model, and the estimated force is used as the external force input of the admittance controller. A compliant control strategy that tracks a given trajectory and dynamically adjusts the power assist is proposed. Finally, through the linear and circular trajectory training experiments, it is verified that the proposed method can realize the compliance control in the upper limb training process.

References

1. Gao, P.C., Tang, F.: Effect of intelligent rehabilitation training system on upper limb and hand function of patients with stroke. Chin. J. Rehabil. Theor. Pract. **26**(10), 1198–1203 (2020). https://doi.org/10.3969/j.issn.1006-9771.2020.10.013
2. Kim, J.S.: Acute vestibular disorders: stroke or not. J. Neurol. Sci. **429**, 117978 (2021). https://doi.org/10.1016/j.jns.2021.117978
3. Fisher, M., Martins, S.: Update of the world stroke organization activities. Stroke **52**(7), e356–e357 (2021). https://doi.org/10.1161/STROKEAHA.121.035357
4. Xiong, J., Zheng, G.H.: Advance in executive function for post-stroke patients. Chin. J. Rehabil. Theor. Pract. **26**(7), 797–801 (2020). https://doi.org/10.3969/j.issn.1006?9771.2020.07.012

5. Ye, H.L., Chen, Q.Y., Peng, X.M.: Investigation and research on the needs of nursing professional support in rehabilitation patients after stroke. Int. Med. Health Guidance News **27**(03), 379–381 (2021). https://doi.org/10.3760/cma.j.issn.1007-1245.2021.03.019
6. Peng, F., Zhang, C., Xu, B.: Locomotion prediction for lower limb prostheses in complex environments via sEMG and inertial sensors. Complexity **28**(7), 1–12 (2020). https://doi.org/10.1155/2020/8810663
7. Li, Q.L., Kong, M.X., Du, Z.J.: 5-DOF upper limb rehabilitation robotic ARM interactive rehabilitation training control Strategy. J. Mech. Eng. **44**(009), 169–176 (2008). https://doi.org/10.3321/j.issn:0577-6686.2008.09.028
8. Wu, J., Jian, H., Wang, Y.: A wearable rehabilitation robotic hand driven by PM-TS actuators. In: International Conference on Intelligent Robotics and Applications, pp. 1154–1159. ICIRA (2010). https://doi.org/10.1016/j.jns.2021.117978

Trajectory Tracking Control Based on RBF Neural Network Learning Control

Chengyu Han, Yiming Fei, Zixian Zhao, and Jiangang Li[✉]

School of Mechanical Engineering and Automation, Harbin Institute of Technology, Shenzhen, China
jiangang_lee@hit.edu.cn

Abstract. In this paper, a radial basis function neural network (RBFNN) learning control scheme is proposed to improve the trajectory tracking performance of a 3-DOF robot manipulator based on deterministic learning theory, which explains the parameter convergence phenomenon in the adaptive neural network control process. A new kernel function is proposed to replace the original Gaussian kernel function in the network, such that the learning speed and accuracy can be improved. In order to make more efficient use of network nodes, this paper proposes a new node distribution strategy. Based on the improved scheme, the tracking accuracy of the 3-DOF manipulator is improved, and the convergence speed of the network is improved.

Keywords: Deterministic learning · 3-DOF manipulator · Trajectory tracking control · RBFNN

1 Introduction

With the rapid development of automation, robots play an increasingly irreplaceable role in industrial manufacturing, medical and health care, daily life, military, aerospace, and other fields.

The robot manipulator is the most widely used automatic mechanical device in robot technology. Although their structures and functions are different, they are all required to track the reference signal accurately and quickly. There are strong uncertainties such as parameter perturbation, external disturbance, and unmodeled dynamics in the manipulator, which affect the trajectory tracking accuracy. Therefore, it is challenging to further improve the manipulator's tracking accuracy.

The model-based adaptive controller can deal with the problem that the plant cannot be modeled accurately. However, it often depends on the system's gain, the increase in gain will affect the robustness of the system and make it more sensitive to noise. Therefore, performing feedforward control of the system based on the identification model is a better choice. The neural network has a higher model approximation ability than other traditional system identification algorithms. With the rapid improvement of computing power, it is possible to use a neural network to design a feedforward controller in the trajectory tracking control process. In [1], Cong Wang proposed a deterministic learning mechanism for identifying nonlinear dynamic systems using RBF networks. When it satisfies the persistent excitation (PE) condition [2] which is proved to be satisfied when the RBFNN is persistently excited by recurrent input signals, its weights can converge to a specific range around the optimal values. The numerical control system or some manipulators in production applications repeat periodic actions. It provides an effective off-line high-precision control method for practical application scenarios.

However, deterministic learning also has some defects and deficiencies in some aspects. One of them is that its training speed is limited by the PE levels, and it often takes thousands of seconds to learn the knowledge of some complex tracking control tasks. The excessive consumption of time makes it difficult to be applied to practical production. This paper points out two standards to measure the training speed and improve the training speed of deterministic learning in two aspects: changing the structure of the RBF network and changing the distribution of nodes. By improving the kernel function in the RBF network, the training structure can meet the PE condition and reduce the amount of calculation. Furthermore, the use of nodes is improved by an optimized node distribution strategy. As a result, each node can better characterize the unknown dynamics while raising the PE levels to improve the training speed.

2   Problem Formulation and Preliminaries

This part will establish the dynamical equation of the 3-DOF manipulator and design a corresponding adaptive RBFNN controller based on the deterministic learning theory. It shows that for any periodic trajectory, the RBFNN can satisfy the PE condition with appropriate parameter selection.

2.1   3-DOF Manipulator Model

The selected three-link manipulator model is shown in Fig. 1. For the link i ($i = 1, 2, 3$), m_i represents the mass, l_i is the length, θ_i represents the angle of each link joint with the vertical direction, J_i is the moment of inertia of each link perpendicular to the XY plane, l_{ci} is the distance from the head joint its center of gravity.

Using Newton-Euler equation, the dynamic equation of three-link manipulator can be expressed as follows:

$$M(\theta)\ddot{\theta} + C\left(\theta, \dot{\theta}\right)\dot{\theta} + G(\theta) = \tau \tag{1}$$

where $M(\theta) \in \mathbb{R}^{3 \times 3}$ is the inertia matrix, which meets the positive definiteness and symmetry, $C\left(\theta, \dot{\theta}\right) \in \mathbb{R}^{3 \times 3}$ is the combination vector of Coriolis force and

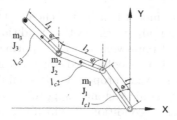

Fig. 1. Structure of three-link manipulator.

centrifugal force; $G(\theta) \in \mathbb{R}^{3\times 1}$ is the gravity matrix. $\ddot{\theta} = \begin{bmatrix} \ddot{\theta}_1 & \ddot{\theta}_2 & \ddot{\theta}_3 \end{bmatrix}^T$ is the angular acceleration vector of the system, and $\dot{\theta} = \begin{bmatrix} \dot{\theta}_1 & \dot{\theta}_2 & \dot{\theta}_3 \end{bmatrix}^T$ is the angular velocity vector of the system, $\tau = \begin{bmatrix} \tau_1 & \tau_2 & \tau_3 \end{bmatrix}^T$ is the control torque vector [3,4].
$M(\theta)$:

$$M(\theta) = \begin{bmatrix} \alpha_{11} & \alpha_{12}C_{21} & \alpha_{13}C_{31} \\ \alpha_{12}C_{21} & \alpha_{22} & \alpha_{23}C_{32} \\ \alpha_{13}C_{31} & \alpha_{23}C_{32} & \alpha_{33} \end{bmatrix} \tag{2}$$

where α, S, C are fixed parameters:

$$\begin{cases} \alpha_{11} = J_1 + m_1 l_{c1}^2 + (m_2 + m_3) l_1^2 \\ \alpha_{12} = (m_2 l_{c2} + m_3 l_2) l_1 \\ \alpha_{13} = m_3 l_1 l_{c3} \\ \alpha_{22} = J_2 + m_2 l_{c2}^2 + m_3 l_2^2 \\ \alpha_{23} = m_3 l_2 l_{c3} \\ \alpha_{33} = J_3 + m_3 l_{c3}^2 \end{cases} \tag{3}$$

$$\begin{cases} S_i = \sin\theta_i, \; S_{ij} = \sin(\theta_i - \theta_j) \\ C_i = \cos\theta_i, \; C_{ij} = \cos(\theta_i - \theta_j) \end{cases} \tag{4}$$

$C(\theta, \dot{\theta})$:

$$C(\theta, \dot{\theta}) = \begin{bmatrix} 0 & -\alpha_{12}\dot{\theta}_2 S_{21} & -\alpha_{13}\dot{\theta}_3 S_{31} \\ \alpha_{12}\dot{\theta}_1 S_{21} & 0 & -\alpha_{23}\dot{\theta}_3 S_{32} \\ \alpha_{13}\dot{\theta}_1 S_{31} & \alpha_{23}\dot{\theta}_2 S_{32} & 0 \end{bmatrix} \tag{5}$$

where g is the gravitational acceleration, and the formation $G(\theta)$ are:

$$G(\theta) = \begin{bmatrix} -\beta_1 S_1 & -\beta_2 S_2 & -\beta_3 S_3 \end{bmatrix}^T \tag{6}$$

where

$$\begin{cases} \beta_1 = (m_1 l_{c1} + m_2 l_1 + m_3 l_1) g \\ \beta_2 = (m_2 l_{c2} + m_3 l_2) g \\ \beta_3 = m_3 l_{c3} g \end{cases} \tag{7}$$

The three-link manipulator model can be built based on the above dynamic equations and parameters.

2.2   RBF Neural Network and Deterministic Learning

RBF neural network has a good approximation ability. Theoretically, with enough neurons it can approximate any Σ-Borel measure nonlinear function with arbitrary precision in the compact set [5]. Generally, an RBF neural network can be expressed as:

$$f_{nn}(Z) = \sum_{i=1}^{N} w_i s_i(Z) = W^T S(Z) \tag{8}$$

where $Z \in \Omega_Z \subset \mathbb{R}^n$ is the input vector of the neural network, N is the number of network nodes, $W = [w_1, w_2, \ldots, w_N] \in \mathbb{R}^N$ is the weight vector, $S(Z) = [s_1(\|Z - \xi_1\|), \ldots, s_N(\|Z - \xi_N\|)]^T$ represents the regressor vector of the neural network, $s_i(\cdot)\,(i = 1, \ldots, N)$ describes the RBF, where $\xi_i\,(i = 1, \ldots, N)$ is the center of each neuron function. The most commonly used RBF is the Gaussian RBF [6], which is expressed as follows:

$$s_i(\|Z - \xi_i\|) = \exp\left[\frac{-(Z - \xi_i)^T (Z - \xi_i)}{\eta_i^2}\right] \tag{9}$$

where η_i indicates the width of the function receptive field.

The single axis of a three-link manipulator is considered, and its order is set as 2. The nonlinear system in Brunovsky form is as follows:

$$\begin{cases} \dot{x}_1 = x_2 \\ \dot{x}_2 = f(x) + u \end{cases} \tag{10}$$

where $x = [x_1, x_2]^T \in \mathbb{R}^2, u \in \mathbb{R}$ is state variable and system input respectively, $f(x)$ is an unknown smooth nonlinear function, which can be approximated by RBF network (8).

Consider the second-order reference model:

$$\begin{cases} \dot{x}_{d_1} = x_{d_2} \\ \dot{x}_{d_2} = f_d(x_d) \end{cases} \tag{11}$$

where $x_d = [x_{d_1}, x_{d_2}]^T \in \mathbb{R}^2$ is the system state, $f_d(\cdot)$ is a known smooth nonlinear function. The system's trajectory starting from the initial condition $x_d(0)$ is denoted by $\varphi_a(x_d(0))$ (also as φ_d for brevity). Assume that the states of the reference model are uniformly bounded, i.e., $x_d(t) \in \Omega_d, \forall t \geq 0$, and the system orbit φ_d is assumed to be a periodic motion [1].

The adaptive neural controller using the Gaussian RBF network is expressed as:

$$u = -z_1 - c_2 z_2 - \hat{W}^T S(Z) + \dot{\alpha}_1 \tag{12}$$

where

$$\begin{cases} z_1 = x_1 - x_{d_1} \\ z_2 = x_2 - \alpha_1 \\ \alpha_1 = -c_1 z_1 + \dot{x}_{d_1} = -c_1 z_1 + x_{d_2} \\ \dot{\alpha}_1 = -c_1 \dot{z}_1 + \dot{x}_{d_2} = -c_1(-c_1 z_1 + z_2) + f_d(x_d) \end{cases} \tag{13}$$

$c_1, c_2 > 0$ is the control gain, $Z = x = [x_1, x_2]^T$ is the network input.

W^* is ideal constant weights and $\hat{W}$ is the estimated value of weights W^* of RBF network. Let $\tilde{W} = \hat{W} - W^*$, and its update rate is:

$$\dot{\tilde{W}} = \dot{\tilde{W}} = \Gamma \left(S(Z) z_2 - \sigma \hat{W} \right) \tag{14}$$

where $\Gamma = \Gamma^T > 0$ is a design matrix, σ is a small positive value.

PE condition is an essential concept in adaptive control systems.In the study of adaptive control, the PE condition played an essential role in the convergence of controller parameters. It is defined as follows:

A piecewise-continuous, uniformly bounded, the vector-valued function S : $[0, \infty) \to \mathbb{R}^n$ is said to satisfy the PE condition if there exist positive constants T_0, α_1 and α_2 such that:

$$\alpha_1 I \le \int_{t_0}^{t_0+T_0} S(\tau) S(\tau)^T d\tau \le \alpha_2 I \tag{15}$$

holds for $\forall t_0 > 0$, where $I \in \mathbb{R}^{n \times n}$ is the identity matrix [2].

It has been proved that almost any periodic or quasi-periodic trajectory can satisfy the partial PE condition of the corresponding RBF regressor vector [7].

When RBF neural network is applied locally, $f(Z)$ can be approximated by a limited number of neurons involved in a particular region of trajectory Z:

$$f(Z) = W_\xi^{*T} S_\xi(Z) + e_\xi \tag{16}$$

$S_\xi(Z) = [s_{j1}(Z), \ldots, s_{j\xi}(Z)]^T \in \mathbb{R}^{N_\xi} (N_\xi < N), |s_{ji}| > \tau (i = 1, \ldots, \xi), \tau > 0$ is a small positive constant, $W_\xi^* = [w_{j1}^*, \ldots, w_{j\xi}^*]^T$, e_ξ is the error caused by approximation. That is to say, $S_\xi(Z)$ is a dimension-reduced subvector of $S(Z)$.

Since the input of the manipulator follows a cyclic (or quasi-cyclic) trajectory, it can be proved in [8] that the RBF neural network satisfies the local PE condition.

In deterministic learning theory, the neural weight estimation $\hat{W}_\xi$ converges to its optimal value W_ξ^*, and the locally accurate $\hat{W}^T S(Z)$ approximation of the dynamic system $f_g(x)$ along the trajectory $\varphi_\zeta(x(T))$ is obtained by reaching the error level e^*.

$$\bar{W} = mean_{t \in [t_a, t_b]} \hat{W}(t) \tag{17}$$

where $[t_a, t_b]$ with $t_b > t_a > T$ represents a time segment after the transient process.

3   Methods to Improve Training Speed

The low training speed is the disadvantage of deterministic learning, and it is caused by the irrational distribution of the neural network. In the process of applying deterministic learning theory, the training speed can be reflected in two aspects:

- Weights Convergence: according to the deterministic learning theory, the weights will eventually converge when the PE condition is satisfied. The earlier the weights join, the faster it can approach the inverse model of the plant, and the tracking error can be reduced to a reasonable range.
- Convergence of tracking error: after the weight has converged or is close to convergence, the tracking error of the plant will generally decrease with the training process. The shorter the tracking error can be reduced to a reasonable range, the faster the training speed will be.

To improve the training speed of deterministic learning, this paper considers two aspects: one is to change the RBF's structure and find a scheme to replace the Gaussian kernel function, the other is to propose a method to calculate the radius of curvature from scattered data, to design the node distribution.

3.1 Change the Structure of the Network

The periodicity of the input signal $Z(t)$ makes $S_\zeta(Z)$ satisfy the PE condition, but this is usually not the PE condition of the entire regressor vector $S(Z)$. According to the adaptive law (14), the whole closed-loop system can be summarized as follows:

$$\begin{bmatrix} \dot{z} \\ \dot{\tilde{W}} \end{bmatrix} = \begin{bmatrix} A & -bS(Z)^T \\ \Gamma S(Z)b^T & 0 \end{bmatrix} \begin{bmatrix} z \\ \tilde{W} \end{bmatrix} + \begin{bmatrix} be \\ -\sigma\Gamma\hat{W} \end{bmatrix} \quad (18)$$

where $z = [z_1, z_2]^T, \tilde{W} = \hat{W} - W^*$ are the states, A is an asymptotically stable matrix expressed as

$$A = \begin{bmatrix} -c_1 & 1 \\ -1 & -c_2 \end{bmatrix} \quad (19)$$

which satisfies $A + A^T = -Q < 0, b = [0,1]^T, (A, b)$ is controllable, $\Gamma = \Gamma^T > 0$ is a constant matrix. Then we have:

$$\dot{\tilde{W}}_{\bar{\zeta}} = \dot{\hat{W}}_{\bar{\zeta}} = \Gamma_{\bar{\zeta}}\left(S_{\bar{\zeta}}(Z)z_2 - \sigma\hat{W}_{\bar{\zeta}}\right) \quad (20)$$

From [9–11], PE of $S_\zeta(Z)$ leads to the exponential stability of $\left(z, \tilde{W}_\zeta\right) = 0$ for the nominal part of the system (18). $\left\| e'_\zeta \right| - |e_\zeta| \right\|$ is small, and $\sigma\Gamma_\zeta\hat{W}_\zeta$ can be made small by choosing a small σ [12].

Selecting $\bar{W}$ according to (17), the convergence of $\hat{W}_\zeta$ to a small neighborhood of W_ζ^* indicates along the orbit $\varphi_\zeta(x(T))$, we have:

$$\begin{aligned} f(x) = f(Z) &= W_\zeta^{*T}S_\zeta(Z) + e_\zeta = \hat{W}_\zeta^T S_\zeta(Z) - \tilde{W}_\zeta^T S_\zeta(Z) + e_\zeta \\ &= \hat{W}_\zeta^T S_\zeta(Z) + e_{\zeta1} = \bar{W}_\zeta^T S_\zeta(Z) + e_{\zeta2} \end{aligned} \quad (21)$$

where $e_{\zeta1} = e_\zeta - \tilde{W}_\zeta^T S_\zeta(Z)$ is close to e_ζ due to the convergence of $\tilde{W}_\zeta$, $\bar{W}_\zeta = [\bar{w}_{j_1}, \ldots, \bar{w}_{j_\zeta}]^T$ is the subvector of $\bar{W}$, using $\bar{W}_\zeta^T S_\zeta(Z)$ to approximate the whole system, then $e_{\zeta2}$ is the error.

After time T, $\|e_{\zeta 2}| - |e_{\zeta 1}\|$ is small. Besides, neurons whose center is far away from the track φ_ζ, $\left|S_{\bar{\zeta}}(Z)\right|$ will become very small due to the localization property of the RBF network. From the law (20) and $\hat{W}(0) = 0$, the small values of $S_{\bar{\zeta}}(Z)$ will make the neural weights $\hat{W}_{\bar{\zeta}}$ activated and updated only slightly. Since many data are small, there is:

$$
\begin{aligned}
f(Z) &= W_\zeta^{*T} S(Z) + e_\zeta \\
&= \hat{W}_\zeta^T S_\zeta(Z) + \hat{W}_{\bar{\zeta}}^T S_{\bar{\zeta}}(Z) + e_1 = \hat{W}^T S(Z) + e_1 \\
&= \bar{W}_\zeta^T S_\zeta(Z) + \bar{W}_{\bar{\zeta}}^T S_{\bar{\zeta}}(Z) + e_2 = \bar{W}^T S(Z) + e_2
\end{aligned}
\tag{22}
$$

It is seen that both the RBF network $\hat{W}^T S(Z)$ and $\bar{W}^T S(Z)$ can approximate the unknown $f(x) = f(Z)$.

From the above process of proving the weights convergence, it can be found that the requirement for the RBF is only its localized structure, so the selection of the RBF can be more extensive. Considering that most of the radial basis functions used in the original RBF network are Gaussian kernels, the deterministic learning theory also continues to use Gaussian kernels when proposed. However, considering the computational complexity, the Gaussian kernel function is not necessarily the optimal solution in all cases.

Quadratic rational kernel is also commonly used radial basis functions:

$$
s_i(\|Z - \xi_i\|) = 1 - \frac{\|Z - \xi_i\|^2}{\|Z - \xi_i\|^2 + c}
\tag{23}
$$

where $Z \in \Omega_Z \subset \mathbb{R}^n$ is the input vector of the neural network, $\xi_i \, (i = 1, \ldots, N)$ is the center of each neuron function.

Since the unknown quantity c in the quadratic rational kernel function is a constant, we have:

$$
s_i(\|Z - \xi_i\|) = 1 - \frac{\|Z - \xi_i\|^2}{\|Z - \xi_i\|^2 + c} = \frac{c}{\|Z - \xi_i\|^2 + c}
\tag{24}
$$

Let $\|Z - \xi_i\| = t$, comparing the computational complexity of (9), (24), it can be found that the computational complexity of quadratic rational kernel function is $o\left(t^2\right)$, while the computational complexity of Gaussian kernel function is $o\left(e^t\right)$. With the increase of t, the computational complexity $o\left(e^t\right) > o\left(t^2\right)$. Therefore, when the number of nodes i is kept constant, the computational complexity of applying the Gaussian kernel function is more than that of the quadratic rational kernel function.

For the quadratic rational kernel function, if the constant n is introduced, there is $s_i(\|Z - \xi_i\|) = 1 - \frac{n * \|Z - \xi_i\|^2}{\|Z - \xi_i\|^2 + c}$. The approximation accuracy of the network is further improved by changing the value of the constant n.

3.2 Change the Distribution Strategy of Nodes

The nonlinear approximation ability of the neural network will be improved with the increase of the node density. On the other hand, an excessive number of nodes will affect the training speed. Therefore, under the same approximation accuracy, reducing the number of nodes can effectively improve the training speed of the RBF network.

In the deterministic learning theory, the reference input of RBF model training is generally selected as the required position information and its first and second derivative information (velocity and acceleration information). A certain point in the three-dimensional space thus constructed can represent their position, velocity, and acceleration information at the current time. The selection of network nodes is based on this three-dimensional space. There are two modes for the distribution of RBF network nodes:

– Distributed by regular lattice: Only the area occupied by the input information of the RBF network in the three-dimensional space needs to be considered, as shown in Fig. 2.
– Distributed along the input signal: This distribution model is evenly distributed along the input track, as shown in Fig. 3, which can better use each nodes.

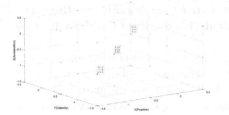
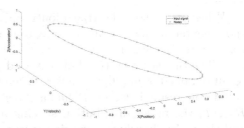

Fig. 2. Nodes are distributed by lattice.

Fig. 3. Nodes are evenly distributed by input.

The curvature information can be used to represent the complexity of input signal. In the space composed of three-dimensional input information, the part where the curve changes sharply is usually the position where the radius of curvature is small. Therefore, more nodes should be distributed around the parts with larger curvature (smaller curvature radius) to improve the approximation accuracy, and the node width can be reduced accordingly.

For curve $y = f(x)$, the commonly used curvature calculation formula is $K = \frac{|\ddot{y}|}{(1+\dot{y}^2)^{\frac{3}{2}}}$, where $\dot{y}, \ddot{y}$ are the first and second derivatives of y to x. However, the limitation of this method is that it is only applicable to continuous functions. The problem with this method is that the curve fitting will lose part of the input signal information, resulting in the decline of approximation accuracy. When calculating the curvature of the local position, it is also easy to receive the interference of noise and other information to produce peaks, which is not conducive to the approximation of the network.

Therefore, consider a new way to define the curvature for the scattered points in space. For three points A, B, C in state space, their time sequence is A passes through B to C. When the angle formed by $\angle ABC$ is an acute angle or right angle, the schematic diagram is as follows:

Since the coordinates of points A, B, C in the input data are known, the size of $|AB|, |BC|, |AC|$ in space can be obtained. Let $|AC| = l_b$, $\angle ABC = \angle\theta$. Let the center of the circumscribed circle passing through the three points be O and the radius be R, thus the radius of curvature obtained from the three points A, B, C in the definition space be the circumscribed circle radius R.

To obtain the size of radius R, connect segment OA, OB, OC, and OH is the vertical line of AC. Then at $\angle\theta \leq 90°$, it can be known from the geometric relationship:

$$\angle ABO + \angle CBO + \angle OAC = 90° \tag{25}$$

where $\angle ABO + \angle CBO = \angle\theta$, can get $\angle AOH = \angle COH = \angle\theta$. In $\triangle AOH$, we can calculate the newly defined radius of curvature of the scatter:

$$R = \frac{l_b}{2\sin(\theta)} \tag{26}$$

When $\angle\theta > 90°$, the transition from $\overrightarrow{AB}$ to $\overrightarrow{BC}$ is smooth and the corresponding radius of curvature is large, the calculation results of the above formula conform to this feature.

When the variation trend of scattered points with time is more intense, the result obtained from (26) is smaller. When the variation trend of spray with time is flat, the result is larger. Define a threshold T, when the radius of curvature $R < T$, the nodes distribution spacing and the scope of action are reduced, and the nodes distribution spacing is increased at other positions to reduce the number of nodes. In this way, the complex signal can be approximated more accurately while maintaining a certain number of nodes, which saves computing power and improves the approximation accuracy (Fig. 4).

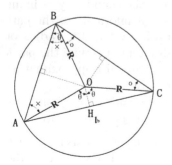

Fig. 4. Calculation of radius of curvature of scattered points.

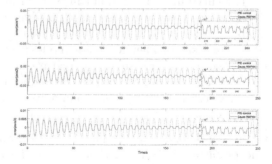

Fig. 5. Tracking error of three-axis manipulator.

4   Experiment and Analysis

4.1   Experimental Result

1) Experiment preparation: Input $x = \sin(t)$; $y = \cos(t)$; $z = \sin(t)$ to the three axes of the three-link manipulator model for training. Figure 5 shows the system's three-axis tracking error comparison data using only PID control and in addition with the original deterministic learning control.

2) Change the RBF network structure: The Gaussian kernel function in the RBF network is replaced by the modified quadratic rational kernel function $s_i(\|Z - \xi_i\|) = 1 - \frac{n*\|Z-\xi_i\|^2}{\|Z-\xi_i\|^2+c}$, and $n = 2.5$; $c = 1.5$ is selected through experimental comparison.

The three-axis input signals are $x = \sin(t)$; $y = \cos(t)$; $z = \sin(t)$ respectively. For axis 3 of the three-link manipulator, Fig. 6 and Fig. 7 show the weights convergence of the Gaussian kernel and the modified quadratic rational kernel. Figure 8 is a comparison diagram of the tracking error between the Gaussian kernel function and the modified quadratic rational kernel function.

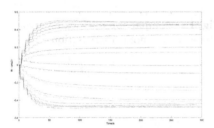

Fig. 6. Axis 3's weights of manipulator using Gaussian kernel.

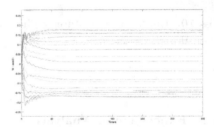

Fig. 7. Axis 3's weights of manipulator using the modified quadratic rational kernel.

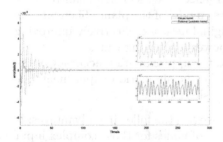

Fig. 8. Axis 3's tracking error comparison.

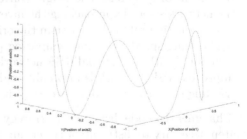

Fig. 9. 3-DOF manipulator input track.

3) Change the distribution strategy of nodes: The crown trajectory is selected as the input of the 3-DOF manipulator, as shown in Fig. 9, where X, Y, Z are the position information of each axis.

In one trajectory period of axis 3, the value of the radius of curvature of the scatter can be obtained, as shown in Fig. 10.

Set the threshold T to 20, and increase the node distribution density when the threshold is less than 20.

Figure 11 shows the error comparison of axis 3 according to two distribution modes when the number of nodes is 41.

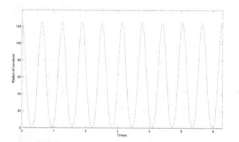

Fig. 10. Curve of curvature radius (axis 3).

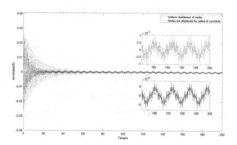

Fig. 11. Comparison of tracking errors between two node distribution methods.

4.2 Experimental Analysis

From the above experimental results, it can be seen that in the simulation with the three-link manipulator model as the plant, compared with the original RBF network, the method of changing the RBF network's kernel function has the following advantages:

– The weight convergence speed of the improved RBF network is faster than that of the original one. The weight convergence speed will significantly affect the network's speed approaching the inverse model of the plant. Therefore, its error reduction rate is higher than the original network, effectively improving the training speed, reducing computing power and saving time.
– Compared with the original RBF network, the approximation accuracy of the improved RBF network is also enhanced. In the simulation experiment, the tracking error can be reduced to 10^{-6} in a short time.

Changing the node distribution strategy also has the following advantages: It is often necessary to distribute a larger number of nodes for those complex input trajectories. This method can optimize the distribution of nodes by applying the same number of nodes, thereby improving the tracking accuracy, on the premise of the same tracking accuracy, it can reduce the number of nodes, speeding up the training.

5   Conclusion

Under the framework of deterministic learning theory, this paper modifies the RBF network structure of the feedforward-feedback control loop part, proposes a modified quadratic rational kernel function to replace the Gaussian kernel function in the RBF network which is suitable for the 3-DOF manipulator. By optimizing the network structure, periodic signals' training speed and tracking accuracy are improved. A new definition of the curvature radius is presented, and the node distribution strategy is optimized on this basis, which can make better use of nodes and save computing power. Experiments verify the effectiveness of the improved strategy.

Acknowledgment. This work was supported by Shenzhen Science and Technology Program under Grant GXWD20201230155427003-20200821171505003.

References

1. Wang, C., Hill, D.: Learning from neural control. In: 42nd IEEE International Conference on Decision and Control (IEEE Cat.No.03CH37475), vol. 6, pp. 5721–5726 (2003)
2. Zheng, T., Wang, C.: Relationship between persistent excitation levels and RBF network structures, with application to performance analysis of deterministic learning. IEEE Trans. Cybern. **47**(10), 3380–3392 (2017)
3. Xin, X., Kaneda, M.: Swing-up control for a 3-DOF gymnastic robot with passive first joint: design and analysis. IEEE Trans. Rob. **23**(6), 1277–1285 (2007)
4. Lai, X.Z., Pan, C.Z., Wu, M., Yang, S.X., Cao, W.H.: Control of an underactuated three-link passive-active-active manipulator based on three stages and stability analysis. J. Dyn. Syst. Meas. Contr. **137**(2), 021007 (2015)
5. Park, J., Sandberg, I.W.: Universal approximation using radial-basis-function networks. Neural Comput. **3**(2), 246–257 (1991)
6. Park, J., Sandberg, I.W.: Approximation and radial-basis-function networks. Neural Comput. **5**(2), 305–316 (1993)
7. Wang, C., Hill, J.D.: Deterministic Learning Theory: For Identification, Recognition, and Control. CRC Press (2018)
8. Wang, C., Hill, J.D., Chen, G.: Deterministic learning of nonlinear dynamical systems. In: Proceedings of the 2003 IEEE International Symposium on Intelligent Control. IEEE (2003)
9. Farrell, J.A.: Stability and approximator convergence in nonparametric nonlinear adaptive control. IEEE Trans. Neural Netw. **9**(5), 1008–1020 (1998)
10. Narendra, K.S., Anuradha, A.M.: Stable adaptive systems. Courier Corporation (2012)
11. Sastry, S., Bodson, M., Bartram, J.F.: Adaptive control: stability, convergence, and robustness, 588–589 (1990)
12. Khalil, H.K.: Nonlinear systems, **38**(6), 1091–1093 (2002)

Intelligent Vision and Learning

A Knowledge-Embedded End-to-End Intelligent Reasoning Method for Processing Quality of Shaft Parts

Teng Zhang[1], Bingbing Li[1], Hao Sun[1], Shengqiang Zhao[1], Fangyu Peng[1,2(✉)], Lin Zhou[3], and Rong Yan[1]

[1] School of Mechanical Science and Engineering, The National NC System Engineering Research Center, Huazhong University of Science and Technology, Wuhan 430074, China
{zhang_teng,sunhao_hust1,d202080293,yanrong}@hust.edu.cn,
zwm8917@263.net

[2] The State Key Laboratory of Digital Manufacturing Equipment and Technology, School of Mechanical Science and Engineering, Huazhong University of Science and Technology, Wuhan 430074, China

[3] The Wuhan Digital Design and Manufacturing Innovation Center Co. Ltd., Wuhan 430074, China
zhoulin@niiddm.com

Abstract. The machining quality of a part is one of the most important factors affecting work effectiveness and service time, and it is closely related to multi-stage manufacturing processes (MMPs). State space model (SSM) is a typical method to analyze error propagation in MMPs, which contains the deep laws of error propagation, but the modeling process is complicated and the perception of quality is afterwards. In actual production, it is difficult to realize the pre-reasoning and control of processing quality. To address the above problems, an end-to-end intelligent reasoning method for processing quality with SSM knowledge embedding is proposed. On the one hand, the knowledge embedded in SSM is used for data simulation, and on the other hand, the end-to-end mapping between measured dimensions and processing quality of each process is realized by an Adaptive Network-based Fuzzy Inference System (ANFIS). In this paper, wall thickness difference (WTD) is used to describe the machining quality of shaft parts, and four sections of four processes are studied. SSM was constructed and validated using workshop data, and the average relative error for the six shafts was 5.54%. In the testing phase of the intelligent reasoning model, the maximum RMSE and MAE of the models for the four processes were 4.47 μm and 3.23 μm, respectively, satisfying the WTD prediction requirements.

Keywords: State space model · Knowledge-embedded · End-to-end intelligent reasoning · Processing quality

1 Introduction

With the development of modern manufacturing technology, the characteristics of parts are gradually complicated. Complex parts are often processed through MMPs. In this

H. Liu et al. (Eds.): ICIRA 2022, LNAI 13458, pp. 425–436, 2022.
https://doi.org/10.1007/978-3-031-13841-6_39

way, the quality of the machining of the part is related to each error source in each process, including fixture error, datum error, machining error and other error sources. It is necessary to study the propagation law of various errors.

The error propagation was studied in the assembly field firstly [1], Zhou et al. [2] applied this method to the machining of parts. On this basis, the research on the MMPs is gradually extensive. Yang et al. [3] summarized relevant research on error propagation modeling and the advantages of Differential Motion Vectors (DMVs) [1] is specifically discussed. Abellan J V et al. [4] proposed a fixture equivalence and datum change method based on positioning surfaces, which extended the applicability of the SMM model. Abellan-Nebot et al. [5] considered spindle thermal errors, tool deformation and tool wear to improve the accuracy of the model calculation.

In addition to the above researches, the error source that causes quality problems is also revealed. Zhou et al. [6] established a linear mixed quality model to describe the mapping relationship between fault information and the final quality. Du et al. [7] achieved the estimation of process control parameters by establishing the relationship between error sources and processing quality. However, for the above study, the machining quality can only be obtained after specifying the error of each process.

Data-driven, as a method to solve the mapping relationship between input and output of complex systems, has made remarkable achievements in engineering fields such as machining error prediction [8] and compensation [9], fault diagnosis [10] and parameter identification [11]. However, the biggest disadvantage of the data-driven method is lack of interpretation. To solve this problem, Sun et al. [12] integrated the simulation data and working condition data to realizing knowledge embedding at the data level. Abdulshahed et al. [13] realized high precision thermal error compensation for CNC milling machines by using the ANFIS.

The content of the article can be summarized as follows. In Sect. 2, the theory of the proposed method is presented. In Sect. 3, State space model (SSM), the simulation of knowledge-embedded data and the end-to-end intelligent reasoning model based on ANFIS are constructed. In Sect. 4, the accuracy of the SSM and four end-to-end inference models are analyzed. In Sect. 5, general conclusions are made.

2 Methodology

2.1 Proposed Method

A knowledge-embedded end-to-end intelligent reasoning method for processing quality of shaft parts includes the following three parts, the construction of SSM, the simulation of knowledge-embedded data and the construction of end-to-end intelligent reasoning models based on ANFIS, as shown in Fig. 1.

For the first part, after analyzing the process of shaft parts and clarifying the process requirements for different processes, the SSM is constructed using differential motion vector and homogeneous transformation matrix. After validation with complete process data from the workshop, the model can accurately describe the error propagation of the part machining process and can also be used for the simulation of knowledge-embedded data. For the second part, the four sections of the four processes are simulated under the tolerance band constraint, and the simulation results are expressed as a vector form

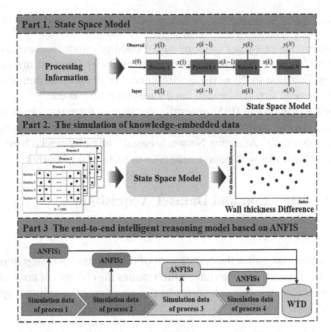

Fig. 1. Overall flow chart of the method proposed in this article

representation in the workpiece coordinate system. The final WTD can be obtained by SSM calculation, which contains the error propagation knowledge of the four processes. For the third part, four ANFIS models between the simulation data of the four processes and the final WTD are constructed as the final end-to-end intelligent inference models.

In this method, the measurement data after the current process can be input into the corresponding end-to-end model, and the final WTD can be obtained in advance to realize the pre-perception of the processing quality.

2.2 State Space Mode

In MMPs, a variety of errors are introduced, such as tool error, fixture error, datum error, machining error and so on [14], which affect the processing quality of parts. After transforming the coordinate system according to the error propagation process, the final error vector can be obtained by the SSM method, which can be expressed as,

$$x(k) = A(k)x(k-1) + B(k)u(k) \quad k = 1, 2, ..., N \tag{1}$$

where $A(k)$ represents the influence of the error of process $k-1$ on the error of process k, which is called system matrix. $B(k)$ represents the influence of various errors introduced in the process k on the characteristic errors of parts after the process k is completed, which is called control matrix. $x(k)$, $x(k-1)$ represent the error vector of process k and process $k-1$ respectively. $u(k)$ represents the error introduced by the process $k-1$.

2.3   Adaptive Network-Based Fuzzy Inference System

Fuzzy inference treats problems in terms of probability rather than events in terms of exact logic. The function that calculates the probability of event occurrence is defined as Membership Function (MF) in fuzzy inference. For manufacturing, absolute values are not sought, instead fuzzy tolerance bands are commonly used.

A fuzzy inference system (FIS) generally consists of three parts in structure: a rule set, a database and an inference mechanism. However, FIS is not able to learn the relevant parameters automatically. Adaptive Network-based Fuzzy Inference System (ANFIS) [15], which combines FIS with neural networks to make it self-learning.

3   Model Construction and Dataset Acquisition

3.1   Construction of SSM and Simulation of Dataset

When parts are processed after the completion of the process $k-1$, step into the process k, it need to be clamped on a new fixture, which results the changes of error measurement benchmark. Therefore, the clamping error in the new fixture coordinate system can be described as follows,

$$x_0(k) = A_1(k)x(k-1) \tag{2}$$

where $A_1(k)$ is the coefficient matrix between the two reference coordinate systems, $x_0(k)$ represents the differential motion vector of the dimension error in the process k.

After the part is installed on the fixture of process k, since the surface processed by process $k-1$ is the benchmark of this process, the error of process $k-1$ is transmitted to this process, which can be described as follows,

$$x_{FCS(k)}^{R(k)} = A_2(k)x_0(k) \tag{3}$$

where $R(k)$ represents the reference coordinate system of process k, and $FCS(k)$ represents the fixture coordinate system of process k, $x_{FCS(k)}^{R(k)}$ refers to the datum error of process k, which describes the error between the coordinate system of the part and the fixture.

Due to fixture wear, there is fixture error named $x_{0FCS(k)}^{FCS(k)}$ between the actual fixture and the ideal fixture coordinate system, which can be described as,

$$x_{0FCS(k)}^{FCS(k)} = A_3(k)u_f(k) \tag{4}$$

where $u_f(k)$ is the dimension deviation vector of the equivalent six-point anchor point of the fixture, which is set to $[0.001, 0.001, 0, -0.001, -0.001, 0.001]'$ in this article.

Tool error includes factors such as tool wear, tool thermal expansion, and part deformation. After considering the fixture error and tool error, the characteristic error of process k can be described as:

$$u_t(k) = A_4(k)x_{0FCS(k)}^{FCS(k)} + u_m(k) \tag{5}$$

where $u_m(k)$ is the tool error, which is set to $[0.015, 0.005, 0.01, -0.002, -0.001, 0.001]'$ in this article, $u_t(k)$ is the total error of the process k, and $A_4(k)$ is the coefficient matrix.

The total error of the characteristic size after processing in process k is influenced by the reference error generated in process k−1 and the error generated in process k. The total error in the process k can be expressed as,

$$x''(k) = A_4(k)x_{FCS(k)}^{R(k)} + u_t(k) \tag{6}$$

Since the machining process may bring the appearance of new dimension characteristics, but only the dimension error in the previous process is transmitted in (2), therefore the new dimension error generated in this process should also be considered. Therefore, the final error can be expressed as,

$$x(k) = x_0(k) + A_5(k)x''(k) \tag{7}$$

where $A_5(k)$ is the selection matrix with a combination of zero and identity matrix.

By combining (2)–(7), the final error can be expressed as (1), where

$$A(k) = [A_1(k) + A_5(k)A_4(k)A_2(k)A_1(k)]$$
$$B(k) = A_5(k)[A_4(k)A_3(k) \quad I_{6\times6}] \tag{8}$$

Error propagation of adjacent processes is shown in (9). The relationship of all errors mentioned above is shown in Fig. 2. It is sufficient to extend the error propagation rules shown in (9) to MMPs.

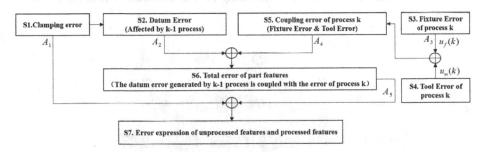

Fig. 2. The relationship of each error source

The processing of shaft parts studied in this article consists of four processes, which are roughing of outer circle, drilling, finishing of outer circle and reaming. The final quality evaluation index is WTD.

Random simulation is carried out on the outer circle and inner hole sizes of the four sections in Fig. 3 for each process. The error between the measured and nominal values is vectorized and expressed as $\Delta P = [\Delta x, \Delta y, \Delta z, \Delta\alpha, \Delta\beta, \Delta\gamma]^T \in R^{6\times1}$, where $\Delta x, \Delta y, \Delta z$ indicates the position error and $\Delta\alpha, \Delta\beta, \Delta\gamma$ indicates the angle error. The actual vector can be obtained by superimposing the error vector onto the nominal vector, which in turn gives the diameter of the inner and outer bore, denoted as D_{Oi}, D_{li}. The wall

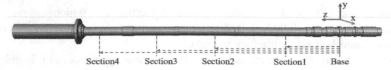

Fig. 3. The four sections of the shaft

thickness of the i-th section can be expressed as $\delta_i = (D_{Oi} - D_{Ii})/2$, where $i = 1, 2, 3, 4$ correspond to the four sections in Fig. 3. The WTD of the final part after processing can be expressed as $\max(\delta_1, \delta_2, \delta_3, \delta_4) - \min(\delta_1, \delta_2, \delta_3, \delta_4)$.

Using the tolerance band of each process as a constraint, 1000 samples of simulated data were randomly generated, where each sample contains four processes and each process contains four sections. The simulation data of each process and the WTD calculated by SSM are combined into the data set. Finally, the samples are divided into training and test sets in a 4:1 ratio.

3.2 End-to-End Intelligent Reasoning Models Based on ANFIS

For the intelligent reasoning of machining quality of shaft parts carried out in this article, the data set of each process is in the form of 4-dimensional input and 1-dimensional output. Before the training stage, max-min normalization is utilized on the data of all dimensions in order to accelerate the convergence of the model, although the data ranges of all dimensions are similar. In this article, the degree function of each dimension of ANFIS in each process is set to 5, and the weighted average defuzzifier is selected. The structure of the end-to-end intelligent reasoning models based on ANFIS for a process is shown in Fig. 4.

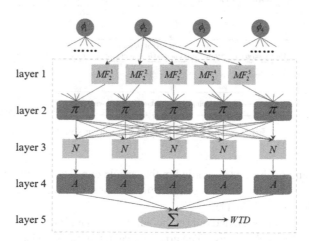

Fig. 4. The structure of the end-to-end intelligent reasoning models based on ANFIS

The first layer is called the fuzzy layer, which is used to calculate each membership function corresponding to each node. The corresponding output can be expressed as,

$$O^1_{MF^i_j} = \mu_{MF^i_j}(\phi_j), \quad i = 1, 2, ..., 5; j = 1, 2, 3, 4 \tag{9}$$

where MF^i_j represents the i-th membership function of the j-th input variable, $\mu_{MF^i_j}(\cdot)$ is the joint Gaussian membership function which can be expressed as,

$$f(\phi_j, \sigma^{i1}_j, c^{i1}_j, \sigma^{i2}_j, c^{i2}_j) = \begin{cases} \exp\left[\dfrac{-(\phi_j - c^{i1}_j)^2}{2(\sigma^{i1}_j)^2}\right] & \phi_j \leq c^{i1}_j \\ 1 & c^{i1}_j \leq \phi_j \leq c^{i2}_j \quad, \quad i = 1, 2, ..., 5; j = 1, 2, 3, 4 \\ \exp\left[\dfrac{-(\phi_j - c^{i2}_j)^2}{2(\sigma^{i2}_j)^2}\right] & \phi_j \geq c^{i2}_j \end{cases} \tag{10}$$

where $\{\sigma^{i1}_j, c^{i1}_j, \sigma^{i2}_j, c^{i2}_j\}$ are the parameters corresponding to the joint Gaussian membership function, called premise parameters, which uniquely determine the expression of the joint Gaussian membership function.

The second layer is called the superposition layer. The multiplication operation is performed. The output of this layer can be expressed as,

$$O^2_m = w_m = \prod_{j=1}^{4} \mu_{MF^i_j}(\phi_j), \quad m = 1, 2, \cdots 5^4 \tag{11}$$

The third layer is called the normalized layer. Normalized operation is performed on the weight calculated in the second layer. The output of this layer can be expressed as,

$$O^3_m = \overline{w_m} = w_m / \sum_{m=1}^{5^4} w_m \tag{12}$$

The fourth layer is called the adaptive layer, and the output can be expressed as,

$$O^4_m = \overline{w_m} f_m \tag{13}$$

where f_m is the linear expression of the rule m defined in terms of the parameters $\{\alpha_{m0}, \alpha_{m1}, \alpha_{m2}, \alpha_{m3}, \alpha_{m4}\}$, which can be can be expressed as, if ϕ_1 is MF^i_1, and ϕ_2 is MF^i_2, and ϕ_3 is MF^i_3, and ϕ_4 is MF^i_4 then $f_m = \alpha_{m0} + \alpha_{m1}\phi_1 + \alpha_{m2}\phi_2 + \alpha_{m3}\phi_3 + \alpha_{m4}\phi_4$.

The fifth layer is called the output layer. The output of this layers can be expressed as,

$$O^5 = \sum_{m=1}^{5^4} \overline{w_m} f_m \tag{14}$$

After the structure is fixed, the end-to-end intelligent reasoning models based on ANFIS can be trained using the knowledge-embedded data sets of each process. The model is trained in the anfisedit toolbox of MATLAB. The error bound and the number of iterations are set to 3 μm and 100, respectively.

4 Results and Analysis

4.1 Results of the SSM for Shaft Parts

The actual machining of the six shafts was carried out according to a predefined technical procedure, and the dimensions of the four sections were measured after each process. The results obtained by the deep-hole measuring machine and the SSM are shown in Table 1.

Table 1. The results of WTD from measurement and SSM calculation.

ID	Measurement	State space model	Absolute relative error
1	42.0	39.8	5.24%
2	38.7	37.0	4.39%
3	29.0	26.3	9.31%
4	33.0	32.4	1.82%
5	22.1	23.8	7.69%
6	27.0	28.3	4.81%

To express the results of the two methods more clearly, a line graph is shown in Fig. 5. It can be seen that there is a small absolute relative error between the measured results of the WTD in the workshop and the results calculated by the SSM. Each absolute relative error is less than 10%, and the average relative error is 5.54%, which proves the high computational accuracy of the constructed SSM.

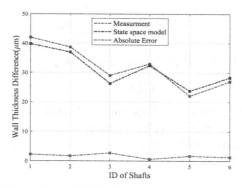

Fig. 5. Comparison of SSM calculation and measurement results

However, for measurement and SSM, processing quality is only available after the machining is completed. To exploit the error propagation law of MMPs embedded in SSM, the model is utilized for the simulation of the knowledge-embedded data.

4.2   Results of the End-to-end Intelligent Reasoning Models Based on ANFIS

The dataset of SSM knowledge embedding can be obtained by using the validated SSM in Sect. 4 and the dataset simulation method introduced in Sect. 3. An end-to-end intelligent reasoning model based on ANFIS is constructed for each of the four processes of the studied shaft parts.

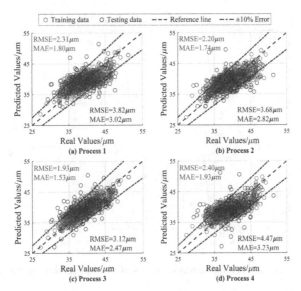

Fig. 6. Training and testing results of the prediction model for the four processes

The models for four processes were trained and tested with RMSE and MAE as evaluation indexes, and the results are shown in Fig. 6. The red color in the figure indicates the training data and the blue color indicates the testing data, the RMSE and MAE indicators are also represented in the same colors.

It is clear from the figure that all four prediction models can accurately predict the WTD. Overall, the RMSE and MAE in the training phase are less than 3 μm and 2 μm, respectively, and the RMSE and MAE in the testing phase are less than 5 μm and 4 μm, respectively, which satisfies the requirement of 50 μm WTD tolerance band.

Among the four prediction models, the prediction model for process 3 is the best, with RMSE and MAE of 3.12 μm and 2.47 μm, respectively, while the prediction model for process 4 is the worst, with RMSE and MAE of 4.47 μm and MAE of 3.23 μm, respectively. Analyzing the causes of the above phenomenon from the machining process of shaft parts, the third process is the finishing of the outer circle with small cutting volume, and this process is the last process of the outer circle, so it directly affects the wall thickness difference. Then when constructing the end-to-end intelligent inference model from process 3 to WTD, there is less redundant data at the data level, therefore the model is more accurate. The fourth process is internal hole reaming, which is the last process of the part, with difficult process and complex error influence relationship.

Therefore, the end-to-end model prediction is poor, but the MAE of 3.23 μm can also meet the prediction accuracy requirement compared to the tolerance band of 50 μm.

In addition to the analysis for the performance of four models, the distribution of the membership function is also analyzed because the end-to-end intelligent inference model used in this paper is ANFIS. Taking the process 3 as an example, the corresponding membership function curves of the four sections after training are shown in Fig. 7.

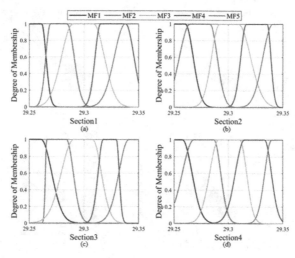

Fig. 7. The membership function curves of the four sections in process 3

The number of membership function for each section in this paper is set to 5. From MF1 to MF5 corresponds to the range of the interval where the variables are located, MF1 corresponds to the lower boundary and MF5 corresponds to the upper boundary of the tolerance band. It can be seen from the Fig. 7, that MF3 in the trained membership function are all located in the middle part of the tolerance band, which reveals the dependence of the part WTD on the intermediate state, i.e., when the diameter of the intermediate process is in the middle of the tolerance band, the corresponding feature state is better and the margin of overrun from the boundary is larger. Analyzing the complete situation of the joint Gaussian membership function in the tolerance band, it can be concluded that for process 3, Sect. 1 should be in the diameter range where MF2 and MF3 are located, Sects. 2 and 4 should be in the diameter range where MF3 and MF4 are located, and Sect. 3 should be in the direct range where MF2-MF4 are located. That is, after the part completes process 3, the quality of the part will be free from the risk of overrun after each section is distributed according to the above interval. By analyzing the membership function curve, it can guide the adjustment of the machining parameters.

5 Conclusions and Future Work

In this article, a knowledge-embedded end-to-end intelligent reasoning method for processing quality of shaft parts is proposed. Using this method, knowledge in SSM can be embedded in simulation data sets. In addition, an end-to-end intelligent inference model based on ANFIS was developed to achieve final WTD pre-awareness based on current measurements. The average training RMSE and MAE for the four process prediction models were 2.21 μm and 1.75 μm, respectively, and the average test RMSE and MAE were 3.77 μm and 2.89 μm, respectively. Finally, by analyzing the MFs, it is possible to specify the appropriate size range for each section, which ensuring that the WTD meets the requirements.

In the future, we will carry out end-to-end quality prediction for more complex parts such as aircraft blades and casing, and introduce other working conditions parameters into the prediction model to improve the prediction accuracy.

Acknowledgement. This research was financially supported by the National Key Research and Development Program of China (Grant No. 2018YFB1701904) and the National Natural Science Foundation of China (Grant No. U20A20294).

References

1. Jin, J., Shi, J.: State space modeling of sheet metal assembly for dimensional control. J. Manuf. Sci. Eng. Trans. **121**(4), 756–762 (1999). https://doi.org/10.1115/1.2833137
2. Zhou, S., Huang, Q., Shi, J.: State space modeling of dimensional variation propagation in multistage machining process using differential motion vectors. IEEE Trans. Robot. Autom. **19**(2), 296–309 (2003). https://doi.org/10.1109/TRA.2003.808852
3. Yang, F., Jin, S., Li, Z.: A comprehensive study of linear variation propagation modeling methods for multistage machining processes. Int. J. Adv. Manuf. Technol. **90**(5–8), 2139–2151 (2016). https://doi.org/10.1007/s00170-016-9490-7
4. Abellan, J.V., Liu, J.: Variation propagation modelling for multi-station machining processes with fixtures based on locating surfaces. Int. J. Prod. Res. **51**(15), 4667–4681 (2013). https://doi.org/10.1080/00207543.2013.784409
5. Abellan-Nebot, J.V., Liu, J., Subirn, F.R., Shi, J.: State space modeling of variation propagation in multistation machining processes considering machining-induced variations. J. Manuf. Sci. Eng. Trans. **134**(2), 1–13 (2012). https://doi.org/10.1115/1.4005790
6. Zhou, S., Chen, Y., Shi, J.: Statistical estimation and testing for variation root-cause identification of multistage manufacturing processes. IEEE Trans. Autom. Sci. Eng. **1**(1), 73–83 (2004). https://doi.org/10.1109/TASE.2004.829427
7. Du, S., Yao, X., Huang, D.: Engineering model-based Bayesian monitoring of ramp-up phase of multistage manufacturing process. Int. J. Prod. Res. **53**(15), 4594–4613 (2015). https://doi.org/10.1080/00207543.2015.1005247
8. Zhang, T., Sun, H., Zhou, L., Zhao, S., Peng, F., Yan, R.: A transfer learning based geometric position-driven machining error prediction method for different working conditions. In: 2021 27th International Conference on Mechatronics and Machine Vision in Practice (M2VIP), pp. 145–150 (2021). https://doi.org/10.1109/M2VIP49856.2021.9665105
9. Fan, W., Zheng, L., Ji, W., Xu, X., Wang, L., Zhao, X.: A data-driven machining error analysis method for finish machining of assembly interfaces of large-scale components. J. Manuf. Sci. Eng. Trans. **143**(4), 1–11 (2021). https://doi.org/10.1115/1.4048955
10. Yuan, Y., et al.: A general end-to-end diagnosis framework for manufacturing systems. Natl. Sci. Rev. **7**(2), 418–429 (2020). https://doi.org/10.1093/nsr/nwz190

11. Sun, H., Zhou, L., Zhao, S., Zhang, T., Peng, F., Yan, R.: A hybrid mechanism-based and data-driven approach for the calibration of physical properties of Ni-based superalloy GH3128. In: 2021 27th International Conference on Mechatronics and Machine Vision in Practice (M2VIP), pp. 151–156 (2021). https://doi.org/10.1109/M2VIP49856.2021.9665158

12. Sun, H., Peng, F., Zhou, L., Yan, R., Zhao, S.: A hybrid driven approach to integrate surrogate model and Bayesian framework for the prediction of machining errors of thin-walled parts. Int. J. Mech. Sci. **192**(106111), 2021 (2020). https://doi.org/10.1016/j.ijmecsci.2020.106111

13. Abdulshahed, A.M., Longstaff, A.P., Fletcher, S.: The application of ANFIS prediction models for thermal error compensation on CNC machine tools. Appl. Soft Comput. J. **27**, 158–168 (2015). https://doi.org/10.1016/j.asoc.2014.11.012

14. Abellan-Nebot, J.V., Liu, J., Romero Subiron, F.: Design of multi-station manufacturing processes by integrating the stream-of-variation model and shop-floor data. J. Manuf. Syst. **30**(2), 70–82 (2011). https://doi.org/10.1016/j.jmsy.2011.04.001

15. Jang, J.R.: ANFIS: adaptive-network-based fuzzy inference system. IEEE Trans. Syst. Man. Cybern. **23**(3), 665–685 (1993)

Robotic Grasp Detection Based on Transformer

Mingshuai Dong, Yuxuan Bai, Shimin Wei, and Xiuli Yu$^{(\boxtimes)}$

School of Modern Post (School of Automation), Beijing University of Posts and
Telecommunications, Beijing 100876, China
yxl@bupt.edu.cn

Abstract. Grasp detection in a cluttered environment is still a great challenge
for robots. Currently, the Transformer mechanism has been successfully applied
to visual tasks, and its excellent ability of global context information extraction
provides a feasible way to improve the performance of robotic grasp detection in
cluttered scenes. However, the insufficient inductive bias ability of the original
Transformer model requires a large-scale dataset for training, which is difficult
to obtain for grasp detection. In this paper, we propose a grasp detection model
based on encoder-decoder structure. The encoder uses a Transformer network to
extract global context information. The decoder uses a fully convolutional neural
network to improve the inductive bias capability of the model and combine features
extracted by the encoder to predict the final grasp configurations. Experiments on
the VMRD dataset demonstrate that our model performs better in complex multi-
object scenarios. Meanwhile, on the Cornell grasp dataset, our approach achieves
an accuracy of 98.1%, which is comparable with state-of-the-art algorithms.

Keywords: Grasp detection · Cluttered environment · Transformer

1 Introduction

The purpose of the deep learning-based grasp detection model is to identify a set of
suitable grasp configurations from an input image. Currently, predicting grasp configurations of objects in cluttered or stacked scenarios remains a challenging task. Firstly,
for grasp detection, it is not only to accurately predict the position of the object but
also to model the pose and contour information of the object to predict the angle and
opening distance of the gripper when the robot is grasping. Secondly, it is challenging to
extract and map the complex and changing robot working environment features, which
requires a large-scale dataset for model training. However, grasp detection datasets are
very expensive to make. Therefore, we need to find an algorithm that can perfectly map
the features of the input image to the grasp configuration through the training on the
limited scale datasets.

In recent works [1–5], researchers have mainly focused on applying deep learning
networks based on convolutional neural networks (CNNs) to grasp detection. They have
achieved satisfactory results in the single object grasp detection task. In objects overlapping and cluttered scenes, however, grasp detection performance still has a lot of

H. Liu et al. (Eds.): ICIRA 2022, LNAI 13458, pp. 437–448, 2022.
https://doi.org/10.1007/978-3-031-13841-6_40

room to improve because of the complex features. [6] proposed a robotic grasp detection approach based on the region of interest (ROI) in the cluttered multi-object scene. The method divides the regions of interest according to the instance information of the object and then predicts the grasp configuration of each region. [7] proposed a two-stage multi-task model, which can simultaneously realize grasp detection, object detection, and object manipulation relationship reasoning. In order to improve the reasoning efficiency of the multi-task model, [8] proposed a one-stage fully convolutional neural network to predict the position, grasp configuration, and manipulation relations of different objects and achieved acceptable results. Most of the above methods use deeper networks and down-sampling mechanisms to increase the receptive field and improve the global feature extraction ability of the model, thus better predicting the object grasp configuration and other attributes. However, with the increase of model depth, some valuable features will disappear, which limits the improvement of model performance.

Recently, Transformer [9] has been widely used in the field of natural language processing and computer vision due to its excellent ability to extract global context features. Transformer, with parallel sequences as input, can better convey the fusion of information across global sequences at the beginning of the model, reducing feature loss and improving feature representation ability. In computer vision, Transformer models represented by DETR [10], Deformable DETR [11] VIT [12], MVIT [13] and Swin [14] have achieved excellent performance in multiple visual tasks. In particular, the Swin-Transformer [14] model outperforms CNNs in image classification tasks and achieves start-of-the-art results. This further demonstrates the Transformer architecture's excellent feature extraction and feature mapping capabilities for specific tasks. However, Transformer has insufficient inductive bias capability compared to CNNs and requires large datasets for training [12].

In this paper, we propose a grasp detection model based on a Transformer and fully convolutional neural network. The model uses attentional mechanisms and sequence input to obtain adequate global feature representation and uses a fully convolutional neural network to enhance the inductive bias of the model so that it can be trained on limited-scale datasets with promising results. The transformer is used as the encoder of the model to extract the features of the input image, and a fully convolutional neural network is used as the decoder to construct the final grasping configuration. In addition, to evaluate our algorithm, we validated the performance of our model in the VMRD dataset [6, 15] and the Cornell grasp dataset [16]. Experimental results demonstrate that the Transformer mechanism can improve the robot's grasp detection performance in cluttering or stacking scenarios.

In summary, the main contributions of this paper are concluded as follows:

1) We propose a grasp detection model combining a Transformer and a fully convolutional neural network, which can be trained on a limited scale of grasp detection datasets and acquire satisfactory results.
2) We proved that our model achieved state-of-the-art results in cluttered or stacked scenarios on the VMRD dataset and achieved comparable results with state-of-the-art algorithms on the single-objective Cornell grasp dataset.

2 Related Work

Robotic grasp detection has always been the focus of research in the field of robotics. Significantly, the application of deep learning technology in the field of robotic grasping makes the process of grasp detection free from manual features. Moreover, the deep learning model can directly predict all possible grasp configurations from RGB or RGB-D images. [1] was one of the earliest works that applied deep learning to grasp detection. They used the local constraint prediction mechanism to directly regression the grasp position in each image grid, thus realizing one-stage Multi-Grasp detection. However, this direct regression method is difficult to train and has inadequate robustness to the environment. Inspired by the Faster-RCNN object detection algorithm, [3, 6] proposed a two-stage grasp detection method. This method transforms the grasp detection problem into the object detection problem and improves the efficiency and accuracy of grasp detection. However, the efficiency of a two-stage network is lower than that of a one-stage network. Therefore, [3] proposed a one-stage fully convolution model to improve the real-time performance of model prediction. In addition, in order to realize the robot grasping specified objects in a multi-objective environment, [6–8, 17, 18], and [19], et al. proposed to add object detection or instance segmentation branches into the grasp detection model to guide the model to recognize the categories of objects in the scene while detecting the grasp configuration. These multi-task models enhance the intelligence level of the robot's perception of the working environment.

From the optimization and improvement process of the grasp detection model, we can find that the development of grasp detection technology heavily follows the progress of computer vision technology. However, grasp detection is more complex than computer vision tasks such as object detection. There are not only countless feasible grasping configurations but also substantial angle restrictions on grasping positions. Therefore, it is necessary to find a better feature extraction method and a relational mapping model so that the robot can better model the global and local features of the object so as to generate a more reasonable grasp configuration.

Recently, Transformer [9], with its self-attention mechanism at its core, has achieved satisfactory results in natural language processing tasks. Moreover, because of its satisfactory global feature extraction ability and long sequence modeling ability, it gradually replaces CNNs and RNNs in NLP and computer vision.

In the application of computer vision, researchers use convolution or patch embedding to encode visual information into sequence data to meet the input requirements of the Transformer. For example, DETR [10] and Deformable DETR [11] proposed the use of convolution operations to encode input images as sequential information; VIT [12], MVIT [13], and Swin-Transformer [14] proposed to split the image into patches as the input of the Transformer model. These Transformer based vision prediction models outperform traditional CNNs models in image classification, object detection, and image segmentation. However, the Transformer mechanism lacks the inductive bias capability inherent in CNNs [12], so the model needs pre-training on large-scale datasets to generalize well and achieve start-of-the-art performance. For grasping detection tasks, dataset making is a very expensive job; so far, there is no grasp dataset as large as ImageNet. Therefore, when the original Transformer is directly applied to the grasp detection model, the model cannot fully fit the relationship between the input image features and the grasp configurations, especially in cluttered or stacking scenes.

Different from previous work, in this paper, we propose a network structure with Swin-Transformer as the encoder and a fully convolutional neural network as the decoder for grasp detection. With this structure, the model has the ability of global feature modeling and the special ability of inductive bias of convolutional neural network, which enables the model to converge rapidly on smaller datasets. Compared with previous works, our model performs better in cluttered multi-object scenes while maintaining comparable results with start-of-the-art in single-object scenes on the basis of guaranteeing real-time performance.

3 Method

3.1 Grasp Representation

Given an RGB image, the grasp detection model should detect not only the grasp position but also the grasp posture of an object. Therefore, [16] has proposed a five-dimensional grasp representation, which can simultaneously represent the position of the center point, rotation angle, and opening size of the parallel plate gripper and has been widely used in other grasp works [1–7]. In our work, we also use this representation. At the same time, in order to increase the representation ability in the multi-object environment and enable the robot to grasp the specified category object, we add a dimension representing the object category on this basis. Therefore, the grasp representation of our model's final output can be expressed as:

$$g = \{x, y, w, h, \theta, c\} \tag{1}$$

where (x, y) is the pixel coordinates of the center point of grasp position, w is the opening size of the parallel plate gripper, h is the width, and θ is the angle between the closing direction of the parallel plate gripper and the horizontal direction, and c is the corresponding object category of the grasp representation.

3.2 Overview

In this paper, the grasp detection model based on the Transformer architecture proposed by us consists of two parts, the encoder with Shifted Windows (Swin) Transformer as the component and the decoder with the convolutional neural network as the component. The overview structure is shown in Fig. 1 (A). Input an RGB image through the patch partition layer and split it into non-overlapping image regions. Each region serves as a token for Transformer input. More detailed, an image with an input size of $I = \mathbb{R}^{W \times H \times 3}$ is split into fixed-size patches $x = \mathbb{R}^{N \times (P \times P \times 3)}$ in its spatial dimension, where $N = (W \times H)/P^2$ represents the number of patches generated by the image split, and $P \times P$ is the size of each image patch. Then position embedding is added into each image patch and fed into the encoder. In the encoder, behind several rounds of attention calculated, the input image patches are mapped to three sets of feature maps with different dimensions. The decoder uses convolution operation, further extracts and fuses the features of the feature map according to the task requirements, and finally, the grasp configuration of the input image is predicted by the grasp detector. The details of the Swin-Transformer-based encoder and convolution-based decoder are described as follows.

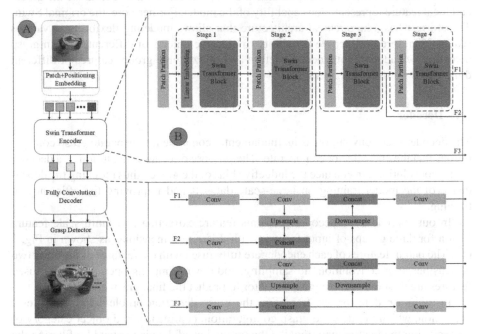

Fig. 1. (A). Overview architecture of our proposed model. (B). Encoder based on Swin-Transformer. (C). Decoder based on fully convolutional neural network.

3.3 Encoder

Inspired by Swin-Transformer [14], the encoder for our model consists of four stages, as shown in Fig. 1 (B), each composed of identical Swin-Transformer blocks. The attention mechanism in each block establishes long-distance interactions across distant pixels at the beginning of the model and establishes global relevance descriptions without feature loss.

The input image token's feature X is linearly transformed to derive the Q, K, and V vectors. The learnable linear transformation process can be defined as follows:

$$Q = XW_Q, K = XW_K, V = XW_V \tag{2}$$

where W_Q, W_K, and W_V are learnable linear transformation matrices. On this basis, the attention calculation method between different image tokens is as follows:

$$\text{Attention}(Q, K, V) = \text{SoftMax}(\frac{QK^T}{\sqrt{d}} + B)V \tag{3}$$

where d is the dimension of Q and B is the relative position encoding of each token.

Because the Swin-Transformer uses a window-based attention calculation method, it has less computation than VIT. In addition, Swin-Transformer assumes the shifted windows attention mechanism to change the scope of attention and enhance the global and local feature representation capability of the model. Furthermore, the original Swin-Transformer has a hierarchical architecture that allows modeling flexibility at various scales. Therefore, to improve the ability to perceive objects of different sizes in grasp detection, we adopt a bottleneck structure and utilize three group features of different dimensions for decoding operation.

3.4 Decoder

The decoder uses convolution as its fundamental component to generate grasp configurations that the end-effector can operate. The purpose of using convolution as a decoder is that convolution can enhance the inductive bias of the model, thus reducing the dependence of the model training on large-scale datasets and improving the efficiency of training.

In our approach, the decoder performs feature extraction and multi-scale feature fusion for three groups of input features with different dimensions, as shown in Fig. 1 (C). The output features of each encoder are fully fused with the features of the other two dimensions after convolution, up-sampling, and down-sampling operations. The fused features are then fed into the grasp detector to predict the final grasp configuration.

In the grasp detector, we transform the grasp detection problem into pixel-level prediction, which predicts the grasp configuration, confidence, and object category of each pixel in the feature map. Finally, the optimal candidate is retained by filtering the grasp configuration through confidence score and IoU. The advantage of this approach is that only a single forward propagation can obtain the optimal grasp configuration in a global scenario.

3.5 Loss Function

In this paper, the final prediction output of the model includes three parts: the position parameter, angle, and object category corresponding to the grasping rectangle. In addition, the angle of the grasping rectangle is predicted by the classification method. Therefore, the loss function of our algorithm consists of three parts, regression loss of grasping position, classification loss of grasping angle, and classification loss of object category.

In this paper, we employ CIoU loss function to supervise the training process of grasp position parameters. This loss function can evaluate the training process and guide the model to converge quickly by evaluating several indexes between the predicted grasp rectangle and the ground truth, such as IoU, the distance of the center point, and the aspect ratio. The realization process of CIoU loss function is as follows.

$$L_{grasp\_pos} = L_{CIoU} = 1 - IoU + \frac{\rho^2(b, b^{gt})}{c^2} + \alpha v \tag{4}$$

$$v = \frac{4}{\pi^2} \left(\arctan \frac{w^{gt}}{h^{gt}} - \arctan \frac{w}{h} \right) \tag{5}$$

$$\alpha = \frac{v}{(1 - IoU) + v} \tag{6}$$

where $\rho(b, b^{gt})$ is the distance between the central points of the predicted grasp rectangle and the ground truth, c is the diagonal length of the smallest enclosing box covering two rectangles and v represents the similarity of the aspect ratio between the predicted grasping rectangle and ground-truth, and α is the weight function.

We use the cross-entropy loss as the loss function of angle and object category prediction. We define the loss function of grasp angle and object category as follows:

$$L_{angle} = L_{obj\_class} = -\sum_{i=0}^{N-1} p_i^{gt} \log(p_i) \tag{7}$$

where N is the number of categories for angles or objects, $p^{gt} = [p_0^{gt}, p_1^{gt}, ..., p_{N-1}^{gt}]$ is the one-hot encoding of the sample's ground-truth; $p = [p_0, p_1, ..., p_{N-1}]$ is the prediction result of the model and represents the probability distribution of the category to which the sample belongs.

In general, the loss function of our algorithm in the training process can be defined as:

$$L_{total\_loss} = \omega L_{grasp\_pos} + \beta L_{angle} + \lambda L_{obj\_class} \tag{8}$$

In the training process of the model, we set ω as 0.05, β as 0.25, and λ as 0.5.

4 Experiment Set

4.1 Dataset

This paper utilizes the Cornell and the VMRD datasets to evaluate our proposed grasp detection algorithm. The single-object Cornell grasp dataset consists of 885 images of 244 different objects, and each image is labeled with multiple grasping positions of corresponding objects. We employ this dataset to evaluate the performance between our proposed algorithm and other start-of-the-art algorithms. In the VMRD dataset, each image contains multiple objects, and the dataset simultaneously labels each object with its category, grasping position, and grasping order. The VMRD dataset contains 4233 training images and 450 testing images, with 32 object categories. We use this dataset to demonstrate the performance of our model in multi-object and cluttered scenarios.

In training, we take advantage of data augmentation, including random clipping, flipping, and random brightness. Thus, in each training iteration, images fed into the model are different from the previous, with a fixed size of (224 × 224). This data enhancement method effectively expanded the diversity of the dataset at different locations and angles, which can reduce the risk of overfitting and enhance the generalization ability of our model in different workspaces.

4.2 Metric

In the single-objective scenario, we adopt a rectangular metric similar to [1–4] to evaluate the performance of our model. In the multi-objective scenario, we also consider adding the category information of the target to the assessment process. We consider that the correct grasp satisfying the rectangle metric is when a grasp prediction meets the following conditions.

1. The difference between the angle of the predicted grasping rectangle and the ground truth is smaller than 30°.
2. The Jacquard coefficient between the predicted grasping rectangle and the ground truth is more significant than 0.25.

The Jacquard index is defined as follow:

$$J(G, G^{gt}) = \frac{G \cap G^{gt}}{G \cup G^{gt}} \tag{9}$$

where G is the grasping configuration predicted by the model, and G^{gt} is the corresponding ground truth.

4.3 Implementation Details

Our algorithms are trained end-to-end on GTX 2080Ti with 11 GB memory, using Pytorch as the deep learning framework. We set the batch size to 64 and the learning rate to 0.001, divided by 10 for every ten iterations. Finally, we use SGD as the optimizer for the model, with momentum set to 0.99.

5 Results and Analysis

5.1 Results for Single-Object Grasp

In this part, we use the Cornell grasp dataset to verify the performance of our proposed model in a single-objective scenario. Verification results on Cornell grasp dataset are demonstrated in Table 1, and Fig. 2.

Table 1. Accuracy of different methods on Cornell grasp dataset.

Author	Backbone	Input	Accuracy (%)	Speed (frame/s)
Lenz [16]	SAE	RGB	75.6	0.07
Redmon [1]	AlexNet	RG-D	88.0	3.31
Guo [2]	ZFNet	RGB	93.2	–
Zhou [3]	ResNet-101	RGB	97.7	9.89
Fu-Jen[4]	ResNet-50	RG-D	96.0	8.33
Zhang [6]	ResNet-101	RGB	93.6	25.16
Liu D [5]	ResNet-50	RGB-D	95.2	21
Ours	Swin-Transformer	RGB	**98.1**	**47.6**

Fig. 2. Detection results on Cornell grasp dataset. The color of the grasp rectangle represents the category information of the grasping angle, and the printed annotation information includes the value and confidence of the angle.

The grasp detection network based on the Swin-Transformer structure proposed by us achieves an accuracy of 98.1% with a speed of 47.6 FPS. Compared with the state-of-the-art model [3], our algorithm improves accuracy by 0.4% and improves reasoning speed five times. In more detail, we can see that compared with the two-stage model of Fu-Jen [4], Zhang [6], and Liu D [5], the one-stage model proposed by us has a better speed advantage. In addition, compared with the traditional backbone network such as AlexNet [1] and ResNet [3–6], our proposed network with Swin-Transformer is more satisfied in obtaining a higher detection accuracy.

5.2 Results for Multi-object Grasp

In order to demonstrate the grasp detection performance of our model in a complex multi-objective environment, we used the VMRD multi-objective dataset to verify our model, and the verified results are shown in Table 2 and Fig. 3. We can see that our model can accurately identify the grasp configuration of each object and its corresponding object category in the multi-object scene. Besides, our model achieves an accuracy of 80.9% on the VMRD dataset when considering categories and grasping configurations simultaneously. Compared with Zhang [6], our proposed algorithm gains 12.7% accuracy. This also proves that Transformer mechanisms can improve the model's grasp detection performance in cluttered scenarios. Compared with other models with object spatial position reasoning, such as Zhang [20] and Park [8], our model achieves higher detection accuracy, but this comparison is not rigorous. We will further improve the function of our model in future work, thus verifying the performance of our model more comprehensively.

Table 2. Performance summary on VMRD dataset

Method	mAPg (%)	Speed (frame/s)
Zhang [6], OD, GD	68.2	9.1
Zhang [20], OD, GD, reasoning	70.5	6.5
Park [8], OD, GD, reasoning	74.6	**33.3**
Ours	**80.9**	28.6

Fig. 3. Experimental results on VMRD dataset. The detection results of the model include the position attribute and the angle information of the grasping rectangle and the object category corresponding to the grasping configuration.

Fig. 4. Grasp detection results in VMRD grasp dataset. The first line is the input image of the model, the second line is the graspable score heatmap of the model, and the last line is the grasp detection result.

Furthermore, in order to determine the areas of our proposed model's attention, we visualized the heatmap of the graspable score, as shown in Fig. 4. From the heatmap, we can see that most of the model's attention focused on the graspable parts of the object, such as the edges and center of the object. This phenomenon proves that our model has accurately modeled the feature mapping from the input image features to the grasp configuration.

6 Conclusion and Future Work

In this paper, we propose a novel one-stage grasp detection algorithm based on the Transformer mechanism. Compared with other CNN-based methods and their variants, the model based on Transformer shows more flexibility for global and local feature representation and feature modeling. This attribute is particularly important for robotic grasp detection, especially in multi-object complex scenes. In addition, in order to enhance the inductive bias capability of the model and reduce the dependence of Transformer-based model training on large-scale datasets, we apply a CNN-based decoder to find reasonable feature mapping relations more quickly according to the requirements of the model. Experimental results in single-object and multi-object scenarios demonstrate that our proposed method outperforms the CNN-based models in the grasp detection performance and inference speed. In the future work, we will devote ourselves to applying the model based on the Transformer mechanism to grasp detection tasks more widely, especially in improving the accuracy of grasp detection in cluttered scenes and predicting the spatial position relationship of objects. Exploit fully the advantages of the Transformer mechanism to improve the adaptability of robots to complex features.

Acknowledgements. This work is supported by the BUPT innovation and entrepreneurship support program (No. 2022-YC-A274).

References

1. Redmon, J., Angelova, A.: Real-time grasp detection using convolutional neural networks. In: 2015 IEEE International Conference on Robotics and Automation (ICRA), pp. 1316–1322. IEEE (2015)
2. Guo, D., Sun, F., Liu, H., Kong, T., Fang, B., Xi, N.: A hybrid deep architecture for robotic grasp detection. In: 2017 IEEE International Conference on Robotics and Automation (ICRA), pp. 1609–1614. IEEE (2017)
3. Zhou, X., Lan, X., Zhang, H., Tian, Z., Zhang, Y., Zheng, N.: Fully convolutional grasp detection network with oriented anchor box. In: 2018 IEEE/RSJ International Conference on Intelligent Robots and Systems (IROS), pp. 7223–7230. IEEE (2018)
4. Chu, F.J., Xu, R., Vela, P.A.: Real-world multiobject, multigrasp detection. IEEE Robot. Autom. Lett. **3**(4), 3355–3362 (2018)
5. Liu, D., Tao, X., Yuan, L., Du, Y., Cong, M.: Robotic objects detection and grasping in clutter based on cascaded deep convolutional neural network. IEEE Trans. Instrum. Meas. **71**, 1–10 (2021)

6. Zhang, H., Lan, X., Bai, S., Zhou, X., Tian, Z., Zheng, N.: ROI-based robotic grasp detection for object overlapping scenes. In: 2019 IEEE/RSJ International Conference on Intelligent Robots and Systems (IROS), pp. 4768–4775. IEEE (2019)

7. Zhang, H., Lan, X., Bai, S., Wan, L., Yang, C., Zheng, N.: A multi-task convolutional neural network for autonomous robotic grasping in object stacking scenes. In: 2019 IEEE/RSJ International Conference on Intelligent Robots and Systems (IROS), pp. 6435–6442. IEEE (2019)

8. Park, D., Seo, Y., Shin, D., Choi, J., Chun, S. Y.: A single multi-task deep neural network with post-processing for object detection with reasoning and robotic grasp detection. In: 2020 IEEE International Conference on Robotics and Automation (ICRA), pp. 7300–7306. IEEE (2020)

9. Vaswani, A., et al.: Attention is all you need. In: Advances in Neural Information Processing Systems, vol. 30 (2017)

10. Carion, N., Massa, F., Synnaeve, G., Usunier, N., Kirillov, A., Zagoruyko, S.: End-to-end object detection with transformers. In: Vedaldi, A., Bischof, H., Brox, T., Frahm, J.M. (eds.) Computer Vision – ECCV 2020, vol. 12346, pp. 213–229. Springer, Cham (2020). https://doi.org/10.1007/978-3-030-58452-8_13

11. Zhu, X., Su, W., Lu, L., Li, B., Wang, X., Dai, J.: Deformable DETR: deformable transformers for end-to-end object detection. arXiv preprint arXiv:2010.04159 (2020)

12. Dosovitskiy, A., et al.: An image is worth 16x16 words: transformers for image recognition at scale. arXiv preprint arXiv:2010.11929 (2020)

13. Fan, H., et al.: Multiscale vision transformers. In: Proceedings of the IEEE/CVF International Conference on Computer Vision, pp. 6824–6835. IEEE (2021)

14. Liu, Z., et al.: Swin transformer: hierarchical vision transformer using shifted windows. In: Proceedings of the IEEE/CVF International Conference on Computer Vision, pp. 10012–10022. IEEE (2021)

15. Zhang, H., Lan, X., Zhou, X., Tian, Z., Zhang, Y., Zheng, N.: Visual manipulation relationship network for autonomous robotics. In: 2018 IEEE-RAS 18th International Conference on Humanoid Robots (Humanoids), pp. 118–125. IEEE (2018)

16. Lenz, I., Lee, H., Saxena, A.: Deep learning for detecting robotic grasps. Int. J. Robot. Res. 34(4–5), 705–724 (2015)

17. Dong, M., Wei, S., Yu, X., Yin, J.: MASK-GD segmentation based robotic grasp detection. Comput. Commun. 178, 124–130 (2021)

18. Jia, Q., Cao, Z., Zhao, X., Pang, L., Yu, Y., Yu, U.: Object recognition, localization and grasp detection using a unified deep convolutional neural network with multi-task loss. In: 2018 IEEE International Conference on Robotics and Biomimetics (ROBIO), pp. 1557–1562. IEEE (2018)

19. Yu, Y., Cao, Z., Liu, Z., Geng, W., Yu, J., Zhang, W.: A two-stream CNN with simultaneous detection and segmentation for robotic grasping. IEEE Trans. Syst. Man Cybern. Syst. (2020)

20. Zhang, H., Lan, X., Wan, L., Yang, C., Zhou, X., Zheng, N.: RPRG: toward real-time robotic perception, reasoning and grasping with one multi-task convolutional neural network, pp. 1–7. arXiv preprint arXiv:1809.07081 (2018)

An Improved Off-Policy Actor-Critic Algorithm with Historical Behaviors Reusing for Robotic Control

Huaqing Zhang[1,2], Hongbin Ma[1,2]([✉]), and Ying Jin[1,2]

[1] School of Automation, Beijing Institute of Technology, Beijing 100081, China
mathmhb@139.com
[2] State Key Laboratory of Intelligent Control and Decision of Complex Systems,
Beijing Institution of Technology, Beijing 100081, China

Abstract. When the robot uses reinforcement learning (RL) to learn behavior policy, the requirement of RL algorithm is that it can use limited interactive data to learn the relatively optimal policy model. In this paper, we present an off-policy actor-critic deep RL algorithm based on maximum entropy RL framework. In policy improvement step, an off-policy likelihood ratio policy gradient method is derived, where the actions are sampled simultaneously from the current policy model and the experience replay buffer according to the sampled states. This method makes full use of the past experience. Moreover, we design an unified critic network, which can simultaneously approximate the state-value and action-value functions. On a range of continuous control benchmarks, the results show that our method outperforms the state-of-the-art soft actor-critic (SAC) algorithm in stability and asymptotic performance.

Keywords: Deep reinforcement learning · Robotic control · A unified critic network

1 Introduction

Deep reinforcement learning (DRL) is a general learning framework that combines the perception ability of deep learning with the decision-making ability of reinforcement learning. It can realize the direct control from the original perception input to the decision-making action output through end-to-end learning. This method has natural applicability for solving many technical problems such as automatic control system, mobile robot control, automatic driving, gaming and so on [2,3,8,17,18]. After the combination of neural networks and reinforcement learning, the DRL methods suffer from brittleness with respect to their hyperparameters. In the domain of robotic control with using DRL, the basic requirement is that the DRL method has high sample efficiency and stability. Therefore, the sample efficiency and the stability of the DRL method used in

© The Author(s), under exclusive license to Springer Nature Switzerland AG 2022
H. Liu et al. (Eds.): ICIRA 2022, LNAI 13458, pp. 449–458, 2022.
https://doi.org/10.1007/978-3-031-13841-6_41

robotic control are key factors that need to be considered when designing a deep RL algorithm.

The on-policy likelihood ratio policy gradient method named trust region policy optimization (TRPO) [14] was derived by making several approximations to the theoretically-justified procedure. It repeatedly optimizes a policy loss function with a KL divergence penalty by exploiting the sampled data of the current trajectory, and obtains theoretically monotonic improvement. The key to success of TRPO lies in that it ensures each update to policy model parameters small enough in policy improvement step. In order to make the algorithm more simpler to be implemented and compatible with complicated neural networks or tasks, the proximal policy optimization (PPO) [15] algorithm achieved first-order policy optimization that emulates the monotonic improvement of TRPO. It uses a novel surrogate objective with clipped probability ratios, which ignores the change in probability ratio when it would make the objective improve, and includes it when it makes the objective worse. TRPO and PPO all make small enough updates to policy parameters, so it will not cause too much difference between the actions sampled from the current trajectory and the policy model.

Value-based DRL methods such as (DQN) [10,11] are only suitable for discrete action space. In the control or decision-making problems of continuous action space, the policy gradient DRL methods need to be used. Off-policy actor-critic algorithms aim at reusing the interaction data sampled from a experience replay buffer to improve sample efficiency. The deep deterministic policy gradient (DDPG) [9] or twin delayed deep deterministic policy gradient (TD3) [4] algorithms optimize a parameterized policy model, which represents the current policy by mapping states to exclusive actions deterministically. The policy model is optimized by applying the chain rule to the expectation of discounted return represented by action-value function Q with respect to the model parameters. The soft actor-critic (SAC) algorithm [6,7] essentially updates policy model parameters by maximizing the expectation of the soft Q-values over actions sampled from current policy. It extends the DDPG style policy gradients to any tractable stochastic policy by using the reparametrization trick. However, whether DDPG, TD3, or SAC, in the policy improvement step, they all sample actions from the current policy model according to the sampled states.

In this paper, under the maximum entropy RL framework, a new off-policy actor-critc method with historical behaviors reusing which we call AC-HBR is proposed in this paper. The contributions of this paper are as follows.

1. In policy improvement step, the actions are sampled simultaneously from the current policy model and the experience replay buffer according to the sampled states. This method can make full advantage of the past experience and motivate the agent to learn a near-optimal policy.
2. In addition, we design a unified critic network, which can predict the state-value and action-value functions at the same time. Through this unified critic network, we can directly obtain the advantage function which is used to calculate the policy gradient.

The performance of AC-HBR is verified with SAC in PyBullet [1] robotic environments. The results show that AC-HBR algorithm has better performance than SAC.

2   Preliminaries

In this section, we briefly introduce the basic notation and the maximum entropy reinforcement learning framework.

2.1   Notation

The AC-HBR algorithm learns maximum entropy policies in continuous action space. The learning process of the agent can be defined as policy search in an infinite-horizon Markov decision process (MDP), which is defined by a tuple $\left(\mathcal{S}, \mathcal{A}, P_{\mathbf{s}_t, \mathbf{a}_t}^{\mathbf{s}_{t+1}}, r, \gamma\right)$. The state space $\mathcal{S}$ and the action space $\mathcal{A}$ respectively represent a finite continuous state set and action set. The state transition probability is defined as $P_{\mathbf{s}_t, \mathbf{a}_t}^{\mathbf{s}_{t+1}} : \mathcal{S} \times \mathcal{S} \times \mathcal{A} \to [0, \infty)$, which represents the probability density of next state $\mathbf{s}_{t+1} \in \mathcal{S}$ given the current state $\mathbf{s}_t \in \mathcal{S}$ and action $\mathbf{a}_t \in \mathcal{A}$. After the agent performs action $\mathbf{a}_t$ and interacts with the environment, the environment gives a reward $r : \mathcal{S} \times \mathcal{A} \to [r_{\min}, r_{\max}]$ on this transition. For simplifying the notation, the reward is abbreviated as $r_t \overset{\Delta}{=} r(\mathbf{s}_t, \mathbf{a}_t)$. The discount factor is defined as γ, and $\gamma \in [0, 1]$. The state marginal of the trajectory distribution induced by a policy $\pi(\mathbf{a}_t|\mathbf{s}_t)$ is defined as $\rho_\pi(\mathbf{s}_t)$.

2.2   Maximum Entropy Reinforcement Learning

By augmenting the standard objective used in reinforcement learning with the expected entropy of the policy over $\rho_\pi(\mathbf{s}_t)$, the infinite-horizon objective of the maximum entropy reinforcement learning can be defined as

$$J(\pi) = \sum_{t=0}^{\infty} \gamma^t \mathbb{E}_{(\mathbf{s}_t, \mathbf{a}_t) \sim \rho_\pi}[r(\mathbf{s}_t, \mathbf{a}_t) + \alpha \mathcal{H}(\pi(\cdot|\mathbf{s}_t))], \tag{1}$$

where the entropy temperature parameter α represents the relative importance of the entropy term compared to the reward, which determines the stochasticity of the policy. $\mathcal{H}(\pi(\cdot|\mathbf{s}_t))$ represents the entropy of the policy $\pi(\cdot|\mathbf{s}_t)$. In SAC [7], α is adjusted according to a gradient-based temperature turning method. The maximum entropy objective can induce the policy not only explore more widely, but also capture multiple modes of near-optimal behaviors.

According to soft Bellman equation, the concepts of action-value function Q and state-value function V in standard reinforcement learning can also be applied to maximum entropy reinforcement learning [5]. The soft Q-function of a stochastic policy π can be defined as

$$Q(\mathbf{s}_t, \mathbf{a}_t) = r(\mathbf{s}_t, \mathbf{a}_t) + \gamma \mathbb{E}_{\mathbf{s}_{t+1} \sim P_{\mathbf{s}_t, \mathbf{a}_t}^{\mathbf{s}_{t+1}}}[V^\pi(\mathbf{s}_{t+1})], \tag{2}$$

where the soft state-value function is given by

$$V^\pi(s_t) = \mathbb{E}_{a_t \sim \pi}[Q(s_t, a_t) - \alpha \log \pi(a_t|s_t)]. \qquad (3)$$

The goal of the maximum entropy reinforcement learning algorithms is to maximize the soft state-value function by optimizing the policy π. There are many maximum entropy reinforcement learning algorithms [5–7,16,19] that were proposed so far. The SAC algorithm [6,7] is the first off-policy actor-critic method in the maximum entropy reinforcement learning framework, which achieves state-of-the-art performance on a range of continuous control benchmark tasks.

3   Main Results

In the paper, a policy gradient method with historical behaviors reusing is designed for continuous action space. The actions are sampled simultaneously from the current policy model and the experience replay buffer. This method improve the learning ability of the agent by using the limited interaction data. In addition, an unified critic network is designed to obtain the advantage functions of the sampled actions. This unified critic network can approximate the state-value and action-value functions at the same time.

3.1   Off-Policy Policy Gradient with Historical Behaviors Reusing

BipedalWalkerHardcore is characterized by completely random terrain generation, which is also a difficult place in this environment depicted in the right picture of Fig. 1. The training model must be very robust to get a high average score. The states of this environment include hull angle speed, angular velocity, horizontal speed, vertical speed, joints position and joints angular speed, legs contact with ground and of 10 lidar rangefinder measurements. The action space in this environment is a 4-dimensional continuous action space, the agent needs to master a series of skills such as running, crossing pits, obstacle climbing, descending stairs and so on. Although the current advanced SAC, TD3, PPO and other deep RL algorithms can solve many challenging tasks, they can hardly solve BipedalWalkerHardcore without using any tricks or long short-term memory (LSTM) neural networks.

Fig. 1. The environment of BipedalWalkerHardcore-v3.

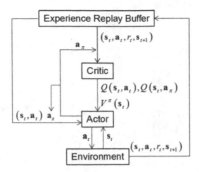

Fig. 2. A Gaussian with mean $\mu = 0$ and standard deviation $\sigma = 0.2$.

The policy gradient with historical behaviors reusing is beneficial for the agent to learn multiple skills. For example, suppose the tuple $(s_d, a_d) \sim E_b$ represents the skill of successfully descending stairs. As long as the agent samples this tuple from experience replay buffer, it will strengthen this skill regardless of whether the agent is still learning other skills in policy improvement step of HBRU-AC. However, if the actions are sampled only from the current Gaussian policy according to the sampled states, the tuple (s_d, a_d) may not be obtained. Then the skill of descending stairs may be forgotten, because the multilayer perceptron neural networks have a tendency of forgetting the past fitting functions. The data flow for this method is shown in Fig. 2, where a_π denotes the action sampled from the current policy model.

The policy model π_ϕ is differentiable to its parameters ϕ. The method of policy gradient with historical behaviors reusing is presented as follow

$$\nabla_\phi J(\phi)$$
$$= \mathop{\mathbb{E}}_{\substack{s_t \sim E_b \\ a_t \sim \pi_\phi}} [\nabla_\phi \log \pi_\phi(a_t|s_t)(Q(s_t, a_t) - \alpha \log \pi_\phi(a_t|s_t) - V^\pi(s_t))]$$
$$- \alpha \mathop{\mathbb{E}}_{\substack{s_t \sim E_b \\ a_t \sim \pi_\phi}} [\nabla_\phi \log \pi_\phi(a_t|s_t)] \tag{4}$$
$$+ \mathop{\mathbb{E}}_{(s_t, a_t) \sim E_b} [\nabla_\phi \mathcal{BC}(\log \pi_\phi(a_t|s_t))(Q(s_t, a_t) - V^\pi(s_t))],$$

where E_b denotes the experience replay buffer; $\mathcal{BC}(\bullet)$ represents Box-Cox transformation [13] that converts the input variables into data subject to an approximate normal distribution. In Eq. (4), $\mathcal{BC}(\log \pi_\phi(a_t|s_t))$ denotes the conversion for the log probabilities of the actions sampled from experience replay buffer E_b in the current policy model.

3.2 A Unified Critic Network Model

To calculate the advantage functions, we design a unified critic network model depicted in Fig. 3, which can approximate both the state-value function $V^\pi(s_t)$ and the action-value function $Q(s_t, a_t)$. The unified critic network mdoel has fewer parameters compared with using two critic network models.

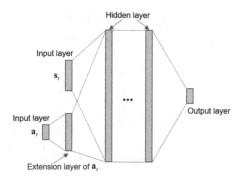

Fig. 3. A unified critic network model.

The critic network is composed of state input layer, action input layer, action expansion layer, hidden layer and output layer of the state-value and action-value functions. When predicting the state-value function $V^\pi(\mathbf{s}_t)$, $\mathbf{a}^e$ is defined to represent a vector with all zero elements and the same shape as $\mathbf{a}_t$. In addition, the outputs of the extension layer are set to zeros when detecting the elements of input layer are all zeros. Hence, we can get the state-value function as follow

$$V^\pi(\mathbf{s}_t) = Q(\mathbf{s}_t, \mathbf{a}^e) \tag{5}$$

We define θ as the parameters of the unified critic network model, and employ the unified critic network model to simultaneously approximate the soft action-value and state-value functions. The parameters θ are updated by using the random gradient descent to minimize the squared residual errors according to the formula

$$\begin{aligned}
&\nabla_\theta J(\theta) \\
&= \nabla_\theta J_V(\theta) + \nabla_\theta J_Q(\theta) \\
&= \nabla_\theta \mathop{\mathbb{E}}_{\mathbf{s}_t \sim E_b} \left[\frac{1}{2} \left(V_\theta^\pi(\mathbf{s}_t) - \mathop{\mathbb{E}}_{\mathbf{a}_t \sim \pi_\phi} [Q_\theta(\mathbf{s}_t, \mathbf{a}_t) - \alpha\log\pi_\phi(\mathbf{a}_t|\mathbf{s}_t)] \right)^2 \right] \\
&\quad + \nabla_\theta \mathop{\mathbb{E}}_{(\mathbf{s}_t, \mathbf{a}_t, \mathbf{s}_{t+1}) \sim E_b} \left[\frac{1}{2} \left(Q_\theta(\mathbf{s}_t, \mathbf{a}_t) - (r(\mathbf{s}_t, \mathbf{a}_t) + \gamma V_{\bar\theta}(\mathbf{s}_{t+1})) \right)^2 \right],
\end{aligned} \tag{6}$$

where $V_{\bar\theta}(\mathbf{s}_{t+1})$ represents the state-value function predicted by target critic network with parameters $\bar\theta$, which are obtained as an exponentially moving average of the parameters θ.

The unified critic network can approximate the action-value and state-value functions with high accuracy by using Eq. (6) to update the parameters. The theoretical basis that the unified critic network can simultaneously approximate the action-value and state-value functions lies in the formula

$$Q(\mathbf{s}_t, \mathbf{a}_t) = V^\pi(\mathbf{s}_t) + A(\mathbf{s}_t, \mathbf{a}_t), \tag{7}$$

where $A(\mathbf{s}_t, \mathbf{a}_t)$ represents the advantage function. According to Fig. 3 and Eq. (7), we can conclude that the action-value functions can be obtained by combining the state-value functions with the actions weighted by the parameters of the extension layer and hidden layers.

3.3   Practical Algorithm

To address the problem of overestimation bias, the clipped double-Q learning trick [4] is used, which learns two Q-functions, and uses the smaller of the two Q-values to form the target in soft Bellman error loss function. Hence, we construct two critic networks, with parameters θ_i ($i = 1, 2$), and train them independently to optimize $J(\theta_i)$. The minimum of the soft Q-functions is used for calculating the advantage functions in Eq. (4) and for the stochastic gradient in Eq. (6).

We also apply an invertible squashing function $\tanh(\cdot)$ to the Gaussian samples [6,7]. The actions sampled from experience replay buffer is converted to the corresponding Gaussian actions according to

$$\mathbf{a}_G = \frac{1}{2} \log \frac{1 + \mathbf{a}_{\text{tanh}}}{1 - \mathbf{a}_{\text{tanh}}}, \tag{8}$$

where $\mathbf{a}_{\text{tanh}}$ represents the sampled actions which has been compressed. In addition, the log probabilities of the sampled actions from experience replay buffer in current policy model is truncated by -30. In addition, the entropy temperature α is adjusted by usning the method proposed in SAC [7].

Parameter	Value
optimizer	Adam
learning rate	3×10^{-4}
discount (γ)	0.98
replay buffer size	10^6
number of hidden layers (all networks)	2
number of hidden units per layer	256
number of samples per minibatch	256
number of steps between training intervals	8
number of training times in each training	8
entropy target	- dim(A)
nonlinearity	ReLU
target network smoothing coefficient(τ)	0.02
target network update interval	1

Fig. 4. Common hyperparameters of our PG-HBR and SAC used in the comparative evaluation.

4   Experiments

We evaluate our algorithm with the state-of-the-art SAC algorithm, and verify the stability and asymptotic performance of them. The hyperparameters used in this experiment for comparative evaluation is presented in Fig. 4, which mainly refers to Stable-Baselines3 [12] and the original paper of SAC. The units in extension layer of the unified critic network is 84. We evaluate the two algorithms in four PyBullet [1] instances with different random seeds.

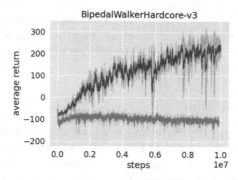

Fig. 5. Average returns on BipedalWalkerHardcore of AC-HBR (blue) SAC (orange).

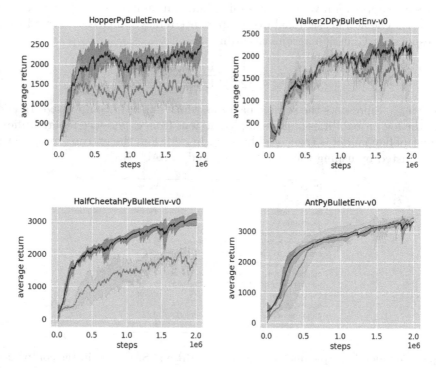

Fig. 6. Average returns on several benchmarks of Pybullet of AC-HBR (blue) SAC (orange). (Color figure online)

Figure 5 presents the average returns for our AC-HBR and SAC on Bipedal-WalkerHardcore. Figure 6 presents the average returns for our AC-HBR and SAC on several Pybullet environments. Based on the experimental results, we can not only conclude that the unified critic network is effective, but also that AC-HBR algorithm has better performance than SAC.

5   Conclusion

Aiming at autonomous behavior policy learning of robots, we presented a polcy gradient method with historical behaviors reusing under maximum entropy RL framework. This method can make full use of past experience. In addition, the experimental results show that our designed unified critic network model can approximate the state-value and the action-value functions at the same time. The experimental results show that our AC-HBR algorithm has more advantages than SAC in the learning of robotic behavior policy model.

Acknowledgments. We sincerely thank the reviewers for their suggestions and pioneers who have made contributions in the deep RL field. This work was partially funded by the National Key Research and Development Plan of China (No. 2018AAA0101000) and the National Natural Science Foundation of China under grant 62076028.

References

1. Coumans, E., Bai, Y.: Pybullet, a python module for physics simulation for games, robotics and machine learning. GitHub Repository (2016)
2. Duan, J., Li, S.E., Guan, Y., Sun, Q., et al.: Hierarchical reinforcement learning for self-driving decision-making without reliance on labelled driving data. IET Intell. Transp. Syst. **14**, 297–305 (2020)
3. Fu, Y., Li, C., Yu, F.R., Luan, T.H., et al.: A decision-making strategy for vehicle autonomous breaking in emergency via deep reinforcement learning. IEEE Trans. Veh. Technol. **69**, 5876–5888 (2020)
4. Fujimoto, S., Hoof, H., Meger, D.: Addressing function approximation error in actor-critic methods. In: International Conference on Machine Learning, pp. 1587–1596 (2018)
5. Haarnoja, T., Tang, H., Abbeel, P., Levine, S.: Reinforcement learning with deep energy-based policies. In: International Conference on Machine Learning, pp. 1352–1361 (2017)
6. Haarnoja, T., Zhou, A., Abbeel, P., Levine, S.: Soft actor-critic: off-policy maximum entropy deep reinforcement learning with a stochastic actor. In: International Conference on Machine Learning, pp. 1861–1870 (2018)
7. Haarnoja, T., Zhou, A., Hartikainen, K., Tucker, G., et al.: Soft actor-critic algorithms and applications. arXiv preprint arXiv (2018)
8. Hoeller, D., Wellhausen, L., Farshidian, F.: Learning a state representation and navigation in cluttered and dynamic environments. IEEE Rob. Autom. Lett. **3**, 5081–5088 (2021)
9. Lillicrap, T.P., Hunt, J.J., Pritzel, A., Heess, N., et al.: Continuous control with deep reinforcement learning. arXiv preprint arXiv (2015)
10. Mnih, V., Kavukcuoglu, K., Silver, D., Graves, A., et al.: Playing atari with deep reinforcement learning. arXiv preprint arXiv (2013)
11. Mnih, V., Kavukcuoglu, K., Silver, D., Rusu, A.A., et al.: Human-level control through deep reinforcement learning. Nature **7540**, 529–533 (2015)
12. Raffin, A., Hill, A., Gleave, A., Kanervisto, A., Ernestus, M., Dormann, N.: Stable-baselines3: reliable reinforcement learning implementations. J. Mach. Learn. Res. **22**(268), 1–8 (2021). http://jmlr.org/papers/v22/20-1364.html

13. Sakia, R.M.: The box-cox transformation technique: a review. J. R. Stat. Soc.: Series D **41**, 169–178 (1992)
14. Schulman, J., Levine, S., Abbeel, P., Jordan, M., et al.: Trust region policy optimization. In: International Conference on Machine Learning, pp. 1889–1897 (2015)
15. Schulman, J., Wolski, F., Dhariwal, P., Radford, A., et al.: Proximal policy optimization algorithms. arXiv preprint arXiv (2017)
16. Toussaint, M.: Robot trajectory optimization using approximate inference. In: International Conference on Machine Learning, pp. 1049–1056 (2009)
17. Vinyals, O., Babuschkin, I., Czarnecki, W.M.: Grandmaster level in starcraft II using multi-agent reinforcement learning. Nature **575**, 350–354 (2019)
18. Wu, X., Chen, H., Chen, C., Zhong, M., et al.: The autonomous navigation and obstacle avoidance for USVS with ANOA deep reinforcement learning method. Knowl. Based Syst. **196**, 105201 (2020)
19. Ziebart, B.D., Maas, A.L., Bagnell, J.A., Dey, A.K.: Maximum entropy inverse reinforcement learning. In: AAAI Conference on Artificial Intelligence, pp. 1433–1438 (2008)

MIA-Net: An Improved U-Net for Ammunition Segmentation

Haiqing Cao[1], Yuning Wang[1(✉)], Meng Li[1], and Huijie Fan[2]

[1] Unit 32681, PLA, Tieling 112609, China
wangyuning0928@163.com

[2] State Key Laboratory of Robotics, Shenyang Institute of Automation, Chinese Academy of Sciences, Shenyang 110016, China

Abstract. The task of destroying all types of scrapped ammunitions has always been extremely dangerous. Effective ammunition image segmentation algorithms can assist in reducing the risk of destruction missions. According to the uniqueness of the ammunition image segmentation task, we proposed an effective method for ammunition image segmentation named MIA-Net based on U-Net deep learning model. The Multi-scale Input Module (MIM) is used to supervise and revise the model at multiple levels, and the Weighted Attention Module (WAM) is used to represent features of different channels. The learning of multi-layer information is weighted and fused, which greatly increases the performance of the segmentation network model. Experiments demonstrate the effectiveness of the proposed method.

Keywords: Ammunition segmentation · Improved U-Net · Multi-scale Input · Weighted Attention

1 Introduction

The task of destroying all types of scrapped ammunitions has always been extremely dangerous. In the case of unknown ammunition types, it is very difficult to manually approach and complete the destruction task, so the research and development of intelligent automatic ammunition segmentation and identification technology is very important. Effective ammunition image segmentation and recognition algorithms can assist in reducing the risk of destruction missions.

1.1 Traditional Object Segmentation Methods

Most of traditional object segmentation methods are simple and effective, and are often used as a preprocessing step in image processing to obtain key feature information of images and improve the efficiency of image analysis. It mainly includes common and classic segmentation methods based on threshold, edge, region, cluster and graph theory.

Threshold-based image segmentation method: The essence is to classify image grayscale histograms by setting different grayscale thresholds. Edge-based image segmentation method: In the image, if a pixel has a large difference in gray value with

H. Liu et al. (Eds.): ICIRA 2022, LNAI 13458, pp. 459–467, 2022.
https://doi.org/10.1007/978-3-031-13841-6_42

its adjacent pixels, it is considered that the pixel may be at the boundary. Region-based image segmentation method [1]: The region-based image segmentation method is to segment according to the spatial information of the image, and classify the pixels through the similarity features of the pixels to form regions. The cluster-based image segmentation method [2] gathers the pixels with feature similarity into the same area, and iterates the clustering results repeatedly until convergence. The image segmentation method based on graph theory converts the segmentation problem into graph division, and completes the segmentation process by optimizing the objective function, including: Graph Cut [3], GrabCut [4] and other common algorithms.

1.2 Object Segmentation Based on Deep Learning

Traditional image segmentation methods mostly use the surface information of images, which are not suitable for segmentation tasks that require a lot of semantic information, and cannot meet actual needs. With the development and introduction of deep learning, breakthroughs have been made in the field of computer vision. Convolutional neural network has become an important means of image processing. Introducing it into the field of image segmentation can make full use of the semantic information of images and realize image processing semantic segmentation. In order to cope with the increasingly complex challenges of image segmentation scenes, a series of deep learning-based image semantic segmentation methods have been proposed to achieve more accurate and efficient segmentation, which further promotes the application scope of image segmentation.

FCN [5] Fully Convolutional Network (FCN) is the pioneering work of deep learning for semantic segmentation, and established a general network model framework for image semantic segmentation (ie, pixel-level classification of objects). PSPNet [6] Pyramid Scene Parsing Network (PSPNet) integrates contextual information, makes full use of global feature prior knowledge, parses different scenes, and achieves semantic segmentation of scene objects. The core of DeepLab [7–10] is to use atrous convolution, that is, the method of inserting jacks in the convolution kernel, which can not only explicitly control the resolution of the response when calculating the feature response, but also expand the feeling of the convolution kernel. Mask R-CNN [11] is a deep convolutional network for image segmentation proposed by He et al. based on Faster R-CNN [12], which achieves high-quality segmentation while performing object detection.

According to the uniqueness of the ammunition image segmentation task, we proposed an effective method for ammunition image segmentation named MIA-Net based on U-Net [13] deep learning model. The Multi-scale Input Module (MIM) is used to supervise and revise the model at multiple levels, and the Weighted Attention Module (WAM) is used to represent features of different channels. The learning of multi-layer information is weighted and fused, which greatly increases the performance of the segmentation network model. The content proposed in this paper technically helps the subsequent projectile matching work, and provides intelligent assistance for the ammunition destruction task.

2 Method

The improved U-Net segmentation network proposed in this paper called MIA-Net, the network structure is shown in Fig. 1, the gray box in the figure represents the multi-channel feature map, and white box represents the feature map copied by bilinear interpolation. The scale size and number of channels for feature maps are in the format W*H*C, where W and H represent the feature map size, and C represents the number of channels.

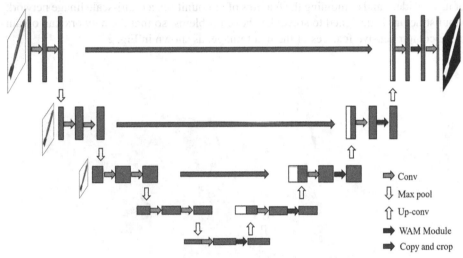

Fig. 1. Illustration of our MIA-Net architecture, which included the main encoder-decoder network with a multi-scale input module (MIM) and weighted attention modules (WAM). The weighted attention module details are introduced at the next part.

The overall structure is based on Resnet18 network, and three images of different scales are introduced into the network as the input of different layers, so that the network retains as much original feature information of the image as possible. At decoder step, adding the weighted channel attention mechanism allows the context extraction to fully fuse global information and local information, and input the fused information to the upsampling network. Finally, in order to balance the overall loss caused by the input of three scales of images, losses are calculated for the three scale prediction maps output after upsampling (bilinear interpolation), and all three losses are added to the overall loss.

2.1 Multi-scale Input Module

Convolutional neural network (CNN) layer deepening process is a process of semantic feature extraction from low-level to high-level. The ammunition images have the characteristics of finer texture distribution and complex contour shapes, and the features extracted by the network at the low level are only some ammunition contour features.

With the deepening of the network, more detailed texture information of ammunition will be added to the feature map, and contour features will be further extracted. However, each layer of the network has limitations in image feature extraction, and cannot extract complete global features. Each time the image passes through a layer of the network, some texture features and contour feature information will be lost, and more texture and contour information will be lost at the last layer.

Sheikh, Y. A. et al. [14] proposed a hierarchical multi-scale attention network based on multi-scale input, using images of different resolutions as network input, and showed good performance on the open source dataset of street view image segmentation. Inspired of its core ideas and combining the features of ammunition, a multi-scale image network input structure is designed to solve the above problems, so that the network can obtain more comprehensive features of the input image, as shown in Fig. 2.

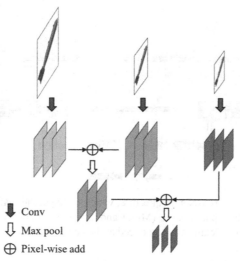

Fig. 2. Illustration of multi-scale input module using images of different resolutions as network input.

The output of Stage1 extracts the features of input 1 and supplements the original image feature information from input 2. Input 1 passes through the stride (stide) of 2, the output of the convolutional layer with the convolution kernel of 7×7 and the output of the input 2 through the convolutional layer with the convolution kernel of 3×3 are both 112×112 feature maps. The number of channels is 64, and the feature map of 112×112 and 128 channels is obtained after the channel feature fusion of the two.

Similarly, the image information from input 3 is supplemented in the output of Stage2. The output of Stage1 is passed through a pooling downsampling layer with a convolution kernel of 2×2, and a feature map of 56×56 and 64 channels is obtained as the input of Stage2. After passing through a convolutional layer with a convolution kernel of 3×3, the output and the output of Stage2 are both 56×56 feature maps, and the number of channels is 64. The channel feature fusion of the two feature maps obtains 56×56 with 128 channels. The fused feature map is passed through a pooling downsampling layer with a convolution kernel of 2×2 to obtain a 28×28 feature map with a channel number of 64, which is used as the input of Stage3.

By introducing images with the same scale and number of channels as the output of the previous layer in different layers as the input of this layer, some global information of the previous layer can be retained and the overall information loss can be reduced. The method of sending images of different scales into the network to extract features of different scales for fusion enables the network to obtain different receptive fields and capture information at different scales, which greatly improves the performance of the entire network.

2.2   Weighted Attention Module

The attention mechanism just like the selective vision of human visual perception, it can capture the key areas you want to focus on accurately after quickly scanning target objects; the attention mechanism can traverse the global feature map as well, and the positioning requires to focus on the key region, give additional attention to the feature information of this region besides a certain proportion of weight, in order to obtain more detailed information of the feature map from key regions, and also suppress other disposable information. Using the attention mechanism can effectively solve the long-term dependency problem in ammunition segmentation and improve the accuracy of the overall model.

In order to adapt to ammunition objects shape and size variations, existing methods tend to along the channel dimension sum up multi-scale outputs for final predictions (e.g., [15, 16]). But in high-level layers, some features are not benefit and cannot activated the recovery of objects. Based on that, we proposed the Weighted Attention Module (WAM) to emphasize the useful features, and fuse multi-scale information learning to improve the ammunition segmentation performance. From Fig. 1 we can see, outputs of each decoder layer are fed into the Weighted Attention Module to highlight the valu-able feature information. The structure of a Weighted Attention module is shown in Fig. 3. In this module, global average pooling is adopted to aggregate the global context feature information of inputs firstly, and then two 1×1 convolutional layers with differ-ent non-linearity activation functions, i.e., ReLU and Sigmoid, are applied to evaluate the layer relevance and generate weights along the channel dimension. After this step, the generated weights are multiplied with the outputs to generate more representative features.

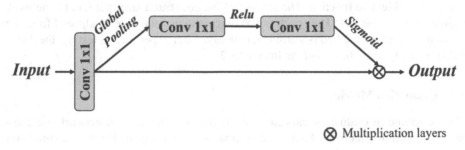

⊗ Multiplication layers

Fig. 3. Illustration of Weighted Attention Module.

Our WAM integrates the features of different scales via a bottom-up pathway, which generates a feature hierarchy consisting of feature maps of different sizes. Finally, the WAM also concatenates multi-scale input image feature representations from the encoder stage, and then applies a 1×1 convolution to extract features.

We adopt Binary Cross-Entropy as our loss function. The total loss function of our MIA-Net is defined as:

$$L_{total} = \sum_{c=1}^{M} y_c \log(p_c) \tag{1}$$

where M represents the number of categories, y_c represents the true label value, a value of 1 represents foreground pixels, a value of 0 represents background pixels, and p_c represents the probability that the predicted sample is ammunition. In the calculation of binary cross-entropy, when the distribution of the actual value and the distribution of the predicted value are closer, the cross-entropy value is smaller.

3 Experiments

3.1 Dataset Construction

The ammunition image data is collected in equal proportions in different weather and different time periods, and the initial data set has a total of 3564 images. In order to prevent the phenomenon of over-fitting, the data set is augmented by rotation, left-right exchange and scaling, and 15,000 images are generated after data augmentation. The dataset is divided into training set, validation set and test set with a ratio of 8:1:1, and the image data used among the three do not overlap each other. According to the two-class problem, the pixels in the image are divided into ammunition pixels and non-ammunition pixels. The pixel value of the ammunition part is set to 1, and the pixel value of the non-aquatic part is set to 0. Labelme software [17] is used to manually label the corresponding ammunition mask label.

3.2 Implementation Details

The environment of this paper is based on the Pycharm platform and the Python language. Coding on the basis of Pytorch1.60 under Ubuntu18.04 system, and used Nvidia RTX2080ti GPU for training. In this paper, the Adam optimizer is used for optimization in the neural network training experiment, and the multi-scale mixed loss function is used as the objective function. The number of images (batch-size) put into the network training at one time is 4; The epoch is 100 times; the learning rate is adjusted from the 20th epoch, and the method is learning rate decay. After experimental testing, the decay value is finally set to 0.92, and the interval is 2.

3.3 Evaluation Metrics

The performance evaluation indicators of the image segmentation network are commonly known as Precision, Mean Intersection over Union (mIoU) and Average Pixel

Precision (mean Pixel Accuracy, mPA). In this paper, the above three indicators are used for comprehensive evaluation and comparative analysis of the segmentation performance of different network aquatic plants images. The final segmentation performance is determined by the value of each indicator. The larger the value of the evaluation indicator is, the better the segmentation results.

3.4 Experimental Results and Analysis

Compared with Other Methods. In order to verify the effectiveness of this method for ammunition segmentation, four more popular segmentation networks are selected, namely FCN (VGG16), UNet (VGG16), U-Net (Resnet18) and Deeplabv3, and the improvements proposed in this paper. The above networks are trained with the ammunition dataset established in this paper, and the performance of the trained models is tested with the test set.

Table 1. Segmentation results compared with different method.

Method	Acc. (%)	mIoU (%)	mPA (%)
FCN	88.26	74.35	85.24
U-Net (VGG16)	89.71	78.28	87.33
U-Net (Resnet18)	91.15	85.23	91.28
DeeplabV3	93.02	86.69	92.81
Our method	**95.67**	**90.24**	**94.88**

After comparing the above segmentation tests with different networks, it can be seen in Table 1 that the method in this paper has better performance in ammunition segmentation. This is because, on the one hand, the improved network extracts the features of the image more fully through multi-scale image input, and on the other hand, the weighted attention mechanism module is added, so that the network can pay more attention to the local key areas, so that the local key areas can be The regional features get a certain weight, and the network extracts the features of key regions more fully, and combines the hole convolution to retain the global useful information, which further strengthens the transmission and utilization of the features by the network, and introduces three kinds of up-sampling images on the loss function. The loss function is used to balance the overall loss of the network brought by the input images of the three scales.

Ablation Study. The evaluation index values of each network segmentation result are shown in Table 2. Due to confidentiality, we cannot disclose the data set and ammunition image display, so there is no visual comparison result.

In order to verify the impact of the improved part on the network segmentation performance, ablation experiments are compared in this summary, and the effects of the multi-scale image input and the weighted attention module on the network performance are analyzed. In order to ensure the experimental effect and reduce the redundancy of the experiment, we conduct experiments on the three cases of baseline U-Net, U-Net+ weighted attention module and U-Net+ multi-scale image input and compare them with the model in this paper. The experiment is carried out on the ammunition dataset established in this paper. From Table 2, compared with a single U-Net (Resnet18), the overall performance of the network has been improved significantly after adding the weighted attention module.

Table 2. Segmentation results of our ablation study.

Method	Acc. (%)	mIoU (%)	mPA (%)
Baseline model	91.15	85.23	91.28
Multi-scale input	93.21	86.49	92.07
WAM module	95.04	88.32	93.78
Our method	**95.67**	**90.24**	**94.88**

4 Conclusion

Effective and intelligent automated ammunition segmentation algorithms can improve the safety and efficiency of ammunition destruction tasks. In this paper, an improved U-Net network is proposed for ammunition segmentation by collecting and making datasets from ammunition images. Compared with other segmentation methods, the network can meet the multi-scale feature fusion, and use the multi-channel focused image features of the weighted attention mechanism. Finally, the mixed loss function is added to help the network return gradient information to achieve the feature expression of the training network. Compared with other models, the accuracy and mIoU of this model are significantly improved. The experimental results show that the proposed method is more accurate for the outline segmentation of ammunition, and shows a better effect on the segmentation of small target ammunition. At present, the data set collected in the laboratory is still expanding, and the next step will continue to carry out research on the improvement of the data set and the identification of ammunition categories.

References

1. Tremeau, A., Borel, N.: A region growing and merging algorithm to color segmentation. Pattern Recogn. **30**(7), 1191–1203 (1997)
2. Achanta, R., Shaji, A., Smith, K., Lucchi, A., Fua, P., Süsstrunk, S.: SLIC superpixels compared to state-of-the-art superpixel methods. IEEE Trans. Pattern Anal. Mach. Intell. **34**(11), 2274–2282 (2012)

3. Boykov, Y.Y., Jolly, M.P.: Interactive graph cuts for optimal boundary and region segmentation of objects in ND images. In: Eighth IEEE International Conference on Computer Vision (ICCV) 2001, vol. 1, pp. 105–112. IEEE (2001)
4. Rother, C., Kolmogorov, V., Blake, A.: "GrabCut" interactive foreground extraction using iterated graph cuts. ACM Trans. Graph. (TOG) **23**(3), 309–314 (2004)
5. Long, J., Shelhamer, E., Darrell, T.: Fully convolutional networks for semantic segmentation. In: IEEE Conference on Computer Vision and Pattern Recognition 2015, pp. 3431–3440 (2015)
6. Zhao, H., Shi, J., Qi, X., Wang, X., Jia, J.: Pyramid scene parsing network. In: IEEE Conference on Computer Vision and Pattern Recognition 2017, pp. 2881–2890 (2017)
7. Chen, L.C., Papandreou, G., Kokkinos, I., Murphy, K., Yuille, A.L.: Semantic image segmentation with deep convolutional nets and fully connected CRFs. arXiv preprint arXiv:1412.7062 (2014)
8. Chen, L.C., Papandreou, G., Kokkinos, I., Murphy, K., Yuille, A.L.: DeepLab: semantic image segmentation with deep convolutional nets, atrous convolution, and fully connected CRFs. IEEE Trans. Pattern Anal. Mach. Intell. **40**(4), 834–848 (2017)
9. Chen, L.C., Papandreou, G., Schroff, F., Adam, H.: Rethinking atrous convolution for semantic image segmentation. arXiv preprint arXiv:1706.05587 (2017)
10. Chen, L.-C., Zhu, Y., Papandreou, G., Schroff, F., Adam, H.: Encoder-decoder with atrous separable convolution for semantic image segmentation. In: Ferrari, V., Hebert, M., Sminchisescu, C., Weiss, Y. (eds.) ECCV 2018. LNCS, vol. 11211, pp. 833–851. Springer, Cham (2018). https://doi.org/10.1007/978-3-030-01234-2_49
11. He, K., Gkioxari, G., Dollár, P., Girshick, R.: Mask R-CNN. In: IEEE International Conference on Computer Vision 2017, pp. 2961–2969 (2017)
12. Ren, S., He, K., Girshick, R., Sun, J.: Faster R-CNN: towards real-time object detection with region proposal networks. In: Advances in Neural Information Processing Systems, vol. 28 (2015)
13. Ronneberger, O., Fischer, P., Brox, T.: U-net: convolutional networks for biomedical image segmentation. In: Navab, N., Hornegger, J., Wells, W., Frangi, A. (eds.) Medical Image Computing and Computer-Assisted Intervention, vol. 9351, pp. 234–241. Springer, Cham (2015). https://doi.org/10.1007/978-3-319-24574-4_28
14. Sheikh, Y.A., Khan, E.A., Kanade, T.: Mode-seeking by medoidshifts. In: 2007 IEEE 11th International Conference on Computer Vision 2017, pp. 1–8. IEEE (2007)
15. Fu, H., Cheng, J., Xu, Y., Wong, D.W.K., Liu, J., Cao, X.: Joint optic disc and cup segmentation based on multi-label deep network and polar transformation. IEEE Trans. Med. Imaging **37**(7), 1597–1605 (2018)
16. Wang, W., Shen, J., Ling, H.: A deep network solution for attention and aesthetics aware photo cropping. IEEE Trans. Pattern Anal. Mach. Intell. **41**(7), 1531–1544 (2018)
17. Russell, B.C., Torralba, A., Murphy, K.P., Freeman, W.T.: LabelMe: a database and web-based tool for image annotation. Int. J. Comput. Vis. **77**(1), 157–173 (2008). https://doi.org/10.1007/s11263-007-0090-8

A Method for Robust Object Recognition and Pose Estimation of Rigid Body Based on Point Cloud

Guiyu Zhao[1], Hongbin Ma[1,2(✉)], and Ying Jin[1]

[1] School of Automation, Beijing Institute of Technology, Beijing 100081,
People's Republic of China
mathmhb@139.com
[2] State Key Laboratory of Intelligent Control and Decision of Complex Systems,
Beijing 100081, People's Republic of China

Abstract. Object recognition and pose estimation of rigid body are important research directions in the field of both computer vision and machine vision, which has been widely used in robotic arm disorderly grasping, obstacle detection, augmented reality and so on. This paper introduces a method for object recognition and pose estimation of rigid body based on local features of 3D point cloud. A new 3D descriptor (MSG-SHOT) is proposed in the disordered grasping of robot, and only the depth information is used to complete the recognition and pose estimation of the object, which greatly improve the accuracy in the scenes full of clutters and occlusions. Firstly, the adaptive voxel filter based on local resolution is used to realize data reduction and keypoint extraction. Secondly, the MSG-SHOT descriptor is used to complete feature calculating and matching, and the preliminary object recognition and pose estimation of rigid body are completed. Finally, the fast non-maximum suppression algorithm based on point cloud is used to complete the screening of candidate objects. The experimental results show that our method has stability and accuracy, and has robustness to the scenes full of clutters and occlusions, which meets the standard of high-precision grasping of manipulator.

Keywords: Object recognition · 6D pose estimation · Local feature · Point cloud · MSG-SHOT

1 Introduction

With the increasing requirements, the technology based on 3D object recognition and 6D pose estimation has been widely studied by scholars. In the process of 3D object recognition, classification takes the size and category of objects as the core to complete the classification task of category level or instance level. 6D pose refers to the pose of an object, especially based on translation vector and rotation matrix. Object recognition and 6D pose estimation are important technologies in many industrial or robotic fields. It provides pose information for the manipulator to complete the recognition of parts and ensure that it can complete accurate and robust grasping. In recent years, object

H. Liu et al. (Eds.): ICIRA 2022, LNAI 13458, pp. 468–480, 2022.
https://doi.org/10.1007/978-3-031-13841-6_43

recognition and 6D pose estimation have become a hot topic in the industry. However, it faces many challenges, such as poor recognition effect when the scenes are full of clutters and occlusions.

Recently, the object recognition of two-dimensional images has been very mature. However, the pose estimation based on two-dimensional image cannot meet the needs of people. The methods of object recognition and 6D pose estimation based on point cloud are gradually developing. However, at the current stage, it still faces many problems and challenges. The existing methods of object recognition and 6D pose estimation based on point cloud are divided into four categories: methods based on feature matching, methods based on template, methods based on point pair voting, and methods of classification and regression based on deep learning. This paper uses the first method, which completes object recognition and 6D pose estimation by local feature matching.

As for the methods based on feature matching, in 2008, Rusu et al. [1] propose the point feature histogram (PFH), which uses the relationship between point pairs in the support region and the estimation of surface normal to describe local features, which is time-consuming. Tombari et al. [2] propose signatures of histograms of orientations (SHOT), which constructs a local coordinate system by using the eigenvalue decomposition (EVD) of the covariance matrix, divides the sphere domain and counts the number of the points in each part of the sphere domain. This method has good invariance of translation and rotation, yet the SHOT descriptor will be greatly affected when encountering occlusions or objects next to each other. In 2014, Tombari et al. [3] added color features on the original basis to improve robustness of object recognition, and this is not suitable to point clouds generated from 2.5D depth images.

In addition to local features, in recent years, some scholars have used point pair features and regression based on deep learning to complete the 6D pose estimation. Drost et al. [4] proposed a point pair feature (PPF) descriptor which completes the description of point pair information by calculating the distance and angle between each group of point pairs. Jianwei Guo et al. [5] proposed the central voting method based on the original PPF, which significantly improved the effect of pose estimation and achieved good performance on many point cloud datasets, yet it is not suitable for depth images. Yang you et al. [6] combined PPF with deep learning and proposed a CPPF network, which can realize 9D pose estimation through voting and regression methods. Yijia Wang et al. [7] Proposed the CAPTRA method, which can realize object recognition and 6D pose estimation through coordinate prediction network and rotation regression network, which can track real-time through video, and extend the rigid objects to articulated objects. Qin et al. [8] propose IPPE-PCR, which improves the accuracy of pose estimation for non-textured workpieces. Jiaze Wang et al. [9] achieve accurate category-level 6D pose estimation via cascaded relation and recurrent reconstruction networks. Ge Gao et al. [10] propose CloudAAE, which only used depth information to complete pose estimation through network training. Wei Chen et al. [11] propose FS-Net with efficient category-level feature extraction for 6D pose estimation.

However, most of the methods have low accuracy in recognition and 6D pose estimation when facing scenes full of clutter and occlusion, and they are not suitable for point cloud constructed only using depth information. Based on the original SHOT descriptor, this paper introduces a new 3D descriptor (MSG-SHOT). And through the innovation and improvement of several other parts, it can solve the problem of inaccurate recognition in the scenes full of clutters and occlusions, and extend the feature matching method based on 3D descriptor to the data type of 2.5D depth image.

The rest of this paper is organized as follows. The second section briefly introduces overall scheme of our method and the SHOT descriptor. The third section develop the three innovations, which introduces the method of this paper in more detail. In the fourth section, we conduct experiments to verify the performance of our method on some public datasets and self-made datasets. Finally, ablation experiments are conducted to test the necessity for our innovations.

2 Overall Scheme

In this paper, a robust method of object recognition and 6D pose estimation based on local features of 3D point cloud is introduced. Our algorithm framework takes local features as the core, and divides the task into four modules: data preprocessing of point cloud, local feature describing, feature matching [9] and matching verification. The data we input is a 3D model object and a scene. Our goal is to recognize and locate the 3D object in the scene, and estimate a 6D pose information. Our method is based on the basic framework of the feature matching of the original 3D descriptor SHOT. In order to make the paper more complete, this section first analyzes and explains the method of feature matching of SHOT to complete object recognition and 6D pose estimation, and then introduces the new method and three innovations proposed in this paper. The overall scheme of our algorithm is shown in Fig. 1.

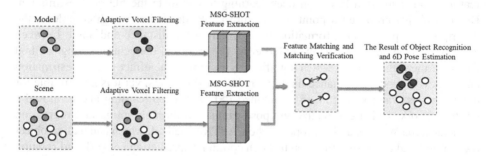

Fig. 1. Overall scheme of our method

2.1 Feature Matching Based on SHOT Descriptor

SHOT [2, 3] is a hybrid descriptor. The main principle of the SHOT descriptor is to establish the local sphere field of the point cloud, count the distribution information of the points in the local field, and use the histogram voting method to describe the spatial distribution information. Its good spatial domain setting enables it to describe local information well; The establishment of its local coordinate frame makes it have good translation and rotation invariance.

First, select keypoints $p_q(q = 1, 2, 3 \ldots\ldots N)$ by down sampling, where N is the total number of keypoints. Taking p_q as the center of the sphere and r as the radius, the sphere domain $U_q(p_q, r)$ is established. Then, query the nearest neighbor in its field $p_q^j(j = 1, 2, 3 \ldots\ldots k)$, where k is the number of nearest neighbors in the domain.

In the sphere domain, with the help of the nearest neighbor points in the domain, the covariance matrix with weight is constructed

$$M = \frac{1}{\sum_{j:d_q^j \leq R}(R - d_i)} \sum_{i:d_q^j \leq R}\left(r - d_q^j\right)\left(p_q^j - p_q\right)\left(p_q^j - p_q\right)^T, \tag{1}$$

where d_q^j is the distance between a point p_q^j in the neighborhood and the spherical center p_q, and we uses distance $r - d_q^j$ measure as the weight of each point in the neighborhood.

The covariance matrix M is decomposed by EVD to obtain three eigenvalues $(\lambda_1, \lambda_2, \lambda_3)$ and three eigenvectors (w_1, w_2, w_3). With p_q as the coordinate origin and eigenvectors (w_1, w_2, w_3) as the direction of coordinate axis, local reference coordinate frame $\mathcal{F}_{U_q}$ of the spherical field $U_q(p_q, r)$ is constructed.

Based on the coordinate system $\mathcal{F}_{U_q}$, establish spherical support area $U_q^*(p_q, r)$. Divide the spherical support area into 32 small areas $U_{q,i}^*(p_q, r)$ which are 2 in the dimension of radius (i.e. inner sphere and outer sphere), 2 in the dimension of latitudinal (i.e. northern hemisphere and southern hemisphere), and 8 in the dimension of longitude. The local sphere domain e $U_q^*(p_q, r)$ is shown in Fig. 2 (a).

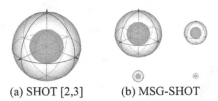

(a) SHOT [2,3]   (b) MSG-SHOT

Fig. 2. Sketch map of descriptors' local sphere domain

For each small region $U_{q,i}^*(p_q, r)$, a bin of the histogram is constructed, and voting is carried out according to the cosine $\cos\theta_q = n_q \cdot z_k$ based on the angle between the normal n_q of the feature point and the z-axis of the local coordinate frame $\mathcal{F}_{U_q}$.

In order to weaken the edge effect, when the nearest neighbor points are voted to the bin of the histogram, perform linear interpolation on its adjacent domain (normal vector cosine interpolation, latitude interpolation, longitude interpolation, radius interpolation).

According to the above description, the local SHOT features of each keypoint in the scene is calculated, and a feature description vector is obtained. Similarly, the local SHOT features of each keypoint of the model is also calculated. Traverse the feature descriptor subsets of the model and scene, and calculate the similarity between two feature descriptors

$$corr\left(f_i^A, f_j^B\right) = \sqrt{\sum_{m=1}^{n}\left(f_i^A(m) - f_j^B(m)\right)^2} \tag{2}$$

where f_i^A and f_j^B are n-dimensional feature vectors of the model and the scene.

Then, with the help of the similarity between two feature descriptors, the points with highly similar feature in the scene and the model are matched and connected to form point pairs, by the method of approximate nearest neighbors. Finally, each group of point pairs is clustered to complete the object recognition. And through the coordinate transformation from the model to the scene, the R and T matrices are output to estimate the pose information.

2.2 Our Key Improvements

Although our algorithm framework is roughly the same as the framework of SHOT feature matching, we have made ingenious improvements in each key step to make the result more robust and accurate when the scene is full of noise, clutters, occlusions, incomplete information and so on.

First, we use a voxel filter based on local resolution of point cloud to adaptively adjust the voxel side length to extract keypoints for the model and the scene, which can greatly solve the problem of inconsistent sparsity of point cloud, and improve the efficiency of feature calculating. Second, by setting multiple different radii to extract multi-scale local feature MSG-SHOT which can improve robustness. Then, the Hough 3D voting method is used to cluster and estimate the preliminary candidate pose of the target. Finally, the non-maximum suppression based on point cloud voting is used to select the final pose.

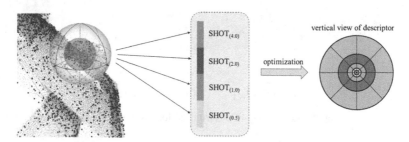

Fig. 3. The overall framework of MSG-SHOT descriptor

3   Methodology

3.1   Adaptive Voxel Filter Based on Local Resolution

Voxel filter is a down sampling algorithm of point cloud. Its basic principle is to set a side length l, construct a voxel grid, and slide the grid in the point cloud. With the sliding of the voxel grid, the points in the voxel grid whose number of points is less than the threshold n are deleted and filtered. Otherwise, the points will be replaced by the center of the voxel grid, which realizes the down sampling and keypoints extraction of the data.

However, traditional voxel filter has a series of problems, because when collecting data, the sparsity of point clouds in different scenes or different areas of the same scene is inconsistent, while the traditional voxel filter only considers the number of point clouds and the length of the interval when setting the voxel grid, and does not respond to the sparse information, which may lead to dense scenes being filtered greatly and sparse scenes not achieving good filtering results. In this paper, the setting of side length l of voxel grid is improved, and the side length l of voxel grid is adaptively adjusted based on the local resolution of point cloud:

$$l = m \times \frac{1}{n} \sum_{j=1}^{n} (\frac{1}{k} \sum_{i=1}^{k} S_i), \tag{3}$$

where m is the conversion coefficient between the side length l and the local resolution, n is the number of points in the scene, and k is the number of points queried by the nearest neighbors of KD-tree, S_i is the distance between the keypoint and the i th nearest neighbor point.

3.2 MSG-SHOT Feature

For some scenes full of a large number of occlusions and clutters, the traditional SHOT feature is used to complete the feature description, and then the feature matching is carried out. Finally, the recognition effect is poor. Many objects are unrecognizable or incorrectly recognized.

According to this problem, a new descriptor (MSG-SHOT) is introduced in this paper to improve the robustness of object recognition in the scenes full of occlusions and incomplete information. MSG-SHOT can also complete the rough estimation of 9D pose, which cannot be achieved by other 3D descriptors. The work of 9D pose estimation will be studied in the future.

Based on the principle of traditional SHOT feature, different sizes of radii 0.5 r, 1r, 2r, 4r are set, and SHOT feature $SHOT_{(4.0)}$, $SHOT_{(2.0)}$, $SHOT_{(1.0)}$, $SHOT_{(0.5)}$ can be obtained, as shown in Fig. 2 (b). By using the method of multi-scale grouping (MSG) [13] to calculate the SHOT features for many times, we can well describe the local domain information in more detail so as to improve the robustness of recognition. However, because the SHOT feature is calculated many times, the computational complexity will be greatly increased and the real-time performance will be poor.

Therefore, we use the idea of integral graph to avoid many repeated calculations. The algorithm framework of the whole MSG-SHOT is shown in Fig. 3 above. With the help of the idea of integral graph, the descriptor is optimized and combined into final MSG-SHOT descriptor whose vertical view is shown on the right of Fig. 3. First, the spatial distribution information of $SHOT_{(0.5)}$ with the minimum radius 0.5r is calculated, and then the distribution information of points in inner and outer spheres of $SHOT_{(0.5)}$ are superimposed to obtain the inner spherical distribution information of $SHOT_{(1.0)}$, which don't require additional calculation. Only the distribution information of the outer sphere of $SHOT_{(1.0)}$ need to be counted to obtain the $SHOT_{(1.0)}$ descriptor. By analogy, the calculations of $SHOT_{(4.0)}$, $SHOT_{(2.0)}$, $SHOT_{(1.0)}$ and $SHOT_{(0.5)}$ are completed, which greatly improves the calculation efficiency.

3.3 Non-maximum Suppression Based on Point Cloud

Table 1. The pseudo code of fast non-maximum suppression based on point cloud.

Algorithm 1: Non-Maximum Suppression Based on Point Cloud

Input:	$Clusterers = \{C_1, C_2, \ldots \ldots C_n\}$, which is the set of candidate objects in the scene, S contains corresponding object scores, N is the NMS threshold
Output:	G, which is the set of final objects in the scene

1	$G \leftarrow \{\}$
2	**While** $Clusterers \neq empty$ **do**
3	$k \leftarrow argmax\, S$ # Arrange the candidate cluster points according to
4	$G \leftarrow C_k \cup G$ # the confidence from large to small
5	$Clusterers \leftarrow Clusterers - C_k$
6	**end for**
7	**For** $i = 1,2,\ldots,n$ **do**
8	**For** $j = i+1, i+2, \ldots, n$ **do**
9	Initialization $hashMap < int, int > set$
10	**For** $point\ p \in G_i$ **do**
11	$set[p]++$
12	**end for**
13	**For** $point\ p \in G_j$ **do**
14	$set[p]++$
15	**end for**
16	Initialization I, U # the Intersection and Union
17	**For** $it \in set$ **do**
18	$I++$
19	**If** $set[it] \geq 1$
20	$U++$
21	**end if**
22	**end for**
23	$IoU = I/U$
24	**If** $IoU \geq N$
25	$G \leftarrow G - G_j$
26	**end if**
27	**end for**
28	**end for**
29	**Return** G

The traditional non-maximum suppression algorithm [14] is proposed for object detection. It has many variant algorithms, which can well solve the screening of candidate boxes for two-dimensional target detection. However, for the 6D pose estimation based on point cloud, because the object has six degrees of freedom. In this case, the traditional non-maximum suppression based on the method of computing intersection over union

(IoU) by volume is used. The effect is not very good, and because the volume intersection is complex, the calculation is complex and the real-time performance is not good. To solve this problem, this paper proposes a fast non-maximum suppression (PFNMS) algorithm for point cloud data. With the help of hash table, the method based on points is used to calculate IoU, which is more efficient. The pseudo code of the algorithm is shown in the Table 1.

First, we get some candidate objects in the scene through feature matching and cluster algorithm. The number of points in the point cloud of each candidate object is taken as the confidence score, and the candidate objects are arranged from large to small. Then, compute the IoU between the candidate objects, uses a hash table to record which points in the scene are indexed. At this time, it is obvious that the point in the hash table with a value greater than 1 is the intersection of two candidate objects, and the point appearing in the hash table is the union of the two candidate objects, so as to we complete the calculation of the IoU. Finally, the candidate objects whose IoUs are greater than the threshold value and ranks are lower are deleted to complete the filtering of the candidate objects.

4 Experiment

In this section, we will verify the superiority and practicability of our proposed algorithm. We test the performance on the public datasets and the self-made datasets, and compare it with other advanced 6D pose estimation algorithms to highlight the advantages of our method. Finally, the ablation studies are conducted to analyze the necessity of our multiple innovations. This experiment is conducted in the Ubuntu 18.04 environment with RTX 3060 laptop, 6 GB video memory, AMD Ryzen 75800h CPU and 16 GB memory.

We use the following formula to calculate the result of feature matching to measure the accuracy of our object recognition and pose estimation:

$$m = \operatorname*{avg}_{\mathbf{x} \in \mathcal{M}} \| (\mathbf{R}\mathbf{x} + \mathbf{T}) - \left(\tilde{\mathbf{R}}\mathbf{x} + \tilde{\mathbf{T}} \right) \| \tag{4}$$

where $\mathbf{R}$, $\mathbf{T}$ are the real pose of the target object, $\tilde{\mathbf{R}}$, $\tilde{\mathbf{T}}$ is our estimated pose, and $\mathcal{M}$ is the set of point clouds of the target object. We give a threshold k and calculate the maximum distance d from the center point of the object to the boundary. The results of correct object recognition and pose estimation need to meet the following formula:

$$m \leq k \times d. \tag{5}$$

4.1 Experiment on Public Datasets

RGB-D Object Dataset [15] is selected as the experimental data. The kitchen scene of RGB-D Object Dataset contains a large number of objects, which block each other and have a lot of clutters. Previously, many scholars have done a lot of research under RGB-D Object Dataset, but most methods have achieved good results only under the use of data types of RGBD. In this paper, experiments will be conducted in the kitchen scene of RGB-D Object Dataset. Two different data types, RGBD and D, are used to test the accuracy of this method, compared with other methods. The results are shown in the Table 2. and Fig. 4.

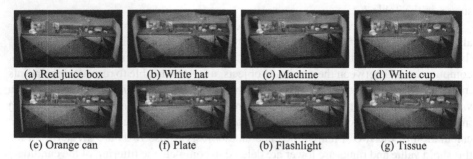

| (a) Red juice box | (b) White hat | (c) Machine | (d) White cup |
| (e) Orange can | (f) Plate | (b) Flashlight | (g) Tissue |

Fig. 4. A part of the results in the kitchen scene of RGB-D object dataset (Color figure online)

Table 2. Comparison of accuracy between the method proposed in this paper and other methods using RGBD data and D data.

Method	D	RGBD
SIFT + texton + color histogram + spin images [15]	64.7	73.9
RGB-D kernel descriptors [16, 17]	70.2	91.2
Convolutional k-means descriptor [18]	80.7	90.4
Hierarchical matching pursuit [19]	39.8	78.9
Unsupervised feature learning [20]	51.7	**92.8**
Feature matching of SHOT [2]	71.0	77.2
Our method: MSG-SHOT	**90.9**	**90.9**

4.2   Experiment on Our Own Datasets

The scenes of this experiment come from the experimental platform of the manipulator grabbing built by our laboratory. The experimental data were self-made datasets taken with depth cameras. The first task is to complete the 3D object recognition and 6D pose estimation of workpieces under occlusions and clutters. And the second task is to complete the 3D object recognition and 6D pose estimation of multi-target for oranges.

Object Recognition and Pose Estimation of Workpieces. The first experiment of the self-made datasets is Object recognition and pose estimation of workpieces. The main objective is to verify that the algorithm proposed in this paper can ensure the robustness and accuracy of object recognition and pose estimation in the face of occlusions, clutters and other problems in the actual scenes of manipulator grasping. By stacking different workpieces, 9 different scenes are set, including three workpiece objects. Each scene is sampled 200 times with a depth camera to obtain 200 depth maps and point cloud data. Experiments are carried out on these 1800 sets of scenes to verify the effectiveness of the proposed algorithm. Our accuracy on the dataset of workpieces reaches 91.2% (Figs. 5 and 6).

Fig. 5. The incomplete workpiece scenes only generated from the depth information

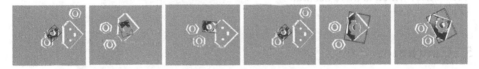

Fig. 6. The results on the experiment of workpieces in different scenes

Object Recognition and 6D Pose Estimation of Oranges. The second experiment of self-made datasets is the experiment of orange multi-target recognition and pose estimation. This experiment is mainly set up to verify the effectiveness and reliability of this method for multi-target recognition. In the manipulator grabbing experimental platform we built, several oranges were put into open cartons, and the depth map was obtained by scanning with a depth camera to form point cloud. Five different scenes were set up. Each scene was sampled 100 times with a depth camera to obtain 100 depth maps and point cloud data. Experiments are carried out on these 500 sets of scenes to verify the effectiveness of the proposed method. Our final accuracy on the dataset of oranges is 88.8%.

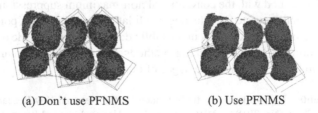

(a) Don't use PFNMS   (b) Use PFNMS

Fig. 7. Multi-target recognition and 6D pose estimation of oranges (Color figure online)

4.3 Ablation Studies

MSG-SHOT. In our experiments, we compared the results of object recognition and pose estimation between the traditional SHOT descriptor and the MSG-SHOT descriptor proposed in this paper. For RGB-D object dataset, the results of object recognition and pose estimation are shown in Table 2. When only the depth information is used to complete object recognition and pose estimation, the accuracy by SHOT descriptor is only 71.0%, while our method can reach 90.9%, which is a great improvement compared with the SHOT.

Fast Non-maximum Suppression for Point Cloud. To verify the effect of our PFNMS. We conducted corresponding ablation experiments and used our self-made multi-target orange dataset for testing. The test results are shown in Fig. 7. The result of unused PFNMS is on the left of Fig. 7. It can be seen from the figure that there are two duplicate candidate objects that have not been filtered. On the right of Fig. 7, the PFNMS are used to filter the repeated candidate objects. Finally, 6 orange objects are recognized, which is more accurate.

5 Conclusion

This paper introduced a method for object recognition and 6D pose estimation based on local features of point cloud. Compared with the original feature matching method based on local features, this method can expand the ability of local features from 3D point cloud to 2.5D depth information, and greatly improve the robustness and accuracy of object recognition and pose estimation.

With local features as the core, the task is divided into four parts: data preprocessing of point cloud, local feature calculating, feature matching, matching verification and candidate object selecting. For data preprocessing of point cloud, this paper introduces an adaptive voxel filter based on local resolution. Compared with traditional voxel filter or other down-sampling methods, this method can well solve the problem of different sparsity of point clouds. After that, based on the SHOT feature, a new descriptor MSG-SHOT is introduced in combination with the idea of multi-scale grouping, which improves the ability to extract local features. In addition, in the part of the selection of candidate object selecting, a fast non-maximum suppression algorithm for point cloud is developed. Compared with the conventional non-maximum suppression algorithm, it is more efficient and accurate for selecting candidate objects based on point cloud.

Finally, experiments are carried out on public datasets and self-made datasets. Compared with traditional feature matching methods based on local features and other advanced methods, we show the advantages of our method.

Acknowledgments. This work was partially funded by the National Key Research and Development Plan of China (No. 2018AAA0101000) and the National Natural Science Foundation of China under grant 62076028.

References

1. Rusu, R., Blodow, N., Marton, Z.: Aligning point cloud views using persistent feature histograms. In: 2008 IEEE/RSJ International Conference on Intelligent Robots and Systems, pp. 3384–3391. IEEE (2008)
2. Tombari, F., Salti, S., Stefano, L.: Unique signatures of histograms for local surface description. In: Daniilidis, K., Maragos, P., Paragios, N. (eds.) Computer Vision – ECCV 2010, vol. 6313, pp. 356–369. Springer, Berlin, Heidelberg (2010). https://doi.org/10.1007/978-3-642-15558-1_26
3. Salti, S., Tombari, F., Stefano, L.: SHOT: unique signatures of histograms for surface and texture description. Comput. Vis. Image Underst. **125**, 251–264 (2014)
4. Drost, B., Ulrich, M., Navab, N.: Model globally, match locally: efficient and robust 3D object recognition. In: 2010 IEEE Computer Society Conference on Computer Vision and Pattern Recognition, pp. 998–1005. IEEE (2010)
5. Guo, J., Xing, X., Quan, W.: Efficient center voting for object detection and 6D pose estimation in 3D point cloud. IEEE Trans. Image Process. **30**, 5072–5084 (2021)
6. You, Y., Shi, R., Wang, W.: CPPF: towards robust category-level 9D pose estimation in the wild. arXiv, preprint arXiv:2203.03089 (2022)
7. Weng, Y., Wang, H., Zhou, Q., Qin, Y., Duan, Y., Fan, Q.: Captra: category-level pose tracking for rigid and articulated objects from point clouds. In: Proceedings of the IEEE/CVF International Conference on Computer Vision, pp. 13209–13218 (2021)
8. Qin, W., Hu, Q., Zhuang, Z., Huang, H., Zhu, X., Han, L.: IPPE-PCR: a novel 6D pose estimation method based on point cloud repair for texture-less and occluded industrial parts. J. Intell. Manuf. 1–11(2022). https://doi.org/10.1007/s10845-022-01965-6
9. Wang, J., Chen, K., Dou, Q.: Category-level 6D object pose estimation via cascaded relation and recurrent reconstruction networks. In: 2021 IEEE/RSJ International Conference on Intelligent Robots and Systems, pp. 4807–4814. IEEE (2021)
10. Gao, G., Lauri, M., Hu, X., Zhang, J., Frintrop, S.: CloudAAE: learning 6D object pose regression with on-line data synthesis on point clouds. In: 2021 IEEE International Conference on Robotics and Automation, pp. 11081–11087. IEEE (2021)
11. Chen, W., Jia, X., Chang, H.J., Duan, J., Shen, L., Leonardis, A.: FS-Net: fast shape-based network for category-level 6D object pose estimation with decoupled rotation mechanism. In: Proceedings of the IEEE/CVF Conference on Computer Vision and Pattern Recognition, pp. 1581–1590. IEEE (2021)
12. Tombari, F., Stefano, L.: Object recognition in 3D scenes with occlusions and clutter by hough voting. In: 2010 Fourth Pacific-Rim Symposium on Image and Video Technology, pp. 349–355. IEEE (2010)
13. Qi, C., Yi, L., Su, H.: PointNet++: deep hierarchical feature learning on point sets in a metric space. In: Advances in Neural Information Processing Systems, vol. 30 (2017)
14. Bodla, N., Singh, B., Chellappa, R.: Soft-NMS—improving object detection with one line of code. In: 2017 IEEE International Conference on Computer Vision (ICCV), pp. 5562–5570. IEEE (2017)
15. Lai, K., Bo, L., Ren, X., Fox, D.: A large-scale hierarchical multi-view RGB-D object dataset. In: 2011 IEEE International Conference on Robotics and Automation, pp. 1817–1824. IEEE (2011)
16. Bo, L., Ren, X., Fox, D.: Depth kernel descriptors for object recognition. In: IEEE/RSJ International Conference on Intelligent Robots and Systems, pp. 821–826. IEEE (2011)
17. Lai, K., Bo, L., Ren, X.: RGB-D object recognition: Features, algorithms, and a large scale benchmark. In: Fossati, A., Gall, J., Grabner, H., Ren, X., Konolige, K. (eds.) Consumer Depth Cameras for Computer Vision, pp. 167–192. Springer, London (2013). https://doi.org/10.1007/978-1-4471-4640-7_9

18. Blum, M., Springenberg, J., Wülfing, J.: A learned feature descriptor for object recognition in RGB-D data. In: IEEE International Conference on Robotics and Automation, pp. 1298–1303. IEEE (2012)

19. Bo, L., Ren, X., Fox, D.: Hierarchical matching pursuit for image classification: architecture and fast algorithms. In: Advances in Neural Information Processing Systems, vol. 24 (2011)

20. Bo, L., Ren, X., Fox, D.: Unsupervised feature learning for RGB-D based object recognition. In: Desai, J., Dudek, G., Khatib, O., Kumar, V. (eds.) Experimental Robotics, vol. 88, pp. 387–402. Springer, Cham (2013). https://doi.org/10.1007/978-3-319-00065-7_27

Machine Learning in Human-Robot Collaboration

Motion Regulation
for Single-Leader-Dual-Follower
Teleoperation in Flipping Manipulation

Haifeng Huang[1], Junbao Gan[1], Chao Zeng[2], and Chenguang Yang[1(✉)]

[1] College of Automation Science and Engineering,
South China University of Technology, Guangzhou 510640, China
cyang@ieee.org
[2] School of Automation, Guangdong University of Technology,
Guangzhou 510520, China

Abstract. In order to organically combine single leader dual follower teleoperation with force information during human-robot interaction (HRI), this paper proposes a single leader dual follower teleoperation system based on force control, which is applied to the common box flipping task in the logistics industry. The relative pose increment method is adopted to realize the leader-follower attitude matching, which is more flexible and reliable than the traditional method, and makes the operator perform the teleoperation task comfortably. Under the background that there is no information sharing between follower arms, a force controller is designed to generate a reference trajectory for the assisting follower robot (AFR) based on the contact force. The AFR can actively move to the desired position corresponding to the required contact force in the process of flipping the box, so as to realize the coordination during HRI.

Keywords: Teleoperation systems control · Force control · Single leader dual follower · Box flipping

1 Introduction

In recent years, teleoperation technology has developed rapidly, which has been widely used in complex unstructured environment operation and is used to solve the problems of weak robot autonomy, uncontrollable interaction with the environment and poor cooperation [9,16]. Its application scope has been expanded from the initial industrial field to manufacturing [12], medical care [3], aerospace [1] and marine exploration [2].

Since Goertz built the first leader-follower remote controller in 1940 [4], the field of remote control has experienced several stages from understanding the

This work was supported in part by Foshan Science and Technology Innovation Team Special Project under Grant 2018IT100322, in part by Industrial Key Technologies R & D Program of Foshan under Grant 2020001006496 and Grant 2020001006308, and in part by the National Nature Science Foundation under Grant 62003096.

H. Liu et al. (Eds.): ICIRA 2022, LNAI 13458, pp. 483–495, 2022.
https://doi.org/10.1007/978-3-031-13841-6_44

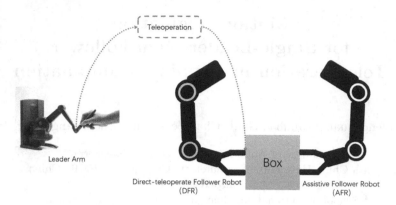

Fig. 1. Single leader dual follower teleoperation system

interaction between human and robot to the field of basic control theory. In teleoperation system, local operator and remote robot play the roles of manipulator and executioner respectively, so it is also called leader-follower mode. In the leader-follower mode, using the characteristics of ergonomic principles for reference, dual arms are used for cooperative teleoperation, which has stronger dexterity, higher reliability, and greater operation space and bearing capacity. This makes the dual arm teleoperation robot not only perform delicate and complex tasks, but also have the ability of coordination and dexterous operation similar to humans. Therefore, the single leader and dual follower teleoperation system provides a solution to the difficulties such as the highly complex and unpredictable working environment and the poor interaction performances between the robot and the environment, which has attracted the discussion and research of experts and scholars in the field of robot. Compared with multi leader and multi follower teleoperation [6,10], using one leader robot for teleoperation task requires less attention of the operator, which is conducive to reducing the burden of the operator; Compared with single leader single follower teleoperation [8] and multi leader single follower teleoperation [7], it can handle more complex tasks due to the cooperation of two follower robots.

The single leader dual follower teleoperation system is usually composed of three robots [13], as shown in Fig. 1. One of them is the teleoperation leader arm, and the other two are the teleoperation follower arm. The teleoperation main arm is controlled by the operator, and the two teleoperation follower arms are operated remotely according to the leader arm. Two follower arms usually play different roles when performing tasks. One is directed-teleoperate follower robot (DFR), and the other one is assistive follower robot (AFR) which provides assistance to DFR.

Most of the above teleoperation methods are based on the matching between leader and follower for position control of the robot. However, in most practical application scenarios (e.g. polishing, grinding, flipping), it is not enough to control the robot's position, what is needed is the precise control of the force.

Therefore, in academic research, we need to consider not only robot position control, but also reasonable control of robot forces. [18] proposes a bionic method to adjust the impedance of the robot. It is combined with an impedance model to control the force of the robot end-effector in real time. [17] proposes a novel learning and control framework that is able to adjust the impedance and force magnitude and reduce the influence of external disturbances during the robot's recurrence process. [14] proposed a sensorless admittance control strategy, which designed a force observer to estimate the external torque. Its control effect is comparable to the ordinary admittance control.

Therefore, this paper proposes a single leader dual follower teleoperation system based on force control, which is applied to the common box flipping task in the logistics industry. We use the method of relative pose increment to match the workspace from teleoperation equipment to manipulator, which can be realized according to some sign events (such as press a button) for the leader-follower pose matching. Compared with the traditional method of teleoperation matching the whole task space, the proposed method makes the teleoperation more flexible and reliable, and enables the operator to perform the teleoperation task comfortably, so as to improve the comfort in the process of teleoperation.

Under the assumption that there is no information sharing between follower arms, a force controller is designed based on the contact force to generate a reference trajectory for AFR. The force received by AFR in the process of box flipping is used to make it actively move to the correct position corresponding to the required contact force, without considering the movement of DFR, unknown parameters of the object and time-varying internal force, so as to realize the coordination between the human user and the robot.

The rest of this paper is organized as follows: In Sect. 2, fundamentals of teleoperation system is introduced. Section 3 introduces the box flipping task based on force control. Section 4 verifies the effectiveness of our proposed method through experiments on a Baxter robot. Section 5 concludes the paper.

2 Fundamentals of Teleoperation System

The teleoperation system adopts leader-follower control structure. It samples the information of the following robot and sends it to the central processing computer. At the same time, it applies feedback force to the haptic device [5]. In this way, the operator can manipulate the object in a remote position according to visual and tactile feedback.

The traditional teleoperation space matching is generally to match the whole task space [15]. This brings two problems: first, the magnification factor from the teleoperation space to the whole task space is fixed, and sometimes it is difficult to meet the delicate operation; Second, the operator's teleoperation experience is not considered. In the process of performing teleoperation tasks, some teleoperation postures are encountered that are not ergonomic or bring uncomfortable feeling to the operator. This requires re-matching the tele-operation task space to enable the operator to continue performing the task comfortably. Therefore, the relative pose increment method is adopted to keep the attitude of the tele-operation equipment consistent with that of the end of the manipulator through coordinate transformation. The matching between the teleoperation equipment and the workspace of the manipulator can be realized according to some flag events (such as buttons), so as to realize the matching of the leader-follower attitude. After each match, the task space can be re-matched, making the tele-operation more flexible and reliable. When some uncomfortable postures are encountered in the process of teleoperation, the task space can be re-matched by marking events, so that the operator can continue to perform teleoperation tasks with comfortable postures.

2.1   Position Matching

The position relationship between teleoperation main boom and DFR is shown in the following formula.

$$^{DE}\triangle X_D = \alpha \cdot ^{DE}_{TE}R \cdot ^{TE}\triangle X_T \tag{1}$$

where DE is the end coordinate system of DFR, TE is the end coordinate system of the teleoperation leader arm, $^{DE}\triangle X_D = [\triangle x_D, \triangle y_D, \triangle z_D]^T$ is the displacement of DFR, $^{TE}\triangle X_T = [\triangle x_T, \triangle y_T, \triangle z_T]^T$ is the displacement of teleoperation leader arm, $\alpha = diag\{\alpha_x, \alpha_y, \alpha_z\}$ is the magnification factor, $^{DE}_{TE}R$ is the rotation matrix from the base coordinates of the teleoperation equipment to the base coordinates of the DFR.

The relative displacement between the teleoperation leader arm and DFR is

$$^{DE}\triangle X_D = ^{DE}X_{D,t} - ^{DE}X_{D,t_0} \tag{2}$$

$$^{TE}\triangle X_T = ^{TE}X_{T,t} - ^{TE}X_{T,t_0} \tag{3}$$

where the subscript t indicates the time index, $^{DE}\triangle X_{D,t}$ is the initial position at time t, and $^{DE}\triangle X_{D,t_0}$ is the initial position of the DFR at time t_0. Similarly, $^{TE}\triangle X_{T,t}$ is the expected position of the teleoperation leader arm at time t and $^{TE}\triangle X_{T,t_0}$ is the initial position of the teleoperation leader arm at time t_0.

Therefore, through the matching of workspace, the displacement of DFR end can be obtained according to the end displacement increment of teleoperation main arm.

$$\begin{aligned}^{DE}X_{D,t} &= ^{DE}X_{D,t_0} + ^{DE}\triangle X_D \\ &= ^{DE}X_{D,t_0} + \alpha \cdot ^{DE}_{TE}R \cdot \left(^{TE}X_{T,t} - ^{TE}X_{T,t_0}\right)\end{aligned} \tag{4}$$

2.2   Direction Matching

In order to enhance the immersion of teleoperation, it is often necessary to control the end attitude of follower arm robot through the end attitude of tele-operation device. The coordinate system of its teleoperation system is shown in

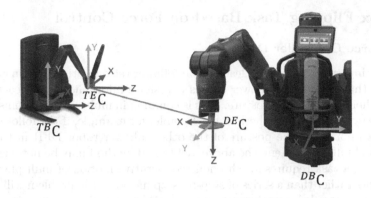

Fig. 2. The coordinate system in a teleoperation system.

Fig. 2. Equation (6) can be deduced according to the relationship between the teleoperation leader arm base coordinate system ^{TB}C, teleoperation leader arm end coordinate system ^{TE}C, DFR base coordinate system ^{DB}C and DFR end coordinate system ^{DE}C.

$$_{TE}^{DE}R = {}_{DB}^{DE}R \cdot {}_{TB}^{DB}R \cdot {}_{TE}^{TB}R \tag{5}$$

where $_{TB}^{DB}R$ is determined by the base coordinate system of teleoperation leader arm and DFR base coordinate system. In the actual physical environment, it is easy to obtain the rotation matrix $_{TB}^{TE}R$ from the base coordinate system of the teleoperation leader arm to the end coordinate system of the teleoperation leader arm and the rotation matrix $_{DB}^{DE}R$ from the DFR base coordinate system to the DFR end coordinate system. Equation (6) can be converted to

$$\begin{aligned} _{TE}^{DE}R &= \left(_{DE}^{DB}R \right)^{-1} \times {}_{TB}^{DB}R \times {}_{TE}^{TB}R \\ &= \left(_{DE}^{DB}R_{t_0} \right)^{-1} \times {}_{TB}^{DB}R \times R_{t_0} \end{aligned} \tag{6}$$

where t_0 is the start time of the remote operation. According to the Eq. (7), as long as the relationship between the posture of the teleoperation leader arm and the posture of the DFR is established at the beginning time t_0, the corresponding relationship between the leader arm and the DFR can be determined. Therefore, some flag events can be displayed in t_0 resets the leader-follower attitude correspondence, so as to realize the overall relative direction matching, which could make the operator perform teleoperation tasks with a comfortable posture continually.

3 Box Flipping Task Based on Force Control

3.1 Force Controller Design

The existing research of single leader dual follower teleoperation system generally assumes that the leader-follower robots can share information with each other, such as their position and posture. This is common in multi robot systems (MRS) [11]. However, if this hypothesis is not tenable, for example, if the follower robot AFR does not know the posture of the other follower robot DFR in the single leader dual follower system, the above mentioned method may be not feasible. In addition, if a task requires synchronous cooperative motion of multiple follower arm robots rather than a series of step-by-step motions, the problem will become more challenging. It is very important to solve these problems in the single leader dual follower teleoperation system, mainly for the following two reasons: firstly, it is very cumbersome to calibrate the communication between follower robots; Secondly, many real-world applications require synchronous cooperative motion between arm robots. In this paper, two follower robots DFR and AFR do not know the posture of their partners, and their cooperation is only based on contact force.

Therefore, a force controller is designed to generate reference trajectory for AFR. Using the force received by AFR in the process of box flipping, AFR can actively move to the correct position corresponding to the required contact force, regardless of the movement of DFR, unknown parameters of the object and time-varying internal force. The force controller is set as follows:

$$M_e(\ddot{x} - \ddot{x}_d) + C_e(\dot{x} - \dot{x}_d) + G_e(x - x_d) = F - F_d \tag{7}$$

where F is the force collected from the sensor from the operator, F_d is the desired force, M_e is the inertia matrix of the environment, C_e is the damping matrix of the environment, G_e is the stiffness matrix, x, $\dot{x}$, $\ddot{x}$ represent position, velocity and acceleration respectively. Let the position error be $e_x = x - x_d$ and the force error be $F_e = F - F_d$, the Eq. (9) can be expressed as:

$$M_e\ddot{e}_x + C_e\dot{e}_x + G_e e_x = F_e \tag{8}$$

The acceleration of the robot end effector is

$$\begin{aligned}\ddot{e}_x &= M_e^{-1}(F_e - C_e\dot{e}_x - G_e e_x) \\ &= M_e^{-1}F_e - M_e^{-1}C_e\dot{e}_x - M_e^{-1}G_e e_x\end{aligned} \tag{9}$$

We could set $x_{t_0} = x_{d,t_0}$ during initialization, and then we get $e_{x,t_0} = \dot{e}_{x,t_0} = \ddot{e}_{x,t_0} = 0$. The force error F_e changes because the influence of human force applied to the robot end effector, which could get the acceleration error $\ddot{e}_x$ under different forces through Eq. (1). By integrating the acceleration error and quadratic integration, we can get the velocity error $\dot{e}_x$ and position error e_x respectively, so we can get the displacement in Cartesian space.

$$\dot{e}_{x,t_n} = \dot{e}_{x,t_{n-1}} + \ddot{e}_{x,t_n} \cdot dt \tag{10}$$

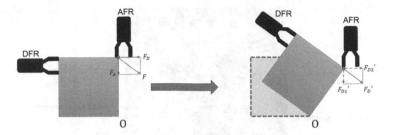

Fig. 3. Force analysis in the flipping task.

$$e_{x,t_n} = e_{x,t_{n-1}} + \dot{e}_{x,t_n} \cdot dt \qquad (11)$$

$$x_{t_n} = x_{t_{n-1}} + e_{x,t_n} \qquad (12)$$

where dt is the integration time, $x_{t_{n-1}}$, $e_{x,t_{n-1}}$, $\dot{e}_{x,t_{n-1}}$ are position, position error and speed error respectively at time t_{n-1} and x_{t_n}, e_{x,t_n}, $\dot{e}_{x,t_n}$ are position, position error and speed error respectively at time t_n.

3.2 Force Analysis of Box Flipping Task

In order to successfully complete the box flipping task, the robot must meet the following assumptions:

Assumption 1: both arms need to coordinate forces to turn the box upward.
Assumption 2: the ends of both arms always keep in contact with the box, and the contact points move in a circle around point O without relative sliding during box flipping.
Assumption 3: the ends of both arms move only on a two-dimensional plane during box flipping.

When operating the manipulator in the task of box flipping, the force analysis is shown in Fig. 3. Before the task starts, AFR needs to contact the box and provide corresponding pressure F_A to fix the box at point O without relative sliding. The position and posture of the DFR are remotely controlled through the teleoperation system to perform the box flipping task and provide thrust F_D, forming an oblique downward resultant force of F. At this time, if assumption 1 is met, the box starts to turn upward. The position and posture of DFR are remotely controlled through the teleoperation system. And we manipulate the DFR to provide force F_D, forming an oblique downward resultant force of F, which meet the hypothesis 1 and make the box start to turn upward. After the box flipping task starts, the ends of both arms always keep in contact with the box and the contact points move in a circle around the point O, which meet the assumption 2. At this time, the box only receives the force F'_D of DFR, and the force decomposition of the force F'_D can obtain F'_{D1} and F'_{D2}. The force F'_{D1} provide power for the flipping task, so that the flipping actions can continue. F'_{D2} is the force received by AFR, which is subtracted from the expected force

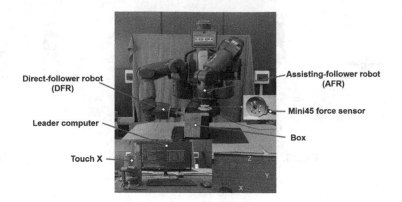

Fig. 4. Experimental setup.

obtained from the previous teaching as the force error F_e. Combined with the Eq. (9) and Eq. (1), AFR can actively move to the correct position corresponding to the required contact force according to the magnitude of the external force. Then it can assist DFR to perform the box flipping task only in the two-dimensional plane, which meets the assumption 3. The above assumptions are met, so the box flipping task can be completed smoothly.

4   Experiment

4.1   Experimental Setup

The experimental setup is shown in Fig. 4. TouchX is used as the leader device, and Baxter is the follower robot in the teleoperation system. The TouchX has six degrees of freedom (DOFs), the first and last three DOFs control the position and orientation of the end-effector, respectively. In addition, a stylus with a button is connected to the end-effector. The right arm of the Baxter robot is used as the DFR, and the left arm is the AFR, which is controlled autonomously by the designed controller. ATI mini45, a force sensor installed at the end of Baxter's left arm, is used to measure the interactive force of the robot arm and taken as a feedback signal. As shown in Fig. 5, we also prepared three different materials (glass, cardboard and sandpaper) to change the operating environment for the box flipping task. The glass has a smoother surface, the cardboard is relatively rougher, and the sandpaper has the largest coefficient of friction.

4.2   Experimental Results

Teleoperation. To improve the ergonomics and the precision of the teleoperation, we proposed the relative pose transformation method. We compare it with the method of matching the whole workspace, taking the box flipping task as the experimental scenario. The process of the experiment is shown in Fig. 7 and Fig. 6.

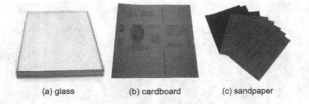

(a) glass   (b) cardboard   (c) sandpaper

Fig. 5. Three different materials.

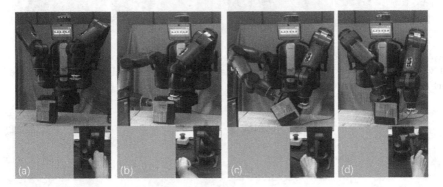

Fig. 6. The method of matching the whole workspace. (a) initial pose; (b) working pose; (c) uncomortably flip the box; (d) final pose.

When the operator teleoperates a follower to flip a box, a more ergonomic and precise teleoperation is achieved by using the proposed method (Fig. 7), compared with the method that matches the whole workspaces (Fig. 6). Specifically, as shown in Figs. 7(c) and 6(c), we can see that when flipping the box, the proposed method provides a more ergonomical operating pose. In addition, it is easier for the operator to manipulate the holding tool of the DFR to fit closely to the box through the proposal method, achieving more effective teleoperation. In the process of teleoperation, the operator's operating feeling will undoubtedly influence the accuracy of the operation. A more ergonomic relative posture matching is obviously better in terms of accuracy. The quality of teleoperation on DFR will influence the effectiveness of AFR assistance to a certain extent, so we can also reflect the difference between the two teleoperation techniques side-by-side from the tracking effect of AFR on force. The force of AFR is shown in Fig. 8. As can be seen from Fig. 8, the force curves under both methods track on the desired force from an overall view, but the force tracking error of the proposed method is smaller, which indicates that the proposed method is more advantageous in terms of operational accuracy.

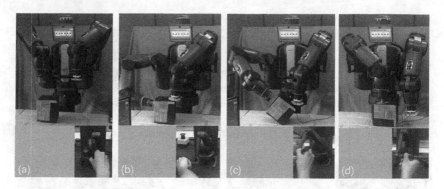

Fig. 7. The relative pose transformation technique. (a) initial pose; (b) working pose; (c) working pose but the operator can re-set an ergonomic initial operating pose to perform the task; (d) final pose.

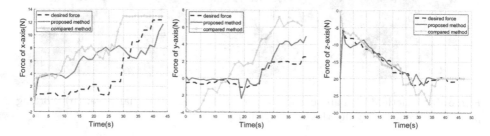

Fig. 8. The measured force signals by using different methods.

Force Control. This step is mainly to verify the effectiveness of the force control method and to observe the performances in different environments. We performed the box flipping task on the glass, on the cardboard and on the sandpaper, respectively. This set of experiments exemplifies the performance of the proposed method on planes with different degrees of smoothness. The experimental result is shown in Fig. 9. As expected, Baxter succeeded in flipping the boxes smoothly and steadily on different planes. With the relative pose transformation technique and the force controller, the end-effectors of Baxter's two arms are able to keep in contact with the box during the flipping process. The force profiles of the AFR is shown in Fig. 10. The track performance of AFR in the three environments is quite good, but there is a certain amount of variation in the tracking error of the force in different environments. Since this is a human-in-the-loop teleoperation system, a certain amount of error is acceptable and adjustable. Overall, the methods proposed in this paper is effective and feasible.

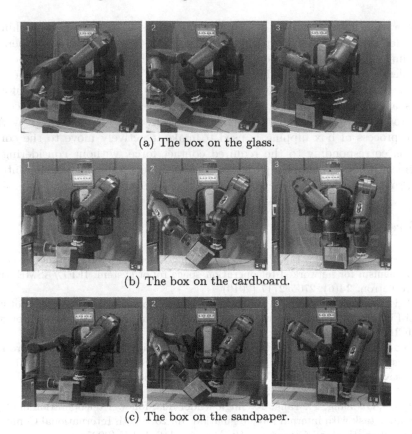

(a) The box on the glass.

(b) The box on the cardboard.

(c) The box on the sandpaper.

Fig. 9. The experimental results of box-flipping on different materials.

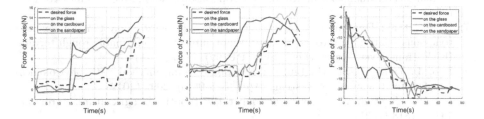

Fig. 10. The force at the end-effector of the AFR in different environments.

5   Conclusion

In this paper, we combine single leader and dual follower teleoperation system with force control and propose a novel teleoperation system that can be used for box flipping. For the common box flipping task in the logistics industry, this paper analyzes the force of dual arm coordinated control, and then adopts the relative pose increment to realize the matching of the workspace from the teleoperation equipment to the manipulator so as to realize the matching of leader-follower attitude. Compared with the traditional method of teleoperation matching the whole task space, the proposed method makes the teleoperation more flexible and reliable, and enables the operator to perform the teleoperation task in a more comfortable way. Under the assumption that there is no information sharing between arms, a force controller is designed based on the contact force to generate a reference trajectory for AFR. The force received by AFR in the process of box flipping is used to make it actively move to the correct position corresponding to the required contact force, without considering the movement of DFR, unknown parameters of the object and time-varying internal force, so as to realize the coordination between the human user and the robot.

References

1. Chen, H., Huang, P., Liu, Z.: Mode switching-based symmetric predictive control mechanism for networked teleoperation space robot system. IEEE/ASME Trans. Mechatron. **24**(6), 2706–2717 (2019)
2. Codd-Downey, R., Jenkin, M.: Wireless teleoperation of an underwater robot using Li-Fi. In: 2018 IEEE International conference on information and automation (ICIA), pp. 859–864. IEEE (2018)
3. Guo, J., Liu, C., Poignet, P.: A scaled bilateral teleoperation system for robotic-assisted surgery with time delay. J. Intell. Robot. Syst. **95**(1), 165–192 (2019)
4. Hokayem, P.F., Spong, M.W.: Bilateral teleoperation: an historical survey. Automatica **42**(12), 2035–2057 (2006)
5. Huang, D., Jiang, Y., Yang, C.: Single-leader-dual-follower teleoperation in object-holding task with internal force regulation. In: 2021 26th International Conference on Automation and Computing (ICAC), pp. 1–6. IEEE (2021)
6. Huang, P., Dai, P., Lu, Z., Liu, Z.: Asymmetric wave variable compensation method in dual-master-dual-slave multilateral teleoperation system. Mechatronics **49**, 1–10 (2018)
7. Li, J., et al.: Dual-master/single-slave haptic teleoperation system for semiautonomous bilateral control of hexapod robot subject to deformable rough terrain. IEEE Trans. Syst. Man Cybern. Syst. **PP**(99), 1–15 (2021)
8. Luo, J., Yang, C., Su, H., Liu, C.: A robot learning method with physiological interface for teleoperation systems. Appl. Sci. **9**(10), 2099 (2019)
9. Lytridis, C., et al.: An overview of cooperative robotics in agriculture. Agronomy **11**(9), 1818 (2021)
10. Minelli, M., Ferraguti, F., Piccinelli, N., Muradore, R., Secchi, C.: An energy-shared two-layer approach for multi-master-multi-slave bilateral teleoperation systems. In: 2019 International Conference on Robotics and Automation (ICRA), pp. 423–429. IEEE (2019)
11. Sanchez, D., Wan, W., Harada, K.: Towards tethered tool manipulation planning with the help of a tool balancer. Robotics **9**(1), 11 (2020)
12. Solanes, J.E., Muñoz, A., Gracia, L., Martí, A., Girbés-Juan, V., Tornero, J.: Teleoperation of industrial robot manipulators based on augmented reality. Int. J. Adv. Manuf. Technol. **111**(3), 1077–1097 (2020)
13. Sun, D., Liao, Q., Loutfi, A.: Single master bimanual teleoperation system with efficient regulation. IEEE Trans. Robot. **36**(4), 1022–1037 (2020)

14. Yang, C., Peng, G., Cheng, L., Na, J., Li, Z.: Force sensorless admittance control for teleoperation of uncertain robot manipulator using neural networks. IEEE Trans. Syst. Man Cybern. Syst. **51**(5), 3282–3292 (2021)
15. Yang, C., Wang, X., Li, Z., Li, Y., Su, C.Y.: Teleoperation control based on combination of wave variable and neural networks. IEEE Trans. Syst. Man Cybern. Syst. **47**(8), 2125–2136 (2016)
16. Yu, X., Zhang, S., Sun, L., Wang, Y., Xue, C., Li, B.: Cooperative control of dual-arm robots in different human-robot collaborative tasks. Assembly Autom. **40**(1), 95–104 (2019)
17. Zeng, C., Li, Y., Guo, J., Huang, Z., Wang, N., Yang, C.: A unified parametric representation for robotic compliant skills with adaptation of impedance and force. IEEE/ASME Trans. Mechatron. **27**(2), 623–633 (2021)
18. Zeng, C., Yang, C., Chen, Z.: Bio-inspired robotic impedance adaptation for human-robot collaborative tasks. SCIENCE CHINA Inf. Sci. **63**(7), 1–10 (2020). https://doi.org/10.1007/s11432-019-2748-x

An Autonomous Obstacle Avoidance Method for Dual-Arm Surgical Robot Based on the Improved Artificial Potential Field Method

Qiao Chen, Yiwei Liu[⊠], and Peng Wang

State Key Laboratory of Robotics and System, Harbin Institute of Technology, West Dazhi Street, Harbin 150001, China
lyw@hit.edu.cn

Abstract. Most surgical robots adopt a simple master-slave control method, and their forms are transitioning from non-autonomous to semi-autonomous states. Motion planning and obstacle avoidance are essential research directions. In this regard, an obstacle avoidance method for a dual-arm surgical robot based on an improved artificial potential field is proposed. First, improve the artificial potential field method. Considering the working posture of the dual-arm surgical robot in the limited workspace, respectively apply the gravitational potential field and the repulsive potential field to each joint to achieve precise control. Secondly, in terms of collision detection, use the convex hull algorithm to convex the model, and use the GJK algorithm to calculate the distance between the obstacle and the equivalent convex body of the manipulator. The distance threshold can be manually set to alert when a collision is imminent. Besides, the motion is steady by using the adaptive step size. An improved splicing path method is proposed to make the manipulator jump out of the local minimum and improve the planning efficiency. Finally, smooth the resulting path and ensure the manipulator doesn't collide. Experiments show that this study can make the dual-arm surgical robot move relatively smoothly on avoiding obstacles, which provides a reference for the automation of surgical robots.

Keywords: Obstacle avoidance · Artificial potential field method · Surgical robot · Dual-arm

1 Introduction

With the continuous development and progress of robotic technology, surgical operations are currently developing from open surgery through regular minimally invasive surgery to robot-assisted minimally invasive surgery, which has advantages of precise operation and vital flexibility [1]. Dual-arm collaborative robots are often used in industry, service, and the military [2]. The dual-arm is complex, so the efficient collision algorithm and trajectory optimization method need further exploration.

H. Liu et al. (Eds.): ICIRA 2022, LNAI 13458, pp. 496–508, 2022.
https://doi.org/10.1007/978-3-031-13841-6_45

Most of the motion control methods of surgical robots are simple master-slave tele-operation control methods. Without the function of autonomous obstacle avoidance, they may not be able to complete the specified surgical work. At present, many surgical robots are developing in the direction of autonomous obstacle avoidance. For example, da Vinci Xi surgical robot [3] uses the ECM motion planner to complete obstacle avoidance. LP Company adopts the robot surgical collision detection system [4]. Tsinghua University aims for an obstacle avoidance planning method and system based on the RRT algorithm [5] for Stereotaxic surgery on the head.

The obstacle avoidance of the manipulator is mostly realized in path planning. The manipulator's path planning algorithm [6] mainly includes the artificial potential field method, A* algorithm, and RRT algorithm. However, the A* algorithm cannot guarantee the optimal path, and the RRT algorithm is difficult to find a path in a narrow environment. Both algorithms need to obtain global information in advance, and the algorithm overhead is high. In comparison, although the artificial potential field method has the local minimum problem, its structure is simple, the algorithm efficiency is high, and it is more suitable for the path planning of multi-joint manipulators.

In recent years, scholars have proposed different improved algorithms based on the artificial potential field method. Reference [7] proposes a randomization method. If the manipulator traps in a local minimum, it will move to a random joint. Some scholars improve the gravitational field coefficient [8], set up virtual target points [9], and use the RRT algorithm to traverse the reachable points in the workspace [10] to escape from the local minimum. However, both the random algorithm and the virtual point increase the calculation amount of the algorithm, and there is a problem with path oscillation.

This study proposes an obstacle avoidance method for a dual-arm surgical robot based on an improved artificial potential field. Potential field act on the six joints to protect the normal operation of the manipulator. Secondly, in terms of obstacle avoidance, unlike the rough calculation, the more accurate GJK algorithm is used to calculate the distance between two convex bodies (the manipulator and the obstacle), which improves the accuracy. In addition, propose a method of splicing paths to jump out of the local minimum, which can adjust the end-posture and enhance the search efficiency. Finally, use an effective trajectory smoothing method to solve the oscillation problem.

2 Modeling

The model establishment is mainly divided into three parts. The kinematic model of the double manipulator is established based on the physical model. The workspace of both arms was analyzed using the Monte Carlo method. Take the end-effector of the surgical robot, the surrounding table, and cameras as obstacles established by using the convex hull algorithm method.

2.1 Kinematics Modeling of Dual Manipulators

The model includes an operating table and two manipulators. The UR3 and UR5 are used as the research objects. The simple model is shown in Fig. 1.

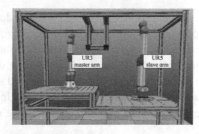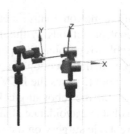

Fig. 1. The image on the left is the simple model, and the image on the right is the dual-arm model established by the D-H method.

The kinematics model of the manipulator is established by the standard D-H method. According to the theory of forward kinematics, the homogeneous transformation matrix between two adjacent links is obtained, and establish the transformation matrix from the end-effector to the base coordinate system.

$$T_n^0(q) = \begin{bmatrix} R_n^0(q) & o_n^0(q) \\ 0 & 1 \end{bmatrix} \tag{1}$$

where q is a vector of joint variables, R_n^0 is the attitude of end-effector attitude, and o_n^0 is the position of end-effector.

$$\xi = J\dot{q} \tag{2}$$

$$\xi = \begin{bmatrix} v_n^0 \\ \omega_n^0 \end{bmatrix} J = \begin{bmatrix} J_v \\ J_\omega \end{bmatrix} \tag{3}$$

J is the Jacobian matrix, ξ is the vector of the linear and angular velocity of the end-effector, $\dot{q}$ is the joint velocity vector.

2.2 Workspace with Dual Robotic Arms

The working space of the manipulators is simulated by the Monte Carlo method [11]. Take 30,000 random points to obtain the point cloud pictures. The simulation shows some overlap in the cooperation process, having the possibility of collision, and the collision problem needs to be considered (Fig. 2).

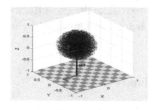

(a) Master arm workspace   (b) Dual-arm workspace

Fig. 2. Workspace point cloud pictures

2.3 Convex Hull Algorithm to Build Obstacle Model

In many cases, the obstacle is irregular, and accurate modeling is cumbersome and unnecessary. The operating table is a common obstacle based on the working environment, so choose a cuboid to simplify the model. Use the convex hull algorithm [12] on the end-effector to reduce the volume of obstacles as much as possible to expand the corresponding movement space. The puncture needle model is as shown in Fig. 3.

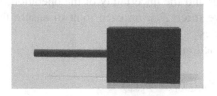
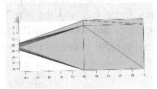

(a) Simplified model of puncture needle   (b) Puncture needle convexity model

Fig. 3. Puncture needle model diagram

Wrap the manipulator with the cylinder, because the cylinder is convex and the points on the circumference can represent its position. According to the established D-H model, seven position-planes (six joints and one base) are selected to make links equivalent to cylindrical surfaces. Figure 4 shows the equivalent cylinder of links diagram.

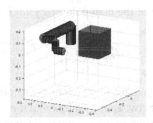

Fig. 4. Schematic diagram of the equivalent cylindrical surface of links

3 Autonomous Obstacle Avoidance

The autonomous obstacle avoidance method for a dual-arm surgical robot in this paper is mainly divided into four aspects. First, build the artificial potential field method. Then, add the adaptive step size to improve the adaptability of the motion of the manipulator. Secondly, propose the improved splicing path algorithm to deal with the local minimum problem. Thirdly, adopt a collision detection strategy with the GJK algorithm to ensure the accuracy of obstacle avoidance. Finally, preprocess the path.

3.1 Improved Artificial Potential Field Method Function

The basic idea of the artificial potential field method [13] is to search for the collision-free path by searching for the descending direction of the potential field function. The potential field is formed by the combined action of the gravitational field built around the target pose and the repulsive force field built around the obstacle.

It is difficult to express the specific position information of obstacles in the joint space. Therefore, the potential field is constructed in the Cartesian space. Considering the limited workspace of the manipulator and the uncertainty of the operation, act the gravitational force F_{att} and the repulsive force F_{rep} on each joint to ensure that the manipulator does not collide with obstacles.

The gravitational potential energy function is established as:

$$U_{att}(q) = \frac{1}{2}K_{att}(p(q) - p_{goal})^2 \tag{4}$$

The gravity function is:

$$F_{att}(q) = -\nabla U_{att}(q) = -K_{att}(p(q) - p_{goal}) \tag{5}$$

In the above equation, K_{att} is the gravitational parameter, p_{goal} is the target position of the joint coordinates solved by positive kinematics, q is the angle of each joint during the movement of the manipulator, and p is the real-time position of joint coordinates solved by forward kinematics.

The repulsive potential energy function between the obstacle and each equivalent cylindrical surface of the manipulator's joint is:

$$U_{rep}^n(i) = \begin{cases} \frac{1}{2}K_{rep}(\frac{1}{d_i^n} - \frac{1}{d_0})^2, & d_i^n < d_0 \\ 0, & d_i^n > d_0 \end{cases} \tag{6}$$

where K_{rep} is the repulsion parameter, i is the joint's number, n is the number of obstacles, d_i^n is the distance between the ith link and the obstacle, d_0 is the set repulsion threshold distance, $U_{rep}^n(i)$ is the repulsion potential energy of the nth obstacle acting on the link i of the manipulator. The repulsion function is:

$$F_{rep}^n(i) = -\nabla U_{rep}^n(i) = \begin{cases} -K_{rep}(\frac{1}{d_i^n} - \frac{1}{d_0})(\frac{1}{d_i^n})^2 \vec{d}_i^n, & d_i^n < d_0 \\ 0, & d_i^n > d_0 \end{cases} \tag{7}$$

where $\vec{d}_i^n$ is the unit vector, and the direction is from the ith link to the closest point on the obstacle's surface (n). Through the principle of virtual work, force and joint moment can be connected by the transposition of the Jacobian matrix as follows:

$$\tau = J^T F^T \tag{8}$$

The resultant force of the above two potential fields is

$$F_{to} = \sum_{i=1}^m F_{att} + \sum_{n=1}^k \sum_{i=1}^m F_{rep} \tag{9}$$

$$F_{total} = [F_{total}, \; nx, \; ny, \; nz] \tag{10}$$

Thus, the resultant moment is obtained as

$$\tau_{total} = \sum_{i=1}^{n} J^T F_{total}{}^T \tag{11}$$

From this, the joint angle at the next moment can be calculated

$$q_{next} = q_{current} + step \frac{\tau_{total}}{\| \tau_{total} \|} \tag{12}$$

From the above formula, the step size is a critical factor in ensuring the stable movement of the manipulator and improving the search efficiency. Therefore, use the adaptive step size to enhance the algorithm. To reasonably avoid obstacles in limited space, choose the distance from the manipulator to the obstacle for planning, and adopt the power function for adaptive optimization.

$$\delta(\theta) = \| d_i^n \| \tag{13}$$

$$Step - min(\alpha \delta(\theta) exp(-\beta \delta(\theta)), Step_{max}) \tag{14}$$

The step size is adjusted by the proportional coefficients α, β (Determine the appropriate value by testing), so that within the workspace and obstacle avoidance range, the farther the distance from the manipulator to the obstacle is, the larger the step size is, otherwise, the smaller. Therefore, the efficiency is improved. And the maximum step size is a fixed value $Step_{max}$, which can play a role in constraining smoothness.

3.2 The Improved Splicing Path Algorithm Handles the Local Minima Problem

First, determine whether to fall into a local minimum and use the heuristic method to identify it. Three consecutive q^i are located in a small region in the configuration space, and there may be a local minimum nearby. ε_m is a small positive number. When the above formula is satisfied, the local minimum is reached.

$$\| q^i - q^{i+n} \| < \varepsilon_m \; n = 1, 2, 3 \tag{15}$$

To escape from the local minimum, we propose a method of splicing paths. The splicing path is added when running to the local minimum point A. The form is as follows: select the target point B as one part of the remaining path, and use the quintic polynomial trajectory to plan the two points A and B. The function is as follows:

$$\begin{cases} q(t) = a_0 + a_1 t + a_2 t^2 + a_3 t^3 + a_4 t^4 + a_5 t^5 \\ \dot{q}(t) = a_1 + 2a_2 t + 3a_3 t^2 + 4a_4 t^3 + 5a_5 t^4 \\ \ddot{q}(t) = 2a_2 + 6a_3 t + 12a_4 t^2 + 20a_5 t^3 \end{cases} \tag{16}$$

Set six initial conditions of joint angle, velocity, and acceleration at the starting and stopping time. Iterate a suitable path that meets the conditions to jump out of the local minimum, output the current joint angle, put them into the improved artificial potential field method, and repeat the above process until the actual target point is reached.

In order to prevent collisions in the splicing path, add the constraint threshold of repulsion and collision detection. If the distance between the joint and the obstacle is less than a certain threshold, it will turn to the original improved artificial potential field method program. In addition, this method can also solve the problem of only constraining the end position instead of the end posture. And the spliced trajectory can solve the problems, such as the moment of the resultant force field to each joint is too small, the manipulator cannot reach the target position quickly, and the algorithm efficiency is low.

3.3 Collision Detection Algorithm

Due to the limited space of the operating table, using traditional bounding box algorithms will result in many pose constraints. It cannot meet the requirements of the precise operation of surgical robots. Therefore, select the Gilbert–Johnson–Keerthi (GJK) distance algorithm for collision detection, which can reduce the unnecessary loss of workspace and improve the accuracy of obstacle avoidance.

The GJK algorithm is suitable for distance detection between two convex bodies.

$$A - B = \{(a - b)|a \in A, b \in B\} \tag{17}$$

A simplex is equivalent to iteratively forming a polyhedron within the Minkowski difference. If it contains the origin, then the Minkowski difference contains the origin, and the objects intersect. Otherwise, calculate the closest distance to the origin of the polyhedron formed by the Minkowski difference.

We adopt an improved GJK algorithm proposed by Montanari in 2017 [14], which transforms the original Johnson sub-algorithm into a distance sub-algorithm with faster speed and accuracy closer to machine accuracy, to reduce the computational time of guiding the GJK algorithm towards a shorter search path.

Based on the GJK algorithm, collision detection is often used to complete path planning in the obstacle avoidance algorithm. First, it is applied in the improved artificial potential field method to calculate the repulsive force. Second, the position point is detected in real-time in the improved splicing path to ensure a certain distance from the obstacle and will not collide due to tremors. Finally, the detection is performed after the processing of the path.

3.4 Trajectory Preprocessing

After planning through the above steps, the trajectory will fluctuate, and the data cannot be directly applied to the real machine. Therefore, to enable the manipulator complete obstacle avoidance planning better and improve the algorithm's feasibility, the above-calculated trajectory needs to be preprocessed before being inputted into the control program.

As the six joints can be independently planned, a joint curve is now selected to analyze and compare various optimization methods, as shown in Fig. 5.

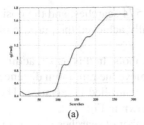 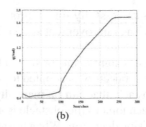 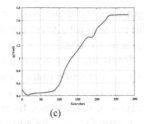

(a)   (b)   (c)

Fig. 5. Optimization curve comparison chart: (a) locally weighted linear regression smoothing, (b) robust locally weighted linear regression smoothing, (c) robust locally weighted quadratic regression smoothing.

The curve in Figure (b) is smoother and reduces fluctuation three times. Therefore, we use the robust local weighted linear regression smoothing algorithm, which uses the weighted linear least-squares method and the first-order polynomial model for local regression. And the algorithm can assign lower weights to outliers in the regression and assign zero weights to data outside the six-mean absolute deviation.

4 Simulation Test

Parameter initialization: $d_0 = 0.10$; initial pose $qStart = [0, 0, 0, 0, 0, 0]$; target pose $qGoal = [pi/2, 0, pi/2, 0, 0, pi/2]$; Repulsion parameter: $K_{rep} = 0.3$; Attraction parameter: $K_{att} = 0.2$; Initialize a fixed-size step in joint space: $Step = 0.01\ rad$; $\alpha = 0.05$, $\beta = 0.05$; Obstacle position: x_min y_min z_min x_max y_max z_max = $[-0.100, -0.100, 0, -0.300, -0.300, 0.500]$ Input the above parameters into the program, adjust the position of the manipulator and obstacles, and carry out an experiment to study the local minimum. The results are shown in Fig. 6:

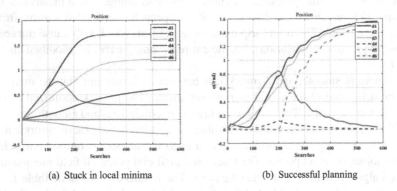

(a) Stuck in local minima   (b) Successful planning

Fig. 6. Joint angle position comparison in obstacle avoidance simulation

Figure (a) shows that the manipulator falls into the local minimum after 205 searches and cannot escape. In Figure (b), after using the improved algorithm and the splicing algorithm, the target position is successfully found through 574 searches, and the position curve is relatively smooth. The improvement successfully achieved the purpose of obstacle avoidance.

Real-time collision detection is significant for surgical robots. In this paper, adding collision detection to the splicing trajectory is adopted to achieve the minimum distance from the manipulator to the obstacle that can be manually controlled in advance. The analysis of the distance from each joint to the obstacle is shown in Fig. 7.

Figure (a) does not add collision detection. When the number of searches is between 100 and 200, although the manipulator does not encounter obstacles, the distance between 3rd, 4th, 6th joints to the obstacle is too close, only 0.01 m. It collides easily affected by the surrounding environment. Figure (b) shows the threshold distance for collision detection is set to 0.05 m. When the distance between the r joint and the obstacle is less than 0.05 m, the manipulator is far away, and the curve has an obvious turning point at 0.05 m. These ensure the feasibility of obstacle avoidance.

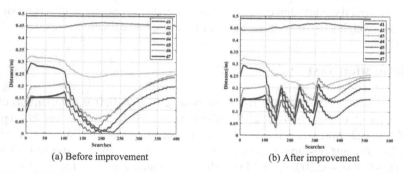

(a) Before improvement   (b) After improvement

Fig. 7. Joint angle position comparison diagram in obstacle avoidance simulation

Due to the algorithm problem, the curve is too oscillating, which means that within the actual 522 search times, the manipulator approaches and moves away from the obstacle three times. The round-trip distance is 0.15 m, which will cause unnecessary time loss in practical applications. So, the entire planning curve is smoothed, as shown in Fig. 8.

The curve is smooth, and 3 round trips become 1, indicating that the manipulator first approaches the obstacle and then moves away. The path is optimized to reduce unnecessary round trips. The curve in Figure (b) is continuous and smooth, and there is no oscillation phenomenon, which is suitable for application in practical surgical work.

Besides, to verify the algorithm, according to the actual operation area, select 20 different points as target points. The traditional artificial potential field method and the improved algorithm are used to plan the arms. The results are shown in Table 1.

It can be seen from the table that the traditional artificial potential field method failed mainly because of the local minimum. Collisions occur during the escape process because the repulsion force is not large enough. The number of searches is large. The manipulator can escape from the local minimum and achieve effective obstacle avoidance with the improved algorithm. The success rate can be greatly increased. Besides, the obstacle

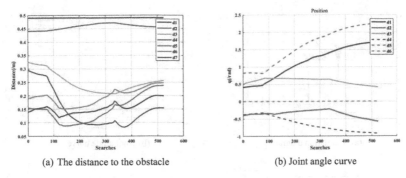

(a) The distance to the obstacle   (b) Joint angle curve

Fig. 8. Figures after using the improved method

avoidance distance can be quantified to the ideal value. Search efficiency is improved, and the curve is optimized. It realizes the possibility of application in natural objects.

Table 1. Experimental data

Algorithm	Planning times	Number of successes	Success rate	Stuck in local minima	The average number of searches
Traditional artificial potential field method	20	5	25%	11	1572
Improved artificial potential field method	20	18	90%	0	886

According to the surgical operation, the required pose is determined by teaching, and the data is input into the program for simulation verification. The results are shown in Fig. 9.

Figure (d) shows that manipulator reaches the target position area after 815 searches and starts to fall into the local minimum at the 332nd time. The curve in Figure (b) is relatively smooth. Figure (c) shows only one large approach to the obstacle, and the minimum distance is 0.22 m beyond the threshold. It will not occur collision, which verifies the feasibility and certainty of the algorithm.

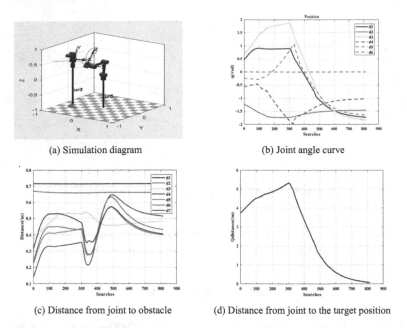

<table>
<tr><td>(a) Simulation diagram</td><td>(b) Joint angle curve</td></tr>
<tr><td>(c) Distance from joint to obstacle</td><td>(d) Distance from joint to the target position</td></tr>
</table>

Fig. 9. Simulation experiment result graph

5 Virtual Machine Experiment

In order to further verify the application of the algorithm, carry out a virtual machine experiment. Use Visual Studio and QT to build a visual control platform and conduct simulation verification on the virtual machine. Initialize URSIM, determine the location of the TCP, and start the simulation. 441 sets of initial points in a pre-planned path are passed into UR3 to make it reach the initial pose. Perform the test, positions and speeds of its six joints are recorded in the process, as shown in Fig. 11 (Fig. 10):

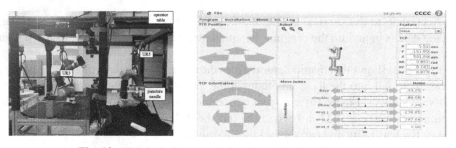

Fig. 10. Physical picture and virtual machine interface picture

The curve is smooth, and the similarity rate with the simulation is as high as 90%. The entire movement takes 44.1 s. The program performs a simple interpolation calculation to speed by input joint angle. The speed and acceleration of the six joints meet the operating

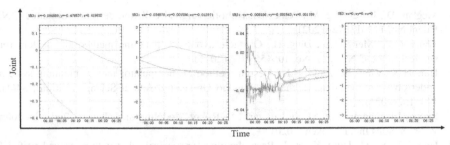

Fig. 11. The position and velocity charts (The first from left to right is the end-position curve. The second is the end-posture curve. The third is the end-velocity curve, the curve fluctuates greatly. After 15 s, the speed gradually slows down and changes. The range is maintained within 0.01 Rad/s and fluctuates slightly at the turning point of splicing trajectory. The last is the curve of the end angular velocity and is always maintained within 0.2Rad/s^2 without major fluctuations)

conditions of the manipulator, and it can reach the target position with relatively smooth motion. It illustrates the feasibility of the algorithm.

6 Conclusion

In this paper, we improve the potential field, which can better control the movement of the manipulator in a narrow workspace. The search efficiency is improved by about 25%. The occurrence frequency of local minimum increases, which causes specific difficulties in the movement of the manipulator. Therefore, propose an improved splicing paths method to solve this problem. After experiments, this method can effectively help the manipulator escape from the local minimum, and the total success rate is increased by 20% applicated in real. However, the transition of the two path splicing needs to be improved.

Collision detection is carried out in multiple steps. The required minimum distance from the manipulator to the obstacle can be manually set. If they collide, an alarm will be issued. Adopt the preprocessing of the trajectory. The entire path is a collection of points found by each search, which has not undergone trajectory and velocity interpolation calculations. In the physical test, use the program to calculate the speed and acceleration to control the manipulator. In the future, detailed planning needs to be improved for each part of the trajectory.

References

1. Yan, Z.Y., Niang, Y.L., Du, Z.J.: A review of the development of robotic technology in laparoscopic surgery. Robot Technique and Application **2**, 24–29 (2020)
2. Zhang, D.M.: Dialogue with Liu Rong: robotic surgery in the era of precision medicine. Chin. Sci. Bull. **62**(26), 2997–2998 (2017)
3. Liang, J.T., Huang, J., Chen, T.C.: Standardize the surgical technique and clarify the relevant anatomic concept for complete mobilization of colonic splenic flexure using da Vinci Xi robotic system. World J. Surg. **43**, 1129–1136 (2019)

4. Meglan, D., Rosenberg, M., Peine, W.: Robotic surgical collision detection systems. C.N. Patent No. 113613852A(2021)
5. Wang, G.Z., Meng, F.L., Ding, H.: Obstacle avoidance planning method and system for surgical robot. C.N. Patent No. 105455901A(2016)
6. Han, H.X., Zhou, S., Zhou, H.B.: Design method of manipulator motion planning system under obstacle condition. Journal of Qingdao University(Natural Science Edition), 34(4), 144–152(2021)
7. Spong, M., Hutchinson, S., Vidyasagar, M.: Robot Modeling and Control, 2nd edn. John Wiley & Sons Inc, Hoboken (2020)
8. Hao, L.J., Ye, C., Du, S.X., et al.: Pose planning for surgical robot with improved artificial potential field method. Control Theory & Applications, http://kns.cnki.net/kcms/detail/44.1240.TP.20211118.0943.002.html, last accessed 2022/05/28
9. Ma, H.N., Zhang, Z.A., Li, Q.L.: Improved artificial potential field method for dual-manipulator path planning algorithm. Journal of Mechanical Transmission **45**(6), 77–84 (2021)
10. He, Z.C., He, Y.L., Zeng, B.: Obstacle avoidence path planning for robot arm based on mixed algorithm of artificial potential field method and RRT. Ind. Eng. J. **20**(2), 56–63 (2017)
11. Li, B.F., Sun, H.X., Jia, Q.X., Chen, G.: Calculation of space robot workspace by using Monte Carlo method. Spacecraft Engineering **20**(4), 79–85 (2011)
12. Chen, M.J., Fang, Y.M., Chen, J.: Influence of initial convex hull on the efficiency of Quickhull algorithm. Science of Surveying and Mapping **41**(7), 23–27 (2016)
13. Yu, Z.Z., Yan, J.H., Zhao, J., et al.: Mobile robot path planning based on improved artificial potential field method. Journal of Harbin Institute of Technology **43**(1), 50–55 (2011)
14. Montanari, M., Petrinic, N., Barbieri, E.: Improving the GJK algorithm for faster and more reliable distance queries between convex objects. ACM Trans. Graph. **36**(3), 1–17 (2017)

UAV Path Planning Based on DDQN
for Mountain Rescue

Yu Wang(✉) ⓘ, Chuanqi Jiang ⓘ, and Tianjun Ren ⓘ

Shenyang Aerospace University, Shenyang 110136, China
wangyu@sau.edu.cn

Abstract. The high calculation cost and low success rate of strategy generation caused by unknown environment and emergencies, highly limited the usage of traditional UAV path planning methods. A path planning method based on DDQN algorithm is proposed to solve the mountain rescue problem in a complex environment. First, the state space and action space of the UAV are determined, then the reward function is designed based on the positional relationship between target, obstacle and UAV, and finally the DDQN reinforcement learning model based on the greedy strategy is established. Simulation experiments in the two scenarios confirm that the DDQN algorithm can not only achieve path planning for rescuing static goals, but also realize fast-tracking of moving targets through quadratic programming. At the same time, compared with the results of the DQN algorithm, it shows that the method has faster network convergence and better path planning ability.

Keywords: Mountain rescue · Path planning · Deep reinforcement learning · DDQN · Dynamic target

1 Introduction

Mountain accident rescue generally occurs in remote and inaccessible places, and conventional rescue methods always take a long time, which will seriously threaten the lives of trapped people. In recent years, the rapid development of UAV technology can provide help for fire rescue personnel to quickly search for trapped people in mountains and assist in commanding the rescue process. In this process, reasonable path planning is particularly important.

Traditional path planning algorithms such as A* algorithm [1, 2], intelligent optimization algorithm [3], artificial potential field algorithm [4], have a large amount of calculation and are easy to fall into local optimal solutions, which greatly reduces the autonomy of UAVs. As a result, when dealing with emergencies and dynamic environment, the success rate of path planning strategy is low, and it is difficult to complete real-time path update.

With the advent of deep reinforcement learning methods, the above problems have been improved. Deep Q-Network (DQN) is firstly proposed by Hassabis, and there are many applications in path planning [5–7].

© The Author(s), under exclusive license to Springer Nature Switzerland AG 2022
H. Liu et al. (Eds.): ICIRA 2022, LNAI 13458, pp. 509–516, 2022.
https://doi.org/10.1007/978-3-031-13841-6_46

However, with the development of the DQN algorithm, the shortcoming that it is prone to overestimation has gradually emerged. To solve this problem and speed up the convergence of the network, Hassabis proposes the Deep Double Q Network (DDQN) [8]. This algorithm inherits the advantages of the DQN algorithm, which can provide more accurate evaluation of value function, is more suitable for path planning problems in complex environments [9–13]. Fei Zhang [9] adopts the DDQN algorithm to train the robot to successfully learn obstacle avoidance and optimize path.

Based on DDQN algorithm, in this paper, a UAV path planning model for mountain rescue is proposed. The model enables the UAV not only to reach the fixed target point accurately and realize the rescue of static targets, but also to track and search the moving targets through quadratic path planning. Compared with DQN algorithm, the effectiveness of DDQN algorithm designed in this paper is verified, and a certain theoretical basis is provided for the autonomous path planning of the UAV.

2   DDQN Configuration for Path Planning in Mountain Rescue

DDQN algorithm has the same basic design concept as the DQN algorithm, which mainly uses the neural network to approximate the value function. The input of the network is the current flight state (s) of the UAV, and the output is the action value function $Q(s, a, \theta)$ of the action (a) taken by the UAV in the current state. DDQN adjusts the neural network parameters to fit the action value function through Q network training. Therefore, the network can accurately predict the action value function in each state and output an optimization strategy in the face of complex environments. The Q network structure is shown in Fig. 1.

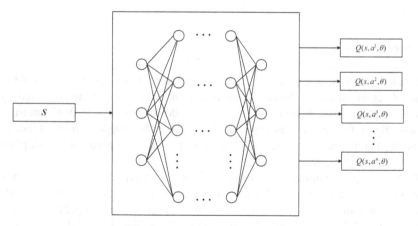

Fig. 1. Structure of the Q network

In order to solve the problem of overestimating the Q value of a certain state in the max operation when the target value of the DQN algorithm is updated, DDQN implements action selection and action evaluation with different action value functions, using the eval network to select actions, and the target network to evaluate actions. By decoupling the two steps of action selection and target value calculation at the next moment, the overestimation problem of DQN is eliminated. Suppose the Q network target value in DDQN be Y_i, the update formula is shown in the Eq. (1).

$$Y_i = \begin{cases} R_i & end \\ R_i + \gamma Q(s_{t+1}, \arg\max_{a'} Q(s_t, a', \theta); \theta^-) & else \end{cases} \quad (1)$$

where, i is the action selection sequence number of the current state; R_i is the reward obtained in the environment when the action is selected; s_{t+1} is the state after taking action a_t in the current state s_t; θ^- is the parameter of the target network and γ is the decay factor of the reward.

The DDQN update model [13] is shown in Fig. 2.

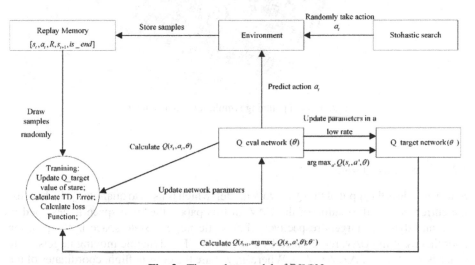

Fig. 2. The update model of DDQN

where a_t is the action taken in state s_t.

During the network training, the DDQN network is trained with random sample data in the replay memory to eliminate the correlation between samples and improve the stability of the algorithm. The loss function of the DDQN algorithm is:

$$Loss = \frac{1}{N} \sum_{i=1}^{N} (Y_i - Q(s_t, a_t, \theta))^2 \quad (2)$$

3 Path Planning Reinforcement Learning Algorithm Design

UAV mountain rescue path planning algorithm is based on the Markov decision process consisting of five-tuples (S, A, P, R, γ). where S is a finite set of states; A is a finite set of actions; $P = 1$ is the state transition probability; R is the reward function; $\gamma = 0.95$ is the decay factor of the reward.

3.1 Environmental Model Construction

In this paper, the peaks function is used to model the UAV mountain rescue environment, as shown in Fig. 3.

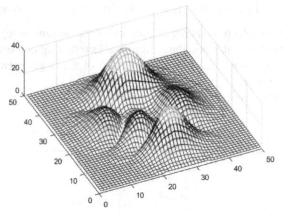

Fig. 3. Path planning simulation environment

3.2 State Space Design

State variable is the input of the Q network model, which is used to quantitatively describe the current state information of the UAV. In this paper, the state space is designed to static and dynamic targets respectively. For static targets: state space is the position coordinates of the UAV, represented by $s = [x, y, z]$. For dynamic moving targets, state space is $s = [x, y, z, \Delta x, \Delta y, \Delta z]$. Where, x, y, z are the current flight coordinates of the UAV; $\Delta x, \Delta y, \Delta z$ are the distance changes between the UAV and the target point in the x-axis, y-axis and z-axis directions, respectively.

3.3 Action Space Design

The UAV action space designed in this paper is divided into six directions of movement: forward, backward, left, right, up, and down, represented by $a^1 - a^6$:

$$a = \left[a^1, a^2, a^3, a^4, a^5, a^6 \right]$$

3.4 Action Strategy Design

The ξ-greedy strategy is adopted for taking actions during the training process of the DDQN model. The method is as follows:

$$\pi(a|s) = \begin{cases} a = \arg\max_a Q(s, a) & \text{if } \eta > \xi \\ a \neq \arg\max_a Q(s, a) & \text{if } \eta < \xi \end{cases} \tag{3}$$

where, when the random number η is greater than the exploration rate ξ, the action with the largest action value function is taken, and when η is less than the exploration rate ξ, a random action is taken. As the number of explorations increases, the probability of taking a random action gradually decreases.

3.5 Reward Function Design

Rewards in reinforcement learning are feedback signals from the environment to the agent to evaluate the behavior of agent. In this paper, a non-sparse reward is used to guide the UAV to move towards the target point, and realize the rescue under the premise of avoiding collision with mountains. The reward function is:

$$R = \begin{cases} C_1 & \text{if } D_t < 2 \\ \lambda(D_{t-1} - D_t) & \text{if } s(x, y, z) = peak(x, y, z) \\ C_2 & else \end{cases} \quad (4)$$

where, $C_1 = 2$ is the positive reward obtained by UAV when it reaches the rescue point and completes the task, while $C_2 = -1$ is the negative reward when the UAV hits a mountain; λ is a positive weight ratio, respectively taken 0.4 and 0.6 in the subsequent experiments 4.1 and 4.2; D_{t-1} and D_t are the distance from the UAV to the rescue point at the last moment and the current moment respectively.

4 Simulation

In order to verify the effectiveness of the proposed model in this paper, two simulation scenarios are constructed in this section, and path planning is carried out for the rescue of a static target and a dynamic moving target respectively. At the same time, in order to prove the advantages of DDQN algorithm in terms of performance, a comparison with the DQN algorithm is carried out.

4.1 Static Target

A static search and rescue scene is constructed: the UAV starts from the starting point with coordinate of [5, 5, 1], and flies to the rescue point with coordinate of [36, 25, 21], moving with a uniform speed. The DQN and DDQN algorithms are used for the path planning training of the UAV, respectively, and the flight trajectories are shown in Fig. 4 (a) and (b).

It can be seen from Fig. 4 that no matter the DQN algorithm or the DDQN algorithm is used for training to static targets, the UAV can cross the mountain peak to the rescue point without collision. In order to verify the speed of convergence of the two algorithms, the cumulative reward curve of DQN and DDQN are drawn respectively, as shown in Fig. 5.

It can be seen clearly from Fig. 5 that the DDQN algorithm can obtain the maximum reward more quickly, and can reach the rescue point to complete the task after 400 times of training. However, the DQN algorithm needs to be trained for about 600 times before it can reach the rescue point. Therefore, DDQN algorithm is better than the DQN algorithm in terms of convergence speed.

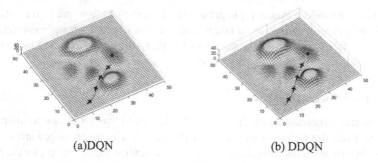

<table>
<tr><td>(a)DQN</td><td>(b) DDQN</td></tr>
</table>

Fig. 4. Static target rescue flight trajectory comparison

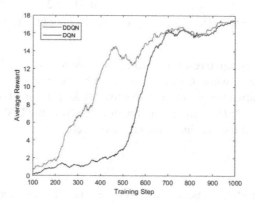

Fig. 5. Comparison of cumulative reward changes to static target rescue

4.2 Dynamic Target

Considering that in the mountain rescue mission, when the UAV flies according to the initial detection target point, the target to be rescued may move. In this experiment, a dynamic path planning scenario in which the target moves at a uniform speed is constructed. The mission is that the UAV needs to reach the first target point through path planning firstly, and then perform quadratic path planning from this point to complete target tracking. The scene setting is as follows: when the UAV first arrives at the initial target point ① ([36, 25, 21]), it searches for the target and finds that the target is moving in a straight line to the position ② ([41, 25, 19]). The flight trajectory planned by DDQN algorithm and DQN algorithm is respectively shown in Fig. 6(a) and (b). It can be seen from the figure that with the two algorithm decisions, the UAV can successfully achieve the quadratic tracking of the dynamic moving target after reaching the initial target point.

Comparing the cumulative reward change curve of the two methods (Fig. 7), it can be seen that after 1000 times of exploration, although the DQN model can complete the task, the convergence effect is far less than that of the DDQN model.

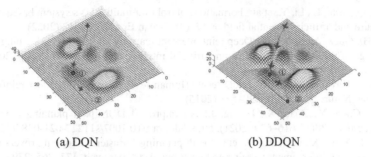

(a) DQN   (b) DDQN

Fig. 6. Dynamic target rescue flight trajectory comparison

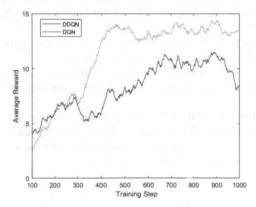

Fig. 7. Comparison of cumulative reward changes for dynamic target rescue

5 Conclusion

In this paper, a path planning model based on DDQN is designed for UAV mountain rescue. Through effective model training, not only the successful rescue of static targets, but also the rapid rescue of dynamic targets is realized through quadratic path planning. Simulation experiments show that compared with DQN algorithm, DDQN algorithm has faster convergence speed and higher learning efficiency, which can better complete the path planning task of rescue in complex environment.

References

1. Zhang, J., Wu, J., Shen, X., et al.: Autonomous land vehicle path planning algorithm based on improved heuristic function of A-Star. Int. J. Adv. Robot. Syst. **18**(5), 1–10 (2021)
2. Liang, C., Zhang, X., Watanabe, Y., et al.: Autonomous collision avoidance of unmanned surface vehicles based on improved A star and minimum course alteration algorithms. Appl. Ocean Res. **113**, 1–11 (2021)
3. Blum, C.: Ant colony optimization: Introduction and recent trends. Phys. Life Rev. **2**(4), 353–373 (2005)

4. Zhen, Q., Wan, L., Li, Y., et al.: Formation control of a multi-AUVs system based on virtual structure and artificial potential field on SE (3). Ocean Eng. **253**, 1–12 (2022)
5. Van, H., Guez, A., Silver, D.: Deep reinforcement learning with double q-learning. In: Proceedings of the AAAI Conference on Artificial Intelligence, vol. 30, no. 1, pp. 2094–2100 (2016)
6. Mnih, V., Kavukcuoglu, K., Silver, D., et al.: Human-level control through deep reinforcement learning. Nature **518**(7540), 529–533 (2015)
7. Li, J., Chen, Y., Zhao, X., Huang, J.: An improved DQN path planning algorithm. J. Supercomput. **78**(1), 616–639 (2021). https://doi.org/10.1007/s11227-021-03878-2
8. Jiang, J., Zeng, X., Guzzetti, D., et al.: Path planning for asteroid hopping rovers with pre-trained deep reinforcement learning architectures. Acta Astronaut. **171**, 265–279 (2020)
9. Zhang, F., Gu, C., Yang, F.: An improved algorithm of robot path planning in complex environment based on double DQN. In: Yan, L., Duan, H., Yu, X. (eds.) Advances in Guidance, Navigation and Control, vol. 644, pp. 303–313. Springer, Cham (2022). https://doi.org/10.1007/978-981-15-8155-7_25
10. Li, S., Chen, X., Zhang, M., et al.: A UAV coverage path planning algorithm based on double deep q-network. J. Phys. Conf. Ser. **2216**(1), 1–10 (2022)
11. Chu, Z., Wang, F., Lei, T., et al.: Path planning based on deep reinforcement learning for autonomous underwater vehicles under ocean current disturbance. IEEE Trans. Intell. Veh. **2002**, 1–13 (2022)
12. Wu, R., Gu, F., Liu, H., et al.: UAV path planning based on multicritic-delayed deep deterministic policy gradient. Wirel. Commun. Mob. Comput. **2022**, 1–12 (2022)
13. Lei, X., Zhang, Z., Dong, P.: Dynamic path planning of unknown environment based on deep reinforcement learning. J. Robot. **2018**, 1–10 (2018)

Online Safe Trajectory Generation of Quadrotors Autonomous Landing in Complex Dynamic Environments

Bo Liu⬤ and Shimin Wei(✉)

Beijing University of Posts and Telecommunications, Beijing 100876, China
wsmly@bupt.edu.cn

Abstract. This paper regards obstacle avoidance and landing as a whole process and proposes a motion planning framework for the quadrotor, which can real-time calculate and enable the quadrotor to avoid obstacles while landing on the mobile platform. Assuming the platform's motion state is known, the Move-RRT and Move-B-RRT sampling algorithms can establish the static and dynamic trees to obtain the collision-free path containing time information. The algorithm adopts proportional sampling to make the time allocation between path points reasonable. We can determine the static obstacles and mobile platform positions and generate the flight corridor according to the position and time information contained in the path points. After optimization, trajectories represented by piecewise Bézier curves satisfying dynamic constraints are obtained. This paper verifies the motion planning framework in a complex simulation environment.

Keywords: Motion planning · Autonomous vehicle navigation · Collision avoidance · Quadrotor autonomous landing on mobile platform

1 Introduction

Due to the mobility and flexibility of quadrotors, they have been widely used in power inspection, agricultural plant protection, express distribution, and other fields. To improve quadrotors' working range and efficiency, they can be deployed on mobile platforms such as unmanned vehicles, ships, and airships. When the quadrotor returns to the unmanned platform, on the one hand, it needs to approach the mobile platform while avoiding the static obstacles. On the other hand, when the quadrotor approaches the mobile platform, it needs to regard the mobile platform structure outside the landing area as a moving obstacle to avoid. As shown in Fig. 1, it is crucial to plan a smooth, collision-free trajectory for the quadrotor.

In the existing research on quadrotor autonomous landing on a mobile platform, [1, 2] used a visual servo algorithm to complete the landing of the quadrotor on the fast-moving platform. However, only considering the fast landing, the research ignores the impact of the time spent crossing the obstacles in the early stage of the actual flight mission. [3] address time-optimal trajectory generation in dynamic environments, e.g.,

© The Author(s), under exclusive license to Springer Nature Switzerland AG 2022
H. Liu et al. (Eds.): ICIRA 2022, LNAI 13458, pp. 517–529, 2022.
https://doi.org/10.1007/978-3-031-13841-6_47

landing on a moving platform, but the algorithm did not consider obstacle avoidance. [4] used the velocity obstacles method to calculate a collision-free trajectory that allows the quadrotor to approach the unmanned ground vehicle, hover above it, and land on it. The algorithm does not consider the interaction between obstacle avoidance and landing. In the virtual environment, when the quadrotor avoids obstacles, the target platform also moves simultaneously. Existing algorithms do not consider static and moving obstacles or consider obstacle avoidance and landing separately. The quadrotor takes too long or fails to land on the mobile platform in complex environments.

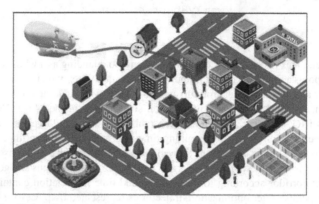

Fig. 1. The red collision-free trajectories of quadrotors fly back to the vehicle-mounted quadrotor automatic airfield or the airship cabin. (Color figure online)

The position of the target points in this paper changes in real-time, and there are fixed and moving obstacles, so the original sampling-based method cannot find a safe path. This paper improves the RRT * algorithm to obtain the Move-RRT and Move-B-RRT algorithms. The path points generated by the new algorithm are composed of position and time information to ensure that the quadrotor does not collide with obstacles and land on the mobile platform. After obtaining the sequence of waypoints, we generate the safe corridor, and then the Bernstein basis is used to represent the trajectory of the piecewise Bézier curves. Through optimization, the trajectory safety and high order dynamics feasibility are guaranteed.

2 Related Work

There has been much academic interest in quadrotors' autonomous landings on mobile platforms. [1, 2] provided the visual-based autonomous landing technologies. [3] proposed a time-optimal aircraft trajectory generation method. This method can deal with arbitrary input and state constraints. It can operate in real-time and land the quadrotor mobile platform in an obstacle-free environment. [4] use the velocity obstacles method to avoid fixed and moving obstacles. Under the condition of ensuring no collision, the quadrotor hovers above the unmanned ground vehicle and then lands on the mobile platform.

The motion planning problem can be divided into front-end feasible pathfinding and back-end trajectory optimization. For the front-end pathfinding, methods ranging from sampling-based to searching-based have been proposed. [5] proposed a typical sample-based method Rapidly-exploring Random Tree (RRT). The asymptotic optimal sampling algorithms [6] are PRM*, RRG, and RRT*. [7] proposed a bidirectional sampling-based method with a time configuration space representation to generate collision-free trajectories in complex and non-static environments. However, the algorithm has to set the renunciation time in advance. Typical searching-based methods include JPS [8], ARA* [9] and hybrid A* [10]. [11–13] proposed a motion planner based on a heuristic search to pick up moving objects smoothly. The back-end optimization module needs to calculate the smooth trajectory with time parameters. Gradient-based methods like CHOMP [14] formulate the trajectory optimization problem as a nonlinear optimization. [15] pioneered a minimum snap trajectory generation algorithm, and the trajectory generation problem is formulated as a quadratic programming (QP) problem. [16–18] all carve a flight corridor consisting of simple convex regions against the environments and confine the trajectory within the corridor. [18] utilized the properties of Bernstein's polynomial basis, the safety and dynamical feasibility constraints are directly enforced on the entire trajectory.

3 Move-RRT and Move-B-RRT Algorithms

The RRT correlated sampling algorithms find an initial path quickly but cannot handle time-indexed constraints. This paper proposes the Move-RRT and Move-B-RRT versions based on time configuration space. Algorithms solve the path planning problems where the target is moving and there are static and moving obstacles. The moving obstacles are at the same speed as the target.

3.1 Sampling Algorithm for Moving Target

The set of states in the configuration space is expressed as $Z \subset R^n$,$n \geq 2$,where n is the dimension and $z \in Z$ is the state of the object. The time configuration space is $S = Z \times [0, +\infty)$, and $s =< z, t >\subset S$ is the state at the time t.$Z_{obs}(t) \subset Z$ is the states that are present in configuration space occupied by the obstacles at the time t. $Z_{free}(t)$ is the traversable states for the robot such that $Z_{free}(t) = Z/Z_{obs}(t)$. $S_{free} = \{\langle z, t \rangle \subset S | z \subset Z_{free}(t)\}$ is the valid region in the time-configuration space. The sampling path from the start state $s_0 =< z_{init}, 0 >$ to the intersection target state $s_1 =< z_{goal\_m}, t_i >$ is expressed as $\tau[0, 1] \rightarrow \{\tau(0) = s_0, \tau(1) = s_1\} \subset S_{free}$, where z_{init} is the initial state of the robot, z_{goal_m} is the state at the intersection time of the robot, and t_i is the intersection time. The following z_{goal} is used to indicate the state of the target state at the initial moment.

Let T represents a Rapidly-exploring Random Tree, where the target is in motion. V and E is the vertices and edges of the tree, such that $T = (V, E) \subset S_{free}$. The algorithms consider the configuration space occupied by the moving obstacles $S_{obs\_move} = \{\langle z, t \rangle \subset S | z \subset Z_{obs\_move}(t)\}$ and the configuration space occupied by the static obstacles Z_{obs_static} separately. As shown in Fig. 2, The actual configuration space is decomposed into the static configuration space Z_{static} and the dynamic configuration space Z_{move}. In the Z_{static}, the target (red point) and the together moving obstacles (gray circle) are regarded as relatively stationary and fixed at the position at the beginning of the planning algorithm, but the static obstacles (black circles) are not considered. In the Z_{move}, which is the state space of the real movement of the robot, only static obstacles are considered.

The tree growth process is similar to RRT* and only carried out in the static space. After getting the new node, it is mapped to the dynamic space to check the collision with the static obstacles. The point is inserted into the trees only if there is no collision between the two spaces. In the algorithm, the displacement of the moving target is regarded as the time measure. A static tree $T_s = (V_s, E_s)$ obtained by sampling and a dynamic tree $T_m = (V_m, E_m)$ obtained by mapping are established in two-state spaces, respectively. V and E of the two trees correspond one-to-one, and the sampling points correspond one-to-one with the displacements of the moving target.

Assuming the motion sampling step of the moving target B_{len} is in a fixed proportion to the robot's motion sampling step U_{len}. That is, the same moving distance of the robot is using the same time. U_{len} is also the step of the dynamic tree. The sampling step S_{len} of the static tree is the combined step of U_{len} and B_{len}. When the robot can move in all directions, the end track of S_{len} forms a sampling circle, and the starting point of S_{len} is the offset center of the sampling circle as shown in Fig. 3. There are forward and reverse sampling circles for sampling tree growth.

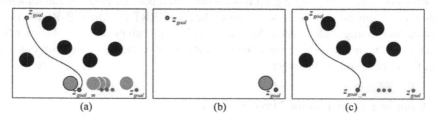

Fig. 2. (a), (b) and (c) are the actual, static, and dynamic configuration spaces.

Fig. 3. Sampling circle. The direction of B_{len} in the forward sampling circle is opposite to the moving target, otherwise it's the reverse sampling circle.

3.2   Move-RRT Algorithm

The sampling relationship of parent-child nodes of T_s and T_m in the Move-RRT algorithm is shown in Fig. 4. When there is no collision between the two spaces' sampling points, the two spaces' sampling points are added to the static and dynamic tree, respectively.

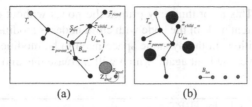

(a)   (b)

Fig. 4. Illustration of the sampling relationship of parent-child nodes of T_s and T_m in the Move-RRT algorithm. (a) is the static configuration space, T_s grows toward the target region Z_{goal}, and z_{parent_s} is the closest point to the random point z_{rand}. z_{parent_s} is the center of the forward standard sampling circle to generate the child node z_{child_s}. The time increment of the parent node to the child node is B_{len}. U_{len} vector is shifted to the dynamic configuration space to obtain the child node z_{child_m} in (b).

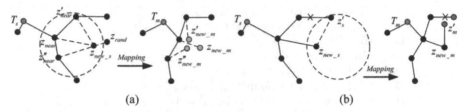

(a)   (b)

Fig. 5. The new node finding parent node process in (a) and the pruning process in (b).

When the point of the static tree reaches the target region Z_{goal}, the sampling stops, and the actual path of the robot is extracted from the dynamic tree T_m.

Alg. 1 summarizes the relevant pseudocode of the Move-RRT algorithm. After initializing T_s and T_m, random sampling point z_{rand_s} is generated in the static configuration space, and the nearest point $z_{nearest\_s}$ in the T_s is found. With $z_{nearest\_s}$ as the center of the bias circle and $\overrightarrow{z_{nearest\_s}z_{rand\_s}}$ as the direction, the intersection point on the forward standard sampling circle is z_{new_s}.

The NeightboringVertices routine finds the neighbor parent node set $Z_{near\_s} = \{z_{near}, z_{near}', z_{near}''\}$ by using the reverse sampling circle with z_{new_s} as the center of the circle expanded by a certain multiple of the radius. The Length routine calculates the cost from parent point to z_{new_s}. The Mapping routine maps z_{new_s} to the dynamic configuration space, and if the parent node of z_{new_s} is different, z_{new_m} is different. In the Z_{near_s}, the node with the least cost from z_{init} to z_{new_s} and no collision between the two configuration spaces is found as the parent node of z_{new_s}. The process of finding the parent node is shown in Fig. 5(a).

The FindPath function finds the path τ_{best} of the least cost. When the new node enters the target region, z_{goal} is projected into the dynamic configuration space to obtain the actual intersection point z_{goal_m} and the actual robot path is extracted in T_m. The NoChildVertices routine finds the node set with no child node set Z_{near_s}' near the z_{new_s} by enlarging the forward sampling circle with z_{new_s} as the center. The RewiringVertices function modifies the parent node of the node set Z_{near_s}'. When collision detection is carried out in two configuration spaces and the cost value of z_s' decreases after reconnection, the connection relation of related child nodes in the T_s and T_m is modified, as shown in Fig. 5(b). This algorithm only prunes the nodes without child nodes. When the corresponding parent node of the node with child nodes is modified, the corresponding child nodes' positions in the dynamic space need to be modified and the collision detection needs to be carried out again, which will increase the amount of calculation.

Algorithm 1 Move-RRT(z_{init}, z_{goal})

1: $V_s \leftarrow z_{init}; E_s \leftarrow \phi;$
2: $V_m \leftarrow z_{init}; E_m \leftarrow \phi;$
3: $T_s \leftarrow (V_s, E_s); T_m \leftarrow (V_m, E_m);$
4: $J(\tau_{best}) \leftarrow \infty;$
5: **for** $i \leftarrow 0$ to N **do**
6:     $z_{rand\_s} \leftarrow$ RandSample(i);
7:     $z_{nearest\_s} \leftarrow$ NearestVertex(T_s, z_{rand_s});
8:     $z_{new\_s} \leftarrow$ Extend($z_{nearest\_s}, z_{rand\_s}$);
9:     $Z_{nearest\_s} \leftarrow$ NeightboringVertices(T_s, z_{new_s});
10:     $BestCost \leftarrow \infty;$
11:     **for** $i \leftarrow 0$ to N **do**
12:         $len \leftarrow$ Length(z_{new_s}, z'_s);
13:         $(z'_m, z_{new\_m}) \leftarrow$ Mapping(z'_s, z_{new_s});
14:         **if** CollisionCheck(z'_m, z_{new_m}) and
15:             CollisionCheck(z'_s, z_{new_s}) **then**
16:             **if** cost(z'_s)+len < BestCost **then**
17:                 $BestCost = $ cost(z'_s)+len;
18:                 $z_{parent\_s} = z'_s; z_{parent\_m} = z'_m;$
19:             **end if**
20:         **end if**
21:     **end for**
22:     **if** z_{parent_s} **then**
23:         $T_m \leftarrow$ VertexIntsert($z_{new\_s}, z_{parent\_m}, T_m$);
24:         $T_s \leftarrow$ VertexIntsert($z_{new\_s}, z_{parent\_s}, T_s$);
25:         $\tau_{best} \leftarrow$ FindPath($z_{new\_s}, z_{new\_m}, T_s, T_m$);
26:         $Z'_{near\_s} \leftarrow$ NoChildVertices(z_{new_s});
27:         $(T_s, T_m) \leftarrow$ RewiringVertices($z_{new\_s}, Z'_{near\_s}, T_s, T_m$);
28:     **end if**
29: **end for**
30: **return** $T_s(V_s, E_s), T_m(V_m, E_m);$

3.3   Move-B-RRT Algorithm

In the Move-B-RRT algorithm, the forward sampling tree T_{a_s} uses forward sampling circles to generate new nodes and backward sampling tree T_{b_s} uses reverse sampling circles. T_{a_s} and T_{b_s} are in the Z_{static}, T_{a_m} and T_{b_m} are the corresponding sampling trees in the Z_{move}. The sampling trees $T_{a\_s}, T_{b\_s}, T_{a\_m}, T_{b\_m}$ are shown in Fig. 6. The forward growing new nodes need to be connected to the sampling tree if there is no collision in both configuration spaces. Reverse growing new nodes perform collision detection only in the static space and map directly to the dynamic space. When T_{a_s}

and T_{b_s} are connected, the related path (blue) is found in T_{b_m}. We translate the path to connect the T_{b_m} and carry out collision detection in the Z_{move}. Alg. 2 summarizes the relevant pseudocode.

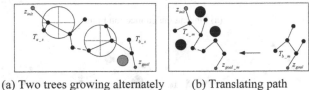

(a) Two trees growing alternately   (b) Translating path

Fig. 6. Illustration of the Move-B-RRT algorithm. When two trees growing alternately in the static space are connected, the corresponding path (blue path) in T_{b_m} is translated to the connection point of T_{a_m} to obtain the robot path. (Color figure online)

Algorithm 2 Move-B-RRT(z_{init}, z_{goal})

1: $V_{a\_s} \leftarrow z_{init}; V_{b\_s} \leftarrow z_{goal}; V_{a\_m} \leftarrow z_{init}; V_{b\_m} \leftarrow z_{goal};$
2: $E_{a\_s} \leftarrow \phi; E_{b\_s} \leftarrow \phi; E_{a\_m} \leftarrow \phi; E_{b\_m} \leftarrow \phi;$
3: $T_{a\_s} \leftarrow (V_{a\_s}, E_{a\_s}); T_{b\_s} \leftarrow (V_{b\_s}, E_{b\_s});$
4: $T_{a\_m} \leftarrow (V_{a\_m}, E_{a\_m}); T_{b\_m} \leftarrow (V_{b\_m}, E_{b\_m});$
5: $J(\tau_{best}) \leftarrow \infty;$
6: **for** $i \leftarrow 0$ in N **do**
7:    $(T_{a\_s}, T_{b\_s}, T_{a\_m}, T_{b\_m}) \leftarrow$
8:        GrowingAtoB($T_{a\_s}, T_{b\_s}, T_{a\_m}, T_{b\_m}$);
9:        SwaoTrees(T_{a_s}, T_{b_s}); SwaoTrees(T_{a_m}, T_{b_m});
10: **end for**
11: **return** $(T_{a\_s}, T_{b\_s}, T_{a\_m}, T_{b\_m}) = (V, E)$

As shown in Alg. 2, after initializing the four trees, the GrowingAtoB function grows the sampling tree T_{a_s} and T_{a_m} towards T_{b_s} and T_{b_m}. After completing once growth, T_{a_s} and T_{a_m} are swapped with T_{b_s} and T_{b_m} by the SwaoTrees function to continued growth. Finally we find a path with the least cost value. The two-tree connection and full path generation process are shown in Fig. 7.

The sampling scale coefficient $rot = U_{len}/B_{len}$ makes the robot's moving step size in the dynamic tree proportional to its time. Assuming there is no obstacle in the space, the rapid generation of motion primitive algorithm in [19] can be used to calculate the intersection point. After the intersection point is found, the trajectory length of the quadrotor L_{uva} and the movement distance of the moving platform L_{move} are calculated to obtain the sampling proportion $rot = L_{move}/L_{uva}$.

4 Flight Corridor and Safe Trajectory Generation

After the collision-free path is obtained through the sampling algorithm, this paper uses a similar method [18] to generate the flight corridor and optimize the trajectory. Merges can

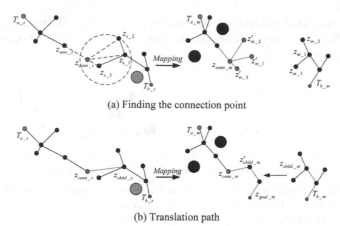

(a) Finding the connection point

(b) Translation path

Fig. 7. Illustration of the connecting process. In (a), we take z_{conn_s} as the center of the sampling circle, the set of adjacent points $\{z_{s\_1}, z_{s\_2}, z_{s\_3}\}$ in the T_{b_s} is found and mapped to the dynamic configuration space is $\{z'_{m\_1}, z'_{m\_2}, z'_{m\_3}\}$. In (b), the child node z_{child_s} is found in the points set by comparing the cost value and collision detection. The corresponding path (blue path) is extracted from T_{b_m} and translated from z_{child_m} to z'_{child_m}. (Color figure online)

be made when the maximum axial volumes generated by adjacent path points coincide. When the path points are close to the moving obstacle, due to the different positions of the moving obstacle at different times, many maximum axial volumes do not wholly overlap. In this paper, if the coincidence degree of the adjacent maximum axial volumes near the moving obstacle is greater than 70%, the maximum axial volumes are combined to reduce the number of the maximum axial volumes. In this paper, the trajectory is represented as the piecewise Bézier curve. The trajectory generation problem can be expressed as a convex quadratic program (QP) and can be solved by general off-the-shelf convex solvers [18]. The entire flight corridor and optimized trajectory are shown in Fig. 8.

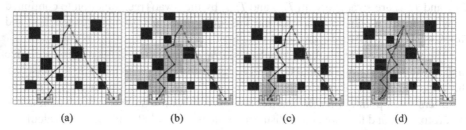

(a)   (b)   (c)   (d)

Fig. 8. Flight corridor and optimization trajectory generation. In (a), the Move-RRT generates the green and black path in the static and kinematic configuration space, respectively. As in (b), nodes away from the moving obstacle generate and merge maximum axis-aligned volumes on the black path. The maximum axis-aligned volumes are generated near the moving obstacle in (c). Finally, the trajectory is optimized to be confined entirely within the flight corridor and satisfy dynamical feasibilities, as shown in the red curve in (d). (Color figure online)

5 Implementation Details and Results

This paper assumes that the moving platform's real-time speed and position are known. This section gives the simulation results of the autonomous landing on a computer equipped with a 3.20 GHz Intel Core i7-8700. Due to the field of view limitation and the updating of mobile platform speed and position information, the sampling algorithms need to be constantly called for replanning. The Planning Strategy is shown in Fig. 9.

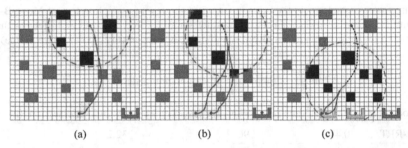

(a)   (b)   (c)

Fig. 9. The planning strategy. We define an execution horizon (the red dotted circle) that only checks the collision state of the current trajectory within the horizon. In the navigation process, the planned trajectory is divided into the execution segment (the green segment) and collision detection segment (the blue segment) in (a). As shown in (b), the replan mechanism will be triggered if a collision occurs in the collision detection section. When the mobile platform is outside the execution horizon, it is treated as a moving point. When the collision detection section enters the mobile platform area, the waypoints are mapped back to the static space to carry out collision detection. The blue square represents the mobile platform entering the event horizon, and the light blue square represents the position of the mobile platform that will collide with the trajectory, as shown in (c). (Color figure online)

5.1 MATLAB Implementation Details

The performance of the front-end sampling algorithm is verified by simulation in MAT-LAB. Randomly generating ten groups of static obstacles in the space of 80 m × 65 m, every algorithm runs 100 times on each map. RRT* directly generates the trajectory to the current target, and after executing one step, the planner is carried out again until reaching the target. Move-RRT and Move-B-RRT plan one time at the starting position to obtain the path. Suppose the quadrotor takes off from the upper left corner of the map with a maximum speed limit of 3.5 m/s. The platform moves horizontally at a constant speed of 1.5 m/s from the lower right corner.

The results of the sampling algorithms are shown in Table 1. Move-RRT has a fast calculation speed, and Move-B-RRT has a high success rate. Each RRT* step requires replanning, so the comparison does not include planning time. There is no target-moving information in RRT*, so it is easy to fall into extremes and has a longer intersection time. The Move-RRT and Move-B-RRT algorithms are shown in Fig. 10.

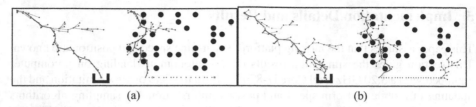

| (a) | (b) |

Fig. 10. Two sampling algorithms generate paths. In (a), Move-RRT computes the light blue intersection point, generates blue sampling points, and finds red time-constrained paths. In (b), there are fewer obstacles near the moving target, so the reverse sampling tree of Move-B-RRT sampling frequency is lower than the forwarding sampling tree. The red and green paths are extracted from the forward and backward sampling trees, respectively. (Color figure online)

Table 1. Comparison of path planning algorithms.

Method	Planning time [s]	Planning success [%]	Optimal intersection time[s]
Move-RRT	0.47	96	32.2
Move-B-RRT	0.94	100	32.2
RRT*	–	86	36.3

5.2 ROS Implementation Details

We use ROS to verify the overall algorithm framework. The environment information is known in MATLAB simulation, while UAV needs to explore the environment in ROS simulation. The simulation randomly generates obstacles on a 40 m × 40 m × 5 m map, assuming that the speed of the moving target is 1 m/s and the maximum speed of the quadrotor is 2 m/s. We use the Move-RRT and RRT* algorithm to generate the initial path. We do not detect the collision between the UAV and the mobile platform when they are more than 10 m. Using Move-RRT and trajectory optimization, the overall process of the UAV trajectory is shown in Fig. 11.

The sampling methods simulation results are shown in Table 2. Since the algorithm is calculated in real-time, we counted the planning time when the UAV is 15 m away from the landing site. There is no time sequence between path points in RRT*, so the planning time is shorter. Move-RRT considers the mobile platform's displacement and has a higher success rate. RRT* moving directly to the target is a greedy strategy. Although it is easy to fall into extreme value, the final intersection time is shorter in the case of an unknown environment.

When the distance between the quadrotor and the mobile platform is 15 m, the average computing time for path searching, corridor generation, and trajectory generation are 3.7 ms, 4.9 ms, and 20.1 ms, respectively. The autonomous landing trajectory is shown in Fig. 12. The framework in this paper can be calculated in real-time within 0.03 s. The rapidly generated path can provide better time allocation for back-end trajectory optimization so that the UAV can land more smoothly and safely.

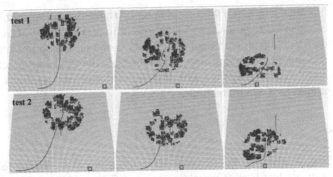

Fig. 11. The UAV senses the local environment in real-time and generates a complete red trajectory in two tests. The purple moving platform moves at a constant speed below the map. (Color figure online)

Fig. 12. The autonomous landing trajectory of the quadrotor in two tests. The trajectory of the moving platform is yellow, the track of the quadrotor is red, and the green arrow and yellow arrow represent velocity and acceleration, respectively. (Color figure online)

Table 2. Comparison of path planning algorithms in ROS.

Method	Planning time [ms]	Success [%]	Actual optimal intersection time[s]
Move-RRT	3.7	93	25
RRT*	2.3	78	22

6 Conclusions

This paper proposes a quadrotor's online motion planning framework to avoid static obstacles and land on a mobile platform. Move-RRT and Move-B-RRT algorithms search the feasible path, and each path point is composed of position and time information. The algorithm adopts proportional sampling to make the time allocation between path points more reasonable, thus improving the success rate of trajectory optimization. Then, the feasible path is expanded to produce a flight corridor to make full use of free space and a safe, dynamic feasible path with hard constraints based on the optimization method. We use the corresponding planning strategy to generate the trajectory quickly, and the framework is simulated to verify the feasibility. We will apply this method to the swarm landing on a mobile platform in the future.

References

1. Jin, S., Zhang, J., Shen, L., Li, T.: On-board vision autonomous landing techniques for quadrotor: a survey. In: Chinese Control Conference CCC, pp. 10284–10289 (2016)
2. Baca, T., et al.: Autonomous landing on a moving vehicle with an unmanned aerial vehicle. J. Field Robot. **36**(5), 874–891 (2019)
3. Beul, M., Behnke, S.: Fast full state trajectory generation for multirotors. In: 2017 International Conference on Unmanned Aircraft Systems (ICUAS) ICUAS 2017, no. June, pp. 408–416 (2017)
4. Battisti, T., Muradore, R.: A velocity obstacles approach for autonomous landing and tele-operated robots. Auton. Robot. **44**(2), 217–232 (2019). https://doi.org/10.1007/s10514-019-09887-8
5. LaValle, S.M.: Rapidly-exploring random trees: a new tool for path planning (1998)
6. Karaman, S., Frazzoli, E.: Incremental sampling-based algorithms for optimal motion planning. Robot. Sci. Syst. **6**, 267–274 (2011)
7. Yang, Y., Merkt, W., Ivan, V., Vijayakumar, S.: Planning in time-configuration space for efficient pick-and-place in non-static environments with temporal constraints. In: IEEE-RAS International Conference on Humanoid Robots, vol. 2018, pp. 893–900 (2019)
8. Harabor, D., Grastien, A.: Online graph pruning for pathfinding on grid maps. In: Proceedings of National Conference on Artificial Intelligence, vol. 2, pp. 1114–1119 (2011)
9. Likhachev, M., Gordon, G., Thrun, S.: ARA*: Anytime A* with provable bounds on sub-optimality. In: Proceedings of Advances in Neural Information Processing Systems (NIPS 2003), pp. 767–774 (2003)
10. Dolgov, D., Thrun, S., Montemerlo, M., Diebel, J.: Path planning for autonomous vehicles in unknown semi-structured environments. Int. J. Robot. Res. **29**(5), 485–501 (2010)
11. Cowley, A., Cohen, B., Marshall, W., Taylor, C.J., Likhachev, M.: Perception and motion planning for pick-and-place of dynamic objects. In: IEEE International Conference on Intelligent Robots and Systems, pp. 816–823 (2013)
12. Menon, A., Cohen, B., Likhachev, M.: Motion planning for smooth pickup of moving objects. In: Proceedings of IEEE International Conference on Robotics and Automation, pp. 453–460 (2014)
13. Islam, F., Salzman, O., Agarwal, A., Likhachev, M.: Provably constant-time planning and replanning for real-time grasping objects off a conveyor belt. Int. J. Robot. Res. **40**, 1370–1384 (2021)
14. Ratliff, N., Zucker, M., Bagnell, J.A., Srinivasa, S.: CHOMP: gradient optimization techniques for efficient motion planning, pp. 489–494 (2009)
15. Mellinger, D., Kumar, V.: Minimum snap trajectory generation and control for quadrotors. In: Proceedings of IEEE International Conference on Robotics and Automation, pp. 2520–2525 (2011)
16. Chen, J., Liu, T., Shen, S.: Online generation of collision-free trajectories for quadrotor flight in unknown cluttered environments. In: Proceedings of IEEE International Conference on Robotics and Automation, vol. 2016, pp. 1476–1483 (2016)

17. Gao, F., Shen, S.: Online quadrotor trajectory generation and autonomous navigation on point clouds. In: SSRR 2016 - International Symposium on Safety, Security, and Rescue Robotics, pp. 139–146 (2016)
18. Gao, F., Wu, W., Lin, Y., Shen, S.: Online safe trajectory generation for quadrotors using fast marching method and Bernstein basis polynomial. In: Proceedings of IEEE International Conference on Robotics and Automation, pp. 344–351 (2018)
19. Mueller, M.W., Hehn, M., Andrea, R.D.: A computationally efficient motion primitive for quadrocopter trajectory generation. IEEE Trans. Robot. **31**(6), 1294–1310 (2015)

Revised Discrete Control Barrier Functions for Safe Control of a Redundant DoF Manipulator

Yufan Zhu[1,2], Silu Chen[1(✉)], Chi Zhang[1], Zhongyu Piao[2], and Guilin Yang[1]

[1] Ningbo Institute of Materials Technology and Engineering, Chinese Academy of Sciences, Ningbo 315201, China
chensilu@nimte.ac.cn
[2] Zhejiang University of Technology, Hangzhou 310023, China

Abstract. The control barrier function provides an efficient tool to ensure the safety of Human-robot interaction. In this paper, we represent the barrier function in the discrete-time form together with the control Lyapunov function for safety operation in human-robot coexisting environment. And we apply it to the kinematic control of the redundant degree-of-freedom manipulator in the task space without disturbing the robot's job. Specially, we revise the definition of the minimum distance from each link to the human so that no collision happens on any link of the robot. The effectiveness of the control method is verified by simulation of controlling a planar three-link manipulator.

Keywords: Human-robot interaction (HRI) · Discrete-time control barrier functions · Redundant DoF robot

1 Introduction

By Human-robot interaction (HRI), the robotized automation lines can be set up with lower cost [9]. As robots and humans are working in fenceless environment, it is important to setup appropriate safety conditions and determine robots' control action promptly for the safety of humans.

Being analogous to the control Lyapunov function (CLF) [2], the control barrier functions (CBF) set up the safety conditions as inequality constraints and aims to maintain the control effort within an invariant safe set [4]. CBF performs better than artificial potential field method in real-time obstacle avoidance [13]. It has been applied to control of UAV [6], adaptive cruising [3], biped walking robot [10] and many other scenes. The discrete-time CBF is proposed (DCBF) [1], and worked with discrete-time control Lyapunov functions

National Natural Science Foundation of China (U20A20282, 51875554, 51705510), Zhejiang Key R&D Plan (2018C01086), Zhejiang Key Lab of Robotics and Intelligent Manufacturing Equipment Technology (2015E10011), Equipment R&D Fund (6140923010102), and Ningbo S&T Innovation Key Project (2018D10010).

H. Liu et al. (Eds.): ICIRA 2022, LNAI 13458, pp. 530–539, 2022.
https://doi.org/10.1007/978-3-031-13841-6_48

(DCLF) [5] for safe control of robots in environment with low-sampling rates. However, the safety constraints, especially the distances between the human to parts of the robot, are not accurately defined, which is a risk for HRI.

In this paper, the distance between a human and every link of the robot is accessed accurately by evaluating whether the projection of a human's position is on a link of robot or on its extension line, rather than only considering the distance to the end effector [14] or the midpoint of each link [7]. Through this, a control method based on DCBF and DCLF is proposed for safe HRI. Specially, this method can be applied to the manipulator with redundant DoF [12], so that the robot can complete its task as normal by varying its configuration to avoid collision with humans. The simulation of a three-degree-of-freedom manipulator in 2D plane verifies the effectiveness of the method.

2 Background

In this section, we will review the content of control Lyapunov and barrier functions in discrete time, and the kinematic control of manipulator in task space.

2.1 Discrete-time Control Lyapunov and Barrier Functions

First, we consider a nonlinear discrete-time system

$$x_{k+1} = f(x_k, u_k), \tag{1}$$

where $x_k \in \mathcal{D} \subset \mathbb{R}^n$ and $u_k \in \mathcal{U} \subset \mathbb{R}^m$ are the system state and control input at each time instant $k \in \mathbb{Z}^+$, and $\mathcal{U}$ is the set of admissible control inputs.

For safe human-robot co-existence, a safe set $\mathcal{C}$ is defined by a continuously differentiable function $h : \mathbb{R}^n \to \mathbb{R}$,

$$\mathcal{C} = \{x \in \mathbb{R}^n : h(x) \geq 0\}, \tag{2}$$
$$\partial\mathcal{C} = \{x \in \mathbb{R}^n : h(x) = 0\}, \tag{3}$$
$$\text{Int}(\mathcal{C}) = \{x \in \mathbb{R}^n : h(x) > 0\}. \tag{4}$$

The h is a control barrier function (CBF) if $\frac{\partial h}{\partial x}(x) \neq 0$ for all $x \in \partial\mathcal{C}$ and there exists an extended class $\mathcal{K}$ function α such that for system (1) satisfies,

$$\exists u \text{ s.t. } \dot{h}(x, u) \geq -\alpha(h(x)), \ \alpha \in \mathcal{K}_\infty. \tag{5}$$

Remark 1. We choose a special case of (5), which uses a scalar γ to simplify the constraint:

$$\exists u \text{ s.t. } \dot{h}(x, u) \geq -\gamma h(x), \ \gamma > 0. \tag{6}$$

The above CBF can be converted to the discrete-time control barrier function (DCBF) $h(x_k)$. And is given by

$$\Delta h(x_k, u_k) \geq -\gamma h(x_k), \ 0 < \gamma \leq 1, \tag{7}$$

where $\triangle h(x_k, u_k) = h(x_{k+1}) - h(x_k)$. When constraint (7) is satisfied, we have $h(x_{k+1}) \geq (1 - \gamma)h(x_k)$ and the control input u_k maintains $h(x_k) \geq 0$, $\forall k \in \mathbb{Z}^+$ given that $h(x_0) \geq 0$. In other words, the set $\mathcal{C}$ is forward invariant and the lower bound of DCBF decreases with the rate $1 - \gamma$. Its proof can be referred to [1].

While ensuring the safe of the system, we also hope that the system can maintain stability under a control Lyapunov function (CLF) $V(x)$. The CLF-based constraints is given as

$$\exists u \text{ s.t. } \dot{V}(x, u) \leq -\alpha(V(x)), \ \alpha \in \mathcal{K}. \tag{8}$$

We can also extend the constraint to discrete-time systems, where the discrete-time control Lyapunov function (DCLF) is introduced:

$$\triangle V(x_k, u_k) \leq -\alpha V(x_k), \ 0 < \alpha \leq 1, \tag{9}$$

where $\triangle V(x_k, u_k) = V(x_{k+1}) - V(x_k)$. Similar to DCBF, the upper bound of DCLF decreases with the rate $1 - \alpha$.

After defining DCBF and DCLF, we can get the admissible set K_{dcbf} and K_{dclf} of control inputs u_k:

$$K_{\text{dcbf}} = \{u_k \in \mathcal{U} : \triangle V(x_k, u_k) + \alpha V(x_k) \leq 0\}, \tag{10}$$
$$K_{\text{dclf}} = \{u_k \in \mathcal{U} : \triangle h(x_k, u_k) + \gamma h(x_k) \geq 0\}. \tag{11}$$

The set K_{dcbf} guarantees the safety of HRI system and the set K_{dclf} ensures the desired trajectory can be tracked.

Given a desired control input $u_d(x, k)$, using K_{dcbf} and K_{dclf} as constraints in a min-norm controller, we can convert the problem into an optimization formula to solve:

$$u_k^* = \text{argmin} \|u_k - u_d\|^2 + p\delta^2 \tag{12a}$$
$$\text{s.t. } \triangle V(x_k, u_k) + \alpha V(x_k) \leq \delta, \tag{12b}$$
$$\triangle h(x_k, u_k) + \gamma h(x_k) \geq 0, \tag{12c}$$
$$u_k \in \mathcal{U}, \tag{12d}$$

where $p > 0$, and $\delta \geq 0$ is a slack variable. When u_k satisfies both DCBF and DCLF-based constraints, δ becomes 0.

2.2   Task-space Kinematic Control for Robotic System

Consider an n-link manipulator with joint displacements $q = [q_1, q_2..., q_n]^T$ moves in 2D, and choose joint velocities $\dot{q} = [\dot{q}_1, \dot{q}_2..., \dot{q}_n]^T$ as the control variables. The coordinates of the end effector and the base are expressed as $p_e \in \mathbb{R}^2$ and $p_0 \in \mathbb{R}^2$ respectively. From this, we can get the relationship between $\dot{q}$ and $\dot{p}_e$:

$$\dot{p}_e = J_{p_e}\dot{q}, \tag{13}$$

where $J_{p_e} \in \mathbb{R}^{2 \times n}$ is the Jacobian. Suppose $p_d(k) \in \mathbb{R}^2$ is the desired position of the end effector at time k, and we can get a feedback controller with a control gain $K_p \in \mathbb{R}^{2 \times 2}$:

$$\dot{p}_e(k) = K_p(p_d(k) - p_e(k)). \tag{14}$$

By (13) and (14) the control inputs $\dot{q}$ can be written as

$$\dot{q}(k) = J_{p_e}^{\dagger} \dot{p}_e(k), \tag{15}$$

where $J_{p_e}^{\dagger}$ is the pseudo inverse of the Jacobian. The vector of joint displacements at time $k + 1$ is

$$q(k + 1) = q(k) + \triangle t \dot{q}(k). \tag{16}$$

Bring (16) into the forward kinematics formula introduced in [8]:

$$T_{0e} = T_{01}T_{12}...T_{(n-1)n}T_{ne}, \tag{17}$$

and the coordinates of each joint p_i at time $k + 1$ can be written as

$$p_i(k + 1) = AT_{0(i+1)}([q_1..., q_i])B, \quad i = 1, ..., n, \tag{18}$$

where $A \triangleq [I_{2 \times 2}, 0_{2 \times 2}]$ and $B \triangleq [0, 0, 0, 1]^T$. A and B are used to extract the Cartesian coordinates of the end effector in (17). In particular, $p_n \equiv p_e$.

3 Construct Constraints for Safe HRI

In this section, we will construct DCBF-based constraints for a redundant DoF manipulator to ensure the safety of HRI, and constructing a DCLF-based constraint to ensure that it can keep the end effector in a constant position through an optimization based controller.

3.1 Distance to a Human on the Link

In order to construct DCBF-based constraints, it is necessary to accurately define the distance between the human h and each link of the manipulator. Denote $p_i^m \in \mathbb{R}^2 (i = 1, ..., n)$ to be the closest point on i-th link to the human, which is denoted by point $h \in \mathbb{R}^2$, while o_i is the projection point from h to i-th link.

The shortest distance d_i^{min} is represented by the red line as in Fig. 1. The distance between the human and the link are calculated according to whether o_i is tallied with p_i^m. This condition is justified by

$$p_i^m = \begin{cases} o_i & \vec{a} \cdot \vec{b} > 0 \wedge -\vec{a} \cdot \vec{c} > 0 \\ p_{i-1} & \vec{a} \cdot \vec{b} < 0 \wedge -\vec{a} \cdot \vec{c} > 0 \\ p_i & \vec{a} \cdot \vec{b} > 0 \wedge -\vec{a} \cdot \vec{c} < 0, \end{cases} \tag{19}$$

where $\vec{a} = \overrightarrow{p_{i-1}p_i}$, $\vec{b} = \overrightarrow{p_{i-1}h}$ and $\vec{c} = \overrightarrow{p_i h}$. In other words, if h is projected on the link, as shown in Fig. 1(a), p_i^m shall be the projection point. Otherwise, p_i^m

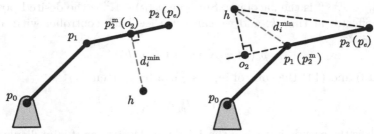

(a) The projection of the human to the second link is on the link

(b) The projection of the human to the second link is outside the link

Fig. 1. Positional relationship between the human and the second link

should be either end point with shorter distance from h to p_i or p_{i-1}. This is shown in Fig. 1(b).

After determining p_i^m, the minimum distance between the human and each link is given by:

$$d_i^{min} = \|h - p_i^m\|, \ i = 1, ..., n. \tag{20}$$

The problem of ensuring safe HRI then turns into the problem of making d_i^{min} be consistently greater than preset safety distance D^{min}.

3.2   Construction of Safety and Stability Constraints

From above, a set of constraints can be designed to define safe set $\mathcal{C}$:

$$h_i(x_k, u_k) = d_i^{min}(k) - D^{min} \geq 0, \ i = 1, ..., n. \tag{21}$$

In order to ensure the forward invariance of $\mathcal{C}$, we can write the DCBF-based constraints as

$$d_i^{min}(k+1) - d_i^{min}(k) \geq \gamma(d_i^{min}(k) - D^{min}), \ i = 1, ..., n. \tag{22}$$

Different from the distance defined in UAV [13] or the scene where only the end effector needs to avoid obstacles [11], the location of p_i^m changes as the relative position between links and h changes with time. As shown in Fig. 2, $p_2^m(k+1)$ is obviously not the same point as $p_2^m(k)$ on Link 2.

However, since the angular velocity $\dot{q}$ is the control variable, whether $o_1, \ldots, o_n$ are on the link are unknown for the future time $k+1$. So the coordinates of p_i^m cannot be determined, which will cause the inaccurate assessment of $d_i^{min}(k+1)$ in (22). In this paper, we solve this problem by assuming that $p_i^m(k+1)$ at time will fall into the same case in (19) as $p_i^m(k)$.

A constraint to keep the end-effector staying at the target point is built as

$$V(x_k) = \varepsilon - d_g(k) > 0, \tag{23}$$

where $d_g(k) = \|p_e(k) - g\|$ and $g \in \mathbb{R}^2$ represents the goal of the robot and ε is a small constant. Similarly, we can write the DCLF-based constraint as

$$- d_g(k+1) + d_g(k) \leq -\alpha(\varepsilon - d_g(k)) + \delta. \tag{24}$$

The flow of the proposed method is summarized in Fig. 3.

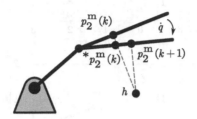

Fig. 2. The closest point to the human on the links p_i^m change with time.

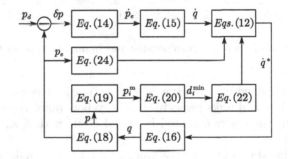

Fig. 3. The flow of DCBF-DCLF-based control of manipulator.

4   Simulation

In this section, we will simulate a planar three-link manipulator to complete the goal achievement task in the plane to verify the effectiveness of the proposed method. All simulations are run on the MATLAB 2020b platform with 2.20GHz Intel Core i7 Processor. In order to solve the optimization results efficiently, we use the fmincon function of MATLAB.

Given the three-link manipulator with initial values of joint angles $q = [\frac{\pi}{2}, -\frac{\pi}{2}, -\frac{\pi}{2}]^T$, and the lengths of the links are set to $l = [1.5, 1.5, 1.5]^T$. The task of the manipulator is to make the end effector reach the target point $g = [2, -1]^T$ and all three links are away from the human $h = [-0.3 + 0.005t; 1]^T$, who is moving at a constant speed.

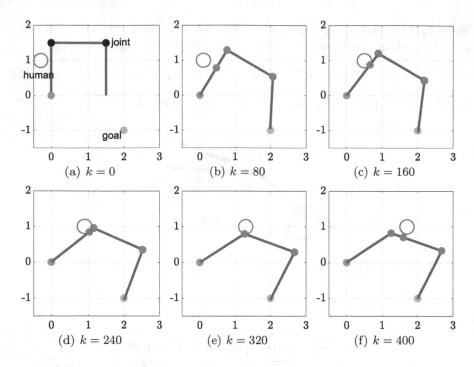

Fig. 4. Snapshots of the manipulator and human at time instant k.

The schematic diagram is shown in Fig. 4(a). Black points and blue lines represent the joints and links respectively, the yellow point represents the goal. The preset safety area is represented by a red circle with h as the center and $D^{\min}$ as the radius.

As we introduced in Sect. 2, we use kinematic control to make the end effector reach the goal. In this simulation, $p_d(k) = g$ is a constant value, so the control law is written as

$$\dot{q}(k) = J_{p_e}^{\dagger} K_p(g - p_e(k)). \tag{25}$$

By introducing the DCBF-based constraints (21) into the optimization formula (12), $\dot{q}_k$ is obtained to drive the robot without collision with human. When the end effector approaches the goal, the DCLF-based constraint (23) is added to (12) to ensure that the end effector can stay at g meanwhile no colliding with the human. Therefore, (12) is rewritten as

$$\dot{q}_k^* = \operatorname{argmin}\|\dot{q}_k - \dot{q}_d\|^2 + p\delta^2 \tag{26a}$$

$$\text{s.t.} - d_g(k+1) + d_g(k) \leq -\alpha(\varepsilon - d_g(k)) + \delta, \text{ when } d_g(k) < \varepsilon \tag{26b}$$

$$d_i^{\min}(k+1) - d_i^{\min}(k) \geq \gamma(d_i^{\min}(k) - D^{\min}), \ i = 1, ..., n, \tag{26c}$$

$$\dot{q}_k \in \mathcal{U}, \tag{26d}$$

$\mathcal{U}$ is set as the joint speed limit in the simulation. The setting of parameters in the formula is shown in Table 1.

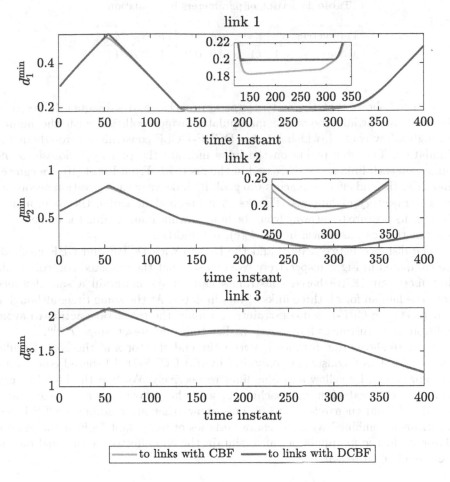

Fig. 5. Distance between links and the human.

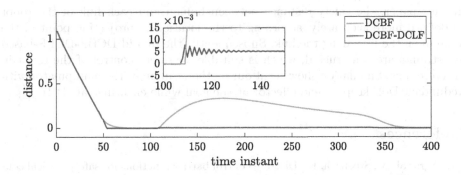

Fig. 6. Distance between the end effector and the human.

Table 1. Setting of parameters in simulation.

Parameters	α	γ	ε	δ	$D^{\min}$	p	K_p	$\dot{q}_{max}$
Value	0.1	0.1	0.1	0	0.2	1	$2.5I$	1

Figure 4 shows that the end effector approaches and subsequently keeps at the goal, meanwhile the whole manipulator avoids collision with the human through safety control, which satisfies DCBF-DCLF constraints throughout the simulation. The blue points on the links indicate the point p_i^{m} closest to the human on each link, as we discussed in the Sect. 3.1. From Fig. 4 (b), we can see that after the end effector reaches the goal, its links vary their position according to the trajectory of humans. Thanks to its redundant DoFs, the manipulator changes its posture to be away from the human while maintaining the end effector stays at the goal, as shown in Fig. 4 (c), (d) and (e).

The distance between links and the human with DCBF and CBF methods are compared in Fig. 5 respectively. We can see that the adjusted control inputs that meet our DCBF-based constraints can always maintain a safe distance from the human for all three links of manipulator. At the same time, although $\dot{q}$ that meets the CBF-based constraints can make the robot take action to avoid collision, their distances have been smaller than the preset range $D^{\min}$.

Figure 6 shows the distance between the end effector and the goal. Results with DCBF-based constraints only and hybrid DCBF-DCLF-based constraints are represented by yellow and blue lines respectively. We find the blue line can remain unchanged after approaching 0, and the yellow line rises again after reaching 0, and then returns to 0. This shows that after adding DCLF-based constraints, combined with the characteristics of redundant DoF of the manipulator itself, the manipulator can maintain the end effector at the goal on the premise of ensuring safety.

5   Conclusions

In this paper, the safety distance between human and each link of the robot is defined more accurately, according to the location of projecting point of the human on the line along the link. Subsequently, the hybrid DCBF-DCLF-based constraints are constructed, which is suitable for safety control of the robot in discrete time. Simulation shows that our method can make the manipulator with redundant DoF keep its end effector at the goal while ensuring safe HRI.

References

1. Agrawal, A., Sreenath, K.: Discrete control barrier functions for safety-critical control of discrete systems with application to bipedal robot navigation. In: Robotics: Science and Systems. vol. 13. Cambridge, MA, USA (2017)

2. Ames, A.D., Galloway, K., Sreenath, K., Grizzle, J.W.: Rapidly exponentially stabilizing control Lyapunov functions and hybrid zero dynamics. IEEE Trans. Autom. Control **59**(4), 876–891 (2014)
3. Ames, A.D., Grizzle, J.W., Tabuada, P.: Control barrier function based quadratic programs with application to adaptive cruise control. In: 53rd IEEE Conference on Decision and Control, pp. 6271–6278. IEEE (2014)
4. Ames, A.D., Xu, X., Grizzle, J.W., Tabuada, P.: Control barrier function based quadratic programs for safety critical systems. IEEE Trans. Autom. Control **62**(8), 3861–3876 (2016)
5. Grizzle, J., Kang, J.M.: Discrete-time control design with positive semi-definite Lyapunov functions. Syst. Control Lett. **43**(4), 287–292 (2001)
6. Hegde, A., Ghose, D.: Multi-UAV collaborative transportation of payloads with obstacle avoidance. IEEE Control Syst. Lett. **6**, 926–931 (2021)
7. Landi, C.T., Ferraguti, F., Costi, S., Bonfè, M., Secchi, C.: Safety barrier functions for human-robot interaction with industrial manipulators. In: 2019 18th European Control Conference (ECC), pp. 2565–2570. IEEE (2019)
8. Lynch, K.M., Park, F.C.: Modern Robotics. Cambridge University Press, Cambridge (2017)
9. Maurtua, I., Ibarguren, A., Kildal, J., Susperregi, L., Sierra, B.: Human-robot collaboration in industrial applications: safety, interaction and trust. Int. J. Adv. Rob. Syst. **14**(4), 1729881417716010 (2017)
10. Nguyen, Q., Hereid, A., Grizzle, J.W., Ames, A.D., Sreenath, K.: 3D dynamic walking on stepping stones with control barrier functions. In: 2016 IEEE 55th Conference on Decision and Control (CDC), pp. 827–834. IEEE (2016)
11. Rauscher, M., Kimmel, M., Hirche, S.: Constrained robot control using control barrier functions. In: 2016 IEEE/RSJ International Conference on Intelligent Robots and Systems (IROS), pp. 279–285. IEEE (2016)
12. Siciliano, B.: Kinematic control of redundant robot manipulators: a tutorial. J. Intell. Rob. Syst. **3**(3), 201–212 (1990). https://doi.org/10.1007/BF00126069
13. Singletary, A., Klingebiel, K., Bourne, J., Browning, A., Tokumaru, P., Ames, A.: Comparative analysis of control barrier functions and artificial potential fields for obstacle avoidance. In: 2021 IEEE/RSJ International Conference on Intelligent Robots and Systems (IROS), pp. 8129–8136. IEEE (2020)
14. Singletary, A., Kolathaya, S., Ames, A.D.: Safety-critical kinematic control of robotic systems. IEEE Control Syst. Lett. **6**, 139–144 (2021)

Multimodal Sensing and Understanding

Precision Peg-In-Hole Assembly Based on Multiple Sensations and Cross-Modal Prediction

Ruikai Liu, Ajian Li, Xiansheng Yang, and Yunjiang Lou[✉]

State Key Lab of Robotics and System, School of Mechatronics Engineering and Automation, Harbin Institute of Technology Shenzhen, Shenzhen 518055, People's Republic of China
louyj@hit.edu.cn

Abstract. Some precision assembly procedures are still manually operated on the industrial line. Precision assembly has the highest requirements in accuracy, which is characterized by a small range of 6D movement, a small tolerance between parts, and is full of rich contacts. It is also difficult to automate because of unintended block of sight, variational illumination, and cumulative motion errors. Therefore, this paper proposes a cross-modal image prediction network for precision assembly to address the above problems. The network predicts the representation vectors of the actual grayscale images of the end-effector. Self-supervised learning method is used to obtain the authentic representation vectors of reference images and actual images during training. Then these vectors will be predicted by combining the reference picture representation, robot force/torque feedback and position/pose of the end-effector. To visualize prediction performance, decoder trained by the above self-supervised network deconvolves the predicted representation vectors to generate predicted images, which can be compared with the original ones. Finally, USB-C insertion experiments are carried out to verify the algorithm performance, with hybrid force/position control being used for flexible assembly. The algorithm achieves a 96% assembly success rate, an average assembly steps of 5, and an average assembly time of about 5.8 s.

Keywords: Peg-in-Hole · Multimodal learning · Cross-Modal prediction

1 Introduction

To realize the automation of electronic product assembly, it is not only necessary to ensure the motion accuracy of the robot, but also to ensure the safety. To better analyze the assembly process, it can be decomposed into multiple simple processes. Each simple assembly process is divided into four steps: identifying the initial position of the part, grabbing the part, moving to the target position and final precision assembly. As the last step of the assembly process, precision assembly is characterized by small-scale operation, six-dimensional pose adjustment, small fitting clearance of parts, uncertain

This work was supported partially by the NSFC-Shenzhen Robotics Basic Research Center Program (No. U1913208) and partially by the Shenzhen Science and Technology Program (No. JSGG20210420091602008).

errors in grasping pose, and unintended block of sight. Therefore, conventional position control is difficult to meet the requirements of precision assembly.

In practical applications, some sensors are easily affected by the external environment, or it is difficult to obtain real data. And if some sensor data can be obtained, and then a model can be trained to predict the mode that is difficult to obtain real data or susceptible to environmental influence, then the dependence on this sensor can be cancelled, and the data generation method can be used to replace the sensor itself. Cross-modal prediction is a method to establish the mapping relationship between modalities. By training the modal information extracted from the existing data, the information of one or more modalities is fused to predict other modal information. At present, cross-modal prediction has a wide range of applications in many aspects, such as establishing the association between images and text, speech synthesis, etc.

In the early days, Hunt et al. [1] used cross-modal mapping in speech synthesis to reproduce sound sequences from text. Kojima et al. [2] utilized a cross-modal prediction method to describe human activities from videos, converting dynamic images into textual descriptions. Rasiwasia et al. [3] studied how to jointly model text and images, where the text is derived from hidden topic model samples and the correlation between the two modalities is learned through canonical correlation analysis. A generative model based on a deep recurrent architecture that combines computer vision and machine translation is proposed in Vinyals et al. [4] to generate natural sentences describing images. Venugopalan et al. [5] also used a deep recurrent neural network to translate video into text.

Nevertheless, cross-modal prediction is rarely used in precision assembly. Li et al. [6] established the link between vision and touch across modalities and used their proposed conditional adversarial model to predict each other for generating realistic images or tactile patterns. Since vision sensors are susceptible to ambient lighting, using other modalities to predict or generate visual information can overcome the effects of unstable illumination and unintended block of sight. Therefore, it is of great significance to use cross-modal for precision assembly.

In this paper, we constructed a precision assembly algorithm structure based on multimodal fusion [7] and cross-modal prediction method, aiming at the problems of environmental illumination instability and unintended block of sight. In order to ensure the safety of contact between the part and the robot during assembly, a compliant control strategy is adopted. We validated our algorithm with USB-C docking on the Franka robot platform, achieving an assembly success rate of 96%.

The main contributions of this paper include,

1) A multimodal fusion algorithm is proposed to extract information about the potential relative poses between parts in the feedback information.
2) A cross-modal image prediction algorithm is proposed to overcome the poor robustness of vision sensors to illumination.
3) For the USB-C assembly target, we established a suitable compliant motion control strategy, and verify the algorithm in robot experiments.

The follow-up content of the article is as follows. In Sect. 2, a multi-modal fusion algorithm is proposed for precision assembly. In Sect. 3, based on the multi-modal fusion algorithm, a cross-modal image prediction algorithm that overcomes the influence of illumination is proposed. Section 4 verifies the proposed algorithm by simulation and experiments. Section 5 concludes the article.

2 Multimodal Fusion Network

Multimodal fusion is responsible for combining information from multiple sensors to perform object prediction. Reasonable processing of multiple modal information can obtain rich features. This paper uses vision and force/sense for fusion decision-making, where the visual information includes RGB images and depth images, and the force sense is the six-dimensional force/torque feedback from the end-effector.

2.1 Self-supervised Learning to Extract Visual and Depth Features

Since there is a certain distance between the camera and the target assembly position, it contains a lot of useless information. We crop the collected RGB map and depth map data, and only focus on the parts related to the assembly process. Nevertheless, the amount of visual data in a single set is still as high as $128 \times 128 \times 3$, which is much higher than the dimension of force perception information, so compression processing is required. The convolutional neural network can reduce the dimension of a large amount of data into a one-dimensional vector with a small amount of data, and can retain the characteristics of the picture, so this paper adopts the CNN structure to extract the image features.

The image data does not have classification labels or fitting targets, so the supervised learning method cannot be used to predict the target. This paper adopts a self-supervised method to automatically extract features. The network structure is divided into two parts: encoding and decoding. According to the dimension of input data, it is determined that the coding network in the self-supervised learning network structure is a four-layer convolutional network structure and a fully connected layer, and the decoding network is a four-layer deconvolution network structure. The convolution kernel size of the convolutional network is 3, the stride is 1, and the padding size is 1. The schematic diagram of the neural network structure of self-supervised learning is shown in Fig. 1, and the length of the feature vector is 32. In order to train the network faster and better, the data needs to be normalized. The range of RGB values is 1–255, which is normalized to 0–1 by dividing all elements by 255.

2.2 Multimodal Decision-Level Fusion Algorithm Framework

Through self-supervised network training, a network model that compresses data dimensions but retains data features can be obtained [8]. Since the picture contains the relative pose information between the parts, the representation vector obtained by the model trained on the picture data will also contain this information. Therefore, the purpose of the self-supervised network is not only to compress the amount of data, but also to facilitate subsequent reinforcement learning training.

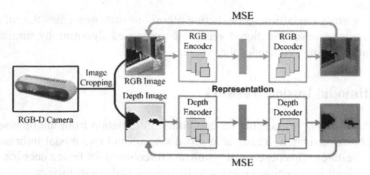

Fig. 1. Self-supervised learning network of RGB and depth images.

The RGB map and the depth map use the same network structure for self-supervised encoding, and then combine the six-dimensional force/torque information at the end of the robot as the environment perception of reinforcement learning, so as to carry out the motion control of the robot. From this, a multimodal fusion algorithm framework based on vision and force perception can be obtained, as shown in Fig. 2. The RGB data and depth map data are first trained by the self-supervised network, and then the encoder parameters are extracted to obtain the representation vector of the actual image as the input to the agent. The agent adopts the algorithm of reinforcement learning, and the motion control of the robot adopts the hybrid control method of force and position. These two parts will be given in Sect. 4.

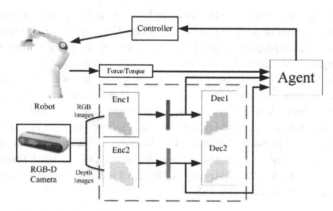

Fig. 2. Multimodal fusion network for precision assembly task.

3   Cross-Modal Prediction Network

Compared with unimodal data, multimodal data increases the dimension and quantity of information. There is a relationship between modal information from different angles for the same object, and one or more of these modalities can be used to predict the other modalities. This can play an important role when certain modes are missing or abnormal. It is also possible to directly discard the sensors corresponding to some modalities and use other modalities to generate the modalities, that is, cross-modal prediction, a method of predicting other modalities with known modalities.

Cross-modal prediction belongs to the multimodal mapping in the multimodal learning task. A modality provides information about some aspect of the object being described. For modalities describing the same object, each modality is directly associated with the object due to the determinism of the object. Therefore, each modal is indirectly related by describing the object. Through this association, we can use some methods to establish the mapping relationship between different modalities.

To overcome the effect of illumination on vision, consider using reference images, forces/torques, and position/pose to predict end-effector real-time images. Different from the multi-modal fusion algorithm, this algorithm discards the depth information, for the depth camera is noisy in actual use, and the obtained depth map is not clear, so it is difficult to extract effective information. In addition to the use of visual sensors for data collection, visual sensors are no longer used in online or offline training, which effectively prevents the effects of unstable ambient lighting and obstructions.

3.1   Reference Image and Image Encoder

Like the previous multimodal fusion algorithm, this chapter still uses Eye-to-Hand instead of Eye-in-Hand to obtain visual information. In addition to reducing the payload of the robotic arm, it is more desirable to obtain a single background of the picture, which is conducive to the mapping between modalities. There are invariable parts and variable parts in the visual information obtained by configuring the camera according to the Eye-to-Hand scheme. The invariant part considers the use of reference pictures for prediction, which is easy to do, that is, to find the mapping relationship between fixed data. The changing part is predicted using force/moment and pose, because for a fixed assembly object, the robot's information is enough to describe the changing part during the assembly process. Therefore, it is logically feasible to predict the real picture by combining the immutable part with the variable part, and it is also the core idea of the algorithm in this chapter.

The collected image dataset first needs to be encoded to obtain a lower-dimensional representation vector containing latent pose information. For the reference picture, the ideal framing position is the photo when the shaft and the hole are close but not touching, i.e., the initial assembly position. By comparing the RGB image and the grayscale image used in Sect. 2, we can find that the grayscale image can completely replace the RGB image without affecting it. Because we don't care about the color of the object, we only need the grayscale value to reflect the difference between pixels. The data volume of the grayscale image is only 1/3 of the RGB data volume, there is only one data channel, and the data dimension is $128 \times 128 \times 1$, which is the same as the depth map dimension used in Sect. 2. The pixel value of the grayscale image can be obtained by RGB value conversion,

$$Gray = 38 \times R + 75 \times G + 15 \times B \gg 7 \tag{1}$$

The range of grayscale values obtained by the above formula is also 1–255. To facilitate self-supervised network learning, all pixel values are divided by 255 to normalize to 0–1, and then used as input to the encoding network. The coding network adopts a four-layer convolutional neural network structure.

3.2 Cross-Modal Image Prediction

Cross-modal image prediction uses supervised learning approach [9]. Directly predicting the representation of the grayscale image instead of the original one can simplify the network structure and computational complexity, so the target of the cross-modal prediction algorithm proposed in this paper is the representation vector of the grayscale image. First, it is necessary to extract the encoding network of the reference picture and grayscale image, and then fix its parameters. Since the reference picture has only one set of data, it can be directly encoded to obtain the reference picture representation Z_r. Each set of grayscale image data *Gray* corresponds to the robot end-effector F/T and *Pose*. The grayscale image is encoded to obtain Z_{real} and used as the target value for cross-modal prediction. And Z_r, F/T and *Pose* are concatenated and used as the input of the prediction network. The prediction network consists of 4 layers of perceptrons, and the output is a vector Z_{rep}, whose dimension is the same as Z_{real}, which has a total of 32 dimensions.

The predicted representation vector can then be used to generate a grayscale image through the trained decoder. The prediction effect can be compared by the original grayscale image and the generated grayscale image, and the pixel point error with physical meaning can be obtained. Figure 3 is a schematic diagram of a network for predicting end real-time images across modalities through reference images, force/torque feedback, and position/pose.

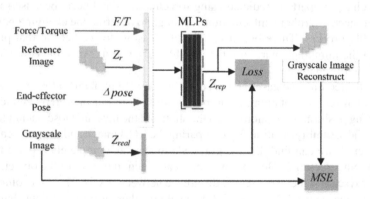

Fig. 3. Cross-modal prediction network for precision assembly task, in order to avoid the problem of unstable ambient illumination or being blocked by obstacles.

3.3 Action-Generation System

Since grayscale images can already be generated, the vision sensor can be discarded in subsequent actual assembly tasks. The information that can be obtained now includes the force/torque of the end of the robot arm, the pose of the end of the robot arm, the reference picture, and the representation vector of the grayscale image jointly generated by the first three. Force perception and pose are two independent state variables, and the generated grayscale representation contains potential part fit information. Therefore, the end-effector force/torque, position/pose and grayscale representation vector are used together as the input state of the action generator.

Reinforcement learning is designed to solve the explicit or implicit mapping relationship between states and policies. It contains two parts, the agent and the environment, which can be understood as the human brain to make corresponding decisions based on the feedback of the environment. The agent can perceive the state of the environment and choose an appropriate action based on the feedback reward to maximize long-term benefits. The environment is evaluated according to the actions selected by the agent, and a quantifiable signal is given back to the agent. In this continuous interaction process, the agent can learn continuously, and finally get the optimal policy. Since the task of this paper is the pose adjustment of 6-dimensional continuous space, the Continuous Q-Learning with NAF algorithm [10] is finally selected. The NAF algorithm is a reinforcement learning algorithm specially proposed for high-dimensional continuous state space and action space. Although DDPG is also designed to solve the problem of continuous action, it is not suitable for scenarios in random environments, especially the motion control of robots. The action-generation algorithm cam be written as the following code (Table 1).

Table 1. NAF algorithm for precision assembly.

Continuous Q-Learning with NAF
Randomly initialize the normalized Q network $Q(s, a \mid \theta_Q)$;
Initialize Target network Q' parameter weights $\theta_{Q'} \leftarrow \theta_Q$;
Initialize the experience playback pool;
for episode = 1~M:
Initialize stochastic process Γ for action exploration;
Get initial state $s_1 \sim p(s_1)$;
for t = 1~T:
Choose action $a_t = \mu(s_t \mid \theta_\mu) + \Gamma_t$;
Execute action a_t to obtain r_t and s_{t+1};
Save (s_t, a_t, r_t, s_{t+1}) into R;
for iteration = 1~I:
Randomly sample a minibatch of size m from R;
Set $y_i = r_i + \gamma V'(s_{i+1} \mid \theta_{Q'})$;
Minimize $Loss = \frac{1}{N}\sum_{i=1}^{N}(y_i - Q(s_i, a_i \mid \theta_Q))^2$ to upgrade θ_Q;
Upgrade target network parameters $\theta_{Q'} \leftarrow \tau\theta_Q + (1-\tau)\theta_{Q'}$;
end **for**;
end **for**;
end **for**;

3.4 Reward Function

In addition to the network structure, the reward function also plays a crucial role. Our goal is to let the robot's end effector find the hole first, and then adjust the posture to move into the hole. Therefore, the principle of reward function design is to encourage movement towards the hole, and the end effector is restricted to a small range of movement. Set the position/pose of the end-effector before & after a single action as

$$P_{prime} = [x_0, y_0, z_0, R_0, P_0, Y_0] \tag{2}$$

$$P_{current} = [x_1, y_1, z_1, R_1, P_1, Y_1] \tag{3}$$

and the target position of the hole as

$$P_{hole} = \left[x_h, y_h, z_h, R_h, P_h, Y_h\right]. \tag{4}$$

Then we set

$$\Delta z = z_1 - z_0 \tag{5}$$

$$\Delta xy = |(x_1, y_1) - (x_h, y_h)| - |(x_0, y_0) - (x_h, y_h)| \tag{6}$$

$$\Delta RPY = |(R_1, P_1, Y_1) - (R_h, P_h, Y_h)| - |(R_0, P_0, Y_0) - (R_h, P_h, Y_h)|. \tag{7}$$

To avoid the end-effector moving too far away from the target area, we also set limitations as

$$\Delta_z = z_1 - z_h \tag{8}$$

$$\Delta_{xy} = |(x, y) - (x_h, y_h)| \tag{9}$$

$$\Delta_{RPY} = |(R, P, Y) - (R_h, P_h, Y_h)|. \tag{10}$$

Then, we set the reward function as the follows.

$$r = \begin{cases} -1, & f > F_{max} \text{ or } \tau > T_{max} \text{ or } \Delta_{xy} > 3 \\ & \text{ or } \Delta_z < 3 \text{ or } \Delta_{RPY} < 5 \\ 1, & \text{for the first time } \Delta_{xy} \leq 0.2 \\ 3, & \text{for the first time } \Delta_z \leq -\frac{d_h}{2} \\ 5, & \Delta_z \leq -d_h \\ -\Delta xy - \Delta z - \Delta RPY, & \text{others} \end{cases} \tag{11}$$

in which d_h is the depth of the hole.

4 Experiments and Results

4.1 Hybrid Position/Force Control

In the previous subsection, we obtained a cross-modal image prediction algorithm model based on the reference image, end-effector force/torque and position/pose, which determined three state quantities for reinforcement learning. After the action is given by the agent, it needs to be executed by the robot, which involves the motion control of the robot. Precision assembly is a contact type task that requires high precision. In the assembly target of this paper, the fitting clearance of the parts is about 0.1 mm, and there is collision during the movement, so the traditional point-to-point position control strategy fails. What we need is a flexible assembly strategy to keep robots and parts safe. The compliance control method of robot motion control is hybrid position/force control, which is a method of independently controlling each dimension through decoupling to perform position control or force control.

The schematic diagram of the force-potential hybrid control used in this paper is shown in Fig. 4, and the task is defined in the Cartesian space. Among them, a constant assembly force is adopted in the z direction to ensure assembly safety. In the x, y, R, P and Y directions, position control is used for pose adjustment. R, P and Y are Euler angles. In position control, the stiffness coefficients for the six dimensions are $\{600, 600, 600, 50, 50, 50\}$ and the force gain coefficients are $\{0.1, 0.1, 0.1, 0.1, 0.1, 0.1\}$. The final S matrix is $diag(1, 1, 0, 1, 1, 1)$. The corresponding position of 1 indicates that the position uses position control, and the corresponding position of 0 indicates that the position uses force control.

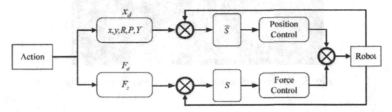

Fig. 4. Hybrid position/force control framework for safe precision assembly.

4.2 Environment Setup

In the experiment, the assembly robot chose Franka Panda, and the vision camera chose Intel RealSense D435i. The force information is fed back by the robot's own force estimation function with a frequency of 1000 Hz. The assembly object is a mobile phone and a USB-C data cable. The minimum depth detection distance of RealSense D435i is 0.2 m, which allows us to obtain data at a closer distance. The maximum resolution of RGB images is 1920 × 1280, and the maximum resolution of depth images is 1280 × 720, and the frame rate is 30 fps. Figure 5 shows the hardware environment of the cross-modal prediction experiment.

4.3 Results and Discussion

Multimodal Fusion Assembly. The RGB-D camera is about 300 mm away from the phone to be assembled. Manually adjust the camera so that the assembly origin is at the center of the camera's vision, and then fix the camera's position and attitude. A black background curtain was arranged around the experimental platform, and a black baffle was also fixed on the background of the camera's field of view to simplify the visual information. In the training phase, we collected 5000 sets of data, of which the test set accounted for 0.1.

In the subsequent online training process, the coding part of the trained model is extracted to encode RGB image data and depth image data, and the representation vector is obtained through the corresponding coding network coding, and then spliced with the end effector force/torque information as the state input of the NAF algorithm. The shaft hole assembly experiment was trained for 200 rounds in total, and the obtained reinforcement learning curve is shown in Fig. 6.

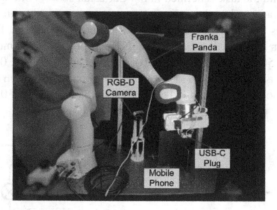

Fig. 5. Experiment setup of USB-C precision assembly.

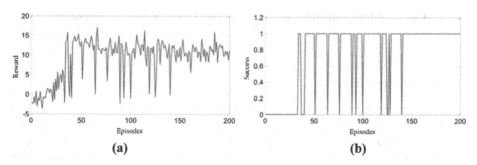

Fig. 6. (a) Achieved reward; (b) insertion success curves of multimodal fusion assembly task.

Cross-Modal Prediction Assembly. Our cross-modal prediction experimental process is the same as the multi-modal fusion part. First, we collected training data, with a total of 6400 groups, and a reference image. Then we trained the self-supervised network and the cross-modal prediction network, with the result as follows (Figs. 7, 8 and 9).

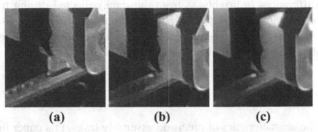

(a)   **(b)**   **(c)**

Fig. 7. (a) Reference image (original/reset point of each episode); (b) one of the actual grayscale image during assembly trials; (c) the corresponding image predicted by the cross-modal prediction network and the decoder, which is much smoother and clearer.

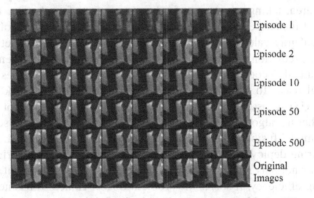

Fig. 8. Comparison of the predicted images and the original ones in different episodes.

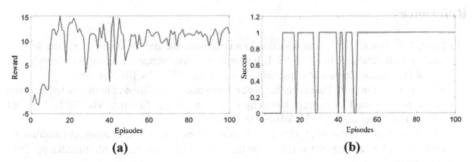

(a)   **(b)**

Fig. 9. (a) Achieved reward; (b) insertion success curves of the assembly task based on cross-modal prediction network.

The results show that precise assembly through cross-modal image prediction is better than using raw images, not only in success rate but also in efficiency. Moreover, multimodal fusion is more robust than single modality because there are complementary and auxiliary roles between modalities. The addition of vision may have a negative effect on network learning because of lighting instability. This is because the acquired images have differences in brightness from the data collected during training due to lighting effects, and thus are encoded with incorrect representations. Cross-modal image prediction does not use vision sensors, and other modalities are not affected by lighting, so the assembly policy can be trained quickly and well.

5 Conclusion

According to the characteristics of precision assembly tasks, this paper first proposes a multimodal fusion network based on RGB images, depth images and force perception. Aiming at the problem of unstable ambient illumination, this paper then proposes a cross-modal image prediction network. With an attached supervised learning block, the network is able to predict the representation vector of the real grayscale image of the assembly area, taking advantage of reference image, force/torque feedback, and position/pose of the end-effector. The authentic representation vectors of the reference image and actual grayscale images are also obtained by self-supervised network. In order to visualize the prediction performance, we decode the predicted representation vectors through the trained decoder to generate the predicted grayscale images and compare it with the real ones. To verify the performance of the whole network, experimental verification of USB-C assembly is carried out on the Franka Panda robot platform. The results show that the algorithm is better not only in success rate, but also in efficiency than the multimodal fusion algorithm. The algorithm does not require the participation of cameras during deployment, nor does it need to process images during actual data processing. This not only reduces the cost of large-scale deployment, but also improves data processing efficiency. It solves the problem of low camera robustness to ambient illumination, and the problem of unintended block of sight during assembly.

References

1. Hunt, A.J., Black, A.W.: Unit selection in a concatenative speech synthesis system using a large speech database. In: 1996 IEEE International Conference on Acoustics, Speech, and Signal Processing Conference Proceedings, vol. 1, pp. 373–376. IEEE (1996)
2. Kojima, A., Tamura, T., Fukunaga, K.: Natural language description of human activities from video images based on concept hierarchy of actions. Int. J. Comput. Vis. **50**(2), 171–184 (2002). https://doi.org/10.1023/A:1020346032608
3. Rasiwasia, N., Costa Pereira, J., Coviello, E., et al.: A new approach to cross-modal multimedia retrieval. In: Proceedings of the 18th ACM International Conference on Multimedia, pp. 251–260 (2010)
4. Vinyals, O., Toshev, A., Bengio, S., et al.: Show and tell: a neural image caption generator. In: Proceedings of the IEEE Conference on Computer Vision and Pattern Recognition, pp. 3156–3164 (2015)

5. Venugopalan, S., Xu, H., Donahue, J., et al.: Translating videos to natural language using deep recurrent neural networks. Comput. Sci. 3–9 (2014)

6. Li, Y., Zhu, J.Y., Tedrake, R., et al.: Connecting touch and vision via cross-modal prediction. In: Proceedings of the IEEE/CVF Conference on Computer Vision and Pattern Recognition, pp. 10609–10618 (2019)

7. Li, A., Liu, R., Yang, X., Lou, Y.: Reinforcement learning strategy based on multimodal representations for high-precision assembly tasks. In: Liu, X.J., Nie, Z., Yu, J., Xie, F., Song, R. (eds.) Intelligent Robotics and Applications, vol. 13013, pp. 56–66. Springer, Cham (2021). https://doi.org/10.1007/978-3-030-89095-7_6

8. Lee, M.A., Zhu, Y., Zachares, P., et al.: Making sense of vision and touch: learning multimodal representations for contact-rich tasks. IEEE Trans. Robot. 36(3), 582–596 (2020)

9. Lee, M.A., Tan, M., Zhu, Y., et al.: Detect, reject, correct: crossmodal compensation of corrupted sensors. In: 2021 IEEE International Conference on Robotics and Automation (ICRA), pp. 909–916. IEEE (2021)

10. Gu, S., Lillicrap, T., Sutskever, I., et al.: Continuous deep q-learning with model-based acceleration. In: International Conference on Machine Learning, pp. 2829–2838. PMLR (2016)

An Improved YOLOX for Detection in Urine Sediment Images

Minming Yu[ID], Yanjing Lei[(✉)][ID], Wenyan Shi[ID], Yujie Xu[ID],
and Sixian Chan[ID]

College of Computer Science and Technology, Zhejiang University of Technology,
Hangzhou 310023, China
leiyj@zjut.edu.cn

Abstract. In clinical medicine, the detection of human urine sediment is usually a basic test. The indicators of test can effectively analyze whether the patient has the disease. The traditional method of chemical, physical and microscopic analysis of samples artificially is time-consuming and inefficient. With the development of deep learning technology, many detectors now can replace traditional manual work and play a good detection effect. So it is of great value to put deep learning technology into the medical field. Usually, the Urine Microscopic Image has challenges for research, in which many detectors can not detect the cells well due to their small scale and heavy overlap occlusion. Therefore, we propose a novel detector for the detection of urine sediment in this paper. Firstly, considering the friendliness of YOLOX to the small objects, we adopt the framework from the YOLOX. Secondly, we add spatial, channel and position attention to enhance the feature information to achieve more accurate detection results. Then, the better Giouloss is also applied to make a better regression of the bounding box. Finally, the experimental results show that our improved model based on YOLOX achieves 44.5% AP_{50-90} and 80.1% AP_{50} on the public dataset Urine Microscopic Image Dataset, which is far better than other detectors.

Keywords: Deep learning · Object detection · Urine sediment · YOLOX

1 Introduction

In clinical medicine, the examination of human urine samples is usually regarded as an important item. The indicators obtained by analyzing the urine sediment in microscopic images play an important role in the prevention and diagnosis of urological and renal diseases. The main indicators include red blood cells (RBCs), white blood cells (WBCs) and epithelial cells. Accurate detection and classification of these cells are essential for the diagnosis and prevention of diseases. The traditional method of having professionals manually distinguish and the count is time-consuming and laborious, it is no longer suitable for use in real-life situations.

H. Liu et al. (Eds.): ICIRA 2022, LNAI 13458, pp. 556–567, 2022.
https://doi.org/10.1007/978-3-031-13841-6_50

Object detection, as a fundamental task in the field of computer vision, has been widely used in satellite remote sensing image processing [23,30], vehicle detection [2,22], face detection [16,35], etc. Meanwhile, with the advancement of deep learning technology in object detection, many excellent detection models and algorithms have been born, such as Faster R-CNN [27], FCOS [29], YOLOX [8] and DETR [5,6], etc. These detectors can play a marvelous detection effect. The urine sediment dataset we used is Urine Microscopic Image Dataset [11]. Most of the cellular objects in this dataset are small scale and some images are very dense with cellular objects, which may result in missed and false detections with conventional detectors.

Therefore, we propose an improved YOLOX for urine sediment detection in this paper. YOLOX is based on one-stage algorithm and anchor-free approach, with CSPDarknet-53 as the backbone network, multi-scale feature fusion using PANet, and adopts the decoupled head method for object detection, which is one of the current high-performance detectors. Then, we add channel and spatial attention modules after dark2 and dark3 of the backbone network CSPDarknet-53. we also add position attention modules after dark5. These attention modules can tell the network to ignore the unimportant regions and focus on those important regions to improve the representation power of CNNs. At the same time, we discard the original Iouloss [33] and use the Giouloss [28] as the regression loss function to achieve a better regression effect of the bounding box.

In summary, our main contributions are as follows:

- We apply the high-performance detector YOLOX to the urine sediment dataset and design the mixed (channel, spatial and position) attention module based on YOLOX to improve the CNNs representation power.
- We replace Iouloss with Giouloss to perform better regression on bounding box. Our improved detector achieves state-of-the-art results on Urine Microscopic Image Dataset

2 Related Work

2.1 Object Detection

The definition of object detection is to give an image and output the classes and position of the objects that have appeared in the training set. Object detection algorithms can be divided into one-stage algorithms and two-stage algorithms. The one-stage algorithm is to directly predict the classes and position of the objects using only one CNN network, such as YOLO [1,3,8,24–26], SSD [21], Retina-net [18], etc. The YOLO algorithm, goes directly from the image pixels to get the anchor box [27] and classification probabilities and can reach a speed of 45 frames per second. The SSD network [21] adopts one-stage idea to improve the detection speed, incorporates the idea of anchors in the network and extracts features in layers to calculate classification and bounding box regression. Thus SSD network is adapted to the detection task of more multi-scale objects. Retina-net [18] mainly proposes Focal loss to solve the problem of unbalanced ratio of positive and negative samples in one-stage object detection. The detector with one-stage algorithm has lower accuracy, but gains the faster detection speed. In contrast, the two-stage algorithm first generates a regional proposal using heuristics (selective search) or Region Proposal Networks(RPN) [27], and then continues to do classification and regression tasks on the regional proposal. The two-stage algorithms are R-CNN [10], Fast R-CNN [9], Faster R-CNN [4,12,27], etc. R-CNN [10] extracts features by generating region proposal and using CNN operation for each region proposal, which causes redundancy in the extracted feature map and the drawback of slow speed. Fast R-CNN [9] is proposed to do the CNN operation after extracting the feature map, which can reduce the redundant CNN operation for all the region proposals. Faster R-CNN [27] is proposed to use RPN instead of selective search to generate regional proposal. We use the one-stage algorithm YOLOX [8] as the framework, which is faster and can achieve the same or higher accuracy than the two-stage algorithm.

2.2 Attention Mechanism

Attention mechanisms are derived from the study of human vision. The human visual system uses a series of partial glimpses to better capture information in a scene and selectively focus on salient parts. Attention mechanisms have since arisen in the field of image processing as well, and have also proven usefully in various computer vision tasks. Attention mechanisms not only tell the network where to focus its attention, but also suppress unnecessary features and improve the representation power of CNNs. Squeeze-and-Excitation Networks (SENet) [14] compresses the channels and proposes channel attention. Selective Kernel Networks (SKNet) [17] is an improved version of SENet, by adding multiple branches, each with a different feeling field. Non-Local Neural Networks [31] is essentially a kind of self-attention, consisting of three branches: query, key and value. The weights are obtained by firstly calculating the similarity between query and key, and then weighting and summing the weights with the corresponding values to obtain the final result. Considering the huge computational effort of Non-Local Neural Networks, Criss-Cross Network (CCNet) [15] is also proposed. This attention module can obtain the contextual information well while reducing the computational effort significantly. In this paper, we propose a mixed attention module that can effectively focus on spatial and channel as well as location information to achieve advanced detection performance.

3   Proposed Approach

3.1   YOLOX

YOLOX based on anchor-free is one of the most advanced detectors, which consists of the backbone, neck and head. Firstly Mosaic [3] and MixUp [34] are used as the data augmentation. CSPDarknet-53 [3] is used as the backbone, which consists of dark2, dark3, dark4 and dark5 parts, to extract features on images. The multi-scale fusion adopts the PANet [20] as the Neck part. PANet uses dark3, dark4 and dark5 as inputs and passes the semantic information of the deep layer back to the shallow layer by top-down fusion, and then bottom-up fusion, which is used to enhance its position information. Finally produces three different scales of outputs into the prediction head. Considering that the classification branch and the regression branch focus and interest on different parts, therefore we propose the classification task separately from the regression task by using the decoupled head. Anchor-free boxes are also used, producing only one prediction box per grid, which reduces hyperparameters and avoids the imbalance between positive and negative samples, while the performance is still comparable to anchor-based ones. The label classification strategy uses SiamOTA [8], which is improved based on OTA [7]. For the loss function, YOLOX calculates classification loss and object score loss with Binary Cross Entropy Loss and bounding box loss with IOULoss [33]. In summary, YOLOX is one of the advanced detectors in terms of detection performance. The structure of our improved model based on YOLOX as shown in Fig. 1.

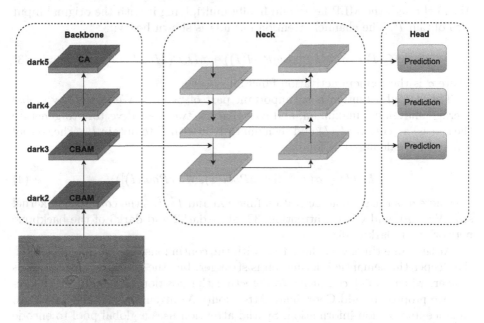

Fig. 1. The general architecture of our proposed improved model is based on YOLOX. For training, our input is a 640×640 size urine sediment image, and we use CSPDarknet-53 as the backbone for feature extraction. We add CBAM attention after dark2, dark3 layers and CA attention after dark5 layer. We use PANet for multi-scale feature fusion to generate prediction heads at different scales, and in the Head section to perform classification and regression tasks, for bounding box regression we use Giouloss

3.2   Attention Module

To better improve the representation power of CNNs, to let the network know 'what' and 'where' to learn in the channel and spatial axes. And to help the flow of information in the network more effectively. We add the Convolutional Block Attention Module(CBAM) [32] attention, which consists of the channel attention and the spatial attention. The calculation formula is as follows:

$$I' = M_c(I) \otimes I \tag{1}$$

$$I'' = M_s(I') \otimes I' \tag{2}$$

For a given feature map $I \in R^{C \times H \times W}$, $M_c \in R^{C \times 1 \times 1}$, $M_s \in R^{C \times 1 \times 1}$, $\otimes$ denotes element-wise multiplication.

The channel attention is focused on the given input image 'what' is meaningful, and consists of Avgpool and Maxpool to aggregate the information in the space. Thus generating different spatial context descriptors to enhance the representation power of CNNs networks, and then summing up the channel attention $M_c(I)$ through the MLP layer, and finally multiplying it with the original input I to obtain I'. The channel attention formula is shown below:

$$M_c(I) = \sigma(MLP(AvgPool(I)) + MLP(MaxPool(I))) \tag{3}$$

where σ is the sigmoid activation function

The spatial attention is an important part of 'where'. We pool I' by global average and global maximum, and convolve the two pooled vectors to generate the spatial attention $M_s(I)$ and then multiply it with I' to obtain I''. The spatial attention is calculated as follows:

$$M_s(I) = \sigma(f^{7 \times 7}([AvgPool(I); MaxPool(I)])) \tag{4}$$

where σ is the sigmoid activation function and $f^{7 \times 7}$ is the convolution kernel size. We only add CBAM attention [32] after dark2 and dark3 of the backbone network CSPDarknet-53.

At the same time, we believe that with the continuous convolution operation, the deeper the semantic information is stronger, but the position information is weaker, which is not conducive to detecting the position of the object. Therefore we propose to add Coordinate Attention(CA) attention [13] after dark5 to enhance its position information. Spatial attention uses a global pool to encode spatial information, which compresses spatial information into the channel, but this tends to lose position information, while CA attention embeds position information into the channel. The specific operation is to first use two 1D global average pooling by width and height in two directions, respectively, to obtain the feature maps in both directions, with the following equation:

$$z_c^h(h) = \frac{1}{W} \sum_{0 \leq u < W} x_c(h, u) \tag{5}$$

$$z_c^w(w) = \frac{1}{H} \sum_{0 \leq v < H} x_c(v, w) \tag{6}$$

Global information is better captured using global averaging pooling, by which we can capture long-range dependencies along one spatial direction while retaining their precise position information along the other direction.

Then the two directions of the special detection map z^h and z^w concat together after downscaling by 1×1 convolution. So that its channel becomes C/r, after normalization and sigmoid activation function processing to obtain f, $f \in R^{C/r \times (H+W)}$, as shown in the following equation:

$$f = \delta \left(F_1 \left([z^h, z^w] \right) \right) \tag{7}$$

Then the number of channels is changed to be the same as the original number of channels using 1×1 convolution to obtain F_h and F_w, $f^h \in R^{C/r \times H)}$ and $f^w \in R^{C/r \times W)}$. The attention weights g^h and g^w in height and width are obtained by the sigmoid activation function, as shown in the following equations:

$$g^h = \sigma \left(F_h \left(f^h \right) \right) \tag{8}$$

$$g^w = \sigma \left(F_w \left(f^w \right) \right) \tag{9}$$

Eventually, we multiply and weight the attention weights obtained on height and width with the original feature map to perform the enhancement of position information with the following equation.

$$y_c(u, v) = x_c(u, v) \times g_c^h(u) \times g_c^w(v) \tag{10}$$

3.3 Loss

The loss function of our detector consists of the following three components, $Loss_{cls}$ is the classification loss, $Loss_{obj}$ is the object score loss, and $Loss_{reg}$ is the edge loss composition.

$$Loss = Loss_{cls} + Loss_{obj} + 5 * Loss_{reg} \tag{11}$$

We calculate the classification loss and object score loss by using the Binary Cross Entropy Loss function with the following formula:

$$BCELoss = -(y \log(p(x)) + (1 - y) \log(1 - p(x))) \tag{12}$$

When we calculate the classification loss, we firstly use one-hot encode to get the true value, y represents the encoded value as 0 or 1, and p(x) represents the confidence value for each category. And when we calculate the object score loss, y represents the foreground or background with a value of 0 or 1, and p(x) represents the confidence value of the foreground and background.

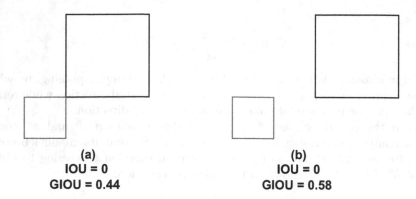

(a)
IOU = 0
GIOU = 0.44

(b)
IOU = 0
GIOU = 0.58

Fig. 2. (a) (b) shows the two cases when the predicted frame does not intersect the real frame. iou for both (a) and (b) is 0, which cannot measure the relative position, but Giou for (a) is 0.44 and Giou for (b) is 0.58.

In terms of bounding box loss, we consider that there is still improvement for the original Iouloss. As shown in the Fig. 2, when the prediction box does not intersect with the ground truth, the concatenation of the two boxes is 0 and Iouloss is 0. There is no consideration of the relative position of the prediction box to the ground truth, and Giouloss can solve this trouble. Therefore, we calculate the bounding box loss by using Giouloss, and the Giouloss formula is as follows:

$$IOU = \frac{I(S_1, S_2)}{U(S_1, S_2)} \tag{13}$$

$$GIOU\,Loss = 1 - \left(IOU - \frac{A - U}{A}\right) \tag{14}$$

$S1$ represents the prediction box and $S2$ represents the ground truth. $I(S1, S2)$ is the area of the intersection of the prediction box and the ground truth, $U(S1, S2)$ is the area of the concatenation of the prediction box and the ground truth, and IOU is $I(S1, S2)/U(S1, S2)$. Giouloss is done by making the minimum outer rectangle of the prediction box and the ground truth. A represents the area of the smallest outer rectangle, and U is the area where the predicted box intersects the ground truth. lower Giouloss indicates a more accurate prediction.

4   Experiments

4.1   Implementation

We use the public dataset Urine Microscopic Image Dataset [11]. We convert the tags in csv format to json to get 268 training images, 60 test images, and 38 val images, and then put them into the model for training.

Our network model is trained on a GPU with two 2080ti's, using python 3.8, pytorch 1.7.1 and cuda 11.0. We use the l-version of YOLOX as the baseline and add the weights already trained on the COCO dataset [19] as our pre-training weights, which can better help the network converge. With an input image size of 640×640. Originally, YOLOX used Mosaic and MixUp data augmentation, but considering that Urine Microscopic Image Dataset is a small dataset, the models trained with these two data augmentation are extremely unstable and cause the accuracy curve to drop, so we turned off the data augmentation during training. A total of 50 training sessions are conducted, the first 5 epochs are warm-up. A stochastic gradient descent strategy is used, the initial learning rate is lr $\times$ batch size /64, $lr = 0.01$, batch size= 4. Weight decay is 0.0005, SGD momentum is 0.9, and the learning rate adjustment strategy is the cosine annealing method.

4.2   Comparison with Other Object Detection Algorithms

We compared our algorithm with other object detection algorithms, such as YOLOV3, YOLOV5, Faster R-CNN, PAN, and FCOS. We trained these networks on the mmdetection framework with two nvidia 2080ti GPUs on hardware devices for one training cycle (12 epochs).

Table 1 shows the comparison between our improved detector and the above detector in terms of AP_{50-90} and AP_{50}. We can find that the AP_{50-90} and AP_{50} metrics of our detector are much higher than the other detectors. Our detector also uses the One-stage algorithm, and compared with YOLOV5, AP_{50-90} and AP_{50} improve by 14.5% and 13.1%, respectively, under the same Backbone. The reason is that our detector has many advantages compared to YOLOV5, such as the use of anchor-free mechanism, decoupled headers, SiamOTA strategy, etc. Compared with the Two-stage classical algorithm Faster R-CNN, our AP_{50-90} and AP_{50} improve by 13.4% and 14%, and we keep the speed fast while the accuracy is far better than Faster R-CNN. Compared with the anchorless detector FCOS, our AP_{50-90} and AP_{50} are also substantially ahead. The above fully demonstrates that our improved model based on YOLOX reaches the sate-of-the-art level. The results of the proposed detection on the urine sediment UMID dataset can be seen in Fig. 3.

Table 1. The comparison of detection performance on the UMID.

Methods	Backbone	AP_{50-90}	AP_{50}
Faster R-CNN [27]	Resnet50	31.1	66.1
YOLOV3 [26]	Darknet-53	18.1	39.0
FCOS [29]	Resnet50	11.5	30.1
PAN [20]	Resnet50	26.8	66.0
YOLOV5 [1]	CSPDarknet-53	30.0	67.0
Ours	CSPDarknet-53	44.5	80.1

4.3   Ablation Study

Ablation Experimental results are shown in Table 2. Using the l-version of YOLOX as the baseline, we replace Iouloss with Giouloss to increase AP_{50-90} and AP_{50} by 0.5% and 1.7%. Respectively, proving that Giouloss can effectively solve the situation that the relative position cannot be measured when the prediction box does not intersect with the ground truth, and can achieve a more effective regression on the bounding box. We add mixed attention to the network. The detail is as follows: the CBAM attention to the backbone network after dark2

Table 2. Ablation experimental performance on the UMID.

Methods	AP_{50-90}	AP_{50}
YOLOX baseline	41.6	74.7
+Giouloss	42.1	76.4
+Mixed attention $(CBAM + CA)$	41.6	75.8
+Giouloss+Mixed attention	44.5	80.1

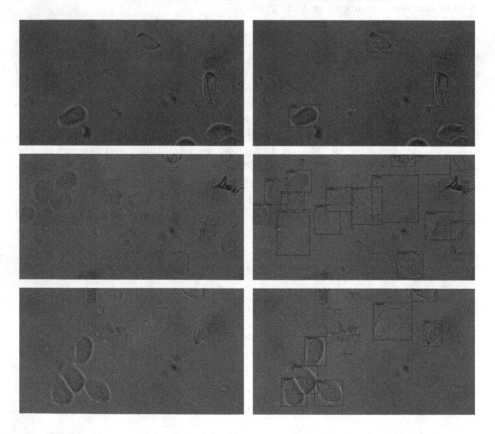

Fig. 3. Here we show the original images and the results after detection.

and dark3, and the CA attention to the backbone network after dark5. AP_{50-90} improves 1.1% compared to baseline, which proves that CBAM attention and CA attention can correctly and effectively tell the network which parts to pay attention to. Finally, based on the baseline, adding Giouloss with CBAM attention and CA attention at the same time, AP_{50-90} and AP_{50} improved by 2.9% and 5.4%. The two innovations were used in combination with a more obvious effect, which proved the feasibility and effectiveness of our two innovations.

5 Conclusion

In this paper, we applied deep learning object detection techniques to the medical field, which would greatly improve efficiency compared to traditional manual processing methods. We proposed an improved detector based on YOLOX and experimentally demonstrated that the mixed attention (CBAM attention and CA attention) mechanisms are very effective with Giouloss. The former could tell the network which parts to learn and suppress the unimportant regions. While the latter could better consider the relative position of the prediction box and the ground truth, which played a better bounding box regression effect. We improved AP_{50-90} and AP_{50} to 44.5% and 80.1%, respectively, in the original baseline, and also substantially exceeded other commonly used detectors. The ablation study proved the effectiveness of the mixed attention and the Giouloss. Finally, we hope that our detector will be applied to the detection of cells in urine sediment to assist medical and nursing staff to improve efficiency, provide assistance to the majority of patients, and promote the development of medical progress.

Acknowledgments. This work was partly supported by the National Natural Science Foundation of China (No. 61873240) and the Foundation of State Key Laboratory of Digital Manufacturing Equipment and Technology (Grant No. DMETKF2022024).

References

1. G.J., et al.: Yolov5 (2021). https://github.com/ultralytics/yolov5
2. Benjumea, A., Teeti, I., Cuzzolin, F., Bradley, A.: YOLO-Z: improving small object detection in YOLOv5 for autonomous vehicles. arXiv preprint arXiv:2112.11798 (2021)
3. Bochkovskiy, A., Wang, C.Y., Liao, H.Y.M.: YOLOv4: optimal speed and accuracy of object detection. arXiv preprint arXiv:2004.10934 (2020)
4. Cai, Z., Vasconcelos, N.: Cascade R-CNN: delving into high quality object detection. In: Proceedings of the IEEE Conference on Computer Vision and Pattern Recognition, pp. 6154–6162 (2018)
5. Carion, N., Massa, F., Synnaeve, G., Usunier, N., Kirillov, A., Zagoruyko, S.: End-to-end object detection with transformers. In: Vedaldi, A., Bischof, H., Brox, T., Frahm, J.-M. (eds.) ECCV 2020. LNCS, vol. 12346, pp. 213–229. Springer, Cham (2020). https://doi.org/10.1007/978-3-030-58452-8_13

6. Dai, Z., Cai, B., Lin, Y., Chen, J.: UP-DETR: unsupervised pre-training for object detection with transformers. In: Proceedings of the IEEE/CVF Conference on Computer Vision and Pattern Recognition, pp. 1601–1610 (2021)

7. Ge, Z., Liu, S., Li, Z., Yoshie, O., Sun, J.: Ota: optimal transport assignment for object detection. In: Proceedings of the IEEE/CVF Conference on Computer Vision and Pattern Recognition, pp. 303–312 (2021)

8. Ge, Z., Liu, S., Wang, F., Li, Z., Sun, J.: YOLOX: exceeding yolo series in 2021. arXiv preprint arXiv:2107.08430 (2021)

9. Girshick, R.: Fast R-CNN. In: Proceedings of the IEEE International Conference on Computer Vision, pp. 1440–1448 (2015)

10. Girshick, R., Donahue, J., Darrell, T., Malik, J.: Rich feature hierarchies for accurate object detection and semantic segmentation. In: Proceedings of the IEEE Conference on Computer Vision and Pattern Recognition, pp. 580–587 (2014)

11. Goswami, D., Aggrawal, H.O., Gupta, R., Agarwal, V.: Urine microscopic image dataset. arXiv preprint arXiv:2111.10374 (2021)

12. He, K., Gkioxari, G., Dollár, P., Girshick, R.: Mask R-CNN. In: Proceedings of the IEEE International Conference on Computer Vision, pp. 2961–2969 (2017)

13. Hou, Q., Zhou, D., Feng, J.: Coordinate attention for efficient mobile network design. In: Proceedings of the IEEE/CVF Conference on Computer Vision and Pattern Recognition, pp. 13713–13722 (2021)

14. Hu, J., Shen, L., Sun, G.: Squeeze-and-excitation networks. In: Proceedings of the IEEE Conference on Computer Vision and Pattern Recognition, pp. 7132–7141 (2018)

15. Huang, Z., Wang, X., Huang, L., Huang, C., Wei, Y., Liu, W.: CCNet: Criss-cross attention for semantic segmentation. In: Proceedings of the IEEE/CVF International Conference on Computer Vision, pp. 603–612 (2019)

16. Li, J., Xie, H., Li, J., Wang, Z., Zhang, Y.: Frequency-aware discriminative feature learning supervised by single-center loss for face forgery detection. In: Proceedings of the IEEE/CVF Conference on Computer Vision and Pattern Recognition, pp. 6458–6467 (2021)

17. Li, X., Wang, W., Hu, X., Yang, J.: Selective kernel networks. In: Proceedings of the IEEE/CVF Conference on Computer Vision and Pattern Recognition, pp. 510–519 (2019)

18. Lin, T.Y., Goyal, P., Girshick, R., He, K., Dollár, P.: Focal loss for dense object detection. In: Proceedings of the IEEE International Conference on Computer Vision, pp. 2980–2988 (2017)

19. Lin, T.-Y., et al.: Microsoft COCO: common objects in context. In: Fleet, D., Pajdla, T., Schiele, B., Tuytelaars, T. (eds.) ECCV 2014. LNCS, vol. 8693, pp. 740–755. Springer, Cham (2014). https://doi.org/10.1007/978-3-319-10602-1_48

20. Liu, S., Qi, L., Qin, H., Shi, J., Jia, J.: Path aggregation network for instance segmentation. In: Proceedings of the IEEE Conference on Computer Vision and Pattern Recognition, pp. 8759–8768 (2018)

21. Liu, W., et al.: SSD: single shot multibox detector. In: Leibe, B., Matas, J., Sebe, N., Welling, M. (eds.) ECCV 2016. LNCS, vol. 9905, pp. 21–37. Springer, Cham (2016). https://doi.org/10.1007/978-3-319-46448-0_2

22. Lu, Z., Rathod, V., Votel, R., Huang, J.: Retinatrack: online single stage joint detection and tracking. In: Proceedings of the IEEE/CVF Conference on Computer Vision and Pattern Recognition, pp. 14668–14678 (2020)

23. Pan, X., et al.: Dynamic refinement network for oriented and densely packed object detection. In: Proceedings of the IEEE/CVF Conference on Computer Vision and Pattern Recognition, pp. 11207–11216 (2020)

24. Redmon, J., Divvala, S., Girshick, R., Farhadi, A.: You only look once: Unified, real-time object detection. In: Proceedings of the IEEE Conference on Computer Vision and Pattern Recognition, pp. 779–788 (2016)

25. Redmon, J., Farhadi, A.: YOLO9000: better, faster, stronger. In: Proceedings of the IEEE Conference on Computer Vision and Pattern Recognition, pp. 7263–7271 (2017)

26. Redmon, J., Farhadi, A.: YOLOV3: an incremental improvement. arXiv preprint arXiv:1804.02767 (2018)

27. Ren, S., He, K., Girshick, R., Sun, J.: Faster R-CNN: towards real-time object detection with region proposal networks. Adv. Neural Inf. Process. Syst. **28** (2015)

28. Rezatofighi, H., Tsoi, N., Gwak, J., Sadeghian, A., Reid, I., Savarese, S.: Generalized intersection over union: a metric and a loss for bounding box regression. In: Proceedings of the IEEE/CVF Conference on Computer Vision and Pattern Recognition, pp. 658–666 (2019)

29. Tian, Z., Shen, C., Chen, H., He, T.: Fcos: fully convolutional one-stage object detection. In: Proceedings of the IEEE/CVF International Conference on Computer Vision, pp. 9627–9636 (2019)

30. Van Etten, A.: You only look twice: rapid multi-scale object detection in satellite imagery. arXiv preprint arXiv:1805.09512 (2018)

31. Wang, X., Girshick, R., Gupta, A., He, K.: Non-local neural networks. In: Proceedings of the IEEE Conference on Computer Vision and Pattern Recognition, pp. 7794–7803 (2018)

32. Woo, S., Park, J., Lee, J.Y., Kweon, I.S.: CBAM: convolutional block attention module. In: Proceedings of the European Conference on Computer Vision (ECCV), pp. 3–19 (2018)

33. Yu, J., Jiang, Y., Wang, Z., Cao, Z., Huang, T.: Unitbox: an advanced object detection network. In: Proceedings of the 24th ACM International Conference on Multimedia, pp. 516–520 (2016)

34. Zhang, H., Cisse, M., Dauphin, Y.N., Lopez-Paz, D.: Mixup: beyond empirical risk minimization. arXiv preprint arXiv:1710.09412 (2017)

35. Zhao, H., Zhou, W., Chen, D., Wei, T., Zhang, W., Yu, N.: Multi-attentional deepfake detection. In: Proceedings of the IEEE/CVF Conference on Computer Vision and Pattern Recognition, pp. 2185–2194 (2021)

Multi-scale Feature Based Densely Channel Attention Network for Vision-Based Haze Visibility Detection

Jie Tao[1], Yaocai Wu[2], Qike Shao[3], and Shihang Yan[3(✉)]

[1] Zhejiang Institute of Mechanical and Electrical Engineering Co., Ltd., Hangzhou 311203, China
[2] Zhejiang Machinery and Electrical Group Co., Ltd., Hangzhou 311203, China
[3] School of Computer Science and Technology, Zhejiang University of Technology, Hangzhou 310023, China
shyan@zjut.edu.cn

Abstract. Due to the problem of reduced visibility caused by haze pollution, it has brought great inconvenience to outdoor activities and traffic travel. Therefore, haze control has become one of the topics closely concerned by all sectors of society. Real time and accurate visibility detection is one of the important links to effectively prevent the impact of sudden fog or haze on driving safety, but the cost performance, accuracy and popularity of existing methods and equipment need to be improved. In this paper, we proposed a vision-based haze visibility detection method that achieves a better balance in the abovementioned aspects. Specifically, an improved AlexNet network with multi-scale feature mechanism is used to capture richer haze spatial details. Then, channel attention is employed to emphasize the characters of the feature maps. Finally, densely connection network is utilized to improve the contribution of the interconnected information flows. The experimental results show that the algorithm is consistent with the human observation, which meets the safety requirements. Moreover, our method achieves 95.6% accuracy with 11.68% improvement.

Keywords: Haze visibility detection · Multi-scale feature · Channel attention · Densely connection network

1 Introduction

As a part of physical meteorology, atmospheric visibility will be reduced due to the occurrence of haze, rain, snow and sandstorm, which often leads to a series of traffic accidents, resulting in property losses and casualties. Therefore, it is particularly important to detect the atmospheric visibility in real time and accurately.

For many years, although the technical means of weather forecast are improving year by year, it is considered extremely difficult to accurately predict visibility. The main reason is that the visibility reduction usually occurs in local areas, which is the microclimate change in this area, and in some cases, the atmospheric visibility will

H. Liu et al. (Eds.): ICIRA 2022, LNAI 13458, pp. 568–578, 2022.
https://doi.org/10.1007/978-3-031-13841-6_51

change many times in a short time. In particular, when such visibility changes occur along the highway, it is very fatal to the driver, which is likely to lead to large-scale vehicle serial collisions. Therefore, low visibility weather is always one of the weather conditions that the public and relevant management departments need to focus on.

At present, the detection methods of atmospheric visibility at home and abroad are mainly divided into three categories: direct estimation method of human eye, instrument detection method and estimation method based on image processing. Among them, human eye direct observation method is a traditional and simple measurement method, but due to the influence of many factors, the observation results have great errors, so it is gradually abandoned. The instrument measurement method adopts visibility detector, including transmission detector and scattering detector. Although the optical measurement method has good performance in haze days, the detection performance of this kind of detection method is not high in rainy and foggy weather or rainy and snowy weather due to variable light scattering coefficient and uneven atmospheric particles.

There are several problems in detecting visibility by optical scattering measurement method: the equipment is a precision instrument, so the cost of large-scale use is too high; both scattering and absorption will reduce the visibility; only considering the influence of scattering will lead to the error of detection results; and the equipment can only measure the visibility near the instrument, if it needs to cover a large area, multiple equipment must be installed, which may greatly increase the total cost of the project. The detection method based on image processing technology originated in the 1940s, when it was still based on black-and-white images [1]. As an alternative to optical scattering measurement, the popularity of digital cameras provides attractive technical support and solutions: a large number of surveillance cameras have been used in various traffic applications, which provides a low-cost solution for visibility estimation; the photosensitive element system of the camera has the same structure as the human vision system; the camera can collect scene information in real time, which is more convenient for detection. Therefore, the vision-based detection method will become the trend in the future, and some progress has been made, which included contrast method, image inflection point method and dark channel prior method.

For haze visibility detection, the detection method based on image processing technology is still in the theoretical research stage, and the research results are still in the initial stage, but it can be seen that accurately obtaining the value of atmospheric extinction coefficient is the key. Based on the optical measurement principle, the local atmosphere is used to replace the whole. In the actual measurement process, the proportion of scattered light intensity in a certain direction in the overall extinction is different. Therefore, the detection results are different, especially for scenes with low visibility, the error is large, and it is not suitable for real-time use. Most of the detection methods are complex, and the stability and accuracy need to be improved. Atmospheric visibility depends on the observation results of human eyes, which has strong subjectivity. It is often affected by various factors, so there is an urgent need for more reliable, practical and stable detection methods.

In this paper, we proposed a vision-based haze visibility detection method (shown in the Fig. 1), which is based on multi-scale feature extraction, channel attention and densely connection network method. Specifically, the multi-scale feature is used to get

Fig. 1. The goal of haze visibility detection is to recognize whether there is a haze. The first row shows the representative haze image, and the haze-like images are shown in second row such as the high beam or wrong camera focal length.

more detail at the low-level, and then we employ the channel attention with the densely connection structure to enhance the interaction among the information flows. The main contributions of this paper as follows:

- We proposed an improved AlexNet* to enhance the performance of vision-based haze detection method, which use the parameter correction method on minimum image entropy.
- Moreover, we use the multi-scale feature extraction and channel attention method with densely connection network to increase the detection accuracy and compress the model size.

2 Related Works

Traditional vision-based haze visibility detection methods include contrast method, image inflection point method and dark channel prior method, which are mainly focus on physical model of atmospheric scattering calculation.

Contrast method [1] is used to photograph the black object in the fog environment by digital cameras, and then the brightness contrast between the black object and its background is used to simply estimate the atmospheric visibility. The edge information with contrast greater than 5% in the collected image is extracted based on wavelet transform [2], and the atmospheric visibility value on the road is estimated, but the camera needs to be calibrated in advance. Wavelet transform and camera self-calibration technology are used to measure the visibility of Expressway [3–5], which is overcomes the shortcomings of the previous method, which requires the erection of auxiliary equipment and targets. In [6], an image contrast method is proposed, which extracts the features reflecting the change of visibility through the edge detection method, and then used the least square method and inverse transform to fit the parameters, finally determines the visibility in the image. According to the visual characteristics of human eyes, the position corresponding to visibility is just the dividing point between visible and invisible when human eyes observe an object; therefore, the visibility value can be obtained by looking for the position of the inflection point of image [7] brightness characteristics. The vanishing point and camera parameters are obtained by camera self-calibration technology [8], and the visibility is estimated by extracting the region of interest and calculating the brightness trend inflection point of the image. The logarithmic linear model [9] is used to estimate fog visibility by local contrast features and dark primary color prior statistics. The haze visibility is detected by combining the fog light transmission theory and geometric optics[10], which calculated the distance from the point on the road to the sampling point, similarly, this method is also based on the method of estimating the transmittance in the image without manual calibration. In [11], the priori data is used to calculated haze visibility by the vehicle camera visibility range and digital map. The feature vector method of scene projection [12] is proposed to improve the quality of night image through high dynamic range image, which is suitable for day and night conditions.

However, these methods generally need to calibrate the camera by place the target object in advance or calibrate the camera, which did not have universal applicability. Moreover, for different camera hardware models and practical application scenarios, the preliminary preparation of this kind of method is extremely cumbersome, so its application to different scenarios is limited.

3 The Proposed Method

AlexNet [13] is a typical convolutional neural network, which has good performance to object detection. To enhance the accuracy of haze visibility detection, we propose an improved AlexNet[*] which is composed of 5-convolution layers and 3-full connection layers. However, the AlexNet convolution structure gets the features with a fixed receptive field, which is difficult to distinguish the haze and haze-like. So, we use the multi-scale feature method to get more detail information, which is with channel attention mechanism to transform the importance of channels into learnable parameters. Finally, the densely connection mechanism is apply to maintain powerful representation.

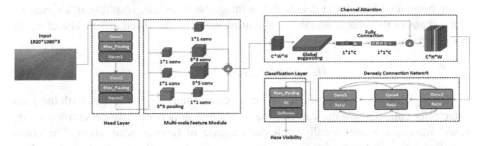

Fig. 2. The structure of our haze visibility detection networks, which includes head layer, multi-scale feature module, channel attention, densely connection network and the classification layer.

3.1 Overview

As shown in the Fig. 2, our network include head layer, multi-scale feature model, channel attention, densely connection network and classification layer. Firstly, the digital camera image is send into the head layers to generated spatial detail features, and the Conv1 and Conv2 are used to enhance the performance. Then, to receive different fields' features, three multi-scale feature modules are used. The channel attention module is applied to get more features detail, which can more effectively with the densely connection network. Finally, haze visibility is detected by the classification layer including Max_Pooling, fully connected layer and softmax function.

3.2 Image Entropy

Image entropy [14] is a mathematical statistical method used to describe the characteristics of histogram. It reflects the average amount of information contained in the image. In general, the one-dimensional information entropy of an image refers to the amount of information represented by the distribution characteristics of its gray histogram. If the image is regarded as a set of many pixels, each pixel x represents a random event, and P_x represents the proportion of the number of pixels with a gray value of x to the total number of pixels. The one-dimensional information entropy of the image is defined as:

$$H = -\sum_{x=1}^{255} P_x log_2 P_x \tag{1}$$

where $0 \leq x \leq 255$ and x is only an integer.

The image entropy corresponding to the brightness distribution of the region with fixed reflectivity in the image is usually very small in sunny weather without haze or slight haze. On the contrary, in severe weather with heavy haze, the image entropy of the same region in the image will be greater than that without haze. Therefore, for the same scenario, the image entropy in haze weather is larger than that in sunny weather, because the appearance of haze makes the histogram distribution of the scene image more balanced.

Assume that the image entropy in sunny weather is H_{sunny}, the light haze weather is $H_{lighthaze}$ and the heavy haze weather is $H_{heavyhaze}$. When there is a slight haze, the image becomes blurred, the details in the image become less, resulting in an increase in the chaos of the image, and the image turns white in the visual effect. Therefore the inequality is:

$$H_{sunny} < H_{lighthaze} < H_{heavyhaze} \tag{2}$$

Through the above analysis, it can be concluded that for the images with the same reflectivity collected by the camera, the one-dimensional information entropy of the image increases monotonically with the increase of haze concentration. The corresponding image entropy of the scene in sunny weather is the smallest, and the haze concentration in the image is approximately 0.

3.3 Multi-scale Feature Method

A multi-scale feature is used to obtain more spatial details, because rich spatial feature detail information is useful for representation and foundation to map in the high-level region of interest areas.

As shown in Fig. 2, we employ 4 different branches. The 1 * 1 convolution (as 1 * 1 conv in figure) is a simple transformation and is used to reduce the dimensionality. Compared with the 1 * 1 convolution, 3 * 3 convolution and 5 * 5 convolution have a larger receptive field to enhance the performance of the spatial details in a wider range. These 4 branches is 3 * 3 max pooling with a stride of 1. As the feature map is defined as:

$$A \in R^{C*H*W} \tag{3}$$

so the 4 different receptive fields feature maps are A_1, A_2, A_3 and A_4, where $A_i \in R^{C_i*H_i*W_i}$, and $C = \sum C_i$. And the mathematical expression of the new integration feature map $A_{new} \in R^{C*H*W}$ can be expressed as:

$$A_{new} = \left[H_{1*1}(A), H_{3*3}(A), H_{5*5}(A), H_{Max\_Pooling}(A)\right] \tag{4}$$

where $H_{Max_{Pooling}}(\cdot)$ indicates 3 * 3 max_pooling, $H_{n*n}(A)$ represents an n*n convolution operation, and [...] is concatenation function.

3.4 Channel Attention Method

As illustrated in Fig. 2, the channel attention method is utilized between the multi-scale feature models and densely connection network, which is efficiently select the features to contribute significantly for the target task. Our channel attention method includes global average pooling, two fully connection layers, and multiplication operation.

The global average pooling is executed to squeeze the feature maps into the 1*1*C vector along the spatial dimension. And then, the vector T_c theoretically has the global receptive filed of the input feature map, which is obtained as:

$$T_c = Global(F_c) = \sum_{i=0}^{H-1} \sum_{j=0}^{W-1} F_c(i,j) \Big/ H * W \tag{5}$$

where $F_c(i,j)$ is the value at (i, j) of the c-th feature map with the H*W input feature size, $Global(\cdot)$ is global pooling function, T_c indicates the output vector.

After two fully connected layers stacked, the vector T_c is transformed into learnable parameters, which is used to recalibrate the features and is obtained as:

$$LP_C = \theta(w_2 \odot \delta(w_1 \odot T_c)) \tag{6}$$

where $\odot$ is the convolution operation, w_1 and w_2 are the weight matrix of the AlexNet[*] network architecture, δ is the ReLU activation function, θ is the sigmoid activation function.

Finally, the output weighted result γ_i parameters T_c of channel i with the final feature can be obtained as:

$$\gamma_i = LP_i \cdot F_i \tag{7}$$

where i ∈ (0, 1, 2, ..., C).

Moreover, the γ_i is used to implement the recalibration of the original features, as the channelize multiplication operation.

3.5 Densely Channel Network

Generally, the haze visibility change is based on time-sequence, as shown in the Fig. 3. In order to get effective approach for improve the interaction among the feature information flows, we use the densely connection network architecture to permit the gradient to flow directly to earlier layers.

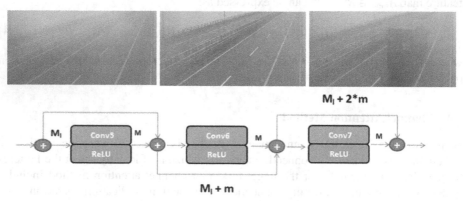

Fig. 3. The haze visibility change is based on time-sequence, and the picture from left to right in first row shows the change process. The second row show the densely connection network architecture, where M_l is the number of input feature maps, the output feature maps is increase by "+" concatenation operation.

The densely channel network architecture is shown in the second row of Fig. 3. The output feature of the l_{th} layer of the densely connection with the input feature m_0 can be obtained as:

$$M_l = \delta_l(M_{l-1}, M_{l-2}, \ldots, M_0) \tag{8}$$

where [...] is the concatenation operation, $\delta_l(\odot)$ is the ReLU activation function. So the each input is the sum of all earlier layers features. For example, the input of the first layer is M_l, then the next output should be $M_l + m$, and so on, after l layer, the output is $M_l + i * m$. In our AlexNet[*] network, we use Conv5, Conv6 and Conv7 as the densely connection network. Moreover, the convolution layer is used to reduce the spatial dimension of the feature map.

4 Experiments

In this section, the detail of our datasets and the evaluation metrics is provided firstly, and then we compared the performance between proposed method with the traditional and existing AlexNet haze visibility detection method.

4.1 Datasets

The visibility value of the image is calculated according to the Image entropy which is self-recorded data form the traffic video, classified and labeled respectively, that is, the mark above 200 m is 0, 100–200 m is 1, the mark at 50–100 m is 2, and the mark at 0–50 m is 3. Set the size of all images to 1920 * 1080, and prepare 3000 pictures for each category. The images of the verification part are also classified according to the above method. This data set is small, with 500 images respectively. In this way, a training and verification data set containing 25000 images for training is obtained. There are 300 pictures in the test data set without labels for each mark level. The detailed statistics of training, validation, and testing are illustrated in Table 1.

Table 1. The detailed statistics of training, validation, and testing

Mark level	Training set	Validation set	Testing set	Total
0	3500	500	300	4300
1	3500	500	300	4300
2	3500	500	300	4300
3	3500	500	300	4300

4.2 Implementation Details

We use Intel I7 8750H CPU, NVidia RTX 3060 graphics card with 16G memory and 512G SSD hard disk as the experimental hardware platform, and we implement our method mainly on Pytorch 1.0 [15], and the Adam optimizer [16] with $\beta_1 = 0.9$, $\beta_2 = 0.98$, and $\epsilon = 10^{-9}$. And the learning rate is set as 0.001 in the first 80 epoch and 0.0001 in the next 20 epoch, the batch size is set to 32 ande training time is set to 100 epochs. Moreover, the cross-entropy loss function is used in the haze visibility detection, which can be set as:

$$\text{loss funciton} = -\left[y\log\hat{f} + (1-f)\log\left(1-\hat{f}\right)\right] \qquad (9)$$

where f and $\hat{f}$ are the ground truth label and prediction.

In this paper, we use the recall, precision, accuracy and F1-score as the common evaluation metrics; the specific description detail is shown as follows.

Recall is the ratio of the number of positive samples that are correctly detected of the total number of positive samples.

$$Recall = {}^{TP}\!/_{(TP + FN)} \tag{10}$$

Precision is the ratio of the number of positive samples that are correctly detected to the total number of detected positive sample.

$$Precision = {}^{TP}\!/_{(TP + FP)} \tag{11}$$

Accuracy measures the overall performance of the model, which is the ratio of the number of samples that are correctly detected to the total number of datasets.

$$Accuracy = {}^{TP + TN}\!/_{(TP + FP + TN + FN)} \tag{12}$$

where TP is the true positive, TN is the true negative, FP is false positive, and FN is false negative.

F1-score is most commonly used to assess the recall and precision synthetically, can be calculated as

$$F1 - score = {}^{Recall * Precision}\!/_{(Recall + Precision)} \tag{13}$$

4.3 Performance Comparison

AlexNet is as the baseline; moreover, our improved network architecture AlexNet* with multi-scale feature (MSF), channel attention model (CAM), and densely connection network (DCN) to enhance the performance of the haze visibility detection.

To verify the performance of the mechanisms, the different settings are conducted the experiments as following:

- AlexNet as the baseline (AlexNet)
- Our improved AlexNet* (AlexNet*)
- Appending the MSF, CAM, and DCN models on AlexNet*

The experimental results are shown in the Table 2, which including the recall, precision, accuracy and F1-score results. Although AlexNet* improves the accuracy to 90.3%, the performance still cannot meet the haze visibility detection requirement.

In particular, our AlexNet* with MSF can achieves 94.2% accuracy which achieves 10.04% improvement; and CAM can achieves 94.3% accuracy with 10.16% improvement as well. When we adopt these two strategies simultaneously, the accuracy performance improves to 93.6%. Moreover, the accuracy can be 95.6% with three methods work together, which the F1-score is the best performance as well.

As shown in Fig. 4, there are some haze-like images in the test dataset, our method can effective detection them.

Table 2. Performance comparison of AlexNet, AlexNet*, MSF, CAM and DCN

Method	MSF	CAM	DCN	Recall	Precision	Accuracy	F1-score
AlexNet				92.5%	82.3%	85.6%	0.863
AlexNet*				96.7%	85.2%	90.3%	0.913
AlexNet*	✓			96.8%	91.2%	94.2%	0.936
AlexNet*		✓		96.9%	91.1%	94.3%	0.937
AlexNet*	✓	✓		98.2%	91.7%	93.6%	0.923
AlexNet*	✓	✓	✓	97.5%	93.2%	95.6%	0.955

(a)   (b)

Fig. 4. Some haze-like image in our test dataset. (a) the high beam, (b) water on the camera

5 Conclusions

We have presented the method with multi-scale feature based densely channel atten-tion connection network. Particularly, we study the problem of the application of haze visibility detection on computer vision. Moreover, compared with AlexNet between the improved AlexNet* network, our method achieves get better tradeoff on accuracy, which can meet the haze visibility detection requirements. More remarkable, we achieve 95.6% accuracy with 11.68% improvement.

References

1. Steffens, C.: Measurement of visibility by photo-graphic photometry. Ind. Eng. Chem. **41**(11), 2396–2399 (1949)
2. Busch, C., Debes, E.: Wavelet transform for analyzing fog visibility. IEEE Intell. Syst. **6**, 66–71 (1998)
3. Chen, Z., Zhou, Q., Chen, Q.: Video visibility detection algorithm based on wavelet transformation. Chin. J. Sci. Instrum. **31**(1), 92–98 (2010)
4. Chen, Z.Z., Chen, Q.M.: Video contrast visibility detection algorithm and its implementation based on camera self-calibration. J. Electron. Inf. Technol. **32**(12), 2907–2912 (2010)
5. Li, B., Dong, R., Chen, Q.M.: Automatic calibration method for PTZ camera. J. Beijing Univ. Posts Telecommun. **32**(1), 24–29 (2010)
6. An, M.W., Guo, Z.L., Li, J., et al.: Visibility detection based on traffic camera imagery. In: International Conference on Information Sciences and Interaction Sciences, pp. 411–414. IEEE (2010)

7. Hautiere, N., Tarel, J.P., Lavenant, J., et al.: Automatic fog detection and estimation of visibility distance through use of an onboard camera. Mach. Vis. Appl. **17**(1), 8–20 (2006). https://doi.org/10.1007/s00138-005-0011-1

8. Chen, Z.: PTZ visibility detection based on image luminance changing tendency. In: International Conference on Optoelectronics and Image Processing (ICOIP), pp. 15–19. IEEE (2016)

9. Graves, N., Newsam, S.: Using visibility cameras to estimate atmospheric light extinction. In: Workshop on Applications of Computer Vision (WACV), pp. 577–584. IEEE (2011)

10. Song, H.J., Gao, Y.Y., Chen, Y.Z.: Traffic visibility estimation based on dynamic camera calibration. Chin. J. Comput. **38**(6), 1172–1187 (2015)

11. Belaroussi, R., Gruyer, D.: Road sign-aided estimation of visibility conditions. In: 2015 14th IAPR International Conference on Machine Vision Applications (MVA), pp. 202–205. IEEE (2015)

12. Varjo, S., Kaikkonen, V., Hannuksela, J., et al.: All-in-focus image reconstruction from in-line holograms of snowflakes. In: 2015 IEEE International Instrumentation and Measurement Technology Conference (I2MTC), pp. 1096–1101. IEEE (2015)

13. Krizhevsky, A., Sutskever, I., Hinton, G.E.: ImageNet classification with deep convolutional neural networks. In: Advance in Neural Information Processing Systems, pp. 1097–1105 (2012)

14. Kikuchi, R., Soffer, B.H.: Maximum entropy image restoration. I. The entropy expression. JOSA **67**, 1656–1665 (1977)

15. Paszke, A., Gross, S., Chintala, S., et al.: Automatic differentiation in PyTorch. In: Workshop on Machine Learning Systems, NIPS (2017)

16. Kingma, D., Ba, J.: Adam: a method for stochastic optimization. In: ICLR (2015)

Generative Unknown-Aware Object Detection

Changhua Wang[1], Bao Li[1], Likang Chen[2], and Qike Shao[2(✉)]

[1] Zhejiang Institute of Mechanical and Electrical Engineering Co. Ltd.,
Hangzhou 311203, China
[2] School of Computer Science and Technology, Zhejiang University of Technology,
Hangzhou 310023, China
sqk@zjut.edu.cn

Abstract. Building object detectors can identify unknown objects, which is critical yet underexplored. An additional discriminative inference pass is generally needed to generate final classification results for "unknown" class on the existing methods of unknown-aware object detection. But human beings can immediately identify unknown objects by themselves without other auxiliary materials. Hence, a stricter task called "Generative Unknown-Aware Object Detection" (G-UAOD) is proposed to constrain the prediction process in this paper. The setting of G-UAOD lays stress on identifying unknown objects by detectors themselves. For achieving this task, we first repair the serious issue of providing inconsistent labels for training by the proposed auto-labelling unknowns methodologies. The inconsistent labels come from the situation that proposals which highly overlap with the same unknown objects may are given distinct labels. Secondly, the overlooked components of known objects are capitalized. The rest proposals which appear strong possibilities that localize the components of known objects are reactivated as "unknown" class. Finally, only the classification loss of the unknown proposals is computed to learn the network but the regression loss of them is left out. Our work improves the U-Recall score remarkably compared to the previous best method while retains the competitive accuracy of detecting known objects.

Keywords: Unknown-aware object detection · Auto-labeling unknowns · Unknown proposals

1 Introduction

Modern object detection models [1–7] have achieved tremendous success in known contexts which are available during training with a supervised manner. Yet, although under a strong assumption that only seen classes should be predicted, they are still likely to suffer from overconfident prediction problems [8,9] for unseen objects in a dynamic world. To relax this closed-world condition, open-world object detection [10–13] considers a more natural scheme that all novel objects in test images should be localized and classified as "unknown". In other words, these works try to teach object detectors to be aware of unknown objects.

To automatically acquire the explicit training samples of unknowns in training set is one of the key challenges for achieving unknown-aware. Because it will be laborious to re-annotate unknown objects in existing datasets [14,15] in which known instances already have been collected. However, it is non-trivial to acquire credible labels for unknown instances without any corresponding annotations.

(a) Inconsistent Labels   (b) A car

Fig. 1. The proposed auto-labeling unknowns approaches produce inconsistent labels (a). Inconsistent labels come from the situations that the proposal (in yellow) with the higher "objectness" score is automatically labeled as "unknown" while the proposal (in green) which highly overlap with the same unknown object still retains its "background" label. The car in (b), whose ground truth is red, is actually made up of many components, tires, front windshield and so on. Thus, the yellow proposals, which localize components of the car also should be labeled as "unknown" in unknown-aware object detection. (Color figure online)

Recently, some auto-labeling unknowns approaches [10,11] were proposed in open-world object detection for acquiring training samples of unknown objects. They employed some exquisite designs to excavate unknown proposals among the buried information under the strong supervision signals of known objects. For instance, inspired by the observation that the degree of the feature activation of some regions of feature maps implies an object appears. The auto-labeling approach in [11] selects few background proposals predicted by DETR [6] whose the strengths of average feature activation within a window are conspicuous as unknown ones.

However, the proposed auto-labelling unknowns approaches give rise to inconsistent labels. Figure 1(a) shows inconsistent labels, the yellow proposal with the higher "obejctness" score (refers to how likely is it to be an unknown object) is chosen as "unknown" class while the green one with the lower "obejctness" score is regard as "background". In fact, these two proposals should share the same label "unknown", because they all localize the most part of the unknown object. Inconsistent labels bring paradoxical information between unknown objects and backgrounds, that severely hinders the detectors' ability of perceiving unknowns.

Besides, the overlooked components of known objects are not well capitalized. The car is displayed in Fig. 1(b) which is actually made up of many components, tires, front windshield and so on. In the general object detection, only the proposals which highly overlap with the red ground truth of the car are considered as positive; this kind of treatment is unsuited in unknown-aware object detection. In unknown-aware object detection, the yellow proposals which localize the components of the car also should be hold and labeled as "unknown" class. Otherwise, the detectors are willing to identify these components as "background" in test phase.

One more thing, the existing frameworks of unknown-aware object detection [8,10,12,13,16,17] suffer the other drawback. Specifically, their pipelines need a additional discriminative inference pass to generate final classification results for "unknown" class. Not to mention the out-of-distribution detection emphasizes to estimate the uncertainty of prediction, which is different from our focus of unknown-aware object detection. And the unknown objects are discriminated can be thought as by-products, because their concern is to obtain the reliable predictions of known objects. In our opinions, the cumbersome discriminative operations actually are remedial actions for the existing detectors' inferior ability of identifying unknowns. Ideally, the detectors should only depend on its inherent ability. Just like human beings who can immediately identify unknown objects by themselves without other auxiliary materials. We call this task as "Generative Unknown-Aware Object Detection" (G-UAOD), which is stricter but more reasonable compared with existing definitions.

In this paper, we re-label the background proposals, which highly overlap with the produced unknown proposals by the proposed auto-labeling approaches, as "unknown" class. This process called as "consistent auto-labeling unknowns" which bring up no conflicting information for training. Alongside, we search unknowns inside ground truths of known objects. Specifically, we firstly pick up the background proposals whose "objectness" scores are conspicuous; "obcjctness" scores are predicted by the region proposal network (RPN) [4]. Then, these proposals whose unknown internal proportions (UIP) exceed the certain threshold are labeled "unknown" class. For one chosen proposal, UIP is defined as the area of intersection divided by its own area; the area of intersection is calculated by the proposal and the corresponding ground truth. Benefit from above steps, the overlooked unknown objects inside ground truths are reactivated.

The contributions are summarized as follows:

- We introduce a stricter task called "Generative Unknown-Aware Object Detection", which lays stress on identifying unknown objects by detectors themselves.
- We propose a consistent auto-labelling unknowns approach that labels the background proposals, which highly overlap with the same chosen unknown objects, as "unknown" class. The consistent auto-labeling unknown approach repairs the issue of providing inconsistent labels by the present auto-labelling unknown approach.
- We capitalize the overlooked components of known objects. Labelling the rest background proposals, in which "objectness" scores are salient and the scores of unknown internal proportion (UIP) exceed the certain threshold, as "unknown" class. These unknown proposals boost the detector's performance of retrieving unknowns.

- Our extensive experiments demonstrate the effectiveness of the proposed method. Specifically, our method outperforms the previous work remarkably on identifying the unknown objects while retains the competitive accuracy of detecting known objects.

2   Related Work

Open-set Object Detection. The object detection is defined as training a detector which can accurately localize and classify all the interested objects in given images. However, although the most advanced object detectors in benchmarks are proactively trained to reject any uninterested class, some works [8] found that they are still likely to erroneously identify unknown objects as know classes with high confidences. Open-set object detection [8,9] provides protocols and metrics to analyze the performance of detectors during encountering unknowns.

Out-of-Distribution Detection. Out-of-distribution underlines the uncertainty of the classifications predictions, which distinguish between the known vs. unknown objects in test phase. Miller et al. [9] demonstrated the Dropout Sampling which is available to judge label uncertainty, and the similar bayesian perspective arises in works [8,18,19]. Liu et al. [20] proved the energy scores is more appropriate in this field than the softmax scores. However, these works draw support from the extra data with weak unknown object supervision. Du et al. [17] distills unknown objects from videos in the wild to regularize model to reshape the decision boundary between in and out-distribution objects. Considering the class-conditional distribution in the feature space, the work [16] proposes a approach which adaptively synthesizes virtual outliers. The primary difference between out-of-distribution and our G-UAOD is that the classifier of model in the former is not responsible for identifying unknowns.

Open-World Object Detection. Recalling unknowns as far as possible in given images is one of tasks in open-world object detection, the other is incremental learning. Joseph et al. [10] obtained a set of pseudo-unknowns for training a Faster R-CNN based object detector ORE through automatically labeling unknowns. Aiding with an energy-based unknown identifier, ORE re-retrieved unknowns from the objects which already classified by the detector before. Gupta et al. [11] believed the above method obtains unknown proposals are biased to the "known" class. So they proposed an attention-driven pseudo-labeling unknowns approach which is better generalized. But their detector still need a foreground objectness branch to separate the unknown objects from the background. Yang et al. [13] provided a unified perspective for solving unknown recognition and incremental learning, i.e.semantic topology. Zheng et al. [12] tried to resolve an issue that discover novel categories in the identified unknowns, which is not our concern in this paper. For identifying unknowns, open-world object detection gives loose definition, but our G-UAOD setting lays stress on recognizing unknown objects by models themselves.

3   Proposed Method

We formally formulate the task of Generative Unknown-Aware Object Detection (G-UAOD). We have a set of known object classes $C_k = \{C_1, C_2, \ldots, C_m\}$ and $C_u = \{C_{m+1}, \ldots\}$, where $C_k \cap C_u = \oslash$. The training dataset contains objects from C_k; and the testing dataset contains object from $C_k \cup C_u$. An object I is represented by $I = [c, x, y, w, h]$, the c denoting the class label and the x, y, w, h denote the center of the object bounding box, width and height respectively. A object detector is trained to detect known objects while simultaneously classifying unknown objects as "unknown" by itself, denoted by a label C_0.

3.1   Method Overview

As our method overview is illustrated in Fig. 2, we first obtain the positive and negative proposals from the RoI head [4], where the positive proposals are considered as "known" and the negative proposals are considered as "background". Given an input image, the RPN [4] generates a set of bounding box predictions (also known as proposals) for foreground instances. Following the RoI head which employs a IoU threshold to distinguish between positive proposals and negative proposals.

Then, we employ the consistently auto-labelling unknowns methodology to provide consistent labels for some background proposals; these background proposals are re-labeled as "unknown". Specifically, we further optimize the auto-labelling unknowns approach in [10] via re-labelling the background proposals which highly overlap with labeled unknown proposals. This process provides labels for chosen unknowns without conflict or confrontation. Finally, we leverage overlooked the components (LOC) of the known objects in training set. We reactive the background proposals which appear strong possibilities that localize the unknown components of known objects; these proposals are also labeled as "unknown" class.

During training, only the classification loss of the unknown proposals is computed but the regression loss of them is left out. Because there are no precise bounding boxes of selected unknown objects, the regression loss of the unknown objects can't be computed.

3.2   Consistently Auto-labelling Unknowns

Try to explore unknown objects in pixel space if at all possible, the proposed auto-labelling steps in [10,11] essentially determine which regions of the given images may conceal unknowns. They designed diverse scores, such as the "objectness" score predicted by region proposal network (RPN) [4], to select the ones with high score from some part of interested proposals. However, they all lose sight of a critical issue that inconsistent labels are generated for same unknowns objects. Concretely, proposals which highly overlap with the same unknown objects may have distinct labels.

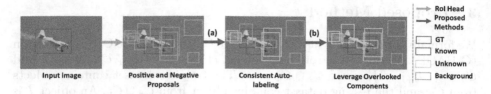

Fig. 2. Overview of our method. We obtain the positive and negative proposals from RoI head, where the positive proposals are considered as "known" and the negative proposals are considered as "background". (a) Then, we employ the consistently auto-labelling unknowns methodology (CALU) to label some background proposals as "unknown". (b) Finally, we leverage overlooked components (LOC) of the known object to label other background proposals as "unknown".

To tackle this issue, we further optimize the existing auto-labelling unknowns approach [10]. Employing the same operations, we simply label the top-k background proposals as "unknown" class according to its "obejctness" scores; these proposals are collected into a set $\mathcal{P}_u = \{p_i\}_i^k$. At present, each proposal belongs to known, unknown or background; the set of background proposals is expressed as $\mathcal{P}_b = \{p_j\}_j^n$. Then, we calculate intersection over union (IoU) for pairs of unknown proposals and background proposals. Let iou_{ij} represents the IoU for the pair of the i-th unknonw proposal and the j-th background proposal.

To providing the inconsistent labels, we apply the IoU threshold α:

$$G_j = \begin{cases} 1 & if \ iou_{ij} \geqslant \alpha, \\ 0 & if \ iou_{ij} < \alpha. \end{cases} \tag{1}$$

where $G_j = 1$ denotes the background proposal p_j highly overlap with the unknown proposal p_i. When the iou_{ij} exceeds the IoU threshold α, we label the j-th background proposal as "unknown" class.

Finally, supposing that there are m background proposals are re-labeled as "unknown", the set of unknown proposals updates to $\mathcal{P}_u = \{p_i\}_i^{k+m}$ and the set of background proposals updates to $\mathcal{P}_b = \{p_j\}_j^{n-m}$.

3.3   Leverage the Overlooked Components

The overlooked components of the known objects are not adequately capitalized for unknown-aware object detection. In the general object detection, the proposals which own inferior intersections of union (IoU) are considered as "background" class for training. The result is that the components of known objects are predicted as "background" in testing phase. For instance, the predicted bounding boxes, which finely localize the components of the cars (such as tires and front windshields which are not labelled in training set), are classified as "background" as expectation. This treatment can be inexpedient for the unknown-aware object detection. Because it will severely devastates the performance of identifying unknown objects.

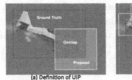

(a) Definition of UIP   (b) The scores of UIP

Fig. 3. (a) Definition of UIP. UIP indicates the ratio of the area belongs to the known object to the proposal, which depends on the area of the intersection (refereed to as Overlap) and the area of the proposal. (b) The scores of UIP for different proposals. For each interested proposal (in yellow), we discover the higher scores of UIP with the ground truths (in red), which are more likely to contain the components of the known objects. The yellow numbers show the scores of UIP for different proposals. (Color figure online)

To leverage the overlooked components of the known objects, we reactivate the proposals which appear strong possibilities that localize them; these proposals are labeled as "unknown" class. From the set of background proposals $\mathcal{P}_b = \{p_j\}_j^{n-m}$, we firstly collect the proposals whose "objectness" scores exceed a threshold β into a set $\mathcal{P}_b' = \{p_j\}_j^h$, where h is smaller than $n - m$. Then, the scores of unknown internal proportion (UIP) are calculated for every proposal in $\mathcal{P}_b'$:

$$u_j = \frac{overlap_j}{area_j} \qquad (2)$$

where $overlap_j$ denotes the intersection area of the proposal p_j and the corresponding ground truth; $area_j$ denotes the area of the proposal p_j; u_j denotes the score of UIP for the proposal p_j. The definition of UIP is illustrated in Fig. 4(a), UIP indicates the ratio of the area belongs to the known objects to proposals, which depends on the area of the intersection and the area of the proposal. The scores of UIP for different proposals are illustrated in Fig. 4(b). The proposals which localize the components of the plane, such the propeller, the nosewheel and the rear, have more significant scores of UIP.

To distinguish between background and unknown proposals, we employ the common thresholding mechanism:

$$G_j = \begin{cases} 1 & if \ u_j \geqslant \beta, \\ 0 & if \ u_j < \beta. \end{cases} \qquad (3)$$

where $G_j = 1$ denotes the proposal p_j belongs to "unknown" class. While u_j is greater than a UIP threshold β, the proposal p_j is re-labeled as "unknown" class.

Lastly, supposing that there are g background proposals are re-labeled as "unknown", the set of unknown proposals updates to $\mathcal{P}_u = \{p_i\}_i^{k+m+g}$. During training, the classification loss of the unknown proposals set $\mathcal{P}_u = \{p_i\}_i^{k+m+g}$ is computed to learn model bu the regression loss is left out.

Table 1. Here we exhibit how our work performs on VOC+COCO test and VOC+COCO val. The comparison is displayed in terms of the known class mAP and unknown class recall (U-Recall). The general mAP metric appraises how well a model to detect the known classes, while evaluating the retrieval ability for the unknown classes by U-Recall. We observe that our method outperforms on both metrics compared with ORE.

Datasets	VOC+COCO test		VOC+COCO val		FSOD	
	U-Recall	mAP	U-Recall	mAP	U-Recall	mAP
Faster-RCNN [4]	–	56.16	–	83.89	–	12.51
ORE−EBUI	5.21	56.37	6.01	82.63	22.42	**13.56**
ORE [10]	8.58	56.21	10.99	82.40	29.05	13.49
Ours	**19.55**	**56.41**	**24.44**	**83.78**	**30.55**	12.46

4   Experiments and Resutls

4.1   Evaluation Protocol

Datasets: We let all classes of Pascal VOC [14] as known and use corresponding data to train our detector. Then we first evaluate our detector on MS-COCO [15] validation set and Pascal VOC [14] test set. MS-COCO have 80 classes in total and the 20 of them exist in Pascal VOC. In order to facilitate comparison with the previous works, we employ the test set and the validation set are split in work [10] denoted by VOC+COCO test and VOC+COCO val respectively. Besides, we also evaluate our detector on FSOD [21]. FSOD contains 1000 categories, that is available to be compact while effective for unknown-aware object detection.

Evaluation Metrics: We use recall as the main metric for the unknown classes as same as the selection in [11], confronting that not all the possible unknown instances are annotated in existing datasets. Besides, the general mean average precision (mAP) is used as the metric for the known classes.

Implement Details: We adopt the standard Faster R-CNN [4] with the backbone of ResNet-50 [22], whose weights are pretrained on ImageNet [23], by utilizing the Detectron2 library [24]. We ran our experiment on a 2 Nvidia 2080Ti GPUs with batch size of 4. We use SGD with a learning rate of 0.01. The trainset is learned for 90k iterations. The k for selecting unknown proposals is set to 2, while the IoU threshold α is set to 0.6. Besides, the threshold δ of unknown internal proportions (UIP) is set to 0.8 and the "objectness" threshold β is set to 0.6.

4.2   State-of-the-Art Comparison

Table 1 shows a comparison of our work with the approach of ORE on VOC+COCO test, VOC+COCO val and FSOD. We also report the performance of the stardard Faster R-CNN framework which only can detect the known classes. For a fair comparison, although the transformer-based OW-DETR [11] have reported better performance, we compare our work with the state-of-the-art faster R-CNN based detector ORE [10]. We also report the ORE without its energy-based identifier (EBUI) (referred as "ORE−EBUI"). The comparison is displayed in terms of the mAP and the U-Recall. The resulting ORE-EBUI framework reaches U-Recall of 5.21, 6.01 and 22.42 on VOC+COCO test, VOC+COCO val and FSOD respectively. And the resulting ORE framework arrives U-Recall of 8.58, 10.99 and 29.05. Our method improves the retrieval of unknown objects, leading to improved performance with significant gains for U-Recall, achieving 19.55, 24.44 and 30.55 on same test sets respectively. Furthermore, our scheme outperforms ORE-EBUI and ORE in term of the known class mAP on VOC+ COCO test and VOC+COCO val. The consistent improvement of our method on identifying the unknown objects, which emphasizes the importance of proposed contributions.

4.3   Ablation Studies

Table 2. We thoroughly ablate each of the composed component of our work. CAL and LOC refers to "Consistent Auto-labelling" and "Leverage the Overlooked Components" respectively.

Row ID	CALU	LOC	U-Recall	mAP
1	×	×	−	56.16
2	×	✓	17.52	56.24
3	✓	×	14.55	**56.47**
4	✓	✓	**19.55**	56.41

Ablating Components: Table 2 shows the contribution of each of the components in our method. The consistent auto-labelling unknowns approach (referred to as CAL) which combined with leverage the overlooked components (referred to as LOC) performs better on identifying unknowns objects (row 4) than either of them separately (row 2 and 3). We can observe that only a slight drop on the mAP scores form row 2 to row 3. The ablation results indicate that each component in our work play a available role to identify unknowns.

Table 3. Ablation study on the top-k and the unknown IoU threshold α. Here we evaluate the detector only trained with CALU.

k	α	U-Recall	mAP
1	0.5	13.19	56.18
1	0.6	9.91	56.03
1	0.7	5.61	56.32
2	0.5	16.64	56.39
2	**0.6**	**14.55**	**56.47**
2	0.7	9.76	56.34
3	0.5	18.81	56.04
3	0.6	16.95	56.12
3	0.7	13.43	55.97

Fig. 4. Visualization of detected objects by ORE (top) and our detector (bottom). **Blue:** Objects are classified as one of the known classes. **Green:** Objects are identified as the unknown class. (Color figure online)

Ablation on the Top-k and the Unknown IoU Threshold α. Table 3 reports the G-UAOD detection results as we vary the top-k and the unknown IoU threshold α for CALU. This ablation shows that the detector indeed benefits from inconsistent labels provided by CALU. The U-Recall generally improves while the unknown IoU threshold α declines on the certain k. However, a smaller α hurts the detection performance for known objects. The results suggest that $\alpha = 0.6$ is appropriate. Besides, we can observe that mAP falls while the k is larger than 2. We assume this is because many redundant proposals are used during training.

Table 4. Ablation study on the UIP threshold δ and the objectness threshold β. Here we set $k = 2$ and the unknown IoU threshold $\alpha = 0.6$.

δ	β	U-Recall	mAP
0.6	0.6	19.38	56.08
0.6	0.7	19.56	56.07
0.6	0.8	19.13	56.09
0.7	0.6	19.57	56.22
0.7	0.7	19.42	56.02
0.7	0.8	19.40	56.32
0.8	**0.6**	**19.55**	**56.41**
0.8	0.7	19.67	55.80
0.8	0.8	19.42	55.44

Ablation on the Unknown UIP Threshold δ and the Objectness Threshold β. Table 4 illustrates the G-UAOD detection results as we vary the UIP threshold δ and the objectness threshold β for LOC. This ablation shows that the detector has better ability for identifying unknown objects when trained with LOC. We can observer that the U-Recall scores considerably raise with only slight drop for mAP. The results suggest that let $\delta = 0.8$ and $\beta = 0.6$ is well-turned for getting the balance of detecting known objects and identifying unknown ones.

4.4 Qualitative Analysis

Here we further present qualitative analysis between ORE and our detector on the instance-level detection results. In Fig. 4, we visualize the predictions on several images from MS-COCO and VOC. The predictions are acquired by the detector from ORE (top) and the detector trained with our method (bottom). We notice that, in comparison to ORE, our method performs much better in identifying unknown instances (in green). Besides, our detector also gives a competitive results on the known objects.

5   Conclusions

In this paper, we introduced a stricter task setting called "Generative Unknown-Aware Object Detection". The G-UAOD lays stress on identify unknown objects by detectors themselves. For achieving this task, we proposed a consistent auto-labelling unknowns approach (CALB) and leveraged the overlooked components (LOC) of known objects. Our detector improves the U-Recall score remarkably compared to the previous best method. We hope that our work will motivate further research on unknown-aware object detection in open setting.

References

1. Redmon, J., Divvala, S., Girshick, R., Farhadi, A.: You only look once: unified, real-time object detection. In: Proceedings of the IEEE Conference on Computer Vision and Pattern Recognition, pp. 779–788 (2016)
2. Redmon, J., Farhadi, A.: YOLO9000: better, faster, stronger. In: Proceedings of the IEEE Conference on Computer Vision and Pattern Recognition, pp. 7263–7271 (2017)
3. Redmon, J., Farhadi, A.: YOLOv3: an incremental improvement. arXiv preprint arXiv:1804.02767 (2018)
4. Ren, S., He, K., Girshick, R., Sun, J.: Faster R-CNN: towards real-time object detection with region proposal networks. Adv. Neural Inf. Process. Syst. **28** (2015)
5. Zhou, X., Wang, D., Krähenbühl., P.: Objects as points. arXiv preprint arXiv:1904.07850 (2019)
6. Carion, N., Massa, F., Synnaeve, G., Usunier, N., Kirillov, A., Zagoruyko, S.: End-to-end object detection with transformers. In: Vedaldi, A., Bischof, H., Brox, T., Frahm, J.-M. (eds.) ECCV 2020. LNCS, vol. 12346, pp. 213–229. Springer, Cham (2020). https://doi.org/10.1007/978-3-030-58452-8_13
7. Tian, Z., Shen, C., Chen, H., He, T.: Fcos: Fully convolutional one-stage object detection. In: Proceedings of the IEEE/CVF International Conference on Computer Vision, pp. 9627–9636 (2019)
8. Dhamija, A., Gunther, M., Ventura, J., Boult, T.: The overlooked elephant of object detection: open set. In: Proceedings of the IEEE/CVF Winter Conference on Applications of Computer Vision, pp. 1021–1030 (2020)
9. Miller, D., Nicholson, L., Dayoub, F., Sünderhauf, N.: Dropout sampling for robust object detection in open-set conditions. In: 2018 IEEE International Conference on Robotics and Automation (ICRA), pp. 3243–3249. IEEE (2018)
10. Joseph, K.J., Khan, S., Khan, F.S., Balasubramanian, V.N.: Towards open world object detection. In: Proceedings of the IEEE/CVF Conference on Computer Vision and Pattern Recognition, pp. 5830–5840 (2021)
11. Gupta, A., Narayan, S., Joseph, K.J., Khan, S., Khan, F.S., Shah, M.: OW-DETR: open-world detection transformer. In: Proceedings of the IEEE/CVF Conference on Computer Vision and Pattern Recognition, pp. 9235–9244 (2022)
12. Zheng, J., Li, W., Hong, J., Petersson, L., Barnes, N.: Towards open-set object detection and discovery. In: Proceedings of the IEEE/CVF Conference on Computer Vision and Pattern Recognition, pp. 3961–3970 (2022)
13. Yang, S., et al.: Objects in semantic topology. arXiv preprint arXiv:2110.02687 (2021)
14. Everingham, M., Van Gool, L., Williams, C.K.I., Winn, J., Zisserman, A.: The pascal Visual Object Classes (VOC) challenge. Int. J. Comput. Vis. **88**(2), 303–338 (2010). https://doi.org/10.1007/s11263-009-0275-4
15. Lin, T.-Y., et al.: Microsoft COCO: common objects in context. In: Fleet, D., Pajdla, T., Schiele, B., Tuytelaars, T. (eds.) ECCV 2014. LNCS, vol. 8693, pp. 740–755. Springer, Cham (2014). https://doi.org/10.1007/978-3-319-10602-1_48
16. Du, X., Wang, Z., Cai, M., Li, Y.: VOS: learning what you don't know by virtual outlier synthesis. arXiv preprint arXiv:2202.01197 (2022)
17. Du, X., Wang, X., Gozum, G., Li, Y.: Unknown-aware object detection: learning what you don't know from videos in the wild. arXiv preprint arXiv:2203.03800 (2022)

18. Miller, D., Dayoub, F., Milford, M., Sünderhauf, N.: Evaluating merging strategies for sampling-based uncertainty techniques in object detection. In: 2019 International Conference on Robotics and Automation (ICRA), pp. 2348–2354. IEEE (2019)
19. Deepshikha, K., Yelleni, S.H., Srijith, P.K., Mohan, C.K.: Monte carlo dropblock for modelling uncertainty in object detection. arXiv preprint arXiv:2108.03614 (2021)
20. Liu, W., Wang, X., Owens, J., Li, Y.: Energy-based out-of-distribution detection. Adv. Neural. Inf. Process. Syst. **33**, 21464–21475 (2020)
21. Fan, Q., Zhuo, W., Tang, C.-K., Tai, Y.-W.: Few-shot object detection with attention-RPN and multi-relation detector. In: Proceedings of the IEEE/CVF Conference on Computer Vision and Pattern Recognition, pp. 4013–4022 (2020)
22. Kipf, T.N., Welling, M.: Semi-supervised classification with graph convolutional networks. arXiv preprint arXiv:1609.02907 (2016)
23. Deng, J., Dong, W., Socher, R., Li, L.J., Li, K., Fei-Fei, L.: ImageNet: a large-scale hierarchical image database. In: 2009 IEEE Conference on Computer Vision and Pattern Recognition, pp. 248–255. IEEE (2009)
24. Wu, Y., Kirillov, A., Massa, F., Lo, W.Y., Girshick, R.: Detectron2 (2019). https://github.com/facebookresearch/detectron2

Super-Resolution Based on Degradation Learning and Self-attention for Small-Scale Pedestrian Detection

Yaocai Wu[1], Hancheng Yu[2], Zhengkai Lv[3], and Shihang Yan[3(✉)]

[1] Zhejiang Machinery and Electrical Group Co., Ltd., Hangzhou 311203, China
[2] Zhejiang Institute of Mechanical and Electrical Engineering CO., LTD., Hangzhou 311203, China
[3] School of Computer Science and Technology, Zhejiang University of Technology, Hangzhou 310023, China
shyan@zjut.edu.cn

Abstract. Recently the object detection algorithms have been widely used in various fields. In the highway monitoring scene, the performance of existing pedestrian detection algorithms degrade rapidly when the size of pedestrian decreased. To enhance the performance of detector, we designed a method named DSANet, which combines super-resolution with object detection algorithm, so that the detection network can capture more detailed features. Compared with the existing super-resolution algorithms, we integrate degeneration learning and self-attention module to make the super-resolution algorithm better fit the pedestrian detection. In particular, we introduce the MSAF module to fuse self attention information of different head numbers. The proposed super-resolution method provides better support for pedestrian detection. The experimental results show that the reconstructed SR image has richer detail features, which improves the accuracy of pedestrian detection.

Keywords: Pedestrian detection · Super resolution · Degradation learning · Self attention

1 Introduction

As a popular field of object detection, pedestrian detection has attracted extensive attention in recent years. As we all know, it is very dangerous for pedestrians to appear on the highway. Pedestrian detection based on video surveillance has been widely used because of its high speed and low cost. Due to the camera on the highway is high and the pedestrian size in view is small, very few features can be captured. The existing pedestrian detection algorithm will miss such samples. On the other hand, there are some false positives with similar characteristics to pedestrians. Super-resolution has shown excellent performance in various visual tasks. In order to improve the accuracy of detection, we add a super-resolution module for object detection. However, the existing super-resolution algorithms

H. Liu et al. (Eds.): ICIRA 2022, LNAI 13458, pp. 592–603, 2022.
https://doi.org/10.1007/978-3-031-13841-6_53

don't have good performances on this task. Because they do not consider contextual information, and cannot adapt to real-world degradation.

In this study, we proposed a DSANet for pedestrian detection, in which we combine the Super Resolution and Object Detection. We improve the super resolution method [1] in two aspects. First, a degradation module is used to inject degradation information into the super-resolution reconstruction process. And we use the SFT [2] module to better fuse features and facilitate stable training. Second, we use the MSAF module based on self-attention to make the network pay more attention to the contextual information. So that the SR results will have more realistic texture details. As will be shown in Sect. 4.1. The experiments show that the enhanced super resolution algorithm is able to provide richer details.

Specifically, We first use an object detection network to get bounding box, and then cropping the image according to the coordinates of the bounding box as LR image. We introduce an enhanced super resolution algorithm to upscale the LR image into 4x size. We add degradation learning to make the network adapt to different degradation forms. The introduced MSAF module guides the network to focus on the contextual information. Our motivation is to make the network adapt to pedestrians of different scales and poses by fusing self-attention with different head numbers. For the fusion of information between different layers, we use the SFT module, which allows the network to adaptively adjust the fusion strategy. Therefore, our method can supplement rich features for blurred small-sized pedestrians, so that the detection network has a better chance to discriminate pedestrians with more robust performance. The architecture of the introduced networks and the loss functions will be presented in Sect. 3.

To sum up, this article makes the following three main contributions: 1) A small-size optimized pedestrian detection network structure named DSANet is proposed. Where the super-resolution network is used to generate pedestrian images with more details. 2) Degradation learning is introduced to make the network better adapted to different degradation types. 3) An self-attention based MSAF module is proposed to integrate the information learned by the network. The motivation is to make the network pay more attention to the key structures of pedestrians. In which self-attention with different head numbers are used.

Finally, we demonstrate the effectiveness of our proposed method in detecting small-scale pedestrians and have a good performance on the challenging dataset.

2   Related Works

Driven by the development of deep learning, A series of deep learning methods have achieved good performances in the pedestrian detection. Compared with traditional methods, deep learning-based methods have high precision, and good generalization ability.

Pedestrian detection algorithms can be mainly divided into three categories: 1) Methods based on handcrafted features: First use the region proposal method represented by sliding window to extract the candidate area, then use the algorithm like histogram of oriented gradients HOG [3] or SIFT [4] to extract the feature descriptor. A classifier is then used to distinguish pedestrians based on the obtained feature descriptors. These handcrafted features usually extract color, texture or edge information. 2) Deep learning based methods: Feature extraction, localization and classification tasks are all done by neural networks. Representative algorithms include YOLOv4 [5], YOLOv5 [6] etc. 3) Hybrid approach: use a region proposal network to extract candidate regions and use traditional methods for classification or swap the position of the two steps. Although the above three methods have achieved impressive performance in some scenarios, there is still room for improvement.

As a sub-task of many vision tasks, super-resolution has received extensive attention in various fields. Dong et al. [7] used deep learning for the first time for super-resolution reconstruction. The proposed method directly uses neural networks to learn the mapping of low-resolution and high-resolution images end-to-end. While achieving good visual performances, it has fewer parameters. Ledig et al. [8] proposed a super-resolution reconstruction method based on generative adversarial network GAN (SRGAN). The idea of confrontation is used to make the high-resolution images generated by the network closer to the real images. For some blurry low-resolution images, a more realistic texture can be recovered. Based on SRGAN, Wang [9] et al. made further enhancements on the problem of generating artifacts. This method (ESRGAN) is able to produce images with sharper visual effects.

Since it is difficult to obtain pairs of high-resolution and low-resolution images in the real world, low-resolution images are often generated using algorithms. The super-resolution algorithm is sensitive to low-resolution training images, and when the used degradation method deviates from the real-world degradation, it will have a large impact on the performance of super-resolution. Bell-Kligler et al. [10] proposed a kernelGAN method, which uses a generative adversarial network to learn the degradation process of images, so that the constructed low-resolution images are closer to real images. Ji et al. [1] proposed an algorithm for real-world super-resolution tasks, which obtains low-resolution images that share a domain with real images by estimating the blur kernel and the distribution of real noise. Zhang et al. [11] combined super-resolution and object detection. Unlike the previous methods, we use a degradation learning method to Incorporate degradation information into the reconstruction process. And then utilize the proposed self-attention-based MSAF module implicitly encode the global context in different scales.

3   The Proposed Method

In this section, we introduce the proposed pedestrian detection method as shown in Fig. 1. We aim to use super-resolution to improve the detection performance. Given a single monitoring image of expressway, we first use an object detection algorithm to get the proposal bounding box. The LR image is obtained by

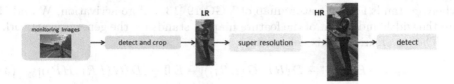

Fig. 1. Framework of the proposed pedestrian detection method.

cropping the image according to the coordinates of the proposal bounding box. Then use the super resolution model to estimate a high-resolution one $\hat{y}$. Further detect $\hat{y}$ to determine whether it is a pedestrian.

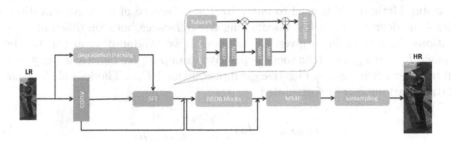

Fig. 2. Structure of the proposed super resolution method. The SFT structure is in the dotted box.

3.1 Super Resolution Model

Based on method [1], we implement an improved SR model as shown in Fig. 2 and train it on the DIV2K dataset [12]. We use SFT structure to fuse the degradation information. The structure of SFT module is in the dotted box. It uses convolution to calculate the weights and biases to dynamically fuse the two features. We use the self-attention based MSAF module to integrate the features before upsampling. The degradation learning and MSAF module will be introduced in Sect. 3.2 and Sect. 3.3. In the training phase, the total loss is the weighted sum of several losses includes pixel loss, perceptual loss, contrastive loss, and adversarial loss:

$$L_{total} = \theta_p \cdot L_{perceptual} + \theta_{ad} \cdot L_{adv} + \theta_{pix} L_{pixel} + \theta_{contra} L_{contra} \qquad (1)$$

where θ_ρ, θ_{ad}, θ_{pix}, θ_{contra} are the weights to tradeoff different loss terms. And $L_{pixel} = E||G(LR) - y||_1$ is the pixel loss that calculate the L1 distance between the generated SR image and the ground truth.

The perceptual loss $L_{perceptual}$ can make the edges sharper. Mathematically,

$$L_{perceptual} = \frac{1}{W * H} \sum_{x=1}^{W} \sum_{y=1}^{H} (\varphi(HR) - \varphi(G(LR)))^2 \qquad (2)$$

where φ stands for the feature map of VGG-19 [13] before activation, W and H are the width and height of the feature map. G stands for the generator network.

The adversarial loss is defined as:

$$L_{adv} = -E\left[\log\left(1 - D\left(HR, G\left(LR\right)\right)\right)\right] - E\left[\log\left(D\left(G\left(LR\right), HR\right)\right)\right] \tag{3}$$

where D stands for the discriminator network.

3.2   Degradation Learning

Aims to enable the super-resolution network to adapt to different degradations. Follow [14], we use an degradation learning network to extract the latent degradation representation D_e from the input LR image. To this end, an contrastive learning Method [15] is used to minimize the difference of the representation of the same degradation, while maximizing the difference between different degradations. In details, for a given LR image L_r, we randomly crop two patches, named L_q and L_{k+}, we take them as positive examples. And we treat the patches from other LR images as negative examples, named L_{k-}. The loss of the degradation learning can be formulated as:

$$L_{contra} = -log\frac{e^{(L_q * L_{k+}/t)}}{\sum_{i=0}^{K} e^{(L_q * L_{k-}/t)}} \tag{4}$$

where K is the number of the negative examples, and t is a hyper-parameter.

In this way, the reconstruction process can take the degraded information into account and be adaptive to different degradations. As shown in Fig. 2, we use the SFT [2] module to fuse the degradation information. So that the network can adaptively adjust the fusion method.

(a)   (b)

Fig. 3. (a) The architecture of the degradation learning encoder. (b) The architecture of the resBlock

The structure of degradation learning encoder is shown in Fig. 3(a). And the structure of resblock is shown in Fig. 3(b). In the inference phase, we only use the output of the first convolution layer in Fig. 3(a) as the degradation features.

3.3   MSAF Module

In order to integrate the features learned by previous modules, we propose a MSAF module. We enhanced the self-attention structure in [16], first, we remove the normalization layer, Because in our experiments, normalization destroys the learned image details, which leads to a drop in super-resolution performance. Bisides, we use self-attention with different numbers of heads to enable the network to fuse context at different scales.

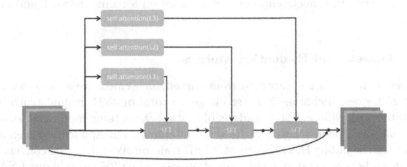

Fig. 4. The architecture of the MSAF module.

As shown in Fig. 4, from a feature X, first it will through three self-attention blocks with different head numbers. Then the SFT module [2] is used to integrate the outputs of the three blocks. In this way, Attention of different scales will be adaptively fused with input features. Then, a residual connection is used to integrate the features of different stages and input features.

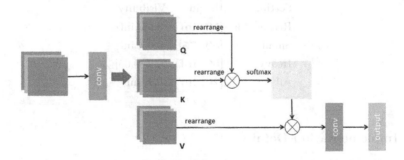

Fig. 5. The architecture of the self-attention block used in the proposed MSAF module.

As shown in Fig. 5, The input features will first pass through a convolution layer, and the obtained feature matrix will be divided into three feature matrices Q, K, and V according to the channel. Then, Q and K are multiplied together, and the result of the product after softmax is multiplied by V, One more convolution to get the final result, Finally, the output is obtained after a convolution.

4   Experiments

In this section, we experimentally validate our method on our dataset and the public citypersons dataset. First, we compare our method against the advanced algorithms on pedestrian detection. Then, we conduct some ablation experiments to verify the effectiveness of our degradation learning network and MSAF module.

4.1   Datasets and Evaluation Metrics

Dataset. Our dataset is captured from surveillance video, we sample an image every 25 frames, including 500 test images, a total of 3521 ground truth boxes annotated with different sizes and visible ratios. It contains many long-distance and small-sized pedestrians, so it is very suitable for our application scenario.

We use the public DIV2K dataset for SR training. We follow the conventional breakdown between training and evaluation sets of DIV2K to train our DSANet.

Evaluation Metrics. We follow the standard miss rate (MR) [17] evaluation metric in experiments, which is calculated in the False Positive Per Image (FPPI) over range [0.01, 1]. The IOU threshold is set to 0.5. We report the results for different sizes and occlusion levels namely, Reasonable, Small, Heavy, All. Definition of each split is shown in Table 1.

Table 1. Experimental settings.

Setting	Height	Visibility
Reasonable	**[50, inf]**	[0.65, inf]
Small	**[50, 75]**	[0.65, inf]
Heavy	**[50, inf]**	[0.2, 0.65]
All	**[20, inf]**	[0.2, inf]

4.2   Implementation Details

Our baseline pedestrian detector is YOLOv5. It should be noted that any exist pedestrian detector can be used as the baseline. In training the super resolution network, we set the tradeoff weights to $\theta_\rho = 1$, $\theta_{ad} = 0.05$, $\theta_{pix} = 0.01$, $\theta_{contra} = 0.05$. We first train 1200 iterations for the degradation learning network, Then the super-resolution network is trained as a whole.

The Adam optimizer [18] is used to optimize the super resolution networks. The learning rate is set to 0.0001, and the total number of iterations is 2400. Our system is implemented in PyTorch on two NVIDIA 2080 Ti GPUs.

In the testing phase, due to objects with high confidence already have enough detailed features and do not need to be supplemented by super-resolution, in addition, objects that are too small do not have basic features, so we only perform super-resolution on bboxes that satisfy the following conditions.

$$B_{conf} \leq 0.55 \tag{5}$$

$$B_{width} \geq 20 \tag{6}$$

$$B_{aspect} \geq 1.7 \tag{7}$$

where B_{conf}, B_{width}, B_{aspect} are the confidence, width and aspect ratio of the bounding box.

After super-resolution, we further detect the high-resolution crop. In order to make the detection effect more stable, we only use the detection results of the bounding box with the highest confidence that meet the following conditions, and the rest retain the results before super-resolution.

$$S_{det}/S_{SR} > 0.6 \tag{8}$$

$$M_{conf} \geq 0.35 \tag{9}$$

$$R_{acpect} \geq 1.6 \tag{10}$$

where S_{det} and S_{SR} are the area of the bounding box and the high resolution crop respectively, M_{conf} is the confidence of the bounding box, and R_{acpect} is the acpect ratio of the bounding box. The reason for setting the area ratio is that in a few cases, a part of the crop image after super-resolution looks like a pedestrian, and we want to avoid false positives in this case. and we found that after super-resolution, the detection results with confidence greater than 0.35 are more stable.

4.3   Ablation Studies

Our Dataset. We performed ablation experiments on our dataset to verify the effectiveness of our method. Firstly, we compare it with the baseline results. As shown in Table 2, Our DSANet significantly improves on both the small and heavy subsets. It should be noted that the reasons why our method is not as

Table 2. Results of our method against the baseline detector YOLOv5. MR^{-2} is used to evaluate the performance. (Lower is better)

Method	Reasonable	Small	Heavy	All
YOLOv5	31.16	73.71	59.25	42.88
DSANet (ours)	33.29	71.95	58.12	45.17

effective as the baseline algorithm in reasonable setup are as follows: (1) For some pedestrians with large sizes, some negative bounding boxes only frame the part of the pedestrian, such as the head or arm etc., in this case, the confidence of the crop after super-resolution will increase, but this will lead to a decrease in the evaluation metric. (2) For pedestrians with a relatively large size, the detailed features required for detection are already available, and super-resolution is not needed to supplement them.

Note that the small and heavy setups are of particular concern to us, this demonstrates the effectiveness of our algorithm for pedestrians with small size and occlusion.

Table 3. Results of ablation learning. MR^{-2} is used to evaluate the performance. (Lower is better)

Method	Degradation	MSAF	Reasonable	Small	Heavy	All
DSANet	No	No	32.62	72.81	58.75	44.61
	Yes	No	33.14	70.60	60.10	45.31
	No	Yes	32.81	72.15	57.60	44.91
	Yes	Yes	33.29	71.95	58.12	45.17

In order to prove the benefit of our DSANet, we replace the enhanced super resolution network with origin realSR algorithm [1]. To verify the effectiveness of degenerate learning, we remove it in ablation experiments. Through performance comparisons, we show that the addition of degenerate learning has a positive effect. We also demonstrate the effectiveness of the MSAF module in the same way.

As shown in Table 3, the four algorithms were trained under the same training settings as mentioned in Sect. 4.2, Algorithm using only degenerate learning performs best on small subset, but doesn't work well on heavy subset, while algorithm using only MSAF module performs best on heavy subset, but doesn't work well on small subset, our DSANet get a balanced performance on both subsets. This result shows that the MSAF module can well integrate context information at different scales, and pay more attention to the local details of pedestrians, so it can greatly improve the occluded pedestrians. The degradation learning enables the network to adapt to different degradations, so it has better robustness for small-sized fuzzy pedestrians. Compared to the original realSR algorithm [1], our DSANet achieves improvements on both heavy and small subsets. So, fusion of the two modules can make the network has a more balanced performance for blurred and occluded pedestrians in long-distance scenes.

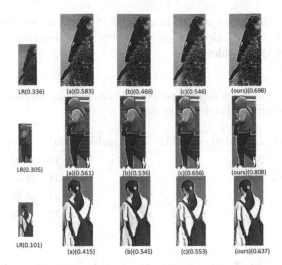

Fig. 6. Comparison of SR images of different algorithms, the left is the low-resolution crop image, the right (a) is the result of the original realSR algorithm [1], (b) is the result of only adding MSAF module, (c) is the result of only adding degradation learning, and d is The results of our DSANet, the corresponding confidence are in parentheses.

We show the performance of different algorithms in ablation experiments as shown in Fig. 6. We can find that the confidence of the results of all four algorithms increases, but our DSANet produces more realistic results with the most confidence increase.

Citypersons Dataset. To further verify the effectiveness of our method, we conduct same experiments on the public citypersons dataset. We found that there are some problems in the annotations of public dataset citypersons [19], for example, using a bounding box to frame several people, besides, some bounding boxes do not have any features of pedestrians at all, which is harmful to the evaluation of our algorithm and does not meet our application scenarios. So we relabeled the citypersons dataset. We removed some samples that don't have any features of pedestrians at all. And we adjusted the coordinates of the bounding box to solve the above problems. In this experiment, we train the model for 12000 iterations. The rest of the settings are the same as above. As shown in the Table 4, Our method improves on both the small and heavy subsets, and the

Table 4. Results of our method against the baseline detector YOLOv5 on citypersons. MR^{-2} is used to evaluate the performance. (Lower is better)

Method	Reasonable	Small	Heavy	All
YOLOv5	21.81	28.51	66.25	37.98
DSANet(ours)	23.59	28.32	64.35	40.01

improvement on the heavy subset is more obvious. And we perform the same ablation experiments on citypersons to verify the effectiveness of degenerate learning and MSAF modules.

Table 5. Results of ablation experiments on the citypersons dataset. MR^{-2} is used to evaluate the performance. (Lower is better)

Method	Degradation	MSAF	Reasonable	Small	Heavy	All
	No	No	25.66	29.48	65.02	41.58
DSANet	Yes	No	23.81	28.54	64.61	39.87
	No	Yes	23.44	28.35	64.22	39.53
	Yes	Yes	23.59	28.32	64.35	40.01

As shown in Table 5, while our method achieves good results on the heavy subset, it performs best on the small subset, which verifies the effectiveness of our method for small-sized pedestrians.

For the problems encountered during the experiment, we will do more experiments in the future, such as super-resolution on the full image to overcome the problems mentioned above.

5   Conclusion

In this article, we have improved the pedestrian detection algorithm for distant and small size pedestrians. In order to achieve this goal, we first use super-resolution to enlarge the detection results, The reconstructed results are then further detected. In order to enable the super-resolution algorithm to recover more detailed information, A degenerate learning network is introduced to provide degradation information for the super-resolution network. In this way, the super-resolution network is able to adapt to specific degradation scenarios. And we propose a self-attention-based MSAF module to let the network pay attention to the contextual information. The experimental results prove the effectiveness of our algorithm. For unresolved issues, we will do more experiments in the future, such as super-resolution on the full image, etc.

References

1. Ji, X., Cao, Y., Tai, Y., Wang, C., Li, J., Huang, F.: Real-world super-resolution via kernel estimation and noise injection. In: Proceedings of the IEEECVF Conference on Computer Vision and Pattern Recognition Workshops, pp. 466–467 (2020)
2. Wang, X., Yu, K., Dong, C., Loy, C.C.: Recovering realistic texture in image super-resolution by deep spatial feature transform. In: Proceedings of the IEEE conference on computer vision and pattern recognition, pp. 606–615 (2018)

3. Dalal, N., Triggs, B.: Histograms of oriented gradients for human detection. In: 2005 IEEE Computer Society Conference on Computer Vision and Pattern Recognition (CVPR 2005), vol. 1, pp. 886–893. IEEE (2005)
4. Lowe, D.G.: Distinctive image features from scale-invariant keypoints. Int. J. Comput. Vision **60**(2), 91–110 (2004). https://doi.org/10.1023/B:VISI.0000029664. 99615.94
5. Bochkovskiy, A., Wang, C.Y., Liao, H.Y.M.: Yolov4: optimal speed and accuracy of object detection (2020)
6. Jocher, G., et al.: Ultralytics/yolov5: v6.0 - YOLOv5n 'Nano' models, Roboflow integration, TensorFlow export, OpenCV DNN support (2021). https://doi.org/ 10.5281/zenodo.5563715
7. Dong, C., Loy, C.C., He, K., Tang, X.: Learning a deep convolutional network for image super-resolution. In: Fleet, D., Pajdla, T., Schiele, B., Tuytelaars, T. (eds.) ECCV 2014. LNCS, vol. 8692, pp. 184–199. Springer, Cham (2014). https://doi. org/10.1007/978-3-319-10593-2_13
8. Ledig, C., et al.: Photo-realistic single image super-resolution using a generative adversarial network. In: Proceedings of the IEEE conference on computer vision and pattern recognition, pp. 4681–4690 (2017)
9. Wang, X., et al.: Esrgan: enhanced super-resolution generative adversarial networks. In: Proceedings of the European Conference on Computer Vision (ECCV) Workshops (2018)
10. Bell-Kligler, S., Shocher, A., Irani, M.: Blind super-resolution kernel estimation using an internal-gan. In: Proceedings of the 33rd International Conference on Neural Information Processing Systems, pp. 284–293 (2019)
11. Zhang, Y., Bai, Y., Ding, M., Xu, S., Ghanem, B.: Kgsnet: key-point-guided super-resolution network for pedestrian detection in the wild. IEEE Trans. Neural Netw. Learn. Syst. **32**(5), 2251–2265 (2020)
12. Agustsson, E., Timofte, R.: Ntire 2017 challenge on single image super-resolution: Dataset and study. In: Proceedings of the IEEE Conference on Computer Vision and Pattern Recognition Workshops, pp. 126–135 (2017)
13. Simonyan, K., Zisserman, A.: Very deep convolutional networks for large-scale image recognition. In: International Conference on Learning Representations (ICLR), pp. 1–14 (2015)
14. Li, B., Liu, X., Hu, P., Wu, Z., Lv, J., Peng, X.: All-in-one image restoration for unknown corruption. In: IEEE Conference on Computer Vision and Pattern Recognition. New Orleans, LA (2022)
15. He, K., Fan, H., Wu, Y., Xie, S., Girshick, R.: Momentum contrast for unsupervised visual representation learning. In: Proceedings of the IEEE/CVF conference on computer vision and pattern recognition, pp. 9729–9738 (2020)
16. Zamir, S.W., Arora, A., Khan, S., Hayat, M., Khan, F.S., Yang, M.H.: Restormer: efficient transformer for high-resolution image restoration. In: Proceedings of the IEEE/CVF Conference on Computer Vision and Pattern Recognition, pp. 5728–5739 (2022)
17. Dollar, P., Wojek, C., Schiele, B., Perona, P.: Pedestrian detection: an evaluation of the state of the art. IEEE Trans. Pattern Anal. Mach. Intell. **34**(4), 743–761 (2011)
18. Kingma, D.P., Ba, J.: Adam: a method for stochastic optimization. In: International Conference on Learning Representations (ICLR), vol. 5 (2015)
19. Zhang, S., Benenson, R., Schiele, B.: Citypersons: a diverse dataset for pedestrian detection. In: Proceedings of the IEEE conference on computer vision and pattern recognition, pp. 3213–3221 (2017)

Context Dual-Branch Attention Network for Depth Completion of Transparent Object

Yutao Hu[1], Zheng Wang[2(✉)], Jiacheng Chen[1], and Wanliang Wang[1]

[1] College of Computer Science and Technology, Zhejiang University of Technology, Hangzhou 310000, Zhejiang, China
[2] School of Computer and Computational Science, Zhejiang University City College, Hangzhou 310000, Zhejiang, China
2560219894@qq.com

Abstract. With the rise in popularity of RGB-D cameras, vision-based robot approaches that rely on the depth information given by RGB-D cameras are gaining favor. However, because of their reflection and refraction features, transparent objects, which are a prevalent part of our daily lives, are difficult to distinguish and locate with an RGB-D camera. To overcome this issue, we present DCTNet, a novel technique for depth completion of transparent objects, in this study. DCTNet is a dual-branch approach that uses a single RGB-D picture to complete the depth of a transparent end-to-end. We apply MSSA, a multi-scale spatial attention technique, to fuse distinct branch feature maps to improve the depth completion results even more. Experiments show that when compared to ClearGrasp, our approach produces much better performance and improves inference speed.

Keywords: Transparent objects · Depth completion · Attention mechanism · Robot grasp

1 Introduction

With the widespread usage of RGB-D cameras, depth information is becoming increasingly relevant in a variety of applications and situations. However, due of the peculiarity of its visual properties such as refraction and specular reflection, obtaining the depth information of transparent objects is difficult. This makes it impossible to apply some current robotics technologies and algorithms that use depth information to transparent objects which is very common class of objects in life. As a result, several robotics technologies and algorithms that use depth information cannot be used for transparent objects, which are fairly common class of objects in life.

Calculating the geometry of transparent objects has frequently been done in controlled situations in the past, such as assuming the shape of the transparent object is known [1,2] and requiring extra devices [3] or fixed backgrounds [4].

H. Liu et al. (Eds.): ICIRA 2022, LNAI 13458, pp. 604–614, 2022.
https://doi.org/10.1007/978-3-031-13841-6_54

ClearGrasp [5] is the first method that uses neural network to complete the depth information of transparent objects and gets good results. In the meantime, it creates a large-scale synthetic dataset for the task of completing the depth of transparent objects. It performs global optimization to complete the depth information by using RGB image-predicted masks, occlusion bounds, and surface normal as input. However, it cannot be employed in real-world applications that have speed demands because of the slow inference time.

In this research, we propose an end-to-end method for depth completion of transparent objects from an RGB-D image that achieves better results and is faster than previous work. Our method is made up of two branches that handle color and depth pictures separately, as well as spatial attention mechanism that fuses the feature maps from the distinct branches. The following two concepts drive our approach.

- Transparent object depth information can be extracted from color and noise depth images separately; various modality datas are complementary. In certain works, dual-branch designs are also developed [6–8] and late fusion can achieve better results compared with early fusion.
- By acquiring global background information, the attention mechanism simulates human perception, which picks significant regions while disregarding irrelevant information. Using the attention mechanism to combine the information from two branches might lead to improved results.

The main contributions of our work are summarized as follows: 1) We propose DCTNet, an end-to-end method for depth completion of transparent objects. 2) We propose MSSA, a multi-scale spatial attention mechanism, to fuse information in different branches. 3) Our approach achieves better results on the ClearGrasp dataset with faster inference times.

2   Related Work

2.1   Depth Completion of Transparent Objects

Recently, depth completion and estimation grows in popularity as study topic, which can be divided into three classes based on the input. Depth maps are estimated directly from RGB images in some methods [9–13]. Because the depth information from RGB images is inherently vague and inaccurate, estimating depth maps from single RGB images is an ill-posed problem. Some other methods complete the dense depth maps based on RGB and sparse depth images [8,14–16]. These methods try to reconstruct high-accuracy depth maps using sparse depth images obtained from less expensive sensors. The third category attempts to complete depth maps using noisy RGB-D images [5,17–19].

Our method belongs to the last class because the depth information in transparent objects' area is usually noisy and unobservable. Zhang et al. [17] complete depth maps using global optimization according to surface normals and occlusion boundaries computed from RGB images. However, the approaches described above are not appropriate for dealing with transparent objects. Based on previous works, Sajjan et al. [5] generate a large-scale dataset for transparent objects depth completion and propose some essential changes to Zhang's pipeline. Nevertheless, its inference time of global optimization is so long that it's unsuitable for robot grasping tasks. Zhu et al. [18] present an end-to-end method that learns a local implicit function using an RGB picture and local depth, and its inference time is 20 times faster than Sajjan's [5]. We propose an end-to-end method that takes color and depth photos as inputs and improves the inference time by a factor of 100 compared to Sajjan's [5].

2.2 Attention Mechanism

In many tasks, attention mechanism that mimics human perception yields great results recently [20–26]. With the help of attention mechanism, the neural network focuses on critical areas dynamically and processes information selectively. Hu et al. [21] first propose channel attention method that combines squeeze module for aggravating global context information with an excitation module for generating a weight vector that depicts channel-wise interactions. However, its squeeze module, which generates global context information through global average pooling, is too simplistic for aggregating complex global information. To improve the ability to aggregate global context information, Gao et al. [23] generate a covariance matrix to model high-order information. Dai et al. [24] present a method that, unlike other methods, uses additional offsets to modify the receptive field of convolution to focus on crucial locations. Wang et al. [25] apply self-attention to computer vision, and yet its applicability is limited by its complexity. Woo et al. [26] model channel-wise interactions as well as concentrating significant regions by combining channel attention and spatial attention in series. We devised spatial attention mechanism that aggregates the features on several receptive fields without the need for additional calculations or parameter numbers.

3 Method

3.1 Overview

We go over our DCTNet in great depth in this part. DCTNet is an end-to-end method for depth completion of transparent objects which consists of two branches as shown in Fig. 1. One branch takes an RGB image $I \in \mathbb{R}^{H \times W \times 3}$ as input and predicts full depth map according to color information. The other branch is depth-dominant, which predicts depth map from noisy depth image $D \in \mathbb{R}^{H \times W \times 1}$, where H and W denotes the input image's size.

The dual-branch backbone is designed to fully use different information from their respective branches, allowing for successful fusion of two modalities by Multi-Scale Spatial Attention blocks. Each branch is UNet [27] encoder-decoder architecture as shown in Fig. 2. We apply a 3×3 convolutional layer to extract

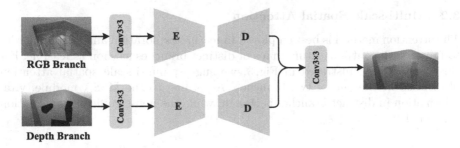

Fig. 1. The overview of our proposed model: DCTNet.

the features from input before being processed by the UNet. Each downsampling step includes context-gated convolution [28] (Sect. 3.3), residual block [29], and max-pooling with stride 2. In contrast to downsampling, the upsampling step replaces max-pooling with bilinear upsample operation.

The multi-scale spatial attention module (Sect. 3.2) fuses the feature maps that output in various branches, and then we apply a 3×3 convolution and ReLU function to output the complete depth map $\hat{D}$. Experiments show that our approach produces good outcomes.

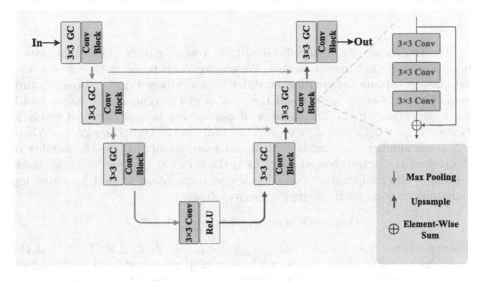

Fig. 2. The encoder-decoder architecture with context-gated convolution layers.

3.2   Multi-scale Spatial Attention

The attention method is best employed in feature exploration and fusion in order to fully use the output feature maps of distinct branches as soon as feasible. For this purpose, as illustrated in Fig. 3, we suggest multi-scale spatial attention block used at the end of two branches. According to the MSSA module, vital information in distinct branches is chosen, while the non-significant information is ignored.

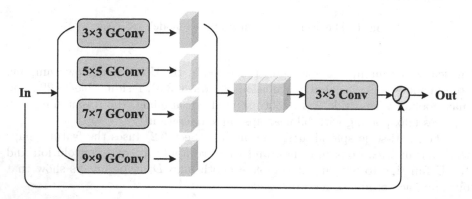

Fig. 3. The multi-scale spatial attention (MSSA) for fusing features from dual-branch.

The traditional 3×3 convolutional layer cannot gather global information because of the small receptive field. We employ convolution with different kernel sizes to capture information on different scales based on the input feature map. The number of factors and the cost of calculation, on the other hand, are unacceptably high. The number of parameters in convolutional layers is $ks \times ks \times C_{in} \times C_{out}$, and it grows exponentially as the kernel size grows. Where C_{in} is the number of channels of the input feature map. C_{out} is the number of channels of the output feature map. ks is the kernel size of convolutional layer. To reduce the computation cost, depth-wise convolution is used for gathering global information from different scales as follows:

$$feat_i = GConv_{i \times i}\left(feat_{in}\right), i \in [3, 5, 7, 9] \tag{1}$$

where i denotes the kernel size of group convolution. $feat_i \in \mathbb{R}^{H \times W \times C}$ has the same size as $feat_{in}$ and refers to the feature map generated by the convolution of a group with kernel size i. The feature maps, generated from different convolutional layers, are concatenated. Finally, the attention map $F_{CA} \in \mathbb{R}^{H \times W \times 1}$ is generated as follows:

$$F_{CA} = \sigma\left(Conv\left(\left[feat_3, feat_5, feat_7, feat_9\right]\right)\right) \tag{2}$$

where $Conv\left(\cdot\right)$ means the ordinary 3×3 convolution. $\sigma\left(\cdot\right)$ denotes the sigmoid function.

3.3 Context-Gated Convolution

Because of the narrow receptive fields, each convolutional operation harvests information exclusively in the local field. To address the aforementioned flaw, we employ Context-Gated Convolution (CGC) [28], whose parameters are dynamically produced based on input attributes. We employ a pooling layer to reduce the resolution of the input feature to $h' \times w'$ to gather the global information and reduce the computation costs, and then we extract a latent representation of the global context for all of the spatial locations for each channel. To project each channel to a latent vector of size d, which we set the vector size as $d = \frac{k_1 \times k_2}{2}$, a linear layer with weight $W_C \in \mathbb{R}^{h' \times w' \times d}$ that is shared across different channels is utilized to output the global information $F_C \in \mathbb{R}^{c \times d}$.

To project feature representations $F_C \in \mathbb{R}^{c \times d}$ to $F_{CI} \in \mathbb{R}^{c_{out} \times d}$ on Channel Interacting, we utilize grouped linear with weight $W_{CI} \in \mathbb{R}^{\frac{c_{in}}{g} \times \frac{c_{out}}{g}}$. The number of groups is denoted by g.

The Gate Decoding takes $F_C \in \mathbb{R}^{c \times d}$ and $F_{CI} \in \mathbb{R}^{c_{out} \times d}$ as inputs and $W_{new} = W \odot F_A$ generates $F_{A1} \in \mathbb{R}^{c_{out} \times k_1 \times k_2}$ and $F_{A2} \in \mathbb{R}^{c_{in} \times k_1 \times k_2}$ using two shared linear layers with weights $W_{DC} \in \mathbb{R}^{d \times k_1 \times k_2}$ and $W_{DO} \in \mathbb{R}^{d \times k_1 \times k_2}$. Specifically, each element is produced by

$$(F_A)_{h,i,j,k} = \sigma \left((F_{A1})_{i,j,k} + (F_{A2})_{h,j,k} \right) \tag{3}$$

Following the preceding functions, we get a mask $F_A \in \mathbb{R}^{c_{in} \times c_{out} \times j \times k}$ of the same size as the convolution kernel size W, and then modulate the weight of a convolution layer according to F_A as follows:

$$W_{new} = W \odot F_A \tag{4}$$

Where the operation $\odot$ means element-wise multiplication. Specifically, We use L1 loss in the training process.

4 Experiments

4.1 Dataset and Implement Detail

In all trials, the input picture resolution was set at 256×256. As with Sajjan's [5], we eliminate the depth information that corresponds to transparent objects as input depth. Our model was trained for 200 epochs with the Adam optimizer and the CosineAnnealingLR scheduler, with lr of 1e−4 to 1e−7. The batchsize parameter has been set to 32.

We complete our model training on the ClearGrasp dataset [5]. Transparent objects are ubiquitous in daily life, but they have distinct visual properties. In cluttered situations, the ClearGrasp dataset includes various supervisions for transparent and opaque objects. It is a large-scale synthetic dataset with almost 50,000 RGB-D images and a realistic test benchmark with 286 RGB-D transparent object images and associated ground truth geometry.

Metrics For depth estimate, The standard metrics specified in [5] are used. Unless otherwise noted, all measurements are calculated on transparent regions using transparent masks. We first resize the prediction and ground-truth to 256×256 resolution, then compute errors in the region of the transparent object using the metrics below:

Root Mean Squared Error(RMSE): $\sqrt{\frac{1}{|\hat{D}|} \sum_{d \in \hat{D}} \|d - d^*\|^2}$

Absolute Relative Difference (REL): $\frac{1}{|\hat{D}|} \sum_{d \in \hat{D}} |d - d^*| / d^*$

Mean Absolute Error (MAE): $\frac{1}{|\hat{D}|} \sum_{d \in \hat{D}} |d - d^*|$

Threshold: the percentage of d_i satisfying:$\max \left(\frac{d_i}{d_i^*}, \frac{d_i^*}{d_i} \right) < \lambda$

The first three metrics are in meters. Where d_i, d_i^* are D, $\hat{D}$'s equivalent pixels. λ is set to 1.05, 1.10 and 1.25.

4.2   Comparison to State-of-the-art Methods

We compare our method with the state-of-the-art method in Table 1. Our method is trained on the same dataset as the baseline method [5]. Cleargrasp is the state-of-the-art approach for completing the depth of transparent objects. We employ the best model for our approach: DCTNet and our method produces the best results. We generate depth maps to color pictures for comparison with ClearGrasp [5], as seen in Fig. 4. Our method can produce more precise depth information for transparent objects.

Table 1. Comparative analysis of state-of-the-art methods. ↓ and ↑ means to "lower is better" and "higher is better." And the best results are highlighted. For more information, please see the text.

Methods	RMSE↓	REL↓	MAE↓	$\lambda_{1.05}$ ↑	$\lambda_{1.10}$ ↑	$\lambda_{1.25}$ ↑
ClearGrasp Syn-known Dataset						
CG [5]	0.044	0.047	0.033	71.23	92.60	98.24
Ours	**0.021**	**0.028**	**0.015**	**86.03**	**94.64**	**99.23**
ClearGrasp Syn-Novel Dataset						
CG [5]	0.040	0.071	0.035	42.95	80.04	**98.10**
Ours	**0.028**	**0.046**	**0.022**	**68.72**	**89.47**	98.05

Inference speed is a significant consideration for implementing the model in real-world applications. We compare our method's inference time with [5]. CG employs a two-stage methodology, but our technology gives an end-to-end solution for completing the scene's depth image. We run both approaches on a system with three NVIDIA 3090 GPUs for training and one for testing, and compute the average time throughout the whole testing set to compare the runtime equitably. Our method takes 0.02 s to process a single image, whereas CG takes 1.81 s, demonstrating that our method is 100 times quicker.

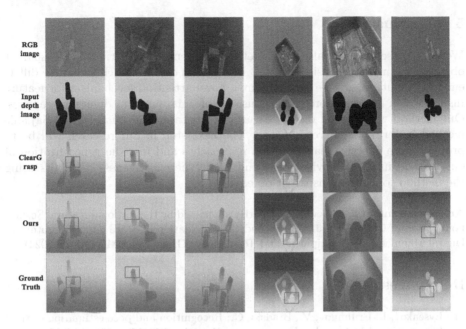

Fig. 4. Qualitative comparison to ClearGrasp on synthetic dataset.

4.3   Ablation Studies

We propose multi-scale spatial attention blocks to achieve better completion performance in detail parts by fusing color features. Vital information in different branches is chosen by the MSSA module, while non-significant information is omitted.

We examine the impact of multi-scale spatial attention blocks in this section. We perform two experiments with and without spatial attention to demonstrate the efficiency of the multi-scale spatial attention blocks. We directly add the feature maps generated by different branches during the experiment without multi-scale spatial attention block. Table 2 illustrates how incorporating multi-scale spatial attention blocks might improve performance. With the MSSA blocks, our method achieve better results.

Table 2. Ablation studies for effect of MSSA.

Methods	RMSE↓	REL↓	MAE↓	$\lambda_{1.05}$ ↑	$\lambda_{1.10}$ ↑	$\lambda_{1.25}$ ↑
ClearGrasp Syn-known Dataset						
w/o MSSA	0.0257	0.0367	0.0194	78.77	91.72	**98.88**
w MSSA	**0.0256**	**0.0370**	**0.0188**	**80.64**	**92.20**	98.43
ClearGrasp Syn-Novel Dataset						
w/o MSSA	0.0411	0.0688	0.0346	53.88	78.40	93.45
w MSSA	**0.0324**	**0.0536**	**0.0270**	**57.85**	**85.73**	**98.62**

5   Conclusion

We have presented a dual-branch method for depth completion of transparent objects. Our method consists of RGB branch and depth branch to handle different type input image. We also present a novel attention mechanism for feature fusion, which enables more efficient use of information from different branches. Our method was trained on the ClearGrasp dataset and outperforms Sajjan's method in terms of inference speed. The next step in our research will be to propose more effective feature fusion approaches and test the generalization of our method in a real environment and verify the effectiveness of robots using the method to grasp transparent objects.

Acknowledgments. This work was partly supported by the National Natural Science Foundation of China (No. 61873240) and the Foundation of State Key Laboratory of Digital Manufacturing Equipment and Technology (Grant No. DMETKF2022024).

References

1. Lysenkov, I., Eruhimov, V., Bradski, G.: Recognition and pose estimation of rigid transparent objects with a kinect sensor. Robotics **273**(273–280), 2 (2013)
2. Phillips, C.J., Lecce, M., Daniilidis, K.: Seeing glassware: from edge detection to pose estimation and shape recovery. In: Robotics: Science and Systems, vol. 3, p. 3 (2016)
3. Han, K., Wong, K.-Y.K., Liu, M.: A fixed viewpoint approach for dense reconstruction of transparent objects. In: Proceedings of the IEEE Conference on Computer Vision and Pattern Recognition, pp. 4001–4008 (2015)
4. Qian, Y., Gong, M., Yang, Y.H.: 3d reconstruction of transparent objects with position-normal consistency. In: Proceedings of the IEEE Conference on Computer Vision and Pattern Recognition, pp. 4369–4377 (2016)
5. Sajjan, S.: Clear grasp: 3d shape estimation of transparent objects for manipulation. In: 2020 IEEE International Conference on Robotics and Automation (ICRA), pp. 3634–3642. IEEE (2020)
6. Van Gansbeke, W., Neven, D., De Brabandere, B., Van Gool, L.: Sparse and noisy lidar completion with RGB guidance and uncertainty. In: 2019 16th International Conference on Machine Vision Applications (MVA), pp. 1–6. IEEE (2019)
7. Hu, M., Wang, S., Li, B., Ning, S., Fan, L., Gong, X.: PENet: towards precise and efficient image guided depth completion. In: 2021 IEEE International Conference on Robotics and Automation (ICRA), pp. 13656–13662. IEEE (2021)
8. Qiu, J., et al.: DeepLiDAR: deep surface normal guided depth prediction for outdoor scene from sparse lidar data and single color image. In: Proceedings of the IEEE/CVF Conference on Computer Vision and Pattern Recognition, pp. 3313–3322 (2019)
9. Eigen, D., Puhrsch, C., Fergus, R.: Depth map prediction from a single image using a multi-scale deep network. In: Advances in Neural Information Processing Systems 27 (2014)
10. Fu, H., Gong, M., Wang, C., Batmanghelich, K., Tao, D.: Deep ordinal regression network for monocular depth estimation. In: Proceedings of the IEEE Conference on Computer Vision and Pattern Recognition, pp. 2002–2011 (2018)

11. Laina, I., Rupprecht, C., Belagiannis, V., Tombari, F., Navab, N.: Deeper depth prediction with fully convolutional residual networks. In: 2016 Fourth International Conference on 3D Vision (3DV), pp. 239–248. IEEE (2016)

12. Chen, W., Fu, Z., Yang, D., Deng, J.: Single-image depth perception in the wild. In: Advances in Neural Information Processing Systems 29 (2016)

13. Eigen, D., Fergus, R.: Predicting depth, surface normals and semantic labels with a common multi-scale convolutional architecture. In: Proceedings of the IEEE International Conference on Computer Vision, pp. 2650–2658 (2015)

14. Ma, F., Karaman, S.: Sparse-to-dense: depth prediction from sparse depth samples and a single image. In: 2018 IEEE International Conference on Robotics and Automation (ICRA), pp. 4796–4803. IEEE (2018)

15. Chen, Y., Yang, B., Liang, M., Urtasun, R.: Learning joint 2d–3d representations for depth completion. In: Proceedings of the IEEE/CVF International Conference on Computer Vision, pp. 10023–10032 (2019)

16. Xu, Y., Zhu, X., Shi, J., Zhang, G., Bao, H., Li, H.: Depth completion from sparse lidar data with depth-normal constraints. In: Proceedings of the IEEE/CVF International Conference on Computer Vision, pp. 2811–2820 (2019)

17. Zhang, Y., Funkhouser, T.: Deep depth completion of a single RGB-D image. In: Proceedings of the IEEE Conference on Computer Vision and Pattern Recognition, pp. 175–185 (2018)

18. Zhu, L.: RGB-D local implicit function for depth completion of transparent objects. In: Proceedings of the IEEE/CVF Conference on Computer Vision and Pattern Recognition, pp. 4649–4658 (2021)

19. Xu, H., Wang, Y.R., Eppel, S., Aspuru-Guzik, A., Shkurti, F., Garg, A.: Seeing glass: joint point cloud and depth completion for transparent objects. arXiv preprint arXiv:2110.00087 (2021)

20. Vaswani, A., et al.: Attention is all you need. In: Advances in Neural Information Processing Systems 30 (2017)

21. Hu, J., Shen, L., Sun, G.: Squeeze-and-excitation networks. In: Proceedings of the IEEE Conference on Computer Vision and Pattern Recognition, pp. 7132–7141 (2018)

22. Hu, J., Shen, L., Albanie, S., Sun, G., Vedaldi, A.: Gather-excite: exploiting feature context in convolutional neural networks. In: Advances in Neural Information Processing Systems 31 (2018)

23. Gao, Z., Xie, J., Wang, Q., Li, P.: Global second-order pooling convolutional networks. In: Proceedings of the IEEE/CVF Conference on Computer Vision and Pattern Recognition, pp. 3024–3033 (2019)

24. Dai, J.: Deformable convolutional networks. In: Proceedings of the IEEE International Conference on Computer Vision, pp. 764–773 (2017)

25. Wang, X., Girshick, R., Gupta, A., He, K.: Non-local neural networks. In: Proceedings of the IEEE Conference on Computer Vision and Pattern Recognition, pp. 7794–7803 (2018)

26. Woo, S., Park, J., Lee, J.-Y., Kweon, I.S.: CBAM: convolutional block attention module. In: Ferrari, V., Hebert, M., Sminchisescu, C., Weiss, Y. (eds.) ECCV 2018. LNCS, vol. 11211, pp. 3–19. Springer, Cham (2018). https://doi.org/10.1007/978-3-030-01234-2_1

27. Ronneberger, O., Fischer, P., Brox, T.: U-Net: convolutional networks for biomedical image segmentation. In: Navab, N., Hornegger, J., Wells, W.M., Frangi, A.F. (eds.) MICCAI 2015. LNCS, vol. 9351, pp. 234–241. Springer, Cham (2015). https://doi.org/10.1007/978-3-319-24574-4_28

28. Lin, X., Ma, L., Liu, W., Chang, S.-F.: Context-gated convolution. In: Vedaldi, A., Bischof, H., Brox, T., Frahm, J.-M. (eds.) ECCV 2020. LNCS, vol. 12363, pp. 701–718. Springer, Cham (2020). https://doi.org/10.1007/978-3-030-58523-5_41

29. He, K., Zhang, X., Ren, S., Sun, J.: Deep residual learning for image recognition. In: Proceedings of the IEEE Conference on Computer Vision and Pattern Recognition, pp. 770–778 (2016)

Bio-inspired Healthcare Robotics and Technology

Theoretical Calculation and Analysis of Microdroplet Evaporation on Micropipette Force Sensor

Huiyao Shi[1,2,3,4], Jialin Shi[1,2,3], Kaixuan Wang[1,2,3], Si Tang[1,2,3], Chanmin Su[1,2,3], and Lianqing Liu[1,2,3(✉)]

[1] State Key Laboratory of Robotics, Shenyang Institute of Automation, Chinese Academy of Sciences, Shenyang, China
lqliu@sia.cn
[2] Institutes for Robotics and Intelligent Manufacturing, Chinese Academy of Sciences, Shenyang 110169, China
[3] University of Chinese Academy of Sciences, Beijing, China
[4] Institute for Stem Cell and Regeneration, Chinese Academy of Sciences, Beijing, China

Abstract. Super-hydrophobic materials and coatings have excellent anti-fogging, self-cleaning and antibacterial capabilities, which has been appeared in both industrial manufacture and scientific research. Methods for quantitative measurement of hydrophilicity and hydrophobicity have attracted much attention. However, for the reason droplet evaporation inevitably exists, the method based on the observation of the contact angle and the force curve contacting by a droplet brings the problem of the inability of the contact angle measurement to be maintained for a long time and the measurement error. In this paper, the relationship between droplet evaporation and time in the constant contact radius (CCR) mode is studied, and a scheme of adaptive pressure regulation through the hierarchical cavity structure is proposed. Numerical calculations show that under specific conditions, the height of the droplet is reduced by 10 nm, and the time required is more than 10^6 s. This method is expected to be used for the measurement of solid-liquid contact mechanics with high stability for a long time.

Keywords: Superhydrophobic · Micropipette · Microdroplet

1 Introduction

Superhydrophobicity is widely found in nature, including lotus leaves [1], water striders [2], and butterflies [3]. Animals and plants achieve their own waterproof, clean, and antibacterial properties through the microstructures covered on the surface. Hydrophobic materials have attracted attention over the world for its potentials ranging from industrial manufacturing to daily life [4]. The micro-nano structure plays a crucial role in this special kind of wetting phenomenon. In addition to the superhydrophobic phenomenon, droplet unidirectional transport and directional transport are all related to the microstructure covering the surface [5, 6].

© The Author(s), under exclusive license to Springer Nature Switzerland AG 2022
H. Liu et al. (Eds.): ICIRA 2022, LNAI 13458, pp. 617–625, 2022.
https://doi.org/10.1007/978-3-031-13841-6_55

The traditional wettability measuring method based on contact angle measurement can only acquire the wettability at the macro scale, but cannot realize the analysis of the related properties at the micro/nanoscale. In recent years, the force curves using a droplet-based on image correlation recognition have received extensive attention [7–9], but in actual measurement, the droplet volume is large and the measurement resolution is limited. At the same time, the evaporation rate of droplets at the micro/nanoscale is fast, which cannot be maintained, and it is difficult to achieve effective measurement. It is urgent to develop a measurement scheme that can maintain the droplet size for a long time at the micro/nanoscale.

In this paper, we propose a method to achieve adaptive control of droplet scale through a hierarchical structure, which replenishes evaporated droplets by maintaining an adaptive balance of droplet surface tension and air pressure. Theoretical analysis shows that um-sized droplets can be maintained for up to 106 s, so as to meet the measurement of solid-liquid contact characteristics with high stability for a long time.

2 Theoretical Analysis

2.1 CCR Model of Droplet Evaporation

Assuming that the surface of the contact substrate is isotropic, homogeneous, and smooth, the horizontal force balance equation at the air-liquid-solid contact line is given as Young's equation [10, 11]:

$$\sigma_{sg} - \sigma_{ls} - \sigma_{lg} cos(\theta) = 0 \tag{1}$$

In which, σ_{sg}, σ_{ls}, and σ_{lg} are the tensions force between "solid-gas", "liquid-solid" and "liquid-gas" interfaces, respectively, and θ is the contact angle of droplet.

When the contact angle is determined, the shape of droplets can be determined by the gravity and surface tension. When the droplet contact radius r is less than the capillary length l_c.

$$r < l_c = \sqrt{\sigma_{lg}/\rho g} \tag{2}$$

where $\rho = 1000$ kg/m^3 and $g = 9.8$ N/kg are liquid density and gravitational acceleration, respectively. In this situation, the gravity of the droplet cannot overcome the surface tension, the surface of the droplet will tend to have a spherical crown shape.

For a spherical-crowned droplet with a radius of r, the evaporation rate of the droplet depends on the diffusion of water molecules on the surface. The evaporation rate formula can be simplified as:

$$\frac{dm}{dt} = \rho \frac{dV}{dt} = -D \int \nabla c dS \tag{3}$$

m is the mass of the droplet, t is the evaporation time, V is the volume of the droplet, D is the diffusion coefficient of the vapor ($D = 2.55 \times 10^{-5}$ m^2/s), c is the vapor concentration, the integral concentration gradient ∇c Taken from the surface dS of the spherical cap.

The droplet boundary (c_0) and the surrounding environment away from the droplet (c_∞) are approximately constant, and the vapor concentration gradient radially outward across the droplet boundary can be described as

$$\frac{\partial c}{\partial h} = \frac{c_\infty - c_0}{r_s} \tag{4}$$

h is the height of the droplet, r_s is the radius of the droplet.

$$c_\infty = Hc_0 \tag{5}$$

H is the relative humidity (RH) in the air.

The volume of the droplet can be calculated as:

$$V = \frac{\pi r_s^3 \left(2 - 3\cos\theta + \cos^3\theta\right)}{3\sin^3\theta} \tag{6}$$

When $\theta = 90°$, the surface evaporation is uniformly distributed.

$$\nabla c = -\frac{D(1-H)c_0}{r_s} \tag{7}$$

Equation 3 can be written as

$$\frac{dV}{dt} = -2\pi r_s \frac{D(1-H)c_0}{\rho} \tag{8}$$

For droplets with the same surface area, the evaporation rates of the droplets are approximately the same despite the large difference in droplet contact radii and contact angles.

For a contact angle of θ, the contact radius r of a hemispherical droplet with the same surface area can be calculated as:

$$\frac{dV}{dt} = -2\pi r_s \frac{D(1-H)c_0}{\rho} \tag{9}$$

Equation 8 can be written as:

$$\frac{dV}{dt} = -2\pi r \frac{D(1-H)c_0}{\rho\sqrt{1+\cos(\theta)}} \tag{10}$$

For the CCR mode, r does not change with time, and the relationship between the droplet contact angle and time is shown as:

$$\frac{\pi r^3}{(1+\cos\theta)^2} \frac{d\theta}{dt} = -2\pi r \frac{D(1-H)c_0}{\rho\sqrt{1+\cos(\theta)}} \tag{11}$$

And

$$\frac{d\theta}{dt} = -2\pi r \frac{D(1-H)c_0}{\rho}(1+\cos(\theta))^{3/2} \tag{12}$$

Integrating over time t gives the contact angle changes with time.

$$t(\theta) - t(\theta_0) = -\frac{\sqrt{2}}{8}\frac{\rho r^2}{D(1-H)c_0}[F(\theta_0) - F(\theta)] \tag{13}$$

where $F(\theta)$ is a function of θ.

$$F(\theta) = \ln\left(tan\left(\frac{\theta}{2}\right)\right) + \frac{(1-cos\theta)}{sin^2\theta} \tag{14}$$

The lifetime of a droplet t_f can be calculated as:

$$t_f = \frac{\sqrt{2}}{8}\frac{\rho r^2}{D(1-H)c_0}F(\theta_0) \tag{15}$$

For a droplet with a contact radius of um, the contact angle changes with time when the contact angle is 150, 90, and 30°, as shown in Fig. 2. Increasing the contact radius will increase the volume of the droplet, and the droplet will evaporate. The time also increases, and for small diameter droplets the evaporation time is on the order of ms (Fig. 1).

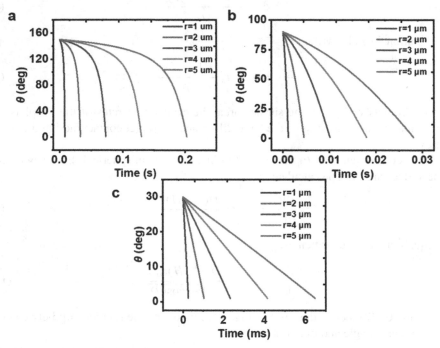

Fig. 1. The relationship between the contact angle of CCR mode droplet evaporation with time under different initial contact angles, (a) $\theta_0 = 150$, (b) $\theta_0 = 90$, (c) $\theta_0 = 30$.

Then the relationship between the lifetime and the contact radius of the droplet is calculated under different contact angles. With the radius increasing, the droplet survival time increases significantly.

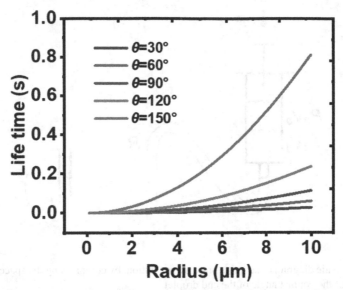

Fig. 2. The relationship between droplet survival time and droplet contact radius under different contact angles.

It can be concluded that at the micro-scale, the survival time of tiny droplets is very short, and cannot be used for the measurement of the solid-liquid contact characteristics at the micro-nano scale without the assistance of a high-speed camera. There is an urgent need to develop methods that can maintain droplet stability at room temperature.

2.2 Adaptive Pressure Regulation Method

Figure 3 schematically illustrated the adaptive pressure regulation method. The concept is connecting a syringe with enough space to the glass micropipettes of variable diameter through a rubber hose. The glass micropipette is perfused with water through capillary action, and the syringe is compressed so that a tiny droplet is generated at the end of the microtube, and the droplet is evaporated in the air. However, the evaporation results in a decrease in the total volume of droplets in the micropipettes. At the same time, the surface tension of the droplet decreases with the decrease of contact angle, the balance between the air pressure in the syringe and surface tension were broken and cannot be maintained with the volume of the compressed. The expanded air squeezed out water in the micropipettes, which eventually causes the droplet evaporation to be replenished by the droplet in the tube, thereby realizing the long-term maintenance of the droplet volume. Here, the air should have enough volume to maintain the slow change of air pressure, and the variable radius micropipettes should have enough diameter difference to prevent the liquid from falling too fast.

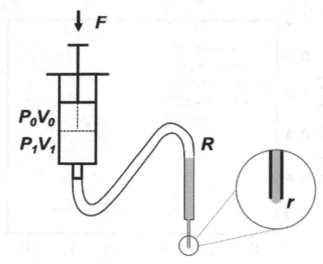

Fig. 3. Schematic diagram of adaptive pressure regulation, by compressing the space to maintain the stability of the contact angle of the end droplet.

2.3 Stability Analysis of Droplet

Consider a capillary, the water rises in the capillary is defined as capillary height H (Fig. 4):

$$H = \frac{2rcos(\theta)}{\rho g R} \tag{16}$$

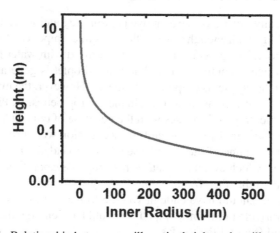

Fig. 4. Relationship between capillary rise height and capillary radius.

Usually, the liquid is completely wet in the capillary, and the contact angle is zero. Under the action of surface tension, microtubules are easily filled.

The contact radius of the hanging droplet is constant. We consider the change in the height of the stable droplet contact angle every time the contact angle decreases by 1°, as shown in Fig. 5.

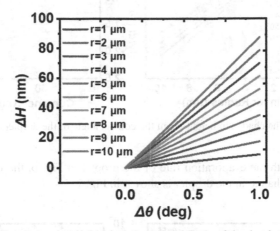

Fig. 5. The change in height when the contact angle of the droplet changes.

The change in height when the contact angle of the droplet changes. It can be observed from Fig. 5 that for a droplet with a radius of 1–10 μm when the droplet contact angle is less than 0.1°, the height variation of the droplet is less than 10 nm.

Considering the mechanical force equilibrium of the micropipettes, the surface tension of the system is equal to the gravity of the liquid height and the pressure in the syringe.

$$\frac{2\sigma}{R} + \frac{2\sigma\cos(\theta)}{r} = \rho g H_r + \rho g H_R + P_1 - P_0 \tag{17}$$

where R is the radius of the upper part of the opening, r is the radius of one end of the small opening, H_R and H_r are the heights of the two sections, P_1 is the pressure in the syringe, P_0 is the atmospheric pressure, and σ is the surface tension coefficient ($\sigma = 7.28 \times 10^{-2}$).

Consider that when H_R and H_r are equal to 1 cm when the droplet contact angle decreases by 0.1°, the new equilibrium state, the change in liquid volume is ΔV.

$$\frac{2\sigma}{R} + \frac{2\sigma\cos\theta'}{r} = \rho g H_r + \rho g H_R' + P_1 - \Delta P - P_0 \tag{18}$$

According to the ideal gas equation of the state

$$P_0 V_0 = P_1 V_1 = (P_1 - \Delta P)(V_1 + \Delta V) \tag{19}$$

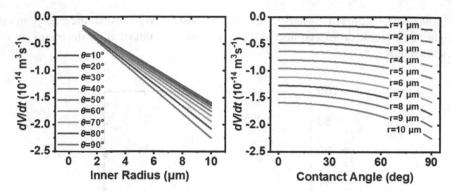

Fig. 6. The change in height when the contact angle of the droplet changes.

Combined with the evaporation rate of the droplet in Fig. 6, the time required for each 0.1-degree change in the droplet is shown in Fig. 7.

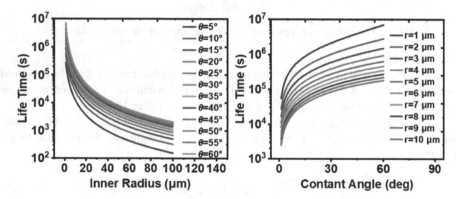

Fig. 7. Time required for each 0.1-degree change in droplet contact angle.

It can be concluded that theoretical calculations show that this method can achieve long-term maintenance of the microdroplet morphology.

3   Conclusion

In this paper, a droplet maintenance method based on the self-adaptive balance between surface tension and compressed air pressure is proposed, the droplet evaporation rate in CCR mode is theoretically calculated, and the method of maintaining droplet shape by air pressure is verified by mechanical balance calculation. The results show that the hanging droplets can be maintained for up to 10^6 s, and this study provides an effective method for studying the properties of solid-liquid contact at the micro/nanoscale.

Funding. Research supported by the Strategic Priority Research Program of the Chinese Academy of Sciences (XDA16021200), National Natural Science Foundation of China (Grant

No. 61925307, 61927805, 61903359, 62127811), Instrument Developing Project of the Chinese Academy of Sciences (Grant No. YJKYYQ20210050), Youth Innovation Promotion Association CAS.

References

1. Yamamoto, M., et al.: Theoretical explanation of the lotus effect: superhydrophobic property changes by removal of nanostructures from the surface of a lotus leaf. Langmuir **31**, 7355–7363 (2015)
2. Koh, J.S., et al.: BIOMECHANICS. Jumping on water: surface tension-dominated jumping of water striders and robotic insects. Science **349**, 517–521 (2015)
3. Zheng, Y., Gao, X., Jiang, L.: Directional adhesion of superhydrophobic butterfly wings. Soft Matter **3**, 178–182 (2007)
4. Wang, D., et al.: Design of robust superhydrophobic surfaces. Nature **582**, 55–59 (2020)
5. Parker, A.R., Lawrence, C.R.: Water capture by a desert beetle. Nature **414**, 33–34 (2001)
6. Wang, T., et al.: Apex structures enhance water drainage on leaves. Proc. Natl. Acad. Sci. **117**, 1890–1894 (2020)
7. Liimatainen, V., et al.: Mapping microscale wetting variations on biological and synthetic water-repellent surfaces. Nat. Commun. **8**, 1–7 (2017)
8. Dong, Z., et al.: Superoleophobic slippery lubricant-infused surfaces: combining two extremes in the same surface. Adv. Mater. **30**, 1803890 (2018)
9. Hokkanen, M.J., Backholm, M., Vuckovac, M., Zhou, Q., Ras, R.H.A.: Force-based wetting characterization of stochastic superhydrophobic coatings at nanonewton sensitivity. Adv. Mater. **33**, 2105130 (2021)
10. Tan, S., Zhang, X., Zhao, N., Xu, J.: Simulation of sessile water-droplet evaporation on superhydrophobic polymer surfaces. Chin. J. Chem. Phys. **20**, 140–144 (2007)
11. Rowan, S.M., Newton, M.I., McHale, G.: Evaporation of microdroplets and the wetting of solid surfaces. J. Phys. Chem. **99**, 13268–13271 (1995)

Evaluation of Muscle Activation Reaction on Fore-Aft Dynamic Interference During Load-Carrying Level Walking

Kai Liu, Kui Xiang, Biwei Tang, Jing Luo, and Muye Pang$^{(\boxtimes)}$

School of Automation, Wuhan University of Technology, Wuhan, Hubei, China
pangmuye@whut.edu.cn

Abstract. Loading-carrying walking is a common and important task. Since carrying load is one of the main functions of wearable robotic devices, studying human responses to the dynamic disturbance of load-carrying can help to design sophisticated control algorithms for wearable robots. However, few studies focus on the effects of for-aft direction load on locomotion and the reaction of human has not been fully analyzed. This paper studies the surface Electromyography (sEMG) reaction under the fore-aft dynamic disturbance. A backpack is designed which can exert disturbance force on fore-aft direction during level walking. Comparison experiments, with and without load backpack, are performed to obtain kinematic and sEMG data from subjects. The muscle synergy is used to evaluate the dynamic responses of subjects to the disturbance. The experimental results indicate that subjects explore new patterns, expressed by different muscles synergies, to adapt to fore-aft interference through adjusting muscle activations. The obtained results may hint that human beings tend to utilize ankle strategy to exert fore-aft disturbance during level walking.

Keywords: Load-carrying · Muscle activations · Fore-aft dynamic disturbance · Muscle synergy

1 Introduction

Load-carrying walking is a common activity of occupational field, such as industrial field, disaster relief, rescue and environmental disinfection. The most specific characteristic of load carriage is that it induces significant peak forces on supported body and affects the original control strategy of carriers. As load-carrying is one of the major functions for wearable robot devices, it is helpful to study how human react to the dynamic interference from load carriage, in order to design sophisticated control algorithms for wearable robots.

So far, load-carrying of up-and-down direction and suspended-load backpack have aroused increasing research interest. Early experimental results regarding to load carriage with compliant poles show that peak vertical ground reaction force is only slightly increased above unloaded levels [1]. Ren et al. [2] have investigated the biomechanical effects of load carriage dynamics on human locomotion performance. Their experimental results show that backpack suspension stiffness and damping have little effects on

H. Liu et al. (Eds.): ICIRA 2022, LNAI 13458, pp. 626–636, 2022.
https://doi.org/10.1007/978-3-031-13841-6_56

locomotion energetics. However, decreasing suspension stiffness contributes to moderate the vertical pack force peak values and lower limb joint loads. To investigate the factors influencing suspended-load carriage, Ackerman and Seipel [3] have used a simple two-degree-of-freedom model to approximate the energetic cost of human walking with a suspended load. Their model shows that a compliant load suspension is more effective in reducing the energetic cost of walking with low suspension damping, high load mass, and fast walking speed. He et al. [4] have designed a disturbance observer-based acceleration control to minimize the inertial force of a lightweight backpack. Their proposed method is able to averagely reduce the load acceleration by 98.5%, the gross metabolic power by 8.0% to 11.0%, compared to load-locked and rucksack conditions, respectively. Yang et al. [5] have propose an orbitally stable event-based control strategy to tune the damper value of a suspended backpack. Their simulation results reveal that the energy efficiency of load carriage has been improved and the load force exerting on carriers could be reduced.

Besides up-and-down direction, the effect of medial-lateral direction load carriage has also been extensively studied. Martin and Li [6] have developed a backpack specifically for allowing a carried mass to oscillate in the horizontal direction. The experimental results show that walking with an oscillating mass is able to reduce the accelerative forces of load carriage in both horizontal and vertical directions. Yang et al. [7] have provided a theoretical analysis and experimental validation on the biomechanical and energetic effect of swinging loads. They have discovered that swinging load has the advantages of reducing fore-aft leg impulses and the mechanical energy of the stance leg, compared to the typical rigid backpack.

Based on our best knowledge, few studies have been reported on effect of fore-aft direction load carriage. Loading carriage of fore-aft direction can be found when human beings work carrying liquid load such as in environmental disinfection during COVID-19 attack (as shown in Fig. 1). In this paper, human muscle activation reaction on fore-aft direction dynamic interference during load-carrying level walking is investigated. The surface Electromyography (sEMG) and muscle synergy technique are adopted to analyze the adaption of locomotion control strategy of human to the dynamic of load carriage.

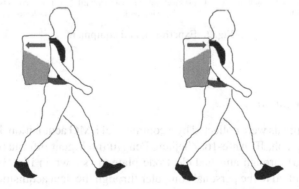

Fig. 1. Sketch picture of fore-aft direction dynamic interference on level walking

2 Methods

2.1 Experiment Protocol

Five able-bodied subjects with normal motor function participated in this experiment. Prior to the experiment, all subjects have signed informed consents approved by the Ethics Committee of Wuhan University of Technology.

This experiment included two tasks. In the first task, subjects were asked to walk on the treadmill without load, as shown in Fig. 2E. In the second task, as displayed in Fig. 2F, subjects were asked to carry a 13 kg weighted load. The load is a backpack containing a cylindrical bucket (diameter 25 cm and height 40 cm, see Fig. 1D) with water, as described in Fig. 2H. The water occupies 60% regarding to the bucket's volume, such that the water in bucket could keep swinging in fore-aft direction during walking to exert dynamic interference to the subject. In both tasks, the speed of the treadmill was set to 4.5 km/h. The subjects were asked to walk for three minutes and then have a five-minute break. Each task was carried out twice.

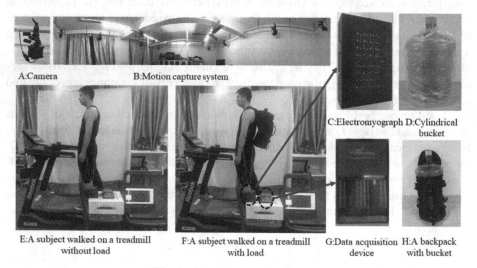

Fig. 2. Experiment and equipment

2.2 Data Acquisition

Surface EMG signals were collected by a commercial EMG acquisition device (16 channel electromyograph, JP-Anfe-16, Zhejiang FengJu Intelligent Information Technology Co., Ltd., China) through attached electrode plate, as shown in Fig. 3A. EMG signal has been transmitted to the personal computer through the data acquisition device (Data acquisition card, Usb5633, Beijing Altay Technology Development Co., Ltd., China), which was displayed in Fig. 2G. sEMG signals were acquired from 5 muscles (Erector Spinae (ES), Biceps Femoris long head (BF), Rectus Femoris (RF), Tibialis Anterior muscle (TA) and Gastrocnemius muscle (GA)). EMG electrode locations were demonstrated in Fig. 3A. The kinematic data were collected by a passive optical 3D motion capture system (Optical 3D motion capture system, MARS series, Beijing NOKOV Technology Co., Ltd., China), as shown in Fig. 2A and Fig. 2B. The system adopted passive infrared light principle design, including 12 sets of cameras, which could record the position information of each marker. A total of 21 marker points were affixed to the shoulder, legs, hips, ankles, thumbs, thumbs and other positions of the subject.

In order to divide a complete gait cycle of the experimenter, the NOKOV optical 3D motion capture system was used to capture the information of the experimenter's motion. The overall data acquisition framework of the experimental system was indicated in Fig. 3B.

All signals were simultaneously recorded and then were imported into MATLAB software (release R2018b, MathWorks Inc., Natick, MA, USA) to be processed offline through custom program.

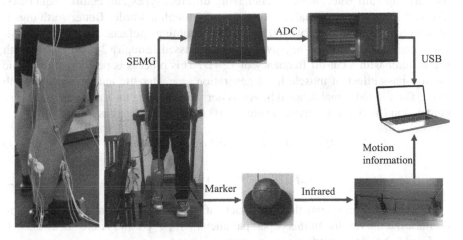

A:EMG electrode locations   B:The overall data acquisition framework of the experimental system

Fig. 3. EMG electrode locations and data acquisition framework

2.3 Data Processing

According to the dynamic capture system, 11 groups of gait cycles are segmented. The segment principle of the 11 gait groups is as follows. Firstly, we capture an entire gait, where the starting point is set at the beginning of right leg push-off phase. The end point of the gait interval is set at the ending of the right leg touch-down phase. Secondly, after five continuous gait cycles are performed, these five gaits are divided into a group. In other words, each group includes 5 complete gait cycles. The interval between two adjacent groups is about 10 s. The sEMG signals are segmented according to the above group dividing method. The above segmentation process is shown in Fig. 4.

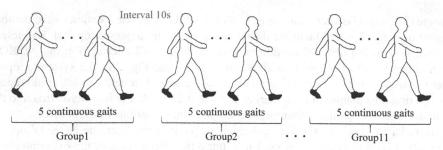

Fig. 4. Interception of 11 groups of gaits

- **Muscle activation processing**

  The muscle activation level (M) is obtained from raw sEMG signals and calculated by the method recommended by Buchanan et al. [8]. The filters used in this paper are zero-lag shift Butterworth filters having different types and cutoff frequencies. The segmented sEMG signals are first passed through a 4-order Butterworth digital filter with a cut-off frequency of 30 Hz to remove motion artefacts. Then, they are full-wave rectified to obtain non-negative signals and passed through a 2-order Butterworth digital filter with a cut-off frequency of 12 Hz. This process is performed to mimic the low-pass effect of muscle force generation characteristic and obtain a smooth trend. The filtered signal denoted by $e(t)$ is normalized using the maximum voluntary contraction (MVC) test activation value. $M(t)$ is then calculated as follows [8]:

  $$u(t) = \alpha e(t - d) - \beta_1 u(t - 1) - \beta_2 u(t - 2) \tag{1}$$

  $$M(t) = (e^{Au(t)} - 1)/(e^A - 1) \tag{2}$$

  Equation (1) represents the muscle activation dynamics. Equation (2) is used to de-linearize the results. In this paper, parameters α, $\beta 1$, $\beta 2$ and A are set as 2.25, 1, 0.25 and -1.5, respectively.

  To analyze the amplitude of EMG signal, parameter that is frequently used is root mean square (RMS). The RMS is calculated as shown in following Equation:

  $$RMS = \sqrt{\frac{\sum\limits_{t=0}^{T} M(t)^2}{T}} \tag{3}$$

  where $M(t)$ represents the muscle activation of each observed muscle and T represents the duration of muscle activation. RMS of muscle activations during 5 consecutive gaits in each group is averaged.

- **Muscle Synergy Extraction**

  Muscle synergies are extracted from the amplitude normalized muscle activations by means of the Non-Negative Matrix Factorization (NNMF) algorithm [9, 10]. NNMF is a factorization algorithm widely used in muscle collaborative extraction. The original muscle activation matrix ($M(t)$) can be decomposed as the linear combination of two different components: the time-dependent activation coefficient ($W(t)$) and the time-independent activation (H) [11] as described in below Equation:

$$M(t) = \sum_{k=1}^{N} W(t)_k H_k + e = M_r(t) + e \tag{4}$$

where N represents the number of muscle synergies required for modeling motion control. e is the reconstruction error. $M_r(t)$ represents the reconstructed sEMG activation of the muscle. The activation coefficient vector $W(t)_k$ represents the time-dependent modulation of the muscles enrolled in the k-synergy (temporal component of the motor control), while the weight vector H_k describes the time-dependent contribution of each muscle to the k-synergy (spatial component of the motor control) [12].

Reconstruction accuracy of the original sEMG activation matrix ($M(t)$) is measured for each number of muscles synergies (N) by means of the total Variance Accounted For ($tVAF$), defined as the uncentered Pearson's correlation coefficient expressed in below Equation:

$$tVAF = (1 - \frac{\sum_{k=1}^{m} (M_k - M_k^R)^2}{\sum_{k=1}^{m} (M_k)^2}) \cdot 100\% \tag{5}$$

where m represents the number of observed muscles, while Mk^R and Mk represents the reconstructed and the original sEMG activation of the k-muscle, respectively.

The optimal number of muscle synergies (N_{opt}) needed to properly reconstruct the original sEMG matrix ($M(t)$) is selected by choosing the least number of muscle synergies ensuring $VAF \geq 90\%$ (global criterion) [13].

- **Calculation of PCC**

To compare muscle synergy between subjects with and without load bearing, Pearson correlation coefficient (PCC) was used to measure the similarity between two muscle synergy vectors. The PCC is calculated by following Equation:

$$r = \frac{N \sum_{i}^{N} x_i y_i - \sum_{i}^{N} x_i \sum_{i}^{N} x_i}{\sqrt{N \sum_{i}^{N} x_i^2 - (\sum_{i}^{N} x_i)^2} \sqrt{N \sum_{i}^{N} y_i^2 - (\sum_{i}^{N} y_i)^2}} \tag{6}$$

where x_i and y_i represent the column vectors of different groups of H matrices, respectively. N also represents the number of muscle synergies.

As there are 55 (5×11) gait circles, a total of 55 pairs of $W(t)$ and H matrices are obtained. To eliminate the influence of transient dynamic of sEMG signals, the final H_f matrices used to evaluate the muscle reaction were acquired by averaging five H matrices in each gait group. In other words, the H_f matric is calculated by the below Equation:

$$H_{f_i} = \frac{H_{i_1} + H_{i_2} + H_{i_3} + H_{i_4} + H_{i_5}}{5} \tag{7}$$

where i represents group number, ranging from 0 to 11.

A total of 11 groups of H_f matrices are obtained. The experimental data processing processes for load-bearing and non-load-bearing are the same. In order to perform an assessment of muscle synergy similarity, the PCC between different H_f matrices are calculated. We assumed that people will reach a state of dynamic equilibrium after walking for a period of time. As a consequence, the last group of H_f matric is taken as the benchmark matric, recorded as H_b. Then the PCC between each matrix H_f and the benchmark matrix H_b are calculated (The PCC are calculated on each synergy). Total of 11 groups of PCC are obtained. We also calculate the PCC between the load-bearing H_f matrix and the non-load-bearing H_f matrix are calculated according to the same time period(group).

3   Experimental Results and Discussions

3.1   Muscle Activation

The muscle activations with and without load bearing after 3 min level ground walking are shown in Fig. 5. The experimental results are calculated from the 11th group of the walking movements, which means the read solid lines are mean values of 5 consecutive gaits and the gray areas are standard deviations of these data.

Due to the fore-aft dynamic interference, control strategy of the subject has changed compared with normal walking. For GA, load-bearing walking resulted in greater peak-to-peak activation and an increase in the overall activation. The role of the GA during walking is to provide the plantar flexion necessary to control the tibia and maintain the stability of the forefoot, and to plantarflex the ankle to store the energy required for lower limb rotation. In order to reduce the adverse effect on the physical balance of the subject, the activation of GA is increased to maintain the stability of the walking movement. Similar to GA, the activation of TA varies more during load-bearing walking and the amplitude of the activation also increased compared to no load walking. The main function of TA is also related to ankle joint control. The changes in the activation of GA and TA indicate that subjects have altered control strategy of the ankle joint due to dynamic fore-aft interference. Compared with normal walking, the activation of ES does not change significantly and has a small decrease in amplitude during load-bearing walking. The ES function is to maintain the body in an upright position and to ensure that the trunk is straight during walking. When fore-aft dynamic interference occurs, the subjects have been pulled backward by the backpack. In order to keep the upper limb upright, some subjects choose to lean forward to resist the fore-aft dynamic interference. As a consequence, the activation of ES decreases to reduce the lean backward trend. Compared with normal walking, the peak-to-peak value of RF activation increases during weight-bearing walking, and the maximum activation level also increases. As part of the quadriceps, the RF mainly controls the knee joint and provides the stability and flexibility needed for walking. The fore-aft interference affects the balance of the body. As a result, the activation of the RF is increased to resist the fore-aft disturbance to maintain the balance of the body. Muscle activation of BF decreases during weight-bearing walking compared to normal walking, even though the activation fluctuations are greater. The BF is part of the hamstrings, and its main function is to flex the knee and prevent the trunk from leaning forward. Due to the gravity, the backpack provides the subject with a continuous backward torque. Therefore, weight-bearing subjects are less likely to lean forward compared to normal walking. As a consequence, the BF does not require much activation to prevent the body from leaning forward compared to normal walking.

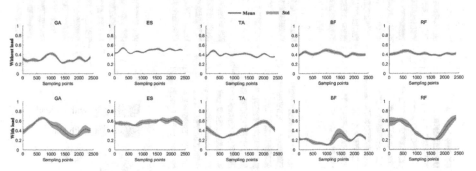

Fig. 5. Muscle activations during five consecutive gaits

3.2 RMS of Muscle Activation

As shown in Fig. 6, compared with normal walking, the change trend of RMS of muscle activation of five muscles in weight-bearing walking is different. For the same muscle, the RMS of muscles activation in different group of gaits is also different. For GA, compared with no load walking, the RMS values of load-bearing walking increases by 115% at most. The GA requires more effort to maintain the balance of the forefoot during walking due to the dynamic fore-aft interference compared with normal walking. When with load, RMS of muscle activation of BF decreased by 133% at most during load-bearing walking compared with no load walking. Since function of BF is to prevent a person from leaning forward, as mentioned above, the likelihood of a person leaning forward during weight-bearing walking is reduced. Therefore, BF does not need much activation to prevent body anteversion when with a backpack. There was no significant difference (t-test, p for TA, RF and ES are 0.42, 0.96 and 0.25, respectively) in RMS of muscle activation of TA, RF and ES between weight-bearing walking and normal walking.

3.3 Pearson Correlation Coefficients

As stated above, the optimal number of muscle synergies(N_{opt}) necessary to properly reconstruct the original sEMG activation is selected by choosing the smallest number of synergies which guarantees $tVAF \geq 90\%$ [13]. When N = 2, the $tVAF$ is 93.0% ± 1.5%. So, the number of muscle synergies is set to 2 in this paper.

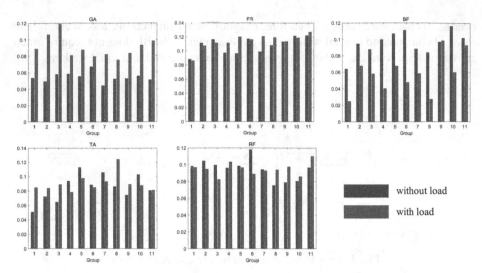

Fig. 6. Average RMS of muscles activations in each group

The PCC(r) between two muscle synergy vectors reflects the difference between muscle synergy. When r ≥ 0.9, we can consider that the muscle synergies are similar. As shown in Fig. 6A, the trend of the PCC between each matrix H_f and the benchmark matrix H_b is asymptotically rising when the subject walks without a backpack. PCC reaches above 0.9 in Group 2 for synergy1 and in Group 3 for synergy2. We conclude that subjects quickly reach a dynamic equilibrium during normal walking. When the subject walks with a backpack, the PCC between each matrix H_f and the benchmark matrix H_b is low at the beginning, as shown in Fig. 6B, but after a period of oscillation and rise, in other words, after walking for a period of time, the PCC reaches above 0.9 at Group 7 (about 100 s passed) for synergy1 and synergy2. We conclude that the subjects gradually adapted to the effects of this fore-aft disturbance through their own continuous adjustment. The PCC between each matric H_f with and without the backpack corresponding to the same time period(group) was also calculated. Figure 6C shows that the changing trend of PCC is similar to a parabola. The PCC is relatively high when the subjects begin to walk. We speculate that this is because the disturbance had not formed when the subject started to walk. Compared with the normal walking, the control strategy of the subject did not change significantly during the beginning of weight-bearing walking. This shows that no matter whether the weight is loaded or not, the control strategy of the subject at the beginning of walking has not changed much. The PCC begin to decrease rapidly after the fore-aft disturbance has an effect. Subject's control strategies begin to change to adapt to the effects of the dynamic disturbance. The subject has gradually adapted to this for-aft interference over time, and the PCC rises, but does not rise to 0.9, indicating that the subject control strategy is similar but not identical compared to no load walking (Fig. 7).

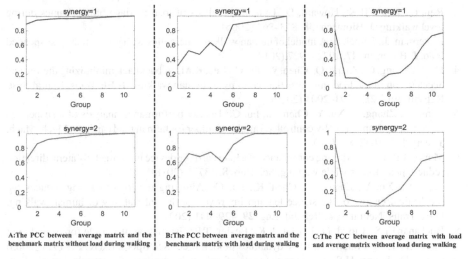

A:The PCC between average matrix and the benchmark matrix without load during walking

B:The PCC between average matrix and the benchmark matrix with load during walking

C:The PCC between average matrix with load and average matrix without load during walking

Fig. 7. Pearson correlation coefficient

4 Conclusion and Future Work

Compared with normal-walking, people will face greater challenges when performing a new task that fore-aft dynamic interference is exerted on their back during walking. In order to study the control reaction of human during fore-aft dynamic interference walking, a water-load bearing walking experiment is designed and the activations of five muscles are analyzed. The experimental results indicate that human will explore a new mode to adapt to this fore-aft dynamic interference through adjusting the muscle activation, mainly focused on ankle related muscle. In other words, people do not passively adapt to this interference, but actively use it by change their control strategies. We assume that high values of the PCC between each matrix H_f and benchmark matrix H_b reveal dynamic stabilization of human motion system. Under this assumption, the gradual process of the adaptation to fore-aft dynamic disturbances of human control system can be observed by muscle synergies. We believe that our study results would provide useful ideas for the control algorithm design of ankle exoskeletons.

In future work, dynamic fore-aft interference will be equivalent to a spring-damping system in the for-aft direction, which can be used for modeling and dynamic analysis. Moreover, an ankle joint exoskeleton prototype will be designed to assist walking during fore-aft dynamic interference.

Acknowledgment. This work was supported by the National Natural Science Foundation of China under Grant 61603284 and 61903286.

References

1. Kram, R.: Carrying loads with springy poles. J. Appl. Physiol. **71**, 1119–1122 (1991)

2. Ren, L., Jones, R.K., Howard, D.: Dynamic analysis of load carriage biomechanics during level walking. J. Biomech. **38**, 853–863 (2005)
3. Ackerman, J., Seipel, J.: A model of human walking energetics with an elastically-suspended load. J. Biomech. **47**, 1922–1927 (2014)
4. He, L., Xiong, C., Zhang, Q., Chen, W., Fu, C., Lee, K.M.: A backpack minimizing the vertical acceleration of the load improves the economy of human walking. IEEE Trans. Neural Syst. Rehabil. Eng. **28**, 1994–2004 (2020)
5. Yang, L., Zhang, J., Xu, Y., Chen, K., Fu, C.: Energy performance analysis of a suspended backpack with an optimally controlled variable damper for human load carriage. Mech. Mach. Theory **146**, 103738 (2020)
6. Martin, J.P., Li, Q.: Altering compliance of a load carriage device in the medial-lateral direction reduces peak forces while walking. Sci. Rep. **8**, 13775 (2018)
7. Yang, L., Xu, Y., Zhang, K., Chen, K., Fu, C.: Allowing the load to swing reduces the mechanical energy of the stance leg and improves the lateral stability of human walking. IEEE Trans. Neural Syst. Rehabil. Eng. **29**, 429–441 (2021)
8. Buchanan, T.S., Lloyd, D.G., Manal, K., Besier, T.F.: Estimation of muscle forces and joint moments using a forward-inverse dynamics model. Med. Sci. Sports Exerc. **37**, 1911 (2005)
9. Lee, D.D., Seung, H.S.: Learning the parts of objects by non-negative matrix factorization. Nature **401**, 788–791 (1999)
10. Torres-Oviedo, G., Ting, L.H.: Muscle synergies characterizing human postural responses. J. Neurophysiol. **98**, 2144–2156 (2007)
11. Zelik, K.E., La Scaleia, V., Ivanenko, Y.P., Lacquaniti, F.: Can modular strategies simplify neural control of multidirectional human locomotion? J. Neurophysiol. **111**, 1686–1702 (2014)
12. Ghislieri, M., et al.: Muscle synergy assessment during single-leg stance. IEEE Trans. Neural Syst. Rehabil. Eng. **28**, 2914–2922 (2020)
13. Clark, D.J., Ting, L.H., Zajac, F.E., Neptune, R.R., Kautz, S.A.: Merging of healthy motor modules predicts reduced locomotor performance and muscle coordination complexity post-stroke. J. Neurophysiol. **103**, 844–857 (2010)

Effects of Different Resistance Schemes Applied by Hip Exoskeleton on Lower-Limb Muscle Recruitment and Coordination

Zilu Wang[1,3,4], Zhihao Zhou[2,3](✉), and Qining Wang[1,2,3]

[1] Department of Advanced Manufacturing and Robotics, College of Engineering,
Peking University, Beijing 100871, China
[2] Institute for Artificial Intelligence, Peking University, Beijing 100871, China
zhouzhihao@pku.edu.cn
[3] Beijing Engineering Research Center of Intelligent Rehabilitation Engineering,
Beijing 100871, China
[4] College of Future Technology, Peking University, Beijing 100871, China

Abstract. Lower-limb exoskeletons are used in a wide range of scenarios. The extensive applications are based on the effective intervention on people, which relies on the understanding of the effect of the exoskeleton intervention on human body. Muscle synergy has been used previously as an important assessment metric to evaluate the intervention effectiveness of exoskeletons on the wearer. However, the exoskeleton has limitations in terms of the type of intervention applied. In this paper, we applied various resistance schemes to the standing phase of the gait cycle and analysed the effect of the hip exoskeleton on neuromuscular synergy and co-contraction. Experimental results indicated that the hip exoskeleton intervention altered muscle recruitment and coordination to some extent. The ankle joint antagonist muscles co-contraction was related to the resistance intervention in the support phase, and intervention results did not show a difference in the synergy complexity. Besides, the muscle synergy weight was discriminated under the interventions. It may help therapists to develop effective gait intervention strategies in the near future.

Keywords: Hip exoskeleton · Muscle synergy · Resistance scheme

1 Introduction

Lower-limb exoskeletons play an important role in protecting workers [1], reducing the metabolic cost of walking [2] as well as medical applications [3]. The widespread use of lower-limb exoskeletons is based on the effective intervention

This work was supported by the National Key R& D Program of China (No. 2020YFC2008803, 2018YFC2001503), the National Natural Science Foundation of China (No. 51922015, No. 91948302, No. 52005011) and PKU-Baidu Fund (No. 2020BD008).

H. Liu et al. (Eds.): ICIRA 2022, LNAI 13458, pp. 637–646, 2022.
https://doi.org/10.1007/978-3-031-13841-6_57

of the exoskeleton on the human being. In the case of medical exoskeletons, for example, exoskeletal interventions for wearers are only therapeutic if the developer fully understands the impact of the intervention on the person. The intervention effectiveness includes kinematic and kinetic index, the EMG signals and many other dimensions [3–5].

Muscle synergy is known as a very important dimension that reflects the influence of the exoskeleton on human intervention. It is defined as groups of muscles with fixed ratios of activation that can be recruited by neural commands to execute a task in a feedforward or feedback manner [6]. It has been suggested that muscle synergies represent a library of muscle actions that can be combined to create movements [7]. The exoskeleton interferes with the muscle synergy and muscle activity of the wearer. Steele et al. aimed to evaluate changes in muscle recruitment and coordination for ten unimpaired individuals walking with an ankle exoskeleton [8]. They evaluated changes in the activity of individual muscles, co-contraction levels, and synergistic patterns of muscle coordination with increasing exoskeleton work and torque. Furthermore, peak time shifting of the performing intervention has also been considered. Wang et al. systematically evaluated the lower leg muscle activities under different ankle exoskeleton assistance conditions [9]. In this study, nine assistance conditions, which combined three peak times (46%, 49%, and 52% of stride time) and three peak torque levels (0.3, 0.5, and 0.7 $N \cdot m \cdot kg^{-1}$), are applied to assist plantarflexion during ankle push-off. The Acosta-Sojo et al. concerned more about the ankle joint muscle activity patterns variation during powered ankle exoskeleton walking [10]. They measured individual muscle activation pattern changes in response to exoskeleton power state, the time within an exoskeleton power state, and across gait cycle phases. Besides the ankle exoskeleton, the intervention of multiple joints exoskeleton has been considered. Li et al. tried to investigate how muscle synergy patterns can be affected by lower-limb exoskeleton systems to assist normal dynamic walking [11].

However, the studies mentioned above mainly use the exoskeletons for walking assistance, instead of providing resistance to the wearer [8–11]. Furthermore, although the intervention involved Peak Time Shifting [9], we wonder the effect of higher amplitude Peak Time Shifting (20% of the stance phase). In addition, the duration and the phase of the intervention may be two of the important factors for muscle synergy performance variation. The proposed study aimed to understand the effect of the hip exoskeleton on neuromuscular synergy and co-contraction by applying resistance to the standing phase of the gait cycle (heel strike to toe off). As shown in Fig. 1(a), the intervention we performed can mainly be divided into three categories: Peak Time Shifting (B-A), Phase Adjustment (C-D), and Duration Variation (B-C).

2   Method

2.1   Test Setup

The volunteer in this study is a healthy adult (male, 25 years old, 187 cm, 80 kg). We used a bilateral hip exoskeleton (Fig. 1(b)) to provide resistance force to the human hip joint. The hip exoskeleton is light-weighted (3.5 kg). Interventions are performed by two "arms", which are fixed together tightly with the wearer's thighs. The exoskeleton can provide a maximum of 10 N·m assistance/resistance torque. In addition, we can design the shape of the output torque curve to meet our experimental requirements.

2.2 Experimental Protocol

The experiment procedure is shown in Fig. 1(c). Firstly, we asked the volunteers to wear the exoskeleton with no-control (baseline). He was asked to walk on the treadmill in a speed of 1.2 m/s. Two intervention group were performed afterwards. In intervention group I, the peak time of the resistance torques shifted from 10% of the stance phase, toward 90%. The desired torque curves were displayed in Fig. 4(d). In intervention group II, the Phase Adjustment and Duration Variation interventions were performed. The desired torque curves are displayed in Fig. 4(e). For all the experiment in each intervention group, we set thirty seconds of initial adaptation before data recording process so that the wearer could get used to the extension torque resistance. After that, data for one minute were recorded and followed by thirty seconds of rest in order to avoid the fatigue influence.

2.3 Data Recording

The interaction torque was recorded with the sensor on the exoskeleton. Muscle recruitment was evaluated by monitoring EMG data collected during each trial (Trigno, Delsys Inc.) from up to ten muscles on the right leg, including medial and lateral gastrocnemius (MG/LG), anterior tibialis (TA), medial and lateral vastus medialis (VM/VL), biceps femoris long head (BF), semitendinosus(SS) and rectus femoris (RF). Electrodes were placed once at the beginning of the experiment and were not adjusted between each trial. The ground reaction force value (collected by force platforms under the treadmill, Arsalls) was recorded simultaneously.

2.4 Data and Statistical Analysis

EMG data were collected at 2000 Hz and then applied with a bandpass filter with cut-offs at 20–450 Hz. After that, the signal was rectified, followed by low-pass filtered 5 Hz (Zero-phase digital filtering). EMG data were qualitatively evaluated to check for signal integrity, noise, and cross-talk, and channels with poor signal quality were excluded from further analysis. As maximum voluntary contractions were not collected as part of this protocol, EMG data for each muscle was normalized to the peak activation during each normalized result. Then the EMG data were normalized to 100 points for each gait cycle (heel-strike to next heel strike) and averaged across all gait cycles from each trial. All data analysis was completed using custom MATLAB programs (2022a, The MathWorks, Inc., Natick, USA).

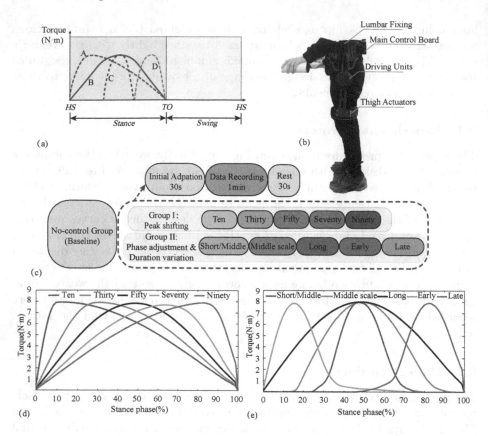

Fig. 1. (a) Peak Time Shifting (B versus A), Phase Adjustment (C versus D), Duration Variation (B versus C). (b) The powered hip exoskeleton can provide resistance torque on the stance phase. (c) Experiment procedure: Group I includes Peak Time Shifting intervention experiments, from 10% of the stance phase duration (Ten) to 90% of the stance phase duration (Ninety); Group II includes Phase Adjustment and Duration Variation experiments. (d) Peak shifting desired torque. (e) Phase Adjustment and Duration Variation desired torque.

We used two methods to evaluate muscle coordination with the hip exoskeleton: the co-contraction index and synergy analysis. The co-contraction Index (CCI) was calculated according to the formula mentioned in [12]:

$$CCI = 2 \cdot \frac{common\ area\ EMG_A\ \&\ EMG_B}{area\ EMG_A + area\ EMG_B} \tag{1}$$

which compares the integrated area of two muscles (agonist and antagonist's muscle), including the overlapping area (common area) and summed-area of each muscle. CCI can range from zero to one-hundred percent, indicating the relative activation of two muscles. In this studying, we calculated five pairs of antagonist muscles' co-contraction index. Two of them are related to the knee joint (BF-RT,

SS-RT), while three of the pairs are related to the ankle joint (MG-TA, LG-TA, LG-TA). We used non-negative matrix factorization (NNMF) to calculate the synergies for each trial. For a given number of synergies (n), muscles (m), and time points (t), NNMF identifies weighted groups of muscles (synergy weights) and their activation patterns (synergy activations) whose product explains the greatest variance in the EMG data [13].

$$EMG_{m \cdot t} = W_{m \cdot n} \cdot C_{n \cdot t} + error \qquad (2)$$

where error represents the EMG data not explained by the specified synergy weights and activation. For all analyses, the number of synergies ranged from one to one less than the number of muscles with EMG data for a given limb.

Firstly, we calculated synergies during the No-control trial. We characterized synergy complexity using the total variance in the EMG data accounted for by n synergies $(tVAF_n)$ as:

$$tVAF_n = 1 - \frac{SSE}{SST} = 1 - \frac{||EMG - W \cdot C||^2}{||EMG||^2} \qquad (3)$$

which compares the sum of squared errors (SSE) to the total squared sum of the EMG data [14]. We directly calculated synergies for each trial walking with the hip exoskeleton and $tVAF_n$ to evaluate synergy complexity. We choose the least synergy number which could explain not less than 90% of the variance for further analysis. Then we evaluated the synergy weights (W) and activations (C) calculated from NNMF for each exoskeleton trial with the chosen number. We compared the synergy weights and activations difference between each experimental group.

3   Results

3.1   Muscle Activity and Co-contraction

We recorded the activities of ten muscles in the lower limb (right) for all the experiments. The lower limb EMG activities (normalized to a gait cycle) are shown in Fig. 2. The calculated Co-contraction index (CCI) for two intervention groups and No-control group is shown in Fig. 3(a)(b). Compared with Group I (Peak time shifts 10%–90% interventions), the No-control group CCI is larger than the intervention group in SS-RT, MG-TA, LG-TA, SL-TA pairs. Most of the CCI index related to ankle flexion and extension muscles decreased with the peak time of the torque delayed. For Group II (Phase Adjustment and Duration Variation), the No-control group CCI is larger than the intervention groups in SS-RT, MG-TA, LG-TA, SL-TA pairs. In LG-TA and SL-TA pairs, the CCI increased with the torque duration enlargement. For SL-TA, CCI decreased with the phase delayed.

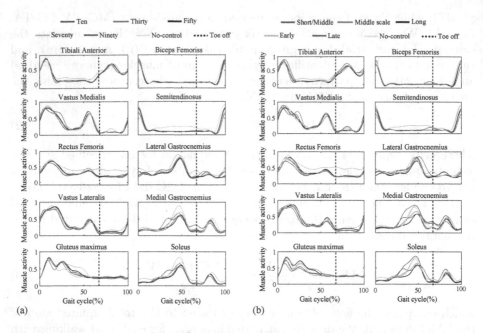

Fig. 2. Lower-limb (right side) muscle EMG activity normalized to a gait cycle for all the experiments. (a) Ten muscle EMG activities for No-control group and intervention Group I (Peak Time Shifting) (b) Ten muscle EMG activities for No-control group and intervention Group II (Phase Adjustment and Duration Variation).

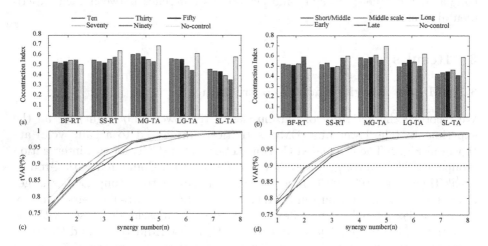

Fig. 3. Co-contraction index (CCI) and total variance in EMG data during each walking trial accounted for (tVAF) for all the experiments. (a) & (c) CCI and tVAF for No-control group and intervention Group I (Peak Time Shifting). (b) & (d) CCI and tVAF for No-control group and intervention Group II (Phase Adjustment and Duration Variation)

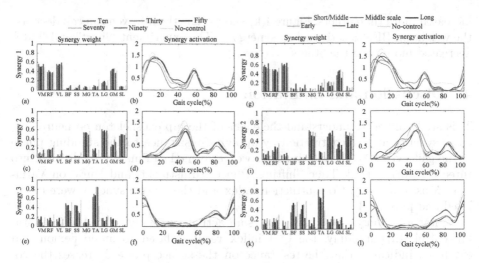

Fig. 4. (a)-(f) Synergy weights and activation for No-control group and intervention Group I (Peak Time Shifting). (g)-(l) Synergy weights and activation for No-control group and intervention Group II (Phase Adjustment and Duration Variation). (a) All the muscle weight activated by synergy 1. (b) Synergy 1 activation. (c) All the muscle weight activated by synergy 2. (d) Synergy 2 activation. (e) All the muscle weight activated by synergy 3. (f) Synergy 3 activation. (g) All the muscle weight activated by synergy 1. (h) Synergy 1 activation. (i) All the muscle weight activated by synergy 2. (j) Synergy 2 activation. (k) All the muscle weight activated by synergy 3. (l) Synergy 3 activation.

3.2 Muscle Synergy

Synergy analysis includes the synergy complexity analysis as well as the calculation of synergy weights and activation. Figure 3(c)(d) demonstrates the synergy complexity for No-control group and intervention experiments. For all experiments, three synergies could describe more than 90% of the variance in EMG data during walking. Figure 4 demonstrate the synergy weights and activation of the experiments. Synergy 1–3 correspond to the functional requirements of walking: propulsion, limb flexion, and swing assistance [15]. Although the functional contributions of the synergies remained similar across all the trials, the weighting of individual muscles or synergy activation changed with different interventions. Figure 4(c) shows that the response of the GM to synergy 2 increase in all intervention groups, with the greatest increase in the weight of experiment "Seventy". Figure 4(e) shows that the intervention can increase the weight on TA activated by synergy 3. TA increased more synergy weight in experiments "Seventy" and "Ninety". In Fig. 4(e), synergy 3 has more weight on BF, SS for the No-control group than all the intervention groups. The weight decrease with the peak time of the planned torque delayed. Figure 4(i) shows that the intervention can increase the weight of GM activated by synergy 2. The experiment "Long" and "Late" increased more than others. Figure 4(k) shows that the intervention can decrease the weight on BF, SS activated by synergy 3. The experiment "Short" and "Late" decreased more than the others.

4   Discussion and Limitation

This study aimed to understand the effect of the hip exoskeleton on neuromuscular synergy and co-contraction by applying resistance to the standing phase of the gait cycle. All the interventions we performed can mainly be divided into three categories: Peak Time Shifting, Phase Adjustment, and Duration Variation. Muscle activity, Co-contraction index and the muscle synergy were calculated and presented.

Antagonist muscle co-contraction is an activity strongly related to joint stability [16]. In our study, the CCI index result related to ankle flexion and extension indicated that the resistance on the stance phase decreases the co-contraction effect. Shifting the torque peak to the end of the stance phase or reducing the torque duration can diminish this effect.

The synergy complexity varies little under all the interventions while the structure or activation was altered to some extent. We hypothesized that the muscle activity related to the hip extension might increase response to the intervention. Unsurprisingly, the result indicates that the resistance during the stance phase increased the synergy weight of GM for synergy 2. A longer duration with the peak time of the torque appearance in the seventy percent of the stance phase seems more effective. Contrary to our initial suspicions, the resistance on the stance phase decreased the synergy weight on BF and SS for synergy 3. Peak and phase delays as well as a shorter duration increased the reduction. What's more, we observed that the synergy weight of TA increased activated by synergy 3 under the intervention. Peak and phase delays, as well as short duration, strengthen the effect.

Limitations exist in this study. Firstly, only one subject was included in the test. Secondly, the intervention time was only 90 s, which may not enough to alter the muscle synergy.

5   Conclusion

In this paper, we applied various resistance schemes to the standing phase of the gait cycle and analyze the effect of the hip exoskeleton on neuromuscular synergy and co-contraction. The result of the experiment indicated that the hip exoskeleton intervention altered muscle recruitment and coordination to some extent. The ankle joint antagonist muscles co-contraction was related to the resistance intervention in the support phase, and intervention results did not show a difference in the synergy complexity. Besides, the muscle synergy weight was discriminated under the interventions. The experiment results may help therapists to develop effective gait intervention strategies in the near future.

References

1. Yan, Z., Han, B., Du, Z., Huang, T., Peng, A.: Development and testing of a wearable passive lower-limb support exoskeleton to support industrial workers. Biocybern. Biomed. Eng. **41**(1), 221–238 (2021)
2. Cseke, B., Uchida, T., Doumit, M.: Simulating ideal assistive strategies to reduce the metabolic cost of walking in the elderly. IEEE Trans. Biomed. Eng. (2022)
3. Lerner, Z.F., Damiano, D.L., Bulea, T.C.: A lower-extremity exoskeleton improves knee extension in children with crouch gait from cerebral palsy. Sci. Transl. Med. **9**(404), eaam9145 (2017)
4. Awad, L.N., et al.: A soft robotic exosuit improves walking in patients after stroke. Sci. Transl. Med. **9**(400), eaai9084 (2017)
5. Kang, J., Martelli, D., Vashista, V., Martinez-Hernandez, I., Kim, H., Agrawal, S.K.: Robot-driven downward pelvic pull to improve crouch gait in children with cerebral palsy. Sci. Robot. **2**(8), eaan2634 (2017)
6. Safavynia, S.A., Ting, L.H.: Task-level feedback can explain temporal recruitment of spatially fixed muscle synergies throughout postural perturbations. J. Neurophysiol. **107**(1), 159–177 (2012)
7. Chvatal, S.A., Ting, L.H.: Voluntary and reactive recruitment of locomotor muscle synergies during perturbed walking. J. Neurosci. Official J. Soc. Neurosci. **32**(35), 12237–50 (2012)
8. Steele, K.M., Jackson, R.W., Shuman, B., Collins, S.H.: Muscle recruitment and coordination with an ankle exoskeleton. J. Biomech. **59**, 50–58 (2017)
9. Wang, W., Chen, J., Ji, Y., Jin, W., Zhang, J.: Evaluation of lower leg muscle activities during human walking assisted by an ankle exoskeleton. IEEE Trans. Industr. Inf. **16**(11), 7168–7176 (2020)
10. Acosta-Sojo, Y., Stirling, L.: Individuals differ in muscle activation patterns during early adaptation to a powered ankle exoskeleton. Appl. Ergon. **98**, 103593 (2022)
11. Li, Z., Liu, H., Yin, Z., Chen, K.: Muscle synergy alteration of human during walking with lower limb exoskeleton. Front. Neurosci. **12**, 1050 (2018)
12. Alexander, R.M.: Biomechanics and motor control of human movement. In: David, A.W. (ed.) Quarterly Review of Biology (1991)
13. Ting, L.H., Chvatal, S.A.: Decomposing muscle activity in motor tasksmethods and interpretation. Motor Control (2010)
14. Torres-Oviedo, G., Macpherson, J.M., Ting, L.H.: Muscle synergy organization is robust across a variety of postural perturbations. J. Neurophysiol. **96**(3), 1530–1546 (2006)

15. Allen, J.L., Neptune, R.R.: Three-dimensional modular control of human walking. J. Biomech. **45**(12), 2157–2163 (2012)
16. Yamazaki, Y., Suzuki, M., Ohkuwa, T., Itoh, H.: Coactivation in arm and shoulder muscles during voluntary fixation of a single joint. Brain Res. Bull. **59**(6), 439–446 (2003)

A Biologically Inspired Lower Limb Cable Driven Exoskeleton

Lingyun Yan[1] , Lei Ren[1] , and Guowu Wei[2(✉)]

[1] Department of Mechanical, Aerospace and Civil Engineering, The University of Manchester, Manchester M13 9PL, UK
{lingyun.yan,lei.ren}@manchester.ac.uk
[2] School of Computing, Science and Engineering, University of Salford, Salford M5 4WT, UK
g.wei@salford.ac.uk

Abstract. The lower limb exoskeleton has been widely applied in different fields, such as rehabilitation, training, and the military, which generally improves the performance of subjects. This paper developed a lower limb cable-driven soft exoskeleton to assist walking called MCR Exo. The exoskeleton is mainly combined by a two-layer structure: passive and active layers. The passive layer is made of elastic material and worn by the users, just like tights. Meanwhile, the active layer is composed of an actuator and Bowden cable attached to the passive layer to supply the assistant force. The two-layer structure is arranged corresponding to the muscle group distribution that produces the largest force in the gait cycle. The exoskeleton can detect five gait events based on artificial neural networks (ANN) and determine the gait cycle. Meanwhile, the MCR Exo would supply a torque up to 10.7 Nm, and the torque profile is designed based on the lower limb muscle force patterns. A human trial experiment is conducted to analyse the performance of the MCR Exo by measuring the surface electromyography (sEMG) of lower-limb muscles during walking. The MCR Exo can achieve the largest muscle activity (%MVIC) reduction at 5.90% in soleus (SO), 2.20% in gastrocnemius medialis (GM) and 2.05% in Gastrocnemius lateralis (GL) compared with walking without Exo.

Keywords: Exoskeleton · Gait events · sEMG · Muscle activity

1 Introduction

The exoskeleton is an external skeleton that supports movement and protects the human body, it's designed to assist in walking, lifting or holding heavy objects. Therefore, robotic exoskeletons have been applied in large number of applications like rehabilitation, assisting and human walking enhancement [1–3]. The rigid exoskeleton was developed and widely applied [4–7]. This type of exoskeleton is usually applied for load carriage, weight support and rehabilitation since it has a rigid structure to support the overall system and the human limb. In the rehabilitation field, some exoskeleton adopted a knee–ankle–foot orthosis structure which could be used to treat crouch gait [5]. Moreover, this type of design provides an assistant torque for knee extension during

© The Author(s), under exclusive license to Springer Nature Switzerland AG 2022
H. Liu et al. (Eds.): ICIRA 2022, LNAI 13458, pp. 647–655, 2022.
https://doi.org/10.1007/978-3-031-13841-6_58

the stance and swing phases. In addition, Argo Medical Inc. proposed a RewalkTM to assist hip/knee motion for paraplegics [8]. Also, the Ekso Bionics proposed a medical exoskeleton (EksoTM) for gait-training, which could deal with different levels of paralysis and hemiparesis [9]. These rigid structure exoskeletons had partially active hip/knee/ankle joints similar to the lower extremities of humans. However, most joints have only two or three degrees of freedom (DOF), limiting the displacement of the related brackets and hindering the natural movement to some extent.

Meanwhile, the soft exoskeleton always adopts a tethered, pneumatic, or spring-clutch drive system, which leads them to abandon rigid frame design and adopt a brace or band to connect their main structure with the human body like "Exosuit" and "Myosuit" [1, 10]. Most soft exoskeletons use flexible materials for limb attachment and tethered drive method to avoid motion interference with the human body [10–12]. Besides, the soft exoskeleton is significantly lighter than the rigid exoskeleton since it abandons the rigid frames or linkage systems. Also, it achieves excellent gait assistance performance because of the high power/weight ratio [13]. This type of compliant structure has achieved good performance, and the metabolic rate could be reduced by 23% using a multi-articular suit architecture when walking with a tethered structure [14]. Furthermore, the textile material attached to the human body contributes to the exoskeleton and can only apply tensile force, which does not restrict the kinematic motion. However, a soft exoskeleton cannot withstand a heavy load without a rigid frame since the wearer's skeletal structure sustains all the compressive forces. In addition, for the tethered drive system, the subjects would absorb some part of the power due to the limited cable speed, which decreases the efficiency.

Moreover, these articles did not provide detailed biological evidence regarding actuation path arrangements since the biomechanical mechanism of walking remains unclear. This study aims to design a biologically inspired soft cable-driven lower-limb exoskeleton based on the analysis of the lower limb muscle activities in the gait cycle that is capable of assisting human walking by reducing muscle activity.

2 Musculoskeletal-Model-Based Simulation and Exoskeleton Design

2.1 Principles of Human Walking Pattern

The exoskeleton and its actuation path structure were designed based on lower-limb muscle patterns analysis. OpenSim® was adopted to build a lower-limb musculoskeletal model to analyse the muscle force pattern during walking. OpenSim 3.3 version was adopted for modelling and simulation. The model adopts a 73 kg male adult to simulate human walking at normal speed (4.2 km/h). Based on the standard open-source biological data of the male subject, this platform runs the simulation and obtains the following results: muscle activation pattern, muscle forces, and ground reaction forces. The simulation results of the right leg muscle force pattern in a complete gait cycle are shown in Fig. 1. Meanwhile, Fig. 1 indicate the muscle activation state, where the blue square represents the muscle in an activated state.

Biomechanical data were evaluated based on the simulation of the musculoskeletal model. The forces of 40 muscles in the lower limbs were calculated using this method.

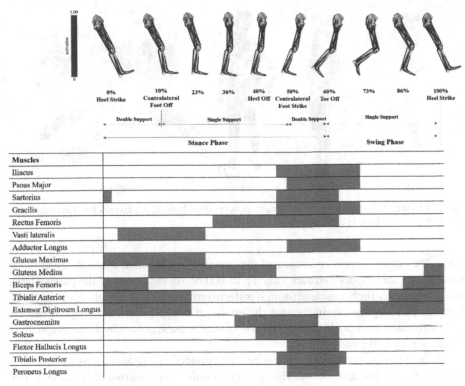

Fig. 1. Right leg muscle activation pattern based on OpenSim result

It indicates that the majority of lower-limb muscles generate the peak power during the push-off stage in a gait cycle. Furthermore, the data showed that several muscles contribute the largest amount of power during walking and the top 8 muscles are the soleus, medial gastrocnemius head, psoas major, iliacus, vastus lateralis, rectus femoris, gluteus medius, and gastrocnemius lateral head, respectively. In addition, it can find that the muscles that contribute the largest force during walking belong to specific muscle groups: triceps surae, quadriceps femoris, and iliopsoas.

2.2 Exoskeleton Structure and Arrangement Design Based on Biomechanical

According to the force analysis of the three muscle groups, exoskeleton assistance should be applied in parallel with the direction of muscle contraction to reduce muscle activation levels and achieve the highest power efficiency. Based on this concept, the actuation path of the exoskeleton should be arranged according to the distribution of the target muscle groups. Figure 2 (a) shows the location and appearance of the target muscle groups in the lower limbs. Also, the actuation path was arranged corresponding to the distribution of these muscle groups, as Fig. 2 (b) indicates.

As Fig. (b–c) indicates, the exoskeleton is mainly divided into the passive and active layers. The passive layer is made of elastic material and worn by the users, just like

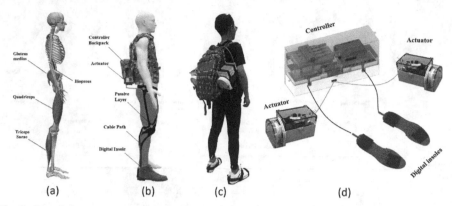

Fig. 2. Exoskeleton arrangement. (a) Target muscles distribution, (b) Exoskeleton arrangement, (c) MCR Exo, (d) Exoskeleton systems.

tights. The active layer is composed of the actuator and Bowden cable attached to the passive layer and supply assistant force up to 200 N. As the layout of the passive layer follows the lower limb muscle activation pattern during walking, it could cooperate with the corresponding muscle. In contrast, the two-layer design's main advantage is that the cable's assistant force could be distributed to desired muscle groups by the corresponding actuation path in the passive layer.

Meanwhile, the exoskeleton system could be divided into control, sensory, and actuator modules, as Fig. 2(d) shows. The sensory module integrates two FSR and IMU into a digital insole that could gather the kinematic data of the subject during walking. In the control module, two Uno R3 boards received the signal data from the digital insole and converted it to the kinematic parameters for x86 mini pc. Then ANN-based gait detection module identifies the gait cycle and sends the torque profile to the actuator. The actuator releases the corresponding assistance to the subject by the Bowden cable attached to the pulley.

3   Gait Detection System

The human motion recognition system plays an essential role in understanding the interaction between humans and the environment. Gait detection systems have been widely applied in exoskeletons because they recognise the walking state and contribute to the control strategy [15, 16]. For instance, the human-robot interaction requires a better understanding of human intention and shorter activity detection time [90, 91]. We had put forward a gait detection algorithm adopts a multilayer perceptron (MLP) model and a rule-based calibration filter to classify kinematic data into five distinct gait events: heel strike (HS), foot flat (FF), heel-off (HO), toe-off (TO), and initial-swing (IS) [19]. Besides, the gait detection algorithm's structure is shown in Fig. 3(a). The MLP model has a complex structure with different constraints, weights, batch sizes, learning rates, and neurons to generate different data patterns. Hyperparameter optimisation searches for the most optimal combination of ANN parameters to achieve the best performance. In this study, a grid search is applied to the MLP model, and it searches for the optimal neuron numbers and batch size. In addition, five-fold cross-validation was applied to evaluate the performance. According to the grid search result in Fig. 3 (b), the optimal hyperparameters of the MLP model could reach 96.25% accuracy with a small SD (0.0202) when this model adopts six neurons in layer1, two neurons in layer2, and a batch size of eight. Adopting the most optimal MLP structure and calibrating by a rule-based calibration filter, the gait detection system could achieve a high accuracy around 99.7%. Moreover, a confusion matrix was used to illustrate the detection accuracy of each gait event in the test dataset as Fig. 3(c) shows. The left figure shows the number of correct detections, whereas the right indicates normalised detection accuracy. The confusion matrix indicates that the customs system has a stable performance for detecting each gait event. The accuracies of HS and FF were 99.4% and 99.7%, respectively. The detection accuracy of the TO and IO events was 100%. Even in the worst-case scenario, the HO event detection accuracy remained at 99.2%.

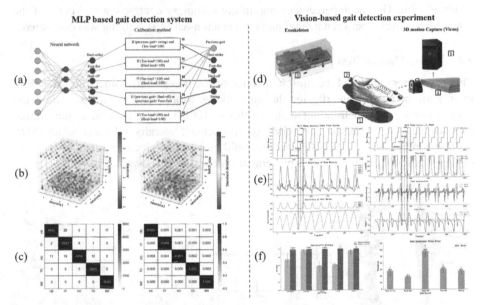

Fig. 3. Gait detection system and vision-based gait detection experiment. (a) MLP based gait detection system, (b) Hyperparameter optimisation result, (c) Confusion Matrix result, (d) Vision based gait detection experiment, (e) kinematic data in gait experiment, (f) gait detection accuracy and time error.

Meanwhile, a gait experiment is proposed to evaluate the performance of the gait detection system in the exoskeleton. The experiment requires the subject to walk with an exoskeleton on the treadmill under a vision-based motion capture system (Vicon), as Fig. 3(d) indicate. Five subjects were required to walk on a treadmill at a normal walking speed (4.2 km/h) under two systems for data collection and gait event classification. The line charts in Fig. 3(e) indicate the detected gait event by the exoskeleton and Vicon system, respectively. The gait detection accuracy and relative time error were estimated by comparing the classified gait events in the exoskeleton with the Vicon system as a reference, which showed in Fig. 3(f). The results indicate that the customs system achieves excellent performance in detecting gait events with an average accuracy of 99.66%. Meanwhile, the time errors amounting to 32 ms appeared on average for the five gait phases relative to the reference signal from the Vicon system.

4 Evaluation of Exoskeleton Performance Through Human Experiment

The performance of the proposed lower-limb cable-driven exoskeleton (MCR Exo) should be emulated by experiment. This study mainly focused on analysing muscle activity because the MCR Exo aims to reduce muscle activation during walking. The exoskeleton human trial investigated the surface electromyography (sEMG) activities of the triceps surae muscle groups during walking. Moreover, the EMG signal was normalised by maximum voluntary isometric contraction (MVIC) for muscle activity quantification. The mean percentage maximum voluntary contraction (%MVC) of the lower limb muscles between natural and exoskeleton-assisted walking was compared.

4.1 MVIC Manual Test

This experiment analysed the muscle activity of the triceps surae since the MCR Exo mainly assists ankle plantarflexion during walking. Moreover, the triceps surae is the major muscle group contributing to plantar flexion [20]. The triceps surae contains three muscles: gastrocnemius medialis (GM), gastrocnemius lateralis (GL) and soleus (SO), as shown in Fig. 4(a). The EMG sensors should monitor the electromyographic activity of these muscles, and the sensor's placement on the skin is shown in Fig. 4(a).

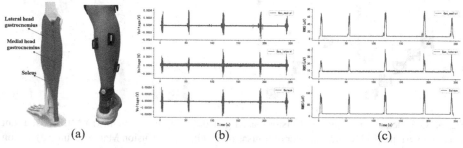

Fig. 4. MVIC based manual test. (a) EMG sensors placement, (b) Raw EMG data, (c) RMS filtered EMG data.

Manual muscle tests are required to obtain reference values during MVIC. Each test was repeated at least thrice and separated by at least 2 min to reduce the influence of muscle fatigue [21]. The maximum RMS values calculated from the sEMG signal during the repeat tests were adopted as reference values for EMG normalisation. In the MVIC manual test, the subject was requested to perform plantar flexion in the prone position, and the raw sEMG signals of the triceps surae were collected using the Delsys® system at 2000 Hz. The raw EMG signal is shown in Fig. 4(b), and the RMS envelope of the EMG is indicated in Fig. 4(c).

4.2 MVIC Treadmill Walking Test

In the treadmill waking test, the subjects were requested to walk on the treadmill at 4.2 km/h. Meanwhile, the sEMG signals of the triceps surae were collected and recorded for more than 15 steps. The recorded data normalised to %MVIC according to the maximum RMS values obtained during the MVIC manual test. The mean %MVIC and SD in 10 consecutive gait steps of four subjects were calculated.

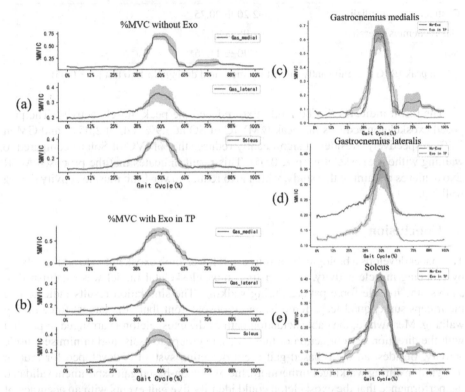

Fig. 5. Average sEMG activity (%MVC) of triceps during treadmill walking test. (a) %MVC of subject when walking without Exo, (b) %MVC of subject when walking with Exo in TP, (c) %MVC comparison of GM between with Exo and without Exo, (d) %MVC comparison of GL between with Exo and without Exo, (e) %MVC comparison of SO between with Exo and without Exo (Color figure online)

The Fig. 5 shows the average %MVC values with SD in a gait cycle that collected under two different walking conditions: walking without Exo and walking with Exo. And the exoskeleton releases the assistance according to the predefined torque profile (TP). Figure 140(a–b) shows the %MVC of the triceps surae when the subject walks without/with the MCR Exo. Figure 140 (c–e) compares the %MVC among three muscles when the blue line represents without Exo and the orange line indicates with Exo. As shown in the figure, subjects walking with Exo could reduce muscle activity in most cases compared with walking without Exo.

The peak %MVIC difference of the treadmill waking test is summarised in Table 1, representing the walking assistance results of Exo. It indicates the mean value and SD of the difference in triceps surae of all participants in the treadmill walking tests.

Table 1. The %MVIC difference between walking with exoskeleton and without exoskeleton

Muscles	Peak %MVIC Difference (Mean ± *SD*)
Gastrocnemius medialis	−2.20 ± 20.75
Gastrocnemius lateralis	−2.05 ± 11.37
Soleus	−5.90 ± 11.76*

*When peak EMG is significantly lower than measured during No-Exo test ($p < 0.05$).

The result indicates the TP mode Exo reduced the peak muscle activity. The proposed exoskeleton reduces the peak %MVIC of SO at 5.9%, GL at 2.05%, and GM at 2.2%, respectively. Besides, it significantly reduces the %MVC of Soleus compared to walking without exoskeleton ($p < 0.05$). This result indicates that the proposed MCR Exo achieves the aim of this study, which is to reduce lower-limb muscle activity during walking.

5 Conclusion

This paper develops a biologically inspired soft lower-limb exoskeleton to assist walking by reducing muscle activity. A lower-limb musculoskeletal model was established to analyse the muscle force pattern during walking. The simulation results indicate that the triceps surae, quadriceps femoris, and iliopsoas contribute the largest force during walking. Meanwhile, the cable actuation path of the exoskeleton is arranged in parallel with the direction of contraction of these muscle groups to assist and minimise muscle activity. Besides, an MLP based gait event detection system is developed for motion recognition during walking. Furthermore, the 3D vision-based gait experiment validated the performance that the exoskeleton could identify five gait events with an accuracy of 99.6% and 32 ms time error.

The performance of the MCR Exo was evaluated by an MVIC based test, which compared the muscle activity between walking with Exo and without Exo. The experiment result indicates that the exoskeleton could reduce the peak %MVIC of SO at 5.9%, GL at 2.05%, and GM at 2.2%, respectively. The result validates that the proposed exoskeleton can assist human walking by reducing the lower limb muscle activity.

References

1. Asbeck, A., De Rossi, S., Holt, K., Walsh, C.: A biologically inspired soft exosuit for walking assistance. Int. J. Robot. Res. **34**(6), 744–762 (2015)
2. Bolus, N.B., Teague, C.N., Inan, O.T., Kogler, G.F.: Instrumented ankle-foot orthosis: toward a clinical assessment tool for patient-specific optimisation of orthotic ankle stiffness. IEEE-ASME Trans. Mechatron. **22**(6), 2492–2501 (2017)

3. Lee, Y., et al.: Biomechanical design of a novel flexible exoskeleton for lower extremities. IEEE-ASME Trans. Mechatron. **22**(5), 2058–2069 (2017)
4. Malcolm, P., Galle, S., Derave, W., De Clercq, D.: Bi-articular knee-ankle-foot exoskeleton produces higher metabolic cost reduction than weight-matched mono-articular exoskeleton. Front. Neurosci. **12**, 69 (2018)
5. Lerner, Z.F., Damiano, D.L., Bulea, T.C.: A lower-extremity exoskeleton improves knee extension in children with crouch gait from cerebral palsy. Sci. Transl. Med. **9**, 404 (2017)
6. Cestari, M., Sanz-Merodio, D., Garcia, E.: Preliminary assessment of a compliant gait exoskeleton. Soft Robot. **4**(2), 135–146 (2017)
7. Jansen, O., et al.: Hybrid assistive limb exoskeleton HAL in the rehabilitation of chronic spinal cord injury: proof of concept. World Neurosurg. **110**, 73–78 (2018)
8. ReWalk Personal System 6.0. http://www.rewalk.com. Accessed 15 May 2022
9. EksoTM robotic exoskeleton. http://www.eksobionics.com/ekso. Accessed 15 May 2022
10. Schmidt, K., et al.: The Myosuit: bi-articular anti-gravity exosuit that reduces hip extensor activity in sitting transfers. Front. Neurorobot. **11**, 57 (2017)
11. Ding, Y., et al.: Biomechanical and physiological evaluation of multi-joint assistance with soft exosuits. IEEE Trans. Neural Syst. Rehabil. Eng. **25**(2), 119–130 (2017)
12. Grazi, L., Crea, S., Parri, A., Lova, R.M., Micera, S., Vitiello, N.: Gastrocnemius myoelectric control of a robotic hip exoskeleton can reduce the user's lower-limb muscle activities at push off. Front. Neurosci. **12**, 71 (2018)
13. Seo, K., Lee, J., Lee, Y., Ha, T., Shim, Y.: Fully autonomous hip exoskeleton saves metabolic cost of walking. In: 2016 IEEE International Conference on Robotics and Automation (ICRA), pp. 4628–4635 (2016)
14. Quinlivan, B.T., et al.: Assistance magnitude versus metabolic cost reductions for a tethered multiarticular soft exosuit. Sci. Robot. **2**(2) (2017)
15. Li, Z.J., Ren, Z., Zhao, K.K., Deng, C.J., Feng, Y.: Human-cooperative control design of a walking exoskeleton for body weight support. IEEE Trans. Ind. Inform. **16**(5), 2985–2996 (2020)
16. Wei, Q., Li, Z.J., Zhao, K.K., Kang, Y., Su, C.Y.: Synergy-based control of assistive lower-limb exoskeletons by skill transfer. IEEE-ASME Trans. Mechatron. **25**(2), 705–715 (2020)
17. Hoai, M., De la Torre, F.: Max-margin early event detectors. Int. J. Comput. Vis. **107**(2), 191–202 (2013). https://doi.org/10.1007/s11263-013-0683-3
18. Ryoo, M.S.: Human activity prediction: early recognition of ongoing activities from streaming videos. In: 2011 IEEE International Conference on Computer Vision (ICCV), pp. 1036–1043 (2011)
19. Yan, L., Wei, G., Hu, Z., Xiu, H., Wei, Y., Ren, L.: Low-cost multisensor integrated system for online walking gait detection. J. Sens. **2021**, 1–15 (2021)
20. Cardona, M., Cena, C.E.G.: Biomechanical analysis of the lower limb: a full-body musculoskeletal model for muscle-driven simulation. IEEE Access **7**, 92709–92723 (2019)
21. Mathiassen, S.E., Winkel, J., Hagg, G.M.: Normalisation of surface EMG amplitude from the upper trapezius muscle in ergonomic studies - a review. J. Electromyogr. Kinesiol. **5**(4), 197–226 (1995)

A Novel Compliant Actuator, ISSA and the Applications on a Robotic Arm

Haosen Yang[1] , Lei Ren[1] , and Guowu Wei[2(✉)]

[1] The University of Manchester, Manchester M13 9PL, UK
[2] University of Salford, 43 Crescent, Salford M5 4WT, UK
g.wei@salford.ac.uk

Abstract. This paper presents the design and development of a novel motor-based soft actuator. i.e. an internal torsion spring soft actuator (ISSA). The mechanical design of the actuator will be first introduced. Its force-displacement relationship will be simulated and validated. By applying the ISSA to a test joint, the actuation workflow and simulation will be discussed, including joint stiffness adjustment, and joint torque control. Prototypes of the ISSA will be developed and evaluated with the application to the test joint. The ISSAs are suitable for applications in soft robots, human-robot interaction, and especially highly biomimetic tendon-driven anthropomorphic robots.

Keywords: Artificial muscle · Biomimetic robotics · Compact soft actuator

1 Introduction

Until the last few decades, hinge joints or universal joints were directly connected to the geared motor in most robots for joint actuation [1–4]. It could deliver advantages including a simplified design process, low cost, precise motion control and convenient maintenance. However, this actuation method showed limitations in several aspects including safety. To provide safety, researchers have proposed different methods to provide compliance to robotics, including algorithmic compliance and mechanical compliance. Algorithmic compliance can keep the robot itself rigid, while the contact force between the robot and the environment can be controlled [5,6]. However, delays in the sensing and control system may make these conventionally stiff actuation systems generally incapable of responding to high-speed transients, especially when the power supply is cut off. Therefore, compliance at the physical level might be important.

Researchers proposed Series Elastic Actuator (SEA) [7–9] to provide mechanical compliance for robotics actuation. The SEA added an elastic element with elasticity and damping to release the coupling between the motor and the end effector.

In recent years, highly biomimetic tendon-driven robots have revolutionised the field of robotics. Motor-based tendon-driven methods are widely used in

H. Liu et al. (Eds.): ICIRA 2022, LNAI 13458, pp. 656–664, 2022.
https://doi.org/10.1007/978-3-031-13841-6_59

highly biomimetic robots [10,11]. In some cases, joint actuation is achieved by remote tendon-driven due to the large actuator size. These robots still fall short of the muscle-driven joints in the human body in terms of appearance, and mass distribution.

Thus, compact motor-based muscle-like actuators are required for highly biomimetic tendon-driven robots. In this paper, a compact tendon-driven internal spring soft actuator (ISSA) will be presented. This actuator is intended for use in safety-critical tendon-driven highly biomimetic robots.

Section 2 will introduce the design principles of the ISSA and its potential advantages and disadvantages. Section 3 will present the actuation workflow by applying the ISSA to a test joint. Important analyses in the workflow will be calculated and modelled. In Sect. 4, prototypes of the ISSA will be developed and applied to the test joint. Finally, there will be conclusions and a future plan in Sect. 5.

2   Design of the ISSA

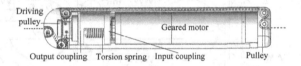

Fig. 1. CAD model of the internal spring soft actuator (ISSA). (Color figure online)

As shown in Fig. 1, the ISSA consists of a geared motor, an input coupling, a torsion spring, an output coupling, five pulleys and tendons.

The tendons on the left (red) and right (blue) sides are fixed to the driving pulley of the output coupling. The left tendon (red) is guided inside the shell and exits from the left side through two pulleys for friction reduction, which can be connected to the driven joint. The right tendon (blue) passes through the internal rails of the shell and leads out through three pulleys and can be attached to the driven joint.

The elastic element consists of a torsion spring, an input and an output coupling. The input coupling is fixed to the motor output shaft and the torsion spring is placed between the output coupling and the input coupling. When the geared motor rotates, the driving pulley attached to the output coupling makes the left tendon (red) and the right tendon (blue) contract at the same time. If the tendon is restricted by external forces, the output coupling and input coupling will rotate relative to each other and deform the torsion spring.

Advantages of the ISSA: 1. The outer diameter of the actuator remains small. Protection of the motor and external environment can be achieved without increasing the overall diameter, only the length is increased compared to the motor. 2. The tendons at both ends are able to contract by the driving pulley at the same time. With the same motor and driving pulley, twice the output speed can be achieved.

Disadvantages of the ISSA: Due to the restricted size of the torsion spring (which is limited to the motor diameter), the available maximum torque is limited. If a torsion spring with a small maximum torque is selected, the torsion spring will reach its maximum deformation before the motor reaches its rated torque, and the actuator will no longer be 'soft'. Therefore, the ISSA is only appropriate for use with high-speed and low-torque motors for high-speed and low-load applications.

3 Workflow

In most tendon-driven robots, the driven joint is actuated by a pair of actuators. The workflow is shown in Fig. 2 and has three steps. In the diagram, the torsion springs and the tendons are simplified as springs.

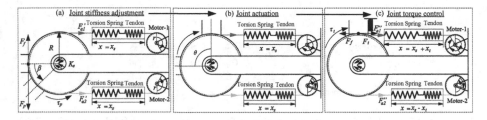

Fig. 2. Workflow of tendon-driven joint actuation by a pair of soft actuators. (a) joint stiffness adjustment; (b) joint angle actuation; (c) joint output torque control.

The first step is joint stiffness adjustment: before driving the joint to rotate (Fig. 2(a)), motor-1 and motor-2 in both actuators rotate at the same angle. The torsion springs deform, generating pre-tension tendon displacements $x = x_s$ (x_s is the result of the torsion spring deformation and tendon material deformation, s means stiffness). This will increase the tension F_a, which in turn provides the joint with a joint stiffness K_s.

The second step is joint rotation actuation (Fig. 2(b)): maintain K_s, the motors in the two actuators rotate at the same angle in opposite directions. If friction and gravity are not considered, the joint will rotate to the target position θ. During this step, the tendon displacement x in both actuators and the joint stiffness K_s remain constant, $x = x_s$.

The third step is joint torque control (Fig. 2(c)), when the joint is restricted, motor-1 continues to rotate to increases the tension on actuator-1 to F''_{a1}. Motor-2 rotate in opposite direction to decrease the tension on actuator-2 to F''_{a2}. F''_{a1} will be larger than F''_{a2}, resulting in a joint torque τ_t.

3.1 Force-Tendon Displacement Relationship

When the ISSA is subjected to a force F_a, the torsion spring and the tendon material will be deformed.

Assuming the tendon displacement is x_{max} when the torsion spring reaches its limited position and the tension is F_{amax}. The deformation of the tendon material is included in x_{max}.

In the first stage, before the torsion spring reach its limited position ($0 \leq x \leq x_{max}$), the torsion spring is deformed and the tendon material is stretched.

The equivalent elastic coefficient of tendon displacement due to the torsion spring deformation is $k_{ts} = k_e \backslash 4r^2$. ($k_e$ is the elasticity coefficient of the torsion spring, r is the radius of the driving pulley). The tendon will cross the pulleys and there will be friction $F_f = \mu_p F_a$, μ_p is the friction coefficient. Assuming the tendon elasticity coefficient is k_t and keep constant.

In the second stage, after the torsion spring reaches the limited position ($x > x_{max}$), the force F_a will stretch the tendon material only. The relationship between x and F_a in the two stages can be deduced as:

$$\begin{cases} x = \frac{(F_a - F_f)}{k_{ts}} + \frac{F_a}{k_t} \\ x = x_{max} + \frac{F_a - F_{amax}}{k_t} \end{cases} \tag{1}$$

Combining the two stages, the relation between F_a and x is:

$$F_a = f_{Fx}(x) \tag{2}$$

3.2 Joint Stiffness-Tendon Displacement Relationship

The actuators can provide joint stiffness before joint rotation (Fig. 2(a)). The simultaneous rotation of the motors in both actuators deforms the torsion springs and the tendon material, producing x_s. According to (2), the tension on the actuator is:

$$F_{aj} = f_{Fx}(x_s)(j = 1, 2) \tag{3}$$

The joint will be loaded with a joint stiffness K_s. To calculate K_s, a virtual external torque $\tau_p = F_p R$ (R is the joint moment arm) is applied to the joint and results in a passive rotation angle β in response (from the solid position to the dashed position in Fig. 2 (a)). K_s can be defined as the difficulty of making a passive rotation angle β by τ_p, which is:

$$K_s = \frac{\tau_p}{\beta} = \frac{F_p R}{\beta} \tag{4}$$

The tendon displacement x on actuator-1 will increase by βR to $x = x_s + \beta R$, and the tension will change from F_{a1} to F'_{a1}. The tendon displacement on actuator-2 will decrease to $x = x_s - \beta R$, and the tension will change from F_{a2} to F'_{a2}. The static frictional torque can be equated to the frictional force acting on the joint $F_f = \mu_s F_{aj} (j = 1, 2)$, μ_s is the static friction coefficient and F_p can be calculated as:

$$F_p = F'_{a1} - F'_{a2} + F_f \tag{5}$$

Combined with (2), F_p can be further expressed as:

$$F_p = F'_{a1} - F'_{a2} + F_f = f_{Fx}(x_s + \beta R) - f_{Fx}(x_s - \beta R) + \mu_s F_{aj} \tag{6}$$

For different x_s, only the stage in which the elastic element is involved are considered. When $\beta R < x_s \leq x_{max} - \beta R$, τ_p causes the torsion spring in actuator-1 further to deform. The torsion spring in actuator-2 resumes partial deformation and will not return to its initial stage. According to (6), F_p is:

$$F_p = 2k_{ts}k_t\beta R/[k_t(1 - \mu_p) + k_{ts}] + \mu_s F_{aj} \tag{7}$$

Combining (3)(4), the joint stiffnesses provided to the driven joints using the ISSA at different x_s can be obtained as:

$$K_s = f_K(\beta, x_s) \tag{8}$$

3.3   Joint Output Torque-Displacement Relationship

As shown in Fig. 2(c), if the joint is restricted, further increasing the tendon displacement will result in a joint torque. This subsection calculates the relationship between the joint output torque τ_t, x_s and x_{tj} (the torque output tendon displacement, $j = 1, 2$).

Motor 1 in actuator-1 continues to rotate and motor 2 in actuator-2 rotates in the opposite direction. The tendon displacement in actuator-1 increases to $x = x_s + x_{t1}$ and the tendon displacement in actuator-2 decreases to $x = x_s - x_{t2}$. The tension on actuator-1 increases from F_{a1} to $F''_{a1} = f_{Fx}(x_s + x_{t1})$ and the tension on actuator-2 decrease to $F''_{a2} = f_{Fx}(x_s - x_{t2})$. The joint outputs a torque:

$$\tau_t = F_t R \tag{9}$$

According to Fig. 2(c) and (2), F_t can be deduced as:

$$F_t = F''_{a1} - F''_{a2} - F_f = f_{Fx}(x_s + x_{t1}) - f_{Fx}(x_s - x_{t2}) - F_f \tag{10}$$

Combining (9)(10), the joint output torque τ_t can be deduced. τ_t is related to x_{t1} x_{t2}, and x_s, denoted as:

$$\tau_t = f_{tx}(x_s, x_{tj})(j = 1, 2) \tag{11}$$

When the actuators are in the torsion spring working stage, i.e. $x_s + x_{t1} \leq x_{max}$ and $x_s - x_{t2} \geq 0$, it is considered as the controllable output torque stage.

4 Prototype and Evaluation

4.1 Prototype

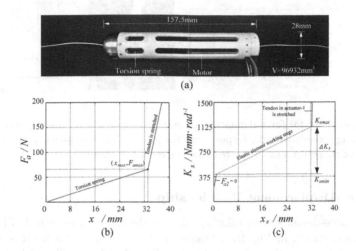

Fig. 3. (a) The prototype of the ISSA; The simulation results of the ISSA: (b) $F_a = f_{Fx}(x)$, $\mu_p = 0.2$; (c) $K_s = f_K(\beta = 0.087, x_s)$, $\mu_s = 0.1$.

Maxon brushless motor (22 mm diameter, 62:1 planetary gearbox, rated torque = 1.6 Nm) with a radius of $r = 5$ mm driving pulley was used for the ISSA. The braided fishing line (1.0 mm outer diameter, maximum force 200 lb, through experiment, $k_t = 30$ N/mm, $L = 200$ mm) was selected for the tendon. The prototype of the ISSA is shown in Fig. 3(a) and its key parameters are listed in Table 1.

Table 1. Performance of the ISSA prototype

Rated force	Rated speed	Diameter	Length	Mass	Volume
125 N	220 mm/s	28 mm	157.5 mm	280 g	96932 mm³

Due to size constraints, a torsion spring with an elasticity coefficient of $k_e = 161.78$ Nmm/rad and maximum deformation of πrad was chosen. The equivalent elasticity coefficient for the tendon displacement is $k_{ts} = k_e/4r^2 = 1.618$ N/mm and the spring is deformed to the limited position when $F_{amax} = 50.8$ N.

According to (1), $F_a = f_{Fx}(x)$ can be obtained as shown in Fig. 3(b). According to (8), $K_s = f_K(\beta = 0.087, x_s)$ is shown in Fig. 3(c).

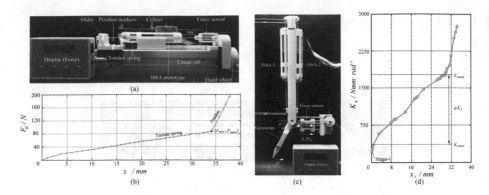

Fig. 4. Experiment for force-displacement relationship with (a) test rig setup and (b) corresponding recorded result; Experiment for joint stiffness-displacement relationship with (c) test rig setup and (d) corresponding recorded result

4.2   Force-Displacement Relationship

First, the force-displacement relationships of the ISSA were tested. The experiment setup is shown in Fig. 4(a). One end of the tendon was fixed to the force sensor (0–50 kg) and the other end is fixed to the slider. The slider can move freely along the linear rail and its position can be adjusted by the handwheel. The motor is powered but stays stationary. The experimental results are recorded as the readings of the force sensor and the calliper at different slider positions. The results is shown in Fig. 4(b).

4.3   Joint Stiffness-Displacement Relationship

Secondly, the variable joint stiffness of a test joint with ISSAs was validated. The experiment set-up is shown in Fig. 4(c). Two ISSAs were applied to the test joint. Motor-3 is able to move the force sensor on the linear rail. The force sensor is connected to the driven arm via a cable and its movement is able to rotate the joint counterclockwise. The joint angle can be recorded by a gyroscope located on the driven arm.

In this experiment, the joint stiffness is tested by the following steps.

Step1: The two ISSAs drive the joint to the target angle (70°) without deforming the torsion spring.

Step 2: Motor-3 rotates and gradually moves the force sensor to the right. The joint will rotate counterclockwise by the external force from the force sensor. Record the external force when the joint reaches the target position (75°). Return the Motor-3 to its original position.

Step 3: Control actuator-1 and actuator-2 to produce different tendon displacements x_s. The joint angle remains the same value as in Step 1. Repeat step 2 to record the forces throughout the process.

The relationship between F_p and x_s, and hence between K_s and x_s, can be obtained from the test, and the result for the ISSA is shown in Fig. 4(d).

4.4   Application on a Biomimetic Robotic Arm

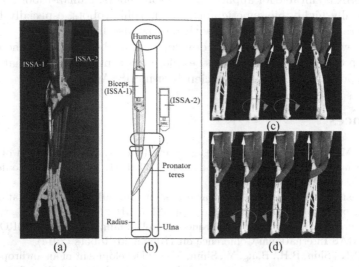

Fig. 5. Application on a biomimetic robotic arm. (a) Biomimetic robotic arm with two ISSAs; (b) Schematic diagrams of the robotic arm actuation; (c) Forearm pronation actuated by ISSA-2; (d) Forearm supination actuated by ISSA-1.

A tendon-driven highly biomimetic robotic arm is shown in Fig. 5(a). This type of robotic arm is the target serving robot by ISSA. Two ISSAs are applied to this robotic arm for forearm rotation actuation. The whole system can be simplified as Fig. 5(b).

ISSA-1 is originally from the humerus and is connected to the radial tuberosity. It actuates the forearm supination (Fig. 5(c)). ISSA-2 is located at the medial humerus, only one tendon is connected to the driving pulley. The tendon passes through the internal rail inside the medial epicondyle and is connected to the anterior surface of the radius. It works as the pronator teres assists the forearm pronation (Fig. 5(d)).

This robotic arm is "soft" due to the application of springs in the actuators. When an external force is applied to the arm, the springs are able to absorb the external force and protect the motor and the surrounding operating environment. The protection is also activated even without a power supply.

5   Conclusion

In this paper, a soft actuator was presented. i.e. an internal torsion spring soft actuator (ISSA). The design of the ISSA was first introduced. Its force-displacement relationships were simulated and validated. By applying the ISSAs to a test joint, the actuation workflow was presented, including joint stiffness adjustment, joint angle actuation, and joint torque control. Prototypes of the ISSAs were developed and evaluated with the application to the test joint.

The ISSA is suitable for applications in soft robots, human-robot interaction, and especially highly biomimetic anthropomorphic robots, especially for joints that require high speed and joints with narrow installation space.

Future work will include further development of the control scheme to realise closed-loop control with sensors, and explore the control strategy that can lead to fast-response safe control for efficiently using ISSAs.

References

1. Fuchs, M., et al.: Rollin Justin-Design considerations and realization of a mobile platform for a humanoid upper body. In: 2009 IEEE International Conference on Robotics and Automation (2009)
2. Grebenstein, M.: The DLR hand arm system. In: 2011 IEEE International Conference on Robotics and Automation, pp. 3175–3182 (2011)
3. Englsberger, J.: Overview of the torque-controlled humanoid robot TORO. In: 2014 IEEE-RAS International Conference on Humanoid Robots (2014)
4. Paik, J.K., Shin, B.H., Bang, Y., Shim, Y.-B.: Development of an anthropomorphic robotic arm and hand for interactive humanoids. J. Bionic Eng. 9(2), 133–142 (2012). https://doi.org/10.1016/S1672-6529(11)60107-8
5. Vischer, D., Khatib, O.: Design and development of high-performance torque-controlled joints. IEEE Trans. Robot. Autom. 11(4), 537–544 (1995)
6. Hyon, S.-H., Hale, J., Cheng, G.: Full-body compliant human-humanoid interaction: balancing in the presence of unknown external forces. IEEE Trans. Rob. 23(5), 884–898 (2007)
7. Hirai, K., Hirose, M., Haikawa, Y., Takenaka, T.: The development of Honda humanoid robot. In: Proceedings IEEE International Conference on Robotics and Automation (Cat. No. 98CH36146) (1998)
8. Yang, H., et al.: A low-cost linkage-spring-tendon-integrated compliant anthropomorphic robotic hand: MCR-Hand III. Mech. Mach. Theory 158, 104210 (2021)
9. Sensinger, J., Weir, R.: Design and analysis of a non-backdrivable series elastic actuato. In: 9th International Conference on Rehabilitation Robotics. ICORR 2005 (2005)
10. Asano, Y., Okada, K., Inaba, M.: Musculoskeletal design, control, and application of human mimetic humanoid Kenshiro. Bioinspiration Biomimetics 14(3), 036011 (2019)
11. Nakanishi, Y., et al.: Design approach of biologically-inspired musculoskeletal humanoids. Int. J. Adv. Rob. Syst. 10(4), 216 (2013)

A New 3D Printed Passive Flexible Prosthesis Based on the Human Foot

Jianqiao Jin[1], Kunyang Wang[1,2(✉)], Lei Ren[1,3(✉)], Zhihui Qian[1,2], Wei Liang[1], Wei Chen[1], Xuewei Lu[3], and Di Zhao[1]

[1] Key Laboratory of Bionic Engineering, Ministry of Education, Jilin University, Changchun 130025, China
{kywang,lren}@jlu.edu.cn
[2] Weihai Institute for Bionics, Jilin University, Weihai 264402, China
[3] School of Mechanical, Aerospace and Civil Engineering, University of Manchester, Manchester M13 9PL, UK

Abstract. The existing passive foot prostheses do not contain all the joints of the foot, so they cannot fully simulate the natural human gait. They can induce various secondary injuries and require extra energy consumption in amputee patients. In this study, a new manufacturing design was used to develop a passive ankle-foot prosthesis, which was used to retain every joint of the foot as far as possible by flexible connections to reproduce the complete mechanical and kinematic performance of the ankle joint. After testing on healthy subjects, using the VICON MX system to capture the motion of the markers, and inserting the data into the OpenSim system to perform musculoskeletal model-driven calculations, the results show that the mechanical and kinematic properties of the ankle joint of the prosthesis were similar to those of a healthy limb, and the performance was greatly improved. Future work includes continuing to test the mechanical and kinematic properties of other joints in the foot, enhancing the mechanical properties of 3D printed materials, and inviting amputees for more comprehensive wearable testing.

Keywords: Passive prosthetic design · 3D printing · Flexible connection · Bionic design

1 Introduction

Feet play an important role in human walking, not only needing to bear the body's weight but also playing a role in movement shock absorption and to support push off [1]. According to one study, of more than 1.6 million Americans, approximately one in 190 have lost a limb, and 62% of these patients had lower limb amputations. By 2050, the number of people with physical disabilities is expected to increase to 3.6 million, of whom more than 1.4 million are under the age of 65. Clinical studies have shown that 68 to 88% of amputees wear prostheses for at least seven hours a day to maintain daily activity [2, 3].

Prosthetics can be classified as active or passive depending on whether they provide external energy. Smarter and faster active prosthetics are the mainstream development trend in the future. In 2019, Erik P. Lamers et al. unveiled a microprocessor-controlled

© The Author(s), under exclusive license to Springer Nature Switzerland AG 2022
H. Liu et al. (Eds.): ICIRA 2022, LNAI 13458, pp. 665–675, 2022.
https://doi.org/10.1007/978-3-031-13841-6_60

prosthetic that mimics as much of the biomechanics of a healthy human foot as possible by controlling the angle of the wearer's ankle [4]. Based on the traditional multicentre structure design, Marco Cempini and others put forward a more efficient design method for an artificial limb, which can not only reduce the distance between the centre of gravity and the centre of rotation but also reduce the requirement for motor torque and the overall mass and size of the prosthesis [5].

However, compared with passive prostheses, active prostheses are heavier and more expensive and encounter many problems, such as software control and hardware maintenance, under different walking conditions. Passive prostheses also have a wide market and audience due to their low cost of production and maintenance as well as good stability. For example, Huy-Tuan Pham et al. designed a passive prosthetic titled MACPA that not only reduces vibration but also converts the body's gravitational potential energy into strain energy that can be stored to propel the body when the toes are off the ground. MACPA synthesizes human biomechanics and the Gait Movement Law, improves the ankle joint self-adaptation inside-out turn, and helps the human body keep walking balance [6]. Osama Abdelaal and others have reverse-engineered a custom-made silicone-rubber partial foot prosthesis (SPFP) that not only looks good in a custom-made match to the amputee's opposite foot but at the same time also plays an active role in promoting the restoration of the human body's natural gait [7].

The complex three-dimensional motion of the joint surface of the human foot consists of several joint axes that influence each other. The motions of different joint axes constitute the natural walking of humans.

However, the designs of many prostheses only consider the independent motion of the sagittal plane and coronal plane, which does not conform to the multiaxis combined motion model of the human foot. This will not only increase the rate of knee joint strain, but also reduce walking speed and step length and increase energy consumption [8]. In addition, most of the existing passive prostheses have single-foot plates. Even with the addition of foot joint movement, they cannot simulate human gait well, which only increases the metabolic rate of prosthetic wearers and reduces their mobility [9].

Therefore, how to enhance symmetrical walking with the healthy side to reduce secondary injuries and be able to better simulate the characteristics of the human foot will be an important direction of future research.

The main functions of the human foot can be summarized into three categories. 1. Adapt to the contour of the ground; 2. Absorb impact. 3. Store and release energy to improve the efficiency of movement.

In human gait, the foot plays a very important role. It not only needs the flexibility of the whole structure to absorb the impact force of the human body but also must provide enough stiffness and propulsion force for when the body moves forward [10], which is largely due to the arch structure of the human foot. The human foot arch can be roughly divided into three parts, the lateral longitudinal arch, the medial longitudinal arch, and the transverse arch, which have different functional characteristics [11] (Fig. 1A). For this reason, the arch should be considered in the design of prostheses. For example, Cristina Piazza et al. introduced a passive prosthesis called SoftFoot, which focuses on the exploration of the adaptability and stability of the prosthesis based on the functions of the foot arch and plantar fascia and has better stability and adaptability to a certain extent [12–15]. Millicent Schlafly et al. developed a passive bionic compliant prosthesis called the CAPA Foot. The CAPA foot can use torsion springs of different parameters to store energy at the joints and imitate the working state of normal human feet, releasing energy to provide thrust during the stepping-off [16–19] (Fig. 1B).

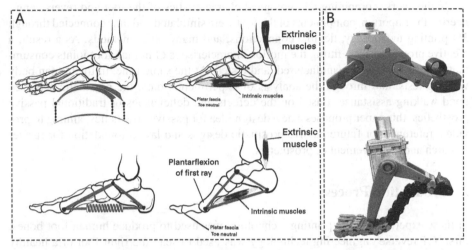

Fig. 1. Introduction to the arch of the foot and two passive bionic prostheses. A, Introduction to the arch of the foot. B, The Soft Foot (top) and the CAPA Foot (bottom)

The human foot can be divided into three functional units: the hindfoot, middle foot, and forefoot. Specifically, it is mainly composed of the ankle joint, subtalar joint, tarsal joint (including the talonavicular joint and calcaneocuboid joint), interarticular joint (including the cuneonavicular joint and cuboid joint), Lisfranc's joint, plantar joint and metatarsophalangeal joint [20]. The coordination of various joints constitutes a complex motion state of the foot so that no single joint can fully reproduce the motion of the foot. Many existing prostheses have concentrated on some areas of the joints. For example, Eric C Honert et al. noticed the action caused by the plantar toe joint on the walking situation of the ankle-foot prosthesis, which has two free degrees, and the test purpose was achieved by changing the different stiffnesses of the spring and toes. The study finally proved that changing the stiffness of the metatarsophalangeal joint in the prosthesis can improve the wearer's motor potential [21].

In addition, the human body's movable joints (synovial joints) mainly contain two parts, an articular cartilage part and a joint capsule. Articular cartilage covers both ends of the bone and between the articular surfaces, which can play a buffer role and disperse the pressure of the articular surface. The main function of the joint capsule is to reduce the friction between the joint surfaces.

At the same time, ligaments are important parts of the joint. Their main function is to protect the joint and avoid excessive movement. However, the existing prosthesis designs do not fully simulate the functions of each joint of the foot, and the bionic simulations of the joint capsule are not perfect.

In summary, from the above foot theory analysis, it can be seen that to achieve a passive prosthesis design that mimics human natural feet, all parts are indispensable, including the articular surfaces of the foot bones, arch, ligaments, cartilage, and joint capsules. Each part has its biological functions that have important roles in human walking. Therefore, it is worth considering how to simulate these characteristics and apply them to the design of passive prostheses.

In this work, combining the biological characteristics of the foot and reverse engineering the important components of the foot were simulated and interconnected through 3D printing technology, flexible connections, and many other methods. As a result, a creative prosthetic foot, fitting the motion characteristics of human foot joints consummately, was designed, manufactured, and tested. At the same time, in the human body wearing tests, and through the analysis of experimental data, the prosthetic achieved good walking assistance. Based on the defects and deficiencies of traditional passive prosthetics, this paper proposes a new design idea for passive prosthetics, aiming to provide a reference for future passive prosthetic designs and lays a foundation for further research and improvement of prosthetics.

2   Production Process

In these experiments, 3D printing technology was used to produce human foot bones. First, CT reverse engineering technology was used to scan the right foot of a healthy 176 cm tall, 75 kg 30-year-old male with no foot disease. Mimics (Version 10.0, Materialise, Belgium) was used to segment and generate the scanned CT image sequence (Fig. 2A).

The STL files generated by the above process were imported into the PolyJet 3D printing device, Stratasys J8509 (Stratasys, Shanghai, China). The fabrication was conducted in a 3D printing studio at Jilin University's Weihai Bionics Institute (Weihai, China). Next, the printed 26-foot bones (except the two sesamoid bones) were divided into three parts, anterior, middle and posterior, according to the biological characteristics of human feet and were connected successively.

In the fabrication of the forefoot, synthetic silicone rubber rings of 2 mm–5 mm were used to connect the adjacent articular surfaces. of The synthetic silicone rubber rings simulated the ligament in the articular capsule. During joint connection, Teflon tape was cut and pasted on the two joint surfaces to simulate the cartilage between joints and play a role in distributing pressure and increasing buffering. The adjacent joined bones were rotated with DP100PLUS soft glue purchased from 3M to simulate connective tissue synovial fluid and fat pads in a joint capsule. After the glue injection was completed, the glue injection site was wrapped with a polyolefin thermal shrinkage sleeve and heated (Fig. 2B), and the synthetic silicone rubber ring was continuously wound externally to simulate the joint capsule and extravasate ligament (Fig. 2C).

In the connection of the middle foot part, adhesive rubber strips were used to adhere each piece relative to the bone according to the position of the human ligament. The next step was as described above. The soft glue is poured first, and then the heat-shrinkable tubes are used for fixation.

In the connection of the hindfoot, the same steps were carried out. First of all, according to the position of the human body, the corresponding joint ligaments of the talus, calcaneus, tibia, fibula (the tibiofibular in the previous 3 d printing process had been made as a single element) were connected with a rubber bar inside an external heat-shrinkable tube placed over the whole package. Finally, the rubber strips were wrapped around the outside for fixation.

It should be noted that the connections between the forefoot and the middle foot (metatarsophalangeal joint) and the middle foot and the hindfoot (tarsal joint) are the same as the connection between the forefoot and the middle foot mentioned above. A viscose plaster bandage was used between the forefoot and the middle foot for overall stabilization, and the final foot bone connection is shown in the figure.

After the bone connections were completed, a small sports ankle protector was used to limit the ankle joint and the subtalar joint, and a viscose plaster bag was used again for the overall stability of the prosthesis, followed by an orthopaedic silica gel heel pad, a silica gel flat foot corrective pad, and a silica gel toe tip cushioning pad.

In these experiments, each part of the prosthesis was positioned, and the silicone shoe cover was placed on the outside to make the prosthesis simple and clean in appearance (Fig. 2).

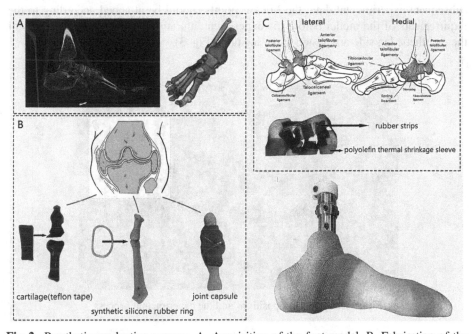

Fig. 2. Prosthetic production process. A, Acquisition of the foot model. B, Fabrication of the bionic joint capsule. C, Selection and fixation of the biomimetic ligaments

3 Experimental Process

3.1 Test Platform Construction and Marking Point Layout

The experimental part of this work was carried out in the Bionic Walking and Health Engineering Laboratory of Jilin University (Chang Chun, China). A Vicon MX system was used to capture the real-time motions of each joint of a prosthetic foot. The Vicon MX 3D Gait Analysis system was designed by Vicon Motion Systems in the UK. By capturing the motion trajectory of Marker points, it can capture the motion of each joint in real time. Double-sided adhesive tape was used to connect each Marker point with the corresponding position of the tester's body, and there were 53 Marker points in the whole system.

During the tests, there were 7 infrared sources. To ensure that all the joint markers of the artificial limb in this experiment could be recognized, the light reflected from each passive Marker was captured by two infrared cameras at the same time, and the acquisition frequency was set at 100 Hz.

The moving ground reaction data of the experimental object were measured by three 200×400 mm Kistler force plates (frequency: 1000 Hz), whose data were subsequently imported into OpenSim software. OpenSim is free and open-source software developed by Stanford University for kinematics and dynamics calculations of walking. In this work, the whole-body skeletal muscle system model proposed by Raabe M E et al. was used as the benchmark for scaling [22]. At the same time, to facilitate the import of subsequent experimental data, the Marker points should be attached according to the requirements of the model before the experiment, among which the Marker points of the prosthetic leg side are pasted at the leg tube (Fig. 3).

Fig. 3. Marker point positions and the experimental process

3.2 Test Subjects

The bone models obtained by CT technology mentioned above were obtained from the experimental subjects. Both of them are the same people who read and signed the consent form before participating in the experiments. The work was conducted following the Declaration of Helsinki, and the test subjects were informed of the test procedures and research methods, which were approved by the Ethics Committee of the First Bethune Hospital of Jilin University.

3.3 Introduction to the Body Wear Test Process

Before the experiments, the subjects were familiarised with the whole operation process in advance and underwent adaptive prosthesis wearing training. To ensure safety, handrails were placed on both sides of the passage of the three force plates (none of the handrail parts were reflective). After an experiment officially began, the test subject passed through the force plate at three speeds: slow (1 m/s), medium (1.3 m/s) and fast (1.5 m/s). It should be noted that to ensure the accuracy of the data, the test subjects should not directly walk up or down the force plate but should walk approximately one metre before and after the force plate and take a half-minute rest after each set of experiments (Fig. 3).

4 Results

At the end of the experiments, data preprocessing was first carried out in the Vicon system, including the interconnection of Marker points, the repair of Marker point motion trajectories, filtering and exporting the static and dynamic data. Because passive Marker reflections confuse the infrared cameras thus generating less information, the Marker point trajectories must be adjusted. At the same time, because the data collected will receive test equipment and signal interference from the outside world, adjustments need to be made again after filtering processing prior to data export.

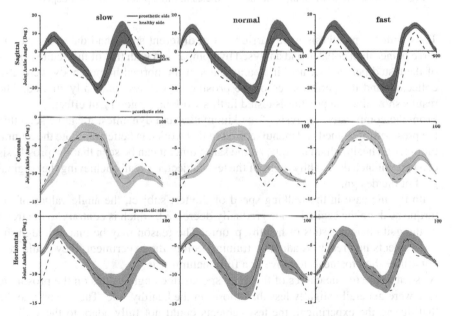

Fig. 4. The ankle joint angle in three planes at different speeds

The test data of the normal human body under three gait rates and three planes were analysed and sorted [23], and the conclusions were drawn by comparing the data processed in these experiments (Figs. 4 and 5).

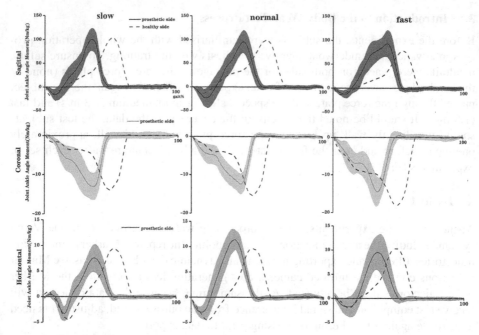

Fig. 5. The ankle joint moment of the prosthesis in three planes at different speeds

1. Tests with the prosthesis were carried out at different speed and data collected in three planes then collated and analysed by comparison with that of the healthy limbs of the tested person. Meanwhile, parameters of the normal human body were also collected, and the performance of the prosthesis was systematically studied. The results show that the prosthesis tested in this work had a good gait effect.

2. From the comparative analysis of the kinematics and dynamics, it can be seen that the prosthetic designed and manufactured in this work can better simulate the natural motion of a healthy human body. At the same time, it can be seen that the prosthesis can better match the healthy limbs of the test subject, basically achieving the original goal of the design.

3. With the increase in the walking speed of the test subject, the angle values of the torque peak on the sagittal plane gradually decreased, which is contrary to the trend of the gait characteristics of healthy people. The reason may be that although the test subjects had received adaptive training before the experiment, they could still not utilize the prosthesis to move in a fully natural gait.

4. As seen in the torque curves of the three speeds, the angle values on the prosthetic side were generally slightly less than those on the healthy side. The reason may be that during the experiment, the test subjects could not fully adapt to the walking process of wearing the prosthetic limb. During the tests, they held onto the railings with both hands to maintain their balance, so the values of the ground return forces were slightly reduced, resulting in deviations of the torque values. Although wearing training was carried out before the tests, the testers wearing the prosthesis were still

unable to apply the leg force used in a normal gait on the prosthesis side due to the unaccustomed walking during the experiments, which led to a problem.

5   Comparative Analysis of Other Prostheses

The CAPA foot designed by Millicent Schlafly et al. was selected as the comparative sample. There were two prostheses prototypes (the large radius and the small radius), which were designed by changing the curvature radius of the spring, described in their paper. They carried out two groups of tests while not performing motion tests at the same speed. Therefore, for convenient analysis, the kinematic results (angle) of the prosthesis side designed by our group were compared with the two CAPA foot prostheses (the large radius and the small radius) [16], and the results are shown in Fig. 6.

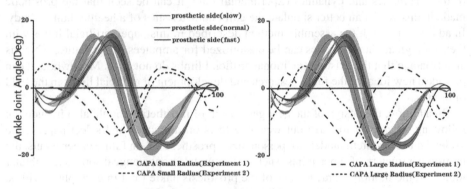

Fig. 6. Comparative analysis of other prostheses

1. The overall motion trends of the prosthesis were similar to those of the CAPA foot prostheses. The motion amplitudes of the prosthesis on the sagittal plane were higher than those of the CAPA foot prostheses. The reason is related to the type of flexible connection of the prosthesis.
2. The prosthesis designed and fabricated in this work retains all the joints of the natural foot structure, so it can move in three spatial planes (sagittal plane, coronal plane and horizontal plane) and exhibit more degrees of freedom and higher adaptability. For long-term prosthetic wearers, the design means less secondary joint damage caused by mobility restraints and better protection of healthy joints. In addition, the advantages of the artificial limb presented in this paper are based on the design concept of personal customization, which uses the shapes of the bones and joints of the healthy limb of the unilateral amputee so that the artificial limb can better restore the normal walking gait of the prosthetic wearer. However, most prostheses currently do not have this design concept.
3. The motion curve trends of the prosthesis were similar not only at different speeds but also among the different devices at the same speed. Therefore, the preferable stability of the new prosthesis was confirmed during these tests.

6 Discussion

A normal foot contains joints that work together with more exercise, however because the existing ankle-foot prosthesis designs are mainly rigid, thus ensuring stability and abandoning flexibility, they cannot guarantee the amputee after wearing prosthetic activities a more natural gait. The consequences of this will not only increase secondary lesions of the amputee's contralateral limb but can also increase the work effort of the prosthetic users at the same time and thus have a negative impact.

The innovation of work presented in this paper lies in the overall reproduction of the human foot and ankle bones based on reverse medical engineering and 3D printing and the selection of suitable flexible materials to connect each of the bones according to the corresponding joint positions, which ultimately retain the movements of each joint of the human body but also effectively reduces the energy consumption. Through the analysis of the kinematics and dynamics experimental data, it can be seen that the prosthetic made in this work can better simulate the gait characteristics of a healthy human body. In addition, through the assembly method described in this paper, artificial limbs with their biological characteristics can be customized for amputees in the future, which is an advantage that the existing traditional artificial limbs do not have. Meanwhile, it can provide a new idea for the future research and development of artificial limbs in the field of bionics.

In addition, the design of the next generation of prosthetics should also include the following. 1. A plan to carry out wearable tests on amputees and select appropriate skeletal muscle system models for personalized prostheses. 2. In future experiments, the motion parameters of other joints, such as the metatarsophalangeal joint and subtalar joint, and the motion characteristics of the prosthesis ankle joint in each plane will be further measured in detail. 3. In addition, more suitable 3D printing materials should be selected to improve the overall mechanical properties of the prosthesis. 4. Gradually optimize the manufacturing process of artificial limbs to improve the production efficiency of artificial limbs.

References

1. Boonpratatong, A., Ren, L.: The human ankle-foot complex as a multi-configurable mechanism during the stance phase of walking. J. Bionic Eng. **7**(3), 211–218 (2010). https://doi.org/10.1016/S1672-6529(10)60243-0
2. Pohjolainen, T., Alaranta, H., Kärkäinen, M.: Prosthetic use and functional and social outcome following major lower limb amputation. Prosthet. Orthot. Int. **14**, 75–79 (1990)
3. Walker, C.R.C., Ingram, R.R., Hullin, M.G., McCreath, S.W.: Lower limb amputation following injury: a survey of long-term functional outcome. Injury **25**, 387–392 (1994)
4. Lamers, E.P., Eveld, M.E., Zelik, K.E.: Subject-specific responses to an adaptive ankle prosthesis during incline walking. J. Biomech. **95**, 109273 (2019)
5. Cempini, M., Hargrove, L.J., Lenzi, T.: Design, development, and bench-top testing of a powered polycentric ankle prosthesis, pp. 1064–1069. IEEE (2017)
6. Pham, H.-T., Le, M.-N., Mai, V.-T.: A novel multi-axis compliant prosthetic ankle foot to support the rehabilitation of amputees, pp. 238–243. IEEE (2016)

7. Abdelaal, O., Darwish, S., Abd Elmougoud, K., Aldahash, S.: A new methodology for design and manufacturing of a customized silicone partial foot prosthesis using indirect additive manufacturing. Int. J. Artif. Organs **42**, 645–657 (2019)
8. Torricelli, D., et al.: Human-like compliant locomotion: state of the art of robotic implementations. Bioinspir. Biomim. **11**, 051002 (2016)
9. Zelik, K.E., et al.: Systematic variation of prosthetic foot spring affects center-of-mass mechanics and metabolic cost during walking. IEEE Trans. Neural Syst. Rehabil. Eng. **19**, 411–419 (2011)
10. Ker, R.F., Bennett, M.B., Bibby, S.R., Kester, R.C., Alexander, R.M.: The spring in the arch of the human foot. Nature **325**, 147–149 (1987)
11. Hashimoto, K., et al.: A study of function of foot's medial longitudinal arch using biped humanoid robot, pp. 2206–2211. IEEE (2010)
12. Piazza, C., et al.: Toward an adaptive foot for natural walking, pp. 1204–1210 IEEE (2016)
13. Birglen, L., Laliberté, T., Gosselin, C.: Underactuated Robotic Hands. Springer, Heidelberg (2008). https://doi.org/10.1007/978-3-540-77459-4
14. Seo, J.-T., Yi, B.-J.: Modeling and analysis of a biomimetic foot mechanism, pp. 1472–1477. IEEE (2009)
15. Bicchi, A., Gabiccini, M., Santello, M.: Modelling natural and artificial hands with synergies. Philos. Trans. R. Soc. B. Biol. Sci. **366**, 3153–3161 (2011)
16. Schlafly, M., Reed, K.B.: Novel passive ankle-foot prosthesis mimics able-bodied ankle angles and ground reaction forces. Clin. Biomech. **72**, 202–210 (2020)
17. Nägerl, H., Kubein-Meesenburg, D., Fanghänel, J., Dathe, H., Dumont, C., Wachowski, M.M.: The upper ankle joint: curvature morphology of the articulating surfaces and physiological function. Acta. Bioeng. Biomech. **18** (2016)
18. Schlafly, M., Ramakrishnan, T., Reed, K.: 3D printed passive compliant and articulating prosthetic ankle foot. Am. Soc. Mech. Eng. 1–5 (2017)
19. Schlafly, M.K., Ramakrishnan, T., Reed, K.B.: Biomimetic prosthetic device (2019)
20. Nordin, M.: Basic Biomechanics of the Musculoskeletal System. Lippincott Williams & Wilkins (2020)
21. Honert, E.C., Bastas, G., Zelik, K.E.: Effect of toe joint stiffness and toe shape on walking biomechanics. Bioinspir. Biomim. **13**, 066007 (2018)
22. Raabe, M.E., Chaudhari, A.M.W.: An investigation of jogging biomechanics using the full-body lumbar spine model: model development and validation. J. Biomech. **49**, 1238–1243 (2016)
23. Winter, D.A.: Biomechanical motor patterns in normal walking. J. Mot. Behav. **15**, 302–330 (1983)

Robot Vision and Applications

The Improved YOLOV5 Algorithm and Its Application in Small Target Detection

Yu Zhao⑩, Yuanbo Shi⑩, and Zelong Wang(✉)⑩

Liaoning Petrochemical University, Fushun 113000, China
329265562@qq.com

Abstract. According to the characteristics of YOLOV5, a method based on YOLOV5 is proposed. First, this method is used for the identification of small objects. Secondly, this paper conducts experiments on the improved YOLOV5 algorithm and conducts experiments on it, and compares the performance of the two methods. In modern detection technology, the most commonly used is the target detection technology. In recent years, small object detection has been an important research topic in industrial inspection. The small target has a small number of pixels, and its features are blurred. Larger targets have lower detection rates and higher false detection rates. In order to improve the accuracy and accuracy of target detection, this paper proposes a method based on depthwise convolution and K-means clustering, which realizes the clustering of the dimension and aspect ratio of the target image. On the basis of CCPD, the YOLOv5 algorithm is optimized and compared with the original YOLOv5 algorithm. Experiments show that the improved YOLOv5 can better detect smaller targets, so that the recall rate and average precision of small targets are significantly improved.

Keywords: Machine vision · Small object detection · YOLOv5 · CCPD dataset · K-means clustering algorithm · Mosaic

1 Introduction

At present, it is widely used in military, civil and other aspects. Small target detection is an important research field at home and abroad. Long-distance targets often have small characteristics. Compared with large targets, this method has the characteristics of less pixels, fuzzy parameters, low detection rate and high false alarm rate.

With the development of deep learning technology, a variety of target detection and tracking algorithms based on deep learning are proposed. Deep convolutional neural network can learn target detection dataset independently and improve the model. With the development of computer hardware, graphics processing unit GPU has been widely used, and the calculation speed has been greatly improved, which ensures extensive and in-depth learning and training.

H. Liu et al. (Eds.): ICIRA 2022, LNAI 13458, pp. 679–688, 2022.
https://doi.org/10.1007/978-3-031-13841-6_61

Deep learning method [1] has become the mainstream method of target detection. Among them, R-CNN algorithm [2] is an improved fast region extraction algorithm based on R-CNN algorithm. The first step of R-CNN algorithm is to extract the region, and the second step is to calculate the boundary gradient feature. However, extraction takes up too much disk space. In order to overcome the shortcomings of R-CNN algorithm, a fast R-CNN algorithm is proposed to solve the problem of task loss in multi-layer ROI. Fast-R-CNN algorithm [3] increases the speed of R-CNN algorithm by embedding the extracted area into the depth of the network by adding another branch in the RPN network. However, the calculation is complex and it is difficult to meet the requirements of real-time engineering. Redmon [4] proposed YOLO V2 and YOLO V3 detection algorithms based on YOLO algorithm. In order to overcome the shortcomings of YOLO V3 and YOLO V4, YOLOV5 algorithm was proposed in References [5–7]. The algorithm is much faster than YOLO V3 and YOLO V4, and can achieve 250F/s on V100GPU. It has a high psychological quality, easy to form the environment.

In order to improve the accuracy and recall rate of small target detection, the structure of YOVO5 was improved based on the one-step target detection algorithm of deep convolution neural network YOLOV5, and it was used for training and target detection in CCPD dataset. Based on the original YOLOv5, the Mosaic-8 data are used to enhance and modify the objective equation to improve the convergence accuracy of the model. The results show that the improved network structure can significantly improve the recall rate and accuracy of small target detection.

2   Introduction to YOLOV5 Network

YOLOV5 is the SOTA (state-of-the-art) [9] of the current YOL0 series algorithms. Like other target detection algorithms, it is composed of input, backbone, feature fusion and prediction structures. YOLOV5 contains four models with different widths and depths, namely YOLOv5s, YOLOv5m, YOLOv5I and YOLOv5x. Using the Efficient Net approach [10], the width and depth of each dimension are balanced by a constant throughout the network. In this study, the YOLOv5s network is the smallest depth and smallest feature width in the YOLOv5 series network. Under the premise of ensuring fast and accurate, YOLOV5 algorithm is the most advanced detection network of YOLO target detection algorithm to minimize the network structure and improve the measurement accuracy. The algorithm integration innovation is carried out on the basis of YOLO v3 and YOLO v4 algorithms, which improves the detection speed. YOLOV5 algorithm draws on the idea of anchor boxes, improves the speed of R-CNN algorithm, abandons the manually selected anchor box, and runs K-means clustering on the dimension of boundary box [11] to obtain better prior values (Fig. 1).

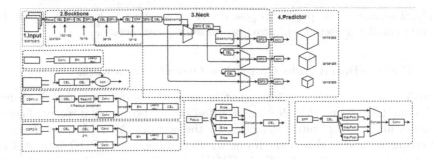

Fig. 1. YOLOV5s network structure.

(1) The input end is composed of Mosaic data enhancement, image size processing and automatic adaptive anchor frame. The input is randomly scaled, cut and arranged by Mosaic data enhancement, and the small target detection effect is better, which is suitable for the detection model in this paper. In the YOLO algorithm, the input image size is changed into a unified size, and then the image is sent to the model for detection. In this paper, the initial setting size is $460 \times 460 \times 3$, and the initial anchor frame of YOLOV5 is [116, 90, 156, 198, 373, 326].

(2) The pillar layer is composed of Focus and CSP. Focus can be cut in the support layer, and the original 608 * 608 * 3 image is segmented into a feature map of $304 \times 304 \times 12$, and then the convolution operation is carried out to obtain the feature map of 32 convolution kernels. YOLOV5 algorithm has two CSP structures. CSPDarknet53 is the basis of YOLOv3 backbone network Draknet. Referring to the pillar layer structure generated by CSPNet in 2019, it can enhance the learning ability of CNN, reduce memory cost and break through the computational bottleneck. With the help of Mish [12] technology, the accuracy of CSP structure can be enhanced. YOLOV5 algorithm and YOLO v4 algorithm adopt the same FPN + PAN structure in the fusion feature layer, but YOLOV5 algorithm adopts CSP2 based on CSPNet, which can strengthen the network feature fusion ability. (3) The fusion feature map adopts the FPN+PAN structure, FPN is top-down, and PAN is the bottom pyramid. FPN uses upsampling to transfer features for feature fusion to obtain feature maps. (4) At the output end, the YOLOV5 algorithm uses GIOU_ Loss as the loss function of the Bounding box. In overlapping target detection, the effect of GIOU_nms is stronger than the traditional nms. At the same time, the YOLOV5 algorithm reasonably uses freebie and specials for tuning processing, AP and The FPS is increased by 7% and 15% respectively, and the optimal target can be obtained.

3   Modified Model of YOLOV5

The focus of this paper is the detection of small targets. The layered grid method of anchor box determined by the original grid method is not suitable for this study. Therefore, this paper proposes a K-means-based clustering method to identify smaller objects by improving the network structure.

3.1   Cluster-Based Data Collection Object Framework

Eurov5 provides us with an idea, that is, an initial candidate block with fixed width and height, and the selection of initial anchor boxes will directly affect the accuracy and speed of target detection by the network. YOLOV5 uses K-means clustering method to cluster the frame width and height of CPDD dataset. Cluster analysis was conducted with AVGIOU as an indicator. Objective Function and Cluster Function of AVGIO.

$$f = \arg\max \frac{\sum\limits_{i=1}^{k} \sum\limits_{j=1}^{n_k} I_{IOU}(b,c)}{n} \tag{1}$$

In the formula: (b) represents the sample, that is, the target of groundtruth; (c) nk represents the number of samples in the kth cluster center, and the number of samples in K cluster centers. (n) represents the total number of samples; (k) represents the number of groups; IOU (b,c) represents the intersection and merging ratio of the center frame and group frames; (i) represents the sample sequence number; j represents the sequence number in the sample set.

Select $K = 1$–9 and compare it with AVGIU to get the correspondence between K and AVGIU, When the value of K increases, its change tends to be stable, and the change of the inflection point can be regarded as the optimal solution. When the K value exceeds 3, the curve begins to become stable, so the anchor boxes number is selected as 3, which can not only accelerate the convergence, but also effectively overcome the error caused by the filter box. The size of the predicted frame is divided into three cluster centers whose width and height are 22, 9, 10, 21, 20, and 19, respectively.

3.2   Improved YOLOV5 Detection Model

In this paper, the YOLOv5 network is improved. The improved overall network structure is shown in Fig. 2, and a 1/4 feature map is added to improve the mining ability of small objects. The loss function uses CIOU [13] to better describe the regression of the target box from three aspects: overlapping area, center distance and aspect ratio. On the basis of the original YOLOv5, Mosaic-8 data is used to enhance and modify the formula of target box regression to improve the convergence accuracy of the model. The Mosaic-8 data enhancement and feature extractor are introduced in detail.

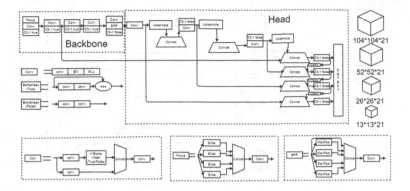

Fig. 2. Improved network structure

Mosaic-8 Data Augmentation

In order to get the neural network model with good performance, a lot of data is needed. However, acquiring new data often requires a lot of time and labor costs, so data enhancement technology emerges as the times require. The advantage of data enhancement is to increase the number of training samples, increase the appropriate noise data, so as to improve the generalization ability of the model. In YOLOv5, besides the basic data enhancement method, we also use Mosaic data enhancement method. The main idea is to randomly cut and amplify the four images, and then randomly arrange and splice them to form images, so as to enrich the data set, increase the small sample target and improve the network training speed. In the standardization process, the data of four images will be calculated at the same time, thus reducing the memory requirements of the model. Mosaic enhancement data processing, using Mosaic 8, Mosaic enhancement technology, eight pictures were randomly cut, randomly arranged, randomly amplified, and merged into a picture to increase the size of the sample. On this basis, we also appropriately introduce some random noise, thereby enhancing the ability to identify small and medium target images, thereby enhancing the generalization performance of the model. Figure 3 shows:

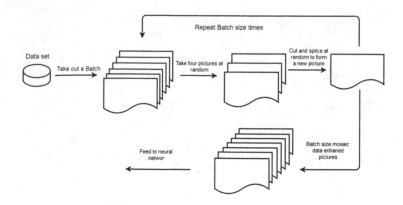

Fig. 3. Mosaic data augmentation process

Feature Extractor

In the backbone network of YOLOv5, three feature maps with different sizes are used to detect targets with different sizes. Among them, eight times of down-sampling, 16 times of down-sampling and 32 times of down-sampling are used to obtain three feature curves with different sizes, and then they are input into the feature fusion network. From the concept of feature pyramid (FPN) [14], although the feature map after deep convolution has a large amount of semantic information, it will lose some position information of the target in multiple convolutions, which is not conducive to the detection of small targets. Through the shallow convolution, the semantic information in the feature map is not much, but the positioning information of the object has high accuracy (Fig. 4).

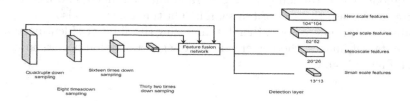

Fig. 4. Original YOLOv5 feature extraction model

Therefore, this paper adds a four-fold down-sampling process to the original input image based on the YOLOv5 backbone network, as shown in Fig. 5. After 4 times down sampling, the original image is sent to the feature fusion network to obtain a new size feature map. The feature map has small receptive field and rich location information, which can improve the detection effect of small targets.

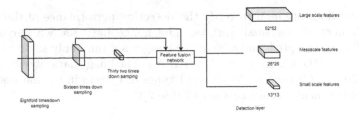

Fig. 5. Improved feature extraction model

4   Experimental Results and Analysis

YOLOv5 performs target detection on multiple tables. This is a representative algorithm that can better consider the target size. Therefore, the improved YOV5 algorithm is compared with the YOV5 target detection algorithm. The improved YOV5 algorithm is compared with the YOV5 algorithm of CCPD dataset. CCPD dataset is the experiment and test of license plate detection and recognition for traditional small dataset. This algorithm is not competent for license plate detection and recognition tasks with environmental changes and angle changes. To this end, a team of China University of Science and Technology established CCPD dataset, which is widely used in domestic vehicle license plate recognition and license plate dataset. The group was also released at the ECCV2018 International Conference.

The data was collected from 7 : 30 a.m. to 10 : 00 p.m. in a parking lot in Hefei. The parking staff used the robot POS machine to photograph the vehicles in the parking lot and manually marked the license plate of the parking lot. License plate images are taken in various complex environments, including blur, tilt, rain, weather, etc. CCPD dataset contains nearly 300,000 images, each of which is $720 \times 1160 \times 3$. Total 8 projects (Table 1):

Table 1. CCPD dataset content table.

Type	Quantity	Explain
ccpd_ base	199998	Normal license plate
ccpd_ base	10006	This more challenging license plate
ccpd_ db	20001	The light is darker or brighter
ccpd_ fn	19999	Far or close to the camera
ccpd_ np	3036	An unlicensed new car
ccpd_ rotate	9998	Horizontal tilt 20–50°, vertical tilt - 10-10°
ccpd_ tilt	10000	The license plate of a rainy day, day, or day
ccpd_ weather	9999	The license plate of a rainy day, day, or day
All: 283037 license plate image		

Two methods are used to verify the detection performance of the improved YOLOV5 network for small targets. The image data set with resolution of $460 \times 460 \times 3$ is adopted, and 80% of the images are randomly selected for training, and 20% of the images are used for testing. The image dataset with resolution of $304 \times 304 \times 12$ is used to detect eight types of targets in the dataset.

The experimental conditions are (Table 2):

Table 2. Experimental equipment content

Name	Environmental parameters
Operating system	Windows10 64 bit
CPU	11th Gen Intel(R) Core(TM) i7-11700F CPU @ 2.50 GHz
GPU	GeForce RTX 3080 Ti
Memory	32 GB
Python	3.8

4.1   Training of the Network

YOLOV5 and YOLOV5 were tested. In the training phase, the learning rate and attenuation factor of beginners are 0.001 and 0.0005 respectively. To further converge, the learning rate is reduced to 0.0001 and 0.00001. By rotating the image and increasing the contrast, the data set can be enhanced and expanded. After 20,000 repeated calculations, each parameter tended to be stable, and the final loss decreased to 0.23. AVGIU gradually approached 1 and hovered around 0.88. Through the parameter convergence analysis of YOLOV5, the effectiveness of the algorithm is proved.

4.2   Network Test

Experiment

Eight minimum targets are classified into one class, and two different networks are tested, and their recall rate and detection accuracy are calculated. The target recovery R and detection accuracy P can be expressed as follows

$$R = \frac{X_{TP}}{X_{TP} + X_{FN}} \tag{2}$$

$$R = \frac{X_{TP}}{X_{TP} + X_{FP}} \tag{3}$$

In the formula: the number of targets measured; represents the number of targets not detected; represents the number of targets detected. In 885 pictures, a total of 1689 measured objects were measured. The CCPD data were measured by two methods, and the R value and P value were obtained, and the corresponding results were given. Comparison of different detection methods in Table 3.

Table 3. Comparison of precision and recall between YOLOV5 and the improved YOLOV5 algorithm

Detection algorithom	X_{TP}	X_{FP}	X_{FN}	P/%	R/%
YOLOV5	367	65	55	84.3	86.5
Improve YOLOV5	400	55	37	87.5	93.1

Compared with YOLOV5 algorithm, the improved YOLOV5 algorithm improves the small target detection accuracy from 84.3% to 87.5%, and the recall rate from 86.5% to 93.1%. The average accuracy of small target detection is calculated by using two networks on CCPD dataset. The average accuracy is measured from the accuracy of corner detection algorithm and recall accuracy. It is a visual evaluation standard for evaluating the accuracy of detection model, and can be used for the analysis of single-class detection effect [15]. The test results show that the target detection accuracy of the improved YOLOV5 network is further improved.

5   Epilogue

Based on the original YOV5 algorithm, this paper adopts the improved YOLOV5 algorithm to improve the data splicing algorithm and the feature extraction algorithm, so as to effectively improve the accuracy of YOV5 network model for small target detection. The detection rate of the improved algorithm is lower than that of the original YOLOv5. Compared with other network models through continuous training of filtering frame, convolution layer and input layer, the improved YOLO-V5 detection training results have higher recognition accuracy and faster recognition speed, and provide better reference effect. Next, we will collect more large-scale data to improve network versatility and achieve better results.

References

1. Leifeng, C., Lisa, H., Lihui, X., et al.: Target behavior knowledge discovery method based on deep learning. Comput. Digital Eng. **50**(03), 532–537 (2022)
2. Shi, L., Jing, M.E., Fan, Y.B., et al.: Segmentation detection algorithm based on R-CNN algorithm. J. Fudan Univ. (Nat. Sci. Ed.) **59**(04), 412–418 (2020)
3. Zhiyong, S., Jiahui, G.: Vehicle target detection based on improved fast R-CNN. Mod. Comput. **20**, 74–79 (2021). https://doi.org/10.3969/j.issn.1007-1423.2021.20.015
4. Denig, W.F.: The international council for science world data system stewardship award 2014 presented to Dr. Robert Redmon of the national geophysical data center. Space Weather **13**(1), 1 (2015). https://doi.org/10.1002/2014SW001136
5. Lei, G., Qiulong, W., Wei, X., et al.: Small target detection algorithm based on improved YOLOv5. J. Univ. Electron. Sci. Technol. **51**(2), 251–258 (2022). https://doi.org/10.12178/1001-0548.2021235

6. Cheng, L.: Research on small target detection algorithm based on improved YOLOv5. Changjiang Inf. Commun. **34**(9), 30–33 (2021). https://doi.org/10.3969/j.issn.1673-1131.2021.09.010

7. Deshuo, K., Wanmi, C., Nan, Y.: Target recognition algorithm of service robot based on improved YOLOv5. Ind. Control Comput. **35**(2), 82–83 (2022). https://doi.org/10.3969/j.issn.1001-182X.2022.02.032

8. Shixiong, W., Mingwu, Y., Zhilian, G., et al.: A photoelastic data acquisition and processing system. J. Hefei Univ. Technol. (Nat. Sci. Ed.), (S1), 71–73 (1993)

9. Krebs, E.E.: VA state of the art (SOTA) conference on non-pharmacological approaches to chronic musculoskeletal pain management. Ann. Behav. Med. **51**(suppl.1), S2364–S2365 (2017)

10. Wang, Z.L.: An effective model detection method based on LTL and petri nets. Comput. Appl. **26**(10), 2490–2493 (2006)

11. Changming, L., Hongchen, Z., Chao, W., et al.: An efficient Yin Yang K-means clustering algorithm. J. Jilin Univ. (Sci. Ed.) **59**(6), 1455–1460 (2021). https://doi.org/10.13413/j.cnki.jdxblxb.2020406

12. Liao, Q., Jiang, Y., Le, Q., et al.: Hot deformation behavior and processing map development of AZ110 alloy with and without addition of La-rich Mish Metal. Mater. Sci. Technol. (Engl. Version) **61**(2), 1–15 (2021)

13. Fengdi, L., Weixing, S., Jiefang, W., et al.: Study on detection method of pine wood nematode disease tree based on YOLOv3 CIOU. J. Shandong Agric. Univ. (Nat. Sci. Ed.) **52**(2), 224–233 (2021). https://doi.org/10.3969/j.issn.1000-2324.2021.02.012

14. Qifan, G., Lei, L., Lei, Z., et al.: Multi-scale feature fusion network based on feature pyramid. J. Eng. Math. **37**(5), 521–530 (2020)

15. Yaqian, L., Chengyuan, G., Cunjun, X., et al.: Target detection network based on refined multi-scale depth features. Acta Electron. Sin. **48**(12), 2360–2366 (2020). https://doi.org/10.3969/j.issn.0372-2112.2020.12.011

Workpiece Detection of Robot Training Platform Based on YOLOX

Siting Chen and Dianyong Yu[✉]

Harbin Institute of Technology, Harbin, China
dyyu@hit.edu.cn

Abstract. The industrial robot training platform is close to the industrial field environment, which enables students to comprehensively learn and master robot application skills, among which machine vision is an important part of industrial robot. Machine vision can be applied to workpiece completion detection. Therefore, based on the YOLOX model, the activation function is improved by multi-scale detection so that the image feature information can be better extracted, so as to train the coupling tooling and distinguish four different tooling. The results show that the mAP value of the improved YOLOX algorithm is 100%, and the accuracy of the improved YOLOX algorithm is obviously improved compared with that before the improvement, indicating that the improved YOLOX algorithm has a good effect.

Keywords: Robot training platform · YOLOX

1 Introduce

Teaching practice platform is a truly, in the service of the practice teaching system of robot application platform construction, set the current robot typical industrial application cases, industrial design, advanced manufacturing, automated industrial equipment, industrial control system completely, close to the industrial field environment, can let students comprehensive skills and control of robot applications. Set digital control, PDM (product data management), MES (processing and Manufacturing execution system), automation control, robot application, industrial configuration software and human-computer interaction, modern logistics and other technologies to ensure the advanced and leading nature of the base. The system adopts modular design, in the actual teaching application, ensure that each module can run separately, convenient for students' cognition - participation - integration of cyclic gradual learning and practice training. Through the construction of the platform and the reasonable integration of different structures, it can be deduced into different elective courses, teaching material construction, training system construction, skill appraisal, etc. At the same time, it can be built into a demonstration innovative teaching platform.

The construction of the platform fully considers the development trend in the next few years, and is in line with the development trend of manufacturing industry, information

---

This paper is based on the national key research and development project (2019YFB1312602).

H. Liu et al. (Eds.): ICIRA 2022, LNAI 13458, pp. 689–699, 2022.
https://doi.org/10.1007/978-3-031-13841-6_62

development and construction, and the goal of training high-skilled personnel, so as to become a leading robot teaching platform in China and play a radiation role.

Machine vision module is an important module on the training platform of industrial robots. This paper conducts deep learning training based on YOLOX network to train and learn the workpiece installed on the robot training platform, detect the completion degree of the workpiece installed, and give feedback to the operator. Make the operator familiar with and master the machine vision module on the robot training platform. YOLO series [1, 2, 4–6] of algorithms perform well in target detection and transform the target detection problem into regression problem. In 2021, Megvii technology Company proposed the YOLOX algorithm, which was improved based on the YOLO series and proposed five standard networks, namely, Yolox-S, Yolox-M, Yolox-L, Yolox-X and Yolox-Darknet53. Two lightweight networks, YOLOX-Nano and YOLOX-Tiny, are proposed. In this paper, yolox-S calibration network is improved and used to identify coupling tooling. In this paper, based on the YOLOX model, the activation function is improved by multi-scale detection so that the image feature information can be better extracted, so as to train the coupling tooling and distinguish four different tooling. The results show that the mAP value of the improved YOLOX algorithm is 100%, and the accuracy of the improved YOLOX algorithm is obviously improved compared with that before the improvement, indicating that the improved YOLOX algorithm has a good effect.

2 YOLOX Algorithm Model

Yolox-S is improved on the basis of YOLOV5-S [2], and consists of four parts: input end, main network, neck end and prediction end. Its network structure is shown in Fig. 1.

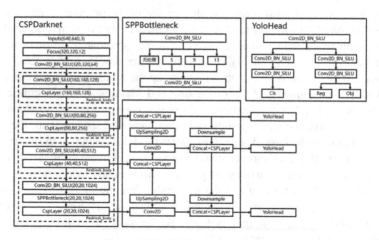

Fig. 1. YOLOX-S structure diagram

2.1 Input

The input terminal of YOLOX-S mainly filters and marks pictures, adjusts them to RGB format, scales them to a fixed size and sends them to the backbone network.

2.2 Trunk Network

The main part mainly adopts Focus network structure, Cross Stage Partial (CSP) network structure and Spatial Pyramid Pooling (SPP) network structure.

Focus. The input image of $640 \times 640 \times 3$ becomes a feature graph of $320 \times 320 \times 12$ through slicing operation, and then becomes a feature graph of $320 \times 320 \times 64$ through 64 convolutional kernels. The structure of Focus network is shown in Fig. 2.

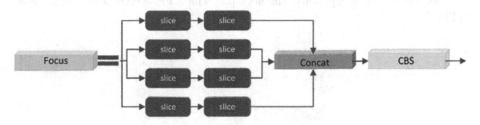

Fig. 2. Focus structure diagram

CSP. Yolox-s designed two kinds of CSP networks, namely CSP1_X [7] structure and CSP2_X structure. The CSP1_X structure is applied to the backbone network, which consists of two branches. One branch is stacked by X Bottleneck modules, and the other branch is only processed by the convolution layer. The two branches are then connected through a convolutional layer to increase the network depth and enhance feature extraction capability. The STRUCTURE of CSP1_X is shown in Fig. 3.

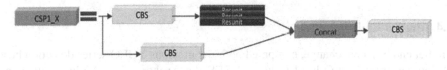

Fig. 3. CSP1_X structure

SPP. SPP [1, 2] structure mainly increases the perceived field of the network through feature extraction in different pooling layers, so as to integrate more feature information. The maximum pooling layer of $1 \times 1, 5 \times 5, 9 \times 9$ and 13×13 scales is mainly used to extract image features. The SPP structure is shown in Fig. 4.

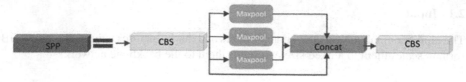

Fig. 4. SPP structure

2.3   The Neck

Feature Pyramid Networks (FPN) structure conveys semantic features from top to bottom through up-sampling and fusion with the underlying features. The bottom-up structure of Pyramid Attention Network (PAN) conveys location features by integrating bottom-up sampling with upper-level features. The simultaneous use of both can enhance the network feature fusion capability. The neck part adopts FPN+PAN structure, as shown in Fig. 5.

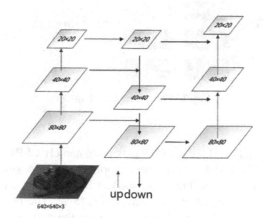

Fig. 5. FPN + PAN structure

2.4   Predict End

Predict end has a big change, compared with the previous YOLO series detection head) Decoupled from YOLO head to head, USES the Anchor - free, Multi positives and SimOTA way.

Decoupled Head. While the O series' backbone and features are being improved, the sensor is still coupled, and it may degrade performance against the YOLOX algorithm coupling head. After changing YOLO head to Goldman sachs head, the two parallel branches, the speed of convergence improved significantly. Decoupled head structure is shown in Fig. 6.

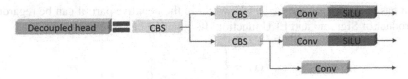

Fig. 6. Decoupled head structure

Anchor Free. Anchor-based is used in both YOLOv3 [6] and YOLOv5, but anchor-based has problems such as designing Anchor points in advance, intensive sampling of images and containing too much negative sample information. YOLOX adopts anchor-free [3, 8, 9] mode to reduce the number of predictions for each position from 3 to 1, and let them simultaneously predict the two offsets in the upper left corner of the grid and the height and width of the prediction box. At the same time, the center of each object is taken as a positive sample, and a range of standard points is defined in advance to determine the FPN level of each object. This method reduces the parameters and Giga Floating-point Operations (GFLOPs) of the detector, and improves the transfer speed and performance.

Many Positives. As the anchor-free allows only one positive sample to be selected for each picture, the number of positive and negative samples may not match. In this study, the 3 × 3 region of the grid with Multi positives was assigned as a positive sample to improve the performance of the model.

SimOTA. SimOTA is an improvement based on Optimal Transport Assignment (OTA) proposed by Kuangshi Technology. OTA solves the problem of unreasonable allocation of different targets with the same number of positive samples by transforming the label allocation process into Optimal Transport (OT). If the Sinkhorn-Knopp algorithm is simplified into a dynamic top-K strategy, the training time can be shortened by 25% and the recognition accuracy can be improved.

3 YOLOX Algorithm Improvement

3.1 Activation Function Improvement

The activation function used in YOLOX is SiLU, an improved version of Sigmoid function, which has no upper bound, lower bound, smooth and non-monotone characteristics. Non-monotone can be distinguished from other activation functions. Its function can be expressed as:

$$y(x) = \frac{x}{1 + e^{-x}} \tag{1}$$

The ELiSH activation function adopts the idea of crossover operator, which can better improve the information flow and avoid the disappearance of gradient. In the positive part, it has the same property as SiLU, while in the negative part, it can be regarded as the product of Sigmoid and ELU function. Its function can be expressed as:

$$y(x) = \begin{cases} \frac{x}{1+e^{-x}}, & x \geq 0 \\ \frac{e^x - 1}{1+e^{-x}}, & x < 0 \end{cases} \qquad (2)$$

Cifar-10 and ImageNet datasets were trained in Resnet56 and VGG-16 networks, and the ELiSH activation function had better results than the SiLU activation function. The ELiSH piecewise mixed activation function combines the SiLU, ELU, and Sigmoid functions, as shown in Fig. 7. It can inherit genes from three activation functions at the same time, and has a better classification effect for DNN.

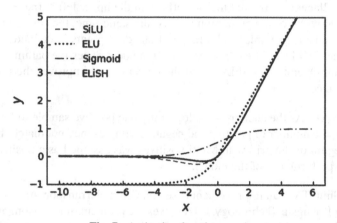

Fig. 7. Activation function graph

As for the Conv2D Batch Normalization Normalization plus activation function of the convolution block CBS (CBS), after replacing the SiLU activation function with ELiSH activation function, the convolution block CBS also becomes the convolution block CBE, as shown in Fig. 8.

Fig. 8. Convolution of the CBE

3.2 Improved Multi-scale Detection

In YOLOX algorithm, the detection scale of pled head is $80 \times 80 \times 256$, $40 \times 40 \times 512$, and $20 \times 20 \times 1024$. In addition to the overall contour, the identification of tomato diseased leaves also needs to better deal with the details of regionalization, that is, to increase the utilization of deep network by adding a scale, so as to improve the identification effect of tomato diseased leaves. The feature detection of the four scales is shown in Fig. 9. At this point, after the SPP module is processed by THE CSP network, the convolution block CBE is used to carry out the convolution standardization plus the activation function. Through the CSP network, the up-sampling, down-sampling and the new feature layer are added for fusion. Four scales of $80 \times 80 \times 256$, $40 \times 40 \times 512$, $20 \times 20 \times 1024$ and $10 \times 10 \times 2048$ were obtained.

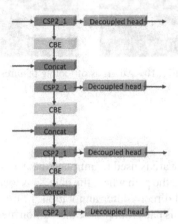

Fig. 9. Feature detection at 4 scales

4 Data Collection and Preprocessing

4.1 The Data Collection

The workpiece data set in this paper is collected from the robot training platform, including images of normal installation, unqualified installation, missing parts and missing tooling. In this paper, 5872 training sets, 653 test sets and 725 verification sets are selected from various images, and a total of 7250 images are selected as the data set of this paper. The selected quantity and label names of each type of workpiece are shown in Table 1.

Table 1. Tooling category, label name and number of images selected

Category	Tag name	Number of pictures/piece
Installation of qualified	Good	1812
Nonconforming installation	Bad	1812
Lack of parts	Lack	1813
Lack of tooling	None	1811

Pictures of different types of workpiece installation are shown in Fig. 10. It can be seen from the figure that parts installation corresponding to different workpiece is different, which is presented on the image in the form of different clearance and missing parts, which is easy to be trained and recognized by the algorithm.

Fig. 10. All kinds of tooling pictures

4.2 Data Preprocessing

In this paper, labelImg software is used to annotate the data set. In this software, the file can be annotated by opening the path where the data set is located, and the corresponding XML file can be generated directly after annotation. In this data set, there is only one state for each workpiece. This paper adopts the annotation method of including the whole workpiece, as shown in Fig. 11, to input the installation features of the workpiece into the network as much as possible, so that the model can better identify the installation state and improve the generalization ability of the network.

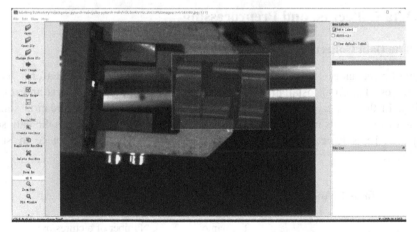

Fig. 11. The workpiece is installed with labelImg annotations

5 Results Analysis

5.1 The Evaluation Index

Generally, mean Average Precision (mAP) and Average Precision (AP) are selected as experimental evaluation indexes for target detection. MAP and AP need to be calculated according to the Precision and Recall of model training samples, and the calculation is as follows:

$$Precision = \frac{TP}{TP + FP} \times 100\% \tag{3}$$

$$Recall = \frac{TP}{TP + FN} \times 100\% \tag{4}$$

In the formula, TP represents positive samples of correct detection, FP represents negative samples of error detection, and FN represents positive samples of error detection. The average accuracy AP is obtained from the area enclosed by p-R curve and coordinate axis, and the calculation formula is as follows:

$$AP = \int_{0}^{1} Precision \; dRecall \tag{5}$$

Average accuracy mAP is the average value of AP of all categories, which can be shown as:

$$mAP = \frac{1}{n} \sum_{i=1}^{n} AP_i \tag{6}$$

where, n is the number of sample categories, and I is the current number.

5.2 Experimental Results and Analysis

The input image size of this training is 640×640, and the initial learning rate is 0.001 and the minimum learning rate is 0.000 1. After 100 iterations of training, the tooling is identified. The results show that the recognition accuracy of four kinds of tooling is high. Through the verification set of 725 pictures, the AP value of the tool recognition is predicted, and the accuracy values of the four types of tools are obtained as shown in Fig. 12. The prediction results show that the accuracy of the four types of tools is above 0.9, indicating that the trained model has good recognition effect.

After the improved YOLOX algorithm is trained on the tooling image, its AP values for the four types of tooling are shown in Fig. 13. According to Formula (6), the mAP value of the improved YOLOX algorithm is 100%, indicating that the performance of the improved YOLOX algorithm is improved.

In order to verify the advanced nature of the improved YOLOX algorithm, EfficientDet, SSD, YOLOv3 and YOLOv4 algorithms were compared on the same training platform with the same data set. The experimental results are shown in Table 2. Table 2 results show that improved YOLOX still performs better than other mainstream algorithms, and AP values of most blades are improved. Its mAP value is 12.37, 8.81, 11.19

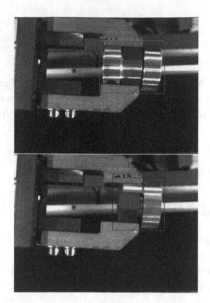
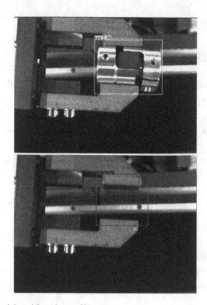

Fig. 12. Four types of tooling identification effects

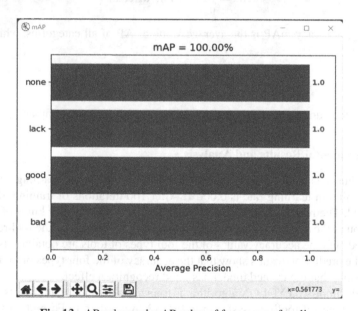

Fig. 13. AP value and mAP value of four types of tooling

and 8.95 percentage points higher than that of YOLOv3, SSD and YOLOv4 algorithms, respectively. In conclusion, the improved YOLOX algorithm can effectively identify the coupling fixture, which can be applied to the robot training platform to help industrial robot learners understand the relevant technology of machine vision.

Table 2. Identification results of four types of tooling by different algorithm models

Algorithm model	Four types of tooling identification results				mAP/%
	Good	Bad	Lack	None	
EfficientDet	88.83	92.49	85.55	83.66	87.63
SSD	88.92	94.16	92.18	89.48	91.19
YOLOv3	94.74	86.94	82.88	90.69	88.81
YOLOv4	93.26	91.76	86.21	92.95	91.05
Improved YOLOX	100	100	100	100	100

6 Conclusion

Based on the data collected by the robot training platform, 7250 pictures are selected as the data set. Based on the Yolox-S algorithm model, YOLOX is improved to improve the accuracy of coupling fixture identification. By introducing a new activation function ELiSH and using four scales to detect the image, the mAP value of the improved YOLOX algorithm is significantly improved compared with the original one, indicating that the improved YOLOX algorithm has a good effect on the workpiece. At the same time, there is still more room for improvement of YOLOX algorithm, and further research is needed to improve the detection speed and accuracy of the algorithm.

References

1. Bochkovskiy, A., Wang, C. Y., Liao, H.Y.M.: YOLOv4: optimal speed and accuracy of object detection. arXiv preprint arXiv:2004.10934 (2020)
2. Jocher, G., et al.: YOLOv5. https://github.com/ultralytics/yolov5 (2021)
3. Law, H., Deng, J.: CornerNet: detecting objects aspaired keypoints. In: ECCV (2018)
4. Redmon, J., Divvala, S., Girshick, R., Farhadi, A.: You only look once: unified, real-time object detection. In: CPPR (2016)
5. Redmon, J., Farhadi, A.: YOLO9000: better, faster, stronger. In: CVPR (2017)
6. Redmon, J., Farhadi, A.: YOLOv3: an incremental improvement. arXiv preprint arXiv:1804. 02767 (2018)
7. Wang, C.-Y., Liao, H.-Y.M., Wu, Y.-H., Chen, P.-Y., Hsieh, J.-W., Yeh, I.-H.: CSPNet: a new backbone that can enhance learning capability of CNN. In: CVPR Workshops (2020)
8. Tian, Z., Shen, C., Chen, H., He, T.: FCOS: fully convolutional one-stage object detection. In: ICCV (2019)
9. Zhou, X., Wang, D., Krähenbühl, P.: Objects as points. arXiv preprint arXiv:1904.07850 (2019)

Detecting Temporal Pain Status of Postoperative Children from Facial Expression

Wenhao Wu[1], Lei Bi[2], Weihong Ren[1], Wei Nie[1], Ruihan Lin[1], Zuode Liu[1], Sufang Li[3(✉)], Xi Lin[4], and Honghai Liu[1(✉)]

[1] School of Mechanical Engineering and Automation, Harbin Institute of Technology, Shenzhen, China
honghai.liu@hit.edu.cn
[2] Operating Theatre, Shenzhen Children's Hospital, Shenzhen, China
[3] Nursing Department, Shenzhen Children's Hospital, Shenzhen, China
[4] School of Materials Science and Engineering, Harbin Institute of Technology, Shenzhen, China

Abstract. Insufficient analgesia during resuscitation of postoperative children may lead to sequelae such as atelectasis and worsening respiratory function, so timely and accurate detection of pain status in children is essential. At present, the pain status of children is mainly judged by nurses based on facial pain expression scales, which is highly subjective. At the same time, with the increasing shortage of medical resources, untimely detection of pain in children often occurs. In this paper, We built an automatic detection system to detect the pain state of children in real-time, which significantly reduced the workload of medical staff. Specifically, we first design a set of highly flexible facial expression acquisition devices, and then we build a children facial pain expression dataset with the help of clinical experts. After that, we propose an end-to-end children pain detection network, which can automatically evaluate the pain status of children in real-time in an end-to-end framework. Experimental results demonstrate that the evaluation accuracy of the proposed network is higher than that of untrained volunteers and is comparable to the results of clinical experts.

Keywords: Children · Postoperative pain · Pain expression · Pain intensity

1 Introduction

After surgery, children will be transferred to the resuscitation room for postoperative observation under the care of nurses. During the resuscitation process, some children will experience the pain of varying degrees. [29] shows that one-third of hospitalized children had moderate and severe pain. [28] reported moderate and higher levels of pain in children in the postoperative period.

Postoperative pain management is essential to improve patient comfort and ensure a better postoperative experience [4]. The main issue with pain management in children is the difficulty involved in evaluating it. When the pain

H. Liu et al. (Eds.): ICIRA 2022, LNAI 13458, pp. 700–711, 2022.
https://doi.org/10.1007/978-3-031-13841-6_63

level of children cannot be accurately assessed, effective analgesia cannot be prescribed [41]. This complication may ultimately lead to an increased hospital stay, reduced quality of life, surgical failure, and immunosuppression because of long-term stress [9,16]. The available literature documents the harmful physiological effects of pain on young patients [11,24], as well as the beneficial results of adequate analgesia in children [26]. So precise postoperative pain detection in children is critical and should employ a structured monitoring approach and frequent reassessment until comfort is achieved.

Currently, the commonly available method for pain assessment is a combination of patient self-report, external observation by medical personnel, and physiological tests [34]. Among them, patient self-report refers to the assessment of pain intensity by patients themselves through various scales, such as the visual analog scale, verbal rating scale and numerical rating scale. These scales are valid, reliable and appropriate for use in monitoring postoperative pain in patients who are able to self-report [3]. Nevertheless, it is unsuitable for neonates and preverbal children who cannot express their pain state as accurately as adults. Meanwhile, physiological tests require the use and possession of sophisticated equipment that may not always be available [21].

Therefore, for children - especially young children - the most simple and intuitive assessment method is for nurses to evaluate the pain status of children according to their facial pain expressions and behaviors, but this method also has drawbacks, its assessment results are highly subjective, so the standard is difficult to unify. Due to this, an automated system for postoperative pain status detection of children could improve safety during resuscitation while reducing the burden on nurses.

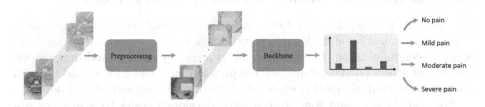

Fig. 1. The overall architecture of the proposed classification network

In this paper, we propose a pain detecting system for postoperative children to realize real-time automatic monitoring of their pain status and promptly notify medical staff when children experience pain. To this end, we first built a set of facial image acquisition equipment. Then, we acquire images of many postoperative children and selected 15 of them to present a new dataset that we call a Facial Pain Expression Dataset of Children (FPE-C). The dataset includes 26070 photos with 4 labels annotated by clinical experts, namely No pain, Mild pain, Moderate pain and Severe pain. Meanwhile, we propose an end-to-end classification network incorporating a multi-head attention mechanism called Pain Detection Network (PDN), which can automatically monitor facial pain expressions of children in real-time and output pain levels, The overall architecture of PDN is shown in Fig. 1.

The main contributions of our work are summarized as follows:

(1) We propose an automatic pain detection system for facial pain expressions of children, which can replace manual detection, thus significantly improving the efficiency and stability.
(2) We create a facial pain expressions dataset of children (FPE-C), containing 28,976 photos of 15 children, all annotated by clinical experts.
(3) The results of the leave-one-out experiment show that our pain detection network can achieve a recognition accuracy of 84.9%, which is higher than that of volunteers, and is comparable to the results of nurses.

The rest of the paper is organized as follows. Section 2 reviews related literature on postoperative pain assessment methods for children and facial pain expression recognition, focusing on the deep learning method. Afterward, Sect. 3 describes the proposed method in detail. Section 4 then presents the experimental evaluation results followed by closing remarks in Sect. 5.

2   Related Works

This section briefly reviews related work in postoperative pain assessment methods for children and facial pain expression recognition using deep neural networks.

2.1   Pain Assessment Method of Children Facial Expression

Facial expressions are the most direct and primary social signals in human emotional communication and play an essential role in pain assessment. As a form of social communication, facial expression can convey distress and may recruit the help of others [7]. Therefore, facial expression has been widely used for pain assessment in clinical practice, especially for nonverbal patients like children.

For many years, numerous studies have developed scales to assess postoperative pain levels in children, and almost all of these include an assessment of facial expressions. For example, the Children's Hospital of Eastern Ontario Pain Scale (CHEOPS) [22] divides the postoperative expressions of one to seven-year-olds into three categories: smiling, composed and grimace. Children and Infants Postoperative Pain Scale (CHIPPS) [5] classifies postoperative expressions of infants and children under five years into relaxed/smiling, wry mouth, and grimace (mouth and eyes). Neonatal Infant Pain Scale (NIPS) also divides the pain expressions of infants into three levels. The Wong-Baker FACES® Pain Rating Scale (Fig. 2) represents 6 faces [35,36], with scores ranging from 0 to 10 [0 = no pain and 3 = strong level of pain]. On this basis, the patient aged three and older choose the face that best describes his/her level of pain. The Oucher Scale [2] also contains 6 pictures of different pain levels, and the scale has the advantage of being available in different ethnic versions, such as examples for white, black, and Hispanic children. Similarly, researchers developed the Face, Legs, Activity, Cry and Consolability (FLAAC) scale [32] for children two months to seven years of age and the Numeric Rating Scale (NRS) [15] for children over eight years old. In addition, the Visual Analogue Scale (VAS) [12] for children over the age of three, the Poker Chip Tool for children over three years of age, Faces Pain Scale-Revised (FPS-R) [14] for children over four years old. In general, various scales are widely used in clinical practice. For children under anesthesia or under the age of five, behavioral scales such as CHEOPS and FLACC should be used because patient self-assessment is not required. For children over five years of age who can describe their pain intensity, scales such as the Oucher scale and the Wong-Baker FACES® scale is recommended [41].

After analyzing the existing pain scales with doctors, we believe that it is more appropriate to classify postoperative pain of children into four levels, which can provide a practical reference for doctors while ensuring the robustness of the network. Therefore, we combine 2 and 4, 6 and 8 in the Wong-Baker FACES® scale to form a four-category scale as the standard for image annotation.

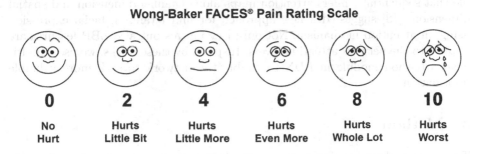

Fig. 2. Wong-Baker FACES pain rating scale

2.2 Deep Facial Pain Expression Recognition

Facial expression recognition (FER) is a technology that uses computers to recognize facial expressions automatically. Recently, Convolutional Neural Network (CNN) has been successfully extended to the identification of facial expression and achieved good performance [6,33]. But most studies aim to analyze and classify a given facial image into several emotion types, such as angry, disgust, fear, happy, sad, and surprise. [10,19,23,27] Of the existing methods of automatic expression analysis, only a few methods focused on pain detection in children. This can be attributed to the lack of publicly-available datasets. Another reason is that the faces of children are not fully developed, so their facial muscle movements are different from adults. [30] used optical flow to estimate motion trajectories of the entire image to determine whether a premature infant has a painful expression [17] implemented detection of uncomfortable expressions in infants using R-CNN and HMM [38] proposed a new pipeline for pain expression recognition in neonates using transfer learning. Most of the above methods are only used to determine whether there is a pain expression but cannot provide a clinical reference. [1] proposed a new enhanced deep neural network framework designed for the effective detection of pain intensity, which can estimate four different levels of pain.

2.3   Multi-head Attention Mechanism

The attention mechanism has been widely used in visual perception in recent years. [25,39,40] In a picture containing massive information, people can quickly locate the regions of interest through the attention mechanism. Inspired by this, researchers introduced the attention mechanism into the convolutional neural network [6,20]. [31] proposed a new simple network architecture based solely on attention mechanisms, called the Transformer. [37] present a module that sequentially infers attention maps along channel dimension and spatial dimension. [18] suggested a new approach for understanding facial expression using an attention mechanism. Not only raw images but also LBP features are applied to the network attention layers. Inspired by these works, we use a multi-head attention module in PDN to enable the network to seek more valuable information.

3   Method

To realize real-time monitoring of pain status, we propose an automatic pain expressions monitoring system for children, including facial image acquisition and pain expression analysis. In this section, we first introduce the acquisition scene and procedure. After that, we detail our proposed analysis algorithm called Pain Detection Network (PDN).

3.1   Facial Image Acquisition

Acquisition Scene. The acquisition process was carried out after the child was transferred to the resuscitation room with a mobile bed, which means that position of the child was not fixed. At the same time, children have different heights and postures, so we have adopted a highly flexible acquisition system. In the acquisition scene, a 2-DOF gimbal camera that can automatically track the face of a child was fixed on a tripod. The system will preprocess the facial image captured by the camera and display it on the side screen so that nurses can check it at any time. At the same time, we set up a Bluetooth controller, and nurses can control the entire acquisition process only through the controller. Finally, there is an alarm to alert the nurse if the child is in pain. This scene is shown in Fig. 3.

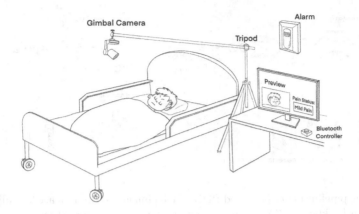

Fig. 3. The acquisition scene

Acquisition Procedure. To automatically monitor the pain status of children and provide timely feedback, specific paradigms and experimental sites were designed. In addition, we have simplified the operation procedure to improve the convenience of the system, which is given as follows.

1) Children are transferred to the resuscitation room and placed in the detecting area. The nurse adjusts the camera to make sure the face of the child is in the center of the frame.
2) The nurse presses the start button on the Bluetooth switch, and the system starts to work. The screen will display the facial image of the child and the corresponding pain status calculated by the detection algorithm in real-time.
3) When the child is in pain, an early warning will be given to notify the nurse to check the pain status of the child.

3.2 Pain Expression Analysis

Our Pain Detection Network (PDN) is built upon CNNs and consists of three crucial parts: i) feature extraction, ii) multi-head attention, and iii) feature classification, as shown in Fig. 4.

Pain expression is localized in the facial region, whereas images contain extensive irrelevant information. Due to this, Face detection is performed first. Next, we use the RetinaFace network to obtain the facial landmarks of children, then align and crop the facial images to the same size according to these facial landmark locations.

Next, we construct a facial feature extractor for the proposed PDN. Since there is a certain similarity between emotional expression recognition and pain expression recognition, we pre-train a facial expression recognition network using ResNet-18 to extract deep features of images.

Since facial pain expressions involve multiple action units, we use a multi-head attention mechanism to get the network to focus on different facial regions

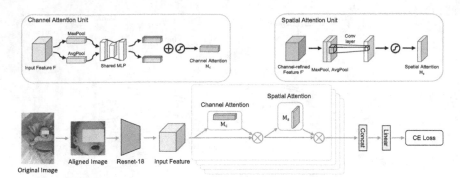

Fig. 4. The pipeline of our proposed PDN. Facial images of children are first aligned and then into a backbone CNN for feature extraction. Multi-head attention module then concerns multiple facial regions concurrently to refine the feature. Next, we concatenate and linearize the features extracted by each attention head. Finally, the cross-entropy loss is used for feature classification

associated with expressions of pain. The advantage of the multi-head attention mechanism is that different types of information can be jointly extracted from multiple representation subspaces.

More concretely, we use four attention heads, each including a channel attention unit and a spatial attention unit. The channel attention focuses on the channel information of a given input image, while the spatial attention focuses on the position information of the information part, which is complementary to the channel attention. As shown in Fig. 4, channel attention unit use both average-pooling and max-pooling operations simultaneously, generating average-pooled features F_{avg}^c and max-pooled features F_{max}^c, both are then fed into a share multi-layer perceptron (MLP). The channel attention map is computed as:

$$M_c(F) = \sigma(W(F_{avg}^c) + W(F_{max}^c)), \tag{1}$$

where σ is a sigmoid function, W are the parameters of MLP.

The spatial attention unit applies average-pooling and max-pooling operations along the channel axis to the input features, resulting in two 2-dimensional maps, $F_{avg}^s \in \mathbb{R}^{1 \times H \times W}$ and $F_{max}^s \in \mathbb{R}^{1 \times H \times W}$, respectively. Then they are concatenated, and a convolution operation with the filter size of 7×7 is performed to obtain the spatial attention map, which can be calculated as:

$$M_s(F) = \sigma(f([F_{avg}^s; F_{max}^s]), \tag{2}$$

where σ is a sigmoid function, f represents the convolution operation.

In general, after inputting a feature map $F \in \mathbb{R}^{C \times H \times W}$, the channel attention module and the spatial attention module will generate a one-dimensional attention map $M_c \in \mathbb{R}^{C \times 1 \times 1}$ and a two 2-dimensional map $M_s \in \mathbb{R}^{1 \times H \times W}$ in sequence, and the refined output of the channel attention module F' and the final refined output F'' can be summarized as:

$$F' = M_c(F) \otimes F, \tag{3}$$

$$F'' = M_s(F') \otimes F', \tag{4}$$

Then, we concatenate the partial representations captured by all attention heads to get the final representation. Then, after linearization and batch normalization, we get the refined deep features of the image, and finally, we use cross-entropy loss to make the output of the network closer to the ground truth.

4 Experiments

In this section, we report our experiments on the children facial pain expression dataset. First we introduced the proposed FPE-C dataset, then describe our experiment setup. Next, we verify that the multi-head attention mechanism contributes to the final performance through ablation studies. Finally, we compare our model with volunteers and quantitatively demonstrate the superiority of the proposed method.

4.1 Datasets

Our proposed Facial Pain Expressions Dataset of Children (FPE-C) dataset is a facial expression database collected in the postoperative resuscitation room. There are currently 26,070 images of 15 children with obvious pain symptoms, all with four-category labels labeled by clinical experts, namely No pain, Mild pain, Moderate pain and Severe pain.

4.2 Experiment Setup

On the FPE-C dataset, after using the RetinaFace [8] model to align facial images, we reshape all images to 224 * 224 pixels. To prevent overfitting, we randomly employ data augmentation methods such as horizontal flipping, random erasing, random cropping, and random rotation up to 40 °C. In addition, the experiment adopts the ResNet-18 [13] model as the backbone. In order to make the model converge faster than the original ResNet-18, we pre-train the model on the MS-Celeb-1M face recognition dataset.

Our experimental code is implemented with Pytorch, and the models are trained on a workstation with 4 RTX 6000 24G GPU. We train our model using the SGD optimization with an adaptive learning rate strategy, and its initial learning rate is 0.1. The batch size is 128, and the model is trained for 40 epochs.

4.3 Ablation Experiment

We conduct an ablation study to verify the effectiveness of the multi-head attention mechanism and choose an appropriate number of attention head.

The number of attention heads affects the performance of the network. Figure 5 shows the variation of accuracy with the number of attention heads. It is obvious that the accuracy of the network using the multi-head attention structure is better than that of single attention. Furthermore, using 4 attention heads maximizes the performance gain.

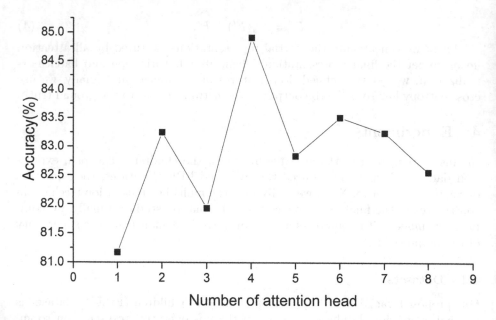

Fig. 5. Ablation test result between number of attention heads and accuracy

4.4 Test Results and Comparison with Volunteers

We carry out a comparative experiment between the model and volunteers to verify the effectiveness of the network. We first test the model by leave-one-out method. After that, we recruit five volunteers, randomly select 100 facial images of children from the database for each volunteer, and ask them to give corresponding pain status according to the pain scale. The results of the comparative test show that our model outperforms untrained volunteers. The experimental results of leave-one-out and volunteers are shown in Table 1.

Table 1. Result of leave-one-out tests and volunteers.

ID	Acc	ID	Acc	ID	Acc	Volunteers	Acc
1	89.11%	6	75.56%	11	95.57%	1	75%
2	80.04%	7	80.08%	12	81.25%	2	79%
3	77.97%	8	91.64%	13	91.02%	3	72%
4	97.98%	9	79.13%	14	92.45%	4	81%
5	78.28%	10	73.83%	15	89.84%	5	79%
				Average	**84.92%**	**Average**	**77.2%**

5   Conclusion

To avoid untimely and inaccurate detection of postoperative pain in children, this paper introduces a new automatic pain detection system, which is used to assist nurses in monitoring children's pain status and giving an early warning when necessary. First, we establish a set of acquisition equipment to get facial images of children and then propose a Pain Detection Network (PDN) to analyze pain status. In particular, we use a multi-head attention mechanism to let the network pay attention to different facial regions. The results of our experiments have shown that the multi-head attention module can promote the performance of our PDN and our model outperforms volunteers.

Our future work will combine physiological signals such as Heart Rate (HR) and blood pressure. This is because children's faces are not fully developed to characterize their pain status adequately so that physiological signals can be measured and used as supplements. In addition, we expect that the two kinds of inputs can complement each other to further improve the expressiveness of our network.

References

1. Bargshady, G., Zhou, X., Deo, R.C., Soar, J., Whittaker, F., Wang, H.: Enhanced deep learning algorithm development to detect pain intensity from facial expression images. Expert Syst. Appl. **149**, 113305 (2020)
2. Beyer, J.E., Denyes, M.J., Villarruel, A.M.: The creation, validation, and continuing development of the Oucher: a measure of pain intensity in children. J. Pediatr. Nurs. **7**(5), 335–346 (1992)
3. Breivik, H.: Assessment of pain. BJA Br. J. Anaesth. **101**(1), 17–24 (2008)
4. Bringuier, S., Macioce, V., Boulhais, M., Dadure, C., Capdevila, X.: Facial expressions of pain in daily clinical practice to assess postoperative pain in children: reliability and validity of the facial action summary score. Eur. J. Pain **25**(5), 1081–1090 (2021)
5. Buttner, W., Finke, W.: Children and infants postoperative pain scale. Paediatr. Anaesth. **10**(3), 303–318 (2000)
6. Chen, L., Ouyang, Y., Zeng, Y., Li, Y.: Dynamic facial expression recognition model based on BiLSTM-attention. In: 2020 15th International Conference on Computer Science & Education (ICCSE), pp. 828–832. IEEE (2020)
7. Craig, K.D., Prkachin, K.M., Grunau, R.E.: The facial expression of pain (2011)
8. Deng, J., Guo, J., Ververas, E., Kotsia, I., Zafeiriou, S.: Retinaface: single-shot multi-level face localisation in the wild. In: Proceedings of the IEEE/CVF Conference on Computer Vision and Pattern Recognition, pp. 5203–5212 (2020)
9. Economidou, E., Klimi, A., Vivilaki, V.G., Lykeridou, K.: Does music reduce postoperative pain? A review. Health Sci. J. **6**(3), 365 (2012)
10. Fard, A.P., Mahoor, M.H.: Ad-Corre: adaptive correlation-based loss for facial expression recognition in the wild. IEEE Access **10**, 26756–26768 (2022)
11. Grunau, R.E., Holsti, L., Peters, J.W.: Long-term consequences of pain in human neonates. In: Seminars in Fetal and Neonatal Medicine, vol. 11, pp. 268–275. Elsevier (2006)

12. Hayes, M.: Experimental development of the graphics rating method. Physiol. Bull. **18**, 98–99 (1921)
13. He, K., Zhang, X., Ren, S., Sun, J.: Deep residual learning for image recognition. In: Proceedings of the IEEE Conference on Computer Vision and Pattern Recognition, pp. 770–778 (2016)
14. Hicks, C.L., von Baeyer, C.L., Spafford, P.A., van Korlaar, I., Goodenough, B.: The faces pain scale-revised: toward a common metric in pediatric pain measurement. Pain **93**(2), 173–183 (2001)
15. Jensen, M.P., Karoly, P., Braver, S.: The measurement of clinical pain intensity: a comparison of six methods. Pain **27**(1), 117–126 (1986)
16. Kehlet, H., Jensen, T.S., Woolf, C.J.: Persistent postsurgical pain: risk factors and prevention. Lancet **367**(9522), 1618–1625 (2006)
17. Li, C., Pourtaherian, A., van Onzenoort, L., a Ten, W.T., de With, P.: Infant facial expression analysis: towards a real-time video monitoring system using R-CNN and HMM. IEEE J. Biomed. Health Inform. **25**(5), 1429–1440 (2020)
18. Li, J., Jin, K., Zhou, D., Kubota, N., Ju, Z.: Attention mechanism-based CNN for facial expression recognition. Neurocomputing **411**, 340–350 (2020)
19. Li, S., Deng, W.: Deep facial expression recognition: a survey. IEEE Trans. Affect. Comput. (2020)
20. Li, X., Jiang, Y., Li, M., Yin, S.: Lightweight attention convolutional neural network for retinal vessel image segmentation. IEEE Trans. Industr. Inform. **17**(3), 1958–1967 (2020)
21. Lucey, P., Cohn, J.F., Prkachin, K.M., Solomon, P.E., Chew, S., Matthews, I.: Painful monitoring: automatic pain monitoring using the UNBC-McMaster shoulder pain expression archive database. Image Vis. Comput. **30**(3), 197–205 (2012)
22. McGrath, P.J.: CHEOPS: a behavioral scale for rating postoperative pain in children. Adv. Pain Res. Ther. **9**, 395 (1985)
23. Minaee, S., Minaei, M., Abdolrashidi, A.: Deep-emotion: facial expression recognition using attentional convolutional network. Sensors **21**(9), 3046 (2021)
24. Mitchell, A., Boss, B.J.: Adverse effects of pain on the nervous system of newborns and young children: a review of the literature. J. Neurosci. Nurs. **34**(5), 228 (2002)
25. Niu, Z., Zhong, G., Yu, H.: A review on the attention mechanism of deep learning. Neurocomputing **452**, 48–62 (2021)
26. Pawar, D., Garten, L.: Pain management in children. Guide to Pain Management in Low-Resource Settings 255 (2010)
27. Pecoraro, R., Basile, V., Bono, V., Gallo, S.: Local multi-head channel self-attention for facial expression recognition. arXiv preprint arXiv:2111.07224 (2021)
28. Smeland, A.H., Twycross, A., Lundeberg, S., Rustøen, T.: Nurses' knowledge, attitudes and clinical practice in pediatric postoperative pain management. Pain Manag. Nurs. **19**(6), 585–598 (2018)
29. Stevens, B.J., et al.: Pain assessment and intensity in hospitalized children in Canada. J. Pain **13**(9), 857–865 (2012)
30. Sun, Y., et al.: Automatic and continuous discomfort detection for premature infants in a NICU using video-based motion analysis. In: 2019 41st Annual International Conference of the IEEE Engineering in Medicine and Biology Society (EMBC), pp. 5995–5999. IEEE (2019)
31. Vaswani, A., et al.: Attention is all you need. In: Advances in Neural Information Processing Systems 30 (2017)
32. Voepel-Lewis, T., Shayevitz, J.R., Malviya, S.: The FLACC: a behavioral scale for scoring postoperative pain in young children. Pediatr. Nurs. **23**(3), 293–7 (1997)

33. Wen, G., Chang, T., Li, H., Jiang, L.: Dynamic objectives learning for facial expression recognition. IEEE Trans. Multimedia **22**(11), 2914–2925 (2020)
34. Werner, P., Al-Hamadi, A., Niese, R., Walter, S., Gruss, S., Traue, H.C.: Automatic pain recognition from video and biomedical signals. In: 2014 22nd International Conference on Pattern Recognition, pp. 4582–4587. IEEE (2014)
35. Whaley, L., Wong, D.: Nursing Care of Infants and Children. CV Mosby Comp 3, 1070, St. Louis (1987)
36. Wong, D.L., Baker, C.M.: Pain in children: comparison of assessment scales. Pediatr. Nurs. **14**(1), 9–17 (1988)
37. Woo, S., Park, J., Lee, J.-Y., Kweon, I.S.: CBAM: convolutional block attention module. In: Ferrari, V., Hebert, M., Sminchisescu, C., Weiss, Y. (eds.) ECCV 2018. LNCS, vol. 11211, pp. 3–19. Springer, Cham (2018). https://doi.org/10.1007/978-3-030-01234-2_1
38. Zamzmi, G., Goldgof, D., Kasturi, R., Sun, Y.: Neonatal pain expression recognition using transfer learning. arXiv preprint arXiv:1807.01631 (2018)
39. Zhao, H., Jia, J., Koltun, V.: Exploring self-attention for image recognition. In: Proceedings of the IEEE/CVF Conference on Computer Vision and Pattern Recognition, pp. 10076–10085 (2020)
40. Zheng, C., Fan, X., Wang, C., Qi, J.: GMAN: a graph multi-attention network for traffic prediction. In: Proceedings of the AAAI Conference on Artificial Intelligence, vol. 34, pp. 1234–1241 (2020)
41. Zieliński, J., Morawska-Kochman, M., Zatoński, T.: Pain assessment and management in children in the postoperative period: a review of the most commonly used postoperative pain assessment tools, new diagnostic methods and the latest guidelines for postoperative pain therapy in children. Adv. Clin. Exp. Med. **29**(3), 365–374 (2020)

Detection of Response to Instruction in Autistic Children Based on Human-Object Interaction

Weibo Jiang[1], Weihong Ren[1(✉)], Bowen Chen[1], Yuhang Shi[1], Hanwei Ma[1], Xiu Xu[2], Qiong Xu[2], and Honghai Liu[1]

[1] School of Mechanical Engineering and Automation, Harbin Institute of Technology, Shenzhen, China
renweihong@hit.edu.cn
[2] Department of Child Health Care, Children's Hospital of Fudan University, Shanghai, China

Abstract. Autism is a childhood developmental disorder characterized by impairments in social interaction, verbal and nonverbal communication, narrow interests, and repetitive stereotypes, starting in infancy and early childhood. Children's Response to Instruction (RTI) is an important protocol in the diagnosis of children with autism. The so-called verbal response refers to a child's response to a doctor's verbal or gestural instructions in the process of performing a specific task. This paper proposes an end-to-end network for detecting Human-Object Interaction (HOI), which can simply, quickly and efficiently evaluate the behaviors of children, doctors, and parents in the RTI protocol. Through behavior analysis, we can determine whether the children's performance in this protocol is normal, and can also give a screening score for autism. In order to verify the proposed method, 16 children aged 5–8 are recruited to take participate in this study. The HOI detection accuracy and autism screening accuracy can reach 81.9% and 89%, respectively, which proves the effectiveness of our method in ASD screening.

Keywords: Human-Object Interaction · Behavior analysis · Autism screening

1 Introduction

The medical treatment for children with autism is mainly based on early screening and intervention. The idea is "early detection, early intervention, and early treatment". The autism screening method that relies entirely on doctors has unavoidable human influences such as strong subjectivity and inconsistent judgment standards. In recent years, considering the introduction of computer vision

Supported by GuangDong Basic and Applied Basic Research Foundation (2021A1515110438).

H. Liu et al. (Eds.): ICIRA 2022, LNAI 13458, pp. 712–722, 2022.
https://doi.org/10.1007/978-3-031-13841-6_64

technology into the screening process of autistic children has become a new research focus. Its rapidity, objectivity and stability have a great auxiliary role in the early screening process of children with autism.

The protocol of RTI is important for judging whether a child is prone to autism. The test process of this protocol is as follows: The child sits in a small chair and plays with toys, and the doctor sits opposite the child and gives instructions in a normal, clear tone. There are four rounds of the test, and the doctor give instructions twice in each round. In the first round, the doctor take out the ball and roll it on the table for the child to play for 2–3 min. The doctor says, "Give the ball to me". After 2 min, the test enters the second round. Based on the first round, the doctor stretch out his/her hand and says, "Give the ball to me". The third and fourth rounds of the test are similar to the first and second rounds, except that the toy balls are replaced with toy turtles. Children who respond are usually shown as follows: they make corresponding actions according to the instructions, for example, when they hear "give the turtle to me", they will put the turtle on the doctor's hand. However, when the children do not respond, they do not make any corresponding actions, such as "just pick up the turtle toy", "look at the adult" or "plays on his own" and so on. For each round of the test, the child receives a score of 0 for response, and a score of 1 for no response. Higher scores represent greater propensity for autism [7] (Fig. 1).

Fig. 1. Autism screening scenario of RTI. The image contains 3 groups of HOI categories, namely: <child, hand over, toy>, <doctor, stretch out to, child>, <parent, hold, child>.

The existing computer vision based methods mostly adopt single modal information such as children's facial expressions [4], eye gaze [14,16], or body and hand postures [15] for autism screening. These methods focus more on the children's response, and ignore the interactive actions or behaviors between children and other participants (e.g., doctors, parent and auxiliary toys), resulting in poor autism screening results. In order to capture the interactions between children and other participants, we propose a method of human-object interaction detection for autism screening. HOI is an important method for action detection in computer vision, which aims to detect the positions of human and objects in an image and also infers the relations between them [18]. The HOI detection output can be expressed as a <human, interaction, object> triplet.

There are some difficulties in applying HOI detection method to the RTI protocol. E.g., the implementation of this protocol involves multiple participants including children, doctors, parents, bystanders, etc., and how to accurately understand the multiple groups of human-object interactions in an image is a challenge. In addition, similar to other action datasets, this protocol contains many few-shot actions, such as "children hand over the toy", "doctors stretch out to children", "doctors talk to children" and so on. The above interactions are important signs to determine whether a child is prone to autism, so how to accurately detect them is also crucial for protocol judgement.

The main contributions of this paper are as follows:

- We propose an end-to-end HOI detection method that focuses on multiple groups of HOI detection in the autism screening scenario, which is helpful for Autism screening.
- A HOI dataset tailed for autism screening is collected, and it contains 16 children aged 5–8 with 90,000 annotated images.

2   Related Work

2.1   Detection of Autistic Children Based on Computer Vision

There is a lot of behavioral information in the screening process of children with autism, and numerous researchers have applied computer vision to the process. [9] put forward a vision-based detection method for children's expression of needs with pointing, which focuses on the evaluation of finger pointing and the analysis of hand movement trends. [16] adopted gaze detection to the diagnosis of autistic children. It first designed a gaze-driven interactive system to capture the eye gaze of the test children, and then derived a cognitive ability index to assess their cognitive levels. The above methods for autism screening focus on the pose or gaze behaviors of the children, and unilaterally predict their actions or emotions without considering the interactions from other participants. It is difficult for these methods to recognize different behaviors when the children exhibit similar actions. Therefore, the existing methods don't perform well in distinguishing actions at a fine-grained level. In addition, some important information of other participants is discarded during the screening process. In order to make full use of global information, it is appropriate to consider introducing HOI detection into the autism screening process.

2.2   Human-Object Interaction

In general, HOI detection methods can be divided into three categories: two-stage HOI detection, one-stage HOI detection and end-to-end HOI detection.

Most of the existing HOI detection methods belong to the two-stage category, which locate humans and objects in the first stage, and then pair them together and feed the corresponding features into a classifier network to predict interactions in the second stage. The second stage has a greater impact on the overall accuracy of HOI detection. Thus, some methods have been proposed to improve the performance of the second stage. Some researchers tried to understand the interaction prediction progress by capturing context information [13]. [1] utilized an instance-centric attention module to facilitate interaction prediction. To solve the problem of sample imbalance and sample indistinguishability, [3] introduced an action co-occurrence prior to improve the prediction accuracy for small samples. Two-stage HOI detection method can achieve satisfactory performance, but it is very time-consuming due to the separate network architectures.

One-Stage HOI detection method has been widely studied, since it has high efficiency and low computation, which is being applied in many fields. The one-stage method detect the human-object pairs and interactions parallelly, and then match them directly. [5] proposed a one-stage PPDM solution to reformulate the HOI detection task as a point detection problem and a matching problem. [17] created a Glance and Gaze Network, which locates the interaction points in the glance step and then infers the exact ActPoints around each pixel in a progressive manner.

End-to-end HOI detection method predicts the HOI in a simpler and faster way. [11] proposed an end-to-end detection method by a LSTM based encoder-decoder network, which is an auto-regressive model that predicts the output sequence at a time. [19] designed a HOI Transformer to tackle human object interaction detection in an end-to-end manner.

The screening process contains various of interactions between children and other participants, and it also has high requirement for running time. Thus, it is very suitable to apply end-to-end HOI detection method to autism screening.

3   Method

3.1   Overview

Different from the previous work, we propose a method that combines Convolutional Neural Network and Transformer to directly output the predictions of HOI in an end-to-end manner. Additionally, since the detection task of RTI is a time-series task, the proposed model also introduces time-series information to fuse temporal context from different frames. The overall architecture of the network is shown in Fig. 2. The backbone generates the feature map containing temporal context from the input images, and then the transformer extracts key features through the encoder and decoder. Finally, these features are projected to HOI instances.

3.2   Feature Extraction

ResNet [2] has powerful ability to extract multi-level features, and has been applied to many applications such as image classification, object detection and

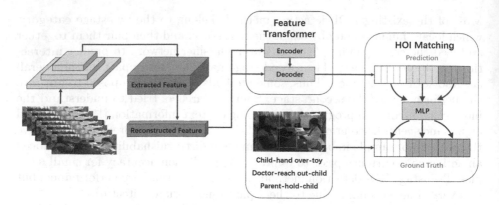

Fig. 2. The Architecture of the HOI detection model. The CNN backbone first performs feature extraction on the input image sequence to obtain feature map, which is reconstructed in the next step. The reconstructed feature map is input into the Feature Transformer architecture for key information extraction through encoding and decoding operations. Finally, the HOI Matching network predicts the output of the model.

natural language processing. In this work, we choose Resnet-50 as our backbone to extract features from the input images. To fuse temporal information, we use a sliding window to crop the input video, forming a video clip as model input. We set the sliding window width as w_d with step size l_s, where w_d is an odd number. Then, the image sequence $(n_1, n_2, \ldots, n_{w_d})$ in a sliding window is input into the HOI detection model at each time, and its label equals to the one of center image $(n_{(w_d-1)/2})$. The shape of the input sequence is $(3 \times w_d, H, W)$, after feature extraction, the feature map of shape (H, W, C) is obtained, which contains high-level semantic concepts. After that, the model reduces the dimension of the feature map to 256 in order to be suitable for Transformer processing. Since the Transformer was first proposed for the task of machine translation [12], the feature input to the Transformer is a two-dimensional word vector group. Thus, a spatial transformation should be performed on the feature map after dimension reduction: the feature map is cropped along the width direction into H small feature maps, marked as $(f_1, f_2, \ldots f_H)$, the shape of each small feature map is $(W, 256)$, then the small feature maps are spliced from left to right in order, and finally get a new feature map of shape $(H \times W, 256)$.

3.3   Feature Transformer

The Transformer architecture is divided into two parts: Encoder and Decoder. The Encoder part aims to guide the network to pay attention to the key areas in the entire feature map, and the Decoder part aims to guide the network to focus on current and previous semantic information. As shown in Fig. 3, The feature map extracted from the backbone is mapped to Input module at first. Then, the model adds timing constraints by performing positional encoding on the Input module to abstract global information.

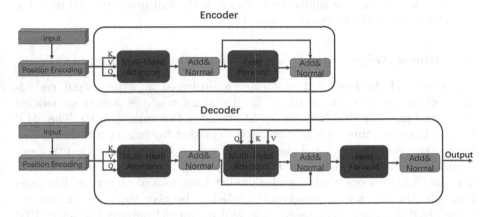

Fig. 3. The Architecture of the Feature Transformer. The position information is added into the Input module through position encoding at first, and then the key information concerned by Encoder is extracted. During the decoding operation, the Decoder module provides Query to extract the Value output from the Encoder, and then outputs the re-focused information with multiple multi-head attention module.

The Encoder part consists of a multi-head self-attention module and a feed-forward network. Similar to using multiple convolutional kernels, multi-head self-attention module implements multiple linear transformations on Q, K and V to get multiple heads, which can be expressed as:

$$Head_i = f(QM_i^Q, KM_i^K, VM_i^V) \tag{1}$$

where M_i^Q, M_i^K, M_i^V stand for the mapping matrices from Q, K, V to a linear layer of $Head_i$, and different heads stand for different attentions of the model. Then, each head performs attention operation in terms of the suitability of Q and K. The attention results of all heads are aggregated through the contact operation. This attention mechanism extracts the Values through different Queries. The output of the multi-head self-attention is finally sent to the feed-forward network with the residual architecture.

The Decoder part consists of two multi-head self-attention modules and a feed-forward network. The first sub-module of the Decoder model is the masked multi-head self-attention module in the original Transformer, which aims to ensure that the model only receive the information before time t. However, for image processing, there is no temporal correlation between each pixel of an image, and thus there is no need to perform a mask operation on the feature map to filter features. Thus, we remove mask from the original multi-head self-attention module, so that the attention scheme will focus all regions of the feature map. Different from the Encoder model, the Queries in the Decoder model come from the first sub-module, while the Keys and Values come from the Encoder model. It is similar to re-focus on the features extracted from the Encoder model with the newly obtained Queries.

3.4 Human-Object Interaction Prediction and Matching

The output of the Feature Transformer is projected into the output embedding, which has a dimension of d_o. Each dimension of the output embedding is decoded into one HOI instance by Multi-Layer Perception(MLP). The MLP has five branches, three of which are used to predict the human confidence (h_c), interaction confidence (i_c) and object confidence (o_c), separately. The other two branches are used to predict the human bounding box (h_b) and object bounding box (o_b). Previous works usually predict humans and objects at first, and then infer the interactions based on the relations between them. In contrast, we regard HOI detection as one-step task, and our model outputs the set of HOI (h_c, i_c, o_c, h_b, o_b) directly.

Our model focuses on multiple groups of HOI instances in the RTI scenario, and the children, doctors and parents are the subjects. The criteria for selecting the final HOI instance from the HOI prediction results is:

$$p_i = \max\{h_{c(i,j)} \times i_{c(i,j)} \times o_{c(i,j)}\} \tag{2}$$

where $i \in (c, d, p)$, stands for children, doctor, parent respectively, and j stands for the predicted HOI instance with i as subject. The loss function is:

$$\mathcal{L}_{hoi} = \sum_{i \in c,d,p} \mathcal{L}_m(p_i, g_i) \tag{3}$$

Here, $\mathcal{L}_m(p_i, g_i)$ is the matching loss between the prediction HOI p_i and the ground truth HOI g_i.

$$\mathcal{L}_m(p_i, g_i) = \alpha_{(i,k)} \sum_k \mathcal{L}_{(i,k)}(p_{(i,k)}, g_{(i,k)}) \tag{4}$$

where $p_{(i,k)}$ stands for five elements of a HOI prediction instance: human category, interaction classification, object category, human bounding box, object bounding box, and $g_{(i,k)}$ stands for the ground truth of these elements. We use focal loss [6] for classification of human, interaction and object, since there exists the imbalanced problem in the RTI dataset. Besides, we use Generalized Intersection over Union (GIoU) [10] loss to calculate the human and object bounding box loss.

4   Experiments

4.1   Dataset and Evaluation Metrics

We collected data from 16 children who took participate in the ASD screening that contains 5 protocols. For this work, we only analyse the test process of RTI protocol which has more HOI instances. In total, we obtain screening videos of 60 min at 25 fps. Based on the advice from clinician, we finally define and annotate 8 actions and 10 HOI categories, forming a HOI dataset of 90,000 frames.

We take accuracy as our criteria for the following experiments. For HOI detection, the accuracy equals to the number of correctly predicted HOI instances divided by the total number of HOI instances. For the screening accuracy in the RTI protocol, it equals to the number of correct predicted rounds divided by the total number of experimental rounds.

4.2   Implementation Details

During training process, we input images in temporal order through the sliding window. We set w_d to 7, l_s to 1, respectively. The input image size is resized to $640 * 360$ for acceleration. We use Adam [8] optimizer with a learning rate 0.00001 for training. For loss calculation, we set $\alpha_{(p,k)}$ to be smaller than $\alpha_{(c,k)}$ and $\alpha_{(d,k)}$ to prevent the model paying too much attention to parents. In total, the model is trained for 100 epoches with batch size 1. For 16 children, we divide them into 4 groups evenly, where three groups are used for training and the left one is used for test. The 4-fold cross-validation is used to verify the effectiveness of our method.

4.3   Results and Discussion

In this part, we discuss the effectiveness of our method from two aspects: the HOI detection accuracy and the screening accuracy. Table 1 shows the accuracy of HOI detection in terms of subject, while Table 2 shows the accuracy of detection in terms of interaction.

Table 1. Results of HOI detection in terms of subject.

Group ID	HOI(Acc_{ave})	HOI(Acc_c)	HOI(Acc_d)	HOI(Acc_p)
1	81.6	79.3	65.4	**100**
2	82.5	78.3	69.2	**100**
3	80.1	76.2	64.1	**100**
4	83.4	78.4	71.8	**100**
ave	**81.9**	**78.1**	**67.6**	**100**

From Table 1, it can be observed that the HOI detection accuracy for parent (denoted as "Acc_p") is 100%, while the accuracy for child and doctor can only reach 78.1% and 67.6%, respectively. The reason is that the categories of different subjects are imbalanced in the RTI protocol. The number of HOI categories for "parent" is the least, while it is the most for "doctor".

Table 2. Results of HOI detection in terms of interaction.

Interaction	Group$_1$	Group$_2$	Group$_3$	Group$_4$	ave
Background	75.1	74.5	72.4	74.6	**74.1**
Play	82.2	83.8	81.5	85.2	**83.2**
Hand over	70.2	71.6	70.8	73.8	**71.6**
Talk to	26.5	28.7	22.3	27.4	**26.2**
Reach out	69.7	71.2	70.4	73.5	**71.2**
Point	/	30.3	/	29.8	**30.1**
Grab	76.2	78.1	75.1	80.3	**77.4**
Hold	**100**	**100**	**100**	**100**	**100**

From Table 2, it can be seen that the accuracy of interaction "talk to" and "point" is lower than that of other interactions. Because the characteristic of "talk to" is not obvious, many experiments were conducted with face masks due to the COVID-19. The interaction of "point" has the lowest accuracy because the sample is too small. Here, "/" indicates that the action did not occur during the test of this group.

In the RTI protocol, the doctor gives verbal instructions to ask the child to hand over the toys in two rounds of the test. Since the visual characteristic of "talk to" is too inconspicuous, we use speech recognition to recognize the doctor's verbal instructions.

Table 3 summaries the result of autism screening in RTI protocol. Round$_i$ $i \in 1, 2, 3, 4$ represents the predicted score of a child in i^{th} round, and Gt$_{Ri}$ is the score of the child marked by the clinician doctor. Values marked in bold indicate that the round was mispredicted. Taking the doctor's score as the standard reference, each child participates in four rounds of the test, and 64 rounds of results can be obtained in total. For our model, it can predict screening results correctly for 57 rounds, with an screening accuracy of 89.1%.

Table 3. Scores of RTI protocol screening

Child ID	$Round_1$	$Round_2$	$Round_3$	$Round_4$	Gt_{R1}	Gt_{R2}	Gt_{R3}	Gt_{R4}
01	0	0	0	0	0	0	0	0
02	0	0	0	0	0	0	0	0
03	0	1	0	0	0	0	0	0
04	1	0	1	0	1	0	1	0
05	0	0	0	1	0	0	0	0
06	0	0	1	0	0	0	0	0
07	1	1	1	0	1	1	1	0
08	0	0	0	0	0	0	0	0
09	1	1	1	1	1	1	1	1
10	0	0	1	1	0	0	0	1
11	0	0	0	0	0	0	0	0
12	1	1	1	0	1	1	1	0
13	1	0	0	0	0	0	0	0
14	1	0	0	0	1	1	0	0
15	1	0	0	0	1	0	0	0
16	1	1	1	1	1	1	1	1

5 Conclusion

In this paper, we are the first to apply HOI detection into autism screening. Our model combines CNN and Transformer to predict HOI in an end-to-end manner, which is very efficient and also effective. For autism screening in RTI protocol, our method can achieve 81.9% detection accuracy for multiple groups of HOIs. Also, it achieves screening accuracy of 89.0% on our own collected dataset. This work will motivate more researchers to focus on interactive actions of autism screening instead of child-centric actions.

Acknowledgment. This research is supported by GuangDong Basic and Applied Basic Research Foundation (2021A1515110438).

References

1. Gao, C., Zou, Y., Huang, J.B.: iCAN: instance-centric attention network for human-object interaction detection, pp. 1–13. arXiv preprint arXiv:1808.10437 (2018)
2. He, K., Zhang, X., Ren, S., Sun, J.: Deep residual learning for image recognition. In: IEEE Conference on Computer Vision and Pattern Recognition, pp. 770–778 (2016)

3. Kim, D.-J., Sun, X., Choi, J., Lin, S., Kweon, I.S.: Detecting human-object interactions with action co-occurrence priors. In: Vedaldi, A., Bischof, H., Brox, T., Frahm, J.-M. (eds.) ECCV 2020. LNCS, vol. 12366, pp. 718–736. Springer, Cham (2020). https://doi.org/10.1007/978-3-030-58589-1_43

4. Li, J., Chen, Z., Li, G., Ouyang, G., Li, X.: Automatic classification of ASD children using appearance-based features from videos. Neurocomputing **470**, 40–50 (2022)

5. Liao, Y., Liu, S., Wang, F., Chen, Y., Qian, C., Feng, J.: PPDM: parallel point detection and matching for real-time human-object interaction detection. In: IEEE Conference on Computer Vision and Pattern Recognition, pp. 482–490 (2020)

6. Lin, T.Y., Goyal, P., Girshick, R., He, K., Dollár, P.: Focal loss for dense object detection. In: IEEE International Conference on Computer Vision, pp. 2980–2988 (2017)

7. Liu, J., Wang, Z., Xu, K., Ji, B., Liu, H.: Early screening of autism in toddlers via response-to-instructions protocol. IEEE Trans. Cybern. **52**, 3914–3924 (2020)

8. Loshchilov, I., Hutter, F.: Decoupled weight decay regularization, pp. 1–8 (2017)

9. Qin, H., et al.: Vision-based pointing estimation and evaluation in toddlers for autism screening. In: Liu, X.-J., Nie, Z., Yu, J., Xie, F., Song, R. (eds.) ICIRA 2021. LNCS (LNAI), vol. 13015, pp. 177–185. Springer, Cham (2021). https://doi.org/10.1007/978-3-030-89134-3_17

10. Rezatofighi, H., Tsoi, N., Gwak, J., Sadeghian, A., Reid, I., Savarese, S.: Generalized intersection over union: a metric and a loss for bounding box regression. In: IEEE Conference on Computer Vision and Pattern Recognition, pp. 658–666 (2019)

11. Stewart, R., Andriluka, M., Ng, A.Y.: End-to-end people detection in crowded scenes. In: IEEE Conference on Computer Vision and Pattern Recognition, pp. 2325–2333 (2016)

12. Vaswani, A., et al.: Attention is all you need. In: Advances in Neural Information Processing Systems, pp. 1–11 (2017)

13. Wang, T., et al.: Deep contextual attention for human-object interaction detection. In: IEEE International Conference on Computer Vision, pp. 5694–5702 (2019)

14. Wang, X., Zhang, J., Zhang, H., Zhao, S., Liu, H.: Vision-based gaze estimation: a review. IEEE Trans. Cogn. Dev. Syst. **14**, 316–332 (2021)

15. Zhang, D., Toptan, C.M., Zhang, G., Zhao, S., Liu, H.: Diversity and complexity of hand movement for autism spectrum disorder intervention. In: International Conference on Advanced Computational Intelligence (2021)

16. Zhang, H., et al.: Gaze-driven interaction system for cognitive ability assessment. In: International Conference on Intelligent Control and Information Processing, pp. 346–351 (2021)

17. Zhong, X., Qu, X., Ding, C., Tao, D.: Glance and gaze: inferring action-aware points for one-stage human-object interaction detection. In: IEEE Conference on Computer Vision and Pattern Recognition, pp. 13234–13243 (2021)

18. Zhou, T., Qi, S., Wang, W., Shen, J., Zhu, S.C.: Cascaded parsing of human-object interaction recognition. IEEE Trans. Pattern Anal. Mach. Intell. **44**, 2827–2840 (2022)

19. Zou, C., et al.: End-to-end human object interaction detection with HOI transformer. In: IEEE Conference on Computer Vision and Pattern Recognition, pp. 11825–11834 (2021)

A Monocular Vision-Based Human-Following Approach for Mobile Robots

Yilong Tan[1], Shuang Wu[1], Wanquan Liu[1]($\boxtimes$), Xiansheng Yang[2], and Hui-Jie Sun[1]

[1] Sun Yat-sen University, Shenzhen 518107, China
liuwq63@mail.sysu.edu.cn
[2] Harbin Institute of Technology, Shenzhen 518055, China

Abstract. The ability to recognize and follow human beings is considered to be a key technology for mobile robots. A vision-based following approach is proposed in this paper. It consists of two parts: the human detection part and the visual servoing part. In the human detection part, the image information is captured by the robot camera and processed by a neural network detection algorithm to extract human position and state information. In the visual servoing part, robot switches between three modes including seeking, following and stopping for human-following. Technically, an algorithm is proposed to calculate the angle between the robot and the human, which is used to control. The innovation of this paper is the use of a full vision-based approach to human-following, where the whole process only requires image information. A series of experiments were conducted to verify the effectiveness of the approach.

Keywords: Vision-based human-following · Monocular camera · Interactive robot · Neural network

1 Introduction

Human-following is an indispensable capability for interactive robots. It is an important task for the robot to follow the human when the position of the human is dynamically changing in the scene. There have been some papers in the past to achieve robot following tasks. They use different kinds of sensors such as ultrasonic sensors, multi-vision cameras, etc. Most of them use the multi-sensor fusion method. Jung et al. [1] proposed a method based on laser rangefinders scanning the environment and detecting humans to accomplish the task. Zhang et al. [2] proposed a visual servoing control method based on image processing assisted by ultrasonic sensor. Feng et al. [3] and Laneurit et al. [4] constructed the robot following system using UWB tag data carried by the target person. Germa et al. [5] designed a multi-sensor-based following strategy based on the tracker outputs and RFID data. Zheng et al. [6] proposed a method by identifying and locating targets in each image frame with binocular cameras. Tsai et al. [7] proposed a real-time tracker that uses a stereo camera to track specific people in different environments. Liu et al. [8], Han et al. [9] and Mi et al. [10] built the human-following system by processing depth image information. Sharma et al. [11] presented a method to detect the location of human using infrared camera to achieve the human-following. Usually, some of these methods require the processing of complex information and have equipment limitations. The implementation of these tasks requires significant computing resources. Vision-based methods have low equipment requirements and only need to process with a single piece of image information, so it is facilitated for deployment on the robot side. Furthermore, the image information contains more semantic information and can be extended to more tasks. Suzuki et al. [12] proposed a method based on face detection. It can perform the task using a small cost, but it does not allow the robot to make accurate turns and cannot track when the face is not in the robot's field of view.

Monocular vision detection can achieve high accuracy and good stability thanks to the rapid development in the field of deep learning in recent years, so vision-based robot tasks are also well supported. Object detection methods basically divide into two categories. The first category is the traditional machine learning based algorithms such as SVM [13]. This type of method is difficult to apply to variable environments due to its reliance on feature extraction. The second category is the deep learning based algorithms. They are usually two-stage algorithms represented by RCNN [14] and single-stage algorithms represented by YOLO [15]. The one-stage algorithms outperform the two-stage algorithms in terms of detection speed due to the fact that the one-stage algorithms generate feature vectors that return both the class of the object and the coordinates of the bounding box. There have also been many recent works based on new feature extraction backbones, such as Transformer [16] and ConvNext [17]. Although they are able to achieve high accuracy, they do not meet the robot's requirements for real-time performance due to too many parameters in the network model. In order to ensure both real-time and accuracy of robot control, the newest YOLOX [18] of YOLO series is selected in this paper.

Benefiting from the fast speed of the YOLOX series, a YOLOX-Nano network is trained as the basic detection algorithm in this paper. The YOLOX-nano is an extremely light-weight network. Compared with the medium model YOLOX-m with 25.3(M) parameters and need 73.8(G) FLOPs, the YOLOX-nano has only 0.91(M) parameters and requires only 1.08(G) FLOPs. The memory requirement of the edge computing device is reduced and the real-time performance of the robot control can be guaranteed. However, due to certain limitations in the accuracy of the light-weight network, we find there are a few missed detection problems in practice. For this issue, this paper designs a method to reduce frame leakage detection, which can effectively ensure the stability of the human-following.

Based on the object detection algorithm, this paper proposes a monocular vision-based human-following approach that can be applied mainly to robotic escorting and human-robot interaction. The significance of this research is that it proposes a purely vision-based idea that simplifies the human-following approach. This approach is characterized by simple image information, low cost, and can be deployed with small size cameras. It is a purely visual information processing approach for the entire route, in which the effective object detection algorithm gives great support. At the end of the paper, the experiment verifies that it can achieve a good human-following effect.

2 Method

The method consists of two steps. Firstly, human information is extracted from the images by means of a neural network. Secondly, the robot's movement modes and control angle are calculated by processing this information. This chapter proposes a solution to target miss detection for light-weight networks and proposes a visual servoing control method for human-following.

2.1 Human Detection

The human detection part uses the YOLOX network. YOLOX is the newest version of the YOLO series. It is a detector that balances accuracy and speed. The network is divided into three parts: backbone, neck, and head.

The object detection process of YOLOX is shown in Fig. 1. First, the images are fed into the backbone network for feature extraction. The backbone network uses an upgraded version of CSP-Darknet53 based on YOLOv5 [19]. In the feature extraction process, the $640 \times 640 \times 3$ size color image is convolved through to produce a feature map of $20 \times 20 \times 1024$ size. Secondly, the Neck framework based on FPN [20] and PAN [21] is used to splice the feature data from different channels to achieve shallow and deep feature fusion. It can enhance human location information on deep features. This results in three different scales of detection feature maps. Finally, the feature data output from the Neck is fed to the Head, which uses a decoupling head to separate the classification and regression tasks and obtain the prediction maps at different scales of size. These prediction maps are concatenated into a matrix of 8400×85 size. Then, the most confident bounding box is selected by decoding this matrix.

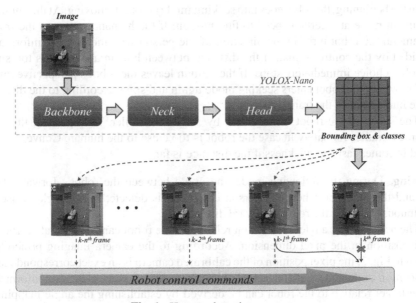

Fig. 1. Human detection process

As YOLOX-nano has fewer network layers for resource-constrained computing reasons. In practice, A small number of missed detections have been found to occur. For the frame miss detection problem, a frame redundancy mechanism is designed in this paper. As shown in Fig. 1. If the human of the kth frame is under-detected, it sends to the robot to continue to execute the last valid command sent in [k-n ~ k] frames. Usually, n is set to a small value that does not affect the safety of the robot. In the experiments of this paper, n is set to one. This method improves the stability of the robot following.

2.2 Visual Servoing Control

This paragraph proposes a visual servoing control method based on bounding boxes. The main aim is to control the robot's actions by the information acquired from vision. The motion modes of the robot can be classified into three main states in the following processes: seeking, following and stopping. The Fig. 2 shows the flowchart of the robot's mode switching.

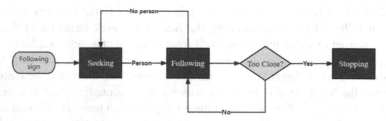

Fig. 2. Transformation of robot states

In the beginning, the robot goes into seeking mode and starts moving. At this moment, it spins in place at a certain speed to find human. If the human appears in the frames of camera, the robot turns in the direction of the person with the steering information provided by the control signal. If the distance between human and robot is too small, the robot choice immediately stops. If the human leaves the robot's perspective during the following, the robot enters seeking mode again and spins according to the direction of the human out of the frame.

The speed of the robot is controlled by a PID controller. The speed of the robot becomes smaller for safety in case the robot is too close to the human. Conversely, the speed becomes fast for quickness if the distance is far.

Steering. During the following mode, the angle between the robot's forward direction and the direction where the person is located is detected. This angle is used to continuously correct the robot's forward direction.

The actual target angle information relative to the robot can be calculated from the pixel position in the pixel dimension. According to the camera imaging principle as shown in Fig. 3, the pixel position of the calibrated camera is an exact correspondence to the position of the flat where the actual object is located. So the orientation information of the target relative to the robot can be derived by establishing the angle mapping of the target angle in the pixel dimension.

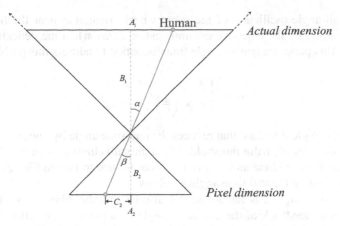

Fig. 3. Camera imaging and dimensional transformation

Where A_1 is the width of the field of view in reality, A_2 is the pixel width of the image. B_1 is the distance of the camera from the target scene, B_2 is the virtual distance in the pixel dimension. C_2 is the distance of the target point from the midpoint of the pixel in the pixel dimension. α is the deflection angle between the target and the camera orientation, and β is the virtual orientation angle in the pixel dimension.

Firstly, a calibration is performed, and the values of A_1 and B_1 in the actual dimension are measured, and based on the imaging principle of the camera, the equation of the size transformation relationship is as follows:

$$\frac{A_1}{B_1} = \frac{A_2}{B_2}. \tag{1}$$

In the pixel dimension, A_2 is set fixed, from which the value of B_2 can be calculated. The offset angle of the target center in pixel dimension can be calculated as follows:

$$\beta = \arctan \frac{C_2}{B_2}, \tag{2}$$

where C_2 is the centre point of human in the pixel dimension, which can be calculated from the following:

$$C_2 = (W_r + W_l)/2 - C_{center} \tag{3}$$

where W_r, W_l are the horizontal coordinates of the left and right boundaries of the bounding box output by the object detection algorithm. β can be calculated by (2), the angle α of the human relative to the robot can be calculated as follows:

$$\alpha = \beta. \tag{4}$$

The small-angle oscillation of the robot wheel orientation near the human-robot midline is caused by the objective communication delay when the deflection angle is very small. This paper designs an angle transformation to address this problem:

$$\hat{\alpha} = \begin{cases} \alpha, & \alpha \geq r_t \\ r_t \times \left(\frac{\alpha}{r_t}\right)^3, & \alpha < r_t \end{cases}, \tag{5}$$

where r_t is the angle threshold that reduces the real-time angle by one magnitude if the real-time angle is less than this threshold. The angle shift eliminates the problem of angle oscillation near the midline and allows the robot to turn to the midline at a smoother speed by calculating the real-time angle feedback.

The deviation angle $\hat{\alpha}$ is calculated in real-time, and the robot adjusts its direction by the real-time feedback of the deviation angle to achieve a very effective result of human-following in real-time.

Stopping. To ensure human safety, stopping judgment is performed when the robot reaches within close range of human. When the robot is close to the human, a command to stop is sent to the robot. In this paper, the size of the human part in the frame is used to determine the distance between the robot and the human. The robot stops moving if the size of the bounding box exceeds a set threshold. The size of human can be calculated as follows:

$$length = W_u - W_b, \tag{6}$$

where W_u and W_b are the vertical coordinates of the upper and lower boundaries of the bounding box of the object detection algorithm. The state pattern of the robot is as follows:

$$Robot\ state = \begin{cases} Stopping, & length > length_t \\ Following, & length \leq length_t \end{cases}, \tag{7}$$

where $length_t$ makes the set threshold value. Compared to using the width of the bounding box to determine distance, the height does not change with the movement of the person's limbs. It also does not decrease when the person is at the edge of the frame. The height of the bounding box is stable when the person is walking normally. In the experiments of this paper, the robot is able to follow the movement of the human in different postures. It has been demonstrated that this method of distance judgement is robust and effective.

The method proposed in this paragraph is based on purely visual information. In general, the real-time image information is taken through two steps to obtain control commands for the robot to act. During the robot's action, the environment is continuously detected and the commands are continuously updated. An adaptive closed-loop system is formed.

3   Experiments

This chapter conducts a series of experiments to verify the method mentioned in the previous chapter in the real situation. The Fig. 4 shows the physical structure of experimental equipment. Among them, camera is used to capture image frames as the original data of the method proposed in this paper. Ranger Mini is a programmable omnidirectional UGV (Unmanned Ground Vehicle) with odometer and other sensors. It has four motion mode including Ackermann, sloping, spinning and sliding to reach the target point, which is flexible enough to meet the demand of the experiment. Nvidia Jetson Xavier communicates directly with UGV through a serial port so that it can send instructions to control the UGV. Intel NUC with Intel Core i5-1135G7 accepts the image frames from the camera and processes them by the human detection algorithm in this paper, which would output the corresponding motion strategy to Nvidia Jetson Xavier. These two edge computing devices communicate with each other under the coverage of LAN signals transmitted by the ASUS router.

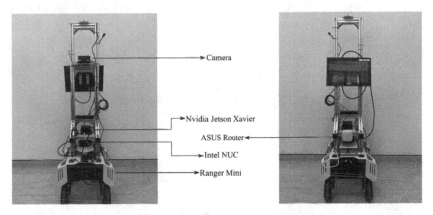

Fig. 4. Experimental equipment

According to the actual application scenario of the method such as eldercare, a series of experiments have been conducted and their results are shown as below. These experiments mainly verify the effectiveness of the approach proposed in this paper through the feedback about velocity, angle and odometer in the actual movement of the robot.

3.1   Velocity of Robot

The first experiment examines the velocity adjustment capability of the robot so that the robot can keep stable when it goes into service. The Fig. 5 shows the robot's velocity variation in different situations during human-following. Experiment records robot's velocity when camera detected standing human in the distance as Fig. 5a. The robot slows down gradually until it stops in front of human form time t_1 to time t_2 due to the shortening of the distance. If human walks to-wards to the robot at the same time, the process of deceleration to zero will be shortened as Fig. 5b. From time t_1 to time t_2 shows the deceleration process of the robot, which is obviously shorter than Fig. 5a. When someone appears in front of robot at a very close distance, emergency stop function would be activated and robot would stop immediately as Fig. 5c for safety reasons. It can be seen that the velocity of the robot drops to zero from time t_1 to time t_2. This part of the experiment proves that the approach meets the needs of rapidity and security. Jitter in the curve is caused by the limitation of sensor measurement accuracy and can be ignored in this experiment.

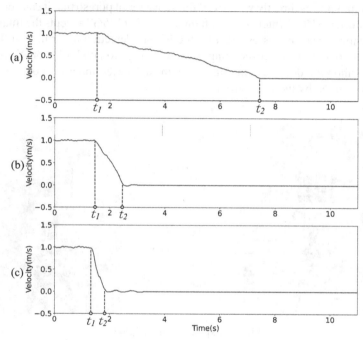

Fig. 5. Velocity variation in different situations

3.2 Angle of Robot

The content of the second experiment is testing the robustness of the human-following approach by recording the robot's angle during human-following. The Fig. 6 shows steering angle variation of robot when human with different postures isn't at the center of the camera frames during human-following. The three curves from top to bottom in the figure represent the situation when robot follows human from a front, side-on and back perspective respectively. In these situations, robot would adjust the direction of movement when human changes the position in the camera frames at time t_1 and time t_3. After rapid adjustment, the approach can turn the direction of the robot to human again at time t_2 and time t_4. Three similar results show that robot has great ability of fast and steady direction adjustment no matter what human gesture is. It can gradually reduce the angle between the direction of the human and the direction of the robot to zero during human-following. This ability effectively reduces the probability of human leaving the camera frame and enhance the robustness of the approach.

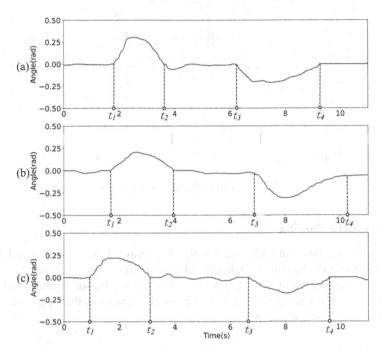

Fig. 6. Angle variation in different situations

If the lateral speed of human is too fast to catch up by the camera, human would leave from the left or right of the camera frame. The approach contains a little trick to record this direction so that the robot can find missing human faster according to this direction. The Fig. 7 shows the efficiency comparison of whether the robot uses the trick to look for human. If human is at the edge of the camera frames, it means that human have a trend to leave. The direction recorded at this moment is just the direction of human leaving the camera frame considering that human can't appear suddenly in another direction. The Fig. 7a represents the trick be used in the approach and the Fig. 7b represents the robot can only seek in a fixed direction. Maintaining an angle of about 0.785 (rad) means the robot is in seeking mode, and its duration is from time t_1 to time t_2. It is clear from the experiment that this trick can reduced the seeking time by approximately 3 s, which shows the effectiveness of the trick.

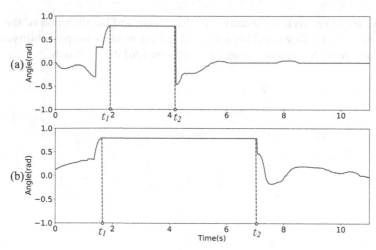

Fig. 7. Seeking efficiency comparison

3.3 Process of Following

In order to ensure the robot with human-following approach works well, a task is given to the robot to follow human to circle around a table in the office without obstacle. The Fig. 8 shows the process of human-following. The robot followed human from point A and move along the red trajectory curve to point B. Pictures in the figure are example scenes during human-following.

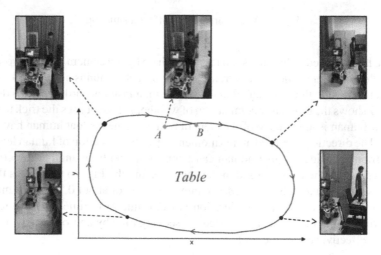

Fig. 8. Moving path of human-following

The trajectory shown above was plotted from displacement data obtained by the robot's odometer. From the experiments it can be seen that the robot's trajectory largely matches that of the human. The robot can run with a steady velocity and keep a distance about 0.7 m during the process, which means that the robot is able to follow the human movement well in real time in an indoor environment. The effectiveness of the approach is proven.

4 Conclusions

In this paper, a vision-based human-following approach is proposed. When human appears in the perspective of the robot, the position of the human in the perspective is obtained by the object detection algorithm. A redundancy method is designed to overcome the problem of missed detection in the object detection phase. After the target information is obtained, a method is proposed to convert the visual signal into a control signal. The control signal is continuously transmitted and updated to the robot to achieve the purpose of real-time following. At the same time, the robot switches to different modes according to the actual situation in the process of human-following. Experimentally, this approach is effective for human-following that can ensure human safety and robustness of following.

For future work, the aim is to build a service-oriented robot system that includes health surveillance, human-robot interaction and other functions. In the short term, the work will continue in the following ways:

(1) The structure of the YOLOX will be modified for the application scenario. The object tracking algorithm will be combined with human detection algorithm to enable the robot to follow a specified person. The stability of human-following will be enhanced.
(2) This approach will be combined with path planning and obstacle avoidance algorithms. When some obstacles are encountered during the following process, the robot is able to avoid the obstacles and continue to follow the human. This makes the robot more capable of handling more complex environments.
(3) The underlying control algorithms of the robot will be improved. More advanced algorithms will be added for speed and angle control. The control will be smoothed even when the bounding box output of the human detection algorithm oscillates.

References

1. Jung, E.J., Lee, J.H., Yi, B.J., et al.: Development of a laser-range-finder-based human tracking and control algorithm for a marathoner service robot. IEEE/ASME Trans. Mechatron. **19**(6), 1963–1976 (2013)
2. Zhang, M.Y., Liu, X.L., Xu, D., et al.: Vision-based target-following guider for mobile robot. IEEE Trans. Industr. Electron. **66**(12), 9360–9371 (2019)
3. Feng, T., Yu, Y., Wu, L., et al.: A human-tracking robot using ultra wideband technology. IEEE Access **6**, 42541–42550 (2018)
4. Laneurit, J., Chapuis, R., Debain, C.: TRACKBOD, an accurate, robust and low cost system for mobile robot person following. In: International Conference on Machine Control & Guidance (2016)

5. Germa, T., Lerasle, F., Ouadah, N., et al.: Vision and RFID data fusion for tracking people in crowds by a mobile robot. Comput. Vis. Image Underst. **114**(6), 641–651 (2010)
6. Zheng, Y.Y., Ge, J.: Binocular intelligent following robot based on YOLO-LITE. In: 2nd International Conference on Computer Science Communication and Network Security, p. 10 (2021)
7. Tsai, T.H., Yao, C.H.: A robust tracking algorithm for a human-following mobile robot. IET Image Process. **15**(3), 786–796 (2021)
8. Liu, H.L., Luo, J., Wu, P., et al.: People detection and tracking using RGB-D cameras for mobile robots. Int. J. Adv. Robot. Syst. **13**(5) (2016). https://doi.org/10.1177/172988141665 7746
9. Han, D., Peng, Y.G.: Human-following of mobile robots based on object tracking and depth vision. In: 3rd International Conference on Mechatronics, Robotics and Automation, pp.105–109 (2020)
10. Mi, W.M., Wang, X.Z., Ren, P., et al.: A system for an anticipative front human following robot. In: International Conference on Artificial Intelligence and Robotics and the International Conference on Automation, Control and Robotics Engineering, pp. 1–6 (2016)
11. Sharma, A.K., Pandey, A., Khan, M.A., et al.: Human following robot. In: 2021 International Conference on Advance Computing and Innovative Technologies in Engineering, pp. 440–446 (2021)
12. Suzuki, S., Mitsukura, Y., Takimoto, H., et al.: A human tracking mobile-robot with face detection. In: 35th Annual Conference of IEEE Industrial Electronics, pp. 4217–4222 (2009)
13. Cortes, C., Vapnik, V.: Support-vector networks. Mach. Learn. **20**(3), 273–297 (1995). https://doi.org/10.1007/BF00994018
14. Girshick, R., Donahue, J., Darrell, T., et al.: Rich feature hierarchies for accurate object detection and semantic segmentation. In: Proceedings of the IEEE Conference on Computer Vision and Pattern Recognition, pp. 580–587 (2014)
15. Redmon, J., Divvala, S., Girshick, R., et al.: You only look once: unified, real-time object detection. In: Proceedings of the IEEE Proceedings of the IEEE Conference on Computer Vision and Pattern Recognition, pp. 779–788 (2016)
16. Liu, Z., Lin, Y.T., Cao, Y., et al.: Swin transformer: hierarchical vision transformer using shifted windows. In: Proceedings of the IEEE/CVF International Conference on Computer Vision, pp. 10012–10022 (2021)
17. Liu, Z., Mao, H., Wu, C.-Y., et al.: A ConvNet for the 2020s. arXiv preprint arXiv:2201.03545 (2022)
18. Ge, Z., Liu, S., Wang, F., Li, Z., et al.: YOLOX: exceeding yolo series in 2021. arXiv preprint arXiv:2107.08430 (2021)
19. Jocher, G., et al.: YOLOv5 (2021). https://github.com/ultralytics/yolov5
20. Lin, T.-Y., Dollar, P., Girshick, R., et al.: Feature pyramid networks for object detection. In: Proceedings of the IEEE Conference on Computer Vision and Pattern Recognition, pp. 936–944 (2017)
21. Liu, S., Qi, L., Qin, H.F., et al.: Path aggregation network for instance segmentation. In: Proceedings of the IEEE Conference on Computer Vision and Pattern Recognition, pp. 8759–8768 (2018)

Learning Grasp Ability Enhancement Through Deep Shape Generation

Junnan Jiang[1], Xiaohui Xiao[2], Fei Chen[3]([✉]), and Miao Li[1,2]([✉])

[1] The Institute of Technological Sciences, Wuhan University, Wuhan, China
miao.li@whu.edu.cn
[2] The School of Power and Mechanical Engineering, Wuhan University,
Wuhan, China
[3] Department of Mechanical and Automation Engineering,
The Chinese University of Hong Kong, Shenzhen, China
feichen@cuhk.edu.hk

Abstract. Data-driven especially deep learning-based approaches have become a dominant paradigm for robotic grasp planning during the past decade [2]. However, the performance of these methods is greatly influenced by the quality of the training dataset available. In this paper, we propose a framework to generate object shapes to augment the grasping dataset and thus can improve the grasp ability of a pre-designed deep neural network. First, the object shapes are embedded into a low dimensional feature space using an encoder-decoder structure network. Then, the rarity and graspness scores are computed for each object shape using outlier detection and grasp quality criteria. Finally, new objects are generated in feature space leveraging the original high rarity and graspness score objects' feature. Experimental results show that the grasp ability of a deep-learning-based grasp planning network can be effectively improved with the generated object shapes.

Keywords: Data augmentation · Grasp planning

1 Introduction

Despite significant progress, it is still a difficult task to plan a grasp for unknown object and robot [2,15]. During the past decade, data-driven especially deep learning-based approaches have demonstrated significant superiority compared with traditional model-based approaches [8]. However, the performance of the deep learning-based approaches is greatly limited by the quality of the available training dataset.

During the past few years, a large number of grasping datasets have been proposed [5,7,9,12,17,21], which can be generally categorized into two classes: CAD

This work was supported by Suzhou Key Industry Technology Innovation Project under the grant agreement number SYG202121. Also thanks Yasemin Bekiroglu for her valuable advice.

H. Liu et al. (Eds.): ICIRA 2022, LNAI 13458, pp. 735–746, 2022.
https://doi.org/10.1007/978-3-031-13841-6_66

(Computer Aided Design) model based datasets [5,17] and sensory model based datasets [9,21]. These datasets play an important role in training and qualifying the performance of different grasp planning algorithms. However, given a new object, a trained grasp planning system can still lead to a bad grasp. Most grasp planning frameworks will normally add these "failed objects" into the training dataset and train the model again. However, this trial and error process can be tedious, non-systematic and expensive.

To address this issue, in this paper we propose a learning-based approach to encapsulate object shape information into a low dimensional feature space. In this feature space, the shapes in the original dataset can be better encoded, interpolated and generated. Moreover, in this low dimensional feature space, two grasp-related metrics are proposed to generate new shapes that can further enhance the grasp ability of the original dataset.

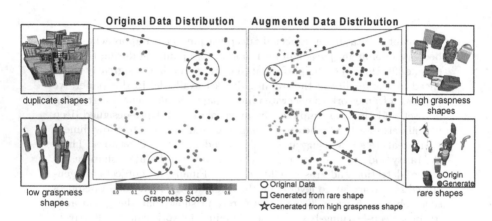

Fig. 1. Original and augmented data distribution comparison. We use t-SNE [16] to project the shapes' feature vectors to a 2D plane, the Euclidean distances between scattered points represent their feature similarity, and the color represents their graspness scores. We generate new data that leveraging the feature of original high rarity and graspness shapes so as to improve the dataset quality.

The main contributions of this paper are two folds:

- An encoder-decoder framework is proposed to map a voxelized shape into a low dimensional feature space.
- A data augmentation method using two new metrics is proposed to enhance the grasp ability

2   Related Work

2.1   Grasping Dataset

With the great success achieved in the data-driven grasp planning methods [2], many grasping datasets have been proposed (Table 1). Among these datasets,

YCB [5] is one of the first datasets that provided high-resolution 3D scans of everyday objects. Later, datasets containing more shapes, more annotated grasps and more sensory information have been proposed one after another. Due to subjective or random shape selection when making these datasets, although existing grasping algorithms can perform well on one dataset, it is still difficult to grasp a new unseen object. To solve this problem, EGAD dataset [18] hopes to scientifically include richer information on shape geometry and grasp complexity. However, since the shapes in EGAD are heuristically generated and do not utilize the existing real-world shapes features, they can only be used for evaluation but is difficult to be applied in the real application.

Table 1. Comparison of publicly available grasping datasets.

Dataset	Data Type	Objects	Annotate Method	Grasps
Cornell [12]	RGB	240	hand	8k
Google Brain [14]	RGB	N/A*	real-robot trials	650k
YCB [5]	CAD	97	N/A**	N/A**
EGAD [18]	CAD	2331	analytical	233k
DexNet [17]	CAD	1500	analytical	6.7M
6DOF-GraspNet [20]	CAD	206	simulator	7.07M
GraspNet [7]	CAD RGBD	88	analytical	1.1B
THU Dataset [11]	RGBD Tactile	17	real-robot trials	1.7k
Object Folder [9]	CAD Tactile Audio	1000	N/A**	N/A**

* around one hundred everyday objects, not provided.
** just single CAD files but no annotations or grasps provided.

2.2 Data Augmentation

Data augmentation [6,22] is a very popular approach in the learning-based methods because it effectively improves dataset quality and reduces network overfitting problems. Handcrafted methods have been widely used in computer vision, such as shifting, scaling and rotating. Similarly, grasping data augmentation by randomly rotating and cropping images [19], or randomly combining different shapes [23] do show some effect. However, except for requiring expert knowledge, these methods can only generate data in instance space, which means that just simply sense the original data multiple times with the original sensor(e.g. camera), but is difficult to combine the feature of grasping into generated data. With the development of generation methods such as AutoEncoder [3] and GAN [10,26], shape features can be better encoded and new shapes can be generated more flexibly. Wang [24] generates adversarial grasp objects which leverage the feature of the difficult-to-grasp object to generate new data, and generated data are difficult to grasp by the grasp planning algorithm. This gives a great motivation for generating new data to expand dataset with original objects' shape and grasp feature.

3 Object Shape Encoding

3.1 Network Architecture

In order to generate new shapes leveraging the feature of the original shapes, we propose an AutoEncoder-Critic network shown in Fig. 2. We use voxel to represent a shape, which maps a shape to a $64 \times 64 \times 64$ binary matrix. The AutoEncoder [3] of AE-Critic contains an Encoder E and a Decoder D. The Encoder maps a voxel x to a 128-dimension feature vector z, containing 5 3D convolution layers and 2 fully connected layers. The convolution layers use $4 \times 4 \times 4$ kernel size and 2 strides, with batch normalization and ReLU layers added in between, mapping the voxel to a $512 \times 4 \times 4 \times 4$ size feature map. The fully connected layers have 32768 and 128 neurons separately, map the feature map to a 128-dim feature vector. The Decoder mirrors the Encoder, maps a 128-dim feature vector to a $64 \times 64 \times 64$ reconstructed voxel $\hat{x}$, and contains 2 fully connected layers and 5 3D transposed convolution layers, the layers configurations are the same as Encoder. Using AutoEncoder, we can generate new shapes leveraging original shapes' feature by changing their feature vectors like interpolation, by changing the interpolation pairs and weights, we can theoretically generate infinite shapes.

In addition, to make the objects generated by interpolation more realistic, we add a Critic C, which aims to estimate the interpolated weight α corresponding to an interpolated shape, to regularize the training process of AutoEncoder [1]. The AE is trained to generate shapes to fool the Critic output lower interpolate weights, which means that the Critic is more willing to think the interpolated input is non-interpolated original shape. And thus, more realistic shapes similar to the original shapes can be generated. The structure of Critic is similar to Encoder, only with one more fully connected layer to map the 128-dim feature vector to a 1-dim interpolated weight.

3.2 Network Training

The Critic is trained to minimize the loss function (1), its first term trains the Critic to recover interpolated weight α from reconstructed voxel $\hat{x}_\alpha$, and its second term ensures the Critic's training process to be more stable.

$$L_C = ||C(\hat{x}_\alpha) - \alpha||^2 + ||C\{\gamma x + (1 - \gamma)D(E(x))\}||^2 \tag{1}$$

The AutoEncoder is trained to minimize the loss function (2), its first term trains the AutoEncoder to generate voxel $\hat{x}$ similar to original voxel x and its second term is to encourage the generated voxel by AutoEncoder to fool the Critic so as to generate more realistic voxel. Here L_B represents binary cross-entropy loss.

$$L_{(E,D)} = L_B \langle x, D(E(x)) \rangle + \lambda ||C(\hat{x}_\alpha)||^2 \tag{2}$$

Finally, we can map a voxel to a 128-dim feature vector. To better visualize the distribution of feature vectors, we use t-SNE [16] to project feature vectors to a 2D plane. The distribution of shapes can be seen in Fig. 1, which shows that similar objects are closer together, indicating that the feature vectors extracted by AE-Critic can be used for clustering or similarity measurement.

AE-Critic

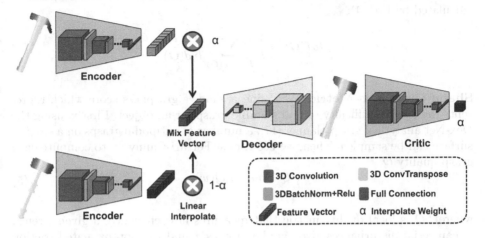

Fig. 2. AE-Critic network architecture. The Critic tries to estimate the interpolated weight α corresponding to an interpolated shape and thus can regularize the AutoEncoder (Encoder+Decoder) to generate more realistic interpolated shapes by fooling the Critic output lower interpolated weight.

4 Data Augmentation

With the AE-Critic network, shapes can be easily generated to expand the dataset, but what kinds of shapes are not sufficient and need to be generated? To let the network learn more diverse data, unseen or rare shapes are definitely what we want. And based on the property of grasping, when random sample grasps pose on an object [17], successful grasps are far less than failed grasps. This lead to the network can not learn many successful grasps, so shapes containing more successful grasps are also what we want to generate. Thus, we define shape rarity and graspness metrics, and new shapes leveraging the feature of original high rarity and graspness shapes are generated to augment the dataset.

4.1 Shape Rarity and Graspness Metrics

Shape Rarity Metric: We assume that rare shapes are those whose features are distinct from others. Thus, we use outlier detection [4] to evaluate each feature vector, for one shape which is rarer, the score of outlier detection is higher. In detail, we use L2 distance to measure two feature vectors' similarity. For one shape O, we select k-nearest shapes $N_k(O)$, and the local reachability density(lrd) can be defined by Eq. (3), which is the reciprocal of the mean of distances between feature vectors from the shape O to its k neighbors.

$$lrd(O) = \frac{1}{\frac{1}{k}\sum_{P \in N_k(O)} dist(O, P)} \tag{3}$$

Then the score of outlier detection defined as local outlier factor(lof) can be calculated by Eq. (4):

$$lof(O) = \frac{1}{k} \sum_{P \in N_k(O)} \frac{lrd(P)}{lrd(O)} \tag{4}$$

Shape Graspness Metric: We define a shape's graspness score which represents the level of difficulty to find a stable grasp for an object. Firstly, using the Dex-Net analytical grasp planner [17], a number of antipodal grasps on a shape's surface can be sampled. Then, we use robust Ferrari-Canny [8] to compute each grasp quality Q:

$$Q = \min_{w} LQ(w) \tag{5}$$

where LQ is local quality metric that measures how efficiently a given wrench w can resist disturbances given applied forces f and the approximated friction cone FC:

$$LQ(w) = \max_{f} \frac{||w||}{||f||} \tag{6}$$
$$\text{s.t.} \quad f \in FC$$

Finally, we use a threshold of 0.002 [13] to distinguish successful and failed grasps, and define the proportion of successful grasps of an object as its graspness score. The lower the graspness score, the harder it is for the object to grasp. The Fig. 3 is the histogram of graspness scores for all objects in the 3dnet dataset [25], the lack of high graspness score objects verifies that they are insufficient and needed to be generated.

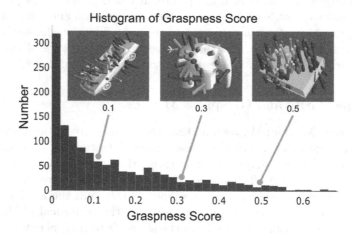

Fig. 3. The graspness score histogram of all objects in the 3dnet. Three objects with different graspness scores are displayed above, each cylinder represents an antipodal grasp, and the color of the cylinder indicates the grasp quality. (Color figure online)

4.2   Shape Generation

Based on AE-Critic network and two defined metrics, we can finally generate
shapes leveraging the feature of insufficient data so as to augment the dataset.
The overall pipeline is shown in Fig. 4.

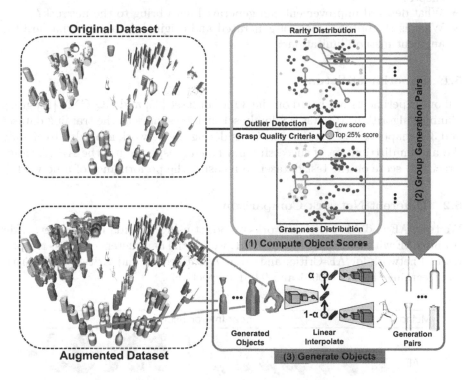

Fig. 4. The whole pipeline of shape generation for grasping dataset augmentation.
Original shapes' rarity and graspness scores are computed through outlier detection
and grasp quality criteria. Then every two high-score nearby objects are grouped as a
generation pair. Finally, the AE-Critic network is used for shape generation through
interpolation between two shapes' feature vectors.

After calculating the rarity and graspness scores of all objects, we only select
each two objects whose scores are higher than $t\%$ of all scores in each metric
as generation pair. Then, to avoid the feature vectors of shapes in generation
pairs being too close cause shapes duplicated or too far cause the intermediate
properties disappear, we group the nearest N-th to $(N + K)$-th neighbors into
generation pairs. With these generation pairs, we finally linear interpolate with
interpolated weight α in each generation pair, and decode the mix feature vector
to a new generated shape.

Up to now, we leverage the feature of high rarity and graspness score shapes
to generate new shapes and get a higher quality grasping dataset. The generated
number of augmented shapes depends on the parameters t, N, K and α.

5 Experiments

The goal of our experiment is to answer the following questions:

- Can Critic regularization help the AutoEncoder generate more realistic shapes?
- What detailed improvement can generated data bring to the network?
- What is the optimal ratio of generated and original data, and what are the augment method limitations?

5.1 Experiment Setup

All our experiments are based on the 3dnet dataset [25] and GQ-CNN [17] grasp planning algorithm. We first randomly select 1000 shapes as the training dataset and 363 shapes as the test dataset. Considering the network is needed to classify the uneven distribution of successful and failed grasps, we use the AP (Average Precision) score on the test dataset to measure the performance of a network.

5.2 Different Network Comparison

We train AE and AE-Critic networks on 3dnet using the Adam optimizer. After training AE with a learning rate of 0.001, we use the parameters of AE as the pre-trained network for AE-Critic, and train AutoEncoder and Critic of AE-Critic with learning rates of 0.0001 and 0.001 respectively.

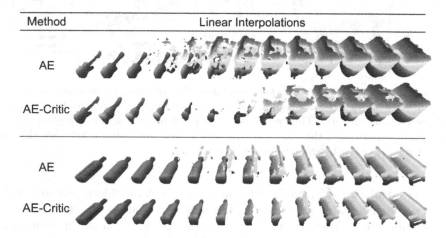

Fig. 5. Example of interpolation data from 3dnet [25], produced by AE and AE-Critic network. AE-Critic generates significantly fewer scattered points and the generated shape is more complete. While the shapes generated by AE are just like a simple addition of two objects.

Figure 5 is the shapes we generated using two networks with 0.1 interval interpolation, The result shows that the shape generated by AE will contain more scattered points, while the shapes generated by AE-Critic are more complete. In our understanding, AE tends to simply remember the voxel distribution corresponding to feature vectors, while AE-Critic tends to learn higher-level semantic information and decode a feature vector into a single object shape.

5.3   Improvement from Generated Data

To see the detailed improvement from generated data, we first randomly select 200 shapes from the training dataset and augment it with 190 and 219 new generated shapes leveraging the feature of the original high rarity or graspness score shapes separately. Then we train GQ-CNN [17] on the original and augmented dataset, and compute their AP score on the test dataset. Finally, we compare the number distribution of selected high-scoring data and generated data on rarity or graspness scores, and the AP score improvement of each object with different scores on the test dataset. The result is shown in Fig. 6, all three kinds of data are normalized for better visualization. It tells that more selected data will result in more generated data in the same score, which means that the generated data have the same property as the original data to a certain extent, and the generated data at the same time will lead to a greater AP score improvement.

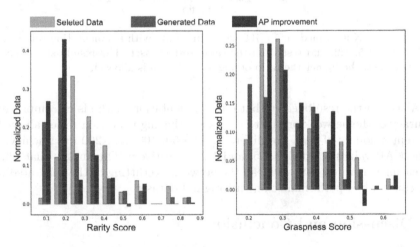

Fig. 6. The distribution between selected high-scoring data, generated data and AP improvement on test dataset with different rarity or graspness scores.

5.4   Augmentation Ratio and Limitation

To find the optimal augmentation ratio and augmentation limitation, we randomly select 50, 100, and 200 shapes from 1000 training datasets, and generate new shapes with augmentation ratios 1:0, 1:0.5, 1:1, 1:1.5, 1:2. This means that for 50 original shapes, 0, 25, 50, 75, and 100 generated shapes similar to both high rarity and graspness scores shapes are used for augmentation, the same as 100 and 200 shapes. Then the whole 15 augmented datasets are used for GQ-CNN training, all the 15 AP scores on the test dataset are shown in Fig. 7.

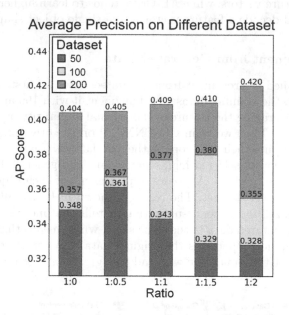

Fig. 7. GQCNN is trained on 50, 100, 200 3dnet data with augmentation ratios of 1:0, 1:0.5, 1:1, 1:1.5, 1:2, and tested on the same test dataset. The results show that the larger dataset, the higher the ratio of augmented data is allowed.

Although the results show that our augmentation methods can improve the accuracy of the network on the test dataset, the augmentation ratios allowed by different amounts of data are different. The 50, 100, and 200 data achieve the highest AP values at 1:0.5, 1:1.5, and 1:2 respectively. This means that blindly increasing generated data will lead the network overfitting to the generated data and cause a bad performance on the original dataset.

6   Discussion and Conclusion

6.1   Discussion

Although the data we generate can play the role of the original object to a certain extent and help the network achieve higher accuracy on the unseen data, there are still some limitations in this paper. First, shape rarity and graspness metrics are not unique. Not considered properties, such as object size or multi-fingers grasp quality evaluation, will also affect the metric score to a certain extent. In addition, in shape generation, the shape representation of voxel, generation pairs selection method and interpolated weight may not optimal. Perhaps new generation methods can enable generated objects to better utilize and extend the characteristic of original data.

6.2   Conclusion

In this paper, we present a general pipeline for grasping dataset augmentation. Objects are encoded into feature vectors using the AutoEncoder-Critic network, and generated objects, leveraging the feature of original high rarity and graspness score objects, are used to augment the original grasping dataset. Experiments show our generated data can play the role of original data to a certain extent, improving the network performance on the test dataset. In the future work, we hope to investigate in more detail about what kind of data can best enhance the robustness of grasp planning algorithms and try new generation methods to reduce the gap between original and generated data.

References

1. Berthelot, D., Raffel, C., Roy, A., Goodfellow, I.: Understanding and improving interpolation in autoencoders via an adversarial regularizer. arXiv preprint arXiv:1807.07543 (2018)
2. Bohg, J., Morales, A., Asfour, T., Kragic, D.: Data-driven grasp synthesis-a survey. IEEE Trans. Rob. **30**(2), 289–309 (2013)
3. Bourlard, H., Kamp, Y.: Auto-association by multilayer perceptrons and singular value decomposition. Biol. Cybern. **59**(4), 291–294 (1988). https://doi.org/10.1007/BF00332918
4. Breunig, M.M., Kriegel, H.P., Ng, R.T., Sander, J.: LOF: identifying density-based local outliers. In: Proceedings of the 2000 ACM SIGMOD International Conference on Management of Data, pp. 93–104 (2000)
5. Calli, B., Singh, A., Walsman, A., Srinivasa, S., Abbeel, P., Dollar, A.M.: The YCB object and model set: towards common benchmarks for manipulation research. In: 2015 International Conference on Advanced Robotics (ICAR), pp. 510–517. IEEE (2015)
6. Cubuk, E.D., Zoph, B., Mane, D., Vasudevan, V., Le, Q.V.: AutoAugment: learning augmentation strategies from data. In: Proceedings of the IEEE/CVF Conference on Computer Vision and Pattern Recognition, pp. 113–123 (2019)
7. Fang, H.S., Wang, C., Gou, M., Lu, C.: GraspNet-1billion: a large-scale benchmark for general object grasping. In: Proceedings of the IEEE/CVF Conference on Computer Vision and Pattern Recognition, pp. 11444–11453 (2020)
8. Ferrari, C., Canny, J.F.: Planning optimal grasps. In: ICRA, vol. 3, p. 6 (1992)
9. Gao, R., et al.: ObjectFolder 2.0: a multisensory object dataset for sim2real transfer. arXiv preprint arXiv:2204.02389 (2022)
10. Goodfellow, I., et al.: Generative adversarial nets. In: Advances in Neural Information Processing Systems, vol. 27 (2014)
11. Guo, D., Sun, F., Fang, B., Yang, C., Xi, N.: Robotic grasping using visual and tactile sensing. Inf. Sci. **417**, 274–286 (2017)
12. Jiang, Y., Moseson, S., Saxena, A.: Efficient grasping from RGBD images: learning using a new rectangle representation. In: 2011 IEEE International Conference on Robotics and Automation, pp. 3304–3311. IEEE (2011)
13. Kappler, D., Bohg, J., Schaal, S.: Leveraging big data for grasp planning. In: 2015 IEEE International Conference on Robotics and Automation (ICRA), pp. 4304–4311. IEEE (2015)

14. Levine, S., Pastor, P., Krizhevsky, A., Ibarz, J., Quillen, D.: Learning hand-eye coordination for robotic grasping with deep learning and large-scale data collection. Int. J. Robot. Res. **37**(4–5), 421–436 (2018)
15. Li, M., Hang, K., Kragic, D., Billard, A.: Dexterous grasping under shape uncertainty. Robot. Auton. Syst. **75**, 352–364 (2016)
16. Van der Maaten, L., Hinton, G.: Visualizing data using t-SNE. J. Mach. Learn. Res. **9**(11) (2008)
17. Mahler, J., et al.: Dex-Net 2.0: deep learning to plan robust grasps with synthetic point clouds and analytic grasp metrics. arXiv preprint arXiv:1703.09312 (2017)
18. Morrison, D., Corke, P., Leitner, J.: EGAD! an evolved grasping analysis dataset for diversity and reproducibility in robotic manipulation. IEEE Robot. Autom. Lett. **5**(3), 4368–4375 (2020)
19. Morrison, D., Corke, P., Leitner, J.: Learning robust, real-time, reactive robotic grasping. Int. J. Robot. Res. **39**(2–3), 183–201 (2020)
20. Mousavian, A., Eppner, C., Fox, D.: 6-DOF GraspNet: variational grasp generation for object manipulation. In: Proceedings of the IEEE/CVF International Conference on Computer Vision, pp. 2901–2910 (2019)
21. Narang, Y.S., Sundaralingam, B., Van Wyk, K., Mousavian, A., Fox, D.: Interpreting and predicting tactile signals for the SynTouch BioTac. Int. J. Robot. Res. **40**(12–14), 1467–1487 (2021)
22. Shorten, C., Khoshgoftaar, T.M.: A survey on image data augmentation for deep learning. J. Big Data **6**(1), 1–48 (2019)
23. Tobin, J., Fong, R., Ray, A., Schneider, J., Zaremba, W., Abbeel, P.: Domain randomization for transferring deep neural networks from simulation to the real world. In: 2017 IEEE/RSJ International Conference on Intelligent Robots and Systems (IROS), pp. 23–30. IEEE (2017)
24. Wang, D., et al.: Adversarial grasp objects. In: 2019 IEEE 15th International Conference on Automation Science and Engineering (CASE), pp. 241–248. IEEE (2019)
25. Wohlkinger, W., Aldoma, A., Rusu, R.B., Vincze, M.: 3DNet: large-scale object class recognition from cad models. In: 2012 IEEE International Conference on Robotics and Automation, pp. 5384–5391. IEEE (2012)
26. Wu, J., Zhang, C., Xue, T., Freeman, W.T., Tenenbaum, J.B.: Learning a probabilistic latent space of object shapes via 3D generative-adversarial modeling. In: Proceedings of the 30th International Conference on Neural Information Processing Systems, pp. 82–90 (2016)

A Grasp Pose Detection Network Based on the DeepLabv3+ Semantic Segmentation Model

Qinjian Zhang[1] , Xiangyan Zhang[1] , and Haiyuan Li[2(✉)]

[1] Beijing Information Science and Technology University, Beijing, China
[2] Beijing University of Posts and Telecommunications, Beijing, China
lihaiyuan@bupt.edu.cn

Abstract. Grasping is an important and fundamental action for the interaction between robots and the environment. However, because grasping is a complex system engineering, there is still much room for development. At present, many studies use regression to solve the problem of grasp detection or use the unstable 3D point cloud as input, which may cause poor results to a certain extent. In this paper, we propose to use semantic segmentation of pixel-level classification to solve the problem of grasp pose detection. We adopt a grasp detection method based on the DeepLabv3+ model, which includes semantic segmentation and post-processing. In the semantic segmentation part, the classification mask of the objects is predicted through the input RGB image, and then the predicted objects of different classifications are fitted with the minimum bounding directed rectangle to obtain the two-dimensional grasp pose, and the final three-dimensional grasping pose is calculated through the conversion of the input depth image. On the validation dataset, we use the indicator of semantic segmentation to evaluate the proposed network and achieve a great result. In addition, the simulation robot experiment further verifies the effectiveness of the network.

Keywords: Grasp pose detection · DeepLabv3+ · Minimum bounding directed rectangle fitting

1 Introduction

Grasping and manipulation are significant forms of interaction between robots and the environment, and grasping is a more fundamental and vital action in the process of interaction. Although in recent years, researchers have carried out plenty of research related to grasping, there is still much room for development in the research of grasping because the grasping process is quite complex, this is reflected not only in the complexity and diversity of grasping scenes but also in the delicacy and difficulty of robot grasping decision-making, path planning and so on.

The traditional mathematical analysis method obtains the reasonable grasp pose through accurate numerical calculation, which will make the analysis and calculation process very complex and difficult to be applied to new objects and scenes [1–3].

© The Author(s), under exclusive license to Springer Nature Switzerland AG 2022
H. Liu et al. (Eds.): ICIRA 2022, LNAI 13458, pp. 747–758, 2022.
https://doi.org/10.1007/978-3-031-13841-6_67

With the development of artificial intelligence and machine vision, data-driven deep learning methods are more and more widely used in grasping research. The typical methods are 2D planar grasp and 6-DoF grasp pose detection. 2D planar grasp is usually represented by an oriented rectangle [4–6]. Typical 2D grasp datasets include the Cornell dataset [4] and the Jacquard dataset [7]. Lenz et al. proposed a convolutional neural network for 2D planar grasp detection [5]. Kumra et al. designed a network using deep convolution to extract features and shallow convolution to predict grasp parameters and to improve accuracy and efficiency [8]. Asif et al. proposed an efficient convolution network based on encoding and decoding structure, which not only maintains a compact structure but also produces high accuracy [9]. 6-DoF grasp can realize the gripper to grasp the object from different angles in three-dimensional space. 3D point cloud data is often used as input for 6-DoF grasp pose detection, and three-dimensional point cloud neural networks, such as PointNet [10] and PointNet++ [11], are used as backbone networks. GPD designs a network structure to generate a set of 6-DOF grasp candidates and realizes the 6-DoF grasp in dense clutter [12]. Liang et al. proposed an end-to-end grasp evaluation model named PointNetGPD [13]. GraspNet uses Approach Network, Operation Network, and Tolerance Network to form an end-to-end grasp detection network to predict and evaluate grasp parameters [14]. Gou et al. proposed the RGBD-Grasp network, which realizes 7-DoF grasp detection with two subtasks [15]. Li et al. built a 6-DoF grasp pose estimation network with the PointNet++ model to encode features and three parallel decoders [16].

In this paper, we designed a grasp detection algorithm based on the semantic segmentation network, which includes a semantic segmentation model and post-processing process. The semantic segmentation network adopts the DeepLabv3+ model with Xception as the backbone [17], which aims to realize the segmentation and location of objects. The post-processing is to fit the predicted semantic segmented objects with the minimum bounding rectangle to obtain the two-dimensional grasp pose and use the depth image to convert it into the final three-dimensional grasp pose.

The proposed grasp detection method has three main advantages. Firstly, semantic segmentation is used to solve the problem of grasp pose detection, which simplifies the problem and improves the prediction accuracy; Secondly, the excellent DeepLabv3+ model is adopted in the network, and the recently proposed large-scale grasp detection dataset GraspNet-1Billion [14] is used; thirdly, the proposed method is verified by simulation.

2 Method

An end-to-end grasp detection network based on image semantic segmentation is proposed, which is illustrated in Fig. 1. The whole network process includes two parts: semantic segmentation network and post-processing of minimum bounding directed rectangle fitting. The semantic segmentation network adopts the DeepLabv3+ model with Xception as the backbone, which is used to segment different objects in the scene according to the input RGB image. In the post-processing process, the minimum bounding directed rectangle of different objects is fitted according to the classification results predicted by the semantic segmentation network, and then the grasp pose parameters are calculated based on the fitted rectangle.

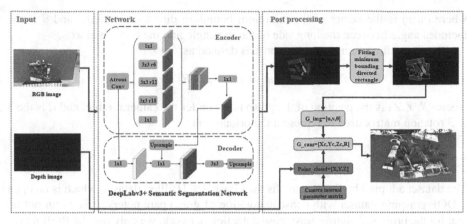

Fig. 1. Overview of the grasp pose detection network

2.1 Representation of Grasp Pose

Grasp pose detection is to obtain the position and orientation of the gripper. In the research, two kinds of representation methods of grasp pose will be adopted: one is the two-dimensional grasp pose under the image frame, and the other is the three-dimensional grasp pose under the camera coordinate system. The two representation methods are embodied in the post-processing stage of the network structure shown in Fig. 1. These two representations are not isolated. The two-dimensional grasp pose will be calculated by fitting the minimum bounding directed rectangle, and then will be converted into the grasp pose in three-dimensional space.

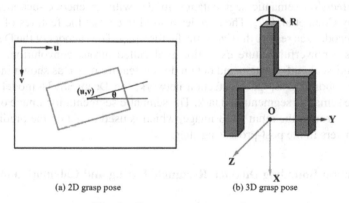

(a) 2D grasp pose   (b) 3D grasp pose

Fig. 2. Grasp pose representation

Figure 2 illustrates the two grasping pose representation methods. The two-dimensional grasp pose is expressed as:

$$G\_img = [u, v, \theta] \tag{1}$$

where (u, v) is the center of the minimum bounding directed rectangle, and θ is the included angle between the long side of the rectangle and the horizontal axis.

The three-dimensional grasping pose is defined as:

$$G\_cam = [X, Y, Z, R] \tag{2}$$

where (X, Y, Z) is the position of the grasp point under the camera frame, and R is the 3 × 3 rotation matrix used to represent the orientation.

2.2 Dataset

The dataset adopted by the research is the GraspNet-1Billion dataset, which is an open 6-DOF grasping dataset with dense annotation of grasp parameters. It is worth noting that for the proposed simple grasp pose detection network, we only use the RGB image and the corresponding semantic segmentation label image in the dataset, rather than the 6-DOF grasp label.

The dataset provides a total of 190 scenes, and each scene contains 256 images taken from different camera views. Of the 190 scenes, 100 scenes are used for model training, and other scenes are used for model verification of different functions. Because the proposed grasp pose detection algorithm is different from the task of 6-DOF grasp detection, in the research, 190 scenes are randomly divided into the training set, test set and verification set according to the ratio of 6:2:2 instead of using the original division rules of the dataset.

2.3 The DeepLabv3+ Semantic Segmentation Network

The adopted grasp pose detection network is based on the DeepLabv3+ model, which is a high-precision semantic segmentation model with an encoder-decoder structure proposed by Chen et al. [17]. The encoder is used to extract the features of the image, while the decoder can restore the size of the feature map. The encoder of the DeepLabv3+ model uses a powerful feature extraction tool called atrous convolution, which can capture multi-scale information and obtain denser feature maps, as shown in Fig. 1.

In the proposed grasp pose detection network, the DeepLabv3+ model is used to perform the semantic segmentation task. The semantic segmentation image of the scene is predicted through the input RGB image, which is used to obtain the predicted grasp pose parameters in the post-processing stage.

2.4 Minimum Bounding Directed Rectangle Fitting and Calculation of Grasp Pose

The post-processing of the network is the process of obtaining the grasp pose under the camera coordinate system by predicting the output image through the semantic segmentation model. It includes two steps: minimum bounding directed rectangle fitting and grasp pose transformation.

The minimum bounding directed rectangle fitting refers to using a directional rectangle to fit and envelope the shapes of different classified objects and then obtaining the two-dimensional grasp pose under the image frame through the fitted rectangle, as shown in Fig. 3.

This process first needs to read the classification of objects in the prediction image, then traverse the classification of each object, find the minimum bounding rectangle of the classified object, and calculate the coordinates of the four corners and center points of the rectangle. The center point of the obtained rectangle is regarded as the grasp point, and the rotation angle is calculated from four corners according to Eq. (3).

$$
\begin{cases}
l_1 = dist(p_1, p_2) \\
l_2 = dist(p_2, p_3) \\
l = \max\{l_1, l_2\} \\
\theta = \begin{cases} \arctan \dfrac{l_v}{l_u} & (l_u \neq 0) \\ \dfrac{\pi}{2} & (l_u = 0) \end{cases}
\end{cases}
\tag{3}
$$

where p_1, p_2 and p_3 are the three corner points obtained in the clockwise direction of the rectangle, $dist$ represents the distance between the two points, l_u and l_v respectively refer to the distance obtained by projecting l in the horizontal and vertical directions. From this, the two-dimensional grasp pose $G\_img = [u, v, \theta]$ is got.

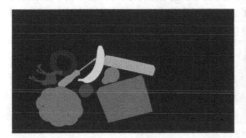 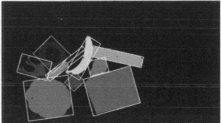

(a) Semantic segmentation mask label   (b) Minimum bounding directed rectangle fitting

Fig. 3. Fitting result

The transformation of the 2D grasp pose to the 3D grasp pose needs the help of the input depth image. Firstly, the depth value of the pixel in the depth image is found by the two-dimensional grasp point, and then the three-dimensional coordinates of the grasp point under the camera coordinate system can be obtained through the conversion of Eq. (4). Finally, the rotation angle is converted into a rotation matrix by Eq. (5).

$$
\begin{cases}
X = (u - c_x) \cdot \dfrac{Z}{f_x} \\
Y = (v - c_y) \cdot \dfrac{Z}{f_y}
\end{cases}
\tag{4}
$$

where u and v are the 2D coordinates of grasp point, X, Y, and Z are the 3D coordinates of grasp point, and f_x, f_y, c_x and c_y are the internal parameters of the depth camera.

$$R = \begin{bmatrix} 0 & 0 & -1 \\ 0 & 1 & 0 \\ 1 & 0 & 0 \end{bmatrix} \bullet \begin{bmatrix} 1 & 0 & 0 \\ 0 & \cos(\theta) & -\sin(\theta) \\ 0 & \sin(\theta) & \cos(\theta) \end{bmatrix} \qquad (5)$$

where θ is the rotation angle in the two-dimensional grasp pose, and R is the rotation matrix in the three-dimensional space. Thus, the predicted grasp pose $G = [X, Y, Z, R]$ is obtained.

3 Experiment

In this part, we first train the semantic segmentation model based on DeepLabv3+, then predict and evaluate the trained model by the verification dataset, and finally further verify the proposed grasp pose detection network through simulation experiments.

3.1 Model Training

The training process of the semantic segmentation network is to input the RGB image and the corresponding semantic segmentation label image into the DeepLabv3+ network and train a series of weight parameters of the model through forward and backward propagation, so that the prediction result can approach the label data as much as possible.

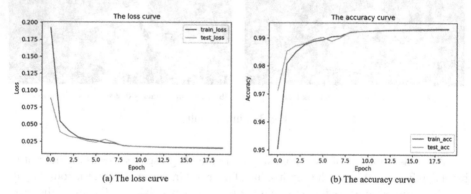

(a) The loss curve   (b) The accuracy curve

Fig. 4. The model training process curve

The dataset used in the training is the data of the Kinect file in the GraspNet-1Billion dataset. After randomly disrupting 48640 samples of 190 scenes, the training set, test set, and verification set are allocated according to the ratio of 6:2:2. The training set and test set are used in the training process, and the verification set is used for the later evaluation model. In order to improve the operation efficiency and training accuracy, firstly, the image is reduced to 224×224 pixels, and then normalize the input image. In data loading, to save computer memory, a data generator is used to load data.

The optimizer used in the training process is the Adam optimizer, the initial learning rate is set to 0.0005, and the set learning rate can be automatically adjusted according to the performance of the test set during the training process. The loss function uses cross-entropy, as shown in Eq. (6).

$$Loss = -\frac{1}{N} \sum_{i=1}^{N} \left[y_i \cdot \ln a_i + (1 - y_i) \cdot \ln(1 - a_i) \right] \tag{6}$$

where N is the number of samples, y is the predicted value and a is the label. The training batch is set to 6 and the epoch is 20.

The training result is shown in Fig. 4. It can be seen from the figure that the curve is stable without obvious fluctuation during the training process, and the training curve is close to the test curve, indicating that there is no problem with over fitting and under fitting. The accuracy curve exceeds 99% after the 10th epoch, indicating that the model training effect is quite superior.

3.2 Prediction and Evaluation

It can be seen from the training curve that the prediction accuracy of the model is very great. In order to further verify the effect of the model, the divided verification set is used to predict and verify the trained model.

Figure 5 shows the prediction of the semantic segmentation network and the effect of using minimum bounding directed rectangle fitting. The four columns from left to right in the figure represent the input RGB image, label image, prediction image, and fitting image respectively. Comparing the prediction results with the label images, it can be seen that the prediction effect is very close to the actual label. It can not only correctly predict the classification of objects, which are represented by different colors, but also basically accurately predict the shape and details of objects. From the fitting image of the minimum bounding rectangle in the fourth column, it can be seen that the proposed fitting method can fit the directed rectangles of different classified objects based on the prediction results, which verifies that the post-processing process of the proposed grasp pose detection network is effective.

Because the proposed grasp pose detection network transforms the grasping problem into a semantic segmentation task, the evaluating indicator of the semantic segmentation network, which includes pixel-wise accuracy and means of class-wise intersection over union, simplified as Pixel Acc. and Mean IoU, is used to verify the trained model on the verification set [18]. Take 6 as the batch, obtain the validation data from the data generator and calculate the values of these two indicators. According to the calculation results on these batches, a boxplot is drawn, as shown in Fig. 6.

The left and right figures show the evaluation results of Mean IoU and Pixel Acc respectively. The green box in the figure represents the evaluation results of the DeepLabv3+ model with Mobilenet as the backbone, while the orange box represents the evaluation results of the DeepLabv3+ model with Xception as the backbone. It can be seen from the two figures that the DeepLabv3+ model with Xception as the backbone performs better than the other one, which is the reason why the grasp pose network chooses the DeepLabv3+ model with Xception as the backbone.

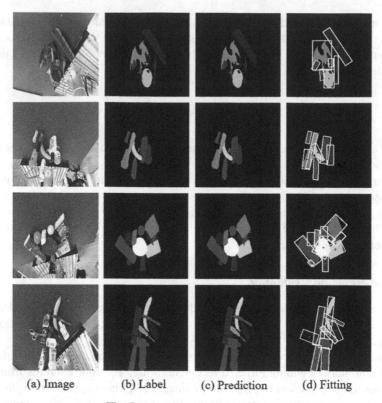

(a) Image   (b) Label   (c) Prediction   (d) Fitting

Fig. 5. Model prediction and fitting

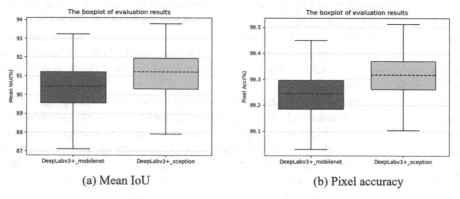

(a) Mean IoU   (b) Pixel accuracy

Fig. 6. The boxplot of evaluation results

The detailed data of the evaluation results can be seen in Table 1. The data in the table is the average value of the calculation results on different batches. It can be seen from the data in the table that the evaluation results of the two methods are excellent. The pixel-wise accuracy of the two methods exceeds 99%, and the mean of class-wise intersection over union also exceeds 90%. In the comparison, it can also be seen that the effect of using Xception as the backbone is better.

Table 1. Evaluation results of the DeepLabv3+ network based on different backbone models

Method	Backbone	Evaluation results	
		Mean IoU (%)	Pixel acc. (%)
DeepLabv3+	Mobilenet	90.25	99.24
	Xception	91.02	99.31

3.3 Grasp Simulation

In order to verify the practicability of the proposed grasp pose detection network, the grasp experiment in the simulation environment is carried out. Coppeliasim software is used in the simulation, which is a cross-platform simulation software with rich functions and powerful performance. The actuator used in the experiment is the UR5 robot equipped with Jaco three-finger dexterous hand, and the depth camera adopts the Kinect camera.

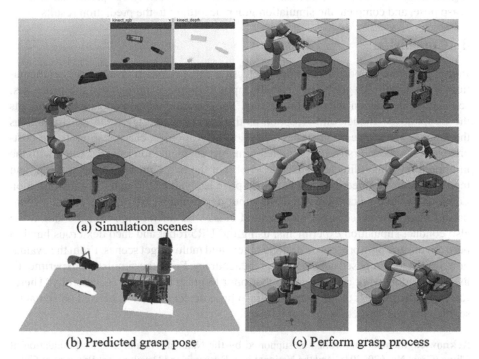

(a) Simulation scenes

(b) Predicted grasp pose   (c) Perform grasp process

Fig. 7. Simulation grasp experiment

Using the joint simulation of Python and Coppeliasim, firstly, import the object model from the dataset and add the depth camera and actuator in the virtual environment, then obtain the image taken by the depth camera and send it to the grasp pose detection network to predict the three-dimensional grasp pose under the camera frame and convert it into the grasp pose under the world coordinate system through Eq. (7), Finally, the actuator reaches the predicted pose and according to the planned path to grasp.

$$T = \begin{bmatrix} R & P \\ 0 & 1 \end{bmatrix}$$

$$\begin{pmatrix} Pw \\ 1 \end{pmatrix} = T \bullet \begin{pmatrix} Pc \\ 1 \end{pmatrix}$$

$$Rw = R \bullet Rc \tag{7}$$

where T is the homogeneous transformation matrix from the camera coordinate system to the world coordinate system, P_c and R_c represent the position and rotation matrix under the camera coordinate system, and P_w and R_w are the position and rotation matrix under the world coordinate system.

The process of simulation grasp is shown in Fig. 7. Figure (a) shows the built simulation scene, figure (b) shows the predicted grasp pose under the camera coordinate system, and figure (c) shows the process of grasp according to the predicted grasp pose. From the simulation results, the proposed grasp pose detection network based on semantic segmentation still has good performance in the new scene, which can predict the desired grasp pose, and complete the simulation grasp according to the prediction results.

4 Conclusion

In this paper, we propose a grasp pose detection network based on semantic segmentation. It predicts the 3D grasp pose from the input RGB image through two sub-processes: semantic segmentation and post-processing. The semantic segmentation network adopts the DeepLabv3+ model with Xception as the backbone and takes the RGB image as the input to predict the semantic segmentation map of object classification. In the post-processing process, firstly, the predicted semantic segmentation image is fitted with the minimum bounding directed rectangle to obtain the two-dimensional grasp pose, and then the predicted three-dimensional grasp pose is obtained through the transformation Equation of the predicted grasp and the input depth image. We achieve model evaluation using pixel-wise accuracy and mean of class-wise intersection over the union. We also conduct simulation experiments, using the UR5 robot and Jaco dexterous hand to perform the grasping process on a single object and multi-target scenes. From the evaluation results, the proposed network has great accuracy. From the simulation experiments, the proposed network can also guide the robot to grasp the object successfully. Therefore, the effectiveness of the proposed grasp pose detection network based on semantic segmentation is verified.

Acknowledgments. This work was supported by the National Natural Science Foundation of China (Grant No. 62003048) and the National Key Research and Development Program of China (Grant No. 2019YFB1309802).

References

1. Bicchi, A., Kumar, V.: Robotic grasping and contact: a review. In: Proceedings 2000 ICRA. Millennium Conference. IEEE International Conference on Robotics and Automation, vol. 1, pp. 348–353. IEEE, San Francisco (2000)
2. Bohg, J., Morales, A., Asfour, T., Kragic, D.: Data-driven grasp synthesis—a survey. IEEE Trans. Rob. **30**(2), 289–309 (2014)
3. Dang, H., Allen, P.K.: Semantic grasping: planning robotic grasps functionally suitable for an object manipulation task. In: 2012 IEEE/RSJ International Conference on Intelligent Robots and Systems, pp. 1311–1317. IEEE, Vilamoura-Algarve (2012)
4. Jiang, Y., Moseson, S., Saxena, A.: Efficient grasping from RGBD images: learning using a new rectangle representation. In: 2011 IEEE International Conference on Robotics and Automation, pp. 3304–3311. IEEE, Shanghai (2011)
5. Lenz, I., Lee, H., Saxena, A.: Deep learning for detecting robotic grasps. Int. J. Robot. Res. **34**(4–5), 705–724 (2015)
6. Pinto, L., Gupta, A.: Supersizing self-supervision: learning to grasp from 50K tries and 700 robot hours. In: 2016 IEEE International Conference on Robotics and Automation, pp. 3406–3413. IEEE, Stockholm (2016)
7. Depierre, A., Dellandréa, E., Chen, L.: Jacquard: a large scale dataset for robotic grasp detection. In: 2018 IEEE/RSJ International Conference on Intelligent Robots and Systems, pp. 3511–3516. IEEE, Madrid (2018)
8. Kumra, S., Kanan, C.: Robotic grasp detection using deep convolutional neural networks. In: 2017 IEEE/RSJ International Conference on Intelligent Robots and Systems, pp. 769–776. IEEE, Vancouver (2017)
9. Asir, U., Tang, J.B., Harrer, S.: GraspNet: an efficient convolutional neural network for real-time grasp detection for low-powered devices. In: 27th International Joint Conference on Artificial Intelligence, Stockholm, pp. 4875–4882 (2018)
10. Qi, C.R., Su, H., Mo, K.C., Guibas, L.J.: PointNet: deep learning on point sets for 3d classification and segmentation. In: 2017 IEEE Conference on Computer Vision and Pattern Recognition, pp. 652–660. IEEE, Honolulu (2017)
11. Qi, C.R., Su, H., Mo, K.C., Guibas, L.J.: PointNet plus plus: deep hierarchical feature learning on point sets in a metric space. In: 31st Annual Conference on Neural Information Processing Systems, Long Beach (2017)
12. Ten Pas, A., Gualtieri, M., Saenko, K., Platt, R.: Grasp pose detection in point clouds. Int. J. Robot. Res. **36**(13–14), 1455–1473 (2017)
13. Liang, H.Z., et al.: PointNetGPD: detecting grasp configurations from point sets. In: 2019 International Conference on Robotics and Automation, pp. 3629–3635. IEEE, Montreal (2019)
14. Fang, H.S., Wang, C., Gou, M., Lu, C.: GraspNet-1Billion: a large-scale benchmark for general object grasping. In: 2020 IEEE/CVF Conference on Computer Vision and Pattern Recognition, pp. 11441–11450. IEEE, Seattle (2020)
15. Gou, M., Fang, H.S., Zhu, Z., Xu, S., Wang, C., Lu, C.: RGB matters: learning 7-DoF grasp poses on monocular RGBD images. In: 2021 IEEE International Conference on Robotics and Automation, pp. 13459–13466. IEEE, Xi'an (2021)
16. Li, Y., Kong, T., Chu, R., Li, Y., Wang, P., Li, L.: Simultaneous semantic and collision learning for 6-DoF grasp pose estimation. In: 2021 IEEE/RSJ International Conference on Intelligent Robots and Systems, pp. 3571–3578. IEEE, Prague (2021)

17. Chen, L.-C., Zhu, Y., Papandreou, G., Schroff, F., Adam, H.: Encoder-decoder with atrous separable convolution for semantic image segmentation. In: Ferrari, V., Hebert, M., Sminchisescu, C., Weiss, Y. (eds.) ECCV 2018. LNCS, vol. 11211, pp. 833–851. Springer, Cham (2018). https://doi.org/10.1007/978-3-030-01234-2_49
18. Zhao, H.S., Shi, J.P., Qi, X.J., Wang X.G., Jia J.Y.: Pyramid scene parsing network. In: 2017 IEEE Conference on Computer Vision and Pattern Recognition, pp. 6230–6239. IEEE, Honolulu (2017)

Topology Reconstruction of High-Reflective Surfaces Based on Multi-modality Data

Xiaohan Pei, Yuansong Yang, Mingjun Ren[(✉)], and Limin Zhu

School of Mechanical Engineering, Shanghai Jiao Tong University, Shanghai 200240, China
renmj@sjtu.edu.cn

Abstract. Fringe projection profilometry (FPP) performs poorly in the three-dimensional (3-D) topology reconstruction of high-reflective surfaces. The missing points are inevitable in the high-reflective regions in the point clouds reconstructed by the FPP. The existing research on the high-reflective problems cannot ensure the accuracy and efficiency of the reconstruction simultaneously. The photometric stereo (PS) technique is introduced into the system to provide additional normal information to solve the problem in this paper. The point clouds measured by the FPP sensor and the normal data measured by the PS sensor are combined into the multi-modality data. The fusion method is formulated as an optimization problem based on two constraints, i.e., the position constraint estimated by the point clouds and the direction constraint estimated by the normal data. Different values of the weight factor are specially designed in the optimization to deal with the constraint reliability difference in the high-reflective regions and the other regions. Not only the missing points in high-reflective regions are complementally reconstructed through the proposed fusion method, but also the accuracy of the reconstructed topology is optimized due to the introduction of the high-accuracy normal data. In addition, the proposed method only needs measuring once without repeated parameter adjustment or any human intervention, which improves the reconstruction efficiency. In the experiment of reconstructing a metal free-form surface, the deviation of the topology error between the proposed fusion method and a coordinate measuring machine is only 10 μm.

Keywords: Topology reconstruction · Fringe projection profilometry (FPP) · Photometric stereo (PS) · High-reflective surfaces · Multi-modality data

1 Introduction

The three-dimensional (3-D) topology reconstruction is widely used in industry, including process control and inspection [1, 2]. The optical methods have developed rapidly recently due to non-contact and high efficiency. Fringe projection profilometry (FPP) is one of the most promising techniques among them [3, 4]. The FPP system mainly consists of a projector and a camera. The projector projects a sequence of designed fringe patterns on the target surface. Simultaneously, the camera captures the fringe patterns deformed by the topology of the target surface, which are used for the reconstruction based on the phase values implied in the fringe patterns. However, the optical property of

© The Author(s), under exclusive license to Springer Nature Switzerland AG 2022
H. Liu et al. (Eds.): ICIRA 2022, LNAI 13458, pp. 759–768, 2022.
https://doi.org/10.1007/978-3-031-13841-6_68

the target surface has a great impact on the reconstruction result. Most target objects are machined metallic workpieces. Their reflectance properties would influence the reconstruction integrity and accuracy due to the intensity saturation of the camera image in the high-reflective regions.

To overcome the high-reflective problem in FPP, many methods have been proposed by the researchers recently. Zhang et al. [5] captured a sequence of images under different exposure times, and the points in high-reflective regions were complementally reconstructed through the images under short exposure time. Likewise, Waddington et al. [6] captured a sequence of images under different projecting intensities. These two kinds of methods are prone to adjust the parameters of the camera or projector. For them, the conflict between the number of the designed parameters and the reconstruction efficiency is hard to compromise. Besides these parameter-based methods, the equipment-based methods are proposed by introducing additional hardware, e.g., the polarizing filters [7], the polarization camera [8], and the light field camera [3]. Additional system errors lead to a low signal-to-noise ratio for these methods, and further reduce the reconstruction accuracy. Therefore, the existing methods cannot ensure both the efficiency and the accuracy to overcome the high-reflective problem.

The high-reflective problem in FPP is caused by the missing information in the high-reflective regions. The information complementary in these regions is critical to overcome this problem. The introduction of the additional sensor is considered. The photometric stereo (PS) is another kind of the optical technique with a great advantage in the estimation of the high-accuracy surface normal [9]. The PS system mainly consists of several designed lighting sources and a camera. A sequence of the images of the target surface are captured under different lighting directions. The normal data are estimated from the images based on the reflectance model. An inverse reflectance model is proposed in our previous work [10], which is robust to the high-reflective surfaces.

A multi-modality sensor system is proposed to tackle the high-reflective problem by integrating FPP and PS in this paper. The FPP sensor obtains the original point clouds of the target surface with the missing points in the high-reflective regions. The PS sensor obtains the intact high-accuracy normal data of the target surface. The point clouds and normal data are combined into the multi-modality data for fusion to improve the reconstruction accuracy. The position error and normal error are respectively estimated by point clouds and normal data. The fusion method is conducted by minimizing the sum of position error and normal error. Different values of the weight factor are designed to deal with the data reliability difference in the high-reflective regions and the other regions. The high-frequency textures on the topology are recoverd by the normal data. Therefore, both integrity and accuracy are improved by the fusion method. Moreover, the intact point clouds are estimated by measuring only once without repeated parameter adjustment and human intervention, which lifts the reconstruction efficiency.

2 Method

2.1 Multi-modality Sensor System

The multi-modality sensor system, including an FPP unit and a PS unit, is developed for reconstruction in this paper. To be specific, the system mainly consists of a camera, a projector and 29 light-emitting diodes (LEDs), as shown in Fig. 1. For the FPP sensor, the projector is used to project a series of fringe patterns on the target surface. For the PS sensor, the LEDs are used to provide multiple lighting directions on the target surface. These two sensors share the same camera to capture multiple images of the target surface when different light sources work.

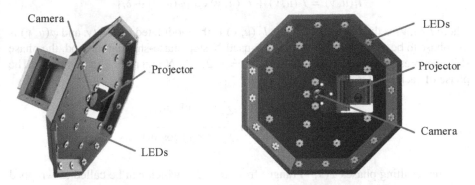

Fig. 1. Schematic diagram of the proposed multi-modality sensor system.

The proposed multi-modality sensor system provides multi-modality data, including the point cloud and normal data, as shown in Fig. 2. To be specific, the FPP sensor reconstructs the original point cloud data except for the points in the high-reflective regions, which can provide the initial topology of the target surface. The PS sensor estimates the intact normal data with high accuracy. If the point cloud of the target surface is directly reconstructed by the normal data based on the integration method, the low-frequency bias would seriously distort the point cloud due to the accumulative errors. Therefore, a new fusion method is proposed to reconstruct the point cloud of the high-reflective surface. For the estimation of each point, the original point cloud data provide the position constraint, and the normal data provide the direction constraint.

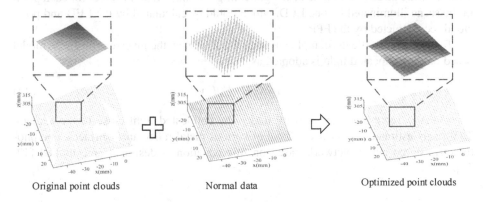

Original point clouds   Normal data   Optimized point clouds

Fig. 2. Schematic diagram of the fusion of multi-modality data.

2.2 Fringe Projection Profilometry

For the FPP, a set of sinusoidal fringe patterns are projected onto the target surface by the projector. For any pixel (u, v) in the image captured by the camera, the intensity is expressed as

$$I_i(u, v) = I'(u, v) + I''(u, v) \cos[\varphi(u, v) + \delta_i] \tag{1}$$

where $I'(u, v)$ is the average intensity, $I''(u, v)$ is the modulated intensity, and $\varphi(u, v)$ is the phase to be estimated. For the widely-used N-step phase-shifting method, the phase shift is represented as $\delta_i = 2\pi i/N$, where $i = 1, 2, \ldots, N$ and $N = 8$ in this paper. The phase of each pixel is estimated by

$$\varphi(u, v) = -\arctan \frac{\sum_i I_i(u, v) \sin(\delta_i)}{\sum_i I_i(u, v) \cos(\delta_i)} \tag{2}$$

The resulting phases $\varphi(u, v)$ ranges from 0 to 2π, which can be called as wrapped phases. To unwrap the wrapped phase map into a continuous phase map, three frequencies are employed in our FPP system. The point clouds are estimated by the unwrapped phase map through the proposed calibration method [11].

2.3 Photometric Stereo

Photometric stereo estimates the surface normal $n \in \mathbb{R}^3$ by inversely solving it from the reflectance model. For any point on the surface, the intensity I captured by the camera could be expressed as

$$I = \rho(l, n, v) l^T n \tag{3}$$

where $\rho(l, n, v)$ is the reflectance function, $l \in \mathbb{R}^3$ is the lighting direction, and $v \in \mathbb{R}^3$ is the viewing direction. For the near-light configuration, I, l, and v differ for each point in the scene illuminated by one LED, which could be calculated by the LED and point cloud reconstructed by the FPP.

To inversely handle the complicated metal reflectance, the inverse reflectance model based on the collocated light is adopted as

$$l^T n = g(I, I_c, l^T v) \tag{4}$$

where the I_c represents the intensity under the collocated light close to the camera. To directly estimate the surface normal of various metal reflectance surfaces, one photometric stereo neural network based on this equation is designed and applied [12, 13].

2.4 Fusion

For the point clouds reconstructed by the FPP, the interpolation algorithm is usually applied to complement the missing points through the neighboring valid points. However, the low-frequency bias would seriously distort the topology in the high-reflective regions due to the accumulative errors. The original noise in the point clouds reconstructed by the FPP would further affect the interpolation accuracy in the high-reflective regions. Therefore, the fusion method is proposed to optimize the topology accuracy with the normal data as the additional cue. The entire process is shown in Fig. 3.

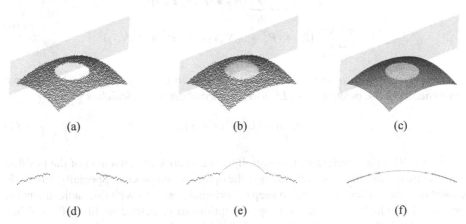

(a)   (b)   (c)

(d)   (e)   (f)

Fig. 3. Schematic diagram of the proposed fusion process. (a) The original point clouds reconstructed by FPP. (b) The point clouds complemented by the interpolation in high-reflective regions. (c) The point clouds optimized by the proposed fusion method. (d) The cross-section map at the position of the green plane in (a). (e) The cross-section map at the position of the green plane in (b). (f) The cross-section map at the position of the green plane in (c). (Color figure online)

The topology connection relations between each point and its neighboring points express the 3-D shape of the reconstructed surfaces in detail. The triangulation meshes of the point clouds are generated based on its natural grid arrangement. Each point in the point clouds serves as the vertex in the corresponding mesh. Each normal serves as the normal vector of the corresponding vertex in the meshes.

The fusion method is conducted through adjusting the position of each point based on the normal data. The 3-D coordinates of vertices obtained by FPP are used as position constraints to limit the adjustment values of these vertices. For a given vertex v, the position error E^P is defined as the sum of squared distances between the optimized vertex positions $P_v = (X, Y, Z)$ and the original vertex positions $P_v^0 = (X_0, Y_0, Z_0)$. In order to prevent intersections of the optimized vertices, the adjustment of vertex is restricted to the respective normal direction N_v. If δ_v denotes the adjustment values by optimization, the adjustment vector should be $\delta_v N_v$. Since the normal N_v is a unit vector, the position error is written as

$$E^P = \sum_v \left\| (P_v - P_v^0) \right\|^2 = \sum_v \|\delta_v N_v\|^2 = \sum_v \delta_v^2 \qquad (5)$$

The normal data of vertices are used as direction constraints to favor them being perpendicular with tangents in corresponding triangular patches. The normal error E^N is defined as the sum of the squared distances of projecting the tangents into the normal direction. To be specific, if u and w are assumed as two neighboring vertices of the given vertex v in a triangular patch, the tangent of the vertex v in this patch can be denoted by the vector from w to u. It is worth noting that the 3-D coordinates of the vertices u and w should already be corrected by δ_u and δ_w. If the optimized vertices are defined as u' and w', the normal error can be expressed as

$$
\begin{aligned}
E^N &= \sum_v \sum_{u,w} [N_v \bullet (P_u - P_w)]^2 \\
&= \sum_v \sum_{u,w} [N_v \bullet (P_u^0 + \delta_u N_u) - N_v (P_w^0 + \delta_w N_w)]^2
\end{aligned}
\tag{6}
$$

In order to optimize the reconstructed surface, an object function is defined as a combination of the position error E^P and the normal error E^N, which is given by

$$
\arg\min_P \lambda E^P + (1 - \lambda) E^N
\tag{7}
$$

where $\lambda \in [0, 1]$ is a weight factor controlling the relative effectiveness of the position constraints and the direction constraints in the optimization process. Specially, when λ is closed to 1, the vertices are prone to keep the original positions with little adjustments in optimization, which means that the proposed optimization method has little effect. When λ is closed to 0, the optimization process tends to depend on the normal map exclusively, which means that the optimization algorithm is prone to correct all the positions based on the normal data. Since the topography reconstructed by FPP is generally well except the high-frequency texture, only very small adjustments are required to correct the positions of the original points cloud in diffuse regions. On the other hand, the topography reconstructed by interpolation is distorted due to the low-frequency errors, so larger adjustments are required to correct the positions in high-reflective regions. Therefore, a single value of the weight factor λ cannot meet the requirement of the different regions. Two different values of the weight factor, λ_1 in the high-reflective regions and λ_2 in the diffuse regions, are proposed to deal with this conflict. Considering the larger errors in point clouds exiting in the high-reflective regions by interpolation than those in diffuse regions by FPP, it is essential to let $\lambda_1 < \lambda_2$. Therefore, if D_h denotes the high-reflective regions of the reconstructed surfaces, the object function is further expressed as

$$
\arg\min_P F(P, N)
$$
$$
F(P, N) = \begin{cases} \lambda_1 E^P + (1 - \lambda_1) E^N & \text{if } P \in D_h, \\ \lambda_2 E^P + (1 - \lambda_2) E^N & \text{else.} \end{cases}
\tag{8}
$$

The optimized positions of all the vertices are solved using the weighted least squares method. The solution of this minimization process is operated as a sparse linear system, which allows the corresponding algorithm to perform efficiently even for large data.

3 Experiment

The multi-modality sensor system is developed to verify the proposed fusion method as shown in Fig. 4. The hardware system mainly consists of a camera (Daheng, MER-2000-19U3C), a projector (SK telecom, SK L-NX), and 29 white LEDs. The camera has a resolution of 5496×3672, and the focal length of the camera lens (Fujinon, CF16ZA-1S) is 16 mm. The projector has a resolution of 1280×720. The target object is aluminum alloy and machined by milling. The reconstructed surface is the upper free-form surface, the size of which is about $100 \times 100 \times 22$ mm. The working distance of the system is 280 mm to 340 mm, and the working range is about 240 mm $\times$ 160 mm. Both the FPP system calibration [11] and the PS system calibration [14] are employed to calibrate the multi-modality sensor system.

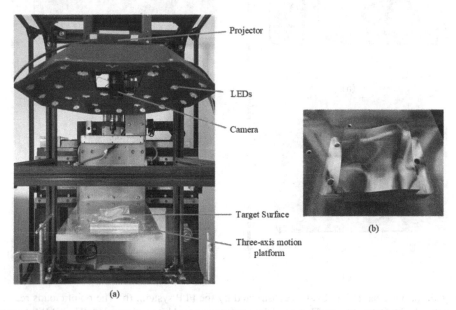

Fig. 4. (a) The diagram of the system setup. (b) The measured object with a free-form surface.

The reconstruction error is the deviation of the reconstructed topology and the real one. There is a difference with the real topology and the designed 3-D model due to the machining error. As the points measured by the coordinate measuring machine (CMM) are much more accurate than those measured by the optical system, the former is considered as the ground truth of the target surface. Many commercial software provides the analysis of the 3-D measurement by compare the measured points and 3-D model. The deviation between the points measured by CMM and the designed 3-D model is considered as the standard. The deviation between the points measured by the proposed multi-modality sensor system and the designed 3-D model is also estimated. The smaller difference between these two deviations means the higher accuracy. Polyworks, a popular commercial software, is used for the evolution. The point clouds reconstructed by the

FPP, linear interpolation, and fusion are compared in the form of error map, as shown in Fig. 5. The root mean square (RMS) of all the points in error map are also computed and listed in Table 1. It is noted that the result of FPP is smoothed by the Gaussian filter. Otherwise, the result is seriously affected by the high-frequency noises and the RMS is in the submillimeter level.

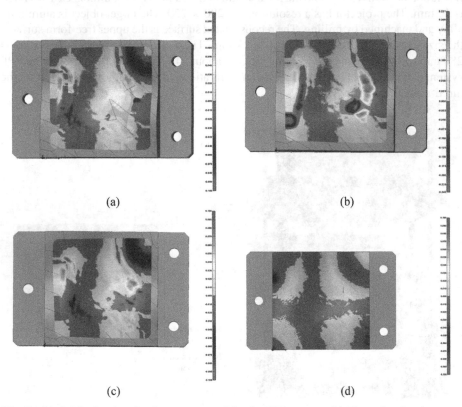

(a)   (b)

(c)   (d)

Fig. 5. (a) Original point clouds reconstructed by the FPP system. (b) The point clouds reconstructed by interpolation. (c) The point clouds reconstructed by the fusion. (d) The CMM data as the ground truth.

Table 1. The errors of point clouds reconstructed by different methods.

Method	FPP	Interpolation	Fusion	CMM
RMS (μm)	38	52	**25**	15

According to Fig. 5 (a), it is obvious that the missing points are existed in the high-reflective regions in the FPP result. Although the intact point clouds are estimated by the linear interpolation, the interpolated points in the high-reflective regions are trapped in the large errors as shown in Fig. 5 (b). The deviation between the RMS of the fused point clouds and the ground truth, i.e., CMM result, is only 10 μm, which is much smaller than FPP and interpolation results. The distribution of the error map shown in Fig. 5 (c) is much closer to that in Fig. 5 (d) than the other error map. The fusion method not only greatly improves the accuracy of the points in the high-reflective regions, but also improves the whole reconstruction accuracy. In summary, the proposed method ensures both the integrity and accuracy of the reconstruction.

4 Conclusion

This paper proposes a fusion method on the multi-modality data to overcome the high-reflective problem in high-reflective surface reconstruction based on the designed multi-modality sensor system. The multi-modality data combined by the point clouds measured by the FPP sensor and the normal data measured by the PS sensor. The fusion method is realized by minimizing the sum of position error and normal error with the weighted least square method. The deviation between the RMS of the fused point clouds and the ground truth is only 10 μm, which not only ensures the reconstruction integrity but also improves the reconstruction accuracy. This method is realized by only measuring once without human intervention, which improves the reconstruction efficiency.

The designed multi-modality sensor system is flexible and portable, which means it can be mounted on mobile robots or the other moving platforms. We will carry the research on the reconstruction of the large workpiece surfaces based on the multi-viewpoint cloud registration in the future.

Acknowledgement. The work was substantially supported in part by the National Natural Science Foundation of China under Grant 91948301 and Grant 52175477.

References

1. Shen, Y., Zhang, W., Zhang, Y., Huang, N., Zhang, Y., Zhu, L.: Distributed particle swarm optimization for the planning of time-optimal and interference-free five-axis sweep scanning path. IEEE Trans. Industr. Inf. (2022). https://doi.org/10.1109/TII.2022.3155159
2. Shen, Y., Zhang, X., Wang, Z., Wang, J., Zhu, L.: A robust and efficient calibration method for spot laser probe on CMM. Measurement **154**, 107523 (2020)
3. Cai, Z., et al.: Structured light field 3D imaging. Opt. Express **24**, 20324–20334 (2016)
4. Zhang, L., Chen, Q., Zuo, C., Feng, S.: High dynamic range 3D shape measurement based on the intensity response function of a camera. Appl. Opt. **57**, 1378–1386 (2018)
5. Zhang, S., Yau, S.-T.: High dynamic range scanning technique. Opt. Eng. **48**, 033604 (2009)
6. Waddington, C., Kofman, J.: Saturation avoidance by adaptive fringe projection in phase-shifting 3D surface-shape measurement. In: 2010 International Symposium on Optomechatronic Technologies, pp. 1–4. IEEE (2010)
7. Chen, T., Lensch, H.P., Fuchs, C., Seidel, H.-P.: Polarization and phase-shifting for 3d scanning of translucent objects. In: 2007 IEEE Conference on Computer Vision and Pattern Recognition, pp. 1–8. IEEE (2007)
8. Salahieh, B., Chen, Z., Rodriguez, J.J., Liang, R.: Multi-polarization fringe projection imaging for high dynamic range objects. Opt. Express **22**, 10064–10071 (2014)

9. Chen, G., Han, K., Wong, K.-Y.: PS-FCN: a flexible learning framework for photometric stereo. In: Ferrari, V., Hebert, M., Sminchisescu, C., Weiss, Y. (eds.) ECCV 2018. LNCS, vol. 11213, pp. 3–19. Springer, Cham (2018). https://doi.org/10.1007/978-3-030-01240-3_1
10. Ren, M., Wang, X., Xiao, G., Chen, M., Fu, L.: Fast defect inspection based on data-driven photometric stereo. IEEE Trans. Instrum. Meas. **68**, 1148–1156 (2019)
11. Pei, X., Liu, J., Yang, Y., Ren, M., Zhu, L.: Phase-to-coordinates calibration for fringe projection profilometry using Gaussian process regression. IEEE Trans. Instrum. Meas. **71**, 1–12 (2022)
12. Wang, X., Jian, Z., Ren, M.: Non-Lambertian photometric stereo network based on inverse reflectance model with collocated light. IEEE Trans. Image Process. **29**, 6032–6042 (2020)
13. Pei, X., Ren, M., Wang, X., Ren, J., Zhu, L., Jiang, X.: Profile measurement of non-Lambertian surfaces by integrating fringe projection profilometry with near-field photometric stereo. Measurement **187**, 110277 (2022)
14. Nie, Y., Song, Z., Ji, M., Zhu, L.: A novel calibration method for the photometric stereo system with non-isotropic LED lamps. In: IEEE International Conference on Real-time Computing and Robotics (IEEE RCAR), pp. 289–294. IEEE (2016)

Position-Pose Measurement Algorithm Based on Geometrical Characteristics

Ben Shi[1] and Xu Zhang[1,2(✉)]

[1] School of Mechatronic Engineering and Automation, Shanghai University, Shanghai, China
zhangxu@hust-wuxi.com

[2] Huazhong University of Science and Technology Wuxi Research Institute, Wuxi, China

Abstract. Based on the geometrical characteristics, this paper proposes a position-pose measurement algorithm with the non-feature point data of the cooperative target. This method only needs to project six parallel laser beams to the target and obtain the range-finding result without knowing the coordinates of measurement points in target system, then the position-pose of target and the object fixed to it can be figured out. This algorithm is verified by establishing the model of the cooperative target and the position-pose measurement system. The experimental results show that the average absolute error of the pose rotation measured by the algorithm is stable within 0.5°, and the movement is within 1 mm.

Keywords: Pose estimation · Laser ranging · Laser target · Geometric features

1 Introduction

Position-pose measurement has a wide range of applications in industrial automation, aerospace, augmented reality, etc. Usually, several feature points are set on the object, then the object is photographed and the feature points are extracted by image processing. The position-pose of the object can be calculated by using the constraint relationship of these corresponding points. Although the solved position-pose has high accuracy, the accuracy of the results depends heavily on the strong geometric features of the target, while the background and lighting in the actual environment are often complex, which has a great impact on feature extraction. At the same time, the feature extraction process involves a large number of matrix operations, causing the high time complexity, which is difficult to meet the real-time requirements [1–5]. More importantly, this type of method must know the coordinates of the feature points under the target object in advance. But in practice, when the measurement space is compact, it may not be able to set the feature cursor points on the object. Naturally, it is impossible to know the coordinates of the feature point in the target object coordinate system.

Fishler et al. proposed a perspective n-point positioning algorithm, which uses the two-dimensional coordinates of the feature points on the image and the three-dimensional coordinates of the feature points in the target coordinate system to calculate the relationship between the target coordinate system and the camera coordinate system [6]. However, the problem has infinitely many solutions when n < 3; Moreno-Noguer F et al.

© The Author(s), under exclusive license to Springer Nature Switzerland AG 2022
H. Liu et al. (Eds.): ICIRA 2022, LNAI 13458, pp. 769–779, 2022.
https://doi.org/10.1007/978-3-031-13841-6_69

proposed a non-iterative PNP pose algorithm called EPnP, which uses the weighted sum of 4 virtual control points for each 3D point representation, then solves the coordinate value of the control point relative to the camera coordinate system, and finally obtains the pose. The calculation efficiency of the algorithm is significantly improved, but it is still necessary to know the coordinates of the feature points under the target object in advance [7]. Halralink proposed an attitude calculation method for a rectangle with unknown spatial size [8]. The algorithm uses four parallel laser beams to obtain the coordinates of four laser points on the reference plane, and does not need the coordinates of the laser points under the object. This algorithm can obtain the pose of the space rectangle, but not its position;

Aiming at the above issues, this paper proposes a position-pose solution algorithm that fuses target non-feature point data. As shown in Fig. 1, this method only needs to fix a cooperative target on the target object and project six parallel laser beams to the target to obtain the range-finding result. Then the rotation and translation data of the target in the six degrees of freedom are obtained by using the geometric features of the reference plane. Finally, the position-pose of current target is obtained. This method addresses the issue that the measuring points must be known in the object coordinate system in the traditional PNP problem. At the same time, it can meet the requirements of compact space and real-time, which can be used for the positioning of space objects.

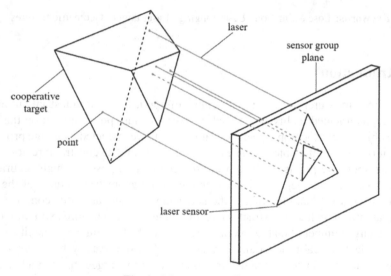

Fig. 1. Measurement diagram

2   Algorithm

2.1   Target Structure

This paper uses the geometric features of the cooperative target to constrain the projected laser points to establish a solution model, and finally calculate the target position-pose. Different from the PNP problem, which requires the coordinates of the feature points in the target coordinate system and the corresponding relationship with the feature points in the measurement coordinate system, this method only needs the coordinates of the laser point in the measurement coordinate system, and six points are required to figure out the position-pose at least. The cooperative target is produced by intercepting a regular triangular pyramid, and the serial number convention of each plane is shown in Fig. 2. The sensor group emits laser beams to the four reference planes of the target through an appropriate layout and obtains the distance to the irradiation point. Since the sensor group has been calibrated to determine the sensor coordinate system, the laser points can be converted into this coordinate system to obtain their three-dimensional coordinates. The three laser points on the plane 1 are p_{11}, p_{12}, p_{13}, and the points on the plane 2, plane 3 and plane 4 are p_2, p_3 and p_4. When these symbols are quoted below, they will be equivalent to the three-dimensional coordinate column vector of the corresponding point.

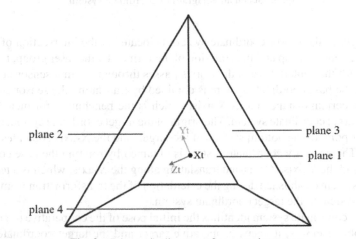

Fig. 2. Schematic diagram of cooperative target

2.2 Coordinate System Conventions

Four coordinate systems are established in the process of solving the target position-pose: sensor coordinate system $O_s - X_sY_sZ_s$, base coordinate system $O_b - X_bY_bZ_b$, auxiliary coordinate system $O_f - X_fY_fZ_f$, and target coordinate system $O_t - X_tY_tZ_t$. The relationship is shown in Fig. 3.

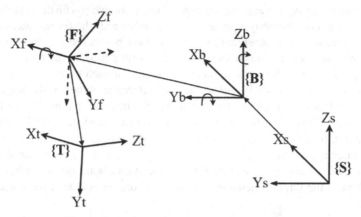

Fig. 3. Schematic diagram of coordinate system

The origin of the sensor coordinate system is located at the intersection of the centerline of the sensor group and the emission plane formed by the laser group, the X-axis coincides with the centerline, and the Z-axis passes through the first sensor laser emission point; The base coordinate system is obtained by translating the sensor coordinate system by a certain distance on its X axis, which is the benchmark for measuring the pose of the target coordinate system; The origin of the target coordinate system is located at the center point of the bottom surface of the target, and the X-axis coincides with the centerline; The auxiliary coordinate system is obtained by rotating the base coordinate system around the Y-axis, Z-axis and translating along the X-axis, which is a temporary coordinate system established during the calculation of the transformation from the base coordinate system to the target coordinate system.

The base coordinate system identifies the initial pose of the cooperative target. When the target object moves, it keeps cooperative target and the target coordinate system moving synchronously, thereby separating from the reference coordinate system. This separation represents the movement of the target in six degrees of freedom, which can be accurately described by the rigid body transformation matrix. At the same time, the laser spots projected on the target are also changing constantly. The special structure of the target ensures that the six laser spots always appear on the four reference surfaces of the cooperative target. The sensor group measures the distance of each laser spot and obtains the distance, and obtains the coordinates in the sensor coordinate system. Then they are converted to the base coordinate system. Finally, the measurement system will use the six laser points in the base coordinate system to figure out the rigid body transformation matrix from the reference coordinate system to the auxiliary coordinate system and the auxiliary coordinate system to the target coordinate system through modeling. Then, the transformation relationship between the reference coordinate system and the target coordinate system is obtained. Finally, the motion data of the cooperative target relative to the starting pose in six degrees of freedom are obtained.

2.3 Transformation from Base Coordinate System to Auxiliary Coordinate System

The sensor collects six laser points projected on the four reference planes of the cooperative target and converts them to the base coordinate system. Since the laser points p_{11}, p_{12} and p_{13} are coplanar, the normalized normal vector of plane 1 can be obtained

$$n_1' = \frac{(p_{11} - p_{13}) \times (p_{12} - p_{13})}{\|(p_{11} - p_{13}) \times (p_{12} - p_{13})\|}, \tag{1}$$

n_1 is the normal of the target plane 1 at the initial pose, and the angle between it and n_1' is

$$\theta_r = \arccos(n_1 \bullet n_1')$$

The rotation of a vector can be represented by a rotation axis and a rotation angle, which is called rotation vector [9]. Considering n_1' is the rotated n_1, the rotation from n_1 to n_1' is equivalent to rotating θ_r around a unit vector in three-dimensional space, and the vector is

$$n_r = \frac{n_1 \times n_1'}{\|n_1 \times n_1'\|} \tag{2}$$

Furthermore, through the Rodrigues formula [10], the rotation matrix can be obtained

$$_f^b R = \cos\theta_r I + (1 - \cos\theta_r)n_r n_r^T + \sin\theta_r n_r^\wedge \tag{3}$$

where $\hat{}$ is the vector to the antisymmetric converter, the formula is

$$n^\wedge = \begin{bmatrix} 0 & -n_z & n_y \\ n_z & 0 & -n_x \\ -n_y & n_x & 0 \end{bmatrix} \tag{4}$$

where $n = [n_x \ n_y \ n_z]^T$.

The rotation transformation matrix $_f^b R$ from the base coordinate system to the auxiliary coordinate system is obtained. It is import that since the degrees of freedom around n_r (that is, the target $O_t - X_t$) have not been constrained, so $_f^b R$ is not fixed. Besides rotation, the relative relationship between the auxiliary coordinate system and the base coordinate system also includes translation. As shown in Fig. 4, the translation from the base coordinate system to the auxiliary coordinate system only exists along the $O_f - X_f$ direction. According to the projection relationship, there are

$$_f^b T_X = n_1' \bullet (p_{11} - o_b) \tag{5}$$

where o_b is the origin of the base coordinate system.

We have

$$_f^bT = \begin{bmatrix} _f^bT_X & 0 & 0 \end{bmatrix}^T \tag{6}$$

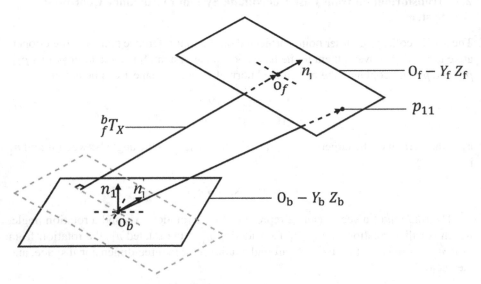

Fig. 4. Schematic diagram of translation

The above fitting has determined the rigid body transformation matrix from the base coordinate system to the auxiliary coordinate system, which constrains two rotations and one translational degrees of freedom from the base coordinate system to the target coordinate system.

2.4 Transformation from Auxiliary Coordinate System to Target Coordinate System

The auxiliary coordinate system moves from the target coordinate system by rotating the w_1 around $O_f - X_f$ and translating (w_2, w_3) in the $O_f - Y_f Z_f$ plane. Let the parameter vector $w = \begin{bmatrix} w_1 & w_2 & w_3 \end{bmatrix}^T$, there are

$$_t^fR = \begin{bmatrix} 1 & 0 & 0 \\ 0 & \cos w_1 & -\sin w_1 \\ 0 & \sin w_1 & \cos w_1 \end{bmatrix}, \quad _t^fT = \begin{bmatrix} 0 \\ w_2 \\ w_3 \end{bmatrix}, \tag{7}$$

These three degrees of freedom constrain the rigid body transformation from the auxiliary coordinate system to the target coordinate system. Taking the target plane 2 as an example, the schematic diagram is shown in Fig. 5, p_2 is the laser point projected on the surface 2, then converted it to the base coordinate system; p_0 is the common point where the target planes 2, 3, and 4 intersect by extension, and n_2 is the normal of the surface 2. Since the size of the target is certain, both of them are known in the target coordinate system.

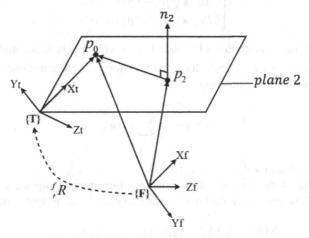

Fig. 5. Rigid body transformation diagram

Using the results of formulas (4) and (5), transform p_2 to the auxiliary coordinate system as

$$^f p_2 = {}_b^f R p_2 + {}_b^f T,\tag{8}$$

Converting the target vertex to the auxiliary coordinate system as

$$^f p_0 = {}_t^f R p_0 + {}_t^f T,\tag{9}$$

Considering that $_t^f R$ only contains rotations about $O_t - X_t$, and p_0 is on the axis $O_t - X_t$ as follows

$$^f p_0 = p_0 + {}_t^f T,\tag{10}$$

Since the point p_0 and the point p_2 are located in the target plane 2, n_2 is the normal of the plane 2. According to the geometric relationship, we have

$$_t^f R n_2 \bullet (^f p_0 - ^f p_2) = 0, \tag{11}$$

Considering that the target vertices are located in the target planes 2, 3, and 4 at the same time, we have

$$\begin{cases} _t^f R n_3 \bullet (^f p_0 - ^f p_3) = 0 \\ _t^f R n_4 \bullet (^f p_0 - ^f p_4) = 0 \end{cases}, \tag{12}$$

Substituting Eq. (7) into Eqs. (11) and (12), and obviously it is a multivariate function about $w = [w_1 \ w_2 \ w_3]^T$, which can be transformed into a nonlinear least-squares problem. Setting objective function

$$\psi(w) = \frac{1}{2} \sum_i^3 f_i^2(w), \tag{13}$$

where $f_i(w) = _b^f R n_{i+1} \bullet (^f p_0 - ^f p_{i+1})$.

The solution of the equation then translates into minimizing the residual sum of squares $\psi(w)$. The first-order Taylor expansion of $f_i(w)$ at w_k is approximated by $\phi_i(w)$

$$\begin{aligned} \phi_i(w) &= f_i(w_k) + \nabla f_i(w_k)^T (w - w_k) \\ &= \nabla f_i(w_k)^T w - (f_i(w_k) - \nabla f_i(w_k)^T w_k) \end{aligned}, \tag{14}$$

Substituting formula (13) into (14), we have

$$\psi(w) = \sum_i^3 \phi_i^2(w) = (\begin{bmatrix} \nabla f_1(w_k)^T \\ \nabla f_2(w_k)^T \\ \nabla f_3(w_k)^T \end{bmatrix} w - \begin{bmatrix} f_1(w_k) - \nabla f_1(w_k)^T w_k \\ f_2(w_k) - \nabla f_2(w_k)^T w_k \\ f_3(w_k) - \nabla f_3(w_k)^T w_k \end{bmatrix})^T$$

$$(\begin{bmatrix} \nabla f_1(w_k)^T \\ \nabla f_2(w_k)^T \\ \nabla f_3(w_k)^T \end{bmatrix} w - \begin{bmatrix} f_1(w_k) - \nabla f_1(w_k)^T w_k \\ f_2(w_k) - \nabla f_2(w_k)^T w_k \\ f_3(w_k) - \nabla f_3(w_k)^T w_k \end{bmatrix}) \tag{15}$$

Let

$$A_k = \begin{bmatrix} \nabla f_1(w_k)^T \\ \nabla f_2(w_k)^T \\ \nabla f_3(w_k)^T \end{bmatrix}, G_k = \begin{bmatrix} f_1(w_k) \\ f_2(w_k) \\ f_3(w_k) \end{bmatrix}, b = A_k w_w - G_k$$

Thereby

$$\psi(w) = (A_k w - b)^T (A_k w - b) \tag{16}$$

Differentiating it and making it 0 to get

$$w - w_k = -(A_k^T A_k)^{-1} A_k G_k \tag{17}$$

We have

$$w_{k+1} = w_k - (A_k^T A_k)^{-1} A_k G_k, \tag{18}$$

To avoid the optimization falling into a local optimum, a reasonable initial value needs to be determined. Since the movement of the target is mainly the rotation around $O_b - X_b$, the remaining five degrees of freedom are only minor disturbances. When the target rotates, the beam emitted by the laser illuminates the three laser spots formed on plane 1, which roughly constitutes a triangle whose centroid are lying on $O_t - X_t$ of the target coordinate system. The centroid coordinates in the auxiliary coordinate system can be obtained as follows

$$^f o'_b = \frac{^f p_{11} + {}^f p_{12} + {}^f p_{13}}{3} = [x_0 \; y_0 \; z_0]^T, \tag{19}$$

Therefore, the initial value $w_0 = [0 \; y_0 \; z_0]^T$ is obtained.

3 Experiments

Based on C++ and Eigen library, the model of the cooperative target was implemented, and the edge length was set to 100 mm and the top side length was 40 mm. The theoretical values of the remaining key parameters are shown in Table 1. The steps of the position-pose solution model are

1. Set the rotation and translation of the cooperative target and get coordinates of six laser points on four reference planes.
2. Set the coordinates to algorithm and get the position-pose of cooperative target;
3. Comparing with the set value to calculate the mean absolute error.

Table 1. Algorithm parameter setting.

Parameter	Value
p_0	$[81.65 \; 0 \; 0]^T$
n_1	$[1 \; 0 \; 0]^T$
n_2	$[0.333 \; 0.816 \; 0.471]^T$
n_3	$[0.333 \; 0 \; -0.943]^T$

Input the rotation angle and translation amount of the target into the target model to obtain the six-point coordinates after the rigid body transformation and transfer it to the base coordinate system. It can be regarded as simulation of collecting the laser points by the laser sensor; Then put coordinates into the pose solution model to obtain the calculated rotation and translation. Finally compare the results with the input of the target model to obtain the MAE (Mean Absolute Error). The results are shown in Table 2. It can be seen that in the proposed algorithm the mean absolute error of the measurement is stable between 0.5° and 1 mm.

Table 2. Experimental results of position-pose measurement

Input of target model		Out of target model	Output of algorithm		
Rotation (°)	Translation (mm)	Coordinate of point	Rotation (°)	Translation (mm)	MAE
Rx = 5 Ry = 10 Rz = 15	Tx = 10 Ty = 20 Tz = 30	(53.777, 40.242, 17.405) (58.454, 31.373, 30.003) (57.859, 22.713, 14.035) (29.069, 38.462, 45.720) (19.319, 31.042, 4.991) (37.020, 5.386, 30.906)	Rx = 5.110 Ry = 10.321 Rz = 15.221	Tx = 10.149 Ty = 20.483 Tz = 30.612	R: 0.217° T: 0.415 mm
Rx = 10 Ry = 15 Rz = 20	Tx = 15 Ty = 25 Tz = 35	(55.710, 48.919, 19.019) (62.315, 39.771, 30.505) (60.527, 31.919, 14.211) (34.445, 43.942, 49.653) (20.765, 37.941, 9.831) (42.858, 12.316, 32.162)	Rx = 10.054 Ry = 14.688 Rz = 20.303	Tx = 15.083 Ty = 25.112 Tz = 34.608	R: 0.223° T: 0.195 mm
Rx = 15 Ry = 20 Rz = 25	Tx = 20 Ty = 30 Tz = 40	(57.171, 57.063, 20.745) (65.558, 47.898, 30.988) (62.393, 40.607, 14.642) (39.845, 49.531, 53.279) (22.108, 44.276, 14.981) (48.048, 19.224, 33.502)	Rx = 15.411 Ry = 20.301 Rz = 25.299	Tx = 20.199 Ty = 29.812 Tz = 40.680	R: 0.337° T: 0.356 mm

4 Conclusion

This paper studies a position-pose-solving algorithm that fuses the non-feature point data of the target. This method address the issue of needing to know the point in the target coordinate system when solving the PNP problem. As long as the Laser Rangefinder emits six parallel beams of light onto the target and obtains the distance measurement results, the position-pose of the target can be calculated. The simulation experiment is carried out by establishing the model of the cooperative target and the pose measurement algorithm. The experimental results show that the average absolute error of the pose rotation measured by the algorithm is stable within $0.5°$, and the movement amount is within 1mm, which can be used for the positioning of space objects.

Acknowledgement. This research was supported by the National Natural Science Foundation of China (Grant No. 51975344).

References

1. Quanl, L.Z.: Linear N-point camera pose deter-minaiton. IEEE Trans. Pattern Anal. Mach. Intell. **21**(8), 774–780 (1999)
2. Hu, Z., Lei, C.: A short note on P4P problem. Acta Autom. Sinica **27**(6), 770–776 (2001)
3. Liuml, W.: Pose estimation using four corresponding points. Pattern Recognit. Lett. **20**, 69–74 (1999)
4. Tang, J.L.: On the number of solutions for the P4P problem. J. Math. **26**(2), 137–141 (2006)
5. Moriyansu, I.M.: Autonomous satellite capture by a space robot. In: Proceedings of the 2000 IEEE International Conference on Robotics & Automation, San Francisco CA, pp. 1169–1174 (2000)
6. Fisher, M.A., Bolles, R.C.: Random sample consensus . Commun. ACM **24**(6), 381–395 (1981)
7. Moreno, N.F., Lepetit, V., Fua, P.E.: An accurate O(n) solution to the PnP problem. Int. J. Comput. Vis. **81**(2), 155–166 (2009). https://doi.org/10.1007/s11263-008-0152-6
8. Haralick, R.M.: Determining camera parameters from the perspective projection of a rectangle. Pattern Recogn. **22**(3), 225–230 (1989)
9. Gao, X., Zhang, T.: Visual Slam14 from theory to practice. Publishing House of Electronics Industry, Beijing
10. Chen, Y., Li, W.: Dual attitude representations based attitude estimation using high order Rodrigues parameter. J. Huazhong Univ. Sci. Technol. **45**(01), 82–86 (2017)

Safety-Oriented Teleoperation of a Dual-Arm Mobile Manipulation Robot

Jiatai Guo[1], Linqi Ye[1], Houde Liu[1(✉)], Xueqian Wang[1], Lunfei Liang[2], and Bin Liang[1]

[1] The Center of Intelligent Control and Telescience, Tsinghua Shenzhen International Graduate School, Tsinghua University, Shenzhen 518055, China
liu.hd@sz.tsinghua.edu.cn

[2] Robotic Institute, Harbin Institute of Technology, Harbin 150001, People's Republic of China

Abstract. Mobile manipulation robots can be deployed to handle various hazardous tasks such as fire fighting, disaster relief, and bomb disposal. Currently, the high-level control of mobile manipulation systems mostly relies on human teleoperation. This paper designs a novel dual-arm mobile manipulation robot and proposes a safety-oriented teleoperation strategy for it. Unlike traditional dual-arm setup which mimics humans, a functional complementary design is adopted by using a longer arm and a shorter arm. The longer arm can achieve a 360° wide-range manipulation around the base, while the shorter arm is aimed at more dexterous manipulation in the front of the base. Then a teleoperation system is designed based on the V-REP software. Three aspects are taken into account to guarantee safety during operation, including the workspace protection based on virtual walls, the self-collision protection based on minimal distance calculation, and the configuration-switch protection based on open motion planning library (OMPL). The effectiveness of the proposed method is verified through simulations and experiments.

Keywords: Dual-arm mobile robot · Teleoperation · Safety-oriented

1 Introduction

In the post-disaster rescue scene and the implementation of specific explosive disposal tasks, mobile robots are put to great use, which can reduce losses and save manpower. But in this situation, the requirement of the robot is very high, it needs to have the capability to cross unstructured terrain, and can respond quickly, stably and safely. At present, the mobile robot is mainly controlled by teleoperation, which allows humans to operate the robot to complete the task without entering a dangerous place. To better complete the task in various scenes, we need to take careful consideration for the structure of each module and the design of the robot control algorithm. The structure of a mobile manipulation robot mainly includes a mobile base and a manipulation system.

According to the structure of the mobile base, the categories of ground mobile robots can be divided into wheeled, tracked, and legged robots. One of the main challenges for ground mobile robots is the movement in complicated environments [1]. Wheeled robots have advantages in moving on smooth ground, which can move at high speed and has good steering flexibility [2]. The control of wheeled robots is simple and the energy consumption is lower than that of tracked and legged robots. However, the wheels need to be designed very large to pass through an uneven road. Legged robots such as Atlas and Spot from Boston Dynamics and MIT cheetah [3] are very famous. Legged robots have a strong capability to deal with unstructured terrains, but the control of the robot is complex [4]. The wheeled-legged hybrid mobile robot combines the advantages of wheeled robots and legged robots, but the cost is very high [5]. Tracked mobile robots have good adaptability to unstructured terrain and are easy to control. There are many excellent tracked mobile robots as can be seen from the RoboCup-Rescue competition, which aims to create rescue robots that can be used after a disaster. In the RoboCup competition of 2013, new tracked mobility apparatuses overcome the alternative version of the stepfield built of concrete blocks [6]. And a tracked robot VIKINGS is introduced in [7], which has mobile flippers that can help the main track to cross more difficult terrains. To sum up, tracked robots (especially when equipped with mobile flippers) can cross large obstacles and is easy to control, which has great potential to be used in complicated environments.

In terms of the manipulation system, a mobile manipulation robot can have single or multiple manipulators. In the 2014 World Cup in Brazil, a mobile robot named "Pack-bots" [8] with a retractable arm and a tactile claw helped deal with security problems. But the range of motion of a mobile robot with one manipulator is usually limited. For the design of multiple manipulators, most of them are in the form of a dual-arm setup that mimics humans. For example, Centauro [9] has a design with wheels at the bottom of its four legs (like a quadruped with wheels), and its head and humanoid arms are connected to the upper torso in a human form. Robots with humanoid arms can achieve coordinated control, but the workspace is still limited, especially for ground objects. It is of great significance to design new types of multi-arm systems that can achieve wide-range operation (like an excavator) as well as coordinated control.

Motivated by the above work, we design a novel dual-arm mobile manipulation robot. The main advantages of our robot are as follows. First, for the mobile base, we adopt tracks along with the front and rear flippers, which allows the robot to have excellent mobility to cross large obstacles and unstructured terrains. Second, for the manipulation system, we adopt a novel dual-arm design with a longer arm and a shorter arm, so it not only has a large workspace but also can perform fine operations. The longer manipulator can grasp objects in a wide range like an excavator, while the short manipulator can perform more precise operations in a close range. Third, we take advantage of the powerful robot simulator V-REP [10] along with a joystick to control the robot. We can use the joystick to control the simulated robot in V-REP and the real robot at the same time, which is more intuitive and effective. We also designed several algorithms including the workspace protection based on virtual walls, the self-collision protection based on minimal distance calculation, and the configuration-switch protection based on the open motion planning library (OMPL) to ensure safety. Simulation and experimental results demonstrate that the proposed methods can guarantee safety effectively during teleoperation.

The rest of this paper is organized as follows. Section 2 introduces related work on robot teleoperation. The overview of the robot design is described in Sect. 3, followed by the teleoperation strategy in Sect. 4. Section 5 describes the simulation and experimental results. Conclusions are given in Sect. 6.

2 Related Work

2.1 Teleoperation Forms

At present, the forms of teleoperation mainly include visual teleoperation, tactile teleoperation, teleoperation by control interface and so on. Reference [11] introduces visual teleoperation based on gesture recognition which explored the similarity of the human arm and robot arm in appearance and anatomy, then enriched the local features of the reconstructed image. But visual teleoperation is based on gesture recognition, the operator may feel uncomfortable in long-time teleoperation, and it is difficult for high-precision tasks. In [12], a telerobot system Rokviss was designed, which provides tactile feedback for ground operators. It has force feedback and can provide more detailed information, but it has a complex structure and high cost. In [13], to control the UR manipulator, an appropriate control interface is designed to have a comprehensive grasp of the task.

In this paper, we take advantage of the powerful robot simulator V-REP and a joystick BTP-2185T2 (Fig. 1) to control the robot, which is convenient and intuitive. We can control the movement of the manipulator in Cartesian space mode with two vertical control rods, control the movement of the tracked vehicle with the left button, and perform special functions and joint space moving through the right and upper buttons.

Fig. 1. Function assignment for the joystick.

2.2 Teleoperation Algorithms

Mobile robots need to have optimized algorithms to better meet the task requirements. Reference [14] considers the trajectory planning to avoid collision. They used a 3D model of the environment based on the OctoMap library. Using the method of reachability planning, the observation configuration of the given target configuration is generated automatically. This method improves the robustness of the robots, but when there are multiple manipulators, we need to further consider the interaction between the manipulators. In [15], Niklas Litzenberger's mobile robots have nuclear sensors, cameras and a mechanical claw. The robot can operate remotely and autopilot to return. It is improved in shape design to prevent the collision, and the arm can ensure safety when disconnected. In [16], there are two control modes for the manipulator of a mobile robot, one is the operation of the twist position based on the cellular coordinate system, the other is an operation based on the hand coordinate system. This design is more convenient for operation.

In this paper, the teleoperation algorithm is designed in the V-REP environment. The teleoperation includes two basic modes. One is the Cartesian space control, which allows the end effector of the manipulator to move in the three axes in 3D space. The other is joint space control, which allows the manipulator to switch between different configurations conveniently. Besides, we also design three algorithms to ensure safety during teleoperation, including workspace protection, self-collision avoidance, and autonomous trajectory planning. The proposed framework offers some advantages compared to other teleoperation algorithms. On one hand, we take advantage of the powerful tools in V-REP, such as inverse kinematics solver and minimum distance calculator, which is easy to implement. On the other hand, the additional protection algorithms can guarantee safety for dual-arm manipulation, so damages can be prevented due to inappropriate operations of the operator.

3 Overview of the Robot Design

As can be seen from Fig. 2, there are several options for the arm design. The first is the single-arm design. For a short arm, the operation range is small and the task it can accomplish is limited. For a long arm, although the operation range is large, it is difficult to perform fine operations near the base. The humanoid dual-arm design can perform some fine tasks and has more flexibility than single-arm design, but its operating range is still small and it is not convenient to operate near the ground. Therefore, we proposed a new dual-arm design (see Fig. 2c), which uses complementary long and short arms. It combines the advantages of the big arm and the small arm. The long arm can achieve a 360° wide-range manipulation around the base, while the short arm is in charge of more dexterous manipulation in the front of the base. A detailed comparison of the three manipulator designs is listed in Table 1.

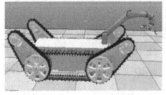

(a) Single-arm design   (b) Humanoid dual-arm   (c) Design with long and short arms

Fig. 2. Comparison of three kinds of manipulator design

The main structure of the proposed robot is shown in Fig. 3. The main track and flippers can have configuration combinations to deal with various complex terrain. The designed robot can be applied to find explosives, extract explosives and carry out bomb removal tasks. Besides, it can help search and rescue in disaster areas. Several cameras are installed on the robot to facilitate teleoperation.

Table 1. Comparison of manipulator design

Type of manipulator	Operation range	Fine operation	Cooperative operation
Single long arm	Wide	Limited	Unavailable
Single short arm	Limited	Fine	Unavailable
Humanoid arms	Limited	Fine	Fine
A longer arm and a shorter arm	Wide	Fine	Moderate

(a) robot in V-rep   (b) robot in the lab

Fig. 3. The main structure of the proposed robot

4   Teleoperation Strategy

To make mobile robots perform tasks more safely, we designed the workspace protection based on virtual walls, the self-collision protection based on minimal distance calculation, and the configuration-switch protection based on open motion planning library (OMPL).

4.1   Teleoperation Framework

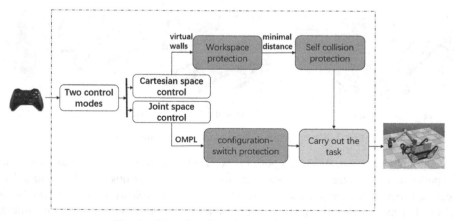

Fig. 4. Control mode and protection measures.

There are two kinds of control modes for the manipulator of the mobile robot. One is Cartesian space mode, the other is joint space mode. Our joystick can control the movement of the mobile robot, the movement of the long and short manipulator, and the switch of the control modes of the manipulator (Fig. 4).

Mode 1: Cartesian Space Mode
In Cartesian space mode, the end of the manipulator can move in a straight line. The space increment of x, y and z directions of the manipulator end is given by the joystick. The manipulator can move by using the inverse kinematics solver in V-REP.

Mode 2: Joint Space Mode
The angle of each joint angle is controlled, the expected value of each joint angle is set in advance, and the value of the current joint angle is obtained. The movement of the manipulator is completed by continuously reducing the difference between the current angle value and the expected angle value of each joint. The start and end of the movement can be controlled by the joystick. The changes of joint angle are as follows:

$$cq[i] = cq[i] + 0.1 \tanh\big[2(cf[i] - cq[i])\big] \qquad (1)$$

where is $cq[i]$ the i-th joint angle, $cf[i]$ is the expected value of the i-th joint angle. Through the above formula, the error between the current angle and the desired angle can be continuously reduced to achieve the desired configuration.

4.2 Workspace Protection

In teleoperation, it is found that when the end of the manipulator approaches the boundary of the workspace, it will not only affect the work task, but also bring potential safety hazards. Therefore, this situation must be avoided (Fig. 5).

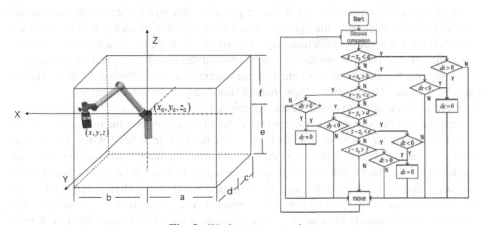

Fig. 5. Workspace protection.

We set a workspace limit. Taking the base of the manipulator as the origin, the distance from the workspace boundary to the origin is set:

$$a \leq x - x_0 \leq b$$
$$c \leq y - y_0 \leq d \tag{2}$$
$$e \leq z - z_0 \leq f$$

$$a, \ b, \ c, \ d, \ e, \ f \in R \tag{3}$$

where $(x_0, \ y_0, \ z_0)$ is the coordinate of the origin, and $(x, \ y, \ z)$ is the coordinate of the end of the manipulator. Because the base of the manipulator is taken as the center origin, the point most likely to exceed the workspace is at the vertex of the cube:

$$|\vec{\alpha}|^2 \leq \max\left\{ b^2 + d^2 + e^2, b^2 + d^2 + f^2, \\ a^2 + c^2 + e^2, a^2 + c^2 + f^2 \right\} \tag{4}$$

where $\vec{\alpha}$ is the vector from the base to the end of the manipulator. Because of the symmetry, we only need to compare the maximum of the four distances.

The six sides of the cube workspace protection are like virtual walls. When the end of the manipulator is in the workspace, it can move freely. Only when the end of the manipulator moves to the boundary of the virtual wall and moves away from the base, the increment of Cartesian space operation will be cleared, which completes the protection of the workspace. The length, width and height of the cube are set according to the task and the workspace of the manipulator.

4.3 Self-collision Protection

When we remotely operate a mobile robot, we don't want the robot arm to touch the robot itself in the process of moving. But in practice, although there is a camera that can detect the movement of the manipulator in real-time, the manipulator may still encounter obstacles in the process of Cartesian space control. We hope to use a simple algorithm to avoid self-collision. When the distance between the manipulator and the obstacle is less than the threshold, the movement of the manipulator is forbidden, so the collision can be avoided. The algorithm flow chart of this design is shown in Fig. 6.

We set three states to complete this function. Firstly, the safety distance is set as the threshold, and the shortest distance between the manipulator and the other parts of the robot is obtained by using the minimal distance calculator in V-REP. When the shortest distance reaches the threshold, it switches to intermediate state 1, and the motion of the manipulator is limited. When the teleoperation signal is detected, it will switch to state 2. According to the shortest distance, it will judge whether it is slightly adjusted under the limit of state 1 or normal operation in state 0. The constant d0 is a value slightly smaller than the threshold value, which is convenient for a slight adjustment in state 1. We confirm that there is no collision when the shortest distance is close to d0.

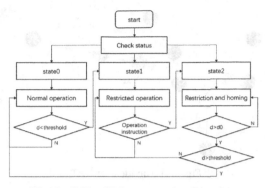

Fig. 6. Self-collision protection flow chart

4.4 Configuration-Switch Protection

As shown in Fig. 7, to make the mobile robot complete the task better through teleopera-tion, we designed several configurations for the robot arm in advance. One configuration is that the mobile robot is easy to move. At this time, the manipulator folds up. The other is the configuration that is convenient to operate the objects on the ground. At this time, the manipulator is extended. Because our mobile robot has two robotic arms, they all have complex postures. Therefore, in the process of configuration switching, it is necessary to ensure that there is no collision between the manipulators.

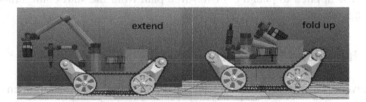

Fig. 7. The configurations of the arms.

To avoid collision, we use the OMPL library, call the RRT-connect algorithm to optimize the path between different configurations: RRT algorithm generates multiple random points according to the step size L at the same time, then selects the best point considering the index of avoiding obstacles and the closest target point. Every step L, we select the best point of a path and then connect them in turn. So we get a collision-free path from the starting point to the endpoint. As an improvement, RRT-connect can generate paths from both sides at the same time, which improves efficiency.

The basic ideas of RRT are shown in Fig. 8. Denote C as the reachable Cartesian space of the robot arm, and (x, y, z) can be used to represent the end position coordinates of the robot space. Let G_k be the workspace random tree of the manipulator with k nodes, x_{start} be the initial state and x_{goal} be the target state. x_{randm} is a random point in C space. Traverse the random tree G_k. L is the search step length, p, $q \in C$, $d(p, q)$ is the geometric distance between two pose in space, if $L \leq d(x_{near}, x_{randm})$, then find

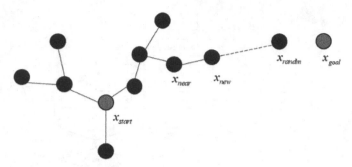

Fig. 8. Basic ideas of RRT.

x_{new} on the line between x_{near} and x_{random}, make $L = d(x_{near}, x_{new})$. If x_{new} exists and there is no collision with obstacles at any point of the connecting line between x_{near} and x_{new}, a new node is added to the random tree. Otherwise, a new set x_{random} is selected and the above process is repeated until the target point is reached. We use RRT connect, which is expanded from both ends of the starting point and the target point [17]. The expansion formula is as follows:

$$x_{new} = x_{near} + L * \frac{(x_{randm} - x_{near})}{\|x_{randm} - x_{near}\|} \tag{5}$$

Based on RRT connect, the obstacle avoidance motion planning algorithm of the manipulator is applied to plan a collision-free path from the start configuration to the target configuration.

5 Simulation and Experimental Results

The effectiveness of the designed algorithm is verified through simulation environment V-REP and experiments. The video of experiments can be found in:

https://www.bilibili.com/video/BV1DY411M7Zp?share_source=copy_web.

5.1 Workspace Constraints

We set up a simple cube as the workspace of the manipulator. The limit length, width, and height of the cube workspace are 2.4 m, 1.3 m, and 1 m respectively.

Make the manipulator move away from the origin. When the end of the manipulator exceeds the workspace, vibration may occur, which may bring danger to the robot and affect the work task. By comparing the situation with and without space protection, as shown in the Fig. 9, the situation with protection can effectively ensure safety.

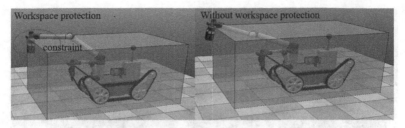

Fig. 9. Space limitation of a manipulator.

5.2 Self-collision Protection

To verify the effectiveness of the algorithm, we control the longer arm in Cartesian space to move towards some objects that are easy to collide, such as the shorter arm, flippers. In Fig. 10, the red circle marks the place where self-collision is likely to occur.

Fig. 10. The most likely part to collide with the longer arm (the flippers, and the shorter arm). (Color figure online)

We set the threshold of the shortest distance to 0.05 m. During the experiment, we move the long arm in the direction of the short arm through the joystick (see Fig. 11). The red arrow is the movement direction of the longer arm. The lower part of the picture corresponds to the state of the joystick of each process. When the manipulator is very close to the easily colliding object, it will stop moving though the joystick continues to output commands. Next, we can make the longer arm move away from it by teleoperation.

Similarly, when the longer arm moves near the flippers, it will stop when it approaches the minimum distance threshold, which proves the effectiveness of the algorithm.

5.3 Configuration Switch

When the robot is performing a task, the manipulator can switch between different configurations. By optimizing the trajectory, we can avoid collisions and interference between the two arms.

We make the manipulator move from a preset configuration to a random configuration and then move to another preset configuration. We design a random value for the joint angle of the longer manipulator and determine whether this configuration is safe so that this configuration is random. This method is repeated many times to verify the effectiveness of the algorithm.

Fig. 11. The process of the longer arm approaching the object easy to collide (Color figure online)

Fig. 12. Trajectory planning with no collision between the two arms

In the experiment, we did a lot of tests. The longer arm switches between the two kinds of pre-designed configurations and random configuration arbitrarily, and there was no collision. One case is listed in Fig. 12, t is the time of the each movement. The first row is the motion planning from extended configuration to random configuration, and the second row is the planning from random configuration to folded configuration.

6   Conclusion

We have designed a dual-arm mobile manipulation robot that can demolish explosives and rescue in a dangerous environment. By using V-REP along with a joystick, an intuitive and effective teleoperation interface is designed. At the same time, the workspace protection based on virtual walls, the self-collision protection based on minimal distance calculation, and the configuration-switch protection based on OMPL can guarantee safety during operation. Through simulations and experiments, it is found that the robot has accomplished the task excellently. We have also applied our algorithms in the A-TEC Advanced Technology & Engineering Challenge (https://atec.leaguer.com.cn/), which has won the second place. Mobile manipulation robots can play a huge role in disaster relief and explosive disposal tasks. The robot we designed has strong locomotion ability and effective algorithms to ensure safety, which makes it promising to be used in real task scenes. In the future, we will optimize the configuration-switch protection, such as the shortest time or the most energy-saving.

Acknowledgements. This work was supported by Shenzhen Science Fund for Distinguished Young Scholars (RCJC20210706091946001), Guangdong Special Branch Plan for Young Talent with Scientific and Technological Innovation (2019TQ05Z111), and National Natural Science Foundation of China (62003188, U1813216).

References

1. Delmerico, J., Mintchev, S., Giusti, A., et al.: The current state and future outlook of rescue robotics. J. Field Robotics 36(7), 1171–1191 (2019)
2. Oliveira, J., Farconi, L., Pinto, A., et al.: A review on locomotion systems for RoboCup rescue league robots. In: Robot World Cup, pp. 265–276 (2017)
3. Bledt, G., Powell, M., Katz, B., et al.: MIT Cheetah 3: design and control of a robust, dynamic quadruped robot. In: 2018 IEEE/RSJ International Conference on Intelligent Robots and Systems (IROS), pp. 2245–2252 (2018)
4. Kostavelis, I., Gasteratos, A.: Robots in crisis management: a survey. In: Dokas, I.M., Bellamine-Ben Saoud, N., Dugdale, J., Díaz, P. (eds.) ISCRAM-med 2017. LNBIP, vol. 301, pp. 43–56. Springer, Cham (2017). https://doi.org/10.1007/978-3-319-67633-3_4
5. Bjelonic, M., SankarMarko, P., Bellicosoet, C., et al.: Rolling in the deep – hybrid locomotion for wheeled-legged robots using online trajectory optimization. IEEE Robot. Autom. Lett. 5(2), 3626–3633 (2020)
6. Pellenz, J., Jacoff, A., Kimura, T., Mihankhah, E., Sheh, R., Suthakorn, J.: RoboCup rescue robot league. In: Bianchi, R.A.C., Akin, H.L., Ramamoorthy, S., Sugiura, K. (eds.) RoboCup 2014. LNCS (LNAI), vol. 8992, pp. 673–685. Springer, Cham (2015). https://doi.org/10.1007/978-3-319-18615-3_55
7. Merriaux, P., Rossi, R., Boutteau, R., et al.: The VIKINGS autonomous inspection robot: competing in the ARGOS challenge. IEEE Robot. Autom. Mag. 26(1), 21–34 (2019)
8. Michael, K., Michael, M.: The PackBots are coming: boosting security at the 2014 FIFA world cup. IEEE Consum. Electron. Mag. 3(3), 59–61 (2014)
9. Kashiri, N., Baccelliere, L., Muratore, L., et al.: CENTAURO: a hybrid locomotion and high power resilient manipulation platform. IEEE Robot. Autom. Lett. 4(2), 1595–1602 (2019)
10. Rohmer, E., Singh, S., Freese. M.: V-REP: a versatile and scalable robot simulation framework. In: 2013 IEEE/RSJ International Conference on Intelligent Robots and Systems, pp. 1321–1326 (2013)
11. Li, S., Jiang, J., Ruppel, P., et al.: A mobile robot hand-arm teleoperation system by vision and IMU. In: 2020 IEEE/RSJ International Conference on Intelligent Robots and Systems (IROS), pp. 10900–10906 (2020)
12. Siciliano, B., Khatib, O.: Springer Handbook of Robotics, pp. 1085–1108. Springer, Heidelberg (2007). https://doi.org/10.1007/978-3-540-30301-5
13. Kim, H., Ha, C., Ahn, J., et al.: User interface design for semi-autonomous teleoperation of manipulator-stage system on flexible beam. In: 2018 15th International Conference on Ubiquitous Robots (UR), pp. 96–102 (2018)
14. Kohlbrecher, S., Stryk, O.V.: From RoboCup rescue to supervised autonomous mobile robots for remote inspection of industrial plants. KI - Künstliche Intelligenz 30(3–4), 311–314 (2016). https://doi.org/10.1007/s13218-016-0446-8

15. Ritzberger, N., Emenshuber, S., Schubert, G., et al.: Mobile robot for exploration and manipulation inside a nuclear power plant. Ann. DAAAM Proc. **28** (2017)
16. Takemori, T., Miyake, M., Hirai, T., et al.: development of the multifunctional rescue robot FUHGA2 and evaluation at the world robot summit 2018. Adv. Robot. **34**(2), 119–131 (2020)
17. Lau, C., Byl, K.: Smooth RRT-connect: an extension of RRT-connect for practical use in robots. In: 2015 IEEE International Conference on Technologies for Practical Robot Applications (TePRA), pp. 1–7 (2015)

Author Index

Printed in the United States
by Baker & Taylor Publisher Services